Introductory PHYCOLOGY

Second Edition

H.D. Kumar
Formerly Professor of Botany
Banaras Hindu University
Varanasi

EWP

Affiliated East-West Press Private Limited
NEW DELHI

Dedicated to
Wilhelm Nultsch
for
1983-84, 1988

Published by:

EWP
Affiliated East-West Press Private Limited
G-1/16, Ansari Road, Darya Ganj,
New Delhi 110002

H. D. Kumar, INTRODUCTORY PHYCOLOGY, 2nd ed.

ISBN 978-81-8593-896-7

Printed in India

Contents

Preface to the Second Edition

The whole book has been thoroughly revised and updated. Several additions have been made in Chapters 1–3, 7, 9, 11–14. Special attention is drawn to the following aspects covered in the revised edition:

- Recent work on the evolution and classification of algae and other lower organisms on the basis of inputs from molecular analyses of rRNA sequences
- Phylogeny of green algae in relation to the ancestry of land plants
- Cavalier-Smith's work on heterokont algae and the new division Chromista
- Origin of the eucaryotic cell: the role of symbiosis
- Chlorarachniophytes
- Phylogenetic significance of secondary metabolites
- Propagules of marine algae
- Photomovements and circadian rhythms
- Life history types and alternation of generations: recent views
- Recent advances in nitrogen fixation and *nif*-genes
- Photosynthetic apparatus of the Cryptophyceae
- Eyespots, reproduction, and life cycles of dinoflagellates
- Molecular phylogeny of diatoms
- Stress physiology and population ecology of fucoids
- Importance of disturbance and turbulence in ecology
- Usefulness of oceans and phytoplankton as sinks for atmospheric CO_2 (including role of iron fertilization)
- Marine agronomy and aquaculture
- Medical phycology and algal pathology
- Algal weeds

I am deeply indebted to Professors G.E. Fogg (Menai Bridge, UK) and W. Wehrmeyer (Marburg, Germany) for constructive criticism of the first edition and for many valuable suggestions for its improvement. I am obliged to Professors M. Ohmori (Tokyo), K. Ueda and T. Noguchi (Nara, Japan), and I. Inouye (Tsukuba, Japan) not only for stimulating discussions but also for providing micrographs, photographs, and other phycological material. Thanks are also due to Professors D.P. Häder (Erlangen, Germany), Dorothy Parker (Oshkosh, Wisconsin), and E. Hase (Tokyo) for continuing friendship and advice, and to my associates Ashok Kumar, J.B. Singh, and L.C. Rai for help in the preparation of this edition.

H.D. Kumar

Preface to the First Edition

Looking back over the last three decades, one can only marvel at the breadth, depth, and quality of the progress made in our understanding of the structure, reproduction, life history, physiology, biochemistry, ecology, and genetics of diverse procaryotic and eucaryotic algae. The phycotechnology and outdoor mass culture of the protein-rich blue-green alga *Spirulina* have made rapid strides and may soon catch up, if not overtake, the older, maturer practices of sea farming and mariculture of *Porphyra*, *Laminaria*, and other seaweeds in Japan, China, and other maritime countries. The algae are also proving useful as experimental organisms in biotechnology, molecular biology, aquatic ecology, and photobiology.

Although a number of textbooks and introductory monographs on phycology have appeared during the last few years, the pace of research progress has been much faster and consequently while many of the existing texts do fill a niche, few, if any, satisfy the needs of the beginner in a well balanced manner. The available books tend to fall into one of two categories: (1) the traditional group, emphasizing the structure, reproduction, and life history of some or many algae, and (2) the more modern kind, dealing largely or entirely with physiology, biochemistry, ecology, genetics or biology of algae in a comparative manner. While realizing the great importance of the modern approach, it is nevertheless felt that a beginner student of phycology cannot strictly avoid or abandon the traditional taxonomic and morphological approach which alone can provide a strong foundation for the overarching edifice of modern phycology. Accordingly, I have chosen to introduce the student to a reasonable diversity of algal taxa by means of brief comparative as well as individual accounts. These accounts have been supplemented with pertinent notes on physiology, biochemistry, cytology, morphogenesis, and genetics. Further, in view of the undisputed, unique position occupied by the algae among primary producers, and in the light of their essentiality, as food organisms, in the economy of freshwater and marine environments, a chapter on ecology has been included to cover the soil algae, phytoplankton, and marine algae. In short, my aim has not been to attempt any phycological bravery, but rather to venture modestly into providing a textbook with a basic matrix of morphology on which have been grafted some applied, experimental, and ecological aspects of current concern so as to attain at least a partially balanced blend of contemporary phycological knowledge.

It appears that most, if not all, authors of algal textbooks face the problem of choosing a suitable system of classification of the algae. Being highly intuitive and subjective, the algal taxonomic processes are strongly influenced by temporal, spatial, and personal factors. There exists a plethora of classification schemes, and it is doubtful if a universally-acceptable classification system will ever become available. In this text, I have avoided the temptation of raising the lesser known, smaller classes, such as Prasinophyceae and Eustigmatophyceae, to the status of independent phyla, preferring to treat them as classes coordinate with the classes from which they were carved out, and placing both the mother and daughter classes in the same phylum. In these and allied matters, my approach, once again, has been one of balanced compromise between the extreme views of the "lumpers" and the "splitters".

Two other features of this book that may enhance its usefulness are the glossary of phycological terms and suggestions for further reading. The latter mostly contains some recent books and monographs, and excludes some of the already too well-known authoritative and encyclopaedic treatises such as those by F.E. Fritsch and G.M. Smith.

Parts of the first draft of the manuscript of this text were reviewed by the late Professor H.A. Von Stosch (Philipps Universität, Marburg, Federal Republic of Germany) and I am extremely indebted to him for his constructive criticism and valuable suggestions. I am much obliged to Professor W. Nultsch (Marburg) and Professor K. Ueda (Nara, Japan) for their kind help and suggestions. A number of phycologists have very kindly provided electron micrographs which are duly acknowledged in the legends. I must specially thank my colleagues Professors Y.B.K. Chowdary and Y.S.R.K. Sarma for their interest and cooperation. Much valuable assistance has been given by my associates and research students, notably, Drs. J.B. Singh, A. Kumar, A.K. Mishra, D. Kumar, M. Jha, and D.V. Singh.

H.D. Kumar

All algae are equal, but some are more equal than others . . .

1 Morphology and Classification

DEFINITION

The algae comprise a large, heterogeneous, and polyphyletic assemblage of relatively simple plants or thallophytes which lack roots, stems, and leaves, and which have little in common except chlorophyll-a as their primary photosynthetic pigment. As in higher green plants, photosynthesis in algae is accompanied by oxygen evolution. However, unlike bryophytes and other higher plants, algae lack a covering or jacket of vegetative cells around their reproductive organs which are mostly unicellular. An exception is the antheridium of the Charophyceae which has a sterile jacket around it. In the brown algae (Phaeophyceae), some reproductive organs are multicellular but all the cells of such an organ are fertile. The algae differ from the other group of thallophytes, viz., the fungi, in having chlorophyll and being photosynthetic.

The algae are predominantly aquatic (marine and freshwater) plants, and there may be fundamental differences between terrestrial and marine plant communities. Most terrestrial plants (e.g., angiosperms) partition vital functions much more than do the mainly aquatic algae. Although there may be some superficial similarities between algal thalli and angiosperm leaves, between algal stipes and plant stems, and between holdfasts and roots, functionally they are quite different. For example, in algae all or most of the thallus functions in photosynthesis, osmotic balance, nutrient uptake, and gas exchange. Algae are about one order of magnitude smaller and shorter-lived than are land plants. Concepts of resource allocation have been shown to be different for marine algae and for terrestrial plants. Thus, Pfister (1992) showed that the kelp *Alaria nana* incurs no measurable cost for its reproductive effort. The most intensive marine herbivores can deforest the tallest canopy-forming algal assemblage (e.g., kelp beds) but this is not so in the terrestrial world. Finally, it is possible that there are no terrestrial counterparts of encrusting coralline algae which are composed of limestone and dominate many zones of highest productivity and disturbance potentials (see Steneck and Dethier, 1995).

Many crustose algae occur in virtually all environments (see Dethier, 1994). Some crusts can be stress-tolerant, others disturbance-tolerant, and yet others may be both.

With the exception of the blue-green algae [Cyanophyta (cyanobacteria)] and *Prochloron*, most others can be sharply distinguished from bacteria. The main difference between the Cyanophyta and bacteria on the one hand, and the remaining groups of algae, fungi, bryophytes, higher plants, and animals on the other, is the procaryotic nature of cells in the former group as contrasted with the eucaryotic nature in the latter. The Procaryota lack organized nuclei, chromatophores, and mitochondria, and possess cell walls containing certain distinctive mucopeptides and muramic acid. All blue-green algae are procaryotic. While most species of the Cyanophyceae resemble the higher green plants in their oxygenic photosynthesis, many strains also have the capability to switch over to the anoxygenic photosynthesis characteristic of the photosynthetic bacteria. In view of their close cytological similarity with bacteria and partial resemblance in respect of facultative anoxygenic photosynthesis with photosynthetic bacteria, the blue-green algae are now popularly designated as "cyanobacteria".

CELL STRUCTURE

There are two basic types of cell in the algae, namely, procaryotic and eucaryotic. The procaryotic cells are characteristic of the Cyanophyceae (cyanobacteria) and *Prochloron,* whereas all other algae have eucaryotic cells. The two basic types of cell are shown in Fig. 1-1, and the distinctions between the two types are listed in Table 1-1.

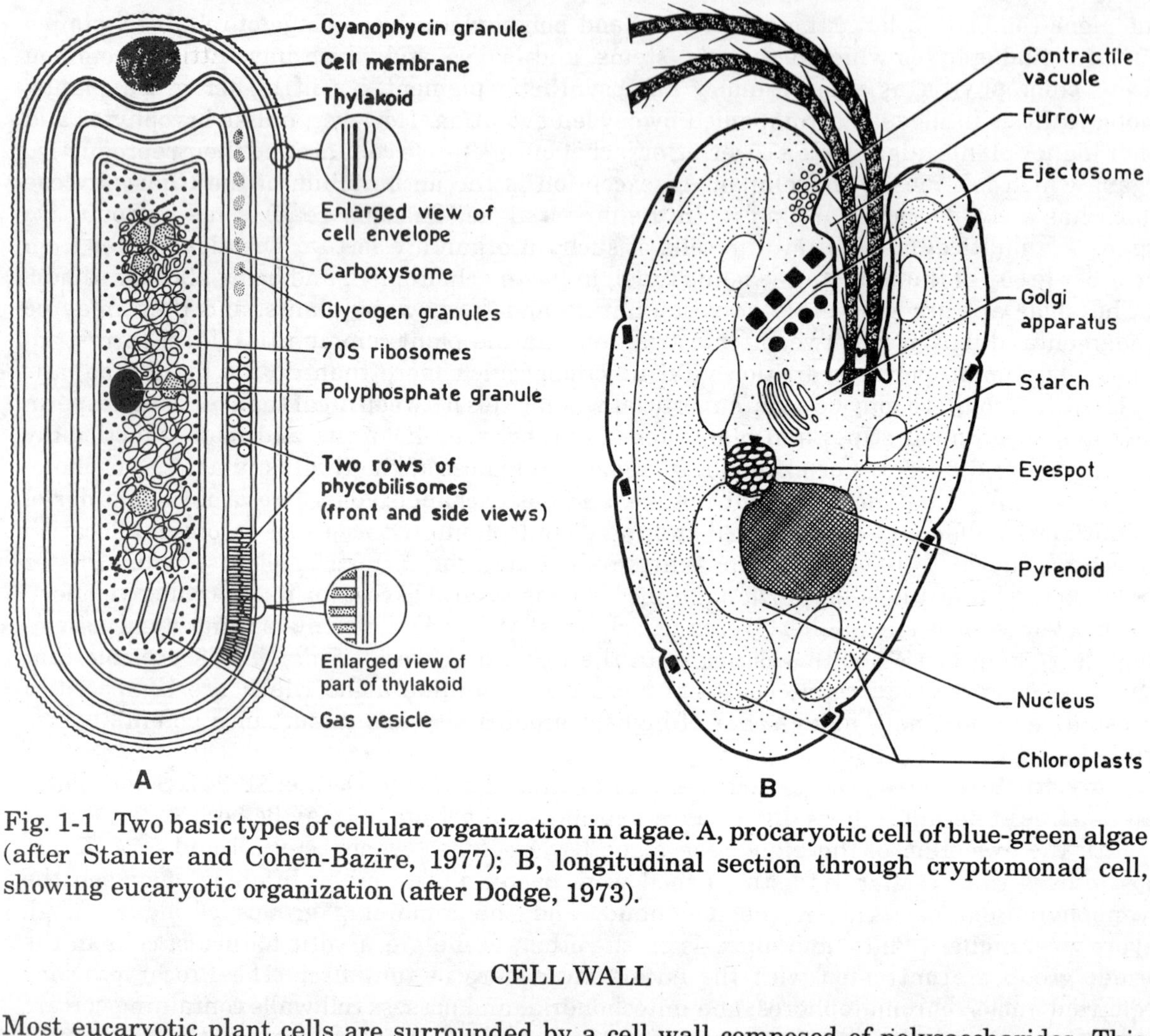

Fig. 1-1 Two basic types of cellular organization in algae. A, procaryotic cell of blue-green algae (after Stanier and Cohen-Bazire, 1977); B, longitudinal section through cryptomonad cell, showing eucaryotic organization (after Dodge, 1973).

CELL WALL

Most eucaryotic plant cells are surrounded by a cell wall composed of polysaccharides. This wall occurs outside the plasma membrane which delimits the protoplasm. Unlike the plasma membrane which is a living structure controlling the absorption and outflow of materials, the cell wall is nonliving and made of a fibrillar component forming the skeleton of the wall, and an amorphous matrix within which the fibrillar part is embedded. Sometimes, the wall contains proteins and may be impregnated with calcium carbonate or chitin. According to their composition, the algal cell walls may be predominantly cellulosic, silicified or mucopolymeric.

Table 1-1 Some general distinctions between procaryotic and eucaryotic algae

Character	Procaryota (Cyanobacteria)	Eucaryota
Cell diameter	Usually less than 15 μm	Usually 10–50 μm
DNA	Present in nucleoplasm; not associated with histones	Present in nucleus, chloroplast, and mitochondria; associated with histones
Ribosomes	70S; sensitive to streptomycin and chloramphenicol, insensitive to cycloheximide	In cytoplasm, 80S (in chloroplast and mitochondria, 70S); insensitive to streptomycin and chloramphenicol, sensitive to cycloheximide
Cell wall	Always present; peptidoglycan; penicillin-sensitive	Occurs only in some groups; has cellulose, silica, calcium carbonate, protein, or other materials; insensitive to penicillin
Vacuoles	Gas vacuoles present in many planktonic forms	Only fluid vacuoles present (contain sap)
Nitrogen fixation and heterocysts	Present in many species	Absent
Tolerance to low O_2 in dark	Can tolerate well	None (obligate aerobes)
Temperature tolerance	High (some species can tolerate 70°C, most can tolerate 40°C)	Low (most cannot tolerate 40°C, exception: *Cyanidium* can tolerate 55°C)

The cellulosic walls are fibrillar, composed of a polymer of glucose residues (β-1,4-glucose) alone or glucose plus some other carbohydrates, e.g., β-1,4-mannan (in some siphoneous green algae). In the Phaeophyceae, the cell wall contains such additional compounds as hemicellulose, alginic acid, fucoidin, and fucin. In diatoms (Bacillariophyceae), the silicified walls lack hemicellulose but contain acidic carbohydrates. These walls have amorphous hydrated silica plus some organic layers and an acidic layer rich in carbohydrates. The dinoflagellates (Dinophyceae) have elaborate cell coverings consisting of several membranes and usually a layer of thecal plates. The cryptomonads (Cryptophyceae) also possess a several-layered periplast with the outermost layer being the plasmalemma. The periplast is usually subdivided into a pattern of squarish or polygonal plates. Some Chrysophyceae possess loricae composed of ordered chitinous microfibrils.

The mucopolymeric cell wall is characteristic of cyanobacteria and *Prochloron*, and contains acetylglucosamine, acetylmuramic acid, diaminopimelic acid, amino acids, and some sugar polymers.

The abutting walls of adjacent cells in several red algae have pit connections traversed by protoplasmic strands known as plasmodesmata which interconnect the protoplasts. As much as two-thirds of the dry matter content of some red algae may be composed of sulphated polysaccharides. In the Rhodophyta, ester sulphate is usually associated with galactans, whereas in the Phaeophyta, it tends to be associated with fucans.

The carrageenans are composed of D-galactose units alternately linked by alpha-1,3 and β-1,4 bonds. Agar, on the other hand, contains equimolar proportions of D- and L-galactose linked in the same way as in carrageenans. Some types of carrageenan become esterified with sulphate. The carrageenans of some members of the Grateloupiaceae are partly methylated, sulphated D-galactans.

The wall polysaccharide of *Porphyridium* spp. appears to be a glucuronoglucoxylogalactan in which galactose and xylose occur in equal proportions and more than 90% of the galactose is L-galactose. This cell wall also contains about 7.5% of sulphate content which may be associated both with galactose and xylose residues (see McCandless and Craigie, 1979).

The cell walls of brown algae contain significant amounts of polyuronide alginate and glycans rich in sulphated L-fucose. *Fucus vesiculosus* seems to lack a discrete fucan sulphate (fucoidin) but developing embryos of *F. distichus* do have fucoidin.

The biosynthesis of the polysaccharide chains as well as their sulphation is thought to occur in the Golgi bodies. The mechanism of deposition of sulphated polysaccharides in algal cells and the functional or metabolic significance, if any, of these polysaccharides is not known. We also know little about the nature of the covalent linkages in the cell wall though the involvement of certain glycoproteins seems likely (McCandless and Craigie, 1979). In *Porphyridium* and possibly other red algae, xylose residues seem to bind to threonine or serine of the wall proteins but, again, the functional significance of such binding, if any, is obscure.

Many flagellates are wall-less. Many flagellate green algae and some prasinomonads have a continuous extracellular wall, with the flagella emerging from pores at the anterior end.

Sporopollenin, a polymer composed of oxidized carotenoids and carotenoid esters, is present in the cell walls of living and fossil diatoms, green algae, and in some fossil prasinophytes. The distribution of sporopollenin appears to go hand in hand with the presence of trilaminar cell wall construction and the presence of certain secondary carotenoids that serve as structural components.

The types of cell walls found in some important classes of algae are shown in Table 1-2.

Table 1-3 gives the distribution of some mono-, di-, and polysaccharides in algae, and Table 1-4 illustrates the distribution of some selected polysaccharide types in various classes.

In some flagellates, e.g., *Chrysochromulina, Micromonas,* and *Pyramimonas*, characteristic scales occur outside the plasmalemma (most flagellates lack cell wall). In *Mallomonas,* the scales are siliceous and bear spines. The scales of different algae are variously ornamented. *Hymenomonas roseola* interestingly deposits scales of several different kinds in the same cell, often in several layers (Manton and Peterfi, 1969). The coccolithophorids (Prymnesiophyceae) produce some of the most elaborate scales known. In these algae, calcite ($CaCO_3$) crystals grow within the Golgi bodies or other vesicles, usually in association with a glycoprotein matrix. The holococcoliths are those which contain many crystals of the same type. The heterococcoliths contain different types of crystal. Both are released to the cell's exterior.

The walls of the prasinophycean flagellate *Tetraselmis* and the chlorophycean *Chlamydomonas* develop by fusion of scales or their precursors (Domozych *et al.*, 1981).

FLAGELLA

Most algal classes except the Rhodophyceae, Cyanophyceae, and Prochlorophyceae include some algae that are either themselves motile or reproduce by means of certain motile cells which bear flagella. Two or more flagella are commonly inserted anteriorly. Usually, one

Table 1-2 Diagnostic characters of 12 algal classes

Class	Chlorophyll*	Biliprotein(s)	Carotenoids†	Number of appressed thylakoids	Main food reserve(s)	Cell wall composition	Flagellum (number and insertion)
PROCARYOTA							
Cyanophyceae		PC, PE	Myxoxanthophyll, zeaxanthin	None	Glycogen, cyanophycin	Diaminopimelic acid, glucosamine, muramic acid	Absent
Prochlorophyceae	b		α-carotene, zeaxanthin, cryptoxanthin	2–10	?	Diaminopimelic acid, glucosamine, muramic acid	Absent
EUCARYOTA							
Rhodophyceae		PE, PC	α-carotene, lutein, zeaxanthin, cryptoxanthin	None	Floridean starch	Cellulose, xylans, galactans	Absent
Cryptophyceae	c	PC	α-carotene, Σ-carotene, alloxanthin	2	Starch	Absent	2, unequal, subapical
Dinophyceae	c		Peridinin, neoxanthin, diatoxanthin, diadinoxanthin	3	Starch, rarely oil	Cellulose or wall absent	2, 1 trailing, 1 girdling
Chrysophyceae	c		Fucoxanthin, α-carotene, zeaxanthin, violaxanthin, neoxanthin, diatoxanthin, diadinoxanthin	3, girdle lamella	Chryso-laminarin, oil	Cellulose or wall absent	1 or 2, unequal or equal, apical
Tribophyceae	c		Vaucheriaxanthin, cryptoxanthin, neoxanthin, diatoxanthin, diadinoxanthin, heteroxanthin	3, girdle lamella may or may not be present	Leucosin, oil		2, unequal, 1 smooth, 1 with stiff hairs
Bacillariophyceae	c		Fucoxanthin, diatoxanthin, diadinoxanthin	3, girdle lamella	Chryso-laminarin, oil	Silica	1, with stiff hairs
Phaeophyceae	c		Fucoxanthin, violaxanthin	3, girdle lamella	Laminarin, mannitol	Cellulose, alginic acid, fucoidin	2, unequal, lateral
Euglenophyceae	b		Diadinoxanthin, heteroxanthin, diatoxanthin, zeaxanthin	3, grana?	Paramylon	Wall absent	1–3, apical, subapical
Chlorophyceae	b		Lutein, siphonein, α-carotene, zeaxanthin	2–6, grana?	Starch	Cellulose	2 or more, apical, smooth
Charophyceae	b		Lutein, α-carotene, zeaxanthin, neoxanthin	2–6, grana?	Starch	Cellulose	2 or more, apical, smooth

*All classes have chlorophyll-a. †All classes have β-carotene. PC, phycocyanin; PE, phycoerythrin.

Table 1-3 Distribution of selected mono-, di-, and polysaccharides in algae (after Ragan and Chapman, 1978)

Saccharide	Cyano-phyceae	Eugleno-phyceae	Rhodo-phyceae	Dino-phyceae	Crypto-phyceae	Bacillario-phyceae	Phaeo-phyceae	Chryso-phyceae	Hapto-phyceae	Tribo-phyceae	Chloro-phyceae	Prasino-phyceae
Arabinose	+		+	+		+			+		+	+
Fructose	+	+		+				+	+		+	
Fucose	+			+		+	+				+	
Galactose	+		+	+		+	+	+	+		+	+
Glucose	+	+	+	+		+	+	+	+	+	+	
Maltose		+	+	+					+		+	+
Mannose	+		+	+		+	+	+	+	+	+	+
Rhamnose	+			+		+		+	+		+	
Sucrose	+	+	+				?	+		+	+	
Trehalose	+	+	+									
Xylose	+		+	+		+	+	+	+	+	+	
Arabans											+	
Fructans	+										+	
Galactans			+								+	
Mannans			+								+	
Polyuronides						+	+					
Xylans			+								+	

All classes contain ribose, deoxyribose, and glucans.

Table 1-4 Distribution of selected polysaccharide types in algae (after Ragan and Chapman, 1978)

Polysaccharide	Cyano-phyceae	Eugleno-phyceae	Rhodo-phyceae	Dino-phyceae	Crypto-phyceae	Bacillario-phyceae	Phaeo-phyceae	Chryso-phyceae	Hapto-phyceae	Tribo-phyceae	Chloro-phyceae	Prasino-phyceae
Alpha-1,4-linked												
Amyloses				+	+						+	+
Amylopectins	+		+	+	+						+	+
Glycogens	+											
β-1,4-linked												
Cellulose	+		+	?	?	?	+	+		+	+	?
β-1,3-linked												
Laminarin							+					
Chrysolaminarin				+		+		+	+	+		
Paramylon		+										
Others												
Agarose			+									
Alginic acid							+					
Fucoidin							+					
Carrageenans			+									
Peptidoglycans	+											

flagellum is better developed than the other; the second may even be vestigial as in chrysophytes and euglenoids. In many dinoflagellates, the flagella are inserted laterally and one of them is ribbon-like. Usually, the Chlorophyceae have two acronematic flagella, whereas in the Phaeophyceae and Tribophyceae, there is one acronematic and one pleuronematic flagellum. In *Cryptomonas*, both flagella are pleuronematic.

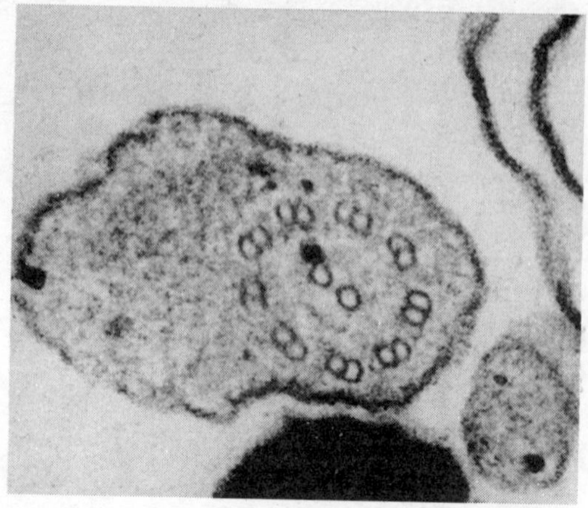

Fig. 1-2 *Euglena*, cross-section of flagellum, showing 9 + 2 arrangement. (×100,000.) *Courtesy* K. Ueda.

In a transverse section examined under the electron microscope, a flagellum (axoneme) is seen to consist of two central microtubules surrounded by a ring of nine doublet microtubules, all being enclosed in a membrane (Fig. 1-2). This basic pattern is called the 9 + 2 arrangement. The outer membrane seems continuous with the plasma membrane of the cell. At the base of the flagellum lies a basal body (Fig. 1-3) and often attached to this body are either some microtubular roots or striated fibrillar roots. The microtubular roots extend into the protoplasm. The striated fibrillar roots are characterized by the presence of groups of fibres having striations along their length.

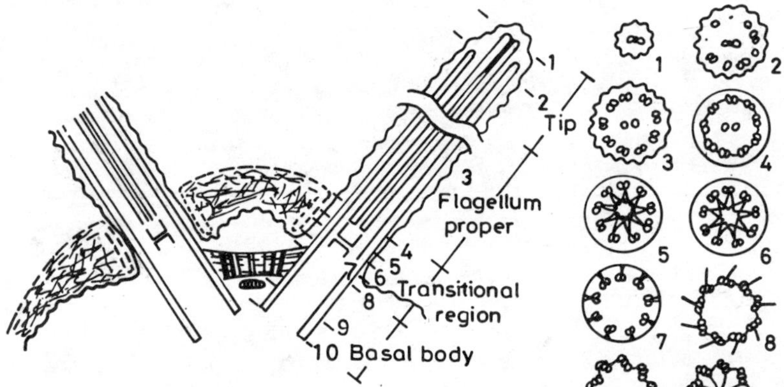

Fig. 1-3 Schematic representation of basal bodies and flagella, showing cross-sections of microtubules at ten levels from flagellar tip to basal body. Note that the two single central microtubules terminate in the transitional region and are not templated by the basal body. In the transitional region, two of the fused triplet microtubules of the basal body become continuous with the fused doublets of the flagellum, and here is situated the stellate structure characteristic of certain plant flagella. (From Pickett-Heaps, 1975.)

The mastigonemes found on some flagella may be of two types, viz., (1) fibrous and solid, and (2) tubular (Fig. 1-4). The fibrous hairs are made of solid fibrils up to 10 nm wide. The tubular (tripartite) hairs are up to 20 nm wide and are composed of a tapering basal region attached to the flagellar membrane, a microtubular shaft, and a few terminal filaments (Bouck, 1971). The flagella of some algae (e.g., *Micromonas*) are covered with scales. In *Chrysochromulina*, an additional flagellum-like structure, called haptonema, is present which can coil and anchor the cell to a substratum.

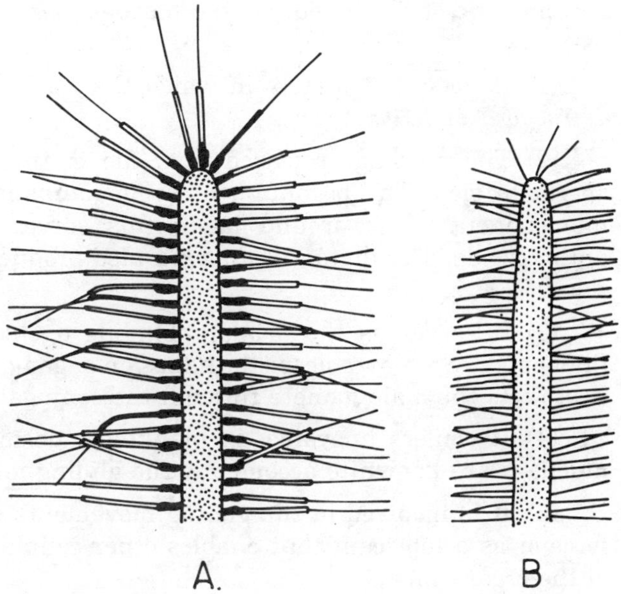

Fig. 1-4 Types of hair on algal flagella. A, tubular hairs on a flagellum of *Ascophyllum* sperm, each hair being composed of a basal region attached to the flagellar membrane, the microtubular shaft, and a terminal fibril; B, fibrillar hairs on a flagellum of a gamete of *Chlamydomonas*.

The flagella of several algae are swollen at their proximal ends. In *Dinobryon,* the flagellar swelling seems to play an important role in the subcellular coordination between light perception and flagellar movement (Kristiansen and Walne, 1977). Indeed, the flagellar swelling rather than the eyespot seems to be the primary photoreceptor in this and many other algae. The eyespot tends to act as a light shield and possibly regulates the optical quality of the transmitted light before this is focussed on the flagellar swelling.

A flavin-like autofluorescent substance occurs in the flagella of euglenoids and brown algae. This substance appears to show some photoreceptive function in phototaxis (Kawai and Inouye, 1989). Kawai and Inouye surveyed several algae containing chlorophyll-a and -c and detected autofluorescence in some members of the Chrysophyceae along the length of the short, smooth flagellum but only when this was associated with an eyespot and a flagellar swelling. The xanthophycean *Botrydiopsis intercedens* showed autofluorescence along both the flagella. However, there was no autofluorescence in the sperm or the synzoospore of *Vaucheria sessilis*. Among the Prymnesiophyceae, fluorescence was seen in the proximal part of one of the isokont flagella in some species but was not detected in many other taxa. No flagellar autofluorescence has been detected in the Bacillariophyceae, Raphidophyceae, Eustigmatophyceae, Dinophyceae, and Cryptophyceae.

On the basis of their extensive survey, Kawai and Inouye (1989) concluded that flagellar autofluorescence occurs only among those algae whose storage products are beta-glucans. The starch-storing algae (i.e., having alpha-linked glucans) do not show such fluorescence. Further, among the β-glucan algae, the autofluorescence is found mostly with the smooth flagellum, but two notable exceptions are euglenoids and *Botrydiopsis*.

MUCILAGE

Mucilage production is a fairly ubiquitous attribute of most algal groups. Many algal mucilages are made up of sulphated polysaccharides. Some common functions of the algal mucilage are as follows:

(1) It acts as a matrix in which the cells of palmelloid stages remain embedded, e.g., *Tetraspora* and *Hydrurus*.

(2) The mucilage released from the mature oogonium of *Vaucheria* serves to trap the spermatozoids. The oogonium of some nannandrous *Oedogonium* spp. secretes a distinct mucilaginous mass around itself; this serves as a trap for the dwarf males or their antherozoids. The diatom *Epithemia* also produces a mucilage enclosure during its conjugation.

(3) It serves as the primary binding agent between the properly aligned conjugating filaments of *Spirogyra* or for the adhesion of gametangial cells in *Sirogonium*. Upon expansion, it projects the male gamete through the conjugation canal.

(4) It confers buoyancy in planktonic desmids, e.g., *Mesotaenium*. Polar secretions of mucilage are known to accompany the gliding movements of desmid cells.

(5) It is involved in the gliding movements of certain cyanobacteria, either as a driving force or as a lubricant that enables other cellular activities to cause a propulsive movement of the organism.

(6) It serves to attach the algal spores to substrata where they can germinate.

(7) Its extrusion accompanies spore discharge in some members of the Rhodophyceae (Boney, 1981), e.g., *Ceramium* and *Palmaria*, and Phaeophyceae (e.g., *Pylaiella littoralis*).

PLASTIDS

There are two types of plastids, the colourless leucoplasts and the coloured chromatophores. Those plastids which contain both chlorophyll-a and -b are usually called chloroplasts. Those that lack chlorophyll-b are termed chromatophores. Typical, well organized chromatophores or chloroplasts are found in most algae except Cyanophyceae in which the photosynthetic pigments are concentrated in the peripheral zone of the protoplasm.

According to its location in a cell, the chromatophore may be parietal or axile. In the cryptomonads, prasinophytes, and motile colonial green algae, only a single chromatophore is usually present in a cell but the members of the Conjugales, Siphonales, Charales, Tribophyceae, some dinoflagellates, and many diatoms generally contain more than one chromatophore per cell. The morphology of the chromatophore varies considerably in different algae (Fig. 1-5) but the following main types can be recognized: (1) cup-shaped, as in *Chlamydomonas*; (2) girdle-shaped, as in *Ulothrix*; (3) discoid, as in *Vaucheria* and *Chara*; (4) reticulate, as in *Oedogonium*; (5) spiral, as in *Spirogyra*; and (6) stellate, as in *Zygnema*.

In some diatoms and the dinoflagellate *Pyrocystis lunula*, the chromatophores can change their shape and location within the cell in response to light. Light induced rotation of a chloroplast, mediated by phytochrome, occurs in the desmid *Mesotaenium*.

The electron microscopy of the algal chromatophore has revealed that it is generally a double-membraned structure composed of a photosynthetic lamellar system traversing the colourless granular matrix, the stroma. The structural unit of the lamellar system is a closed double-membrane disc termed thylakoid. A thylakoid membrane consists of a central lipid layer covered on both sides with protein particles, the lipid layer containing the fat-soluble photosynthetic pigments. The water-soluble pigments (phycoerythrin and phycocyanin) of the Rhodophyceae and Cyanophyceae are located in characteristic particles, termed phycobilisomes, which are found linearly arranged along the surface of each thylakoid.

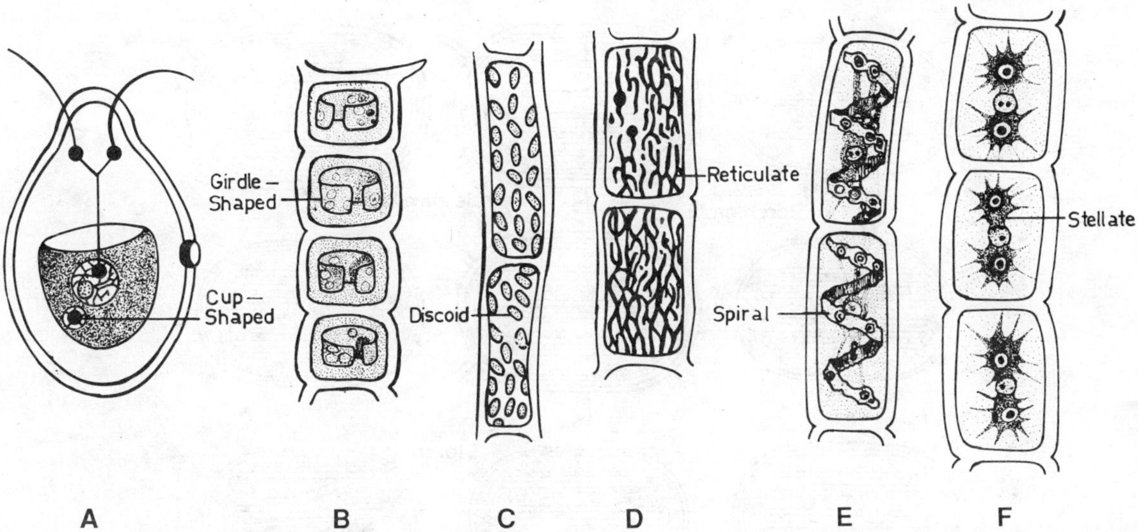

Fig. 1-5 Chromatophore shapes. A, *Chlamydomonas*; B, *Ulothrix*; C, *Tribonema*; D, *Oedogonium*; E, *Spirogyra*; F, *Zygnema*. (After Fritsch, 1935.)

The chromatophore envelope is double-membraned in the Rhodophyceae, Chlorophyceae, and Charophyceae. In most other classes of eucaryotic algae, it is surrounded by one or two membranes of the chloroplast endoplasmic reticulum, which has ribosomes attached to the outer surface of the membrane. In the Cryptophyceae, Chrysophyceae, Prymnesiophyceae, Bacillariophyceae, Tribophyceae, Eustigmatophyceae, and Phaeophyceae, the chloroplast endoplasmic reticulum is two-membraned with the outer membrane usually being continuous with the outer membrane of the nuclear envelope. The Cryptophyceae is unique in possessing a nucleomorph, ribosomes, and storage granules in the compartment between the chloroplast and chloroplast endoplasmic reticulum (Gillott and Gibbs, 1980).

In the Rhodophyceae, the thylakoids are widely separated and occur singly (Fig. 1-6) like cyanophycean thylakoids. In all other classes, they are stacked together into bands. The Phaeophyceae generally contain a band of three thylakoids. In the Chlorophyta and Euglenophyceae, a band of 4–6 thylakoids predominates.

The chromatophores of most algae have electron-translucent areas containing DNA fibrils. In algae with a girdle band, e.g., *Ochromonas*, the plastid DNA is located in a peripheral circular nucleoid inside the chromatophore, but in algae lacking girdle bands (Table 1-2), in general, the DNA areas are randomly scattered in the chromatophore matrix. Another characteristic feature of the chromatophore which is of some taxonomic or phylogenetic significance concerns the location and storage of starch grains. In the green algae, starch grains are stored within the chloroplast; in the dinoflagellates and red algae, in the cytoplasm outside the chromatophores; but in the Cryptophyceae, they are stored between the wall of the chromatophore and the sac of endoplasmic reticulum present around the plastid. Figure 1-6 illustrates a few types of chloroplast found in various classes.

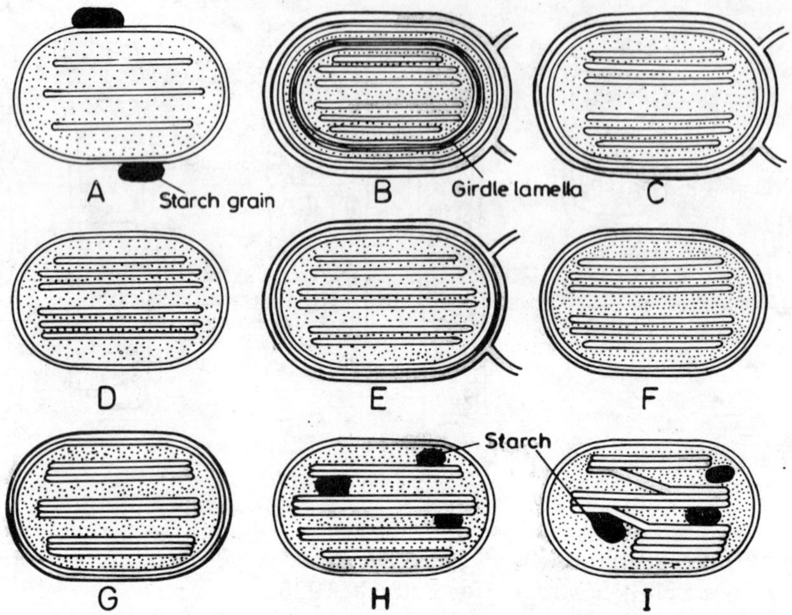

Fig. 1-6 Chromatophore structure in various algal groups. A, Rhodophyceae, with extraplastic starch and single thylakoids; B, Chrysophyceae, Xanthophyceae, Bacillariophyceae, Phaeophyceae, Raphidophyceae, with girdle lamella; C, Haptophyceae, lacking girdle lamella; D, Eustigmatophyceae; E, Cryptophyceae; F, Dinophyceae, 3-membraned envelope; G, Euglenophyceae; H, Chlorophyceae, no grana formation; I, Chlorophyceae, Prasinophyceae, with grana formation. (After Taylor, 1977.)

The chromatophores are genetically semiautonomous systems containing histone-free DNA, messenger RNA, transfer RNA and ribosomes. Besides, new chloroplasts always arise from pre-existing ones. These features have made it highly probable that chromatophores are subcellular symbionts which had their origin in free-living photosynthetic procaryotes.

Colourless Algae

Some algae are colourless, probably through loss of pigments during evolution. A few algae, e.g., *Polytoma uvella, Polytomella agilis, Prototheca zopfii,* and *Astasia longa*, are incapable of synthesizing chlorophylls but are capable of carotenoid biosynthesis. However, these species do possess some plastid-like structures. Some others, e.g., *Oxyrrhis marina, Crypthecodinium cohnii, Katodinium glandulum,* and *Paraphysomonas vestita,* seem to lack any plastidic structure. The colourless cryptomonad *Chilomonas paramecium*, though not synthesizing any pigments, does retain some proplastid-like organelles. Figure 1-7 illustrates two colourless algae.

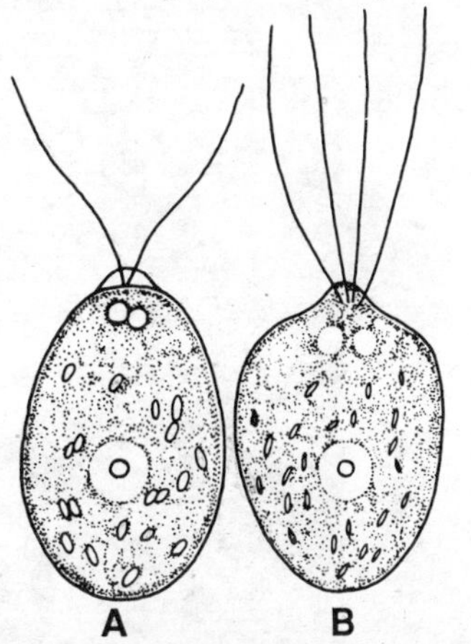

Fig. 1-7 Two colourless Chlorophyceae. A, *Polytoma papillatum*; B, *Polytomella* sp.

PYRENOIDS

These proteinaceous organelles occur within the chromatophores of most eucaryotic algae. The main chemical constituent of most pyrenoids is the enzyme ribulose bisphosphate carboxylase (Rubisco). Their general function is to convert the early (soluble) products of photosynthesis to storage products. Thus, they store starch in the green algae and concentrate some related food reserve in other algae. In some algae, however, the pyrenoids do not seem to be visibly associated with reserve polysaccharides.

NUCLEI AND CHROMOSOMES

Most eucaryotic algae have typical, organized nuclei, nucleoli, and chromosomes. In dinoflagellates, a nuclear membrane is present; during mitosis, the chromosomes of dinoflagellates attach to the nuclear membrane rather than to the spindle directly, and they lack centromere.

The nucleus is bounded by two unit membranes of which the outer is continuous with the membranes of the endoplasmic reticulum. The nucleus envelope is traversed by numerous pores. In the Tribophyceae, Chrysophyceae, Bacillariophyceae, and Phaeophyceae, the nuclear envelope is intimately associated with a sac of the endoplasmic reticulum found around the chromatophores but no such plastid endoplasmic reticulum is met with in the Chlorophyta and Rhodophyceae. The interphase nuclei of most eucaryotic algae contain uncoiled and expanded chromosomes, but in the Euglenophyceae and Dinophyceae, the chromosomes, which lack centromeres, remain condensed. According to Leedale (1970), the persistence of the nuclear wall during mitosis, the attachment of chromosomes to the nuclear wall, the lack of centromeres, and the absence of a compact spindle are primitive features.

The cells of most algae are uninucleate but those of the Cladophorales, Siphonales, Heterosiphonales, and Charales are multinucleate. The position, shape, and size of the nuclei are quite variable.

The nucleoli and chromosomes remain suspended in the granular matrix of the nucleus. In general, there is a single nucleolus per nucleus but in the Conjugales, for instance, there may be several nucleoli in a nucleus.

In the Euglenophyceae, the nuclear membrane and nucleolus persist throughout the division cycle, whereas in most other algae, the nucleoli break up during division and are reorganized after the completion of the nuclear division by a nucleolar organizing chromosome.

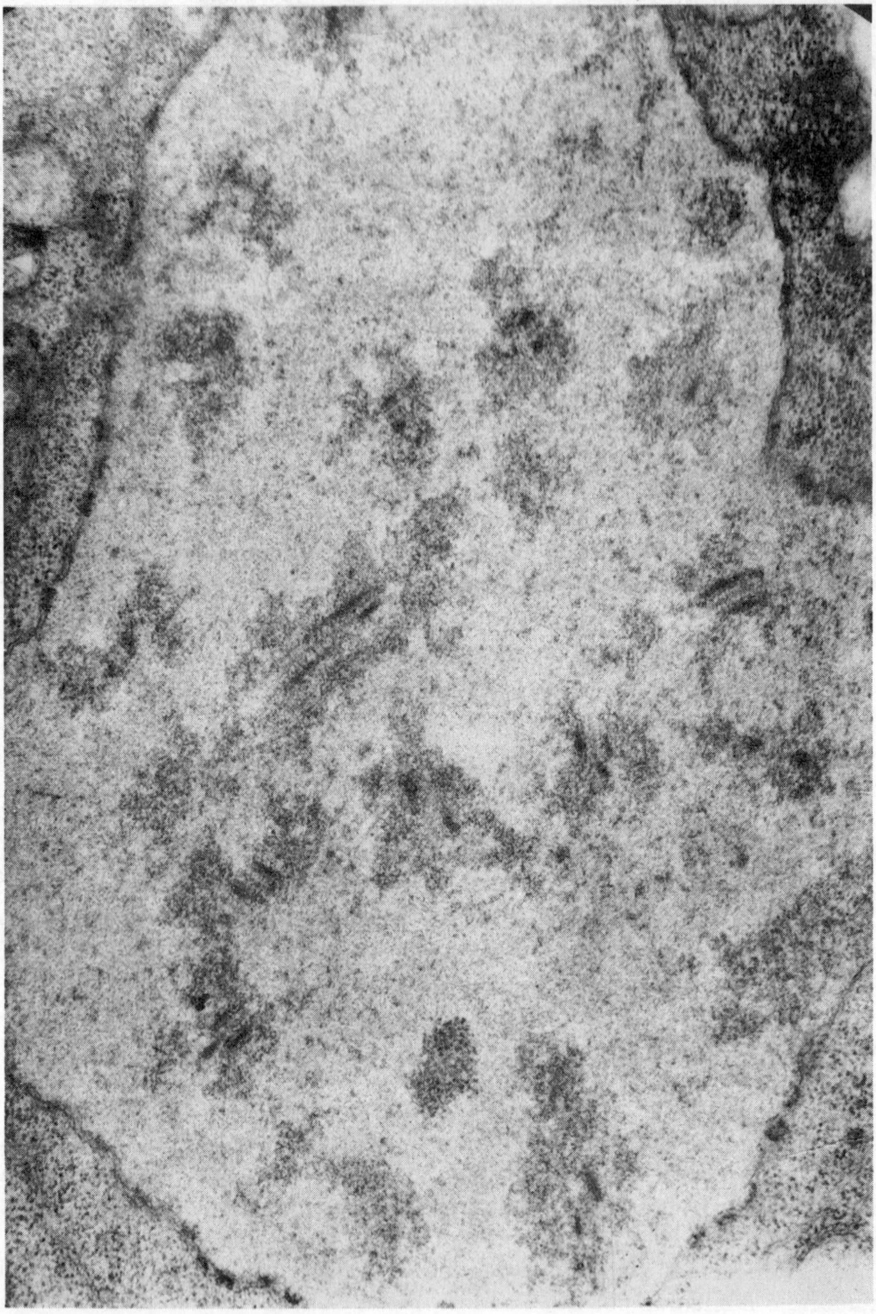

Fig. 1-8 *Janczewskia gardneri,* section through nucleus of tetraspore mother cell showing synaptonemal complexes. (Approx. ×50,000.) *Courtesy* P. Kugrens..

In some species of *Spirogyra* and *Zygnema*, the nucleolar organizing chromosomes are associated with satellite chromosomes. The nuclear division may or may not be accompanied by wall formation. In the Conjugales, the chromosomes have diffused centromeres.

Characteristic synaptonemal complexes occur in the meiotic nuclei of some red and brown algae. Under the electron microscope, a synaptonemal complex consists of two lateral longitudinal rods (Fig. 1-8) which give rise transversely to minute fibrils extending inward. Each such complex is believed to correspond to a bivalent. The existence of synaptonemal complexes is the most reliable evidence for meiosis not only in algae but also in higher plants.

KARYOLOGY

As a group, the algae show a wide range of variation in the shape, size, and organization of the interphase nuclei. Three kinds of nuclei, viz., dinocaryotic, nocticaryotic, and eucaryotic, occur within a single class Dinophyceae (Sarma, 1983). The dinocaryotic nucleus has condensed chromosomes at interphase, whereas the nocticaryotic nuclear chromosomes are relaxed at interphase. The vegetative cells of *Noctiluca* have nocticaryotic nucleus, whereas its gametes have dinocaryotic nucleus. In the binucleate cells of *Glenodinium foliaceum* and *Peridinium balticum,* one nucleus is dinocaryotic and the other eucaryotic. A unique aspect of the dinocaryon is the lack of histones in the chromosomes.

The algal nuclei may or may not exhibit chromocentres. The greatest variation in nucleolar structure occurs in the desmids.

The chromosomes of the Charales, Oedogoniales, and Cladophorales are fairly large, having localized centromeres. Most members of the Volvocales, Chlorococcales, Ulothrichales, Siphonales, and Bacillariophyceae have quite small, dot-shaped chromosomes.

The smallest chromosome number ($n = 2$) is reported in *Spirogyra* and the largest ($n = 600$) in a species of *Gymnodinium*. The Cladophorales and Charophyceae tend to show mostly euploid chromosome numbers ($x = 6$ or $x = 3$ or 7 respectively), aneuploidy being exceptional in the former and uncommon in the latter.

The variety of mitotic patterns seen in diverse eucaryotic algae is quite large and complex. Nuclear division involves a microtubular spindle which is associated with one or more microtubule organizing centres. In the dinoflagellates and some colourless flagellates, the spindle remains extranuclear throughout mitosis. In other eucaryotic algae, the spindle remains within the nucleoplasm during some part of mitosis. The green algae have spindles of two basically different types, viz., (1) those that persist at telophase, and (2) those that collapse at telophase. In the diatoms, the spindle originates outside the nucleus and later sinks into the nucleus (Tippit and Pickett-Heaps, 1977).

Sometimes, quite distinct patterns are seen in different taxa belonging to the same class. Thus, in the Prasinophyceae, *Pedinomonas minor* shows a completely intranuclear division as its nuclear envelope remains intact; in *Platymonas subcordiformis*, the envelope is interrupted by polar fenestrae; and in *Pyramimonas parkeae,* mitosis is open as the nuclear envelope breaks down. Other examples of algae showing open mitosis include *Klebsormidium*, *Coleochaete*, and *Prymnesium*, and of those showing closed mitosis are *Vaucheria* and *Vacuolaria*.

In the Euglenophyceae, the nucleolus (endosome) persists throughout mitosis. In many other algae, it degenerates by the end of prophase.

The centrioles seem to act as centres for the origin of spindle microtubules in many algae.

Some algae show clear association of microtubules with nuclear envelope and, in some Dinophyceae, cytoplasmic microtubules penetrate into some nuclear tunnels.

MITOCHONDRIA

All eucaryotic algae contain mitochondria. *Micromonas* has one large mitochondrion per cell but most algae have several mitochondria per cell. A mitochondrion is a double-membraned organelle, the inner membrane being variously infolded, forming papillae or cristae (Fig. 1-9) which project into the lumen. In the Cryptophyceae, the cristae are typically flattened. Mitochondria are rich in respiratory enzymes and generate energy in the form of ATP (adenosine triphosphate). Like chloroplasts, they contain DNA and are genetically autonomous.

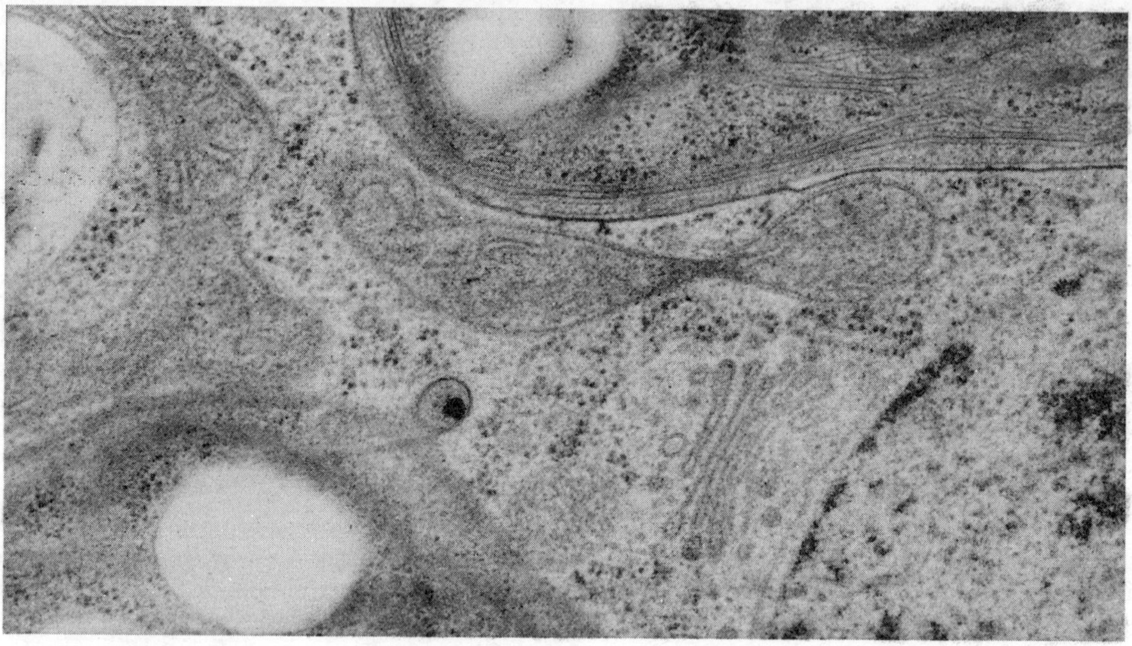

Fig. 1-9 *Scenedesmus acuminatus*, part of cell showing mitochondria, Golgi body, chloroplasts, and a portion of the nucleus, in freeze-substituted cell. (×54,000.) *Courtesy* K. Ueda.

Depending on their behaviour during the cell division cycle, the algal mitochondria can be classified into the following three types:

(1) Those that show drastic form change, appearing as a large, reticular structure at one stage and as minute rods at another stage of the cell cycle. Examples occur in *Euglena gracilis*, *Chlamydomonas reinhardii,* and *Chlorococcum infusionum* (Chida and Ueda, 1986).

(2) Those that are (a) small, spherical, (b) thread-like, branched, and (c) large, reticulated, and coexist through the entire cycle. The best known example is *Polytoma*.

(3) Those that remain single, conspicuous, and reticular all through the cycle. Examples include *Chlorella, Pyramimonas*, and *Friedmannia*.

GOLGI BODIES

Structurally, the Golgi apparatus is an association of stacks of smooth lamellae or cisternae in which each stack is referred to as a dictyosome and consists of 2–20 cisternae. In cells having a single dictyosome, the Golgi apparatus is equivalent to one dictyosome. The dictyosomes may be located near the chromatophore, the flagellar base, or the nucleus. Very prominent dictyosomes occur along the periphery of the chloroplast in some desmids (Fig. 1-10).

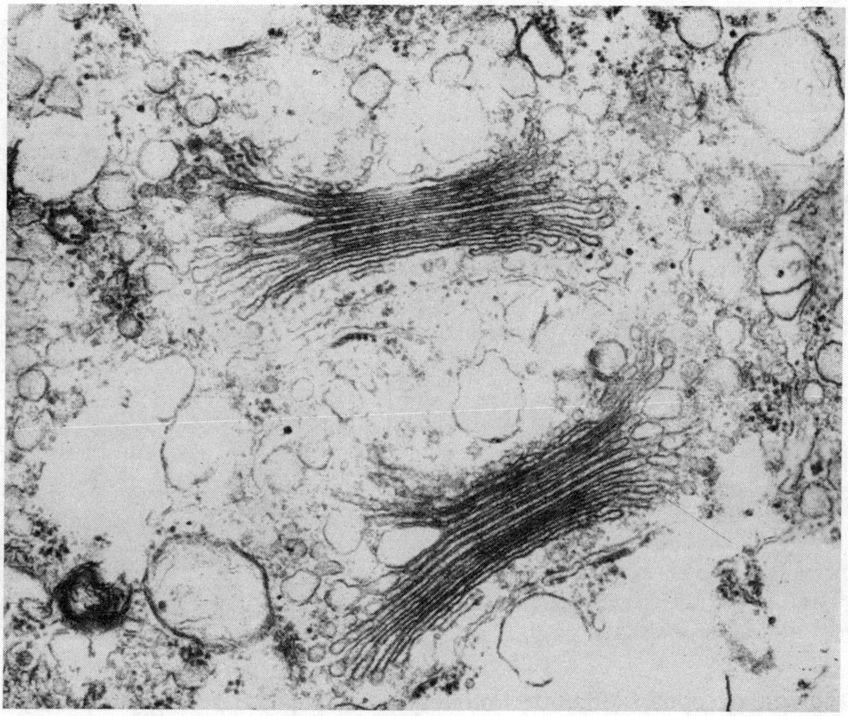

Fig. 1-10 *Micrasterias crux-melitensis*, part of cell showing dictyosomes. (×37,500.) *Courtesy* K. Ueda.

The Chrysophyceae typically have a single, large, compact Golgi body which lies closely against the nuclear envelope with its distal end directed towards the flagellar basal bodies. The dictyosomes are involved in the formation of the scales in some green algae, Chrysophyceae, and Prymnesiophyceae, and also in the formation of wall in Chrysophyceae and Bacillariophyceae.

The Golgi bodies of red algae display a high level of structural organization. Those of *Corallina* and *Jania* are unique in that there is close apposition of the membranes of adjacent cisternae. There are also some indications of the occurrence of fusions between the outer portion of the adjacent cisternal membranes.

EYESPOT (STIGMA)

The motile, flagellated cells of algae have a pigmented organelle called the eyespot. The eyespot is a tight assemblage of orange coloured lipid globules. The eyespot of *Chlamydomonas reinhardii* consists of two parallel rows of globules (Fig. 1-11), and between the two rows are two thylakoids running longitudinally through the eyespot and continued into the thylakoids of the chloroplast. These globules shade the photoreceptor which is commonly a rod-shaped or crystalline area near the flagellar axoneme. The photoreceptor is involved in the phototactic response.

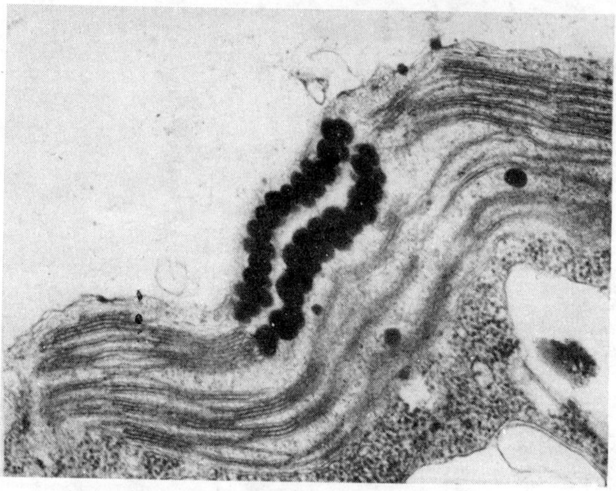

Fig. 1-11 *Eudorina*, eyespot. (×35,000.) *Courtesy* K. Ueda.

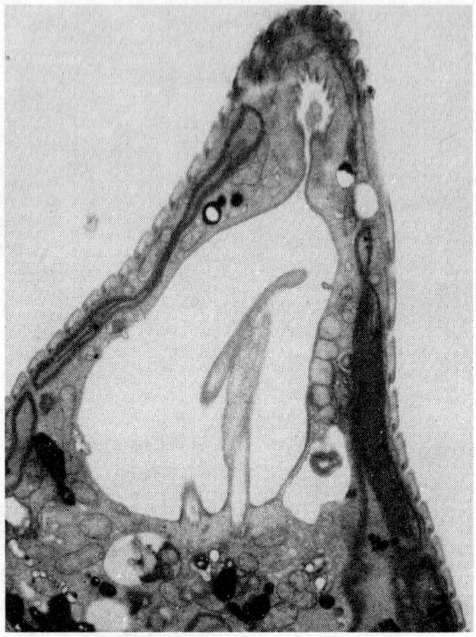

Fig. 1-12 *Euglena*, reservoir, eyespot, flagella, and vacuoles. (×7000.) *Courtesy* K. Ueda.

The eyespot in the Chlorophyceae, Cryptophyceae, Chrysophyceae, Tribophyceae, and Phaeophyceae lies embedded within the chloroplast. In the Euglenophyceae and Eustigmatophyceae, it exists independently and outside the chloroplast in the cytoplasm.

In the Dinophyceae, three types of simple eyespot occur. *Woloszynskia coronata* has an independent eyespot which is not membrane-bound. In *Glenodinium foliaceum*, the eyespot is an independent structure but is surrounded by three membranes. In *Peridinium cinctum* and several other dinoflagellates, the eyespot forms part of a chloroplast (Dodge, 1984), adjacent to the flagella, as in Chrysophyceae. In all cases, the eyespot is situated behind the longitudinal groove of the dinoflagellate and there is a strand of microtubules between the eyespot and the cell covering (theca).

ENDOPLASMIC RETICULUM

A system of tubules and vesicles traversing the cytoplasm and termed the endoplasmic reticulum is present in all eucaryotic algal cells. These tubules appear to have some ribosomes disposed along their surface. The function of these ribosomes is to synthesize proteins or enzymes.

VACUOLES

The mature cells of eucaryotic algae have one or more vacuoles bounded by distinct membranes. These vacuoles play an important role in osmotic relations and the absorption of solutes and water.

In motile algae, two types of vacuolar apparatus are recognized, namely, (1) the simple vacuoles, called contractile vacuoles, which contract periodically and expel their contents to the exterior as in the green algae; and (2) the complex apparatus, which consists of a cytopharynx (canal), a reservoir, and a group of vacuoles of varying size (Fig. 1-12) as is characteristic of the Euglenophyceae and Dinophyceae and some members of the Chrysophyceae. The smaller vacuoles feed their contents into one larger vacuole which then empties and releases the contents into the reservoir. A periodical contraction of the reservoir then expels the contents to the outside through the cytopharynx. In some holozoic algae, the cytopharynx functions as a gullet (for ingesting food particles) besides being an emptying canal for the vacuoles.

EJECTISOMES

Many flagellates contain ejectile organelles. Some of these are sac-like bodies that produce and release mucilage. *Chattonella* (Chloromonadophyceae) produces some mucus which contains palmitic acid and can kill fish. Others may be discoidal or rolled up ribbons. The ejectile bodies of the dinoflagellate *Nematodinium* are so elaborate that they resemble the nematocysts of coelenterates and may possibly function in prey capture. This idea is supported by the presence of distinct ocelli which partly resemble the "eyes" of lower invertebrates.

The ejectisomes of *Chilomonas* and other cryptomonads typically occur in two sizes. The smaller ones, prior to ejection, occur in close association with the plasma membrane of the outer body surface. In contrast, the larger ejectisomes are associated with the gullet membrane. The two types further differ in respect of their intramembrane particle distribution. In small ejectisomes, the portion of the membrane in contact with the cell's plasmalemma has a rosette of fine particles; these ejectisomes and the plasma membrane both contain clumps of particles a short distance from the site of contact (called the docking site). The larger ejectisomes seem to lack rosettes (Grim and Staehelin, 1984). The particle clumps of *Chilomonas* broadly resemble the clusters of intramembrane particles of *Tetrahymena*; these latter particles are involved in the attachment of mucocysts to the plasma membrane.

SEPTA

The cross walls between adjacent cells of filamentous or parenchymatous thallus are known as septa. Each septum consists of a central core, the middle lamella, and a peripheral primary wall. The cell division usually takes place by transverse furrowing of the cytoplasm midway between the two extremities of a cell. Within the furrow, a transverse wall of pectic substance, known as the middle lamella, is first laid down; over this, the subsequent apposition layers (primary wall), consisting chiefly of cellulose, are deposited.

Septa may be complete or incomplete. The former are mainly of five types, viz., (1) plane, (2) replicate, (3) semireplicate, (4) colligate, and (5) unduliseptate (Fig. 1-13). The plane type has a homogeneous contour as in *Ulothrix*. In some species of *Spirogyra*, the middle lamella shows circular infoldings. If each of the adjoining cells has two infolds in opposite directions, then the septum is called replicate, and if less there is only a single infold in alternate positions, it is semireplicate. The colligate septum is an H-shaped cross wall as seen in *Microspora*. In the unduliseptate type, the middle lamella is much expanded and has a wavy, undulating margin, as in *Spirogyra undulisepta*.

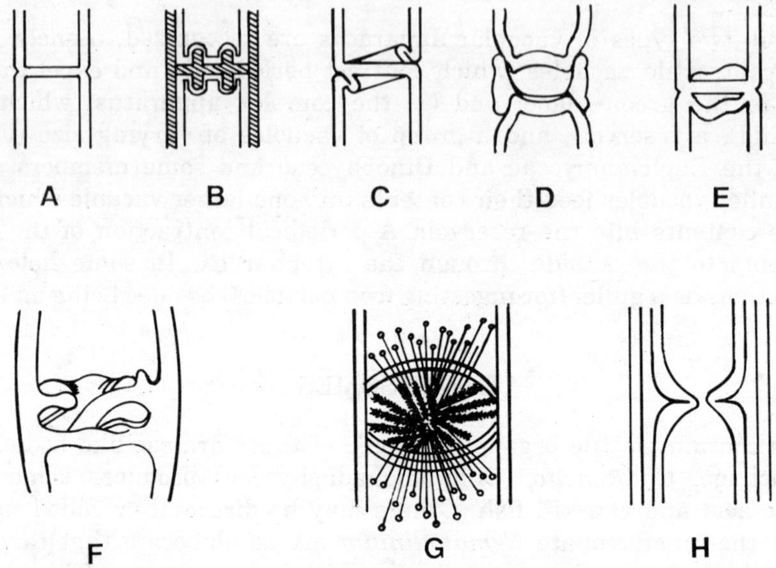

Fig. 1-13 Types of septa. A, plane; B, replicate; C, semireplicate; D, colligate; E, unduliseptate; F, *Sphaeroplea*, thick septum showing finger-shaped processes; G, *Sphaeroplea*, septum in surface view showing central opening; H, pitted septum. (Figs. A–E after Randhawa, 1959, F–H after Fritsch, 1935.)

The incomplete septum is found in most Rhodophyceae and Cyanophyceae. It has a central opening called a pit through which the cytoplasm of adjacent cells remains connected (Fig. 1-13). In *Sphaeroplea* (Chlorophyceae), the septa are made of radiating ingrowths of side walls which fail to meet in the centre and form a central opening (Fig. 1-13). During cell division in *Oedogonium*, a septum is laid down across the middle of the cell and remains unconnected with the side walls (i.e., free-floating) for some time.

Except for the plane septa, the other septa are thought to assist in the fragmentation of the filaments. An alteration in the turgor pressure inside the cell leads to the development of a shearing strain in the cross wall which finally ruptures, resulting in fragmentation of the filament.

Algae range in size from single cells just 1 μm in diameter to giant kelps over 30 metres long. Unicellular algae may be solitary or colonial, free-living or attached, with or without a protective cover, and motile or nonmotile. Colonies may be irregular or with some distinctive pattern; the latter are called coenobia and may be motile or nonmotile. Multicellular algae may form packets, filaments, laminae, or complex pseudoparenchymatous or parenchymatous thalli which may have structures resembling roots, stems, and leaves. Some algae are coenocytic; they range from microscopic spheres (e.g., *Botrydium*) to large macroscopic thalli having fairly complex anatomical differentiation of tissues.

While many algae are microscopic, quite a few are macroscopic. Macroalgae belong mostly to the benthic, marine forms of Rhodophyceae, Phaeophyceae, and Chlorophyceae. Though freshwater, all Charophyceae are macroscopic. Most other algal classes are dominated by microalgae but there are several exceptions: *Hydrurus* (Chrysophyceae), *Tribonema* and *Vaucheria* (Xanthophyceae), *Navicula ulvacea* (Bacillariophyceae), *Hydrodictyon, Draparnaldiopsis*, and *Cladophora* (Chlorophyceae) are a few examples of macroalgae.

Algal life histories range from binary fission in some unicells to a sequence of four multicellular somatic phases in several red algae, involving highly specialized reproductive organs. Some algae are highly plastic in respect of life history in the sense that they can bypass one or other stage by recycling, apogamy, apospory, pedogenesis, parthenogenesis, and vegetative propagation; they sometimes produce special microscopic stages in response to seasonal or occasional changes in the environment (Wynne and Loiseaux, 1976). Some benthic marine algae resort to different patterns of life history in different parts of their geographical range, probably being influenced by temperatures and light regimes.

RANGE OF THALLUS STRUCTURE

The organization of thallus in algae is basically of two types, the unicellular and the multicellular. The wide range of forms that algae exhibit arises from a modification or elaboration of these types. The cells of a multicellular thallus may be loosely held together by a mucilaginous matrix or cemented together through middle lamellae. During its growth cycle, an alga passes through two phases, the vegetative or developmental, and the reproductive or multiplicative. In unicellular algae, the growth in size constitutes the vegetative phase, whereas the increase in cell numbers by cell division constitutes the reproductive phase. In multicellular thalli, both the vegetative and the reproductive phases involve cell division and cell growth.

UNICELLULAR HABIT

All phyla except the Phaeophyta include unicellular forms which may be motile or nonmotile. The motile type is of two kinds, the flagellated kind, moving by means of flagella (found in all phyla except the Cyanophyceae, Prochlorophyceae, and Rhodophyceae), and the rhizopodial kind, having the fine protoplasmic projections (the rhizopodia) and showing an amoeboid movement (Tribophyceae and certain other algae; Fig. 1-14). The cell envelope of the rhizopodial forms is characteristically periplastic and rather soft, thus permitting extensive changes in the shape and size of the thallus. The flagellated forms may be periplastic, e.g., *Euglena* (Fig. 1-12), or may be provided with a definite cell wall, e.g., *Chlamydomonas*. External to the periplast, some flagellates have a special envelope which is provided with pores for the protrusion of the flagella. The calcareous envelope is separated from the cell proper by a space (Fig. 1-15). Such forms are known as the encapsulated forms. In some of these forms, the capsule may become calcareous.

The nonmotile or coccoid type includes forms of diverse shape and size. They are provided with a rigid cell wall and are nonflagellated. Some typical examples are *Chlorella* (Chlorophyta; Fig. 12-30) and *Synechocystis* (Cyanophyta). In *Spirulina* (Cyanophyta), the cell is elongated into a helical filament (Fig. 14-16). The smallest known eucaryotic alga is probably *Micromonas pusilla* (about 1.0 × 1.5 μm).

The dinoflagellates provide good examples of complex, unicellular habit (Fig. 1-16), especially those species which have laterally inserted flagella. The two dinokont flagella occur in surface furrows. One of these passes around the cell. The ribbon-like (transverse) flagellum is placed in this furrow, which is called the cingulum or girdle. The second furrow (termed the sulcus) runs posteriorly and is associated with the longitudinal flagellum. The edges of these grooves in thecate dinoflagellates are usually raised into flanges (called lists). These lists are especially well developed and elaborately patterned in dinophysoid dinoflagellates in which they are modified into wings,

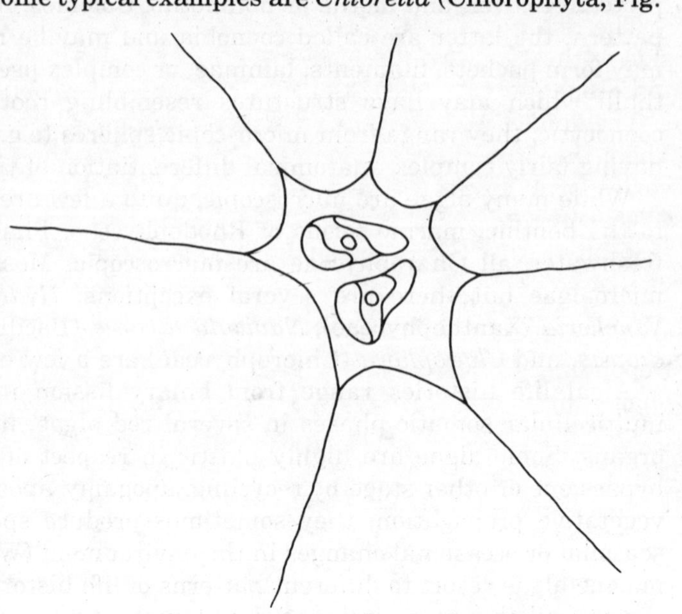

Fig. 1.14 *Rhizochrysis dofleinii*, rhizopodia.

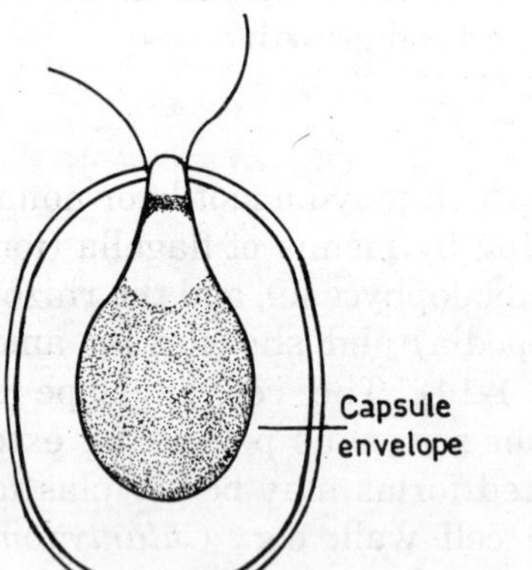

Fig. 1-15 *Phacotus*, cell showing motile encapsulated habit (after Fritsch, 1935).

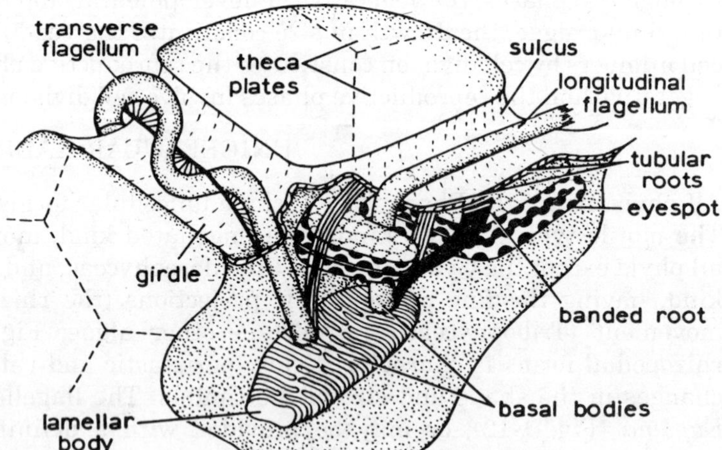

Fig. 1-16 Cell structure of dinoflagellate, showing complexity of organization.

keels, collars, or even chambers which house certain symbiotic, coccoid cyanobacteria (Taylor, 1976).

The placement of the girdle and sulcus in many dinoflagellates is asymmetrical: the left side of the girdle tends to be anteriorly displaced with reference to the right side. According to LeBlond and Taylor (1976), this asymmetry increases forward propulsion in the cells.

The dinoflagellates form some of the most elaborate internal walls known among the algae. Their theca (wall) is made of numerous plates perforated with pores. The plate thickness varies inversely with the number of plates formed. Outside the plates, certain peripheral vesicles occur in many species and are called amphiesmal vesicles. Many or all pores may be associated near the base with a trichocyst.

MULTICELLULAR HABIT

Depending on the manner in which cells are produced and arranged during the vegetative phase, three principal types of habit are recognized—colonial, filamentous, and siphoneous.

COLONIAL HABIT

A colony is a group of separate cells generally similar in structure and function and aggregated by a mucilaginous envelope. On the basis of morphology, there are four main types of colonial organization—coenobial, palmelloid, dendroid, and rhizopodial. A coenobium has a definite number of cells arranged in a particular manner which is determined at the juvenile stage and does not increase during its subsequent growth even though the cells enlarge. The coenobium may be motile or nonmotile. In the motile kind, the cells are flagellated, e.g., *Volvox*. In the nonmotile type, the cells are coenocytic, e.g., *Hydrodictyon* (Fig. 1-17 A).

Unlike the coenobium, the palmelloid, dendroid, and rhizopodial types of colony are not of constant shape and size and their cells divide, leading to an increase in the size of the colony. In the palmelloid colonies, the vegetative cells are nonmotile and remain embedded in a mucilaginous matrix of irregular shape and size (Fig. 1-17 B). They become motile during

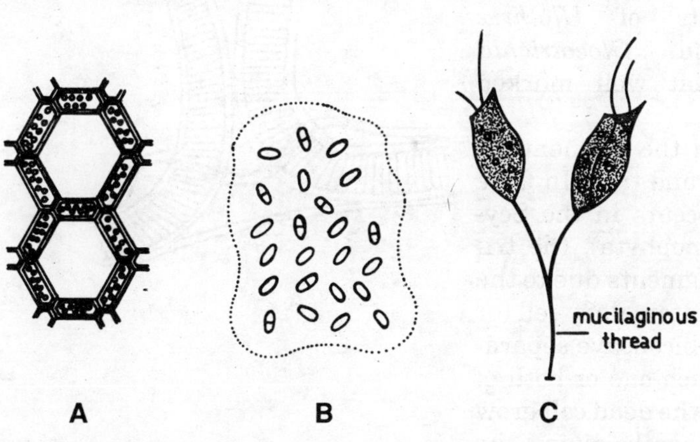

Fig. 1-17 Some colonial algae. A, *Hydrodictyon*, part of nonmotile colony; B, *Aphanothece*, palmelloid colony; C, *Chrysodendron,* dendroid colony (after Fritsch, 1935).

reproduction. The matrix is formed from the walls of individual daughter cells which gelatinize and mix together with the gelatinized walls of daughter cells embedded in the common matrix. Examples of palmelloid habit are met with in *Aphanothece* (Cyanophyta) and *Tetraspora* (Chlorophyta).

In the dendroid colonies, the cells are united in a branching manner by localized production of mucilage at the base of each cell (Fig. 1-17 C). The whole colony looks like a tree in habit. Such an organization is found in *Ecballocystis* (Chlorophyta) and *Chrysodendron* (Chrysophyta).

The cells of rhizopodial colonies are united through rhizopodia, as in *Chrysidiastrum* (Chrysophyta).

Many colonial algae are strongly phototactic as they swim rapidly and respond immediately to changes in light direction. These algae can swim at speeds much faster than the speed of those unicellular algae that are comparable to the individual cells of the colony. The basis of the increased speed is the Stokes law which states that the speed of a body in a viscous medium is directly proportional to the propulsive force and inversely proportional to the viscous resistance. The propulsive force is proportional to the number of flagellated cells in the colony (i.e., to its area). Since the area is known to increase as the square of the radius, and the viscosity increases only as the first power of the radius, the swimming speed will increase as the radius of the colony increases.

FILAMENTOUS HABIT

A uniseriate row of cells joined end to end in a transverse plane through middle lamellae constitutes a filament. Such a habit arises as a result of vegetative divisions being restricted to the transverse plane. In the Cyanophyta, a filament includes both the trichome (i.e., the uniseriate row of cells) and its sheath. The filaments may be unbranched or branched. The unbranched filaments of *Ulothrix* (Chlorophyta) and *Gloeotrichia* (Cyanophyta) exhibit well marked polarity.

The branching of the filaments is of two kinds—false and true. In false branching, which occurs in the Scytonemataceae (Cyanophyta), the trichome generally fragments due to the degeneration of an intercalary cell (or by the formation of biconcave separation discs) after which one or both of its ends adjacent to the dead cell grow out of the parent sheath, giving the semblance of branching (Fig. 1-18 A). Sometimes, false branching may

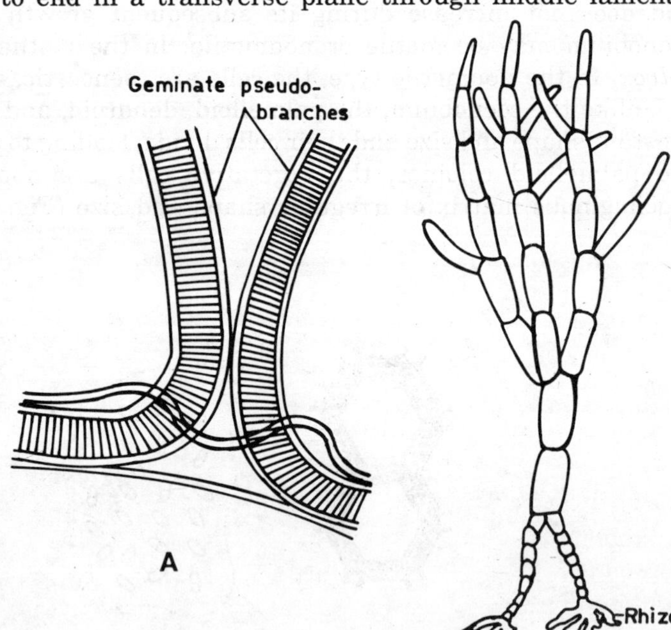

Fig. 1-18 Branched filamentous algae. A, *Scytonema*, pseudobranching; B, *Cladophora*, true branching.

arise through loop formation. In this method, a group of intercalary cells of the trichome becomes meristematic and for a time continues to divide at two localized points, leading to the formation of a loop. The top (middle) cell of the loop finally degenerates, setting free the two arms of the loop as a pair of pseudobranches.

True branching results from repeated transverse divisions of the lateral outgrowths produced by a few or many scattered cells of the main filament. The truly branched thalli are of four types, namely, (1) simple branched filament, e.g., *Cladophora* (Fig. 1-18 B); (2) heterotrichous, in which the thallus is differentiated into an erect and a prostrate system of branched filaments (Fig. 12-58); (3) parenchymatous; and (4) pseudoparenchymatous, in which the thalli show uniaxial or multiaxial construction.

The heterotrichous habit is the most highly evolved type of filamentous construction in algae. During its development, a system of branched creeping filaments is produced first and functions as the holdfast. These creeping filaments give rise to a system of erect branched filaments. More or less equally well developed prostrate and erect systems are found in *Stigeoclonium* (Chlorophyta) and *Ectocarpus* (Phaeophyta). The more advanced heterotrichous thalli show a progressive reduction or elimination of either the prostrate system (e.g., *Draparnaldiopsis*) (Fig. 1-19) or the erect system (e.g., *Coleochaete scutata*) (Fig. 1-20).

The parenchymatous habit is a further variant of the filamentous construction and results from vegetative divisions taking place in more than one plane followed by the failure of the division products to separate. Examples are met with in *Ulva* (Fig. 1-21), *Prasiola* (Chlorophyceae), and *Porphyra* (Rhodophyceae). Some of the largest known algae, e.g., the kelps (Laminariales, Phaeophyta), which can be as large as 60 m, are parenchymatous.

The pseudoparenchymatous habit results from a close juxtaposition of the branched filaments of a single or many axial filaments. If branches from a single filament are involved, as in *Batrachospermum*, the thallus construction is spoken of as uniaxial. If branches of many axial filaments aggregate, the thallus is multiaxial, e.g., *Nemalion*.

The vegetative growth by cell division of filamentous and parenchymatous thalli occurs in five ways—diffuse, intercalary, trichothallic, apical, and basal. In simple filamentous forms such as *Ulothrix* and *Nostoc*, the growth of the thallus is diffuse because each vegetative cell is potentially capable of growth and division. A good example of intercalary growth is furnished by the Laminariales in which the growth of the thallus is brought about by the activity of a meristem located at the junction of the stipe and the blade. The trichothallic growth is also intercalary but the meristem is located at the base of a terminal hair, e.g., in the Rivulariaceae and Cutleriales. The thalli of the Charophyceae, Dictyotales, and certain other algae grow by the activity of a single or a group of apical cells. *Bulbochaete* (Chlorophyta) exemplifies basal growth.

SIPHONEOUS HABIT

A siphoneous thallus is multinucleate and lacks septation except during the formation of reproductive organs. The simplest form of such an organization is found in *Protosiphon* (Chlorophyceae) and *Botrydium* (Tribophyceae), both having a vesicular, unicellular thallus attached to the substratum by a simple or branched rhizoid. In *Vaucheria* (Fig. 1-22), the siphoneous filament is branched; advanced members of the Siphonales (Chlorophyceae) show uniaxial and multiaxial forms.

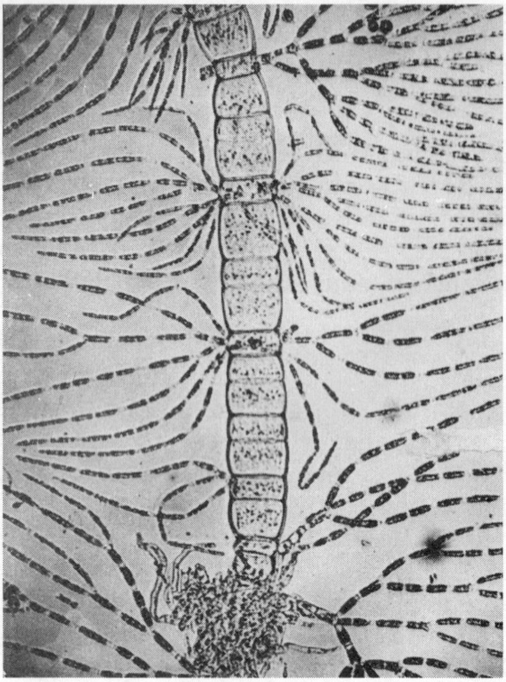

Fig. 1-19 *Draparnaldiopsis indica*, branches, nodal and internodal cells, and cortication of main axis. *Courtesy* Y.B.K. Chowdary.

Fig. 1-20 *Coleochaete scutata*, material from nature showing reniform outline of thallus. *Courtesy* Y.B.K. Chowdary.

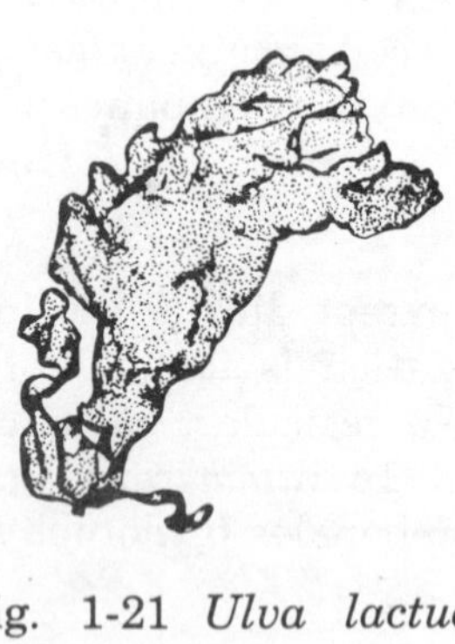

Fig. 1-21 *Ulva lactuca*, habit.

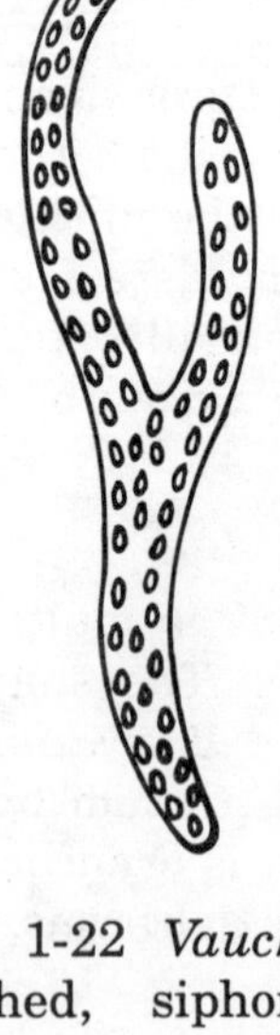

Fig. 1-22 *Vaucheria*, branched, siphoneous habit.

CLASSIFICATION, EVOLUTION, AND PHYLOGENETIC RELATIONS

Before the advent of electron microscopy in the 1950s, the algae were studied with optical light microscopes and classified primarily on the basis of their photosynthetic pigments, storage products in vegetative cells, chemical nature of cell walls, and the morphology (as seen with light microscopes) of the motile reproductive cells. Unlike bryophytes and higher plants, the morphology of the mature vegetative stages did not afford a reliable criterion for distinguishing different classes or phyla of algae. Consequently, several examples became known where morphologically similar algae are placed in different classes or phyla because of their varying physiological and biochemical characters (Table 1-5). Such a classification of morphologically similar but physiologically dissimilar forms in different classes is based on the view that there has been a parallelism in their evolution.

The great range of diversity of the algae has hampered the definition, characterization, and classification of these organisms in any universally acceptable taxonomic manner. Consequently, there now exist perhaps as many different systems of classification (i.e., the numbers and kinds of classes, phyla, and supraphyletic assemblages) as there are the leading phycologists.

The structural diversity ranges from the simple unicellular motile or nonmotile green algae to the gigantic thalloidal-branched brown algae. Nutritionally, the algae range from free-living autotrophic forms containing a variety of photosynthetic pigments (Table 1-2) or heterotrophic forms to some saprotrophic and truly parasitic forms. Figure 1-23 shows some of the nutritional modes encountered in algae (and also other microorganisms) and also how organisms use the available energy sources. In reproduction (Chapter 2), a rather simple binary fission or complicated polymorphic life cycles with budding or spore formation may be met with. Meiosis may be gametic, zygotic or sporic.

One of the best known systems was proposed by Fritsch (1935, 1945) who divides the algae into 11 classes. Bold and Wynne (1978) recognize the following divisions: Cyanochloronta, Chlorophycophyta, Charophyta, Euglenophycophyta, Phaeophycophyta, Chrysophycophyta, Pyrrhophycophyta, Cryptophycophyta, and Rhodophycophyta. Van den Hoek and Jahns (1978) classified the algae into 9 divisions, namely, Cyanophyta, Rhodophyta, Heterokontophyta (including Phaeophyceae, Chrysophyceae, Xanthophyceae, Bacillariophyceae, and Chloromonadophyceae), Haptophyta, Eustigmatophyta, Cryptophyta, Dinophyta, Euglenophyta, and Chlorophyta (including all green plants; green algae are treated as a subdivision Chlorophytina).

When the results of electron microscopic studies of many algae were published, several then unknown details of the fine structure and organelles were revealed and taken into account by modern phycologists in proposing newer systems of classification based on a combination of classical criteria and ultrastructural aspects. It has also been realized that micromorphological characters are much more conservative, in the evolutionary sense, than characters associated with macromorphology (i.e., the whole organism). Among the algae, the classification of the lower taxa (up to the family level) tends to be based heavily on the macromorphological attributes, whereas the conservative micromorphological characters tend to be used more in the primary classification of the orders, classes, and divisions.

A few of the proposals which take micromorphological characters also into account are now given.

Table 1-5 Parallelism in evolution in algal construction

Habit	Chlorophyceae	Tribophyceae	Chrysophyceae	Cryptophyceae	Dinophyceae	Cyanophyceae	Phaeophyceae	Rhodophyceae
Motile unicell	*Chlamydomonas*	*Heterochloris*	*Chromulina*	*Cryptomonas*	*Gymnodinium*			
Motile colony	*Eudorina*		*Synura*		*Polykrikos*			
Dendroid colony	*Ecballocystis*	*Mischococcus*	*Dinobryon*					
Palmelloid colony	*Tetraspora*	*Botryococcus**	*Phaeocystis*		*Gloeodinium*	*Aphanocapsa*		
Coccoid	*Chlorococcum*	*Chlorobotrys*	*Chrysosphaera*	*Tetragonidium*	*Cystodinium*	*Chroococcus*		*Porphyridium*
Simple filament	*Ulothrix*	*Tribonema*	*Nematochrysis*		*Dinothrix*	*Oscillatoria*		*Erythrotrichia*
Branched filament	*Cladophora*	*Monocilia*	*Phaeothamnion*			*Mastigocladus*		
Heterotrichous	*Stigeoclonium*					*Hapalosiphon*	*Ectocarpus*	
Siphoneous	*Protosiphon*	*Botrydium*						
Pseudoparenchymatous								
Uniaxial							*Spermatochnus*	*Batrachospermum*
Multiaxial	*Codium*						*Leathesia*	*Nemalion*
Parenchymatous	*Ulva*						*Punctaria*	*Porphyra*

**Botryococcus* is now commonly placed in the Chlorophyceae.

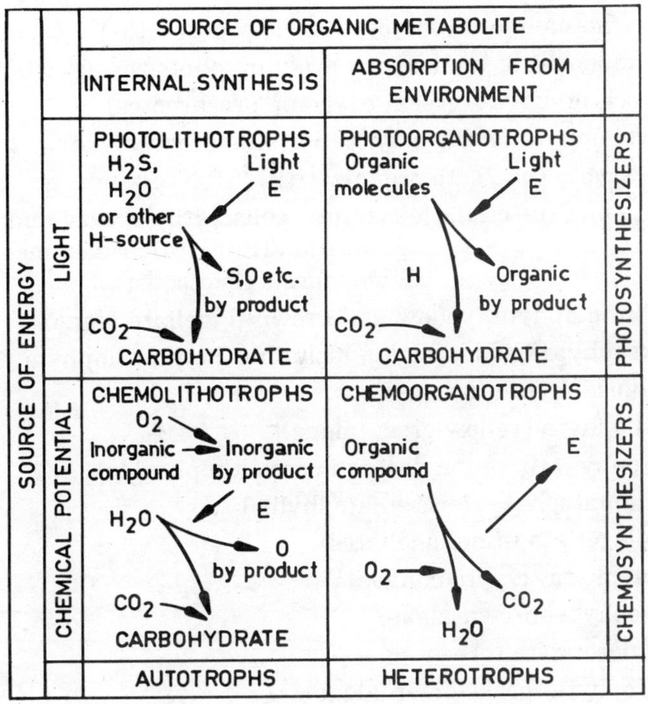

Fig. 1-23 Illustration of various nutritional types, and how organisms exploit energy sources.

Round (1973) recognized the following algal groups: Cyanophyta, Euglenophyta, Chlorophyta, Charophyta, Prasinophyta, Xanthophyta, Eustigmatophyceae, Dinophyta, Bacillariophyta, Chrysophyta, Phaeophyta, Rhodophyta, and Cryptophyta.

Lee (1980) classified the algae into the following six divisions: (1) Cyanophyta (Cyanophyceae); (2) Glaucophyta; (3) Chromophyta (Euglenophyceae, Dinophyceae, Cryptophyceae, Chrysophyceae, Prymnesiophyceae, Bacillariophyceae, Raphidophyceae, Xanthophyceae, Eustigmatophyceae, and Phaeophyceae); (4) Rhodophyta (Rhodophyceae); (5) Chlorophyta (Chlorophyceae); and (6) Charophyta (Charophyceae). Lee's classification relies heavily on the fine structural aspects of such organelles as chloroplast, endoplasmic reticulum, flagellum, eyespot, and nucleus.

In their monumental compilation, Rosowski and Parker (1982) recognize the following 16 classes: (1) Cyanophyceae, (2) Prochlorophyceae, (3) Rhodophyceae, (4) Cryptophyceae, (5) Euglenophyceae, (6) Dinophyceae, (7) Chrysophyceae, (8) Prymnesiophyceae, (9) Bacillariophyceae, (10) Raphidophyceae (Chloromonadophyceae), (11) Tribophyceae (Xanthophyceae), (12) Eustigmatophyceae, (13) Phaeophyceae, (14) Prasinophyceae, (15) Chlorophyceae, and (16) Charophyceae.

Larkum and Barrett (1983) adopted the views of Whittaker and Margulis (1978) with some modifications. Their scheme is as follows:

Kingdom: Monera (procaryotic cells)
  Superphylum: Photomonera (photosynthetic procaryotes)
    Phylum: Photobacteria (nonoxygen-evolving photosynthetic bacteria)
    Phylum: Prochlorophyta (green, oxygenic procaryotes)
    Phylum: Cyanophyta or Cyanobacteria (blue-green algae)
Superkingdom: Eucaryota (nucleate organization)
  Kingdom: Protista or Protoctista [eucaryotic cells with solitary and colonial unicellular organization (Protista) or also including simpler multicellular forms (Protoctista)]
  Superphylum: Chromophyta (yellow and brown flagellate algae)
    Phylum: Chrysophyta (golden algae, including Prymnesiophyta and Chloromonadophyta
    Phylum: Bacillariophyta (diatoms)
    Phylum: Xanthophyta (yellow-green algae)
    Phylum: Haptophyta (haptophytes and coccolithophorids)
    Phylum: Eustigmatophyta (eustigmatophytes)
    Phylum: Dinoflagellata (dinoflagellates)
    Phylum: Cryptophyta (cryptomonads)
    Phylum: Phaeophyta (brown algae)
  Superphylum: Chlorophyta (green algae)
    Phylum: Chlorophyta (grass-green algae)
    Phylum: Siphonophyta (siphonaceous green algae)
    Phylum: Prasinophyta (prasinophytes)
    Phylum: Zygnematophyta (conjugating green algae)
    Phylum: Charophyta (stoneworts)
    Phylum: Euglenophyta (euglenoid flagellates)
  Superphylum: Rhodophyta (red algae)

At least the two classes, Eustigmatophyceae and Prymnesiophyceae, owe their creation substantially to the electron microscopic studies of their flagella.

Corliss (1987) places the algal protists in the following six series: (1) Chlorophyte, (2) Chromophyte, (3) Euglenozoa, (4) Pyrrhophyte, (5) Rhodophyte, and (6) Cryptophyte.

Series 1 (Chlorophyte) comprises both flagellated and nonmotile groups of green algae, including unicellular, coenobial, coenocytic, filamentous, and multicellular forms. This series contains the phyla Chlorophyta, Prasinophyta, Conjugatophyta, Charophyta, and (?) Ulvophyta. All these phyla share the following characters: chlorophyll-a and -b; flattened mitochondrial cristae; cellulosic cell walls; motile cells; true starch in plastids; arrangement of thylakoids in several layered grana; chloroplasts bounded by a double membrane; motile cells showing stellate structure in flagellar transition region; and cruciate flagellar root system. Sexuality is common and most groups are largely freshwater. Except for the Charophyta, the other phyla typically form a phycoplast in cytokinesis; in Charophyta, the phycoplast is replaced by a phragmoplast.

Series 2 (Chromophyte) is larger than the Chlorophyte. The motile members are typically biflagellated with one hairy and one smooth flagellum, but two exceptions to the typical condition are seen in diatoms and haptophytes. In fact, many diatoms altogether lack any flagellated stage in their life cycle. The phyla included in this series are Chrysophyta, Haptophyta, Bacillariophyta, Xanthophyta, Eustigmatophyta, Phaeophyta, and Raphidophyta. The common characters of these phyla are: chlorophyll-a and -c (only chlorophyll-a in Eustigmatophyta); tubular mitochondrial cristae; typically (exception: Phaeophyta) no cell walls but often scales; often silicified cysts; pair of heterokont flagella in the motile members; various storage reserves, e.g., chrysolaminarin; thylakoids grouped in threes; plastids bounded by three or four membranes; basal body transitional region showing helical structure; uncommon sexual reproduction; and predominantly marine in distribution.

Series 3 (Euglenophyte) is characterized by the following: chlorophyll-a and -b (though many species are colourless); unique pellicle underlaid by interlinked microtubules; single large mitochondrion having discoidal cristae; paraxial rod in flagella; nucleus with prominent endosome, permanently condensed chromosomes, and intranuclear spindle; presence of cytostome and a contractile vacuolar system; absence of cellulosic cell wall, storage starch, and probably also of sexuality.

Series 4 (Pyrrhophyte) has a distinctive nuclear apparatus, cortical alveoli, tubular mitochondrial cristae, trichocysts, and pusules. The series includes the dinoflagellates and pyrrhophytes. The members have chlorophyll-a and -c, with plastids generally covered by three membranes. They have two uniquely positioned, heterodynamic flagella.

Series 5 (Rhodophyte) includes the red algae and are characterized by the presence in their plastids of chlorophyll-a plus phycoerythrin and phycocyanin, with floridean starch as the storage product in the cytoplasm, and plastids being bound by two membranes and containing single thylakoids. In these algae, there is total absence of centrioles, basal bodies, and flagellated states. Their mitochondrial cristae are lamellar; cell walls are microfibrillar and gelatinous. Sexuality is common and meiosis is zygotic. These algae are distributed in both freshwater and marine habitats.

Series 6 (Cryptophyte) is characterized by the presence of chlorophyll-a and -c and phycobilins. The members are typically biflagellate with both flagella bearing tubular hairs. Their starch producing organelles, nucleomorphs, and plastids are collectively confined within a membrane system. Their mitochondrial cristae are lamellar. The cryptomonads have a distinct gullet and unique ejectisomes (also called extrusomes). Their mitosis is usually open (Corliss, 1987).

The system followed in this book is modified and partly adapted from several schemes including those of Silva (1980), Rosowski and Parker (1982), Parker (1982), Larkum and Barrett (1983), and Corliss (1987). However, contrary to the views of most contemporary phycologists, it is felt that some of the less studied or smaller classes, created largely or entirely on the basis of fine structural criteria, may, for the time being, be treated as classes rather than as independent phyla. Another scheme of classifying the algae is shown in Fig. 1-24.

Table 1-2 compares the diagnostic characters of some more important classes.

Far-reaching dramatic changes in the primary and secondary classification of living organisms have taken place during the past few years mainly as a consequence of strong inputs from molecular analyses of ribosomal RNA sequences. Also, contrary to the widely accepted classification of cellular organisms into procaryota and eucaryota, the living world is now usually divided into three superkingdoms, viz., Archaea (formerly archaebacteria); Eubacteria (including cyanobacteria or blue-green algae); and Eukarya (formerly eucaryota).

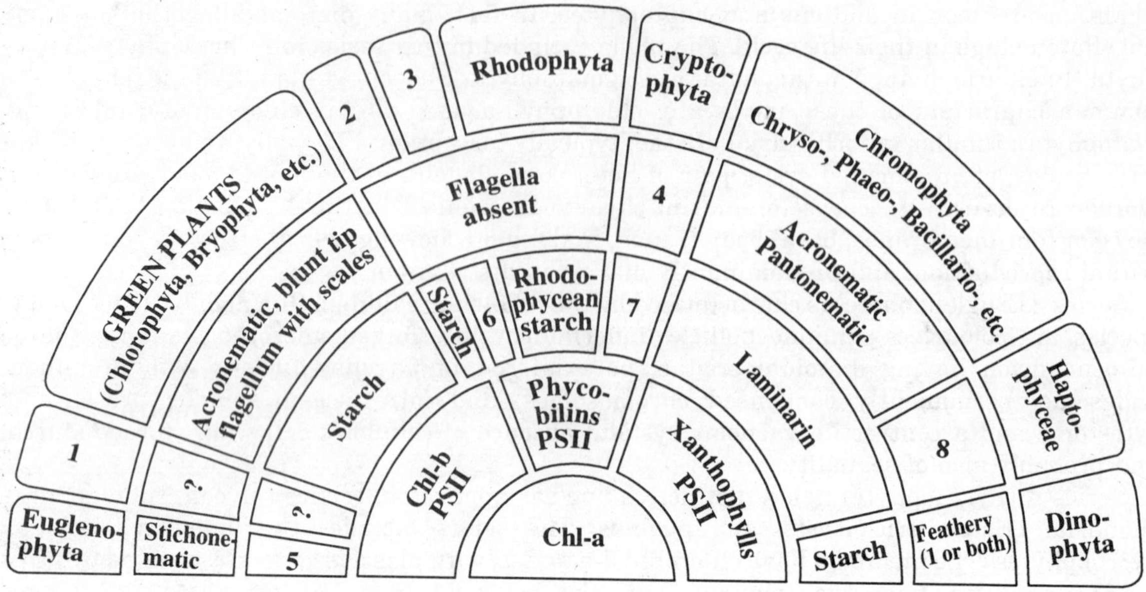

Fig. 1-24 Algal classification. 1, Chlorarachniophyceae (phyta); 2, Prochlorophyceae; 3, blue-green algae; 4, pantonematic + stichonematic; 5, Paramylon; 6, cyanophycean starch; 7, cryptophycean starch; 8, acronematic + haptonema.

Data of molecular analyses from several algae and other lower organisms have further complicated the already confused state in respect of the numbers and delimitations (contents) of various taxonomical categories (kingdom, division/phylum, class, order, etc.) and has created new and difficult problems about which taxa should or should not be placed in which assemblage. Not only the numbers of classes, orders, and divisions proliferated but in some cases organisms that were earlier believed to be fairly unrelated have been brought together in the same group in view of similar rRNA sequences. For instance, the new kingdom Chromista includes not only heterokont algae but also some fungi (Labyrinthulales, oomycetes, hyphochytrids). Since these developments have great significance not only for the study and classification of the algae but also for several lower and higher organisms, they are described in more detail in the pages that follow.

Technology is now available to use sequences of molecules from living organisms to infer sequences that were present in their common ancestors. It is also possible to synthesize these presumed components of extinct organisms, enabling one to study the physico-chemical properties of these molecules and to make inferences about their functions. Ancestral sequences that encode biologically active molecules, some with unexpected properties, have already been reconstructed (see Stewart, 1995).

Ancestral sequences are reconstructed through logical inference upon an evolutionary tree, the process being termed parsimony analysis. If the modern sequences are not too divergent and the tree has enough branches, reconstructions can usually be made without serious ambiguities, and such parsimonious reconstructions (on correct phylogenies) tend to be fairly accurate. One can never be certain that any given reconstructed sequence was actually present in the genome of an extinct organism, but we can ask if the recreated molecules are reasonable ancestors from what is known about their modern homologues.

Biochemical, ultrastructural, and molecular studies have shown algae to belong to several evolutionary lineages (some even including certain protozoa and fungi) that arose in the distant past from symbiotic events involving plastids, mitochondria and some archaic or ancient host cell. Evolutionary relationships of algae are highly confused both because classifications are based on characteristics of host cell as well as of symbionts and because the procaryotic organisms such as the blue-greens and prochlorophytes have usually been treated as algae till recently.

MAJOR EVOLUTIONARY TRANSITIONS

It has been generally believed that evolutionary lineages increase in complexity with time, but there is no actual evidence that they do so. Nevertheless, eucaryotic cells are more complex than procaryotic ones, and animals and plants are more complex than protists. This increase in complexity may have been achieved as a result of a series of major evolutionary transitions which involved changes in the way information is stored and transmitted. Table 1-6 gives the major evolutionary transitions (see Maynard Smith and Szathmary, 1995). Common features recur in many of the transitions:

(1) Entities that were capable of independent replication before the transition can only replicate as parts of a larger unit after it. For example, free-living bacteria evolved into organelles.

(2) Increased efficiency can result from task specialization. For example, in ribo-organisms, nucleic acids acted both as genetic material and enzymes, whereas today most enzymes are proteins.

(3) There have been changes in information storage and transmission. Examples include the origin of the genetic code and of sexual reproduction (see Szathmary and Maynard Smith, 1995; Jablonka and Lamb, 1995; Pinker, 1994).

Two possible measures of biological complexity are the number of protein-coding genes, and the richness and variety of morphology and behaviour. Table 1-7 lists the sizes of the coding regions of various organisms. Eucaryotes have a larger coding genome than procaryotes. Higher plants and invertebrates have a larger genome than protists, and vertebrates a larger genome than invertebrates. Complexity may also be measured in terms of the variety of behaviour: complexity increases with the diversity of actions an organism can carry out. The number of different cell types in an organism can also be taken as a measure of its complexity.

Three possible mechanisms whereby the quantity of genetic information can increase are duplication and divergence, symbiosis, and epigenesis.

Cavalier-Smith (1981) has grouped together Labyrinthulea, oomycetes, and hyphochytrids with the heterokont algae in the division (phylum) Heterokonta within the relatively new kingdom Chromista. This kingdom is fundamentally distinct from the classical kingdoms Fungi, Plantae, and Protozoa (Cavalier-Smith, 1986; 1989): the other chromist phyla (divisions) are the Haptophyta, Cryptista, and Chlorarachniophyta (Cavalier-Smith, 1993a). The phylum Heterokonta also includes numerous chromophyte algae (e.g., brown algae and diatoms) as well as the oomycetes (Cavalier-Smith *et al.*, 1994).

Table 1-6 The major transitions

Replicating molecules to populations of molecules in compartments
Unlinked replicators to chromosomes
RNA as gene and enzyme to DNA and protein (genetic code)
Procaryotes to eucaryotes
Asexual clones to sexual populations
Protists to animals, plants, and fungi (cell differentiation)
Solitary individuals to colonies (nonreproductive castes)
Primate societies to human societies (language)

Table 1-7 Genome size and DNA content

Organism	Genome size (base pairs $\times 10^9$)	Coding DNA (%)
Bacterium (*E. coli*)	0.004	100
Yeast (*Saccharomyces*)	0.009	70
Nematode (*Caenorhabditis*)	0.09	25
Fruitfly (*Drosophila*)	0.18	33
Newt (*Triturus*)	19.0	1.5–4.5
Human	3.5	9–27
Lungfish (*Protopterus*)	140.0	0.4–1.2
Flowering plant (*Arabidopsis*)	0.2	31
Flowering plant (*Fritillaria*)	130.0	0.02

The three unique characters common between Heterokonta and Haptophyta are fluorescent carotenoid in one of the two cilia; fucoxanthin in their chloroplasts; and absence of nucleomorphs in the periplastid space. Hence, they can be classified together in the infrakingdom Chromobiota (Cavalier-Smith, 1993a). It seems probable that the ancestral chromobiote and heterokont were both photophagotrophs possessing fucoxanthin-containing chloroplasts located within a smooth periplastic membrane in the lumen of the perinuclear cisterna. If so, then all plastidless heterokonts must have lost their chloroplasts. Such loss probably occurred independently in the ancestors of labyrinthists and pseudofungi. (Pseudofungi include the oomycetes and hyphochytrids, see Cavalier-Smith *et al.*, 1994.) According to Cavalier-Smith *et al.*, the chloroplasts have probably been lost at least four times within the Heterokonta.

Total loss of plastids (as opposed to the conversion of chloroplasts to nonphotosynthetic leucoplasts as in nonphotosynthetic chrysophytes) is only possible if the host has not yet become dependent on them for some function other than photosynthesis. This is why they are never lost from green plants (Cavalier-Smith, 1993b) because they are the only sites for synthesis of fatty acids, starch, and certain amino acids.

The algae have a central significance in any scenario describing the origin of eucaryotic organisms (Lipscomb, 1991). Recent studies of molecular evolution (Bhattacharya *et al.*, 1992) and reinterpretations of fine structure (Patterson and Sogin, 1993) point to the polyphyletic nature of algae and indicate that the first eucaryotes initially lacked both mitochondria and plastids. These organelles have descended from bacterial and cyanobacterial endosymbionts that formed associations with established, archaic eucaryotes (Leipe *et al.*, 1993). Mitochondria came from a lineage related to purple non-sulphur bacteria whereas plastids were derived from cyanobacteria (Douglas and Turner, 1991).

Bhattacharya *et al.* (1993) found that tree topologies from phylogenetic analyses of rRNA sequences and actin coding regions tend to be congruent and reveal two distinctive evolutionary patterns between heterotrophic and photosynthetic eucaryotes. One pattern is typified by green algae, land plants, and red algae. Neither of these organisms are closely related to any heterotrophic ancestor and their radiation began after they had established a symbiotic relationship with a photosynthetic organism (Leipe *et al.*, 1994). The second pattern involves the radiation of eucaryotic algae which had chlorophyll-a and -c (viz., dinoflagellates, cryptomonads, and haptophytes) as the major photosynthetic pigments. These are strongly and clearly related to several heterotrophic taxa. For instance, dinoflagellates include several photosynthetic and heterotrophic taxa. Molecular analyses bring out a strong affinity between autotrophic organisms having tripartite tubular hairs and fungal-like heterotrophic protists, the oomycetes (Ariztia *et al.*, 1991). Ultrastructural comparisons bring together many chromophytes (i.e., algae having chlorophyll-a and -c), the oomycetes, and some colourless protists, into a complex evolutionary group called the stramenopiles (Patterson, 1989; Leipe *et al.*, 1994), whose common ancestor was probably some heterotroph that happened to acquire its plastid independently of other algal groups. But, according to Cavalier-Smith (1986, 1989), it is conceivable that colourless stramenopiles could have descended from chromophyte algae by secondary loss of their plastids. Recent work of Leipe *et al.* (1994) on 16S rRNA sequences supports the former hypothesis, viz., that stramenopiles evolved from a colourless flagellate and that other taxa with chloroplasts containing chlorophyll-a and -c represent independent evolutionary lines that acquired their chloroplasts separately from the endosymbiotic event leading to the autotrophic stramenopiles.

Fusion of two different eucaryotic cells into a single more complex cell created novel groups of protists. By engulfing an algal cell and exploiting its photosynthesis, heterotrophic protozoans became autotrophic. Drastically reduced, the engulfed cell now exists as an organelle in the host cell. Such blending of lineages was perhaps a driving force in early eucaryotic diversification.

Biologists know that a plant/animal dichotomy breaks down at the level of the protists, some of which can simultaneously be photosynthetic, mobile, and phagotrophic. Yet even for protists, there has been a tendency to divide them into groups based on the presence or absence of a chloroplast. Chloroplast-containing organisms have usually been known as the algae. Algae constitute a heterogeneous and artificial group: certain *algae* are in fact technically protozoans and acquired their chloroplasts from bonafide algae.

During early evolution, the archaic photosynthetic procaryotes lost their dependence on scavenging organic nutrients from the environment and started proliferating, eventually becoming a food supply for heterotrophs. The oxygen, released in photosynthesis, gradually accumulated in the atmosphere, some of it as ozone that provided a radiation shield essential to the colonization of the land. This oxygen also began to serve as an electron acceptor for the oxidation of food molecules during aerobic respiration allowing vast increases in metabolic efficiency. It was somewhere during these events that the eucaryotes arose. Apparently lacking

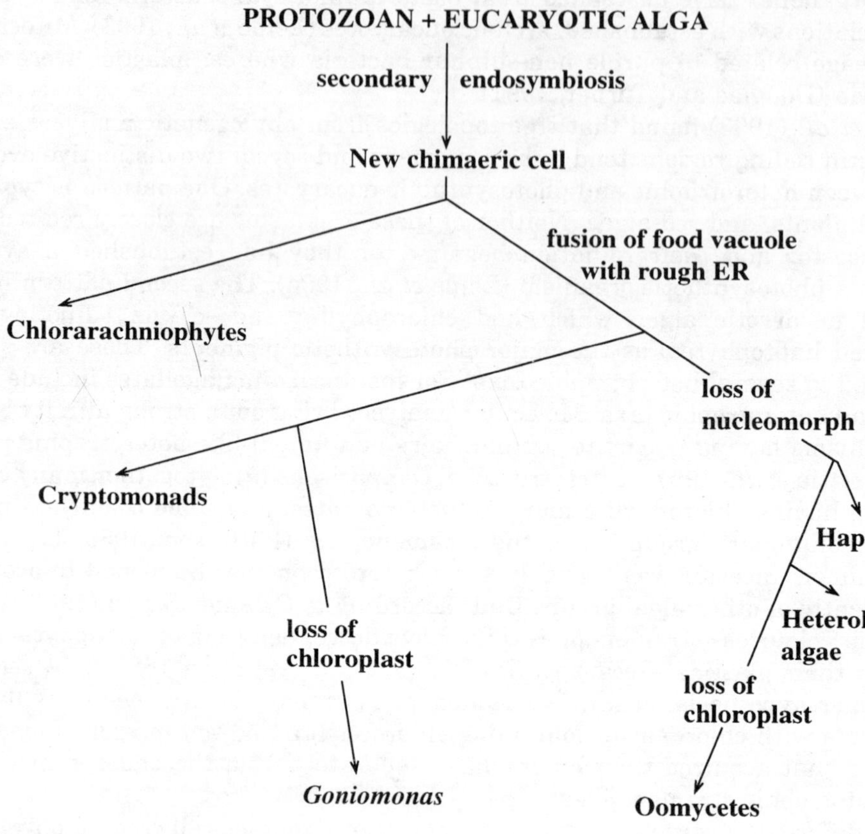

Fig. 1-25 Probable origin of kingdom Chromista by secondary endosymbiosis. Chlorarachniophytes were an early stage in an evolutionary series leading to the heterokont algae and haptophyte algae, plus the oomycetes. A fusion between the food vacuole and the rough ER transferred the endosymbiont into the lumen of the rough ER, where it is found in cryptomonads. The diatoms, brown algae, and coccolithophorids which also have a chloroplast located within the lumen of the rough ER and are thus bound by four membranes, probably originated from a cryptomonad-like ancestor by the loss of the nucleomorph. The oomycetes and their allies (water moulds and downy mildews) which are undoubtedly related to the heterokont algae, and are not true fungi may have originated by loss of the chloroplast. There may have been independent losses of pigments from a hypothetical eucaryotic algal endosymbiont having chlorophyll-a, -b, and -c plus phycobilins to produce the different pigment complements observed in the descendants. (After McFadden and Gilson, 1995.)

photosynthesis, the early eucaryotes may have lived as phagotrophs. Later some of these eucaryotic lineages entered into symbiotic partnerships with photosynthetic procaryotes and the chloroplast originated. This partnership, in which a photosynthetic procaryote was engulfed and retained by a phagotrophic eucaryote, was a *primary endosymbiosis* (McFadden and Gilson, 1995). The endosymbiont became gradually reduced, and lost its autonomy (including some of its genome) to its eucaryote host (Margulis, 1993). Green plants and the green algae have been the outcome of this primary endosymbiosis. The double membrane surrounding their chloroplasts appears to represent the two membranes of a photosynthetic Gram negative bacterium akin to modern cyanobacteria and prochlorophytes. As for the other photosynthetic eucaryotic algae, more data are required to decide whether their chloroplasts (containing various pigments) are monophyletic or polyphyletic.

In at least two groups of algae (the cryptomonads and the chlorarachniophytes, Fig. 1-25; Table 1-8), the chloroplasts are believed to have been acquired laterally via a *secondary endosymbiosis* (McFadden and Gilson, 1995).

Table 1-8 Differences between chlorarachniophytes and cryptomonads (nucleomorph is embedded in pyrenoid, in some species of both groups; there are dense globules in the nucleomorph of some species of both groups)

Character	Chlorarachniophytes	Cryptomonads
Main cell form	Amoeboid	Flagellate
Mitochondrial cristae	Tubular	Plate-like
Flagella number	1	2
Chlorophylls	a and b	a and c
Carotenoids	Neoxanthin, violaxanthin, lutein, beta-carotene, loroxanthin, dodecanoate	Alpha-carotene, beta-carotene, crocoxanthin, alloxanthin, monadoxanthin
Phycobilins	Absent	Present
Nucleomorph karyotype	3 chromosomes all with rRNA genes 95 kb, 140 kb, 145 kb	3 chromosomes all with rRNA genes 175 kb, 180 kb, 195 kb
Storage material	Nonstarchy, in host cytoplasm	Starch, in endosymbiont cytoplasm
Ejectisomes	Absent	Present

In this process, a double-membraned endosymbiont that subsequently became a chloroplast within a red or green algal eucaryote was itself engulfed by another phagotrophic eucaryote (Fig. 1-26). Instead of digesting the engulfed algal cell the phagotroph harboured the photosynthetic guest thereby establishing a secondary endosymbiosis. This type of chloroplast has four bounding membranes: two from the original procaryotic endosymbiont, a third from the plasma membrane of the primary host, and a fourth from the food vacuolar membrane of the secondary host (Fig. 1-26). The nucleus and cytoplasm of the endosymbiont here come to be located between the second and third membranes.

Certain biflagellate cryptomonads contain chloroplasts with four membranes, and also have a small nucleus-like organelle (termed nucleomorph) hitchhiking on the chloroplast sandwiched between the second and third membranes; it might represent the vestigial remains of a eucaryotic nucleus. Another case of secondary endosymbiosis was the finding of a green chloroplast, complete with four membranes and a nucleomorph, in some amoeboid organisms known as chlorarachniophytes. Recent researches in cytochemistry and molecular biology have confirmed that the nucleomorph may indeed be the remnant nucleus of an endosymbiont. Thus, rather than being just a chloroplast, the cryptomonad, and chlorarachniophyte photosynthetic organelles are really greatly modified photosynthetic eucaryotic endosymbionts (McFadden and Gilson, 1995).

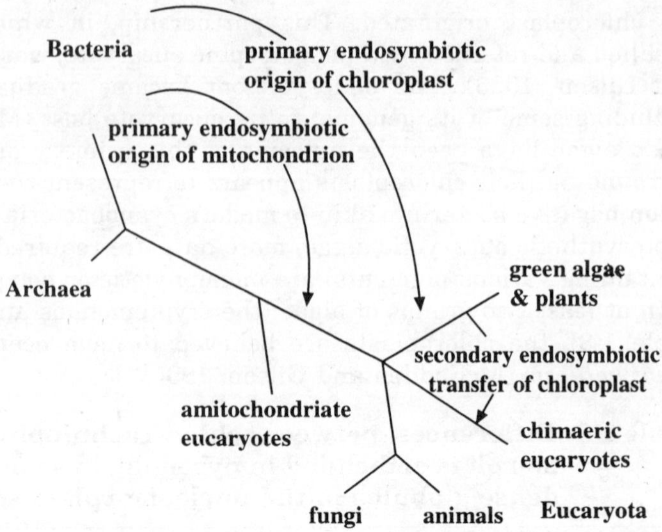

Fig. 1-26 Tree of life showing origin of mitochondria and chloroplasts from two independent primary endosymbioses between bacteria and eucaryotes. Lateral transfer of chloroplasts occurred between eucaryotes by secondary endosymbiosis. (After McFadden and Gilson, 1995.)

The nucleomorph contains DNA and has a nucleolus-like region rich in rRNAs, raising the possibility that the nucleomorph encodes rRNA components for the ribosomes surrounding the nucleomorph—the ribosomes having come from the endosymbiont cytoplasm.

That the nucleomorph is indeed a foreign genome has been confirmed by showing that nucleomorph genes have very different nucleotide sequences from corresponding nuclear genes. The problem of isolating two different versions of the same gene from one cell was solved by means of the polymerase chain reaction (PCR) to amplify genes for the small subunit rRNA. This technique has revealed that cryptomonads contain genes from two remote eucaryotic lineages, thus strongly supporting the secondary endosymbiosis hypothesis. Further confirmation has come from recent studies on isolated nucleomorphs (McFadden and Gilson, 1995).

It can now be stated confidently that the chloroplast is a reduced eucaryotic endosymbiont complete with vestigial nucleus and cytoplasm (McFadden and Gilson, 1995). There is some evidence to suggest that chlorarachniophytes and cryptomonads may have been derived from one secondary endosymbiosis, meaning that cryptomonads and chlorarachniophytes, which are morphologically and biochemically very different (Table 1-8), have diverged from the same host-endosymbiont partnership.

In most plants, euglenoids, green algae, and red algae, most chloroplast proteins are nuclear-encoded. Transcripts of these nuclear genes are translated on cytoplasmic ribosomes and the proteins transported into the chloroplast. To maintain the acquired chloroplast permanently, the secondary host in cryptomonads and chlorarachniophytes may well have retained that part of the endosymbiont's nuclear genome which encoded the chloroplast proteins. The other components of the endosymbionts, such as the mitochondrion, cytoskeleton, endomembrane system, and any surface covering being apparently redundant, were not so retained.

What still remains to be determined is how the nucleomorph divides and whether it ever undergoes meiosis or is merely inherited cytoplasmically like other organelle genomes.

Interestingly, each of the cryptomonad nucleomorph chromosomes as well as the chlorarachniophyte nucleomorph chromosomes carries rRNA genes. Conceivably, only chromosomes carrying rRNA genes are retained in nucleomorphs. The rRNA genes are always retained on chloroplast and mitochondrial genomes, probably because there is no mechanism for transporting such large RNAs across membranes into organelles. The same principle may hold good for the nucleomorph genome with rRNA genes being permanently trapped within the compartment in which they function.

Endosymbiont versus Organelle

Since the endosymbionts in cryptomonads and chlorarachniophytes are about the same size as a chloroplast, should they be termed as an endosymbiont or an organelle? Some corals, jellyfish, clams, hydras, and various protists also harbour algal endosymbionts, but they are not nearly so reduced as those of cryptomonads and chlorarachniophytes. More importantly, the endosymbionts tend to be excluded from the hosts during the reproductive phase and then reintroduced from a pool of free-living forms at a later stage in the host's life cycle (Margulis, 1993). An endosymbiont may be considered to have become an *organelle* when it becomes semiautonomous by the transfer of a part of its genome to the host's nucleus. In the case of the chlorarachniophytes and cryptomonads, these genes could come from either the chloroplast genome or the nucleomorph. This raises the interesting point of genes moving twice, i.e., once from the chloroplast to the nucleomorph predecessor after the primary endosymbiosis, and again from the nucleomorph to the nucleus after the secondary endosymbiosis. The fact that several chloroplast proteins are encoded by the host nucleus in both cryptomonads and chlorarachniophytes, points to the likelihood of the endosymbiont being a bonafide organelle.

According to Cavalier-Smith *et al.* (1995), cryptomonads and chlorarachniophytes represent early stages in the emergence of a new eucaryotic kingdom, Chromista (with brown algae, diatoms, golden flagellates, and oomycetes), that may have developed from a secondary endosymbiosis producing cryptomonads and chlorarachniophytes (Fig. 1-25). The presence of four bounding membranes around the chloroplasts of algae in the kingdom Chromista is the fundamental basis of this theory as these membranes may be the same as those around cryptomonad and chlorarachniophyte chloroplasts, and that the nucleomorph and, in the case of the oomycetes, the entire chloroplast, may have been lost (Fig. 1-26). According to this theory, secondary endosymbiosis has been a most significant event in cellular evolution, comparable to the divergence between procaryotes and eucaryotes or the acquisition of mitochondria or chloroplasts through primary endosymbioses (see Cavalier-Smith *et al.*, 1995).

Universal phylogenetic trees, e.g., the one in Fig. 1-27, cover all organisms from bacteria to mammals. Their construction requires examination of genes that, although intrinsically variable, are highly conserved. This is achieved by comparing sequence similarities of genes encoding for rRNAs.

The distribution among living organisms of a restricted variety of secondary metabolite types, grouped according to functions (e.g., pheromones, neurotransmitters, and hormones)

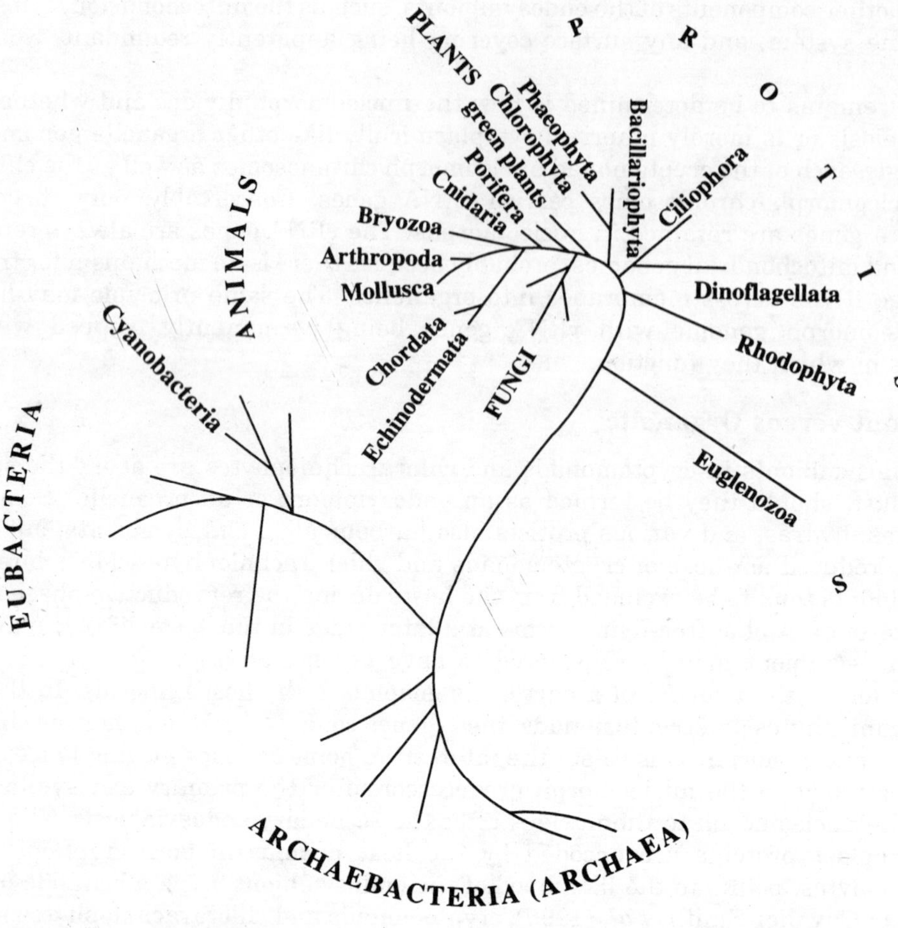

Fig. 1-27 Unrooted multikingdom tree where procaryotic and organellar eucaryotic phylogenies, from bacteria to animals, have been inferred from small subunit (16S-like) rRNA sequence similarities. Only some groups of organisms are included. (After Pietra, 1995.)

has not been of wide utility in constructing phylogenies (Chadwick and Whelen, 1992). This is because secondary metabolites, though having their enzymes encoded in basically the same way as primary metabolites, are limited in this respect, firstly because they have typically restricted distribution among living organisms and secondly because they have adaptive roles and are thus subjected to variability in response to environmental selective pressure. It is just these properties that turn out to be useful, however, when short evolutionary distances are considered (Pietra, 1995). Distribution of secondary metabolites can give good phylogenetic clues that are difficult to obtain otherwise.

Secondary metabolites may also sometimes characterize higher level taxonomic categories such as families or orders notwithstanding the common belief that phylogenetically distant organisms tend to produce structurally unrelated secondary metabolites. This is particularly borne out from a comparison of marine and land organisms, and reflects the scarcity or absence of certain groups of marine organisms on land, apart from different lifestyles. However, sometimes identical secondary metabolites are exceptionally found in phylogenetically distant organisms, even in the absence of any metabolite exchange among them.

Bacteria

As bacteria have successfully penetrated all eucaryotic organisms (see Margulis, 1993), they may be involved in the production of metabolites that either accumulate in the host or enter the host's secondary metabolic pathways. The former is exemplified for the neurotoxic alkaloids tetrodotoxin and saxitoxin, found not only in pure cultures of marine bacteria but also in various marine and terrestrial eucaryotes. But the presence of a tumour promoter lyngbyatoxin A in a marine cyanobacterium and a land actinobacterium is likely to reflect a common ancestry.

According to Pietra (1995), it seems that in contributing to the construction of metabolic machineries, marine bacteria may be responsible more for cytoplasmic growth than for secondary metabolism of the eucaryotes. The biosynthesis of isoprenoid building blocks by bacteria along routes different from those used by eucaryotes is in accord with this suggestion.

Euglenoids and Dinoflagellates

The euglenoids are primitive eucaryotes that biosynthesize 4-methylsterols like certain methane-oxidizing bacteria and the dinoflagellates. This is perhaps an evolutionary transition from the primitive synthesis of triterpenes by early bacteria to that of typical sterols by more advanced eucaryotes.

Certain prostaglandins occur in both euglenoids and red algae, accompanied by their biosynthetic precursor, arachidonic acid, which also occurs in dinoflagellates. Prostaglandins are formed in mammals *via* a cyclooxygenase route. Presumably in euglenoids and red algae, an 8-lipoxygenase route may be followed instead.

The dinoflagellates also produce harman (Fig. 1-28), a simple beta-carboline alkaloid, as do bryozoans and terrestrial angiosperms.

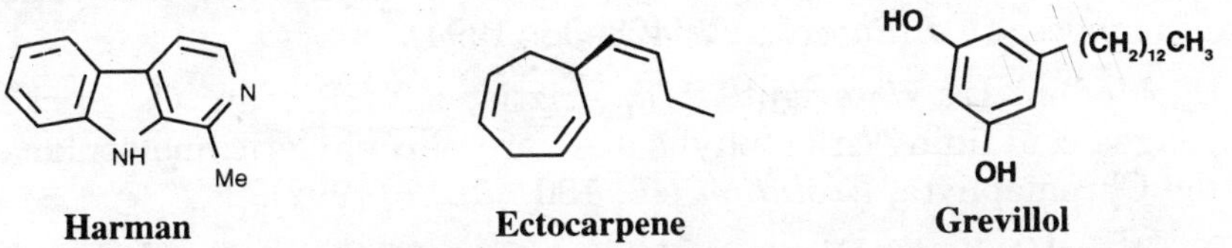

Fig. 1-28 Certain secondary metabolites produced by algae.

Rhodophyta

Transfer of the whole genome in an endosymbiotic event has been invoked to rationalize production of phycoerythrobiliproteins by both cyanobacteria and red algae.

Palythine acts as a filter against UV-B radiation for marine invertebrates and seaweeds. Adaptively, production of this amino acid is elicited by light. Structural analogues of palythine occur in certain fungi and are called mycosporines.

Phaeophyta

Fucalean brown algae are rich in certain phenolic compounds which also occur in other organisms. Thus, grevillol (Fig. 1-28) also occurs in terrestrial angiosperms.

Many brown algae produce ectocarpene (Fig. 1-28) as an attractant for conspecific male gametes. Ectocarpene is also produced by some land plants, e.g., *Senecio isatideus*, for no known purpose (Pietra, 1995).

Chlorophyta

16S-like rRNA sequence similarities indicate that green plants have evolved phyletically from green algae. This is reflected in the similarity of secondary metabolites in these two groups of organisms. Thus, the triterpenoids friedelin, taraxerol, and 31-norcycloartanes occur in both green seaweeds and terrestrial angiosperms.

Pietra's comparative analysis and review of marine secondary metabolites has thrown important light on the evolution of the functions for these metabolites, such as from defensive agents to hormones. While the latter serve in only trace amounts, so as to be rapidly switchable on and off, defensive compounds are needed in much greater amounts. It is not surprising therefore that different biosynthetic routes were selected for the two classes of agents. Perhaps it may be a general consequence of the different organization of phylogenetically distant organisms that in biosynthesizing identical secondary metabolites phylogenetically close organisms use the same pathways, while phylogenetically distant organisms use different pathways (Pietra, 1995).

Another conclusion concerns the scarce contribution of marine bacteria to genetic information for secondary metabolites in eucaryotes. This fits the slowness of phenotypic evolution before the Cambrian period but is in contrast with the emphasis that horizontal transfer and endosymbiotic events are currently receiving. Critical studies of marine bacteria may help clarify the situation.

REFERENCES

Ariztia, E.V., Andersen, R.A., and Sogin, M.L., A new phylogeny for chromophyte algae using 16S-like rRNA sequences from *Mallomonas papillosa* (Synurophyceae) and *Tribonema aequale* (Xanthophyceae), *J. Phycol.*, **27**, 428–36 (1991).

Bhattacharya, D., Medlin, L., Wainright, P.O., Ariztia, E.V., Bibeau, C., Stickel, S.K., and Sogin, M.L., Algae containing chlorophylls a + c are paraphyletic: molecular evolutionary analysis of the Chromophyta, *Evolution*, **46**, 1801–1817 (1992).

Bhattacharya, D., Stickel, S.K., and Sogin, M.L., Isolation and molecular phylogenetic analysis of actin coding regions from *Emiliania huxleyi*, a prymnesiophyte alga, by reverse transcriptase and PCR methods, *Molecular Biology and Evolution*, **10**, 689–703 (1993).

Bold, H.C. and Wynne, M.J., Introduction to the Algae: Structure and reproduction, Prentice-Hall, Englewood Cliffs, New Jersey (1978).

Boney, A.D., Mucilage: the ubiquitous algal attribute, *Brit. Phycol. J.*, **16**, 115–32 (1981).

Bouck, G.B., The structure, origin, isolation, and composition of the tubular mastigonemes of the *Ochromonas* flagellum, *J. Cell Biol.*, **50**, 362–84 (1971).

Cavalier-Smith, T., The kingdom Chromista: origin and systematics. *In* Round, F.E. and Chapman, D.J. (eds.) Progress in Phycological Research, Vol. 4, 309–47, BioPress, Bristol (1986).

Cavalier-Smith, T., The kingdom Chromista. *In* Green, J.C., Leadbeater, B.S.C., and Diver W.L. (eds.) The Chromophyte Algae: Problems and perspectives, 379–405, Clarendon Press, Oxford (1989).

Cavalier-Smith, T., Kingdom Protozoa and its 18 phyla, *Microbiol. Rev.*, **57**, 953–94 (1993a).

Cavalier-Smith, T., The origin, losses and gains of chloroplasts. *In* Lewin, R.A. (ed.) Origins of Plastids: Symbiogenesis, prochlorophytes, and the origins of chloroplasts, 291–349, Chapman and Hall, New York (1993b).

Cavalier-Smith, T., Allsopp, M.T.E:P., and Chao, E.E., Thraustochytrids are chromists, not Fungi: 18s rRNA signatures of Heterokonta, *Phil. Trans. Roy. Soc.* (London) B., **346**, 387–97 (1994).

Cavalier-Smith, T., Allsopp, M.T.E.P., Chao, E.E., and Mathews, G., *Proc. Natl. Acad. Sci.* (USA) (1995).

Chadwick, D.J. and Whelen, J. (eds.), Secondary Metabolites: Their function and evolution, Ciba Foundation Symposium, Vol. 171, Wiley, New York (1992).

Chida, Y. and Ueda, K., Mitochondrial number and form change during autospore formation in *Chlorococcum infusionum* (Schrenk) Meneghini (Chlorococcales, Chlorophya), *Phycologia,* **25**, 503–509 (1986).

Corliss, J.O., Protistan phylogeny and eukaryogenesis, *Internat. Rev. Cytol.*, **100**, 319–70 (1987).

Dethier, M.N., The ecology of intertidal algal crusts: variation within a functional group, *J. Exp. Mar. Biol. Ecol.*, **177**, 27–71 (1994).

Dodge, J.D., The Fine Structure of Algal Cells, Academic Press, London (1973).

Dodge, J.D., The functional and phylogenetic significance of dinoflagellate eyespots, *Bio-Systems*, **16**, 259–67 (1984).

Domozych, D.S., Mattox, K.R., and Stewart, K.D., Development of the cell wall in *Tetraselmis*: role of the Golgi apparatus and extracellular wall assembly, *J. Cell Sci.*, **52**, 351–71 (1981).

Douglas, S.E. and Turner, S., Molecular evidence for the origin of plastids from a cyanobacterium-like ancestor, *Journal of Molecular Evolution*, **33**, 267–73 (1991).

Fritsch, F.E., The Structure and Reproduction of the Algae, Vol. I, Cambridge University Press, London (1935).

Fritsch, F.E., The present day classification of algae, *Bot. Rev.*, **10**, 233–77 (1945).

Gillott, M.A. and Gibbs, S.P., The cryptomonad nucleomorph: its ultrastructure and evolutionary significance, *J. Phycol.*, **16**, 558–68 (1980).

Grim, J.N. and Staehelin, L.A., The ejectisomes of the flagellate *Chilomonas paramecium*: visualization by freeze fracture and isolation techniques, *J. Protozool.*, **31**, 259–67 (1984).

Jablonka, E. and Lamb, M.J., Epigenetic Inheritance and Evolution: The Lamarckian dimension, Oxford University Press, Oxford (1995).

Kawai, H. and Inouye, I., Flagellar autofluorescence in forty four chlorophyll-c containing algae, *Phycologia,* **28**, 222–27 (1989).

Kristiansen, J. and Walne, P.L., Fine structure of photo-kinetic systems in *Dinobryon cylindricum* var. *alpinum* (Chrysophyceae), *Brit. Phycol. J.*, **12**, 329–41 (1977).

Larkum, A.W.D. and Barrett, J., Light harvesting processes in algae, *Adv. Bot. Res.*, **10**, 1–219 (1983).

LeBlond, P.H. and Taylor, F.J.R., The propulsive mechanism of the dinoflagellate transverse flagellum reconsidered, *BioSystems*, **8**, 33–39 (1976).

Lee, R.E., Phycology, Cambridge University Press, London (1980).

Leedale, G.F., Phylogenetic aspects of nuclear cytology in the algae. *In* Fredrick, J.F. and Klein, R.M. (eds.) Phylogenesis and morphogenesis in the algae, *Ann. N.Y. Acad. Sci.*, **175**, 429–53 (1970).

Leipe, D.D., Wainright, P.O., Gunderson, J.H., Porter, D., Patterson, D.J., Valois, F., Himmerich, S., and Sogin, M.L., The stramenopiles from a molecular perspective: 16S-like rRNA sequences from *Labyrinthuloides minuta* and *Cafeteria roenbergensis, Phycologia*, **33**, 369–77 (1994).

Leipe, D.D., Gunderson, J.H., Nerad, T.A., and Sogin, M.L., Small subunit ribosomal RNA of *Hexamita inflata* and the quest for the first branch in the eukaryotic tree, *Molecular and Biochemical Parasitology*, **59**, 41–48 (1993).

Lipscomb, D., Broad classification: the kingdoms and the protozoa. *In* Kreier, J.P. and Baker, J.R. (eds.) Parasitic Protozoa, 2nd edn., 81–136, Academic Press, San Diego (1991).

Manton, I. and Peterfi, L.S., Observations on the fine structure of coccoliths, scales and the protoplast of a freshwater coccolithophorid, *Hymenomonas roseola* Stein, with supplementary observations on the protoplast of *Cricosphaera carterae, Proc. Roy. Soc.*, **172B**, 1–15 (1969).

Margulis, L., Symbiosis in Cell Evolution, 2nd edn., Freeman, New York (1993).

Maynard Smith, J. and Szathmary, E., The Major Transitions in Evolution, Freeman, Oxford (1995).

McCandless, E.L. and Craigie, J.S., Sulfated polysaccharides in red and brown algae, *Ann. Rev. Plant Physiol.,* **30**, 41–53 (1979).

McFadden, G. and Gilson, P., Something borrowed, something green: lateral transfer of chloroplasts by secondary endosymbiosis, *TREE*, **10**, 12–17 (1995).

Parker, S.P. (ed.), Synopsis and Classification of Living Organisms, McGraw-Hill, New York (1982).

Patterson, D.J., Stramenopiles: chromophytes from a protistan perspective. *In* Leadbeater, B.S.C. and Diver, W.L. (eds.) The Chromophyte Algae, 357–79, Clarendon Press, Oxford (1989).

Patterson, D.J. and Sogin, M.L., Eukaryote origins and protistan diversity. *In* Hartman, H. and Matsuno, K. (eds.) The Origin and Evolution of Prokaryotic and Eukaryotic Cells, 13–46, World Scientific Publishing, New Jersey (1993).

Pfister, C.A., Costs of reproduction in an intertidal kelp: patterns of allocation and life history consequences, *Ecology*, **73**, 1586–96 (1992).

Pietra, F., Structurally similar natural products in phylogenetically distant marine organisms, and comparison with terrestrial species, *Chem. Soc. Revs.*, 65–71 (1995).

Pinker, S., The Language Instinct: The new science of language and mind, Penguin, London (1994).

Ragan, M.A. and Chapman, D.J., A Biochemical Phylogeny of the Protists, Academic Press, New York (1978).

Randhawa, M.S., Zygnemaceae, Indian Council of Agricultural Research, New Delhi (1959).

Rosowski, J.R. and Parker, B.C. (eds.), Selected Papers in Phycology, Phycological Society of America, Lawrence, Kansas (1982).

Round, F.E., The Biology of the Algae, 2nd edn., Edward Arnold, London (1973).

Sarma, Y.S.R.K., Algal karyology and evolutionary trends. *In* Sharma, A.K. and Sharma, A. (eds.) Chromosomes in Evolution of Eukaryotic Groups, Vol. 1, 177–233, CRC Press, Cleveland (1983).

Silva, P.C., Names of classes and families of living algae, *Regnum Vegetabile*, **103**, 1–156 (1980).

Smith, G.M., Cryptogamic Botany, Vol. I, Algae and Fungi, 2nd edn., McGraw-Hill, New York (1955).

Stanier, R.Y. and Cohen-Bazire, G., Phototrophic prokaryotes: the cyanobacteria, *A. Rev. Microbiol.*, **31**, 225–74 (1977).

Steneck, R.S. and Dethier, M.N., Are functional classifications different for marine vs terrestrial plants?: a reply to Grime, *Oikos*, **73**, 122–24 (1995).

Stewart, C.B., Active ancestral molecules, *Nature*, **374**, 12–13 (1995).

Szathmary, E. and Maynard Smith, J., The major evolutionary transitions, *Nature*, **374**, 227–32 (1995).

Taylor, F.J.R., Dinoflagellates from the International Indian Ocean Expedition, *Bibliotheca Bot.*, **132**, 1–234 (1976).

Taylor, F.J.R., Flagellate phylogeny: a study in conflicts, *J. Protozool.*, **23**, 28–40 (1977).

Tippit, D.H. and Pickett-Heaps, J.D., Mitosis in the pennate diatom *Surirella ovalis*, *J. Cell Biol.*, **73**, 705–27 (1977).

Van den Hoek, C. and Jahns, H.M., Algen: Einführung in die Phykologie, George Thieme, Stuttgart (1978).

Whittaker, R. and Margulis, L., Protist classification and the kingdoms of organisms, *Bio-Systems*, **10**, 3–18 (1978).

Wynne, M.J. and Loiseaux, S., Recent advances in life history studies of the Phaeophyta, *Phycologia,* **15**, 435–85 (1976).

2 Reproduction and Life History

INTRODUCTION

Reproduction is a process by which a living organism propagates and multiplies the number of its individuals. The algae generally reproduce in three ways—vegetative, asexual, and sexual.

Vegetative propagation does not involve rejuvenation of the protoplasts, and the cell walls of the reproductive units are either entirely parental, or partly parental and partly new. Asexual reproduction, however, involves rejuvenation of the protoplasts, and the reproductive bodies are either naked or provided with a newly synthesized wall of their own. Further, asexual reproduction is accomplished by using specially differentiated cells that are capable of directly multiplying the alga. Both the vegetative and asexual reproduction are accessory means of propagation and are not concerned with bringing together in one cell lineage the genes from different cell lineages.

In contrast to vegetative propagation and asexual reproduction, the sexual reproduction involves alternation of syngamy (fusion of male and female gametes) and karyogamy (fusion of gametic nuclei) on the one hand, and meiosis on the other. This leads to the creation of new combinations of genes by pooling together in one line of descent the genes derived from two different parents, thus resulting in a reshuffling of the gene material. The recombinants so produced can then be subjected to natural selection. In procaryotic organisms, recombinants are formed by such processes as conjugation, transformation, and transduction, none of which involves true karyogamy and meiosis. This genetic recombination in bacteria and the blue-green algae accordingly falls short of the true and complete definition of sexuality in the sense adopted here, even though it fulfils the same function as true sexuality.

VEGETATIVE PROPAGATION

Vegetative propagation is very common in algae and takes place in a variety of ways. In unicellular algae, flagellates, desmids, and diatoms, a cell may divide into two halves to produce new individuals. In multicellular forms, the thallus often breaks into small fragments each of which then grows into a new plant. *Dictyosphaerium* and *Aphanothece* multiply by a splitting of their colonies. The proliferation of filamentous thalli involves two methods—fragmentation and hormogone formation. The fragmentation of the filaments may be due to either the mechanical pressure exerted on them or the dissolution of the cross walls caused by the shearing strains which develop from differences in turgor pressure between adjoining cells. In such algae as *Stichococcus*, the tendency to fragment is so pronounced that filaments longer than a few cells each are seldom found (Fig. 2-1).

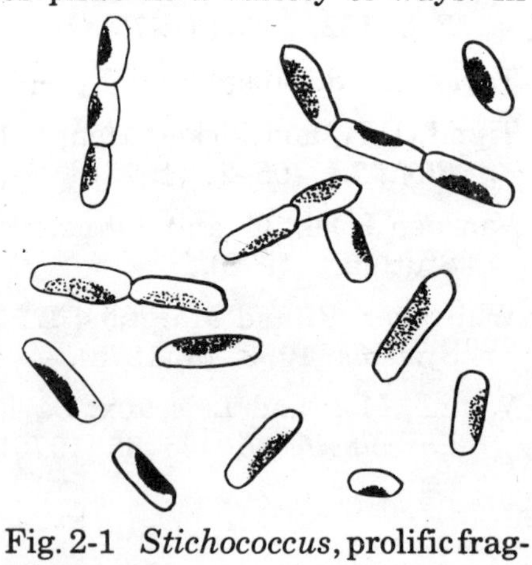

Fig. 2-1 *Stichococcus*, prolific fragmentation.

Most motile green algae have heteropolar cells. The

extremity commonly bearing the flagella is called the anterior (apical) end, whereas the opposite pole is the posterior (antapical) end. The typical division of the green algal flagellates is longitudinal. In walled flagellates, e.g., *Chlamydomonas*, the division occurs inside the wall of the mother cell. The plane of division in these flagellates is mostly longitudinal but, in many cases, before or during division, the protoplast rotates through a right angle, giving the appearance of a transverse division. *Chlorogonium* and *Haematococcus* are examples of flagellates whose cells undergo true transverse division. Ettl (1988) distinguishes the following four types of cell division in motile green algae:

(1) The schizotomous longitudinal division of naked motile cells into two morphologically equal sister cells, the flagella being distributed among the sisters.

(2) The schizogonous (multiple) longitudinal division of some walled Chlamydomonadaceae and Volvocaceae into morphologically equal sister cells whose number is a power of two. The flagella are retracted or discarded.

(3) The semitransverse division of some walled Chlamydomonadaceae into morphologically unequal parts of the protoplast whose number is a power of two. The protoplast rotates after the first division, but the old flagella remain attached with the rest of the mother cell.

(4) The true transverse division, without rotation, of the protoplast into morphologically unequal parts. The number of daughter protoplasts is a power of two, but one of them represents the remains of the mother cell. The old flagella remain attached with the mother cell. This kind of division is known in only a few genera (Ettl, 1988).

The filamentous blue-green algae propagate vegetatively through a specialized process known as hormogone formation. The hormogones, which are short fragments of a trichome, are produced either as a result of fragmentation or by the formation of biconcave, intercalary

Fig. 2-2 *Oscillatoria princeps*, filament showing several separation discs.

separation discs (Fig. 2-2) spaced quite a few cells apart from each other. The vegetative cells lying between two separation discs constitute a hormogone. Devoid of a sheath and endowed with the power of movement, the hormogones constitute an efficient and quick method of vegetative propagation and dispersal of the species during environmentally favourable growth periods.

Some algae reproduce by means of adventitious thalli as in *Dictyota* or by the formation of a few-celled branches, known as propagules, which become detached from the parent and subsequently develop into new plants. In *Sargassum natans*, small parts of the plant get detached and float away, growing into new plants. *Bryopsis* propagates by abscission of older pinnules which then grow into mature thalli. In *Protosiphon*, vegetative propagation takes place by budding of the vesicle. In species of *Trentepohlia* (Fig. 2-3), cells of the prostrate system form a powdery mass which is dispersed by the wind and can give rise to new plants.

In dinoflagellates, the parental thecal plates are shared by the daughter cells, but since the cell usually divides obliquely, one daughter receives most of the epithecal plates and only a few hypothecal plates, whereas the other daughter receives most of the hypothecal plates and a few of the epithecal plates. Because of this, the two daughters look unlike each other for a short while after their birth. Later, they synthesize the missing plates and hence become like each other and the mother cell.

In desmids, the mother cell separates in the isthmus between the two semicells. The isthmus contains the nucleus. A new semicell comes out from the isthmus to match the existing half cell. During the process, some chloroplasts and mitochondria move into the new semicell which also produces a primary and then a secondary cell wall (Pickett-Heaps, 1975). Sexual reproduction in desmids occurs by cell conjugation, with the formation of a large quantity of mucilage, and the migration of an amoeboid (nonflagellate) gamete through a hole formed in the isthmus. The resulting zygote forms a thick wall which sometimes bears long spines (e.g., in *Staurastrum*).

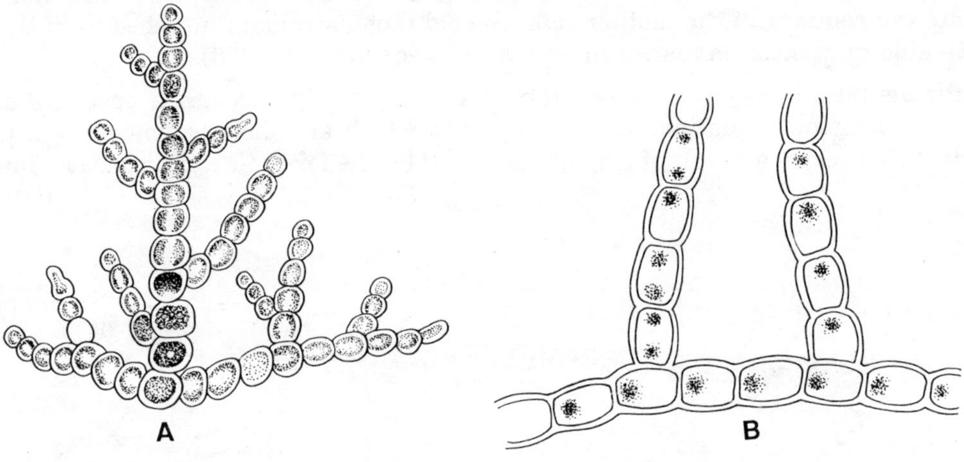

Fig. 2-3 *Trentepohlia*, prostrate and upright systems. A, *T. umbrina*; B, *T. annulata*.

In diatoms, new wall material is formed within vesicles bounded by the silicalemma. This silicalemma pumps silica into the vesicles. The formation of the new wall occurs within the confines of the parent wall; the epitheca acquires a new hypotheca and the parental hypotheca becomes the epitheca to a new hypotheca. This means that the two daughter cells are unequal in size. The epithecal daughter is as big as the mother cell, but the hypothecal daughter is slightly smaller.

CIRCADIAN RHYTHMS

Circadian rhythms have been known to occur in several eucaryotic algae. For instance, in the marine dinoflagellates, photosynthesis is most active around midday, whereas light as bioluminescence is emitted only at night when it can be seen. The timing of these processes does not depend directly on the day-night cycle; it can also be shown in constant light or darkness and at a constant temperature and accordingly must be innate. The timer responsible is termed a circadian clock.

Though widespread in many eucaryotic organisms, circadian timing has till recently remained undetected in procaryotes. Recently, certain nonheterocystous cyanobacteria containing an oxygen-sensitive nitrogenase have been shown to fix nitrogen only at night when there is no photosynthetic oxygen evolution (Stal and Krumbein, 1985). Sweeney and Borgese (1989) have demonstrated a circadian rhythm in cell division in a marine strain of *Synechococcus* under conditions where the generation time is: longer than a day, entrained by a light-dark cycle, and persists for at least four cycles in continuous light and constant temperature with a maximum at about 24 hr intervals. Thus, this cyanobacterium appears to satisfy the criteria for the existence of a true temperature-compensated circadian clock (Sweeney and Borgese, 1989).

Several cyanobacteria also show circadian rhythms and have the cellular machinery (biological clock) that generates these rhythms (see Grobbelaar *et al.*, 1986; Sweeney and Borgese, 1989; Kondo *et al.*, 1993; Huang *et al.*, 1994). Much of this work has been done on the unicellular organism *Synechococcus* which can fix nitrogen and take up leucine rhythmically under constant environmental conditions after undergoing some adaptation to a diurnal light/dark cycle. In *Synechococcus* RF-1 the rhythms can also be established by small temperature changes, in either a raised- or a lowered-temperature cycle, within the growth-permissive range. The circadian oscillator controls. besides the nitrogenase, the rate of synthesis of several polypeptides. The overt rhythms have fixed phase relationships, though the phase is dependent on the particular induction stimulus (Huang and Grobbelaar, 1995). A *clock* consisting of a molecular complex which can respond differentially to different induction conditions has been hypothesized by Huang *et al.* (1994).

In some algae, e.g., the dinoflagellate *Gonyaulax*, cell division, photosynthesis, and bioluminescence show rhythmic patterns with a period of *about* (*not exactly*) 24 hr even in the absence of environmental day and night (Sweeney, 1981). It seems that in this and certain other algae, e.g., *Chlamydomonas*, the circadian timing is intracellular. The two general and common properties of circadian rhythms are (1) persistence in constant conditions, and (2) little change in the period at different temperatures and light intensities, but strong time-dependent responses to light pulses.

Since in *Gonyaulax* the rhythms of bioluminescence, cell division, and photosynthesis have the same period under similar conditions, it seems probable that each cell contains only a single circadian oscillator.

Recent experiments using various metabolic inhibitors as probes have indicated that proteins synthesized on cytoplasmic ribosomes (80S, *not* 70S) are components of the "clock". It seems very likely that membranes and their components are important in temporal regulation.

ASEXUAL REPRODUCTION

Asexual reproduction involves the formation of one or more of the following types of spores: zoospores, aplanospores, autospores, hypnospores, carpospores, tetraspores, endospores, and exospores. These may be formed in any vegetative cell [*Ulothrix* (Fig. 2-4)] or in specially differentiated cells called sporangia (*Trentepohlia*, *Ectocarpus*, and *Dictyota*). Spores are cells that germinate without fusion to produce new individuals. The nonmotile spores are called aplanospores. If the aplanospore, while still within the mother cell, appears like the mother cell in all respects except size, it is spoken of as an autospore. The endospores and exospores of the Cyanophyta are analogous to the aplanospores of the Chlorophyta but not homologous because the term aplanospore connotes a derivation from the motile zoospores which are not met with in the blue-green algae.

The zoospore, which probably constitutes the most important kind of asexual spore, is a motile body equipped with one or more flagella and commonly contains a chromatophore, a nucleus, and an eyespot. Many zoospores show a phototactic response, moving towards or away from light. The zoospores may be biflagellate (e.g., *Ectocarpus*), quadriflagellate (e.g., macrozoospores of *Ulothrix*), or multiflagellate (e.g., *Oedogonium* and *Vaucheria*). During zoospore formation in *Oedogonium*, the entire protoplast assumes a pear shape and escapes from the cell and develops a ring of flagella around a colourless circular area towards its anterior end. In other algae, e.g., *Cladophora*, the protoplast of a cell may give rise to 8, 16, 32, or more zoospores by undergoing repeated divisions either after the completion of all nuclear divisions (simultaneous division) or after each nuclear division (successive division).

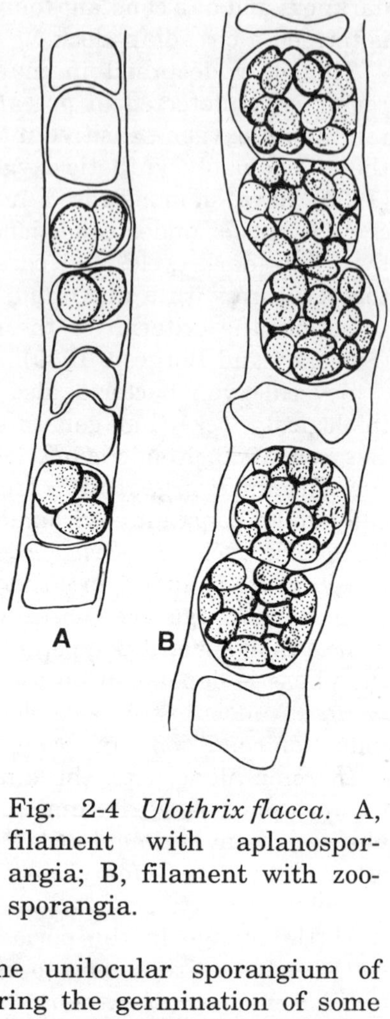

Fig. 2-4 *Ulothrix flacca*. A, filament with aplanosporangia; B, filament with zoosporangia.

Aplanospores are produced in *Ulothrix, Microspora*, and certain other algae, and may be formed either from the entire protoplast of a cell, or a single cell may give rise to many aplanospores. Autospore formation occurs in many members of the Chlorococcales, e.g., *Chlorella*. Hypnospores are aplanospores with a greatly thickened cell wall.

The asexual spores produced by meiotic division in the unilocular sporangium of *Ectocarpus*, in the tetrasporangium of *Polysiphonia*, and during the germination of some zygotes are known as meiospores or gonospores. Such spores are unlike those produced by mitotic division (mitospores) in that they are haploid and are concerned with the perpetuation of only the haploid thalli. The mitospores may be either haploid or diploid and accordingly perpetuate the haploid or diploid generation.

Zoosporogenesis in most algae is influenced by light, temperature, nutrients, osmotic shock, and hydrostatic pressure (Dring, 1974).

PROPAGULES OF MARINE MACROALGAE

Clayton (1992) has discussed the central question of what characters do macroalgal propagules possess that make them uniquely adapted to their essential functions, i.e., to disperse, settle and attach, survive, and eventually regenerate a new individual. Most macroalgal propagules are spores, zygotes or gametes capable of parthenogenesis. They are naked cells bounded by a plasma membrane, and in some species covered by a layer of mucilage. Some propagules are highly specialized, e.g., those produced by *Sphacelaria* spp. (see Table 2-1).

Table 2-1 Propagule characters in some marine brown and green algae (after Clayton, 1992)

Taxon	Propagule	Eyespot	Phototaxis	Flagella
Ectocarpus siliculosus	Zoospore	+	Positive	2
	Gametes	+	Positive	2
Sphacelaria rigidula	Zoospore	+	?	2
	Male gamete	+	Positive	2
	Female gamete	+	?	2
Dictyota diemensis	Spore	–	–	–
	Egg	–	–	–
Prasiola stipitata	Male gamete	–	–	2
	Female gamete	–	–	–
	Zygote	–	–	–
Enteromorpha intestinalis	Zoospore	+	Positive	4
Cladophora vagabunda	Female gamete	+	?	2

Cell Size and Flagella

Cell size and motility exert a strong effect on dispersal (Norton, 1991). Size determines sinking rate: small propagules sinking more slowly than larger ones of a similar density. Algal reproductive cells range in size from 2 μm to more than 250 μm in diameter. The size ranges and also presumably the dispersal characteristics of propagules of the Rhodophyta, Phaeophyta, and Chlorophyta overlap substantially. Some examples of very large reproductive cells are the stephanokont zoospores of Derbesiales, carpospores and tetraspores of the Rhodomelaceae, and the zygotes of some Fucales.

Some flagella terminate in a hairpoint or acronema, a slender extension of varying length containing a continuation of one or more microtubules. The acronema of the anterior flagellum of brown algal motile cells has adhesive properties and is believed to initiate contact leading to attachment. In male gametes of brown algae and in green algal gametes the acronema also appears to be important in mating.

Golgi bodies are usually quite conspicuous in algal reproductive cells and generally consist of a few cisternae lying approximately 10 nm apart. Their cis (forming) face is usually closely associated with the endoplasmic reticulum, nuclear envelope and in red algae, with mitochondria and ER (Pueschel, 1990). Small cells often have a single Golgi body, but larger reproductive cells, such as eggs of the Fucales and spores of the Dictyotales, can have numerous Golgi bodies.

Golgi bodies in algal propagules have been implicated in the synthesis of cell wall polysaccharides, adhesives, and mucilage (Clayton, 1992).

Endoplasmic Reticulum

In higher plant cells ER functions in lipid synthesis and in the regulation of cytosolic Ca^{2+} concentration (Quader, 1990) as well as providing membranes and proteins to the Golgi cisternae.

Mucilage vesicles are produced directly from ER during sporogenesis in some red algae, and ER is closely associated with developing starch grains during sporogenesis and in mature spores in several species of these algae.

In *Durvillaea potatorum* ER appears to be involved in pheromone synthesis and secretion.

Mucilage

Mucilage is perhaps the most ubiquitous of all substances associated with algal propagules. Many algal propagules have a coating of transparent, sticky material containing various polysaccharides and sometimes proteins. Among the varied functions attributed to mucilage are: spore discharge, lubrication (during discharge), spermatozoid entrapment, desiccation resistance, increased buoyancy, adhesion, and defence (Clayton, 1992).

Mucilage functions as a "sex aid", a device that helps promote successful fertilization in some brown algae. In *Fucus spiralis*, oogonial packets are released from the conceptacle in a slime which sticks them to the receptacles until the eggs are fertilized and drop off. Species of *Sargassum* have a highly specialized fertilization mechanism in which eggs are retained attached to the conceptacle surrounded by a mucilaginous layer derived from the oogonial wall. Spermatozoids become trapped in the sticky surface, and are able to penetrate the coating and effect fertilization (May and Clayton, 1991).

Chloroplasts and Mitochondria

Even the smallest algal reproductive cells contain at least one chloroplast and mitochondrion. The early stages of sporogenesis and gametogenesis typically involve a phase of chloroplast multiplication and sometimes also involve differentiation from proplastids. Energy reserves are generally laid down as the reproductive cells mature.

Photosynthesis has been shown to occur in the zoospores of *Laminaria hyperborea*, *Macrocystis pyrifera*, and *Nereocystis luetkeana* and eggs, sperms, and zygotes of *Fucus serratus* and *Hormosira banksii*.

Microclimate

Propagules exist in a world dominated by viscous physical forces because of their very small size and relatively slow swimming speeds. The planktonic and benthic environments are heterogeneous physically, chemically, and biologically when viewed on the spatial scale of a macroalgal propagule. Algal propagules coexist in the plankton with a wide diversity of other microscopic organisms. The layer of water near the bottom where propagules attach is called the boundary layer and is physically, chemically, and biologically distinct from the water above it. Many physical and chemical properties of the boundary layer environment are consequences of the metabolic or secretory activities of the organisms which inhabit the microbial film, but some properties are also affected by abiogenic factors (see Amsler *et al.*, 1992). Nutrient concentrations in some patches are likely to be much higher than those measured in the water column using standard techniques. Chemical morphogens or toxins may also be produced by bacteria and other microorganisms in the boundary layer. Once a macroalgal propagule firmly attaches to the bottom, competition with other algae becomes more likely than in the plankton, and interspecific competition involving germlings can be very important in regulating macroalgal assemblages. Also, recently settled macroalgal spores and germlings are preyed upon by diverse benthic grazers. Motile propagules can influence their position in the microenvironment through behaviours such as phototaxis, chemotaxis, settlement stimulation, and active selection of surface depressions (Amsler *et al.*, 1992).

PROPAGULE DISPERSAL

The dispersal of propagules is of fundamental biological importance in restoring populations, maintaining species distributions, and promoting genetic diversity. The distance over which propagules can successfully colonize new sites depends on processes that increase the time they remain competent while being dispersed. Competency may be prolonged through processes that either decrease the amount of metabolic energy expended by a propagule or increase the amount of metabolic energy available to a propagule during its dispersal phase. At least some algal spores can contribute to their own nutrition (via photosynthesis) during dispersal. Amsler and Neushul (1991) and Reed *et al.* (1992) explored the dispersal potential of *Macrocystis pyrifera* in laboratory experiments by examining (1) how long the spores can swim, (2) the contribution of energy derived from photosynthesis to spore swimming duration, and (3) the ability of spores to germinate and attach after they stop swimming. They noted that under photosynthetically saturating irradiance, no spores swam longer than 120 hr; 10% of the spores were still swimming after 72 hr. When placed in the dark, spores did not swim longer than 72 hr; 10% remained swimming after 48 hr. Spores did not die after they stopped swimming; most germinated in the water column and retained their capacity to produce viable sporophyte recruits. The viable planktonic stage is not necessarily restricted to the spore but may include later life history stages. These results show that the spores and germlings of this kelp can remain competent in the plankton for fairly long periods of time and that their dispersal can occur over greater distances than previously thought possible (Reed *et al.*, 1992).

Many seaweeds can disperse over hundreds of kilometres (Santelices, 1990). Possibly such long-distance dispersal occurs via detached thallus fragments that release spores or gametes after being set adrift. Colonization from the dispersed spores has been established over distances of at least 35 km (Amsler and Searles, 1980); this suggests that at least some algae form spores that remain competent for prolonged periods. In general, small, ephemeral, opportunistic algae have larger dispersal shadows than larger, longer-lived species (Amsler and Searles, 1980).

Kelps (order Laminariales) are large, mostly long-lived, brown algae, which are prominent in temperate reef communities throughout the world. The ability of kelps to disperse is critical because many species occur in highly disturbed habitats and have unstable population structures due to frequent local extinctions and recolonizations (Foster, 1982; Dayton, 1985). Dayton (1985) and Santelices (1990) stated that effective spore dispersal in kelps is limited to a few metres and that recolonizations result from spores being released from drifting fertile plants.

The Effects of Water Motion

Most seaweeds rely chiefly on small propagules for reproduction, proliferation, and dissemination. They are released into the apparent chaos of the waves. They are immotile or, at best, their powers of locomotion are negligible in relation to the forces that they have to contend with. Although swimming can influence the chances of propagules being resuspended by turbulence and be beneficial in the final moments of settlement in the sluggish water boundary layer close to the rock (see Amsler *et al.*, 1992), motility appears to be more useful for finding a nearby mate than for finding a home in the vast sea (Norton, 1992).

The fate of propagules is determined largely by the water flow. Current flow differs in velocity and/or direction, with depth. In deeper water the surface flow tends to be unidirectional for prolonged periods, although the direction may reverse with the tide. In contrast, near the shore and close to the substratum the flow is chaotic or mainly to and fro. In several species dispersal is greatly increased by storms.

Water motion casts propagules downwards or carries them away, sometimes extending the range of the species.

The height from which the propagules are released influences the type of flow in which the propagules find themselves and the distance they are likely to be carried. The dispersal range of very few species is known at present and this makes it difficult to relate plant height and dispersal range (Norton, 1992).

Whereas small seaweeds release their propagules quite close to the substratum, the larger seaweeds are adept at long distance dispersal, as their fronds reach up into the unidirectional flow just below the surface. However, they often have features that can reduce dispersal range. *Macrocystis* and *Alaria* have their reproductive sporophylls situated basally, just above the holdfast. Hence, the dispersal range of an isolated plant of *Macrocystis* or *Alaria* is only a few metres.

Even a metre tall *Sargassum muticum* having reproductive receptacles developed from base to tip surprisingly shows a fairly limited dispersal.

If the water flow is not too turbulent, propagules released in a sustained stream tend to drift downstream in a progressively diluted plume. Alternatively, if they are released suddenly in a batch, for example, when stimulated by the returning tide, they often form a cloud. The oft-observed patchiness of propagules both in the water and when newly settled on the rock points to the existence of spore clouds. The cloud can form from the release from a single plant, or synchronized liberation from many thalli.

A spore cloud is usually displaced laterally by currents and progressively diluted at the edges by turbulent mixing. The degree of dispersion seems to depend on the time during which dispersion has occurred rather than the distance over which the cloud has drifted. A spore cloud 1 m across will be little affected by eddies 1 cm in diameter, whilst a 100 m vortex will simply transport the cloud *en masse* (Norton, 1992).

According to Ngan and Price (1983), taxa with large propagules usually inhabit the lower shore, and shed at a different time from the smaller-spored algae of the higher shore.

If a cloud drifts far enough, slow sedimentation of the propagules tends to occur. Spores of different sizes drift in large, almost discrete clouds, with larger spores at lower altitudes.

Propagules sink, swim, and drift (Norton, 1992). The relative velocity of these three processes influences dispersal.

Negative phototaxis (as in *Enteromorpha* and *Ectocarpus*) may compensate for the low release height resulting from the plant's small stature.

The terminal sinking velocity of algal propagules in stationary water is related to the square of the propagule's radius, and its density. Large spores, or clusters of spores, tend to sink faster than small or solitary spores.

If propagules are to travel far they need to be sustained during their journey by a store of energy, or have a capacity to replenish their supplies, with sufficient energy remaining to allow establishment. The potential range of a drifting propagule is commonly related to its longevity. The longer it lasts, the further it can be transported.

Animal Vectors

Algal spores have been observed on the legs and shells of amphipods and other invertebrates (Buschman and Bravo, 1990; Santelices, 1990). Some invertebrates eat algal reproductive tissues (Buschman, 1992; Santelices, 1990). Some spores of opportunistic species often survive digestion (Santelices, 1992).

The fact that invertebrate grazers break into algal reproductive organs and thereby release some spores may mean that they facilitate dispersal.

Man is also an effective vector of long distance dispersal. Transplanted oysters appear to have extended the geographical distribution of *Sargassum muticum* and *Laminaria japonica* (Hay, 1990).

The ecological benefits of dispersal seem to involve escape from competition with the parent plants and siblings more than reaching some distant favourable site. The restricted zones occupied by many seaweeds means that dispersal up or down the shore is wasteful, but the propagules have no means of directing their dispersal sideways along their natural zone.

SEXUAL REPRODUCTION

Typical or conventional sexuality consisting of karyogamy and meiosis is brought about by a variety of methods invariably involving the union of the male and female sexes. The reproductive units participating in the sexual fusion (see Allen, 1959) are variously named, according to the morphology, behaviour, and nature of the organs in which they are produced. The dictionary meaning of the term gamete is "a germ cell carrying with it the implication of either sex", and for sexual reproduction to occur, the gametes of opposite sexes must be present.

Eucaryotic sex involves an alternation of haploid and diploid nuclear phases. The extent of the vegetative phase (the number of mitotic divisions) between the two events of sexual reproduction, meiosis and syngamy, defines three different kinds of life cycle: diploid, haploid, and haplo-diploid with alternation of generations.

The question of the origin of the alternation of haploid and diploid phases is tightly linked with that of the origin of alternation of mixis (fertilization) and meiosis, and therefore with the problem of the origin of eucaryotic sex. It is generally agreed that diploidy evolved from an ancestral haploid life cycle (see Valero *et al.*, 1992). Because of this general consensus on the evolutionary trend from haploidy towards diploidy, the question is: 'what are the advantages of diploidy?'

Five different kinds of life cycle have been observed in eucaryotes: (1) diploid; (2) haploid;

(3) haplo-diploid with alternation of generations; (4) haplo-diploid with haploid males (arrhenotoky); and (5) haplo-dicaryotic (i.e., after syngamy—fusion of gametes—cells containing the two haploid nuclei undergo simultaneous mitosis; karyogamy—fusion of the nuclei—occurs just before meiosis). The last two life cycles are very rare while the first three are quite common (see Valero *et al.*, 1992).

When syngamy rapidly follows meiosis, the life cycle is called a diploid life cycle. Gametes are produced by meiosis. For unicellular organisms, this definition implies that there is no mitosis between meiosis and syngamy. For multicellular organisms, the definition is less restrictive; individuals are diploid, and only gametes (and possibly the tissues around them) are haploid. This kind of cycle is found in some Protoctista (ciliates, diatoms), multicellular animals, and higher plants, where the gametophyte is reduced to a few cells (see Fig. 2-5).

When meiosis rapidly follows syngamy, the life cycle is called a haploid life cycle. Gametes are produced by mitosis. For unicellular organisms in this category there is no mitosis between syngamy and meiosis. In multicellular organisms, individuals are haploid, and only the zygote (and possibly the tissue around it) is diploid. This kind of life cycle is found in some Protoctista (most green algae) and bryophytes where the sporophyte is small and heterotrophic (see Fig. 2-5).

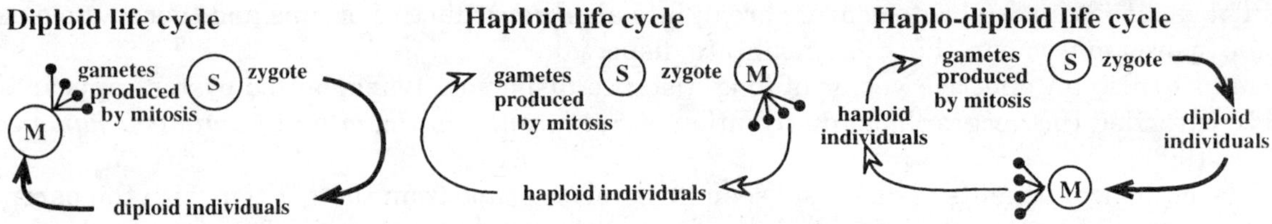

Fig. 2-5 Three common types of life cycle. S, syngamy; M, meiosis; thin arrows, haploid phase; thick arrows, diploid phase. (After Valero *et al.*, 1992.)

When meiosis and syngamy are separated in time and space, the life cycle is described as haplo-diploid. Gametes are produced by mitosis in haploid individuals; meiosis occurs in diploid individuals. For unicellular organisms, this means that mitosis occurs between syngamy and meiosis, and between meiosis and syngamy. For multicellular organisms, the life cycle shows an alternation of haploid and diploid autotrophic individuals. This kind of cycle is found in most red algae, some ferns, some club mosses, and horsetails (see Fig. 2-5; Valero *et al.*, 1992).

The advantage of diploidy in masking deleterious mutations has been tested in multicellular haplo-diploid red algae with an alternation of isomorphic haploid and diploid individuals. In *Gracilaria tikvahiae*, isogenic haploid and diploid individuals had the same growth rates in cultivation. In two species of *Iridea*, when a difference in response was found it was to the benefit of the haploid generation. Furthermore, comparisons of haploid and diploid cells cultivated *in vitro* with toxic or mutagenic agents reveal that haploid cells are sometimes more resistant than expected (see Wakes and Scatkin, 1983; Buss, 1987).

The costs and benefits of the respective positions of meiosis and syngamy within the life cycle are as follows:

(1) In haploid life cycles, few or no mitotic divisions occur between fertilization and

meiosis and each zygote can give only a few (four or a multiple thereof) genetically distinct spores. Consequently, genetic variability will not be distributed in the same manner within and among offspring; in particular, the variability within offspring (or gametes) induced by a diploid life cycle should be far greater than that resulting from a haploid life cycle (Buss, 1987).

It has been suggested that haploidy and diploidy may have evolved from an original undifferentiated haplo-diploid life cycle.

(2) The mixing of vertically transmitted parasites at syngamy, which increases parasite diversity within the host cell and allows recombination, points out a new cost of sex. Rapid divisions of the zygote may be a response of the host to minimize parasite mixing. In diploid life cycles, mitosis follows zygote formation, whereas in haploid life cycles, zygote formation is followed by meiosis. As meiosis is a longer process than mitosis, it is suggested that diploidy evolved from haploidy.

(3) In the evolution of life cycles in plants, the development of the sporophyte is correlated with the migration into the terrestrial environment, the gametophyte being forced to remain in an aquatic environment. This results in a greater difference in function between the two reproductive phases: the haploid phase produces gametes that are motile and require water to swim and to fuse at fertilization, while the diploid phase produces meiospores that permit dispersal in the terrestrial environment (Valero *et al.*, 1992).

It is difficult to explain the maintenance of a haplo-diploid life cycle when there is no difference between the ecological niches of the two generations and when the haploid and diploid stages are isomorphic.

In algae, variation in life cycles among species, among populations of the same species and even within populations has been recorded (Valero *et al.*, 1992). Neither constraints nor disruptive selection can always be invoked to explain the maintenance of a haplo-diploid life cycle, particularly when it is isomorphic (Valero *et al.*, 1992).

If the male and female gametes are flagellated and motile, they are termed zoogametes. Aplanogametes are nonflagellated and may show amoeboid movement. The antheridia and oogonia are the well differentiated gametangia producing, respectively, the male and female gametes which differ in morphology and behaviour. The gametes produced in antheridia are the flagellated, motile antherozoids (or spermatozoids), whereas the gamete produced in the oogonium is the nonmotile, nonflagellated egg or ovum. In the Rhodophyta, the oogonium having a swollen base (containing the egg) and a slender projecting neck, the trichogyne, is called a carpogonium, and the nonmotile, nonflagellate male gamete is termed spermatium, the structure producing it being known as a spermatangium.

True sexuality has been established for most members of the Chlorophyta, Phaeophyceae, and Rhodophyceae and for some members of the Tribophyceae, Bacillariophyceae, Dinophyceae, and Chrysophyceae. In the Cyanophyceae, true sexuality in the sense of karyogamy and meiosis is lacking but a parasexual phenomenon involving the recombination of genes in a single line of descent from two genetically distinct parents has been reported in some genera.

In unicellular forms, sexual fusion may take place between male and female (or minus and plus) gametes produced either by division of the protoplasts of the parent cells, or by fusion of the mature individuals themselves. The latter phenomenon, known as hologamy, occurs in a few species of *Chlamydomonas*. Besides, three other modes of sexual reproduction based on the morphology and behaviour of the mating gametes are known. These are isogamy, anisogamy, and oogamy. In isogamy, the gametes of a fusing pair are morphologically as well as physiologically alike and in dioecious species, are distinguishable genetically as plus or minus mating types. In anisogamy, the gametes differ in size and motility, the smaller, more active gametes being male and the larger, less active being female. In oogamy, the gametes of the two sexes are sharply differentiated and, with a few exceptions, are produced in specialized organs known as the antheridium and the oogonium. Both in isogamy and anisogamy, the gametes of opposite sexes mate outside the parent cells except in the Conjugales in which mating is facilitated by the formation of a conjugation tube and may occur either within the conjugation canal itself, e.g., *Zygnema*, or in the cell containing the female (plus) gamete, in which case the male gamete moves to the female through the conjugation tube, e.g., *Spirogyra*. In the majority of oogamous green algae, the egg is not liberated from the oogonium and fertilization takes place inside the oogonium. Sometimes, different species of the same genus, e.g., *Chlamydomonas*, may reproduce sexually by isogamy, anisogamy, or oogamy.

Isogamy, anisogamy, and oogamy are stages of a progressive series in the differentiation of gametes and this series seems to have evolved independently in different classes. Thus, the Chlorophyceae, Phaeophyceae, Tribophyceae, and Bacillariophyceae include forms ranging from isogamy through anisogamy to oogamy. In diatoms, Centrales are oogamous, the younger Pennales isogamous, and some Araphids anisogamous. However, in diatoms, isogamy is secondary and oogamy is primitive. The members of the Rhodophyceae are characteristically oogamous. In the Bacillariophyceae, only those forms as show a progressive decrease in cell size during vegetative multiplication form auxospores which, in most cases, are sexually formed zygotes that, by swelling, serve as a device to offset reduction in cell size resulting from continued vegetative propagation.

Sexually reproducing thalli may be homothallic (monoecious), showing fusion between gametes derived from a single parent individual, or heterothallic (dioecious), permitting fusion between gametes of different parentage.

The conjugating gametes of many Volvocales bear certain papillae which facilitate the initiation of plasmogamy. In *Pandorina*, *Gonium pectorale* (Fig. 12-23), *Volvulina*, and *Astrephomene*, both the conjugants bear a mating papilla. In *Chlamydomonas reinhardii* and *Gonium sociale*, only one of the two conjugants bears a papilla, whereas the other conjugant lacks it (Fig. 12-23).

In desmids, conjugation usually takes place only in shallow stagnant water after a sufficiently dense population has built up to facilitate a close mutual mating. In this conjugation, chemotactic responses appear to be involved. In *Cosmarium botrytis*, a unidirectional displacement of cells as a sexual response has been demonstrated by means of time-lapse cinematography (Brandham, 1967). In this case, heterothallic mating occurred between clonal biradiate and triradiate strains. Chemotaxis is also involved in the mating of *Closterium ehrenbergii* (Coesel and de Jong, 1986). In this species, there is a one way directional displacement of cells from one mating type towards the other. Some sexual attractant appears to be secreted by the cells of at least one mating type.

Many groups of planktonic algae, including diatoms, dinoflagellates, and green algae show fairly rigid patterns of reproductive strategy, with gametogenesis as well as perennation generally requiring some physiological stress that limits the continued growth of the vegetative cell population. In these algae, therefore, the production of the resistant resting stage commonly follows the period of peak vegetative growth. In contrast, some chrysophycean flagellates show a potentially plastic and quite flexible reproductive strategy. For instance, in *Dinobryon* spp., encystment can follow several dynamic patterns and statospores can be produced either during the exponential phase of population growth or during stationary phase. In many natural populations of chrysophytes, physiological stress does not seem to be a prerequisite for initiation of either sexual or asexual encystment (Sandgren, 1981).

Unlike asexual reproduction, sexual reproduction requires the meeting and fusion of two different cells, the gametes. Any means by which gametes are concentrated in space or time increases the probability of fertilization. This probability will depend upon the following factors: (1) the numbers of gametes produced within a population, (2) the synchrony of their production and release within a population, (3) the mixing and dilution of gametes by water motion, and (4) the ability of gametes to exhibit taxis (Brawley and Johnson, 1992).

PHENOLOGY

Reproductive seasonality can result from variation in the environmental factors that meet the physiological requirements for reproduction or from the use of environmental cues to coordinate reproduction. Such coordination can (1) cause reproduction to occur when environmental conditions are favourable for the establishment of new individuals, (2) produce resting stages in the face of deteriorating conditions, (3) trigger reproduction when conditions favourable to growth are declining, and (4) ensure that mature gametes are available for synchronous release.

In macroalgae, light plays a major role in the induction of reproduction (Santelices, 1990). Photoperiod is a reliable cue for gametogenesis in long-lived algae. Gametogenesis can be induced by both short-day and long-day conditions. Examples of short-day species include the red algae *Audouinella purpurea*, *Delesseria sanguinea*, and *Gigartina acicularis* and the brown alga *Fucus distichus*. Long-day species are exemplified by *Callithamnion hookeri* and *Sphacelaria rigidula*. Blue light is essential for gametogenesis in some kelps. *Dictyota* requires red light. Both photoperiod and total daily irradiance determine the timing of gametophyte production in the freshwater red alga *Batrachospermum boryanum* (Hambrook and Sheath, 1991).

Low temperatures directly induce gametogenesis in some kelp species (Lüning, 1980). In *Bonnemaisonia hamifera* there are different temperature requirements for gametogenesis in male and female plants; maturation in males begins at lower temperatures than in females (Breeman *et al.*, 1988). Thermal shocks induce sexuality in *Derbesia tenuissima*.

Nutrient depletion is an important stimulus for gametogenesis, especially in unicellular algae. Dinoflagellates produce gametes when grown under limiting levels of nitrogen, phosphorus or iron. In several freshwater algae, nitrogen limitation stimulates gametogenesis. In *Ulva*, low levels of nitrogen induce gametogenesis whereas high levels induce asexual reproduction (Mohsen *et al.*, 1974). Rapid changes in environmental factors such as salinity and pH can induce gametogenesis. There are also pH optima for reproduction (e.g., pH 7–9 in *Spirogyra*).

There are indications for a periodic and synchronous production and release of gametes. In some species reproduction occurs and resting stages are produced when environmental conditions deteriorate. Such observations point to environmental coordination of reproduction (Brawley and Johnson, 1992). This is further supported by the timing of gamete production and release relative to that of asexual propagules. Fertilization success may be expected to be increased if male and female gametes are released at the same time. In contrast, asexual reproduction can occur even if spores are released in small numbers at any one time.

In *Dictyota*, a lunar or semilunar periodicity of egg release has been observed but no such rhythmicity has been seen in the production and release of spores. Likewise, the release of gametes was periodic in *Enteromorpha*, whereas that of zoospores was not (Pringle, 1986). In *Ulva*, both gametes and zoospores are periodically released but gametes are released over a shorter period than zoospores (Brawley and Johnson, 1992).

The reproductive thalli of multicellular algae generally release gametes in response to a different cue from the one that confers an overall seasonality to the life history (Brawley and Johnson, 1992). Thus, gametes may be released on a lunar or semilunar cycle, often in relation to tidal height rather than strictly to a lunar phase.

THE ECOLOGICAL ROLE OF PHEROMONES

A reproductive adaptation that enhances fertilization success is the use of pheromones to synchronize gametogenesis, release gametes and/or attract male gametes to the female gamete. Pheromones have been isolated from many algal eggs, chemically characterized, and unequivocally demonstrated to function in attracting the sperm to the egg. Pheromones occur in green and brown algae, and also some diatoms, chrysophytes, and xanthophytes.

REPRODUCTIVE ADAPTATIONS OF RED ALGAE

Recently, spermatia of several species have been found to have extracellular projections, which may modify the transport characteristics of the spermatium and/or attach the spermatium to the trichogyne (West and Calumpong, 1989; Broadwater *et al.*, 1991). These modifications of the spermatial extracellular envelope appear after spermatial release, as the result of secretion of the polysaccharide components of spermatial vesicles. Possibly, lectin-like interactions (see Mirelman, 1986) help the essentially nonmotile spermatium attach to the carpogonial trichogyne, and the projections from some spermatia, or the post-release secretions around other, evenly-contoured spermatia may constitute one component of such a "lock and key" mechanism for attachment (Brawley and Johnson, 1992).

AGGLUTININS AND OTHER ADHESIVE STRUCTURES

Agglutination reactions between opposite mating types of gametes have been well studied in *Chlamydomonas*. The agglutinins are glycoproteins on the flagellar surface. An agglutination reaction ensures that a random encounter leads to gamete fusion, and has obvious ecological benefits in most algal habitats.

THE ROLE OF WATER MOTION

Water movements mix the male and female gametes, increasing the probability of fertilization. On the other hand, most water movements dilute the concentration of gametes, thereby decreasing the probability of fertilization.

The common occurrence of pheromones in several brown and green algae points to the likelihood that sexual reproduction will be enhanced in habitats or at times where water motion is low.

ORIGIN OF SEX

The origin of sex is inherently related to the origin of gametes which are thought to have been derived from asexual zoospores that had become too small or too weak to produce healthy new plants by themselves (Fig. 2-6). In forms such as *Chlamydomonas* and *Ulothrix* with isogamous sexual reproduction, the gametes are very much like the zoospores except for the difference in size. In the isogamous algae, both plus and minus gametes resemble the zoospores, whereas in the anisogamous or oogamous species, only the motile gametes (antherozoids) show this resemblance. The zoospores and gametes differ fundamentally in the way they give rise to new plants; the former germinate directly into new plants, whereas the latter copulate in pairs to form the zygote whose division products ultimately develop into new plants. How a mere variation in size can account for such a fundamental difference in their behaviour is the basic question. The larger zoospores contain the minimum level of factors that help them grow individually into new plants. Comparatively, the smaller zoospores are not self-sufficient and therefore fail to grow. The chance fusion of such zoospores in pairs is considered to restore the factors to optimum level for subsequent development. The precise nature of the factors is not known but it is likely that chemical, hormonal or electrical components may be involved.

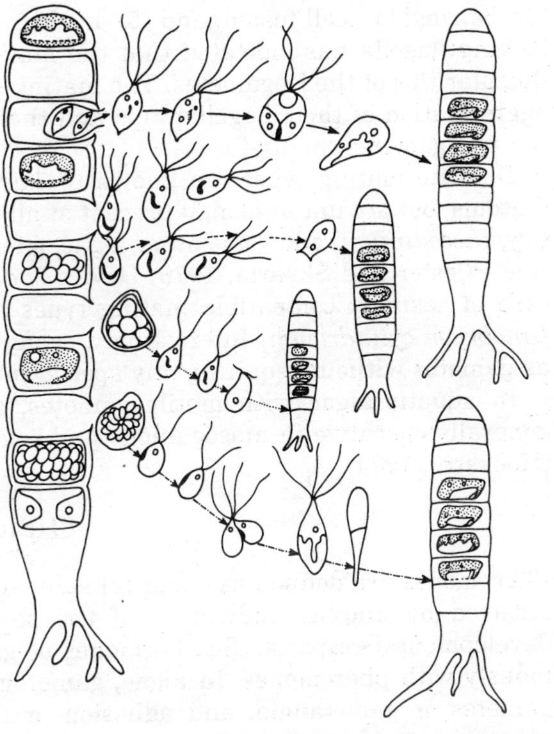

Fig. 2-6 Hypothetical diagram illustrating how sex might have originated in such forms as *Ulothrix*. (Note four types of swarmers—indicated by different kinds of arrows—and their fate, and also relative sizes of germlings produced.)

The difference in size of the larger and weaker zoospores which can potentially act as gametes results from the number of divisions the parent protoplast undergoes. If this number is small, the products are large and behave as zoospores, and if the number is large, the resulting cells are small and behave as gametes. This view is supported by the observation that under certain conditions if the gametes fail to copulate they can act like zoospores. All these facts indicate that the gametes are derived from zoospores and that sex in algae has originated as a result of accidental fusions between small-sized, weaker zoospores.

The origin of gametes (and hence the sex) from zoospores is a hypothesis developed mostly from observations made on materials collected from nature, and it has yet to receive conclusive experimental support. To our knowledge, neither genetical nor physiological factors that might be involved in regulating the zoospore-gamete balance sheet have been experimentally verified.

In heterothallic and isogamous species of *Chlamydomonas*, gametogenesis is induced by a variety of environmental factors such as light, temperature, nitrogen content, and pH. The mating reaction between gametes proceeds through a number of distinct phases, namely, (1) morphological and physiological differentiation, leading to gamete formation; (2) clumping; (3) pairing; (4) cell fusion; and (5) nuclear fusion. The work on mutants of *Chlamydomonas* lacking flagella has indicated that the mating type or sexual substances are located on the flagellar tips of the isogametes. The mating reaction between such gametes is initiated by the agglutination of their flagellar tips and then gradually proceeds downward till the bodies of the two gametes finally fuse.

Discrete mating types are known to exist in the Volvocales, in some dinoflagellates and diatoms, but are uncommon, if present at all, among the planktonic algae. In *Chlamydomonas*, *Crypthecodinium*, and some other algae, gametogenesis must be induced by a special medium (see Pfiester and Skvarla, 1979; Davies *et al.*, 1980). Sandgren (1981) has reported the first case of sexually compatible mating types and a mating group in the chrysophycean alga *Dinobryon cylindricum*. Interestingly, sexually compatible clones of this chrysophyte can act as gametes without requiring any special medium.

In aquatic algae with motile gametes, a pheromonal gamete attraction mechanism is generally operative in anisogamous and oogamous species but absent in isogamous systems (Hoekstra, 1984).

PHEROMONES

Pheromones are defined as chemical substances secreted to the outside by an individual and received by another individual of the same species in which they elicit some definite developmental response. Sex hormones or gamones are two other terms often used synonymously with pheromones. In algae, gametogenesis, chemotaxis or chemotropism of different gametes or gametangia, and adhesion or fusion of gametes are known to be affected by pheromones.

The gametes of *Chlamydomonas moewusii* produce a small, volatile, heat stable substance which attracts the gametes of the opposite sex. The female gametes of *Fucus serratus* release fucoserraten which attracts the male gametes. The corresponding pheromone produced by the female gametes of *Ectocarpus siliculosus* is called ectocarpen and performs the same function as fucoserraten. Multifidene is produced by the female gametes of *Cutleria multifida*. All these pheromones are volatile and attract their corresponding male gametes. The pheromone produced by eggs of *Oedogonium cardiacum* is water-soluble, whereas that formed by coenobia of *Volvox carteri* is a glycoprotein which induces differentiation of females.

Mature eggs of *Fucus vesiculosus*, *F. serratus*, and *F. spiralis* produce a cross-reactive pheromone which can attract male gametes. The species-specificity of most algal hormones is not very pronounced as, for example, male gametes of *Cutleria* can also show some response to ectocarpen, and *Ectocarpus* can likewise respond to multifidene.

The sex attractants of Phaeophyceae are recognized by the antherozoids through their specific binding sites, shaped to satisfy the spatial and steric requirements of the messenger molecules (Boland *et al.*, 1981). Whereas most pheromones (e.g., of insects and ferns) have at least one functional hetero (N-, O-, etc.) group, the algal sexual substances do not have such a group but are mostly unsaturated alicyclic hydrocarbons. In these algal substances, the relative positions of the double bonds seem to function in molecular interactions.

PHOTOPERIODISM

The seasonal development of several marine red, brown, and green algae is under photoperiodic control. The formation of sporangia on the *Conchocelis* phase (sporophyte) of *Porphyra tenera* can be significantly increased by cultivation in a short-day regime and prevented in an interrupted-night regime. *Bonnemaisonia hamifera* is the prominent gametophyte which alternates with a filamentous tetrasporophytic phase called *Trailliella*. The pathway leading to tetrasporangium formation on this *Trailliella* is activated during short-day conditions only within a rather narrow temperature range of 13–18°C (see Lüning, 1981).

In the case of the brown alga *Scytosiphon lomentaria*, short days induce formation of erect thalli (the main plants), whereas long days promote formation of the crustose phase which is a kind of perennating stage. In *Petalonia zosterifolia*, erect thalli are formed from a prostrate system only in short days, and a flash of light given during the night completely inhibits the above response. There is also some unconfirmed evidence that the formation of receptacles in *Fucus distichus* might possibly be under photoperiodic control (Lüning, 1981).

Short-day conditions also induce the formation of reproductive stages in some heteromorphic green algae such as *Monostroma grevillei*. The *Codiolum* phase of this alga becomes reproductive only in short-day conditions.

Blue light induces some photomorphoses in marine algae (see Table 2-2). For instance, *Acetabularia* requires blue light for cap formation. *Dictyota dichotoma* requires blue light for normal growth and differentiation; on the other hand, oogonial formation in this species is stimulated by red light.

Table 2-2 Some photomorphoses in seaweeds that are mediated by blue light (after Lüning, 1981)

Alga(e)	Blue light	Green or red light
Acetabularia spp.	Cap formation, normal growth	No caps formed; growth decreases
Scytosiphon lomentaria	Formation of hairs and 2-dimensional crusts	Growth filamentous; no hairs
Dictyota dichotoma	Normal growth; many hairs	Decreased growth; very few hairs
Laminaria spp.	Reproductive gametophytes	Vegetative gametophytes

PHOTOMOVEMENTS

CYANOBACTERIA

Whereas the trichomes of the Oscillatoriaceae rotate around their long axis during movement, the motile forms and stages of the Nostocaceae do not rotate.

In *Phormidium*, phototaxis is the result of a change of the autonomous rhythm of forward and backward movements. Under unilateral illumination, where individuals are in a more or less parallel position to the light beam, the movement toward the light source is prolonged, while, movement away from it is shortened during positive phototaxis and *vice versa* during negative phototaxis. In contrast, in the Nostocaceae, phototaxis is brought about by a true steering act. At low fluence rates the trichomes bend and move toward the light source and at high fluence rates, away from it. Whereas the action spectrum of positive phototaxis shows that effective radiation is absorbed by the photosynthetic pigments chlorophyll-a, phycoerythrocyanin, C-phycocyanin, and allophycocyanin, in negative phototaxis, in addition to the spectral range absorbed by the pigments mentioned above, wavelengths between 500 nm and 560 nm and between 700 nm and 750 nm are also effective (Nultsch and Häder, 1988).

EUCARYOTES

Photomotile responses are widespread among eucaryotes and show a great diversity in spectral sensitivity, sensory transduction, and motor responses. The diversity of the motor responses is mainly due to the variety of movement mechanisms, such as gliding by slime extrusion, amoeboid movement, or flagellar movement. Figure 2-7 shows the action spectra of phototaxis in three flagellates.

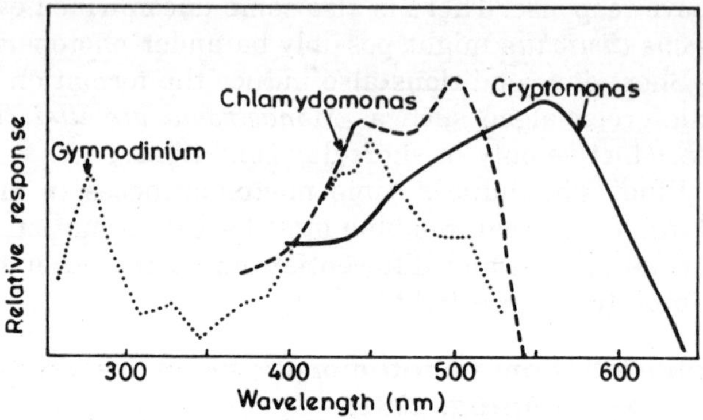

Fig. 2-7 Action spectra of phototaxis in three flagellates.

Desmids

Micrasterias and *Cosmarium* show a gliding movement powered by slime secretion from apical pores. In addition to net forward gliding, fine swaying movements occur during photoorientation. Chlorophyll-a and -b appear to be involved in photomovement.

In *Cosmarium*, switching on of actinic light causes a large fraction of previously immotile cells to start moving while switching it off suddenly stops most of the motile cells. Concomitantly, switching the actinic light on induces an increase in the electric membrane potential and switching it off causes a decrease of about the same amplitude.

Cryptomonas

Repetitive light pulses are as effective as continuous light in causing positive phototaxis in *Cryptomonas* provided that the dark interval is shorter than 60 ms. When the dark interval exceeds 250 ms the responses drastically decrease even at higher fluence rates (Watanabe and Furuya, 1978). A periodic shading mechanism might be involved in the phototactic orientation.

Role of the Stigma

The stigma consists of carotenoid-containing lipid granules which are arranged in one or more parallel layers. Though the stigma is apparently not the photoreceptor site, there is no doubt that it plays an important role in phototactic orientation. Certain eyespotless mutants of *C. reinhardii* which were at least stigma-defective, displayed less straight swimming paths and less well directed orientation than the wild type with an intact stigma.

In order to explain the role of the stigma in phototactic orientation Foster and Smyth (1980) proposed the so-called *quarter-wave-stack* hypothesis. These authors suggested that the stigma acts as a quarter wave interference reflector, consisting of a stack of alternating layers with high and low refractive indices. In such a quarter-wave stack, light reflected at high-to-low-refractive-index interfaces does not change the phase. The authors calculated the pattern of irradiance within and near the stigma at different angles of incident 480 nm light. If the photoreceptor were located between the stigma and the cell surface according to the suggestions by Melkonian and Robenek (1980), light shining on this surface would produce an irradiance at the photoreceptor molecules that is the sum of both the incident and the reflected irradiances. During rotation of the cell light is modulated by strong fluctuations in the irradiance which produces a directional antenna scanning of the environment.

Since, according to this hypothesis, the photoreceptive structure is not located between the stigma and the longitudinal axis of the cell, the phototactic orientation of *Chlamydomonas* appears to be the result of a periodic irradiation rather than of a periodic shading.

Sensory Transduction

According to Melkonian and Robenek (1984), the photoreceptor molecules are located in the plasmalemma area overlying the stigma in the cell equator. This means that a signal transmission from the photoreceptor to the effector (the flagellar apparatus) is necessary. Accordingly, the stimulus perceived has to be transformed into a transmittable signal which acts on flagellar bases where it triggers the motor response, e.g., a change of the flagellar beat. It appears that calcium ions and electrical potential changes are involved in the sensory transduction chain (Nultsch and Häder, 1988).

Calcium is necessary for phototaxis of *C. reinhardii*. Phototaxis decreases greatly when the cells are deprived of calcium. The calcium effects on motility and phototaxis of *C. reinhardii* have recently been studied by Dolle *et al.* (1987) using a fully automated and computerized population system. They have shown that both motility and phototaxis depend on calcium, but differ quantitatively in their calcium requirement. Moreover, Ca^2 dependence is a function of the fluence rate. At low fluence rates higher Ca^2 concentrations are necessary than at higher fluence rates for optimal reactivity. If the organisms are irradiated at high external Ca^2 concentrations the phototactic optimum is shifted to higher fluence rates. The calcium dependence of both phototaxis and motility suggests the involvement of calcium channels in both processes. Figure 2-8 shows a model of sensory transduction in *Euglena*.

There is some indirect evidence for the involvement of electric membrane phenomena in signal transmission.

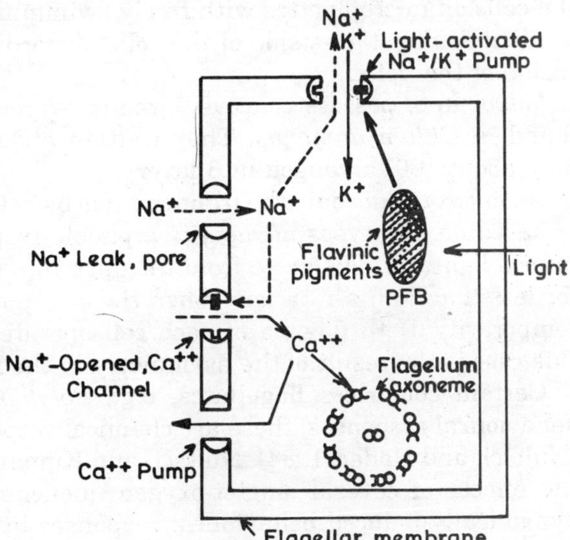

Fig. 2-8 A model for the sensory transduction in *Euglena gracilis* (after Häder, 1987).

A model of the phototactic reaction chain in *C. reinhardii* was proposed by Nultsch (1983). According to this model the absorption of photons by the photoreceptor molecules causes a permeability increase for Ca^2 due to the transient opening of calcium channels and, hence, a Ca^2 influx through the plasmalemma, causing a local membrane depolarization. The assumed subsequent electronic spread causes a transient opening of calcium channels in the flagellar membrane which should be different from the ones mentioned above. The following regenerative influx of Ca^2 activates an axonemal component, causing a change in the flagellar beat. Since the Ca^2 influx into the cell as well as into the flagella would increase the internal Ca^2 concentration, it is necessary that the Ca^2 ions are pumped out again. Thus, some energy-dependent, outward-directed calcium pumps may be present in *Chlamydomonas* cells and flagella.

Motor Response

During normal forward swimming *Chlamydomonas* cells move with their anterior, flagella-bearing end toward the direction of motion. Rüffer and Nultsch (1985) have shown that during forward movement *C. reinhardii* cells rotate counterclockwise about their long axis and that the rotation is caused by a lateral component of the three-dimensional flagellar beating. This lateral deviation starts at the tips of the flagella and proceeds proximally during the effective stroke. Thus, the rotation of *Chlamydomonas* cells during forward movement which is a prerequisite for the periodic illumination of the photoreceptor is out of the question now (Nultsch and Häder, 1988).

Studying *Chlamydomonas* cells sucked to micropipettes, Rüffer and Nultsch (1987) observed that most of the flagellar beats are synchronous but not symmetrical, as the *cis*- and the *trans*-flagella appear to beat in a slightly different manner. They suggested that the helical swimming of *Chlamydomonas* is due to these beat asymmetries. Comparing the beating of the cells on micropipettes with freely swimming ones these beat symmetries make it possible to identify the stigma side of the cells. According to Rüffer and Nultsch the stigma faces the inside of the helix.

Volvox spp. possess concave, circular stigmata which are much larger in size than those found in *Chlamydomonas*. They contain about 2000 pigment globuli (*Chlamydomonas* has only about 100) arranged in 6 layers.

In *Volvox tertius* only the front end has been found to be light sensitive. The photoorientation is based on two types of repetitive phobic responses. When during rotation of the colony in lateral light the cells move from the dark into the light the flagellar beat frequency decreases for less than half a rotation. When the cell moves from light to dark, the frequency increases temporarily. Both flagella of each cell operate synchronously; the phototactic orientation in this case is the result of the asymmetry in the flagellar activity of opposite sides of the colony.

Certain colourless flagellates, e.g., *Polytomella magna*, show photodynamically-induced behavioural responses; these are chemical responses to a photodynamically generated product (Nultsch and Häder, 1984). Nultsch and Kumar (1984) and Kumar and Nultsch (1985) studied the effects of several singlet-oxygen quenchers and free-radical scavengers on the photodynamically-induced behavioural responses in *Polytomella*. It was found that singlet oxygen quenchers either did not influence the photodynamic action of riboflavin or showed only slight quenching at high concentrations. On the other hand, the radical quencher 1,4-benzo-quinone was more effective than the singlet oxygen quenchers. These results suggest the involvement of hydrogen peroxide.

LIFE HISTORIES

The zygote is a diploid cell resulting from gametic fusion and is provided with a thin or thick wall or no wall (at least for a few days, e.g., in spp. of *Gymnodinium*). The thin-walled zygotes often germinate directly, without undergoing any resting period, as in most marine algae. The thick-walled zygotes generally have their walls differentiated into three layers and such zygotes (zygospores or oospores) normally remain dormant for a while before germination. Both karyogamy and meiosis may take place in the zygote which on germination produces a haploid plant. If these processes become separated in time and space, the zygote merely remains a place for karyogamy and its germination gives rise to a diploid plant. It is during sporogenesis by the diploid plant that meiosis occurs. The interpolation of a diploid somatic phase between karyogamy and meiosis probably makes the individuals more stable genetically and physiologically with the consequent attainment of greater adaptability and survival.

The growth and development of an alga proceed through a number of distinct morphological and cytological stages. The sequence of these orderly changes is termed the life cycle or life history. The term life history means the sum total of all developmental and reproductive stages occurring during life in individuals, populations, or species. The important events in a life history are fertilization and meiosis, and the associated processes of formation of gametes and meiospores. Any asexual and vegetative reproduction of the gametophyte and sporophyte generations are also important. Besides the essential features of a life history, there are certain other noteworthy characteristics such as the longevity of each generation, its reproductive span, the relative frequency of sexual and asexual (or vegetative) reproduction, and the seasonality of growth and reproduction (Clayton, 1988). Accordingly, a life cycle has two aspects, the somatic or morphological, and the cytological or chromosomal. The life cycle of sexually reproducing algae tends to belong to one of three basically different patterns. In type I, the free-living alga is haploid, producing gametes which fuse to form a zygote. Meiosis occurs when the zygote germinates (Fig. 2-9). Thus the zygote constitutes the only diploid stage in the life history. Examples: *Oedogonium*, *Coleochaete*, *Ulothrix*. This kind of meiosis is called zygotic meiosis. In type II, the free-living alga is diploid and meiosis occurs during gametogenesis (gametic meiosis). The gametes are haploid. They fuse to form the zygote which by repeated mitotic divisions gives rise to the diploid thallus. Examples: *Fucus*, *Melosira* (Fig. 2-10). Both these types of life history are collectively described as haplobiontic. In type

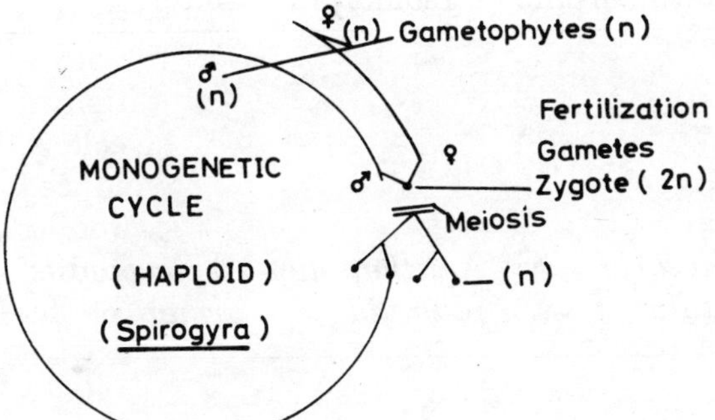

Fig. 2-9 Monogenetic haploid life cycle.

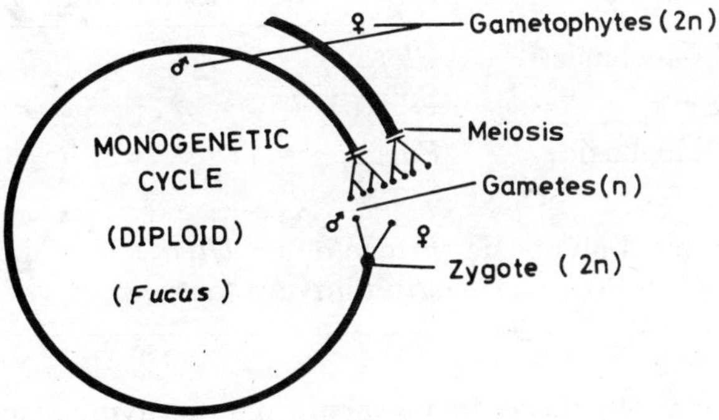

Fig. 2-10 Monogenetic diploid life cycle.

III, there are two independent multicellular free-living generations called the gametophyte and sporophyte generations. The gametophyte generation is haploid and forms gametes. These fuse to form the diploid zygotes. The zygote divides mitotically to develop into the sporophyte generation which is diploid. It produces spores by meiosis (sporic meiosis). These haploid spores develop into the haploid gametophytes. This kind of life cycle is called diplobiontic. In some algae, e.g., *Dictyota* and *Stigeoclonium*, both the gametophytic and sporophytic plants are morphologically alike, hence this type of alternation of generations is described as being isomorphic (Fig. 2-11 A) or homologous. In *Laminaria* and *Cutleria*, for example, there is a pronounced morphological dissimilarity between the gametophytic and sporophytic plants and hence the alternation of generations is stated to be heteromorphic or antithetic (Fig. 2-11 B). Table 2-3 shows examples of life cycle in algae.

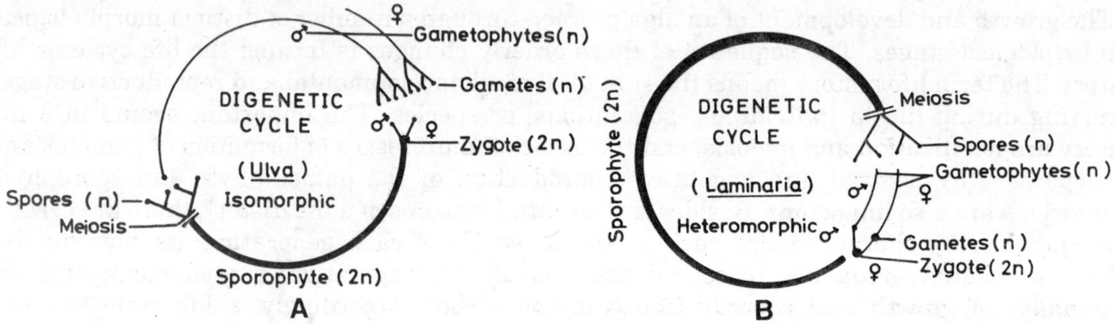

Fig. 2-11 Digenetic life cycles. A, isomorphic; B, heteromorphic.

Table 2-3 Some life cycles in algae

Phase	Generation				
	Cycle				
	Monogenetic	Digenetic		Trigenetic	
		Isomorphic	Heteromorphic	Isomorphic	Heteromorphic
Haplophasic cycle	*Ulothrix*, *Spirogyra*				
Diplophasic cycle	*Fucus*, *Sargassum*				
Haplo-diplophasic cycle	*Prasiola stipitata*	*Ulva lactuca*	*Laminaria digitata*	*Antithamnion plumula*	*Asparagopsis armata*

Life histories in flowering plants, gymnosperms, pteridophytes, and bryophytes follow a single basic pattern. A haploid gametophyte normally gives rise to a diploid sporophyte, the term *alternation of generations* being used to describe the alternation between the two phases. It is misleading to use the term for many algae since the classical picture of a strict alternation of a haploid and diploid generation is not always applicable (John, 1994). In some algae genetic and morphological alternation may not be obligate as each phase can reproduce itself several times without producing an alternate one. The term *life history* should therefore be preferred to *life cycle* to describe recurrent morphological and nuclear phases. Another argument against the use of *alternation* is that many algal life histories involve more than two phases. For example, several members of the red algal Florideophycidae basically show a two-phase life history into which is inserted an additional phase, the carposporophyte.

Much complexity and flexibility occurs in algal life histories having two or more nuclear and/or morphological phases and a considerable intraspecific variability exists in these life history pathways. Indeed, the existence of such high variability in life histories of algae has prompted Guiry and Womersley (1993) to question the practice of assigning names to algal life history types.

The life histories of many algae cannot be interpreted properly because of lack of knowledge about the ploidy levels of different phases. Without such data one cannot know whether an uncoupling of the morphological and genetic components of a life history has taken place. In some algae (e.g., *Scytosiphon lomentaria* and *Petalonia* sp.), heteromorphy is unlinked to changes in ploidy level, and also in view of some isomorphic life histories where meiosis and syngamy are not evident (see Wynne and Loiseaux, 1976). In some brown algae, the life history is complicated by heteroblasty, a phenomenon whereby zooids show different germination modes and develop into different morphs independent of external conditions or sexuality (Pedersen, 1981). Vegetative diploidization also occurs in brown algae and involves a diploid macrothallus developing directly on a haploid microthallus (John, 1994).

Some red algae show an unusual condition involving the production of male and female reproductive organs on the tetrasporangial phase. Such *mixed-phase* reproduction is common in the family Ceramiaceae, where it seems to result from mitotic recombination in the tetrasporophyte leading to paired islands of homozygous male and female tissue (Maggs, 1988). It appears that in several brown and green algae, factors other than ploidy level determine whether an individual functions as a gametangial or a sporangial phase (John, 1994). In some cases, parthenogenetic development of a gamete (without sexual fusion) into an adult plant might suppress a phase giving rise to a direct and single-phase life history. Apomictic reproductive structures are often morphologically indistinguishable from those produced in sexual life histories, and it appears that few algal species are *obligate* apomicts (i.e., those in which all populations reproduce completely asexually). The chief advantage of apomixis is that it enables a morph to survive well in a particular environment. In contrast, sexual reproduction often yields some morphs exposed to a selective disadvantage. Apomixis is probably more important in highly disturbed habitats where selective pressures differentially act against one type of morph compared to another.

GENERALIZED ALGAL LIFE CYCLES

Algal life cycles vary in the position of meiosis relative to syngamy. Meiosis may be gametic (Fig. 2-12) or sporic (Fig. 2-13).

Figure 2-14 illustrates the life cycle and alternation of generations in three genera of Phaeophyceae.

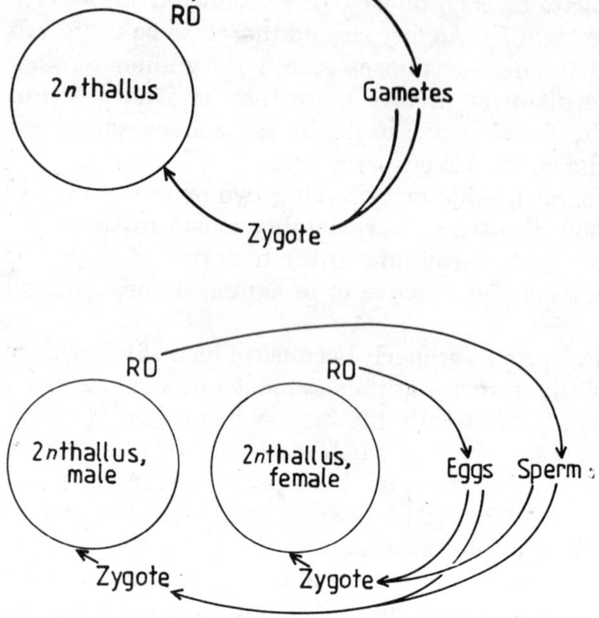

Fig. 2-12 Life histories of algae with gametic meiosis. RD, reduction division; upper figure, gametes are produced by one individual; lower figure, sexes are separate.

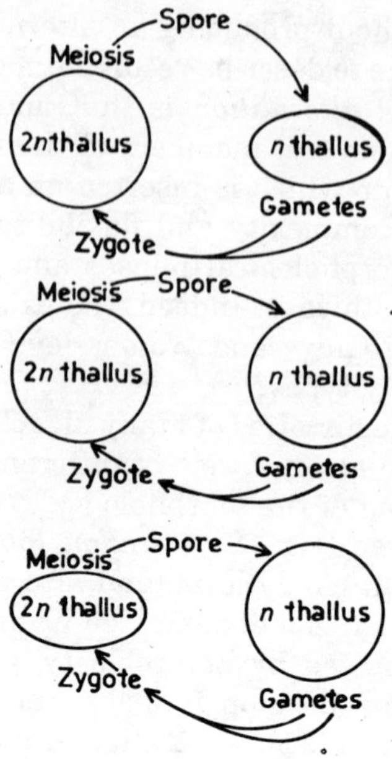

Fig. 2-13 Life histories of algae with sporic meiosis. Circle denotes the adult thallus, the area indicating the size that the individual may achieve (relative). In the middle figure, the haploid and diploid thalli are isomorphic; in the upper and lower figures, they are heteromorphic.

When meiosis immediately follows syngamy and zygote formation, it is called zygotic, the resulting free-living organism is haploid, and the life cycle is termed haploid. Meiosis is sometimes delayed relative to syngamy by the interposition of repeated mitotic divisions and the subsequent generation of a free-living diploid phase (Table 2-4). The diploid phase eventually produces meiotically derived spores that settle and undergo repeated mitosis to generate a free-living haploid phase. Meiosis in this case is termed sporic and the life cycle is haplo-diploid (Klinger, 1993).

Meiosis can be removed further from syngamy by the production of a second diploid phase. Here, the zygote undergoes multiple mitotic divisions, while still retained on the haploid parent, producing many diploid spores. Upon release the spores give rise to a free-living diploid generation that eventually produces haploid spores by meiosis. The haploid spores in turn produce a free-living haploid generation. This life cycle is a special case of the haplo-diploid life cycle, and is restricted to the Rhodophyta.

When syngamy immediately follows meiosis the diploid is the sole free-living phase. This is the case in the familiar diploid life cycle of vertebrates; meiosis here is termed gametic. This type of life history occurs in the Fucales.

TYPES

Generalizations are at present possible for only three classes of algae, namely, Chlorophyceae, Phaeophyceae, and Rhodophyceae. Many earlier generalizations have had to be abandoned in the face of new information, especially in view of the fact that several algae show much intraspecific variation in their life history patterns (e.g., see Maggs, 1988).

The three basic algal life history types are related to differences in the degree of morphological elaboration of the phases. One type has a single free-living haploid or diploid phase, and the other two types have more than one phase. Type I (diplontic life history) occurs in such morphologically advanced orders as the Fucales in which the single phase is diploid, producing (by meiosis) haploid gametes. Some algae have a single haploid phase with meiosis taking place on germination of the zygote. Such

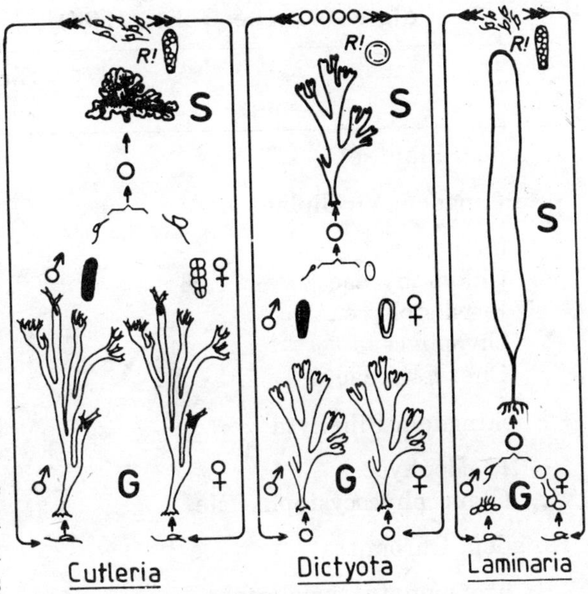

Fig. 2-14 Life cycle and alternation of generations in three genera of brown algae. Haploid phases are drawn in thin lines, diploid in thick. G, gametophyte; S, sporophyte; O, zygote; R!, reduction division.

Table 2-4 Comparison of some algal life cycles

Haploid life cycle	Haplo-diploid life cycle	Haplo-diploid life cycle (Rhodophyta)	Diploid life cycle
Syngamy ↓	Syngamy ↓	Syngamy ↓	Syngamy ↓
Zygote formation ↓	Zygote formation ↓	Zygote formation ↓	Zygote formation ↓
		Diploid retained on haploid parent ↓	
		Spore formation ↓	
	Free-living diploid ↓	Free-living diploid ↓	Free-living diploid ↓
Meiosis ↓	Meiosis ↓	Meiosis ↓	Meiosis ↓
Free-living haploid ↓	Free-living haploid ↓	Free-living haploid	
Gamete formation	Gamete formation		Gamete formation

Table 2-5 Distribution of single or two or more phase life histories in eucaryotic algae (source: John, 1994)

	Single phase: somatic cells diploid or haploid	Two phases: different and/or same ploidy level
Kingdom Plantae*		
Subkingdom Viridiplantae		
Chlorophyta**	+	+
Chlorophyceae	+	−
Prasinophyceae	+	+
Ulvophyceae	+	−
Charophyceae		
Subkingdom Biliphyta		
Rhodophyceae	+	+
Glaucophycocystophyceae	+	−
Kingdom Chromista		
Chromophyta *sensu lato*		
Bacillariophyceae	+	−
Chrysophyceae	+	−
Cryptophyceae	+	−
Eustigmatophyceae	+	−
Phaeophyceae	+	+
Prymnesiophyceae (=Haptophyceae)	+	+
Raphidophyceae	+	−
Synurophyceae	+	−
Xanthophyceae	+	−
Kingdom Protozoa*		
Euglenophyceae	+	−
Dinophyceae	+	−

*Classification into kingdoms follows Cavalier-Smith (1981, 1983, 1989).
**Classification mainly follows the class-level system for Chlorophyta proposed by Mattox and Stewart (1984).

a haplontic life history occurs, for instance, in the Charales. The genus *Coleochaete* has properties in common with what might be considered to be the immediate ancestors of embryophytic plants (see Graham, 1985; Graham *et al.*, 1991). The *direct type* or monophasic life history found in most algal classes (Tables 2-3, 2-4, and 2-5) appears to be the most primitive (John, 1994).

The following basic life histories have been recognized in the Chlorophyceae, Phaeophyceae, and Rhodophyceae: (1) monophasic, a diploid or haploid phase; (2) two or more phases, most commonly an alternation of an isomorphic or heteromorphic haploid gametangial phase and a diploid sporangial phase; and (3) three phases (unique to florideophyte Rhodophyceae), with a diploid spore-producing phase (carposporophyte) developing on the gametangial phase, a diploid phase (tetrasporophyte if meiosis is sporic) and a haploid gametangial phase (John, 1994). In many algae there is an uncoupling of the morphological and nuclear phases. The dominance of one phase and suppression of another may be due to the common occurrence in algae of apogamy, apomeiosis, and parthenogenesis.

Evolution of the carposporangial phase in red algae may conceivably be a way of achieving zygotic amplification to compensate for the infrequency of syngamy. Such amplification allows the production of a large number of propagules from a single fertilization. The direct development of a free-living tetrasporangial phase may be another mechanism for achieving amplification. In freshwater red algae the growth of an upright phase from a perennial microscopic one appears to be an adaptation for maintaining their upstream position (John, 1994).

Algal life history patterns are controlled by subtle environmental influences such as photoperiodism, temperature, light quality, and nutrients. Herbivory is an important selective force suppressing some morphs and promoting the seasonal dominance of others. Differential resistance of morphs to herbivory in environments where grazing intensity is predictable may lead to the selective maintenance of heteromorphy (John, 1994).

Seasonality appears to be crucial in the evolution of life histories where there is more than one ecologically distinct phase (Istock, 1966). The converse may be true, with direct or isomorphic life histories at a selective advantage in constant or stable environments. This may explain why dictyotalean brown algae having isomorphic life histories tend to be so common in tropical shores (Clayton, 1988). In these habitats, brown algae with heteromorphic life histories are quite poorly represented.

Haplo-diploidy

Many of the major algal groups have originated independently. There exists much variation among the different groups in the position of meiosis relative to syngamy, with consequent differences in the proportion of the life cycle spent in haploid versus diploid modes. Haplo-diploidy is common among marine macroscopic algae (seaweeds), but is not typical of most microalgal groups (Klinger, 1993).

Haplo-diploid Life Cycles

Haplo-diploid life cycles are common in the marine Rhodophyta, Chlorophyta, and Phaeophyta. In this life cycle, there is spatial and temporal separation of meiosis and syngamy and the resultant partitioning of the life cycle into free-living haploid and diploid phases. The haploid and diploid phases commonly undergo an alternation of generations, but there are some exceptions to this. Within species, haploids and diploids can be isomorphic or heteromorphic. Among the latter either the haploid or diploid phase can be the more conspicuous.

Isomorphic haploid and diploid phases may or may not share a common habitat. Heteromorphic phases sometimes occupy ternate habitats. For example, in *Macrocystis*, the haploid is a benthic microscopic filamentous phase, while the diploid phase is a large, complex thallus that reaches the water surface. In *Porphyra*, the foliose haploid phase commonly grows on rocky substrata, while the filamentous diploid phase grows in or on animal shells of calcium carbonate. Heteromorphic phases can show strong seasonal differences in recruitment, growth, and reproduction, with the reduced filamentous or crustose phases resistant to environmental stresses such as desiccation and grazing (Klinger, 1993).

Many red seaweeds maintain two distinct, sequential diploid phases in addition to the haploid phase, thereby conferring an even greater separation between meiosis and syngamy. In other red algae, haploid males are isomorphic with the diploid phase, and are large compared with the very reduced heteromorphic females (Klinger, 1993).

Some genera (e.g., *Ulva*, *Ectocarpus*, and *Gracilaria*) show facultative auxiliary reproductive cycles that can include parthenogenetic development of apomeiotically or apomictically derived spores or gametes, in addition to vegetative proliferation. These auxiliary cycles can alter the expression of haploidy relative to diploidy in the life cycle (Klinger, 1993).

Pleiomorphism involves change in morphology independent of ploidy. Thus, haploids and diploids of *Padina jamaicensis* are normally isomorphic but both phases can change morphologically in response to grazing, with no accompanying change in ploidy.

Thus, among the seaweeds, sequential generations can undergo changes in ploidy with no associated change in morphology, changes in ploidy with an obligate change in morphology, or changes in morphology with no change in ploidy (Klinger, 1993). Closely related taxa sometimes show widely variant life cycles, and a single species may show differences in its life cycle across various spatial and temporal scales.

Polyphasic

Sporic life histories typically consist of a spore-producing phase (usually diploid) alternating with a gamete-producing phase (usually haploid). An alternation of two nuclear phases constitutes a biphasic or diplohaplontic life history. The morphological phases linked to the nuclear phases may be either isomorphic (e.g., some Ulvales, Cladophorales, Ectocarpales, Sphacelariales, and Dictyotales) or heteromorphic (e.g., Derbesiales, Laminariales, and Bangiales). The diploid phase either forms haploid spores by meiosis (i.e., meiosis is sporic), or diploid spores which on germination undergo meiosis (e.g., conchospores of *Porphyra*). Alternatively, meiosis occurs in somatic cells giving rise directly to the haploid phase. The haploid phase may be monoecious or dioecious and usually produces gametes by mitosis.

A diplohaplontic life history involving alternation of morphologically identical haploid and diploid plants (isomorphic life history) is very common. In some brown algae (see Clayton, 1988) the sporangial phase can better survive a wider range of conditions than the gametangial phase. In *Ectocarpus*, *Dictyota*, and *Ulva* the haploid phase is monoecious.

The sporangial phase is dominant in four algal classes (see Tables 2-3, 2-4, 2-5) possessing heteromorphic life histories. In several orders of brown algae (e.g., Laminariales, Desmarestiales, and Sporochnales) the sporangial phase is diploid, quite large and long-lived, and regularly alternates with a diminutive, short-lived, haploid phase. In a few brown algal genera (*Cutleria*, *Scytosiphon*, and *Petalonia*) the haploid phase is dominant (John, 1994). Biphasic heteromorphic life histories are found in *Ulothrix*, *Monostroma*, and in *Bangia* and *Porphyra* (see Fig. 2-15). In some algae the different phases are morphologically so dissimilar that until recently they were thought to belong to different species or genera. Indeed in a few cases, genera were even placed in separate families or orders.

In some life histories the two phases are intimately associated. In the green algae *Prasiola meridionalis* and *P. stipitata* the free-living phase is diploid and monostromatic. The gametangial phase develops on it by some cells undergoing meiosis to form paired male and female areas of polystromatic tissue. The gametangial areas form gametes by mitosis and syngamy gives rise to a zygote that germinates into the free-living diploid phase. Other species of *Prasiola* have both heteromorphic and zygotic life histories (John, 1994).

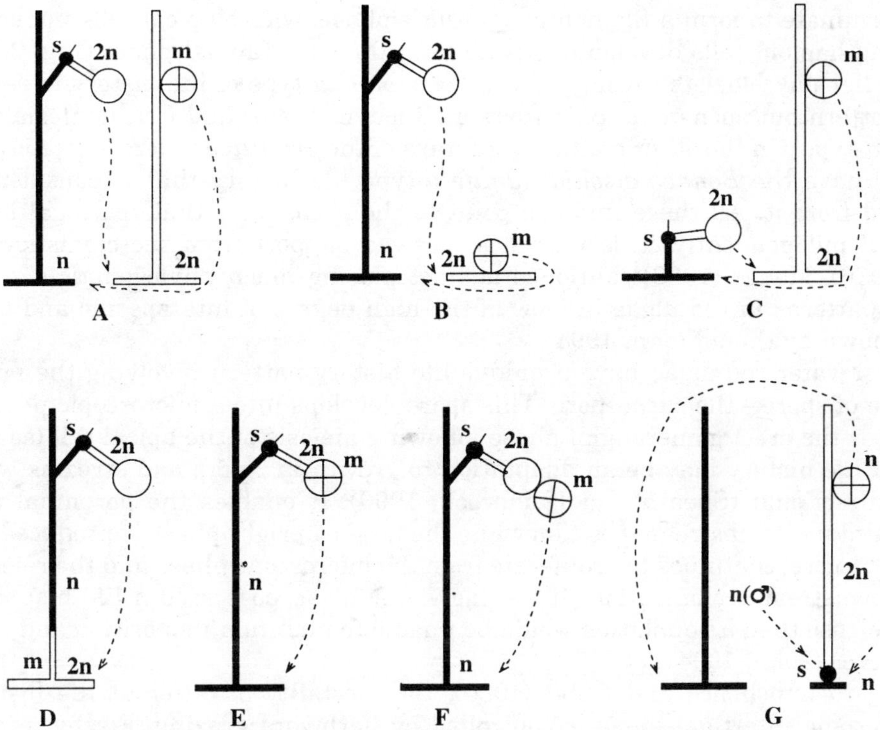

Fig. 2-15 Some life histories in the Rhodophyceae. s, position of syngamy; m, position of meiosis; n, haploid; 2n, diploid. (After Dixon, 1982.)

Triphasic Life Histories in Rhodophyceae

These occur in most orders of the subclass Florideophycidae, except the Palmariales. Typically the life history consists of a gametangial phase and two morphologically-distinct spore-producing phases, the tetrasporangial (tetrasporophyte) and carposporangial (carposporophyte) phases, the latter differing morphologically from the female gametangial phase on which it develops and depends. The carposporangial phase forms spores mitotically. These produce the sporangial phase which usually produces tetrasporangia (less commonly, bisporangia or polysporangia). The sporangial phase is either free-living or develops on the female gametangial phase.

The typical pattern involves two free-living phases (gametangial and tetrasporangial) and a dependent carposporangial phase. In red algae, life histories with isomorphic free-living phases (Fig. 2-15 A, *Polysiphonia*-type) are more common than those with heteromorphic phases. The gametangial phase tends to be more conspicuous (Fig. 2-15) than the tetrasporangial which is usually crustose or sometimes forms tufts of branched filaments (e.g., *Liagora* and *Asparagopsis*). In the Acrochaetiales, the tetrasporangial phase is more conspicuous than the gametangial phase. If one considers the carposporangial phase as being equivalent to other life history phases then all red algae possessing it would be heteromorphic (John, 1994).

In *Batrachospermum* and *Lemanea*, a tetrasporangial stage is absent. The diploid carpospores germinate to form a filamentous *juvenile* phase, whose apical cells undergo meiosis. The resulting haploid cells develop *in situ* to form the gametangial phase (Fig. 2-15).

Many earlier phycologists considered the *Polysiphonia*-type of life history to represent the ancestral pattern but such *advanced* orders as Rhodymeniales and Ceramiales also have the *Polysiphonia*-type. On the other hand, several taxa of the *primitive* orders (e.g., Acrochaetiales, Nemaliales) have the *Bonnemaisonia hamifera*-type life history that is considered to have been derived from it. All these findings point to the probability that red algal life histories have evolved independently. This view has received support from the cladistic analysis by Garbary (1986). Maggs (1988) cautioned against placing much phylogenetic significance on life history patterns in red algae in view of the high degree of interspecific and intraspecific variation shown by them (John, 1994).

Many freshwater red algae have a unique life history pattern involving the production of but one type of spore—the carpospore. This spore develops into a microscopic phase which in turn produces the erect gametangial phase following meiosis of the apical cell (see Fig. 2-15). This type of life history may be an adaptation to growth in rivers and streams where water flow is unidirectional (Sheath and Hambrook, 1990). It enables the perennial microscopic phase to maintain its upstream position while the larger upright phase is produced seasonally. The alga, therefore, continues to proliferate from the microscope phase and the released spores allow for downstream colonization. If flowing-water algae possessed a life history involving just spore release then a population would be unable to maintain its position and so gradually shift downriver (John, 1994).

According to Lubchenco and Cubit (1980), the mortality of different life history phases (morphs) of some intertidal algae is controlled by herbivore grazing. Fleshy upright stages tend to be selectively removed by seasonally-intense grazing whereas crustose or substrate-penetrating morphs are usually resistant to grazing.

Algae having heteromorphic life histories appear to be at an adaptive advantage if the main selective agent(s) is variable rather than constant. Lubchenco and Cubit (1980) noted that if grazing was constant, algae having an *obligate* alternation of different free-living morphs would be at a selective disadvantage due to competition eliminating one morph. Under relatively constant conditions isomorphy appears to be advantageous whereas under variable conditions, heteromorphy predominates. Conceivably, greater fitness accrues to those algae which synchronize the production of the morph which is most likely to survive (e.g., grazing-resistant morphs during season of intense herbivory). For the evolution of synchronization the selective agent(s) must be predictable and the appropriate morph produced in response to environmental cues such as photoperiod and/or temperature.

PERENNATION

When the environmental conditions become unfavourable, many algae form resting stages for perennation, i.e., for tiding over adverse periods. In many Chlorophyceae, the only perennating stage in the life cycle is the thick-walled zygospore or oospore that commonly has a highly viscous protoplast containing an orange or red oily pigment known as haematochrome. They can tolerate unfavourable environmental conditions without any adverse effects.

Many terrestrial or subaerial blue-green algae can perennate as such, i.e., without any apparent modification of the vegetative cell or filament. The thick, stratified or gelatinous sheaths around their cells or trichomes, the gel-like consistency and viscosity of their protoplast, and the virtual universal absence of vacuoles in their cells are probably some features that enable them to endure and survive unfavourable conditions without much structural modification.

Perennation in other algae involves the formation of specially differentiated resting cells. Common examples follow.

Akinetes

These are enlarged vegetative cells which become thick-walled and store abundant reserve food material (Fig. 2-16). With the advent of unfavourable conditions, the ordinary vegetative cells die, whereas the akinetes successfully endure the harsh climate. When favourable conditions recommence during the next spring or rainy season, the akinete germinates and produces a vegetative filament, e.g., *Pithophora*, *Gloeotrichia*, and *Cylindrospermum* (Fig. 2-16). Akinete formation is widespread in the nitrogen-fixing blue-green alga, *Aulosira fertilissima*, which occurs abundantly in tropical rice fields. Here, the vegetative filaments become transformed into chains of akinetes when the stagnant water in the fields begins to dry up, and it is in this sporulating condition that the alga tides over dry and hot periods.

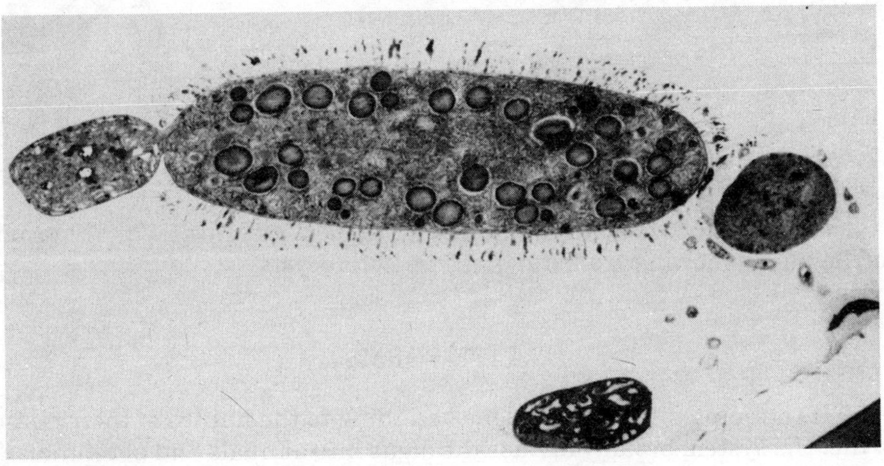

Fig. 2-16 *Cylindrospermum*, part of filament showing heterocyst, akinete, and vegetative cell. (×3200.) *Courtesy* K. Ueda.

Hypnospores or Cysts

Like akinetes, these too are thick-walled but, as a rule, are formed by repeated divisions of the protoplast rather than by the modification of a cell into a single akinete as in *Acetabularia* (Fig. 2-17). *Protosiphon botryoides* and *Sphaerella lacustris* also furnish good examples of cyst formation. During conditions of drought or light of high intensity, their cytoplasm breaks up into a number of thick-walled hypnospores which in *Sphaerella* may remain embedded in a common gelatinous matrix.

In *Fritschiella tuberosa* and *Botrydium*, cysts are formed in the subterranean parts. When favourable conditions recur, the cysts either grow direct into a new cell or give rise to zoospores.

Hormocysts

These are hormogonia which, instead of being liberated from the parent filaments, remain *in situ* and become thick-walled. They may also be regarded as many-celled akinetes. Typical hormocysts are met with in the blue-green alga *Westiella* (Fig. 2-18).

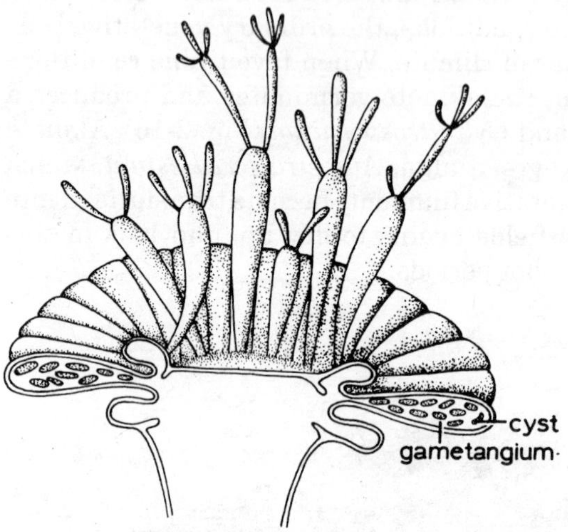

Fig. 2-17 *Acetabularia*, vertical section through fertile disc, showing gametangial rays and cysts.

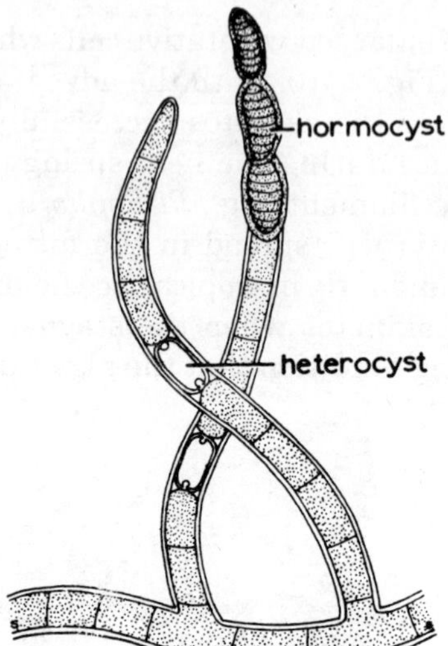

Fig. 2-18 *Westiella*, hormocysts and heterocysts.

LIFE-FORMS

Feldmann (1937) attempted to classify algae according to the nature of their resting stage and duration of life. His system broadly divides the algae into annuals and perennials. The annuals are further classified into (1) true annuals (algae having one reproductive season per year, e.g., *Codium* and most Dictyotales); (2) eclipses (algae surviving the unfavourable season as a minute stage and having a single short or long luxuriant growth period each year, e.g., many Heterogeneratae and *Conchocelis* phase of Bangiophyceae); and (3) ephemerals (algae having in a year two or more generations following each other, and with reproductive cells and gemmae growing immediately into short-lived macroscopic bodies, e.g., species of *Enteromorpha*, *Cladophora*, *Polysiphonia*, *Sphacelaria*, and *Ectocarpus*).

The perennials are further subdivided into the following categories: (1) algae having a perennial basal part or holdfast, e.g., spp. of *Chondrus*, *Gracilaria*, *Rhodomela*, and *Sargassum*; (2) algae in which the holdfasts as well as the main axes of the thallus are perennial, e.g., many Laminariales and Sargassaceae; and (3) algae with perennial fronds, e.g., spp. of *Gelidium* and *Ahnfeltia*.

VIRUSES OF EUCARYOTIC ALGAE

Over 40 taxa of freshwater and marine eucaryotic algae contain viruses or virus-like particles (VLPs) (Table 2-6). Most but not all of the VLPs are polyhedra with diameters varying from 20 nm to 400 nm (Van Etten *et al.*, 1991). Commonly the particles have an external, multilaminate shell which encloses the core. This shell resembles a membrane, at least superficially, but there is no direct evidence that the particles have a bonafide external membrane. Usually a species contains only one type of VLP, but some species of *Cryptomonas*, *Gyrodinium*, *Paraphysomonas*, and *Pyramimonas* contain two sizes of VLPs often in the same cell. *Paraphysomonas corynephora* even harbours three sizes of VLPs (Preisig and Hibberd, 1984). VLPs may occur in the nucleus, in the cytoplasm, or in both. Infected cells often lack a nucleus and it is likely that the VLPs may be formed at the expense of the nucleus (Van Etten *et al.*, 1991). As a general rule, vegetative cells of multicellular algae lack VLPs, and the particles are seen only in the reproductive cells or the germlings. It appears that in several algae the infection with VLPs occurs at the zoospore stage; the zoospores are usually wall-less. In most algae, only about 5% of the cells are infected but the percentage of infected cells is greater in *Platymonas* species (Pearson and Norris, 1974). This rather low frequency of infection in the vast majority of algae, coupled with the observation that the VLPs are present only in some differentiated cells which usually lack infectivity, has prompted many investigators to suggest that the VLPs represent a latent infection. This suggestion is strengthened by the fact that the infected cells usually do not lyse or die. However, there is as yet no direct evidence for lysogeny either.

Gibbs *et al.* (1975) and Stoknicki *et al.* (1976) isolated and characterized the first infectious virus in the eucaryotic alga *Chara corallina* and named it CCV. CCV contains single-stranded RNA and resembles tobacco mosaic virus. Its particles are rigid helical rods that are about double the size of TMV. CCV replicates inside *Chara corallina*.

Dodds and Cole (1980) studied a large, noninfectious VLP from *Uronema gigas*. In this species only about 1% of cells in the germling harbour VLPs; cells of the adult filaments are free from these particles. The particles contain ds DNA.

Mayer and Taylor (1979) described a virus which infects the marine flagellate *Micromonas pusilla*. This flagellate is wall-less. The virus attaches to the cell and has ds DNA.

Viruses or VLPs have also been recorded from *Chlorella*, *Ectocarpus*, *Feldmannia*, *Chlorococcum minutum*, *Cylindrocapsa geminella*, and several other algae (Table 2-6). At least some of these viruses, especially those that infect Phaeophyceae, tend to be expressed only in meiotic cells, suggesting highly specific coordination between the virus and the host's life cycle (Van Etten *et al.*, 1991).

Hydromechanical factors ranging from molecular motion to ocean currents influence the adaptation of phytoplankton to suspension in water. The picoplankton (0.2–2.0 μm) are the best adapted to the physico-chemical environment of the open waters of seas and lakes and, other things being equal, can outcompete the larger forms. The picophytoplankton are an autotrophic component in a microbial community, the ultraplankton, which also includes bacteria and flagellates up to about 20 μm in linear dimensions. This community is a highly dynamic and self-contained equilibrium system operating within a domain dominated by molecular diffusion (Fogg, 1991). Within the photic zone it is not usually limited by nutrient supply but by predator-prey relationships. It is cosmopolitan, has a fairly constant species composition and biomass concentration, and contributes small amounts of organic carbon to

Table 2-6 Viruses and virus-like particles of selected eucaryotic algae (condensed and modified from Van Etten *et al.*, 1991)

Host	Virogenic stroma in			Nucleic acid			Particle character(s)	Remarks*
	Nucleus	Cytoplasm	?	DNA*	RNA	?		
Porphyridium purpureum	+	+				+	Polyhedral, 40 nm**	
Sirodotia tenuissima		+				+	Polyhedral, 50–60 nm	
Cryptomonas sp.	+	+				+	Dimorphic particles in same cell: polyhedral, 99 nm; stalked with head 240 nm × 120 nm	
Gymnodinium uberrimum		+				+	Polyhedral, 385 nm	
Chromophysomonas cornuta		+				+	Two polyhedral particles, 50–60 nm and 150–180 nm	
Mallomonas sp.		+				+	Polyhedral, 175 nm	
Chrysochromulina sp.			+			+	Polyhedral, 22 nm	
Monodus sp.	+					+	Polyhedral, 400 nm	
Ectocarpus fasciculatus	+					+	Polyhedral, 170 nm	Leads to cell lysis
E. siliculosus		+		+			Polyhedral, 130 nm	Infects swimming zoospores
Feldmannia sp.	+			+			Polyhedral, 150 nm	Replicates only in meiotic sporangia
Heteromastix	+					+	Polyhedral, 320 nm, with complex membranes	
Micromonas pusilla		+		+			Polyhedral, 130–135 nm	Virus adheres to host cell surface

Table 2-6 Viruses and virus-like particles of selected eucaryotic algae (condensed and modified from Van Etten *et al.*, 1991) (cont.)

Host	Virogenic stroma in			Nucleic acid			Particle character(s)	Remarks*
	Nucleus	Cytoplasm	?	DNA*	RNA	?		
Chlorella spp.			+			+	Polyhedral head, 41 nm in diameter with a 24-nm-long 10-nm-broad tail	
Chlorella strain NC64A		+		+			Polyhedral, 150–190 nm	Attaches specifically to host walls and uncoats at surface
Chlorococcum minutum		+		+			Polyhedral, 180–220 nm, having a tail	Virus infects only zoospores, progeny viruses released by lysis of cell in about 8 hours
Cylindrocapsa geminella	+	+		+			Polyhedral, 200–300 nm, with a membranous coat	Particles may lead to cell lysis
Chara corallina		+			+ (ssRNA)		Tubular rods, 523 nm long 18 nm broad, with basic pitch of 2.75 nm	Can be injected artificially into uninfected *Chara* cells and then causes chlorosis and death in 10–12 days
Coleochaete scutata	+					+	Polyhedral, 41 nm	

?, unknown.
*Wherever present, it is double-stranded.
**Unless otherwise stated, the dimensions are for diameter.

higher trophic levels. There appears to be a fundamental divide in form and function between this and the microplankton; the latter consists of organisms larger than about 20 μm and can only develop when nutrient levels are in excess of the concentrations required by the picoplankton. Microplankton is opportunistic, nonequilibrium in its dynamics, and highly variable in floristic composition and biomass concentration. Its life processes are dominated by turbulence (Fogg, 1991). Nutrient supply is largely determined by turbulent eddy diffusion and movement of the organisms relative to the water mass. The microphytoplankton can be broadly divided into two classes: one is exemplified by the diatoms and depends on turbulence to maintain it in the photic zone; the other class is exemplified by the dinoflagellates and colonial cyanobacteria and relies on motility or buoyancy control to orient it in a relatively stable water column so as to have optimum access to light and nutrients. Whereas the waxing and waning of microplankton populations is largely determined by hydrography, their floristic compositions are regulated by the interaction of the rhythms of the organisms with the periodicities in the environment. In contrast to the ultraplankton, microplankton shows marked differences in geographical distribution.

REFERENCES

Allen, R.D., The moment of fertilization, *Scient. Am.*, **201**, 124–34 (1959).

Amsler, C.D. and Neushul, M., Photosynthetic physiology and chemical composition of spores of the kelps *Macrocystis pyrifera, Nereocystis luetkeana, Laminaria farlowii,* and *Pterygophora californica* (Phaeophyceae), *J. Phycol.*, **27**, 26–34 (1991).

Amsler, C.D. and Searles, R.B., Vertical distribution of seaweed spores in a water column offshore of North Carolina, *J. Phycol.*, **16**, 617–19 (1980).

Amsler, C.D., Reed, D.C., and Neushul, M., The microclimate inhabited by macroalgal propagules, *Brit. Phycol. J.*, **27**, 253–70 (1992).

Boland, W., Jakoby, K., and Jaenicke, L., Receptor specificity and threshold concentration in chemotaxis of the phaeophyte *Cutleria multifida*, *Zeit. Naturforsch.*, **36C**, 262–71 (1981).

Brandham, P.E., Time-lapse studies of conjugation in *Cosmarium botrytis*. II. Pseudoconjugation and an anisogamous mating behaviour involving chemotaxis, *Can. J. Bot.*, **45**, 483–93 (1967).

Brawley, S.H. and Johnson, L.E., Gametogenesis, gametes and zygotes: an ecological perspective on sexual reproduction in the algae, *Brit. Phycol. J.*, **27**, 233–52 (1992).

Breeman, A.M., Meulenhoff, E.J., and Guiry, M.D., Life history regulation and phenology of the red alga *Bonnemaisonia hamifera*, *Helgolander Meeresunters*, **42**, 535–51 (1988).

Broadwater, S.T., Scott, J.L., and West, J.A., Spermatial appendages of *Spyridia filamentosa* (Ceramiaceae, Rhodophyta), *Phycologia*, **30**, 189–95 (1991).

Buschman, A.H., Amphipod food preference and *Iridaea* spp. (Rhodophyta) spore release and dispersal, *J. Mar. Biol. Ass.* (U.K.), **71**, 891–97 (1992).

Buschman, A.H. and Bravo, A., Intertidal amphipods as potential dispersal agents of carpospores of *Iridaea laminarioides* (Gigartinales, Rhodophyta), *J. Phycol.*, **26**, 417–20 (1990).

Buss, L.W., The Evolution of Individuality, Princeton University Press, Princeton (1987).

Cavalier-Smith, T., Eukaryotic kingdoms: seven or nine, *BioSystems*, **44**, 461–81 (1981).

Cavalier-Smith, T., A 6-kingdom classification and a unified phylogeny. *In* Schenk, H.E.A. and Schwemmler, W. (eds.) Endocytobiology II, 1027–34, Walter de Gruyter, Berlin (1983).

Cavalier-Smith, T., The kingdom Chromista: origin and systematics, *Prog. Phycol. Res.*, **4**, 309–347 (1986).

Cavalier-Smith, T., The kingdom Chromista. *In* Green, J.C., Leadbeater, B.S.C., and Diver, W.L. (eds.) Systematics of Chromophyta, 379–405, Clarendon Press, Oxford (1989).

Clayton, M.N., Evolution and life histories of brown algae, *Bot. Mar.*, **31**, 379–87 (1988).

Clayton, M.N., Propagules of marine macroalgae: structure and development, *Brit. Phycol. J.*, **27**, 219–32 (1992).

Coesel, P.F.M. and de Jong, W., Vigorous chemotactic attraction as a sexual response in *Closterium ehrenbergii* Meneghini (Desmidiaceae, Chlorophyta), *Phycologia*, **25**, 405–408 (1986).

Davies, C.O., Hollibaugh, J.T., Seibert, D.L.R., Thomas, W.H., and Harrison, P.J., Formation of resting spores by *Leptocylindricus danicus* (Bacillariophyceae) in a controlled experimental ecosystem, *J. Phycol.*, **16**, 296–302 (1980).

Dayton, P.K., Ecology of kelp communities, *Ann. Rev. Ecol. Syst.*, **16**, 215–45 (1985).

Dixon, P.C., Life histories in the Florideophyceae with particular reference to the Nemaliales *sensu lato*, *Bot. Mar.*, **25**, 611–21 (1982).

Dodds, J.A. and Cole, A., Microscopy and biology and *Uronema gigas*: a filamentous eukaryotic green alga, and its associated tailed virus-like particle, *Virology*, **100**, 156–65 (1980).

Dolle, R., Pfau, J., and Nultsch, W., Role of calcium ions in motility and phototaxis of *Chlamydomonas reinhardii*, *J. Plant Physiol.*, **126**, 167–73 (1987).

Dring, M.J., Reproduction. *In* Stewart, W.D.P. (ed.) Algal Physiology and Biochemistry, 814–37, Blackwell, Oxford (1974).

Ettl, H., Different division courses in the phytomonads (Chlorophyta), *Arch. Protistenk.*, **135**, 85–101 (1988).

Feldmann, J., Recherches sur lá vegetation marine de lá Mediterrannee la cote des Alberes, *Rev. Algol.*, **10**, 1–339 (1937).

Foster, K.W. and Smyth, R.D., Light antennas in phototactic algae, *Microbiol. Rev.*, **44**, 572–630 (1980).

Foster, M.S., The regulation of macroalgal associations in kelp forests. *In* Srivastava, L. (ed.) Synthetic and Degradative Processes in Marine Macrophytes, 185–205, Walter de Gruyter, Berlin (1982).

Gabrielson, P.W. and Garbary, D.G., Systematics of red algae (Rhodophyta), *CRC Critical Review of Plant Science*, **3**, 325–66 (1986).

Gibbs, A., Stoknicki, A., Gardiner, J.E., Walker, E.S., and Nollings, M., A tobamovirus of a green alga, *Virology*, **64**, 245–57 (1975).

Grobbelaar, N., Huang, T.C., Lin, H.Y., and Chow, T.J., Dinitrogen-fixing endogenous rhythm in *Synechococcus* RF-1, *FEMS Microbiol. Lett.*, **37**, 173–77 (1986).

Guiry, M.D. and Womersley, H.B.S., *Capreolia implexa* gen. et sp. nov. (Gelidiales, Rhodophyta) in Australia and New Zealand: an intertidal mat-forming alga with an unusual life history, *Phycologia*, **32**, 266–77 (1993).

Häder, D.P., Movement. *In* Senger, H. (ed.) Blue Light Responses: Phenomena and occurrence in plants and microorganisms, Vol. I, 101–30, CRC Press, Cleveland (1987).

Hambrook, J.A. and Sheath, R.G., Reproductive ecology of the freshwater red alga *Batrachospermum boryanum* Sirodot in a temperate headwater stream, *Hydrobiologia*, **218**, 233–46 (1991).

Hay, C.H., The dispersal of sporophytes of *Undaria pinnatifida* by coastal shipping in New Zealand and implications for further dispersal of *Undaria* in France, *Brit. Phycol. J.*, **25**, 301–13 (1990).

Hoekstra, R.F., Evolution of gametic motility differences. II. Insertion with the evolution of anisogamy, *J. Theor. Biol.*, **107**, 71–83 (1984).

Huang, T.C. and Grobbelaar, N., The circadian clock in the prokaryote *Synechococcus* RF-1, *Microbiology*, **141**, 535–40 (1995).

Huang, T.C., Chen, H.M., Pen, S.Y., and Chen, T.H., Biological clock in the prokaryote *Synechococcus* RF-1, *Planta*, **193**, 131–36 (1994).

Istock, C.A., Some theoretical considerations concerning life history evolution. *In* Dingle, H. and Hegmann, J.P. (eds.) Evolution and Genetics of Life Histories, 1–250, Springer-Verlag, New York (1966).

John, D.M., Alternation of generations in algae: its complexity, maintenance and evolution, *Biol. Rev.*, **69**, 275–91 (1994).

Klinger, T., The persistence of haplodiploidy in algae, *TREE*, **8**, 256–58 (1993).

Kondo, T., Strayer, C.A., Kulkarni, R.D., Taylor, W., Ishiura, M., Golden, S.S., and Johnson, C.H., Circadian rhythms in prokaryotes: luciferase as a reporter of circadian gene expression in cyanobacteria, *Proc. Natl. Acad. Sci.* (USA), **90**, 5672–76 (1993).

Kumar, H.D. and Nultsch, W., Effects of saffron extract and carotenoid preparations on the photodynamically induced chemotactic response of *Polytomella magna*, *Photobiochem. Photobiophys.*, **9**, 39–42 (1985).

Lubchenco, L. and Cubit, J., Heteromorphic life histories of certain marine algae as adaptations in herbivory, *Ecology*, **61**, 676–87 (1980).

Lüning, K., Critical levels of light and temperature regulating the gametogenesis of three *Laminaria* species (Phaeophyceae), *J. Phycol.*, **16**, 1–15 (1980).

Lüning, K., Photomorphogenesis of reproduction in marine macroalgae, *Ber. Deutsch. Bot. Ges.*, **94**, S401–17 (1981).

Maggs, C.A., Intraspecific life history variability in the Florideophycidae (Rhodophyta), *Bot. Mar.*, **31**, 465–90 (1988).

Mattox, K.R. and Stewart, K.D., Classification of the Green Algae: a concept based on comparative cytology. *In* Irvine, D.E.G. and John, D.M. (eds.) Systematics of the Green Algae, 29–72, Academic Press, London (1984).

May, D.I. and Clayton, M.N., Oogenesis, the formation of oogonial stalks and fertilisation in *Sargassum vestitum* (Fucales, Phaeophyta) from southern Australia, *Phycologia*, **30**, 243–56 (1991).

Mayer, J.A. and Taylor, F.J.R., A virus which lyses the marine nanoflagellate *Micromonas pusilla*, *Nature*, **281**, 299–301 (1979).

Melkonian, M. and Robenek, H., Eyespot membranes of *Chlamydomonas reinhardii*: a freeze-fracture study, *J. Ultrastruct. Res.*, **72**, 90–102 (1980).

Melkonian, M. and Robenek, H., The eyespot apparatus of flagellated green algae: a critical review. *In* Round, F.E. and Chapman, D.J. (eds.) Progress in Phycological Research, Vol. 3, BioPress, Bristol (1984).

Mirelman, D., Microbial Lectins and Agglutinins, Wiley, New York (1986).

Mohsen, A.F., Khaleata, M.A., Hashem, M.A., and Metwalli, A., Effect of different nitrogen sources on growth, reproduction, amino acid, fat and sugar contents in *Ulva fasciata* Delile, *Bot. Mar.*, **27**, 218–22 (1974).

Ngan, Y. and Price, I.R., Periodicity of spore discharge in tropical Florideophyceae (Rhodophyta), *Brit. Phycol. J.*, **18**, 83–95 (1983).

Norton, T.A., Algal dispersal, *J. Phycol.*, **27**, 53 (1991).

Norton, T.A., Dispersal by macroalgae, *Brit. Phycol. J.*, **27**, 293–301 (1992).

Nultsch, W., The photocontrol of movement of *Chlamydomonas*. *In* Cosens, D.J. and Vince-Price, D. (eds.) The Society for Experimental Biology Symposium XXXVI, 521–39, Society for Experimental Biology, Great Britain (1983).

Nultsch, W. and Kumar, H.D., Effects of quenching agents on the photodynamically-induced chemotactic response of the colorless flagellate *Polytomella magna*, *Photochem. Photobiol.*, **40**, 539–43 (1984).

Nultsch, W. and Häder, D.P., Photomovement in motile microorganisms-II, *Photochem. Photobiol.*, **47**, 837–69 (1988).

Nultsch, W. and Häder, M., Light-induced chemotactic responses of the colorless flagellate, *Polytomella magna*, in the presence of photodynamic dyes, *Arch. Microbiol.*, **139**, 21–27 (1984).

Pearson, B.R. and Norris, R.E., Intranuclear virus-like particles in the marine alga *Platymonas* sp. (Chlorophyta, Prasinophyceae), *Phycologia*, **13**, 5–9 (1974).

Pedersen, P.M., Phaeophyta: life histories. *In* Lobban, C.S. and Wynne, M.J. (eds.) The Biology of Seaweeds, 194–217, Blackwell Scientific Publications, Oxford (1981).

Pfiester, L.A. and Skvarla, J.J., Heterothallism and thecal development in the sexual life history of *Peridinium volzii* (Dinophyceae), *Phycologia*, **18**, 13–18 (1979).

Pickett-Heaps, J.D., Green Algae: Structure, reproduction and evolution in selected genera, Sinauer Associates, Sunderland, Mass. (1975).

Preisig, H.R. and Hibberd, D.J., Virus-like particles and endophytic bacteria in *Paraphysomonas* and *Chromophysomonas* (Chrysophyceae), *Nordic J. Bot.*, **4**, 279–85 (1984).

Pringle, J.D., Swarmer release and distribution of life-cycle phases of *Enteromorpha intestinalis* (L.) (Chlorophyta) in relation to environmental factors, *J. Exp. Mar. Biol. Ecol.*, **100**, 97–111 (1986).

Pueschel, C.M., Cell structure. *In* Cole, K.M. and Sheath, R.G. (eds.) Biology of the Red Algae, 7–41, Cambridge University Press, Cambridge (1990).

Quader, H., Formation and disintegration of cisternae of the endoplasmic reticulum visualized in live cells by conventional fluorescence and confocal laser scanning microscopy: evidence for the involvement of calcium and the cytoskeleton, *Protoplasma*, **155**, 166–75 (1990).

Reed, D.C., Amsler, C.D., and Ebeling, A.W., Dispersal in kelps: factors affecting spore swimming and competency, *Ecology*, **73**, 1577–85 (1992).

Rüffer, U. and Nultsch, W., High-speed cinematographic analysis of the movement of *Chlamydomonas*, *Cell Motility Cytoskeleton*, **5**, 251–63 (1985).

Rüffer, U. and Nultsch, W., Comparison of the beating of *cis* and *trans* flagella of *Chlamydomonas*, *Cell Motility*, **7**, 87–93 (1987).

Sandgren, C.D., Characteristics of sexual and asexual resting cyst (statospore) formation in *Dinobryon cylindricum* Imhof (Chrysophyta), *J. Phycol.*, **17**, 199–210 (1981).

Santelices, B., Patterns of reproduction, dispersal and recruitment in seaweeds, *Oceanogr. Mar. Biol. Ann. Rev.*, **28**, 177–276 (1990).

Santelices, B., Digestion survival of algae: an overview. *In* John, D.M., Hawkins, S.J., and Price, J.H. (eds.) Plant-Animal Interactions in the Marine Benthos, 363–84, Oxford University Press, Oxford (1992).

Sheath, R.G. and Hambrook, J.A., Freshwater ecology. *In* Cole, K.M. and Sheath, R.G. (eds.) Biology of the Red Algae, 423–53, Cambridge University Press, Cambridge (1990).

Stal, L.J. and Krumbein, W.E., Oxygen protection of nitrogenase in the aerobically nitrogen-fixing, non-heterocystous cyanobacterium, *Oscillatoria* sp., *Arch. Microbiol.*, **143**, 72–76 (1985).

Stoknicki, A., Gibbs, A., and Wrigley, N.G., Further studies on *Chara corallina* virus, *Virology*, **75**, 457–68 (1976).

Sweeney, B.M., Circadian timing in the unicellular autotrophic dinoflagellate, *Gonyaulax polyedra*, *Ber. Deutsch. Bot. Ges.*, **94**, S335–45 (1981).

Sweeney, B.M. and Borgese, M.B., A circadian rhythm in cell division in a prokaryote: the cyanobacterium *Synechococcus* WH 7803, *J. Phycol.*, **25**, 183–86 (1989).

Valero, M., Richerd, S., Perrot, V., and Destombe, C., Evolution of alternation of haploid and diploid phases in life cycles, *TREE*, **7**, 25–29 (1992).

Van Etten, J.L., Lane, L.C., and Meints, R.H., Viruses and viruslike particles of eukaryotic algae, *Microbiol. Rev.*, **55**, 586–620 (1991).

Wakes, D.B. and Scatkin, M.W. (eds.), Evolution of Sex Determinism Mechanisms, Benjamin-Cummins, Menlo Park (1983).

Watanabe, M. and Furuya, M., Phototactic responses of cell population to repeated pulses of yellow light in a phytoflagellate *Cryptomonas* sp., *Plant Physiol.*, **61**, 816–18 (1978).

West, J.A. and Calumpong, H.P., On the reproductive biology of *Spyridia filamentosa* (Wulfen) Harvey (Rhodophyta) in culture, *Bot. Mar.*, **32**, 379–87 (1989).

Wynne, M.J. and Loiseaux, S., Recent advances in life history studies of the Phaeophyta, *Phycologia*, **15**, 435–53 (1976).

3 Cyanophyta and Prochlorophyta

These two divisions contain procaryotic algae which are now usually called bacteria in view of their cell structure being very similar to eubacteria. Thus Cyanophyta (=Cyanophyceae; blue-green algae) are called cyanobacteria and Prochlorophyta (=Prochlorophyceae) are termed prochlorobacteria.

DIVISION CYANOPHYTA (CYANOBACTERIA)

GENERAL CHARACTERS

The phylum Cyanophyta (Myxophyceae, blue-green algae) differs from other algae in having a procaryotic cell organization, i.e., it lacks organized double-membraned nuclei, chromatophores, and mitochondria, and possesses characteristic photosynthetic pigments including biliproteins and myxoxanthophyll in addition to chlorophyll-a and β-carotene. No flagellated cells are formed and the movement of motile stages is brought about by a characteristic gliding action. However, certain specialized cells, known as heterocysts, are produced in many species. True sexuality, defined as alternating karyogamy and meiosis, does not occur but genetic recombination, which fulfils the function of sex, is known in some members. The recent trend among microbiologists is to call these organisms cyanobacteria in order to emphasize their close relationship with bacteria (see Stanier and Cohen-Bazire, 1977). In fact, they are best defined as microorganisms that contain, within a typically procaryotic cell, a photosynthetic apparatus structurally and functionally similar to that located within chloroplasts of the eucaryotic red algae. One general attribute of most cyanobacteria is that they are morphologically (cell structure, heterocysts, reproduction) quite conservative but metabolically (nitrogen fixation, photosynthetic metabolism) versatile. In this respect, they contrast with most eucaryotic algae which tend to be structurally versatile but metabolically conservative.

OCCURRENCE AND ECOLOGICAL AMPLITUDE

The blue-green algae are perhaps the most widely distributed algal organisms, especially in tropical countries. They are ubiquitous and cosmopolitan, found in clean and polluted waters of lakes, ponds, and reservoirs, in fresh- and salt water, and in stagnant and flowing waters. They occur in the spray zone of seacoasts as well as the surface water of oceans, and are widespread on or beneath tropical soils of diverse kinds. One of the most characteristic and favourite habitats is the tropical paddy field. Other conspicuous places include microaerobic or reducing habitats (mangroves, marshes, hypersaline lakes, marine littoral sediments), limestone rocks in the high rainfall tropics, tree barks, rocks and stones, footpaths, and plant pots. Recently, certain minute *Synechococcus*-like cyanobacterial cells have been found to constitute a significant component of the phytoplankton crop of temperate and tropical oceans (Waterbury *et al.*, 1979).

The blue-green algae form a significant part of the free-floating population of microscopic organisms which constitute the plankton (Fig. 3-1) of eutrophic (organically rich) lakes and oceans. They are frequently associated with waters rich in hydrogen sulphide. They are also found in the benthos of lakes and ponds and are largely responsible for the high fertilizing qualities of the bottom muds of dried ponds and tanks. In tropical countries, the ponds that are heavily polluted and exposed to high temperatures and intense sunlight provide optimum conditions for the growth of the blue-green algae. Species of *Microcystis* and certain other planktonic blue-greens multiply so prolifically in such conditions that they impart a bluish-green colour to the pond water which appears like "pea soup". Such water blooms in tropical ponds are more or less perennial but similar blooms, though ephemeral, are also formed in temperate climates either sporadically or annually.

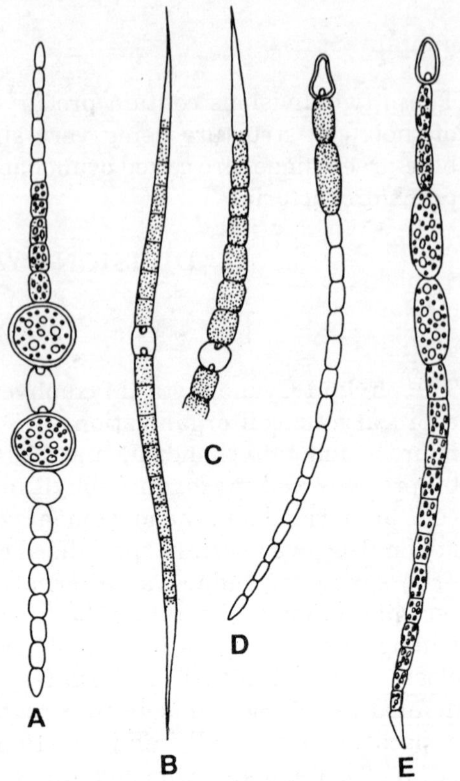

Fig. 3-1 Some planktonic cyanobacteria. A, *Aphanizomenon aphanizomenoides*; B, C, *A. tropicalis*; D, E, *Cylindrospermum raciborskii*.

Various species of cyanobacteria form virtually unialgal blooms in eutrophic lakes in summer, and unialgal cyanobacterial mats occur frequently in benthic habitats. High growth rates, desiccation tolerance, and the production of allelochemicals are some of the factors that lead to massive growths of cyanobacteria.

Some cyanobacteria produce secondary chemicals that are algicidal. Cyanobacterin is a secondary metabolite of *Scytonema hofmanni* that inhibits PSII activity in green algae. The hapalindolinones of *Fischerella* inhibit arginine vasopressin binding (Schwartz *et al.*, 1987). *F. muscicola* synthesizes some antibiotic that kills related algae (Flores and Wolk, 1986). This antibiotic has been named "fischerellin" (Gross *et al.*, 1991).

F. muscicola is a benthic cyanobacterium. Its fischerellin not only inhibits other cyanobacteria but also some green algae, but eubacteria are not inhibited. Fischerellin inhibits the photosynthetic but not the respiratory electron transport of cyanobacteria and green algae. Its site of action is PSII (Gross *et al.*, 1991).

Except for certain bacteria (and, of course, the archaea!), the blue-green algae are the only organisms that grow in adverse and harsh environments. While most of them thrive in biologically normal habitats, some can successfully endure extremes of temperature, light intensity, desiccation, and high or low concentrations of dissolved nutrients. Species of *Mastigocladus* and *Phormidium* are important members of the flora of hot water springs and can tolerate temperatures as high as 75°C. On the other hand, species of *Phormidium* are found in the frigid arctic lakes, and certain others, collected from the Antarctic, have experimentally been shown to survive freezing. A tolerance of extremes in light intensity is illustrated by species found in caves which are virtually dark, on bare rocks exposed to intense sunlight, or those species growing in tropical deserts. Certain species of *Nostoc* and *Chlorogloea* have remained viable after prolonged storage in a calcium chloride desiccator. Likewise, some blue-greens thrive in waters of highly polluted ponds or of non-polluted mountain streams.

The cyanobacteria are pioneer colonizers of bare rocks and virgin lands and grow luxuriantly in alkaline or saline soils. Several species grow in or on calcareous strata. Some have been found in oil field sump ponds and in samples of floating tarry scums.

Symbiotic Associations

Certain blue-greens form intracellular and extracellular symbiotic associations with other organisms. In addition to algae and fungi, these include associations with bryophytes, a pteridophyte, a gymnosperm division, and an angiosperm. The cyanobacterium is almost invariably a *Nostoc* spp. Formation of hormogonia filaments by *Nostoc* spp. is a primary systematic criterion provisionally distinguishing *Nostoc* from *Anabaena* and nearly all symbiotically competent cyanobacteria produce these small-celled, highly motile filaments at some stage of their association with green plants (Campbell and Meeks, 1989). The gliding motility of hormogonia perhaps combined with a chemotactic response appears to play a rôle in the establishment, or maintenance, of the functional symbioses. In contrast to the legume-*Rhizobium* and actinorhizal associations, where infection by the procaryote alters development of plant tissue such that nodules are produced, the structures occupied by the symbiotic cyanobacteria are not a consequence of infection. Minor changes may occur in specific structures believed to facilitate metabolite interchange but the primary structures differentiate and develop in each host plant in the absence of the cyanobacterium. The structures occupied by the cyanobacterium contain a mucilaginous material and the host plants generally have an appreciable phenolic content but the role of the mucilage or phenolics is not known.

Examples of intracellular symbioses occur in certain organisms which harbour cyanobacteria as integral components within their cells. Thus, an *Aphanothece*-like cyanobacterium occurs endophytically within an *Oocystis*-like green algal cell, the resulting obligate symbiont being designated *Glaucocystis nostochinearum* (Fig. 3-2). The symbiont resembles a chlorococcalean green algal cell in most respects except that its "chloroplasts" are not typically green algal but are represented by the blue-green alga. These chloroplasts lack a typical wall and divide by means of median constriction. The chloroplasts, however, lack any cyanophycin granules, gas vacuoles, or other subcellular organelles characteristic of cyanobacteria.

Most symbiotic associations involving cyanobacteria are not obligatory as the cyanobacterium can be isolated and grown in culture in the absence of its partner.

A *Nostoc* occurs intracellularly in hyaline cells of *Sphagnum* (a moss growing in nutrient rich habitats) (Basilier, 1979). When the moss grows submerged in water, the cyanobacterial growth is mainly epiphytic, but both epiphytic and endophytic growths occur in moss plants growing out of water. *Nostoc* is the only endophytic cyanobacterium in this case; epiphytic growths include *Nostoc* plus other cyanobacteria. The *Nostoc* in the association fixes nitrogen.

That there may be some relationship between symbiosis and genome size is suggested by the fact that the symbiotic cyanobacteria can be broadly divided into two types, depending on genome size. Type 1 have genomes ranging in size from 1.6×10^9 daltons to 8.6×10^9 daltons; these species can usually be isolated and grown outside their host. (These genome sizes are broadly similar to those of free-living forms.) Type 2 show a modified cell wall structure though

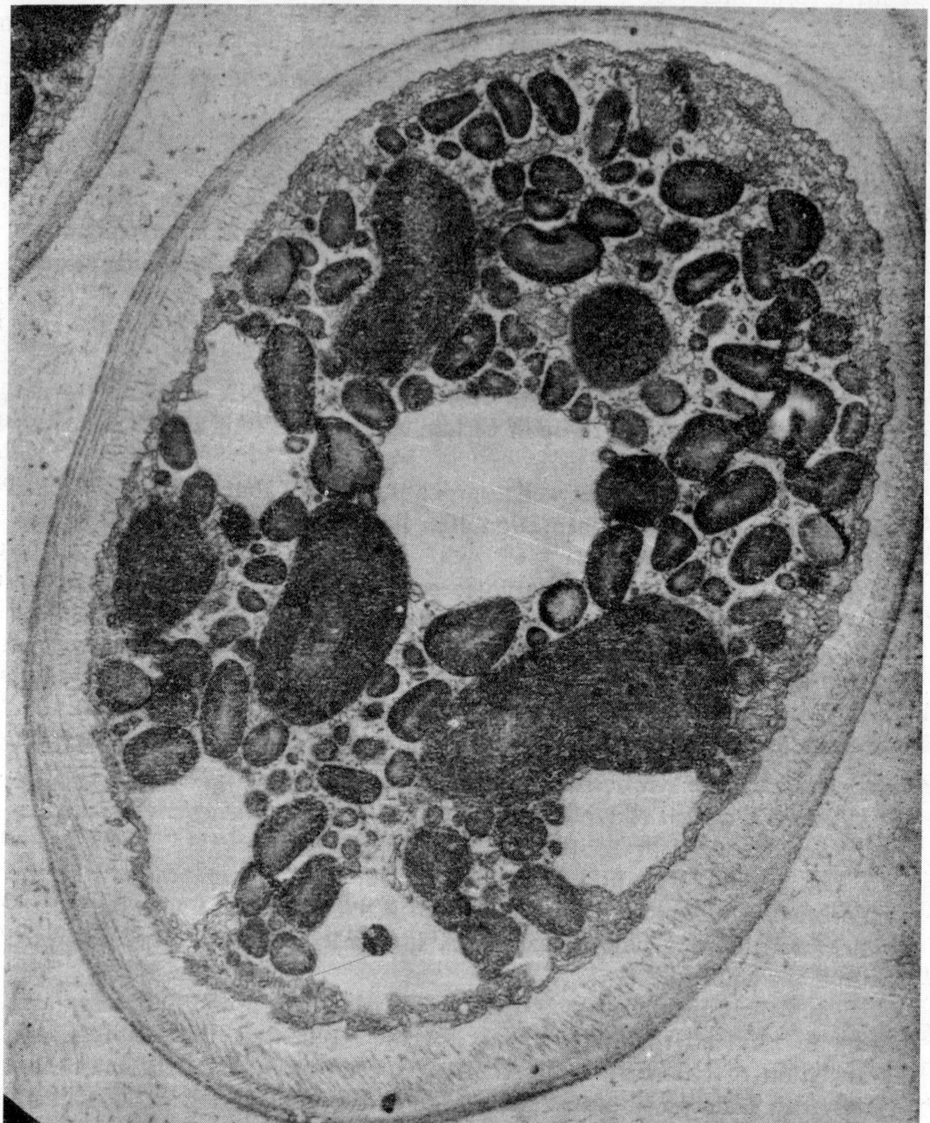

Fig. 3-2 *Glaucocystis nostochinearum*. (×12,000.) *Courtesy* W.T. Hall.

retaining the peptidoglycan layer, and broadly resemble cyanobacteria but contain multiple copies of a small genome (around 1.17×10^8 daltons). In respect of their small genomes, these species resemble the chloroplasts; the genetic information carried by them is too small to permit growth outside the host. A good example of this latter type is the cyanelles of *Cyanophora paradoxa*.

Azolla

The heterosporous aquatic ferns comprising the genus *Azolla* are the only pteridophytes known to exist in symbiosis with a N_2 fixing cyanobacterium. They also are the only plant cyanobacteria symbiosis used in agriculture and have been the subject of several recent reviews (Nierzwicki-Bauer, 1990; Plazinski, 1990). The genus is distributed in tropical and temperate regions. Currently, seven species are generally recognized: *A. caroliniana*, *A. filiculoides*, *A. mexicana*, *A. microphylla*, and *A. rubra* in the section Euazolla and *A. pinnata* and *A. nilotica* in the section Rhizosperma. All species normally harbour a symbiotic cyanobacterium, known historically as *Anabaena azollae* Strass. The cyanobacterium is intimately associated with *Azolla* spp. throughout their life cycle. It grows in concert with the vegetative sporophytes, occupying cavities formed in the dorsal leaf lobes, and during sporogenesis it is packaged into sporocarps such that continuity of the symbiosis is maintained during sexual reproduction.

Azolla sporophytes have multibranched, prostrate floating stems which bear deeply bilobed, alternately arranged, overlapping leaves, and adventitious roots. The growth of the cyanobacterial symbiont and fern is tightly coupled. The symbiont forms heterocysts and fixes N_2. In mature cavities where nitrogenase activity is maximal, cells of the symbiont are enlarged, cell division is greatly diminished, and heterocysts account for about 20–30% of the total cell population. Both heterocysts and vegetative cells contain phycobiliproteins which capture light energy to drive photosynthesis and nitrogen fixation. An interchange of nutrients and metabolites occurs between the partners.

Azolla appears to be unique among the plant-N_2 fixing procaryote symbioses; it maintains the symbiont during sporulation and sexual reproduction precluding the need for a free-living growth state of the cyanobacterium.

Azolla species are heterosporous, producing male and female sporocarps. The male microsporocarps are noticeably larger than the female megasporocarps at maturity. Both sporocarp types contain akinetes of the symbiont. The incorporation of the symbiont is reminiscent of the inoculation of the developing leaf cavity. At the very onset of sporulation a distinct set of branched epidermal trichomes develop near the sporangial initial on the apical symbiont colony and filaments become entangled among them. The sporangial primordium along with the branched trichomes and entwined filaments of the symbiont are then displaced ventrally. Only the symbiont cells enclosed in the megasporocarp are important to continuity of the symbiosis. In the mature megasporocarps akinetes are packaged into the apical portion in a chamber near the indusial pore.

Removal of the apical cap is a means of obtaining symbiont-free *Azolla* (Reddy and Fisher, 1988). The symbiont in the cap of *A. microphylla* can re-establish the symbiosis when positioned on decapitated megasporocarps of *A. filiculoides* and vice versa (Lin *et al.*, 1988). Initially, monoclonal antibodies reacting only with the symbiont from *A. filiculoides* were used to verify that the symbiont in the re-established symbiosis was indeed the one present in the donor apical cap. Subsequently DNA probes specific for the symbiont in *A. filiculoides*, the symbiont in *A. microphylla*, and the symbiont in different strains of both species, have been used to verify symbiont origin in nine such re-established symbioses attained with various strains of these two *Azolla* species (Plazinski *et al.*, 1989).

Early Evolutionary History

There exist significant detailed similarities in cellular morphology between Precambrian and extant cyanobacteria. A substantial fraction of known Proterozoic oscillatoriacean and chroococcacean cyanobacteria has living species-level morphological counterparts, and almost all such fossils can be referred to living cyanobacterial genera. For several taxa, ancient and modern cyanobacteria are essentially indistinguishable in salient characteristics. It appears that the morphology and physiology of diverse taxa belonging to major cyanobacterial families evolved little over hundreds of millions of years. In comparison with the later history of life, such a pronounced occurrence of the so-called hypobradytely is indeed surprising. Whereas bradytelic (i.e., slow-evolving) stasis has been quite rare in Phanerozoic evolution, in the Precambrian it seems to have been a general phenomenon characteristic of a group of procaryotic microorganisms that dominated the Earth's biota, possibly even as early as 3.5 billion years ago. Three reasons that may possibly explain such notable lack of evolutionary change in cyanobacteria may be their predominant asexual reproduction (limiting genetic variability), large population sizes, and ecologic versatility including a high adaptation to some ecological position or zone with broad, selective limits.

The wide ecologic tolerance of cyanobacteria is almost certainly a product of their early evolutionary history. Fossil evidence suggests that oscillatoriaceans and chroococcaceans lived as early as 3.5 billion years ago. They must have originated in an oxygen-deficient environment that lacked an effective UV-absorbing ozone layer. In such an environment, the ability to photosynthesize at low light intensities coupled with the presence of gas vesicles to control buoyancy would have permitted planktonic cyanobacteria to avoid harmful UV by inhabiting the deep oceanic photic zone, just as some *Synechococcus* strains do today. Likewise numerous characteristics of living benthic mat-building cyanobacteria—effective DNA repair mechanisms, synthesis of UV-absorbing scytonemin, secretion of copious extracellular mucilage, phototactic motility, adherence to substrates, stromatolitic mat formation—initially may have been adaptations to cope with a high UV flux in near-shore shallow water settings (Schopf, 1994).

The remarkable hardiness of cyanobacteria, e.g., ability to survive wide ranges of light intensity, salinity, temperature, pH, prolonged desiccation, and intense radiation may be the outcome of their great success in competing for photosynthetic space with other early-evolving microbes. Unlike the oxygen-producing photosynthesis based on chlorophyll-a in cyanobacteria, that in all other photoautotrophic procaryotes is anoxygenic and based on bacteriochlorophyll. Since biosynthesis of bacteriochlorophyll is inhibited by molecular oxygen, oxygen-producing cyanobacteria would have rapidly outcompeted anoxygenic photoautotrophs throughout much of the global photic zone. As a result of the ease of their global dispersal and their success in competing for photosynthetic space, cyanobacteria may have rapidly expanded into a wide range of niches evolving to become exceptional ecologic generalists.

In contrast with the shorter and more recent history of life in Phanerozoic eon, much of the earlier and longer Precambrian history of life was characterized by the hypobradytelic evolution of dominantly microscopic, asexual, metabolically diverse, and commonly ecologically versatile procaryotes, especially cyanobacteria (Schopf, 1994). Evolutionary innovations were biochemical and intracellular. Extinction occurred rarely among procaryotic ecologic generalists, evidently becoming a significant evolutionary force only late in the Precambrian and primarily affecting ecologically relatively specialized, large-celled eucaryotic phytoplankters (Schopf, 1994).

Buoyancy Regulation

The regulation of buoyancy in the larger planktonic cyanobacteria is a complex process involving not only the production and collapse of gas vesicles but the accumulation and depletion of reserves of protein and carbohydrate which act as ballast (Oliver and Walsby, 1984). The response to a buoyancy change depends on size; thus individual filaments of *Oscillatoria* move up or down only slowly whereas colonies of *Microcystis* can float or sink at a rate of nearly 40 μm sec^{-1} (Reynolds, 1973). Populations in a stable water column usually poise themselves at a particular depth in response to light intensity and nutrient availability. Buoyancy is lost at low intensities if the cells are depleted of nutrients or gained if these are in good supply. The population thus becomes placed in optimum conditions for growth. Investigations of ten planktonic strains of *Oscillatoria* by Utkilen *et al.* (1985) suggested that they fell into three distinct groups according to their strategies for optimizing use of the natural light field. Green-coloured strains, which might be expected to exploit higher irradiance, have weak gas vesicles that may be regulated by turgor pressure as a means of controlling buoyancy in shallow water. Secondly, red-coloured strains adapted to utilize the predominantly green light deeper in the photic zone have stronger gas vesicles. The third type lacks gas vesicles, exhibits chromatic adaptation, and thus would be expected to adjust light absorption according to the light available at the depth to the cyanobacterium itself. These different strategies permit the different species to occupy different limnetic niches. The large colonies of *Microcystis*, and probably those of *Anabaena* and *Aphanizomenon*, alter their buoyancy so as to achieve a diel vertical migration, which like that of *Ceratium* may assist in more efficient photosynthesis and replenishment of nutrient supplies (Fogg, 1991).

RANGE OF THALLUS STRUCTURE

The unicellular, colonial (palmelloid), filamentous, and heterotrichous forms are common, whereas the more elaborate macroscopic thalli are rare. The products of cell division, instead of being liberated as distinct individuals, often remain united in an assemblage of cells (a colony). Such colonies may be definite (e.g., *Merismopedia*) or irregular and indefinite (e.g., *Aphanothece*). The actual shape of a colony is largely determined by the number of planes in which the cells divide.

A filamentous blue-green alga consists of a number of cells arranged end to end. The simple, unbranched, uniseriate filaments are characteristic of *Lyngbya*, *Anabaena*, and many other genera of the Nostocales (Fig. 3-3). Here, the term filament includes the row of cells as well as the surrounding gelatinous sheath; if it consists of cells without a distinct sheath, it is designated trichome. The mucilage sheath is also found around unicellular and colonial forms. Most filaments have a single trichome each, but in some more than one trichome is so disposed within the common sheath (Fig. 3-4) that the filament appears to be branched. This phenomenon is known as pseudo- or false-branching and is characteristic of such genera as *Scytonema* and *Tolypothrix*. It is caused either by the growth of free ends of some trichomes through the sheath of the parent filament or by the degeneration of the top cell in a loop, leading to the division of an originally single and continuous trichome into two independent pseudobranches. In some genera, true (lateral) branching occurs (Fig. 3-5).

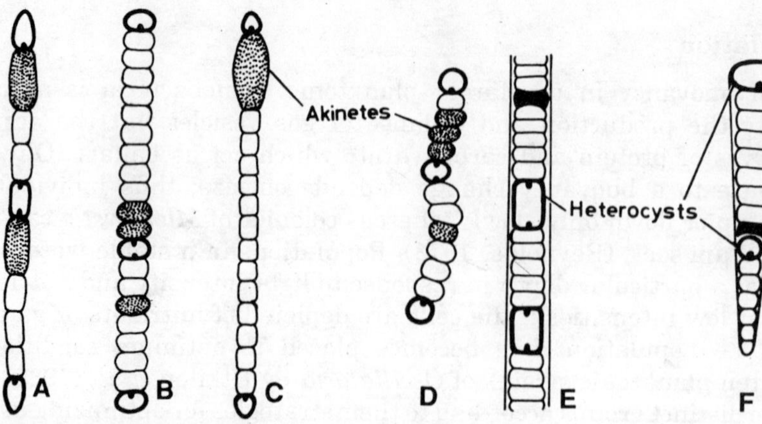

Fig. 3-3 Some genera of Nostocales. A, *Anabaena*; B, *Nodularia*; C, *Cylindrospermum*; D, *Nostoc*; E, *Scytonema*; F, *Calothrix*.

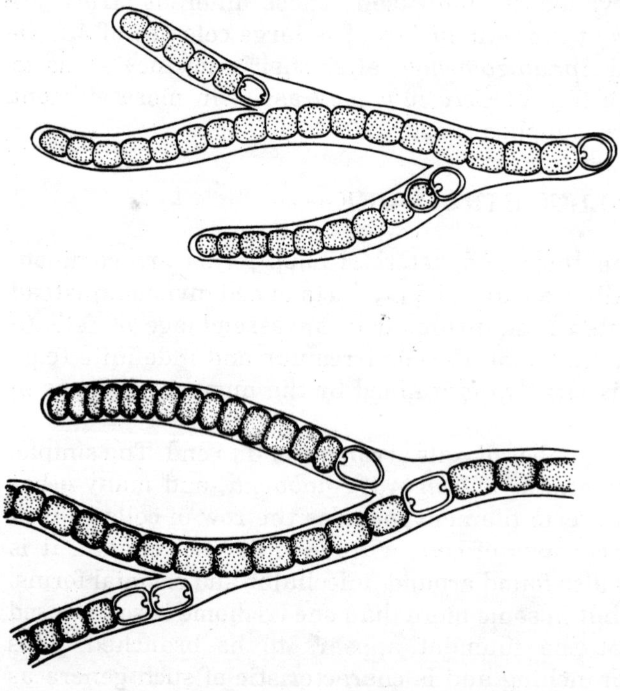

Fig. 3-4 *Tolypothrix*, pseudobranches by the side of heterocyst.

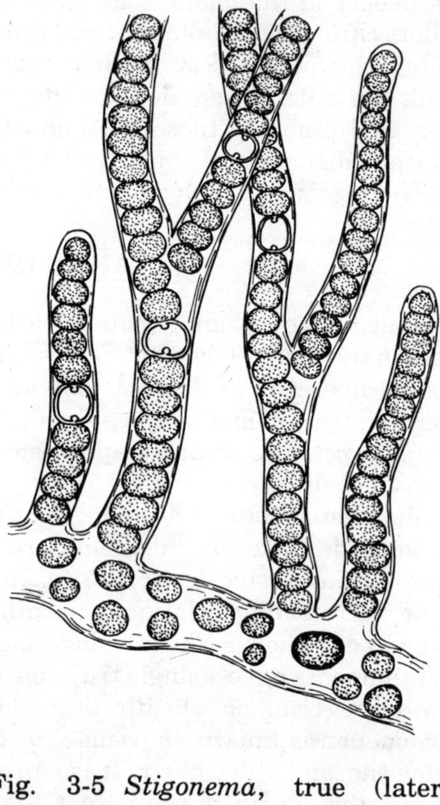

Fig. 3-5 *Stigonema*, true (lateral) branches.

CELL STRUCTURE

The most striking difference in the cell structure of the blue-green algae and other algae is the lack of differentiation of parts in the former. There are no organized nuclei, chromatophores, pyrenoids, mitochondria or true vacuoles. The only prominent structures seen within the blue-green algal cell under the light microscope are the different kinds of granules (Fig. 3-6) whose number and size vary in different genera and depend on physiological and nutritional factors. These are proteinaceous and are called cyanophycin granules. Reserve food is also stored in the form of glycogen. Other storage products are trehalose or sulpholipid.

In addition to the cyanophycin granules, the healthy cells of many planktonic blue-green algae contain numerous small bodies of irregular shape, known as pseudovacuoles or gas vacuoles. These appear black under low power and reddish under high power of a microscope. Under an electron microscope, the gas vacuoles appear to consist of packed arrays of cylindrical vesicles, each with conical ends and bound by a single membrane. Fogg's (1970) study on the biology of gas vacuoles proves that they contain metabolic gases and therefore serve as a mechanism for buoyancy regulation. The gas vacuoles are produced in low light intensity and disappear in high light intensity. In bright light, there is a greater production of sugars through photosynthesis, resulting in an increase in osmotic pressure of the cells, which causes the collapse of gas vacuoles. The ecological significance of this finding is that the blue-green algae growing below the water surface receive less light and form gas vacuoles, thus increasing their buoyancy. Such cells then rise to the surface where they receive more light and develop higher cellular osmotic pressure which leads to the collapse of gas vacuoles. This results in a reduction in buoyancy and consequently the cells sink to deeper layers of the water.

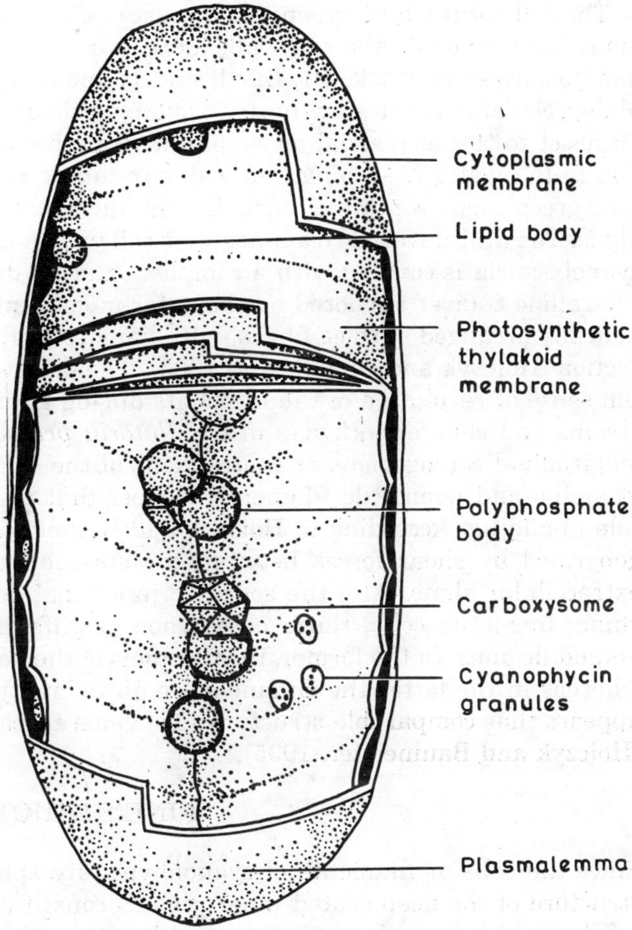

Fig. 3-6 *Agmenellum quadruplicatum*, overall three-dimensional architecture. Thylakoids are depicted as solid sheets, each representing a pair of closely-apposed unit membranes. Various kinds of granules are seen (nuclear material and ribosomes not shown). (After Nierzwicki-Bauer *et al.*, 1983.)

The core or central region of a blue-green algal cell appears somewhat transparent and contains most of the genetic material. There are no nuclei or nucleoli. Since DNA is not associated with protein material (histones or protamines), no organized or firm chromosomes, characteristic of the higher plants and animals, are found in the blue-green algae. RNA is present in addition to DNA.

The cells of the blue-green algae possess a wall that is differentiated into an inner and an outer layer. Outside the cell wall, there is a gelatinous sheath which is either homogeneous and colourless or thick, stratified, and pigmented. Such a sheath is characteristic of those blue-green algae that grow in dry or xerophytic habitats. A firm, pigmented sheath is indeed an asset to the terrestrial or subaerial forms because it enables them to perennate. This is due to the water absorbing and water retaining capacity of the sheath. The cell wall of the blue-green algae contains muramic acid and other components which are not found in other algae. The multilayered Gram negative cell wall of certain gliding filamentous oscillatoriacean cyanobacteria is covered with a complex external double layer. The first layer is a tetragonal crystalline S-layer anchored on the outer membrane. The second array is formed by parallel, helically arranged surface fibrils with diameters of 8–12 nm, which appear serrated in cross-section (Hoiczyk and Baumeister, 1995). The orientation of the surface fibrils correlates with the sense of revolution of the filaments during gliding, being clockwise in some *Phormidium* strains and counterclockwise in *Oscillatoria princeps* and *Lyngbya aeruginosa*. The lack of longitudinal corrugations or contractions of the surface fibrils and the identical appearances of motile and nonmotile filaments suggest that this structure plays a passive screw thread role in gliding. According to Hoiczyk and Baumeister, the necessary propulsive force may be generated by shear forces between the surface fibrils and the continuing flow of secreted extracellular slime. Also the so-called junctional pores seem to be the extrusion sites of the slime. In motile cells, these pores show a different staining behaviour than that seen in nonmotile ones. In the former, the channels of the pores are filled with electron-dense material whereas in the latter the channels are quite empty, highly contrasting the peptidoglycan. It appears that comparable structures are general features of the cell walls of gliding microbes (Hoiczyk and Baumeister, 1995).

FINE STRUCTURE

Since the cells or filaments of cyanophytes are spherical or cylindrical rather than flat, the structure of the deep seated inner regions constituting the core of the sphere cannot usually be observed by merely mounting the alga on a slide and examining it under the microscope. Only the outer or peripheral parts can be observed in this way. For examining the inner or central regions, sections must be cut. Ultrathin sections of a typical cyanophycean cell studied under an electron microscope at magnifications of about 25,000 times reveal many important details (Pankratz and Bowen, 1963) which are diagrammatically represented in Figs. 3-7 and 3-8 and are described here.

Sheath and Cell Wall

The gelatinous sheath of cyanophytes consists of three layers of microfibrils disposed reticulately within an amorphous matrix. The chemical nature of these microfibrils is not known but recent studies indicate that cellulose is absent. Inside the sheath is a double-layered cell wall whose inner layer contains mucopeptide and muramic acid. This inner layer is homogeneous, whereas the outer layer has the fine structure of a unit membrane. Under the electron microscope, the plasmalemma is seen to be surrounded by a cell wall differentiated into four layers, L_I–L_{IV}, which in turn may be surrounded by one or more additional envelope

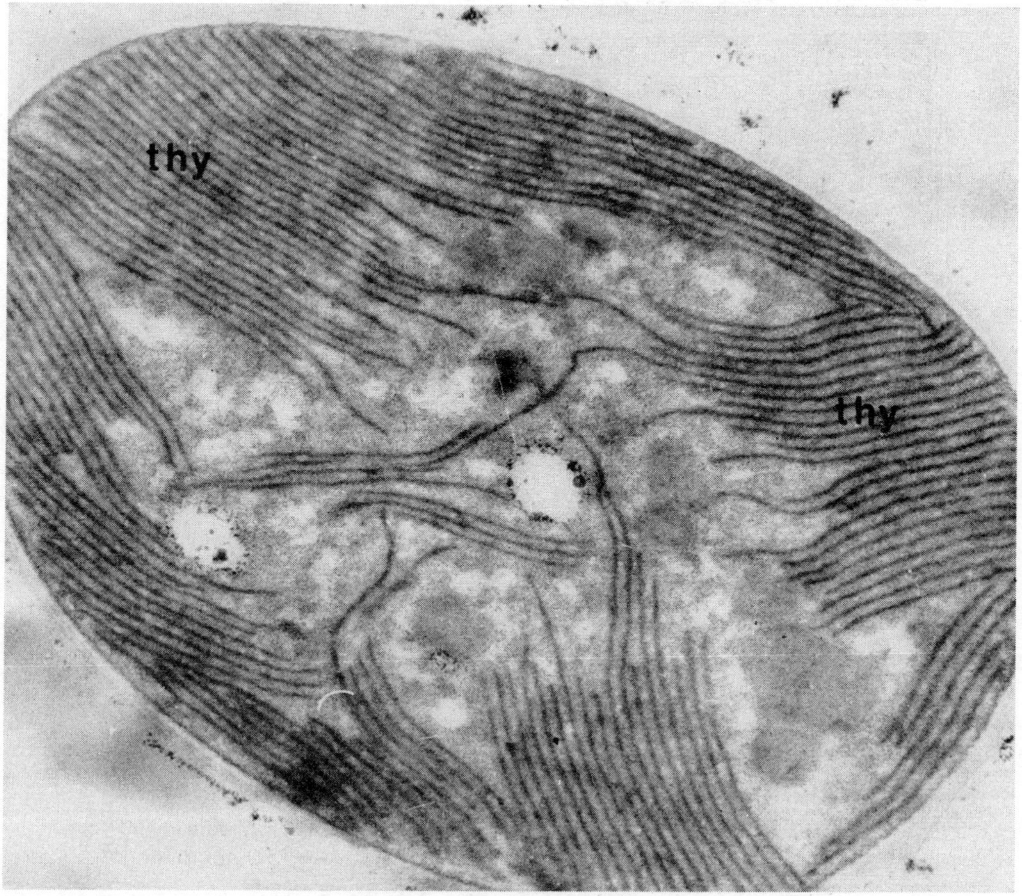

Fig. 3-7 *Phormidium uncinatum*, transverse section of filament, showing thylakoid membranes (thy) arranged mostly perpendicular to cell wall. (×38,700.) *Courtesy* M. Lefort-Tran.

layers. The L_{II} layer has mainly peptidoglycan. Between this layer and the membrane, there is often an electron-transparent gap which is generally construed as a distinct wall layer (L_I). The outermost wall layer (L_{IV}) contains both lipopolysaccharides and proteins. The sheaths of many filamentous blue-greens apear to have a fibrous-fine structure; they are usually tubular with open ends. The wall of several species (e.g., *Oscillatoria*) is perforated. In some strains, one ring of pores occurs near the cross wall. In some others (e.g., *Spirulina*), pores are distributed along partial circles, and in *Pseudanabaena*, the pores are distributed in several concentric rings (Guglielmi and Cohen-Bazire, 1982a).

The cytoplasmic membrane is found inside the cell wall and generally consists of two electron-opaque layers separated by a translucent layer.

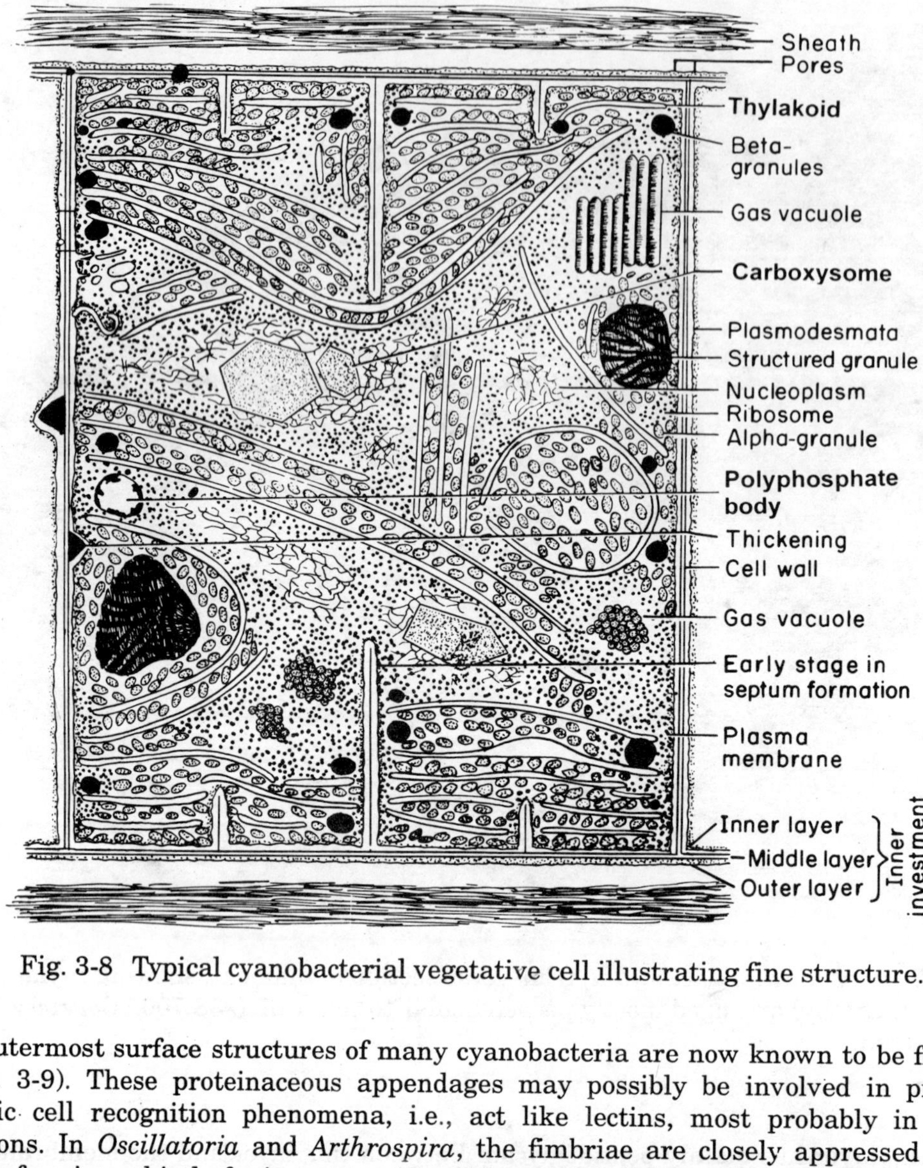

Fig. 3-8 Typical cyanobacterial vegetative cell illustrating fine structure.

The outermost surface structures of many cyanobacteria are now known to be fimbriae or pili (Fig. 3-9). These proteinaceous appendages may possibly be involved in procaryotic-eucaryotic cell recognition phenomena, i.e., act like lectins, most probably in symbiotic associations. In *Oscillatoria* and *Arthrospira*, the fimbriae are closely appressed along the trichome, forming a kind of microcortex (Guglielmi and Cohen-Bazire, 1982b).

Lamellae

Much of the peripheral region of the cell is traversed by a large number of lamellae or thylakoids which are either arranged regularly in two or more parallel stacks or disposed irregularly. A lamella appears as an elongated, flattened sac and consists of two unit membranes, each about 75 Å thick. The thylakoids act as the sites for both photosynthesis and respiration. However, in *Gloeothece violaceus*, which lacks thylakoids, these activities occur at the plasma membrane. Adjacent thylakoids are characteristically separated one from

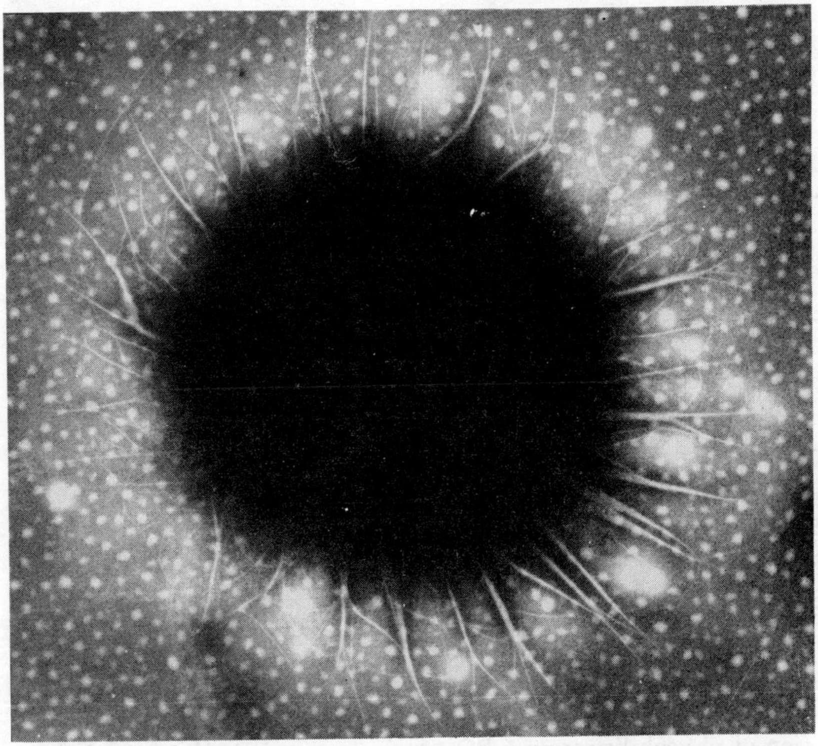

Fig. 3-9 *Synechocystis* CB3 cell negatively stained with 2% phosphotungstic acid in 0.1 M sodium phosphate buffer, pH 6.5. The pili attach together and form bundles around the cell. (×20,000.) *Courtesy* T. Vaara.

the other by a space of 50 nm which is occupied by contiguous rows of discoidal phycobilisomes. The phycobilisomes (Fig. 3-10) have a triangular core of allophycocyanin assembled from three stacks of discoidal subunits. Three rods radiate from each of the two sites of the core. These rods are 12 nm in diameter and contain the phycocyanin and, wherever present, the phycoerythrin.

Granules

The various kinds of subcellular organelles observed in different cyanophycean cells include the cyanophycin granules, gas vacuoles, polyhedral bodies, ribosomes, polyglucoside bodies, polyphosphate bodies, and structured granules. The ribosomes are involved in protein synthesis. The cyanophycin granules are regarded as reserve food. In planktonic forms, pseudovacuoles are found. (Their ultrastructure has been described earlier.) The polyphosphate bodies are sites of phosphorus storage. The polyhedral bodies (now called carboxysomes) contain the important enzyme ribulose diphosphate carboxylase. The structured granules are storehouses of nitrogen. Cyanophycin granules are copolymers of arginine and aspartic acid

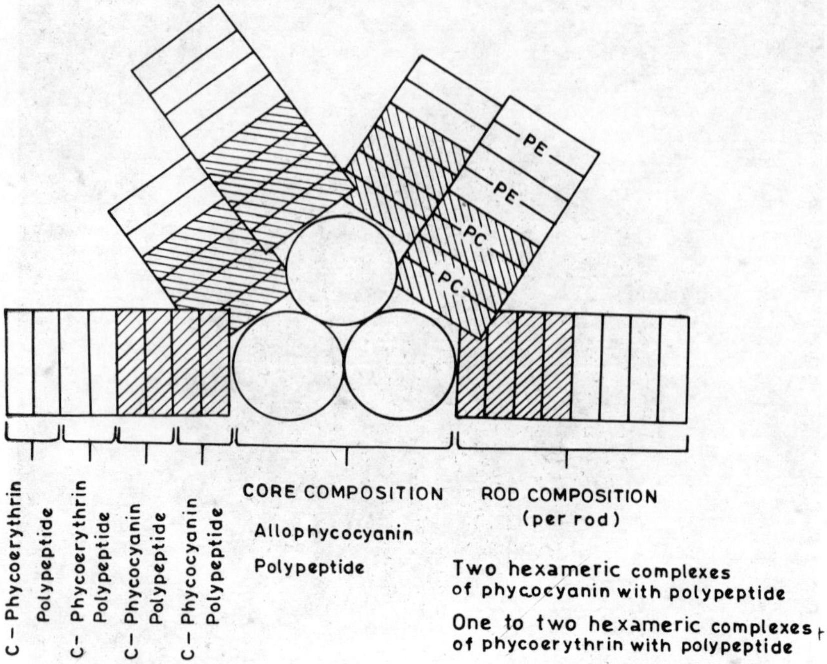

Fig. 3-10 *Synechocystis* PCC 6701, phycobilisome showing location of phycobiliproteins. PC, phycocyanin; PE, phycoerythrin. (After Gingrich *et al.*, 1982.)

(aspartate) in equimolar proportion. These granules tend to accumulate in the cell as a result of phosphate deficiency.

CENTRAL REGION OF CELL

The genetic material, consisting of DNA fibrils, is concentrated in the centre of the cell and this region is also traversed by a few thylakoids.

HETEROCYSTS

Heterocysts are specialized cells which differ from ordinary vegetative cells in having a thickened wall and one or two pores. Usually, they are slightly larger than the vegetative cells and, under the light microscope, appear as markedly distinctive cells. A recent study of heterocyst development with the electron microscope has shown that the general sequence of events during the differentiation of a vegetative cell into a heterocyst includes cell enlargement, synthesis of a many-layered, noncellulosic polysaccharide wall, gradual loss of photosynthetic pigments, decrease in granular inclusions, and reorientation of the photosynthetic lamellae into a complex reticulate pattern (see Lang, 1968). A three-layered envelope—the outer layer being fibrous, the middle one homogeneous, and the inner one laminated—develops outside the vegetative cell wall (see Fig. 3-11). The laminated layer consists of glycolipids which reduce the rate of diffusion of oxygen into the heterocyst. The middle and outer layers

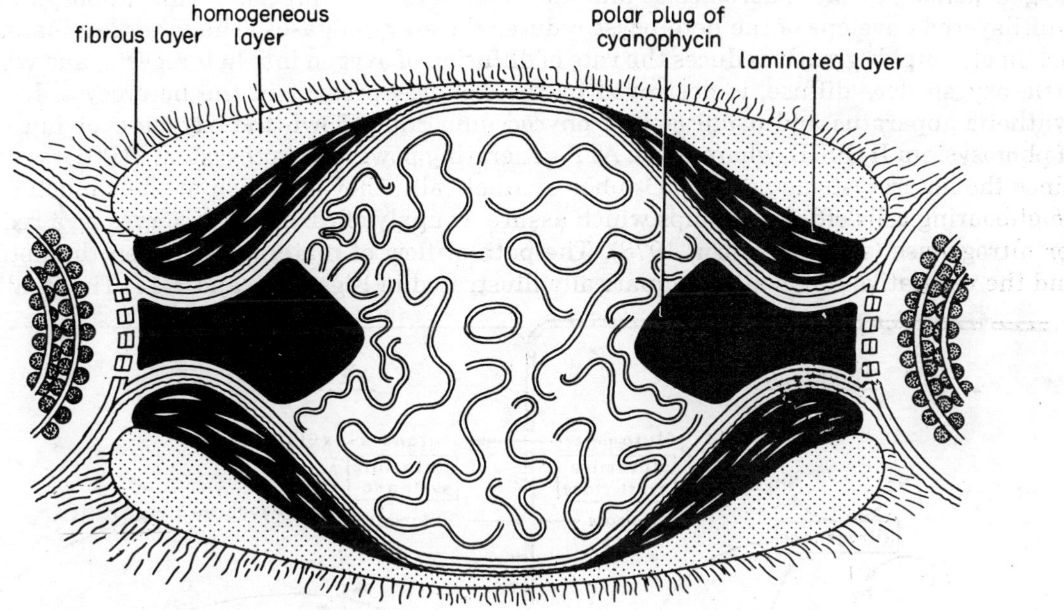

Fig. 3-11 Structure and content of mature heterocyst.

of heterocyst wall consist of polysaccharides which may protect against degradation of the glycolipid layer. The mature heterocysts of most temperate-zone cyanobacteria contain chlorophyll-a but lack phycocyanin. In contrast, the heterocysts of several tropical species do contain some phycocyanin and sometimes also have cyanophycin granules. Generally, mature heterocysts lack carboxysomes. One of the best materials for the study of heterocyst formation and development in tropical cyanobacteria is *Camptylonema lahorense* Ghose (Fig. 3-12) (Kumar, 1962a).

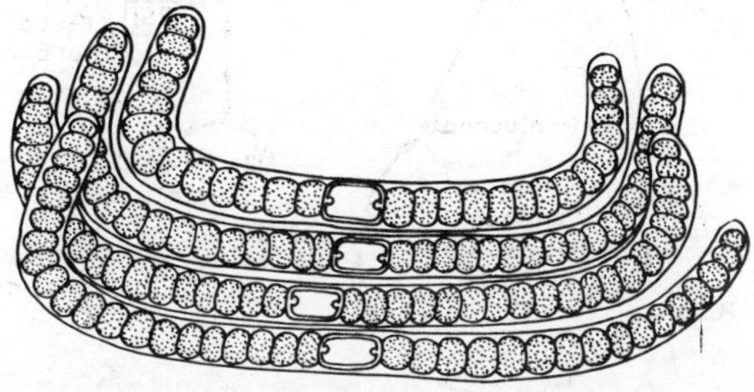

Fig. 3-12 *Camptylonema lahorense*, material from nature showing crescent-shaped filaments with median heterocyst.

Heterocysts are found in many but not all filamentous blue-green algae belonging to the orders Nostocales and Stigonematales, generally as a response to the onset of nitrogen deficiency in the ambient medium. They may occur either terminally or in an intercalary position in the trichome.

It is now conclusively established that, at least under aerobic conditions, the heterocyst is the main site of nitrogen fixation in most blue-green algae. The heterocyst functions as an anaerobic factory for nitrogen fixation under external aerobic conditions. When the algae grow under anaerobic conditions, vegetative cells (of both heterocystous and nonheterocystous species) also may fix nitrogen. The enzyme nitrogenase is very sensitive to oxygen. When unprotected from oxygen, this enzyme becomes inactivated. It becomes active only under oxygen deficiency or anaerobiosis, and the heterocyst has precisely this atmosphere. The multilayered envelope of the heterocyst reduces the entry of gases. The inner laminated layer rich in glycolipids greatly reduces the rate of diffusion of oxygen into heterocysts, and whatever little oxygen does diffuse, is destroyed by the oxidases present in the heterocyst. Its photosynthetic apparatus and usual lack of phycocyanin shuts down the oxygen-evolving activity of photosystem II (PSII), whereas the ATP-generating power of photosystem I (PSI) is retained. Since the heterocysts do not fix CO_2 photosynthetically, they establish at their junctions with neighbouring cells efficient pumps which assure a supply of carbon that serves as a reductant for nitrogenase (see Haselkorn, 1978). The path of flow of materials between the heterocyst and the vegetative cell is diagrammatically illustrated in Figs. 3-13 and 3-14. The localization

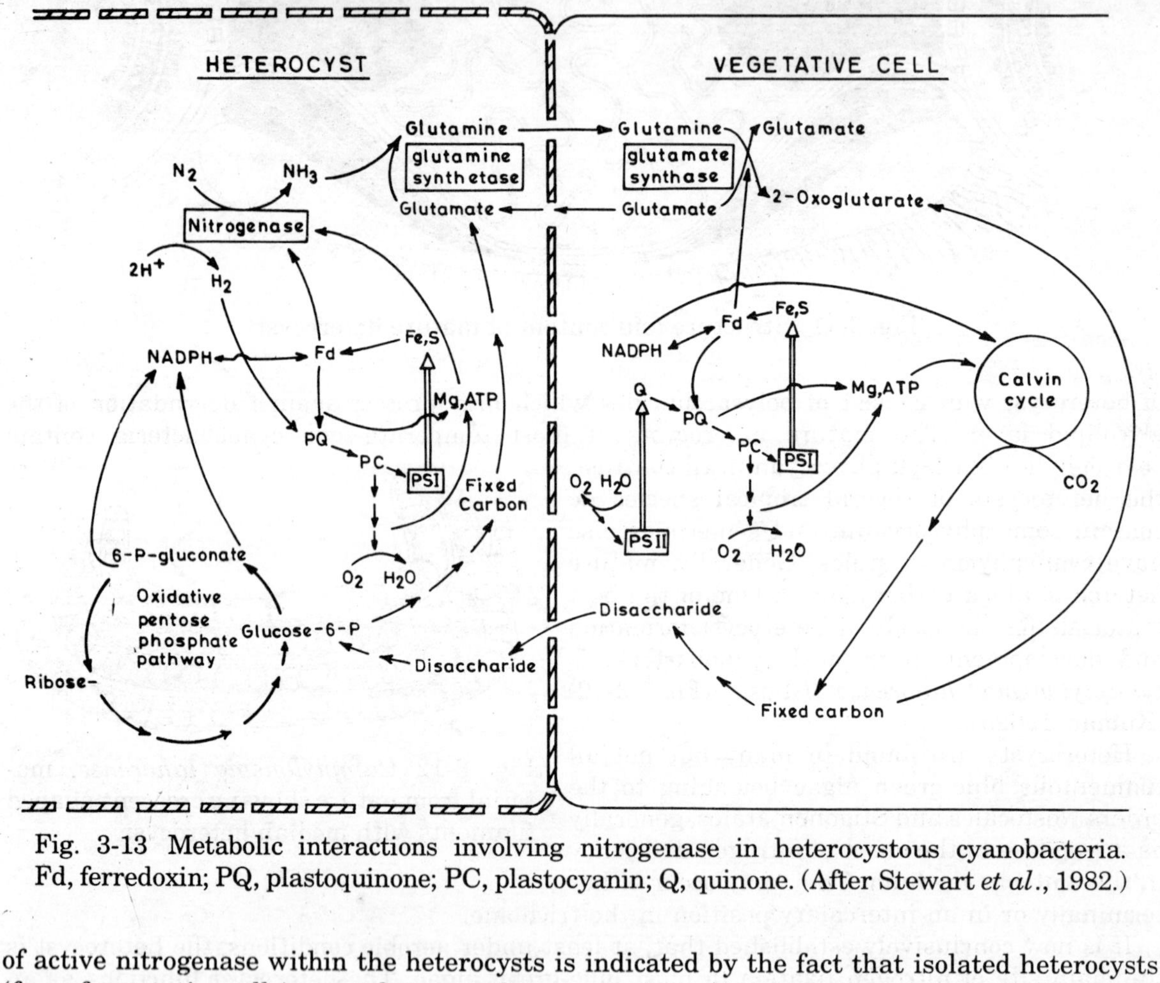

Fig. 3-13 Metabolic interactions involving nitrogenase in heterocystous cyanobacteria. Fd, ferredoxin; PQ, plastoquinone; PC, plastocyanin; Q, quinone. (After Stewart *et al.*, 1982.)

of active nitrogenase within the heterocysts is indicated by the fact that isolated heterocysts (free of vegetative cells) can reduce acetylene to ethylene when supplied with a reducing agent (sodium dithionite) and an energy source, ATP.

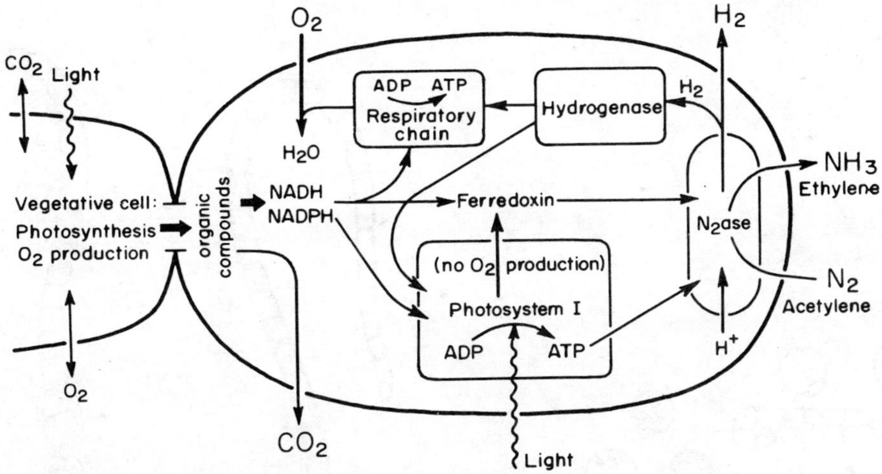

Fig. 3-14 Probable interactions of bioenergetic pathways in heterocysts supporting nitrogenase reaction. (Note that nitrogen fixation is always accompanied by hydrogen production, and H_2 so produced is reutilized by an uptake hydrogenase.)

AKINETES

These are thick-walled specialized cells meant for perennation. They are generally larger than the vegetative cells from which they develop. They appear granular under the microscope (Fig. 3-15 A, B). They may be spherical (e.g., *Anabaena*), discoidal (*Nodularia*), or elongated [*Gloeotrichia*, *Cylindrospermum* (Fig. 3-16)]. In these latter two genera, the akinetes occur adjacent to the heterocysts. In some species of *Anabaena*, the akinetes develop midway between two intercalary heterocysts in nitrogen-fixing cultures. When the alga is grown in nitrate-supplemented medium, the akinetes are formed in the absence of any heterocysts.

Fixed nitrogen and phosphate availability appear to control the onset of akinete development. The akinetes usually lack polyphosphate bodies, and it is believed that phosphate deficiency may trigger akinete formation in some but not all cyanobacteria (see Rai *et al.*, 1985). Light is another important factor influencing akinete development, with akinete frequency usually increasing with decrease in light intensity.

Young and developing akinetes are metabolically active but their metabolism slows down as they mature. According to Thiel and Wolk (1983), the akinetes of *Nostoc spongiaeforme* carry on protein synthesis, respiration, and photosynthesis. The akinetes of most cyanobacteria do not show any nitrogenase activity.

The akinetes are more resistant to environmental stresses than are the vegetative cells. The vegetative cells and akinetes have nearly the same type of thylakoid arrangement. The heterocyst development, however, is accompanied by extensive reorganization of thylakoids in a reticular fashion at its two poles. In addition, the heterocysts contain, near each junction with a vegetative cell, an osmiophilic polar nodule. The mature heterocysts differ from the vegetative cells in that they contain nitrogenase which has a higher level of glutamine synthetase and a lower level of glutamine oxoglutarate amido transferase (GOGAT) (see

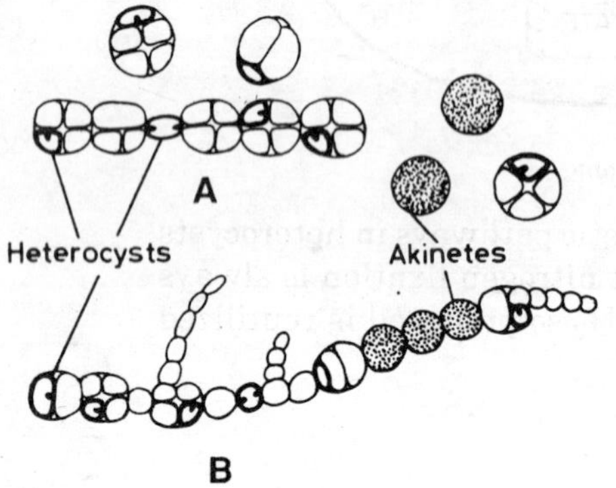

Fig. 3-15 Akinetes. A, *Chlorogloea*; B, *Fischerella*.

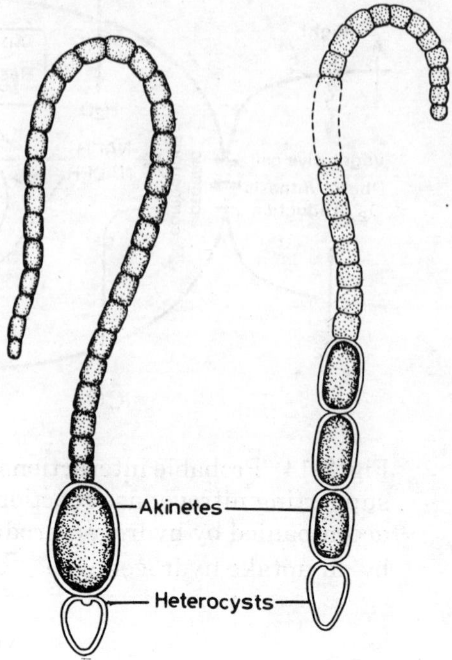

Fig. 3-16 *Cylindrospermum*, elongated akinetes.

Haselkorn, 1978). Further, the ratio of glutamate to aspartate is high in heterocysts and low in vegetative cells. In comparison with vegetative cells, the number of various granules is larger in akinetes (Fig. 3-17) and smaller in heterocysts. Polyphosphate granules, which function both as an energy source and inorganic phosphate reserves, are found in vegetative cells as well as akinetes but not in heterocysts. The lipid composition of the three cell types differs (see under Heterocysts). The vegetative cells contain a variety of photosynthetic pigments, e.g., chlorophyll-a, phycocyanin, β-carotene, myxoxanthophyll, and other carotenoids. The heterocysts mostly have chlorophyll-a and β-carotene; in comparison with vegetative cells, they are weakly pigmented and seem to contain less of DNA. The DNA distribution is more diffuse in the heterocyst than in the vegetative cell. In *Anabaena variabilis*, the heterocyst contains more RNA and nearly as much DNA as a vegetative cell.

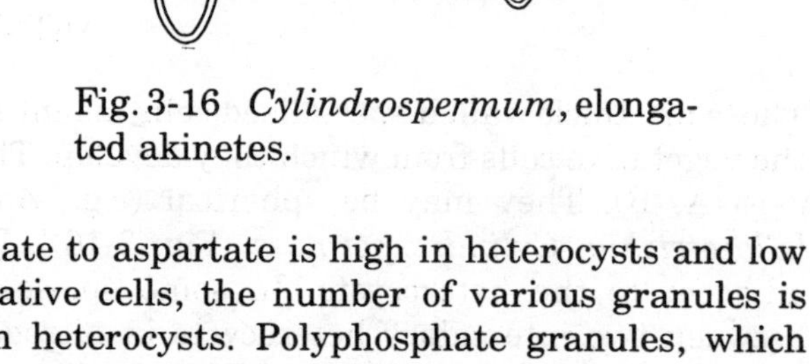

Fig. 3-17 *Nostoc*, diagrammatic sketch of electron microscopic structure of akinete.

Generally, the heterocysts show higher activities of two enzymes of the oxidative pentose phosphate pathway (viz., glucose-6-phosphate dehydrogenase and 6-phosphogluconate dehydrogenase) than the vegetative cells. Sulphate reduction is restricted to vegetative cells, whereas sulphide, cysteine, and glutathione are present in heterocysts (Wolk, 1982). The akinetes seem to be even more deficient in pigments than heterocysts. The distribution of pigments in these cell types is highly significant in their metabolic activities.

The akinetes of *Anabaena doliolum* and *Fischerella mucicola* (Fig. 3-15 B) can germinate in nonphotosynthetic light (Kaushik and Kumar, 1970) but not in the dark; those of *Anabaenopsis arnoldii* require photosynthetic light for germination (Rai *et al.*, 1985).

Some workers have used the term "spore" for the akinetes of cyanobacteria.

COMPARATIVE ORGANIZATION OF VEGETATIVE CELLS, HETEROCYSTS, AND AKINETES

Recent cytological and biochemical studies reveal that heterocysts and akinetes differ in structure, composition, and function (Lang, 1968). Both develop from vegetative cells. As compared with vegetative cells, the wall of the heterocyst includes an additional layer lacking true cellulose, whereas that of the akinete has several additional sheath layers with the outermost one or two layers often variously sculptured.

The vegetative cells carry out the aerobic type of photosynthesis characteristic of other algae and generate both the reducing power, NADPH (reduced nicotinamide adenine dinucleotide phosphate) and the energy source (ATP). The heterocysts include only photosystem I and therefore can have only the anaerobic type of photosynthesis as found in photosynthetic bacteria. The akinetes have been shown to be metabolically active, synthesizing at least some of their own proteins and fats (Thiel and Wolk, 1983). However, the rates of photosynthesis and respiration in akinetes are generally lower than in vegetative cells.

The heterocysts fix nitrogen when the organism is grown aerobically. When grown anaerobically, the vegetative cells may also fix nitrogen. The akinetes do not fix nitrogen at least aerobically.

Simon (1979) has made a comparative study of the macromolecular composition of filaments (which have mostly vegetative cells), heterocysts, and spores of *Anabaena variabilis*. His findings are summarized in Table 3-1.

Table 3-1 Macromolecular composition of *Anabaena variabilis* in grams/cell × 10^{14} (after Simon, 1979)

Cell type	Protein	Chlorophyll	DNA	RNA
Filaments	899	15.2	5.1	66.7
Heterocysts	680	24.6	4.5	263.0
Spores	1051	17.8	5.0	304.0

METABOLIC COMPARTMENTATION

In filamentous, heterocystous forms, the fixation of CO_2 occurs in vegetative cells which have both PSI and PSII and which contain Rubisco (ribulose bisphosphate carboxylase) and other

Calvin cycle enzymes. Heterocysts lack PSII and Rubisco, and cannot fix CO_2. In aerobically grown material, nitrogenase is mainly confined to heterocysts which reduce dinitrogen to ammonia. Fixed nitrogen is thought to be transported to the vegetative cells (Fig. 3-13) in the form of glutamine.

Giddings *et al.* (1981) have further shown that sulphur metabolism is mainly located in the vegetative cells where sulphate ions are activated and some reduced form of sulphur, e.g., the sulphide ion, is transported from vegetative cells to heterocysts. Heterocysts lack ATP sulphurylase which is present in vegetative cells. The enzyme glutamate synthase is restricted to the vegetative cells, whereas glutamine synthetase occurs in heterocysts as well as vegetative cells.

When grown under air-equilibrated CO_2 concentrations, many cyanobacteria behave phenotypically as C_4 plants despite the fact that they have a C_3 type biochemistry (see Raven, 1980). This is thought to be a result of the activity of a 'CO_2-concentrating mechanism' which, by increasing the CO_2 level at the active site of Rubisco, represses the oxygenase function of Rubisco (this enzyme can also act as an oxygenase under certain conditions) as well as the photorespiration.

The current position about whether or not cyanobacteria lack metabolic regulation can be stated as follows. Since most cyanobacteria are obligate phototrophs, there would be little evolutionary demand for end product regulation in response to substrates entering the cells. Bassham (1982) has reported a regulation of the cyanobacterial CO_2 reduction cycle similar to that in higher plant chloroplasts. It seems that the cyanobacteria may not lack metabolic regulation; rather, as obligate phototrophs there was no selective advantage for them to have that part of regulation associated with utilization of exogenous substrates.

PIGMENTS AND CHROMATIC ADAPTATION

The chief pigments are chlorophyll-a, β-carotene, and phycobiliproteins (phycocyanin, allophycocyanin-A, and allophycocyanin-B). These are not located in any chromatophore but are found in photosynthetic lamellae (thylakoids). Smaller amounts of c-phycoerythrin, zeaxanthin, echinone, and myxoxanthophyll may also be found. However, their proportion, especially of phycocyanin (blue) and phycoerythrin (red), varies greatly under different habitat conditions. Forms exposed to bright sunlight are rich in phycocyanin and appear a deep bluish-green; those growing in low light intensity generally have more phycoerythrin so that they appear reddish. The filamentous alga *Trichodesmium erythraeum*, which grows in the plankton of the Red Sea, is an extreme example where the phycoerythrin content is so high, and phycocyanin so low, that it appears distinctly reddish even though it is actually a blue-green.

In contrast to other pigments which are fat-soluble, phycocyanin and phycoerythrin, collectively known as biliproteins, can be extracted in water after cell disruption and are proteinaceous.

While the photosynthesis of most cyanobacteria is oxygenic (as in higher plants), many strains, e.g., *Oscillatoria limnetica*, can shift between anoxygenic bacterial-type photosynthesis and oxygenic photosynthesis. These facultatively anoxygenic strains tend to be distributed in those water bodies in which the prevailing conditions fluctuate between aerobic and anaerobic phenomena.

In some species of the Cyanophyta, especially those having phycoerythrin, the pigmentation seems to be determined by the quality of light in which they are grown (see Bogorad, 1975). For instance, some species of *Oscillatoria* can assume a green colour in red light, a reddish hue in green light, and a bluish-green in yellow light. Such a capacity to change colour complementary to that of the light is known as chromatic adaptation or the Gaidukov phenomenon. This adaptation is of definite advantage since it enables the alga to maximally absorb the light for photosynthesis. In some species, the rate of phycoerythrin synthesis (being lower in red light than in green light) is the chief determining factor in chromatic adaptation. In others, both phycoerythrin and phycocyanin syntheses are subject to regulation by light, and the relative rate of phycoerythrin synthesis is higher in green light and lower in red light, whereas that of phycocyanin is higher in red light and lower in green light (see Bogorad, 1975).

Phycobilisomes are unique light-harvesting complexes found in cyanobacteria and red algae. They are made of stacks of pigment proteins (phycobiliproteins) linked together by colourless proteins, called linkers, in an orderly array. In both cyanobacteria and red algae, the phycobiliproteins make up about 85% of the phycobilisome complex, and occur in three major forms, viz., phycocyanin (PC), phycoerythrin (PE), and allophycocyanin (APC). The phycobilisome of cyanobacteria can modulate its constituent polypeptides in response to the colour of the light it is exposed to. This chromatic adaptation enables these organisms to use effectively whatever wavelength of light is prevalent in the environment (Gantt, 1981).

We may classify cyanobacteria into three groups depending on responses of their phycobilisomes to light. Group I organisms synthesize constant levels of PE and PC, irrespective of light colour. In group II, PE is regulated by light quality in the sense that green light produces higher levels whereas red light produces lower levels of PE. There is no such change in PC. The organisms belonging to group III show elevated levels of PC and reduced levels of PE in response to red light, but just the reverse in green light.

Phycobilisomes are located on the external surface of the thylakoid membrane pair. They appear like large ribosomes and are not surrounded by membranes. They are disposed in both short and long extensive rows with a regular spacing pattern. They may range in shape from disc-shaped to globular. Most cyanobacteria have disc-shaped phycobilisomes, whereas those of the red algae tend to be globular.

Structurally, phycobilisomes of cyanobacteria are commonly thick, hemidiscoidal in shape, and are attached to the thylakoid membranes by proteinaceous material. Each phycobilisome has six stacked rods fanning out from a core. The core is made of allophycocyanin. This is surrounded by phycocyanin molecules which in turn are covered by phycoerythrin (Fig. 3-10).

Scheibe (1972) isolated a phytochrome-like photoreversible pigment from *Tolypothrix tenuis*. The absorption maxima for the two photoreversible forms of this pigment lie in the green and red, instead of in the red and far-red, portions of the spectrum (red and far-red are characteristic of the higher plant phytochrome). In cyanophytes, this new pigment may possibly control several morphogenetic phenomena, including chromatic adaptation.

MOVEMENTS

Flagella, cilia, or other similar means of propulsion are absent in cyanobacteria. However, many species do exhibit a gliding movement which involves a rather slow and smooth movement of the cell, hormogonium, or filament. In some cases, the movement is jerky or oscillatory, or it may involve rotation, bending, and swaying (Häder, 1987).

The cells glide only when in contact with some surface, commonly solid, which does not cause any observable change in the organism's shape.

The two types of movement known in cyanobacteria are (1) the phototactic gliding movement, characteristic of those species which attach to surfaces; and (2) the light-regulated buoyancy changes, characteristic of planktonic species suspended in standing bodies of water.

Recent studies have indicated the existence of two types of phototaxis in cyanobacteria. These are (1) the nostocacean type, in which the filaments move either towards or away from light; and (2) the oscillatoriaceous type, where, instead of a direct steering towards or away from light, the filaments orient themselves by a technique involving "three steps forward, one step back" (Walsby, 1980). It is thought that photosynthetically-generated electrical potentials may be involved in controlling the direction of movement.

Most microbiologists believe that the gliding movement is brought about by the production of contractile waves in one of the surface layers of the cell wall; this is often accompanied by some mucilage secretion through pores in the cell wall. The mucilage is thought to be secreted in a directional manner towards one end of a filament or the other. Upon contacting a solid surface, the mucilage sticks to it and some continued secretion of more mucilage behind the already stuck mucilage causes a relative displacement or movement of the filament with reference to the solid object. In some cases, the direction of gliding movement can be reversed. Some cyanobacteria form rings of mucilage around their cross wall regions and, according to Walsby (1968), the gliding mechanism operates all around the filaments, rather than in a particular band or line. The source of energy for gliding is believed to be ATP.

In some cyanobacteria, the gliding speed increases or decreases with increase in light intensity (Nultsch and Häder, 1979, 1988). This process is photokinesis. In a photophobic response, a rapid temporal change in light intensity produces a transient change in motility.

Gliding of the nonpolar, filamentous cyanobacteria appears as a slow uniform motion and is sometimes interrupted by reversals (Häder and Hoiczyk, 1992). No wriggling, contraction or peristaltic alterations of the filamentous trichomes can be detected by light microscopy. Members of the Oscillatoriaceae translocate in a highly coordinated manner. Translational movements are usually accompanied by revolution around the long axis of the filament. While moving, the trichomes secrete slime which is left behind as a twisted and collapsed thin tube. The sense of revolution is unique and species-specific as seen from the handedness of the rotation (Hoiczyk and Baumeister, 1995).

Some unusual structures have been described which may or may not be related to this peculiar type of motility. These include spinning discs, fibrils within the cell or the cell wall, chain-like strands, anchorage sites of the cell surface, contractile surface appendages, cellular inclusions (rhapidosomes), and extracellular material (see Hoiczyk and Baumeister, 1995).

Several views have been expressed about the functional significance of the gliding movement. These are briefly mentioned here:

(1) It may enable the organism to respond suitably to light. Such a function can involve orientation with reference to the direction of incident light, responses to temporal alterations in light intensity independent of the direction of incident light, or filament aggregation (see Nultsch, 1965).

(2) It may help maintain the diffusion gradients of dissolved nutrients at an optimal level in the organisms growing attached in fast-flowing streams or rain-splashed surfaces.

(3) It may rid the organism of its eubacterial contaminants which adhere to the mucilaginous sheaths that tend to be left behind when the organism glides off.

(4) It sometimes aids the organisms in forming aggregates, clumps, or ropes through which the individuals can glide off (Fig. 3-18).

(5) It enables the organism to exhibit some slow movement while still remaining fixed to some solid surface, e.g., *Oscillatoria* which shows a pendulum-like swaying movement while remaining attached to its substratum in a water body.

(6) It can bring about significant positional changes of the organism in sediments, rock crevices, and thermal springs.

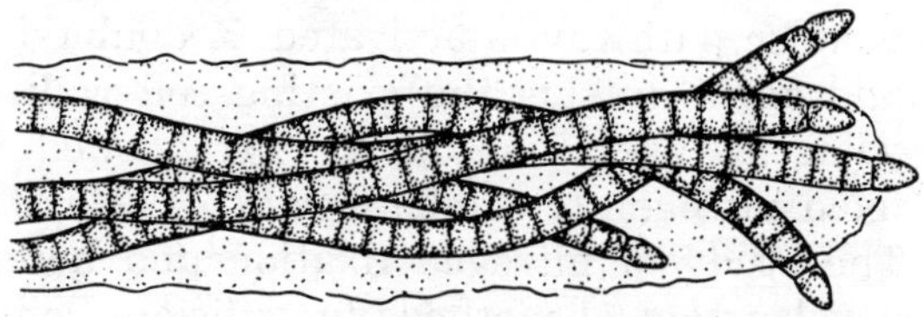

Fig. 3-18 *Microcoleus*, occurrence of several trichomes in a common sheath with some trichomes gliding out.

Filamentous forms such as *Microcoleus* and *Oscillatoria* that show gliding movement are often found in some muds where gradients of light intensity, oxygen concentration, sulphide concentration, pH, and water potential vary significantly with depth and time. All these factors influence the growth of cyanobacteria, which are likely to show not only phototaxis but also directional responses to chemicals or gases. In fact, Malin and Walsby (1985) have demonstrated that an *Oscillatoria* isolated from a salt marsh shows chemotaxis to CO_2 and to O_2.

NITROGEN FIXATION

Numerous strains of cyanobacteria possess the capacity to convert or fix elementary nitrogen (dinitrogen gas) found in the air into useful nitrogenous compounds which can be assimilated. This property makes them truly autotrophic plants in the sense that they can fix not only the atmospheric CO_2 but also the gaseous nitrogen. The cyanobacteria which fix nitrogen can be broadly classified into three types. Type 1 includes unicellular forms such as *Aphanothece* and *Gloeocapsa* which can fix nitrogen both in aerobic and anaerobic (microaerophilic) conditions. Type 2 includes certain nonheterocystous filamentous forms, e.g., *Oscillatoria*, which can fix it only under microaerophilic conditions but not when grown in air. Type 3, the most important group, contains many heterocystous filamentous forms which can fix nitrogen both aerobically and anaerobically. Examples are given in the discussion that follows.

The nitrogen-fixing power is particularly conspicuous in certain filamentous species such as *Aulosira*, *Tolypothrix*, *Anabaena*, *Cylindrospermum*, *Nostoc*, and *Mastigocladus* which possess heterocysts. Certain nonheterocystous filamentous algae, e.g., *Plectonema boryanum*, can also fix nitrogen under anaerobic conditions but not in air. The heterocystous species contribute greatly to the fertility of rice fields in tropical countries. In temperate regions also, nitrogen fixation seems to be mainly a cyanophycean, rather than a bacterial, process. A number of blue-green algae are found in symbiotic association with other plants and the nitrogen fixed by them may be largely responsible for the success of the partnership.

Cyanobacteria have the following requirements for nitrogen fixation: synthesis of the nitrogenase complex and its cofactors, a source of ATP and low-potential electrons, and an environment protected from oxygen. Unique among diazotrophs, cyanobacteria evolve oxygen in the light. Filamentous strains such as *Anabaena* solve the problem of oxygen sensitivity of nitrogenase by differentiating specialized cells called heterocysts at regular intervals along the filament. In the heterocyst, the oxygen-evolving reaction of PSII is turned off, CO_2 fixation stops, nitrogenase, cofactors, and electron donor proteins are synthesized, and the oxidative pentose pathway is activated. A double-layered envelope of polysaccharide and glycolipid is laid down outside the existing cell wall. New connections between the heterocyst and the adjacent vegetative cells are established: these mediate the transport of carbohydrate and of fixed nitrogen (Haselkorn *et al.*, 1991). These changes require differential gene expression. The study of nitrogen fixation and heterocyst differentiation has been stimulated by the development of methods for efficient conjugation of DNA from *E. coli* into *Anabaena* (Wolk *et al.*, 1984). With these methods it has been possible to isolate developmentally significant genes by complementation of mutants, to inactivate genes by targetted insertional mutagenesis, to perform random mutagenesis with transposons, and to create fusions with certain reporter genes to estimate gene expression at the single cell level. Most of our knowledge of the organization of the genes required for nitrogen fixation (*nif*) in *Anabaena* is based on physical mapping, relying on sequence similarity to known *nif* genes of *Klebsiella* and *Azotobacter*. Such studies additionally showed that several large DNA elements (11 kb and 55 kb) interrupt the *nif* genes in *Anabaena* vegetative cells and that these elements are excised during heterocyst differentiation (Golden *et al.*, 1985).

A new approach to the study of genes required for heterocyst differentiation is based on the conjugation system developed by Elhai and Wolk (1988); this has three components: a shuttle vector built from a cryptic plasmid capable of replication in *Anabaena* fused to part of pBR322, a broad host range plasmid to make the apparatus for conjugal transfer of DNA, and a third plasmid that mobilizes the shuttle vector for conjugal transfer. The shuttle vector contains cloning sites for inserted fragments of *Anabaena* DNA. A recent improvement includes genes encoding methylase activities, capable of protecting DNA against the *Ava* restriction enzymes, in the *E. coli* strain in which the shuttle vector is maintained. Additionally, a low copy number shuttle vector with a *cos* site and a multiple cloning site flanked by termination sequences that block transcription into the cloned insert has been constructed. These principles have been applied to study the timing and the spatial distribution of transcripts of several genes expressed only in heterocysts.

In the bacterium *Klebsiella pneumoniae*, which has served as a model of *nif* gene organization, all the known genes uniquely required for nitrogen fixation are clustered within 24 kb. Genes in the *nif* cluster that encode proteins with related functions are transcribed together. The *nifHDK* genes, which encode the components of the nitrogenase complex and the *nifEN* genes, which encode a structure required for synthesis of the Fe-Mo cofactor, comprise operons. The *nifUSV* genes are also cotranscribed. The functions of *nifU* and *nifS* are not yet known; *nifV* encodes homocitrate synthase and homocitrate is a part of the Fe-Mo cofactor. The *nifL* and *A* genes, both participating in regulation of transcription of the other *nif* genes, are cotranscribed. Finally, *nifB* and *Q*, both required for Fe-Mo cofactor synthesis, also comprise an operon (Orme-Johnson, 1985).

The first studies of *Anabaena nif* genes indicated that their organization was different. The *nifD* and *K* genes were not contiguous and the *nifS* gene was 5′ to *nifHD* rather than 3′ as in *Klebsiella*. Moreover, these *nif* genes appeared to be interspersed with and surrounded by DNA that was not transcribed under nitrogen-fixing conditions and therefore not likely to contain other *nif* genes. Subsequent work showed that although this description fits the situation in *Anabaena* vegetative cells, it is not the case in heterocysts. During heterocyst differentiation, two rearrangements occur in this region of the *Anabaena* chromosome. Both are excisions of DNA elements that interrupt the reading frames of *Anabaena nif* genes in vegetative cells. One excision results in the deletion of an 11-kb element from the *nifD* coding region, leading to the formation of *nifHDK* operon very similar to that of *Klebsiella*. The second excision removes a 55-kb element to the 5′ side of the *nifS* gene that interrupts the reading frame of a gene called *fdxN*. This results in the formation of another operon, *NifB-fdxN-nifS-NifU* (Haselkorn *et al.*, 1991). Each excision is the result of recombination between directly repeated short sequences at the ends of the interrupting element. These short sequences differ for the two elements. Excision of the 11-kb element requires the product of a gene, *xisA*, located just inside the left end of the element (see Fig. 3-19). Following the excision reaction, the excised 11-kb element is circular and it contains one copy of the short terminal repeat. The other identical copy of the short repeat remains inside the *nifD* coding region. The *xisA* gene product catalyzes the precise excision reaction when the element is propagated as part of a plasmid in *E. coli* as well. The *xisA* gene has been cloned, sequenced and expressed in *E. coli* but the recombination reaction has not yet been observed *in vitro*. In terms of the sites and protein requirement for excision, the element resembles a lysogenic virus. As yet, no advantage has been found to be conferred on vegetative cells carrying the element.

Figure 3-19 shows the *Klebsiella nif* gene map and the surrounding region of the *Anabaena* chromosome. The operon to the extreme right in the diagram is *rbcLS*, encoding the large and small subunits of RuBP carboxylase. These genes are transcribed in vegetative

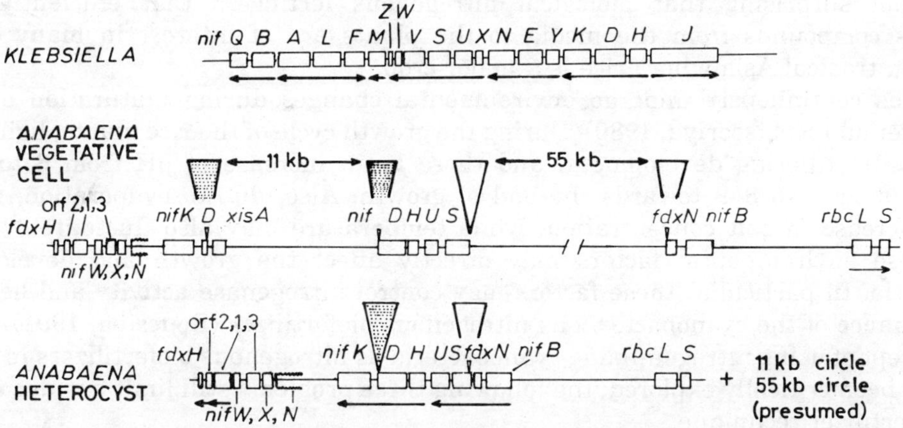

Fig. 3-19 Organization of the *nif* gene region of *Klebsiella*, *Anabaena* vegetative cells, and *Anabaena* heterocysts after excision of the 11-kb and 55-kb elements. Shaded triangles indicate the location of short direct repeats within which the recombination events leading to excision occur. Horizontal arrows below each map indicate transcription units. Sizes of the transcripts produced by genes between *nifW* and *nifK* have not been determined. Sequencing of the *nifN-nifK* region has not been completed. (From Haselkorn *et al.*, 1991.)

cells but not in heterocysts. The 10 kb between *rbcLS* and *nifB* have not been characterized in terms of sequence or transcripts yet (Haselkorn *et al.*, 1991).

The precise roles of some of the genes in *Anabaena* nitrogen fixation are not known.

Immediately following the *nifB* operon is the *nifHDK* operon. This operon produces three transcripts that correspond to *nifH*, *NifHD*, and *nifHDK* in size. The start site for transcription of this operon was mapped by S1 nuclease protection and primer extension and the 5′-flanking sequence of the transcript family was determined. This sequence is not easily related to the characteristic *nif* gene promoter of *Klebsiella*.

Following the *nifHDK* operon there are several kb of DNA for which we do not yet have sequence information.

Large scale production of nitrogen-fixing cyanobacteria was aimed originally at expanding the traditional application of diazotrophic heterocystous cyanobacteria as a source of fixed nitrogen, in rice paddies. Production was confined to nonlined open ponds, in which the resulting algal product contained a high percentage of soil, and the productivity was highly unpredictable in terms of the amount and kind of algal biomass that could be produced.

Interest in the mass culture goes beyond their use as a nitrogenous biofertilizer. The cyanobacteria also constitute a source of valuable products such as phycobiliproteins, polysaccharides, and protein for feed and food. Boussiba (1988, 1991) investigated the potential production of nitrogen-fixing cyanobacteria in outdoor cultures for application as nitrogenous fertilizer and as a source of biochemicals. The lack of available chemical fertilizers, especially nitrogenous, at affordable prices, is a basic problem facing agriculture in developing countries. Nitrogenous chemicals account for about one-fourth of the total fertilizers needed for crops and are often acting as limiting factors in food production in developing countries. It is therefore not surprising that biological nitrogenous fertilizers that efficiently transfer nitrogenous compounds from the media to the plants are of interest in many countries, especially in tropical Asia where rice is a major crop.

Rice fields continuously undergo environmental changes during maturation of the rice plants (Roger and Kulasooriya, 1980). During the growth cycle of the rice plants, light becomes limiting due to tillering development, and there is an increase of pH from 6 to 7 in the inoculation stages, to 8–9 towards the end of growth. Also, due to evaporation, there is a constant increase in salt concentration, while temperature may also fluctuate over a wide range. These environmental factors may directly affect the growth and development of cyanobacteria. In particular, these factors may control nitrogenase activity and hence affect the performance of the cyanobacteria as nitrogenous biofertilizer (Boussiba, 1991).

The concept of using nitrogen-fixing cyanobacteria as nitrogenous biofertilizers in rice fields has not yet been critically explored; the following three problems still limit a wider utilization of this biofertilizer technique:

(1) Lack of understanding of the environmental conditions prevailing in paddy fields which can affect the growth or survival of the native or inoculated cyanobacteria.

(2) Inability to produce good-quality inocula in sufficient quantities at economical price.

(3) The low efficiency of the transfer or utilization of the fixed nitrogen by the cyanobacteria to the rice plants.

An important stage when considering application of nitrogen-fixing cyanobacteria as biofertilizer is mass production of high quality inoculum of the desired strains. The reported rates of inoculum production are quite low (around 6–8 gram m^{-2} day^{-1}).

The rice field ecosystem provides favourable conditions for the development of a large variety of free-living cyanobacteria and symbiotic strains which are capable of fixing atmospheric nitrogen. The nutrients fixed by cyanobacteria are made available to the rice plants through exudation autolysis and decomposition. Under field conditions, however, only a part of the fixed nitrogen is available to the rice plant, some being either reincorporated by the microflora or volatilized. Under these circumstances it becomes difficult to control the flow of nitrogenous compounds needed for the development of rice plants. One approach to this problem is to develop strains which release ammonium continuously. An ammonium-excreting mutant (SS1) of *Anabaena siamensis* has been isolated after ethyl methanesulphonate mutagenesis by selection on L-methionine-DL-sulphoximine (MSX) (Thomas *et al.*, 1990). SS1 can grow both in the presence and absence of MSX at a rate comparable to that of the wild type strain. The rate of ammonium release by SS1 depends on cell density. Prolonged release of ammonium is achieved by maintaining SS1 under continuous cultivation at low chlorophyll levels when nitrogen fixation in the mutant is much higher than that in the wild strain.

Fertilization of rice plants under laboratory conditions by application of another MSX-resistant mutant (SA1) of *Anabaena variabilis* has also been fairly successful (Latorre *et al.*, 1986). The shorter doubling time of SS1 and the lack of a lag phase at the beginning of the growth cycle, as compared with SA1 (Spiller *et al.*, 1986) which does show a lag, are a few obvious advantages for mass cultivation of the strain SS1.

Gloeotrichia natans is common in paddy fields in the Philippines. It appears to be a good source of phycobiliproteins (Palaepac *et al.*, 1990). The red and blue pigments together constitute about 15 per cent of the algal dry weight and can be used as colouring agents for food and cosmetics, and as immunofluorescence probes in medical research.

The enzyme involved in nitrogen fixation is nitrogenase whose properties are now listed.

The nitrogen fixed by the blue-green algae can be assimilated by themselves as well as by other organisms. Substantial amounts of soluble nitrogenous compounds are liberated from the healthy cells of nitrogen-fixing blue-green algae either into the culture medium or in their natural habitats. Besides, when the algae die, their nitrogenous materials decay and form ammonia which may then be transformed into nitrates by nitrifying bacteria, thus enriching the fertility of the habitat.

The pathway of nitrogen fixation in algae has been followed by a variety of biochemical and radioactive tracer techniques. Dinitrogen is first reduced to ammonia by the enzyme nitrogenase. Ammonia is rapidly metabolized to glutamine by the enzyme glutamine synthetase (GS), and glutamine to glutamate by the enzyme GOGAT. Glutamine and glutamate are involved in various transamination reactions leading to the biosynthesis of other amino acids. Nitrogenase and GS are coupled in the heterocyst and their product (glutamine) is transported to the vegetative cell where GOGAT catalyzes the formation of glutamate. The various steps involved are outlined in Fig. 3-20. Hydrogen gas is a good electron donor to nitrogenase in heterocysts in the light, and it can serve as electron donor to the nitrogenase only in the light. This means that H_2 donates its electrons to PSI in heterocysts.

The cyanobacteria show three types of hydrogenases, viz., (1) a nitrogenase, which produces hydrogen; (2) a classical, reversible, hydrogenase; and (3) an uptake hydrogenase, which can reduce O_2. Most of these hydrogenases seem to be active in the heterocysts.

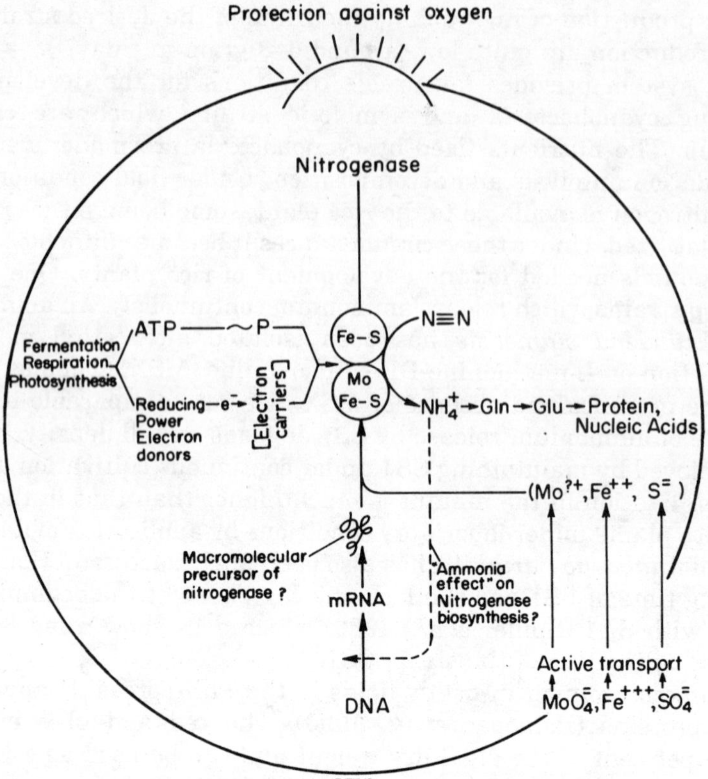

Fig. 3-20 Nitrogen-fixation mechanism (as proposed by Streicher and Valentine, 1973). Gln, glutamine; Glu, glutamic acid.

Properties of Nitrogenase

Nitrogenase uses 34 iron (Fe) atoms and 2 molybdenum (Mo) atoms to catalyze the reaction

$$N_2 + 16MgATP + 8e^- + 8H^+ \rightarrow 2NH_3 + 16MgADP + 16P_i + H_2$$

where MgATP is magnesium adenosine 5′-triphosphate and P_i is inorganic phosphate. Two proteins are responsible for the reaction, the Fe-protein and the MoFe-protein (Fig. 3-21).

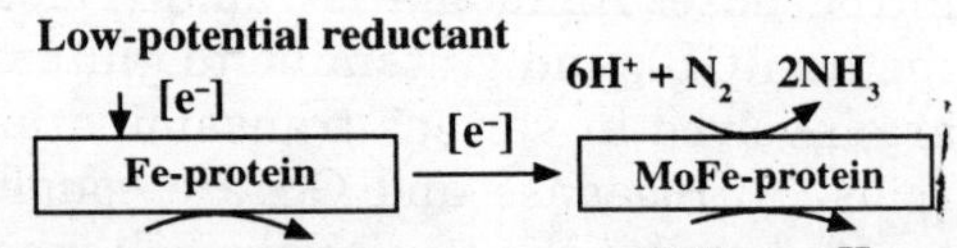

Fig. 3-21 Reactions catalyzed by subunits of nitrogenase.

The Fe-protein has two subunits and a single Fe_4S_4 unit with the atoms at the corners of a cube (a cubane structure) and can be understood on the basis of the structures of ferredoxins, a well-described class of low-potential Fe-S electron-transfer proteins. The Fe-protein binds two MgATP units per molecule that are then hydrolyzed when an electron is transferred to the MoFe-protein. The Fe-protein bears at least part of the machinery needed for reductive dephosphorylation or transduction of ATP hydrolysis energy into strongly negative electron potentials that initiate the saturation of the triple bond in N_2. The initial $2e^-$ reduction is thought to be endothermic by about 49 kcal/mol; the overall reaction is exothermic by about 63 kcal/mol (Orme-Johnson, 1992).

The MoFe-protein is believed to be made of four subunits in an $\alpha_2\beta_2$ arrangement.

Much recent work has been done on the structural characterization of isolated nitrogenase cofactor, as well as the functions of all *nif* genes. In trying to understand the structures of the nitrogenase clusters synthetic chemists have contributed greatly to our knowledge of metal-dinitrogen and metal-calcogenide cluster chemistry. Nitrogenase is still the only natural substance known to react with the major "inert" constituent of the atmosphere at atmospheric pressure and room temperature (Orme-Johnson, 1992).

This enzyme catalyzes the reduction of N_2, from a valency state of zero, to NH_3, i.e., a valency state of minus 3. It is a multi-subunit iron sulphur and molybdenum containing enzyme complex. It is composed of two chief protein types, viz., protein I, which contains iron, sulphur, and molybdenum, and protein II, which has only iron and sulphur. Both proteins I and II are sensitive to oxygen. The nitrogenase also seems to be cold-labile. Its activity requires anaerobic conditions, an electron donor (ferredoxin), magnesium ions, and fairly high amounts of ATP.

The heterocystous species have a nitrogenase that is active under aerobic and anaerobic conditions. *Gloeothece* is unique among nonheterocystous cyanobacteria in having aerobic nitrogenase activity. Most other nonheterocystous species show nitrogenase activity only under anaerobic or microaerobic conditions.

The nitrogenase enzyme can also act as an ATP-dependent hydrogenase which generates H_2 from water and sunlight in air.

NUTRITION

Cyanophytes have a greatly restricted range of nutrition and in this respect they differ sharply from most other procaryotes. With the exception of some strains of *Nostoc*, *Tolypothrix*, and *Chlorogloea*, most of them are obligate photoautotrophs and cannot grow in darkness even in the presence of organic substrates. The biochemical basis of their obligate phototrophy is still not clear. Three hypotheses have been put forward to explain this phototrophy. One suggests that since the key respiratory enzymes, α-ketoglutarate dehydrogenase and nicotinamide adenine nucleotide (NAD) oxidase, are absent from the blue-green algae, the incomplete functioning of the tricarboxylic acid cycle might be responsible for their phototrophic behaviour (Hoare *et al.*, 1970). The second hypothesis implicates the lack of the enzyme repression control mechanism in the tricarboxylic acid cycle and amino acid metabolism as the principal causative feature for the obligate phototrophy (Carr, 1970). The enzyme repression control operates at the transcription (cistron) level, and acts by stopping the synthesis of biosynthetic enzymes in response to the exogenous availability, or overproduction, of their end products. The inhibition of enzyme synthesis is termed repression, and its release, derepression (see also the discussion that follows).

The third view (see Stanier and Cohen-Bazire, 1977) emphasizes the facts that the oxidative pentose phosphate cycle is a universal pathway of endogenous respiration and that cell-free extracts of the obligate photoautotrophs do have hexokinase activity, and, on the basis of these facts, their failure to grow in the dark, at the expense of exogenous glucose or any other sugar, is attributed to the absence of sugar permeases. One other factor that could also cause obligate photoautotrophy in certain cyanophytes is the low rate of respiratory ATP synthesis; this low rate has actually been recorded in a *Synechocystis*.

The extremely great flexibility of some cyanobacteria is further highlighted by their ability to thrive with limited heterotrophic or mixotrophic means in addition to their photoautotrophic mode of life. Some species can utilize their stored polyglucose reserves for survival in the dark by means of respiration, fermentation to lactic acid, and anaerobic respiration with elemental sulphur. The planktonic gas-vacuolate species are uniquely adapted to withstand high oxygen concentrations. These forms are quite resistant to photooxidation and a mechanism of this kind of resistance involves their remarkable ability to maintain high levels of superoxide dismutase activity of the manganese type. *Oscillatoria limnetica* is known to adapt to high oxygen concentrations by increasing its superoxide dismutase content.

REPRODUCTION, GENETICS, AND LIFE CYCLE

In many unicellular and colonial forms, the chief method of reproduction is by division of a parent cell into two daughter cells, or by fragmentation of a colony into two or more colonies. Sometimes, in addition to cell division or fission, nonmotile spores (endospores or exospores) are produced; each of these gives rise to a new plant. The spores are commonly produced in ordinary vegetative cells rather than in differentiated sporangia. Unlike eucaryotic algae, mitosis and meiosis are not involved in cell division or sporogenesis.

The filamentous forms belonging to the Nostocales and Stigonematales regularly multiply by the breaking of their trichomes into hormogonia which are generally motile and later mature into filaments. Some forms produce akinetes which function as reproductive or perennating cells. Differentiation of akinetes seems to be triggered by energy limitation. Cyanophycin granules and carboxysomes accumulate and then a multilayered extracellular envelope and a thick wall are formed. The thick akinete walls of *Anabaena cylindrica* contain the same polysaccharide material that comprises the outer layer of the heterocyst wall, i.e., 1,3-linked glucosyl-mannosyl (3 : 1), with xylosyl and galactosyl residues occurring as side branches. In contrast, the akinete wall of *Cylindrospermum* sp. has a largely 4-linked galactose and a polymer of aromatic groups (Cardemil and Wolk, 1981).

The genome size of various blue-green algae varies widely, being very small (about 2.5×10^9 daltons) in the Chroococcales and larger (3.5×10^9 daltons to 4.6×10^9 daltons) in the remaining orders. However, the range of genome size in the Cyanophyta has been found to be very high, i.e., 1.6×10^9 daltons to 7.6×10^9 daltons (see Stanier and Cohen-Bazire, 1977).

The genome of *Anabaena variabilis* has been isolated as a folded, circular chromosome, and recent research suggests that genome replication in *Anacystis nidulans* is bidirectional (Herdman, 1982).

How is gene expression regulated in cyanophytes? In bacteria, end product repression of the enzymes catalyzing amino acid biosynthesis is very common. There is now evidence that at least some enzymes, involved in nitrogen metabolism, hydroxamate siderophore production, phosphorus metabolism, and phycoerythrin synthesis, are subject to transcriptional control.

True sexuality does not exist but a kind of parasexual phenomenon, known as genetic recombination, first reported in *Anacystis nidulans* by Kumar (1962b), has since been confirmed by other workers (Bazin, 1968). Genetic transformation (a mode of gene transfer leading to genetic recombination) for antibiotic resistance characters has been demonstrated in *A. nidulans* (Shestakov and Khyen, 1970). Genetic recombination differs from true sexuality in that it is not attended by syngamy or meiosis, and yet the function of true sexuality (namely, to bring about gene recombination) is achieved. Besides *Anacystis nidulans*, genetic recombination has been reported in *Cylindrospermum majus* (Singh and Sinha, 1965) and *Anabaena doliolum*.

Lazaroff and Vishniac (1962) claim that under certain conditions different filaments of *Nostoc muscorum* can actually fuse in a manner reminiscent of the heterocaryotic phenomenon in certain fungi. According to them, the alga passes through a life cycle involving alternation between a heterocystous and a sporogenous phase (Fig. 3-22). The former occurs in the presence of light and the latter when the alga is grown heterotrophically in the dark. It appears that the fusion of short nonheterocystous filaments from the dark-grown cultures, which takes place after exposure to light, initiates the heterocystous phase of development.

The genetic systems involved in recombination in the Cyanophyta have become fairly well-known during the last few years. Conjugation (Fig. 3-23) has been demonstrated in *Anacystis nidulans* (Kumar and Ueda, 1984) as in bacteria. Recent studies demonstrating the susceptibility of some blue-green algae to a virus (known as cyanophage, phycovirus or blue-green algal virus) warrant the possibility that gene recombination may also be caused by transduction, a process in which the virus (as prophage) acts as a vector of certain genes, transferring them from donor to recipient cells. In *A. nidulans*, gene transfer can also occur

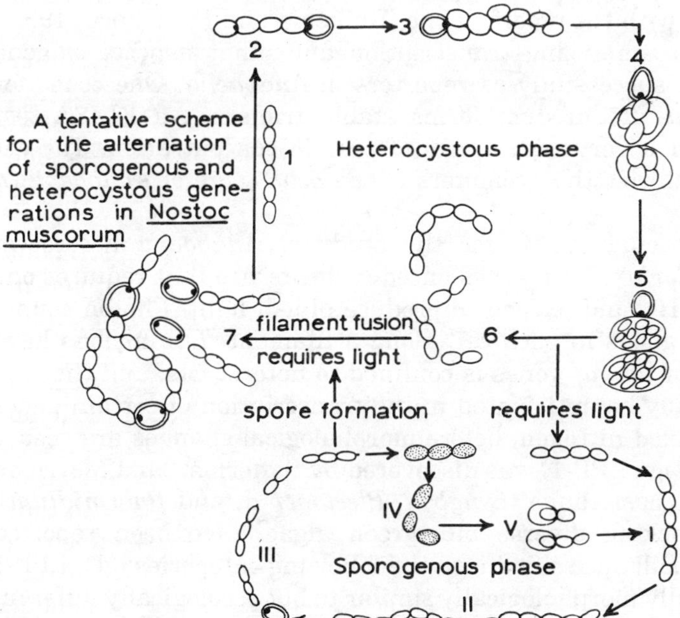

Fig. 3-22 *Nostoc muscorum*, life cycle and alternation of heterocystous and sporogenous phases (after Lazaroff and Vishniac, 1962).

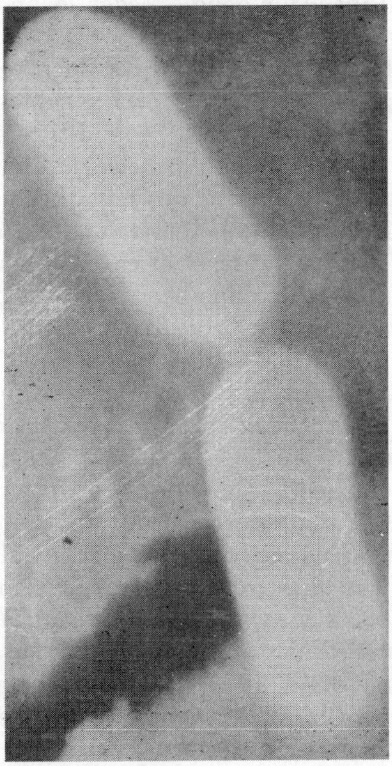

Fig. 3-23 *Anacystis nidulans*, conjugating cells. (×1100.)

as a result of transformation by nucleic acids released into the medium; this has been shown by using the classical U-tube of Davis (1950) (see Herdman, 1982).

Wolk *et al.* (1984) devised an efficient conjugation system for nitrogen-fixing cyanobacteria. The shuttle vector for conjugation consists of an *Anabaena* replicon, an *E. coli* replicon containing an origin of transfer, a *cos* site, antibiotic resistance genes for selection in *Anabaena*, and a multiple cloning site flanked by terminators of transcription. The shuttle vector and its *Anabaena* DNA insert must be protected from host *AvaI* and *AvaII* restriction by suitable methylation in *E. coli* prior to transfer of the DNA to *Anabaena*. Methylation of Tn5 seems to be sufficient to permit it to transpose to the *Anabaena* chromosome following conjugation in a vector that does not replicate in *Anabaena*.

Thiel and Poo (1989) have successfully used electroporation to transform *Anabaena*. As in conjugation, the transforming DNA must be methylated to avoid restriction.

Genetic manipulations require efficient methods for both positive and negative selection, the first to obtain transformants or exconjugants, the second to get rid of unwanted parts of the vectors used for the first. The conventional positive selection markers for bacterial crosses are genes conferring resistance to antibiotics. For *Anabaena* 7120, good selections are achieved with neomycin, streptomycin, spectinomycin, or chloramphenicol.

The most widely used negative selection for *Anabaena* 7120 is the *sacB* gene of *Bacillus subtilis*. This gene encodes levan sucrose, a harmless enzyme for cells growing on the usual cyanobacterial media. On plates containing 5% sucrose, however, the enzyme produces a toxic substance, possibly levan. Inclusion of the *sacB* gene in the vectors used for conjugation and gene inactivation allows selection for those cells in which two recombination events have occurred, replacing the wild-type gene with the modified one (Buikema and Haselkorn, 1993).

Gene fusions are powerful tools for analyzing transcription and other aspects of gene regulation. Two genes have been used successfully as reporters in *Anabaena*. One codes for chloramphenicol acetyltransferase, *cat*. Its product forms stable trimers. An ELISA test measures the level of cat antigen over a very wide range of protein concentration. The cat gene reporter has been used to characterize the promoters of the *psbB* gene of *Anabaena in vivo* (Lang and Haselkorn, 1991).

The other reporter system of particular value for the study of *Anabaena* heterocyst differentiation is the *lux* genes from *Vibrio*. These genes encode a luciferase that requires one of several long chain aldehydes, $FMNH_2$, and oxygen to produce bluish light. Photon counts can give an idea of the expression of genes in each cell along a filament. *Lux* fusions have been used to show that transcription of the *nif* genes is confined to heterocysts, and that the pattern of heterocyst differentiation may be anticipated in the transcription of certain genes expressed early after the removal of fixed nitrogen, before morphological changes are seen.

The blue-green algal virus, cyanophage LPP-1, was discovered by Safferman and Morris in 1963. It was named so to indicate its host range (*Lyngbya*, *Plectonema*, and *Phormidium*). Since then, many more viruses attacking diverse blue-green algae have been reported (Safferman, 1973), and can now be broadly classified into the following categories: (1) LPP-1 virus; (2) LPP-2 virus, which is generally morphologically similar to but serologically different from the LPP-1 virus; (3) SM-1 virus (on hosts *Synechococcus* and *Microcystis*), which is polyhedral and has much shorter tail than the tails of LPP viruses; (4) N-1 virus (on host *Nostoc*), which has a general structure similar to LPP-1 but with a contractile tail; (5) AS-1 virus (on hosts *Anacystis* and *Synechococcus*), which is the largest phycovirus described so far and is morphologically similar to LPP-1 but with a much larger particle size (head diameter

90 nm and tail length about 245 nm) and a contractile tail as in N-1; and (6) miscellaneous phycoviruses, infecting certain species of *Cylindrospermum*, *Anabaenopsis*, *Raphidiopsis*, and *Anabaena*. Of the miscellaneous viruses, A-1 and A-2 are cyanophages that attack *Anabaena variabilis*. The virion of the latter has a long contractile tail and a lipid containing head, and is one of the most complex viruses of cyanobacteria (Gromov, 1983). The capsid (diameter 60 nm) of A-1 virus has a hexagonal projection and is connected to the contractile tail (83 nm) by a narrow neck.

Although the nucleic acid and protein components of some of the above phycoviruses have not been analyzed in detail, available information (mostly on LPP-1) suggests that cyanophages contain double-stranded DNA.

A study of the replication cycle of LPP-1 in *Plectonema boryanum* revealed the following stages: (1) attachment of virus to the host cell wall by means of the tail; (2) injection of viral DNA into the algal cell; (3) replication of viral DNA in the nucleoplasm of the host cell and breakdown of the host cell DNA; (4) migration of replicating viral DNA from the nucleoplasm to the photosynthetic thylakoids, leading to a slight displacement of the latter, and (5) synthesis of protein coats and their enclosure around the DNA particles, leading to virus assemblage.

Apart from cyanophages, certain bacteria and fungi can also cause diseases of the blue-green algae. In water bodies, the abundance of lytic viruses or lytic bacteria generally correlates directly with that of phytoplankton. Whenever this equilibrium is disturbed by changes in environmental factors in favour of algae, water blooms become conspicuous, but when in favour of their pathogens, the water blooms disappear.

Plasmids

Many blue-greens contain “excess” or “redundant” DNA. Some of it occurs as extra-chromosomal particles called plasmids. *Agmenellum quadruplicatum* has six different sizes of covalently closed circular DNA (Roberts and Koths, 1976). Now, many different species of cyanobacteria are known to contain such plasmids. These plasmids exhibit an unusually wide range of size (1.9–75 megadaltons). The base composition of these plasmids differs from that of chromosomal DNA.

The functional significance of cyanobacterial plasmids is unknown (see Kumar and Tripathi, 1985).

CLASSIFICATION

The taxonomy of the blue-green algae has long been in a highly confused state. An enormous number of new species and genera have been created by different workers on trivial grounds, and borderline forms are extremely difficult to classify. Two biotic characteristics have contributed a great deal to the present state of confusion. One is the way in which various morphological features vary with differences in ecological conditions. The second is the variability of the physiological and biochemical response observed under different conditions. This may merely be the physiological counterpart of the morphological variability or may represent genetically determined responses.

A few attempts have been made to produce a rational and orderly system of classification or taxonomic delimitation by reducing the number of genera and species but these have either been drastic or confined to a study of only one or two families rather than the entire phylum.

A satisfactory solution can be found only after a combined approach involving a thorough study of the physiology, cytology, and genetics of different taxa has been made. This seems a distant goal.

Fritsch (1945) divided the blue-green algae into five orders, namely:

(1) Chroococcales Unicellular or colonial (palmelloid) forms; reproduction by cell division and by endospore formation.

(2) Chamaesiphonales Unicellular or colonial lithophytes or epiphytes exhibiting marked polarity; reproduction by endospores or exospores.

(3) Pleurocapsales Heterotrichous filamentous forms lacking heterocysts; reproduction by endospores; hormogonia absent.

(4) Nostocales Nonheterotrichous filamentous forms often showing false branching; heterocysts commonly present; reproduction mostly by hormogonia and akinetes.

(5) Stigonematales Heterotrichous filamentous forms, mostly with heterocysts, showing true branching and usually pit connections between adjacent cells; multiplication mostly by hormogonia and rarely by hormocysts and akinetes.

In a very important contribution, Rippka *et al.* (1979) have proposed a radical new scheme of classifying cyanobacteria. They recognize 22 genera placed in five sections, each distinguished by some particular structural and developmental characters. Section I includes unicellular forms reproducing either by binary fission or by 'budding'. *Gloeobacter*, *Gloeothece*, *Synechococcus*, *Chamaesiphon*, *Gloeocapsa*, and *Synechocystis* are the 6 genera included in this section.

Rapid binary fission of a vegetative cell within a fibrous wall layer, unaccompanied by growth, leading to formation of small, spherical bodies called 'baeocytes', is characteristic of the organisms placed in Section II which includes *Dermocarpa*, *Xenococcus*, *Dermocarpella*, *Myxosarcina*, *Chroococcidiopsis*, and *Pleurocapsa*.

Sections III to V include filamentous or trichomatous forms. The trichome in Section III is made up solely of vegetative cells and is uniseriate. The members of Sections IV and V are collectively distinguished from Section III by their ability of cellular differentiation leading to the formation of heterocyst and akinetes. *Lyngbya, Phormidium, Plectonema, Oscillatoria,* and *Spirulina* are included in Section III (Fig. 3-24), but some workers (see Stam, 1980) propose the merger of some of these genera into smaller number.

Section IV includes *Anabaena* (Fig. 3-25), *Nodularia* (Fig. 3-26), *Cylindrospermum*, *Nostoc*, *Scytonema*, and *Calothrix* (Fig. 3-27).

PHYLOGENETIC RELATIONSHIP

The blue-greens are the most primitive of algal organisms. They have existed on the surface of the earth since the early Precambrian. Fossil evidence indicates that unicellular cyanophytes had developed by the early Precambrian, and that filamentous (including heterocystous) forms probably originated in the middle Precambrian (see Schopf, 1970). It appears that the evolution of cyanophytes occurred most rapidly prior to the development of the oxygenic atmosphere but slowed down significantly after the build-up of oxygen concentration in air when other organisms surpassed them.

Most schemes of algal evolution envisage the evolution of all algal lines from an ancestral

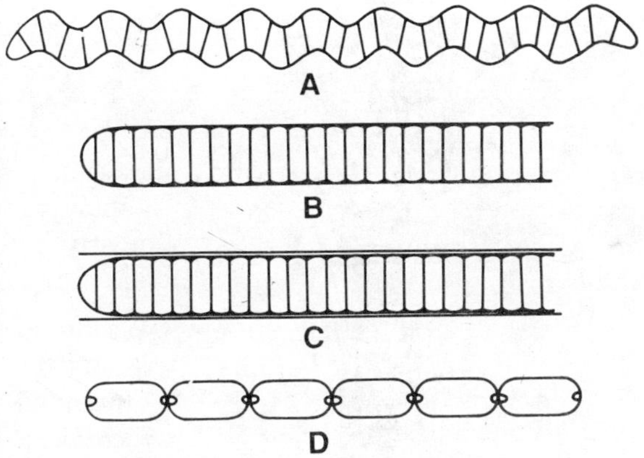

Fig. 3-24 Unbranched, filamentous cyanobacteria. A, *Spirulina*; B, *Oscillatoria*; C, *Lyngbya*; D, *Pseudanabaena*. (After Rippka *et al.*, 1979.)

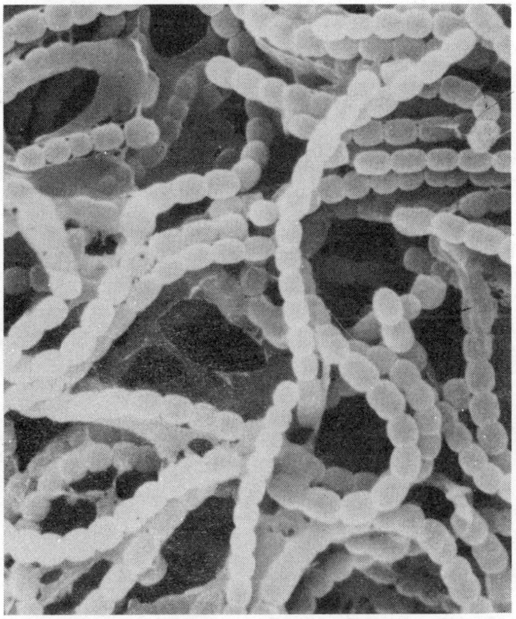

Fig. 3-25 *Anabaena variabilis*. (×400.)

cyanobacterium (Fig. 3-28). Dodge (1979) has proposed multiple, serial symbioses from some groups with a view to explaining the presence of four membranes around the chloroplasts of chromophyte (including cryptophyte) algae and also the existence of two types of chloroplast in some dinoflagellates. However, one drawback of this proposal is the difficulty with the evolution of chromophytes from the Rhodophyceae, i.e., the loss of phycobiliproteins and the acquisition of chlorophyll-c.

In their general cytology, genetics, and morphology as well as procaryotic nature, they seem closely related to bacteria but differ from them in their photosynthetic metabolism and lack of flagellated cells. If the view that chloroplasts are cellular symbionts is accepted, the relationship to be considered is not that between the procaryotic blue-green algae and the eucaryotic algae but between the former and the chloroplasts of the latter. Thus, the blue-green algae as a whole can be compared only with the chloroplasts of the Rhodophyta or Cryptophyta. Some affinity with the red algae is indicated by the presence of phycoerythrin and pit connections and the lack of flagellated structures. Further, the blue-green and red algae have a common pattern of fatty acid formation which differs from other plants in that the lipid content does not increase as the thallus grows. In these algae, nitrogen starvation also is not a factor in fatty acid accumulation (see Klein and Cronquist, 1967).

The resemblance between the blue-green algae and bacteria appears stronger and more

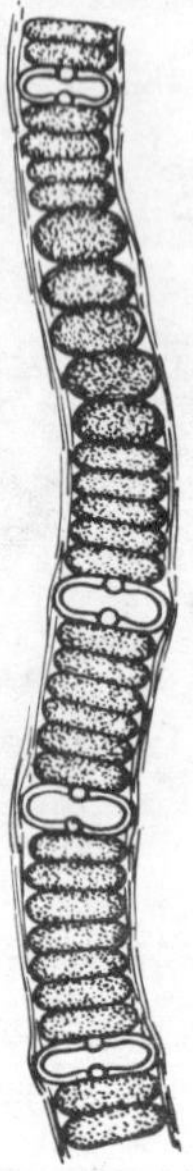

Fig. 3-26 *Nodularia spumigena*, typical discoidal cells and heterocysts.

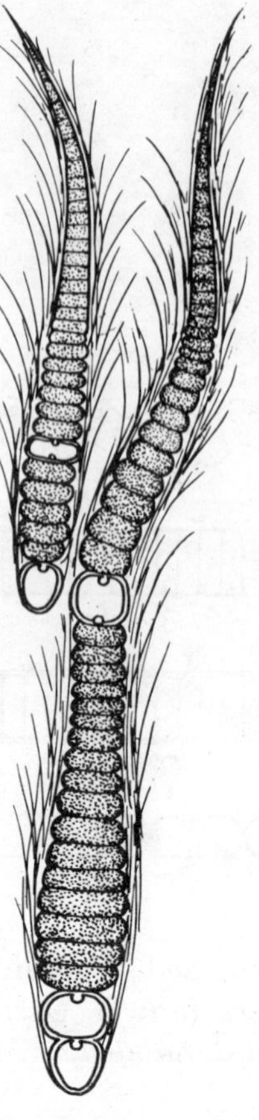

Fig. 3-27 *Calothrix* sp., polar filaments with heterocysts.

fundamental than that between the blue-green and red algae. The chemical composition and ultrastructure of their cell wall and cytoplasm, the organization of photosynthetic apparatus, and aspects of hydrogen, nitrogen, and sulphur metabolism link the blue-green algae with the rest of the Schizomycophyta via the photosynthetic bacteria. Clearly, the blue-green algae and the bacteria are two groups of the same kingdom, Procaryota (Klein and Cronquist, 1967).

SELECTED GENERA

Classification
[According to Fritsch (1945)]

Order: CHROOCOCCALES
Family: Chroococcaceae
Genus: *Gloeocapsa*

Classification
[According to Rippka *et al*. (1979)]

Section I

Gloeocapsa is a terrestrial or subaerial alga generally found on rocks, walls or soils. It is a palmelloid, colonial form. Each colony consists of a few cells (Fig. 3-29) which are more or less

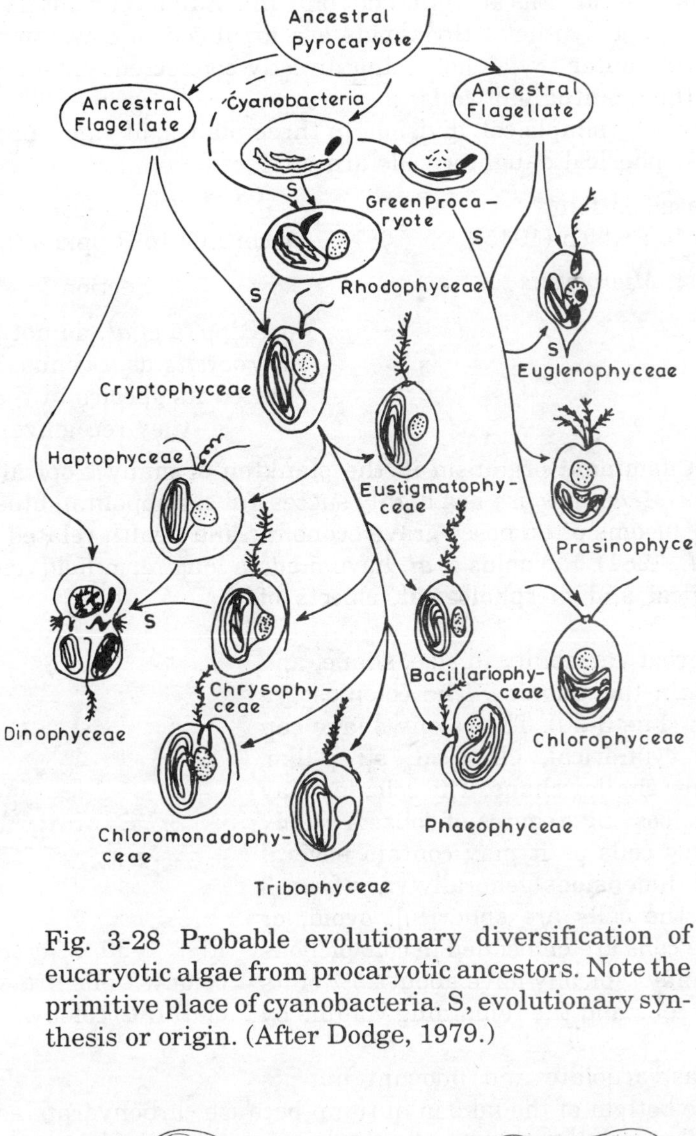

Fig. 3-28 Probable evolutionary diversification of eucaryotic algae from procaryotic ancestors. Note the primitive place of cyanobacteria. S, evolutionary synthesis or origin. (After Dodge, 1979.)

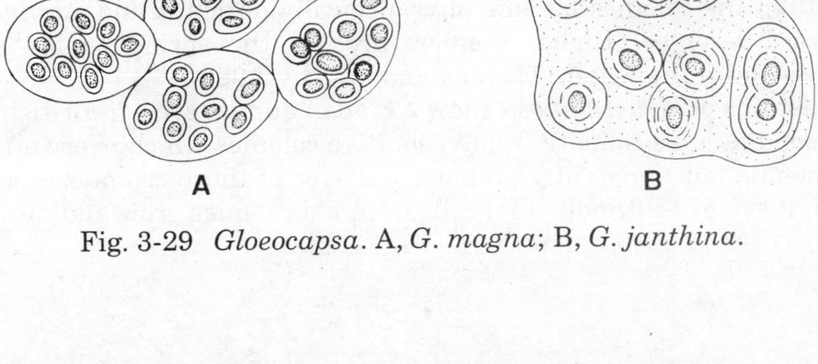

Fig. 3-29 *Gloeocapsa*. A, *G. magna*; B, *G. janthina*.

spherical and have conspicuous, coloured, stratified, and concentrically lamellate gelatinous sheaths around them. The sheaths surround not only individual cells but also the entire colony. In most species, the photosynthetic thylakoids are arranged in rows at right angles to the plasma membrane, the outer thylakoids being directly connected with it; but in *G. alpicola*, they lie parallel to the longitudinal walls.

Reproduction occurs by simple cell division, in three planes, at right angles to one another, so that more or less spherical daughter cells are produced.

Classification [According to Fritsch (1945)]	Classification [According to Rippka *et al.* (1979)]
Genus: *Microcystis*	Section I
	(Rippka *et al.* do not accept *Microcystis* as a genus, and have placed its species in the genera they recognize)

This alga is often a dominant organism in the plankton of many tropical ponds, temperate lakes, and reservoirs. *M. aeruginosa* is a highly successful cosmopolitan blue-green alga whose abundance in water blooms often poses grave economic and health related problems (Collins, 1978; Reynolds *et al.*, 1981). Reynolds *et al.* have made a long-term field and laboratory study of the ecophysiological and morphological aspects of *M. aeruginosa*.

The alga shows great variability in size, shape, and cell disposition within the colonies. The colonies are commonly clathrate (Fig. 3-30). The colony shape can be irregular-ovoid, cylindrical, elliptical, strap-like, subspherical, or other similar shape. The colonies may be quite compact or loose aggregates of cells. A colony may have only a few cells or it may contain several thousands. The cell dimensions generally vary from 3 μm to 10 μm and the cells are spherical, ovoid, or capsule-shaped. The cells are embedded in conspicuous mucilage. A colony may typically have about 25% of its volume occupied by cells and the remaining volume by mucilage.

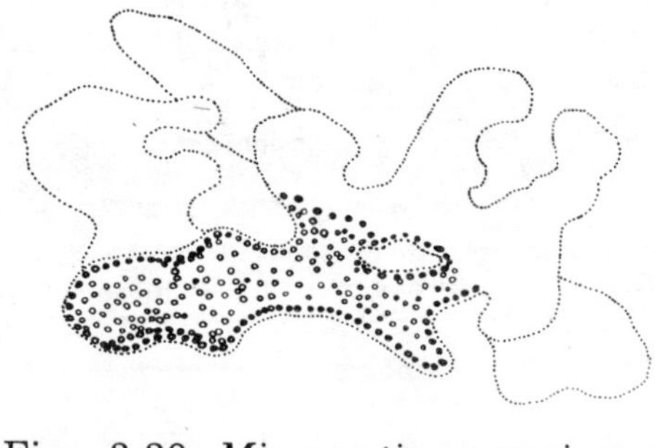

Fig. 3-30 *Microcystis aeruginosa*, colony. Cells are shown in a part of clathrate colony.

Microcystis is gas-vacuolate and buoyant but its colonies settle to the bottom of the lake in autumn because carbohydrate accumulation raises their density and, in some lakes at least, they entrap a dense colloidal precipitate rich in ferric hydroxide which forms in the water when it becomes fully oxygenated in the autumn overturn. Once on the bottom the colonies become physiologically dormant and survive the winter on their carbohydrate reserves. Higher temperatures in the spring enable them to regain buoyancy and recolonize the water (Thomas and Walsby, 1986).

Natural populations of *M. aeruginosa* show a kind of annual cycle in British lakes. Summer bloom-forming populations originate from vegetative colonies which overwinter or perennate on bottom sediments, but apparently no mass transfer of these colonies occurs to the water column; instead, it seems that individual cells from old colonies grow and multiply, producing new colonies. This growth of individual cells is stimulated when the dissolved oxygen content in bottom water falls but when the light availability is increased. Reynolds *et al.* found that optimum growth and multiplication of young colonies occur at initial oxygen concentrations of 1–4 mg/l and that the colonies are adversely affected at oxygen concentrations outside this optimum range. The growth of new colonies is also stimulated by moderate increase in water temperature.

Another factor influencing the success of *Microcystis* populations is grazing by zooplankton. *Microcystis* does not form the major food of crustaceans at least in temperate lakes though the smaller colonies do constitute a fraction of the food ingested by *Daphnia hyalina* (Lam and Silvester, 1979).

After the attainment of seasonal maximum growth, the concentration of suspended colonies declines in the autumn every year. This happens as a result of the sinking and settlement of old colonies at the bottom sediments. These colonies become negatively buoyant and migrate en masse to the bottom where they overwinter, thus completing the annual cycle. According to Reynolds *et al.* (1981), *M. aeruginosa* is biologically well-adapted to the cycles of thermal and chemical stratification, especially with respect to seasonal anoxia of hypolimnia and deep-water sediments. Its wide dispersal and success in eutrophic lakes and its ability to survive and perennate in such environments are mainly responsible for its persistence and for its frequent association with accelerated cultural eutrophication of lakes.

Order: NOSTOCALES
Family: Oscillatoriaceae

The algae placed in this family possess unbranched, more or less cylindrical and torulose trichomes which may either be naked or may lie in a mucilaginous matrix or within more or less discrete sheaths. Except for the apical cells which may taper, bend, or have calyptra, the remaining cells in a trichome are fairly uniform in diameter. No heterocysts are formed. Fragmentation or hormogone formation, usually after death or degeneration of a cell, seems to be the sole method of reproduction.

Rarely, the trichomes, instead of being cylindrical, may be flattened. *Starria* Lang is an interesting alga having trichomes which are triradiate in section. *Spirulina* (Fig. 3-24) is an exceptionally valuable alga having tremendous economic importance in view of its high protein content. It has helically twisted trichomes.

These algae usually occur in those water bodies that are well buffered by high bicarbonate concentrations, with pH values around 8 to 9 or more.

Classification [According to Fritsch (1945)]	Classification [According to Rippka *et al.* (1979)]
Genus: *Oscillatoria*	Section III

Oscillatoria is common and widespread in polluted waters, temporary rain-water pools, drains, and streams. *O. rubescens* forms dense deep-water blooms in temperate lakes and ponds and its migration and colonization in deep-water lakes are often associated with a high level of eutrophication. Also characteristic of highly eutrophic waters are the populations of certain species having very narrow trichomes (less than 3 μm in diameter). Some species are marine. In the living state, many species exhibit a characteristic swinging oscillatory movement of their trichomes. In streams, so long as the trichomes continue to move, they are not attacked by protozoan predators but once movement ceases, the trichomes are invaded and devoured by protozoa.

It is an unbranched trichomatous alga. The trichome consists of a number of simple, undifferentiated cells which are generally more broad than long (Fig. 3-31). There are no constrictions between adjacent cells, no recognizable base or apex, but the end cell in some species may be round, conical or dilated with its outer surface sometimes covered by a thickened hood known as the calyptra. The end of the trichome is occasionally bent on one side. No heterocysts or spores are found in *Oscillatoria*.

The cells exhibit a typical cyanophycean structure, and prominent pseudovacuoles are formed in planktonic forms.

O. tenuis has straight, unbranched trichomes which commonly occur aggregated or mixed with other algae. Trichomes are nontapered and noncapitate and the end cells are broadly rounded. Very slight constrictions may occur at cross walls. This species is mostly tychoplanktonic.

When examined under the light microscope, most species of *Oscillatoria* seem to lack a

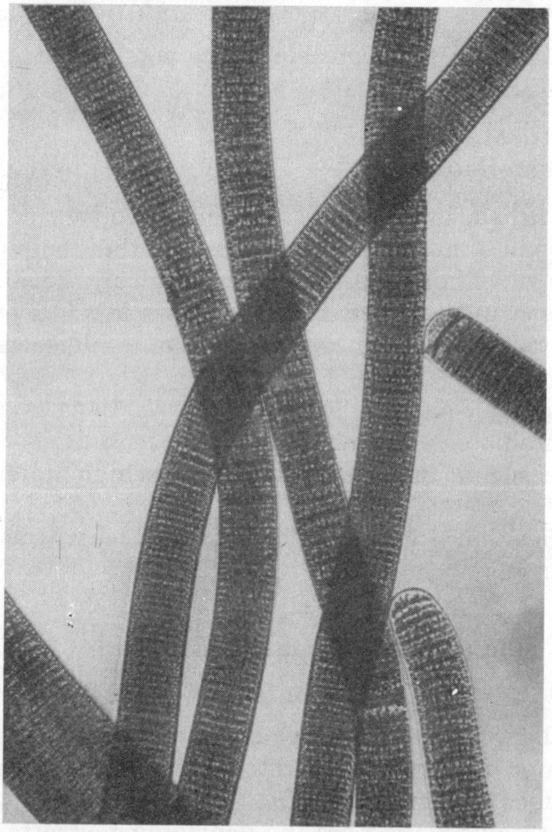

Fig. 3-31 *Oscillatoria princeps*, field material.

Fig. 3-32 *Oscillatoria princeps*, part of filament showing three distinct (dark) separation discs.

distinct sheath, but their examination by means of Nomarski interference microscopy reveals a thin but definite sheath.

O. agardhii is a common bloom forming alga in shallow eutrophic lakes in Holland. It also generally forms blooms not on the surface but in the intermediate water layers in stratified lakes. It can clog filters in drinking water reservoirs and taints the water with an earthy taste and bad flavour. Sometimes, it is distributed throughout the epilimnion.

Whitton and Peat (1969) have studied the developmental variability of *O. redekei* grown in unialgal culture. They observed that gas vacuoles, a trichome sheath, and terminal cells having pointed ends were present at certain stages but absent at others. Their presence or absence depended on physiological and environmental conditions. Furthermore, at certain states in its development, *O. redekei* could not be distinguished from certain other species of *Oscillatoria*.

Reproduction in most species is brought about by the breaking up of the trichome into hormogonia as a result of the formation of biconcave separation discs (Fig. 3-32) at certain points along the trichome.

Family: Nostocaceae

Drouet (1973) concluded that the gelatinous sheaths, excreted as colloids from the cells of the nostocacean trichomes, are subject to great modifications and variability under environmental influences. Hence, the nature of the sheath cannot serve as a good taxonomic marker in this family. As in Oscillatoriaceae, only the characters of the trichome were found to be reliable. Drouet has recognized *Scytonema*, *Calothrix*, and *Raphidiopsis* (Fig. 3-33) as the three genera of Nostocaceae with cylindrical trichomes.

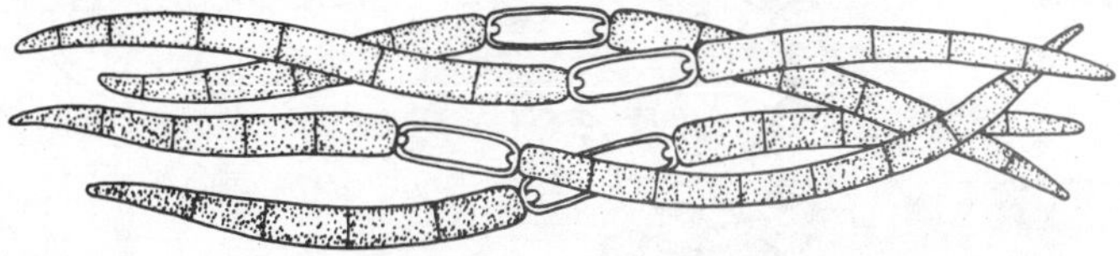

Fig. 3-33 *Raphidiopsis* sp., filaments with heterocysts.

The family (*sensu* Fritsch) has unbranched trichomes with some heterocysts and/or akinetes. Commonly, conspicuous constrictions occur between cells, so that the filaments look moniliform.

Classification [According to Fritsch (1945)]	Classification [According to Rippka *et al*. (1979)]
Genus: *Nostoc*	Section IV

Nostoc is a freshwater or terrestrial alga, abundantly found in paddy fields. Some species grow on moist soil intermingled with mosses and lichens, whereas others may constitute the algal components of lichens or occur as endophytes in higher plants. *N. sphaericum* forms a close symbiotic association with the phycomycetous fungus *Geosiphon pyriforme*. The capacity for nitrogen fixation has been established in bacteria-free cultures of *Nostoc* sp. isolated from lichens and it has been shown that in the lichen *Peltigera aphthosa*, the nitrogen fixed by *Nostoc* is utilized by its fungal partner.

An interesting feature concerning the association of *Nostoc* with the angiosperm *Gunnera* is that the filaments are intracellular rather than intercellular, are devoid of sheath, but are enveloped by a layer of host cell cytoplasm.

It is a filamentous form and the filaments are often aggregated into ball-like gelatinous colonies which vary a great deal in size and shape, some being as large as a hen's egg. The filaments are usually contorted and twisted in various ways. Like *Oscillatoria*, they are always unbranched but the cells have prominent constrictions between them. Consequently, they seem to be arranged like beads on a string (Fig. 3-34). Such a habit is called moniliform. Unlike *Oscillatoria*, the filaments regularly form heterocysts and occasionally also akinetes (Fig. 3-35). The heterocysts are commonly two-pored and intercalary but rarely one-pored and terminal.

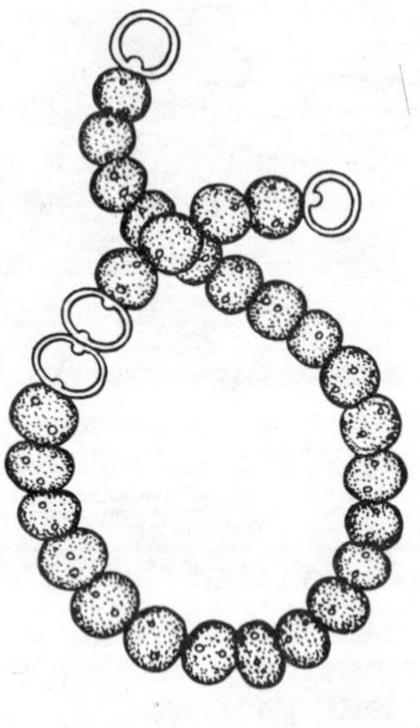

Fig. 3-34 *Nostoc* sp., moniliform filament with heterocysts.

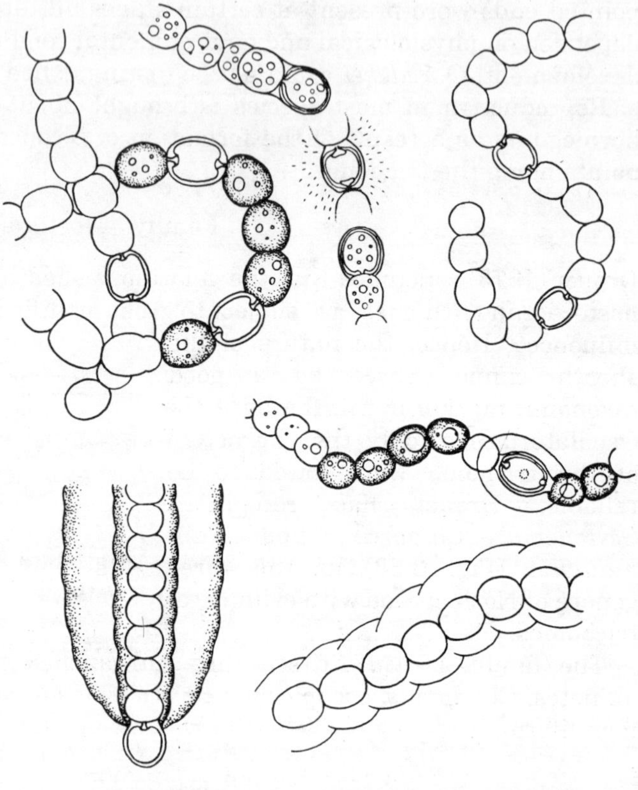

Fig. 3-35 *Nostoc* sp., filaments showing vegetative cells, heterocysts, and akinetes. Some filaments are embedded in mucilage.

The sheaths of adjoining trichomes may coalesce to form a common gelatinous matrix of the colony. The cell structure is typically cyanophycean.

Reproduction takes place by hormogonia and akinetes. Lazaroff and Vishniac (1962) have also reported the occurrence of fusions and anastomoses between different filaments.

Based on developmental patterns, the various species of *Nostoc* may be broadly classified into three groups, namely, (1) the *commune* type, in which the colonies have a firm pellicle; (2) the *piscinale* type, in which the firm pellicle is absent; and (3) the *punctiforme* type, in which filamentous organization is lost and an aseriate form results.

The essentiality of bacteria in the formation of normal colonies of *N. sphaericum* has been established by Schwabe and Mollenhauer (1967). When grown in the absence of bacteria, only minute colonies were formed instead of the normal, macroscopic colonies formed in bacterized cultures.

Classification [According to Fritsch (1945)]	Classification [According to Rippka *et al.* (1979)]
Genus: *Anabaena*	Section IV

It is common in freshwater lakes and ponds and in rice fields. It forms unbranched filaments (Fig. 3-25) broadly resembling *Nostoc* but differs from the latter in not usually forming gelatinous colonies and also not showing the developmental cycle typical of *Nostoc*. The *trichomes* of most *Anabaena* strains are typically straight (not contorted) and motile (gliding movement). In *Nostoc*, on the other hand, only the hormogonia are motile.

Cells are spherical, ovoid, or cylindrical and have cyanophycin granules. Planktonic strains also have gas vacuoles (Fig. 3-36).

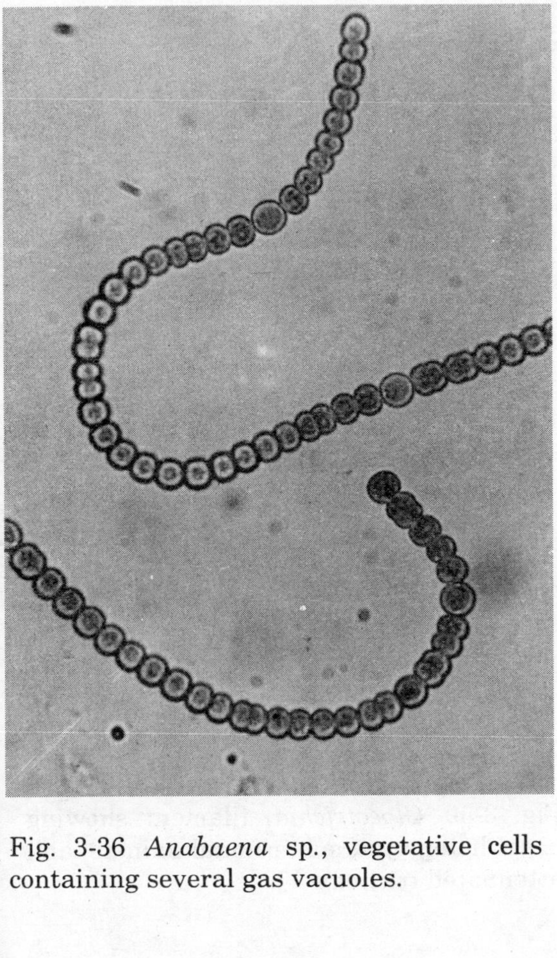

Fig. 3-36 *Anabaena* sp., vegetative cells containing several gas vacuoles.

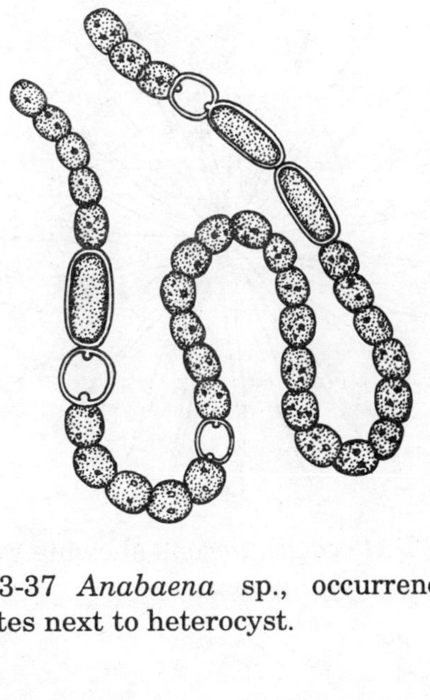

Fig. 3-37 *Anabaena* sp., occurrence of akinetes next to heterocyst.

Heterocysts occur both in intercalary and terminal positions. They are sites of nitrogen fixation.

Reproduction occurs by random filament breakage, and by hormogonia formation.

Some strains form conspicuous akinetes either next to heterocysts (Fig. 3-37) or midway between two heterocysts; in *Nostoc*, no akinetes occur next to the heterocyst, and the akinetes are often produced in chains.

Classification [According to Fritsch (1945)]	Classification [According to Rippka *et al.* (1979)]
Family: Rivulariaceae	
Genus: *Gloeotrichia*	Section IV

Gloeotrichia has unbranched filaments which taper from base to apex. The filaments tend to be arranged radially in more or less globular balls (Fig. 3-38), lying embedded in relatively soft colonial mucilage, with their bases at the centre of the ball and apices near the circumference. The globose colonies grow epiphytically on aquatic plants, forming brownish or greenish blue gelatinous masses. *G. natans* is common in rice fields.

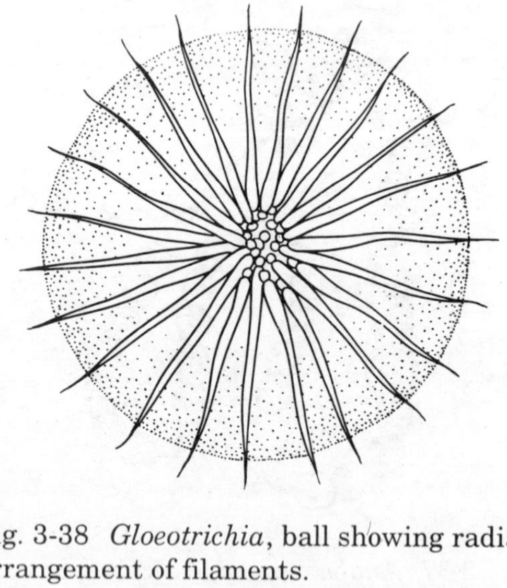

Fig. 3-38 *Gloeotrichia*, ball showing radial arrangement of filaments.

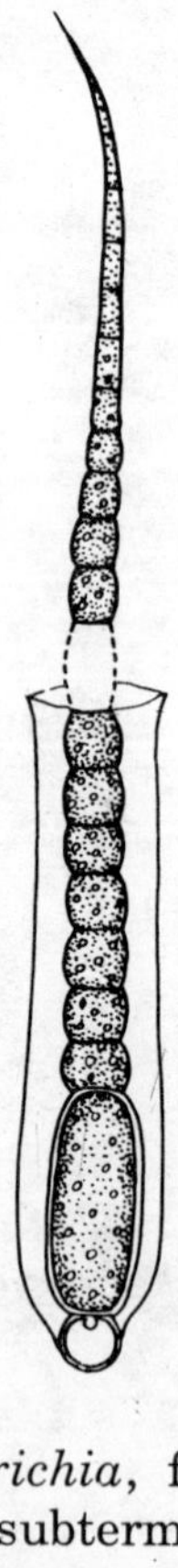

Fig. 3-39 *Gloeotrichia*, filament showing basal heterocyst, subterminal akinete, and attenuated trichome.

The filaments (Fig. 3-39) have basal or terminal heterocyst (at the broader end), then a prominent akinete, followed by vegetative cells. The akinete and some adjoining cells are usually enclosed by a sheath. The narrow end of the filament often ends in a hair, beneath which a few cells are meristematic. It is in this meristematic region that hormogonia are formed; they are released when the hair is detached.

In *G. echinulata*, the cells located towards the basal end are barrel-shaped or cylindrical, whereas those towards the apex tend to be long and cylindrical.

When the filaments grow crowded in dense cultures, they can transform into long, helical, and nonpolar form. Sometimes, even double helices may be formed in such conditions.

Gloeotrichia, *Rivularia*, and other blue-greens whose filaments terminate in long hairs are widespread in lakes, streams, and the upper marine intertidal zone. Species of these algae seem to be associated with environments especially deficient in phosphate and possibly also iron. The presence or absence of nitrogen in the medium seems to affect tapering of trichomes in several species of Rivulariaceae (Sinclair and Whitton, 1977). When grown in nitrogen deficient medium, the trichomes of *Gloeotrichia* were markedly tapered but they became untapered when transferred to medium containing nitrate or ammonia. The heterocystous members of this family were also observed to have lost both the heterocysts and the trichome polarity.

Singh and Tiwari (1970) observed frequent heterocyst germination in *G. ghosei* when the alga was grown in medium containing ammoniacal nitrogen. The latter did not inhibit heterocyst differentiation in this species.

Classification [According to Fritsch (1945)]	Classification [According to Rippka *et al.* (1979)]
Family: Scytonemataceae	
Genus: *Scytonema*	

Scytonema occurs in fresh- and salt water, terrestrial and subaerial habitats, grass lawns, on tree barks, and on a wide variety of other substrata.

It differs from *Oscillatoria* and *Nostoc* in having branched filaments. The branching is false, and both single and double pseudobranches may be formed. Typically, however, two false branches are produced remote from two intercalary heterocysts (Fig. 3-40 A). A filament or its branches may have a few or several heterocysts though these are usually two-pored and intercalary. The trichomes are not moniliform and the cells are more or less quadratic, i.e., as long as they are broad. The filaments have distinct mucilage sheaths (Fig. 3-40 B) which are thick, stratified, and variously pigmented in terrestrial species.

The false branches arise from the degeneration of a cell in the trichome (see Fig. 3-41) which is followed by the outgrowth of one or both ends of the interrupted trichome through the parent sheath as branches. Alternatively, they may arise by loop formation (Fig. 3-42).

Reproduction occurs by hormogonia which are commonly liberated through the extremities of the filaments or branches.

Order: STIGONEMATALES (*sensu* Fritsch)

This order includes truly branched, heterocystous algae having pit connections between cells. The growth is mostly apical and these algae occur in terrestrial, subaerial, or freshwater habitats.

The Nostochopsidaceae and Stigonemataceae show lateral (true) branching. The former

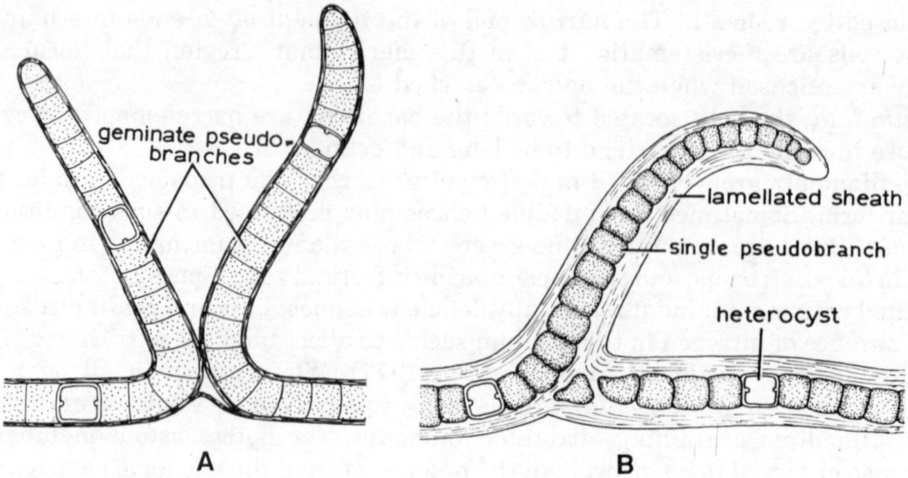

Fig. 3-40 *Scytonema*. A, *S. ocellatum*; B, *S. insigne*.

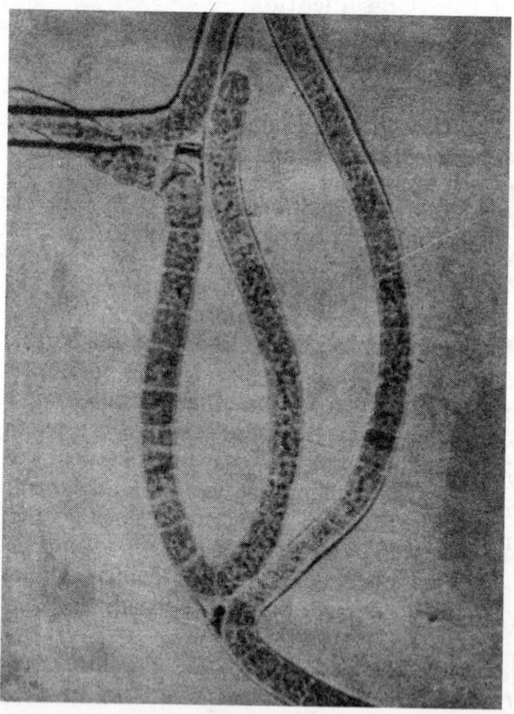

Fig. 3-41 *Scytonema hofmanni*, pseudobranches and degenerated cell. (×500.)

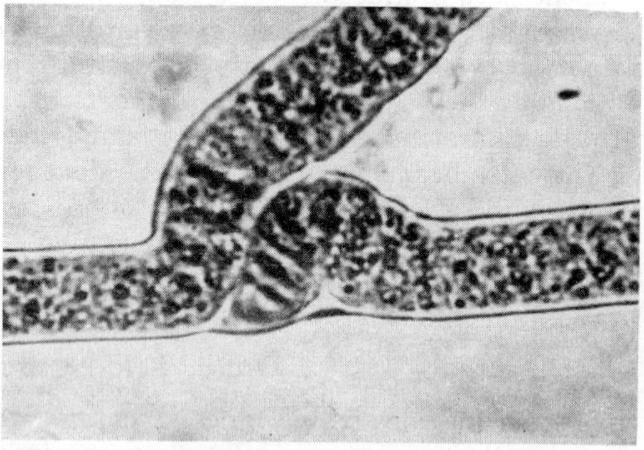

Fig. 3-42 *Scytonema* sp., origin of pseudobranches by loop formation. (×700.)

family is specially distinguished by the possession of two kinds of branches, viz., (1) elongate, and (2) short, 1- to 4-celled, terminating in a heterocyst. In this family, the members are uniseriate and nonheterotrichous. *Nostochopsis* and *Mastigocladus* are two representative examples of this family. *Mastigocladus* is a typical thermophile. *Nostochopsis* is widely distributed in stagnant and flowing waters.

Rippka *et al*. (1979) recognize only two genera (*Chlorogloeopsis* and *Fischerella*) in their Section V, merging all the Stigonematales *sensu* Fritsch in these genera. In *Chlorogloeopsis*, the heterocysts develop in terminal and intercalary positions, whereas in *Fischerella*, they develop exclusively in an intercalary position.

Family: Stigonemataceae

This includes some of the largest and most elaborate, heterotrichous blue-green algae that show a marked tendency towards a multiseriate construction. The upright system of filaments is sparingly branched and these filaments have narrower, longer cells as compared to those of the prostrate system. Hormogonia are formed only by the erect filaments, whereas akinetes develop in the prostrate system. Most members show apical growth and have distinct pit connections.

In *Fischerella*, the erect filaments are uniseriate and the prostrate filaments are multiseriate. In *Hapalosiphon*, the prostrate system is virtually uniseriate but can become biseriate (Fig. 3-43) here and there. *Westiella* is uniseriate throughout.

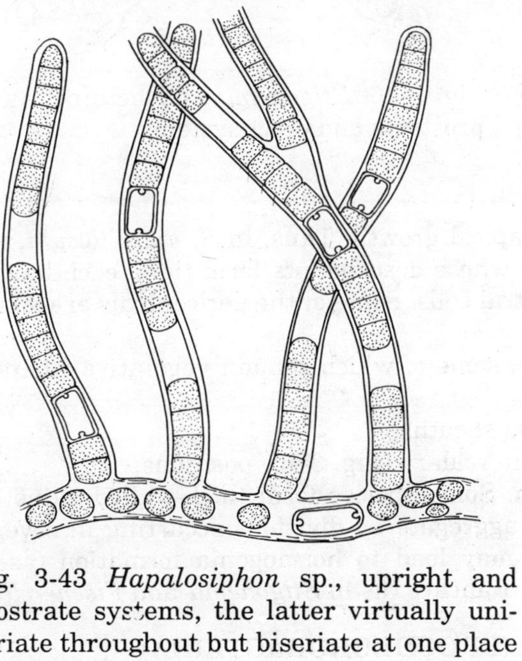

Fig. 3-43 *Hapalosiphon* sp., upright and prostrate systems, the latter virtually uniseriate throughout but biseriate at one place near the right side.

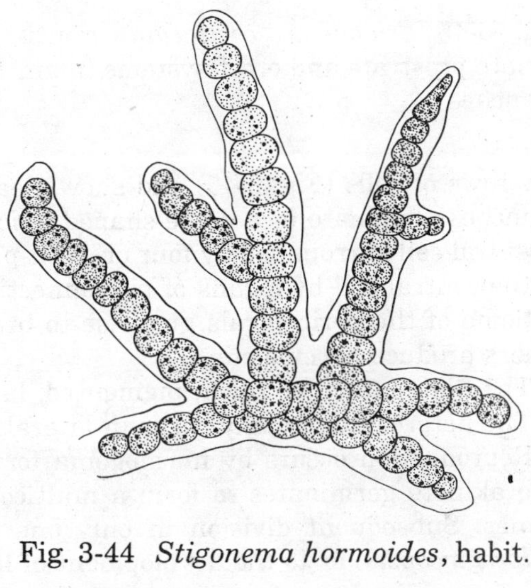

Fig. 3-44 *Stigonema hormoides*, habit.

Genus: *Stigonema*

Most species are subaerial and are common on dripping rocks. *S. hormoides* (Fig. 3-44) and *S. ocellatum* are uniseriate. In most other species, the principal filaments are made up of a

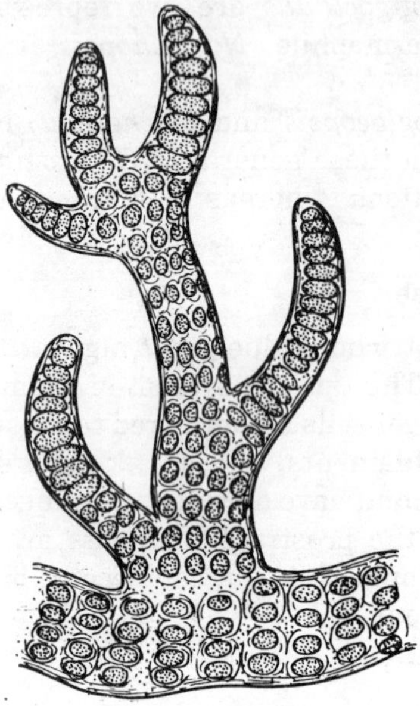

Fig. 3-45 *Stigonema ocellatum*, multiseriate prostrate and erect systems (main branches).

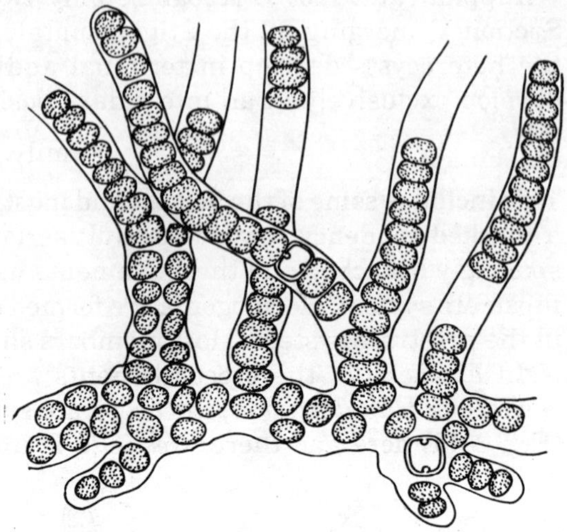

Fig. 3-46 *Stigonema* sp., heterocysts in prostrate and erect systems.

few rows of cells (Fig. 3-45) and show clear-cut apical growth. Thus, in *S. mamillosum*, the branches terminate in a dome-shaped apical cell whose descendants form tiers, each having a central cell surrounded by four or eight pericentral cells. Some of the pericentrals are joined to the central cell by means of pit connections.

Some of the pericentrals give rise to branches, some of which remain vegetative whereas others produce hormogonia.

The filaments have thick, pigmented, lamellose sheaths.

The heterocysts usually occur in lateral and intercalary (Fig. 3-46) positions.

Reproduction occurs by hormogonia formation. Some species form thick-walled akinetes. The akinete germinates to form a multicellular aggregate by divisions occurring in several planes. Subsequent division in only one plane may lead to hormogonia formation (as in *Chlorogloeopsis*) or to the development of lateral branches (as in *Stigonema* and *Fischerella*).

DIVISION PROCHLOROPHYTA (PROCHLOROBACTERIA)

GENERAL CHARACTERS

This division was established by Lewin (1976, 1977) to accommodate certain unicellular, green, procaryotic algae associated with marine didemnid ascidians. *Prochloron didemni* is a typical prochlorophyte. It resembles the cyanobacteria in its general cell structure but differs in lacking phycobiliproteins as well as phycobilisomes. It contains both chlorophyll-a and -b in addition to beta-carotene, in this way resembling the (eucaryotic) green algae and the green plant chloroplasts.

Prochloron is one of the largest known unicellular procaryotes, with spherical cells measuring up to 30 µm in diameter. *Prochloron* cells are not endosymbiotic but appear to be obligate symbionts in colonies of some tropical and subtropical didemnid ascidians, where they are intimately integrated with the tissues of their hosts. *Prochloron* is not normally found as free-living cells in nature but can survive when associated with the larvae of symbiotic didemnids (Lewin and Cheng, 1989; Lewin, 1994). *Prochloron* is also quite abundant in coral reefs where it is associated with colonies of *Lissoclinum patella* which is the largest symbiotic didemnid known; in this, the *Prochloron* cells occur aggregated in cloacal cavities.

When alive, the cells of *Prochloron* are highly turgid and highly refractile. Upon death, they shrink, become translucent, and release a pinkish exudate absorbing maximally around 334 nm (a wavelength absorbed maximally by certain UV-B absorbing compounds such as palythine, palythinol, and mycosporine) and also having a refractive index greater than that of sea water (Lewin, 1994). Cells have one or more vacuoles which occupy the major part of the cell. They have stacked thylakoids (see Fig. 3-47), again reminiscent of green algal and plant chloroplasts. Recent molecular analyses indicate that prochlorophytes may have evolved chlorophyll-b and stacked thylakoids independently of the green algae and land plants (see

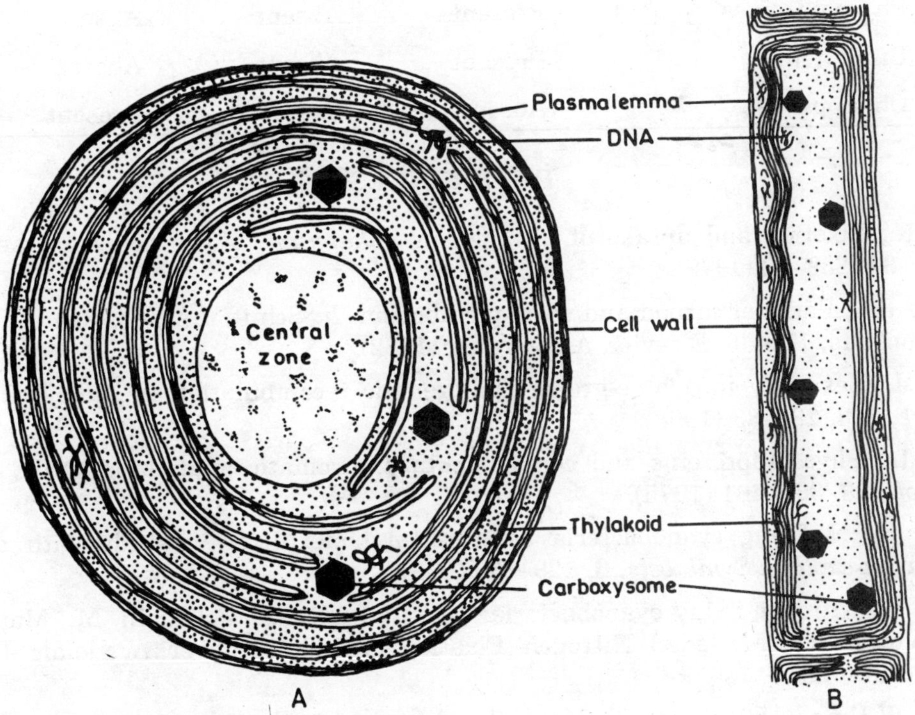

Fig. 3-47 Cytology of prochlorophytes. A, *Prochloron*; B, a free-living filamentous prochlorophyte.

Lewin, 1993). Indeed, the current consensus seems to be that the prochlorophytes may not even be a natural assemblage, their members being scattered throughout the cyanobacteria; they might have evolved chlorophyll-b, and lost phycobilins, on multiple occasions during evolution. Cavalier-Smith (1982) described prochlorophytes as 'green herrings' that have no special significance in the evolution of the chloroplasts.

According to Lewin (1994), glucose or maltose found in the vacuolar sap of *Prochloron* may be responsible for sustaining the symbiotic association whereby *Prochloron* transfers photosynthetically fixed carbon to its host.

Table 3-2 compares the general characters of prochlorophytes with those of cyanophytes and green algae.

Table 3-2 Distinctions among Cyanophyta, Prochlorophyta, and Chlorophyta (after Lewin, 1979)

Characters	Cyanophyta	Prochlorophyta	Chlorophyta
Cell (including nuclear) organization	Procaryotic	Procaryotic	Eucaryotic
Plastids	Absent	Absent	Present
Thylakoids	Single	Paired	Paired
Phycobilisomes	Present	Absent	Absent
Biliproteins	Present	Absent	Absent
Chlorophyll-b	Absent	Present	Present

REFERENCES

Basilier, K., Fixation and uptake of nitrogen in *Sphagnum*: blue-green algal associations, *Oikos*, **34**, 239–42 (1979).

Bassham, J.A., Paths of carbon and their metabolism. *In* Schiff, J.A. (ed.) On the Origins of Chloroplasts, 117–30, Elsevier, Amsterdam (1982).

Bazin, M.J., Sexuality in a blue-green alga: genetic recombination in *Anacystis nidulans*, *Nature*, **218**, 282–83 (1968).

Bogorad, L., Phycobiliproteins and complementary chromatic adaptation, *Ann. Rev. Plant Physiol.*, **26**, 369–401 (1975).

Boussiba, S., N_2-fixing cyanobacteria as nitrogen biofertilizer: a study with the isolate *Anabaena azollae*, *Symbiosis*, **6**, 129–38 (1988).

Boussiba, S., Nitrogen-fixing cyanobacteria: potential uses. *In* Polsinelli, M., Materassi, R., and Vincenzini, M. (eds.) Nitrogen Fixation, 467–80, Kluwer Academic Publishers, Dordrecht (1991).

Buikema, W.J. and Haselkorn, R., Molecular genetics of cyanobacterial development, *Ann. Rev. Plant Physiol. Mol. Biol.*, **44**, 33–52 (1993).

Campbell, E.L. and Meeks, J.C., Characteristics of hormogonia formation by symbiotic *Nostoc* spp. in response to the presence of *Anthoceros punctatus* or its extracellular products, *Applied and Environmental Microbiol.*, **55**, 125–31 (1989).

Cardemil, L. and Wolk, C.P., Polysaccharides from the envelopes of heterocysts and spores of the blue-green algae *Anabaena variabilis* and *Cylindrospermum licheniforme*, *J. Phycol.*, **17**, 234–40 (1981).

Carr, N.G., Metabolic regulation and autotrophic hebaviour in blue-green algae, Proceedings of the First International Symposium on Taxonomy and Biology of Blue-green Algae, University of Madras, Madras (1970).

Cavalier-Smith, T., *Biol. J. Linn. Soc.*, **17**, 289–306 (1982).

Collins, M., Algal toxins, *Microbiol. Rev.*, **42**, 725–46 (1978).

Davis, B.D., Non-filterability of the agents of genetic recombination in *E. coli*, *J. Bacteriol.*, **60**, 507–508 (1950).

Dodge, J.D., The phytoflagellate: fine structure and phylogeny. *In* Levandowsky, M. and Hutner, S.H. (eds.) Biochemistry and Physiology of Protozoa, Vol. 1, 2nd edn., 7–58, Academic Press, New York (1979).

Drouet, F., Revision of the Nostocaceae with Cylindrical Trichomes, Hafner Press, New York (1973).

Elhai, J. and Wolk, C.P., Conjugal transfer of DNA to cyanobacteria, *Methods in Enzymol.*, **167**, 747–54 (1988).

Flores, E. and Wolk, C.P., Production by filamentous, nitrogen-fixing cyanobacteria of a bacteriocin and of other antibiotics that kill related strains, *Arch. Microbiol.*, **145**, 215–19 (1986).

Fogg, G.E., Gas-vacuoles and their ecological significance, Proceedings of the First International Symposium on Taxonomy and Biology of Blue-green Algae, University of Madras, Madras (1970).

Fritsch, F.E., The Structure and Reproduction of the Algae, Vol. II, Cambridge University Press, London (1945).

Gantt, E., Phycobilisomes, *Ann. Rev. Plant Physiol.*, **32**, 327–47 (1981).

Giddings, T.H., Wolk, C.P., and Shomer-Ilan, A., Metabolism of sulfur compounds by whole filaments and heterocysts of *Anabaena variabilis*, *J. Bacteriol.*, **146**, 1067–74 (1981).

Gingrich, J.C., Blaha, L.K., and Glazer, A.N., Rod substructure in cyanobacterial phycobilisomes: analysis of *Synechocystis* 6701 mutant low in phycoerythrin, *J. Cell Biol.*, **92**, 261–68 (1982).

Golden, J.W., Robinson, S.J., and Haselkorn, R., Rearrangement of nitrogen fixation genes during heterocyst differentiation in the cyanobacterium *Anabaena*, *Nature*, **314**, 419–23 (1985).

Gromov, B.V., Cyanophages, *Ann. Microbiol.*, **134B**, 43–59 (1983).

Gross, E.M., Wolk, C.P., and Juttner, F., Fischerellin: a new allelo-chemical from the freshwater cyanobacterium *Fischerella muscicola*, *J. Phycol.*, **27**, 686–92 (1991).

Guglielmi, G. and Cohen-Bazire, G., Structure et distribution des pores et da perforations de l'enveloppe de peptidoglycane chez quelques cyanobacteries, *Protistologica*, **18**, 151–65 (1982a).

Guglielmi, G. and Cohen-Bazire, G., Etude comparee de' la structure et de la distribution des filaments extracellularies on fimbriae chez quelques cyanobacteries, *Protistologica*, **18**, 167–77 (1982b).

Häder, D.P., Photosensory behavior in procaryotes, *Microbiol. Rev.*, **51**, 1–21 (1987).

Häder, D.P. and Hoiczyk, E., Gliding motility. *In* Malkonian, M. (ed.) Algal Cell Motility, Chapman and Hall, New York (1992).

Haselkorn, R., Heterocysts, *Ann. Rev. Plant Physiol.*, **29**, 319–44 (1978).

Haselkorn, R., Basche, M., Bohme, H., Borthakur, D., Borthakur, P.B., Buikema, W.J., Mulligan, M.E., and Norris, D., Nitrogen fixation in filamentous cyanobacteria. *In* Polsinelli, M., Materassi, R., and Vincenzini, M. (eds.) Nitrogen Fixation, 359–65, Kluwer Academic Publishers, Dordrecht (1991).

Herdman, M., Evolution and genetic properties of cyanobacterial genomes. *In* Carr, N.G. and Whitton, B.A. (eds.) The Biology of Cyanobacteria, 263–305, Blackwell, Oxford (1982).

Hoare, D.S., Hoare, S.L., and Smith, A.J., Heterotrophic potentialities of the blue-green algae, Proceedings of the First International Symposium on Taxonomy and Biology of Blue-green Algae, University of Madras, Madras (1970).

Hoiczyk, E. and Baumeister, W., Envelope structure of four gliding filamentous cyanobacteria, *J. Bacteriol.*, **177**, 2387–95 (1995).

Kaplan, D. and Peters, G.A., Interaction of carbon metabolism in the *Azolla-Anabaena* symbiosis, *Symbiosis*, **6**, 53–68 (1988).

Kaushik, M.B. and Kumar, H.D., The effect of light on growth and development of two nitrogen-fixing blue-green algae, *Arch. Microbiol.*, **74**, 52–57 (1970).

Klein, R.M. and Cronquist, A., A consideration of the evolutionary and taxonomic significance of some biochemical, micromorphological and physiological characters in the thallophytes, *Q. Rev. Biol.*, **42**, 105–296 (1967).

Kumar, H.D., Observations on the developmental variability of *Camptylonema lahorense* Ghose, *Hydrobiologia*, **20**, 356–66 (1962a).

Kumar, H.D., Apparent genetic recombination in a blue-green alga, *Nature*, **196**, 1121–22 (1962b).

Kumar, H.D. and Tripathi, A.K., Mutagenic and plasmid-eliminating action of acridine orange in the cyanobacterium *Nostoc*, *Curr. Sci.*, **54**, 845–52 (1985).

Kumar, H.D. and Ueda, K., Conjugation in the cyanobacterium *Anacystis nidulans*, *Molec. Gen. Genet.*, **195**, 356–57 (1984).

Lam, C.W.Y. and Silvester, W.B., Growth interactions among blue-green (*Anabaena oscillarioides*, *Microcystis aeruginosa*) and green (*Chlorella* sp.) algae, *Hydrobiologia*, **63**, 135–43 (1979).

Lang, J.D. and Haselkorn, R., A vector for the analysis of promoters in the cyanobacterium *Anabaena* spp. strain PCC 7120, *J. Bacteriol.*, **173**, 2729–31 (1991).

Lang, N., The fine structure of blue-green algae, *Arch. Microbiol.*, **102**, 171–73 (1968).

Latorre, C., Lee, J.H., Spiller, H., and Shanmugam, K.T., Ammonium ion excreting cyanobacterial mutant as a source of nitrogen for growth of rice: a feasibility study, *Biotechnol. Lett.*, **8**, 507–12 (1986).

Lazaroff, N. and Vishniac, W., The participation of filament anastomosis in the developmental cycle of *Nostoc muscorum*: a blue-green alga, *J. Gen. Microbiol.*, **28**, 203–10 (1962).

Lewin, R.A., Prochlorophyta as a proposed new division of algae, *Nature*, **261**, 697–98 (1976).

Lewin, R.A., *Prochloron*: type genus of the Prochlorophyta, *Phycologia*, **16**, 217 (1977).

Lewin, R.A., Progress in prochlorophyte research (1977–79), Abstract E15, III Internat. Sympos. Photosynthetic Prokaryotes, Oxford (1979).

Lewin, R.A. (ed.), Origins of Plastids: Symbiogenesis, prochlorophytes and origins of chloroplasts, Chapman and Hall, London (1993).

Lewin, R.A., The cell sap of *Prochloron* (Prochlorophyta), *Phycologia*, **33**, 71–76 (1994).

Lewin, R.A. and Cheng, L., Collection and handling of *Prochloron* and its ascidian hosts. *In* Lewin, R.A. and Cheng, L. (eds.) *Prochloron*: A Microbial Enigma, 9–18, Chapman and Hall, New York (1989).

Lin, C., Watanabe, I., Liu, C.C., Zheng, D.Y., and Tang, L.F., Reestablishment of symbiosis to *Anabaena*-free *Azolla*. *In* Bothe, H., de Bruijn, N.J., and Newton, W.E. (eds.) Nitrogen Fixation: Hundred years after, 223–27, Gustav Fischer, Stuttgart (1988).

Malin, G. and Walsby, A.E., Chemotactic responses of *Oscillatoria* sp. to gradients of atmospheric gases, *Brit. Phycol. J.*, **20**, 189 (Abst.) (1985).

Nierzwicki-Bauer, S.A., Balkwill, D.L., and Stevens, S.E. (Jr.), Three dimensional structure of a unicellular cyanobacterium, *J. Cell Biol.*, **97**, 713–22 (1983).

Nierzwicki-Bauer, S.A., The *Azolla-Anabaena* symbiosis: use in agriculture. *In* Rai, A.N. (ed.) Handbook of Symbiotic Cyanobacteria, 119–36, CRC Press, Boca Raton (1990).

Nultsch, W., Light reaction systems in Cyanophyceae, *Photochem. Photobiol.*, **4**, 613–19 (1965).

Nultsch, W. and Häder, D.P., Photomovement of motile microorganisms, *Photochem. Photobiol.*, **29**, 423–37 (1979).

Nultsch, W. and Häder, D.P., Photomovement in motile microorganisms-II, *Photochem. Photobiol.*, **47**, 837–69 (1988).

Orme-Johnson, W.H., Molecular basis of biological nitrogen fixation, *Annu. Rev. Biophys. Chem.*, **14**, 419–59 (1985).

Orme-Johnson, W.H., Nitrogenase structure: where to now?, *Science*, **257**, 1639–40 (1992).

Palaepac, N.M., Martinez, M., and Boussiba, S., Mass cultivation of the nitrogen-fixing cyanobacterium *Gloeotrichia natans*, indigenous to rice fields, *J. Appl. Phycol.*, **2**, 319–25 (1990).

Pankratz, H.S. and Bowen, C.C., Cytology of blue-green algae. I. The cells of *Symploca muscorum*, *Am. J. Bot.*, **50**, 387–99 (1963).

Peters, G.A., *Azolla* and other plant-cyanobacteria symbioses: aspects of form and function.

In Polsinelli, M., Materassi, R., and Vincenzini, M. (eds.) Nitrogen Fixation, 377–88, Kluwer Academic Publishers, Dordrecht (1991).

Plazinski, J., The *Azolla-Anabaena* symbiosis. *In* Gresshoff, P.M. (ed.) Molecular Biology of Symbiotic Nitrogen Fixation, 51–75, CRC Press, Boca Raton (1990).

Plazinski, J., Zheng, Q., Taylor, R., Rolfe, B.G., and Gunning, B.E.S., Use of DNA/DNA hybridization techniques to authenticate the production of new *Azolla-Anabaena* symbiotic associations, *FEMS Microbiol. Lett.*, **65**, 199–204 (1989).

Polsinelli, M., Materassi, R., and Vincenzini, M. (eds.), Nitrogen Fixation, Kluwer Academic Publishers, Dordrecht (1991).

Rai, A.N., Rao, V.V., and Singh, H.N., The biology of cyanobacterial (blue-green algal) akinetes (spores), *Jour. Pl. Sci.*, **1**, 1–20 (1985).

Raven, J.A., Nutrient transport in microalgae. *In* Rose, A.H. and Morris, J.G. (eds.) Advances in Microbial Physiology, 47–226, Academic Press, New York (1980).

Reddy, P.M. and Fisher, R.W., A new simple method to produce *Anabaena*-free *Azolla* by *in vitro* fertilization of micromanipulated megasporocarps, *Plant Cell Rep.*, **7**, 430–33 (1988).

Reynolds, C.S., Jaworski, G.H.M., Cmiech, H.A., and Leedale, G.P., On the annual cycle of the blue-green alga *Microcystis aeruginosa* Kutz. emended by Elenkin, *Phil. Trans. Roy. Soc.* (London), **293**, 419–77 (1981).

Rippka, R., Deruelles, J., Waterbury, J.B., Herdman, M., and Stanier, R.Y., Generic assignment, strain histories and properties of pure cultures of cyanobacteria, *J. Gen. Microbiol.*, **11**, 1–61 (1979).

Roberts, T.M. and Koths, K.E., The blue-green alga *Agmenellum quadruplicatum* contains covalently closed DNA circles, *Cell*, **9**, 551–57 (1976).

Roger, P.A. and Kulasooriya, S.A., Blue-green Algae and Rice, International Rice Research Institute, Los Banos, Philippines (1980).

Safferman, R.S., Phycoviruses. *In* Carr, N.G. and Whitton, B.A. (eds.) The Biology of Blue-green Algae, 214–37, Blackwell, Oxford (1973).

Safferman, R.S. and Morris, M.E., Algal virus: isolation, *Science*, **140**, 679–80 (1963).

Scheibe, J., Photoreversible pigment: occurrence in a blue-green alga, *Science*, **176**, 1037–39 (1972).

Schopf, J.W., Precambrian microorganisms and evolutionary events prior to the origin of vascular plants, *Biol. Rev.*, **45**, 319–52 (1970).

Schopf, J.W., Disparate rates, differing fates: tempo and mode of evolution changed from the Precambrian to the Phanerozoic, *Proc. Natl. Acad. Sci.* (USA), **91**, 6735–42 (1994).

Schwabe, G.H. and Mollenhauer, R., Über den Einfluss der Begleitbäkterien auf das Lägerbild von *Nostoc sphaericum*, *Nova Hedwigia*, **13**, 77–80 (1967).

Schwartz, R.E., Hirsch, C.F., Springer, J.P., Pettibone, D.J., and Zink, D.L., Unusual cyclopropane-containing hapalindoles from a cultured cyanobacterium, *J. Org. Chem.*, **52**, 3704–3706 (1987).

Shestakov, S.V. and Khyen, N.T., Evidence for genetic transformation in a blue-green alga *Anacystis nidulans*, *Molec. Gen. Genet.*, **107**, 372–75 (1970).

Simon, R.D., Macromolecular composition of heterocysts and spores from *Anabaena variabilis*, Abstracts Third International Symposium on Photosynthetic Prokaryotes, Oxford (1979).

Sinclair, C. and Whitton, B.A., Influence of nitrogen source on morphology of Rivulariaceae (Cyanophyta), *J. Phycol.*, **13**, 335–40 (1977).

Singh, R.N. and Sinha, R., Genetic recombination in blue-green alga, *Cylindrospermum majus*, *Nature*, **207**, 782–83 (1965).

Singh, R.N. and Tiwari, D.N., Frequent heterocyst germination in the blue-green alga *Gloeotrichia ghosei* Singh, *J. Phycol.*, **6**, 172–76 (1970).

Spiller, H., Latorre, C., Hassan, M.E., and Shanmugam, K.T., Isolation and characterization of nitrogenase derepressed mutant strains of cyanobacterium *Anabaena variabilis*, *J. Bacteriol.*, **165**, 412–19 (1986).

Stam, W.T., Relationships between a number of filamentous blue-green algal strains (Cyanophyceae) revealed by DNA-DNA hybridization, *Arch. Hydrobiol.*, Suppl., **56**, 347–51 (1980).

Stanier, R.Y. and Cohen-Bazire, G., Phototrophic prokaryotes: the cyanobacteria, *A. Rev. Microbiol.*, **31**, 225–74 (1977).

Stewart, W.D.P., Rowell, P., Hawkesford, M., Jose, M., Sampaio, A.M., and Ernst, A., Nitrogenase and aspects of its regulation in cyanobacteria, *Israel J. Bot.*, **31**, 168–89 (1982).

Streicher, S.L. and Valentine, R.C., Comparative biochemistry of nitrogen fixation, *A. Rev. Biochem.*, **42**, 279–302 (1973).

Thiel, T. and Wolk, C.P., Metabolic activities of isolated akinetes of the cyanobacterium *Nostoc spongiaeforme*, *J. Bacteriol.*, **156**, 369–74 (1983).

Thiel, T. and Poo, H., Transformation of a filamentous cyanobacterium by electroporation, *J. Bacteriol.*, **171**, 5743–46 (1989).

Thomas, S.P., Zaritsky, A., and Boussiba, S., Ammonium excretion by a sulfoximine-resistant mutant of the rice field cyanobacterium *Anabaena siamensis*, *Applied and Environmental Microbiol.*, **56**, 3499–3504 (1990).

Walsby, A.E., Mucilage secretion and the movements of blue-green algae, *Protoplasma*, **65**, 223–38 (1968).

Walsby, A.E., Movements of cyanobacteria in light intensity gradients, Abstracts Second International Congress on Microbial Ecology, pp. 8–9, Coventry (1980).

Waterbury, J.B., Watson, S.W., Guillard, R.R.L., and Brand, L.E., Widespread occurrence of a unicellular marine planktonic cyanobacterium, *Nature*, **277**, 293–94 (1979).

Whitton, B.A. and Peat, A., On *Oscillatoria redekei* Van Goor, *Arch. Microbiol.*, **68**, 362–76 (1969).

Wolk, C.P., Heterocysts. *In* Carr, N.G. and Whitton, B.A. (eds.) The Biology of Cyanobacteria, 359–86, Blackwell, Oxford (1982).

Wolk, C.P., Vonshak, A., Kehoe, P., and Elhai, J., Construction of shuttle vectors capable of conjugative transfer from *E. coli* to nitrogen-fixing filamentous cyanobacteria, *Proc. Natl. Acad. Sci.* (USA), **81**, 1561–65 (1984).

4 Rhodophyta

GENERAL CHARACTERS

The phylum Rhodophyta includes the two classes Bangiophyceae and Florideophyceae. These are dealt with jointly here.

The Rhodophyta (red algae) owe their colour to the presence of excess of r-phycoerythrin in their chromatophores and this red pigment masks the colour of other photosynthetic pigments. The Rhodophyta are characterized by six main features:

(1) The flagellated motile stages are totally absent.

(2) The sexuality is highly specialized. The male gamete, called the spermatium, is motionless and, at the time of fertilization, is passively transported to and lodged on the trichogyne of the female carpogonium. Also, there are distinct postfertilization developments not found in any other algal phyla.

(3) Chlorophyll-d, biliproteins (r-phycoerythrin and r-phycocyanin), and the xanthophyll taraxanthin are the characteristic pigments; besides, the chromatophores generally contain chlorophyll-a, α- and β-carotene, lutein, zeaxanthin, neoxanthin and, rarely, other xanthophylls.

(4) The reserve foods are floridean starch and galactoside floridosides and these do not accumulate within the chromatophore but outside it, in the cytoplasm.

(5) The cell wall contains polysulphate esters of carbohydrates in addition to cellulose and pectin.

(6) The transverse walls in multicellular forms are generally provided with pits which permit cytoplasmic connection between adjacent cells. A pit connection contains a distinct lens-shaped plug locked in a septal aperture.

OCCURRENCE

The unicellular red alga *Porphyridium* grows in damp soil. Except for a dozen genera that are freshwater forms, e.g., *Batrachospermum* and *Lemanea*, others are exclusively marine and grow mostly in the intertidal and sublittoral regions. The members of the Rhodophyta grow in almost all marine habitats but their greater concentration occurs in the warmer seas.

Porphyridium tends to be common on habitats rich in animal excretions, especially urine. The alga cannot, however, be described as urophilous because experiments on axenic cultures have shown that urine is toxic to the alga. It is not the urine, but one of its decomposition products, that exerts a stimulating or nutritive effect. In nature, the alga is always accompanied by bacteria that degrade urine (Rieth, 1964).

Some of the calcareous algae, e.g., *Corallina* and *Lithothamnion,* possess stony thalli and are to some extent responsible for the formation of coral reefs.

Visible light, particularly its blue and red regions, which are mainly effective in photosynthesis (Fig. 4-1), seems to play a somewhat important role in the ecological distribution of the sublittoral marine algae since with an increase in the depth of water there is a corresponding

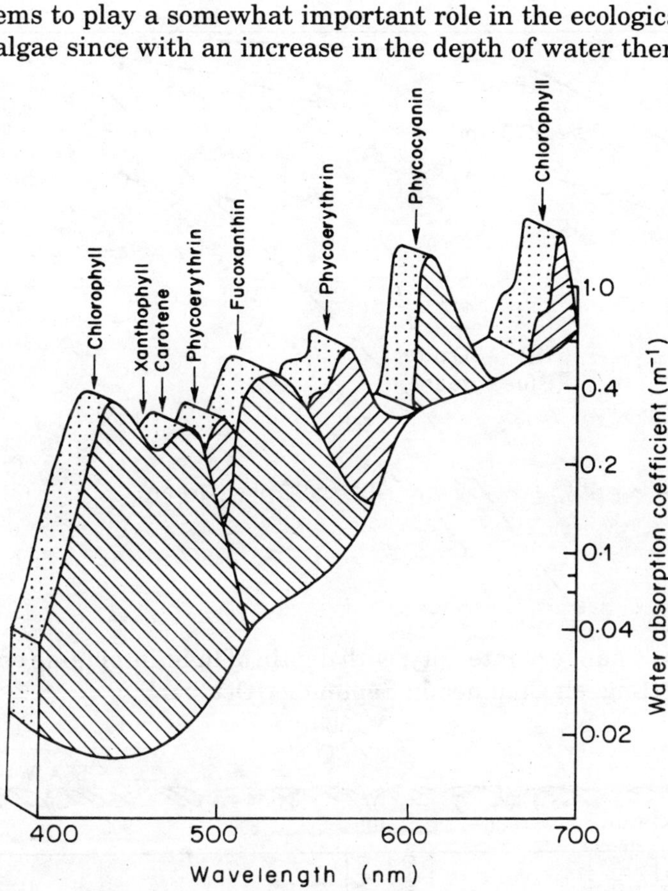

Fig. 4-1 Absorption of light of different wavelengths by various pigments of algae, and 'windows' of clarity in water absorption (after Yentsch, 1980).

decrease in the quantity and quality of incident light. At a depth of about 10 metres, only 10 per cent of the blue-green and 1 per cent (Fig. 4-2) of red light are received. At still deeper levels, a further reduction in the quantity of these spectral regions takes place. Under such light conditions, mainly the rhodophycean members can photosynthesize because the r-phycoerythrin present in them can efficiently absorb the available blue-green light (Fig. 4-3). They also exhibit complementary chromatic adaptation so that the colour of the incident light induces the development of a particular photosynthetic pigment which has maximum absorption of the incident light. Possibly, these are the reasons for the growth of the red algae at depths where few others can subsist.

Parasitic Tendency

Certain parasitic red algae lack pigments (or have very deficient pigmentation), penetrate

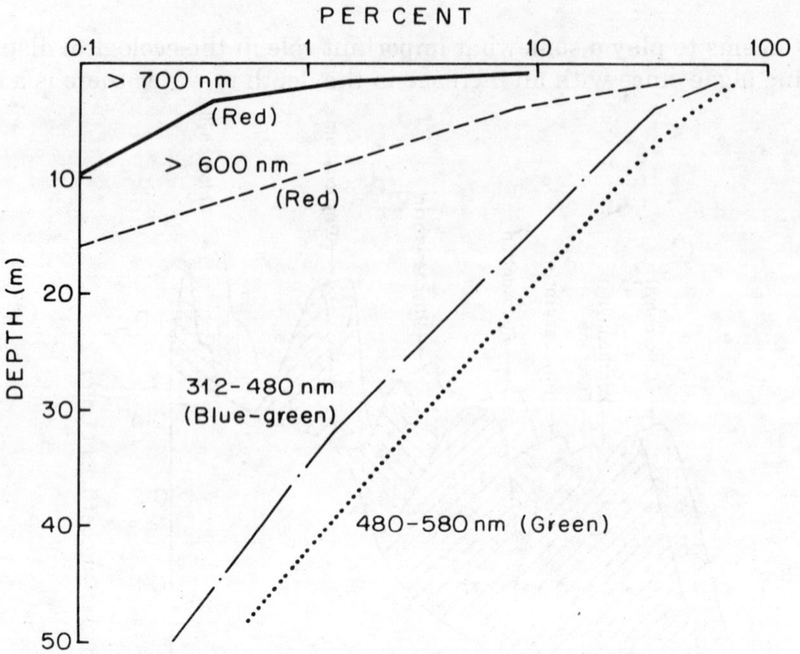

Fig. 4-2 Change of intensity, with depth, of light impinging on sea surface (English Channel, in September/October).

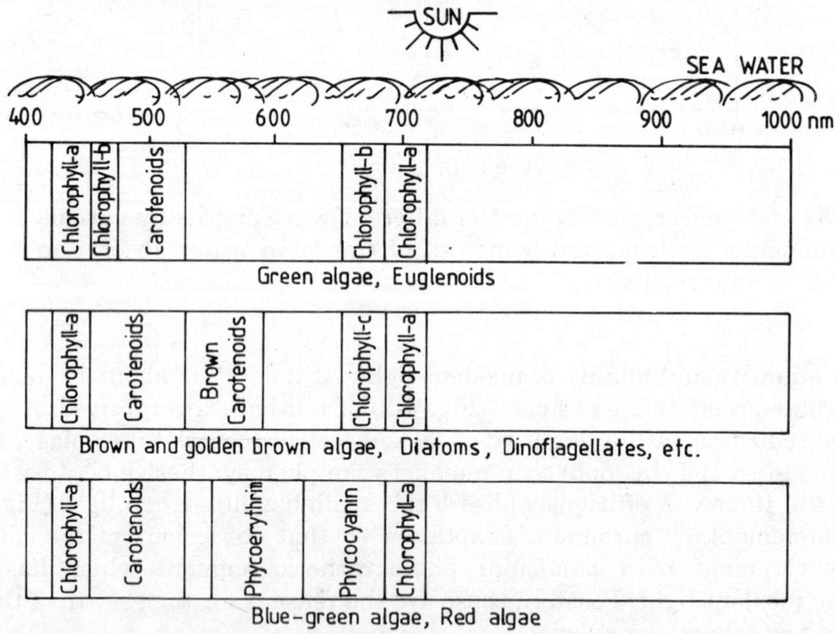

Fig. 4-3 Absorption by photosynthetic pigments in various groups of organisms in relation to ocean depth. Note the 'windows' where certain groups of organisms are transparent, allowing light to pass through to others. (After Schiff, 1981.)

'host' tissues, and show a reduction in their thallus size (Fig. 4-4); however, the nutritional relationships between the host and parasite have not yet been critically investigated biochemically. The parasitic red algae occur chiefly among the orders Gigartinales (e.g., *Gardneriella tuberifera* on *Agardhiella coulteri* and *Ceratocolax hartzii* on *Phyllophora truncata*), Cryptonemiales (e.g., *Choreonema thuretii* on *Corallina* sp.), and Ceramiales (e.g., *Janczewskia* spp. on *Laurencia* spp., *Levringiella gardneri* on *Pterosiphonia* sp., and *Syringocolax macroblepharis* on *Gelidium cartilagineum*). Some of these parasites (called adelphoparasites) are taxonomically very closely related to their hosts (e.g., *Gardneriella* on *Agardhiella*), whereas others (alloparasites) are unrelated to their hosts (e.g., *Syringocolax*). Most parasites lack pigments but contain degenerate plastids. Many parasites are highly host-specific (see Evans *et al.*, 1978).

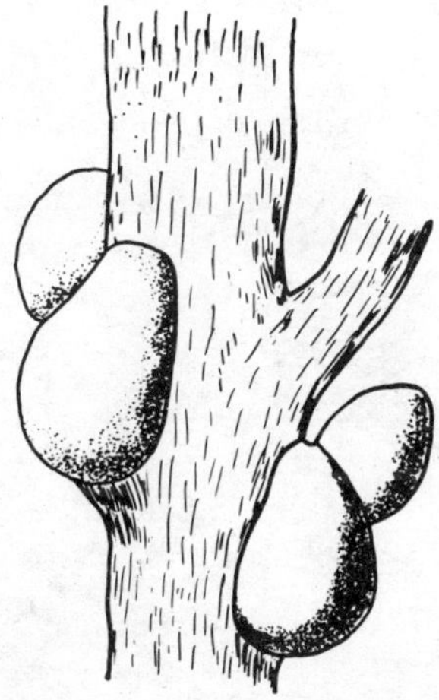

Fig. 4-4 Cystocarpic thalli of *Harveyella mirabilis* parasitic on *Rhodomela subfusca*.

RANGE OF THALLUS STRUCTURE

The Rhodophyta are perhaps the most beautiful and most showy (Fig. 4-5) of the marine algae. Forms such as *Plocamium* and *Delesseria* are a real delight to behold and collect. When mounted on a herbarium sheet and dried, a specimen of *Plocamium* looks like the creation of a painter. Generally not as large as the brown algae, the red algae are more delicate in texture and more slimy and softer to the touch.

The subclass Bangioideae, with the single order Bangiales, comprises unicellular (*Porphyridium*), filamentous (*Goniotrichum*), and parenchymatous (*Porphyra*) forms. The thalli of the Florideae are more elaborate, with two main types of organization—uniaxial and multiaxial—and in both a pseudoparenchymatous thallus results from the coalescence of filament branches. The uniaxial thalli have a single central or axial filament, which may be corticated, with a number of richly branched laterals organized to form a pseudoparenchymatous structure, e.g., *Dumontia* and *Batrachospermum*. In the multiaxial types, there are several central or axial filaments which, together with their branches, form the pseudoparenchymatous thallus, e.g., *Helminthocladia*.

The growth of thallus in the Bangioideae is diffuse, whereas, with a few exceptions, in the Florideae, apical growth is the rule. An apical cell, by consecutive divisions, forms a transverse series of cells, each of which may further divide tangentially to produce a group of pericentral cells that surround a central cell. The pericentral cells may not divide further (as in the Rhodomelaceae) or may divide vertically to form a cortex or the initials of the lateral branches which coalesce to form a compact structure with internal differentiation into an outer photosynthetic zone, an inner food storing cortex, and a central medulla containing vertically elongated hyphae, e.g., *Gelidium* and *Gloiosiphonia*.

The foliose red algae generally develop from a prostrate system of filaments which usually form a compact cushion-like growth adherent to the substratum, the holdfast. This gives rise to one or more upright laminate thalli that are the fruiting bodies of the thallus.

Many red algae produce hairs. Table 4-1 gives a comparison of hairs and hair-producing cells of 5 representative taxa.

Fig. 4-5 Four common red algae from Okha (Gujarat) coast. *Courtesy* A. Tewari.

Table 4-1 Comparison of hairs and hair-producing cells of selected marine red algae (condensed from Oates and Cole, 1994)

	Gelidium vagum	*Gracilaria pacifica*	*Ceramium rubrum*	*Nemalion helminthoides*	*Palmaria palmata*
Hair					
Distribution	Subapical	Thallus	Subapical	Apical	Tufted
Length, μm	290	725	485		
Diameter, μm	3.7	4.9	4.5		4.8
Density, mm	147	162			
Surface increase, %	50	180			
Basal constriction	No	Yes	Yes	No	No
Collar	Yes	No	Yes	No	No
Pit plug	Asymmetric	Asymmetric	Asymmetric	Asymmetric	Present
Position	Surface	Embedded			Surface
Nucleus	Single	Multiple	Single	Single	
Position	Apical	Throughout	Apical	Apical	
Chloroplasts	Absent	Absent	Absent	Absent	
Hair-producing cell					
Cell type	Cortical	Cortical	Cortical	Apical/axial	Cortical
Nucleus	Single	Multiple		Single	Single
Chloroplasts	Small	Very small		Large/single	
Thylakoids	Well-formed	Absent		Well-formed	
Autofluorescence	Yes	No			

CELL STRUCTURE

The red algae are truly eucaryotic. They have microtubules but lack centrioles or flagella. Some forms (e.g., *Porphyridium*) do show some kind of gliding motility, caused perhaps by polar expulsion of mucilaginous material.

The cell walls of most Rhodophyceae show a typical fibrillar structure under the electron microscope and are generally thought to consist of a cellulose framework in a mucopolysaccharide matrix.

The pit connections are lenticular plugs with several-layered caps and these pit connections occupy a central position in the septa between adjacent cells. Open communications do not occur between cells of the red algae. The liberation of spermatia, tetraspores, and carpospores occurs via apertures from which pit connections have been displaced, in the walls of the parent algae (Duckett and Peel, 1978). However, this kind of displacement of pit connections does not seem to occur in the case of apically-located spores or spermatia.

The red algal cell walls characteristically resemble the cell walls of higher fungi in many ways. The rhodophycean pit connections are very similar to septal plugs of fungi. The popular view of the red algal ancestry of higher fungi is strongly supported by the production of apoplastic cells by a process which completely excludes all plastid material from specific cells at cytokinesis (Duckett and Peel, 1978).

The Bangiophyceae tend to have single stellate or lobed plastids containing a single pyrenoid but lacking an inner limiting disc. Most Florideophyceae possess several discoid plastids per cell. These plastids have an inner limiting disc but lack pyrenoids. An exception is *Nemalion* where both pyrenoids and inner limiting disc coexist. The red algal chromatophores are double-membrane organelles having widely separated single thylakoids.

In the red algal cells, the endoplasmic reticulum is one of the most important organelles. Its functions are diverse and manifold, including (1) septal plug formation, (2) fibrous vacuole formation, (3) spermatial vacuole formation, (4) vesicle formation in spores, (5) starch polymerization, (6) mucilage production by fusion cells, (7) microbody formation, and (8) cleavage channel formation and wall secretion during cytokinesis (Kugrens and Koslowsky, 1981).

Golgi bodies are probably the most distinctive and most highly organized of the subcellular organelles of red algal cells (Fig. 4-6). The Golgi-derived vesicles play a major role in cell wall formation and in the production of various internal storage products. Three chief kinds of vesicles found in the red algal Golgi bodies are fibrillar, cored, or striated.

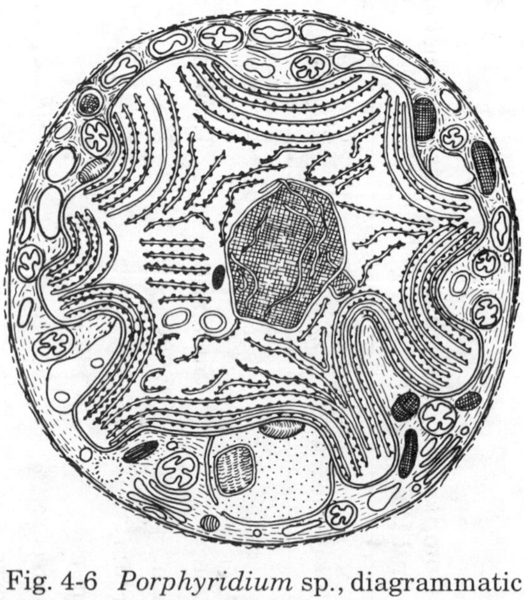

Fig. 4-6 *Porphyridium* sp., diagrammatic sketch of electron micrograph of transverse section of cell. (Note that the pyrenoid in *P. cruentum* is not surrounded by a membrane.)

The red algae show considerable variation in the shape, size, and number of nuclei. The cells of the Bangiophyceae are uninucleate with a single nucleolus; those of the Florideophyceae are more complex. In general, if the apical cells are uninucleate, the segments derived from them will also be uninucleate. The shape of the nucleus varies depending on its position in the cell. Thus, it is spherical when centrally situated, and flat when parietally located. The nuclei may migrate from one cell to another through a pit connection. Some red algae, e.g., *Porphyra*, show a diurnal periodicity in their nuclear division.

The light microscopic observations on red algal mitoses have suggested that the nuclear envelope breaks down during mitosis, but this conclusion is not supported by recent ultrastructural studies which have revealed that open spindles are absent in these algae and that except for polar fenestrae in *Porphyridium, Membranoptera*, and a few other genera, the nuclear envelope remains intact during mitosis (Bronchart and Demoulin, 1977). *Porphyridium* is unusual in having a single large microbody at each spindle pole.

The presence of polar fenestrae indicates that the mitosis is not completely intranuclear. In *Membranoptera*, a distinctive group of chromosomes-to-poles microtubules are interestingly attached by structured kinetochores; such attachment is uncommon in plants (see Heath, 1974).

An electron microscopic study of *Porphyridium* sp. (Fig. 4-6) has revealed the presence of particles, called phycobilisomes, which contain phycoerythrin and phycocyanin. The phycobilisomes are arranged as rows and pillars on the surface of the photosynthetic lamellae, fixed by a foot-like structure; those containing phycoerythrin are usually spherical (but *Rhodella violacea* has hemidiscoidal phycobilisomes containing B-phycoerythrin, C-phycocyanin, and allophycocyanin), whereas those with phycocyanin are usually discoid. Many scattered grains of floridean starch occur in the cell cytoplasm.

Galactose as an intercellular substance in red algae forms various viscous polysaccharides, or galactans, which are all acidic and which include sulphate esters. Hot water can extract them from algae fronds. The resulting liquid is viscous and, if allowed to stand, gels. The gelation power of agar is strong, whereas that of funoran and carrageenan, which are used as glues, is weak. The amount of sulphate ester in the polysaccharide determines its gelation capacity: no coagulation occurs when the sulphate-ester content exceeds 10 per cent. This content varies from species to species: 20 per cent in *Gigartina*, 4–6 per cent in *Ceramium*, and less than 3 per cent in *Gelidium*. The red algae in which a 1 per cent solution gelates at a temperature of 15°C to 20°C are used as agar materials. The ones that do not gelate at these temperatures are used for glues (Arasaki and Arasaki, 1983).

The floridean starch differs from the chlorophycean starch in being devoid of amylose. In some respects, the floridean starch resembles the amylopectin of higher plants but in some other ways it tends to resemble the animal polysaccharide, glycogen.

Floridoside is widely distributed amongst many red algae except Ceramiales, with levels up to 10 per cent of the tissue dry weight. The Ceramiales contain diageneaside (O-alpha-D-manno-pyranosyl) glycerate in place of floridoside.

Floridoside not only acts as the metabolically active photoassimilatory reproduct but is also involved in osmoregulation in marine red algae. Reed (1985) has shown that in *Bangia atropurpurea* floridoside concentration varies directly with external salinity in the manner typical for an osmotic effector. The changes in floridoside concentration are thought to compensate to some extent for changes in external osmolality.

Mitochondria have recently been reported in *Batrachospermum moniliforme*. A discrete organelle unique to some red algae, e.g., *Polysiphonia harveyi*, is the fibrous vacuole associated organelle. This organelle is involved in early stages of fibrous vacuole formation (Broadwater and Scott, 1983).

REPRODUCTION

The unicellular forms propagate vegetatively. In multicellular forms, asexual or sexual reproduction is more common.

The Red Sea alga *Centroceras clavalutum* produces missile-shaped vegetative propagules. These are carried away along ocean currents and settle on leaves of seagrasses where they develop into new individual plants of *Centroceras* (Lipkin, 1977).

Nonflagellate

Asexual reproduction is brought about by nonmotile spores which are given different names depending on the nature of the cells from which they are produced and their number within each sporangium. Accordingly, there are four chief types of asexual spores, namely, (1) monospores (Fig. 4-7), formed singly in monosporangia, as in the Bangioideae; (2) neutral spores, formed by the direct transformation of vegetative cells into spores; characteristic of the Bangioideae; (3) carpospores, formed either directly from the division products of the zygote, as in the Bangioideae, or indirectly from the cells of certain filaments, termed gonimoblasts, arising from the fertilized carpogonium or from an auxiliary cell containing the zygote nucleus; and (4) bispores, tetraspores, and polyspores, produced, respectively, in twos, fours, and multiples of fours within a sporangium of the diploid tetrasporophyte. Except for some red algae that form haploid carpospores growing into sexual plants, most other red algae form diploid carpospores which on germination give rise to

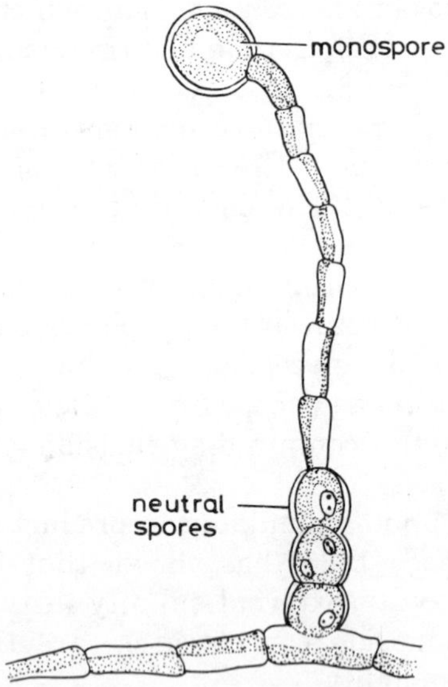

Fig. 4-7 *Porphyra* sp., *Conchocelis* stage with monospore and neutral (?) spores.

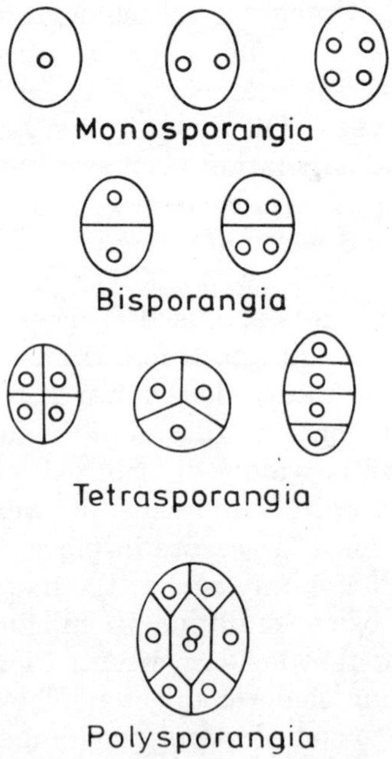

Fig. 4-8 Some sporangial types found in Florideae.

sporophytes or diploid plants, bearing diploid sporangia from which bispores, tetraspores or polyspores are produced after meiosis. These spores are therefore haploid and germinate to form gametophytes or haploid plants.

A tetrasporangium may be cruciate if the two divisions of the cell are at right angles to each other, tetrahedral if the two divisions are oriented in such a manner as to form a group of four tetrahedrally disposed spores, or zonate if there are three parallel transverse divisions. Figure 4-8 illustrates some sporangia.

Proliferation is a widespread phenomenon in the red algae (Fig. 4-9 A, B). Many Nemaliales show carposporangial proliferation. Proliferation has also been reported for hair cells, monospores, spermatia, and tetrasporangia (Ramm-Anderson and Wetherbee, 1982). As a rule, those species which form amoeboid spores tend to have sporangial regeneration. Sporangial regeneration is usually absent in Ceramiales.

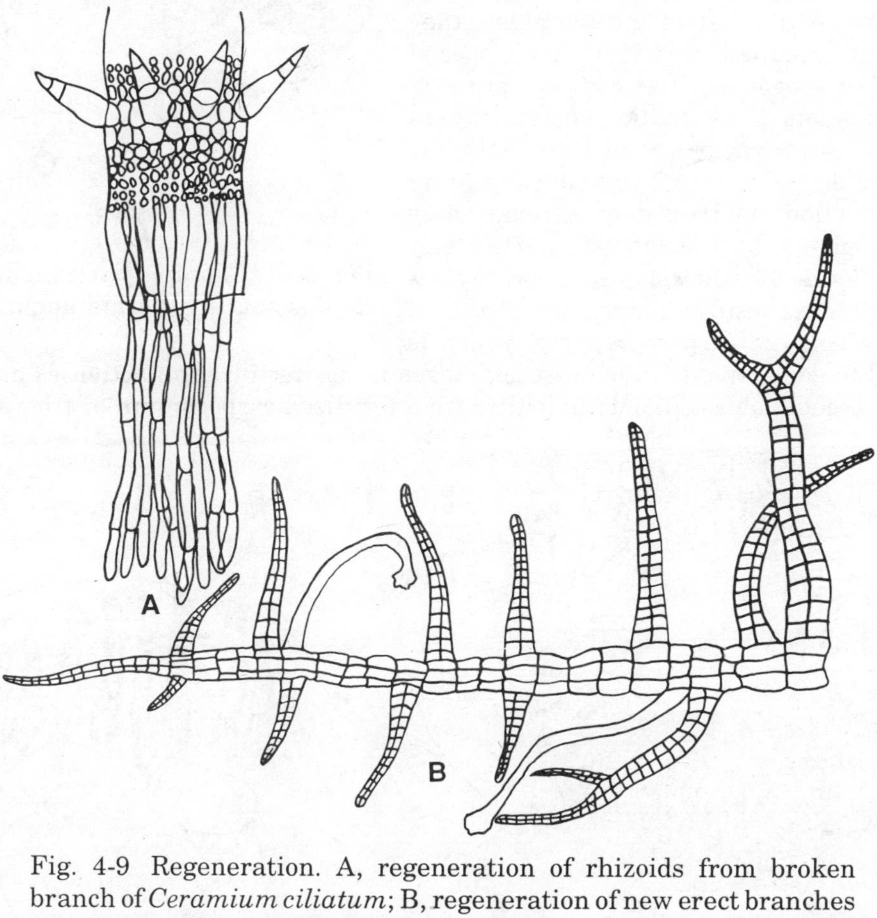

Fig. 4-9 Regeneration. A, regeneration of rhizoids from broken branch of *Ceramium ciliatum*; B, regeneration of new erect branches from a detached branch of *Polysiphonia* sp.

Spores Some species of *Cryptopleura* and *Neoagardhiella* produce a wide range of spore sizes, whereas most red algae produce spores of a fairly constant size. *Bangia fusco-purpurea* produces rather small spores, around 10 μm in diameter, whereas the spores of *Cryptopleura* *violacea* generally exceed 50 μm. In a given species, the carpospores tend to be larger than the tetraspores. The smaller spores tend to sink more slowly than the larger spores.

Sexual

The motionless male cells or spermatia of the Rhodophyta are formed singly within spermatangia (Figs. 4-10 and 4-11 A, B) produced in clusters either on special branches, as in *Polysiphonia*, or in definite sori, as in *Apoglossum*. The female cell, designated carpogonium, is a flask-shaped cell with a neck-like protuberance, the trichogyne (Fig. 4-12 A). The egg nucleus is restricted to the basal portion. In the Bangioideae, carpogonia are sessile, but in the Florideae, they are stalked and produced terminally on a special branch, the carpogonial filament or procarp. During fertilization, a spermatial nucleus passes down through the trichogyne and fuses with the nucleus of the egg. The sexual reproduction, from sex organ formation to fertilization, is remarkably uniform throughout the Rhodophyta, particularly the subclass Florideae, which shows elaborate postfertilization changes resulting in the production of a new generation, the carposporophyte, which is parasitic on the gametophyte. Such distinct stages in postfertilization activities as the place of formation of gonimoblast filaments [either from fertilized carpogonium or from generative

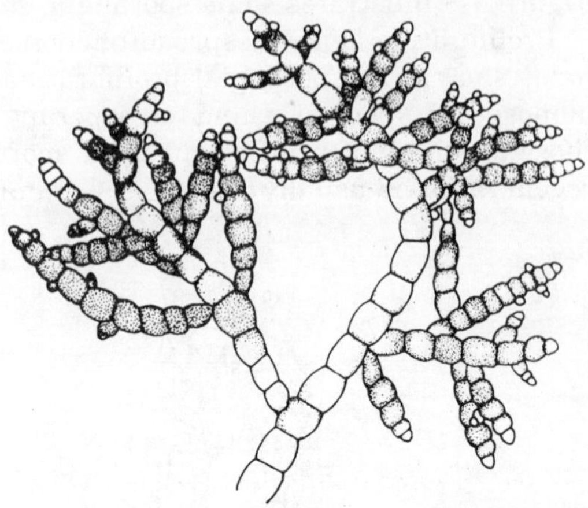

Fig. 4-10 *Champia parvula*, part of male thallus bearing spermatangial sori.

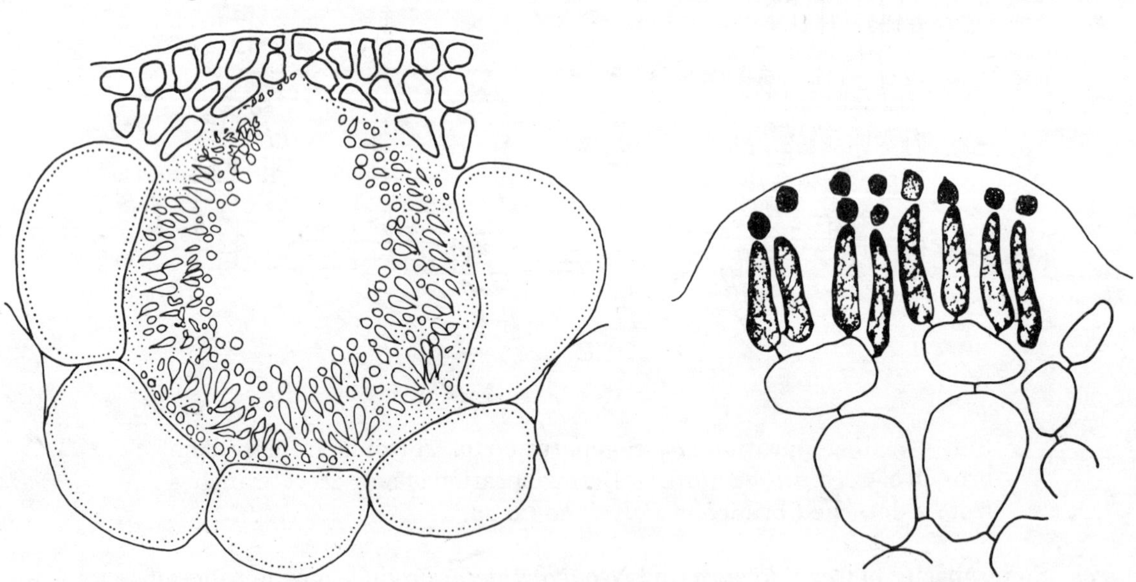

A B

Fig. 4-11 Spermatangia of red algae. A, *Gracilaria verrucosa*; B, *Gelidium* sp.

auxiliary cell and, in the latter case, the position and time of formation, if before or after fertilization of the auxiliary cell (see Fig. 4-12 B–D)] are so important and significant that they have provided the main basis for the classification of the Florideae into various orders.

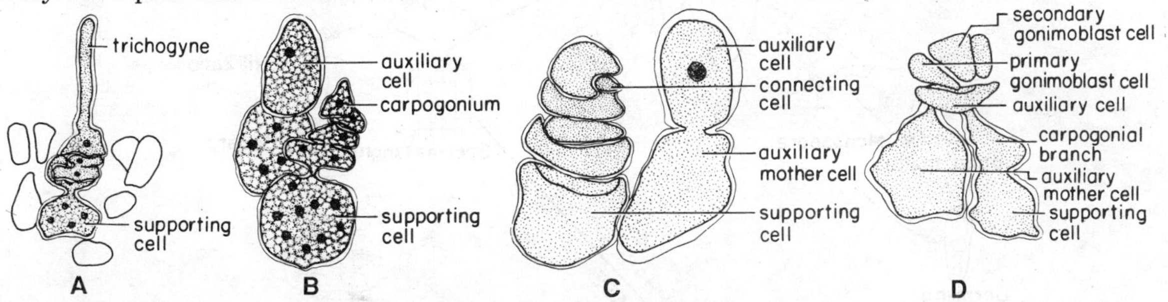

Fig. 4-12 *Champia parvula*. A, supporting cell and carpogonial branch; B, enlargement of auxiliary cell branch; C, delimitation of a cutting cell from carpogonium; D, cutting off of a few gonimoblasts, degenerating fused carpogonial branch, and supporting cell. (After Lee, 1978.)

The spermatia seem to be extruded in some mucilage but it is not definite whether the individual spermatia are coated with mucilage. The spermatia show some amoeboid or gliding movement. Water motion plays an important role in the fertilization of red algae. Neushul (1972) proposed that the release of spermatia in spermatial strands facilitates fertilization in some red algae; this mechanism was at variance with the commonly held belief that individual spermatia are passively carried to the trichogyne by water currents.

Fetter and Neushul (1981) observed that in *Tiffaniella snyderae* the spermatia are released from the exposed spermatangial heads in a spermatium-plus-strand unit which remains joined to the spermatangial head. The spermatial strands contract or extend and rotate as the water velocity past the alga is changed, and in still water the strands retract into a clump on the spermatangial head surface. The release from the spermatangia occurs through tears in the spermatangial head in the exposed spermatangia. An important view expressed by Fetter and Neushul is that spermatial strands seem to possess elastic and spring-like properties which may aid extension, contraction, or rotation. These traits may play some hitherto unknown role in red algal fertilization. Fetter and Neushul (1981) also observed that in this alga the spermatium is not attached terminally on the strand but tangentially.

In the Bangioideae, no new generation, like carposporophyte, is produced but the zygote divides directly into carpospores which germinate to form a *Conchocelis*-like vegetative phase. The general opinion among phycologists is that the mature plants of the Bangioideae, e.g., *Porphyra, Bangia,* and others, are diploid and it is during the formation of carpospores that meiosis occurs. These carpospores produce haploid *Conchocelis*-like plants. Since there is no unequivocal cytological evidence for the occurrence of meiosis, whether during germination of the zygote or formation of the monospores or neutral spores, the controversy about the diploidy or haploidy of *Porphyra* or *Bangia* thalli is yet to be resolved. Some recent evidence (see Fig. 4-13) indicates that *Conchocelis* may be diploid (Von Stosch, personal communication). Morphologically, *Conchocelis* is regarded as the prostrate system and *Porphyra* thallus as the erect system of an originally heterotrichous alga.

In some Florideae, the gametophytes are haploid and the zygote nucleus may divide meiotically or more often mitotically in the carpogonium itself (Knaggs, 1969). In the majority,

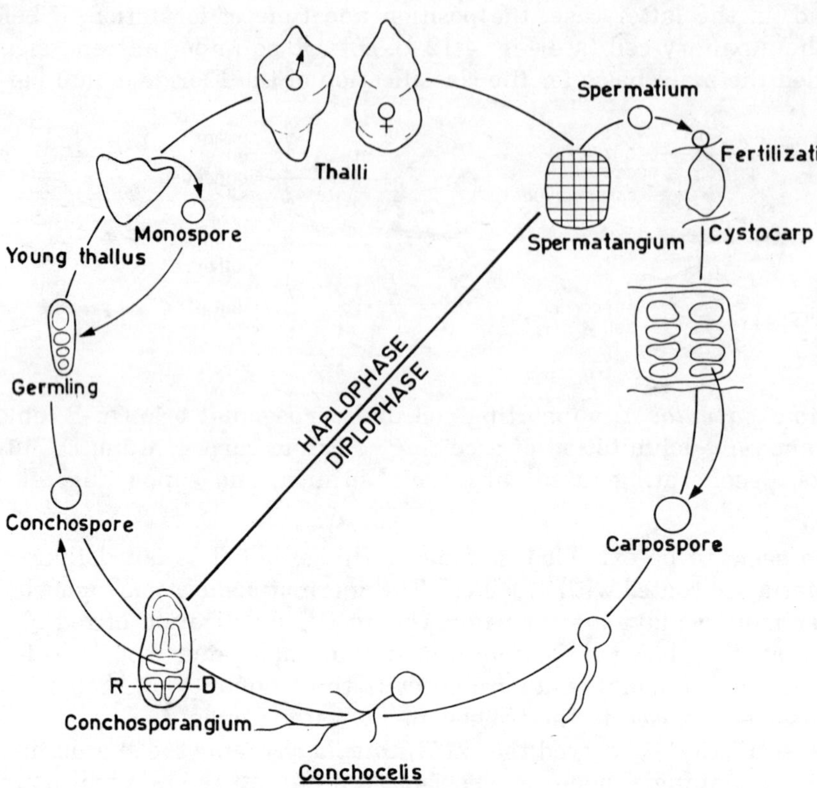

Fig. 4-13 *Porphyra tenera*, life cycle.

however, the zygote nucleus migrates into a well differentiated cell, known as the auxiliary cell (Fig. 4-12 B–D), either through pit connections or through a tubular connection, the ooblast, specially established for this purpose between the carpogonium and the auxiliary cell. The division of the zygote nucleus in the auxiliary cell is always mitotic; hence, all the gonimoblast filaments produced are diploid and so also are the resulting carposporophytes. The gonimoblast filaments produced from the carpogonia after meiosis are haploid but in the others they are diploid. Accordingly, the carposporophytic generation of the former is haploid, whereas that of the others is diploid. Either terminal cells or all the cells of a gonimoblast filament may function as carposporangia (Fig. 4-14). Each carposporangium forms a single carpospore which may be haploid or diploid depending on the nature of the carposporophyte. Both the carposporophyte and tetrasporophyte formed by the germination of the carpospores constitute the asexual generations.

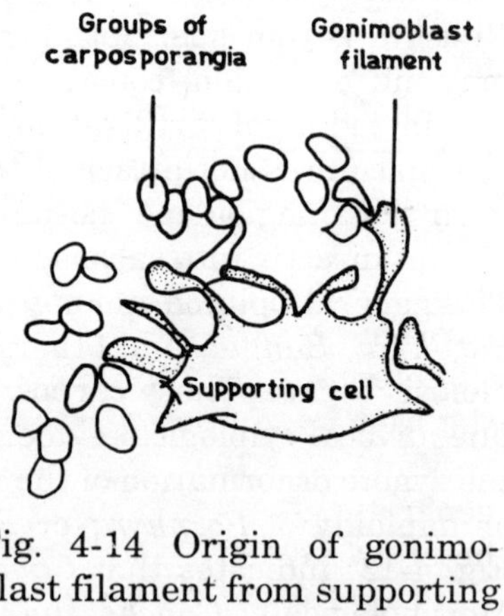

Fig. 4-14 Origin of gonimoblast filament from supporting cell; groups of carposporangia are also shown (after Edelstein *et al.*, 1974).

The early stages of carposporophyte development in the Florideophyceae are characterized by the formation of a centrally located, irregular-shaped fusion cell (Figs. 4-15 and 4-16). This

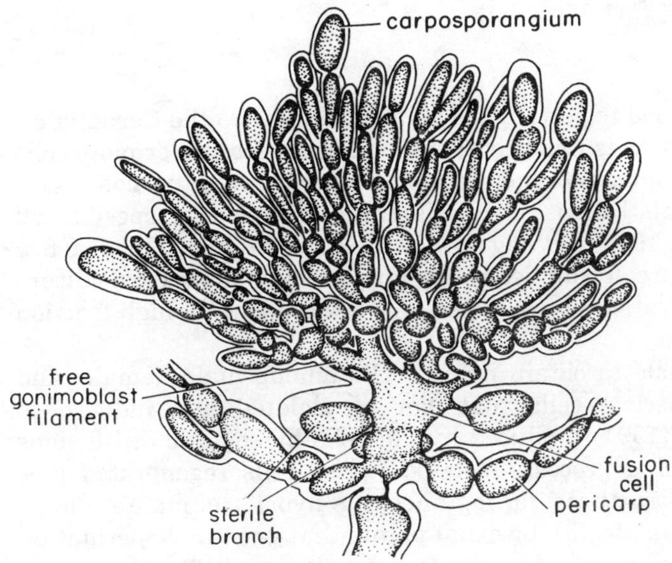

Fig. 4-15 *Scinaia forcellata*, mature cystocarp with fusion cell, showing free gonimoblast filaments, carposporangia, and sterile branches on hypogynous cell (after Huisman, 1985).

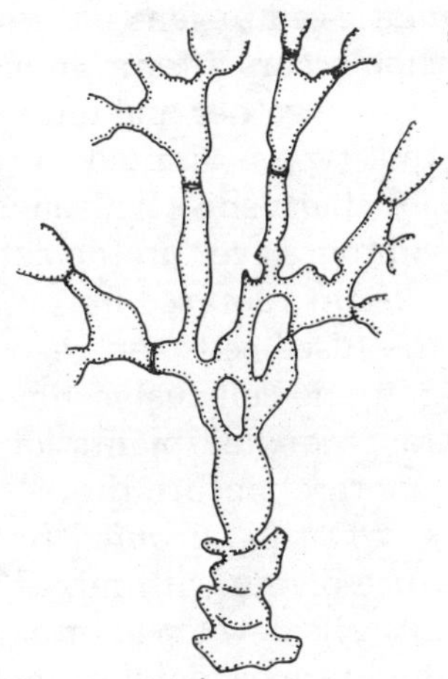

Fig. 4-16 *Champia parvula*, fusion cell in mature cystocarp (after Lee, 1978).

cell results from cytoplasmic fusions of haploid and diploid cells and is multinucleate, containing both haploid and diploid nuclei. Commonly, the haploid nuclei degenerate and only diploid nuclei participate in the subsequent carposporophyte development, which involves the formation of gonimoblasts from the fusion cell, followed by the differentiation of many of the gonimoblast cells into carpospores. The fusion cells are thought to provide nutrients to the developing gonimoblasts and carpospores. In *Asterocolax gardneri*, some gonimoblast cells are continually incorporated into the growing fusion cell and the so enlarged fusion cell may create additional space that could support more gonimoblast filaments and carpospores (Kugrens and Arif, 1981). Another possible function of the fusion cell is secretion of mucilage which surrounds the entire carposporophyte.

Recent researches indicate that meiosis occurs in the developing apex of young plants of the Nemalionales and not in the fertilized carpogonium.

Many phycologists (e.g., T.V. Desikachary and G.F. Papenfuss) believe the carposporophyte generation to be a parasite. Some have even succeeded in growing the carposporophyte as a heterotrophic unit *in vitro*.

The production of parasexual hybrids of *Griffithsia tenuis* after somatic cell fusion between vegetative cells of male and female thalli has been reported by Waaland (1978) who has also achieved successful regeneration of new plants from the hybrid cells. Such somatic hybrids are capable of forming reproductive structures and in this respect differ from hybrids between vegetative cells of the same sex, either male or female, which are incapable of forming reproductive bodies. Careful experiments have further indicated that in the cells of this alga (which are multinucleate) separate male and female nuclei coexist and act in concert, probably in the same way as in many fungal heterokaryons.

Somatic Cell Fusions

Somatic cell fusions have been accomplished in certain red algae belonging to the Ceramiales. Fusion occurs after a wound-healing reaction is induced; this reaction causes two or more cells to grow together and undergo fusion. In contrast to the protoplast-fusion technique, cell fusion of this type is limited to conspecific plants because it is influenced by a species-specific cell fusion hormone (Watson and Waaland, 1983; Hwang *et al.*, 1991). Cell fusion has a few advantages over protoplast fusion: neither cell wall degrading enzymes nor the special culture conditions required for protoplast regeneration are required, and a significantly high fraction of the fused cells can regenerate.

Somatic cell fusion has made it possible to obtain hybrid cells among male, female, and tetrasporangial plants of the same species—cells that can be isolated and induced to regenerate mature thalli. Hwang *et al.* (1991) produced hybrid cells by somatic cell fusions in *Griffithsia japonica* by a wound-healing process. Isolated fusion cells regenerated new mature plants with mixed reproductive structures; for instance, the hybrids of male × female plant cells developed into (1) male; (2) female; (3) bisexual plants that produced spermatangial and carpogonial branches on the same plant; (4) mixed-phase plants with spermatangia and tetrasporangia; or (5) bisexual/mixed-phase individuals with spermatangial, carpogonial branches and tetrasporangia. Many of the plants resulting from the male/female hybrid formed tetrasporangia that were always formed with spermatangia on a single cell. Plants regenerated from a hybrid cell between male and tetrasporangial thalli developed into spermatangiate, tetrasporangiate, or mixed-phase plants bearing spermatangia and tetrasporangia (Hwang *et al.*, 1991). Likewise, plants regenerated from the female × tetrasporangiate hybrid developed into carpogonial, tetrasporangial, or mixed-phase plants bearing carpogonial branches and tetrasporangia.

Other workers have also reported the occurrence of anomalous types of reproduction, e.g., bisexual plants, mixed-phase plants, or bisexual/mixed-phase plants in red algae belonging to the Gracilariales and Ceramiales; two notable examples are West and Hommersand (1981), and Oliveira and Plastino (1984).

CLASSIFICATION

Most phycologists divide the class Rhodophyceae into two subclasses, viz., (1) the Bangioideae (or Bangiophyceae), comprising only the order Bangiales; and (2) the Florideae (or Florideophyceae), with six orders—the Nemalionales, Gelidiales, Cryptonemiales, Gigartinales, Rhodymeniales, and Ceramiales.

The Bangioideae includes those forms that have simple thalli with uninucleate cells containing single, axile chromatophores and are normally devoid of pit connections. The zygote divides directly into diploid carpospores. The thallus of the Bangioideae shows diffuse growth in contrast to the apical growth of the Florideae.

The division of the Florideae into six orders is based on features of its postfertilization development. Except for some Nemalionales, which do not have a free-living diploid generation, all the other orders have two diploid generations—the carposporophytic and the tetrasporophytic—the first parasitic on the gametophyte, the second free-living. The Nemalionales and Gelidiales have been segregated due to their lack of auxiliary cells. In some Nemalionales, e.g., *Nemalion*, carpospores are produced directly by a gonimoblast without a preceding fusion of the carpogonium with another cell; in others, the carpogonium may first fuse with a cell of the carpogonial branch and that cell may give rise even to gonimoblasts. The Cryptonemiales and Gigartinales form auxiliary cells before fertilization whereas the Ceramiales develop them after fertilization. The auxiliary cell in the Gigartinales is often interpreted as a vegetative cell (see Lebednik, 1977). It is either a supporting cell of the carpogonial branch or a cell in an unrelated branch. Most of these algae, except *Calosiphonia,* have tubes or cells derived from the carpogonium fusing directly with the auxiliary cell. In the exceptional genus *Calosiphonia,* the connecting filament originates from the carpogonium in spite of such fusions. In the Rhodymeniales, a cell or tube emanating from the carpogonium undergoes direct fusion with an auxiliary cell (i.e., a vegetative cell) in a related branch; the auxiliary cells differentiate before fertilization but develop well and become easily recognizable only after fertilization. In the Cryptonemiales, the auxiliary cell is located either within a receptive carpogonial branch system or within a reduced (i.e., accessory) carpogonial branch system (Lebednik, 1977). The Cryptonemiales differ from the Gigartinales because their carpogonial branches always arise from special accessory branches whereas in the Gigartinales they are merely unmodified ordinary branches. Further, as compared with the Cryptonemiales, there is much greater development of sterile gonimoblast tissue and also more frequent direct connection of such tissues with the adjoining vegetative cells in the Gigartinales (Lebednik, 1977). In the Rhodymeniales, the auxiliary cell develops from the outer cell of a two-celled branch, but in the Ceramiales, it is formed from the supporting cell.

In materials collected from nature, which lack the carpogonia and associated structures, it becomes impossible to correctly identify the algae. The resulting taxonomic confusion has been particularly serious in the Nemalionales, Gigartinales, and Cryptonemiales. Guiry (1978) has advocated the use of sporangial and spermatangial characters in the ordinal classification of Florideophyceae. Most sporangia so far described (tetrasporangia, carposporangia, bisporangia, and polysporangia) have meiotic and mitotic homologues. According to Guiry (1978), a cruciate disposition of spores within tetrasporangia is the basic type which has later given rise to the zonate and tetrahedral types. Tetrasporangia undergo either successive cleavage (all orders of Florideophyceae), or simultaneous cleavage (mainly in Ceramiales) (see Fig. 4-17 A, B).

Like all commercial crops, *Porphyra* is susceptible to several parasitic and nonparasitic

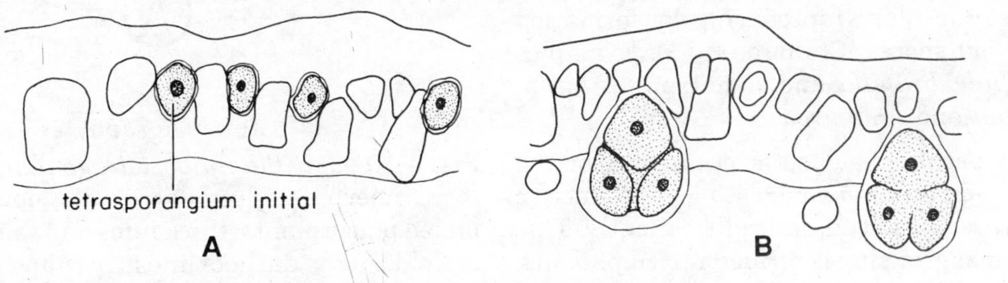

Fig. 4-17 *Champia parvula*. A, early stage of tetrasporangial development; B, late stage of tetrasporangial development.

diseases. A species of *Pythium* causes the red rot disease of *Porphyra*, its hyphae penetrate the algal cells and kill them. A chytrid also parasitizes the alga. The faded rot and perforated rot diseases are caused by nutritional disorders.

The *Conchocelis* stage is attacked by such physiological diseases as yellow spot, green spot, turtle shell pattern, and shark skin (Ogata, 1975).

LIFE HISTORY (FLORIDEOPHYCEAE)

Chihara (1975) described six general types of life history in the Florideophyceae:

(1) *Polysiphonia*-type Very common; has three consecutive phases—haploid gametophyte, diploid carposporophyte, and diploid tetrasporophyte; gametophyte and tetrasporophyte morphologically identical.

(2) *Asparagopsis*-type Involves triphasic alternation of generations (haploid gametophyte, diploid carposporophyte, and diploid tetrasporophyte); tetrasporophyte much smaller than gametophyte. Found in *Bonnemaisonia hamifera* and some species of *Asparagopsis.*

(3) *Ptilonia*-type Has biphasic alternation of generations involving large haploid gametophyte and small haploid carposporophyte. Found in *Bonnemaisonia asparagoides, Ptilonia okadii,* some species of *Delisea, Naccaria wiggii*, and others.

(4) *Phyllophora*-type Biphasic alternation between haploid gametophyte and diploid tetrasporophyte. An example is *P. brodiaei.*

(5) *Liagora*-type Incompletely known, but may be bi- or possibly triphasic; large haploid gametophyte generation and small diploid *Acrochaetium*-like carposporophyte generation known; carposporophyte produces tetraspores by meiosis and monospores by mitosis; monospores seem to repeat *Acrochaetium* phase. Examples are *Liagora farinosa* and *Nemalion vermiculare.*

(6) *Hildenbrandia*-type Sexual reproductive organs not recorded; tetrasporophyte phase known and presumably nuclear divisions within tetrasporangium apomeiotic. This kind of life history is thus monophasic, the plant reproducing by formation of diploid spores (Chihara, 1975). Examples are *Hildenbrandia* and some spp. of *Lithophyllum* and *Amphiroa*.

In several red algae, the occurrence on the same individual of contrasting reproductive structures has been noticed frequently. This abnormal grouping is termed mixed phasing. In *Gracilaria tikvahiae*, mitotic recombination is the mechanism that leads to gameto-

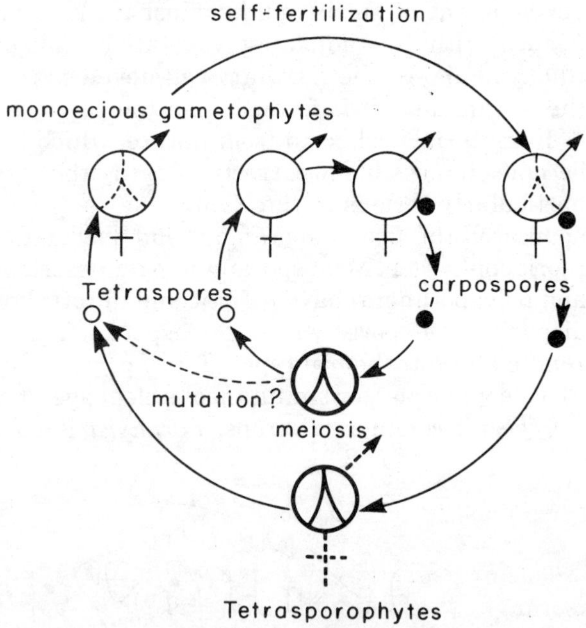

Fig. 4-18 *Callithamnion tetragonum*, life history. Inner circle, regular plants; outer circle, mixed phase plants; thick lines and solid circles, diploid state; dashed lines, perhaps nonfunctional structures. (After Rueness and Rueness, 1985.)

phytic structures on diploid tetrasporophytes (Van der Meer and Todd, 1977). In *Spermothamnion repens* also, gametangia have been seen on diploid tetrasporophytes. Van der Meer (1981) could cross both haploid and diploid gametophytic thalli of *Gracilaria tikvahiae,* obtaining polyploids. Rueness and Rueness (1985) have demonstrated that some plants of the monoecious alga *Callithamnion tetragonum* bear both gametangia and tetrasporangia. The tetraspores from such plants produce monoecious gametophytes with carposporophyte development following self-fertilization. Invariably, the carpospores again give rise to mixed phase tetrasporophytes (Fig. 4-18). The gametangia produced together with functional tetraspores do not develop into carposporophytes, and the tetrasporangia borne on functional gametophytes are always abortive.

Kraft and Robins (1985) suggest a merger of the order Cryptonemiales with Gigartinales as the two orders are quite closely related, the only difference being whether or not an "accessory" auxiliary cell filament is present. Kraft and Robins redefine the merged order Gigartinales as "Auxiliary cells present in various locations before or in absence of fertilization, diploidized by fusion with carpogonium via an external connection (connecting cells, tubes, or filaments), not merely by breakdown of intervening pit connections; pit plugs between somatic cells naked".

Table 4-2 summarizes the occurrence of various types of sporangia in the Florideophyceae.

Table 4-2 Types of sporangia *commonly found* in *most* members of various orders (exceptions apart) (after Guiry, 1978)

Order	Tetrasporangium			Polysporangium	Monosporangium
	Cruciate	Zonate	Tetrahedral		
Nemaliales	+	–	–	–	+
Cryptonemiales	+	+	–	–	+
Gigartinales	+	+	–	–	–
Rhodymeniales					
Rhodymeniaceae	+	–	+	–	–
Champiaceae	–	–	+	+	–
Ceramiales	±	–	+	+	+?

Some Ceramiaceae have parasporangia. Seirosporangia are monosporangia formed in chains on thalli other than carposporophytes and have been reported from Ceramiaceae, Dumontiaceae, and Acrochaetiaceae. Bisporangia have been recorded from Acrochaetiaceae, Corallinaceae, and Ceramiaceae.

The mitosporangial equivalents of tetrasporangia (i.e., tetraspores giving rise to tetrasporangial plants) are now known in *Callithamnion corymbosum, Rhodochorton concrescens, Acrochaetium proskaueri,* and several other species (see Guiry, 1978). Mitotic bisporangia (e.g., in Corallinaceae) and mitotic polysporangia (e.g., *Gastroclonium coulteri*) are also known.

While the majority of Florideophyceae form carpospores which develop into diploid tetrasporophytes, in some taxa of the Gigartinales, the sporangia developing from female reproductive organs have been shown to have the same ploidy level as the parent thallus. Thus, the occurrence of carposporangial plants derived from carpospores has been reported inter alia in *Gigartina stellata* (Fig. 4-19 A, B), *G. papillata*, *G. ochotensis*, and *Gymnogongrus leptophallus* (see Guiry, 1978).

Some members of the Ceramiaceae produce stalked tetrasporangia. A distinctive kind of stalk cell is also formed in the tetrasporangia of *Palmaria*.

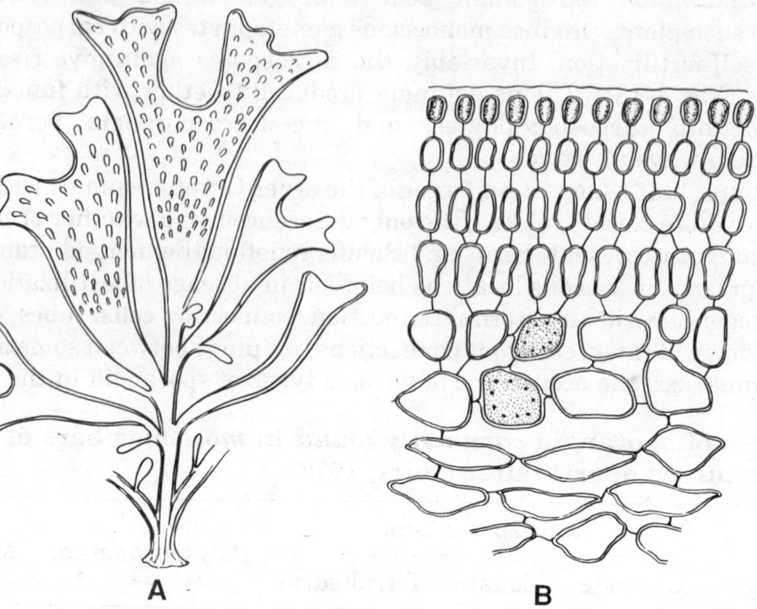

Fig. 4-19 *Gigartina stellata*. A, habit; B, section of thallus.

PHYLOGENY

A fairly homogeneous, well circumscribed group, the Rhodophyta apparently show a much closer relationship with the Cyanophyta than with any other algal phyla. The features shared by the two phyla are (1) the absence of flagellated structures; (2) the formation of similar biliproteins (phycocyanin and phycoerythrin) as the accessory photosynthetic pigments; (3) the presence of pit connections; (4) the accumulation of fairly similar food reserves, e.g., floridean starch in the Rhodophyta and cyanophycean starch in the Cyanophyta; (5) the production of chemically similar mucilages in the blue-green algae and in some Bangioideae and Nemalionales; and (6) similar patterns of fatty acid synthesis, which differ from those of other algae in that the fat content does not increase with increase in the age of the thallus, and that the nitrogen starvation is not a factor in fatty acid accumulation (Fogg and Collyer, 1954; see also Table 4-3).

However, the biliproteins of the Rhodophyta differ from those of the Cyanophyta in their spectral properties. The Cryptophyceae too are now known to possess biliproteins. The biliprotein allophycocyanin is probably identical with the phytochrome of higher plants, and future research may indicate the presence of this or other biliproteins in algal phyla other than the Rhodophyta and Cyanophyta. In view of these, too much phylogenetic importance should not be attached to the biliproteins (see also Table 4-4).

Table 4-3 Resemblances between Rhodophyta and Cyanophyta

Both have water-soluble phycobilins, located on phycobilisomes, as accessory pigments
Both have free trehalose and galactose
Linoleic acid and α-linoleic acid present
Neither nitrogen starvation nor aging of thallus has any effect on pattern of fatty acid accumulation
Xylans are major components in cellulose microfibrillar walls
Sulphated galactoses, uronic acids, glucose, and xylose are principal constituents of mucilage
Organization of photosynthetic thylakoids is similar, i.e., they occur singly and are widely separated
Patterns of isoenzymes involved in elaboration of polyglucosides are similar
Both lack flagellated stages
Both susceptible to viral infection

Table 4-4 Differences between Rhodophyta and Cyanophyta

	Red algae	Blue-green algae
Cell structure	Eucaryotic	Procaryotic
Pigments	Chlorophyll-a and -d, zeaxanthin, neoxanthin	Chlorophyll-a, myxoxanthin, myxoxanthophyll, oscillaxanthin
Cell wall	Cellulose and other carbohydrates present	Mucopolymers main component in certain forms
Motile stages	None	Nonflagellate multicellular motile stages, i.e., hormogonia formed in many forms; mature individuals of some species also motile though nonflagellate
True sexuality	Present in most members	Absent; a primitive type of parasexuality, i.e., genetic recombination, occurs in some members
Chromosomes	Typically eucaryotic	True chromosomes not known, DNA fibrils not associated with histones but present in nucleoplasm
Golgi bodies	Present	Absent
Endoplasmic reticulum	Present	Absent
Heterocysts and nitrogen fixation	None	Many species have heterocysts and can fix atmospheric nitrogen

The stacking together of photosynthetic thylakoids into distinct bands is regarded as an advanced feature and in this respect the Rhodophyta is the most primitive phylum among eucaryotic algae since in the red algae the photosynthetic lamellae are single, unorganized, widely separated, and not stacked into bands or multiple lamellae. Nonetheless, the phylum Rhodophyta is morphologically as complex as the Chlorophyta. Regarding the ancestry of the Rhodophyta, the two alternatives that have been suggested (see Klein and Cronquist, 1967) are that (1) they originated from some simple procaryotic blue-green algae, and (2) they were derived from some archaic eucaryotic algae which themselves originated from the blue-green algae. The fundamental disparity between the eucaryotic and procaryotic cellular organizations seems to rule out the existence of any direct link between the red and blue-green algae. It would seem more plausible to speculate that the former originated from some primitive nonflagellated eucaryotic ancestor possessing biliproteins.

SELECTED GENERA

Class: BANGIOPHYCEAE
Order: BANGIALES
Family: Bangiaceae
Genus: *Porphyra*

Occurrence

Porphyra grows attached to rocks in intertidal and sublittoral zones in shores from polar to tropical seas. Though particularly abundant in the North Pacific Sea, it has a worldwide distribution.

Morphology

It is a thalloid, blade-like or membranous marine alga. In some species, the blades may be over 70 cm long. The plant grows attached by rhizoids to rocks and other algae (or, attached to bamboo poles in sea farming in Japan).

The frond is parenchymatous and resembles the leaf of lettuce or thallus of *Ulva*. Some species have monostromatic (one cell layer thick) blades having one chromatophore per cell. Others have monostromatic blades with two chromatophores per cell. Still others have distromatic blades with a single chromatophore per cell. The chromatophores are stellate, with a pyrenoid. The cells are uninucleate. The growth of thalli is diffuse.

Some thalli have a small, inconspicuous, cuneate stipe (e.g., *P. miniata*). In this species, many thalli have deep folds but some are devoid of folds.

Reproduction

Vegetative In some species, the parent thallus gives rise to new foliar thalli directly.

Asexual and Sexual At maturity, the foliose thalli of most species of *Porphyra* show spores (Fig. 4-20 A, B) or reproductive units of two different sizes along their apices and edges. The larger spores are termed alpha-spores and are pigmented. The smaller, colourless spores are called β-spores. The β-spores mainly occur along the outer edges of the thallus. The vegetative cells enlarge and undergo two longitudinal intersecting divisions followed by a transverse division to form 8 daughter protoplasts. These may constitute alpha-spores and shed as such or may undergo further divisions and be released as small β-spores. *P. hawkes* and some other species also produce prolific monospores which germinate directly into new plants.

There is considerable variability in sexual reproduction and life history of different species. Most species show an alternation of heteromorphic phases. For instance, *P. umbilicalis* has a foliose thallus which may alternate with a filamentous (Fig. 4-7) *Conchocelis* phase, but the alternation of phases is not universal or obligatory.

P. gardneri, P. angusta, P. crispata, P. papenfussii, and some other species have slight protuberances (called protrichogynes) on their carpogonia, but *P. linearis* and *P. dentata* lack such protrichogynes. Functionally, the protrichogynes are homologous with the trichogynes of Florideophyceae.

Hawkes (1978) has proved the existence of sexual reproduction in *P. gardneri*. He has observed the attachment of a spermatium to a protrichogyne and the subsequent transfer of spermatial contents to the carpogonium.

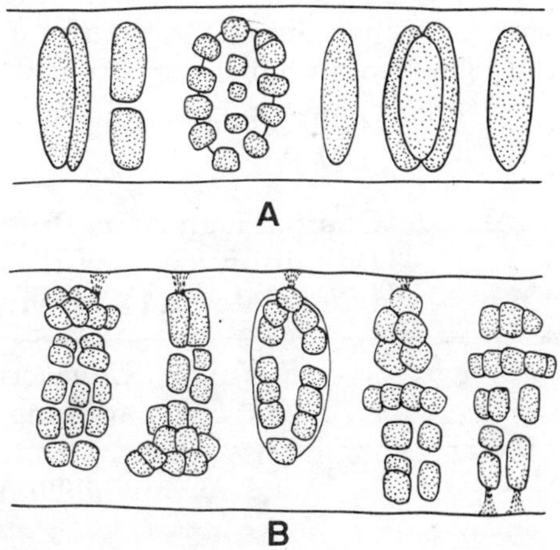

Fig. 4-20 *Porphyra*, transverse section through thallus. A, early stages in spore formation; B, late stages in spore formation.

In *P. miniata*, the carpospores tend to be formed in groups of fours in a marginal zone. The spermatangia are generally intermixed with the carposporangia. In most species, the carpospores upon liberation drift and sink in the sea where some of them settle on molluscan shells or shell fragments, giving rise to the *Conchocelis phase*.

It is believed that the alpha-spores develop into the *Conchocelis* phase, whereas the β-spores tend to disintegrate in culture, and hence their function in nature is obscure.

The foliose thallus seems to be haploid. The *Conchocelis* phases of some species are diploid but those of some other species of *Porphyra* are haploid (see Mumford and Cole, 1977). The *Conchocelis* phase of *P. gardneri* has pit connections. In this species, the photoperiod seems to influence the induction of alpha- and β-spores. The pit connections in the *Conchocelis* phase of *P. columbina* are formed as irregular ingrowths from lateral walls, associated with the presence of lomasomes.

The *Conchocelis* phases of many species can reproduce in a variety of ways, both to replicate the *Conchocelis* itself and to give rise to the succeeding generation of the foliose thallus. Sometimes, the monospores are formed on the *Conchocelis* and they replicate it. In other cases, the monospores produced by the *Conchocelis* give rise to the foliose phase.

Specialized branches, called conchosporangial branches (Fig. 4-13), develop on a mature *Conchocelis* and produce conchospores that develop into bipolar sporelings; these latter can grow into the foliar phase.

We still know very little about the various kinds of habitats occupied by the perennating *Conchocelis*; shells are perhaps its principal habitat.

Some forms of *Porphyra* do not produce a *Conchocelis*. Two main variations may occur in such species, namely, the carpospores may develop (1) directly into the typical *Porphyra* thalli; and (2) into diminutive, miniature *Porphyra* thalli which propagate by formation of spores; these spores germinate and develop into mature *Porphyra* thalli.

Table 4-5 compares the cell structure of adult thallus and *Conchocelis* phase of the bangiophycean algae (including *Porphyra*) with that of adult thallus of the Florideophyceae. Since the cell structure of the *Conchocelis* phases strikingly resembles that of the Florideophyceae but differs from that of the macroscopic phases of the Bangiophyceae, the *Conchocelis* phase might well serve as an evolutionary link between the Bangiophyceae and the Florideophyceae.

Table 4-5 Comparison of cell structure of adult thallus and *Conchocelis* phase of Bangiophyceae with that of adult thallus of Florideophyceae (modified from Cole and Conway, 1975)

Character	*Conchocelis* phase of Bangiophyceae	Adult thallus of Florideophyceae	Adult thallus of Bangiophyceae
Habit	Filamentous	Filamentous	Foliose, rarely filamentous
Mode of growth	Apical or intercalary	Apical	Diffuse or intercalary
Chromatophore(s)	1 or more, commonly ribbon-shaped, rarely parietal or stellate	Several, ribbon-shaped, discoid or parietal	Single, central, stellate
Plugged pit connections	Present	Present	Absent
Central vacuole	Present	Present	Absent
Pyrenoid in chromatophore	Present	Absent	Present
Peripheral thylakoids in chromatophore	Present	Present	Absent

Pathology

Porphyra is a valuable crop in maritime countries such as Japan where it is grown for food as "nori". Like other crops, it is susceptible to several parasitic and nonparasitic diseases. A species of *Pythium* causes the red rot disease of *Porphyra*. The hyphae of *Pythium* penetrate the algal cells and kill them. "Akagusare" or the red wasting disease is caused by *Pythium porphyrae*. Its symptoms include small, rapidly coalescing lesions on algal fronds. The pathogen penetrates by appressoria formation, both inter- and intracellularly. The "Ryokuhan-byo" or green spot rotting disease is caused by species of *Pseudomonas* and *Vibrio*. This disease is endemic in Japanese nori farms. It causes greenish spots and discolourations on the fronds of *Porphyra* (Andrews, 1976). A chytrid also parasitizes the alga. The diseases called faded rot and perforated rot are caused by physiological or nutritional deficiencies or disorders. The shell-inhabiting *Conchocelis* phase often suffers from such common physiological diseases as yellow spot, green spot, turtle shell pattern and shark skin (Ogata, 1975).

Family: Compsopogonaceae
Genus: *Compsopogon*

Occurrence

Compsopogon is a freshwater red alga distributed in tropical and subtropical regions.

Morphology

The thallus consists of a cluster of ramelliferous caespitose, fine branches (ramelli) (Fig. 4-21 A). The young ramelli consist of single linear series of cylindrical or discoidal cells, the apical cell being generally small and pointed. Both the young and older branches have a 1–3 cell layer thick cortical investment of polygonal cells which are commonly elongated. Several discoidal or elongate chromatophores occur in each cell.

The lower ends of cells of some branches give off two or more tubular outgrowths which become cut off from the axial cells by septa, grow downwards, and divide and redivide to form a cellular investment around the underlying axial cell.

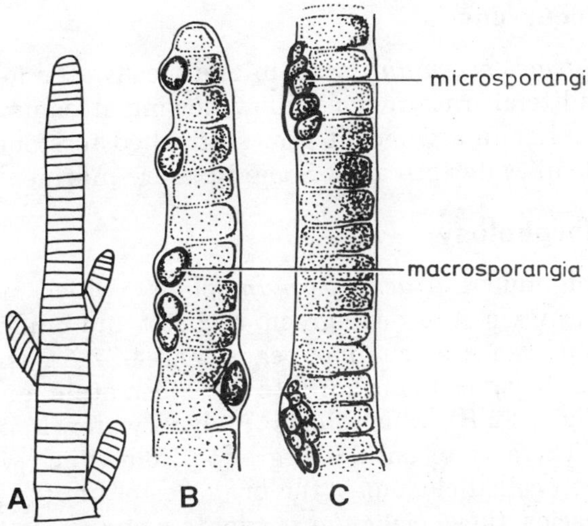

Fig. 4-21 *Compsopogon caeruleus*. A, tip of filament; B, filament with macrosporangia; C, filament with microsporangia.

Reproduction

Asexual and Sexual Spherical monosporangia are generally formed on the cortical portions of old filaments, rarely on the uncorticated parts of young filaments. A parental cell divides unequally by an oblique wall, cutting off a spore. These spores are called monospores. They germinate, giving rise to new individuals.

Some strains of *C. caeruleus* tend to form slightly dimorphic microsporangia (Fig. 4-21 B) and macrosporangia (Fig. 4-21 C). The fate of these sporangia is obscure.

Though primary pit connections are diagnostic features of all red algae in the class Florideophycidae, they have also been reported in a few genera (such as *Porphyra, Bangia, Rhodochaete*, and *Compsopogon*) of the Bangiophycidae (Scott *et al.*, 1988).

There has been some uncertainty regarding the systematic position of *Compsopogon* within the Rhodophyta. Because of its complex macroscopic thallus organization whereby axial cells develop cortication and because of the ability of apical cells to divide and contribute to filament elongation, the genus has attracted comparison with some advanced genera of the class Florideophycidae (Dixon, 1973). However, since it has been reported to lack a sexual cycle, pit connections, and predominantly apical growth (Bold and Wynne, 1985), it is usually placed in the less advanced class Bangiophycidae. The work of Scott *et al.* (1988), reporting the presence of pit connections in *C. caeruleus*, has cast doubt on the assignment of the genus in the Bangiophycidae. According to Scott *et al.*, pit connections are consistently located between axial cells, between axial and cortical cells, and between cortical cells, in *C. caeruleus*. These pit connections resemble those seen in *Rhodochaete* in being extremely small and in possessing pit plugs that lack both plug caps and cap membranes. It appears that the pit connections of *Compsopogon* and *Rhodochaete* may be the simplest known among the red algae.

Class: FLORIDEOPHYCEAE
Order: NEMALIONALES
Family: Batrachospermaceae
Genus: *Batrachospermum*

Occurrence

Batrachospermum is an inland freshwater form widely distributed in tropical, subtropical, and temperate regions. Slow flowing streams, waterfalls, and oligotrophic lakes are some of the habitats where it grows attached to stones. Most species prefer relatively well aerated 'clean' water streams. Some taxa are marine.

Morphology

The adult *Batrachospermum* plants, which may be up to 15 cm long, are generally bluish-green, violet or olive-green, and soft and mucilaginous. To the naked eye, each plant appears as a branching chain of beads (Fig. 4-22 A). The alga is differentiated into a prostrate system which serves to anchor it to the substratum, and an erect branched system, made up of whorls (Fig. 4-22 B), which floats freely in water. Many species are attached by rhizoids.

The axes of unlimited growth from which whorls of branches of limited growth arise have been called cladomes, the branches of limited growth being designated as pleuridia. In most species, these cladomes originate as buds on the simple erect filaments of the heterotrichous

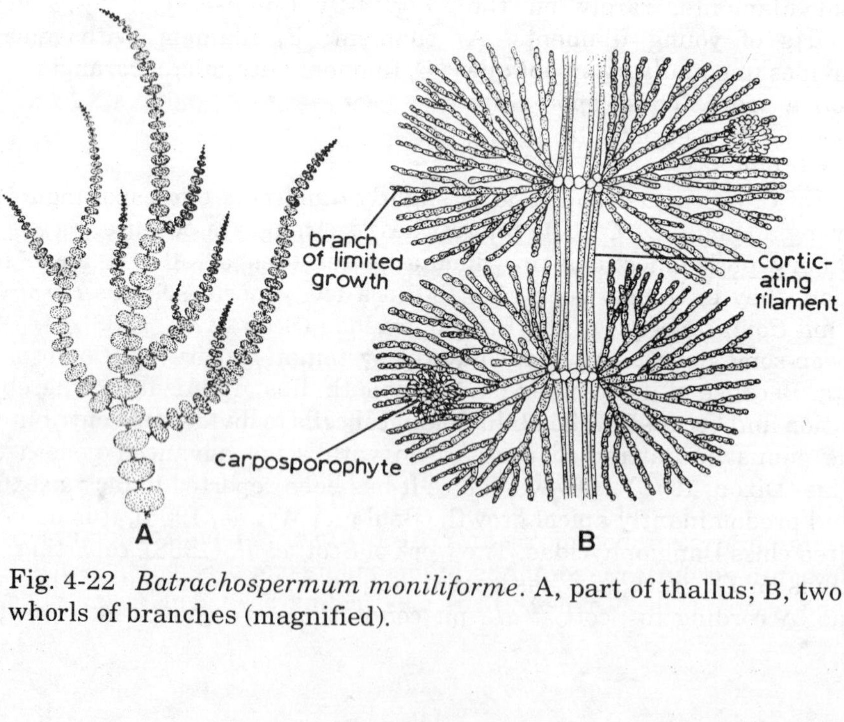

Fig. 4-22 *Batrachospermum moniliforme*. A, part of thallus; B, two whorls of branches (magnified).

Chantransia stage (some phycologists have renamed *Chantransia* as *Pseudochantransia* now; see Von Stosch and Theil, 1979). Since long it has been the general belief that the gametophyte (cladomes), the carposporophyte, as well as the *Chantransia* stage are haploid, but recent researches have established that the carposporophyte and the *Chantransia* stages, both in *Batrachospermum* and the closely related freshwater genus *Lemanea*, are diploid (Eikhorst-Hurdlebrink, 1973; Magne, 1967).

Von Stosch and Theil (1979) have shown that the adult *Batrachospermum* phase does not originate from the erect filaments of the *Chantransia* stage but arises directly from a crustose, prostrate, prothallus-like structure. It seems that a few lowermost segments of the gametophytic cladomes may be diploid whereas the remaining segments may be haploid. This kind of situation has a parallel in the green alga *Prasiola*.

The nodal branches of limited growth are composed of moniliform cells and arise from just below the septa of the axial filament, or from branches of unlimited growth whose cells are much longer than those of branch whorls. The cells are uninucleate (Fig. 4-23 A) and contain several parietal chromatophores, each with a single pyrenoid.

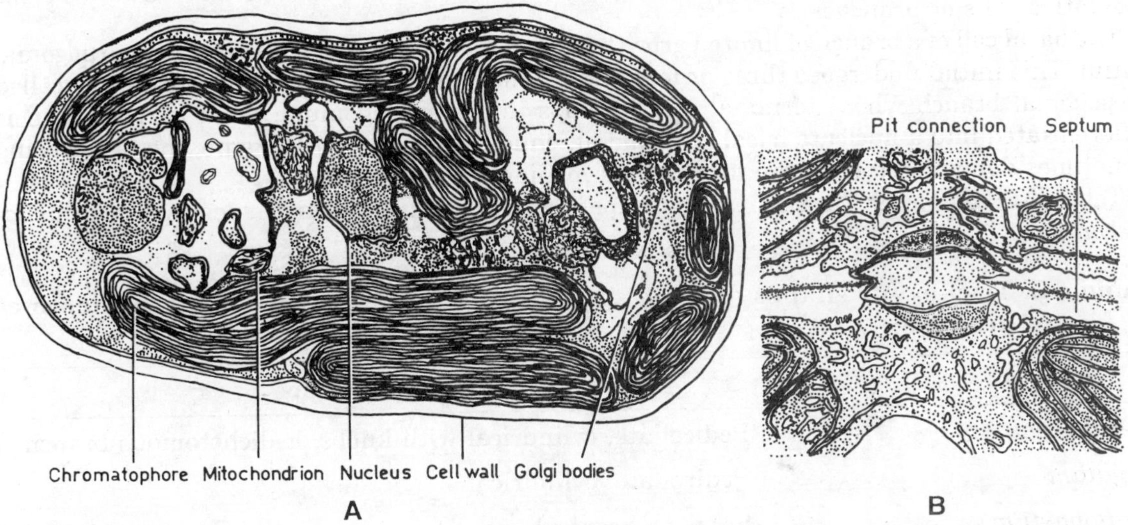

Fig. 4-23 *Batrachospermum*. A, diagrammatic sketch of electron micrograph of transverse section of cell; B, diagrammatic sketch of electron micrograph of septum region.

The growth of the axial filament and of the branches of unlimited growth occurs by means of an apical cell which cuts off segments transversely and produces a uniseriate row of cells. From each cell, there arise near the septum 4–6 lateral projections which soon become separated from the parent cell by a wall and function as initials of branches of limited growth. After the formation of the lateral branches, their basal cells give rise to corticating filaments. A branch of unlimited growth may also develop from one of these basal cells. A characteristic feature is the presence of a closely appressed cortex around the central axis of this genus (and also of other genera belonging to the Family Batrachospermaceae).

The thallus is composed of three major cell types which develop as a result of three different modes of cell division. The apical cells have a distally located nucleus. When this divides, one remains distal whereas the other migrates to the proximal end of the cell. When a pericentral cell develops from an axial one, the nucleus remains within the latter, migrates near the junction of the two cells and there divides; one daughter nucleus then migrates to the lateral initial whereas the other moves back into the axial cell. The nucleus remains in the mother cell when a pleuridial cell initial grows and expands.

Recently, a new type of vegetative pit connection (Fig. 4-23 B) in the main axis of *B. sirodotii* has been described by Aghajanian (1977). It is made of a rivet-like plug which occludes a pore in the pit-ring. This pit plug seems to be derived from the endoplasmic reticulum and Golgi apparatus.

Reproduction

Asexual and Sexual *Batrachospermum* reproduces sexually by the formation of spermatia and eggs, and asexually by carpospores.

The plants are monoecious or dioecious. The terminal or subterminal cells of branches of limited growth constitute the spermatangial initials. Each initial produces one or two spermatangia which are generally colourless and can therefore be easily distinguished from vegetative cells or branches.

The basal cell of a branch of limited growth cuts off a segment which is called the carpogonial initial. This initial undergoes three or four transverse divisions and forms a four-to-five-celled carpogonial branch whose terminal cell develops into a carpogonium. Each carpogonium is differentiated into a nucleate basal part and an enucleate neck or trichogyne, the latter being sometimes demarcated from the former by a median constriction.

Table 4-6 compares the trichogyne shapes of some representative species of *Batrachospermum.*

Table 4-6 Trichogyne shapes of some species of *Batrachospermum* (after Sheath *et al.*, 1986)

Species	Trichogyne shape
caerulescens	Pedicellate, cylindrical with knobs or dichotomous branch
virgatum	Pedicellate, cylindrical
keratophytum	Sessile, obconical
boryanum	Sessile, elliptical-clavate
moniliforme	Sessile, clavate-lageniform
carpocontortum	Sessile, with protrusions and bends

The spermatia are probably carried passively along water currents to the carpogonia. During fertilization, the spermatium nucleus, after migrating through the trichogyne, fuses with the egg nucleus (Fig. 4-24 A, B) of the carpogonium. After fertilization, the trichogyne shrivels and the zygote nucleus divides meiotically to form four haploid nuclei. At this time, the fertilized carpogonium develops several small protuberances. Each of the four nuclei divides mitotically and one of the two resulting nuclei migrates into a protuberance which then becomes separated from the carpogonium and starts functioning as an initial of a gonimoblast filament. Thus, a number of branched gonimoblast filaments (Fig. 4-24 C) arise from the base of the carpogonium. The terminal cells of the gonimoblasts later differentiate into carposporangia within which the diploid carpospores are formed singly. The cluster of

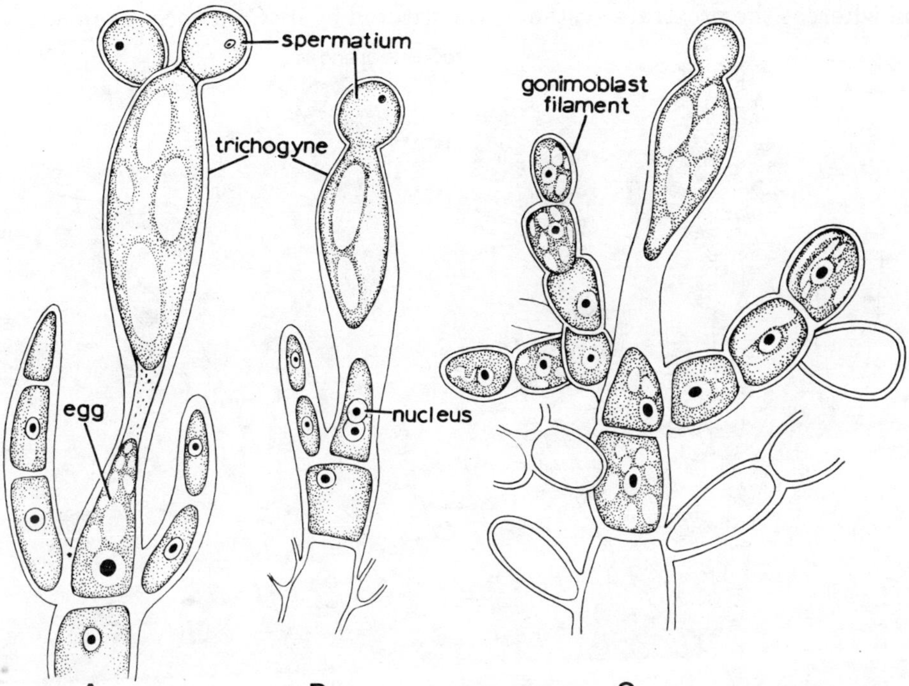

Fig. 4-24 *Batrachospermum moniliforme*. A–C, fertilization and post-fertilization stages.

gonimoblast filaments, along with the associated carposporangia, constitutes the carposporophyte which grows as a parasite on the female gametophyte. Since meiosis occurs during the division of the zygote nucleus, the carposporophyte and carpospores are haploid. Some of the vegetative cells surrounding the carpogonium grow in the meanwhile and form a loose sheath of sterile branches that encloses the carposporophyte which, along with the sheath, forms a characteristic fruit body known as the cystocarp.

Each carpospore on germination forms a branched, heterotrichous protonema-like filament. This constitutes a juvenile stage in the life history of *Batrachospermum* and was previously believed to be an independent algal genus *Chantransia*. Many freshwater species of *Chantransia* have been found to be the juvenile stage (Fig. 4-25 A) of *Batrachospermum*. The *Chantransia* thalli reproduce either asexually by means of monospores formed singly in the monosporangia (Fig. 4-25 B) or by their apical cells being transformed into a meiocyte, three spores of which degenerate; the fourth spore, however, remains attached to the sporophyte and gives rise to the haploid *Batrachospermum* cladome. Thus, the monospores merely serve as an accessory means of multiplication of the *Chantransia* stage. The *Batrachospermum* plant arises from the *Chantransia* stage as a lateral outgrowth. Interpreted in terms of the heterotrichous habit, both the *Batrachospermum* phase and the *Chantransia* phase constitute the two systems of a heterotrichous plant, the former representing the erect system and the latter the prostrate system. A parallel situation is found in another red alga *Porphyra* which itself represents the erect system, whereas the prostrate system is constituted by its *Conchocelis* phase.

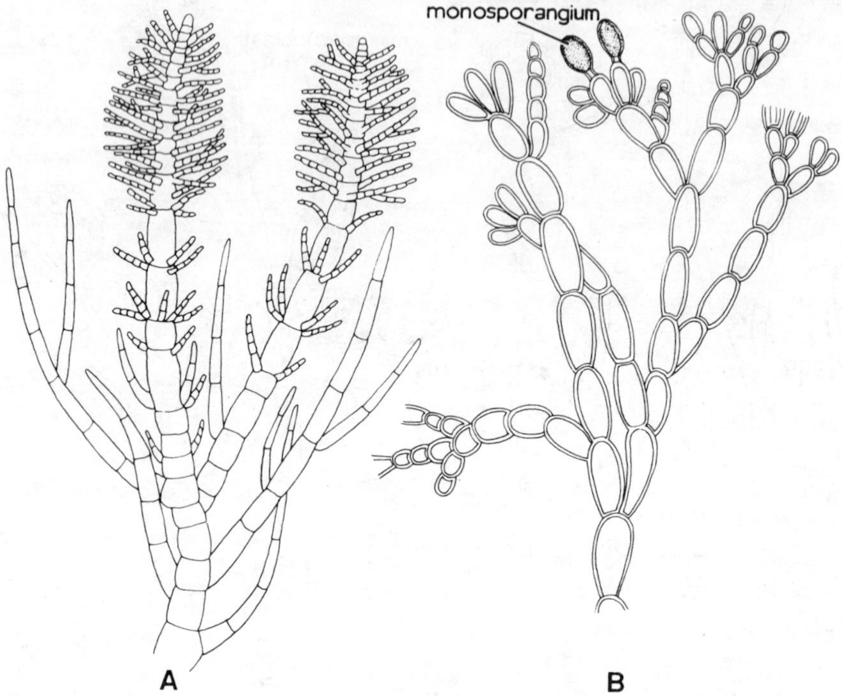

Fig. 4-25 *Batrachospermum.* A, *B. ectocarpum, Chantransia* stage; B, *B. lochmodes,* monosporangia.

Batrachospermum breutelii found commonly in South Africa forms gonimoblast propagules which are zonately septated into 4–6 unequal uninucleate chambers. The propagule initials are single-celled, invariably associated with the fertilized carpogonium and borne on one-celled gonimoblast filaments and divide by simultaneous infurrowing. Mature propagules are thick-walled; each chamber contains numerous chloroplasts, mitochondria, lipid globules, starch granules, and small vacuoles. The chloroplasts have single thylakoids with a peripheral encircling thylakoid. Septations between chambers have pit plugs with two cap layers, the outer of which is domed and unevenly stained. The propagules are released in their entirety and one or more chambers germinate into one or two unbranched *Chantransia*-phase filaments (Sheath and Whittick, 1995). These filaments may wrap around the parent gametophyte or attach to it. The *Chantransia*-phase filaments appear to act as a basal stage of the gametophyte. *Chantransia*-phase cells have an ultrastructure similar to the propagule chambers. The chromosome number is $n = 5$ for spermatangial initials and $2n = 10$ for *Chantransia*-phase filaments (Sheath and Whittick, 1995).

Life Cycle

Batrachospermum includes three kinds of haploid somatic phases in its life cycle, viz., (1) the free-living gametophytic phase, (2) the parasitic carposporophytic phase, and (3) the free-living *Chantransia* phase. The gametophytes reproduce sexually through the formation of spermatia and eggs which unite to form zygotes. The zygote germinates mitotically, forming a large number of branched gonimoblast filaments with their terminal cells functioning as carposporangia. Thus, a diploid carposporophyte parasitic on the gametophyte results from germination of the zygote. The carposporophyte in turn gives rise to the *Chantransia* phase and *Chantransia* gives rise to *Batrachospermum* by reduction division. Both the carposporophytic and *Chantransia* phases are asexual, and the latter perpetuates asexually by monospores.

Cytologically, the life cycle of the alga is diplohaplontic, and morphologically trimorphic because of the succession of three distinct morphological phases.

Family: Nemalionaceae
Genus: *Nemalion*

Occurrence

It is a lithophyte in the intertidal and littoral zones.

Morphology

It forms slender, multiaxial, worm-like thalli which are sometimes sparingly branched (Fig. 4-26 A). The thallus is made of intertwined branching filaments which give off tufts or whorls of lateral branching filaments of limited growth. These latter are composed of moniliform, photosynthetic cells. The tips of some out-turned branches bear a colourless hair.

Reproduction

Vegetative Vegetative proliferation may occur by means of detached branches.

Sexual Reproductive cells differentiate in the tufts of photosynthetic branches. The carpogonium occurs terminally on the carpogonium branch (4-celled) formed within the tuft (Fig. 4-26 B).

Spermatangia are borne on a conspicuous filament arising from the ultimate cells of an assimilatory filament. Each spermatangial filament has 4–5 cells and is sparsely provided with one- to several-celled branches. Except for the one or two lowermost cells, all cells of the filament produce one or two spermatangia (Fig. 4-26 C).

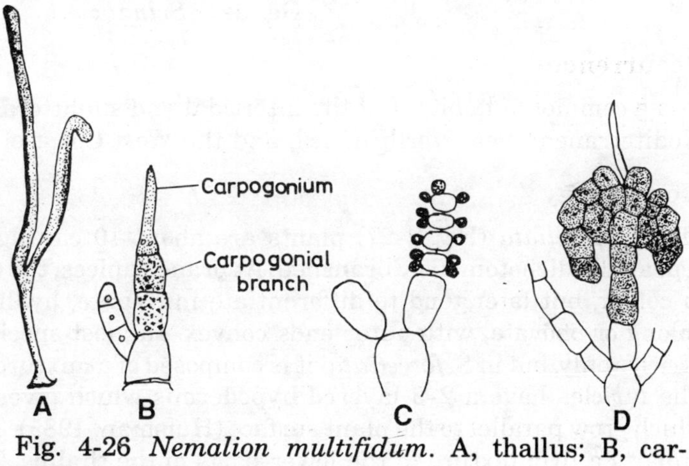

Fig. 4-26 *Nemalion multifidum*. A, thallus; B, carpogonial branch; C, spermatangial branch; D, gonimoblast development.

After fertilization, the zygote divides mitotically. The gonimoblasts develop (Fig. 4-26 D) and form cystocarp. The apical cells of gonimoblasts release carpospores which germinate into a sporophyte which is, in some species, an *Acrochaetium*-like plant.

There is some indication that the tetrasporophytes of *N. vermiculare* arise best in long-day conditions. Sometimes, the *Acrochaetium* phase produces both monosporangia and tetrasporangia. Masuda and Umezaki (1977) have reported that liberated tetraspores grow into filamentous plants resembling carpospore germlings. The monospores develop in the same manner as tetraspores and form erect *Nemalion* thalli.

In *N. helminthoides*, the carposporophyte differentiates into four distinct regions, viz., (1) the fusion cell, (2) the sterile gonimoblast cells, (3) the carposporangial mother cells, and (4) the carposporangia (Ramm-Anderson and Wetherbee, 1982). The gonimoblast is produced by apically-dividing, monopodial filaments of limited growth which sometimes become pseudodichotomous. The gonimoblast sometimes shows sympodial growth. Successive carposporangia are occasionally proliferated from a mother carposporangium after the carpospores have been released. As the carposporophyte matures, the gonimoblast initial, the stalk cell, the hypogynous and subhypogynous cells fuse. Except for this fusion cell, all other cells of the carposporophyte show organelle polarity and contain a distally located, lobed chloroplast and a proximal nucleus.

The erect, cylindrical axes of the gametophytes of *N. helminthoides* are multiaxial whereas the tetrasporophytes are entirely uniaxial and prostrate. The species is heteromorphic with tetraspores being formed under short-day conditions on the prostrate tetrasporophytes and giving rise to uniaxial prostrate growths that are morphologically similar to the uniaxial tetrasporophytes. The induction of multiaxial erect axes on these uniaxial, tetraspore-derived thalli is a long-day photoperiodic response (Cunningham and Guiry, 1989).

The carposporophyte of *Nemalion* is generally much smaller than that of *Polysiphonia*. The gonimoblast of *Nemalion* mostly grows monopodially but may show some sympodial growth later. In contrast, that of *Polysiphonia* shows extensive sympodial growth.

Family: Galaxauraceae
Genus: *Scinaia*

Occurrence

It is a common inhabitant of the intertidal and sublittoral zones in north western Europe, the Mediterranean Sea, North Africa, and the West Coast of India.

Morphology

The *S. forcellata* (Fig. 4-27) plants are about 10 cm high, terete, cylindrical, irregularly or repeatedly dichotomously branched. At branch apices, the cortical cells are at first small and red in colour, but later tend to differentiate into large, hyaline utricles. Utricles (Fig. 4-28) are oblong or obovate, with outer ends convex. In most species, the cortex is made up of inflated utricles only, but in *S. forcellata*, it is composed of a mixture of inflated utricles and smaller cells. The utricles have a 2–3 layered hypodermis which gives off secondary, unbranched rhizoids which grow parallel to the plant surface (Huisman, 1985). They constitute a tangled mass which imparts a firm texture to the lower parts of the thallus. The branches of *S. moniliformis* and *S. indica* are regularly constricted so that they become moniliform (Fig. 4-29).

In surface view, the cortex of most species looks like a rosette.

Reproduction

Vegetative Vegetative propagation may occur from detached branches. The coloured cortical cells bear monosporangia singly or in clusters.

Sexual The plants of *S. forcellata* are monoecious.

The spermatangial branches arise from hypodermal cells. They are 3–4 celled and penetrate between the utricles. A spermatangial mother cell bears 1–3 spermatangia.

Three-celled carpogonial branches emanate from subcortical cells. Before fertilization, the basal cell of the branch gives off many short branches which make up the pericarp around the developing cystocarp. The second cell (=hypogynous) of the carpogonial branch cuts off a one-celled and a two-celled branch (Fig. 4-30). The carpogonium bears a long trichogyne which shrivels off after fertilization. The fertilized carpogonium directly produces 3–4 gonimoblast initials (Fig. 4-31) which then produce compact gonimoblasts (Huisman, 1985). A fusion cell comprised of the carpogonium, hypogynous cell, and basal cell of the carpogonial branch is then formed. The fusion cell expands. The free gonimoblasts project into the pyriform cystocarp cavity (Fig. 4-15).

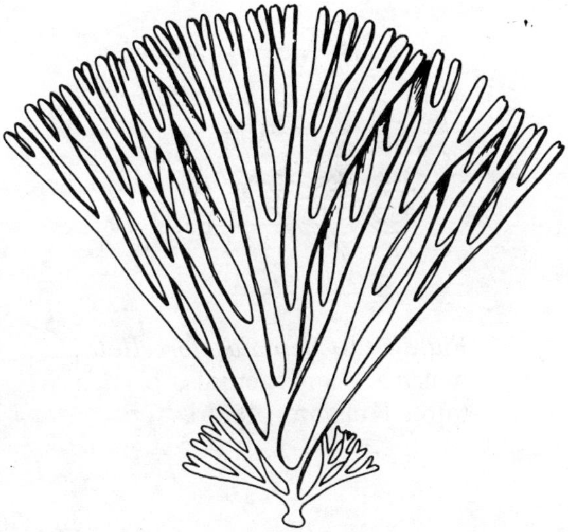

Fig. 4-27 *Scinaia forcellata*, habit.

The carposporangia are borne in chains at the ends of gonimoblasts.

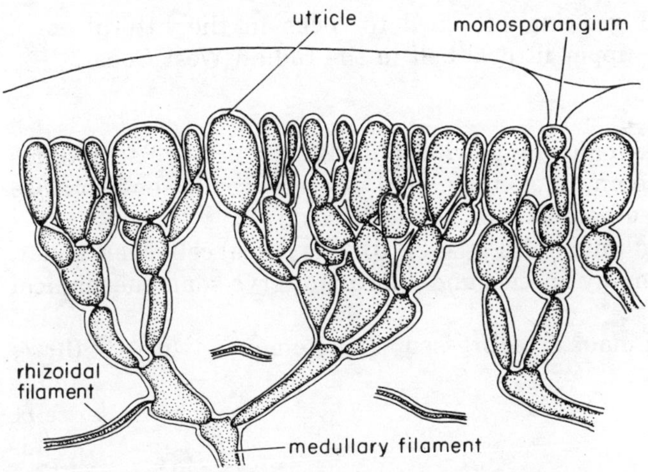

Fig. 4-28 *Scinaia forcellata*, section through part of thallus, showing immature cortex with several coloured cortical cells (after Huisman, 1985).

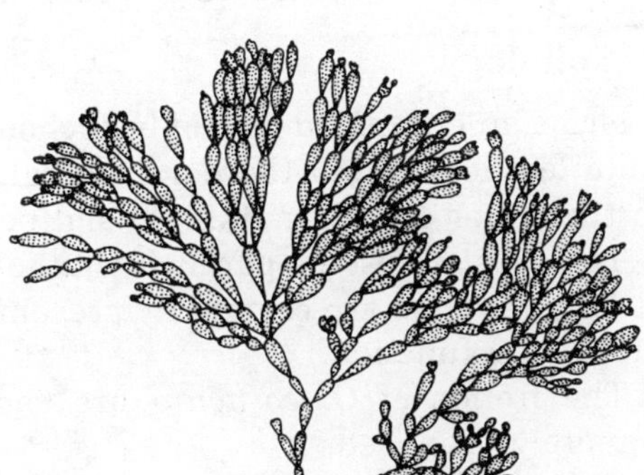

Fig. 4-29 *Scinaia indica*, part of thallus.

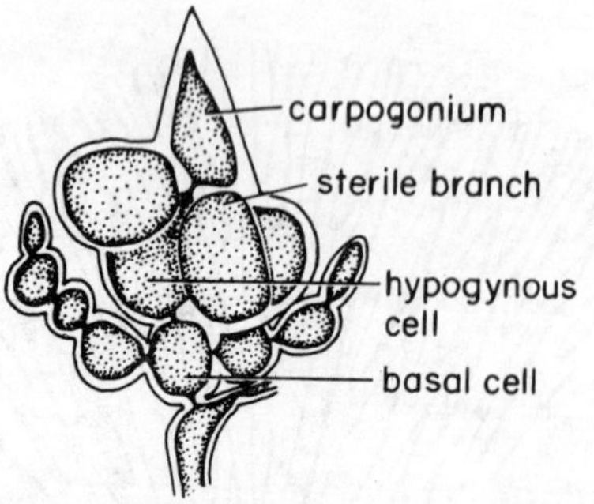

Fig. 4-30 *Scinaia forcellata*, mature carpogonial branch (after Huisman, 1985).

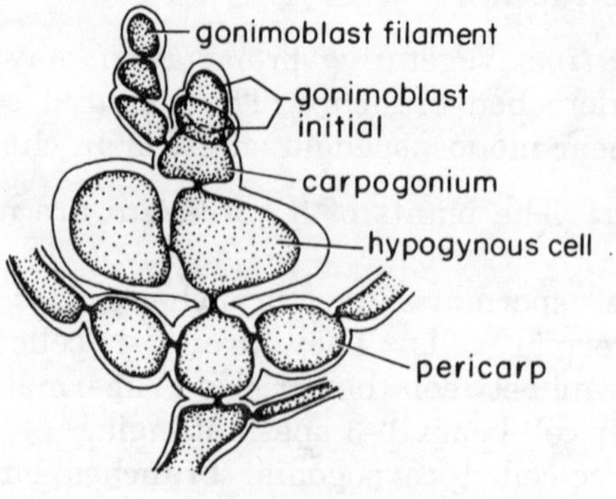

Fig. 4-31 *Scinaia forcellata*, formation of three gonimoblast initials from fertilized carpogonium.

Order: GELIDIALES

The members placed in this order are uniaxial, lacking distinct auxiliary cells. The carpogonial filament is one-celled and this cell itself constitutes the carpogonium. The tetrasporangia are cruciate.

Family: Gelidiaceae
Genus: *Gelidium*

Occurrence

It is a widely distributed small seaweed growing attached to rocks in the littoral zone. *G. corneum* grows on rocks in pools in the upper littoral belt in the Indian West Coast.

Morphology

It forms an entangled mat of branched anastomosing polymorphic axes, which are sometimes quite leathery. From the dorsiventral, creeping stolon, clusters of erect fronds tend to arise on the upper side (Fig. 4-32 A) and peg-like holdfasts on the lower side.

The axes are pseudoparenchymatous and uniaxial (Fig. 4-32 B). The apical cell is lenticular. Internal hyphae are commonly present in many species and appear to serve some mechanical supporting function.

The fronds of *G. corneum* are cartilaginous, compressed, dichotomous, twice or thrice pinnately branched.

Reproduction

Vegetative Vegetative propagation occurs from detached parts of fronds or stolons.

Sexual The spermatangia (Fig. 4-33) and carpogonia (Fig. 4-34) are formed from the cortical cells of upright fronds. The cystocarps occur near the terminal portions of the thalli or in specialized club-shaped lateral branches of limited growth. The cystocarp-bearing branches of *G. corneum* are swollen.

Fig. 4-32 *Gelidium pulchellum*. A, part of thallus; B, section of apical region.

Cruciately dividing tetrasporangia (Fig. 4-35) are located terminally in unmodified vegetative blades or in clavate structures borne marginally on these blades.

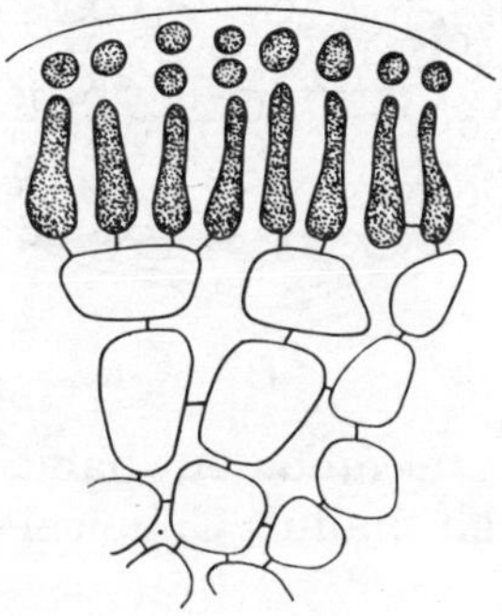

Fig. 4-33 *Gelidium* sp., spermatangia.

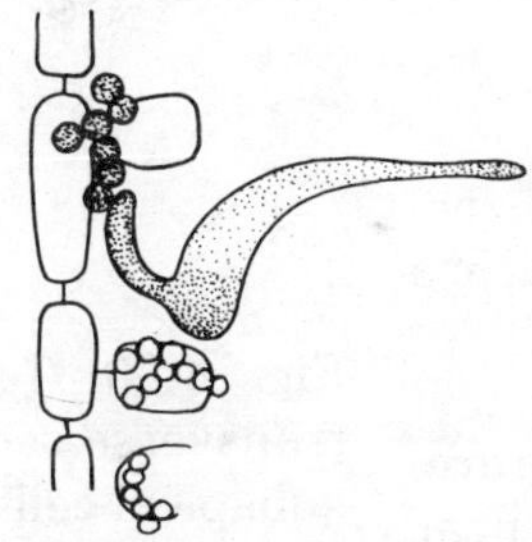

Fig. 4-34 *Gelidium* sp., carpogonium and its fusion with nurse cells.

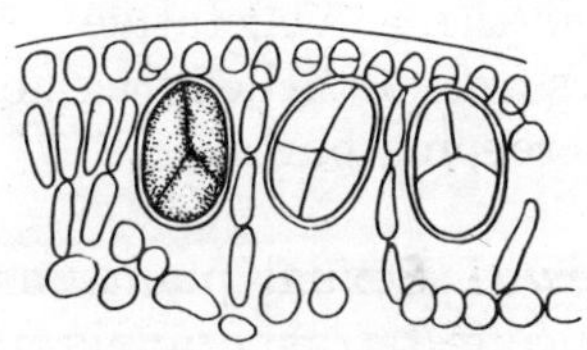

Fig. 4-35 *Gelidium* sp., formation of tetrasporangia.

In *G. robustum*, both tetrasporangial and carposporangial plants exhibit rhythmic activity in spore discharge. The carposporangial plants release more spores than do tetrasporangial plants, and they also remain active over a longer duration of time as compared to the tetrasporangial plants.

In *Gelidium pteridifolium* nutritive filaments are initiated prior to carpogonial elongation; functional carpogonia are intercalary; a fertilized carpogonium becomes multinucleate as it cuts off gonimoblast initials; nuclei in the cortical filaments borne on the carpogonium divide and enlarge following fertilization and pit plugs break down forming channels between the carpogonium and adjoining cortical filaments (Hommersand and Fredericq, 1988). In this species, terminal gonimoblast cells first fuse with the terminal cells of nutritive filaments and later unite with the fusion cells themselves. Unfused, uninucleate gonimoblast cells cut off the first carposporangia, and multinucleate fusion cells later produce a second series of carposporangia (Hommersand and Fredericq, 1988). According to these workers, auxiliary cells are absent in the Gelidiaceae but that particular fusions occurring in this family represent an early evolutionary stage that might potentially give rise to an independent auxiliary cell system.

Genus: *Gelidiella*

Occurrence

It is a lithophyte in the littoral zone.

Morphology

It grows as low tufts of entangled, anastomosing, branching, wiry thalli (Fig. 4-36 A) up to 2 cm high. The erect fronds bear distichously arranged opposite to subopposite pinnae. The thallus construction is pseudoparenchymatous (Fig. 4-36 B) and the growth occurs by an apical cell (Fig. 4-36 C).

Unlike *Gelidium, Gelidiella* commonly lacks internal hyphae.

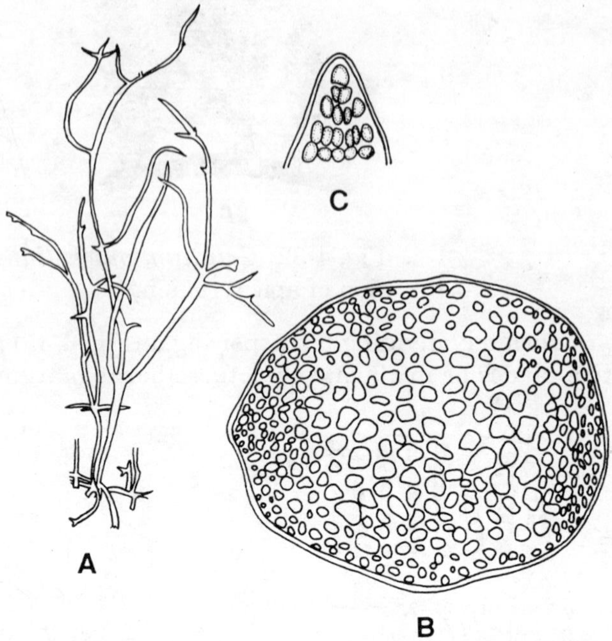

Fig. 4-36 *Gelidiella myrioclada*. A, habit; B, transverse section through thallus; C, apical and subapical cells.

Reproduction

Vegetative Vegetative propagation occurs from detached fragments of branches or creeping parts.

Sexual Sexual plants are rather rare. Cruciate tetrasporangia are formed near the apical portion of vegetative pinnae which then metamorphose into spathulate stichidia.

Order: GIGARTINALES

This is a large order of fairly large and usually fleshy red algae. It includes several families sharing the primary distinguishing character of the auxiliary cell not being borne on any accessory or special filament. The auxiliary cell is a large, intercalary cell of an ordinary vegetative filament and is differentiated and observable prior to fertilization.

Some members, e.g., *Turnerella*, produce a crustose tetrasporophyte and a foliose gametophyte which alternate in the life cycle.

Family: Gracilariaceae
Genus: *Gracilaria*

Occurrence

Gracilaria is commercially one of the more valuable red algae. The genus includes over 90 species widely distributed in temperate and tropical seas. *G. verrucosa* is quite common in intertidal zones; it is attached by a perennial disc which produces several upright cylindrical branches every year. This species thrives in turbid, shallow lagoons near freshwater inflows rich in nutrients.

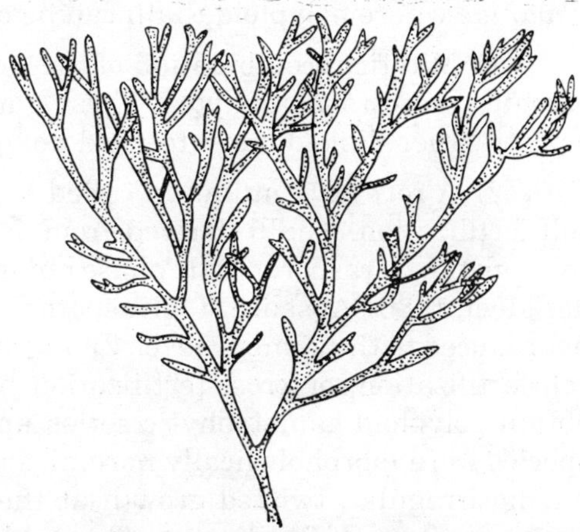

Fig. 4-37 *Gracilaria mammillaris*, part of thallus showing mode of branching.

Morphology

The alga grows as tangled clumps of irregularly, dichotomously, or trichotomously branched, cylindrical, terete (Figs. 4-37 and 4-38 A) or flattened thalli with a cartilaginous texture. The main axis may or may not be crozier-like and may possess or lack certain sinusoidal constrictions.

The thallus is uniaxial, though this is not quite obvious in *G. verrucosa* (Fig. 4-38 B, C). A single apical cell terminates each branch tip. The germlings have single apical cells but, instead of cutting off a series of cells to form an axial filament, a solid cylinder of isodiametric cells is built up. Some species form unilateral branchlets disposed in rows along the main axis. Some species have hair cells.

G. epihippisora (Fig. 4-39) is highly polymorphic. Its fertile thalli are much stronger than sterile plants.

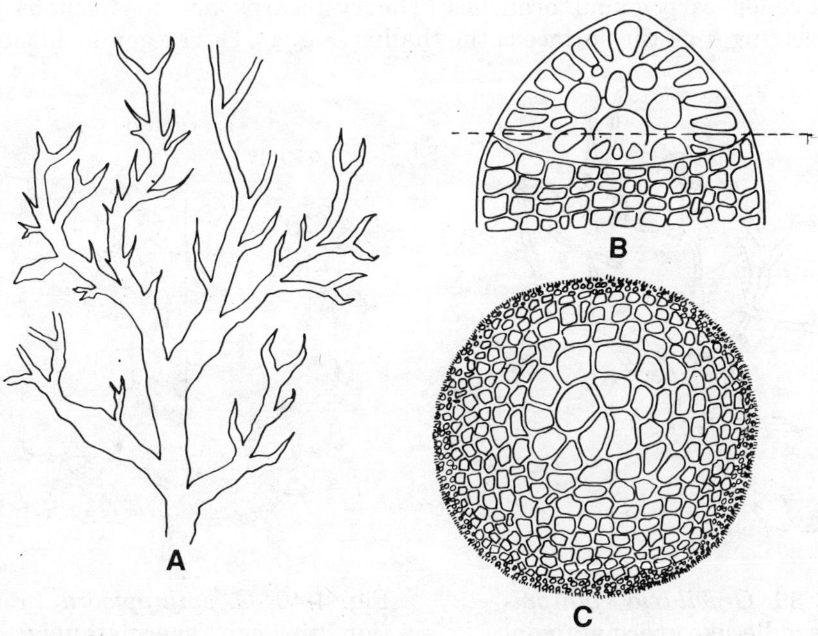

Fig. 4-38 *Gracilaria* sp. A, habit; B, *G. verrucosa*, apical region; C, *G. verrucosa*, transverse section of thallus.

One of the best examples of polyploidy in Rhodophyta is that reported for *Gracilaria tikvahiae* where polyploid thalli can be obtained through sexual crosses in two different ways:

(1) Mitotic recombination of the sex-determining alleles leads to the formation of diploid gametes on tetrasporophytes. These gametes can fuse either with normal (haploid) gametes or with other diploid ones, to yield polyploid tetrasporophytes.

(2) A recessive mutation called *bi* converts males into bisexual thalli that can undergo self-fertilization. Thalli derived from self-fertilized carpogonia fail to complete the life cycle through the tetrasporophytic phase but instead develop into diploid bisexual gametophytes (Van der Meer, 1986). Absence of tetrasporophyte and meiosis means that the chromosome number is not reduced to the gametic level. Zhang and Van der Meer (1988) have reported that by repeated self-fertilization, or cross-fertilization between bisexuals in *G. tikvahiae*, they were able to obtain polyploid gametophytic series up to the $4n$. Haploid and diploid gametophytes of this species were morphologically normal, sexually fertile, bisexual plants. Triploids were stunted, having irregular, twisted growth at the apices, and their cystocarps released no viable carpospores after self-fertilization. Tetraploids were highly abnormal, greatly stunted, and failed to reproduce. The size of cortical cells increased progressively from the haploid to tetraploid gametophytes, even though the size of the thalli decreased (Zhang and Van der Meer, 1988).

Reproduction

Vegetative Vegetative propagation may occur by detachment of branches which grow into new thalli.

Sexual The male plants produce spermatia in shallow depressions (Fig. 4-40). The female plants bear 2-celled carpogonial branches. The cystocarps are conspicuous hemispherical structures projecting from the surface of the thallus (Fig. 4-41). The gonimoblasts develop from

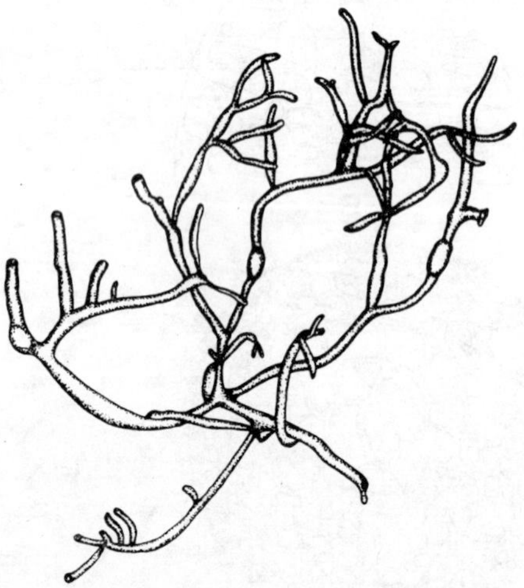

Fig. 4-39 *Gracilaria epihippisora*, saddle-like spermatangial sori.

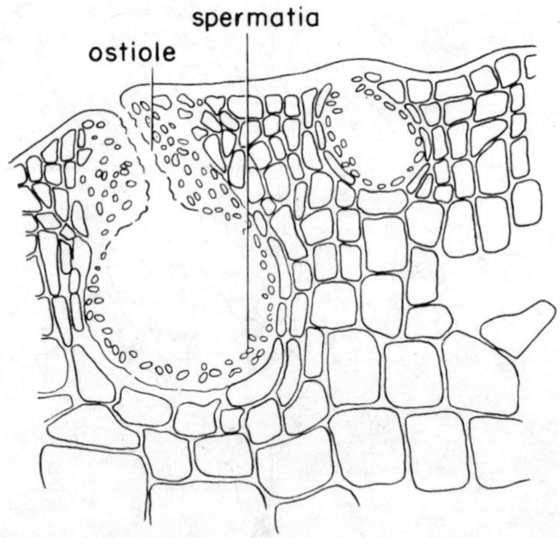

Fig. 4-40 *G. epihippisora*, cross-section through spermatangial sorus; spermatia can be seen in ostiolate pits (after Hoyle, 1977).

the carpogonium after the latter has fused with the auxiliary cell. They develop towards the exterior of the thallus and are covered by a pericarp. The cystocarps have an ostiole through which the carpospores are released. The cystocarp also contains several nutritive filaments.

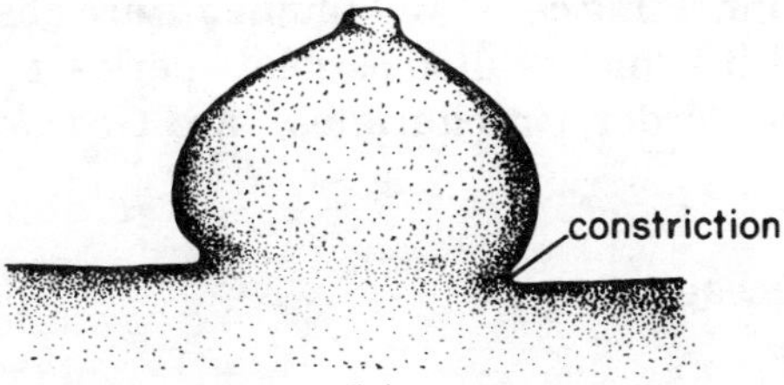

Fig. 4-41 *G. epihippisora*, dome-shaped cystocarp with basal constriction (after Hoyle, 1977).

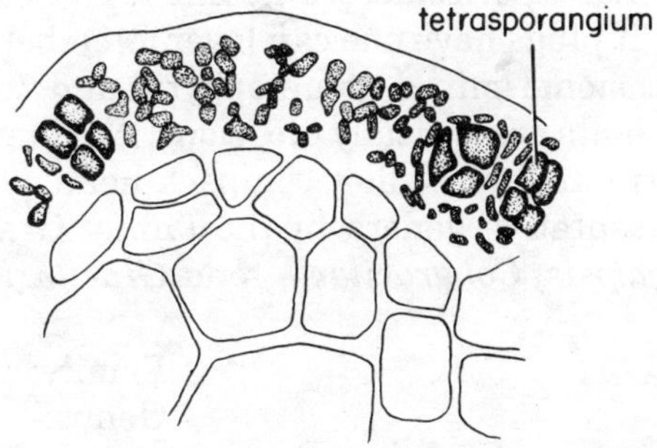

Fig. 4-42 *G. epihippisora*, section through fertile branchlet, showing cruciate tetrasporangia (after Hoyle, 1977).

In *G. epihippisora*, the branches of the tetrasporic plants are constricted at the base. The tetrasporangia, which are ovoid and divide cruciately (Fig. 4-42), are borne in sori. In this species the male gametophytes are very characteristic in bearing a unique kind of swollen or saddle-shaped spermatangial sori [called nemathecia (Fig. 4-39)]; these swellings are borne on one side of a branch. The female gametophytes bear small, dome-shaped cystocarps.

G. blodgetii bears tetrasporangia in nemathecial swellings above the constricted base of the ultimate branchlets. The branchlets sometimes become swollen after the development of groups of antheridia. The projecting cystocarps have occasional radial trabeculae connecting the carposporophyte to the pericarp.

G. verrucosa is characterized by a supporting cell of intercalary origin that bears a 2-celled carpogonial branch flanked by two sterile branches, direct fusion of cells of sterile branches onto the carpogonium, and formation of an extensive carpogonial fusion cell through the incorporation of additional gametophytic cells prior to gonimoblast initiation (Fredericq and Hommersand, 1989). In this species, gonimoblast initials are produced from fusion cell lobes. The cystocarp cavity develops schizogenously; and inner gonimoblast cells produce tubular nutritive cells which fuse with cells of the pericarp or floor of the cystocarp. There is no cytologically modified tissue in the floor of the cystocarp. The carposporangial initials are produced in clusters or irregular chains. Spermatangial parent cells are generated in filaments from intercalary cortical cells that line an intercellular space forming a pit or conceptacle. Tetrasporangial initials are transformed from terminal cells derived by division of an outer cortical cell. Tetrasporangia divide cruciately.

Gracilaria is the only nonparasitic genus of the Gracilariaceae in which an inner pericarp consisting of a cytologically modified nutritive tissue in the floor of the cystocarp is absent (Fredericq and Hommersand, 1989).

On the basis largely of the developmental morphology of the male and female reproductive systems in *G. verrucosa*, Fredericq and Hommersand (1989) have removed the family

Gracilariaceae from the order Gigartinales and transferred it to the newly-created order Gracilariales. The new order appears to have its closest relatives in the order Gelidiales.

The new order Gracilariales includes free-living pseudoparenchymatous thalli ranging from terete to flattened, fleshy to cartilaginous, unbranched or branched, with main axes arising from a single discoid or coalesced holdfast. Growth is uniaxial but the central axis tends to be concealed. Pit plugs have one cap layer. Members typically exhibit a *Polysiphonia*-type life history with occasional mixed gametophytic and tetrasporophytic stages found on a single thallus. Sexual plants are typically dioecious. Auxiliary cells, connecting cells, and filaments are absent. Cystocarps are protruding, compact, hemispherical, with a thick-walled ostiolate pericarp.

Representative genera in the family Gracilariaceae (order Gracilariales): are *Gracilaria, Gracilariopsis*, *Congracilaria*, and *Gracilariophila*.

Family: Gigartinaceae
Genus: *Chondrus*

Occurrence

Chondrus crispus, popularly called "Irish moss" and one of the most important seaweeds of commerce, grows as a lithophyte in the littoral and sublittoral zones of the Atlantic Coast of North America and Canada, and in Ireland, England, and other coastal areas. It ranges in distribution from Norway to Spain and from Newfoundland to New Jersey. It is also abundant in Japan.

It is a typical eurythermal alga as it can tolerate a wide range of temperatures. It is a plant of the subarctic to warm temperate zones. It usually occurs from near low water to about 20 metres below the low water. It also shows a wide tolerance to different light intensities and salinity levels. It grows most luxuriantly on semiexposed coastal sites and estuaries where strong tidal currents are present.

The alga is susceptible to attack by certain fungi, bacteria, and animals which affect its growth and survival. An *Anisolpidium*-like fungus parasitizes cultured carpospores but not the germlings. The cystocarps in natural material are attacked by the ascomycetous species *Didymosphaeria danica*. As many as 50 species of invertebrates are known to occur upon or around the thalli of *C. crispus*.

Morphology

The thallus is made up of a large clump of perennial, firm fronds which extend upward from a perennial cushion-like holdfast crust (Fig. 4-43). The fronds range from small terete branches to large, profusely dichotomously branched, flat fans. The alga is highly polymorphic. The cell wall contains carrageenan as the major constituent. Characteristic villus-like outgrowths occur in the outer medullary cells and it is likely that such "plasmalemma villi" are involved in cell wall formation.

The male gametophytic plants tend to be narrower above, and have spermatangial sori near the apices. The female thalli are slightly broader at the apices and, after development of carposporophytes, show a characteristic ovate convexity on one side matched by a corresponding concavity on the other. The tetrasporophytes have ovate tetrasporan-

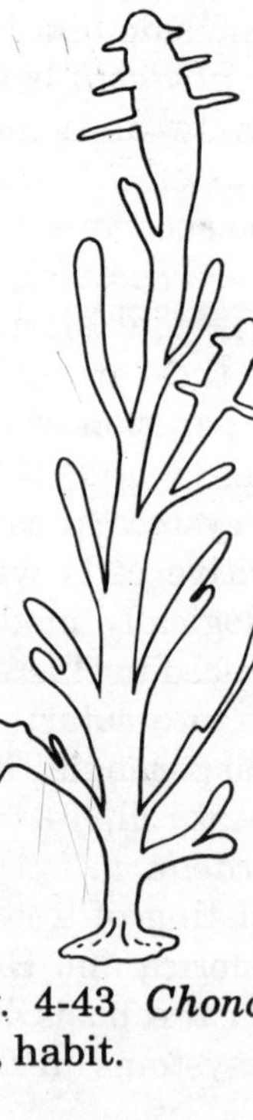

Fig. 4-43 *Chondrus* sp., habit.

gial sori which bulge from both surfaces near the apices. The male, female, and tetrasporophytic thalli are morphologically quite similar to each other; male plants are more rarely encountered in nature than the female and tetrasporophytic plants.

Anatomy

Chondrus is multiaxial. A central medullary region has hyaline cells elongated parallel to the long axis of the plant. These cells have thick, gelatinous walls, and a reticulate leucoplast.

From the medulla, loose filaments radiate outward to form the cortex, whose cells (in the inner cortical layers) are rich in floridean starch.

The cells are irregular, thick-walled, and have prominent pit connections. The cells of the outer layers of the cortex have normal chloroplasts and are photosynthetic. The thallus is covered by a thick cuticular sheath, which can peel off. Some thalli may form hyaline hairs.

Reproduction

Vegetative Vegetative propagation is mostly by regeneration from old holdfasts.

Sexual The spermatangia occur in sori on the apex of the male gametophytic plants.

In the female plant, a large supporting cell bears a 3-celled carpogonial branch developed within the cortex. The supporting cell is connected both to the filament in which it develops and to the nearby vegetative cells by pit connections. It also serves as the auxiliary cell after fertilization.

After fertilization and fusion of the carpogonial branch with the auxiliary cell, the procarp bears elongated gonimoblasts. These penetrate amongst the medullary cells, forming carposporangia in sori on one side of the thallus. The carpospores can grow over a wide range of salinities.

In the tetrasporophytic thalli, the tetrasporangia are formed in the medullary region. The tetraspores are cruciately arranged. Tetrasporangial sori develop on both surfaces of the frond.

Life History

In culture, there occurs a sequence of isomorphic plants consisting of gametophytes, carposporophytes, and tetrasporophytes. The carposporophyte is parasitic on the female gametophyte. The tetraspores germinate into gametophytes, whereas the carpospores develop into tetrasporophytes.

Order: RHODYMENIALES

This order includes a distinctive group of multiaxial algae generally characterized by the fact that the procarp bears one or two auxiliary-cell branches composed of two (rarely three) cells that are initiated directly from the supporting cell before fertilization. These cell branches, however, become distinguishable only after fertilization. The thallus tends to be saccate, cylindrical, flattened, or hollow and has apical or marginal meristems. The tetrasporangia are terminal or intercalary in the cortical layer, and divide cruciately or tetrahedrally. The cystocarps are enveloped by an ostiolate pericarp. The members commonly show a *Polysiphonia*-type of triphasic haplodiplontic life history.

The order may be divided into four families, viz., Rhodymeniaceae, Palmariaceae, Lomentariaceae, and Champiaceae (Lee, 1978). The Rhodymeniaceae lack inner filamentous cells in the medulla, have cruciate tetrasporangia (except in *Hymenocladia* in which they are tetrahedral), and 3-celled carpogonial branch not forming any large fusion cell. In the Palmariaceae (Guiry, 1974), the tetrasporangium has a stalk cell and the female gametophyte is absent. Another feature is that the superficial wall of spermatangial sori is shed during spermatangium formation and the spermatangial mother cells are formed separately unlike in other families in which they are formed seriately.

The Lomentariaceae have longitudinal filamentous cells, 3-celled carpogonial branch, terminal formation of tetrasporangia, and conversion of almost all cells of gonimoblasts into carposporangia. The fusion cell is typically columnar.

The Champiaceae possess filamentous cells in the medulla, intercalary tetrasporangia, and 4-celled carpogonial branch which forms a large fusion cell during cystocarp formation. Only the superficial cells of gonimoblasts are converted into carposporangia.

Family: Palmariaceae
Genus: *Palmaria*

Occurrence

It is a lithophyte in the lower tidal zone.

Morphology

P. palmata has a multiaxial, palmately lobed solid or flattened thallus. Its cortex has up to about 15 layers of cells. The medulla contains large, hyaline, fairly isodiametric loosely-cohering cells arranged in monostromatic rows. The plants are attached to rocks by means of discoidal or flat holdfasts (Fig. 4-44 A, B).

Reproduction

Vegetative Vegetative propagation is by regeneration of new fronds from old fronds (Fig. 4-44 C).

Sexual In *P. palmata*, tetrasporangial plants and spermatangial plants are common but carpogonial and carposporangial plants are extremely rare or unknown.

During spermatangial development, the outermost cortical cells divide periclinally to form two hemispherical cells. The outermost of these cells then divides anticlinally to form two spermatangial mother cells; these elongate and produce a spermatangial initial that gives rise to a spermatangium (see Guiry, 1974). The spermatia are borne singly in a spermatangium; each spermatangial mother cell forms a pair of spermatangia and each spermatangium contains a single spermatium.

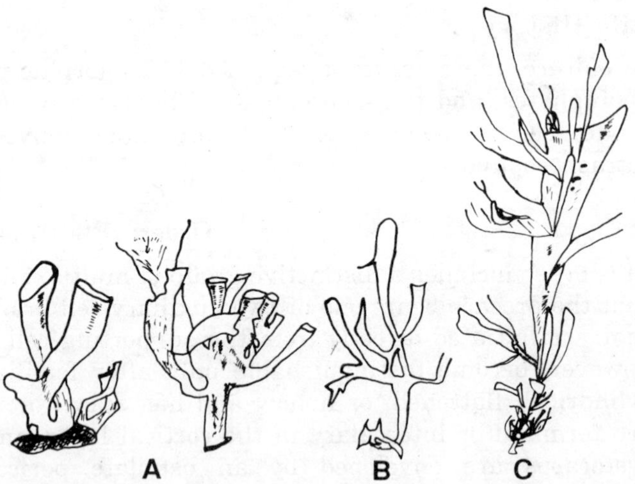

Fig. 4-44 *Palmaria palmata*. A, two plants with holdfasts; B, *P. marginicrassa*, plant with holdfast; C, *P. marginicrassa*, regeneration of new fronds.

Tetrasporangial sori may be formed on most of the thallus and the sori are interspersed with patches of large sterile cortical cells. The terasporangial development begins by the enlargement of a cortical cell which undergoes one periclinal division to form two unequal cells; out of the two, the innermost becomes a stalk cell and the outermost the tetrasporangial mother cell. The latter grows in size, elongates, and divides at first periclinally and then anticlinally to form the tetrasporangium. The stalk cell flattens. The tetrasporangium becomes enveloped by surrounding filaments which form paraphyses.

Family: Champiaceae
Genus: *Champia*

Occurrence

It grows mostly in lower tidal zone in rather calm habitats which are more or less well sheltered from violent waves. *C. parvula* also occurs at places exposed to open sea, is epiphytic on other seaweeds, or lithophytic. *C. wrightii* is mostly lithophytic. *C. parvula* forms globular tufts when growing in calm place and expanded masses at exposed habitat.

Morphology

The thallus forms tufted, tangled masses of articulated, tender, cylindrical, gelatinous branches, the whole tuft being attached by means of a discoid or flat holdfast. There is no perceptible stipe. The thallus branches 3–4 times repeatedly. Some lower branches give off rhizoids. Most or all parts of the thallus are prominently constricted (Fig. 4-45 A, B).

The branches are irregular, verticillate, alternate or opposite, sometimes rather flattened but usually cylindrical. The ultimate branches are much constricted at their bases. The thallus tends to be pyramidal, being narrow at base and apex and broader in the middle.

The frond in section is single-layered with a central cavity traversed by diaphragms (Figs. 4-46 and 4-47 A). Some gland cells occur here and there (Fig. 4-47 B).

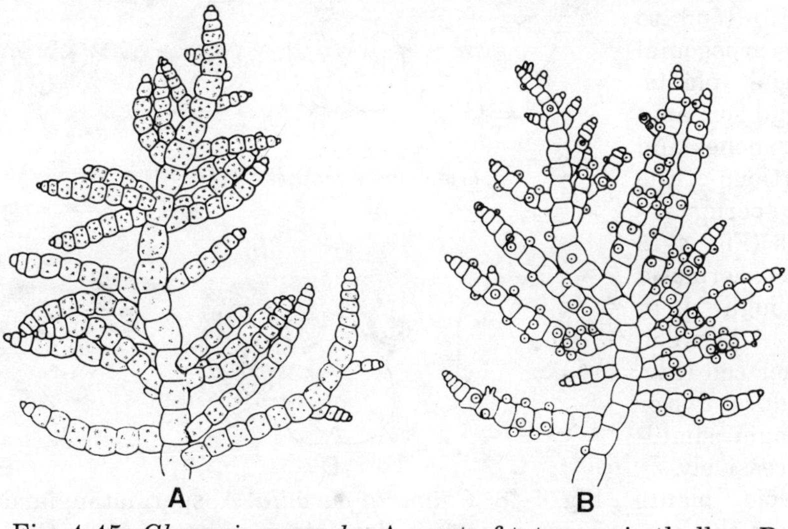

A B

Fig. 4-45 *Champia parvula*. A, part of tetrasporic thallus; B, part of cystocarpic thallus.

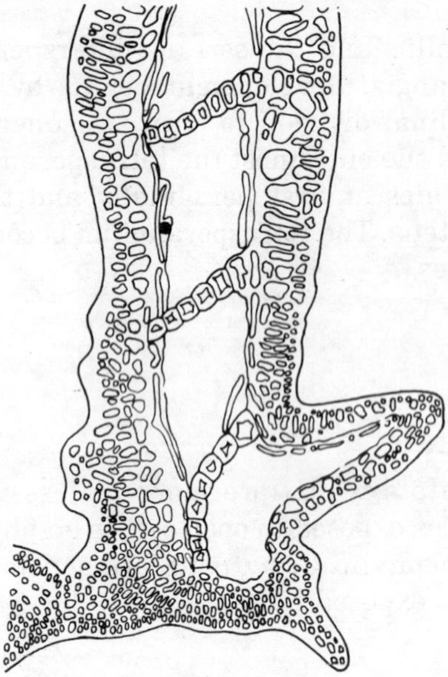

Fig. 4-46 *Champia parvula*, part of thallus showing diaphragm (after Lee, 1978).

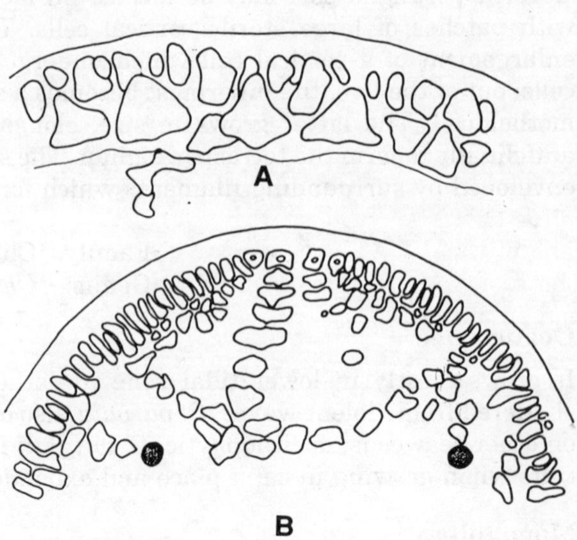

Fig. 4-47 *Champia parvula*. A, transection of mature thallus; B, development of diaphragm and gland cells. (After Lee, 1978.)

The cells are polygonal. Some long filaments attach to these cells and run through the frond.

Reproduction

Vegetative Vegetative propagation may occur from detached branches.

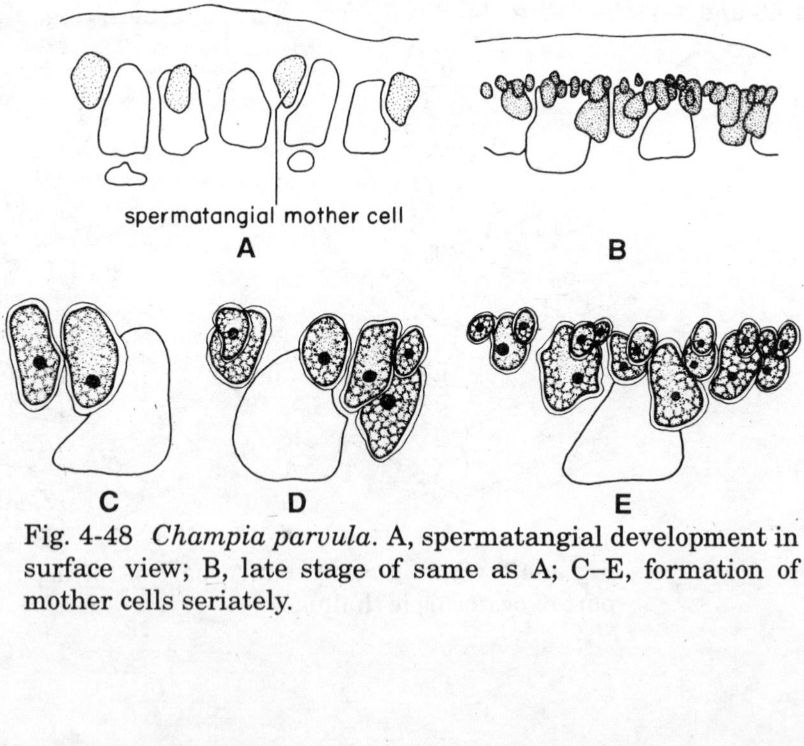

Fig. 4-48 *Champia parvula*. A, spermatangial development in surface view; B, late stage of same as A; C–E, formation of mother cells seriately.

Sexual The spermatangial plants (Fig. 4-10) tend to be smaller than carpogonial or tetrasporangial plants. The spermatangial sori appear on lateral branches and in the upper portions of the main axis. The spermatangial mother cells (Fig. 4-48 A–E) cut off the spermatia transversely, though there are pit connections between the two. A mother cell (Fig. 4-48 B) often produces two or three spermatangia simultaneously or successively.

The cystocarpic plants (Fig. 4-45 B) bear the cystocarps on branches and upper portions of the main axis, either solitary or in groups on septa or internodes (Fig. 4-45 B). The cystocarps are sessile but somewhat raised above the thallus surface.

The carpogonial branch is 4-celled (Fig. 4-49 A). The supporting cell is tetragonal or polygonal (Fig. 4-49 B, C), multinucleate and centrally vacuolate. The terminal cell of the carpogonial branch acts as the uninucleate carpogonium provided with a clear trichogyne. All 4 cells of the branch have conspicuous pit connections.

After fertilization, a 2-celled auxiliary branch becomes discernible. The auxiliary mother cell is uninucleate. The auxiliary cells increase in volume after fertilization (Fig. 4-49 C). The cells of the carpogonial branch fuse together and also with the auxiliary cell (Fig. 4-49 D). The fusion cell later disappears, but the supporting cell and the auxiliary mother cell grow and enlarge (Fig. 4-49 D). The auxiliary mother cell becomes connected with the surrounding

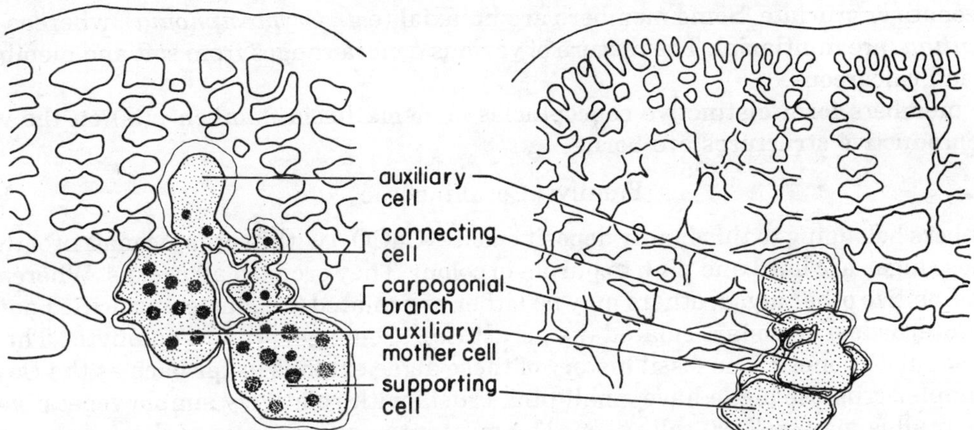

Fig. 4-49 *Champia parvula*. A, fusion between auxiliary cell and connecting cell (note coalescence of cells of carpogonial branch); B, pericarp development, showing greatly modified inner cells; C, young carposporophyte, developing later gonimoblast; D, mature cystocarp. (After Lee, 1978.)

sterile cells, forming gonimoblasts (Fig. 4-49 D). The young carposporophyte is oblong in outline. The carposporangia develop from superficial cells of the gonimoblasts.

A 4–5 layered pericarp is formed around the carposporophyte (Fig. 4-49 D).

The tetrasporangial sori develop in the branches, especially the lower branches. The tetrasporangia divide tetrahedrally.

Order: CRYPTONEMIALES

In this order, the auxiliary cells differentiate before fertilization and are borne in special accessory branches which may be near or away from the carpogonial branches. The latter also arise from special accessory filaments. Following fertilization, certain tubular outgrowths, called ooblasts, develop and help connect the carpogonium to the auxiliary cell while also facilitating ready migration of the carpogonial nucleus to the auxiliary cell. The tetrasporangia may be zonate or cruciate. Some members are uniaxial (e.g., *Cryptosiphonia*), whereas others, e.g., *Corallina*, are multiaxial. The texture of various genera ranges from soft and membranous to hard and calcareous.

Many members form distinctive conceptacles or nemathecia (sunken pits) on the walls of which reproductive structures are borne.

Family: Corallinaceae

The members belonging to this family deposit calcite ($CaCO_3$) within organic matrix of their cell walls; these algae are hard and pink to purple in colour. They occur in all oceans. Whereas some species parasitize other algae, others may be either articulated (i.e., have uncalcified nodes and calcified internodes) or nonarticulated (i.e., crustose). Some genera are epiphytic. The family includes about 45 genera. The fossil history of these algae extends as far back as the Devonian.

The simpler crustose algae have small pink crusts with relatively simple vegetative structure. The thallus may be 2–20 cells deep. The most interesting aspect of these crustose forms is that they combine a simple vegetative organization with complex or well developed reproductive organs; such interesting algae may well represent some neotenic or regressive forms. The thallus of the epiphytic crustose genera (e.g., *Melobesia*) is a polysiphonous filamentous structure with the filaments organized into three cell layers.

The corallinaceous algae reproduce by the formation of large, red, and spherical spores (carpospores, tetraspores, or bispores) which germinate and form a disc consisting of 16 or more small cells. Further developments give rise to an articulated or nonarticulated thallus. The nonarticulated thallus may be thickly crustose having a smooth surface, a thickly crustose form with certain protuberances, a free-living branched or unbranched nodule, a delicate crust, an endoparasite with only its reproductive bodies projecting out, or a filamentous endoparasite (Johansen, 1976).

The thallus is made of narrow-celled filaments which appear like strings of beads, the cells being interconnected by primary pit connections, and joined together by calcite-laden cell walls. Additionally, the cells in neighbouring filaments may also be joined by secondary pit connections. *Fosliella* gives rise to enlarged cells, called trichocytes, from its cortical tissue and these trichocytes produce ephemeral hairs. *Melobesia* lacks trichocytes.

Mature plants, which are commonly dioecious, produce tetrasporangia (or bisporangia) or spermatangia and carpogonia. Sexual cells in most Corallinaceae originate in small clusters. The surrounding sterile tissue grows up and over the cells and forms the roofs of conceptacles which open by pores.

After fertilization, the zygote nucleus passes into the supporting cell. A number of supporting cells then fuse and form a large, plate-like fusion cell. The latter may either give rise directly to gonimoblast filaments or bear connecting filaments (e.g., *Melobesia*). The latter join with the supporting cell near the chamber periphery and then grow into gonimoblast filaments. The gonimoblasts bear carposporangia.

Some good examples of the articulated genera are *Corallina, Jania*, and *Amphiroa*. *Amphiroa* has secondary pit connections which are not found in the other two genera. *Melobesia* (no secondary pit connections; sporangial plugs present), *Lithophyllum* (sporangial plugs absent; secondary pit connections present), and *Choreonema* (both secondary pits and sporangial plugs absent) exemplify the nonarticulated or crustose series.

Genus: *Corallina*

Occurrence

It occurs on rocky shores in the intertidal and sublittoral zones, sometimes at depths of over 60 metres. It is distributed in warm as well as cold seas.

Morphology

It is superficially like an erect, jointed coral, with several branched cylinders (Fig. 4-50) or flattened segments. The upright parts arise from prostrate, calcified sections. The upright portions show pinnate or opposite branching.

Anatomy

The jointed fronds are multiaxial. Many dichotomously branched filaments constitute a central cable. These filaments are made of long cells having lateral connections. At some points, the branches out-turn, forming nodes; the ultimate cells of these branches make up a cortex. The outer cells are encrusted with $CaCO_3$ except at the joints.

Reproduction

Vegetative Vegetative propagation may sometimes occur from detached portions of prostrate or upright thallus.

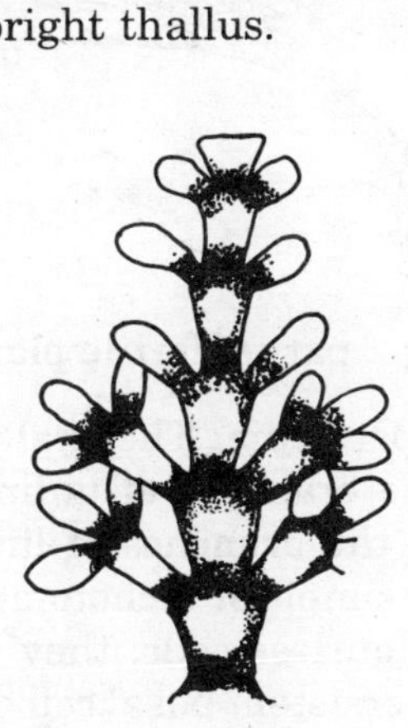

Fig. 4-50 *Corallina* sp., habit.

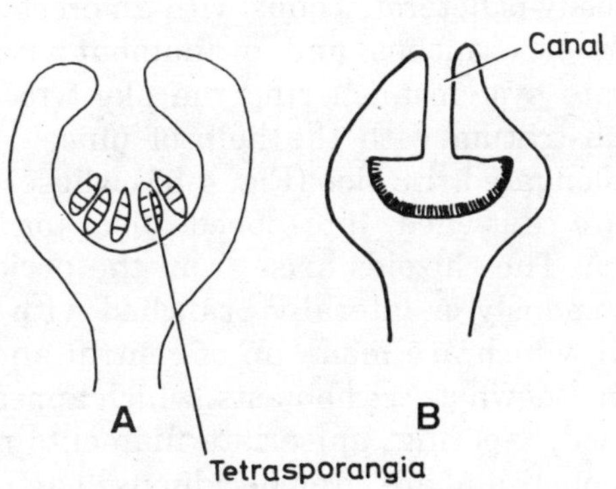

Fig. 4-51 *Corallina* sp. A, roof formation in tetrasporangial conceptacle; B, male conceptacle.

Sexual Species may be monoecious or dioecious. Two-celled carpogonial branches arise from the terminal cells of the filaments lining the nemathecia (Fig. 4-51 A, B). The terminal cell functions as the carpogonium. The spermatangia are borne on clusters of short branches in sori in the male conceptacle (Fig. 4-51 B). The spermatia have a hairy stalk by which they remain attached for some time to the inner wall of the spermatangium. The tetrasporic plants bear conceptacles (Fig. 4-51 A) in which large, stalked tetrasporangia divide meiotically to form a tier of tetraspores.

Order: CERAMIALES
Family: Rhodomelaceae
Genus: *Polysiphonia*

Occurrence

Polysiphonia grows extensively in the intertidal belt and sublittoral region. Most species are epiphytic on the Fucaceae and other large marine algae. *P. fastigiata* grows attached to the fronds of *Ascophyllum nodosum*; this species may be a semiparasite in view of the destruction of some of the host cells near the point of its attachment. Some common species on the West Coast of India are *P. variegata, P. urceolata*, and *P. platycarpa*. The plants grow in dense tufts (Fig. 4-52).

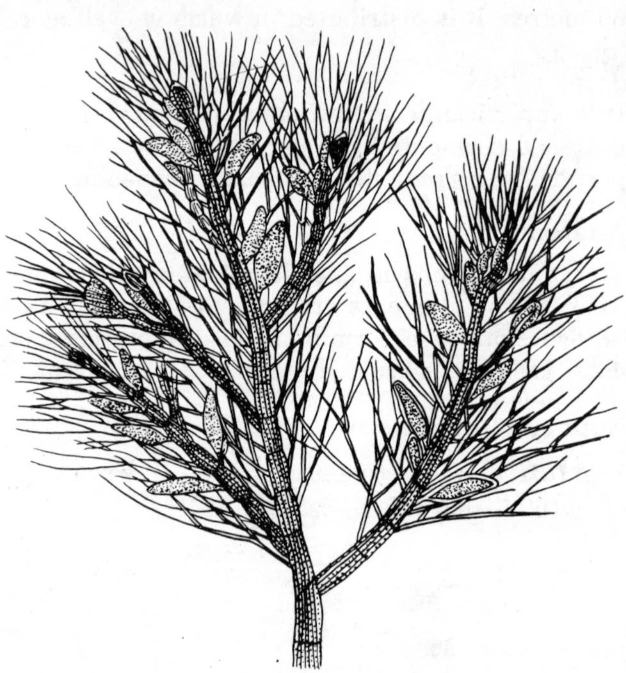

Fig. 4-52 *Polysiphonia* sp., part of fertile plant.

Morphology

The genus *Polysiphonia* derives its name from the polysiphonous nature of its thallus which has an axial row of central siphons (Figs. 4-53 and 4-54) surrounded by a layer of 4–24 pericentral siphons. The plant body is heterotrichous with an erect system of branches and a filamentous prostrate system anchoring the plant to the substratum with the help of unicellular elongated rhizoids (Fig. 4-55) whose tips are flattened into lobed discs or haptera. The rhizoids arise from the pericentral cells facing the substratum. The thallus is dichotomously or laterally branched with two kinds of branches: the branches of unlimited growth, which are made up of central and pericentral siphons; and the branches of limited growth, known as trichoblasts, which appear like hairs and are either simple or dichotomously branched, tapering, uniseriate filaments made up of uninucleate colourless cells; they arise exogenously and are often deciduous, leaving a scar cell, which is the persistent basal cell of the trichoblast. Sometimes, new branches, termed cicatrigenous branches, are given off by these

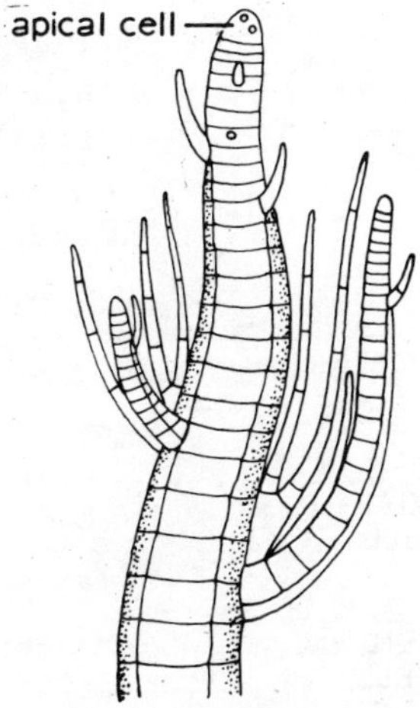

Fig. 4-53 *Polysiphonia sertularioides*, thallus apex.

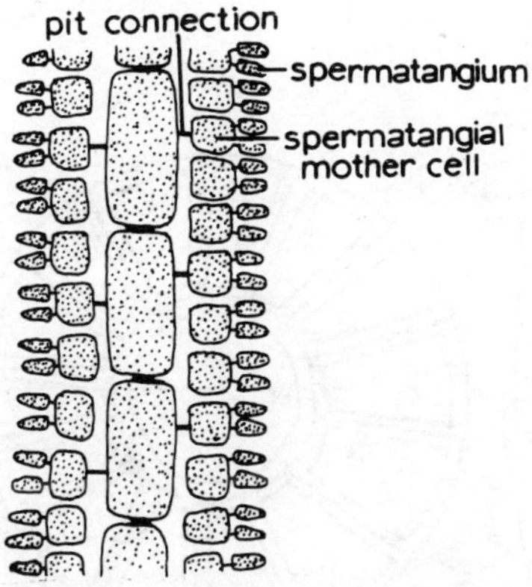

Fig. 4-54 *Polysiphonia sertularioides,* spermatangia as seen in section through fertile trichoblast; central and pericentral cells and pit connections are also seen.

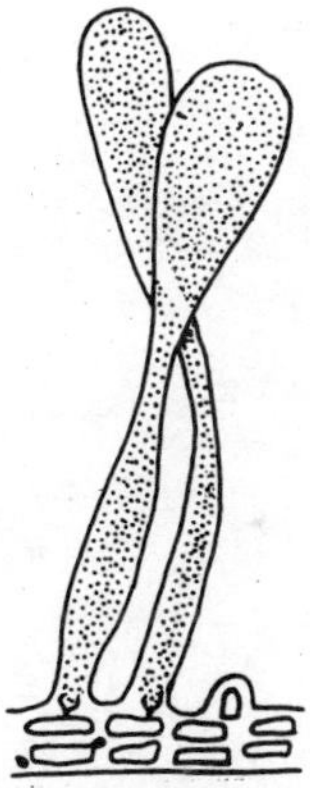

Fig. 4-55 *Polysiphonia* sp., unicellular rhizoids.

scar cells. Pit connections occur in between and among the central and pericentral siphons (Fig. 4-54). The older parts of the thallus are generally corticated with cells cut off *periclinally* by the pericentral cells of those regions. In surface view, under low magnification, the thallus of *Polysiphonia* seems to consist of a number of polysiphonous tiers. The orderly manner in which the tiers are arranged suggests a differentiation of filaments into nodes and internodes.

The thallus grows by means of an apical cell (Fig. 4-56 A) which by repeated divisions forms a row of axial cells. All axial cells excluding the first few cells undergo tangential vertical divisions and form a peripheral layer of a specific number of pericentral cells around the axial row of central cells (Fig. 4-56 B). Both the central and pericentral cells elongate into their respective siphons which have the usual pit connections. The trichoblast initial arises from an axial cell, four or five cells away from the apical meristem, even before the pericentral cells are formed. Branches of unlimited growth also arise similarly but, unlike the trichoblast initial, the initials of these branches behave exactly like the apical cell of the main axis and produce at first a transverse file of axial cells from which the peripheral layer of pericentral cells later arises. A branch of unlimited growth may sometimes arise in the axil of a trichoblast in which case its basal cell serves as the branch initial.

In vegetative cell of *P. harveyi*, polar rings persist near the nucleus in pairs at variable distance from one another, and longitudinally arranged microtubules surround the nucleus (Scott *et al.*, 1981).

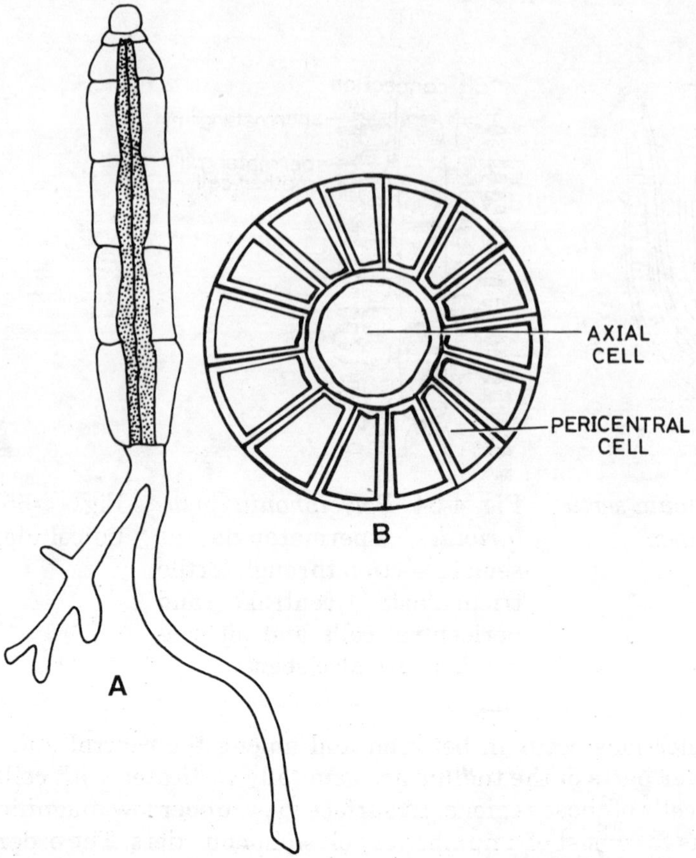

Fig. 4-56 *Polysiphonia*. A, sporeling showing initiation of pericentral cells (the apical cell is distinct); B, *P. lanosa*, transverse section showing 14 pericentral cells.

Mitosis

It has a closed but fenestrated spindle, perinuclear ER, metaphase chromosome plate, conspicuous layered kinetochores, chromosomal and nonchromosomal microtubules, and polar rings (nucleus associated organelles) occurring singly in ribosome-free zones of exclusion at division poles in late prophase. Paired polar rings are present in interphase cells and these rings attach themselves to the nuclear envelope during mitosis. A single polar ring migrates, establishing the division axis. At late prophase, the nuclear envelope commonly protrudes at both division poles. At prometaphase, the polar rings split up into proximal and distal portions. Another interesting novel feature involves the reconstitution of postmitotic nuclei by separation of an elongated interzonal nuclear midpiece during telophase (Scott *et. al.*, 1980). It has also been shown that during cytokinesis, cleavage furrows cut into a central vacuolar region between the two nuclei and pit connections are then formed (Scott *et al.*, 1980). Morphologically, the polar rings of *Polysiphonia* resemble the ring-shaped nucleus associated organelles described in several zygomycetous fungi. This lends support to some phylogenetic relationship between higher fungi and red algae.

Reproduction

Asexual *Polysiphonia* is generally heterothallic or dioecious and includes three kinds of morphologically similar plants: the male gametophyte, the female gametophyte, and the tetrasporophyte (see Fig. 4-57 A–C). The female plant also bears the diploid parasitic

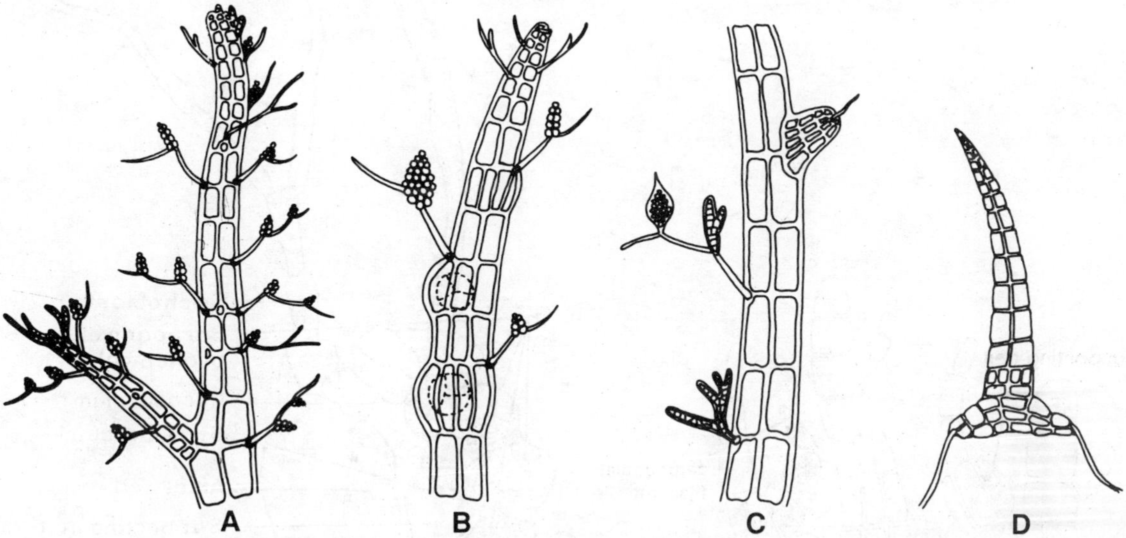

Fig. 4-57 *Polysiphonia ferulacea*. A, male gametophyte; B, tetrasporophyte; C, female gametophyte; D, propagule germling one day after release from parent thallus. (After Kapraun, 1977.)

carposporophyte. Both the carposporophyte and tetrasporophyte reproduce asexually by the formation of carpospores and tetraspores, respectively.

During the formation of monospores in *P. gardneri,* increased Golgi activity produces fibrous vesicles which may play some role in spore release (Hawkes, 1980).

Polysiphonia ferulacea seems exceptional among the red algae in that it regularly propagates itself asexually by producing specialized, spermatangium-like asexual reproductive branches. Unlike bonafide spermatangia, however, these asexual propagules (Fig. 4-57 D) can arise on male, female, and tetrasporophytic plants, and they simply recycle the particular phase on which they are borne (Kapraun, 1977).

Sexual The male and female organs are borne on different trichoblasts, which are exogenous branches since they arise from a subapical cell before the pericentral cells are cut off from the axial cell. The spermatangia and carpogonia occur on small fertile trichoblasts. The male trichoblast, after becoming 2–3 cells long, forks; generally one, rarely both, of the branches so produced participates in the formation of spermatia. If only one branch forms spermatia, the remaining sterile branch repeatedly divides dichotomously. All the cells except the two basal cells of the fertile branch divide and form central and pericentral cells. The latter function as spermatangial mother cells and each produces one or a few spermatangia along its free surfaces. The developing spermatia of *P. hendryi* become polar with rough ER forming a large fibrillar posterior vacuole which is later excluded (exocytosed). The dictyosomes form and deposit a spermatial wall, severing the mother cell pit connection. When younger spermatia expand, the older, maturer spermatia are squeezed out from the spermatial branch (Kugrens, 1980).

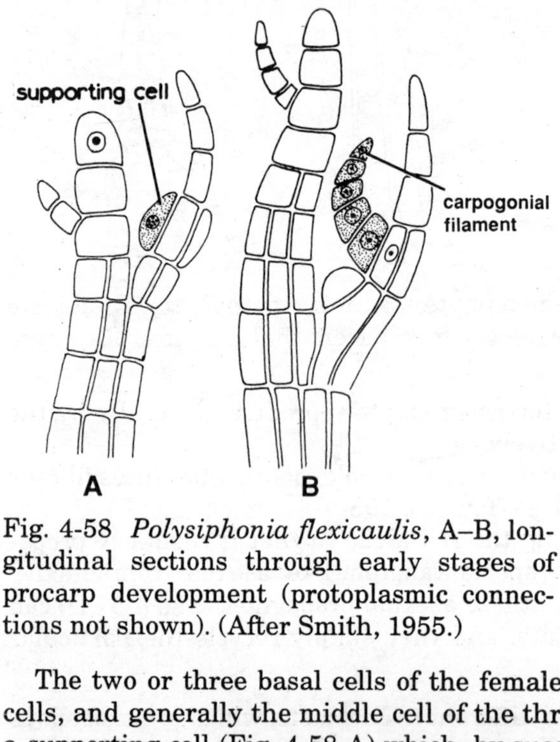

Fig. 4-58 *Polysiphonia flexicaulis*, A–B, longitudinal sections through early stages of procarp development (protoplasmic connections not shown). (After Smith, 1955.)

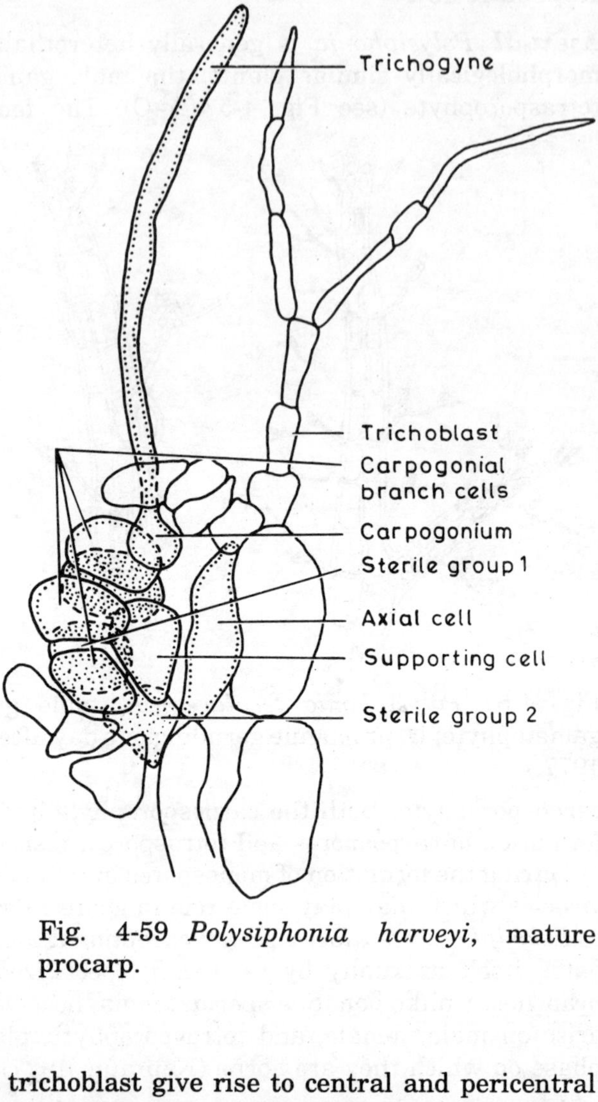

Fig. 4-59 *Polysiphonia harveyi*, mature procarp.

The two or three basal cells of the female trichoblast give rise to central and pericentral cells, and generally the middle cell of the three adaxial pericentrals produces on its free side a supporting cell (Fig. 4-58 A) which, by successive transverse divisions, organizes a four- or five-celled carpogonial branch (Fig. 4-58 B), the procarp (Fig. 4-59). The terminal cell of the procarp transforms into a carpogonium with a swollen base containing a uninucleate egg and a long drawn-out enucleate trichogyne (Fig. 4-60 A, B). Meanwhile, the supporting cell also cuts off two sterile cells, one towards its base and the other towards its side. Both these cells form a few-celled sterile filaments (Fig. 4-60 C). Following these developments, fertilization occurs and a spermatium nucleus passes down the trichogyne and fuses with the egg nucleus

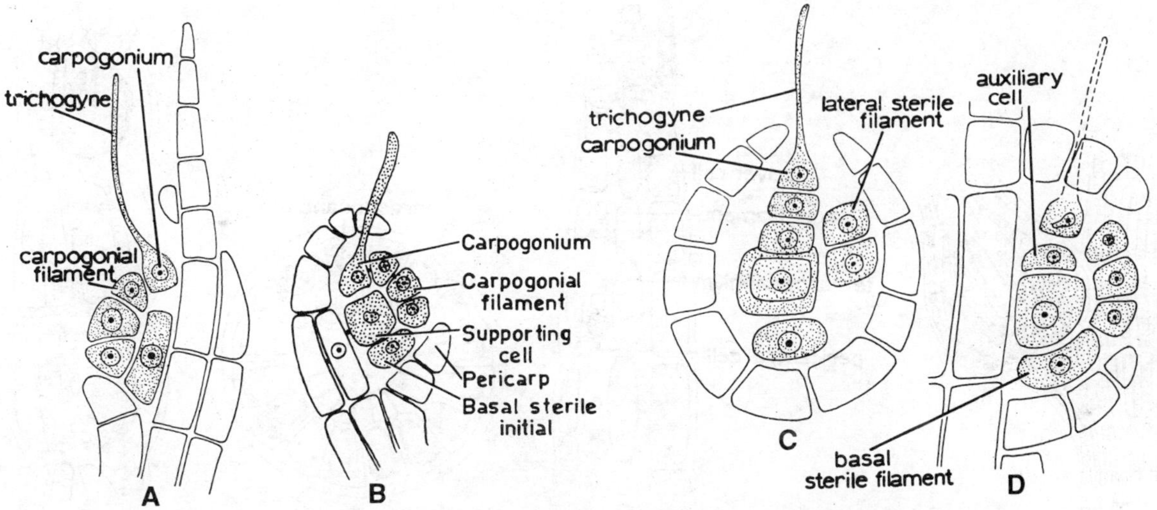

Fig. 4-60 *Polysiphonia flexicaulis*. A, B, longitudinal sections through intermediate stages of procarp development; C, D, longitudinal sections through later stages of procarp development. (After Smith, 1955.)

in the swollen base of the carpogonium (Fig. 4-60 D). This is accompanied by the cutting off of an auxiliary cell by the supporting cell of the carpogonium towards its upper side (Fig. 4-60 D). Soon, a tubular connection is established between the auxiliary cell and the carpogonium base. The zygote nucleus then migrates to auxiliary cell through this tube. By this time, the trichogyne degenerates and the two pericentral cells of the trichoblast adjacent to the supporting cell start producing a sterile sheath, known as the pericarp, around the developing carposporophyte; the pericarp has a terminal opening, the ostiole.

The divisions of the zygote nucleus in the auxiliary cell are always mitotic and a mass of uninucleate gonimoblasts grows out from the upper side of the auxiliary cell. The terminal cells of gonimoblasts then form carposporangia. Meanwhile, the auxiliary cell, the supporting cell, and the sterile filaments fuse to form a large placental cell which nourishes the developing carposporophyte. The carposporophyte with the pericarp and placental cell is known as the cystocarp (Fig. 4-61 A).

The carpospores are diploid and are produced singly within the carposporangia. The carpospore germinates into a new diploid free-living plant, the tetrasporophyte. During germination, it divides transversely to form a four-celled uniseriate filament whose lowermost cell develops into a rhizoid and uppermost cell forms an apical initial of the tetrasporophyte. The tetrasporophyte initial functions exactly like the apical cell of the sexual plants, giving rise to a branched thallus composed of central and pericentral cells (Fig. 4-61 B). The tetrasporophyte forms stalked tetrasporangia from certain pericentral cells (Fig. 4-61 C); the pericentral cell divides vertically into an outer cover cell and an inner sporangial mother cell. The former may not divide further, but the latter segments transversely into a lower stalk cell and an upper sporangial cell. The sporangial nucleus undergoes reduction division followed by cleavage of the sporangial protoplast into four tetrahedral uninucleate spores, called tetraspores (Fig. 4-61 D).

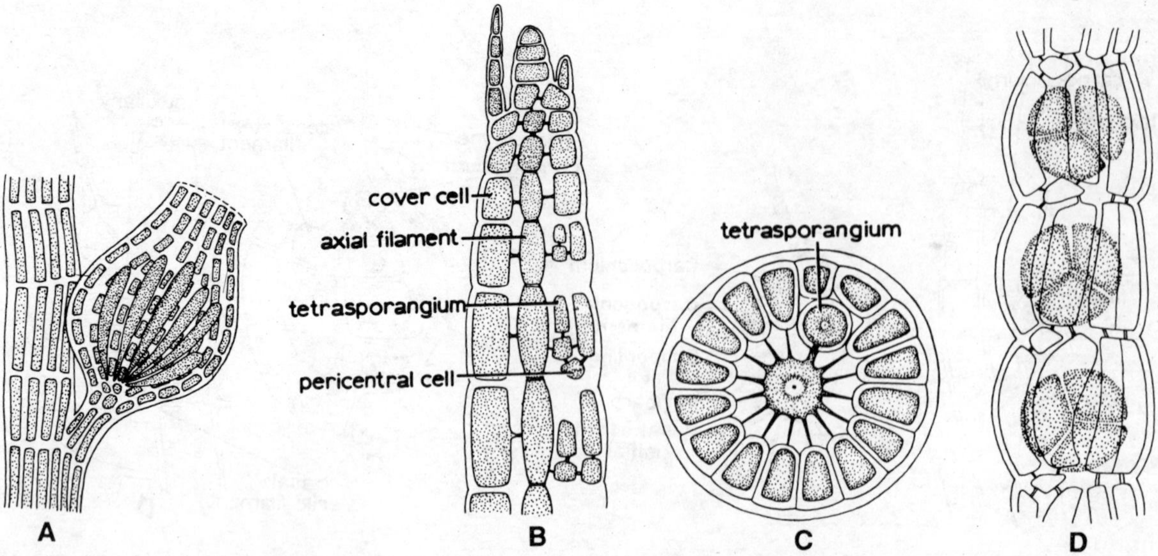

Fig. 4-61 *Polysiphonia.* A, *P. nigrescens*, cystocarp; B, section through apex of tetrasporophyte; C, *P. fastigiata*, transverse section of developing tetrasporangium; D, old tetrasporophyte in surface view showing tetrasporangia. (Figs. B, D after Smith, 1955.)

In *Polysiphonia*, there is a pair of sex-determining allelic genes. The alleles segregate at the first meiotic division and give rise to spores, one-half of which form male plants and the other half female plants.

Life Cycle

The sequence of somatic phases in the life cycle of *P. denudata* has been studied in cultures (Edwards, 1968). The plants are dioecious, and the diploid parasitic carposporophyte results from mitotic divisions of the zygote nucleus in the auxiliary cell. The carpospores germinate into diploid tetrasporophytes which are free-living and are morphologically identical with sexual plants. Each tetrasporangium of the tetrasporophyte forms four haploid spores by reduc-

Fig. 4-62 *Polysiphonia*, life cycle.

tion division; two of these spores produce male plants and the other two give rise to female plants. On the basis of alternation between morphologically identical free-living generations, the life cycle of *Polysiphonia* (Fig. 4-62) is isomorphic. Cytologically, it is diplobiontic and, according to the number of generations, including the parasitic carposporophyte, it is trigenetic.

Family: Ceramiaceae
Genus: *Ceramium*

Occurrence

Ceramium is a common epiphyte in intertidal and sublittoral zones in tropical waters, including the West Coast of India.

Morphology

Ceramium is a filamentous alga showing arbuscular branching. The creeping parts of the thallus are attached to substrata by means of rhizoids (Fig. 4-63). The axial filament shows apical growth (Fig. 4-64 A) with cortications developing at nodes (Fig. 4-64 B). The plants look beaded. Most species have a pair of tong-like (hooked) dichotomous forkings at the tips of their branches (Fig. 4-64 B). In fact, the two most important characteristics of this genus are the nodal banding and the forcipate (claw-like or pincer-like) apices.

The pericentral cells arise from the axial cells (Fig. 4-65 A, B). Figure 4-65 C shows the development of pericentral cells in the nodal regions.

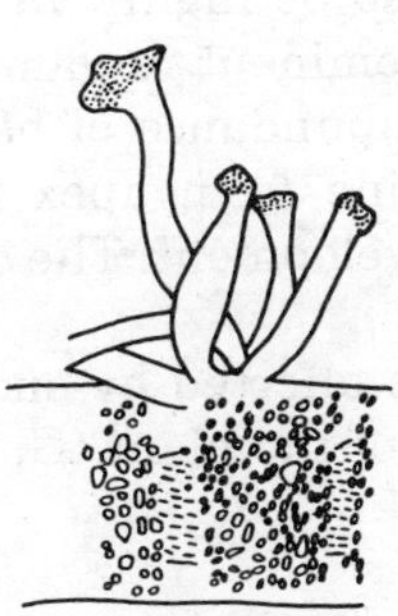

Fig. 4-63 *Ceramium truncatum*, rhizoids arising from creeping part.

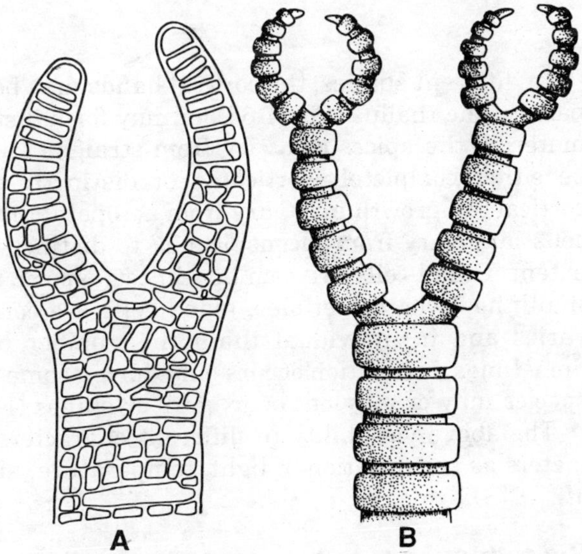

Fig. 4-64 *Ceramium*. A, *C. deslongchampsii*, apex of branch; B, *C. diaphanum*, apex of branch.

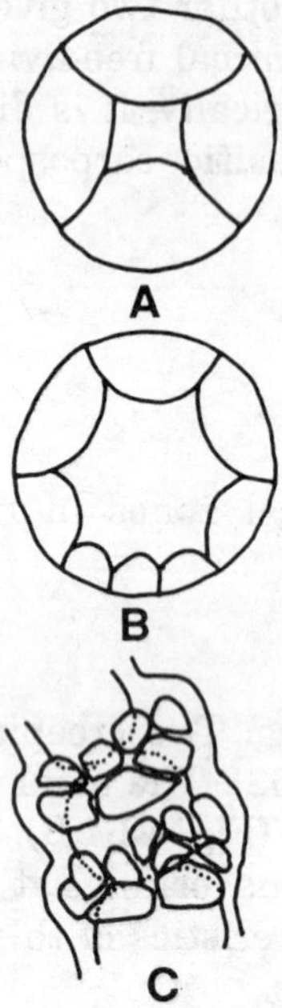

Fig. 4-65 *Ceramium*. A, B, sections of thallus showing origin of pericentral cells from axial cell; C, development of pericentral cells in nodal regions of thallus.

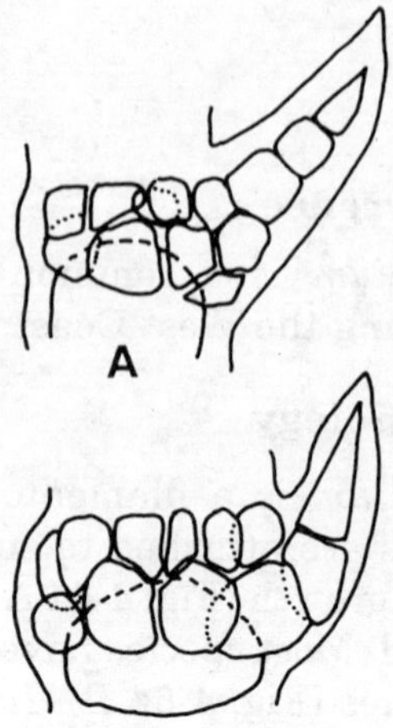

Fig. 4-66 *Ceramium*, spines. A, *C. echionotum*; B, *C. shuttleworthianum*.

In different species, the cortical bands may be confluent throughout, confluent only in some parts of the thallus (Fig. 4-64), or may form distinct bands along the entire plant. (In cultured material, the apices can vary from straight to tightly curved.) The plants of *C. rubrum* may be either completely corticated or distinctly uncorticated at internodes; their direction of cortical cell growth may vary from acropetal to basipetal, the filamentous nature of its cortical cells may vary from inconspicuous to distinct; its branching may also be highly variable in extent. Gland cells are common in tetrasporic thalli but are more prominent in gametangial thalli; however, sometimes, gland cells are completely lacking. The abundance of hairs also varies and in individual thalli the number of hairs tends to decline from apex to base. Sometimes, cortication occurs only during some particular phase of development. The different species may or may not bear hairs or spines (Fig. 4-66 A, B).

The above variability in different characters has been found to be affected by such parameters as the duration of light, temperature, and the nuclear phases of the plant (Garbary *et al.*, 1978).

Reproduction

Vegetative Regeneration of plants from detached branches propagates them vegetatively.

Sexual *Ceramium* is dioecious. The spermatangia occur as dense sori on the surface of corticating cells. The auxiliary cell develops, after fertilization, directly from the supporting cells of the carpogonial branch. Fusion of the carpogonium with the auxiliary cell stimulates the development of gonimoblasts from the procarp.

After fertilization, the zygote nucleus divides twice within the carpogonium. Either a capping cell or an extruded nucleus is produced after the first division. The second division either produces a connecting process or a connecting cell that transfers the diploid nucleus to the auxiliary cell. Sometimes, the two divisions of the zygote nucleus form two connecting cells and a residual 2-celled or 2-nucleate carpogonium. From the carpogonium, a connecting cell or connecting process may grow and join with an auxiliary cell, or the latter may send out a process which fuses with the connecting cell. Figure 4-67 A, B shows the cystocarpic and tetrasporophytic plants of *C. truncatum*.

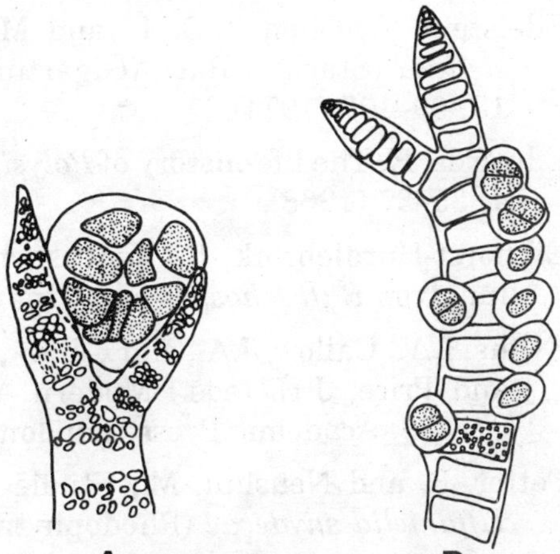

Fig. 4-67 *Ceramium truncatum*. A, part of thallus showing cystocarp; B, part of thallus bearing tetrasporangia.

Ceramium appears to have a *Polysiphonia*-type life history. The gametophytes and tetrasporophytes are morphologically distinct, with the tetrasporophytes being larger but less profusely branched than the gametophytes, and the female plants being larger than the males.

REFERENCES

Aghajanian, J.G., The fine structure of the pit connection of *Batrachospermum sirodotii, J. Phycol.*, Suppl. Abst. No. 5, p. 3 (1977).

Andrews, J.H., The pathology of marine algae, *Biol. Rev.*, **51**, 211–53 (1976).

Broadwater, S. and Scott, J., Fibrous vacuole associated organelles (FVAOS) in the Florideophyceae: a new interpretation of the apparei cinetique, *Phycologia*, **22**, 225–33 (1983).

Bronchart, R. and Demoulin, V., Unusual mitosis in the red alga *Porphyridium purpureum, Nature*, **268**, 80–81 (1977).

Chihara, M., Life-history of algae (Rhodophyta). *In* Tokida, J. and Hirose, H. (eds.) Advance of Phycology in Japan, 137–50, W. Junk, The Hague (1975).

Cole, K.M. and Conway, E., Phenetic implications of structural features of the perennating phase in the life history of *Porphyra* and *Bangia* (Bangiophyceae, Rhodophyta), *Phycologia*, **14**, 239–45 (1975).

Cunningham, E.M. and Guiry, M.D., A circadian rhythm in the long-day photoperiodic induction of erect axis development in the marine red alga *Nemalion helminthoides, J. Phycol.,* **25**, 705–12 (1989).

Duckett, J.G. and Peel, M.C., The role of transmission electron microscopy in elucidating the taxonomy and phylogeny of the Rhodophyta. *In* Irvine, D.E.G. and Price, J.H. (eds.)

Modern Approaches to the Taxonomy of Red and Brown Algae, 157–204, Academic Press, London (1978).

Edelstein, T., Chen, L.C.M., and McLachlan, J., The reproductive structures of *Gigartina stellata* (Stackh.) Batt. (Gigartinales, Rhodophyceae) in nature and culture, *Phycologia*, **13**, 99–107 (1974).

Edwards, P., The life-history of *Polysiphonia denudata* (Dillwyn) Kützing in culture, *J. Phycol.*, **4**, 35–37 (1968).

Eikhorst-Hurdlebrink, L., Untersuchungen Über den kernphasenwechsel und zur Entwicklung von *Batrachospermum*, Inaugural Dissertation, Giessen (1973).

Evans, L.V., Callow, J.A., and Callow, M.E., Parasitic red algae: an appraisal. *In* Irvine, D.E.G. and Price, J.H. (eds.) Modern Approaches to the Taxonomy of Red and Brown Algae, 87–109, Academic Press, London (1978).

Fetter, R. and Neushul, M., Studies on developing and released spermatia in the red alga *Tiffaniella snyderae* (Rhodophyta), *J. Phycol.*, **17**, 141–59 (1981).

Fogg, G.E. and Collyer, D.M., The accumulation of fats as a characteristic of certain classes of algae, Proceedings of the VIII International Botanical Congress, 28 (1954).

Fredericq, S. and Hommersand, M.H., Proposal of the Gracilariales ord. nov. (Rhodophyta): based on an analysis of the reproductive development of *Gracilaria verrucosa, J. Phycol.*, **25**, 213–27 (1989).

Garbary, D.J., Grund, D., and McLachlan, J., The taxonomic status of *Ceramium rubrum* (Huds.) C. Agardh (Ceramiales, Rhodophyceae) based on culture experiments, *Phycologia*, **17**, 85–94 (1978).

Guiry, M.D., A preliminary consideration of the taxonomic position of *Palmaria palmata* (Linnaeus) Stackhouse: *Rhodymenia palmata* (Linnaeus) Greville, *J. Mar. Biol. Ass.* (U.K.), **54**, 509–28 (1974).

Guiry, M.D., The importance of sporangia in the classification of the Florideophyceae. *In* Irvine, D.E.G. and Price, J.H. (eds.) Modern Approaches to the Taxonomy of Red and Brown Algae, 111–44, Academic Press, London (1978).

Hawkes, M.W., Sexual reproduction in *Porphyra gardneri* (Smith et Hollenberg) Hawkes (Bangiales, Rhodophyta), *Phycologia*, **17**, 329–53 (1978).

Hawkes, M.W., Ultrastructure characteristics of monospore formation in *Porphyra gardneri* (Rhodophyta), *J. Phycol.*, **16**, 192–96 (1980).

Heath, I.B., Genome separation mechanism in prokaryotes, algae and fungi. *In* Buch, H. (ed.) The Cell Nucleus, Vol. II, 487–515, Academic Press, New York (1974).

Hommersand, M.H. and Fredericq, S., An investigation of cystocarp development in *Gelidium pteridifolium* with a revised description of the Gelidiales, *Phycologia*, **27**, 254–72 (1988).

Hoyle, M.D., *Gracilaria epihippisora* sp. nov. (Rhodophyta, Gigartinales, Gracilariaceae): a new species from the island of Hawaii, *Phycologia*, **16**, 259–64 (1977).

Huisman, J.M., The *Scinaia* assemblage (Galaxauraceae, Rhodophyta): a re-appraisal, *Phycologia*, **24**, 403–18 (1985).

Hwang, M.S., Kim, H.S., and Lee, I.K., Regeneration and sexual differentiation of *Griffithsia japonica* (Ceramiaceae, Rhodophyta) through somatic cell fusion, *J. Phycol.*, **27**, 441–47 (1991).

Johansen, H.W., Current status of generic concepts in coralline algae (Rhodophyta), *Phycologia*, **15**, 221–44 (1976).

Kapraun, D.F., Asexual propagules in the life history of *Polysiphonia ferulacea* (Rhodophyta, Ceramiales), *Phycologia*, **16**, 417–26 (1977).

Klein, R.M. and Cronquist, A., A consideration of the evolutionary and taxonomic significance of some biochemical micromorphological and physiological characters in the thallophytes, *Q. Rev. Biol.*, **42**, 105–296 (1967).

Knaggs, F.W., A review of Florideophycidean life histories and of the culure techniques employed in their investigation, *Nova Hedwigia*, **18**, 293–330 (1969).

Kraft, G.T. and Robins, P.A., Is the order Cryptonemiales (Rhodophyta) defensible?, *Phycologia*, **24**, 67–77 (1985).

Kugrens, P., Electron microscopic observation on the differentiation and release of spermatia in the red alga *Polysiphonia hendryi* (Ceramiales, Rhodomelaceae), *Am. J. Bot.*, **67**, 519–28 (1980).

Kugrens, P. and Arif, I., Light and electron microscopic studies of the fusion cell in *Asterocolax gardneri* Setch. (Rhodophyta, Ceramiales), *J. Phycol.*, **17**, 215–25 (1981).

Kugrens, P. and Koslowsky, D.J., Electron microscopic studies on a unique cytokinetic structure in tetrasporocytes of red alga *Harveyella* sp. (Cryptonemiales, Choreocolaceae), *Protoplasma*, **108**, 197–209 (1981).

Lebednik, P.A., Postfertilization development in *Clathromorphum, Melobesia* and *Mesophyllum* with comments on the evolution of the Corallinaceae and the Cryptonemiales (Rhodophyta), *Phycologia*, **16**, 379–406 (1977).

Lee, I.K., Studies on Rhodymeniales from Hokkaido, *Jour. Fac. Sci.*, **11**, 1–194 (1978).

Lipkin, Y., *Centroceras*: the missile-launching marine red alga, *Nature*, **270**, 48–49 (1977).

Magne, F., Sur le deroulement et le lieu de la meiose chez les Lemaneaces (Rhodophycees, Nemalionales), *C.R. Acad. Sci.* (Paris), **265**, 670–73 (1967).

Masuda, M. and Umezaki, I., On the life history of *Nemalion vermiculare* Suringar (Rhodophyta) in culture, *Bull. Jap. Soc. Phycol.*, **25**, 129–36 (1977).

Mumford, T.F. and Cole, K.M., Chromosome numbers for fifteen species in the genus *Porphyra* (Bangiales, Rhodophyta) from the West Coast of North America, *Phycologia*, **16**, 373–77 (1977).

Neushul, M., Functional interpretation of benthic marine algal morphology. *In* Abbott, I.A. and Kurogi, M. (eds.) Contribution to the Systematics of Benthic Marine Algae of the North Pacific, 47–71, Japanese Phycological Society, Kobe, Japan (1972).

Oates, B.R. and Cole, K.M., Comparative studies on hair cells of two agarophyte red algae, *Gelidium vagum* (Gelidiales, Rhodophyta) and *Gracilaria pacifica* (Gracilariales, Rhodophyta), *Phycologia*, **33**, 420–33 (1994).

Ogata, E., Physiology of *Porphyra*. *In* Tokida, J. and Hirose, H. (eds.) Advance of Phycology in Japan, 151–60, W. Junk, The Hague (1975).

Oliveira, E.C. and Plastino, E.M., The life history of some species of *Gracilaria* (Rhodophyta) from Brazil, *Jap. J. Phycol.*, **32**, 203–208 (1984).

Ramm-Anderson, S.M. and Wetherbee, R., Structure and development of the carposporophyte of *Nemalion helminthoides* (Nemalionales, Rhodophyta), *J. Phycol.*, **18**, 133–41 (1982).

Reed, R.H., Osmoacclimation in *Bangia atropurpurea* (Rhodophyta, Bangiales): the osmotic role of floridoside, *Brit. Phycol. J.*, **20**, 211–18 (1985).

Rieth, A., Einige Überlegungen zur derzeitigen Situation von Taxonomie und Ökologie in der Algenkunde, *Limnologica* (Berlin), **2**, 267–79 (1964).

Rueness, J. and Rueness, M., Regular and irregular sequences in the life history of *Callithamnion tetragonum* (Rhodophyta, Ceramiales), *Brit. Phycol. J.*, **20**, 329–33 (1985).

Schiff, J.A., Evolution of the control of pigment and plastid development in photosynthetic organisms, *BioSystems*, **14**, 123–47 (1981).

Scott, J., Borco, C., Schornstein, K., and Thomas, J., Ultrastructure of cell division and reproductive differentiation of male plants in the Florideophyceae (Rhodophyta): cell division in *Polysiphonia*, *J. Phycol.*, **16**, 507–24 (1980).

Scott, J., Phillips, D., and Thomas, J., Polar rings are persistent organelles in *Polysiphonia*, *Phycologia*, **20**, 333–37 (1981).

Scott, J., Thomas, J., and Saunders, B., Primary pit connections in *Compsopogon caeruleus* (Balbis) Montagne (Compsopogonales, Rhodophyta), *Phycologia*, **27**, 327–33 (1988).

Sheath, R.G., Morison, M.O., Cole, K.M., and Vanalstyne, K.L., A new species of freshwater Rhodophyta, *Batrachospermum carpocontortum*, *Phycologia*, **25**, 321–30 (1986).

Sheath, R.G. and Whittick, A., The unique gonimoblast propagules of *Batrachospermum breutelii* (Batrachospermales, Rhodophyta), *Phycologia*, **34**, 33–38 (1995).

Smith, G.M., Cryptogamic Botany, Vol. I, Algae and Fungi, 2nd edn., McGraw-Hill, New York (1955).

Van der Meer, J.P., Genetics of *Gracilaria tikvahiae* (Rhodophyceae). 7. Further observations on mitotic recombination and the construction of polyploids, *Can. J. Bot.*, **59**, 787–92 (1981).

Van der Meer, J.P. and Todd, E., Genetics of *Gracilaria* sp. (Rhodophyceae, Gigartinales). 4. Mitotic recombination and its relationship to mixed phases in the life history, *Can. J. Bot.*, **55**, 2810–17 (1977).

Van der Meer, J.P., Genetics of *Gracilaria tikvahiae* (Rhodophyceae). XI. Further characterization of a bisexual mutant, *J. Phycol.*, **22**, 151–58 (1986).

Von Stosch, H.A. and Theil, G., A new mode of life history in the freshwater red algal genus *Batrachospermum*, *Am. J. Bot.*, **66**, 105–107 (1979).

Waaland, S.D., Parasexually produced hybrids between female and male plants of *Griffithsia tenuis* C. Agardh: a red alga, *Planta*, **138**, 65–68 (1978).

Watson, B.A. and Waaland, S.D., Partial purification and characterization of a glycoprotein cell fusion hormone from *Griffithsia pacifica, Plant Physiol.*, **71**, 327–32 (1983).

West, J.A. and Hommersand, M.H., Rhodophyta: life histories. *In* Lobban, C.S. and Wynne, M.J. (eds.) The Biology of Seaweeds, 133–93, Blackwell, Oxford (1981).

Yentsch, C.S., Light attenuation and phytoplankton photosynthesis. *In* Morris, I. (ed.) The Physiological Ecology of Phytoplankton, 95–127, Blackwell, Oxford (1980).

Zhang, X. and Van der Meer, J.P., Polyploid gametophytes of *Gracilaria tikvahiae* (Gigartinales, Rhodophyta), *Phycologia*, **27**, 312–18 (1988).

5 Cryptophyta

GENERAL CHARACTERS

Popularly called recoiling algae, these are eucaryotic, mostly unicellular and flagellated (rarely coccoid or palmelloid) algae which have green, blue, and red pigments including phycocyanin and phycoerythrin. The chloroplasts are parietal, commonly olive brown in colour. The motile stages have two somewhat unequal flagella borne laterally and apically and both the flagella are covered with stiff hairs. Several genera are animal-like in their morphology and nutrition, with the cell surface near the flagellar base being invaginated to form a large gullet (Fig. 5-1) which, especially in several colourless and saprophytic forms, functions as a means of ingestion of food particles. The reserve photosynthate is starch. The pigment spectrum includes chlorophyll-a and -ç, phycocyanin, phycoerythrin, β-carotene, ε-carotene, zeaxanthin, diatoxanthin, cryptoxanthin, dinoxanthin, and diadinoxanthin. Peridinin is conspicuously absent (see Chapman, 1966).

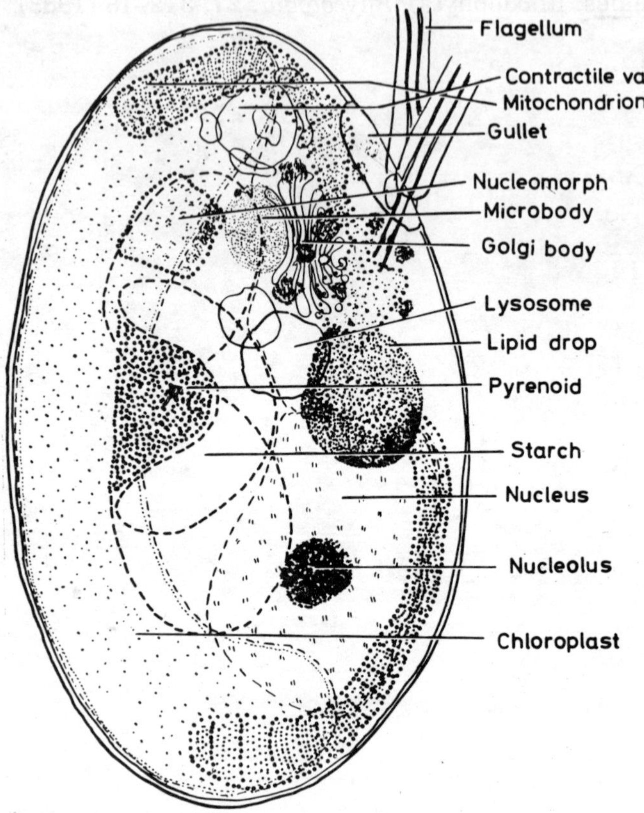

Fig. 5-1 *Hemiselmis rufescens*, cell structure (after Santore and Greenwood, 1977).

The cryptomonads are found in abundance in many habitats and quite frequently are the most abundant phytoflagellates in freshwater habitats.

MORPHOLOGY

Most cryptophytes are naked, motile, unicellular flagellates found in both marine and freshwater habitats. Their cells are generally ovoid slipper-like, being flattened dorsiventrally. *Cryptomonas* and several other genera have a prominent, tubular gullet. *Hemiselmis* has reniform cells with the flagella borne laterally; in lateral view, *Hemiselmis* is broadly hemispherical with a rounded posterior and a more acute anterior end. In many genera, however, the flagella are borne apically. In some species, the presence of fibrous rhizoplasts, which connect one of the blepharoplasts to the nucleus or the centrosome, has been established.

Most cryptophytes have two large parietal chloroplasts per cell (Fig. 5-2) but a few species have several discoid plastids. The endosymbiont of *Mesodinium rubrum* contains more than two chloroplasts per cell. Some cryptophytes have a single, lobed chloroplast per cell. Several pyrenoid-like structures are present within the cell. The cells also have Golgi bodies, mitochondria, and usually a single contractile vacuole at the anterior end. The cells are commonly uninucleate with the nucleus being typically eucaryotic. The chromosomes are nonmoniliform and the chromatin is granular. In holozoic cryptomonads, e.g., *Cyathomonas*, trichocysts line the gullet; in other species, they may line the gullet region as well as the cell periphery.

Species of *Cryptomonas* commonly have small and large trichocysts of identical morphology. The smaller ones are arranged in a regular fashion beneath the periplast; such subperiplastal location of trichocysts causes a regular indenting of the cell surface. The larger ones (about 10 times larger than the small trichocyst) line the inner surface of the gullet (see Lucas, 1970). The trichocysts are contained within single-membraned sacs.

The cryptophytan trichocysts differ somewhat in structure and mode of ejection from those found in the Pyrrhophyta. These cryptophytan trichocysts act as a means of escape and also as buffers against adverse conditions.

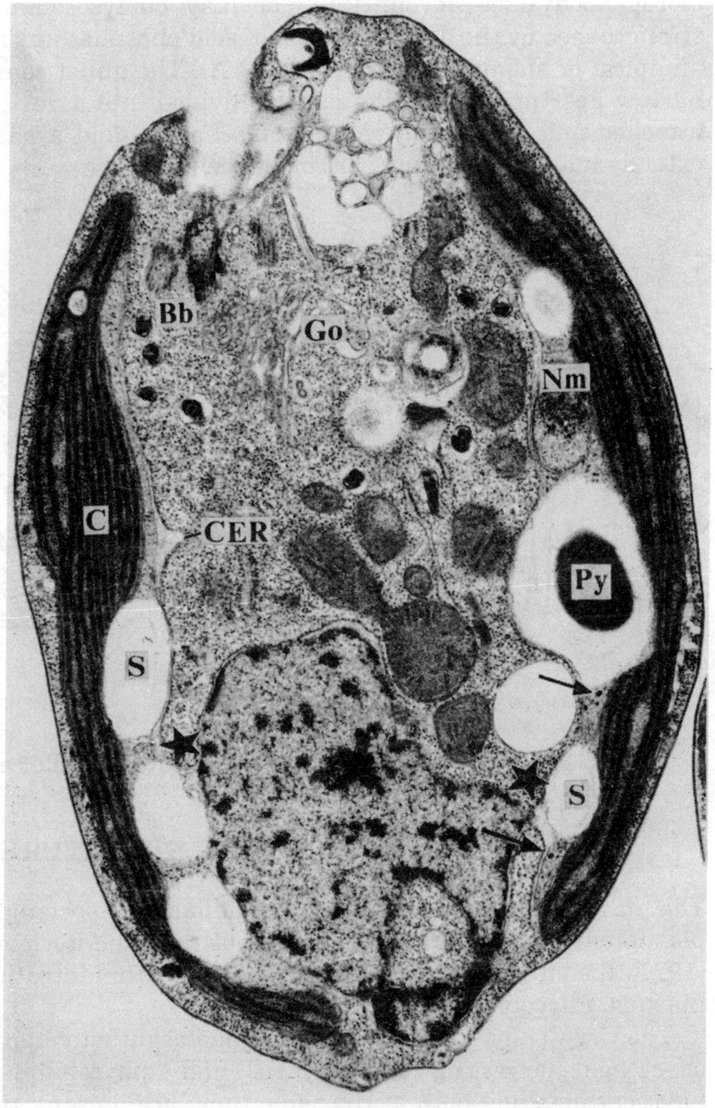

Fig. 5-2 *Cryptomonas* sp., longitudinal section through early preprophase cell, showing presence of starch grains, ribosomes, dense globules, and nucleomorph in periplastidial compartment. Bb, basal bodies; C, chloroplast; S, starch; arrows, dense globules; Nm, nucleomorph; CER, chloroplast ER; stars, nuclear envelope; Go, Golgi; Py, pyrenoid. (×18,800.) (After McKerracher and Gibbs, 1982.) *Courtesy* S.P. Gibbs.

Some cryptomonads possess roughly spherical structures, usually two per cell, between the Golgi apparatus and the chloroplast. These structures are called *Corps de Maupas* and are sometimes visible even under the light microscope. Functionally, they may represent a food storage body (see Joyon, 1963) or may be lysosomal (Lucas, 1970). The latter view is strengthened by the demonstration of acid phosphatases in the cells. Many cryptomonads have an apical or subapical gullet (Fig. 5-3 A). The gullet consists of a tubular invagination and a narrow aperture. The gullet can be divided into a vestibular region (where the flagella are attached and contractile vacuoles discharge), and a channel (lined with trichocysts) which extends into the posterior part of the cell.

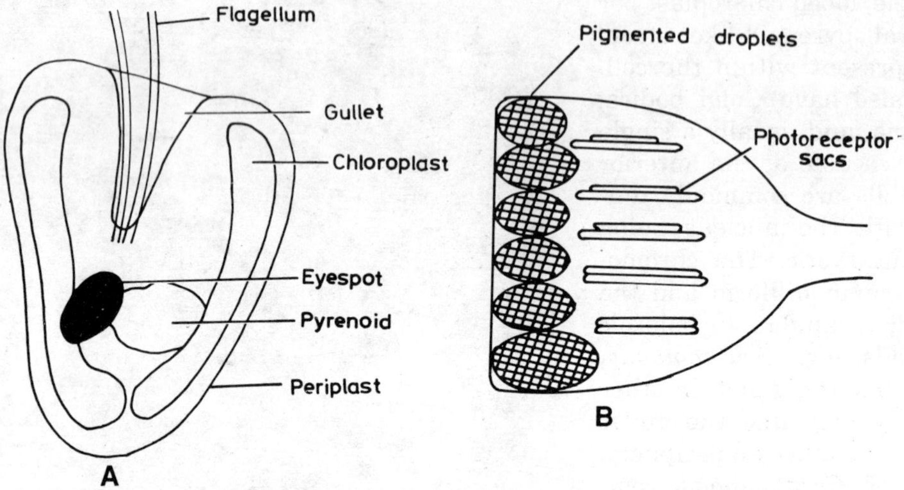

Fig. 5-3 *Chroomonas*. A, whole cell, showing gullet and other structures; B, eyespot.

FINE STRUCTURE

The plastids contain thylakoids predominantly associated in pairs, traversing the stroma. The plastid envelope is generally continuous with the nuclear envelope. According to Gantt *et al.* (1971), the biliprotein pigments are located within intrathylakoidal spaces in the cryptophytan plastids. Phycobilisomes are lacking.

The Cryptophyceae have a unique photosynthetic apparatus in which both a chlorophyll-a or -c2 light-harvesting complex (LHC) and a phycobiliprotein antenna (either phycocyanin or phycoerythrin, not both at the same time) are present; the biliprotein plays the major role in harvesting light (Spear-Bernstein and Miller, 1989). This protein pigment appears to be located in the intrathylakoidal space (Fig. 5-4) and not on the outer surface of the thylakoid as part of a phycobilisome as in red algae and cyanobacteria. Such a location of the chief light-harvesting pigment on the "wrong" side of the otherwise quite normal thylakoids is unexpected and unique to the cryptophytes and appears not to impair the photosynthetic abilities.

Three types of pyrenoid are known in the Cryptophyta, viz., single stalked, multiple stalked, and invaginated. The single stalked pyrenoids are covered by a sheath or cap or reserve

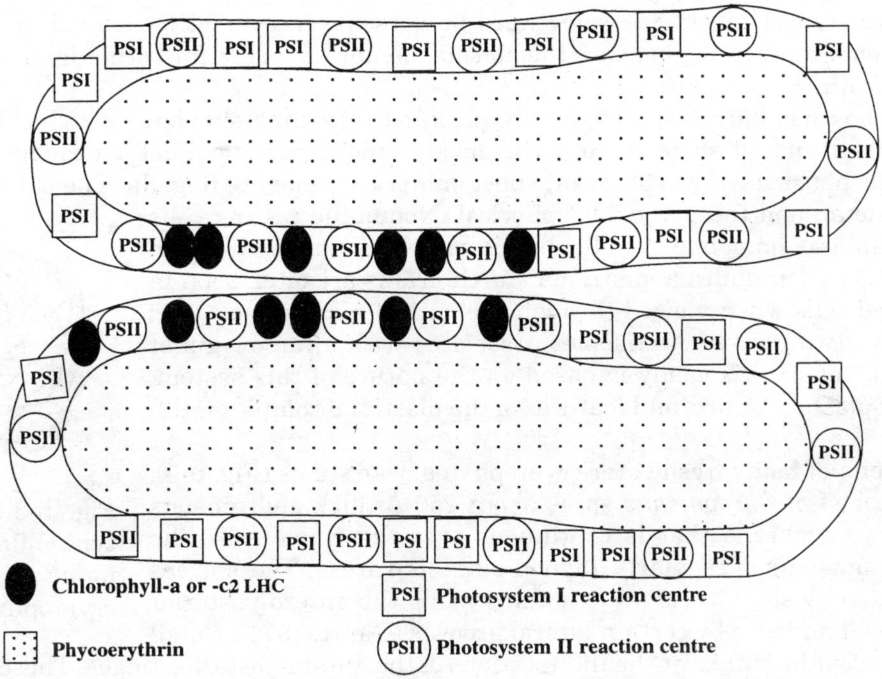

Fig. 5-4 *Rhodomonas lens*. Possible organization of thylakoid components in the cryptophytes (after Spear-Bernstein and Miller, 1989).

polysaccharide; the cap is located between the ER sheath and the pyrenoid envelope and the intervening cavity often also harbours starch grains. Two or more starch grains surround the pyrenoid in some species of *Cryptomonas*; in other species of the same genus, finger-like cytoplasmic processes invaginate the pyrenoid.

Eyespots (Fig. 5-3 B) are uncommon in this phylum and form part of a chloroplast but not obviously associated with the flagella. A shallow, cup-shaped stigma is situated in the chloroplast just below the end of the gullet in *Cryptomonas rostrella*.

The mitotic process in the Cryptophyceae seems to be unique (see Dodge, 1973). Microtubules are present in the cytoplasm outside the nucleus before the commencement of mitosis. The nuclear membrane breaks down by metaphase and the chromosomes form a dense plate on the equator at metaphase. Numerous spindle tubules pass through the metaphase plate and some of them may be attached to it. Distinct centrioles seem to be lacking. The cryptophycean mitosis resembles in some respects that of the Chrysophyceae and the Haptophyceae, but is entirely different from that of the Dinophyceae. The mitotic spindle in this class is generally barrel-shaped, wider than long, and located near the anterior end of the cell with its axis being perpendicular to the long axis of the cell. During spindle formation, microtubules reorientate through 90° angle so as to align themselves in parallel with the spindle. The flagellar bases and associated material appear to act as microtubule nucleating centres but do not have any role in ordering microtubules into a parallel array (Oakley, 1978).

The cells are covered by a peculiar proteinaceous periplast with regularly disposed thin plate thickenings. The periplast consists of a continuous outer membrane on the outer side of which another outer layer may sometimes be present. A layer of hexagonal or rectangular plates or membranes occurs beneath the plasma membrane. A few microtubules are occasionally seen beneath the periplast.

Chroomonas has barrel-shaped, rarely acuminate (comma-shaped) cells that look bluish-green in colour and, at some stage, form thickly mucilaginous palmelloid colonies. The cells in the motile phase have two anterior, subequal, briskly moving flagella. The chloroplasts are simple, parietal, and the pyrenoids spherical. Nonmotile resting cells split up into 1–4 immobile gonidia by successive divisions. Certain minute refractive granules and stroma starch grains are often seen in cryptomonad cells when viewed through the optical microscope.

Cells have two rows of ejectisomes associated with a furrow-gullet system. The generic taxonomy is based on the nature of this system, besides periplast structure, and features of the plastidial complex (Hill, 1991).

The flagella of many freshwater cryptophytes bear scales (Fig. 5-5).

Fig. 5-5 A common type of flagellar scale found in freshwater cryptophytes.

The periplast of *Chroomonas* sp. is about 250 Å thick and consists of a plasma membrane that is continuous over the whole cell. The periplast is made up of regularly aligned plate-like areas. These areas are delineated by shallow ridges extending along the antero-posterior axis of the cell and also by certain lateral grooves (Gantt, 1971). Small trichocysts occur as bumps at the intersections of the antero-posterior ridges. These trichocysts seem to form part of the periplast.

Unlike other algae having chloroplast ER, the space between the chloroplast envelope and the chloroplast ER in the Cryptophyceae contains diverse structures including a small double-membrane limited body called nucleomorph (Figs. 5-6 and 5-1). The nucleomorph might represent a vestigial nucleus of a eucaryotic symbiont. Gibbs (1981) believes that the red algae invaded the colourless cryptomonads and the eucaryotic symbiont became progressively reduced during evolution until all that remained was the chloroplast, a small rudimentary nucleus (=nucleomorph), 80S ribosomes, starch grains, and some tubules and vesicles.

In many Cryptophyceae such as *Chilomonas, Rhodomonas*, and *Cyathomonas*, the contractile vacuole occupies a fixed position in the cell lying adjacent to the flagellar groove/pocket. A small region of the flagellar pocket is invaginated so that the plasmalemma lies close to the membrane of the contractile vacuole. This region behaves as a pore through which the vacuolar contents are voided to the exterior. The discharge of the contents follows the fusion of the contractile vacuole membrane with the plasmalemma (Fig. 5-7) of the pore (Patterson and Hausmann, 1981). Filling initially involves the fusion of small vacuoles that emerge around the contractile vacuole immediately prior to the discharge of its contents. These vacuoles undergo fusion and filling can continue by the accretion of small vesicles which constitute the spongiome surrounding the contractile vacuole. Two types of vesicles exist in the spongiome, namely, type 1, which plays a role in the filling of the contractile vacuole, and type 2, which is involved in the retrieval of membrane from the filling vacuole. Type 1 seems to be formed by fragmentation of the contractile vacuole membrane during the discharge of the vacuolar contents (Patterson and Hausmann, 1981).

Hemiselmis rufescens represents one of the simplest species of Cryptophyceae. The cells possess a single, large, excentric, parietal chloroplast whose outer surface lies close to the periplast. Two flagella are inserted towards the anterior edge of the cell. Pennick (1981) has reported the presence of flagellar scales in the two species *H. virescens* and *H. brunnescens*. The long flagellum in these species bears two rows of mastigonemes each of which terminates

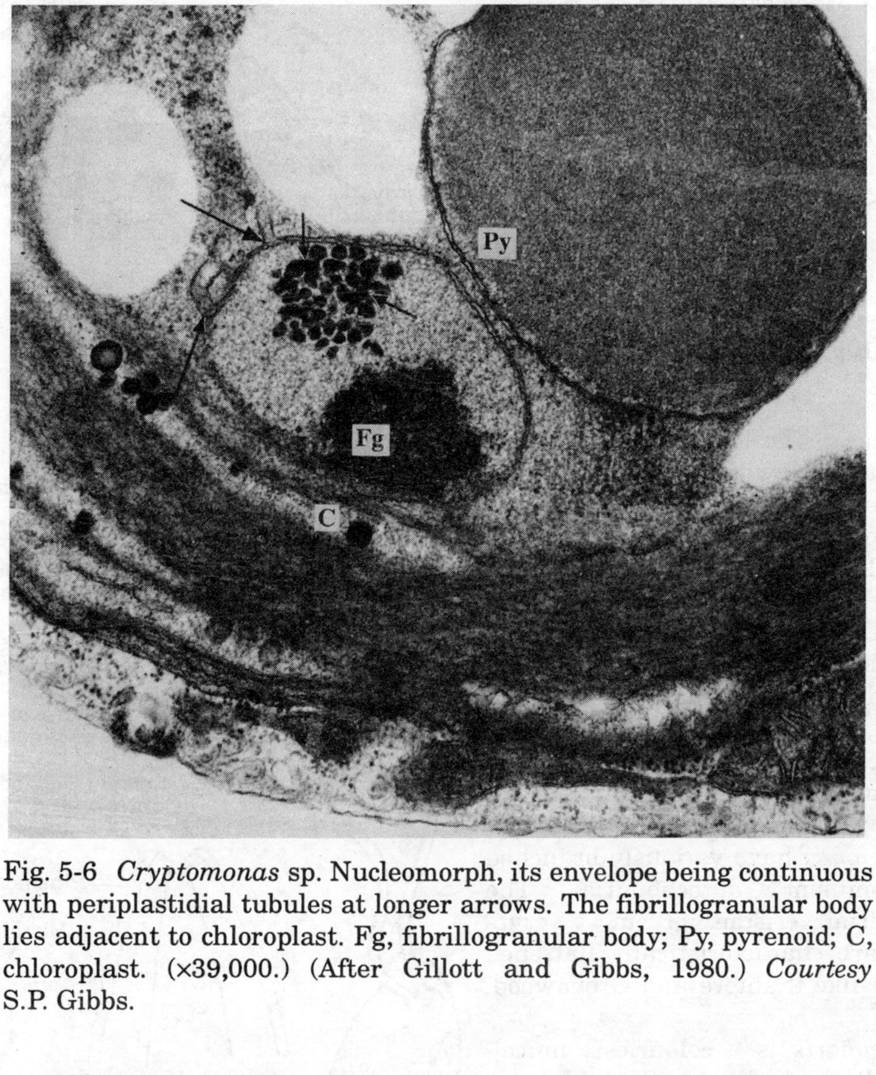

Fig. 5-6 *Cryptomonas* sp. Nucleomorph, its envelope being continuous with periplastidial tubules at longer arrows. The fibrillogranular body lies adjacent to chloroplast. Fg, fibrillogranular body; Py, pyrenoid; C, chloroplast. (×39,000.) (After Gillott and Gibbs, 1980.) *Courtesy* S.P. Gibbs.

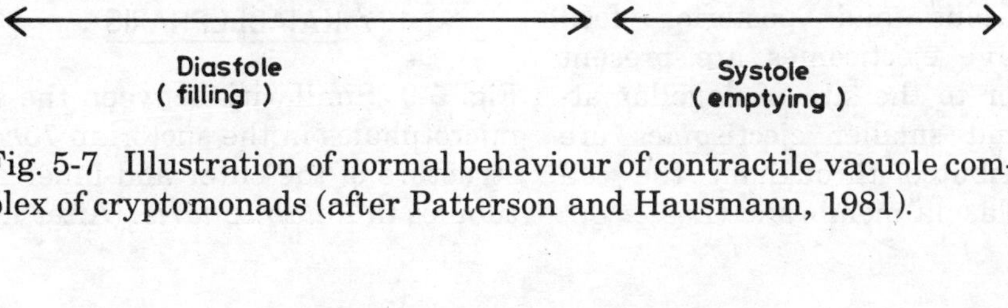

Fig. 5-7 Illustration of normal behaviour of contractile vacuole complex of cryptomonads (after Patterson and Hausmann, 1981).

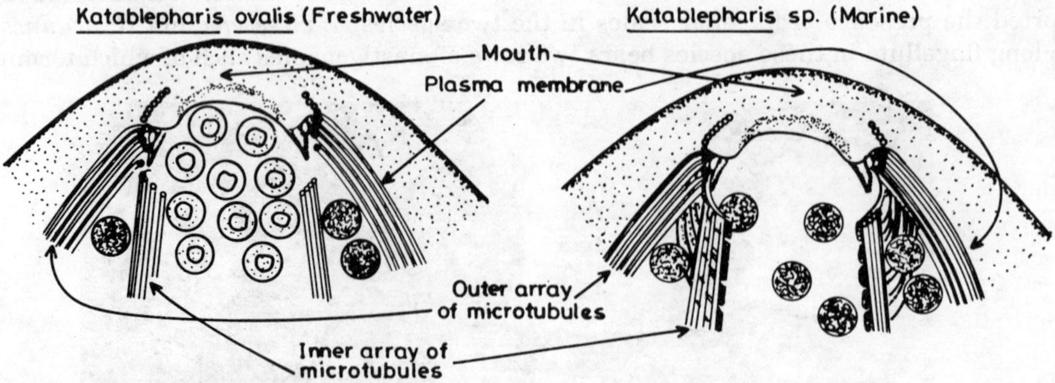

Fig. 5-8 *Katablepharis*. Anterior part of cell of *K. ovalis* and *K.* clone G-2. (After Lee *et al.*, 1991.)

in a filament. The longer flagellum also bears some narrower, shorter filaments. The shorter flagellum bears a single row of mastigonemes, each with a terminal filament. The surfaces of both flagella are covered with an imbricate layer of fine, 7-sided scales. A conspicuous pyrenoid and starch sheath project inwards from the plastid. The mitochondria occur in the cytoplasm, mostly near the flagellar bases. Generally, an unbranched vermiform mitochondrion is found in *H. rufescens*, whereas *Chroomonas* and spp. of *Cryptomonas* have variously branched and prominent mitochondria. The mitochondrial cristae of most cryptophytes are characteristically flattened and finger-like (Santore and Greenwood, 1977).

Katablepharis is a colourless, unicellular flagellate which occurs in freshwater (*K. ovalis*) and marine (clone G-2) habitats. The biflagellate cells have a central nucleus and posterior food vacuole. Large ejectisomes are present just posterior to the site of flagellar attachment and smaller ejectisomes are evenly distributed throughout the cell under the plasma membrane (Lee *et al.*,

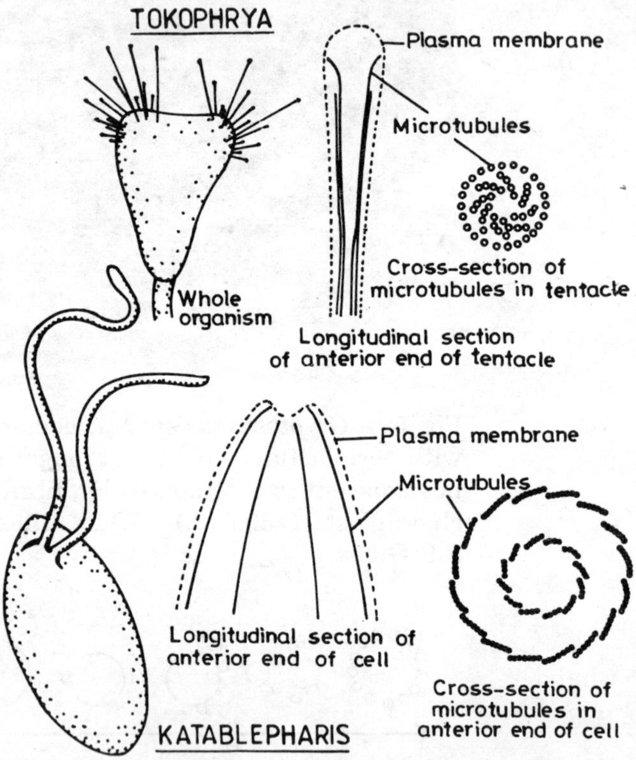

Fig. 5-9 Similarity between the structure of the microtubules in the suctorian *Tokophrya*, and the structure of the outer and inner arrays of microtubules in *Katablepharis*. (After Lee *et al.*, 1991.)

1991). Small microbes are taken in at the mouth and pass through a feeding apparatus to the food vacuole where they are digested. Figure 5-8 illustrates the anterior part of the cells of *K. ovalis* and *K.* clone G-2.

The feeding apparatus of these two species consists of inner and outer oval-shaped arrays of microtubules that begin at the anterior end of the cell and pass into its posterior. Each array of microtubules contains groups of microtubules with 2–8 microtubules per group depending on the position of the array in the cell. The mouth is at the anterior end of the cell. It is oval and has a raised ridge surrounding a central depression. The anterior end of the microtubules of the inner and outer arrays supports the raised ridge of the mouth (Lee *et al.*, 1991). Three small membrane cisternae occur on the protoplasmic side of the plasma membrane in the area of the mouth. Certain vesicles are associated with the microtubular arrays.

Both the inner and outer microtubular arrays of *Katablepharis* are quite similar to the microtubular arrays in the tentacles of the suctoria (Fig. 5-9). In the latter, the tentacular microtubules consist of an outer cylinder of tubules surrounding an inner circle. In both suctoria and *Katablepharis*, the microtubular arrays function in capturing the prey.

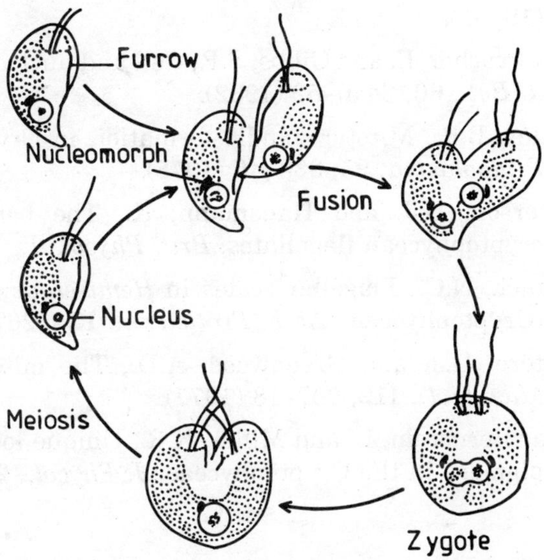

Fig. 5-10 The life cycle of *Cryptomonas* sp.

REPRODUCTION

Cell division is the most common method of multiplication. The motile unicellular cryptomonads divide longitudinally (Fig. 5-10) and the division proceeds even when the organisms are still motile.

The palmelloid forms, e.g., *Phaeococcus*, produce biflagellate zoospores. Zoospore formation has also been recorded in the coccoid alga *Tetragonidium*. These zoospores metamorphose to form the typically tetragonal vegetative cells.

Sexuality does not seem to have been reported in any cryptophyte.

REFERENCES

Chapman, D.J., Three new carotenoids isolated from algae, *Phytochemistry*, **5**, 1331–33 (1966).

Dodge, J.D., The Fine Structure of Algal Cells, Academic Press, London (1973).

Gantt, E., Micromorphology of the periplast of *Chroomonas* sp. (Cryptophyceae), *J. Phycol.*, **7**, 177–84 (1971).

Gantt, E., Edward, M.R., and Provasoli, L., Chloroplast structure in the Cryptophyceae: evidence for phycobiliproteins within intrathylakoidal spaces, *J. Cell Biol.*, **48**, 280–90 (1971).

Gibbs, S.P., The chloroplast endoplasmic reticulum: structure, function and evolutionary significance, *Internat. Rev. Cytol.*, **72**, 49–95 (1981).

Gillott, M.A. and Gibbs, S.P., The cryptomonad nucleomorph: its ultrastructure and evolutionary significance, *J. Phycol.*, **16**, 558–68 (1980).

Hill, D.R.A., *Chroomonas* and other blue-green cryptomonads, *J. Phycol.*, **27**, 133–45 (1991).

Joyon, L., Contribution a l'etude cytologique de quelques protozoaires flagellés, *Ann. Fac. Sci. Univ. Clermont. Biol.*, **22**, 1–96 (1963).

Lee, R.E., Kugrens, P., and Mylnikov, A.P., Feeding apparatus of the colorless flagellate *Katablepharis* (Cryptophyceae), *J. Phycol.*, **27**, 725–33 (1991).

Lucas, I.A.N., Observations on the fine structure of the Cryptophyceae, *J. Phycol.*, **6**, 30–38 (1970).

McKerracher, L. and Gibbs, S.P., Cell and nucleomorph division in the alga *Cryptomonas*, *Can. J. Bot.*, **60**, 2440–52 (1982).

Oakley, B.R., Mitotic spindle formation in *Cryptomonas* and *Chroomonas* (Cryptophyceae), *Protoplasma*, **95**, 333–46 (1978).

Patterson, D.J. and Hausmann, K., The behaviour of contractile vacuole complexes of cryptophycean flagellates, *Brit. Phycol. J.*, **16**, 429–39 (1981).

Pennick, N.C., Flagellar scales in *Hemiselmis brunnescens* Butcher and *H. virescens* Droop (Cryptophyceae), *Arch. Protistenk.*, **124**, 267–70 (1981).

Santore, U.J. and Greenwood, A.D., The mitochondrial complex in Cryptophyceae, *Arch. Microbiol.*, **112**, 207–18 (1977).

Spear-Bernstein, L. and Miller, K.R., Unique location of the phycobiliprotein light-harvesting pigment in the Cryptophyceae, *J. Phycol.*, **25**, 412–19 (1989).

6 Euglenophyta

GENERAL CHARACTERS

The euglenoids are mostly unicellular eucaryotic organisms exhibiting some plant-like and some animal-like characters. The absence of firm cell walls, their motility, their holozoic (along with holophytic) nutrition, and their animal-like gullet, cytopharyngeal apparatus, and contractile vacuoles make them resemble many protozoans. However, most euglenoids are photosynthetic having such pigments as chlorophyll-a and -b, β-carotene, lutein, neoxanthin, antheraxanthin, and astaxanthin. These pigments are located in discoid, rod-shaped, ribbon-like, or stellate chloroplasts. Paramylum, wax, and oil are the usual storage reserves, with paramylum (a β-1:3-linked glucan) occurring as several discrete granules in the cells. Phospholipid vesicles and lysosomes are also known to occur in euglenoid cells. A cellulosic cell wall is lacking and the cells have only a soft or rigid periplast. The cell surface is often helical, and has knobby or warty projections. The organisms having a soft pellicle, e.g., *Euglena*, exhibit a characteristic contractile (flowing) type of motility, whereas those having a firm pellicle, e.g., *Phacus*, have a fixed shape and lack flexibility. The cells of *Trachelomonas* (Fig. 6-1) and a few other genera are loricate. The cells are anteriorly biflagellate but only one flagellum (the longer one) emerges out from the anterior invagination, whereas the other, shorter one, stops short, is non-emergent, and is generally fused with the basal part of the long flagellum. Some genera are colourless and these may have 1, 2 or 3 flagella. All euglenoids have two or more blepharoplasts. The euglenoids reproduce by longitudinal fission and seem to lack sexuality.

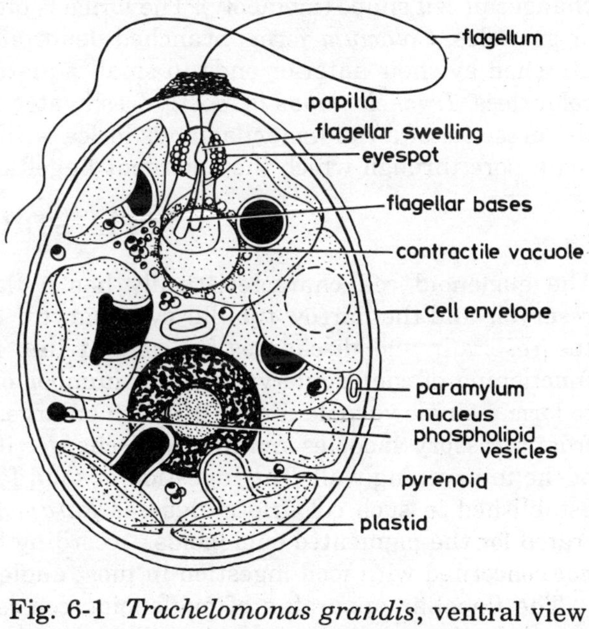

Fig. 6-1 *Trachelomonas grandis*, ventral view of cell structure (after Leedale, 1967).

OCCURRENCE

The euglenoids occur in freshwater, brackish water, marine and terrestrial habitats, and are common in polluted ponds and temporary pools rich in organic matter. They occur only sparsely in the phytoplankton of freshwater lakes.

MORPHOLOGY

Euglena, Trachelomonas, Phacus, Astasia, and several other genera are unicellular. *Colacium* is colonial (dendroid or palmelloid). The cells may be spindle-shaped, fusiform, cylindrical or discoid. They are often flattened and may also be curved or twisted.

The genus *Colacium* is epibiotic and can exist in any of three distinct stages during its life cycle, namely, (1) the free-swimming, flagellate stage, (2) the attached or stalked, nonflagellate stage, and (3) the palmelloid stage. The transition of the flagellated motile stage to the nonmotile, stalked stage occurs in three phases, viz., (1) initial attachment, presumably by means of the flagellum, (2) formation of attachment disc, when the anterior end of the cell comes in contact with the substratum, and (3) extension of the mucilaginous stalk material. Immediately after the initial attachment, the stalk may be resorbed or degraded. The polysaccharide derived from within the intracellular cisternae initially accumulates in the reservoir, then collects in the canal, finally becoming incorporated in the growing stalk (Ward and Willey, 1981). The actual extension of stalk material through the canal is facilitated by metaboly.

Phacus has broadly oval, trilobed cells which have a tail at the posterior end. *Trachelomonas* includes *Euglena*-like cells enclosed in a shell or lorica; like *Euglena*, this alga also exhibits changes in cell shape (metaboly). The lorica is often beautifully ornamented with warts, spines or granules. *Colacium* forms branched dendroid colonies in which *Euglena*-like cells remain attached by their anterior ends to small aquatic animals. *Astasia* resembles *Euglena* but is colourless. *Trachelomonas* is mostly freshwater. Cytologically, it resembles *Euglena* except for the presence of a rigid, mucilaginous lorica with an anterior neck-like construction surrounding a pore through which the emergent flagellum extends.

CELL STRUCTURE

The euglenoid cell characteristically has a flask-shaped gullet which includes the basal reservoir and the narrow tubular cytopharynx. One (or more) contractile vacuole occurs near the reservoir and discharges its content into it. Figure 6-2 illustrates the likely mode of functioning of contractile vacuoles. A number of small accessory vacuoles (Fig. 6-2) coalesce to form a single vacuole (Fig. 6-2) which enlarges (Fig. 6-2) as a result of intake of more fluids from accessory vacuoles and finally discharges its contents into the reservoir after breakdown of the intervening wall. The ingestion of solid food particles through the gullet has been well established in such colourless algae as *Paranema*, but does not seem to have been demonstrated for the pigmented euglenoids. According to Leedale (1967), the anterior invagination is *not* concerned with food ingestion in most euglenoids.

The flagellar apparatus of euglenoids consists of two functional basal bodies and three unequal microtubular roots subtending the reservoir. A fourth group of microtubules arises from one of the flagellated roots and lines the reservoir membrane (Farmer and Triemer, 1988). Some euglenoids also have additional basal bodies, striated roots (rhizoplasts), fibrous roots, and striated connecting fibres between basal bodies. Most euglenoids are biflagellate though one of the two flagella may be shorter or reduced.

A very distinctive feature of the euglenoid flagellar apparatus is a cytoplasmic pocket called cryptic cytostome. This is present in such phototrophic species as *Euglena mutabilis*. In this species, as the ventral flagellar root proceeds anteriorly, it branches off from the lining of the reservoir into the cytoplasm, and forms a small cytoplasmic pocket which is lined on one side by the microtubules of the ventral root. The pocket extends some distance into the cytoplasm before terminating.

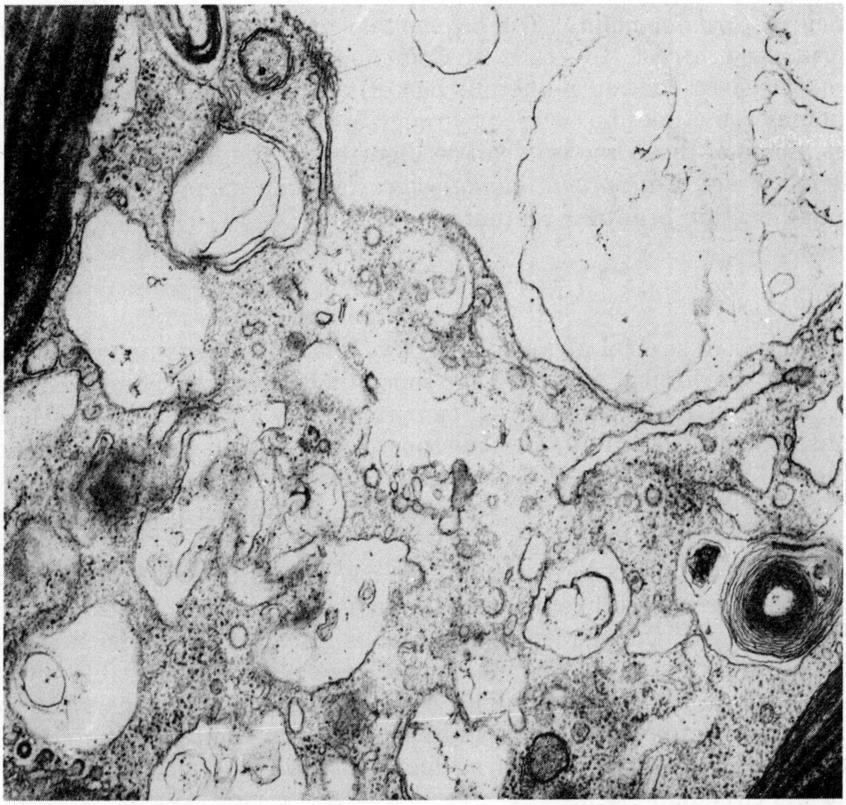

Fig. 6-2 *Euglena*, contractile vacuole, coated vesicles, and other large vesicles. (×23,050.) *Courtesy* K. Ueda.

The cells are commonly uninucleate. The spindle is absent and the metaphase plate is incomplete. The nucleolus divides independent of the chromosomes; such a nucleolus, which is also persistent, and is not apparently associated with nucleolar organizing chromosomes, is called endosome. In *Astasia* and *Trachelomonas*, the flagellar bases seem to act like centrioles. The chromatids seem to lack centromeres. During mitosis, the nuclear envelope remains intact and the nucleolus persists and divides. The chromosomes remain condensed during the entire nuclear cycle. Even during interphase, the euglenoid chromosomes are significantly more highly condensed and distinct than in other eucaryotes. The occurrence of meiosis, though reported by Leedale (1962), has not yet been convincingly demonstrated and is certainly not common.

In normal mitosis of other eucaryotes, a spindle, consisting of *continuous microtubules* (from plate to plate) and *chromosomal microtubules* (from centromeres to poles), is organized. The chromosomal microtubules seem to be absent in *Euglena* (Leedale, 1970). In euglenoids, microtubules are formed only in the nucleus. In some species, even cytoplasmic microtubules are absent (see Leedale, 1970). The nucleoplasmic microtubules is a characteristic feature of the Euglenophyta.

Some species of *Strombomonas, Trachelomonas,* and *Euglena spirogyra* harbour endonuclear bacteria. In contrast, the cells of *Colacium vesiculosum, Euglena mutabilis,* and *Eutreptiella eupharyngea* contain numerous bacteria in their cytoplasm (Walne *et al.*, 1986). These bacteria may sometimes be covered by rough endoplasmic reticulum, forming lysosome-like structures. Some of these bacteria can be digested by the host.

Some euglenoids, e.g., *Eutreptiella eupharyngea*, contain some elongate mucocysts which are vacuolate and contain granular contents.

CELL DIVISION CYCLE

The cell division cycle of several algae such as *Euglena, Chlamydomonas, Acetabularia*, and others seems to be some kind of a clock in the sense that there is a sequence of environmental conditions. The cell division cycle may itself be regulated by a programmable clock that, under some conditions, generates circadian periodicities by interaction with a circadian pacemaker. It is believed that these clocks insert time segments into the algal cell division cycle and that such insertion generates the observed variability in cell generation times (Edmunds and Adams, 1981).

According to Edmunds and Adams (1981), the sequential events of the cell division cycle do not constitute the chronometer controlling the temporal spacing of these events by a simple stoppage and restarting of the sequence; this means that the cell division cycle itself is not the clock. They visualize that a kind of cytochron (a separate programmable entity) is involved in the interpretation of the environmental signals, leading to the insertion or deletion of appropriate time loops, of specified sign and specified duration, into the cell division cycle. The work done on some mutants of *Euglena* has indicated that the cytochron is functionally independent of the circadian clock.

The effect of light on many euglenoids appears to be regulated by a biological clock: these algae show a phototactic response to light during normal daylight hours but fail to respond either positively or negatively during normal dark periods, even when exposed to light.

FINE STRUCTURE

The chloroplast lamellae mostly have three thylakoids each, but bands of 2, 4, 5, and 6 thylakoids are also sometimes present (see Gibbs, 1970). Adjacent thylakoids often seem to be firmly adherent. Unlike Chlorophyceae and Prasinophyceae, no starch is synthesized within the chloroplasts. The chloroplast envelope of euglenoids consists of three membranes. The euglenoid plastids can divide either synchronously with or independent of cell division. Considerable biochemical and genetical work has been done on the nucleic acids of euglenoid plastids and on the genetic continuity and information content of these plastids.

Most euglenoids have a large eyespot which does not form part of a chloroplast but which is situated adjacent to the flagella (Fig. 6-3) and the reservoir. Even though there is a marked correlation between the action spectrum of phototaxis and the absorption spectrum of the eyespot, the eyespot seems to function as an intermittent light screen for the flagellar swelling which (swelling) is thought to be a real photosensory organ (see Buetow, 1968). The eyespot contains all or some of the following pigments: echinenone, euglenanone, hydroxyechinenone, astaxanthin, β-carotene, cryptoxanthin, and lutein.

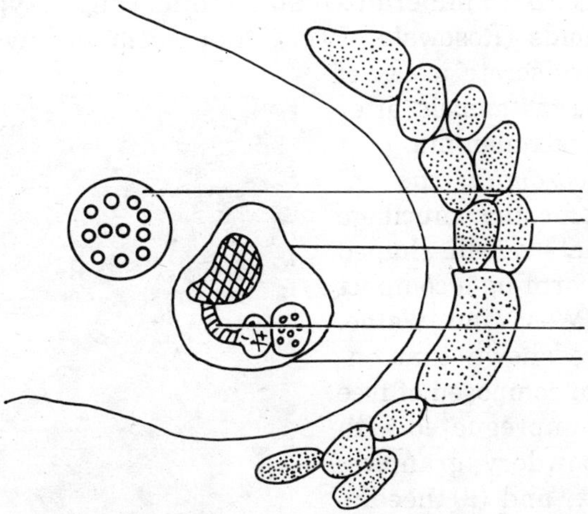

Fig. 6-3 *Euglena*, anterior view of cross-section through eyespot apparatus (after Kivic and Vesk, 1972).

In *Euglena gracilis*, the photoreceptor pigment involved in phototaxis is a flavoprotein, not a carotenoid or rhodopsin as is likely in green algae. The paraflagellar body is a swelling at the base of the flagellum (see Fig. 6-4) and is believed to be the photoreceptor. The stigma is a small pigmented mass which lies in the cytoplasm on one side of the paraflagellar body and serves as a kind of screening device for light. The stigma contains carotenoid pigments located in minute granules with no stalked layers. The paraflagellar body is connected to the paraflagellar rod and lies within the membrane of the emergent flagellum in front of a large screen of pigmented droplets. The overall design of the eyespot apparatus is one of a detector abutting a shading device.

The periplast is made of numerous flat, articulating, proteinaceous segments (see Arnott and Walne, 1967; Schwelitz *et al.,* 1970) disposed spirally around the whole cell and covered by means of an outer plasmalemma. These interlocking strips fuse into one another at each end of the cell. The periplastic strips of *E. spirogyra* have continuous ridges which face outward and which articulate in a groove along the overlapping edge of the adjacent strip. Some sideways movement can occur between two adjoining strips by the sliding action of the ridge in the groove and by stretching and compression of pellicular material. Regularly disposed microtubules occur beneath the periplast segments. Frequently, certain muciferous bodies occur adjacent to the periplastic grooves and are connected with them by pores (see Dodge, 1973). The muciferous bodies are formed from the peripheral part of the endoplasmic reticulum. It is likely that these bodies provide lubrication for the sliding action of ridges and grooves. All euglenoid flagellates excrete mucilage and are covered with a thin slimy layer which sometimes accumulates as a tail at the posterior end of the cell. *Colacium* has characteristic stalks and envelopes made of mucilage. The stalk of *C. mucronatum* is composed primarily of a cylindrical shaft (which is the main structural element), an inner core, and a diffuse peripheral cortex. The stalk seems to be mainly made of carbohydrate material. All members of this class produce some extracellular polysaccharide or mucilage. Creeping species of *Euglena* secrete abundant mucilage. Both mineralized and unmineralized types of mucilage are known to be formed by euglenoids (Rosowski, 1977); they seem to have a distinctive structure since they originate from discrete areas of individual strands which undergo anastomosis after release to the outer surface of the plasmalemma.

In *Trachelomonas hispida* var. *coronata,* the envelope is made of 20 nm anastomosing mucilage threads plus powdery, crystalline, needle-shaped granular mineral deposits, together forming a compact layer that has pores and spines (West and Walne, 1980). West and Walne (1980) have shown that envelopes of *Trachelomonas hispida* are composed of free and anastomosing mucilage strands impregnated with two types of minerals, viz., (1) powdery granules, dispersed within the organic matrix, and (2) needle-shaped microcrystallites, forming axial cores within the mucilage strands. The frequently observed variability in envelope colour, ornamentation, and micromorphology of several species of *Trachelomonas* grown in laboratory cultures may perhaps be the result of environmental factors. West and Walne have also demonstrated that manganese is deposited in the envelopes of *Trachelomonas*.

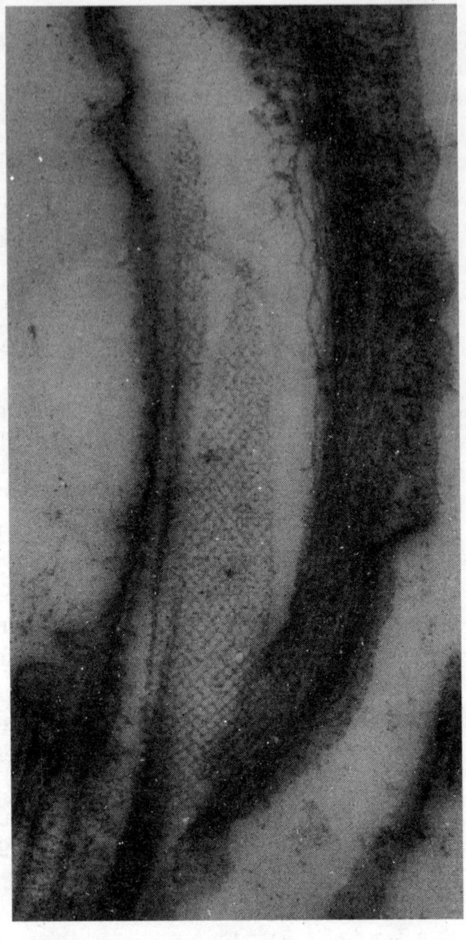

Fig. 6-4 *Trachelomonas*, paraflagellar rod in flagellum. (×42,000.) *Courtesy* K. Ueda.

Species of *Trachelomonas* show a biphasic pattern of envelope development that involves the deposition of mucilage and minerals (chiefly iron) on transitory or permanent primary skin. The envelopes of *T. bulla* have a granular microarchitecture with iron as the major element. Those of *T. zorensis* contain variable proportions of spatially segregated iron and manganese; in these, the Fe-rich regions are granular, whereas the Mn-rich regions are needle-like (Barnes *et al.*, 1986).

The envelopes of *Strombomonas conspersa* are ornamented. When unmineralized, the envelopes appear colourless but when mineralized (mostly with Mn), they are darker. The presence of coarse mucilage strands imparts a rough appearance to the envelopes.

Some euglenoids have a compound internal pyrenoid through which the plastid lamellae (two thylakoids each) run more or less in a parallel manner. Others, e.g., *Colacium* and *Trachelomonas*, have single-stalked pyrenoids having 2-thylakoid plastid lamellae inside them. Some species of *Euglena* have multiple-stalked pyrenoids having a paramylum sheath.

A single row of long fine hairs occurs along the emergent portions of euglenoid flagella. A felt of fibrous material coats the whole length of both locomotory and nonlocomotory flagella in many species (see Leedale, 1967). The locomotory flagellum of *Euglena spirogyra* also has stiff hairs at its tip. The larger flagellum of *Euglena, Trachelomonas, Phacus*, and a few others bears a lateral swelling just opposite the eyespot. The functional significance of such swelling is obscure.

A well developed endoplasmic reticulum occurs in the euglenoid cell and develops into such elements as the muciferous bodies, the nuclear wall, and certain irregular tubular extensions of the perinuclear space. The tubular smooth ER occurs mainly around the nuclear region, is itself free from ribosomes, but is connected to ribosomal (rough) ER by means of certain vesiculate connections. The Golgi bodies are also intimately associated with ER. In *Distigma proteus* and some other euglenoids, the Golgi bodies divide by fission.

The euglenoid mitochondria have an undulating outer membrane and ovoid or circular cristae whose bases are typically constricted. The cristae from opposite sides generally fail to overlap or meet in the middle of the mitochondrion. The colourless euglenoids seem to have larger numbers of mitochondria as compared to the photosynthetic species.

CELL SHAPE CHANGES

In *E. gracilis*, the cell shape changes involve longitudinal (antero-posterior) contractions, or peristaltic waves (see Fig. 6-5 A, B). The latter appear as a ring of contraction advancing slowly from the posterior to the anterior end of the cell. The euglenoid movement may also take the form of lateral bendings as are commonly observed in *E. ehrenbergii, E. terricola,*

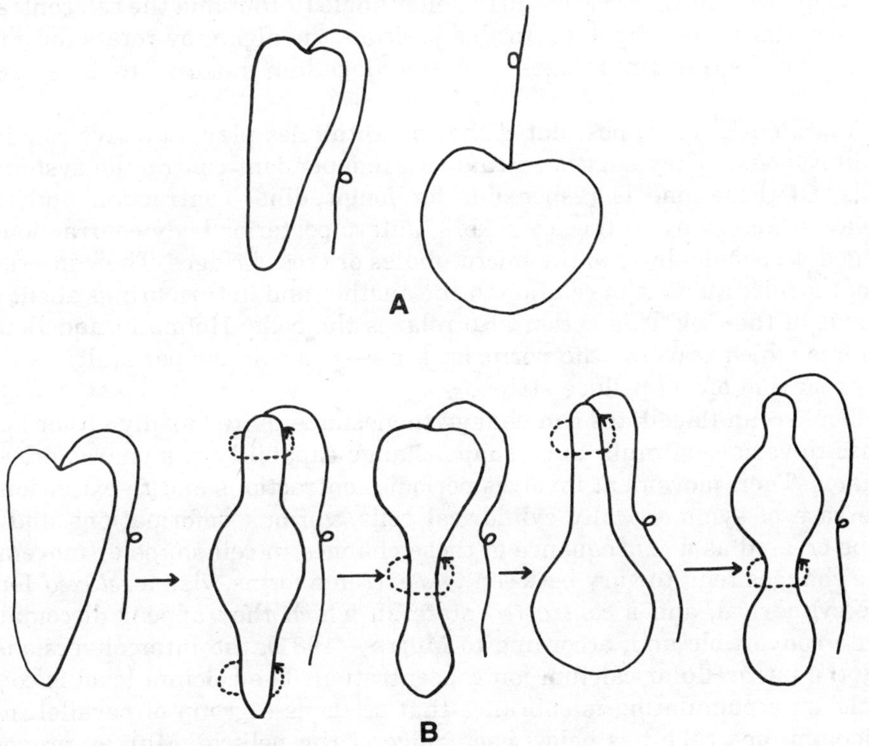

Fig. 6-5 *Euglena gracilis*, two types of cell shape changes. A, longitudinal contraction; B, peristaltic waves (arrows) showing contraction zone. (After Mikolajczyk and Kuznicki, 1981.)

E. limosa, and others. Sometimes the antero-posterior contractions are followed by peristaltic waves.

E. granulata and *E. mutalutis* exhibit strong euglenoid movements. Moderately rigid euglenoid movements are characteristic of *E. agilis* and *E. gracilis*. *E. acus* and *E. tripteris* exemplify almost rigid movements. Completely rigid movements occur in *Phacus* and a few other euglenoids (Mikolajczyk and Kuznicki, 1981). Those euglenoids which have a thick periplast tend to show a very limited range of movements.

According to Mikolajczyk and Kuznicki, longitudinal and lateral changes in the cell shape in euglenoids are evoked by contraction of the fibrillar continuous structure (fibrillar sac) which lies immediately beneath the periplast strips. Contraction occurs as a result of reorientation of the locomotory flagellum. The flagellum takes up a phobic position and this produces some deformation in the reservoir shape which in turn induces contraction of the fibrillar sac. The fibrillar structures beneath the periplast along with the microtubules become stressed during contraction and the periplast reverts to its original cigar shape. These stresses may also play an essential role in peristaltic movement.

In *E. gracilis*, the maximum reorientation is often followed by antero-posterior cell contractions. Light or other stimuli induce a reorientation of the locomotory flagellum in the motile cells, from its normal position along the cell body (Fig. 6-6) which is at right angle to the long axis of the cell. This arrests the forward swimming movement and the alga starts to tumble. This is followed by increase of the flagellar angle to 180° and the cell contracts strongly, assuming a discoidal shape (Fig. 6-6). In this position, the alga may rotate for a few minutes, but gradually the contraction relaxes and the flagellum returns to its normal position (Fig. 6-6).

Hofmann and Bouck (1976) postulated that microtubules play an active role in changes of body shape in *Euglena*. They suggested that two independent contractile systems operate in *Euglena* cells. Of these, one is responsible for longitudinal contraction and the other for peristaltic waves. According to these workers, antero-posterior body contractions are due to fibrils arranged perpendicularly to the microtubules or cross bridges. Their interaction results in a sliding of the microtubules in relation to one another and in turn brings about a shortening of the long axis of the cell. This action also relaxes the cells. Hofmann and Bouck proposed that some fibres which traverse the periplast are responsible for peristaltic waves and they also induce expansion of the pellicle strips.

The euglenophycean flagellates can change their shape quite rapidly either spontaneously or in response to various stimuli. Such shape change capability is a characteristic feature of these flagellates. Their movement involves periodic contractions and re-extensions of the cell. Even in the case of symmetrically cylindrical cells, various deformations and asymmetric shapes can be created as a consequence of these changes in cell shape or movement.

The shape changes tend to vary between two extreme forms, viz., a *relaxed* form, in which the cells are cylindrical, and a *contracted* state, in which they appear discoidal. These two forms are interconvertible and, according to Murray (1981), the interconversions are chiefly regulated by the intracellular calcium ion concentration. The calcium level is controlled by a system of calcium-accumulating membranes that occur as a group of parallel tubes of endoplasmic reticulum; one tube lies below each ridge of the pellicle. Murray proposes that the ridges along with their associated endoplasmic reticulum tubes and microtubules may act as independent motors. He visualizes that a local activation of some of these motors by calcium ions is brought about by the arrangement of the reticulum which can sequester calcium ions,

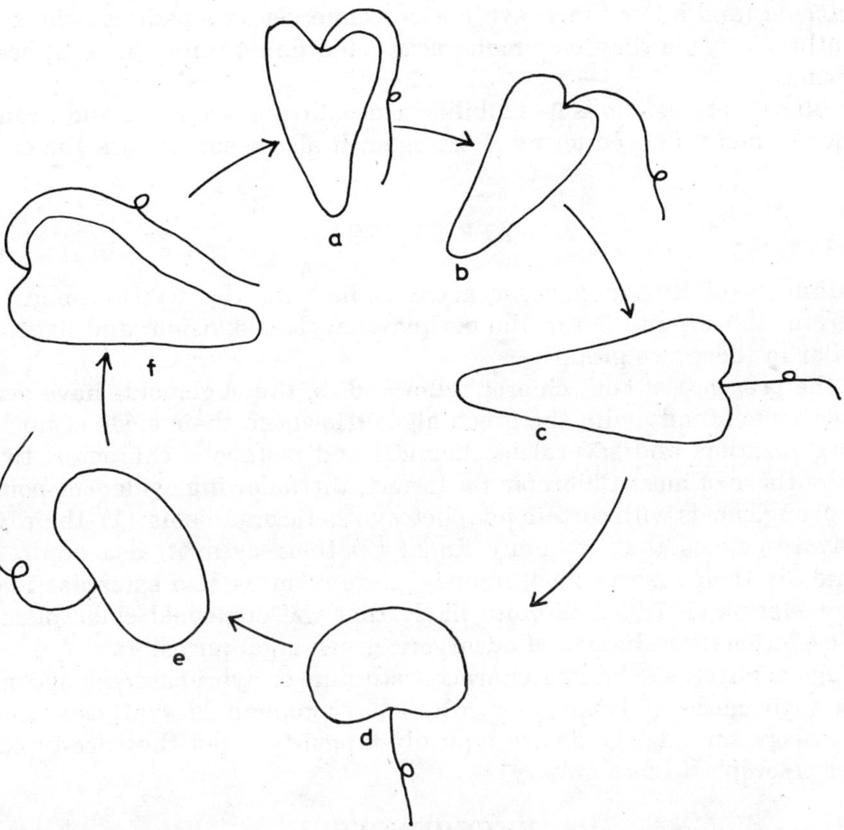

Fig. 6-6 *Euglena gracilis*, relationship between flagellar response and longitudinal contraction (after Mikolajczyk and Kuznicki, 1981).

thereby producing the typical squirming movement of the cell. In contrast to the activation of only some motors, a uniform activation or suppression of all the motors is thought to produce the two extreme types of shape.

REPRODUCTION

Longitudinal cell division constitutes the usual method of reproduction. Sometimes, before division the cells become enclosed by a mucilaginous matrix.

Many species can survive adverse conditions by producing thick-walled cysts. These germinate, forming motile cells, when favourable conditions recur.

Some species of *Euglena* and *Colacium* form palmelloid stages akin to those of the Volvocales. In these, nonflagellate cells remain embedded together in a gelatinous matrix for long or short periods, only to resume motility afterwards.

Sexuality seems to be absent.

METABOLISM

Certain euglenoids show novelties in their nitrogen metabolism. In contrast to most other organisms, *Euglena* (and a few fungi) synthesize lysine via aminoadipic acid; the remaining organisms synthesize it via diaminopimelic acid. This finding may have interesting phylogenetic significance.

Another peculiarity of *Euglena* is its inability to use nitrate (see Klein and Cronquist, 1967); instead, it requires more reduced forms of nitrogen. It also seems to lack the enzyme nitrate reductase.

AFFINITIES

The closest affinities of Euglenophyceae seem to lie with the trypanosomes, as flagellar insertion, microtubular orientation in the periplast, nuclear division, and flagellar structure are fairly similar in these two groups.

Because of the presence of both chlorophyll-a and -b, the euglenoids have generally been thought to have some affinity with the green algae. However, their mode of nuclear division, cytoskeletal organization, and several biochemical and metabolic characteristics differ fundamentally from those of most Chlorophyta. In fact, the following evidences point to a much closer affinity of euglenoids with certain nonphotosynthetic organisms: (1) their lysine biosynthesis pathway resembles that in many fungi, (2) their eyespot also occurs outside the chloroplast, and (3) their reserve food, namely, paramylon, is also extraplastidic. According to Stewart and Mattox (1975), it is quite likely that the euglenoid chloroplasts may have descended by evolutionary reduction of eucaryotic green algal ancestors.

The class Euglenophyceae exhibits a characteristic dual or hybrid assemblage of biochemical characters. In their mode of lysine biosynthesis, tryptophan biosynthesis, and shikimate pathway enzymology, the euglenoids are typically fungal-type but they are typically algal in respect of their chloroplast biochemistry.

REFERENCES

Arnott, H.J. and Walne, P.L., Observations on the fine structure of the pellicle pores of *Euglena granulata*, *Protoplasma*, **64**, 330–44 (1967).

Barnes, L.S.D., Walne, P.L., and Dunlap, J.R., Cytological and taxonomic studies of the Euglenales. I. Ultrastructure and envelope elemental composition in *Trachelomonas*, *Brit. Phycol. J.*, **21**, 387–97 (1986).

Buetow, D.E. (ed.), The Biology of *Euglena*, Academic Press, New York (1968).

Dodge, J.D., The Fine Structure of Algal Cells, Academic Press, London (1973).

Edmunds, L.N. and Adams, K.J., Clocked cell cycle clocks, *Science*, **211**, 1002–1013 (1981).

Farmer, M.A. and Triemer, R.E., Flagellar systems in the euglenoid flagellates, *BioSystems*, **21**, 283–91 (1988).

Gibbs, S.P., The comparative ultrastructure of the algal chloroplast. *In* Fredrick, J.F. and Klein, R.M. (eds.) Phylogenesis and morphogenesis in the algae, *Ann. N.Y. Acad. Sci.*, **175**, 454–73 (1970).

Hofmann, C. and Bouck, G.B., Immunological and structural evidence for patterned intussusceptive surface growth in a unicellular organism: a postulated role for submembranous proteins and microtubules, *J. Cell Biol.*, **69**, 693–715 (1976).

Kivic, P.A. and Vesk, M., Structure and function in the euglenoid eyespot apparatus: the fine structure and response to environmental changes, *Planta*, **105**, 1–14 (1972).

Klein, R.M. and Cronquist, A., A consideration of the evolutionary and taxonomic significance of some biochemical, micromorphological and physiological characters in the thallophytes, *Q. Rev. Biol.,* **42**, 105–296 (1967).

Leedale, G.F., The evidence for a meiotic process in the Euglenineae, *Arch. Microbiol.,* **42**, 237–45 (1962).

Leedale, G.F., Euglenoid Flagellates, Prentice-Hall, Englewood Cliffs, New Jersey (1967).

Leedale, G.F., Phylogenetic aspects of nuclear cytology in the algae. *In* Fredrick, J.F. and Klein, R.M. (eds.) Phylogenesis and morphogenesis in the algae, *Ann. N.Y. Acad. Sci.*, **175**, 429–53 (1970).

Mikolajczyk, E. and Kuznicki, L., Body contraction and ultrastructure of *Euglena, Acta Protozoologica* (Warsaw), **20**, 1–24 (1981).

Murray, J.M., Control of cell shape by calcium in the Euglenophyceae, *J. Cell Sci.*, **49**, 99–117 (1981).

Rosowski, J.R., Development of mucilaginous surfaces in euglenoids. II. Flagellated, creeping and palmelloid cells of euglenoids, *J. Phycol.*, **13**, 323–28 (1977).

Schwelitz, F.D., Evans, W.R., Mollenhauer, H.A., and Dilley, R.A., The fine structure of the pellicle of *Euglena gracilis* as revealed by freeze etching, *Protoplasma*, **69**, 341–49 (1970).

Stewart, K.D. and Mattox, K.R., Comparative cytology, evolution and classification of the green algae with some consideration of the origin of other organisms with chlorophylls a and b, *Bot. Rev.*, **41**, 104–35 (1975).

Walne, P.L., Moestrup, O., Norris, R.E., and Ettl, H., Light and electron microscopical studies of *Eutreptiella eupharyngea* sp. nov. (Euglenophyceae) from Danish and American waters, *Phycologia*, **25**, 109–26 (1986).

Ward, K.A. and Willey, R.L., The development of a cell-substrate attachment system in a euglenoid flagellate, *J. Ultrastruct. Res.*, **74**, 165–74 (1981).

West, L.K. and Walne, P.L., *Trachelomonas hispida* var. *coronata* (Euglenophyceae). II. Envelope substructure, *J. Phycol.*, **16**, 498–506 (1980).

7 Pyrrhophyta (Dinophyta)

GENERAL CHARACTERS

These algae are mainly marine with some forms occurring in freshwater, terrestrial, estuarine, and brackish habitats. They are mostly unicellular flagellates (popularly called dinoflagellates) but rarely colonial, coccoid, palmelloid, amoeboid, or filamentous. Their pigments include chlorophyll-a and -c together with several carotenoids out of which dinoxanthin and peridinin are not reported from algae belonging to any other phyla. The reserve products are stored mainly as starch and oil. A cellulosic cell wall may or may not be present in various species, and when present, it may be sculptured into plates. The motile members have two flagella (one acronematic and one band-shaped) oriented in two different planes, and both lie in grooves. The flagella may be equal or unequal in length. The cells have eyespots, trichocysts (see Fig. 7-1), contractile vacuoles, discoid or band-shaped chromatophores, a large central vacuole, and a large, prominent, and characteristic nucleus. Another characteristic feature of most dinoflagellates is the presence of conspicuous membrane-bound vacuoles, called pusules, which lack contractile activity. The chromosomes remain condensed between divisions so that they are observable at any stage. They lack histones. The nutritional patterns range from free-living holophytic to holozoic, saprophytic, parasitic, or symbiotic, with most species being

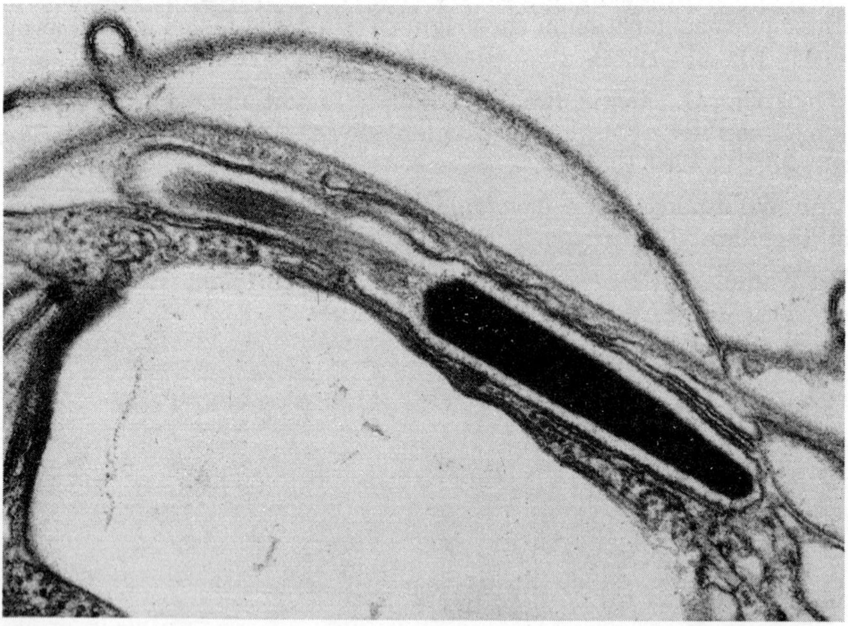

Fig. 7-1 *Amphidinium cryophilum*, depicting trichocyst just beneath amphiesma. (×58,000.) *Courtesy* L.W. Wilcox.

photoautotrophic. Some species of *Pyrocystis* are thought to be the free-living states of parasitic dinoflagellates.

The phylum has two classes, Desmophyceae and Dinophyceae, differing from each other in cell wall morphology and mode of flagellar insertion. The Desmophyceae either lack a cell wall or have a cellulose wall composed of two watch glass-like halves, and their two flagella are anteriorly inserted. The Dinophyceae include flagellate cells with transverse and longitudinal grooves, containing the two flagella. The dinophycean cell is organized into two hemispherical parts separated by an equatorial (transverse) girdle, called cingulum (Fig. 7-2), which harbours the band-like flagellum. The lower hemisphere likewise has a longitudinal furrow, called sulcus, which harbours the other, acronematic, flagellum whose posterior end trails behind the rotating motile cell (Fig. 7-2).

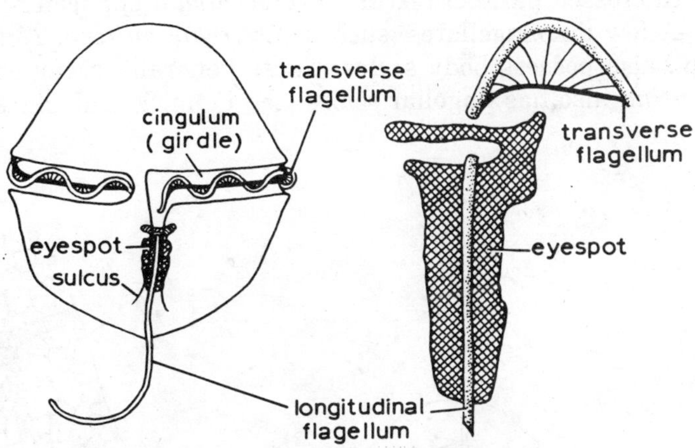

Fig. 7-2 Typical dinoflagellate cell structure.

The members of both the classes have a neuromotor apparatus consisting of centrosomes at or near the nuclear envelope with rhizoplasts which connect it to the blepharoplasts (Steidinger and Cox, 1980). As in the Euglenophyta, the Pyrrhophyta have a cytopharyngeal apparatus and associated contractile vacuoles which empty into this gullet.

The dinoflagellates may be armoured (thecate, i.e., having rather thick wall) or unarmoured (nonthecate, i.e., either lacking a wall or provided with only a thin wall). The Desmophyceae are mainly armoured, whereas the Dinophyceae include both armoured and unarmoured forms. The armoured members of Dinophyceae have their thecae composed of numerous articulated and variously sculptured plates (Fig. 7-3). The cell covering in most dinoflagellates consists of peripheral vesicles underlying a continuous outer membrane.

Ceratium and *Peridinium* (Fig. 7-4) have thick cellulosic plates in their thecal vesicles which can be observed even with a light microscope. *Woloszynskia* has delicate polygonal plates but these are not seen in *Gymnodinium* and *Amphidinium* (with a light microscope). Three types of thecal plate (pore plate, cover plate, or canal plate) are involved in the formation of apical pores in several marine dinoflagellates (Dodge and Hermes, 1981).

The dinoflagellate amphiesma (theca) has a pellicular layer in most genera, and most of these pellicles probably have sporopollenin (Morrill and Loeblich, 1981). External to the pellicle lies a single layer of amphiesmal vesicles often containing thecal plates and then an outer membrane. Another membrane, which bounds the cytoplasm, lies beneath the pellicle in some dinoflagellates. Likewise, in some species, there are present delicate organic scales outside the outer membrane (see Morrill and Loeblich, 1981). Bujak and Williams (1979) have reviewed dinoflagellate evolution. They suggest thecal development by plate fragmentation. The Palaeozoic forms had two anterior flagella and two large valves, the Triassic species had transverse and longitudinal flagella and fragmentation of valves into numerous polygonal plates. Possibly, some influence of flagellar furrows may have led to decrease in number of plates in the modern dinoflagellates (Bujak and Williams, 1979).

The dinoflagellate cell walls (e.g., *Pyrocystis* sp.) contain alpha-cellulose arranged in fibrils with crossed parallel texture. *Prorocentrum* spp. contain many pores in their valves.

A few dinoflagellates, such as *Oxyrrhis marina, Heterocapsa triquetra*, and *Glenodinium* sp., also possess body scales. These generally occur external to the thecal plates. *Oxyrrhis marina* also has flagellar scales (see Pennick and Clarke, 1977).

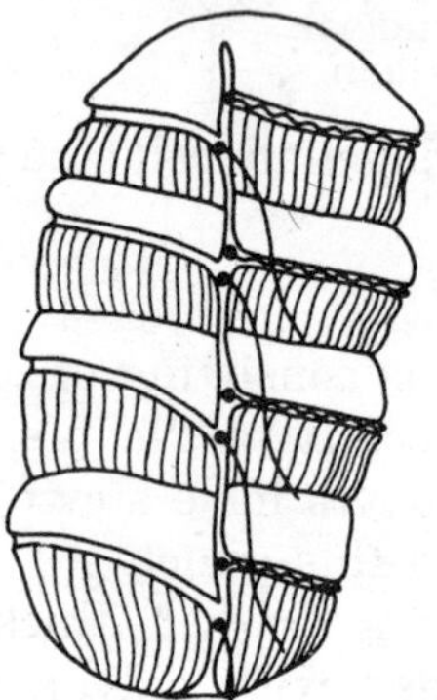

Fig. 7-3 *Polykrikos,* an armoured dinophycean alga.

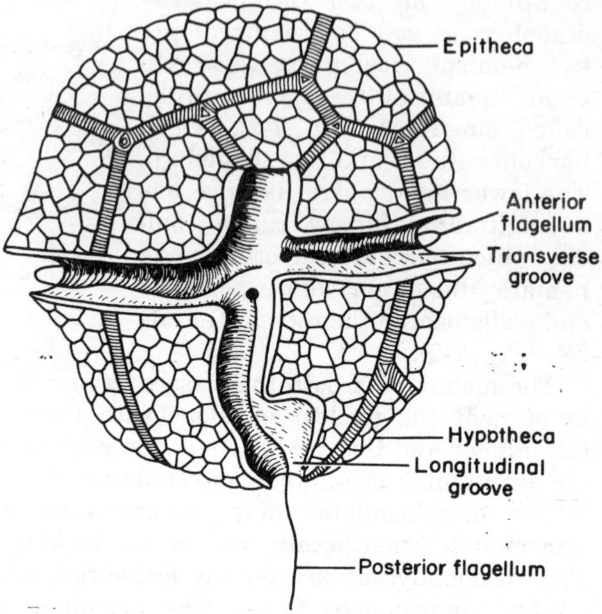

Fig. 7-4 *Peridinium cinctum*, cell structure.

PIGMENTS

Most members possess chlorophyll-a and -c2, in contrast to the Phaeophyceae and Bacillariophyceae which have chlorophyll-a, -c1, and -c2. Their carotenoid content is also disinctive, with peridinin being a specific and major pigment of the Dinophyceae. Peridinin complexes with chlorophyll-a and protein in a water-soluble light harvesting complex which has maximum absorbence at 480–520 nm. Durand and Berkaloff (1985) have reported an unusual pigment composition of *Gambierdiscus toxicus* which causes the ciguatera disease. While it has peridinin as the major carotenoid, it also contains both chlorophyll-c1 and -c2, in addition to chlorophyll-a. Furthermore, its photosynthetic apparatus is fairly complex, with the chloroplasts divided into two parts; towards the periphery of the cell, each chloroplast section has numerous thylakoids but no girdle lamellae. The more internal parts of the chloroplast, on the other hand, lack thylakoids but show a girdle-like structure (Durand and Berkaloff, 1985).

NUCLEAR STRUCTURE AND MITOSIS

The dinoflagellates have highly unusual nuclear characteristics. These include permanently condensed chromosomes, absence of conventional nucleosomes (Herzog and Soyer, 1981), absence of histone, pronounced substitution of thymine with 5-hydroxymethyluracil, and absence of the typical trilamellar arrangement in the kinetochores.

The cells of all dinoflagellates have a nucleus (called dinocaryotic nucleus) with permanently condensed chromosomes and quite rich in its P, Ca, Fe, Ni, Cu, and Zn content. Besides the dinocaryotic nucleus, another nucleus (called supernumerary) is present in *Peridinium balticum* and *Glenodinium foliaceum*; this supernumerary nucleus completely lacks Fe and Ni and has permanently dispersed chromatin, thus resembling the interphase nucleus of eucaryotic cells (Sigee and Kearns, 1981).

The work of Spector *et al.* (1981a, b) suggests that the dinoflagellate chromosome contains a single chromonema composed of helically arranged DNA strands. The unwound chromosome has two important characteristics, viz., (1) it is symmetric along its main axis, and (2) its cross-section and longitudinal section are markedly different.

The nuclear structure and mode of nuclear division in both Desmophyceae and Dinophyceae are broadly identical. Most species possess a nuclear envelope within which several conspicuously fibrillar, helical chromosomes remain intact in a condensed state, even during interphase. During mitosis, no centromeres or spindle are discernible but the nuclear membrane persists intact. Most species have a typical and normal nucleolus; however, in *Oxyrrhis marina* and a few other species, the nucleolus is abnormal since it persists intact through the various stages of mitosis. The chromosomes of the Pyrrhophyta are moniliform and seem to lack histones.

Kubai and Ris (1969) studied nuclear division in the marine *Gyrodinium cohnii* and described several interesting features for this alga as well as for *Woloszynskia micra*. The commencement of the mitotic division is marked by the splitting of the chromosomes into pairs of chromatids. During this splitting, the entire nucleus enlarges and becomes somewhat rectangular. A complex process of invagination of the intact nuclear envelope occurs at one side of the nucleus, resulting in the formation of parallel, cylindrical, cytoplasmic tunnels through the nucleus. These invaginations contain bundles of microtubules, each bundle lying in a cylindrical tunnel. There are never any microtubules within the nucleus and there is no microtubular contact with the chromosomes. The microtubules run through the nucleus into the cytoplasm but do not seem to connect with any other organelle. Such a lack of association between these extranuclear microtubules and the chromosomes is interesting and makes it unlikely that, in this particular alga, the microtubules play any direct role in chromosome movement as do conventional spindle microtubules in normal mitosis. Constriction of the nucleus takes place at right angles to the cytoplasmic tunnels.

The nucleus of *Amphidinium cryophilum* (Fig. 7-5) is about 10 μm long and contains at least one nucleolus and numerous chromosomes. It has an elaborate envelope which gives off vesicular structures sandwiched between the inner and outer membranes of the envelope (Wilcox *et al.*, 1982). Certain pores perforate these vesicles on the inner side whereas the ER connects them on the outer side. Like the Golgi bodies, the nucleus is also surrounded by a vesicular reticulum.

The dictyosomes of *A. cryophilum* are composed of 10–15 cisternae which have fenestrations at their margins. These fenestrae bleb off coated vesicles. Individual dictyosomes are separated

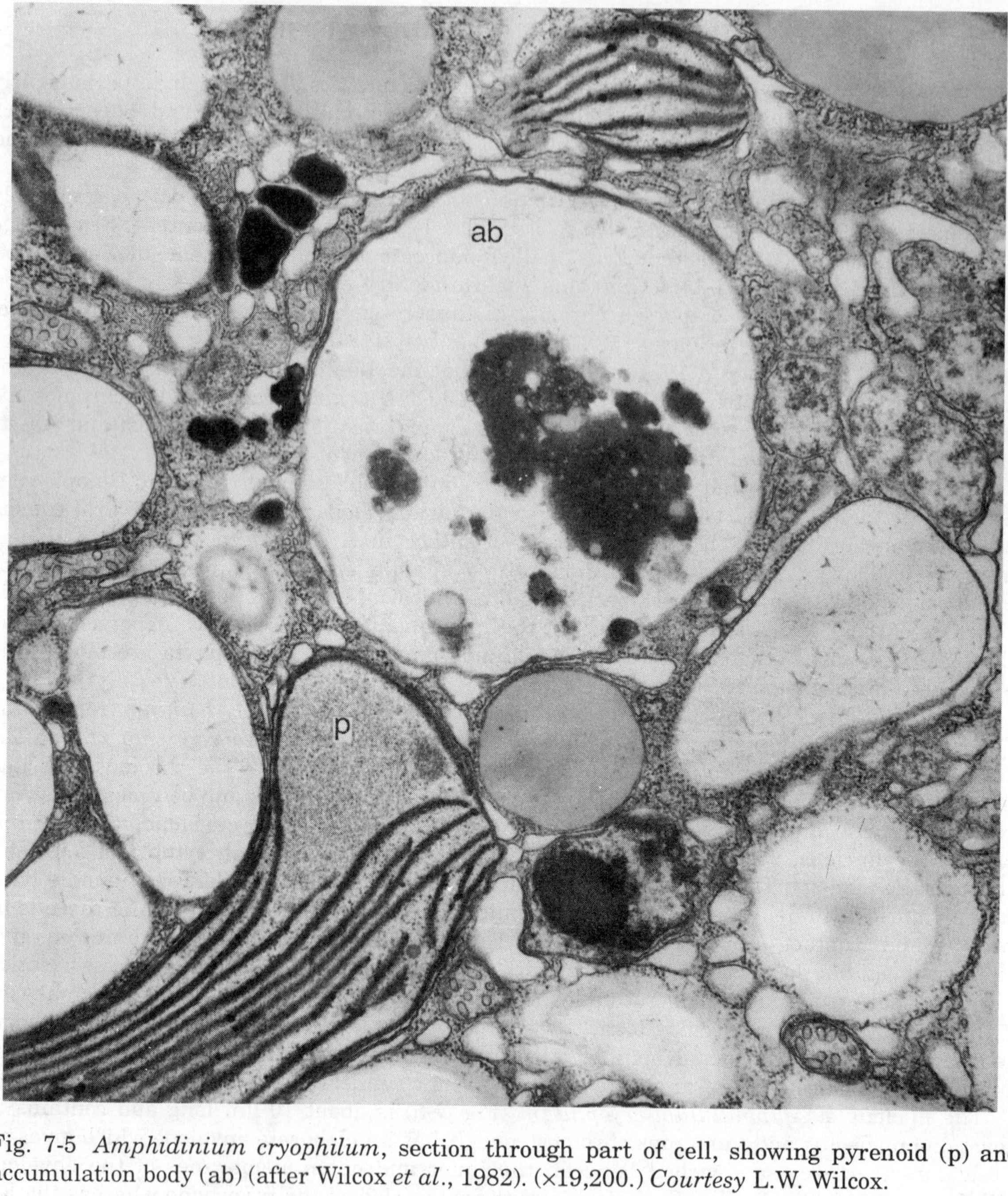

Fig. 7-5 *Amphidinium cryophilum*, section through part of cell, showing pyrenoid (p) and accumulation body (ab) (after Wilcox *et al*., 1982). (×19,200.) *Courtesy* L.W. Wilcox.

by interconnected vesicles, and each dictyosome seems to have one or two large vesicles near its maturing face which contains fibrillar material.

The nuclear and mitotic characteristics of dinoflagellates suggest that these organisms are eucaryotes but which also have certain procaryotic features of chromosomal chemistry and ultrastructure. The dinoflagellate nucleus possibly represents an intermediate type in the evolution of the typical eucaryotic nucleus.

According to Dodge (1973), the spindle-equivalent (i.e., the microtubules) in dinoflagellates is entirely cytoplasmic and in this respect contrasts with most other organisms (except euglenoids) where it is partly cytoplasmic and partly nuclear; in euglenoids, it is entirely intranuclear.

The procaryotic characteristics seem to coexist with a eucaryotic nucleus in the dinoflagellates. The pyrrhophytan chromosomes resemble large genophores and have the same chemistry (i.e., no histones), the same fine structure (2.5 nm microfibrils), direct division, and no centromeres. Further, the likely attachment of pyrrhophytan chromosomes to the nuclear envelope during mitosis is similar to the attachment of bacterial genophores to the cell membrane (Ryter, 1968).

FINE STRUCTURE

The dinophycean algae may or may not contain chloroplasts. When present, these chloroplasts are covered with three membranes. In common with many other algal classes, the dinophycean chloroplasts have their thylakoids predominantly arranged in threes. Most dinoflagellates have peridinin, instead of fucoxanthin, as the dominant carotenoid, but some species have neither fucoxanthin nor peridinin. The pyrenoids may or may not be embedded in the chromatophore lamellae. A great variety of eyespots occurs in various dinoflagellates with some species having complex eyespots consisting of a lens, pigment cup, canal, and retinoid (see Dodge, 1974).

Some members of the Dinophyceae have scaly flagella. The transversely oriented flagellum is hairy, whereas the acronematic, trailing flagellum is mostly hairless.

The complex cell covering of the armoured species consists of microtubules of flattened vesicles. These vesicles may be empty, or may contain delicate polygonal plates, or may enclose cellulosic plates.

According to Dodge (1984), four types of eyespots are known in dinoflagellates, ranging from the simple type consisting of a cluster of pigmented lipid droplets as in *Woloszynskia coronata* to the highly complex organelle, called ocellus, found in the family Warnowiaceae. Horiguchi and Pienaar (1994a) have reported that a marine tidal pool *Gymnodinium natalense* possesses a highly organized eyespot whose structure is unique among dinoflagellates. This eyespot is rectangular in ventral view, C-shaped in apical view, and is located posterior to the sulcus. It is independent of the chloroplast and consists of typically six layers of hemicylindrical walls which are concentrically arranged with narrow spacing between them. Each hemicylindrical wall is enclosed by a single unit membrane and is composed of many regularly arranged rectangular crystalline bricks produced in small vesicles which are formed in the invaginations of the chloroplast. The vesicles containing newly formed crystalline bricks are then transported to the sulcal area where the eyespot is assembled (Horiguchi and Pienaar, 1994a). The crystalline bricks are arranged in a neat row within the vesicle termed "eyespot forming vesicle" (EFV), which is located near the sulcus. The hemicylindrical wall is constructed within the EFV. Based on the structure of the eyespot (viz., consisting of concentric multilayered walls), the eyespot is thought to act as a quarter-wave-stack antenna (Horiguchi and Pienaar, 1994a).

The trichocysts occur in most species of the Dinophyceae. They are ejectile organelles made of an elongated proteinaceous body that is spontaneously and forcibly ejected out through a neck to form solid banded threads. The trichocysts of *Gonyaulax* spp. consist of a long crystalline shaft and head of numerous fibres. Each trichocyst is bounded by a single membrane and is squarish in cross-section. Several microtubule-like structures occur near the sides of the shaft.

The pusules, found in many dinoflagellates, are composed of a plexus of vacuolar membranes associated with plasmalemma invaginations. The pusules apparently do not occur in *Gonyaulax* spp. The pusule of *Amphidinium cryophilum* is a complex organelle composed of highly convoluted tubules bound by a single membrane. Some of these tubules are 300 nm in diameter and are unbranched. These connect with the longitudinal flagellar canal near the emerging flagellum. Others are surrounded by a network of 80 nm branches. The entire pusule system is surrounded by a reticulum (Wilcox *et al.*, 1982).

In *Ceratium hirundinella* which lacks the usual longitudinal sulcus, an abnormal type of sulcus, termed sulcal aperture, opens into a large central chamber at the cell centre. The two flagella are attached at one side of this chamber. A very characteristic and unusual type of microtubular strand lies between the nucleus and the flagellar bases but does not join them. This species is phagotrophic. A large number of food vacuoles occur in the vicinity of the central chamber with the remaining food vacuoles occurring elsewhere in the cell. The vacuoles contain food material in the process of digestion and the food particles seem to enter the cell by way of the central chamber which is free from plates and which is lined only by membranes (Dodge and Crawford, 1970). *C. hirundinella*, unlike other dinoflagellates, has lipid material as the chief food reserve. In keeping with this fact, it also lacks pyrenoids. The pusules are also absent in this species. These cells have a long blunt anterior horn and two or three pointed posterior horns. The cells are dorsiventrally compressed with the ventral side concave and the dorsal convex. The main body of the cell is covered with thick plates. Many trichocysts are situated mainly along the edges of the cell and in the horns. These trichocysts appear diamond-shaped in transection.

In *Gonyaulax* sp., the Golgi bodies are disposed in a ring around a central vesicle in close association with the nucleus. In this alga, the major area of the cell is occupied by fibrous vacuoles with or without a dense granular centre (see Gaudsmith and Davies, 1972). Sometimes, certain coated vesicles are also seen in the cell centre within the ring of Golgi bodies. *Pyrodinium bahamense* seems to have unique type of circular or semicircular mitochondria (Gaudsmith and Davies, 1972).

The naked alga *Gymnodinium splendens* has its external surface covered with rounded projections anchored by numerous fine filaments. Its transverse flagellum is semihelical, whereas the longitudinal flagellum projects posteriorly from the anterior end of the sulcus. At the point of emergence, the long flagellum is swollen and forms a cap over the exit (Herman and Sweeney, 1977a). This basal swelling seems anchored to the theca in the sulcus by flagellar fibres. This flagellum, on emergence from the sulcus, curves back on itself to form a characteristic loop which is enclosed in a membrane. Whereas the longitudinal flagellum is devoid of flagellar fibres, the transverse flagellum has them.

Plastid Ultrastructure

An extensive survey of plastid ultrastructure (see Dodge, 1975) has revealed the existence of five main types of chloroplasts in the Dinophyceae, viz., (1) those having parallel lamellae, e.g., *Ceratium* spp. and *Gymnodinium fuscum*; (2) those with parallel lamellae plus occasional peripheral lamellae, e.g., *Gonyaulax tamarensis*; (3) those having girdle lamellae and internal pyrenoid, e.g., *Glenodinium foliaceum*; (4) those having fusion of thylakoids to envelope and internal pyrenoid, e.g., *Gymnodinium veneficum*; and (5) those having radially arranged lamellae, e.g., *Gymnodinium simplex*.

The plastids of type (3) in *Glenodinium foliaceum* and in the binucleate alga *Peridinium balticum* greatly resemble those of the Chrysophyta and, instead of the usual carotenoid peridinin, have fucoxanthin. Peridinin is also replaced by fucoxanthin in plastids of type (4).

Discoid plastids occur in such species as *Amphidinium britanicum, Ceratium hirundinella, Glenodinium foliaceum, Gonyaulax tamarensis*, and *Woloszynskia* sp. Other dinoflagellates, e.g., *Amphidinium carterae* and various species of *Prorocentrum*, have reticulate plastids. In some species, e.g., *Gonyaulax polyedra, Gymnodinium veneficum, Scrippsiella* sp., and *Woloszynskia tylota*, both reticular and discoid plastids are found.

Photosynthetic dinoflagellates usually have chloroplasts that are bound by three membranes and contain stacks of three thylakoids. Some dinoflagellates contain eucaryotic photosynthetic endosymbionts, derived from chrysophycean algae or diatoms, from chlorophycean algae or from cryptomonads. These various associations, exemplified by *Peridinium balticum, P. foliaceum*, and *Gymnodinium acidotum*, are considered to represent intermediate stages in the endosymbiotic evolution of chloroplasts from eucaryotic cells (Schnepf and Elbrachter, 1988). *Amphidinium wigrense* contains bluish-green chloroplasts with the typical fine structure of cryptophycean chloroplasts, i.e., stacks of two thylakoids and an electron-dense thylakoid lumen (Wilcox and Wedemeyer, 1985). These chloroplasts are covered by three membranes and may have descended from a cryptomonad endosymbiont, the other organelles of which have been lost. Schnepf and Elbrachter (1988) have observed that phototrophic species of *Dinophysis* have an orange primary fluorescence indicating the presence of phycobilins. The chloroplasts of these species are very similar to those of the Cryptophyceae which characteristically have pairs of thylakoids and electron dense material in the thylakoid lumen. In contrast to the bluish-green chloroplasts of *Amphidinium wigrense*, those of *Dinophysis* spp. are bound by only two membranes.

Pyrenoid Types

The following types of pyrenoids occur in the pyrrhophytes: (1) simple and internal, e.g., *Gymnodinium foliaceum*; (2) simple and compound, e.g., *Prorocentrum* spp.; (3) stalked and single, e.g., *Glenodinium hallii*; (4) stalked and multiple, e.g., *Amphidinium carterae* and *Scrippsiella sweeneyae*; and (5) stalked and invaginate, e.g., *Heterocapsa triquetra* [this species may also have type (4) pyrenoids, viz., stalked and multiple].

According to Dodge (1975), the presence of peridinin plus stalked pyrenoids is an advanced feature in dinoflagellates and also that truly photosynthetic species are more advanced than such heterotrophic species as *Oxyrrhis marina* and *Peridinium depressum*.

Gonyaulax polyedra has a novel giant mitochondrion apparently formed by fusion of several small mitochondria (see Herman and Sweeney, 1977b). The giant mitochondrion contains condensed chromosomes resembling nuclear chromosomes.

ECOLOGY AND PHYSIOLOGY

Though encountered in completely mixed water bodies, the dinoflagellates are particularly characteristic of stratified waters. They constitute a major component of the marine phytoplankton. Both freshwater and marine dinoflagellates show a marked tendency to be patchily distributed. Wind, water movement, and vertical migration interact to produce patchy distribution patterns of dinoflagellates. Sometimes, they occur so prolifically in coastal waters that the water becomes reddish brown and the phenomenon is popularly called "red tide". Such red tides are mainly caused by blooms of toxic dinoflagellates and often impart a red, pink, brown or yellowish-green colour to the sea. Species of *Gonyaulax* and *Gymnodinium* seem to be the chief causative agents. Red tides have frequently resulted in massive fish kills and contamination of shellfish with consequent death of marine birds which feed on such fish.

Little is known about the factors controlling the sudden appearance of such red tide blooms. Even during periods when the numbers of dinoflagellates are quite low, they are eaten by shellfish. The shellfish themselves are immune to the toxin produced by these algae, but the shellfish which have fed on toxic dinoflagellates are hazardous to human beings who eat the shellfish. Though the toxin is of no apparent advantage to the dinoflagellates, it may well be a factor in producing blooms. The toxin kills fish and other animals which degenerate and release nutrients which in turn may stimulate the growth and multiplication of dinoflagellates.

There is some indication that the disappearance of dinoflagellate blooms in nature may be brought about by certain bacteria; several marine dinoflagellates are known to harbour bacteria endosymbiotically (see Gold and Pollingher, 1971).

Certain marine dinoflagellates, e.g., *Ceratium* and *Prorocentrum*, migrate vertically towards or away from light both in nature and in laboratory cultures, and some of them can even migrate both up and down even in complete darkness. According to Eppley *et al*. (1968), the combination of vertical migration and the ability to assimilate nitrogenous compounds in the dark may be responsible for conferring a competitive advantage on the red tide or bloom dinoflagellates over diatoms and other organisms when upwelling occurs.

Some planktonic species of *Peridinium*, e.g., *P. quinquicorne*, show a distinctive locomotory behaviour suggestive of a highly evolved pattern of migration related to the tides in the sea. This dinoflagellate forms blooms in certain eutrophic shallow waters. During periods of very intense sunlight, it moves into a distinct near-surface layer during the incoming tide (Horstmann, 1980). The individuals later disappear shortly before high tide, and such disappearance is not dependent on any particular type of light intensity (whether high or low). Horstmann has shown that when the light intensity is reduced, this alga migrates out of the water column and attaches itself to solid substrate away from the light. This attachment is thought to involve some secretion of a mucilaginous substance and the site of adherence seems to be the apical region of the cell.

A worldwide increase in toxic phytoplankton blooms over the past 20 years has coincided with increasing reports of fish diseases and deaths of unknown cause. Several estuaries have been associated with unexplained fish kills. A new toxic dinoflagellate with 'phantom-like' behaviour has been identified as the causative agent of a significant portion of the fish kills in these estuaries (Burkholder *et al*., 1992). The alga requires live finfish or their fresh excreta for excystment and release of a potent toxin. Low cell densities cause neurotoxic signs and fish death, followed by rapid algal encystment and dormancy unless live fish are added. This dinoflagellate was abundant in the water during major fish kills in local estuaries, but only while fish were dying. Within several hours of death where carcasses were still present, the flagellated vegetative algal population had encysted and settled back to the sediments. Isolates from each episode were highly lethal to finfish and shellfish in laboratory bioassays. Given its broad temperature and salinity tolerance, and its stimulation by phosphate enrichment, this toxic phytoplankter may be a widespread but undetected source of fish mortality in nutrient-enriched estuaries (Burkholder *et al.*, 1992).

The alga represents a new family, genus, and species within the order Dinamoebales.

Flagellated, photosynthetic toxic vegetative cells excyst after live fish or their fresh excreta are added to aquaria cultures under low light. The lag period for excystment ranges from minutes to days and increases with dormancy period or cyst age. The cells appear athecate but have thin cellulosic deposits beneath outer membranes that obscure the plate arrangement required for formal speciation. This dinoflagellate completes its sexual cycle while killing fish. Vegetative cells produce poorly pigmented, anisogamous gametes; the male is smaller, and its extended longitudinal flagellum is five-to-six times longer than the cell. The vegetative cells can also form large amoeboid stages with unknown role in the life cycle. Gamete fusion results in planozygote formation followed by production of additional toxic vegetative cells if live fish are present. Without live fish, the planozygotes lose their flagella and form thick-walled cysts but remaining gametes continue to multiply especially under phosphate enrichment. No stimulatory effects were observed with either nitrate or ammonium. A ciliated protozoan, *Stylonichia* sp., is common in estuarine waters and consumes both toxic vegetative cells and cysts. But a pigmented, toxic amoeboid stage of the alga in turn attacks the protozoan predator (Burkholder *et al.*, 1992).

Each flagellated vegetative algal cell forms a peduncle or pseudopodium shortly after excystment. The peduncle becomes fully extended during toxic activity at the optimal salinity of 15%. The lethal agent is some excreted neurotoxin. The alga does not attack fish directly. It rapidly increases its swimming velocity to reach flecks of sloughed tissue from dying fish, however, using its peduncle to attach to and digest the tissue debris. Within several hours of fish death, toxic vegetative cells encyst in the presence or absence of fish carcasses.

During the past century, cultural eutrophication has probably shifted the habitat to more favourable conditions for algal growth and toxic activity. Unlike other toxic phytoplankton, however, this dinoflagellate is ephemeral in the water column. The lethal flagellated vegetative cells move from the sediment surface to the water in response to lingering finfish which become lazy from the toxin. The alga kills the organisms which stimulate it and then rapidly descends (Burkholder *et al.*, 1992).

Many Dinophyceae occur as symbionts in marine animals. Often, the cells are devoid of flagella in the symbiotic state. The algae impart a brown, olive, or green colour to the host animal. The term *zooxanthella* (plural zooxanthellae) has been applied to the symbiotic algae in animals. Zooxanthellae are tiny unicellular algae, mainly *Gymnodinium microadriaticum*. The algal cells are embedded in the tissue of the stony corals, in fire corals, gorgonians, and other corals. The algae live within a solid spiny skeleton surrounded by stinging cells and get protection. They use the coral's metabolic and excretory products such as CO_2, nitrate, and phosphate as nutrients which are otherwise scarce in sea water. In return, the corals get oxygen from the algae and also obtain sugars and certain other metabolites from the algae. The importance of the coral/algal symbiosis lies in accelerating the process of skeleton formation. Without symbiosis between reef-building corals and zooxanthellae, the formation of coral reefs would become impossible (Kühlmann, 1988).

Animal-algal symbioses are ubiquitous and typically dominant features of shallow tropical seas. Of the several kinds of unicellular algal participants the most abundant are certain coccoid yellow-brown dinoflagellates called zooxanthellae. Most zooxanthellae are placed in the dinoflagellate genus *Symbiodinium* as one or several species that are not easily distinguished. Rowan and Powers (1992) compared *Symbiodinium* and nonsymbiotic dinoflagellates using small ribosomal subunit RNA sequences. Surprisingly, small ribosomal subunit RNA diversity within the genus *Symbiodinium* was comparable to that observed among different orders of nonsymbiotic dinoflagellates. These data reinforced the conclusion that *Symbiodinium*-like zooxanthellae represent a collection of distinct species and provide a precedent for a molecular genetic taxonomy of the genus *Symbiodinium* (Rowan and Powers, 1992).

Horiguchi and Pienaar (1994b) described a new sand-dwelling dinoflagellate, *Gymnodinium quadrilobatum,* from South Africa. The species contains 20–30 peripherally arranged chloroplasts, and a conspicuous eyespot. The motile cell is directly transformed into a nonmotile cell and cell division is restricted to the nonmotile phase. The motile cell is typically gymnodinioid in organization. The nonmotile cell has a thick cell wall and develops the characteristic clover-leaf cell shape. The chloroplasts of *G. quadrilobatum* belong to an endosymbiotic chromophyte alga whose cytoplasm is separated from the host (dinoflagellate) cytoplasm by a single unit membrane. Other organelles contained in the endosymbiont cytoplasm are the nucleus, ribosomes, and mitochondria. The eyespot is bounded by a triple membrane and is situated in the host cytoplasm. The species shows broad similarities in its ultrastructure with species of the thecate dinoflagellate *Peridinium* which also possesses a similar endosymbiont.

A central aspect of symbiosis between corals and zooxanthellae is the ability of the latter to remove net quantities of dissolved inorganic nutrients from sea water at low environmental concentrations (Wilkerson and Trench, 1986). In this process, the algal endosymbionts are believed to play a key role because the uptake is usually light-dependent and the symbiont-free animals are unable to effect uptake (D'Elia, 1977). D'Elia (1977) postulated that for uptake of dissolved nutrients by invertebrate-algal symbioses, zooxanthellae act as sites of active transport for nutrients and deplete the animal tissue of nutrients, creating a concentration gradient through which additional nutrient diffuses passively into the animal tissue from sea water.

The general view among phycologists is that the cellular periodicity and migration pattern of dinoflagellates depend more on tidal changes than on the light regimes and some even believe that light regime may not have anything to do with migration (see Eppley *et al.*, 1968).

The call of the sea has attracted man since time immemorial. It is a sheer delight to behold the sea surface at night, when points of light more numerous and brilliant than the stars may be seen in the form of tiny flashes. These flashes usually emanate from luminous cells of dinoflagellates. When their cell density is high, every disturbance of the water, every breaking wave or darting fish, produces a brilliant bluish-green flash. Mariners and nonmariners alike have marvelled at the displays of bioluminescence that accompany large populations of dinoflagellates, and bioluminescence has been recorded from every ocean. Swift and Taylor (1967) have studied bioluminescence in *Pyrocystis lunula* and found that its cysts, but not the swarmers, exhibit bioluminescence, the bioluminescent emission spectrum maximum being at about 480 nm. The light seems to originate from the protoplasm in the centre of the cysts. When placed in the dark, the chromatophores within the cysts contracted distally and expanded with a persistent circadian rhythm. When placed in intense light, the plastids moved to the centre of the cysts; at moderate light intensity, the plastids were expanded, and when the cysts were placed in darkness, they exhibited brilliant bioluminescence.

Hastings (1964), Palmer *et al.* (1964), and Kelly and Katona (1966) have reported on endogenous circadian rhythms in photosynthesis, cell division, spontaneous flashing, and bioluminescence in various dinoflagellates. However, bioluminescence is by no means a universal phenomenon in dinoflagellates; only a few marine species exhibit this phenomenon, the brightest bioluminescence being reported for *Pyrocystis noctiluca*. Though the functional significance of bioluminescence is not clear, it may be used to upset or blind predators or to signal the presence of predators to certain fish which prey on these predators.

Gonyaulax polyedra, Ceratium furca, and *Glenodinium* sp. exhibit circadian rhythms in photosynthesis, the maximum photosynthetic capacity (i.e., rate of oxygen evolution) being reached generally around midday (Prezelin *et al.*, 1977). In *C. furca*, the endogenous photosynthetic rhythm shows a three-fold change during the course of a day. Prezelin *et al.* suggest that the regulation of photosynthesis by the biological clock in *Gonyaulax* may be mediated through the membrane-bound light reactions; ion fluxes between the plastid, nucleus, and cytoplasm and their influence on membrane properties may determine the activity and phasing of each rhythm (Prezelin and Sweeney, 1977).

Certain organic carbon sources enhance the growth of the freshwater *Peridinium cinctum* in both light and dark (Carefoot, 1968), indicating thereby the heterotrophic nature of this species. In nature, *P. gregarium* and *P. sociale* occur in gregarious groups of large populations forming dense cloud-like masses held together by mucilaginous matrix. Both these species have an eyespot and have radiating elongate chloroplasts which change colour (see Lombard and Capon, 1971).

The binucleate species *Peridinium balticum* and *P. foliaceum* are interesting forms which harbour a eucaryotic nucleus and mesocaryotic nucleus within the same cell. Recent research has shown that the eucaryotic nucleus really belongs to a chrysophycean alga which exists endosymbiotically within the dinoflagellate cell. This speculation is supported by the following observations:

(1) The eucaryotic nucleus, chloroplasts, and ribosomes are delimited by a membrane from the rest of the dinoflagellate cell.

(2) The triple-membrane-enclosed eyespot (characteristic of pyrrhophytes but not of chrysophytes), mesocaryotic nucleus, and trichocysts are located within the dinoflagellate cytoplasm outside the endosymbiont.

(3) Fucoxanthin (characteristic carotenoid of chrysophytes but not of the Pyrrhophyta) is the major carotenoid of both *P. foliaceum* and *P. balticum*. In fact, both these species have been shown to have the full complement of typical chrysophycean pigments such as chlorophyll-a and -c, β-carotene, ε-carotene, diatoxanthin, diadinoxanthin, astaxanthin, and fucoxanthin. On the other hand, the characteristic pyrrhophyte xanthophylls peridinin and dinoxanthin seem to be absent in the two species (Jeffrey and Vesk, 1976). The electron microscopic observations and pigment analyses thus seem to strongly indicate that these two species are colourless heterotrophic dinoflagellates which harbour a chrysophycean endosymbiont.

Noctiluca miliaris, which occurs commonly in Southeast Asia, harbours the prasinophycean flagellate *Pedinomonas noctilucae* as an endosymbiont. On the other hand, some dinoflagellates, e.g., *Gymnodinium microadriaticum*, themselves occur as endosymbionts in certain corals, e.g., *Sarcothelia edmondsoni*.

The dinophycean algae occur commonly as endosymbionts within coelentrates and other animals. Schmitz and Kremer (1977) have studied the physiology of symbioses, and the symbionts, called zooxanthellae, have been isolated and studied *in vitro* by Deane *et al*. (1979).

REPRODUCTION

Binary fission is the normal method of reproduction in free-living dinoflagellates. The nucleus divides and the cell undergoes cytokinesis to form two daughters. In many armoured dinoflagellates, the amphiesmal (thecal) plates are shed, with each daughter cell synthesizing an entire new thecal covering. This behaviour occurs in *Peridinium, Scrippsiella, Woloszynskia,* and some others.

A second type of division, called desmoschisis, involves the retention of the mother theca and its partition between the two daughters which later synthesize only the missing parts. Examples occur in such unarmoured genera as *Amphidinium* and *Gymnodinium* and in the armoured genera *Ceratium, Ceratocorys,* and *Gonyaulax* (Dodge, 1988).

In some species of dinoflagellates, smaller cells have sometimes been observed in addition to typically normal-sized vegetative cells (Silva, 1971). Pfiester and Anderson (1987) showed that several dinoflagellates form gametes that are significantly smaller than the vegetative cells. While gametogenesis is induced or triggered by unfavourable conditions, the formation of small cells in several species occurs under seemingly optimal conditions (Silva, 1969). Partensky and Vaulot (1989) have reported the occurrence of two subpopulations differing essentially by their mean cell size in *Gymnodinium* cf. *nagasakiense* (synonymous with *Gyrodinium aureolum*). "Large" cells are the typical form. "Small" cells have nuclei in which the DNA is much more condensed during interphase, as compared to the DNA of large cells. Both large and small cells can divide. The large form generates a small cell by an atypical budding-like division, whereas the small form gives back a large form by simple enlargement and growth following the cessation of division. In contrast to the gametes of most other dinoflagellates, the small cells of *G. nagasakiense* can divide asexually (Partensky and Vaulot, 1989). Under standard conditions, the small cells usually divide quicker than the large ones. The relationships between the two cell forms are summarized in Fig. 7-6. The protoplast of a mother cell divides into two daughter cells. The theca of the mother cell either splits obliquely into two halves or it dissociates at the cell centre along the girdle region. In the former case, one-half of the parental wall is retained by each of the two daughter cells and the missing half is

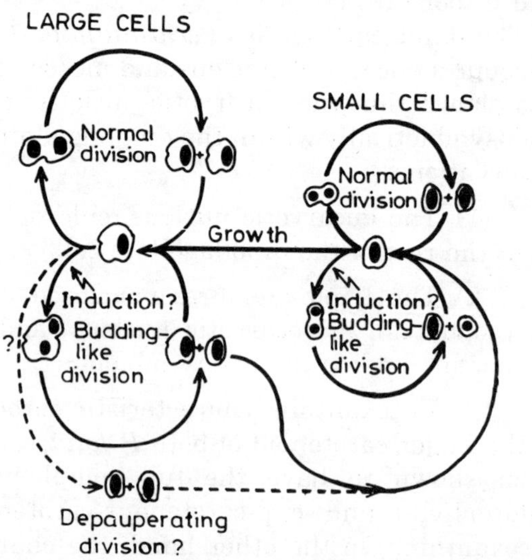

Fig. 7-6 *Gymnodinium* cf. *nagasakiense*. Typical and atypical division modes in "large" and "small" cells. The dashed arrow shows a possible division process, not actually observed. Solid arrows correspond to observed atypical division modes, which probably need induction. (After Partensky and Vaulot, 1989.)

synthesized afresh by the daughters; in the latter case, there is the emergence of a naked protoplast following thecal dissociation, and the emerged, thecaless protoplast divides to form two daughter cells which synthesize their own thecae.

The asexual reproduction in *Pyrocystis* species has been described by Swift and Durbin (1971). The protoplasts shrink and pull away from the parental cell wall, may or may not divide, and differentiate into reproductive cells. Certain species produce either one or two aplanospores or zoospores inside a parent cell wall. These daughter cells swell up soon after their formation and become transformed into new vegetative cells; the swelling process is accompanied by the migration of the centrally located nucleus to a peripheral position in the cell. The nonmotile cells of *P. lunula* divide internally to produce up to 32 crescent-shaped daughter cells. Upon release, these crescent-shaped cells give rise to up to 8 *Gymnodinium*-like naked swarmers.

Sweeney and Hastings (1962) have reviewed the rhythmic patterns in the division of dinoflagellates and have shown that various species divide at different times of the day in nature as well as in culture. *Pyrocystis lunula* tends to produce swarmers at the end of the dark period and the end of the light period.

Until a few years ago, no sexual reproduction was recorded for dinoflagellates but it is now known to occur in such genera as *Amphidinium*, *Ceratium*, and *Noctiluca* (Von Stosch, 1965). Haplontic life cycles are known for *Amphidinium, Ceratium*, and *Coccidinium*, whereas the life cycle of *Noctiluca* seems to be diplontic (Zingmark, 1970). Whereas the gametes of *Noctiluca* are isogamous, those of *Ceratium* are anisogamous. The mode of swimming in *Noctiluca* gametes is peculiar to dinoflagellates; the posterior flagellum beats with sinuous waves, but the body of the gamete does not rotate or gyrate as does that of other dinoflagellates (Zingmark, 1970). Nitrogen deficiency has been demonstrated to induce sexual reproduction in a number of dinoflagellates, e.g., *Peridinium willei*, *P. cinctum*, *Woloszynskia apiculata* (Von Stosch, 1973), and *Glenodinium* sp. (Pfiester, 1976). Both *P. cinctum* and *P. willei* are covered with thin, thecal plates. In both cases, fusion is lateral, the zygotes enlarge and become warty. Fertilization involves the formation of a tube. But whereas the zygote of *P. willei* is uninucleate, that of *P. cinctum* is binucleate.

The sexual life cycles of about 30 species of dinoflagellates have been studied so far (Walker, 1984; Xiaoping *et al.*, 1989). During sexual reproduction vegetative cells divide mitotically to produce gametes which fuse in pairs to form motile zygotes, termed planozygotes. Planozygotes of some species are larger than normal vegetative cells and have two longitudinal flagella. Being products of gametic fusion and precursors to the hypnozygotes or resting cysts, planozygotes play an important role in the sexual life cycle of dinoflagellates.

In species producing hypnozygotes, encystment occurs after the planozygote loses motility. The conversion of planozygotes to thick-walled hypnozygotes involves the replacement of the theca by a thick wall, the rapid increase of starch and lipid, and the reduction in size or disappearance of cytoplasmic structures.

Pellicular and resting (hypnozygotic) cysts form under conditions of nutrient stress (Taylor, 1984). The former are temporary and result from ecdysis (an asexual process) whereas the latter are products of sexual reproduction. In the toxic red tide organism *Alexandrium tamarense* (synonymous with *Protogonyaulax tamarense*), iron stress induces formation of both the types of cysts (Doucette *et al.*, 1989). According to Doucette *et al.*, sexuality induction in this species may be associated with iron limitation rather than the total depletion of biologically available iron. Pellicular cysts are more susceptible to short-term iron stress effects than are hypnozygotes. The pellicular cysts maintain viability over brief periods whereas hypnozygotes maintain it over prolonged spells of adverse conditions.

The planozygote of *Scrippsiella* sp. is armoured and has two longitudinal flagella and one transverse flagellum (Xiaoping *et al.*, 1989). Unlike the vegetative cell, the planozygote has two pairs of basal bodies, large numbers of starch granules, and many vesicles containing electron dense granules (Table 7-1). The build-up of storage products and the reduction in size and number of the organelles in the cytoplasm are prerequisites for encystment and take place in the planozygote.

According to Xiaoping *et al.* (1989), in *Scrippsiella*, the theca is shed at a very early stage of encystment before wall formation. During encystment the cell is covered by three layers of membranes. The cyst wall is laid between the middle and the inner membrane and thickens due to the deposition of wall material on the inward side of the middle membrane. Mucofibrous material is seen between the outer and the middle membranes. Bundles of the mucofibrous material are raised to form protrusions which become calcified with the progress of encystment. Possibly the mucofibrous material plays some important role in the formation and calcification of these protrusions (Xiaoping *et al.*, 1989).

Table 7-1 Comparison of planozygote and vegetative cells of *Scrippsiella* (after Xiaoping *et al.*, 1989)

	Vegetative cell	Planozygote
Size (μm)	20 × 15	24 × 20
Nucleus	Ovoid, smaller	Ovoid, larger
Chromosomes	Condensed, rod-shaped	Condensed, rod-shaped
Chloroplasts	About 12, enclosed by three membranes; lamellae parallel to each other and consisting of three closely appressed thylakoids	More than 12, similar in structure to those in vegetative cell
Mitochondria	Tubular and branched	Tubular and branched
Golgi bodies	Three, consisting of a stack of around 10 flattened cisternae	More than three, similar in structure to those in vegetative cell
Basal body (pairs)	One	Two
Vesicles containing electron-dense particles	None	Many
Starch granules	A few, almost all close to pyrenoids	Many, scattered in cytoplasm
Flagella	One transverse, one longitudinal	One transverse, two longitudinal

According to Walker (1984), over 20 species of Dinophyceae have sexual cycles, with all except *Noctiluca miliaris* being zygotic. Most are isogamous. The gametes tend to be smaller than the vegetative cells. The gametes of armoured dinoflagellates are usually naked. The generalized life cycle of a typical free-living dinoflagellate is illustrated in Fig. 7-7.

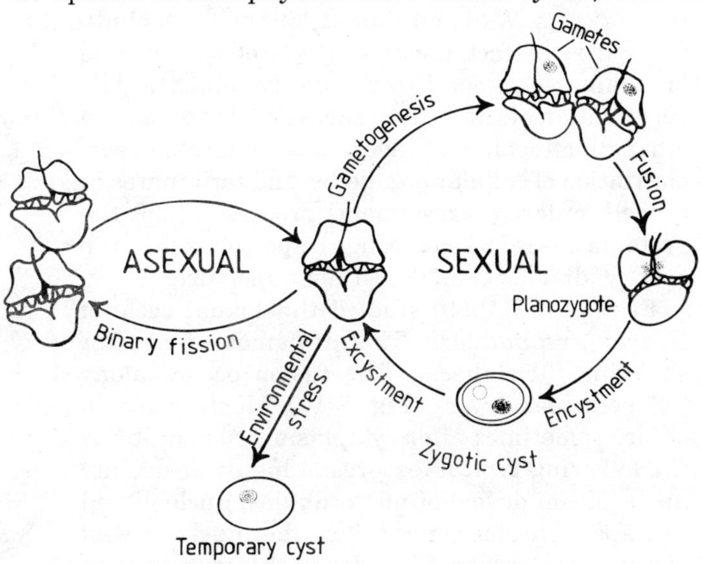

Fig. 7-7 Life cycle of a typical free-living dinoflagellate (after Walker, 1984).

Encystment and Excystment

In sexually reproducing dinoflagellates, the cyst represents the nonmotile zygote stage. However, the cyst of *Ceratium hirundinella* does not seem to be zygotic since it excysts to produce only a single cell (Chapman *et al.*, 1981). In this alga, the cyst is probably a resting stage.

Cyst formation (Figs. 7-8 and 7-9) and spore germination (excystment) seem to be fairly common in dinoflagellates. Whereas in most organisms encystment occurs in response to adverse growth conditions, in dinoflagellates it is favoured by optimal growth conditions. After the cysts have undergone a resting period, they germinate (excyst) in optimal growth conditions.

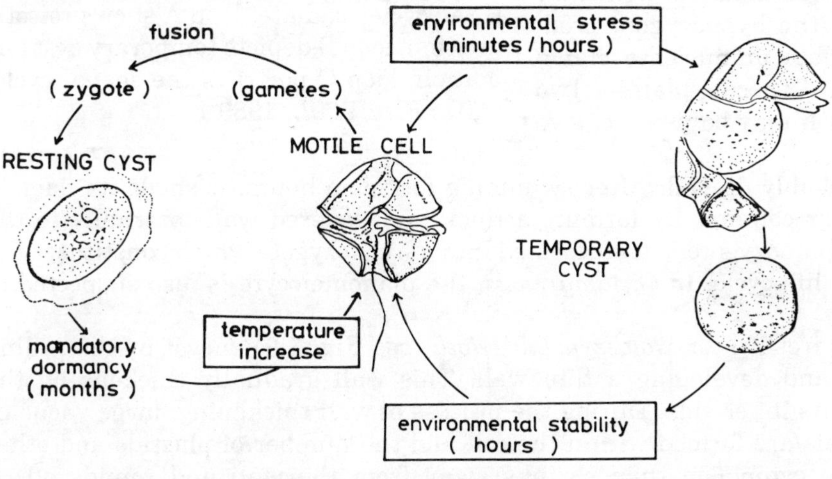

Fig. 7-8 *Gonyaulax excavata*. Cyst development, showing resting cyst, motile cell, temporary cyst. Changes in environmental factors which stimulate formation and conversion of cysts (encystment and excystment) are indicated. (After Yentsch and Incze, 1980.)

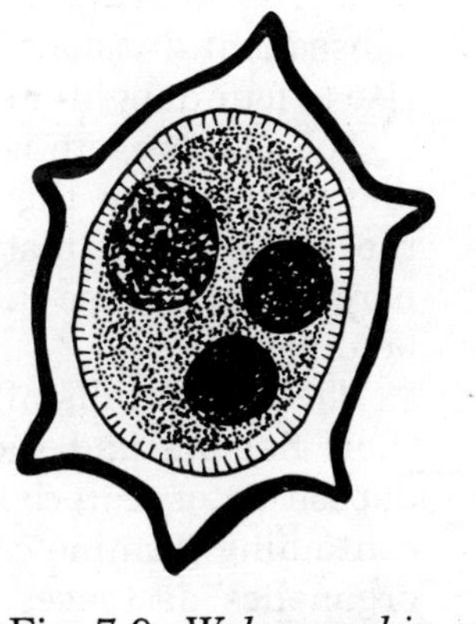

Fig. 7-9 *Woloszynskia tylota*, cyst.

Several armoured dinoflagellates, e.g., *Gonyaulax* and *Peridinium*, are known to produce resting cysts. Wall and Dale (1969) have concluded that the hystrichosphere *Hemicystodinium zoharyi* is in fact the cyst stage of the marine bioluminescent alga *Pyrodinium bahamense.* The germination of the resting spores of this alga (and other dinoflagellates) involves considerable reorganization of cellular organelles and terminates in a well ordered excystment process when the protoplast is released through a specific area in the spore wall to form an excystment aperture.

Fritz *et al.* (1989) studied the sexual cycle of *Gonyaulax tamarensis*. Thecate gametes fuse after shedding their thecae. The fusion occurs along the pellicular layers (Fig. 7-10). Nuclear fusion occurs sometimes after cytoplasmic fusion; it has the following typical features: a highly vesiculate nucleoplasm devoid of microtubules; nucleoli and V-shaped chromosomes abut the nuclear wall distal to the region of nuclear contact; and each chromosome has a longitudinal line termed the central chromosomal axis. As a result of fusion, a planozygote is formed which soon changes into a nonmotile, nonthecate, thick-walled hypnozygote (Fritz *et al.*, 1989). The young hypnozygote characteristically bears numerous minute papillae on its outer surface. The wall of the mature hypnozygote is three-layered, the outermost being the pellicular layer. Upon germination, the hypnozygote produces a large quadriflagellate uninucleate planomeiocyte bearing several thecal plates. Two subsequent divisions, which may be meiotic, give rise to four daughter cells.

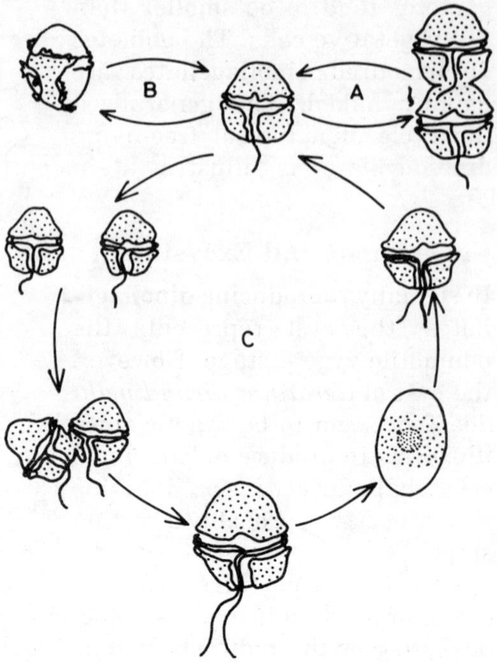

Fig. 7-10 *Gonyaulax tamarensis*, life cycle. From the central vegetative cell, three cycles radiate: loop A shows mitotic division; loop B depicts temporary cyst formation; loop C portrays the sexual cycle. (After Fritz *et al.*, 1989.)

The planozygote is probably diploid. After swimming for some hours, it sheds its flagella and settles from the water column. By forming a thick multilayered wall internally to the thecal plates, the resting planozygote is transformed into a hypnozygote which constitutes the perennating phase in the life cycle. In *G. tamarensis*, the planomeiocyte is also suspected to be diploid.

The motile cells of the freshwater *Woloszynskia tylota* (see Fig. 7-9) encyst by discarding their flagella and theca and developing a thin wall. This wall gradually thickens by the deposition of material on its inner side. During the process of wall thickening, large vacuoles containing guanine crystals are formed within the cell and the number of plastids and other organelles decreases. The cytoplasm then shrinks away from the wall and rounds off. A single layer of lipid droplets forms beneath the plasmalemma. The cyst perennates in this state.

Calcareous cysts are produced by several marine dinoflagellates, both living and fossil. The spinose cysts of the living alga *Peridinium trochoideum* are made of calcite (Wall *et al.*, 1970).

The genus *Pyrocystis* which occurs prolifically in surface waters of the Indian Ocean is a peridinioid dinoflagellate in which the cyst stages of distinctive morphology are dominant. Its motile state is thecate. The motile cells commonly arise singly or in pairs within secondary cysts which in turn arise from large primary cysts (see Taylor, 1972). *P. fusiformis* produces thecate motile stages which resemble a *Gonyaulax*.

Dinoflagellate cysts preserve well as fossil and have been recorded as such from the Silurian onwards. They serve as good stratigraphic markers.

Gymnodinium catenatum is a toxic, chain-forming species. Blackburn *et al.* (1989) cultured it from vegetative cells and benthic resting cysts isolated from estuarine waters. Log-phase cultures form long chains of up to 64 cells each whereas stationary-phase cultures are mostly unicellular.

The species is heterothallic. Sexuality can be induced by growing compatible strains in a nutrient-deficient medium. Gametic fusion produces a large, biconical, posteriorly biflagellate planozygote (double longitudinal flagellum) which after a few days loses one of these two flagella and becomes subspherical. Within about a fortnight, the planozygote encysts into a roundish, brown resting cyst called hypnozygote. After some dormancy period, the resting cyst gives rise to a single posteriorly biflagellate germling cell called planomeiocyte (Blackburn *et al.*, 1989). This then divides to form a chain of two cells, which in due course re-establish a vegetative population.

Figure 7-11 summarizes the life cycle of *G. catenatum*.

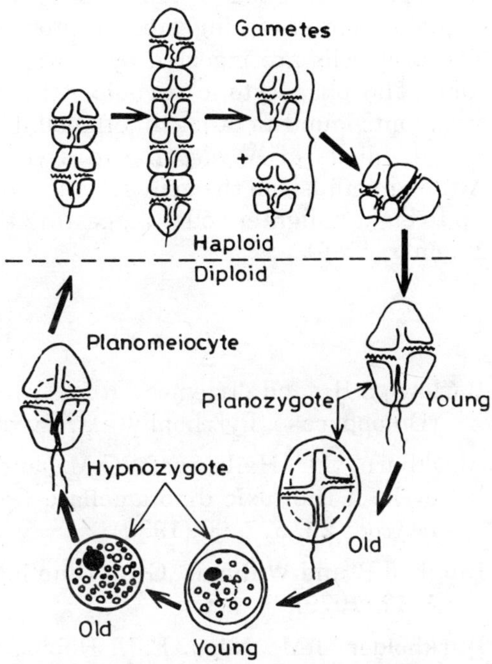

Fig. 7-11 *Gymnodinium catenatum*, sexual cycle in culture. Motile planktonic vegetative cells divide mitotically to form chains, producing + and – gametes, which fuse to form a planozygote. This loses motility to form a benthic hypnozygote. Excystment yields a planomeiocyte which divides meiotically to restart the planktonic vegetative stage. (After Blackburn *et al.*, 1989.)

Amphidinium

Members of this genus are unarmoured dinoflagellates with a greatly reduced epicone, the girdle anteriorly displaced, and most commonly dorsiventrally flattened. They occur in both freshwater and marine environments, in tide pools, and on sand flats all over the world.

Vegetative cells are usually biflagellate, with a transverse flagellum encircling the epicone and the second, longitudinally directed flagellum trailing behind the cell. In *A. klebsii,* Barlow and Triemer (1988) observed cells with one enlarged nucleus and two epicones oriented at 90° to 180° relative to each other. These cells appear to be planozygotes. Later, the two epicones fuse to form a pigmented cell exhibiting the normal vegetative cell morphology but possessing two trailing flagella. These latter cells enlarge and show rotation of the contents of the nucleus. This rotation has been linked to meiosis I in the zygotes of some other dinoflagellates.

A. poecilochroum was described as possessing a few bluish-green or yellowish-green chloroplasts (Larsen, 1985). More recent and critical observations (Larsen, 1988) show that this species is phagotrophic and that the supposed chloroplasts are in fact phagocytotic vacuoles containing ingested cryptophytes. This dinoflagellate feeds on small cryptophytes. The prey cells are ingested by myzocytosis. A weakly developed peduncle forms the feeding tube. The phagocytotic vacuole with its contents is ultrastructurally similar to the endosymbionts found in other dinoflagellates (Larsen, 1988).

Individuals of *A. klebsii* can cycle between a free-living stage and an encysted stage. Although mitosis in the genus *Amphidinium* normally occurs in the motile stage, cysts contain up to eight daughter cells, suggesting that the cysts are vegetative division cysts (Barlow and Triemer, 1988).

REFERENCES

Barlow, S.B. and Triemer, R.E., Alternate life history stages in *Amphidinium klebsii* (Dinophyceae, Pyrrhophyta), *Phycologia*, **27**, 413–20 (1988).

Blackburn, S.I., Hallegraeff, G.M., and Bolch, C.J., Vegetative reproduction and sexual life cycle of the toxic dinoflagellate *Gymnodinium catenatum* from Tasmania, Australia, *J. Phycol.,* **25**, 577–90 (1989).

Bujak, J.P. and Williams, G.L., Dinoflagellate diversity through time, *Mar. Micropaleontol*, **4**, 1–12 (1979).

Burkholder, J.M., Noga, E.J., Hobbs, C.H., and Glasgow, H.B. (Jr.), New 'phantom' dinoflagellate is the causative agent of major estuarine fish kills, *Nature*, **358**, 407–10 (1992).

Carefoot, J.R., Culture and heterotrophy of the freshwater dinoflagellate *Peridinium cinctum* f. *ovoplanum* Lindeman, *J. Phycol.*, **4**, 129–31 (1968).

Chapman, D.J., Livingstone, D., and Dodge, J.D., An electron microscopic study of the excystment and early development of the dinoflagellate *Ceratium hirundinella, Brit. Phycol. J.*, **16**, 183–94 (1981).

D'Elia, C.F., The uptake and release of dissolved phosphorus by reef corals, *Limnol. Oceanogr.*, **22**, 301–15 (1977).

Deane, E.M., Duxbury, T., and O'Brien, R.W., Growth cycle of free-living *Gymnodinium microadriaticum* from *Tridacna maxima, Brit. Phycol. J.*, **13**, 189–95 (1979).

Dodge, J.D., The Fine Structure of Algal Cells, Academic Press, London (1973).

Dodge, J.D., Fine structure and phylogeny in the algae, *Sci. Prog.*, Oxford, **61**, 257–74 (1974).

Dodge, J.D., A survey of chloroplast ultrastructure in the Dinophyceae, *Phycologia*, **14**, 253–63 (1975).

Dodge, J.D., The functional phylogenetic significance of dinoflagellate eyespots, *BioSystems*, **16**, 259–67 (1984).

Dodge, J.D., An SEM study of thecal division in *Gonyaulax* (Dinophyceae), *Phycologia*, **27**, 241–47 (1988).

Dodge, J.D. and Crawford, R.M., The morphology and fine structure of *Ceratium hirundinella* (Dinophyceae), *J. Phycol.*, **6**, 137–49 (1970).

Dodge, J.D. and Hermes, H.B., A scanning electron microscopical study of the apical pores of marine dinoflagellates (Dinophyceae), *Phycologia*, **20**, 424–30 (1981).

Doucette, G.J., Cembella, A.D., and Boyer, G.L., Cyst formation in the red tide dinoflagellate *Alexandrium tamarense* (Dinophyceae): effects of iron stress, *J. Phycol.*, **25**, 721–31 (1989).

Durand, M. and Berkaloff, C., Pigment composition and chloroplast organization of *Gambierdiscus toxicus* Adachi and Fukuyo (Dinophyceae), *Phycologia*, **24**, 217–23 (1985).

Eppley, R.W., Holm-Hansen, O., and Strickland, J.D.H., Some observations on the vertical migration of dinoflagellates, *J. Phycol.*, **4**, 330–40 (1968).

Fritz, L., Anderson, D.M., and Triemer, R.E., Ultrastructural aspects of sexual reproduction in the red tide dinoflagellate *Gonyaulax tamarensis, J. Phycol.*, **25**, 95–107 (1989).

Gaudsmith, J.T. and Davies, C.J., The ultrastructure of several dinoflagellates with emphasis on *Gonyaulax polyedra* Stein and *G. monilata* Davis, *Phycologia*, **11**, 123–32 (1972).

Gold, K. and Pollingher, U., Occurrence of endosymbiotic bacteria in marine dinoflagellates, *J. Phycol.*, **7**, 264–65 (1971).

Hastings, J.W., The role of light in persistent daily rhythms. *In* Giese, A.C. (ed.) Photophysiology, Vol. 1, 333–59, Academic Press, New York (1964).

Herman, E.M. and Sweeney, B.M., Scanning electron microscopic observations of the flagellar structure of *Gymnodinium splendens* (Pyrrhophyta, Dinophyceae), *Phycologia*, **16**, 115–18 (1977a).

Herman, E.M. and Sweeney, B.M., Formation of giant mitochondria in *Gonyaulax polyedra*: ultrastructural observations, *J. Phycol.*, Suppl. Abst. No. 160, p. 29 (1977b).

Herzog, M. and Soyer, M.O., Distinctive features of dinoflagellate chromatin: absence of nucleosomes in a primitive species, *Prorocentrum micans, Europ. J. Cell Biol.*, **23**, 295–302 (1981).

Horiguchi, T. and Pienaar, R.N., Ultrastructure and ontogeny of a new type of eyespot in dinoflagellates, *Protoplasma*, **179**, 142–50 (1994a).

Horiguchi, T. and Pienaar, R.N., Ultrastructure of a new marine sand-dwelling dinoflagellate, *Gymnodinium quadrilobatum* sp. nov. (Dinophyceae) with special reference to its endosymbiotic alga, *Europ. J. Phycol.*, **29**, 237–45 (1994b).

Horstmann, U., Observations on the peculiar diurnal migration of a red tide Dinophyceae in tropical shallow water, *J. Phycol.*, **16**, 481–85 (1980).

Jeffrey, S.W. and Vesk, M., Further evidence for a membrane-bound endosymbiont within the dinoflagellate *Peridinium foliaceum, J. Phycol.*, **12**, 450–55 (1976).

Kelly, M. and Katona, S., An endogenous diurnal rhythm of bioluminescence in a natural population of dinoflagellates, *Biol. Bull.*, **131**, 115–26 (1966).

Kubai, D.F. and Ris, H., Division in the dinoflagellate *Gyrodinium cohnii, J. Cell Biol.*, **40**, 508–28 (1969).

Kühlmann, D.H.H., The sensitivity of coral reefs to environmental pollution, *Ambio*, **17**, 13–21 (1988).

Larsen, J., Algal studies of the Danish Wadden Sea. II. A taxonomic study of psammobious dinoflagellates, *Opera Bot.*, **79**, 14–37 (1985).

Larsen, J., An ultrastructural study of *Amphidinium poecilochroum* (Dinophyceae): a phagotrophic dinoflagellate feeding on small species of cryptophytes, *Phycologia*, **27**, 366–77 (1988).

Lombard, E.H. and Capon, B., *Peridinium gregarium*: a new species of dinoflagellate, *J. Phycol.*, **7**, 184–87 (1971).

Morrill, L.C. and Loeblich, A.R. III, The dinoflagellate pellicular wall layer and its occurrence in the Division Pyrrhophyta, *J. Phycol.*, **17**, 315–23 (1981).

Palmer, J.D., Livingstone, L., and Zusy, F.D., A persistent daily rhythm of photosynthetic capacity, *Nature*, **203**, 1087–88 (1964).

Partensky, F. and Vaulot, D., Cell size differentiation in the bloom-forming dinoflagellate *Gymnodinium* cf. *nagasakiense, J. Phycol.*, **25**, 741–50 (1989).

Pennick, N.C. and Clarke, K.J., The occurrence of scales in the peridinian dinoflagellate *Heterocapsa triquetra* (Ehrenb.) Stein, *Brit. Phycol. J.*, **12**, 63–66 (1977).

Pfiester, L.A., Sexual reproduction of *Peridinium willei, J. Phycol.*, **12**, 234–38 (1976).

Pfiester, L.A. and Anderson, D.M., Dinoflagellate reproduction. *In* Taylor, F.J.R. (ed.) The Biology of Dinoflagellates, 1–48, Blackwell, Oxford (1987).

Prezelin, B.B., Meeson, B.W., and Sweeney, B.M., Characterization of photosynthetic rhythms in marine dinoflagellates. I. *Plant Physiol.*, **60**, 384–87 (1977).

Prezelin, B.B. and Sweeney, B.M., Characterization of photosynthetic rhythms in marine dinoflagellates. II. *Plant Physiol.*, **60**, 388–92 (1977).

Rowan, R. and Powers, D.A., Ribosomal RNA sequences and the diversity of symbiotic dinoflagellates (zooxanthellae), *Proc. Natl. Acad. Sci.* (USA), **89**, 3639–43 (1992).

Ryter, A., Association of the nucleus and the membrane of bacteria: a morphological study, *Bot. Rev.*, **32**, 39–45 (1968).

Schmitz, K. and Kremer, B.P., Carbon fixation and analysis of assimilates in a coral dinoflagellate symbiosis, *Mar. Biol.* (Berl.), **42**, 305–13 (1977).

Schnepf, E. and Elbrachter, M., Cryptophycean-like double membrane bound chloroplast in the dinoflagellate, *Dinophysis* Ehrenb.: evolutionary, phylogenetic, and toxicological implications, *Botanica Acta,* **101**, 196–203 (1988).

Sigee, D.C. and Kearns, L.P., X-ray microanalysis of chromatin-bound Period IV metals in *Glenodinium foliaceum*: a binucleate dinoflagellate, *Protoplasma*, **105**, 213–23 (1981).

Silva, E.S., Cytological aspects on multiplication of *Goniodoma* sp., *Bot. Mar.*, **12**, 233–43 (1969).

Silva, E.S., The "small" form in the life cycle of dinoflagellates and its cytological interpretation. *In* Farinacci, A. (ed.) *Proc. 2nd Plankton Conf.*, 1157–67, Tecnisienza, Rome (1971).

Spector, D.L., Pfiester, L.A., and Triemer, R.E., Ultrastructure of the dinoflagellate *Peridinium cinctum* f. *ovoplanum*. II. Light and electron microscopic observations on fertilization, *Am. J. Bot.*, **68**, 34–43 (1981a).

Spector, D.L., Vasconcelos, A.C., and Triemer, R.E., DNA duplication and chromosome structure in the dinoflagellates, *Protoplasma*, **105**, 185–94 (1981b).

Steidinger, K.A. and Cox, E.R., Free-living dinoflagellates. *In* Cox, E.R. (ed.) Phytoflagellates, 407–432, Elsevier, New York (1980).

Sweeney, B.M. and Hastings, J.W., Rhythms. *In* Lewin, R.A. (ed.) Physiology and Biochemistry of the Algae, 687–700, Academic Press, New York (1962).

Swift, E. and Durbin, E.G., Similarities in the asexual reproduction of the oceanic dinoflagellates: *Pyrocystis fusiformis*, *P. lunula*, and *P. noctiluca, J. Phycol.*, **7**, 89–96 (1971).

Swift, E. and Taylor, W.R., Bioluminescence and chloroplast movement in the dinoflagellate *Pyrocystis lunula, J. Phycol.*, **3**, 77–81 (1967).

Taylor, F.J.R., Unpublished observations on the thecate stage of dinoflagellate genus *Pyrocystis* by the late C.A. Kofoid and Josephine Michener, *Phycologia*, **11**, 47–55 (1972).

Taylor, F.J.R., Toxic dinoflagellates: taxonomic and biogeographic aspects with emphasis on *Protogonyaulax*. *In* Ragelis, E.P. (ed.) Seafood Toxins, *Amer. Chem. Soc. Sympos.*, Ser. No. 262, 77–97 (1984).

Von Stosch, H.A., Sexualität bei *Ceratium cornutum* (Dinophyta), *Naturwissenschaften*, **5**, 52–53 (1965).

Von Stosch, H.A., Observations on vegetative reproduction and sexual life cycles of two freshwater dinoflagellates: *Gymnodinium pseudopalustre* Schiller and *Woloszynskia apiculata* sp. nov., *Brit. Phycol. J.*, **8**, 105–45 (1973).

Walker, L.M., Life histories, dispersal and survival in marine, planktonic dinoflagellates. *In* Steidinger, K.A. and Walker, L.M. (eds.) Marine Plankton Life Cycle Strategies, 19–34, CRC Press, Cleveland (1984).

Wall, D. and Dale, B., The hystrichosphaerid resting spore of the dinoflagellate *Pyrodinium bahamense, J. Phycol.*, **5**, 140–49 (1969).

Wall, D., Guillard, R.R.L., Dale, B., and Swift, E., Calcitic resting cysts in *Peridinium trochoideum* (Stein) Lemmermann: an autotrophic marine dinoflagellate, *Phycologia*, **9**, 151–55 (1970).

Wilcox, L.W., Wedemeyer, G.J., and Graham, L.E., *Amphidinium cryophilum* sp. nov. (Dinophyceae): a new freshwater dinoflagellate. II. Ultrastructure, *J. Phycol.*, **18**, 18–30 (1982).

Wilcox, L.W. and Wedemeyer, G.J., Dinoflagellate with blue-green chloroplasts derived from an endosymbiotic eukaryote, *Science*, **227**, 192–94 (1985).

Wilkerson, F.P. and Trench, R.K., Uptake of dissolved inorganic nitrogen by the symbiotic clam *Tridacna gigas* and the coral *Acropora* sp., *Mar. Biol.*, **93**, 237–46 (1986).

Xiaoping, G., Dodge, J.D., and Lewis, J., An ultrastructural study of planozygotes and encystment of a marine dinoflagellate, *Scrippsiella* sp., *Brit. Phycol. J.*, **24**, 153–65 (1989).

Yentsch, C.S. and Incze, L.S., Accumulation of algal biotoxins in mussels. *In* Luts, R. and Incze, L.S. (eds.) Mussel Culture in North America, 223–46, Elsevier, New York (1980).

Zingmark, R.G., Sexual reproduction in the dinoflagellate *Noctiluca miliaris* Suriray, *J. Phycol.*, **6**, 122–26 (1970).

8 Chrysophyta

GENERAL CHARACTERS

The Chrysophyta, popularly known as golden brown algae, have been variously delimited by different phycologists to include either the single class Chrysophyceae or an assemblage of some or all of the classes Haptophyceae (Prymnesiophyceae), Chrysophyceae, Xanthophyceae (Tribophyceae), Eustigmatophyceae, and Bacillariophyceae. As treated in this book, they include the two classes Chrysophyceae and Prymnesiophyceae (Haptophyceae). These two classes seem to share similar pigmentation (chlorophyll-a and -c; β-carotene, fucoxanthin, diatoxanthin, diadinoxanthin, neofucoxanthin) and food reserves but seem to differ in respect of flagellation, chloroplast and eyespot characteristics, and certain features of the cell wall (Fig. 8-1). No true starch is synthesized in these two classes and uncharacterized lipids in the form of oil droplets seem to be the common storage product along with leucosin and granules of certain polyglucans with β-1:3 and β-1:6 linkages (Klein and Cronquist, 1967).

Many silica-scaled chrysophytes (Mallomonadaceae and Paraphysomonadaceae) are important constituents of freshwater plankton; they sometimes form blooms, making the water unfit for drinking. Most reports of these algae have been from the waters of temperate and subarctic zones of the northern hemisphere (see Kristiansen, 1981). *Mallomonas* and *Synura* have also been recorded from India, Burma (now Myanmar), and Malaysia (see Saha and Wujek, 1989). Saha and Wujek (1989) have taken recourse to electron microscopy to search for the existence of scale-bearing chrysophytes in tropical waters. Electron microscopic examinations of water samples from diverse ponds, rivers, and even thermal springs of north-eastern India (mostly Bihar) have revealed the occurrence of 27 such taxa. Twenty of these were species of *Mallomonas*; some examples of the more common and widely distributed species being *M. morrisonensis, M. peronoides, M. portae-ferreae, M. cyathellata* var. *kenyana*, and *M. costata*. Three taxa belonged to *Synura* and two to *Spiniferomonas*. The two remaining species were *Paraphysomonas vestita* and *Chrysosphaerella longispina*. Most of the 27 taxa occurred in water bodies that were eutrophic and nutrient rich. The majority of the taxa were collected during April through July (summer) when water temperatures were high. This contradicts the hitherto popular belief that silica-scaled chrysophytes are mainly confined to cold, oligotrophic, and mesotrophic waters. Indeed, *M. portae-ferreae* has even been recorded from thermal springs having water temperature exceeding 45°C (Saha and Wujek, 1989).

The motile stages of Chrysophyceae possess two equal or unequal anteriorly inserted flagella of which the longer one has stiff hairs (Fig. 8-2) and the shorter one is smooth and hairless. The Haptophyceae commonly have two anterior equal and smooth flagella plus a characteristic flagellum-like appendage, the haptonema (Fig 8-1), which is also inserted anteriorly. The haptonema has a sticky tip by means of which the alga attaches itself to the substratum. The internal structure of the haptonema differs from that of a true flagellum in having only 7 tubules surrounded by a jacket of two or three concentric membranes; these membranes seem to be extensions of the endoplasmic reticulum. In many large-celled species, a cross-banded and massive flagellar root system extends from the basal bodies deep into the cell; the root branches off as it spreads over and attaches firmly to the nucleus (Hibberd, 1977a). In contrast, those microtubular roots which run from the basal bodies under the cell surface are quite small and are composed of 2–7 microtubules.

The chrysomonads usually have large and deeply lobed chloroplasts. In both classes, the

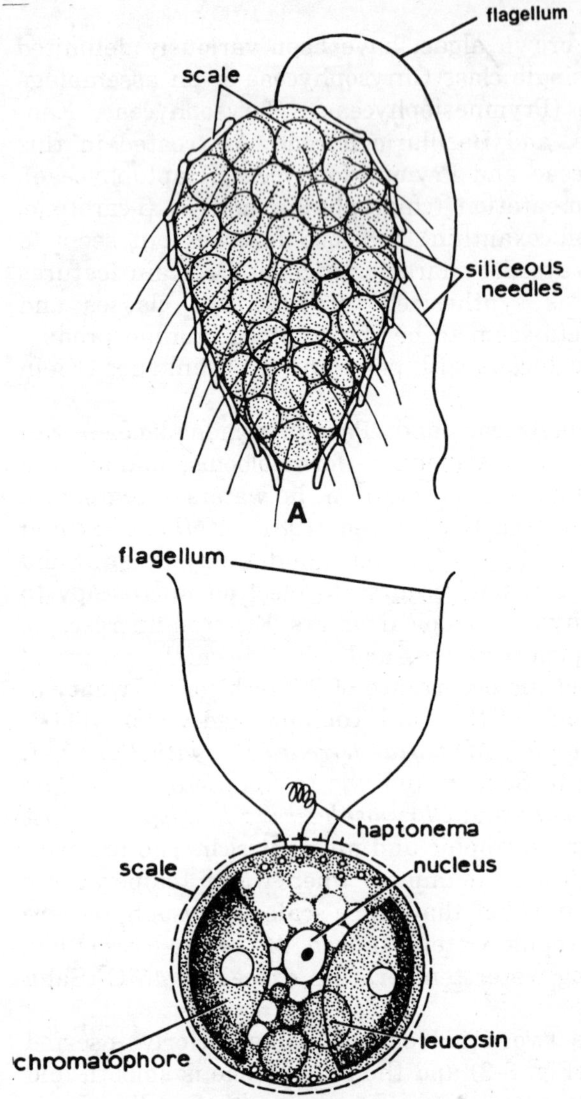

Fig. 8-1 Two typical chrysophytes. A, *Mallomonas*; B, *Chrysochromulina.*

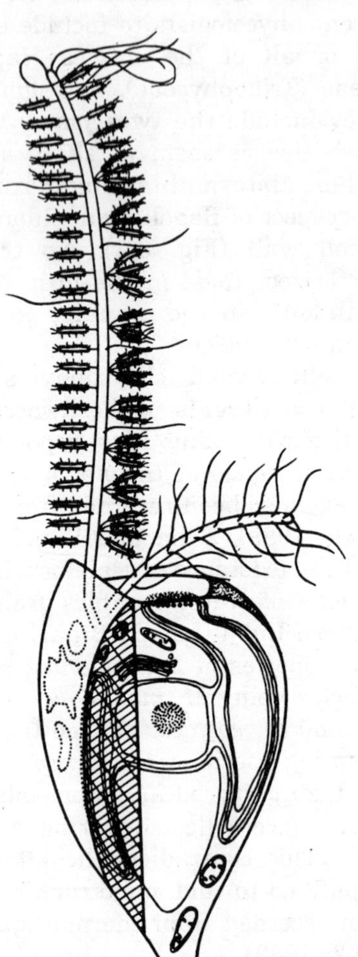

Fig. 8-2 *Ochromonas*, fine structure showing arrangement of hairs on two flagella. The anterior flagellum is seen to have thick hairs covered with lateral filaments. (After Bouck, 1971.)

chloroplast envelope consists of 4 membranes of which the two inner ones constitute the basic chloroplast envelope whereas the outer two are continuous with the ER and usually also enclose the nucleus. They also resemble each other in respect of their chloroplast lamellae being arranged in groups of three thylakoids each. The thylakoids of the Chrysophyceae occasionally anastomose and most members of this class also usually have a distinctive lamella, termed the girdle lamella, which encircles and encloses the remaining lamellae. No such girdle lamella is known in the Haptophyceae.

In the Chrysophyceae, the eyespot forms part of a chloroplast, being situated at its anterior end, adjacent to the flagella. Most members of the Haptophyceae seem to lack an eyespot.

A typical chrysophyte cell has two lateral chloroplasts (Fig. 8-3). The chloroplasts of many chrysophytes possess conspicuous pyrenoids which are traversed by a complex system of membranes. In *Chrysochromulina*, the pyrenoid is attached to the plastid by means of a short neck. The nuclei of the Chrysophyta are typically eucaryotic with a double nuclear membrane, centrosomes, and nucleoli. The cells are generally uninucleate. The Golgi apparatus is highly developed. Unlike most Chrysophyceae, the cells of *Chrysonebula holmesii* have about 8 curved Golgi bodies each, and these lie with convex faces adpressed to the nucleus. An ultrastructural study of cell division in *Ochromonas danica* has revealed several unusual features (Slankis and Gibbs, 1972). During interphase, the basal bodies of the two flagella replicate and the chloroplast constricts between its two lobes. The rhizoplast, which is a fibrous striated root attached to the basal body of the long flagellum, runs under the Golgi body along the surface of the nucleus in interphase cells. One unique feature of mitosis in this species is that the two rhizoplasts form the poles of the spindle, with the spindle microtubules inserting directly on to the rhizoplasts. Whereas some microtubules of the spindle extend from pole to pole, others seem to attach to the chromosomes. Thus, the rhizoplast plays an important role in spindle formation in this alga.

There is a characteristic association between the chloroplast ER and the nuclear envelope in this species; the chloroplast ER persists intact during mitosis. The mode of re-establishment of the characteristic association between the plastid ER and the nuclear wall at anaphase is also interesting and somewhat unique. The part of the nuclear envelope which encloses (along with

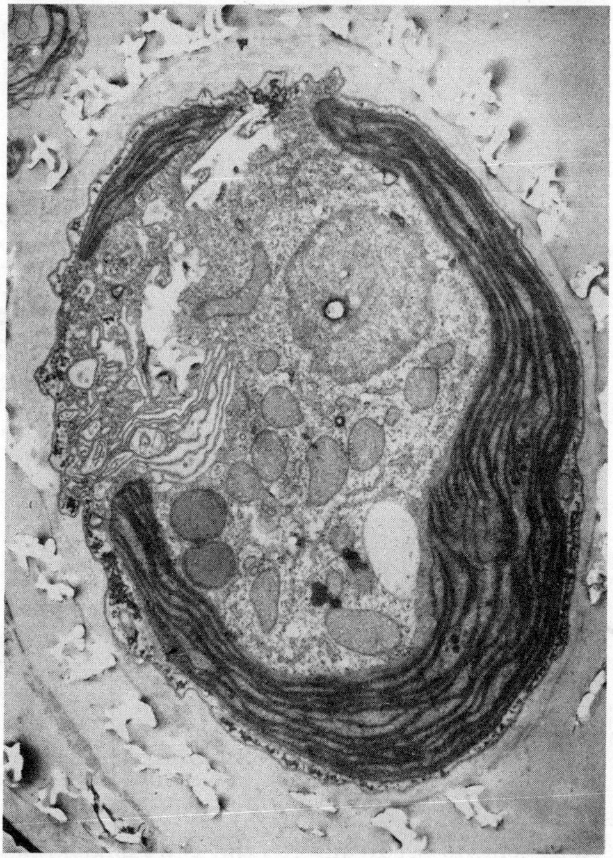

Fig. 8-3 *Cricosphaera roscoffensis*, section of cell showing two lateral chloroplasts. (×9750.) *Courtesy* P. Gayral.

ER) the plastid persists throughout mitosis. At late anaphase, the reforming pieces of the nuclear wall seem to fuse with the outer ER membrane surrounding the plastid, thereby leading to the incorporation of a part of the plastid ER as an integral part of the new nuclear wall (see Slankis and Gibbs, 1972). It certainly seems as if the ultrastructural aspects of mitosis in *Ochromonas* are distinctly different from those in any other algal class. The light microscopic observations on such other chrysophytes as *Synura, Paraphysomonas*, and *Hydrurus* seem to suggest that the same pattern of mitosis as observed in *Ochromonas danica* may be applicable to many other members of the Chrysophyta.

One feature common to many members of both classes is the presence of characteristic scales (Fig. 8-1) on the outside of the plasma membrane. These scales are much smaller than the coccoliths produced by many coccolithophorids, and are visible only under an electron microscope. These scales may be silicified as in *Synura* and *Mallomonas* (Fig. 8-1) or nonsilicified as in (Fig. 8-4) *Chromulina placentula* and *Sphaleromantis tetragona*; in some cases, e.g., *Synura* (Fig. 8-4), even the flagella may be covered with scales. The siliceous

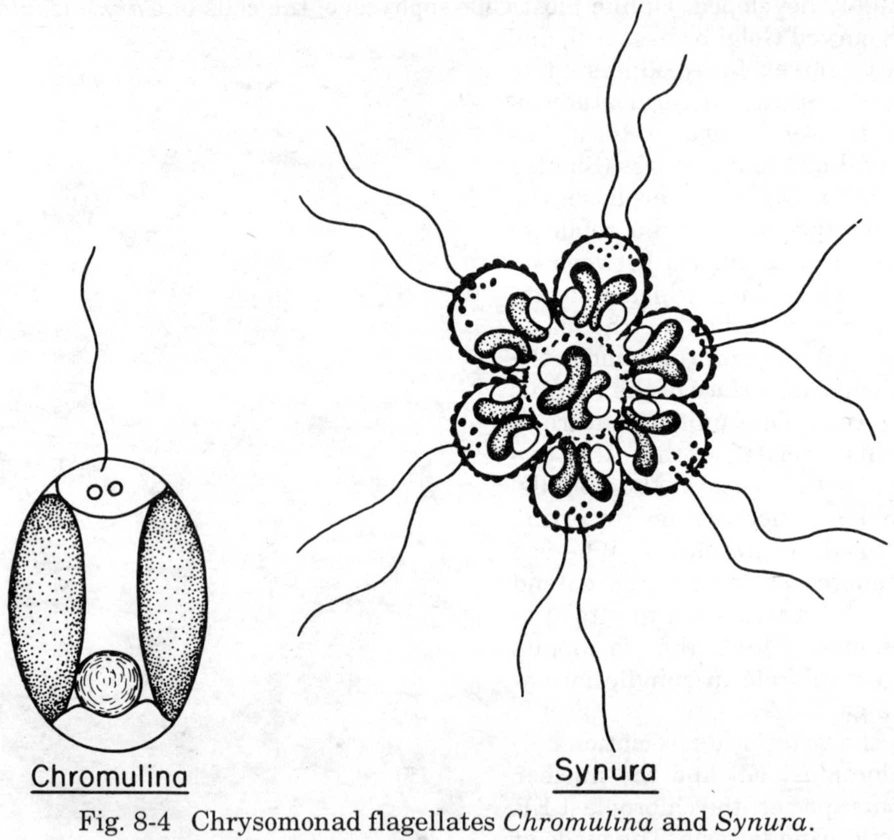

Fig. 8-4 Chrysomonad flagellates *Chromulina* and *Synura*.

scales tend to occur only in the Chrysophyceae. The cells of many Haptophyceae are more like those of the Prasinophyceae. However, certain haptophytes produce the elaborate and conspicuous outer scales, called coccoliths (Fig. 8-5) visible under the light microscope, which are made up of calcium carbonate (calcite). Diverse coccolithophorids have variously patterned and ornamented coccoliths. Outka and Williams (1971) have given an account of the various stages in coccolith formation in *Hymenomonas.* The formation of scales and parts of coccoliths begins in the cisternae of the conspicuous and large Golgi body, whereas the stages in coccolith assembly are seen in certain vesicles which become detached from the Golgi body. The assembly process involves the following stages:

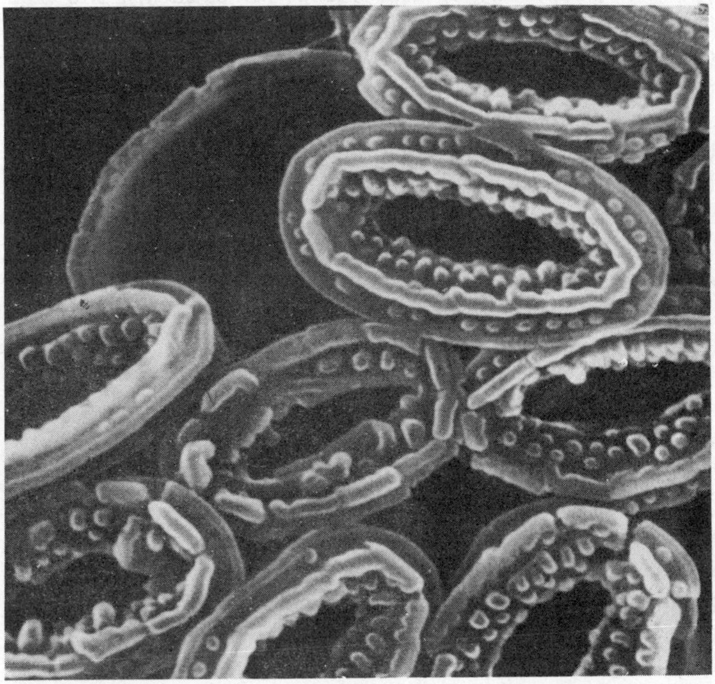

Fig. 8-5 *Cricosphaera roscoffensis*, coccoliths. (×20,000.) *Courtesy* P. Gayral.

(1) The formation of delicate oval base plates made of organic material and patterned with spokes radiating from a line passing through the long axis of the plates.

(2) The formation, around the developing base plates, of a large number of small vesicles, each of which contains coccolithosomes (a coccolithosome is composed of about a dozen granules of approximately 6–8 nm in size).

(3) The release of coccolithosomes into the base vacuole followed by their association with the rim of the plate and gradual formation of an outline of the anvil-shaped subunits which finally make up the rim. The coccolithosomes are used up during the process of coccolith development, presumably as precursors for the material of the rim.

(4) The acquisition by the coccolith rim of its typical shape and its calcification as a result of crystallization of calcium carbonate in the rim matrix (Outka and Williams, 1971).

Coccolithogenesis appears to be one of the most complicated of Golgi functions.

Out of about half-a-dozen coccolithophorids studied under the electron microscope so far, only the motile stage of *Coccolithus pelagicus* shows extracellular mineralization of the organic matrix scale; the others, e.g., *C. huxleyi* and *Hymenomonas* species, exhibit intracellular mineralization (Pienaar, 1969). Pienaar (1971) has studied the mode of coccolith formation in *Hymenomonas carterae.* This alga produces its delicately sculptured coccolith plates on an organic base plate within the Golgi cisternae.

Species of *Mallomonas* bear silica bristles which are tubular elements fastened to the scales. In *M. caudata*, the bristles, like the scales, are deposited in a vesicle budding from the parietal side of the chloroplast ER. They originate as flat sheets which later become rolled up as tubes, leaving a slit on one side of the bristle. They are then extruded from the cell. Each bristle has a foot at its proximal end by means of which it attaches itself to the scale. In many species except *M. caudata*, the bristle foot fits into a special dome on the scale. The foot is articulated into the dome like a socket, permitting the bristle to move freely. The bristle shaft may be smooth or serrated. The distal part of the bristle may be variously elaborated; thus, it is lanceolate in *M. intermedia* and hooked in *M. heterospina*.

Glider and Rosowski (1976) have made a detailed study of the scales, bristles, and spines of *Mallomonas*. This alga bears species-specific siliceous scales. *M. lychenensis* bears anterior circular bristle-bearing scales and rounded rhomboidal body scales, and its posterior scales have spines. All scale surfaces have rows of uniformly-shaped papillae and rows of depressions which contain smaller pores. *M. caudata* produces ovoid to elliptical scales; its bristles are produced from flat siliceous sheets which fold to form hollow, serrated tubes. Three types of scales are produced in *M. tonsurata*, viz., (1) anterior, bristly scales, consisting of a dome, a shield, and a flange; (2) domeless body scales; and (3) domeless posterior scales, which bear a short spine.

The scales of the marine alga *Paraphysomonas foraminifera* are perforated by many pores. The scales of this species as also those of *P. imperforata* have a central dome, bearing a long spine, and a shallow annular fold with a radius one-half of that of the scale.

The basal part of the flagellar axoneme of the motile, coccolith-bearing cells of *Pleurochrysis carterae* contains a spiral structure (a helical band) and the transition region (Fig. 8-6) consists of a distinctive axosome and at least five tiers of transitional rings (Beech and Wetherbee, 1988). The longer flagellum is the left (posterior) flagellum of accepted prymnesiophyte nomenclature. The microtubular flagellar roots are generally similar to those in other species of the genus (Inouye and Pienaar, 1985) but in *P. carterae*, the root

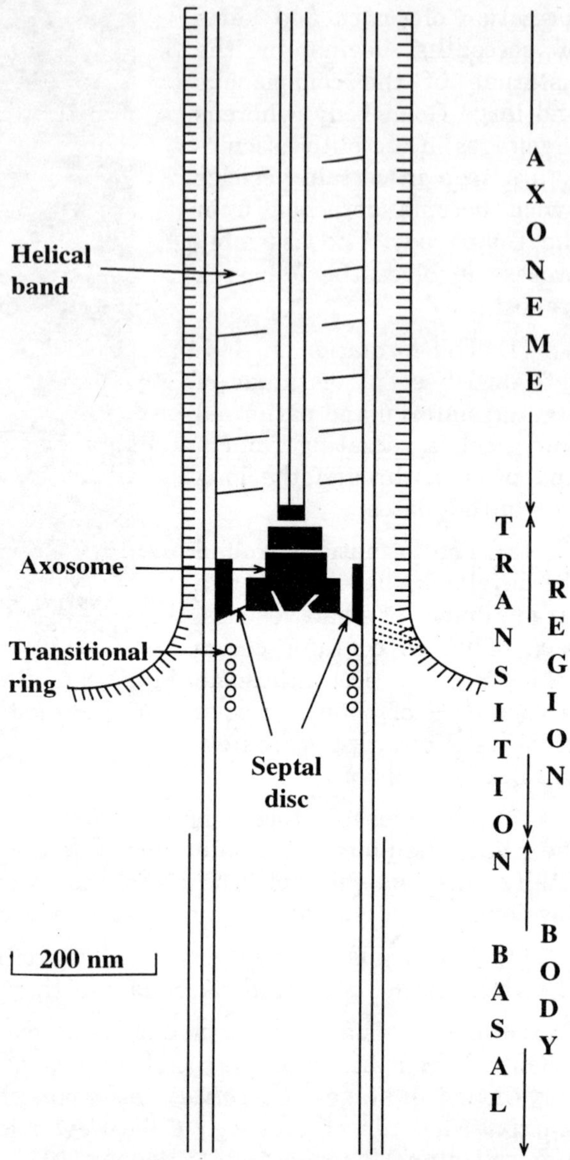

Fig. 8-6 Sketch of a median longitudinal section through the axoneme, transition region, and basal body of a flagellum of *P. carterae*. The helical band is shown as it would appear in a tangential section of a flagellum. (After Beech and Wetherbee, 1988.)

that consists of a broad sheet of microtubules is associated, at its proximal end, with the forming face of the Golgi body and then becomes partially enveloped by peripheral endoplasmic reticulum as it extends for the entire length of one side of the cell; this whole structure is called a cytoplasmic tongue (Beech and Wetherbee, 1988). The peripheral ER shows a characteristic ornamentation at specific points on its membrane surface (Fig. 8-7). This ornamentation and the peripheral ER may possibly have some role in scale/coccolith secretion and the endocytosis of particulate material from the medium.

The species *Chrysochromulina pringsheimii* has an elaborate cocoon-like scaly casing from which the monad can readily disengage itself and swim away, leaving behind the intact empty case. Four different kinds of scales, viz., large and small plates and large and small spines, occur in this species. The alga can resort to phagotrophic feeding both in the presence

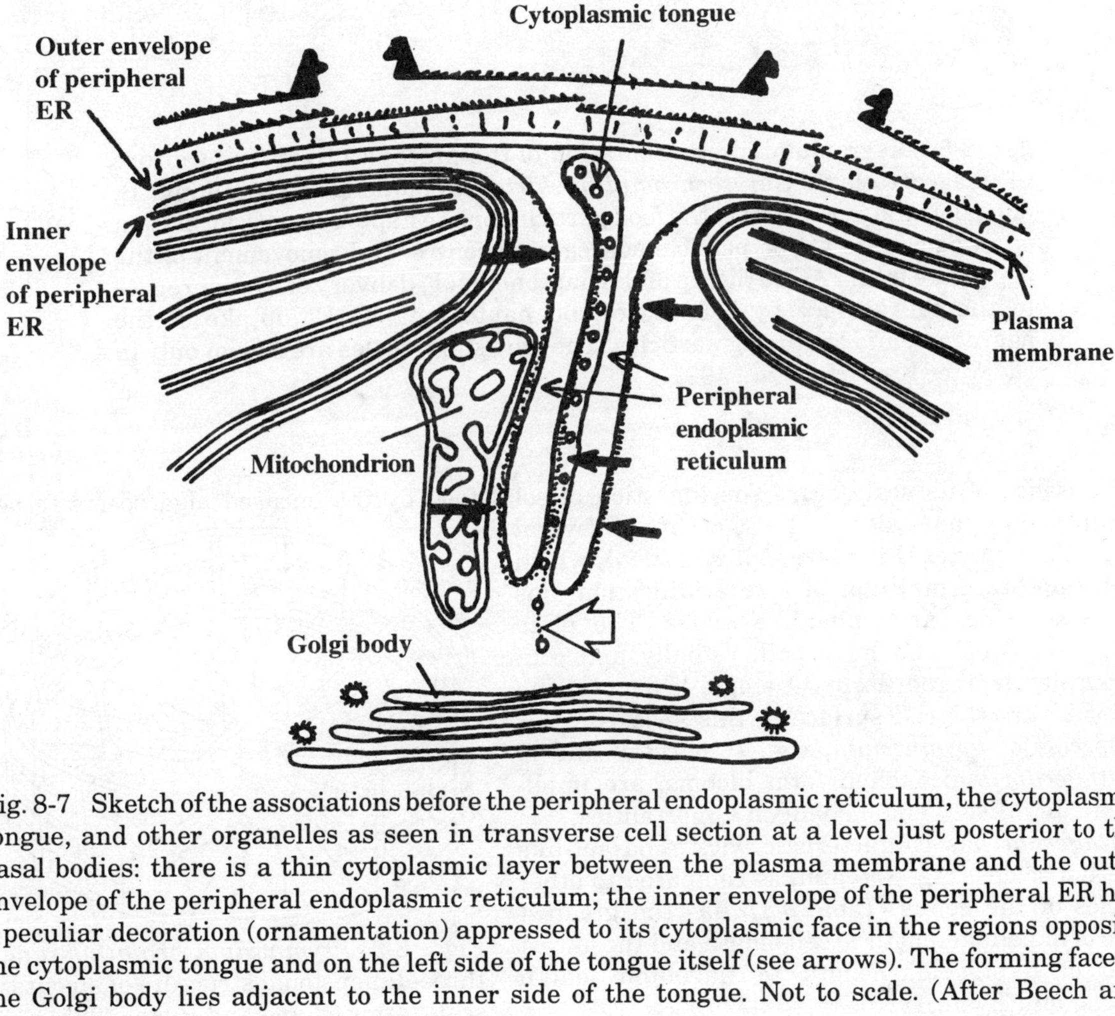

Fig. 8-7 Sketch of the associations before the peripheral endoplasmic reticulum, the cytoplasmic tongue, and other organelles as seen in transverse cell section at a level just posterior to the basal bodies: there is a thin cytoplasmic layer between the plasma membrane and the outer envelope of the peripheral endoplasmic reticulum; the inner envelope of the peripheral ER has a peculiar decoration (ornamentation) appressed to its cytoplasmic face in the regions opposite the cytoplasmic tongue and on the left side of the tongue itself (see arrows). The forming face of the Golgi body lies adjacent to the inner side of the tongue. Not to scale. (After Beech and Wetherbee, 1988.)

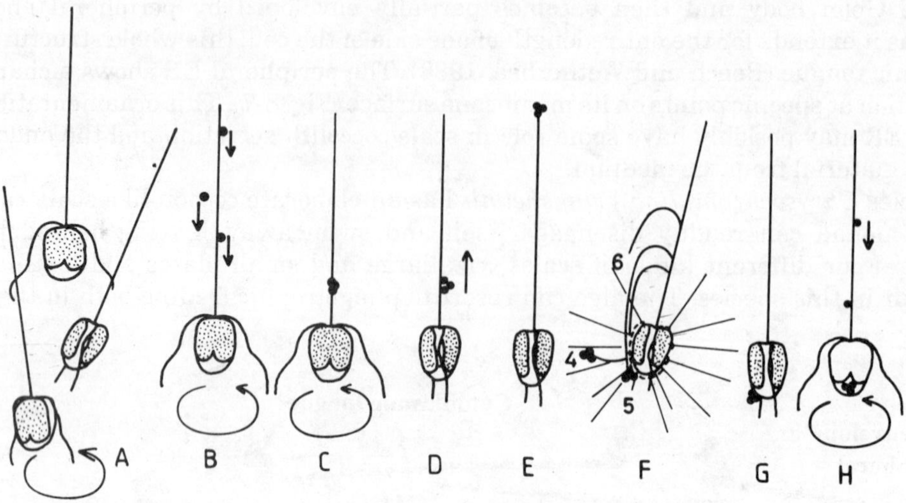

Fig. 8-8 Diagrammatic representation of the processes from food capture to phagocytosis in *Chrysochromulina hirta*. A, motions of swimming; B, adhesion and movement of the food particles on the haptonema; C, formation of an aggregate at the particle aggregating centre; D–E, movement of the aggregate from PAC to the tip of the haptonema; F, delivery of the aggregate to the cell surface by bending of the haptonema; G–H, uptake of the aggregate, and capturing particles. The long spine scales are shown only in H. (After Kawachi *et al.*, 1991.)

and absence of its scaly case. The ingestion of solid food by the encased alga seems to be unimpeded by the scales, and also occurs in several other chrysophytes (Fig. 8-8). *C. breviturrita*, which is an important indicator of lake acidification, has plate-like scales and spine-like scales. The plate scales are ovoid and have both radially and concentrically arranged fibrils. A single layer of spine scales covers the cell surface in this species.

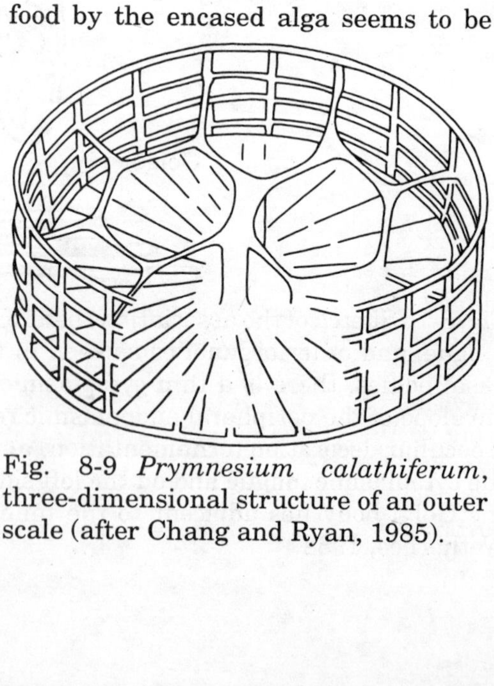

Fig. 8-9 *Prymnesium calathiferum*, three-dimensional structure of an outer scale (after Chang and Ryan, 1985).

Species of *Prymnesium*, e.g., *P. parvum* and *P. calathiferum* which often form blooms, are implicated in fish and shellfish mortalities. *P. calathiferum* has characteristic wicker basket-like external scales (Fig. 8-9) and, as compared to other species of the genus (Table 8-1), has the greatest ratio of flagellum length to cell length and the lowest ratio of haptonema length to flagellum length (Chang and Ryan, 1985).

Table 8-1 Comparison of flagellar, haptonemal, and scale characteristics of some species of *Prymnesium* (after Chang and Ryan, 1985)

Species	Range of cell length, cell width (μm)	Flagellum length:cell length ratio	Haptonema length:flagellum length ratio	External scales	
				Type	Height:length ratio
parvum	8–11, 4–6	1.42	0.30	Flattened	
patellifera	6–12, 3.5–8	1.45	0.33	Raised rim	0.22
annuliferum	10–14, 6.5	1.8	0.26	Raised rim	0.19
zebrinum	10–12, 5.5	1.41	0.19	Raised rim	0.18
calathiferum	6–10, 4–8	2.2–3.0	0.16	Raised rim	0.31
saltans	11–18, 5–7.5	2.0			
sinutum	6–8.5, 3.5	1.7	0.23		

RANGE OF THALLUS STRUCTURE

The Chrysophyceae include a wide variety of mostly freshwater (some marine) algae which are most commonly planktonic (Fig. 8-10) and unicellular or colonial but sometimes filamentous or thalloid. The unicellular and colonial forms may be motile (flagellated) or nonmotile, rhizopodial, or palmelloid (e.g., *Chrysocapsa* and *Hydrurus*) and occasionally the same species may assume more than one of these habits during its life cycle (Allen, 1969). The flagellated cells of *Dinobryon* and *Chrysococcus* may be fully or partly enclosed within a shell or lorica. The colonies of *Dinobryon* (Fig. 8-11) show a dendroid arrangement of open, vase-shaped loricas each of which has a single, flagellate cell. The lorica is chiefly cellulosic. *Ochromonas* (Fig. 8-2) is a naked, motile unicell. *Mallomonas* (Fig. 8-1) has solitary cells and is characterized by its armour with bristles hinged to the scales. It is biflagellate, though sometimes one of the two flagella is greatly reduced or absent. The shorter flagellum is sometimes transformed into a photoreceptor lying very close to the eyespot (Hibberd, 1976). *Synura* (Fig. 8-4) forms more or less spherical colonies, consisting of many cells united posteriorly. It has no bristles, but the scales are

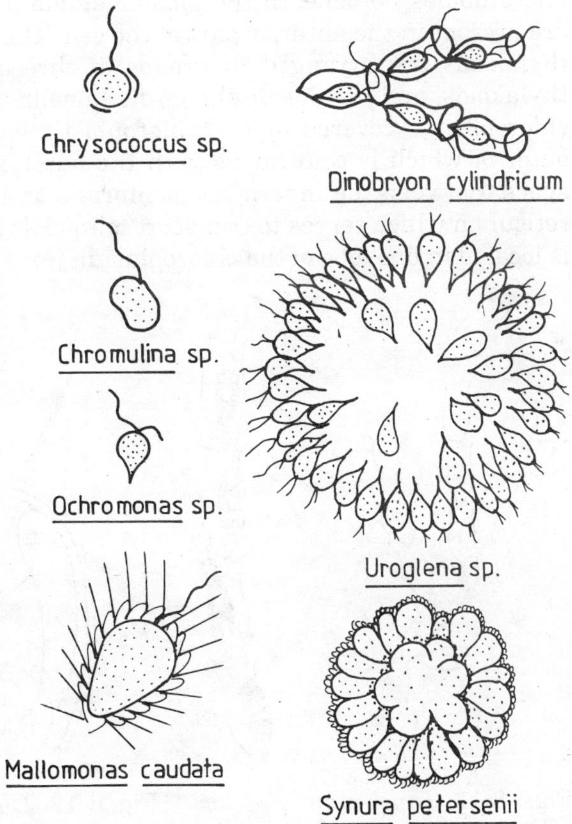

Fig. 8-10 Some common planktonic chrysophyte flagellates.

provided with variously developed distal spines. The shorter flagellum is sometimes transformed into a photoreceptor lying very close to the eyespot (Hibberd, 1976). The rhizopodial species may be either loricate or naked. The chrysophycean loricas are made of cellulosic microfibrils formed *in situ* outside the cell. The filamentous forms are exemplified by *Nomatochrysis* and *Phaeothamnion*.

Chrysosphaerella (Fig. 8-12) is colonial. *Spiniferomonas* and *Paraphysomonas* are solitary, the latter being colourless. In these three genera (belonging to the family Paraphysomonadaceae), the scale types encountered are plate scales, crown scales, and spine scales.

Ochromonas (Fig. 8-2) may be taken as a simple representative of the Chrysophyceae. It is a noncolonial, freshwater flagellate. *O. viridis* has phagotrophic nutrition and can survive in the dark, but most other species are phototrophic. Most species have naked cells, devoid of cell wall, that show amoeboid movement. They are biflagellate. The longer, anterior flagellum is flimmer and the shorter, posterior one is smooth. The flimmer flagellum has two rows of tripartite hairs (mastigonemes). These mastigonemes have a base, a shaft, and a terminal filament. In addition, some very thin hairs are often present on both the flagella. The shorter, smooth flagellum is swollen proximally (Kristiansen, 1986). The flagella are borne on basal bodies which are connected with the outer nuclear membrane by means of a rhizoplast. Several microtubules lie beneath the plasmalemma and impart shape to the cell. Pulsating vacuoles are present in the anterior part of the cell. The cell normally has one bilobed chloroplast whose thylakoids are arranged in groups of threes. A girdle lamella surrounds all the anterior thylakoids, and just inside the girdle lamella the ring-shaped chloroplast DNA is located. The chloroplast is covered by two chloroplast membranes and also by two more membranes, the outer of which is continuous with the outer nuclear membrane and defines the perinuclear space. Between the innermost membrane and the chloroplast membrane is the periplastidial reticulum which serves to transport materials between cytoplasm and chloroplast. The eyespot is located in one lobe of the chloroplast in juxtaposition to the swelling of the smooth flagellum.

Fig. 8-11 *Dinobryon pediforme.*

Fig. 8-12 *Chrysosphaerella brevispina*. Diagrammatic illustration of the cell and its surfaces. The anterior surface has long and short flagella and is towards the top of the diagram. D, dorsal; L, left; R, right; V, ventral. (After Andersen, 1990.)

A single, prominent dictyosome is located near the nucleus. A large vacuole containing chrysolaminarin, and a few oil drops are located in the cytoplasm.

Hydrurus (Fig. 8-13) occurs in clean-water fast-flowing mountain streams in Kashmir and Kulu valleys. It has a foetid smell. A large number of naked cells are embedded in long cylindrical gelatinous strands and the alga occurs in the form of elaborate, feathery tufts, a few mm long. It has apical growth. The single apical cell divides transversely, with one-half becoming the new apical cell whereas the other elongates to form a new vegetative cell.

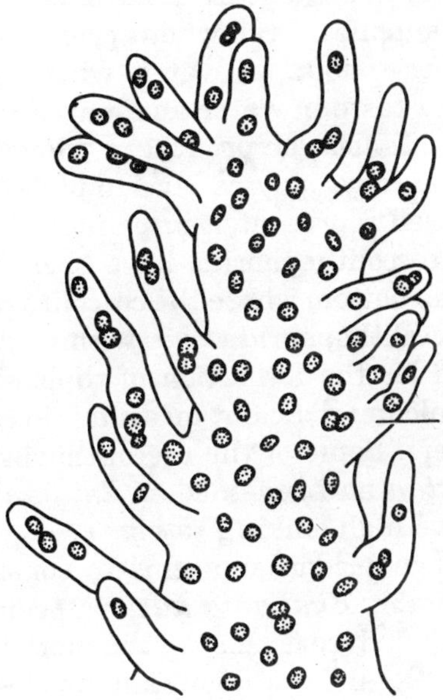

Fig. 8-13 *Hydrurus foetidus*, habit.

Many chrysomonads require such vitamins as B_{12}, thiamine, and biotin for their growth. Their heterotrophic nutritional tendency is demonstrated by the widespread ability to use organic nitrogen and phosphorus sources. A number of chrysomonads, including even some coccolithophorids, are phagotrophic and can meet their carbon requirements from organic sources. *Ochromonas danica* has been reported to synthesize certain vitamins and also to secrete these into its environment (Aaronson *et al.*, 1971). These vitamins include ascorbate, B_6, nicotinate, riboflavin, pantothenate, vitamins A, E, but not B_{12}. *O. danica* is one of the few Chrysophyceae which does not require or synthesize metabolically active vitamin B_{12}.

Among the algae, the coccolithophorids seem unique in respect of their calcium carbonate metabolism. Rahat and Spira (1967) have shown that *Prymnesium parvum* (Haptophyceae) is capable of growth in darkness, but only in the presence of high concentrations of glycerol. This species sometimes produces toxic blooms in fish ponds. Its toxin (prymnesin) has been isolated and is proteinaceous.

In the Coccolithophoridaceae, the conspicuous nucleus is centrally located in the cell. The nuclear envelope, the outer envelope of chloroplast, and the endoplasmic reticulum are interconnected. The endomembrane system, which comprises the Golgi apparatus, is an important part of the cell since coccoliths are formed inside Golgi vesicles or in the endoplasmic reticulum. Also, it has been shown that cellulose biosynthesis can occur in the Golgi region of *Pleurochrysis scherffeii*; this discovery is new for all plants (see Klaveness and Paasche, 1979). There are one or two parietal chloroplasts having a pyrenoid. The latter is traversed by one or a few chloroplast lamellae. The chloroplast lamellae usually have three thylakoids each. Each cell has several, elongated mitochondria with tubular cristae.

The motile stages have two smooth equal or unequal flagella and sometimes also a haptonema. *Emiliania huxleyi* lacks a haptonema. The flagellar bases (kinetosomes) are often associated with bundles of microtubules.

Many marine haptophycean flagellates produce characteristic organic surface scales which are morphologically species-specific. They are often beautifully ornamented with spines, rims, horns, etc.

The calcification in coccolithophorids is strongly dependent on light. The bicarbonate ions seem to be a source of carbon in photosynthesis as well as in calcification.

Some members of the Chrysophyta, e.g., *Dinobryon sertularia*, are known to clog filters in water works plant. Others are notorious producers of foul tastes and obnoxious smells in drinking water supplies. Even when occurring in low numbers, *Synura* produces a "muskmelon or ripe cucumbery odour" in water; when more abundant, it imparts a fishy smell. It also produces a bitter taste in water and leaves a persistent dry metallic sensation on the tongue. *Mallomonas* and *Dinobryon* produce a "violet" odour and leave a slick sensation on the tongue. In general, many chrysophytes tend to prefer relatively clean waters for their growth and the phylum is not well represented in polluted habitats.

The marine coccolithophorids have been responsible for the formation of extensive chalk beds on the ocean bottom where the coccoliths are deposited. These members seem to constitute the family Coccolithophoridaceae within the class Haptophyceae. The coccolithophorids require calcium for the formation of their coccoliths. In culture, coccolith formation can be inhibited in a calcium-deficient medium; there is no evidence of calcium deficiencies occurring in natural waters. Some of the coccolithophorids, especially the nonflagellate forms such as *Coccolithus huxleyi* now renamed as *Emiliania huxleyi* (Lohm.) Hay and Mohler, have a high density and have high sinking rates.

The Coccolithophoridaceae seems to constitute a heterogeneous group since some coccolithophorids, notably *Emiliania huxleyi*, seem to be more closely related to certain genera of noncalcified Haptophyceae than to the more typical coccolithophorids. Besides, cell types that produce no $CaCO_3$ are the dominant phases in the life cycle of some species. Some coccolithophorids, e.g., *Syracosphaera,* have two layers of different coccoliths, a phenomenon designated as dithecatism (Klaveness and Paasche, 1979). In rare cases, coccoliths of two different species or genera may be found on a single cell.

The members belonging to the order Pavlovales of the Prymnesiophyceae show the following distinctive features: (1) anisokont flagella; (2) knob scales on the longer flagellum, sometimes also on the cell body and haptonema; and (3) a canal entering the cell close to the flagellar insertion and penetrating deeply. In the remaining Prymnesiophyceae, the flagella are isokont.

A silicon requirement for the growth of *Synura petersonii* has been established by Klaveness and Guillard (1975). It is not known whether or not silicon is also required for the growth of nonscale-bearing Chrysophyta.

The motile cells and zoospores of most freshwater species and some marine species of the Chrysophyta have pulsating vacuoles occurring in pairs and pulsating alternately. One pair of such vacuoles is found per cell. These vacuoles generally occur near the apical (anterior) end of the cell near the flagella, but their location is equatorial in *Dinobryon* and basal in *Chrysopyxis*. Some of the motile stages possess a gullet, or even cytopharynx, into which the vacuoles empty; the flagella emerge from this cytopharynx. In *Chromulina*, the gullet is lined by trichocysts.

In some chrysophytes, biomineralization occurs by two different processes, viz., (1) as silica deposited inside the cells within a silica deposition vesicle, or (2) as iron, manganese or calcium deposited outside the cells (Lee and Kugrens, 1989). Silicification occurs by structures such as stomatocysts (Sandgren, 1980) or scales or spines (Andersen, 1987). On the other hand, Fe, Mn, and Ca are deposited on the extracellular mucilage of stalks, loricas, and cysts (Thomsen, 1988).

REPRODUCTION

One of the most characteristic features of the Chrysophyceae is the formation (commonly endogenous) of distinctive resting cysts or statospores (also called stomatocysts) which have a silica wall with a single small pore; the pore becomes closed at maturity by the formation of a partly silicified plug. Frequently, the pore becomes surrounded by a collar. The cysts may be spherical ovate or ellipsoid but are usually flask-shaped, and their outer surface may be smooth or variously ornamented. In *Ochromonas tuberculata*, the cysts are produced within a cytoplasmic silica deposition vesicle whose membrane seems to be formed by the coalescence of Golgi bodies (Hibberd, 1977b). The cyst is a perennating structure formed as a result of asexual or sexual reproduction. The morphology of asexual statospores is similar to the sexually produced statospores. Such common planktonic genera as *Ochromonas, Uroglena, Mallomonas*, and *Synura* (Fig. 8-14) produce asexual statospores, whereas the loricate genera *Kephyrion, Chrysolykos* and others reproduce sexually; in these, the loricate vegetative cells themselves fuse by their anterior ends (hologamous isogamy). In some cases, gametic fusion occurs at the posterior rather than anterior ends, as for instance in *Mallomonas caudata*. In these cases of posterior fusion, the resulting zygospore is a siliceous statospore.

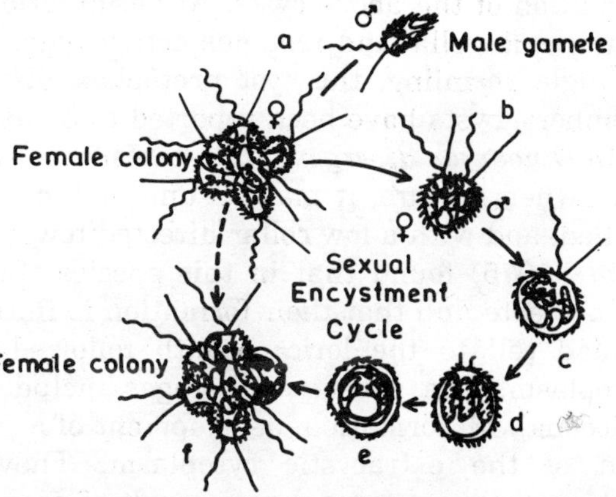

Fig. 8-14 Copulation and zygotic encystment in *Synura petersonii*. a, initial contact of a solitary male gamete with a female gamete within a colony; b, an early stage in plasmogamy characterized by the lateral fusion of cells, each with active flagellar pairs; c, a biflagellate planozygote stage with the fusion cell containing four plastids, two nuclei, and two chrysolaminarin starch vesicles; the planozygote is completely covered with scales; d, an early stage in zygotic encystment during which the remaining flagella are lost and significant rearrangement of cytoplasmic organelles establishes a symmetrical orientation, chrysolaminarin vesicles fuse, and the nuclei associate with the inner margins of the plastids; e, a mature zygotic statospore containing four reduced plastids and two nuclei, some cytoplasm and the vegetative scale layer remain outside the cyst wall; f, a completely mature zygotic statospore as it ultimately appears, taking the place of the female gamete in the colony. (After Sandgren, 1988.)

Some chrysophytes produce both uni- and binucleate statospores (see Sandgren, 1980). The general belief is that asexual statospores are uninucleate, whereas sexual statospores may be binucleate, with the 2 nuclei fusing at some stage.

The common planktonic species *Dinobryon cylindricum* forms three types of statospores, namely, (1) uninucleate, asexual, (2) binucleate, asexual; and (3) binucleate, sexual (Sandgren, 1981). Type (3) statospores are formed as a consequence of anisogamous heterothallic fusion which involves a gametogenic hormone, called erogen, released from female cells. The statospores in this species can be produced not only by old or resting cells but also by younger active cells. Sandgren is of the opinion that statospores represent a more flexible reproductive strategy than the resultant zygospores produced by various other planktonic microalgae.

Apart from longitudinal cell division, the Chrysophyceae reproduce asexually by the formation of the above cysts. At germination, the protoplast emerges through the cyst pore, acquires flagella, and resumes active vegetative growth. In some species, instead of forming a single germling, the cyst protoplast divides to produce two or four zoospores. In some members, cysts have been reported to be formed as a result of isogamous reproduction.

In *Dinobryon divergens*, the statospore (Fig. 8-15) is produced at the apical end of the lorica and, when mature, it may be uni- or binucleate, spherical, smooth-walled, and with a low collar directed toward the lorica base. Sheath *et al.* (1975) found that in this species the statospores are mostly uninucleate and that their formation is initiated by migration of the monad cell to the lorica mouth followed by rounding up of the cytoplasm. The subsequent stages included an unequal cleavage, siliceous wall formation, development of a pore plug, and disintegration of the extracystic cytoplasm. They concluded that these statospores were formed as a result of asexual reproduction. Sheath *et al.* have proposed that the chrysophycean statospores arising asexually and endogenously should be recognized as distinct structures from those which are produced isogamously but not necessarily endogenously; the latter type of statospores, which are produced as a result of sexual reproduction, should be called zygospores.

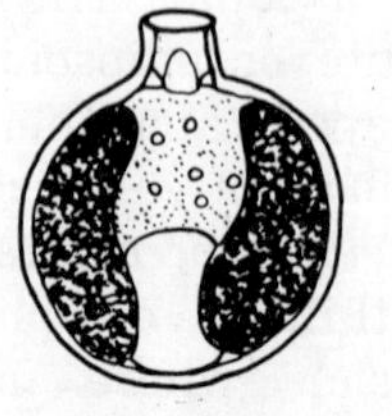

Fig. 8-15 *Dinobryon*, statospore.

Sphaeridiothrix compressa, which occurs in saline ponds, reproduces asexually by the formation of flagellated zoospores (Andrews, 1970).

Certain chrysophytes are known to reproduce sexually. In *Kephyrion* and *Calycomonas*, the protoplasts of two vegetative cells undergo fusion. *Ochrosphaera neapolitana* produces motile isogametes. The zygote in most cases seems to be transformed into a resting cyst. At germination, the zygote nucleus seems to divide meiotically to form four daughter cells.

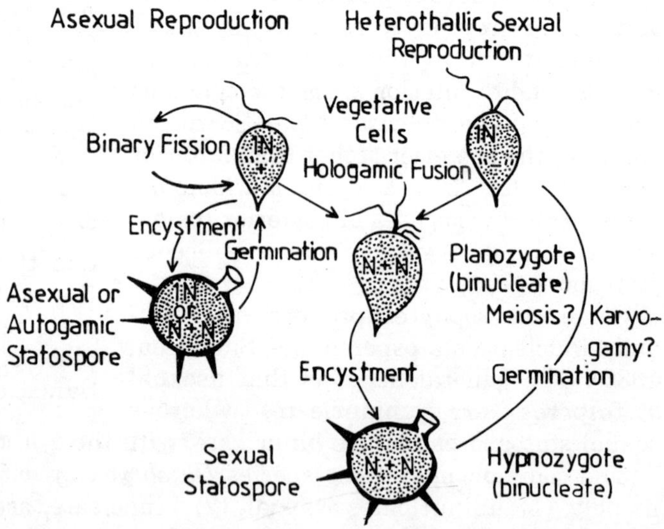

Fig. 8-16 Generalized life cycle diagram for planktonic chrysophytes. Ploidy level of various stages is indicated. (After Sandgren, 1988.)

LIFE HISTORY

The information on life history in the Chrysophyta is meagre and cytological phases are poorly known. Figure 8-16 shows a generalized life cycle of planktonic chrysophytes. Some recent researches in France have shown that many Haptophyceae, which have a pseudofilamentous benthic form and a naked or coccolith bearing unicellular form, are heteromorphic. *Coccolithus pelagicus* and *Emiliania huxleyi* produce a nonmotile coccolithophorid phase alternating with a motile flagellate stage. The motile phase of *E. huxleyi* bears uncalcified organic scales only.

The life history of *Hymenomonas coronata* seems to include a benthic, nonmotile stage, and a biflagellate motile stage. No fusion of motile cells has been observed (see Mills, 1975). Both motile and nonmotile cells bear coccoliths as well as scales.

The dominant phase in *Pleurochrysis* is nonmotile and consists of sessile colonies of cells. These vegetative cells do not produce coccoliths but profusely form organic scales. These cells may form one or the other of two morphologically different flagellate cell types, one of which bears coccoliths and the other bears organic scales but no coccoliths.

One feature of special significance is the frequent appearance of nonmotile forms in clonal culture of motile coccolithophorids. For *Cricosphaera carterae*, a haploid benthic phase has been obtained from a diploid coccolithophorid (Boney and Burrows, 1966). In this species, the motile phase is diploid, and the nonmotile phase haploid.

There seems to be a basic difference between the species that inhabit coastal waters and those that exist in mid-ocean. In the coastal species, the free-swimming phases seem to alternate with filamentous or other sessile forms that colonize rocky substrata; the oceanic species occurring away from the seashore seem to form cyst-like resting stages which are nonmotile, do not require a solid substratum, and can remain suspended in the surface layers of sea water.

The life history of *Hymenomonas* (formerly *Syracosphaera*) *carterae* is biphasic (Fig. 8-17) involving an alternation between a *Hymenomonas* stage and an *Apistonema* stage (Von Stosch,

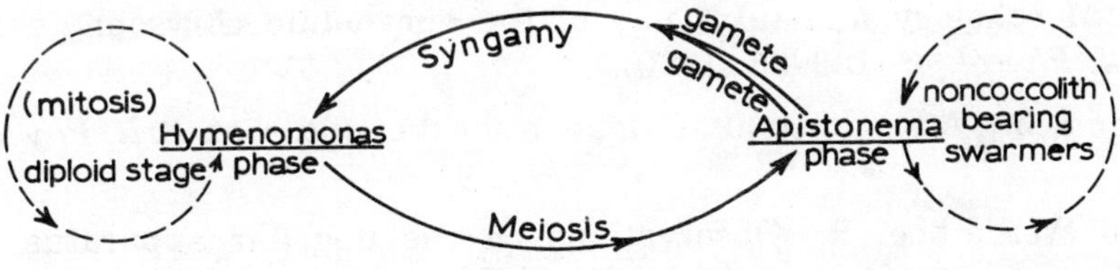

Fig. 8-17 *Hymenomonas carterae*, life history.

1967). The *Hymenomonas* phase propagates itself by mitosis, and after some time divides meiotically to produce the haploid *Apistonema* stage which produces swarmers lacking coccoliths (see Fig. 8-17). Both asexual zoospores and sexual gametes (motile) can be formed by *Apistonema*. The gametes fuse to form the *Hymenomonas* stage.

FEED VALUE

Several prymnesiophytes, e.g., *Isochrysis galbana* and *Pavlova lutheri*, are grazed by juvenile stages of turbot, fish larvae, and molluscs. These algae are rich in polyunsaturated fatty acids (Baynes and Scott, 1979). Their importance as animal feed arises from the fact that marine animals have only a limited capacity for synthesizing higher polyunsaturated fatty acids.

FOSSIL COCCOLITHOPHORIDS

Most coccolithophorids are well preserved as fossils and are known from the Lower Jurassic onwards. They occur abundantly in many Mesozoic and Tertiary rocks. Ordinary chalk often contains innumerable little rosettes of calcite crystals (about 1 μm in diameter); these crystals represent the fossil coccoliths. Most of the earlier known species are more simply constructed than the more recently evolved forms. The Cretaceous species *Braarudosphaera bigelowi* seems unique in having survived to the present day; most other Cretaceous coccolithophorids seem to have become extinct by the end of the Cretaceous itself, with various new species evolving in the Tertiary. The Tertiary rocks often harbour a very interesting group of fossils, called discoasters, which are believed to be closely related to coccoliths, but which have not been reported from rocks of any other age. These discoasters are mostly circular discs having 6, 8, or more rays (see Black, 1965).

REFERENCES

Aaronson, S., DeAngelis, B., Frank, O., and Baker, H., Secretion of vitamins and amino acids into the environment by *Ochromonas danica, J. Phycol.*, **7**, 215–18 (1971).

Allen, M.B., Structure, physiology and biochemistry of the Chrysophyceae, *A. Rev. Microbiol.*, **23**, 29–46 (1969).

Andersen, R.A., Synurophyceae classis nov.: a new class of algae, *Am. J. Bot.*, **74**, 337–53 (1987).

Andersen, R.A., The three-dimensional structure of the flagellar apparatus of *Chrysosphaerella brevispina* (Chrysophyceae) as viewed by high voltage electron microscopy stereo pairs, *Phycologia*, **29**, 86–97 (1990).

Andrews, H.T., Morphology and taxonomy of the euryhaline chrysophyte *Sphaeridiothrix compressa, J. Phycol.*, **6**, 133–36 (1970).

Baynes, S.M. and Scott, A.P., Unicellular algae in the diet of turbot, *Brit. Phycol. J.*, **14**, 19–20 (1979).

Beech, P.L. and Wetherbee, R., Observations on the flagellar apparatus and peripheral endoplasmic reticulum of the coccolithophorid, *Pleurochrysis carterae* (Prymnesiophyceae), *Phycologia*, **27**, 142–58 (1988).

Black, M., Coccoliths, *Endeavour*, **24**, 131–37 (1965).

Boney, A.D. and Burrows, A., Experimental studies on the benthic phases of Haptophyceae. I. Effects of some experimental conditions on the release of coccolithophorids, *J. Mar. Biol. Ass.* (U.K.), **46**, 295–319 (1966).

Bouck, G.B., The structure, origin, isolation, and composition of the tubular mastigonemes of the *Ochromonas* flagellum, *J. Cell Biol.*, **50**, 362–84 (1971).

Chang, F.H. and Ryan, K.G., *Prymnesium calathiferum* sp. nov. (Prymnesiophyceae): a new species isolated from Northland, New Zealand, *Phycologia*, **24**, 191–98 (1985).

Glider, W. and Rosowski, J.R., The morphology of scales, bristles and spines of three species of *Mallomonas, J. Phycol.*, Suppl. Abst. No. 45, p. 18 (1976).

Hibberd, D.J., The ultrastructure and taxonomy of the Chrysophyceae and Prymnesiophyceae (Haptophyceae): a survey with some new observations of the ultrastructure of the Chrysophyceae, *Bot. J. Linn. Soc.*, **72**, 55–80 (1976).

Hibberd, D.J., The cytology and ultrastructure of *Chrysonebula holmesii* Lund (Chrysophyceae), with special reference to the flagellar apparatus, *Brit. Phycol. J.*, **12**, 369–83 (1977a).

Hibberd, D.J., Ultrastructure of cyst formation in *Ochromonas tuberculata* (Chrysophyceae), *J. Phycol.*, **13**, 309–20 (1977b).

Inouye, I. and Pienaar, R.N., Ultrastructure of the flagellar apparatus in *Pleurochrysis* (class Prymnesiophyceae), *Protoplasma*, **125**, 24–35 (1985).

Kawachi, M., Inouye, I., Maeda, O., and Chihara, M., The haptonema as a food-capturing device: observations on *Chrysochromulina hirta* (Prymnesiophyceae), *Phycologia*, **30**, 563–73 (1991).

Klaveness, D. and Guillard, R.R.L., The requirement for silicon in *Synura petersonii* (Chrysophyceae), *J. Phycol.*, **11**, 349–55 (1975).

Klaveness, D. and Paasche, E., Physiology of coccolithophorids. *In* Levandowsky, M. and Hutner, S.H. (eds.) Biochemistry and Physiology of Protozoa, Vol. 1, 2nd edn., 191–213, Academic Press, New York (1979).

Klein, R.M. and Cronquist, A., A consideration of the evolutionary and taxonomic significance of some biochemical, micromorphological and physiological characters in the thallophytes, *Q. Rev. Biol.*, **42**, 105–296 (1967).

Kristiansen, J., Distribution problems in the Synuraceae (Chrysophyceae), *Verh. Intern. Verein. Limnol.*, **21**, 1444–48 (1981).

Kristiansen, J., The ultrastructural bases of Chrysophyte systematics and phylogeny, *CRC Crit. Rev. Plant Sciences*, **4**, 141–211 (1986).

Lee, R.E. and Kugrens, P., Biomineralization of the stalks of *Anthophysa vegetans* (Chrysophyceae), *J. Phycol.*, **25**, 591–96 (1989).

Mills, J.T., *Hymenomonas coronata* sp. nov.: a new coccolithophorid from the Texas coast, *J. Phycol.*, **11**, 149–54 (1975).

Outka, D.E. and Williams, D.G., Sequential coccolith morphogenesis in *Hymenomonas carterae, J. Protozool.*, **18**, 285–97 (1971).

Pienaar, R.N., The fine structure of *Hymenomonas* (*Cricosphaera*) *carterae*. II. Observations on scale and coccolith production, *J. Phycol.*, **5**, 321–31 (1969).

Pienaar, R.N., Coccolith production in *Hymenomonas carterae, Protoplasma*, **73**, 217–24 (1971).

Rahat, M. and Spira, Z., Specificity of glycerol for dark growth of *Prymnesium parvum, J. Protozool.*, **14**, 45–48 (1967).

Saha, L.C. and Wujek, D.E., Scale-bearing chrysophytes from tropical Northeast India, *Nordic J. Bot.*, **10**, 343–54 (1989).

Sandgren, C.D., Resting cyst formation in selected chrysophyte flagellates: an ultrastructural survey including a proposal for the phylogenetic significance of interspecific variations in the encystment process, *Protistologica*, **16**, 289–303 (1980).

Sandgren, C.D., Characteristics of sexual and asexual resting cyst (statospore) formation in *Dinobryon cylindricum* Imhof (Chrysophyta), *J. Phycol.*, **17**, 199–210 (1981).

Sandgren, C.D., The ecology of chrysophyte flagellates: their growth and perennation strategies as freshwater phytoplankton. *In* Sandgren, C.D. (ed.) Growth and Reproductive Strategies of Freshwater Phytoplankton, 9–104, Cambridge University Press, Cambridge (1988).

Sheath, R.G., Hellebust, J.A., and Sawa, T., The statospore of *Dinobryon divergens* Imhof: formation and germination in a subarctic lake, *J. Phycol.*, **11**, 31–38 (1975).

Slankis, T. and Gibbs, S.P., The fine structure of mitosis and cell division in the chrysophycean alga *Ochromonas danica, J. Phycol.*, **8**, 243–56 (1972).

Thomsen, H.A., Ultrastructural studies of the flagellate and cyst stages of *Pseudopedinella tricostata* (Pedinellales, Chrysophyceae), *Brit. Phycol. J.*, **23**, 1–16 (1988).

Von Stosch, H.A., Haptophyceae. *In* Ruhland, W. (ed.) Encyclopaedia of Plant Physiology, Vol. 18, 646–56, Springer-Verlag, New York (1967).

9 Bacillariophyta

GENERAL CHARACTERS

The Bacillariophyceae, popularly called diatoms, comprise a homogeneous assemblage of unicellular and colonial forms which differ generally from other algae in possessing highly sculptured and symmetrically ornamented cell walls. The main characters that collectively differentiate the Bacillariophyta from other phyla are (1) the diploid nature of vegetative cells; (2) the presence of chlorophyll-c and -a, together with fucoxanthin, diatoxanthin, and diadinoxanthin, in the chromatophores, the usual brown colouration being due to the preponderance of carotenoid pigments over chlorophylls; (3) the silicified nature of the cell walls which consist of two highly perforated overlapping pieces, sometimes bearing such structures as spines and bristles; (4) the storage of oil and chrysolaminarin and not starch in food reserves; and (5) the reduction in cell size occurring during vegetative multiplication, which is compensated for by the production of spores known as auxospores.

OCCURRENCE

Cosmopolitan and ubiquitous in distribution, the diatoms form a major component of the planktonic vegetation. They are very important as primary producers in the food web of aquatic ecosystems. The most common genera of freshwater habitats are *Synedra, Melosira, Navicula, Nitzschia*, and *Asterionella*. Species of *Cocconeis, Gomphonema*, and *Eunotia* grow epiphytically on certain freshwater algae such as *Cladophora* and *Oedogonium*. *Triceratium* and *Hyalodiscus* occur in the littoral and sublittoral zones as epiphytes on seaweeds.

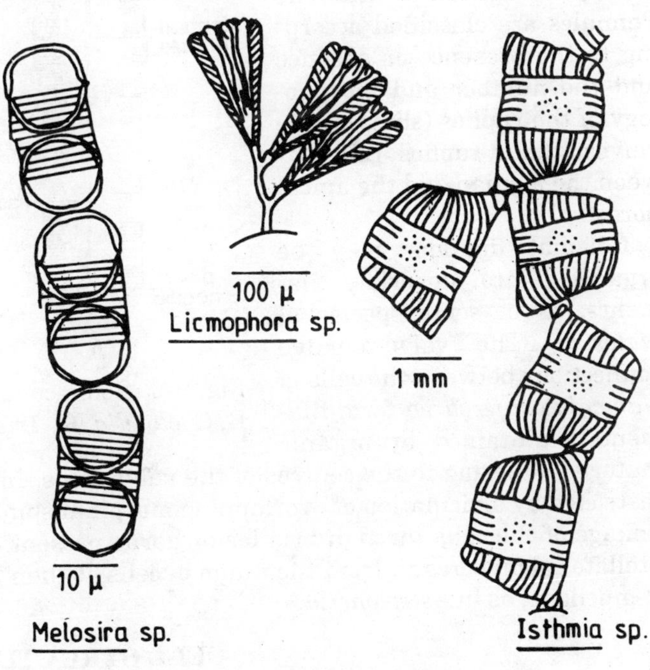

Fig. 9-1 Three common benthic diatoms.

The planktonic diatoms have a variety of structural features which can aid them in counteracting the added burden of their siliceous frustules. These features are of four basic types:

(1) Bladder-like, quite large cells having very little cytoplasm as a peripheral lining. The major part of the cell volume consists of a vacuole. An example is *Ethmodiscus*.

(2) Ribbon-like colonies, with the

narrow cells closely joined together by their valves to look like a ribbon. An example is *Fragilaria*.

(3) Narrow, elongated, hair-like cells or colonies. An example is *Rhizosolenia*.

(4) Branched individual cells (since they bear long spines or horns) or elongate colonial cells, projecting out at various angles. Examples are *Chaetoceros* and *Asterionella*.

The benthic diatoms (Fig. 9-1) may occur on rocks, sand or mud, or be epiphytic, epizoic or endozoic (e.g., *Licmophora*).

MORPHOLOGY

The thalli of the diatoms are unicellular, colonial or filamentous. In respect of their shape and valve morphology, the unicellular diatoms have been classified into two orders, the pennate diatoms (Pennales) with isobilateral symmetry, e.g., *Pinnularia* (Fig. 9-2 A), and the centric diatoms (Centrales) with radial symmetry, e.g., *Cyclotella* (Fig. 9-2 B). *Triceratium* (Fig. 9-2 C) has three planes of mirror symmetry. A further classification of the Centrales is based on the presence or absence of bristles or horns on the cell surface. The Pennales are classified according to the presence or absence and the number and morphology of the raphes (slits) on the valves; these raphes run between the median and the apical pores.

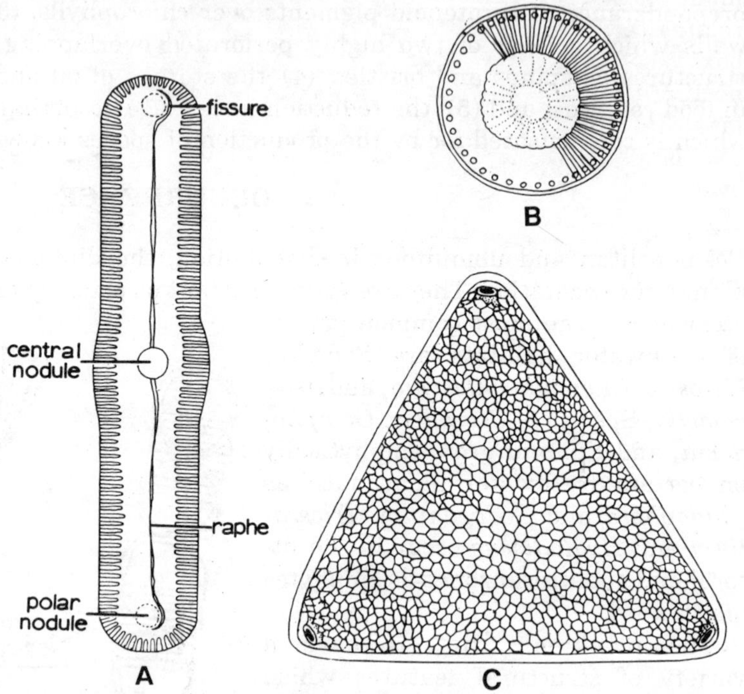

Fig. 9-2 Some common diatoms. A, *Pinnularia*, valve view; B, *Cyclotella*; C, *Triceratium*.

Colonial diatoms may be organized into uniseriate filaments, as in some species of *Melosira* The valve-to-valve connections between the cells of *Navicula confervacea* form filaments maintained by organic material adhering to the centres of the valve faces. In this species, filament bending becomes restricted by articulation of overlapping marginal spines. Sometimes, a colony results from the linkage of the cells through bristles or horns present on the valve surface, as in *Chaetoceros*. Stellate colonies result from the union of cells at their basal ends through localized production of mucilage, as in *Asterionella*.

CELL STRUCTURE

The cell wall (frustule) of the diatoms consists of two overlapping halves, the upper half, known as the epitheca, and the lower, the hypotheca. Each theca is further divided into two parts—the main surface and its incurved margins which are termed the valve and the connecting band, respectively (Fig. 9-3 A, B). The term girdle is applied to the side pieces collectively. The epitheca and hypotheca can be compared to a box, the lid corresponding to the former and the main body to the latter. The two connecting bands represent the incurved sides of the lid and the main body, whereas the valve relates to the top or bottom of the box. When fitted together, the connecting band of the epitheca overlaps that of the hypotheca and the two bands remain united in the overlapping region by a cementing organic substance present between them. Accordingly, a cell can be seen from two different aspects, the valve view and the girdle view. Most diatoms appear rectangular in the girdle view but in the valve view their shape is variable. Most pores are located in the valves.

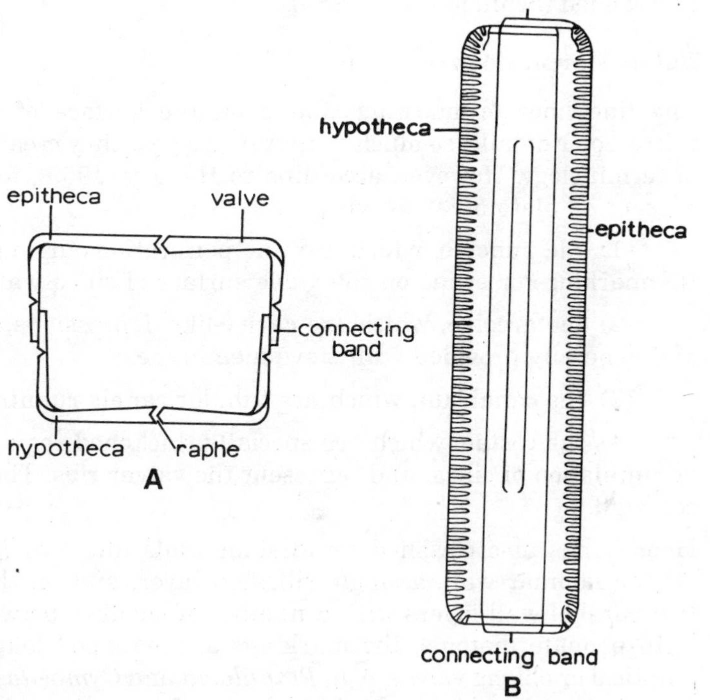

Fig. 9-3 *Pinnularia*. A, transverse section showing relative position of epitheca, hypotheca, connecting band, valve, and raphe; B, girdle view showing relative position of epitheca and hypotheca.

The cell wall (frustule) is enriched with amorphous silica and is formed in internal vesicles surrounded by a specialized membrane, called silicalemma, which becomes extracellular at the end of cell division. In some species, the frustule has a delicate organic coat and organic layers are also sometimes laid down on the inner surface of the wall after it has been formed (Duke and Reimann, 1977).

The cells of *Eunotia* and certain other pennate diatoms have conspicuous chromocentres, and the extent of development of constitutive heterochromatin is exceptionally high in *Navicula radiosa* (Geitler, 1979). In this species, the heterochromatin forms a giant central compound chromocentre. However, this extensive chromocentre becomes dispersed and loose in the auxospores.

In most diatoms, the dictyosomes are localized exclusively in the plasma packet containing the nucleus, but in *Synedra*, they lie in a plasmatic ribbon-like structure extending over the whole length of the cell.

In many genera, the two plate-like chromatophores split transversely during cell division, but in *Nitzschia*, they split longitudinally in coordinated synchrony with the progress of mitosis and cell division.

Chloroplasts are completely enclosed by a cisterna of the ER. Many diatoms have bilobed chloroplasts which round up under unfavourable conditions. Consequently the ratio between the surface enveloping membranes and volume alters and the thylakoidal system becomes rearranged (Schnepf *et al.*, 1988).

Valve Morphology

The fine lines or markings found on the surface of diatom valves vary widely in their microscopic details, so much so that in the past they created much confusion in the formulation of terminology. However, according to Hendey (1959), four types of secondary structures are present on diatom valves, viz.,

(1) the punctae, which are fine perforations arranged in regular rows corresponding to the markings or striae on the valve surface of silica walls;

(2) the areolae, which are cavity-like depressions, coarser and larger than the punctae and generally provided with sieve membranes;

(3) the canaliculi, which are tubular canals running through the valve surface; and

(4) the costae, which are specially thickened regions of the valve, resulting from heavy accumulation of silica, and represent the valvar ribs. The ribs constitute the backbones of the cell wall.

Hendey has also classifed the diatom walls into two types based on their nature, namely, (1) the laminar wall, a single silicified layer; and (2) the locular wall, basically made up of two parallel wall layers with a number of loculi in between them.

In pennate diatoms, the markings are arranged longitudinally, one on either side of the elliptical or oblong valves, e.g., *Pinnularia* and *Cymbella* (Fig. 9-4), whereas in centric diatoms they are distributed concentrically with reference to a central point on the more or less circular valves, e.g., in *Arachnoidiscus* (Fig. 9-5).

In *Pinnularia*, which is an oblong unicell, the valve view presents two planes of isobilateral symmetry—the apical and the transapical. The apical axis joins the two poles of the valve and the transapical axis passes along the transverse axis of the valve. In the axial area of some pennate diatoms, e.g., *Navicula*, there is a longitudinal slit, termed the raphe, which is interrupted in the middle by a central nodule formed by internal thickening of the valve (Fig. 9-6). Each pole of the valve also contains a nodule (polar nodule) which is formed in the same manner as the central nodule (Fig. 9-6). The centric diatoms lack a raphe.

Navicula, like *Pinnularia* (Fig. 9-7), is isobilaterally symmetrical with valve markings consisting of fine pores bridged from the inside by sieve membranes containing numerous fine pores. The raphe situated in the central rib is also called the apical rib. The rows of pores situated on the lateral sides of the apical rib and separated one from the other by solid silica ribs are termed transapical ribs. The pores within a row are separated by siliceous connections which link the adjacent transapical ribs (Fig. 9-8). In valves that lack a raphe, the axial area may give the appearance of a false raphe or pseudoraphe. *Navicula* and *Pinnularia* possess two raphes each, one on each valve, whereas in *Achnanthes*, only one of the two valves has a raphe. A pseudoraphe is characteristic of *Synedra* and *Fragilaria*.

Figure 9-9 shows the raphe system in diatoms.

In some genera, the frustules bear one or more projections, termed the labiate processes, which are merely openings through the valve. Each labiate process projects inward and terminates in a flattened tube which has a longitudinal slit with two lips (Fig. 9-10; see Hasle,

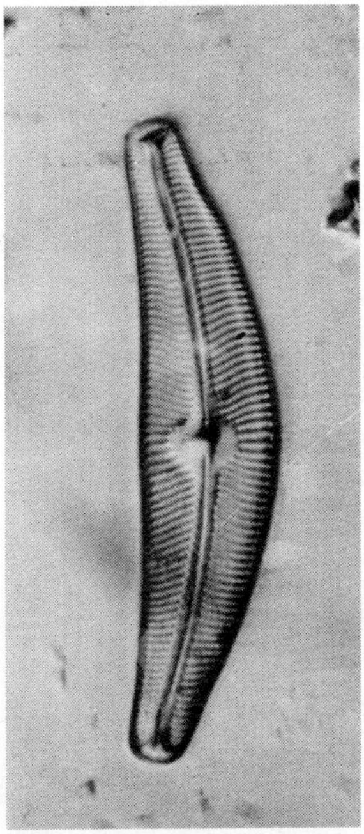

Fig. 9-4 *Cymbella tumida*. (Approx. ×200.) *Courtesy* K. Ueda.

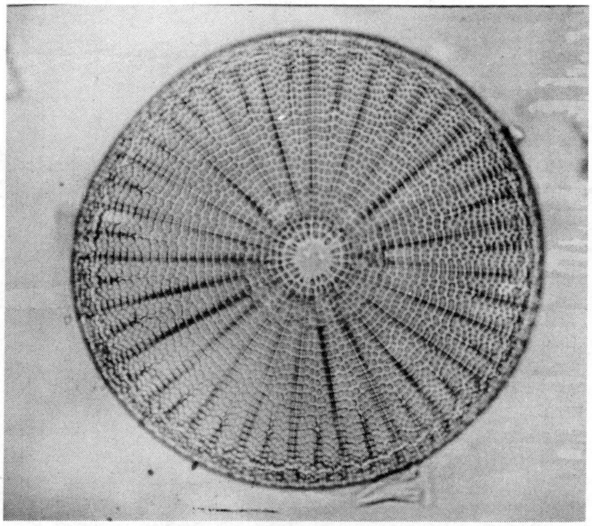

Fig. 9-5 *Arachnoidiscus ehrenbergii*. (Approx. ×200.) *Courtesy* K. Ueda.

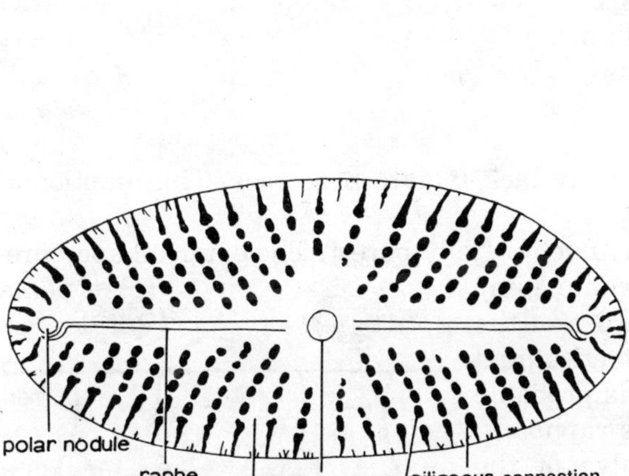

Fig. 9-6 *Navicula*, valve view detailing cell wall structure (after Reimann *et al*., 1966).

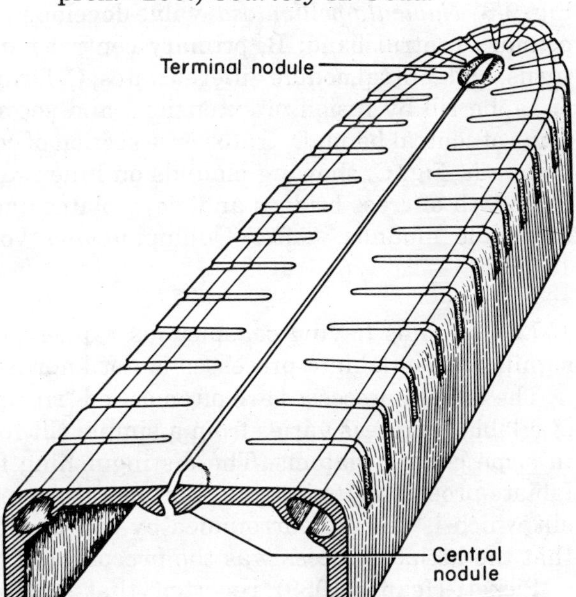

Fig. 9-7 *Pinnularia*, valve view of frustule structure (only one-half shown).

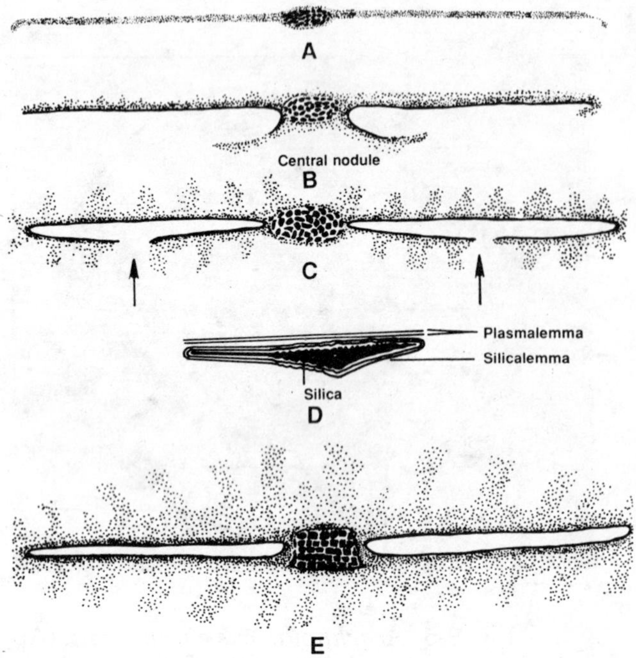

Fig. 9-8 *Navicula pelliculosa*, valve development. A, primary central band; B, primary central band inturns, and central nodule differentiates; C, formation of raphe rib by fusion of extensions and secondary arms of central band; D, transverse section of central nodule in Fig. C, showing mounds on inner surface; E, growth of cross bridges and sieve plates and loss of nodule mounds. (After Chiappino and Volcani, 1977.)

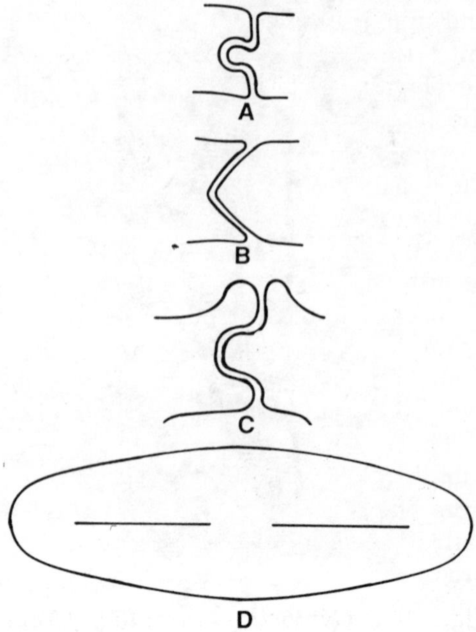

Fig. 9-9 Diatom raphe system. A–C, cross-section; D, surface view (the two halves of raphe can be seen clearly as two long slits).

1972). Diatoms having conspicuous raphes generally lack labiate processes. The functional significance of labiate processes is not known.

The labiate processes are often called "rimoportulae" or "jelly-pores". The external aperture of a labiate process varies from a simple slit to ornate spiny in some centric diatoms. The distinguishing feature of the labiate process is its internal flattened tube or longitudinal slit which is usually surrounded by two lips. It is probable that the labiate process was the precursor of the raphe.

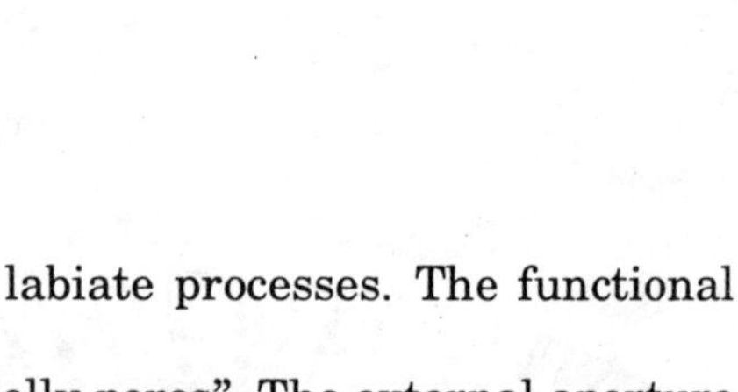

Fig. 9-10 *Thalassiosira bioculata*, labiate processes (after Hasle, 1972).

Pickett-Heaps (1989) reported that each valve of the araphid *Diatoma* has a labiate process at one end; in a frustule, these processes are at diagonally opposite ends. After the completion of mitosis, an elongated dense body detaches from the spindle pole and moves to one end of the daughter cell, always diagonally opposite the labiate process of the parental valve. This dense body trails a cone-shaped array of microtubules (Fig. 9-11). The new valve forms within the silica deposition vesicle. The dense body reaches the cell's end, moves back slightly, finally settling onto the silica deposition vesicle and developing a layered substructure on it; the labiate process of the new daughter valve differentiates immediately beneath the dense body. The dense object appears to be the evolutionary homologue of the "fibrous labiate process apparatus" recorded in some centric diatoms. Pickett-Heaps' demonstration of its presence in an araphid pennate diatom points to the probability that the raphe might have evolved from the labiate process.

The frustules of *Thalassiosira* bear a tubular extension projecting outward from the wall; this tubular structure is called the strutted process. Strutted processes form chitin which may help bind the cells together.

Table 9-1 compares some characters of selected genera of raphed diatoms.

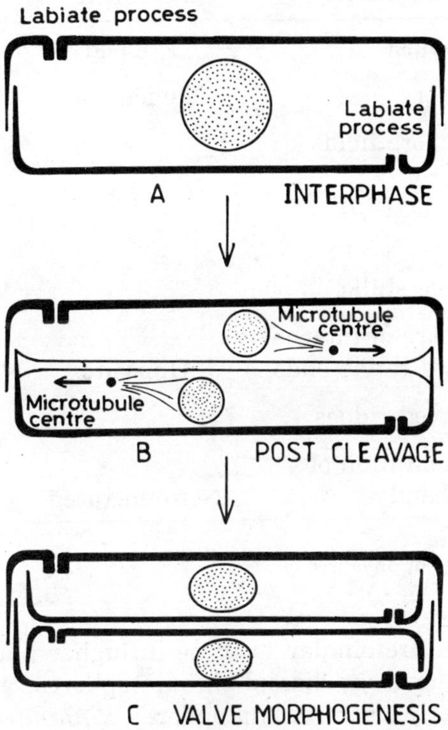

Fig. 9-11 The labiate process location and the position of the microtubule centres during valve morphogenesis. A, at interphase, the labiate processes are at opposite ends of the frustule; B, following cytokinesis, the microtubule centre becomes detached from each spindle pole and moves to the end of each daughter cell, see arrows; the centres are always located as if moving in opposite directions and invariably away from the labiate process in the parent valve; C, the differentiating labiate process in each new frustule is at the end opposite to the old process. (From Pickett-Heaps, 1989.)

Protoplast

The cytoplasm of the diatoms is bounded by a membrane and surrounds a central vacuole. The cells are uninucleate. In the Pennales, the nucleus in most species lies in a massive plasmatic bridge which separates the vacuoles; in the Centrales, it normally occupies a position within the peripheral layer of the cytoplasm. Nuclear division shows the following two interesting features: (1) the spindle formation is intranuclear and the metaphase chromosomes arrange themselves in an equatorial ring rather than on an equatorial plate, and (2) the spindle is an elongated cylinder with flattened ends, a feature common to the Chrysophyta and Pyrrhophyta. In *Lithodesmium undulatum*, certain plate-like structures constituting a spindle precursor are found along the nuclear membrane. During mitotic prophase in sperm producing cells, a mitotic spindle consisting of long microtubules appears between the precursor plates and the nuclear wall. Gradually, the nuclear wall degrades and a compact spindle is formed. The subsequent stages in nuclear

Table 9-1 Comparison of four raphed diatoms (after Kociolek and Stoermer, 1986)

Character	*Cocconeis*	*Mastogloia*	*Achnanthes*	*Gomphonema*
Chloroplast	1, lobed	2 bands	1, curved	1, curved
Symmetry	Naviculoid*	Naviculoid*	Naviculoid*	Gomphonemoid**
Apical pore fields	–	–	–	+
Raphe	1	2	1	2
Locules	+**	+**	–*	–*
Mucilage stalks	–*	–*	+**	+**
Curvature of internal proximal raphe ends	Opposite	Straight	Opposite	Together
Reinforced ridges	+	+	–	–
Ornamentation of girdle band	Nonpunctate*	Punctate**	Nonpunctate*	Punctate**

*Primitive.
**Derived or advanced.

division are similar to those in higher plants. The Centrales (e.g., *Coscinodiscus*) generally have numerous discoid chromatophores, and the Pennales have one or two large plate-like frequently lobed chromatophores. *Pinnularia* has one or two plate-like chloroplasts which may or may not be axile. Single-lobed or H-shaped chloroplasts occur in *Cocconeis* and *Gomphonema*. Naked pyrenoids occur in some diatoms, e.g., *Nitzschia*. The electron microscopy of the diatom cell has demonstrated the presence of endoplasmic reticulum, Golgi bodies, and mitochondria.

Pickett-Heaps and Tippit (1980) have studied the cell division in two large pennate diatoms, *Nitzschia* and *Hantzschia*. At prometaphase, the relatively small spindle elongates and this is accompanied by very active oscillations of the chromosomes. Independently, each pair of chromatids attaches to the other pole, its oscillations stop, and it stretches across the central spindle. Later, the chromatids split synchronously and then start their poleward movements at late metaphase. In *Hantzschia* and many other diatoms, the half spindles become coarsely striated near the poles, and the elongated central spindle maintains its maximum length, until broken by the cleavage furrow, when the broken halves disassemble. In contrast, the half spindles in *Nitzschia* lack striations, and after reaching maximum elongation, its spindle breaks down before cleavage (Pickett-Heaps and Tippit, 1980).

LOCOMOTION

Movement is virtually restricted to those diatoms which have a raphe. Most diatoms possessing a raphe are motile and are also capable of anchorage (Harper and Harper, 1967) to the substratum by means of the raphe. Both motility and anchorage involve the secretion of some mucopolysaccharide material through the raphe slit. This material adheres to the substratum

(Fig. 9-12 A, B) and by further secretion of this continuous strand, the cell pushes itself forward. According to Edgar (1979), the movement is characterized by rapidly fluctuating velocity and the mechanism of locomotion is one which involves a series of forward thrusts rather than smooth, gliding motion. Edgar has suggested that the driving force for locomotion is not steady but intermittent and that this is the cause of velocity changes in the movement of the diatom itself and also in the movement of particles streaming along its dorsal raphe. The computer assisted analysis of particle streaming along the raphe slit suggests that the ventral and dorsal raphe activity may somehow be coordinated and that the driving force may vary along the length of a single raphe slit. Medlin and Crawford (1986) have shown that in the centric diatom *Actinocyclus subtilis*, the movement is directional and is achieved by the production of mucopolysaccharides through the labiate process. Labiate processes are widely distributed among the centric diatoms. During movement, the cells of *A. subtilis* rotate and, in keeping with this behaviour, the labiate processes in this species are disposed around the circumference of the cell.

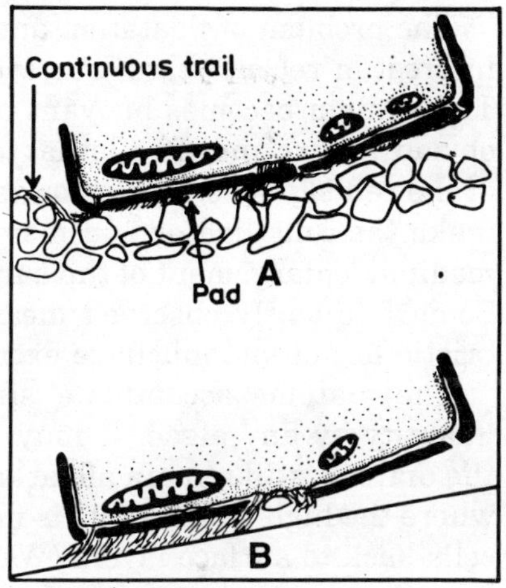

Fig. 9-12 Diatom raphe systems during locomotion. A, longitudinal section through two raphe systems of ventral valve of a naviculoid diatom moving over particulate substratum; B, longitudinal section as in Fig. A, the diatom moving over smooth substratum.

Whereas *Navicula* moves in a straight path, *Amphora* follows a curved path, and *Nitzschia* curves in two different radii.

Some diatoms move actively by a smooth or jerky gliding motion. Until recently, motility has been thought to be restricted to those pennate diatoms which have the raphe. Motility may be due to mucilage secretion through the raphe fissure, associated with the activity of bundles of actin filaments that line the cell membrane immediately adjacent to the raphe.

In 1986 two centric diatoms, viz., *Odontella* and *Actinocyclus*, were shown to exhibit motility (Pickett-Heaps *et al.*, 1986; Medlin *et al.*, 1986). In both these, movement occurs by mucilage secretion through the labiate processes. Pickett-Heaps *et al.* (1991) have reported active gliding motion in a marine pennate diatom *Ardissonea* (formerly called *Synedra*) that has neither a raphe nor any labiate process. This diatom shows smooth, jerky, and rolling movements. The motion is associated with the secretion of trails of mucilage from one end of the cell. Sometimes when one end of the cell ceases to secrete mucilage and the other end starts secreting it, the direction of movement becomes reversed.

SINKING

The diatoms are seldom continuously resident in lake phytoplankton. A bloom is invariably followed by a period of population decline in which a large part of the biomass sediments to the lake bottom. According to Wiseman and Reynolds (1981), the sinking rate of live diatoms is regulated physiologically. Increased sinking rates do not necessarily indicate a loss of viability but a response to unfavourable conditions of nutrient availability and carbon metabolism.

Jaworski *et al.* (1981) have found that limitation of CO_2 uptake either by CO_2 depletion or the addition of an inhibitor of photosynthesis (e.g., DCMU) increases the sinking rate of *Asterionella formosa* cells from 0.3 m to 1 m per day.

The problem of floatation and sinking of planktonic diatoms has also aroused considerable interest in recent years. *Coscinodiscus concinnus* has repeatedly caused oil slicks in the sea. This diatom becomes buoyant by synthesizing large quantities of oil. Yet, this mechanism is obviously rare and often lethal to the cells. An alternative would be to lower the specific gravity of the cell sap by exclusion of heavy ions, as Gross and Zeuthen (1948) suggested. This would make the cells lighter and may even make them float. In diatoms heavier than the ambient medium, enlargement of the surface area relative to cell volume can decrease the sinking rate. Some frequently observed means to achieve this include large vacuoles, elongated shapes, bristle formation, mucilage excretion, or colony formation.

The diatoms accumulate silica which is the heaviest substance accumulated in large quantity by any algae. It may seem strange that, having accumulated this heavy material, the diatoms still remain afloat in water. But most diatoms thrive in fairly turbulent conditions where the high sinking rate is nullified by the turbulence which periodically brings the sinking cells back to surface layers (Walsby and Reynolds, 1980).

ECOLOGY, PALAEOECOLOGY, AND STRATIGRAPHY

Some diatoms grow endosymbiotically inside the Foraminifera. Others occur in springs, estuaries, sediments, and oceanic phytoplankton.

Some marine diatoms are parasitized by the dinoflagellate *Paulsenella*. The food uptake by a *Paulsenella* sp. parasitic on *Streptotheca thamesis* has been studied by Drebes and Schnepf (1982). When a *Paulsenella* dinospore attacks a host cell, the cytoplasm is sucked up and enclosed in food vacuoles. When the host's chloroplasts pass through the parasite's food tube, they become deformed. Nonetheless, the chloroplasts soon recover their normal shape and structure inside the food vacuole. Even the chloroplast ER is somewhat preserved. During their passage through the parasite's feeding tube, at least several thylakoids of the diatom chloroplast remain intact (Schnepf *et al.*, 1988).

Stephanodiscus niagarae grows in various lakes. Recent observations relate its character variation to lake trophic status (see Mann, 1984). The more eutrophic the water, the finer the areolation.

Chaetoceros spp. occur in various inland arid, saline habitats. *C. muelleri* var. *subsalsum* is a typical mesohalobe.

The diatoms have been employed for ascertaining the marine, brackish, or freshwater origin of clays used for making prehistoric pottery.

Diatom communities have been used as indicators of a variety of environmental conditions in freshwater environments, including nutrient status, alkalinity, and pH, to assess long-term changes in lakes due to shifts in climate and human disturbances such as modifications of watershed and acid precipitation.

Diatoms are useful indicators of ionic composition and salinity in athalassic (nonmarine) saline lakes (Blinn, 1990; Fritz, 1990). Some diatoms isolated from these saline environments produce significant quantities of cellular storage lipids and may be valuable for alternative fuel applications.

Blinn (1993) has examined the relationships between diatom assemblages and physico-chemical factors in many American saline lakes. Sodium was the overwhelmingly dominant cation in the lakes examined; lakes above 47° latitude were dominated by SO_4^{-2}, and lakes below 47° were dominated by CO_3^{-2} and Cl^{-1}. This latitudinal gradient for anions was correlated with the distribution and community structure of diatoms. Sixty-two taxa comprised > 85% of the total diatom relative abundance in the saline environments. There were strong negative correlations between specific conductance and diversity and species richness. Cluster analyses identified diatom assemblages along specific conductance and major anion gradients. Indices for specific conductance and major anions were also developed for 62 diatom taxa. Greatest diversity occurred in habitats with ionic concentrations < sea water and ion composition similar to marine environments (Blinn, 1993). Principal components analyses comparing loadings for major cations and anions, ionic concentration, and diatom community structure suggested that shallow saline lakes may have provided evolutionary pathways for speciation of marine pennate diatoms into athalassic (nonmarine) environments (Blinn, 1993).

REPRODUCTION

There are well documented evidences for the occurrence of vegetative and sexual reproduction in diatoms. Although the production of nonmotile or biflagellate zoospores for some members of the Centrales, e.g., *Biddulphia*, has been claimed, there is still some doubt as to whether the spores are actually formed by the diatoms or whether the spores in question are in fact only chytrids that parasitize the diatoms. If indeed they are spores, their fate is unknown.

Vegetative

The two thecae of the parent cell slightly gape apart before division. The nucleus divides mitotically and karyokinesis is followed by cytokinesis of the protoplast into two uninucleate parts along the valvar plane. Soon, new valves and, later, connecting bands are deposited along the freshly formed protoplasmic surfaces. The parental hypotheca serves as the epitheca of one of the two daughter cells, whereas the parental epitheca remains as the epitheca of the other daughter cell (Fig. 9-13). Accordingly, the newly formed wall pieces always serve as hypotheca. Such a division leads to the production of two daughter cells of unequal size; the cell containing the parental hypotheca as the epitheca is always smaller than its sister cell by about twice the thickness of the connecting band. Thus, the progenies of a diatom become progressively smaller during successive cell divisions.

The vegetative phase of most diatoms is diploid, and meiosis occurs at gametogenesis.

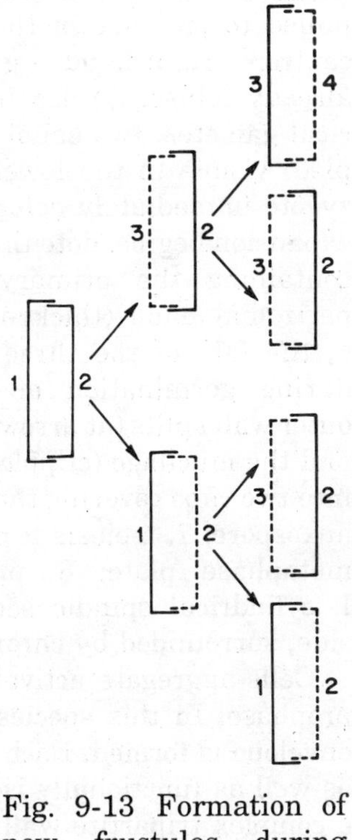

Fig. 9-13 Formation of new frustules during asexual multiplication of pennate diatoms.

Sexual

All sexually-reproducing diatoms are diplonts, but they do show considerable variety in the modes of pairing, gametogenesis, fertilization, and development of the zygote.

Navicula is a bilaterally symmetrical raphid diatom. The sexual reproduction in *N. oblonga* (see Fig. 9-14) has been described by Mann and Stickle (1989). In this figure: 1, 2, cell in interphase: valve view (1) and girdle view (2), note the central nucleus surrounded by dictyosomes (dashes); two plastids, one against each side of the girdle; and the special vacuoles, capped by dense material and containing volutin granules; 3, cell at mitotic anaphase, in girdle view; the ingrowing cleavage furrow is seen in profile; note the absence of volutin granules and the irregular shape of the collapsed special vacuoles; the plastids (stippled) have moved beneath the valves and have divided transversely; 4, paired gametangia; left-hand gametangium at meiosis II, with undivided plastids pulled to one side of the cell at the centre; right-hand gametangium already dehisced, releasing two spherical gametes; two equal nuclei (stippled) visible in the lower gamete; 5, zygote immediately before auxospore expansion begins; note thin inner wall containing the primary transverse perizonial band (thickening of line); 6, the fate of the three wall layers during germination of zygote; the outer wall splits (at arrows) unequally and the mucilage (stippled) separates into two caps covering the poles of the auxospore; 7, meiosis I: polar view of metaphase plate; 8, prometaphase I: cylindrical spindle seen from the side, surrounded by chromosomes.

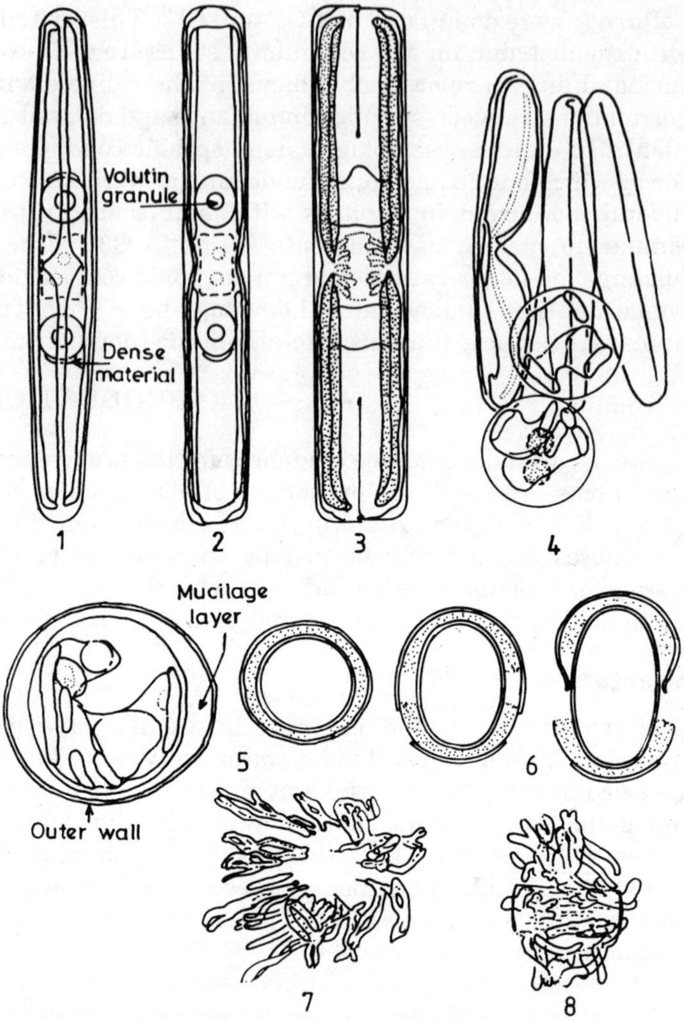

Fig. 9-14 *Navicula oblonga* (after Mann and Stickle, 1989).

Cells aggregate actively and lie side-by-side, contacting each other as they enter meiotic prophase. In this species the gametangia do not subsequently separate, and no copulation envelope is formed. Each gametangium produces two gametes. *N. oblonga* is morphologically as well as functionally isogamous. The newly produced auxospores are spherical and secrete a complex tripartite wall, containing a wide central layer of mucilage. This layer and a thin outer layer separate into two halves as the auxospore expands, remaining as caps over the auxospore ends. A silicified perizonium is formed and covers the rest of the auxospore. After meiosis, all four haploid nuclei survive in each gametangium, so that the gametes are binucleate; only after plasmogamy there is degeneration of the superfluous nuclei, and the two surviving gametic nuclei fuse to form the diploid zygotic nucleus.

During synapsis the chromosomes shrink into a knot that rotates around the interior of the expanded ellipsoidal nucleus. This appears to be the first report of nuclear cyclosis during diatom meiosis (Mann and Stickle, 1989). Similar movements of chromosomes during zygotene and early pachytene are also known to occur in some dinoflagellates (Von Stosch, 1973).

In *Navicula cuspidata* and *N. halophila*, gametangial (mother) cells pair with one another and are covered together by a mucilaginous coat. The pairing cells undergo two meiotic divisions, only one of which is followed by cleavage. Two haploid gametes are thus formed. Upon release from the mother thecae, these fuse with other gametes, forming diploid, spherical zygotes, termed auxospores. The latter secrete a polysaccharidic wall. The auxospores undergo bipolar elongation, breaking the above wall and secreting a special silicified wall, termed the perizonium, which consists of multiple overlapping bands (Cohn *et al.*, 1989). Within the perizonium, two vegetative-type valves are formed one after another, producing an initial cell. The latter breaks open the perizonium and emerges out. The initial cell is much larger than the original gametangial cells. By undergoing normal vegetative divisions, it completes the sexual cycle.

Cohn *et al.* (1989) found that the perizonium of *N. cuspidata* consists of concentric overlapping bands, laid down sequentially at the tips of the expanding biconical auxospore during its elongation. The central perizonial band is more rigid than the distal bands. During auxospore elongation, the chromatophores oscillate between the two ends of the cell; the oscillation stops when the elongation is complete. In contrast to the raphes in gametangial and vegetative valves which are covered by a smooth axial area, the raphes in initial valves lie within a raised ridge that runs along the apical axis of the valve. The distance between striae is significantly longer in initial valves than in gametangial valves. Vegetative interstriae spacing as well as the planar morphology of the valve face tends to be regained at the first division of the initial cell (Cohn *et al.*, 1989).

Another closely related genus is *Gyrosigma*. Table 9-2 compares *Navicula* and *Gyrosigma* in respect of many traits.

Most diatoms are homothallic and sexual reproduction can occur within individuals of the same clone. In the Pennales, an enlarged spore, termed the auxospore, develops from the zygote which results from the union of two amoeboid gametes. In the Centrales, however, the fusion of a flagellated sperm occurs with a nonmotile egg (Fig. 9-15 A–C). Consequently, sexuality in the former is generally isogamous and that in the latter oogamous. Since the zygote enlarges to become an auxospore, the production of auxospores is a compensatory measure for the vegetatively reproducing diatoms in regaining their normal size.

In the Pennales, two cells come to lie very close together with their girdle views facing each other (Fig. 9-16 A–C). A secretion of mucilage then envelops the conjugating pair. The diploid nucleus of the copulating cells undergoes meiosis and produces three or four haploid nuclei of which generally one or two form gametes and the others degenerate. The gametes move out of the parent cells and gametic union takes place in the mucilaginous envelope (Fig. 9-17 A–G). If each cell of the copulating pair gives rise to one gamete, a single zygote results; when two gametes are produced from each partner, then two zygotes are formed. Sometimes, physiological anisogamy occurs; in this case, one gamete is mobile and the other stationary, one zygote being formed within each member of the copulating pair.

Table 9-2 Comparison between *Navicula* and *Gyrosigma* (after Mann, 1989)

	Navicula	*Gyrosigma*
Apical axis	Straight	Sigmoid
Areola structure	Simple	Loculate
Orientation of opening of internal raphe fissure	Lateral	Lateral
Do central internal raphe endings lie in a small lanceolate boss?	Yes	Yes
Shape of central internal raphe endings	Straight	Straight
Presence of ridge on primary internal side of raphe-sternum	Yes	Yes
Number of plastids per cell	2	2
Shape of pyrenoid during interphase	Rod-like	Rod-like
Does pyrenoid lose shape during plastid division?	No	No
Number of pyrenoids per plastid	1	Many
Is pyrenoid penetrated by tubular invaginations?	No	No
Plastid division	Symmetrical	Symmetrical
Is plastid division arrested before completion and remains so throughout interphase?	No	No
Interphase position of nucleus	Central	Central

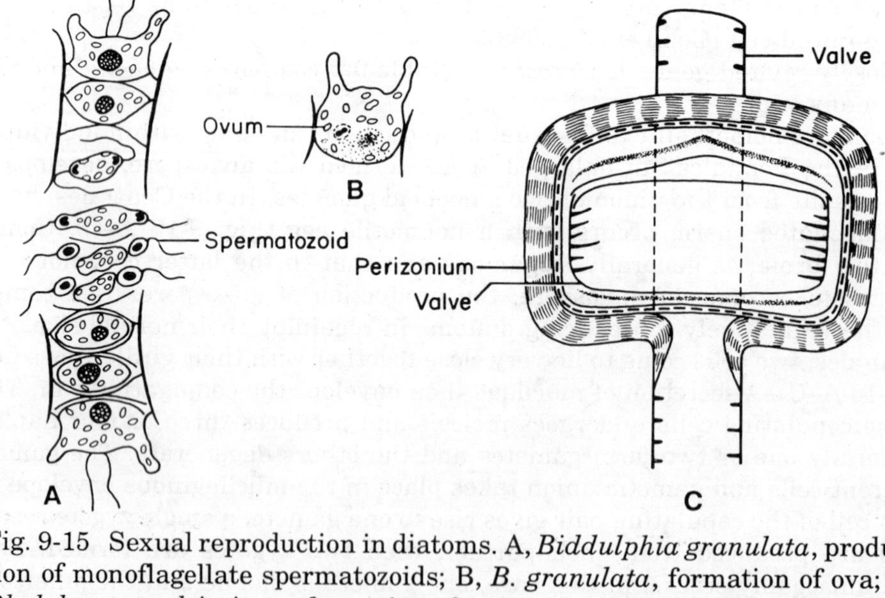

Fig. 9-15 Sexual reproduction in diatoms. A, *Biddulphia granulata*, production of monoflagellate spermatozoids; B, *B. granulata*, formation of ova; C, *Rhabdonema adriaticum*, formation of auxospores. *Courtesy* H. Von Stosch.

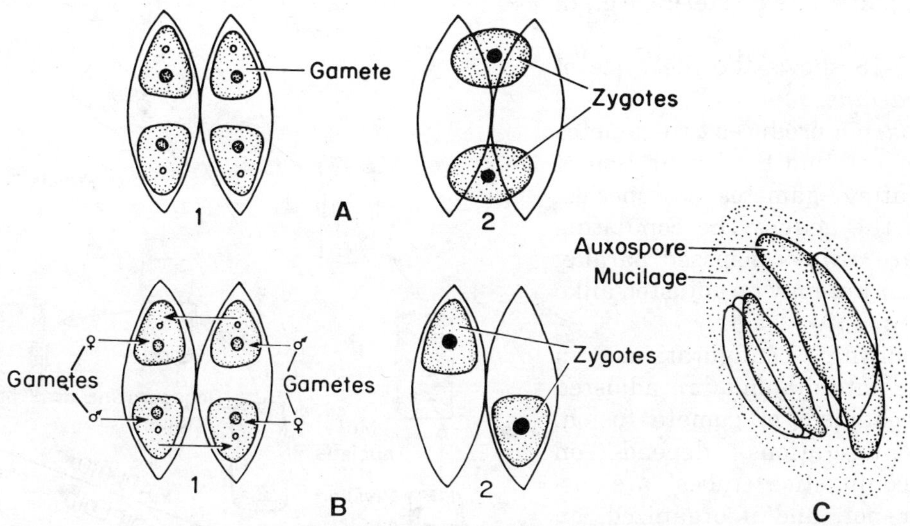

Fig. 9-16 Sexual reproduction in pennate diatoms. A (1, 2), isogamous fusion and zygote formation; B (1, 2), anisogamous fusion, leading to formation of one zygote in each conjugant; C, formation of auxospores embedded in copious mucilage.

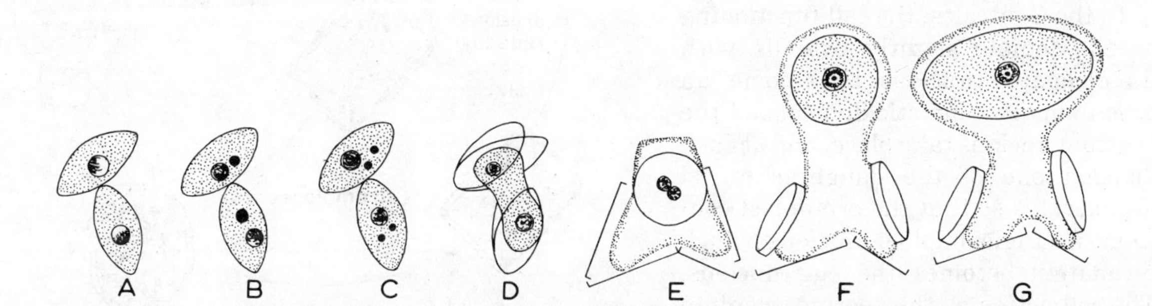

Fig. 9-17 Sexual reproduction in diatoms. A–G, *Cocconeis*, stages in auxospore formation (after Smith, 1955): A–C, meiosis and degeneration of all nuclei except one in each frustule; D, fusion of gametes; E, zygote; F–G, development of auxospore from zygote. H–Q, *Melosira*, auxospore formation in centric diatoms (after Von Stosch, 1951; Smith, 1955): H–L, formation of antherozoids; M–Q, stages in fertilization and formation of auxospore.

In pennate diatoms, the disposition of the hypotheca and epitheca plays a crucial role in gametogenesis. When the thecae are not properly aligned, as much as 50 per cent of the copulating pairs may be sterile, e.g., in *Cocconeis*.

Figure 9-18 shows the life cycle of *Melosira varians*.

Gomphonema produces two gametes per mother cell and the orientation of the copulating gametes is species-specific in the genus. The copulating partners are always disposed parallel to each other but may lie adjusted alike or inversely.

The pairing configurations in various pennate diatoms are adjusted to the mechanism of gamete fusion. These configurations depend on whether conjugation tubes are organized or not, and if organized, on their number (whether 1 or 2). In *Surirella*, the mating cells contact each other only at the poles.

Some gametes of such genera as *Cymbella* and *Amphora*, which fail to copulate, can develop parthenogenetically into haploid auxospores.

In the Centrales, the cell functioning as the female slightly extends with its elongated nucleus to become an oogonium. Two meiotic divisions of the oogonial nucleus take place, and at each division one of the daughter nuclei degenerates so that the protoplast contains a single haploid nucleus which ultimately becomes the egg nucleus. The cell acting as the spermatogonium divides meiotically to produce four uniflagellate spermatozoids. In *Cyclotella tenuistriata*, a vegetative cell functions directly as a spermatogonium but in *Melosira varians* a vegetative cell divides mitotically to produce 4–8 spermatogonia (Fig. 9-17 H–L).

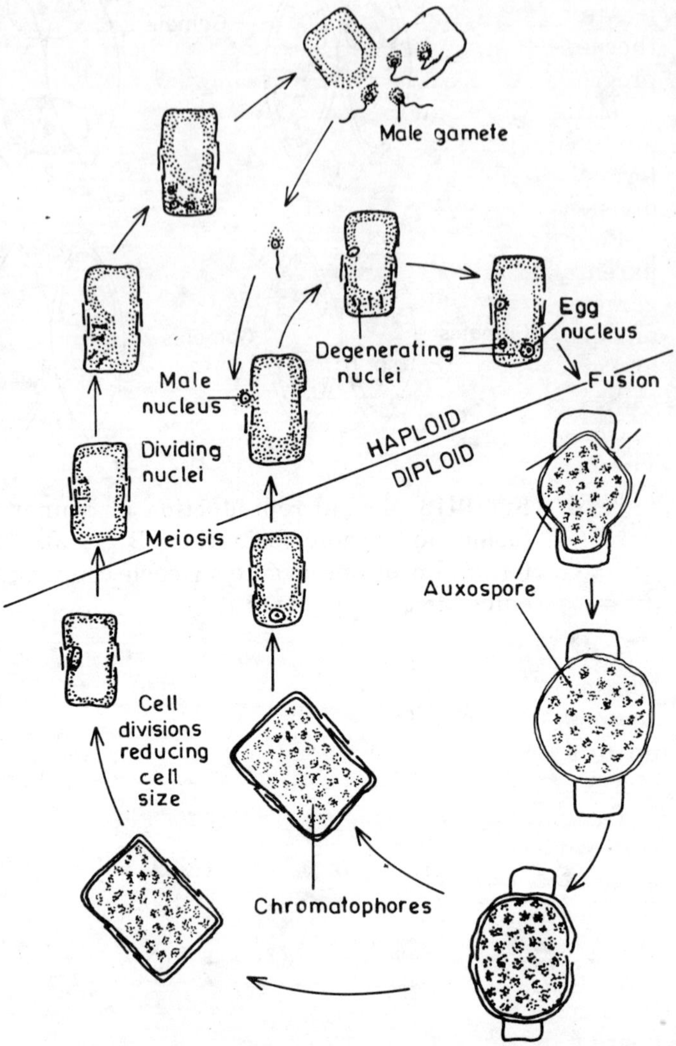

Fig. 9-18 Life cycle of *Melosira varians*.

At the time of fertilization, the spermatozoids congregate around an oogonium and one of them fuses with the egg. The zygote escapes from the female cell, enlarges to a characteristic size, and becomes an auxospore which secretes a new wall and is now a diploid vegetative cell (Fig. 9-17 M–Q).

Schultz and Trainor (1968) have recorded auxospores and uniflagellate and biflagellate spermatozoids in cultures of *Cyclotella meneghiniana* and *C. cryptica* and found that spermatogenesis and auxospore formation are stimulated with increasing concentrations of sodium. Both light and temperature have been reported to regulate sexuality in some diatoms.

After each vegetative cytokinesis, diatoms form new valves entirely within the parental thecae. Each daughter theca is usually slightly smaller than its mother theca. There is a progressive decrease in size over a few generations. The limits of such decrease are overcome by resorting to sexual reproduction during which haploid gametes fuse to produce a diploid auxospore which enlarges until it is quite larger than its mother cells. The mature auxospore forms a primary vegetative-type cell called the initial cell, which undergoes normal vegetative divisions to produce a progeny of larger cells. In this way, sexuality helps regain cell size.

Four different patterns of auxospore formation occur in various diatoms, viz., (1) each parental cell produces one gamete and, hence, one auxospore; (2) each parental cell forms two gametes and, hence, two auxospores; (3) the two haploid nuclei from a single cell fuse to form an auxospore autogamously; and (4) the parent cell nucleus divides without undergoing meiosis and gives rise to auxospores, i.e., the auxospores may develop apogamously or parthenogenetically.

Chaetoceros bears lateral auxospores (Fig. 9-19 A) in the girdle region of the mother cell. The pervalvar axis of the lateral auxospore lies transverse to the mother cell. In contrast, *Thalassiosira* produces intercalary auxospores (Fig. 9-19 B) which remain attached to the valves of the mother cells.

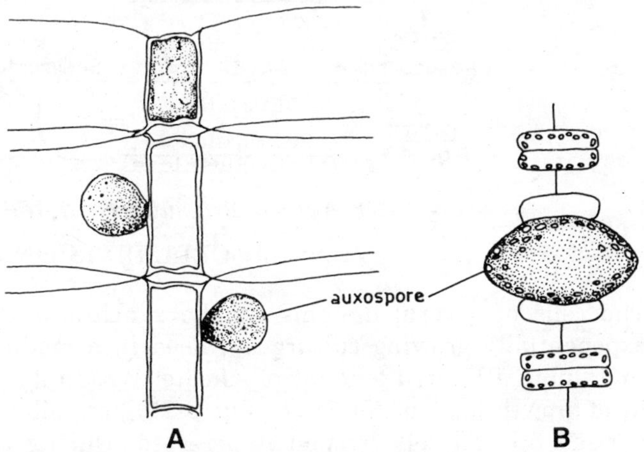

Fig. 9-19 Auxospores. A, lateral auxospores of *Chaetoceros*; B, intercalary auxospore of *Thalassiosira*.

The life cycle of the centric diatom, *Aulacoseira subarctica* in Lough Neagh, Northern Ireland, has been studied by Jewson (1992). Cell numbers can reach up to 17,000 per millilitre in spring. Most cells sediment to the bottom after silica limitation and go into a resting state during summer. The inoculum in autumn partly comes from resuspension, with the surviving cells (up to about 5%) continuing to grow through the winter and doubling every one to two weeks. The population goes through a size reduction and regeneration cycle linked to sexual reproduction. Gametes are only produced in narrower cells, usually after interruptions in growth caused by low light conditions but availability of nutrients, especially silica and nitrogen, is also important. Even the highest densities of auxospores (20 ml^{-1}) represent only a small proportion of the total cells present. Size regeneration results in initial cells with diameters about three times those of the parent. Larger parent cells usually give rise to larger initial cells. Subsequently, cell division leads to a decrease in population diameter, because of the way new valves are laid down below the girdle bands. Reductions are largest in broader cells and gradually decrease as cells get narrower. Occasionally large reductions follow periods of environmental stress. In Lough Neagh, the cells reach a sexually inducible size in 4–6 years. The interaction of certain other environmental factors, when combined with intermittent sexual reproduction at low frequencies, results in a relatively stable population size distribution, where there are always some cells in the size range in which sexual differentiation can be induced (Jewson, 1992). Figure 9-20 illustrates the life cycle.

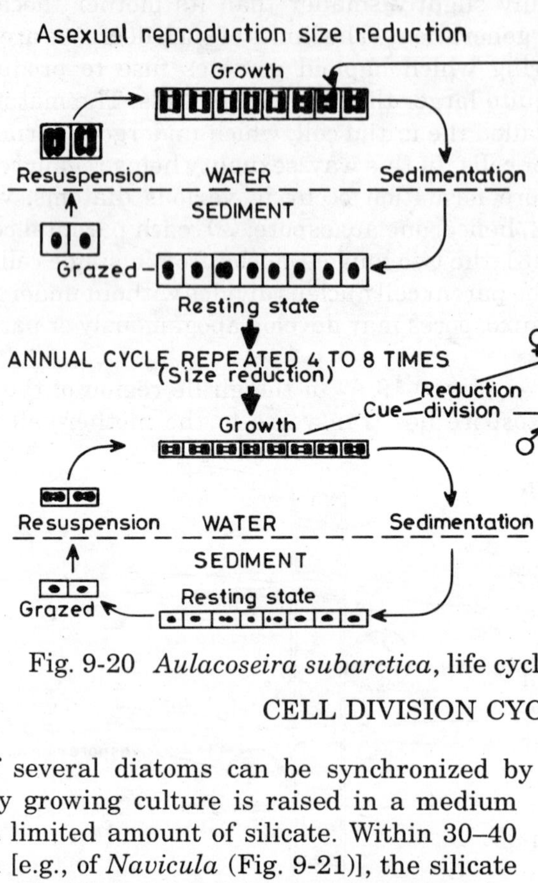

Fig. 9-20 *Aulacoseira subarctica*, life cycle (after Jewson, 1992).

CELL DIVISION CYCLE

The cells of several diatoms can be synchronized by the silica starvation technique. An exponentially growing culture is raised in a medium containing a limited amount of silicate. Within 30–40 hr of growth [e.g., of *Navicula* (Fig. 9-21)], the silicate is used up and cell division is arrested. During the following 12–14 hr period of starvation, the protoplasts and nuclei divide and then the daughter cells begin to form incipient cell walls. At this stage, sodium silicate is supplied to these cells which absorb it rapidly, enabling them to complete the synthesis of the cell wall material. The subsequent 3 hr period includes a synchronous division of over 90 per cent of the cells. Figure 9-21 illustrates the stages in the cell cycle of *Navicula* as studied in synchronous cultures.

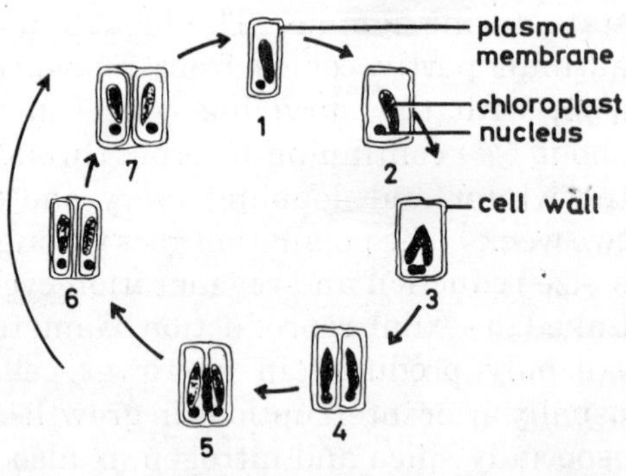

Fig. 9-21 *Navicula pelliculosa*, cell cycle synchronized by silica starvation. 1–5, growth periods in silica-free medium; 6–7, growth periods in silica-supplemented medium.

McDonald-Pfitzer Rule

This rule relates to the occurrence of *gradual* size

reduction in diatoms during vegetative cell division as a result of valve design and morphogenesis (Round, 1972). This phenomenon is the principal factor involved in the generation of a wide range of sizes for a given diatom species. Bellinger (1977) suggested that this phenomenon has ecological implications concerning cell sinking rates and nutrient absorption. Lewis (1984) postulated that the gradual size reduction serves as a chronometer for controlling the timing of sexual reproduction (i.e., a 'sex clock') in diatoms.

Another less well-known phenomenon is the *abrupt* size reduction which occasionally occurs in diatoms in addition to the gradual reduction explained above. Roessler (1988) has described abrupt size reduction in *Synedra ulna*. In this species, conspicuously shorter cells are derived from the normal cells in a single abrupt step. These short cells may be some 50–60% shorter than the mother cells and sometimes may be as short as one-fifth of the mother. Abrupt size reduction may possibly be significant in relation to such ecological processes as sinking rate and size-specific predation.

PERENNATION

Certain benthic centric diatoms form characteristic resting spores singly, in pairs or in groups of fours. These spores develop from the protoplasm of the parent cell by the secretion of a thick siliceous wall and, being heavy, they sink to the bottom and perennate there. The resting spore typically lacks a girdle and has only the two valves. It may be formed endogenously, i.e., completely enclosed within the parent cell, or may be exogenous.

Some biddulphioid diatoms produce resting spores that are morphologically distinct from vegetative cells.

Resting spores should not be confused with auxospores; the latter are never resting or perennating structures.

PHYLOGENY

Because of the siliceous nature of the diatom cell walls, well preserved fossils of the Bacillariophyta are available. The Centrales have been reported from the Jurassic and the Pennales from the early Tertiary. The fossil evidence therefore suggests that the Centrales are more primitive and that the Pennales might have originated from them. The fact that most of the centric diatoms are marine planktonic forms in contrast to the Pennales, which are predominantly freshwater, also indicates a centric ancestry for the Pennales.

The presence of fucoxanthin and chlorophyll-a and chlorophyll-c links the Bacillariophyta with the Phaeophyta, and the characteristic food reserves relate the diatoms to the Xanthophyta and the Chrysophyta.

Sorhannus *et al.* (1995) have made a molecular phylogeny of the diatoms from the nucleotide sequence of two domains of the nuclear-encoded large subunit ribosomal RNA in four centric and four pennate species. Distance and parsimony analyses support the monophyly of the diatoms and their closeness to the chrysophytes. The radially symmetrical Centrales appear to be paraphyletic: the centric *Lithodesmium undulatum* is associated with the pennate lineage. In the bilaterally symmetrical Pennales the araphids are also paraphyletic. These phylogenetic inferences closely agree with those previously obtained from 18S rRNA data (Bhattacharya *et al.*, 1992; Medlin *et al.*, 1993).

Phylogenetic relationships within the diatoms have remained controversial. Their fossil record points to a diversification progressing from centric to pennate forms. The first deposits of the Pennales appear in the Late Cretaceous about 70 My ago after the Centrales (Early Jurassic, around 180 My). Palaeontological data suggest that the raphid diatoms may have been derived from the araphids. Various evolutionary models are now being tested with molecular sequence data. The small and the large subunit of ribosomal RNA are promising sources of information in systematic studies of eucaryotic microorganisms (Sogin *et al.*, 1986) and, in diatoms, phylogenetic schemes based on 18S rRNA data have given new insights into diatom evolution (Bhattacharya *et al.*, 1992; Medlin *et al.*, 1993). These first molecular data suggest that the centric and the araphid pennates may not be monophyletic groups.

REFERENCES

Bellinger, E.G., Seasonal size changes in certain diatoms and their possible significance, *Brit. Phycol. J.*, **12**, 233–39 (1977).

Bhattacharya, D., Medlin, L., Wainright, P.O., Aritzia, E.V., Bibeau, C., Stickel, S.K., and Sogin, M.L., Algae containing chlorophyll a+c are paraphyletic: molecular evolutionary analysis of the Chromophyta, *Evolution*, **46**, 1801–1817 (1992).

Blinn, D.W., The diatom flora of Lake Eyre South: a large episodically filled salt lake in South Australia, *Hydrobiologia*, **210**, 101–104 (1990).

Blinn, D.W., Diatom community structure along physico-chemical gradients in saline lakes, *Ecology*, **74**, 1246–63 (1993).

Chiappino, M.L. and Volcani, B.E., Studies on the biochemistry and fine structure of silica shell formation in diatoms. VII. Sequential cell wall development in the pennate *Navicula pelliculosa*, *Protoplasma*, **93**, 205–21 (1977).

Cohn, S.A., Spurck, T.P., Pickett-Heaps, J.D., and Edgar, L.A., Perizonium and initial valve formation in the diatom *Navicula cuspidata* (Bacillariophyceae), *J. Phycol.*, **25**, 15–26 (1989).

Drebes, G. and Schnepf, E., Phagotrophy and development of *Paulsenella* cf. *Chaetoceratis* (Dinophyta): an ectoparasite of the diatom *Speptotheca thamesis*, *Helgolander Meeresunters.*, **35**, 501–15 (1982).

Duke, E.L. and Reimann, B.E.F., The ultrastructure of the diatom cell. *In* Werner, D. (ed.) The Biology of Diatoms, 65–109, Blackwell, Oxford (1977).

Edgar, L.A., Diatom locomotion: computer assisted analysis of cine film, *Brit. Phycol. J.*, **14**, 83–101 (1979).

Fritz, S.C., Twentieth-century salinity and water-level fluctuations in Devils Lake: test of a diatom-based transfer function, *Limnol. Oceanogr.*, **35**, 1771–81 (1990).

Geitler, L., On some peculiarities in the life history of pennate diatoms hitherto overlooked, *Am. J. Bot.*, **66**, 91–97 (1979).

Gross, F. and Zeuthen, E., The buoyancy of plankton diatoms: a problem of cell physiology, *Proc. Roy. Soc.*, **135B**, 382–89 (1948).

Harper, M.A. and Harper, J.F., Measurements of diatom adhesion and their relationship with movement, *Br. Phycol. Bull.*, **3**, 195–207 (1967).

Hasle, G.R., Two types of valve processes in centric diatoms, *Beihefte Nova Hedwigia*, **39**, 55–78 (1972).

Hendey, N.I., The structure of the diatom cell wall as revealed by the electron microscope, *J. Quekett Microsc. Club*, **5**, 147–75 (1959).

Jaworski, G.H.M., Talling, J.F., and Heaney, S.I., The influence of CO_2 depletion on growth and sinking rate of two planktonic diatoms in culture, *Brit. Phycol. J.*, **16**, 395–410 (1981).

Jewson, D.H., Size reduction, reproductive strategy and the life cycle of a centric diatom, *Phil. Trans. Roy. Soc.* (London), **B336**, 191–213 (1992).

Kociolek, J.P. and Stoermer, E.F., Phylogenetic relationships and classification of monoraphid diatoms based on phenetic and cladistic methodologies, *Phycologia*, **25**, 297–303 (1986).

Lewis, W.M., The diatom sex clock and its evolutionary significance, *Am. Nat.*, **123**, 73–80 (1984).

Mann, D.G., The diatom genus *Sellaphora*: separation from *Navicula, Brit. Phycol. J.*, **24**, 1–20 (1983).

Mann, D.G. (ed.), Proceedings of the VII International Diatom Symposium, Otto Koeltz, Koenigstein (1984).

Mann, D.G. and Stickle, A.J., Meiosis, nuclear cyclosis, and auxospore formation in *Navicula sensu stricto* (Bacillariophyta), *Brit. Phycol. J.*, **24**, 167–81 (1989).

Medlin, L.K., Crawford, R.M., and Andersen, R.A., Histochemical and ultrastructural evidence for the function of the labiate process in the movement of centric diatoms, *Brit. Phycol. J.*, **21**, 297–301 (1986).

Medlin, L.K., Williams, D.M., and Sims, P.A., The evolution of the diatoms (Bacillariophyta). I. Origin of the group and assessment of the monophyly of its major division, *Europ. J. Phycol.*, **28**, 261–75 (1993).

Pickett-Heaps, J.D., Morphogenesis of the labiate process in the araphid pennate diatom *Diatoma vulgare, J. Phycol.*, **25**, 79–85 (1989).

Pickett-Heaps, J.D. and Tippit, D.H., Light and electron microscopic observations on cell division in two large pennate diatoms, *Hantzschia* and *Nitzschia, Europ. J. Cell Biol.*, **21**, 1–11 (1980).

Pickett-Heaps, J.D., Hill, D.R.A., and Wetherbee, R., Cellular movement in the centric diatom *Odontella sinensis, J. Phycol.*, **22**, 234–39 (1986).

Pickett-Heaps, J.D., Hill, D.R.A., and Blaze, K.L., Active gliding motility in an araphid marine diatom, *Ardissonea* (formerly *Synedra*) *crystallina, J. Phycol.*, **27**, 718–25 (1991).

Reimann, B.E.F., Lewin, J.C., and Benjamin, V.E., Studies on the biochemistry and fine structure of silica shell formation in diatoms. II. The structure of the cell wall of *Navicula pelliculosa* (Breb.) Hilse, *J. Phycol.*, **2**, 74–84 (1966).

Roessler, P.G., Characteristics of abrupt size reduction in *Synedra ulna* (Bacillariophyceae), *Phycologia*, **27**, 294–97 (1988).

Round, F.E., The problem of reduction of cell size during diatom cell division, *Nova Hedwigia*, **23**, 291–303 (1972).

Schnepf, E., Meier, R., and Drebes, G., Stability and deformation of diatom chloroplast during food uptake of the parasitic dinoflagellate, *Paulsenella* (Dinophyta), *Phycologia*, **27**, 283–90 (1988).

Schultz, M.E. and Trainor, F.R., Production of male gametes and auxospores in the centric diatoms *Cyclotella meneghiniana* and *C. cryptica, J. Phycol.*, **4**, 85–88 (1968).

Smith, G.M., Cryptogamic Botany, Vol. I, Algae and Fungi, 2nd edn., McGraw-Hill, New York (1955).

Sogin, M.L., Elwood, H.J., and Gunderson, J.H., Evolutionary diversity of eukaryotic small subunit rRNA genes, *Proc. Natl. Acad. Sci.* (USA), **83**, 1383–87 (1986).

Sorhannus, U., Gasse, F., Perasso, R., and Tourancheau, A.B., A preliminary phylogeny of diatoms based on 28S ribosomal RNA sequence data, *Phycologia*, **34**, 65–73 (1995).

Von Stosch, H.A., Entwicklungs geschichtliche Untersuchungen an Zentrischen Diatomeen. I. Die Auxosporenbildung von *Melosira varians*, *Arch. Microbiol.*, **16**, 101–135 (1951).

Von Stosch, H.A., Observations on vegetative reproduction and sexual life cycles of two freshwater dinoflagellates, *Gymnodinium pseudopalustre* Schiller and *Woloszynskia apiculata* sp. nov., *Brit. Phycol. J.*, **8**, 105–34 (1973).

Walsby, A.E. and Reynolds, C.S., Sinking and floating. *In* Morris, I. (ed.) The Physiological Ecology of Phytoplankton, 371–412, Blackwell, Oxford (1980).

Wiseman, S.W. and Reynolds, C.S., Sinking rate and electrophoretic mobility of the freshwater diatom *Asterionella formosa, Brit. Phycol. J.*, **16**, 357–61 (1981).

10 Xanthophyta and Chlorarachniophyta

CLASS: TRIBOPHYCEAE

GENERAL CHARACTERS

The phylum Xanthophyta includes two classes, viz., Tribophyceae and Eustigmatophyceae. The latter class has been carved out of the former on the basis of some differences in the fine structure of the cell.

Commonly known as the yellow-green algae, the Tribophyceae (Xanthophyceae) are characterized by the following general features:

(1) the photosynthetic pigments consist of chlorophyll-a and -e, β-carotene, and xanthophylls; of these, β-carotene is usually present in fairly high concentrations;

(2) the food reserves are oil, lipid, and a glucose polymer termed leucosin or chrysolaminarin;

(3) the cell walls when present are generally composed of two equal or overlapping halves, e.g., *Tribonema* (Fig. 10-1), and are composed mainly of pectic substances with smaller amounts of cellulose; in some members, the cell walls may be silicified; and

(4) the flagellated cells possess two anteriorly inserted flagella of unequal length, the longer being pantonematic and the shorter acronematic.

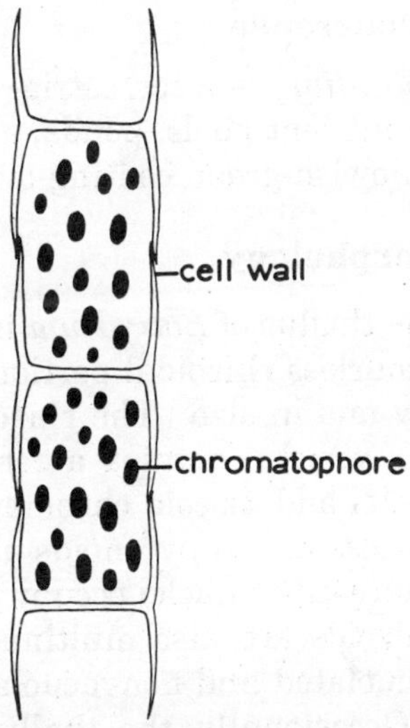

Fig. 10-1 *Tribonema*, part of filament showing cell wall made of overlapping H-pieces, and discoid chloroplasts.

The Tribophyceae are widely distributed in aquatic, terrestrial, and subaerial habitats but the maximum representation is in freshwater habitats.

The Tribophyceae exhibit well marked parallelism with the Chlorophyceae in thallus structure. Thus, both these classes include motile, palmelloid, dendroid, filamentous, and siphoneous forms. However, the yellow-green algae in general do not reach the level of evolutionary development attained in the green algae. Thus, the advanced, elaborate pseudoparenchymatous and parenchymatous habits met with in the Chlorophyta are not evident in the Xanthophyta.

The usual methods of propagation and reproduction are vegetative, asexual, and sexual. Sexuality is rather rare and has been established in only three genera. In *Tribonema*, fusion takes place between two biflagellated zoogametes one of which discards its flagella and becomes nonmotile during or shortly before fusion, thus indicating a sort of oogamy. In *Botrydium*, both isogamous and anisogamous forms of sexuality are known. *Vaucheria* is oogamous.

The formation of flagellated structures during the life cycle of most of the Xanthophyceae, together with the occurrence of predominantly flagellated unicells in primitive members of the class, suggests a flagellated ancestry for the Xanthophyceae.

The Xanthophyceae resemble the Chrysophyceae in their flagellation, amoeboid habit, and food reserves, and the Bacillariophyceae in food reserves and cell wall composition. The class is unique in having a preponderance of pectic substances in the cell wall and the presence of chlorophyll-e in some members. Bold (1967) considered the Xanthophyceae, Chrysophyceae, and Bacillariophyceae to be closely related and accordingly included them in a single phylum, the Chrysophycophyta.

SELECTED GENERA

Order: HETEROSIPHONALES
Family: Botrydiaceae
Genus: *Botrydium*

The most primitive genus of siphoneous Xanthophyceae, *Botrydium* strongly resembles the green alga *Protosiphon* in its habit and habitat. *B. granulatum* and *B. tuberosum* are common in India.

Occurrence

Botrydium is a terrestrial alga found in muddy or damp soils near the banks of temporary or permanent pools, ponds, and streams. It grows as pinhead vesicles which often form a thick, yellowish-green coating over the soil surface.

Morphology

The thallus of *Botrydium* is unicellular, coenocytic, and consists of a lower profusely branched, colourless rhizoidal portion and an upper, globose or cylindrical vesicle which may measure a few mm in size. The rhizoids are subterranean and serve the function of thallus anchorage. The vesicle contains a central vacuole and a peripheral protoplasm with numerous minute nuclei and discoid chromatophores (Fig. 10-2). The chromatophores possess naked pyrenoids and lie next to the cytoplasmic membrane, whereas the nuclei occupy a position internal to the chromatophores. Rhizoids are also multinucleate with nuclei lying scattered in the vacuolated and nonvacuolated cytoplasm.

Occasionally, the thalli become heavily encrusted with calcium carbonate. The cell wall is composed chiefly of cellulose. The photosynthetic food reserves are normally oil and leucosin.

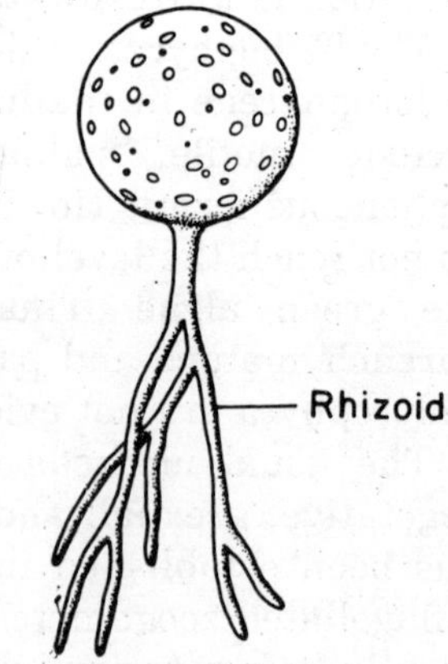

Fig. 10-2 *Botrydium granulatum*, habit.

Reproduction

Vegetative This reproduction is rare and may be brought about by the budding of mature vesicles.

Asexual Reproduction takes place by means of biflagellate zoospores or by the formation of aplanospores or hypnospores. High humidity and free water both stimulate zoospore formation. The vesicular coenocytic protoplast fragments into uninucleate parts, each developing into a pyriform biflagellate zoospore. The flagella are anteriorly inserted, the longer being pantonematic and shorter acronematic.

Generally, the zoospores differentiate directly into vegetative thalli. Sometimes, their behaviour is facultative and they may also act as gametes. Under certain conditions, uninucleate or multinucleate aplanospores are formed instead of zoospores. During adverse environmental conditions, aplanospores transform into uninucleate or multinucleate hypnospores. Both uninucleate and multinucleate aplanospores germinate directly into new thalli. On the other hand, the uninucleate hypnospores behave like aplanospores in respect of germination but the multinucleate hypnospores produce uninucleate aplanospores or zoospores which then give rise to new thalli.

Sexual Biflagellate zoogametes, morphologically identical with zoospores, are formed in the same way as the zoospores. The fusing gametes may be similar or dissimilar and accordingly the sexuality is either isogamous or anisogamous. The zygote is believed to germinate meiotically. Normally, four haploid biflagellate zoospores are produced from a germinating zygote and each of these gives rise to a new *Botrydium* plant. The life cycle involves a haploid multicellular vegetative phase and a diploid unicellular zygote.

Family: Vaucheriaceae
Genus: *Vaucheria*

Vaucheria represents the climax of siphoneous habit among the Xanthophyta. Asexual reproduction in this alga occurs through the formation of synzoospores (compound zoospores), whereas sexual reproduction is of a specialized oogamous type. These reproductive features, together with the branched, filamentous, siphoneous thallus, form the basis of its placement as a separate monogeneric family, the Vaucheriaceae. Previously, *Vaucheria* was included in the order Siphonales of Chlorophyta but the revelation of certain features, such as the absence of chlorophyll-b, presence of chlorophyll-e, excess of carotenoids over the chlorophylls, storage of food reserves in the form of oil, and unequal length of the paired flagella of the compound zoospores, led to its transference from the green algae to the Xanthophyceae.

Occurrence

Species of *Vaucheria* occur widely in stagnant and flowing freshwaters, in shaded terrestrial habitats, in damp soil, and on walls. The alga may occasionally exhibit a thick, deep green felt-like growth on moist soils. Some species are marine. Many species are amphibious on damp mud.

Morphology

The thallus of *Vaucheria* is generally a sparingly branched, cylindrical tube lacking cross walls or septa (Fig. 10-3), except during reproduction. In terrestrial species, anchorage to the substratum is brought about by rhizoid-like branches. The thallus contains an outer cellulosic cell wall, a central vacuole which runs continuously from one end of the thallus to the other (Fig. 10-4), and a continuous layer of protoplast with the peripheral region containing many discoid chromatophores devoid of pyrenoids. Numerous minute nuclei lie internal to the chromatophores (Fig. 10-5) which exhibit phototactic response, i.e., back and forth movement

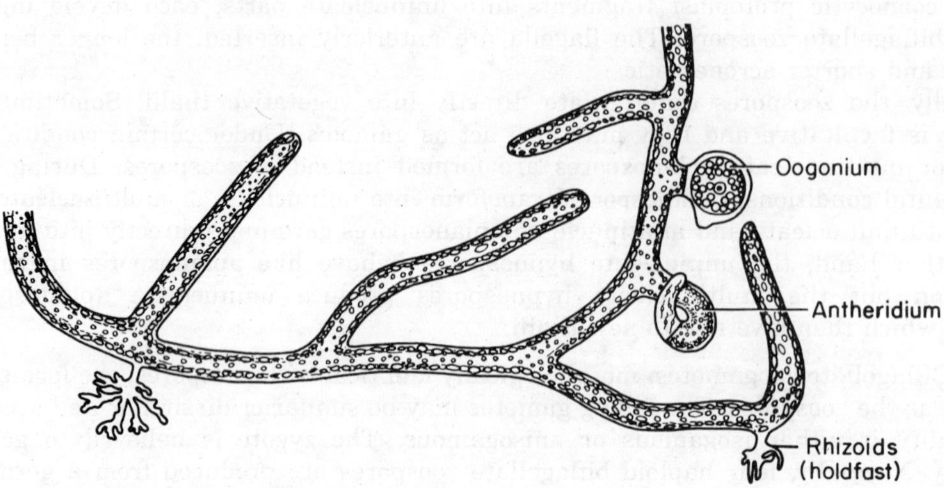

Fig. 10-3 *Vaucheria*, thallus structure, oogonium, and antheridium.

in response to weak, unilateral illumination. When the light intensity is strong, they show a lateral movement away from the light source (see Haupt, 1962). In other words, the phototactic response is regulated in such a way as to permit maximum absorption of photosynthetic light by chromatophores, simultaneously protecting them against excessive photodamage.

The thallus grows in length by a simple elongation of the terminal portions of the branches.

Ott and Brown (1972) have shown that during mitosis the nuclear envelope remains intact and surrounds the spindle; there are no gaps in the nuclear envelope of *Vaucheria*. Both *Vaucheria* and certain phycomycetous fungi, e.g., *Saprolegnia* and *Catenaria*, have a closed, centric spindle lacking polar fenestrae, with the centriole situated outside the nuclear envelope at the poles. Furthermore, in both *Vaucheria* and *Saprolegnia,* each Golgi body is characteristically appressed to a mitochondrion with a part of endoplasmic reticulum being sandwiched between the two organelles (Ott and Brown, 1974).

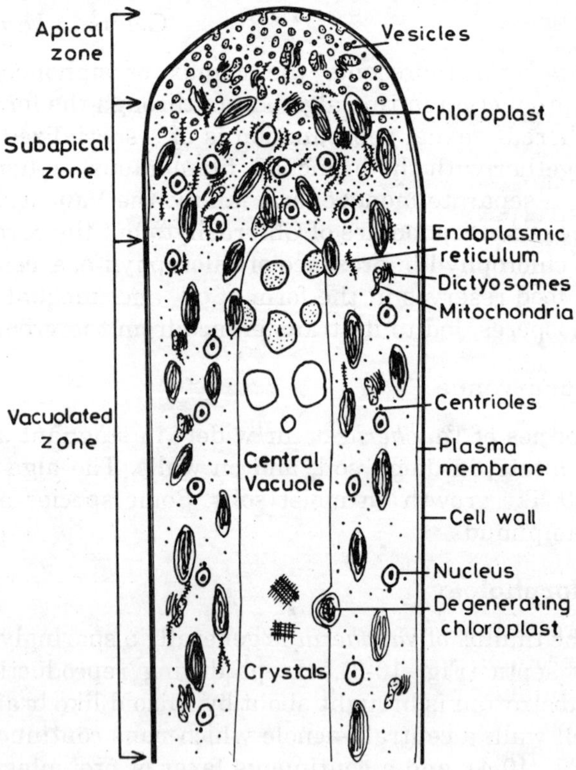

Fig. 10-4 *Vaucheria dillwynii*. Sketch of part of filament end. (After Ott and Brown, 1974.)

Reproduction

Asexual A variety of environmental factors affect zoospore formation (see Erben, 1962). High humidity, transfer from running to still water, low light intensity or darkness, and dilution of the growth medium which causes a reduction in the concentration of nutrients hasten or induce sporulation. Light-controlled, diurnal periodicity in the induction of sporulation has also been reported in *V. sessilis*. It has further been observed that low light intensity enhances sporulation.

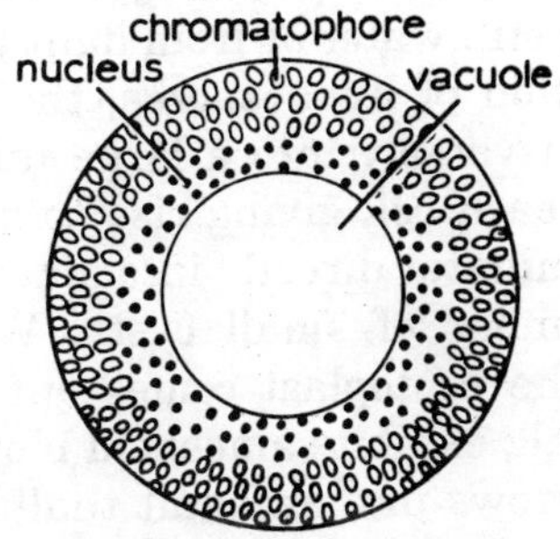

Fig. 10-5 *Vaucheria*, transverse section of vegetative filament showing relative position of chloroplasts and nuclei.

At the time of zoospore formation, apices of branches become delimited from the rest of the thallus by a septum and each of them develops into a club-shaped sporangium (Fig. 10-6 A). Subsequently, the nuclei and chromatophores exchange their position so that the nuclei which were originally placed internal to the chromatophores now come to lie external to the chromatophores (Fig. 10-6 B). The sporangial protoplast then shrinks slightly and a pair of flagella of somewhat unequal length develops opposite each nucleus (Fig. 10-6 C). Both the flagella seem to be acronematic. The zoospores are formed singly within the sporangia. At the time of liberation of the zoospore, an apical pore is formed by gelatinization of the sporangial wall and the zoospore gently glides out through this opening (Fig. 10-6 C). The naked zoospores move freely for some time, settle down on a suitable substratum, discard their flagella, and secrete a new wall. The germinating zoospore forms one to several germ tubes which develop into the *Vaucheria* plant. The substances responsible for the differentiation of polarity, which leads to the appearance of the germ tube, are believed to reside in the peripheral cytoplasm of the germinating zoospore.

The multiflagellate zoospore of *Vaucheria* is regarded as a compound zoospore or synzoospore (Fig. 10-6 B) resulting from failure of the sporangial protoplast to segment into biflagellate uninucleate zoospores, as is the case in many zoosporic Xanthophyceae.

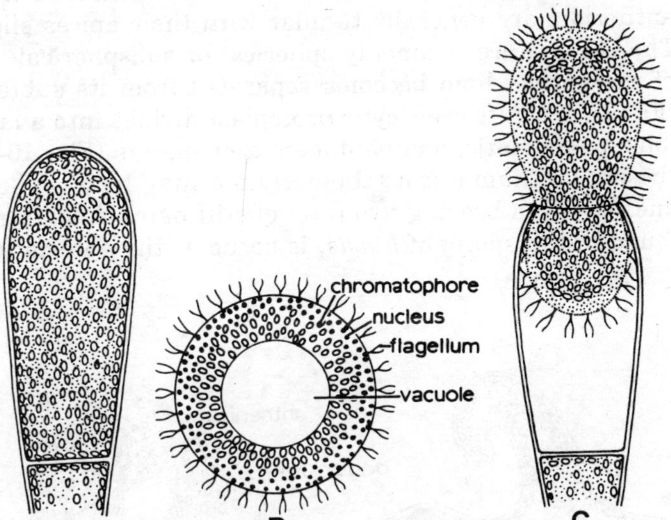

Fig. 10-6 *Vaucheria*. A, club-shaped zoosporangium; B, transection of compound zoospore or synzoospore showing relative position of chloroplasts and nuclei; C, liberation of synzoospore. (Figs. A, C after Smith, 1955.)

The terrestrial species commonly reproduce by the formation of nonmotile aplanospores or hypnospores.

The aplanospores are formed singly in club-shaped aplanosporangia (Fig. 10-7 A) and are liberated through apical pores (Fig. 10-7 B). Occasionally, the aplanospore formation may even be induced in aquatic species by their transference from running to still water or from light to darkness. During the formation of hypnospores, the entire thallus segments transversely into a large number of coenocytic cells with each cell giving rise to a hypnospore which either germinates directly into a new thallus or divides into a number of small cysts. When the cyst germinates, the protoplast comes out through a pore in the cyst wall, exhibits amoeboid movement for a while, and then grows into an adult thallus.

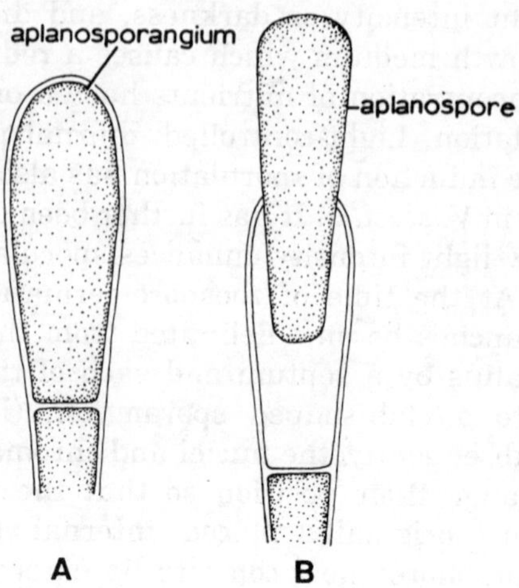

Fig. 10-7 *Vaucheria piloboloides*. A, club-shaped aplanosporangium; B, liberation of aplanospore.

Sexual Sexually reproducing species of *Vaucheria* are either homothallic or heterothallic and bear well differentiated antheridia and oogonia. Sex organs may be sessile or stalked. In *V. geminata*, a homothallic species, sex organs are borne on special reproductive branches, producing a central curved antheridium surrounded by a peripheral group of 3–4 oogonia. Both antheridia and oogonia originate as protuberances (Fig. 10-8) which gradually grow in size and accumulate a large number of nuclei and chromatophores. The antheridia are generally tubular with their apices slightly curved or coiled (Fig. 10-8 A, B). The oogonia are commonly spherical or subspherical. At maturity, the apical, curved portion of the antheridium becomes separated from its subtending branch by a transverse septum (Fig. 10-8 C). Its coenocytic protoplast divides into a large number of uninucleate, biflagellate (one acronematic, one pantonematic) sperms (Fig. 10-8 C) which are usually liberated from the antheridium during the early morning hours. The sperms are laterally biflagellate with one flagellum bearing two rows of stiff hairs. A tongue-like emergent process, similar to that found in the sperm of *Fucus*, is borne at the anterior end of the sperm.

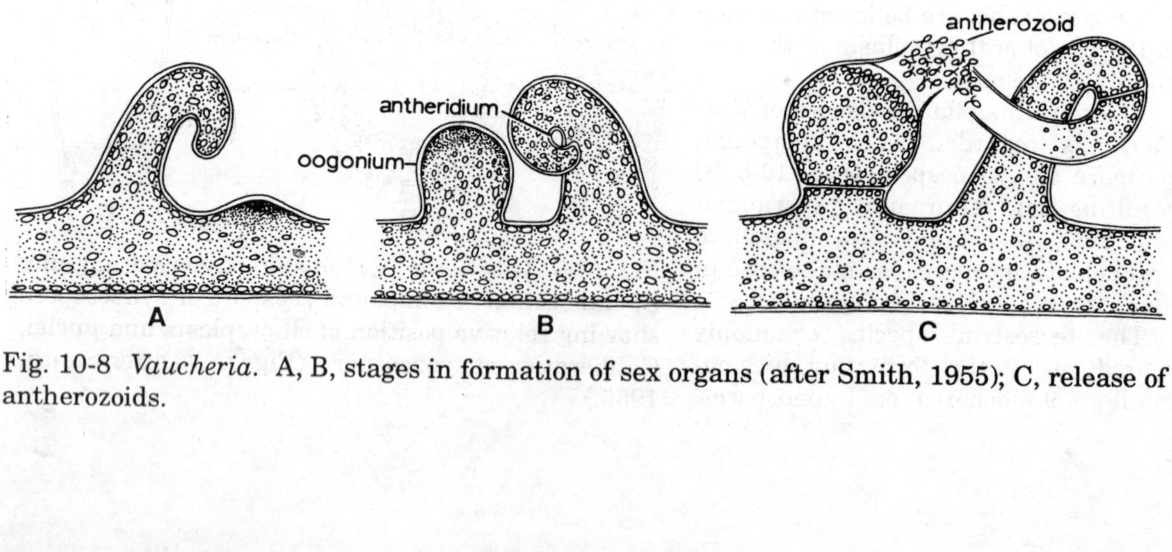

Fig. 10-8 *Vaucheria*. A, B, stages in formation of sex organs (after Smith, 1955); C, release of antherozoids.

As an oogonium matures, all the nuclei except one migrate from the oogonium back to the main filament. Soon a transverse septum is laid down between the oogonium and the filament or the branch bearing it. Subsequently, it develops a receptive region with an opening through which a sperm enters the oogonium.

Homothallic species produce both kinds of sex organs in close proximity but generally do not mature simultaneously; thus, self-fertilization is prevented. The zygotes are thick-walled structures, rich in oil, and are commonly detached from the parent plant along with the oogonial walls. Occasionally, the zygote is liberated from the oogonial wall while the latter is still attached to the parent plant. It is believed that zygotic germination in *Vaucheria* is meiotic and directly gives rise to a new thallus. The life cycle of *Vaucheria* seems to resemble that of *Botrydium*.

CLASS: EUSTIGMATOPHYCEAE

GENERAL CHARACTERS

On the basis of their electron microscopic studies, Hibberd and Leedale (1970) proposed that some unicellular, coccoid algae, previously classified in the Xanthophyceae, should be transferred to a new class, named Eustigmatophyceae, because of the unusual and unique organization of their motile cells. This new class has been created almost entirely on the basis of ultrastructural aspects. It is characterized collectively by the following diagnostic features:

(1) The motile cells have at their anterior end a large, prominent eyespot which lies outside the chloroplast and acts as a shade and reflector.

(2) Most commonly, the zoospores have only one emergent flagellum inserted subapically, but a second basal body is present. The flagellum bears two rows of stiff hairs. The flagellum has a swelling at its proximal end; this swelling contains some paracrystalline material. A button-shaped extension of the flagellum abuts an aggregation of pigment droplets of the eyespot. This extension looks T-shaped in cross-section (Figs. 10-9, 10-10). It abuts the eyespot, and is irregular in shape.

(3) The chloroplast is generally single and elongate (Fig. 10-11). It has three-thylakoid lamellae but lacks girdle lamella. The chloroplast is bounded by the endoplasmic reticulum which, however, is not directly associated with the nuclear wall.

(4) The Golgi bodies occur in vegetative cells but not in the motile cells.

(5) The vegetative cells have a unique type of polygonal pyrenoid which projects from the inner face of the lobed chloroplast on a short stalk. No thylakoids enter the matrix of the pyrenoid. The motile cells or zoospores lack pyrenoids.

(6) The pigments include chlorophyll-a, β-carotene, violaxanthin, and vaucheriaxanthin ester. The food reserves appear as refractile plates surrounding the pyrenoid in vegetative cells, and as rod-like structures lying free in the cytoplasm of zoospores as well as vegetative cells.

Reproduction occurs by means of zoospores or by the formation of up to 4 autospores per cell. Sexuality is not known (Hibberd, 1980).

Some typical examples of the eustigmatophycean algae include *Ellipsoidion*, *Polyedriella*, and *Vischeria*. In contrast, the true Xanthophyceae are exemplified by such algae as *Mischococcus*, *Ophiocytium*, *Tribonema*, *Botrydium*, and *Bumilleria*. The true Xanthophyceae differ from the new class Eustigmatophyceae in the following ways:

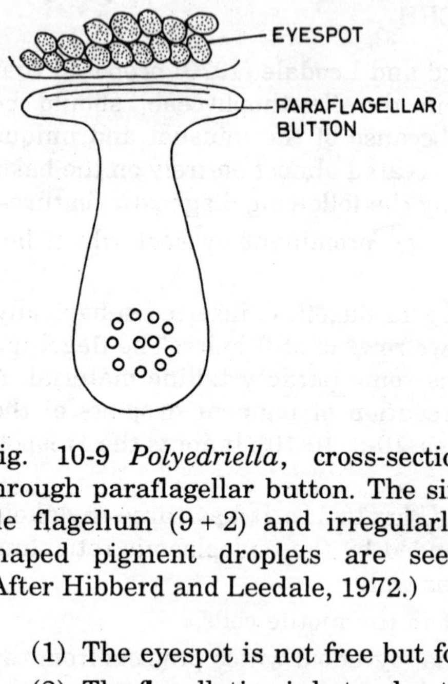

Fig. 10-9 *Polyedriella*, cross-section through paraflagellar button. The single flagellum (9 + 2) and irregularly-shaped pigment droplets are seen. (After Hibberd and Leedale, 1972.)

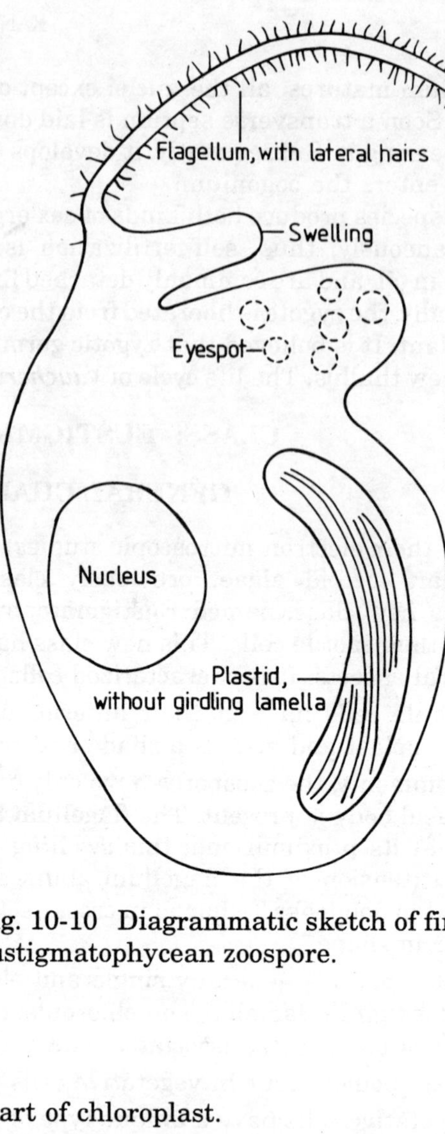

Fig. 10-10 Diagrammatic sketch of fine structure of eustigmatophycean zoospore.

(1) The eyespot is not free but forms part of chloroplast.

(2) The flagellation is heterokont with one anterior hairy flagellum and a posterior smooth swollen flagellum.

(3) The chloroplasts are two or more in number and a girdle lamella is present. The sheath of chloroplast ER is continuous with the nuclear envelope.

(4) Both motile and vegetative cells have Golgi bodies.

(5) The pyrenoids are rare but when present occur both in vegetative cells and motile stages. The thylakoid lamellae from the chloroplast enter the pyrenoid matrix.

(6) The major xanthophyll pigment is antheraxanthin.

CHLORARACHNIOPHYTA

Members belonging to this division were earlier classified in the Xanthophyceae. The new

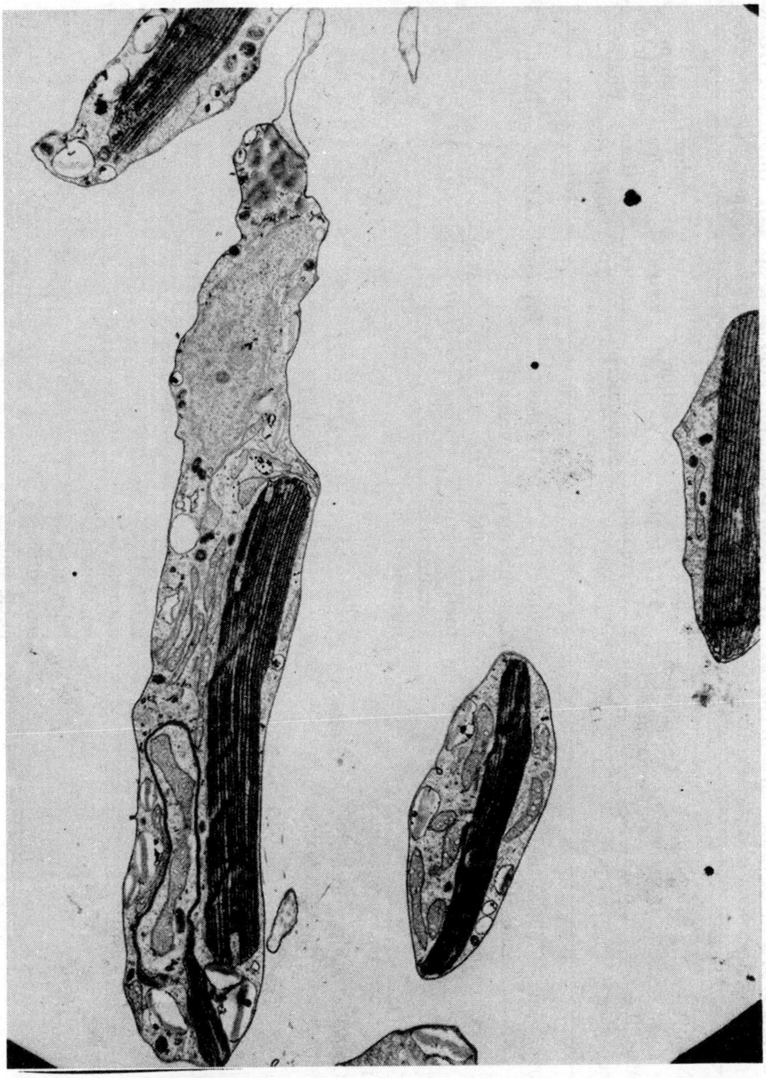

Fig. 10-11 *Eustigmatos*, cell showing elongate chloroplast. (×7500.) *Courtesy* D.J. Hibberd.

division was separated from the Xanthophyceae on the basis of cytological features of the amoeboid cells and zoospores, by Hibberd and Norris (1984) following their work on the type species *Chlorarachnion reptans*. The division has the following general characters. Cells are typically amoeboid with radially extending filopodia, and they form reticulate colonies. Each cell has several chloroplasts containing chlorophyll-a and -b. Each chloroplast is covered by two pairs of membranes and has a conspicuous projecting pyrenoid and a periplastidial compartment containing cytoplasm, ribosomes, and a nucleomorph. Zoospores are uniflagellate, the flagellum coiling posteriorly around the cell body during swimming. Grell (1990) showed that *C. reptans* reproduces sexually involving fusion between coccoid female and amoeboid male gametes.

Table 10-1 Comparison of *Chlorarachnion reptans*, *Cryptochlora perforans*, and *Chlorarachnion globosum* sp. nov. (modified from Ishida and Hara, 1994)

Species	Amoeboid cell	Vegetative coccoid cell	Next cell stage after the zoospore	Swimming manner of the zoospore	Periplastidial compartment (PC)	Extension of PC into the pyrenoid matrix	Location of the nucleomorph	Extru-somes	Periphera vesicles of the zoospore	Mito-chondrial cristae
Chlorarachnion reptans	Present	Absent	Amoeboid	Flagellum coiling helically around the cell body	Present	Wide Does not divide the pyrenoid matrix Contains the nucleomorph	In the pyrenoid	Present	Absent	Tubular
Cryptochlora perforans	Present	Present	Coccoid	Flagellum coiling helically around the cell body	Present	?	?	?	?	?
Chlorarachnion globosum	Absent	Present	Coccoid	Flagellum coiling helically around the cell body	Present	Thin Divides the pyrenoid matrix completely Does not contain the nucleomorph	Beside the pyrenoid base	Absent	Present	Tubular

All three species are uniflagellate. They contain both chlorophyll-a and -b, and lack eyespot. None has starch as the storage product. In all species, 4 membranes surround the chloroplast. Nucleomorph is present in all three taxa.

Chlorarachnion globosum is mostly coccoid with a distinct wall. Amoeboid cells are absent. A thin extension of the periplastidial compartment bisects the pyrenoid matrix into two longitudinal halves and the nucleomorph is located at the base of the pyrenoid (Ishida and Hara, 1994).

Another member, *Cryptochlora perforans* has walled coccoid cells with large vacuoles and mainly solitary amoeboid cells. Table 10-1 compares the above three taxa of chlorarachniophytes.

Chlorarachniophytes represent an interesting new combination of symbiosis between a eucaryotic host and a eucaryotic photosynthetic symbiont (McFadden, 1990; Ishida and Hara, 1994). The presence of chlorophyll-b shows some affinity with the green algae and euglenoids. Like the cryptomonads, chlorarachniophytes appear to be evolutionary chimaerics.

REFERENCES

Bold, H.C., Morphology of Plants, 2nd edn., Harper and Row, New York (1967).

Erben, K., Sporulation. *In* Lewin, R.A. (ed.) Physiology and Biochemistry of the Algae, 701–707, Academic Press, New York (1962).

Grell, K.G., Some light microscope observations on *Chlorarachnion reptans* Geitler, *Archiv für Protistenkunde,* **138**, 271–90 (1990).

Haupt, W., Intracellular movements. *In* Lewin, R.A. (ed.) Physiology and Biochemistry of the Algae, 567–71, Academic Press, New York (1962).

Hibberd, D.J., Eustigmatophytes. *In* Cox, E.R. (ed.) Phytoflagellates, 319–34, Elsevier, New York (1980).

Hibberd, D.J. and Leedale, G.F., Eustigmatophyceae: a new algal class with unique organisation of the motile cell, *Nature*, **225**, 758–60 (1970).

Hibberd, D.J. and Leedale, G.F., Observations on the cytology and ultrastructure of the new algal class Eustigmatophyceae, *Ann. Bot.*, **36**, 49–71 (1972).

Hibberd, D.J. and Norris, R.E., Cytology and ultrastructure of *Chlorarachnion reptans* (Chlorarachniophyta divisio nova, Chlorarachniophyceae classis nova), *J. Phycol.*, **20**, 310–30 (1984).

Ishida, K.I. and Hara, Y., Taxonomic studies on the Chlorarachniophyta: I. *Chlorarachnion globosum* sp. nov., *Phycologia*, **33**, 351–58 (1994).

McFadden, G.I., Evolution of algal plastids from eukaryotic endosymbionts. *In* Harris, N. and Williams, D.G. (eds.) *In situ* Hybridization: Application to developmental biology and medicine, 143–56, Cambridge University Press, Cambridge (1990).

Ott, D.W. and Brown, R.M. (Jr.), Light and electron microscopical observations on mitosis in *Vaucheria litorea* Hofmann ex C. Agardh, *Brit. Phycol. J.*, **7**, 361–74 (1972).

Ott, D.W. and Brown, R.M. (Jr.), Developmental cytology of the genus *Vaucheria*. I. Organization of the vegetative filament, *Brit. Phycol. J.*, **9**, 111–26 (1974).

Smith, G.M., Cryptogamic Botany, Vol. I, Algae and Fungi, 2nd edn., McGraw-Hill, New York (1955).

11 Phaeophyta

CLASS: FUCOPHYCEAE

GENERAL CHARACTERS

The phylum Phaeophyta includes the single class Fucophyceae, formerly known as Phaeophyceae.

Popularly called the brown algae, the Fucophyceae/Phaeophyta are characterized by the following five chief distinguishing features:

(1) The photosynthetic pigments include chlorophyll-a and -c, β-carotene, fucoxanthin, violaxanthin, diatoxanthin, and other xanthophylls, the carotenoids, in general, being in excess of the chlorophyll pigments. Fucoxanthin is present in a sufficient quantity to mask the green colour of the chlorophylls and to impart its own brown colour to these algae.

(2) The excess photosynthate is commonly stored in the form of mannitol, occasionally as laminarin, rarely as fat droplets. Monosaccharides are usually absent.

(3) Certain whitish granules, called fucosan vesicles, are usually present in the cell.

(4) The cell wall is composed of cellulose, fucinic acid, and alginic acid.

(5) The flagellated structures have a pair of laterally inserted unequal flagella, the larger of which is anterior and pantonematic, whereas the smaller one is posterior and acronematic.

OCCURRENCE

With a few exceptions, e.g., *Pleurocladia, Heribaudiella, Bodanella,* and a few species of *Ectocarpus* which are freshwater forms, all other brown algae are marine. They generally inhabit the colder waters but members of the Encoeliaceae (Ectocarpales) and Dictyotales and *Sargassum* are markedly warm-water forms. Fucoids are conspicuous components of the seaweed biomass in arctic, temperate, tropical, and antarctic marine waters. *Sargassum muticum* has become a nuisance after its introduction into North America and Europe.

Depending on the topographical features of the land-sea boundary, the littoral region is divided into three major zones: sublittoral—always submerged, the approximate maximum depth being 100 metres; intertidal—submerged during high tide and exposed during low tide; and supralittoral—not very well defined, the highest tides or tide sprays rarely reaching beyond its boundary. According to the nature of the shore, tides, and algal associations, the intertidal belt is further divided into three minor zones—upper, middle, and lower.

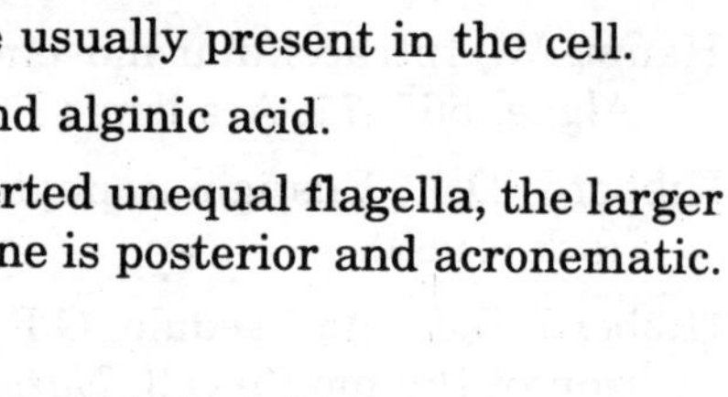

Fig. 11-1 *Colpomenia sinuosa*, habit.

The sublittoral zone includes thick forest of such algae (kelps) as *Laminaria*, with subflora of *Dictyota, Cutleria, Alaria, Himanthalia,* and *Desmarestia*. In the intertidal belt, the rockweeds (Fucaceae) grow in the upper zone, *Colpomenia* (Fig. 11-1), *Iyengaria, Sphacelaria, Leathesia,* and others in the middle zone, and most of the Laminariales in the lower zone. Species of *Ectocarpus* form the subflora of the supralittoral zone.

Kelp forests are among the most productive plant communities in the world. *Laminaria* and *Macrocystis* have very high rates of primary production, being capable of achieving an annual net production of up to 2000 gram carbon/m^2 (Mann and Chapman, 1975). In the North Atlantic, *Laminaria* grows rapidly in late winter and early spring, followed by a quiescent period in late summer. Anderson *et al.* (1981) recorded maximum growth of *L. longicruris* (3.5 cm/day) in June and minimal (0.18 cm/day) in December-February, when ice cover limits light availability. They estimated that 40 gram carbon/yr is the total carbon produced per plant.

STRESS PHYSIOLOGY

Salinity is one of the major abiotic factors controlling the growth of algae. It is expressed as grams of salt per kilogram of solution (%o S). Salinity exerts osmotic stress on cells. Fucoids have to maintain turgor by keeping the internal osmotic potential more negative than that of sea water. Excessive salinity of sea water reverses this differential, resulting in net loss of water from cells. On the other hand, too low a salinity floods the cells with water and can burst them.

Fucoids often live in environments of fluctuating salinity, being very common in estuaries where there are often rapid changes from full strength sea water to freshwater. On rocky coasts exposed to sea water, intertidal fucoids suffer salinity stress during low water when it may rain or during dehydration when evaporation produces hypersaline conditions (Chapman, 1995).

Three primary responses to changes in salinity are: alteration of cell volume, and/or turgor; adjustment of the content and concentration of inorganic ions; and changes in the concentration of organic solutes. K^+ and Cl^- ions are the chief intracellular substances used to regulate osmotic potentials of fucoid cells.

Salinity has an important role in algal distribution. *Fucus ceranoides* occurs only in estuaries and is exposed to undiluted freshwater for part of the tidal cycle. *F. ceranoides* adapts well to life in estuarine habitats with alternating flows of sea water and freshwater. It sheds gametes only during daytime (high salinity) high tides (Brawley, 1992). Its eggs are fertilized within 2 hr of release, after which they can withstand immersion in freshwater. Furthermore, release of gametes during high tides reduces the incidence of polyspermy, which is fatal in fucoids (Brawley, 1992). There appears to be a Na^+-dependent block to polyspermy which is most effective in sea water. The germlings of *Sargassum muticum* fail to grow at less than 20% salinity. In the field, *S. muticum* is restricted to sites where salinity exceeds 24%o.

Fucoids found in the intertidal zone suffer desiccation at low water. *Pelvetia canaliculata* seems to require periodic drying out as under continuous immersion it disintegrates and dies. In *Fucus distichus* (a high-shore species), photosynthesis in air may be several times higher than in water. *Ascophyllum nodosum* also photosynthesizes faster in air than in water.

Eventually, high-shore fucoids become so desiccated that the metabolic processes shut down. *Fucus distichus* plants can be exposed to air for up to 18 hr during low tide periods, whereas *P. canaliculata* is exposed for several days during neap tides. Exposure to air for long periods can be a stress, yet fucoids appear to have no mechanism for retaining water as there are no analogues to the cuticle/stomatal system of higher plants.

It appears that fucoids tolerate drought but do not avoid or resist it. Drought tolerance may be important in the zonation of species on the shore as high-shore species tolerate drought for longer periods without injury than lower-shore species. Thus *P. canaliculata*, occurring highest on European shores, can survive air dryness for 4–6 days, *Fucus spiralis*, found in an immediately contiguous lower zone, survives 1–2 days' in dry air, while the lower-shore *A. nodosum* and *F. vesiculosus* survive only a few hours.

Both the photosynthetic apparatus and the phosphate uptake are sensitive to drying out. Plants were dehydrated to different extents, then re-immersed in sea water and phosphate uptake measured. The rate of uptake in *P. canaliculata* seems unrelated to the extent of previous tissue dehydration. It appears that the sensitivity of the phosphate uptake mechanism is somehow related to the position of fucoids on the shore gradient (Chapman, 1995), high-shore species having less sensitive mechanisms than low-shore species.

The smallest stages in the life history may be more susceptible to desiccation than are large plants. The zygotes and embryos of fucoids have much greater surface area to volume ratios than adults and hence would be expected to dehydrate much more quickly.

A major determinant of seaweed biogeography is temperature tolerance, but there are very few data concerning fucoids. Fucoids are photoautotrophic and require light for their synthetic processes.

Both too little and too much of light are likely stresses. Under sublittoral conditions in turbid waters, fucoids suffer from light deficiency. Fucoids can often adapt their total photosynthetic pigment content and pigment ratios according to the amount of light received. Plants suspended in 4 metre deep water or collected from naturally shady habitats contain more pigments than those exposed to strong light. The fucoxanthin : chlorophyll-a ratio decreases with depth or shade, with the result that shade-adapted plants have higher photosynthetic rates than light-adapted plants.

Fucoids are more sensitive to light quality than to light quantity. They tend to survive long periods in the dark and, conversely, have a protection mechanism against damage from high light. But yellow-green or orange light is lethal for young fucoids exposed for 4–6 weeks at a photon fluence rate of 100 $\mu mol\ m^{-2}\ sec^{-1}$ (McLachlan and Bidwell, 1983). Treatment with long or short wavelengths reverses the effects of mid-wavelengths. Interestingly, the lethal wavelengths are those which penetrate best in turbid waters, and at 10 metres mostly damaging colours of light are usually available.

RANGE OF THALLUS STRUCTURE

The thalli of the brown algae range in structure from heterotrichous filamentous types through pseudoparenchymatous uniaxial forms to true parenchymatous forms. Neither unicellular nor simple filamentous brown algae are known and the simplest thallus organization in this phylum is the branched, heterotrichous filament. Phenotypic plasticity is widespread in this class.

The vegetative body of the Laminariales and Fucales shows well marked morphological and anatomical differences. In *Laminaria*, the thallus is morphologically distinguishable into holdfast, stipe, and blade (Fig. 11-2). A transverse section of the stipe or blade shows the distinction of vegetative tissue into three regions: an outer epidermis, a middle zone of several-layered cortex, and multicellular central medulla. Some cells of the medulla produce vertically elongated hyphae, known as trumpet hyphae (Fig. 11-3), which lack chloroplasts and discharge the function of water and nutrient conduction. *Nereocystis* and *Pelagophycus*

(Laminariales) have certain cells that are similar to the sieve tubes of higher plants but are devoid of companion cells (Parker and Huber, 1965).

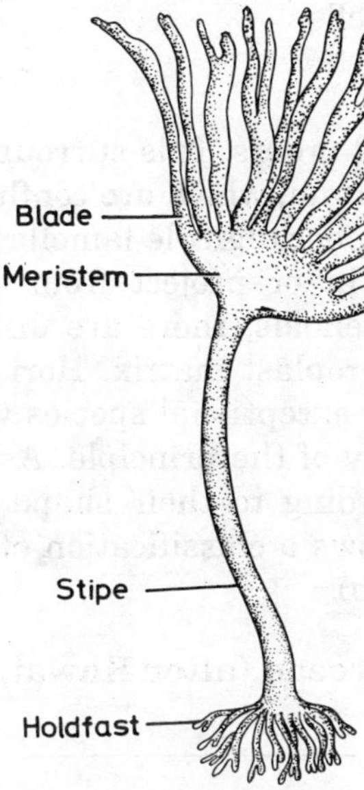

Fig. 11-2 *Laminaria hyperborea*, sporophyte structure showing differentiation into holdfast, stipe, and blade.

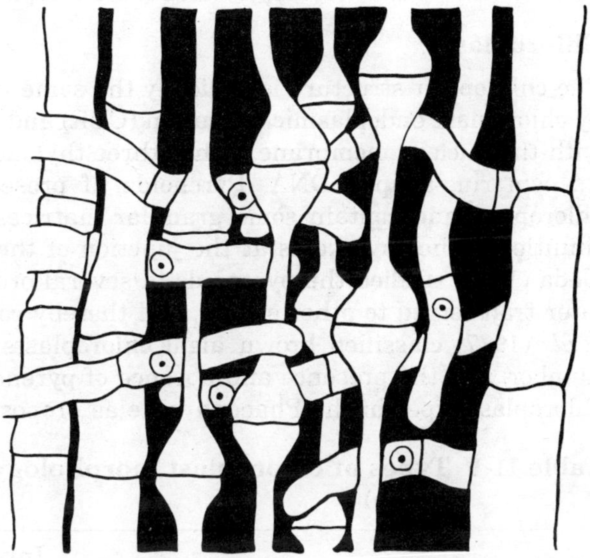

Fig. 11-3 *Laminaria saccharina*, longitudinal section of medullary region showing trumpet hyphae and medullary filaments. The blackened areas denote mucilage.

The vegetative thallus usually grows by intercalary or apical meristems. Trichothallic growth is characteristic of most Ectocarpales, Desmarestiales, Cutleriales, and Sporochnales. Intercalary growth characterizes the Laminariales, which has its meristem located at the junction of the stipe and the blade. The Sphacelariales, Dictyotales, and Fucales show apical growth.

CELL STRUCTURE

Papenfuss (1951) recognized four groups among the Phaeophyceae, namely, isomorphic parenchymatous, heteromorphic pseudoparenchymatous, heteromorphic parenchymatous, and another independent line of Fucales derived from Ectocarpales. Scagel (1966) suggested classification of the Phaeophyceae into Cyclosporidae (i.e., Fucales) and Phaeophycidae (including all other orders). Clayton (1990) also followed this scheme and placed each order in four major lines. On the other hand, recent investigations have revealed some contradictions in such schemes (Kawai, 1992a). For example, Desmarestiales, Sporochnales, and Laminariales, though being heteromorphic pseudoparenchymatous and heteromorphic parenchymatous are sometimes considered to have much closer similarities in features such as life history pattern, morphology of vegetative and reproductive structures of the sporophyte and gametophyte, and nature of sexual pheromones (Clayton, 1990). In the Cutleriales, *Cutleria* is heteromorphic while *Zanardinia* shows isomorphic life history. Therefore, the phylogeny of brown algae cannot be interpreted in terms of life history and thallus construction as being the basic characteristics. Kawai (1992a) has suggested emphasizing cytological characteristics such as the types of chloroplasts and the morphology of flagellate cells.

Chloroplasts

The chloroplast structure is basically the same in many brown algal orders. It is surrounded by chloroplast endoplasmic reticulum (CER) and periplastidial reticulum, which are confluent with the nuclear membrane. It has three thylakoid lamellae, a peripheral girdle lamella and its own ring-shaped DNA. Pyrenoids, if present, are immersed in or project from each chloroplast and contain some granular matrices. In projecting pyrenoids, there are discontinuities of the thylakoids at the junction of the pyrenoid and chloroplast matrix. Hori and Ueda (1975) studied the pyrenoids in several orders. Many of these exceptional species were later transferred to other orders, and thereby confirmed the validity of the principle. Asensi *et al.* (1977) classified brown algal chloroplasts into 8 types according to their shape and number, and the presence and absence of pyrenoids. Table 11-1 shows a classification of the chloroplast types in the Phaeophyceae as proposed by Kawai (1992b).

Table 11-1 Types of chloroplast morphology in the Phaeophyceae (after Kawai, 1992b)

Chloroplast(s)	Location	Pyrenoid	Invagination of pyrenoid	Examples
Single	Parietal	+	–	Scytosiphonales
Single	Parietal	–	–	Ralfsiaceae
Single	Axial	+	+	*Splachnidium*, *Scytothamnus*
Multiple	Spread	+	–	Ectocarpales, Chordariales, Dictyosiphonales
Multiple	Spread	–	–	Cutleriales, Sphacelariales, Dictyotales, Tilopteridales, Sporochnales, Desmarestiales, *Fucales

*Pyrenoid occasionally observed in reproductive cells.

Flagellated Cells

Flagellated cells (swarmers) in the Phaeophyceae include asexual zoospores, isogametes, anisogametes, and sperms. They usually have two heterokont flagella, one anterior hairy and the other posterior smooth. All zoospores and many of the gametes have a longer anterior flagellum (Fig. 11-4 A). Each flagellum has a terminal thin whiplash called acronema. The anterior acronema, which is very long, may be involved in anchoring during sexual reproduction. The anterior flagellum is locomotory by means of its undulating beating and presence of rigid mastigonemes, which thrust the cell forward (Kawai, 1992b). The posterior flagellum steers as a rudder. A rather complicated movement of posterior flagellum occurs in the chemotaxis of *Laminaria* sperm (Maier and Müller, 1990). The acronema of the posterior flagellum is relatively short. Anterior flagellar spines occur in some sperms of Fucales and Dictyotales (Phillips *et al.*, 1991).

Zoospores are structurally uniform while gametes are not so, probably because phototaxis is involved in the oriented movement in asexual zoospores, and its receptive mechanism is common in all brown algae (Kawai *et al.*, 1991). In contrast, the diverse morphologies of gametes can be explained as a result of evolutionary adaptation to sexual reproduction mediated by pheromones.

Most phaeophycean zoospores have a single chloroplast with a reflective stigma and a flagellar swelling on the basal part of the posterior flagellum (Kawai *et al.*, 1990; Kreimer *et al.*, 1991). Exceptionally, zoospores of some Laminariales (Laminariaceae, Lessoniaceae, Alariaceae), which do not show phototaxis, lack both stigmata and flagellar swellings. Some gametes show both phototaxis and chemotaxis, whereas there is no phototaxis in some chemotactic members. Flagellar basal bodies are joined with the nucleus and are associated with the chloroplasts. Female gametes of Cutleriales, Sphacelariales, and *Giffordia* have several chloroplasts. In such cases, only one of the chloroplasts is associated with the flagellar base and has a stigma. The sperms of most of the Laminariales have several small dispersed chloroplasts not associated with the flagellar base (Fig. 11-4 G, H), while those of some Fucales share the longer posterior flagellum but have a chloroplast with or without a stigma (Fig. 11-4 I). Green flagellar autofluorescence is widely distributed in the posterior flagellum of brown algae, and appears to be the photoreceptor. It is not seen in the sperms of Desmarestiales and Laminariales, which lack phototaxis.

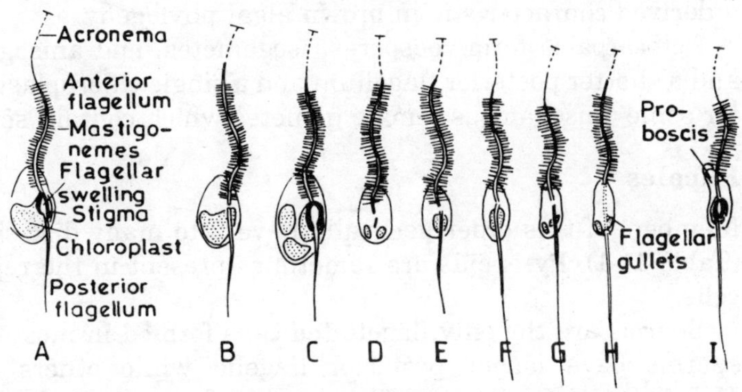

Fig. 11-4 Morphology of flagellated cells in the Phaeophyceae (presence or absence of pyrenoids is not indicated). A, typical (primitive) type of swarmer having longer anterior and shorter posterior flagellum (all zoospores excluding those of advanced Laminariales, most isogametes and male anisogametes); B, zoospore of advanced Laminariales lacking stigma and flagellar swelling; C, female anisogametes in Ectocarpales, Dictyosiphonales, Cutleriales, and Sphacelariales, normally flagellated as in type A but containing several chloroplasts; D, dictyotalean sperm without or with remnant posterior flagellum; chloroplasts are fragmented and lacking stigmata; E, sperm of primitive Fucales, normally flagellated but having a reduced chloroplast; F, sperm of Sporochnales, of *Saccorhiza*, and Desmarestiales having slightly longer posterior flagellum and a chloroplast lacking stigmata and flagellar swellings; G, sperm of Laminariales having longer posterior flagellum and several fragmented chloroplasts not associated with nucleus; H, sperm of Laminariales almost same as type G but having deep flagellar gullets; I, fucalean sperm having longer posterior flagellum, a chloroplast with a stigma and flagellar swelling and anterior proboscis. (After Kawai, 1992b.)

The flagellar rootlet system is broadly similar among phaeophycean flagellated cells, composed of bypassing rootlets which pass through the flagellar bases longitudinally, and four kinds of rootlets (MAR, mar, MPR, mpr) that issue from the flagellar bases (O'Kelly, 1989). However, laminarialean sperms lack MPR (Motomura, 1989). In fucalean sperm a bundle of the MAR forms a proboscis (Fig. 11-4).

Members of the Ectocarpales have disc- and ribbon-shaped, 2 to 3 or more chloroplasts in each cell. This order is usually regarded as the most primitive in the Phaeophyceae, because of the uniseriate thalli and isomorphic life history. However, this concept is questionable since several to many chloroplasts per cell is unlikely to be the most primitive condition in the Phaeophyceae. For example, the ribbon-shaped chloroplasts of *Ectocarpus* are very complicated, and furthermore, the species is not truly morphologically isomorphic. *Giffordia*, which also has many disc-shaped chloroplasts, shows obvious anisogamy, which is considered to be a derived characteristic in brown algal phylogeny.

Ectocarpales form zoospores, isogametes, and anisogametes, all having a longer anterior and a shorter posterior flagellum and a single chloroplast with a pyrenoid and a stigma, except for some anisogamous female gametes which contain several chloroplasts.

Fucales

Members of this order generally have 2 to many disc-shaped chloroplasts lacking pyrenoids (Table 11-1). Pyrenoids are sometimes present in the reproductive cells but not in vegetative cells.

Sperms are the only flagellated cells formed in most of the members of the Fucales. Some sperms have longer posterior flagella while others have longer anterior flagella (e.g., *Halidrys* and *Cystoseira*). The sperms of many are stigmatic.

In the Phaeophyceae, the occurrence of many chloroplasts lacking pyrenoids is regarded as a derived condition, because anisogamous or oogamous orders with elaborate thalli (e.g., Laminariales and Fucales) contain this type of chloroplast. On the other hand, a single chloroplast with a pyrenoid appears to be the most primitive because no obvious anisogamy or oogamy occurs in the order having this type of chloroplast (e.g., Scytosiphonales). Accordingly, the most primitive member of the Phaeophyceae may be found in the order Scytosiphonales, despite its heteromorphic life history and parenchymatous organization of thallus in the known taxa. Asensi *et al.* (1977) believed that the single chloroplast having an invaginated pyrenoid (e.g., in *Splachnidium* and *Scytothamnus*), is the most primitive type in the Phaeophyceae, because such pyrenoids show certain morphological similarities with some chrysophycean pyrenoids.

The cell wall of the brown algae is made up of an outer mucilaginous layer containing alginic and fucinic acids, and an inner cellulosic layer.

The brown algae produce three main types of polysaccharides, viz., laminarin (1,3-linked β-glucan), alginic acid (a polymer of alternating units of D-mannuronic acid and L-guluronic acid), and fucan (a sulphated polymer containing L-fucose plus some D-xylose and D-glucuronic acid). The relative proportions of these three components vary widely. The highest content of fucan (up to 25 per cent on dry weight basis) occurs in *Pelvetia canaliculata* and *Himanthalia elongata*, whereas the lowest content (up to about 2 per cent) has been found in *Desmarestia firma*.

Alginic acid forms a prominent constituent of the brown algal cell walls. Indeed, quantitatively, it is the major polysaccharide of the brown seaweeds.

Fucans appear to protect the plants from desiccation (Percival, 1979).

The ratio of mannuronic acid to guluronic acid residues in the alginates of various genera may range from less than 0.7 in *Dictyosiphon* and *Desmarestia* to more than 1.0 as in several Laminariales and Fucales (Percival, 1978).

The cytoplasm generally contains many small vacuoles and a few refractile bodies of an unknown nature termed the fucosan vesicles which are usually present at the site of high metabolic activity. The chromatophores are mostly parietal, frequently with more than one chromatophore per cell, except in *Pylaiella fulvescens* which contains axile stellate chromatophores. The Ectocarpales show wide variation in the shape of their chromatophores which may be plate-like, ribbon-shaped or discoid. Projecting pyrenoids lacking photosynthetic thylakoids are present in some members of the Ectocarpales, Sphacelariales, and Dictyosiphonales. The chromatophore lamellations in the Phaeophyta result from a rather close aggregation of generally three, rarely four, thylakoids which do not cohere into stacks or bands but run parallel to each other (Evans, 1966). In the biflagellate cells, the two basal granules, each with one flagellum, are laterally connected and in addition the anterior flagellum and the nucleus are joined together through a fibrous structure comparable to a rhizoplast. *Dictyota* has monoflagellate sperms with two basal granules of which the posterior one does not give rise to a flagellum (Manton, 1965). The phaeophycean swarmers are commonly equipped with an eyespot and a chromatophore devoid of pyrenoids. Most Dictyotales, Laminariales, and Fucales, which show oogamous reproduction, lack pyrenoids. In many other brown algae (mostly the primitive forms), the usual pyrenoid commonly found is 1.5–3.0 μm broad and 1.5–2.5 μm long. The pyrenoid of *Cutleria cylindrica*, however, is 0.9 μm long and 0.5 μm wide. The egg plastids of *Fucus* also have a rudimentary pyrenoid.

The cells are uninucleate, with one or two nucleoli. Some members, e.g., *Fucus*, have in their resting nucleus many Feulgen-positive bodies called chromocentres which arrange themselves linearly along the chromosome during late prophase but their identity is lost with the progressive contraction of chromosomes during metaphase; this state is maintained until the next interphase and prophase. The chromocentres are characteristic of only the Phaeophyta, but nothing is known of their function. Another feature is the presence of centrosomes at the poles of a dividing nucleus. The chromosome organization has advanced to such an extent that members of the Laminariales possess well differentiated *X* and *Y* sex chromosomes. Other subcellular organelles such as mitochondria, Golgi bodies, and endoplasmic reticulum are also present. Synaptonemal complexes have recently been reported in the meiotic nuclei of a few brown algae.

Henry and Cole (1982a, b) have studied the fine structure of the zoospores and antherozoids of several brown algae. The zoospores contain a single chloroplast but lack both an eyespot and any swelling at the flagellar base. The antherozoids are elongate, and contain 2–3 chloroplasts lacking eyespots.

OSMOREGULATION

Most brown algae are capable of osmotic adjustment, involving partial or complete turgor regulation over a fairly wide range of external salinities. Turgor regulation in these algae is achieved by means of changes in the intracellular concentrations of K^+, Na^+, Cl^-, NO_3^-, and mannitol. Of these, the inorganic osmotic ions are confined to the vacuole whereas mannitol acts as a cytoplasmic osmoticum.

Mannitol concentration in many brown algae shows a marked correlation with salinity

(Reed *et al.*, 1985). This suggests an important osmoregulatory role for mannitol, especially in response to changes in external water status. Reed *et al.* advocate a predominantly osmotic, rather than respiratory, role for mannitol in brown algae. This view is strengthened by the observation that mannitol is an effective osmoticum for the maintenance of viable chloroplasts from *Fucus*, whereas NaCl is not.

REPRODUCTION

Vegetative

The commonest method of reproduction is by fragmentation of a thallus into two or more parts, each of which regenerates into a mature new plant. In the Sphacelariales, special reproductive branches known as propagules are formed; after detachment from the parent, the propagules give rise to new plants.

Asexual

With the exception of the Tilopteridales, Dictyotales, and Fucales, in all the Phaeophyta zoospores are produced in well defined sporangia borne on the sporophyte. The Ectocarpales and Sphacelariales produce unichambered or unilocular as well as multichambered or plurilocular sporangia. During the formation of zoospores, the diploid nucleus of the unilocular sporangium divides by meiosis, followed by a series of mitotic divisions of the resulting four haploid nuclei. Finally, the cytoplasm becomes segmented into a number of uninucleate portions, each of which subsequently acquires a pair of laterally inserted flagella. The zoospores produced from unilocular sporangia are haploid and on germination give rise to haploid, gametophytic plants.

Both unilocular zoosporangia and paraphyses develop from the meristoderm cells of the sporophytic plants. The sporangia and paraphyses occur in groups or sori. Three kinds of sorus development take place in different genera:

(1) The meristoderm cell of the mature plant divides periclinally into a lower and an upper cell. The latter grows into a unicellular paraphysis. The lower cell forms a projection between the paraphyses. Its nucleus divides and one of the daughter nuclei migrates into the projection. Some plastids also go into the projection which is then delimited from the subtending lower cell by means of a septum. The delimited projection constitutes the zoosporangial mother cell. This mode is exemplified in *Laminaria japonica*, *Ecklonia stolonifer*, *Undaria pinnatifida*, and *Alaria* sp.

(2) The protuberance from the lower cell does not develop into the sporangial mother cell but into a second sterile paraphysis. The sporangial mother cell arises from a second projection from the lower meristoderm cell. This mode is exemplified by *Alaria crassifolia*.

(3) The meristoderm cell divides into upper and lower cells. Since the cuticle covering the meristoderm does not correspondingly stretch, the meristoderm cell is directly exposed to the exterior. The upper cells elongate and separate from each other. The lower cell produces a protuberance that grows between the upper cells. The latter grow into unicellular paraphyses. The protuberance then forms a septum and becomes delimited from the lower cell. The chief characteristic of this mode of sorus development is the stripping-off of the cuticle at an early stage of sorus formation. This mode occurs in *Chorda filum*, *Ecklonia kurome*, and *Eckloniopsis radicosa*.

In plurilocular sporangia, the nuclei never divide meiotically and therefore the zoospores are always diploid and serve as an accessory means of perpetuation of the sporophyte or the gametophyte. Other zoosporic Phaeophyta bear only unilocular sporangia. In the Dictyotales, the sporophyte forms tetrasporangia, and reduction division of the sporangial nucleus in these results in the formation of four haploid, uninucleate aplanospores or tetraspores. The Tilopteridales form single, quadrinucleate aplanospores, termed monospores, in each sporangium. Both tetraspores and monospores give rise to gametophytic plants. The Fucales lack asexual reproduction.

Sexual

The gametophytes bear only multichambered organs, the plurilocular gametangia, which form gametes that resemble zoospores in morphology. The Ectocarpales and Sphacelariales are mostly isogamous but the Punctariaceae, Cutleriales, and possibly Tilopteridales are distinctly anisogamous. Several brown algae, e.g., the Fucales, Laminariales, and Dictyotales, are oogamous. In the Dictyotales, the antheridia and oogonia occur in sori but in the Fucales they are produced in cavity-like depressions (conceptacles) on a fertile blade (receptacle).

A marked lunar periodicity in sexual reproduction has been observed in certain marine brown algae. The ova are released around the first quarter of the moon but there is no such rhythmicity for sporogenesis.

Environmental factors such as temperature, photoperiod, and wavelength of light profoundly influence the structure and reproduction in many brown algae (Wynne and Loiseaux, 1976). In *Ectocarpus*, the formation of unilocular and plurilocular sporangia seems to be determined by the ambient temperature with low (about 13°C) temperature favouring the development of unilocular sporangia, and high (about 19°C) temperature that of plurilocular sporangia. In *Sphacelaria*, the reproductive behaviour is influenced by both day length and temperature (Fig. 11-5). Gametophytic maturation in the Laminariales seems to be controlled by the wavelength of light.

Sexual reproduction is mediated by hormone-like substances which are secreted by female gametes and attract the male gametes. *Ectocarpus*, *Dictyota*, and *Cutleria* synthesize mono-

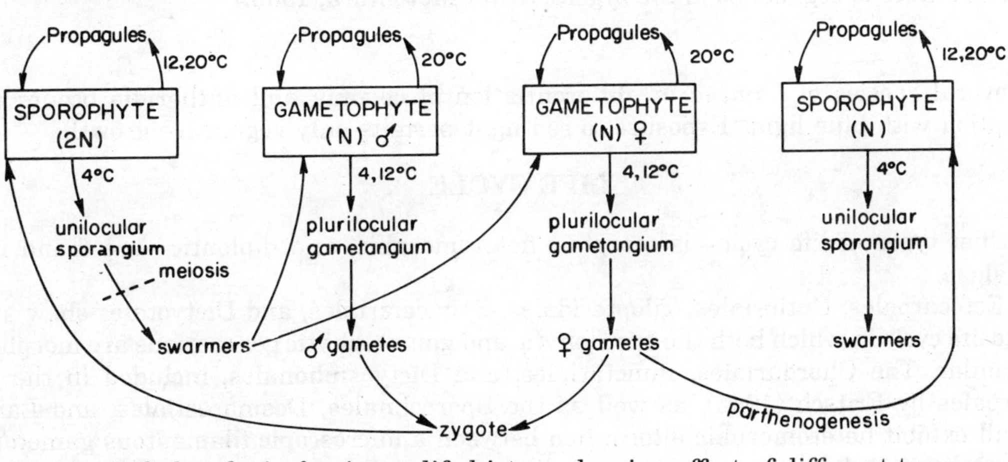

Fig. 11-5 *Sphacelaria furcigera*, life history showing effect of different temperatures (after Van den Hoek and Flintermann, 1968).

cyclic unconjugated C_{11} olefins. *Fucus* produces a conjugated C_8 alkene. *Sargassum horneri* also releases some male-attracting substance called fucoserraten.

The eggs of *Laminaria digitata* secrete a hormone ($C_{11}H_{14}O$) into the ambient medium. This hormone initiates the discharge of antherozoids from the antheridia as well as their subsequent attraction towards the ova (Müller and Gassmann, 1980). Figure 11-6 illustrates cytoplasmic inheritance of mitochondria, chloroplasts, and centrioles in the zygote of *Laminaria*. After plasmogamy, sperm nucleus, mitochondria, chloroplasts, and centrioles are incorporated into the egg cytoplasm. Before and after karyogamy, mitochondria are enclosed by a membrane. After that, they are completely digested in the membrane. Chloroplasts persist but do not increase in size. Sperm centrioles remain whereas egg centrioles disappear after karyogamy. Sperm centrioles duplicate and migrate to each mitotic pole in early mitotic stage.

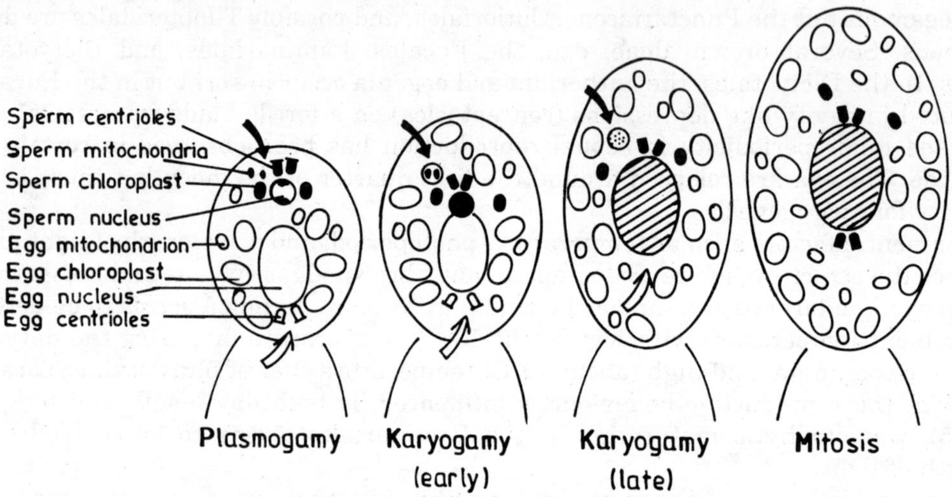

Fig. 11-6 *Laminaria angustata*. Diagrammatic sketch of cytoplasmic inheritance of organelles in the zygote. (After Motomura, 1990.)

In several species of *Laminaria*, differentiation of oogonia and antheridia occurs under illumination with blue light. Exposure to red light permits only vegetative growth.

LIFE CYCLE

Three chief types of life cycle—isomorphic, heteromorphic, and diplontic—are found in the brown algae.

The Ectocarpales, Cutleriales, Tilopteridales, Sphacelariales, and Dictyotales show an isomorphic life cycle in which both the sporophytic and gametophytic generations are morphologically similar. The Chordariales, Punctariales, and Dictyosiphonales, included in the order Ectocarpales by Fritsch (1945), as well as the Sporochnales, Desmarestiales, and Laminariales, all exhibit heteromorphic alternation between a microscopic filamentous gametophyte and an elaborate, often macroscopic sporophyte. In the Chordariales, the zygote germinates into a filamentous structure, designated protonema if it generates the sporophyte as a lateral outgrowth, and plethysmothallus if it forms zoospores in plurilocular sporangia for its own propagation. In the Fucales, the plants are diploid and lack an alternation of generations. The only haploid stage in the life cycle is confined to the gametes. There is no independent, free-living multicellular gametophyte in the Fucales.

It has commonly been believed that the life histories of such algae as *Ectocarpus* and *Sphacelaria* involve the alternation of isomorphic generations. However, recent researches have shown that the basic pattern in *E. siliculosus* and *S. furcigera* is a heteromorphic diplohaplontic life history. In the latter species, the gametophytes are unisexual and somewhat smaller than the sporophytes (see Van den Hoek and Flintermann, 1968). Wynne (1969) has reported the existence of heteromorphic developmental patterns without sexuality in some brown algae. It has also been claimed that haploid sporophytes can develop by the parthenogenetic germination of unfertilized gametes. Such haploid sporophytes produce only unilocular sporangia in *S. furcigera* but both unilocular and plurilocular sporangia in *E. siliculosus*. Müller (1972) too has conducted research which has indicated the existence of diploid gametophytes and tetraploid sporophytes (Fig. 11-7) in *E. siliculosus*. Müller (1975) has found that, contrary to the widely-held notion, the swarmers produced by unilocular sporangia do not fuse, and that there is no such thing as 'relative sexuality' in *Ectocarpus*.

Many Dictyotales show a numerical dominance of sporophytes in the wild populations, the gametophytes being rather rare. In Australia, sporophytes and male and female gametophytes of *Dictyota dichotoma*, *Padina fraseri*, and *Dictyopteris* spp. occur simultaneously in wild populations (Phillips, 1988). Gamete release occurs at monthly intervals in *Dictyota* spp., once every week in *Dictyopteris muelleri*, and once a fortnight in *Padina fraseri*. Ova and sperms are released after the onset of the light period (in the laboratory) for two consecutive days. In *Dictyota* spp., gamete release occurs synchronously some 3–4 days before the new moon; all the gametangia on thalli within the population are at a comparable developmental stage (Phillips, 1988).

It certainly seems that the life histories of the Phaeophyceae are much more flexible than hitherto believed.

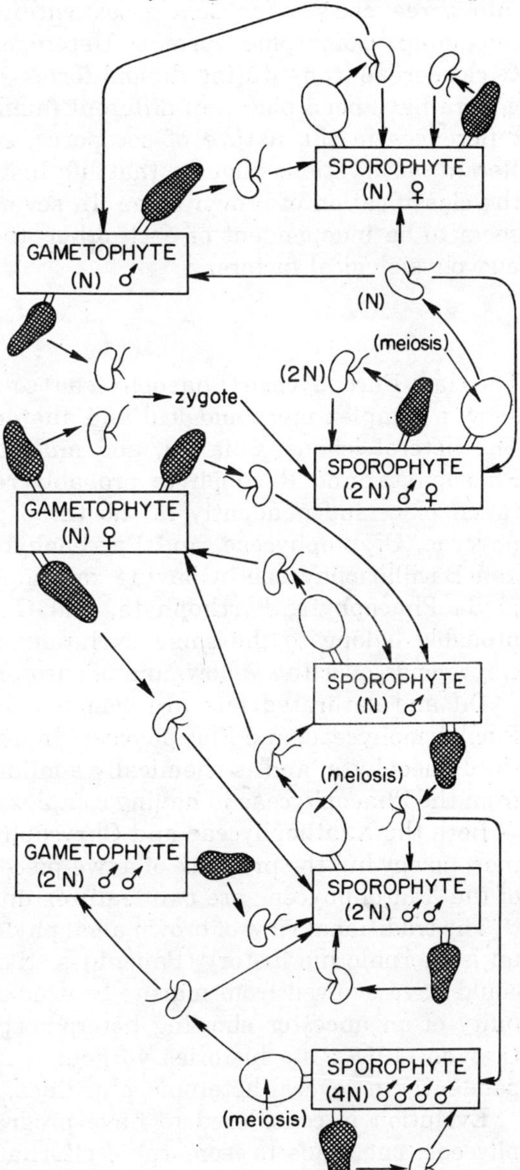

Fig. 11-7 *Ectocarpus siliculosus*, life history (after Müller, 1967).

CLASSIFICATION

The Phaeophyta includes the single class Phaeophyceae. On the basis of vegetative organization and sexual reproduction, Fritsch (1945) divided the Phaeophyceae into nine orders: Ectocarpales, Tilopteridales, Cutleriales, Sporochnales, Desmarestiales, Laminariales, Sphacelariales, Dictyotales, and Fucales.

Most other phycologists emphasize the three types of life cycle, and divide the Phaeophyta into three classes (or subclasses within the class Phaeophyceae), namely, Isogeneratae (including isomorphic forms), Heterogeneratae (comprising heteromorphic forms), and Cyclosporeae (constituting diploid forms). Within the Isogeneratae and Heterogeneratae, the genera have been placed in different families, and families in different orders on the basis of differences in the nature of zoospores, sexuality, organization, and growth of the thallus. Recent observations suggest that life histories may be difficult to use as reliable criteria in the classification of brown algae. In several instances, morphological and cytological phases seem to be independent of each other, their variations mostly depending on environmental and physiological factors.

PHYLOGENY

The class Fucophyceae (Phaeophyceae) comprises a group of multicellular algae some of which show a complex morphological and anatomical differentiation not seen in other algal phyla. The heterotrichous, uniaxial, and multiaxial types of thalli met with in the Chlorophyta, Phaeophyta, and Rhodophyta probably represent the parallel course of evolution that has taken place independently in the three phyla. The Phaeophyceae resemble the Bacillariophyceae, Cryptophyceae, and Pyrrhophyta in having chlorophyll-c; and the Chrysophyceae and Bacillariophyceae in having xanthophylls, fucoxanthin, and neofucoxanthin. The three phyla Phaeophyta, Pyrrhophyta, and Chrysophyta (class Bacillariophyceae, in particular) probably belong to the same evolutionary line, showing a predominance of the brownish carotenoids over the yellow, and of carotenoid pigments over the chlorophylls.

Oil and saturated fats are common food reserves in the Tribophyceae, Chrysophyceae, Bacillariophyceae, and Fucophyceae. In addition, laminarin is a distinctive reserve product of the Phaeophyta, and is chemically similar to leucosin. The Bacillariophyceae however differ from the Phaeophyceae in having complex cellular morphology, with a two-piece silicified wall.

Both the Xanthophyceae and Chrysophyceae resemble the Phaeophyceae in their flagellar morphology but the presence of a two-piece silicified wall and chlorophyll-e in certain members of the Xanthophyceae are two features unknown in the Phaeophyceae.

The traditional view of brown algal phylogeny has visualized an ectocarpoid ancestor having an isomorphic life history (Papenfuss, 1953). A recent hypothesis suggests that brown algae could have evolved from marine benthic chrysophytes (O'Kelly and Floyd, 1985). The possibility of an ancestor showing heteromorphic life history cannot be ruled out. According to Clayton (1988), life histories without a free-living gametophyte may have originated independently in several heteromorphic lines.

Evolution is considered to have progressed along two different lines within the Phaeophyceae: one leads to isomorphic alternation of generations accompanied by an advance in sexuality from isogamy to oogamy and, in vegetative organization, from simple to complex thalli; the other, which has a heteromorphic alternation of generations, shows a similar progression in reproduction and vegetative organization. The diploid Fucales are assumed to represent the evolutionary climax in the heteromorphic series, with the gametophyte reduced to the single-celled stage, i.e., the gamete.

SELECTED GENERA

Order: ECTOCARPALES

The Ectocarpales has been differently delimited by various phycologists. Fritsch (1945) included in this order filamentous, pseudoparenchymatous, and parenchymatous types derived from a heterotrichous filament. Emphasis on the heterotrichous character led to the inclusion of forms exhibiting an isomorphic as well as heteromorphic alternation of generations in the order. Most other phycologists have however considered the life cycle of greater importance than the heterotrichous habit and have consequently raised to the rank of orders those families in the order Ectocarpales *sensu* Fritsch that exhibit heteromorphic alternation. This has led to the restriction of the Ectocarpales to the single family Ectocarpaceae characterized by simple, heterotrichous members exhibiting isogamous sexuality and isomorphic alternation of generations.

In general, the prostrate system of the Ectocarpaceae grows by an apical meristem but the development of the erect system is highly variable—*Ectocarpus siliculosus* shows diffuse growth, *E. lucifugus* apical growth, and *E. paradoxus* trichothallic growth. *Pylaiella*, an alga related to *Ectocarpus*, frequently shows longitudinal septation in its filaments as a result of which the thallus tends to become parenchymatous. *Streblonema* lacks an erect system.

Family: Ectocarpaceae
Genus: *Ectocarpus*

Occurrence

Worldwide in distribution, *Ectocarpus* grows in the littoral and supralittoral regions. In India, it is mostly found in the supralittoral zone along the West and East Coasts.

Morphology

The thallus of *Ectocarpus* is made up of uniseriate filaments and is generally differentiated into a much branched erect system (Fig. 11-8) and a prostrate system which is sparsely or profusely branched. Each branch generally arises from just below a septum. The main branches and their branchlets most often terminate in hairs consisting of numerous elongated, tapering, hyaline, and much vacuolated cells. The plants are attached to the substratum by branched rhizoids produced from lower cells of lower branches and, in some cases, these descending rhizoids form a corticating layer around the lower cells of the main axis.

The cells are uninucleate and have an irregular band-shaped chromatophore or many discoid chromatophores with a smooth margin (Fig. 11-9). The chromatophore contains a projecting pyrenoid from which a new pyrenoid may develop by budding (Evans, 1966).

Mature, healthy cells have numerous large vacuoles as well as some small vesicles. These vesicles are more abundant in younger cells and seem to originate from the endoplasmic reticulum. They fuse with one another as well as with the larger vacuoles. In young cells,

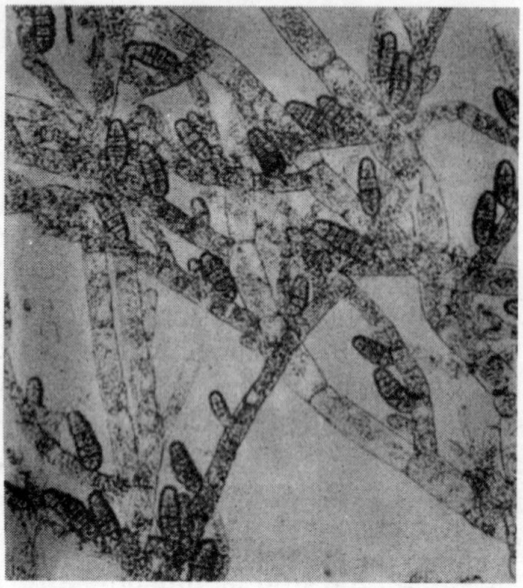

Fig. 11-8 *Ectocarpus*, habit and plurilocular sporangia.

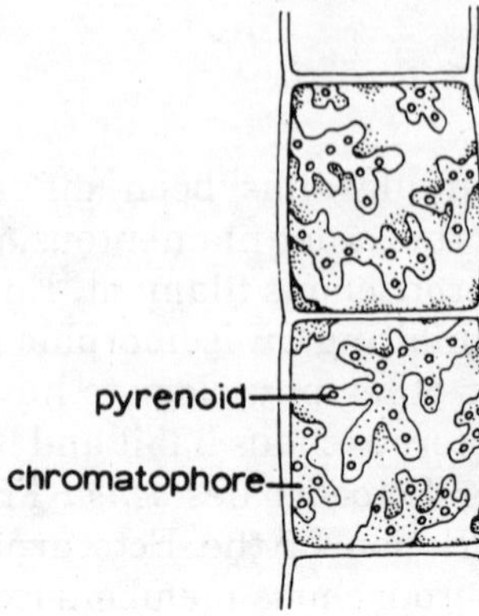

Fig. 11-9 *Ectocarpus siliculosus*, cell structure.

certain membranous projections or cisternae of the endoplasmic reticulum isolate and delimit pockets of cytoplasm. Subsequent dilation and separation of the isolating membranes lead to the formation of a vacuole-like structure which has a few vesicles (Oliviera and Bisalputra, 1977). Another method of partitioning-off and isolation of cellular materials involves the invagination of the vacuolar membrane in the region of contact with the material to be isolated. However, the foregoing two methods of autophagy do not seem to operate in one and the same cell. Autophagy in *Ectocarpus* is invariably associated with an intense reaction for acid phosphatase activity (i.e., lysosomal activity) and results in the formation of residual inclusions inside the vacuoles.

Like many other brown algae, the cells of *Ectocarpus* possess certain characteristic vacuoles, called physodes, which contain polyphenols and are thought to be lysosomal in function.

The growth and nutrition of *Ectocarpus confervoides* have been studied in unialgal, bacteria-free cultures (Boalch, 1961). The alga, which is obligately photoautotrophic, remains viable for over a year in the presence of light but for only about three months in darkness. Potassium nitrate, potassium phosphate, manganese chloride, and a mixture of organic substances stimulate its growth in natural sea water medium in the presence of light.

Reproduction

Asexual The sporophyte produces unilocular as well as plurilocular sporangia (Fig. 11-10) terminally and singly on small branchlets. During the development of a unilocular sporangium, the terminal cell of a branchlet enlarges considerably and assumes a globose or ellipsoid shape (Fig. 11-10 A–C) with numerous chromatophores. Meanwhile, the diploid nucleus of the unilocular sporangium undergoes a meiotic division and then many mitotic divisions until 32–64 haploid nuclei are formed. After nuclear divisions, the sporangial protoplast divides into a number of uninucleate segments, each with a single chromatophore corresponding to the number of haploid nuclei. Each segment is finally transformed into a haploid, biflagellate, pyriform zoospore in which the anterior longer flagellum is pantonematic and the posterior shorter flagellum is acronematic. After the protoplast of a sporangium has been used up in the formation of zoospores, a second sporangium may sometimes regenerate from within the wall of the first sporangium.

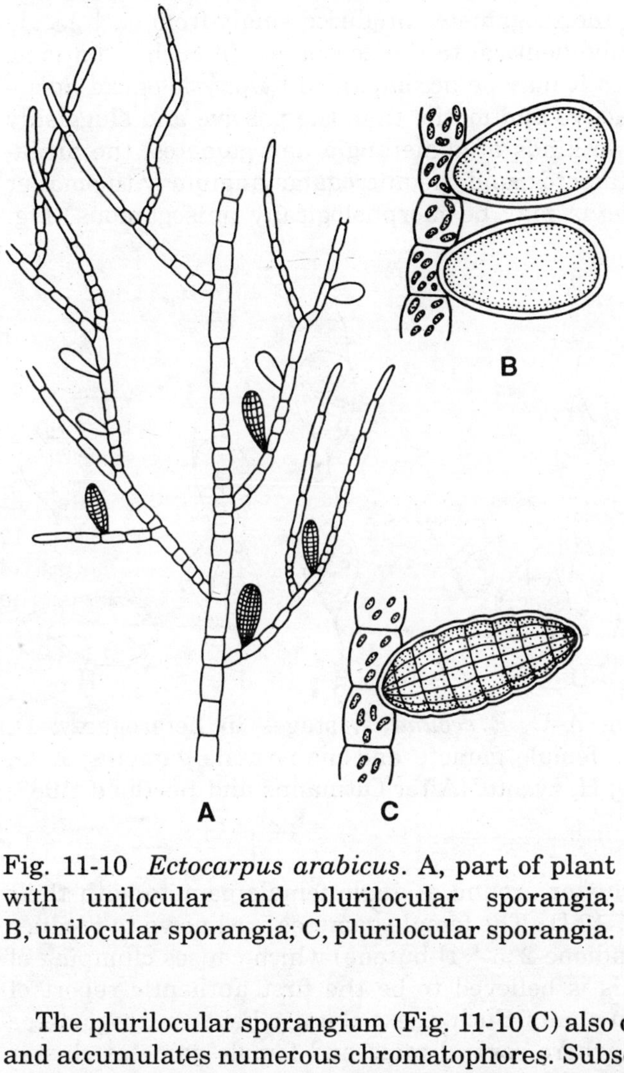

Fig. 11-10 *Ectocarpus arabicus*. A, part of plant with unilocular and plurilocular sporangia; B, unilocular sporangia; C, plurilocular sporangia.

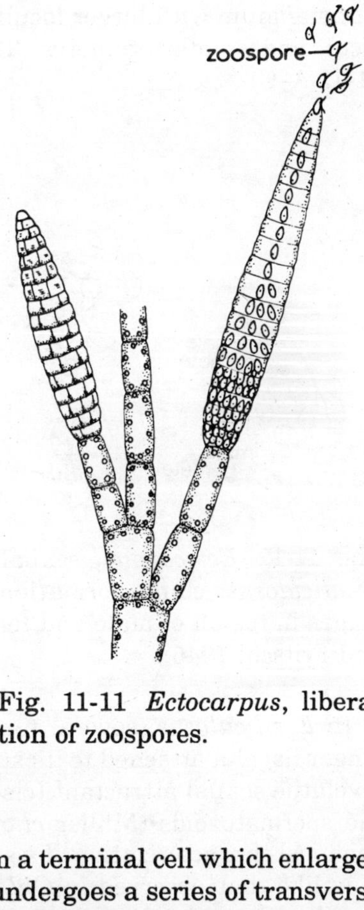

Fig. 11-11 *Ectocarpus*, liberation of zoospores.

The plurilocular sporangium (Fig. 11-10 C) also develops from a terminal cell which enlarges and accumulates numerous chromatophores. Subsequently, it undergoes a series of transverse and vertical mitotic divisions, producing several hundred small cubical cells arranged in definite tiers. Each cubical cell is diploid, uninucleate, and forms a single biflagellate zoospore identical to the zoospores produced from a unilocular sporangium, except that it is diploid. The haploid zoospores from unilocular sporangia are liberated en masse through a terminal pore but those from plurilocular sporangia generally come out one by one, in a rather orderly fashion, through a terminal (Fig. 11-11) or lateral pore. After moving freely for some time, the zoospores settle on some solid substratum and, with their anterior end still attached to some object, grow into new plants. The haploid zoospores from unilocular sporangia form gametophytes or sexual plants, whereas the diploid zoospores from a plurilocular sporangium produce sporophytes or asexual plants.

Sexual The plurilocular gametangia arise in a manner similar to the plurilocular sporangia of the diploid sporophyte. In *E. siliculosus*, which is heterothallic, the loculi of all the gametangia are of equal size. Consequently, the zoogametes produced singly from each locule are also of equal size and are morphologically identical to the zoospores. In such situations, the sexuality is isogamous though sometimes it may be accompanied by physiological anisogamy since the male gamete may be more active and motile than the passive and sluggishly motile female gamete. *E. secundus* forms two kinds of gametangia and gametes, the megagametangium with larger loculi and larger gametes, and the microgametangium with smaller loculi and smaller gametes. Thus, *E. secundus* may be morphologically anisogamous (Fig. 11-12 A–C).

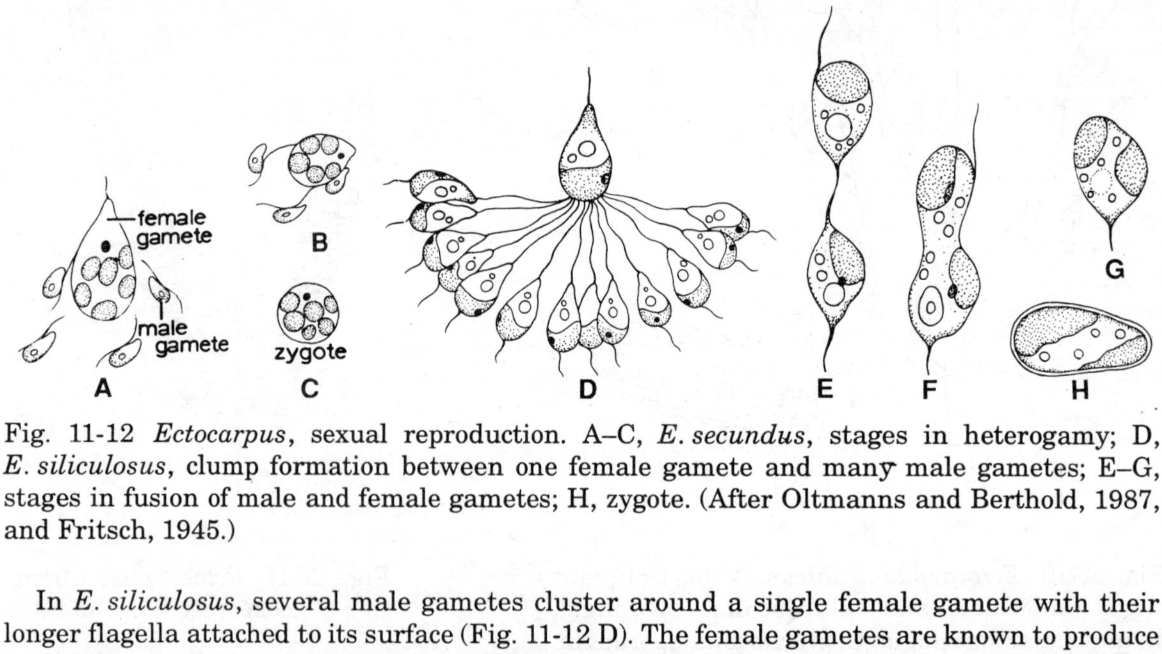

Fig. 11-12 *Ectocarpus*, sexual reproduction. A–C, *E. secundus*, stages in heterogamy; D, *E. siliculosus*, clump formation between one female gamete and many male gametes; E–G, stages in fusion of male and female gametes; H, zygote. (After Oltmanns and Berthold, 1987, and Fritsch, 1945.)

In *E. siliculosus*, several male gametes cluster around a single female gamete with their longer flagella attached to its surface (Fig. 11-12 D). The female gametes are known to produce a volatile sexual attractant (cis-1-[cycloheptadiene-2′,5′-y1]-butene) which causes clumping of the spermatozoids (Müller *et al.*, 1971). This is believed to be the first authentic report of chemical characterization of a sex hormone in plants. Such a sexual union between zoogametes is unlike that observed in *Chlamydomonas* where several male and female gametes cluster together through the agglutination of their flagellar ends. Ultimately, one of the male gametes fuses with the female (Fig. 11-12 E, F). The zygote (Fig. 11-12 G, H) always germinates directly into a new plant and during its germination no reduction division occurs. The resulting plant is therefore diploid and represents the asexual sporophyte. If a gamete fails to unite with another gamete, it may germinate directly into a new plant.

Müller (1979) has studied sexual compatibility in *E. siliculosus* in various geographic areas. Specimens collected from Norway and other parts of Europe, the Mediterranean, and

Australian and American shores were found to be highly or completely interfertile. Local populations of this species seem to be related closely enough to permit plasmogamy on a worldwide basis.

Alternation of Generations

Sexual plants of *Ectocarpus* are dioecious and form only plurilocular gametangia. The zygotes upon germination do not divide meiotically. Hence, the plants produced from germinating zygotes are all diploid, and bear both unilocular and plurilocular sporangia which always form diploid zoospores. Since meiosis does not occur during their formation, they invariably produce diploid sporophytic plants and serve as an accessory means of asexual reproduction. But during the formation of zoospores in unilocular sporangia, the first nuclear division is always meiotic and therefore such zoospores are haploid and germinate into haploid gametophytic plants.

The gametophytic and sporophytic generations of *Ectocarpus* are morphologically alike and indistinguishable and therefore its life cycle is isomorphic. However, recent researches have indicated that the life history may be much more flexible and variable than hitherto assumed. Müller's (1967) work on *E. siliculosus* has established that its life cycle is somewhat heteromorphic-diplohaplontic rather than strictly isomorphic. The germination of unfused gametes gives rise to haploid sporophytes which bear both unilocular and plurilocular sporangia. Similarly, diploid gamctophytes and tetraploid sporophytes may also arise under certain conditions.

Order: SPHACELARIALES

The algae belonging to the order Sphacelariales are markedly heterotrichous, have apical growth, and show a characteristic blackening of the cell walls when treated with bleaching liquor (eau de Javel).

Family: Sphacelariaceae
Genus: *Sphacelaria*

Occurrence

Sphacelaria occurs commonly as epiphyte in intertidal habitats. *S. fluviatilis* is freshwater.

Morphology

The thallus is made up of branched, heterotrichous filaments having prominent, dark apical cells, richly laden with fucosan granules. The apical cell (Fig. 11-13) cuts off primary segments parallel to its base. Each primary segment then divides to form two equal secondary segments. A further division of these segments produces the mature thallus in which the cell number increases but is not accompanied by increase in cell size (Fig. 11-13). Lateral branches arise from some outer cells of the segments (Fig. 11-13). The characteristic feature of *Sphacelaria* is the lack of growth or enlargement of the cells with the consequence that the diameter of the lateral branches remains about the same as that of the original apical cell, thereby producing the *leptocaulus* plant form.

The pattern of branching in *Sphacelaria* may be distichous, helicoid, or irregular. The laterals are generally determinate and may differ from the main axes in diameter and growth.

The daughter cells cut off from the apical cell also undergo vertical divisions so that a regular parenchymatous habit results (Fig. 11-13). By such vertical divisions, tiers of up to about 20 cells can be formed. Since these cells do not increase in size, the filament diameter remains more or less the same throughout. However, in some species, cortication occurs, leading to increase in girth of the filaments.

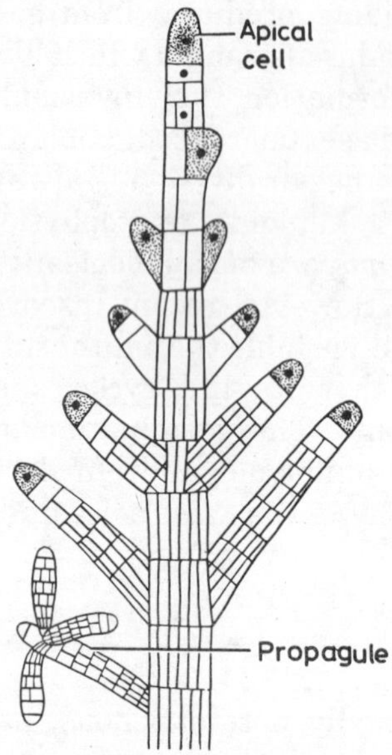

Fig. 11-13 *Sphacelaria*, habit and propagule formation.

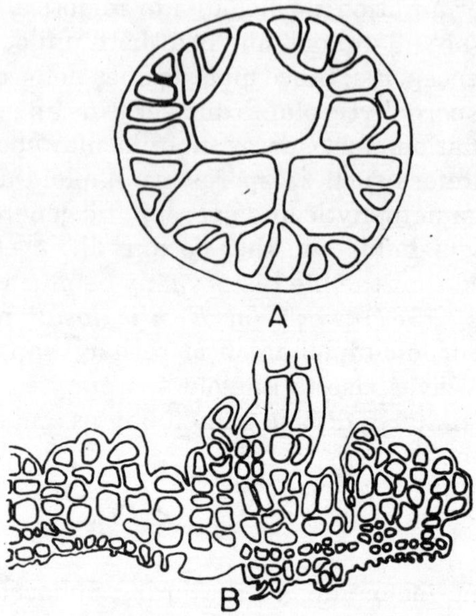

Fig. 11-14 *Sphacelaria californica*. A, transverse section of the middle portion of an erect filament; B, vertical section of the holdfast.

The hairs in this genus may be solitary or in bundles. Some species have distinct, dormant branch-initials, called pericysts.

In some species, the rhizoids arise regularly from the axis; in others, they arise in all directions, or irregularly. Most species are attached by means of a basal disc or by rhizoids. A few species may even be parasitic. In some cases, a species may be epiphytic on one alga, endophytic in another, and epilithic on the stones in between (Prudhomme van Reine, 1978).

S. californica is widely distributed in the Pacific Ocean and on the Japanese coast (Kitayama *et al*., 1991).

Thalli are epilithic or epiphytic and brown in colour. They form erect tufts up to 1.6 cm in height. The holdfasts are discoid and polystromatic (Fig. 11-14). Some are epiphytic on *Codium fragile*; these become rhizoidal and penetrate into the host tissues. The erect thalli are pinnately branched and composed of main axes and laterals. The main axes are straight and terete. The laterals are denser in the upper parts of the thalli, but sparser in the lower parts. Laterals are formed unilaterally or bilaterally. The apical cells of main axes and laterals are 45–60 μm in diameter and 90–200 μm long. The secondary segments are divided radially into several cells in transverse section (Fig. 11-15).

In a surface-lateral view, 3–10 longitudinal walls can be observed in a large secondary segment. The peripheral cells of the secondary segments are rectangular in surface view. The secondary transverse cell walls often occur in the peripheral cells of the segments. Phaeophycean hairs are at times observed to form adaxially. The propagules are borne adaxially on the laterals. They are ellipsoidal when young, becoming tribuliform as they develop. Mature propagules have three apical cells, containing abundant discoid chloroplasts without pyrenoids.

Figure 11-15 illustrates some propagules at various stages of development and germination.

S. britannica has fairly small, narrow, and virtually unbranched filaments. *S. fluviatilis* produces an irregular pseudoparenchymatous prostrate system from which uniseriate hairs as well as erect branches arise. The erect branches bear several lateral branches. The growth of both prostrate and erect systems is apical. The filaments become bi- or quadriseriate.

The fine structure of vegetative cells of *S. tribuloides* was studied by Galatis *et al.* (1977). They have reported numerous digitate ingrowing (Fig. 11-16) processes of the plasmalemma; these ingrowths project into the cytoplasm and partially enclose mitochondria. The fully developed portion of the thallus of this species shows 8 wedge-shaped cells in transection. These cells also possess distinct microbodies, generally associated with mitochondria. Sometimes, complex and wider associations between ER, chromatophores, mitochondria, microbodies can also be detected. The dictyosomes in *S. tribuloides* may be either perinuclear or scattered in the cytoplasm. The transverse walls between cells have numerous plasmodesmata.

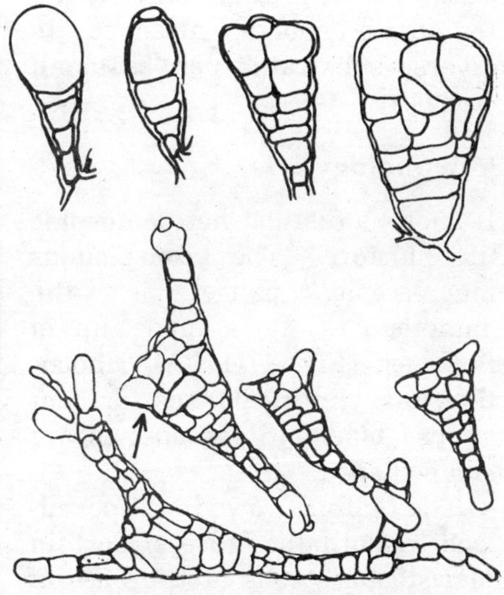

Fig. 11-15 *Sphacelaria californica* in culture (10°C, long day). Various stages of development and germination of propagules showing occasional divisions of the lateral apical cells (arrow). (After Kitayama *et al.*, 1991.)

Reproduction

Vegetative Vegetative propagation occurs by detachment of filament fragments and by the unique mode of formation of specialized triradiate or quadriradiate multicellular stalked branches, called propagules (Fig. 11-13). These detach and settle elsewhere, giving rise to a new plant.

Sexual *S. furcigera* is anisogamous. It has dioecious gametophytes which are slightly bigger than the sporophytes. Some species show isomorphic alternation of generations but *S. furcigera* is slightly heteromorphic.

Order: CUTLERIALES

This includes three genera of parenchymatous brown algae which show trichothallic growth and anisogamous reproduction.

Family: Cutleriaceae
Genus: *Cutleria*

Occurrence

Cutleria occurs commonly in the intertidal belt in spring and summer in subtropical and temperate shores, attached to diverse substrata such as small stones.

Morphology

It shows a distinct heteromorphic life history. The conspicuous macroscopic phase is the gametophyte. It is made up of flattened (Fig. 11-17 A), ribbon-like, or cylindrical axes, or fan-shaped blades. Some species are strap-shaped.

The thallus grows by a specialized trichothallic process. Certain meristematic cells at the base of hairs divide to give outer daughter cells and inner daughter cells. The former increase the length of the hair, whereas the inner cells undergo longitudinal divisions to increase the length of the main frond. The mature plant consists of larger inner cells bounded by small surface (cortical) cells.

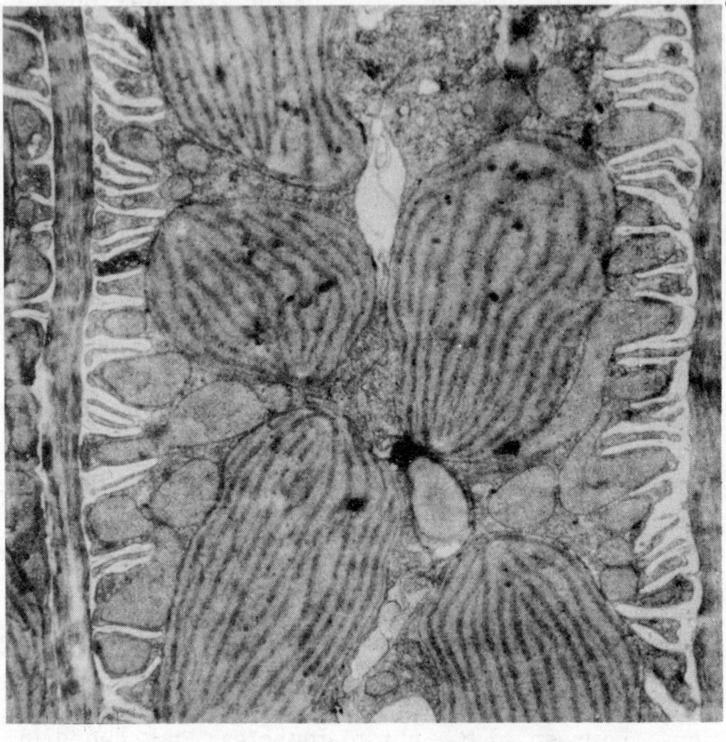

Fig. 11-16 *Sphacelaria tribuloides*, longitudinal section of part of cell. Note the finger-like infoldings associated with mitochondria, and formed by the plasmalemma along its walls. The infoldings form cytoplasmic pockets which are occupied by mitochondria. (×49,000.) *Courtesy* B. Galatis.

Reproduction

Vegetative Vegetative propagation occurs from detached fragments or branches.

Sexual The gametophyte bears anisogamous, plurilocular gametangia (Fig. 11-17 B, C). The chambers of the larger, female gametangium are bigger than those of the smaller, male gametangium. Each chamber produces a laterally biflagellate gamete, the gametes being anisogamous. Several male gametes may cluster around a female gamete before one of them fuses with the female. The zygote develops into the sporophytic phase.

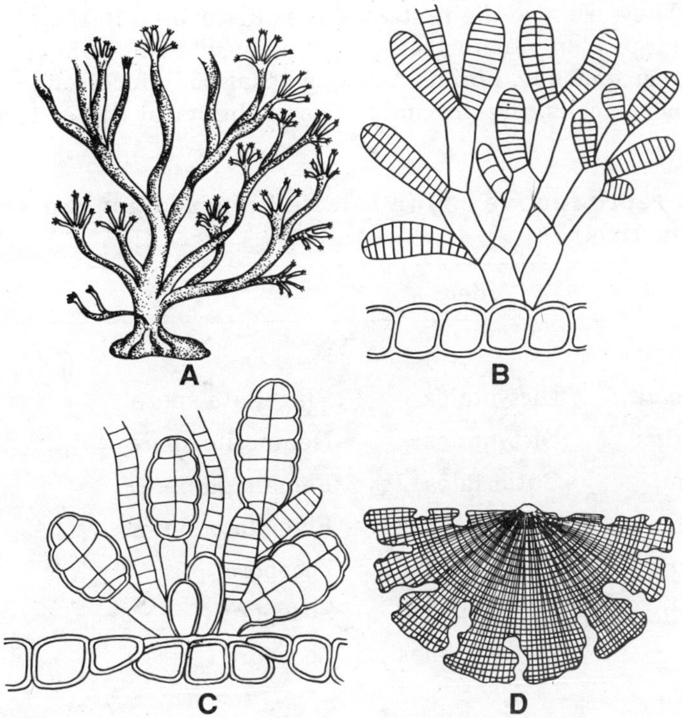

Fig. 11-17 *Cutleria multifida*. A, habit of gametophyte; B, male gametangia; C, female gametangia; D, *Aglaozonia* stage (sporophyte).

The sporophytic phase of *Cutleria* is a perennial, disc-like, parenchymatous, benthic or sublittoral alga, now named as the *Aglaozonia* stage (Fig. 11-17 D) of *Cutleria*. It grows by a marginal meristem. When mature, it bears clusters of unilocular sporangia over its surface. Meiosis occurs in these sporangia, resulting in the production of haploid zoospores which give rise to the gametophytic phase.

Order: DICTYOTALES

This includes tropical and subtropical marine brown algae characterized by apical growth, alternation of isomorphic phases, and pronounced oogamous reproduction, the gametophytes being unisexual. A unique feature of the order Dictyotales is the formation of four or, less commonly, eight (e.g., *Zonaria*) large nonflagellate spores. In most brown algae, spores are typically small (up to 15 μm long), pear-shaped, heterokont and motile; a few exceptions include *Haplospora globosa* (Tilopteridales) and some species of the Ectocarpales which release large, nonmotile spores. Table 11-2 compares the sizes of reproductive cells in selected macroalgae.

Much work has been done on the structure of mature sporangia in the Dictyotales (e.g., Tanaka, 1991) but very little on the released spores. Phillips and Clayton (1994) have reported that the biflagellate spores of *Homoeostrichus olsenii* are the largest motile reproductive cells for any macroalga. They are also the first zoospores discovered in the Dictyotales. Zoospores of *H. olsenii* have a large, elongate nucleus, very long basal bodies (indeed some of the longest for any alga) and a conspicuous, fibrous, nucleus-basal body interconnector. Unlike in most other brown algal motile cells, the proximal ends of the basal bodies terminate close to the nucleus.

Table 11-2 Size of reproductive cell in selected macroalgae (after Phillips and Clayton, 1994)

Species	Order	Type	Size (μm)
Brown algae			
Homoeostrichus olsenii	Dictyotales	Flagellate spore	46**
Dilophus fastigiatus	Dictyotales	Nonmotile spore	165* × 83
Cutleria multifida	Cutleriales	Female gamete	26*
Laminaria angustata	Laminariales	Flagellate ovum	25**
Zanardinia collaris	Cutleriales	Zoospore	22*
Ectocarpus sp.	Ectocarpales	Zoospore	10–12*
Alaria tenuifolia	Laminariales	Zoospore	7*
Green algae			
Derbesia clavaeformis	Derbesiales	Multiflagellate zoospore	30–40**
Ulva rigida	Ulvales	Zoospore	11* × 7

*Length.
**Diameter.

Family: Dictyotaceae
Genus: *Dictyota*

Occurrence

Species of *Dictyota* are common inhabitants of rock pools and of sublittoral habitats. *D. dichotoma* is widely distributed in tropical, subtropical, and temperate waters. *D. divaricata, D. indica*, and *D. maxima* are a few of the species common in India and Sri Lanka. *D. dichotoma* is common in Dwarka and Okha.

Morphology

Dictyota has a flattened, much divided thallus consisting of dichotomously branched, bushy, erect fronds (Figs. 11-18 A, B; 11-19 A). The plants are attached by a tuft of rhizoids. In some species, the branching is pinnate rather than dichotomous. The tips of the fronds bear a prominent apical cell which cuts off transverse segments proximally. Divisions of these segments form walls parallel to the surface. This results in a primary medullary cell and a primary cortical cell on each surface. The cortical cells undergo anticlinal divisions. Thus, the fronds become parenchymatous, having three cell layers of which the middle (medullary) layer has larger cells lacking chromatophores and a surface layer on either side having smaller cells containing numerous discoid chromatophores.

D. dichotoma grows by means of a single lenticular or elliptical apical cell. This cell undergoes two distinct types of division: one perpendicular to the thallus axis, giving rise to a new apical cell and a discoid derivative, and one parallel to the thallus axis, producing two apical cells and thereby initiating a dichotomous branching of the plant (Katsaros and Galatis, 1985).

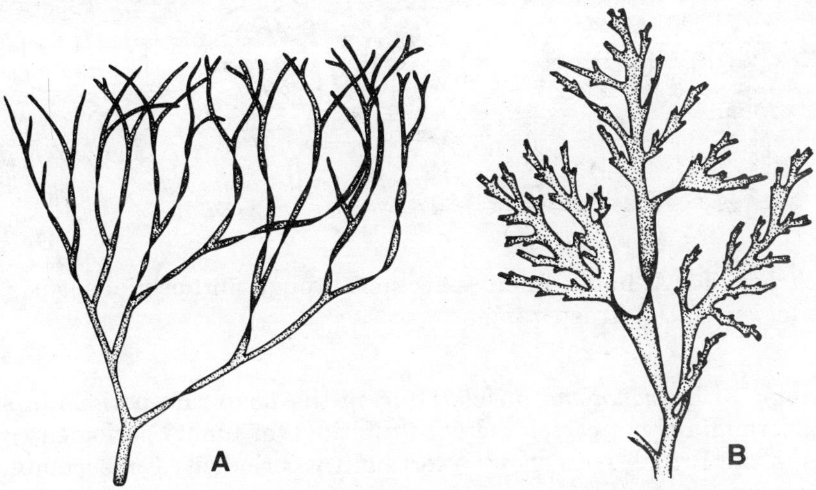

Fig. 11-18 *Dictyota*, habit. A, *D. indica*; B, *D. dentata*.

The descendants of the initial epidermal cells show greater meristematic activity than those of the initial medullary cell and grow mainly by synthesis of protoplasm. During differentiation, they retain a highly secretory ribosomal cytoplasm and contain active plastids, microbodies, and mitochondria. Later, the epidermal cells lose their secretory properties and become more active in photosynthesis. In contrast, the medullary cells grow mainly by vacuolation, lack distinct plastids, and their cytoplasm is structurally much simpler. These cells become parenchymatous and are not so active photosynthetically. They are involved more in storage function (Katsaros and Galatis, 1985).

D. dichotoma has an entire margin but *D. ciliolata* has dentate margin.

Some species occurring in stressful habitats, or habitats subject to much herbivory, grow as a colonial turf rather than as individual thalli. In a turf, the upright branches are packed together in such a way that each branch is in contact with its neighbours. Besides *Dictyota*, many other seaweeds growing in tropical and temperate intertidal habitats, especially in shallow reefs, show tufted growths. The turf-forming species produce both upright and prostrate branches and they show considerable morphological plasticity (Hay, 1981). Turf-forming seaweeds appear to suffer less physiological damage during desiccating low tides and also lose less biomass to herbivores, as compared to nonturf-forming species.

Reproduction

Vegetative Some fronds may detach and then regenerate new thalli.

Sexual Reproductive structures are well developed on the lower portions and along the margins of fronds, and usually occur together in sori or patches.

Sexual reproduction in *Dictyota* is strongly controlled by light and the tidal rhythms. Thus,

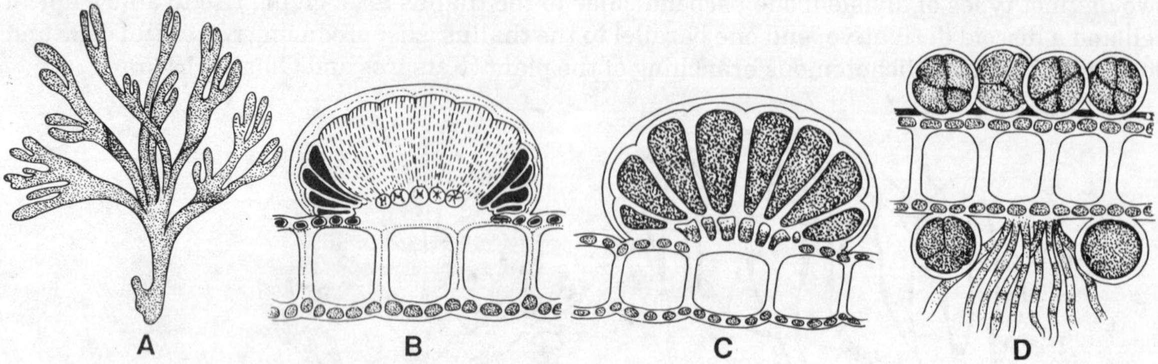

Fig. 11-19 *Dictyota dichotoma*. A, habit; B, cross-section through antheridial sorus; C, cross-section through oogonial sorus; D, tetrasporangia.

in Wales, the gametangia of *D. dichotoma* develop during the neap tide periods in summer, but the formation of sporangia is not correlated with the tidal (or lunar) periodicity. Gametic release of this species in the British Isles shows a fortnightly periodicity corresponding to the interval between successive spring tides.

The male gametophytes bear plurilocular antheridia arranged in sori (Fig. 11-19 B) on both surfaces of the blade. Each chamber of an antheridium produces a uniflagellate spermatozoid. Some vegetative cells near a sorus divide to form a protective involucre over the antheridia.

The oogonia also occur in sori (Fig. 11-19 C) but each oogonium produces a single nonmotile oosphere. The egg cell enclosed in gelatinous matrix is released from oogonium and then escapes from the matrix. It is then fertilized by the spermatozoid. The zygote attaches itself to a substratum and germinates into the diploid sporophyte.

Life History

The diploid plants resemble the haploid gametophytes morphologically. They bear superficial tetrasporangia (most probably homologous with unilocular sporangia). The tetrasporangia occur scattered singly or in small groups (Fig. 11-19 D). Each tetrasporangium produces four nonmotile, haploid tetraspores by meiosis. Two of the four tetraspores give rise to male gametophytes and the other two develop into female gametophytes.

Order: LAMINARIALES

Popularly called kelps, these seaweeds exemplify the largest and most highly differentiated algae known. They often constitute the dominant algal flora of some coastal waters. *Ecklonia stolonifer* has been collected from a depth of about 200 metres below the surface. This is a world record for a marine alga. Many kelps form forests in the ocean. Figure 11-20 illustrates a generalized food web for a kelp forest. In nature, growth and reproduction of perennial kelps are seasonal being low or absent in summer and fairly rapid in winter.

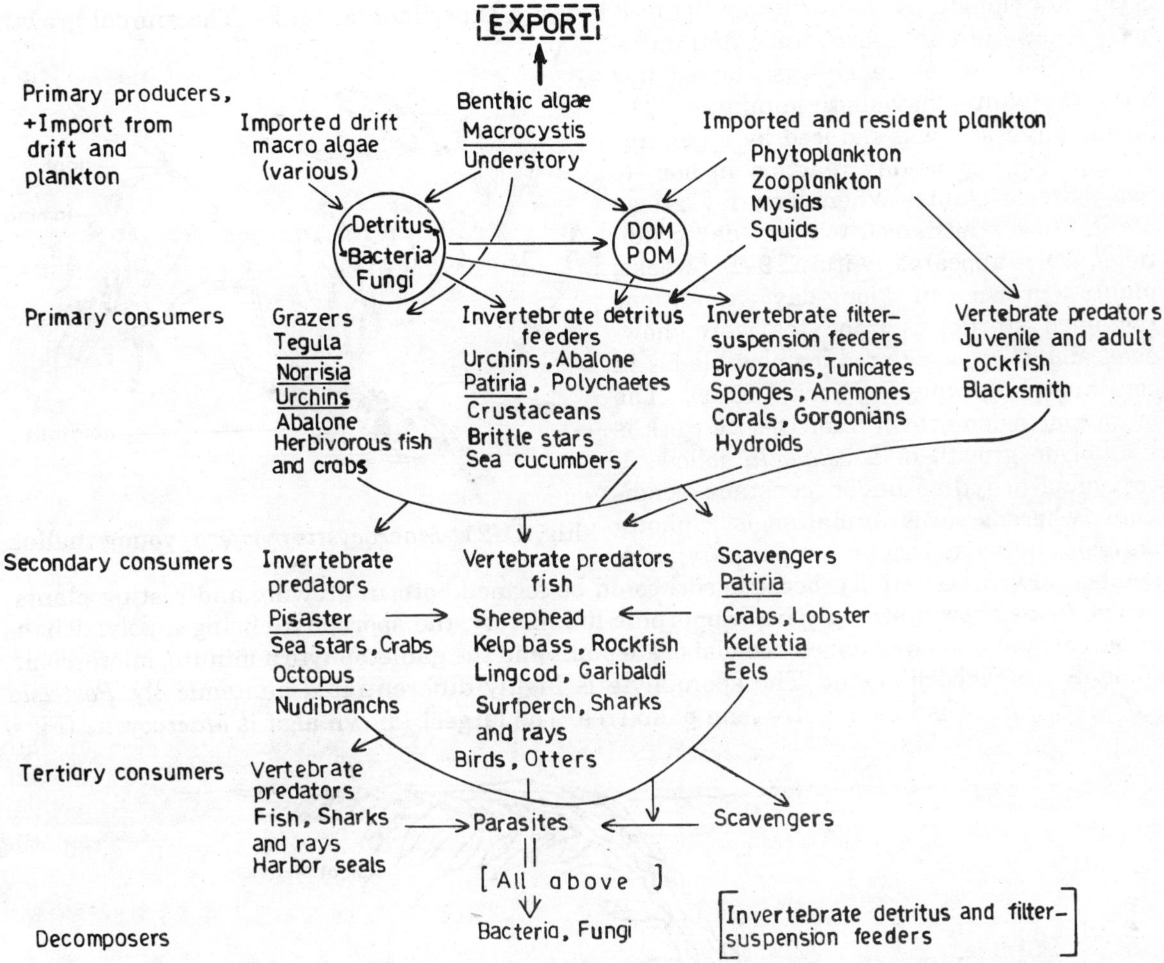

Fig. 11-20 A generalized food web for a kelp forest. Arrows indicate the direction of energy flow. DOM, dissolved organic matter; POM, particulate organic matter.

Nitrogen and other nutrients appear to modify the seasonal growth cycle. The growth cycle may also be controlled by daylength or endogenous rhythms. Lüning (1986, 1988) reported the formation of the new blades in *Laminaria hyperborea* and the formation of sori in *L. saccharina* under short-day conditions.

L. setchellii forms annual rings in its stipe and is deciduous, implying an annual growth/rest cycle. Dieck (1991) studied the significance of photoperiod in growth and reproduction of this kelp in a tank system with controlled conditions of daylength, temperature, and certain nutrients. There was indefinite growth of frond in short-day conditions but in continuous long-day and night-break conditions the growth was rhythmic. The growth rhythm of individual plants could be synchronized by a simulated annual cycle of daylength with a period of one year. The four seasons were simulated at the same time by phase shifting the annual cycle of daylength by 3, 6 or 9 months in 3 out of 4 experimental tanks. The annual growth cycle followed these phase shifts, and initiation of the new blade always started just after the winter daylength minimum. The formation of sori was induced by a genuine photoperiodic short-day reaction in one- to two-year old-plants. When long-day grown plants were transferred to short-day conditions, sori appeared within 9–14 weeks; plants grown in long-day conditions remained sterile. Sporophytes were, however, able to grow or produce new blades in continuous darkness (Dieck, 1991). The main conclusion drawn from Dieck's work is that blade growth of *L. setchellii* follows a circannual rhythm under constant conditions, whereas sorus formation is a photoperiodic short-day reaction apparently independent of growth activity, because sori could be formed both in growing and resting plants.

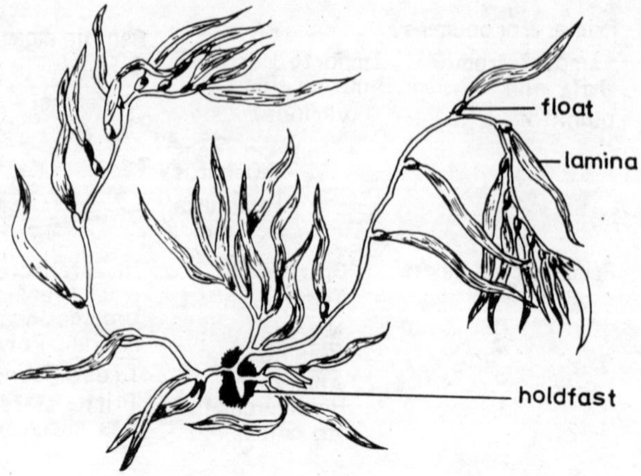

Fig. 11-21 *Macrocystis pyrifera*, young thallus.

The kelps show a strongly heteromorphic life history, the sporophyte being a polystichous or parenchymatous well developed elaborate plant and the gametophyte a minute, microscopic, sparsely branched filament. The sporophyte is highly differentiated anatomically. *Postelsia palmaeformis* looks like a metre long palm tree. The largest known alga is *Macrocystis* (Figs.

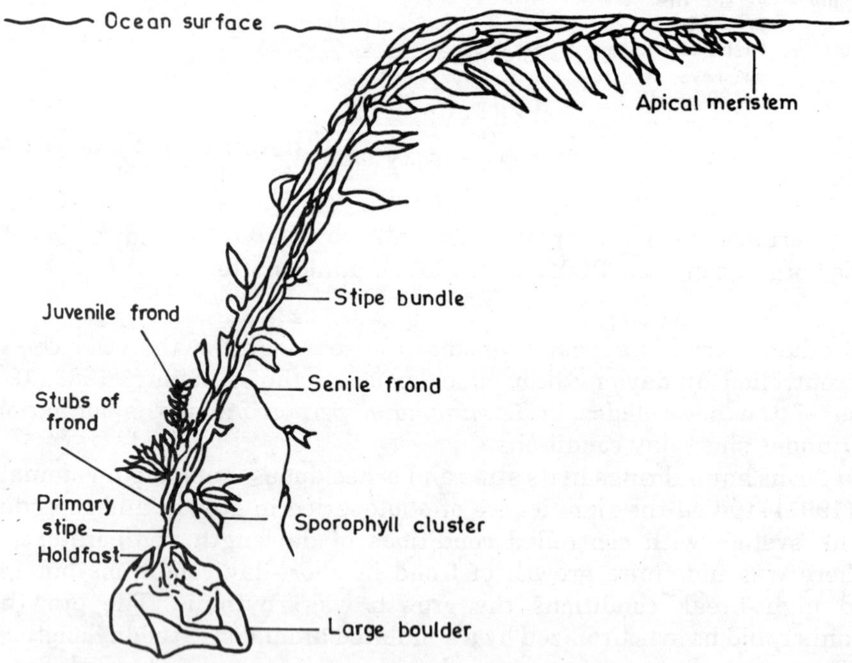

Fig. 11-22 *Macrocystis pyrifera*, adult plant.

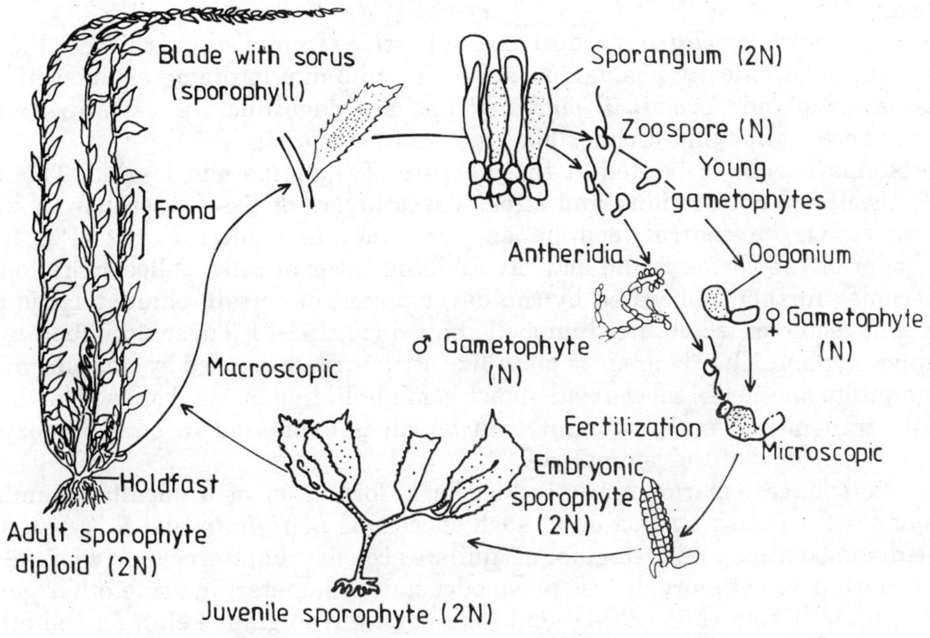

Fig. 11-23 *Macrocystis pyrifera*, morphology and life history.

11-21, 11-22, 11-23), reaching over 30 metres length. In contrast, the simplest member of the order is represented by the genus *Chorda* which has a long, hollow, cylindrical or tubular sporophyte generation. The sporophyte of *C. tomentosa* increases in girth by repeated anticlinal divisions in a superficial meristematic layer, the meristoderm. The whip-like thallus is covered with several multicellular photosynthetic hairs. The thallus is differentiated into a discoid holdfast, a narrow stipe, and an elaborate hollow tube. The inconspicuous stipe lacks hairs. *Chorda* plants are annuals.

Family: Laminariaceae
Genus: *Laminaria*

Occurrence

It grows in sublittoral forests, and is extensively farmed in China and Japan. It is mainly a cold water alga and is rare in the Indian Coast.

Morphology

The plant is differentiated into a holdfast, stipe, and blade or lamina (Fig. 11-2).

The holdfast is a sucker-like organ bearing several haptera which regenerate readily and anchor the plant firmly to the substratum.

The haptera adhere very closely to the crevices of the substratum. The initial fixation of an hapteron to the substratum is brought about by the production of rhizoid-like outgrowths from the outer cells of the meristoderm. These cells fill up all the microcrevices in the substratum until an exact impression of the profile of the substratum is built up. They also secrete mucilage which helps cement them to the substratum as well as to the adjoining rhizoidal cells.

Some species, e.g., *L. sinclairii*, produce multiple stipes from a single rhizome-like holdfast. This species characteristically has narrow stipes (up to 3 mm in diameter) as well as narrow blades (less than 50 mm broad). *L. sinclairii* has mucilage ducts in its stipe, whereas *L. longipes* has shorter stipe and broader blades than *L. sinclairii*.

The meristematic zone is located at the juncture of the stipe and lamina. This meristem contributes tissues to both lamina and stipe. Three layers of tissue result from this meristematic activity, viz., a central medulla and an inner and outer cortex (Fig. 11-3). The outermost layer of the cortex is the actively dividing layer of cells, called meristoderm. The medulla becomes further elaborated by the development of certain characteristic cross-connecting hyphae, some of which are dumbbell-shaped (Fig. 11-3). These dumbbell hyphae are called trumpet hyphae. They bear sieve plate-like structures traversed by cytoplasmic strands.

The nondigitate species *L. saccharina* shows some bullation on its fronds. This bullation is a genetically transmitted and dominant trait which is expressed in both homozygous and heterozygous conditions of the sporophyte.

Some workers have experimentally induced the formation of a cucullate lamina under conditions of shelter from wave action in such species as *L. digitata* and *L. hyperborea*.

The long distance transport system for assimilates consists of interconnected sieve elements which have sieve pores of more or less plasmodesmatal diameter; in some other genera, e.g., *Nereocystis* [the bull kelp (Fig. 11-24)] and *Macrocystis* (the giant kelp), on the other hand, the sieve elements are much wider, more specialized, and have large pores. The chief translocates in most Laminariales are mannitol and several amino acids. In different genera, the translocation velocities range from 10–50 cm/hr and the velocity seems to depend on the diameter of the sieve pores.

The lamina bears sori of unilocular sporangia. These sporangia are club-shaped and associated with numerous paraphyses. Each sporangium produces about 32 pyriform, laterally and unequally biflagellate zoospores meiotically. In England, the sporophytes of *L. hyperborea* produce sori from September to April. Long lived gametophytes and small sporophytes exist under the algal cover and can start growing when sufficient light becomes available. The gametophytes particularly can survive in the dark for long periods. The fast growing period in this species starts in November, partly from reserves, and new fronds are formed by the spring when adequate light is available; these fronds can live and grow right through the brightest months of the year. These fronds do not bear sori during periods of high light intensity. The end of the fertile season coincides with the loss of old fronds.

The sporophytes of *L. sinclairii* and *L. longipes* bear sori in patches on both sides of the blade.

The free-swimming zoospores of *Laminaria* have numerous scales containing mucopolysaccharides or glycoproteins. These scales occur around the cytoplasm. After settling and attachment, most of the zoospores germinate but the remaining few become converted into thick-walled resting spores. The germinating zoospores withdraw their flagella and develop their cell walls and germ tubes simultaneously.

Reproduction

Vegetative It occurs from detached pieces of lamina or from old holdfasts. *L. sinclairii* mostly reproduces by proliferation of new stipes from its holdfast.

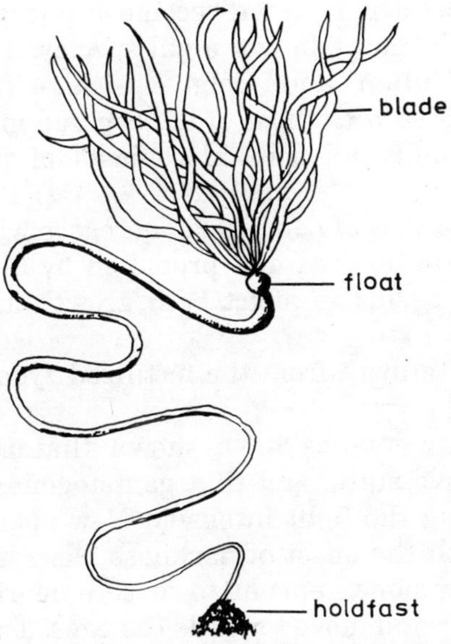

Fig. 11-24 *Nereocystis luetkeana*, habit.

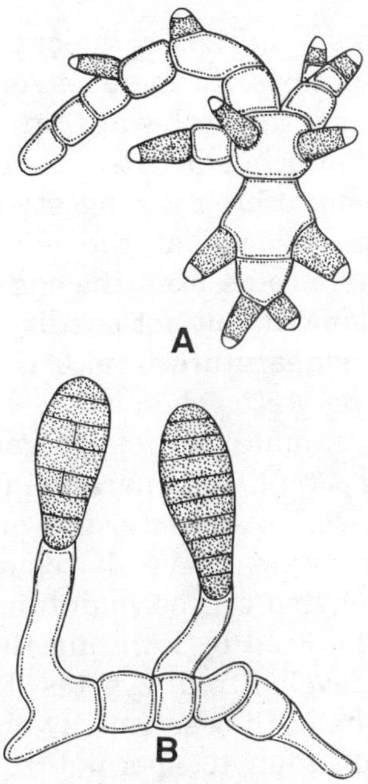

Fig. 11-25 *Laminaria*, gametophytes. A, male gametophyte; B, female gametophyte, bearing young sporophyte.

Sexual The male and female gametophytes develop from germinating zoospores. These gametophytes are microscopic, sparingly branched, ectocarpoid filaments (Fig. 11-25 A, B). In male gametophytes, the antheridial cytoplasm rounds off during its conversion into the male gamete and the Golgi bodies secrete mucilage which aids in the bursting of the antheridium, leading to the release of gametes (Fig. 11-26). The male gametophytes of *L. sinclairii* are branched and have smaller but more numerous cells than female gametophytes which are also sparsely branched. Dimorphism of gametophytes is much less conspicuous in *L. longipes*. *Laminaria* is oogamous.

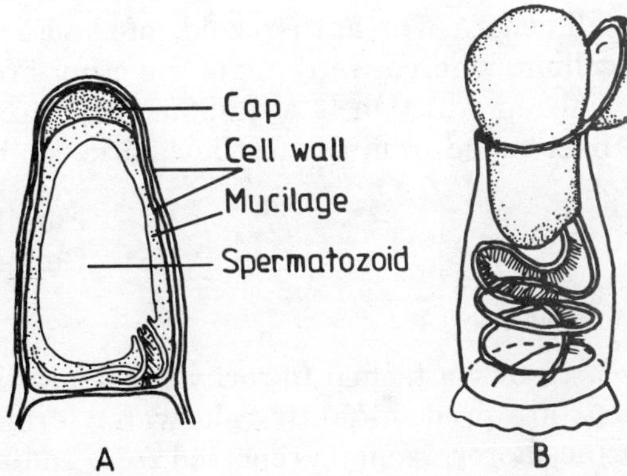

Fig. 11-26 Antheridium of *L. digitata*. A, mature antheridium; B, release of spermatozoid. The cap is pushed away and the sperm is forced out of the antheridium.

In *Laminaria angustata*, wall formation of the zygote is initiated immediately after plasmogamy. The zygote elongates, chloroplasts move from the centre to the periphery, and the sperm nucleus moves towards the egg nucleus (Motomura, 1990). Karyogamy occurs when both the male and the female nuclei are in interphase stage. At this time the male nucleus is rich in heterochromatin whereas the female nucleus is rich in euchromatin. In the early zygote of this species, there occur two pairs of centrioles, originating from the egg and sperm. Later, the egg centrioles disappear and only the sperm centrioles remain. At zygotic mitosis, the members of the surviving pair of centrioles separate and become duplicated as they migrate poleward, in a manner typical of mitosis in many brown algal species. The sperm mitochondria are enclosed by endoplasmic reticulum and Golgi vesicles. The mitochondria are soon digested. The sperm plastids do not fuse with those of the egg and may be detected even at the bicelled sporophyte stage. Virtually all the chloroplasts of the sporophyte come from the egg (Motomura, 1990).

The growth, but not fertility, of male and female gametophytes of *L. digitata* increases with rise in temperature from 0°C to 20°C. Fertility is mainly influenced and promoted by blue light. The water chemistry, especially the SO_4^{--}/Cl^- ratio, seems to affect both growth and fertility of male and female gametophytes.

The sporophyte generation develops as a filamentous outgrowth from the fertilized zygote (Fig. 11-25 B), and later grows into the adult plant.

Most species have dioecious gametophytes. The culture studies have shown that the gametophytes can be maintained indefinitely in a vegetative state, and that gametogenesis can be induced by lowering the temperature and increasing the light intensity. New sporophytes develop from zygotes. Lüning (1981) found that with the onset of darkness, eggs are released and they secrete a volatile pheromone. If this pheromone happens to reach a nearby male gametophyte, spermatozoids are ejected from the latter and move towards the eggs. This pheromone, named lamoxirene, has been identified as a compound $C_{11}H_{14}O$ with the structure 1-(1′2′-cis-epoxibut-3′-enyl)-cyclohepta-2,5-diene (Müller *et al.*, 1985).

Order: FUCALES

The Fucales are characterized by the absence of alternation between multicellular sporophytic and free-living multicellular gametophytic generations in the life cycle. The plants are all sporophytic or diploid. The gametophytic or haploid phase is restricted to the unicellular sperms and eggs produced within unicelled reproductive organs termed antheridia and oogonia.

The number of eggs produced inside an oogonium ranges from one, two, four to eight in various genera, but that of antherozoids within an antheridium is constant, being nearly 64 for all genera. The antherozoids of the Fucales have a shorter anterior and a longer posterior flagellum, whereas in those of the other brown algae the arrangement is just the reverse. The sexual reproduction is oogamous and at the time of fertilization eggs and antherozoids are both extruded from the fertile cavities or the conceptacles.

Family: Fucaceae
Genus: *Fucus*

Occurrence

Fucus grows attached to rocky substrata in the intertidal belt of the littoral zone. Species of *Fucus* are predominantly cold water forms and grow luxuriantly in the North Atlantic and Pacific shores. None is reported from India.

The typical habitat of *Fucus vesiculosus* is the mid-littoral of a moderatcly exposed rocky shore bathed by water of up to 35‰ salinity. The alga is usually benthic but also occurs free-floating in salt marshes. It grows attached to the bottom in the eulittoral in less saline waters in estuaries, marshes, and as a sublittoral haptophyte in the Baltic Sea.

Morphology

Fucus, commonly less than 0.5 metre in length (the length depends on the degree of exposure), has a complex vegetative organization. Externally, each plant is differentiated into a basal discoid holdfast which anchors it to the substratum, a short stipe, and a flattened, dichotomously branched frond or blade (Fig. 11-27). The thallus is generally dark brown, and slimy to the touch. The stipe is continued in the form of a midrib in the frond of many species, though it never reaches the frond apex. *F. vesiculosus* contains a number of air bladders in pairs and these give buoyancy to the submerged plants. The mature thallus is in some respects similar to animal cartilage, the cells being embedded in a biphasic matrix composed of rigid fibres of alginic acid and cellulose.

The swollen tips of fertile branches harbour a large number of small, somewhat raised, flask-shaped cavities—the conceptacles (Fig. 11-28 A)—which contain the antheridia and

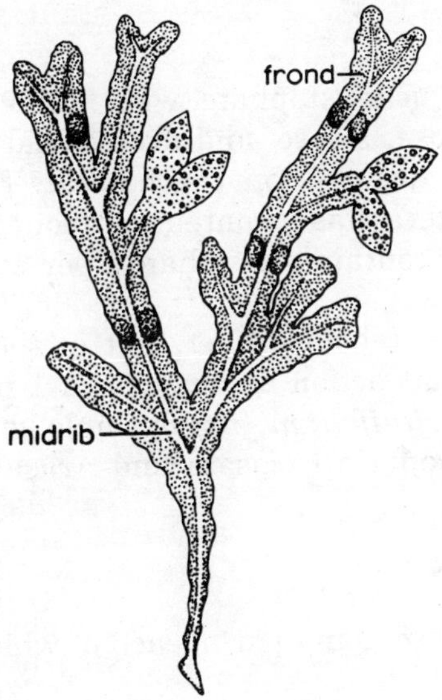

Fig. 11-27 *Fucus vesiculosus*, thallus morphology.

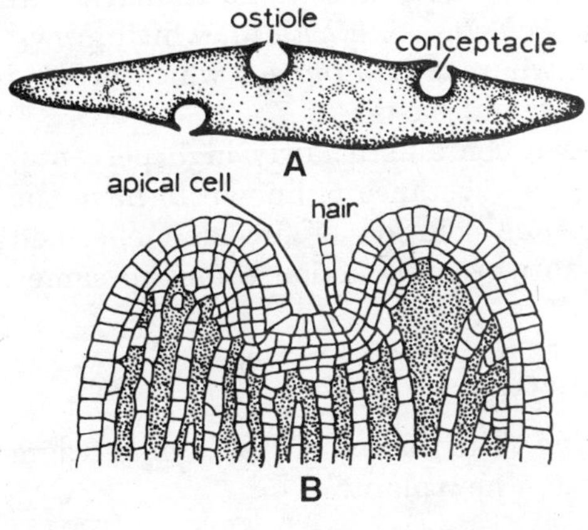

Fig. 11-28 *Fucus*, sections through male receptacle and apex. A, *F. serratus*, transverse section through male receptacle; B, *F. vesiculosus*, vertical section through apex.

oogonia and open to the exterior through an ostiole. Lateral to the midrib are formed flat, wing-like expansions of the thallus with sterile conceptacles, called cryptoblasts or cryptostomata.

Internally, the thallus is differentiated into three distinct regions—an outer single-layered epidermis called the meristoderm, a central many-layered cortex, and an inner several-layered medulla. The cells of the medullary region are loosely arranged, some of them forming an anastomosing network of hyphae. These first-formed hyphae are smooth-walled and are called primary hyphae which may develop secondary thickening at maturity. The region of the cortex close to the medulla has much elongated mucilaginous cells but the outer cortical cells and those of the epidermis are provided with chromatophores.

The growth of the thallus is initiated by an apical cell (Fig. 11-28 B) situated in the hollow depression at the branch apex. The apical meristem is like a truncated pyramid with three cutting faces—two lateral and one basal. The lateral segments derived from the meristem initially divide periclinally; of the resulting two cells, the outer one, by repeated divisions in various planes, organizes the epidermis and the cortex, whereas the inner one, in association with the basal segment cut off by the apical meristem, forms the medulla. The epidermal layer as well as the inner cells of the cortex retain meristematic potentiality; the former, by cell divisions in the vertical plane, increases the girth, and the latter gives rise to secondary hyphae. Thus, in addition to primary growth, the alga exhibits secondary growth.

In respect of functional differentiation, the epidermis and the chromatophore containing cortical region are photosynthetic; the inner cortical region stores food reserves, and the medullary cells are conductive in nature. The primary and secondary hyphae serve a mechanical function.

Fucoidan

Isolated from *Fucus vesiculosus*, fucoidan is a polymer of fucan sulphate with units of L-fucose-4-sulphate and may contain small amounts of galactose, xylose, and uronic acid in some cases. Fucoidan content changes with the season and depends on the habitat. For instance, *Pelvetia canaliculata*, which grows in fairly deep waters, has a content of about 23 per cent, whereas *Laminaria*, which grows in littoral regions, contains less than 7 per cent on a dry weight basis.

Fucoidan contains a fairly high percentage of sulphate ester (about 30 per cent in some cases). This substance is known to have the same anticoagulant action as heparin. A 1 per cent aqueous solution of fucoidan obtained from *Sargassum linifolium*, for example, has greater antithrombic action than the same concentration of heparin (Arasaki and Arasaki, 1983).

Reproduction

Vegetative The thallus of *Fucus* may fragment or dissociate into many parts, each of which grows into a new plant.

Sexual *Fucus* is monoecious (*F. spiralis*) or dioecious (*F. vesiculosus*). It may bear both antheridia and oogonia in the same or in different conceptacles on the same plant in the monoecious species, and in separate conceptacles on different plants in the dioecious species.

Interspecific hybridization occurs rather readily in certain monoecious species of *Fucus*. It is rare or absent in dioecious species of *Fucus*, or in *Ascophyllum* (Bolwell *et al*., 1977). In these latter taxa, certain barriers prevent both interspecific and intergeneric hybridization. Intergeneric hybridization seems to be fairly common in some members of the Lessoniaceae (Sanbonsuga and Neushul, 1980).

A conceptacle develops from a superficial cell whose rate of growth and cell division slow down in comparison with those of neighbouring cells. Consequently, this apical cell comes to lie at the base of a flask-shaped cavity (Fig. 11-29 A). This development is followed by transverse division of the apical initial into two cells, a lower basal cell and an upper tongue cell (Fig. 11-29 B). The latter may develop into a hair or degenerate. The basal cell, by a series of vertical divisions, gives rise to a layer of chromatophore-containing cells which line the floor

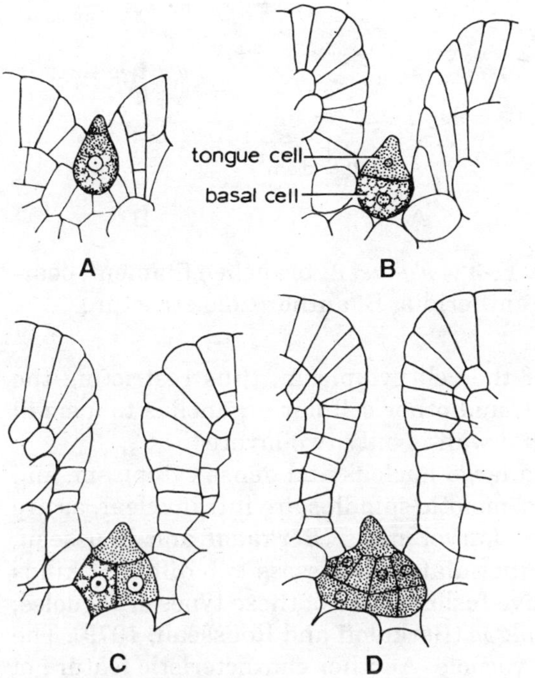

Fig. 11-29 *Fucus serratus*. A–D, early stages in development of conceptacle.

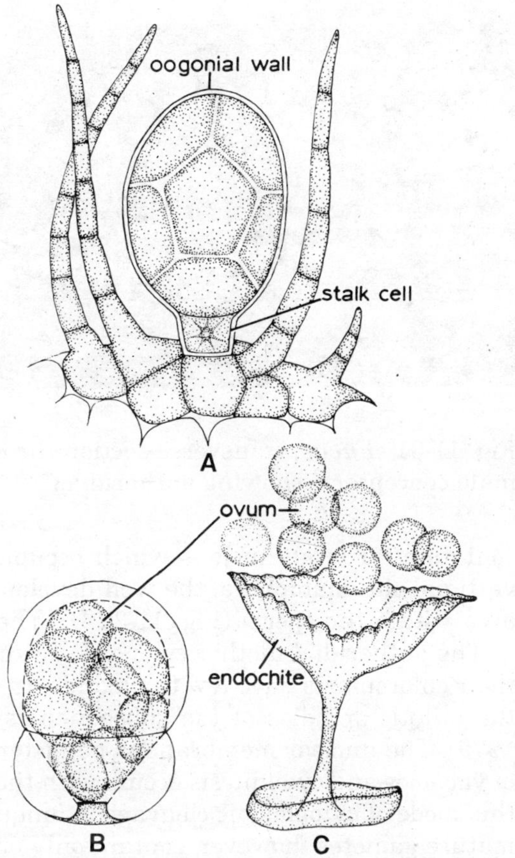

Fig. 11-30 *Fucus vesiculosus*. A, oogonium; B, C, formation and liberation of ova.

of the cavity. These cells undergo one or two transverse divisions and form 2–3 layers (Fig. 11-29 C, D) of which the superficial layer is always fertile, giving rise to antheridia or oogonia, or both.

The superficial cells which start functioning as oogonial mother cells divide into a lower stalk cell and an upper oogonial cell (Fig. 11-30 A). The first two divisions of the oogonial nucleus are always meiotic, invariably followed by a mitotic division of all the four haploid nuclei. The eight-nucleate oogonial protoplast cleaves into eight uninucleate eggs (Fig. 11-30 B, C) enclosed inside a three-layered oogonial wall. The remaining cells of the superficial layer which fail to act as oogonial mother cells develop into multicellular hairs. Some of the peripheral cells near the ostiole also form unbranched hair-like appendages which emerge from the ostiole in the form of a tuft.

The antheridia are formed on lower branches (Figs. 11-31, 11-32 A) of the hairs produced from the superficial cells lining the cavity. Like the oogonial nucleus, the antheridial nucleus also divides meiotically, followed by four consecutive mitotic divisions of the four haploid nuclei. Then after the completion of nuclear division, the antheridial protoplast fragments into 64 uninucleate, phototactic antherozoids bearing two lateral flagella of unequal length and

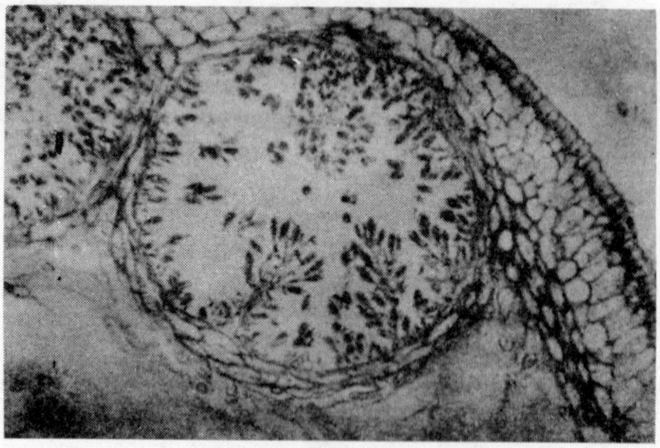

Fig. 11-31 *Fucus*, transverse section through male conceptacle showing antheridia.

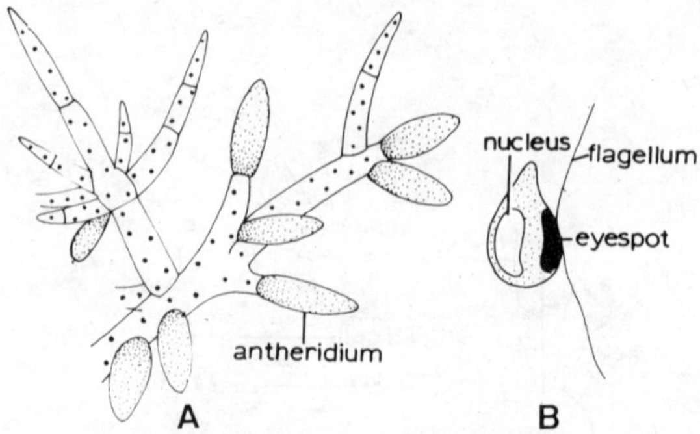

Fig. 11-32 *Fucus*. A, branched filament, bearing antheridia; B, antherozoid structure.

containing a large nucleus which occupies most of the cell cytoplasm, thus restricting the vestigial chromatophore, the well developed eyespot, and other cellular organelles to a small area within the sperm (Fig. 11-32 B). The antheridial wall is only two-layered.

The antheridial mother cells of *F. serratus* have a large nucleus and dense cytoplasm, and their chloroplasts have few thylakoids. In these cells, meiotic spindles are intranuclear, as are the mitotic spindles of the subsequent synchronous karyokinesis (Berkaloff and Rousseau, 1979). The nuclear membrane is persistent. The antheridial cells possess two different kinds of vacuoles and cytokinesis occurs with the progressive fusion of one of these types of vacuoles; this mode of cytoplasmic cleavage is unique among algae (Berkaloff and Rousseau, 1979). The mature gametes, however, contain only one kind of vacuole. Another characteristic feature of *Fucus* (and other Fucales) is the nature and composition of the antheridial wall; the mature antheridium has two definite dense fibrillar walls separated by a clear area.

During antherozoid development, the eyespot originates *de novo* as the vegetative cells do not have any eyespots. In a detailed study of the eyespot of *F. vesiculosus*, Bouck (1970) observed the following stages of development: (1) appearance of electron-opaque granules along the chromatophore; (2) increase in size of the granules; (3) shifting of chromatophore, along with the eyespot, from the centre of the cell towards its periphery, followed by fusion with the plasma membrane. Four distinct microtubules and a few fibrils arise near the base of the posterior flagellum between the chromatophore and the plasma membrane. It is believed that the granules of the eyespot arise from these microtubules and fibrils. Bouck (1970) considers that light is reduced in intensity by a shading device (the eyespot) and brought into focus by a focussing device (the flagellar base), and the photoreceptor is probably sandwiched between these two structures and bound to the plasma membrane.

A unique feature of *Fucus* is the initial generation of a new nuclear envelope on only that surface of the sperm nucleus that faces the egg nucleus.

The internal structure of the sterile conceptacles (cryptoblasts) is similar to that of the fertile conceptacles, except that the former do not bear sex organs. The hairs show either basal or diffuse growth and are unbranched. The cavity contains some mucilage.

The wall layers of the antheridia and oogonia are hydrophilic. They imbibe water at the time of liberation of the antherozoids or eggs as a result of which the outer wall layer swells up and bursts, expelling to the exterior the antherozoids or eggs through the hairs and ostiole. The remaining wall layers also become dissolved in the surrounding water and liberate the antherozoids or eggs. In cultures, the clustering of antherozoids around a single egg has been seen (Fig. 11-33 A); it results from a chemical stimulus provided by a hydrocarbon (probably n-hexane) present in the eggs of *Fucus*. After the attachment of the sperm flagella to the egg surface, the beating of the sperm flagella makes the egg rotate for some time. Ultimately, one of the antherozoids finds its way into the egg, leading to the formation of the zygote.

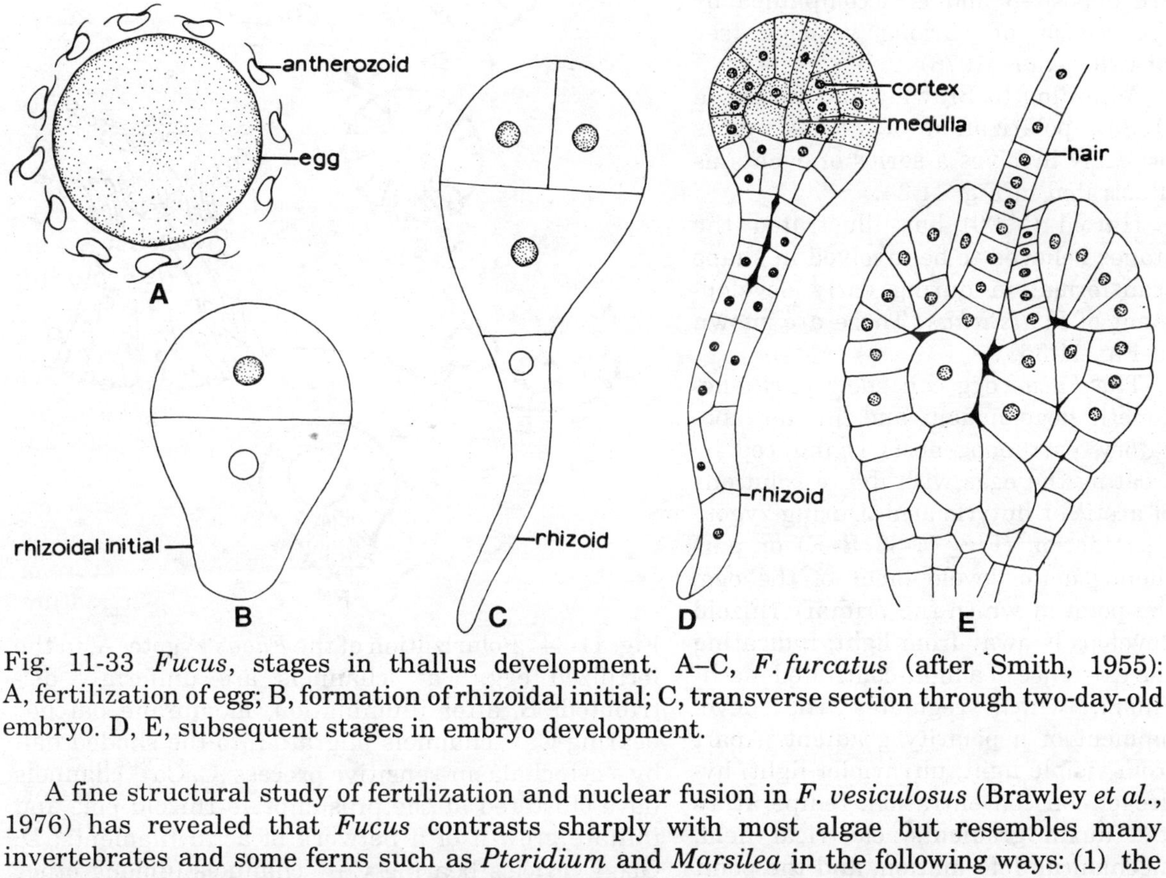

Fig. 11-33 *Fucus*, stages in thallus development. A–C, *F. furcatus* (after Smith, 1955): A, fertilization of egg; B, formation of rhizoidal initial; C, transverse section through two-day-old embryo. D, E, subsequent stages in embryo development.

A fine structural study of fertilization and nuclear fusion in *F. vesiculosus* (Brawley *et al.*, 1976) has revealed that *Fucus* contrasts sharply with most algae but resembles many invertebrates and some ferns such as *Pteridium* and *Marsilea* in the following ways: (1) the chromatin of its sperm nucleus is highly condensed; (2) the nuclear envelope of its sperm disintegrates after gametic fusion; (3) its eggs have nuclear pores but the free-swimming sperms lack such pores; and (4) the nuclear envelope of its egg is highly convoluted in an asymmetric manner; this convolution is mostly localized in the zone facing the advancing sperm nucleus.

Soon after the eggs are liberated from the oogonium, the smooth endoplasmic reticulum produces certain large vesicles which accumulate fibrillar material. After fertilization, the hitherto inactive Golgi bodies, located near the plasmalemma, become activated and give rise to other, thicker vesicles having radiating fibrils and irregularly distributed contents.

In *F. vesiculosus*, the eggs are apolar and the axis is not established in the zygote until about 14 hr after fertilization. During this period of 14 hr, the axis may be induced and reoriented by altering the direction of a unilateral light gradient (Evans *et al.*, 1982). The unfertilized ovum lacks a cell wall and has a highly convoluted nuclear envelope and vesicular contents. The wall formation begins immediately after fertilization when fucans are deposited and is accompanied by the fusion of various vesicles (see Brawley *et al.*, 1976).

According to Brawley and Robinson (1985), polarization of *Fucus* zygote probably involves a series of events as illustrated in Fig. 11-34.

Harold (1990) has illustrated the stages believed to be involved in shape transformation during early development of *F. distichus*. These are shown in Fig. 11-35.

The *Fucus* egg can show parthenogenetic development and, in the laboratory, parthenogenesis is induced by treating the eggs with dilute solutions of acetic or butyric acid. During zygote germination (Fig. 11-33 B–E) or parthenogenetic development of the egg, the point at which the primary rhizoid develops is away from light, indicating the existence of a light-controlled mechanism, which regulates the development of a polarity gradient. Apart from visible light, ultraviolet light, hydrogen-ion concentration, temperature and auxin gradients, electrical field, mechanical deformation, and the point of entry of the spermatozoid, all seem to control the development of polarity, leading to the formation of rhizoids. A CO_2-pH gradient seems to control the auxin concentration and the region rich in auxin activity differentiates the rhizoid.

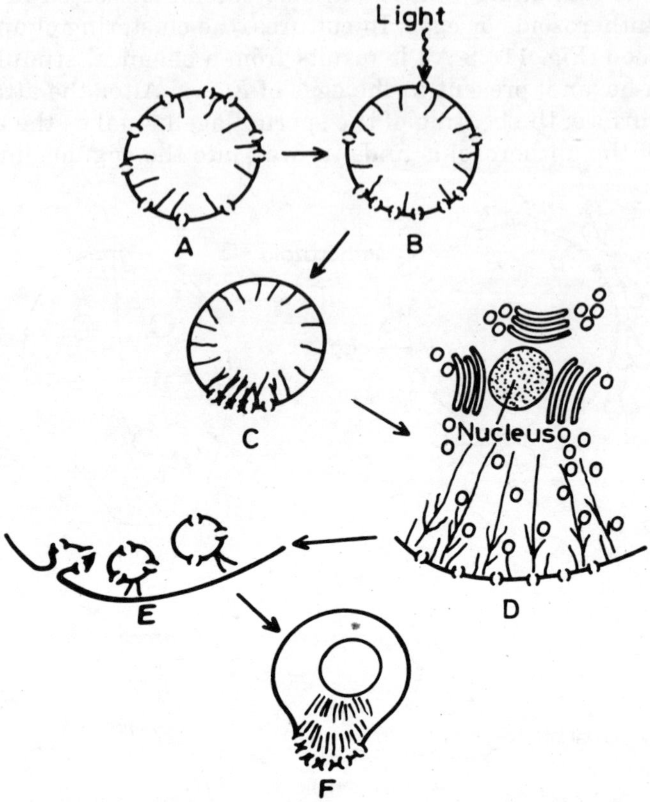

Fig. 11-34 Polarization of the *Fucus* zygote. A, in the fertilized egg, Ca^{2+} channels are uniformly distributed; B, after illumination, membrane patches bearing Ca^{2+} channels migrate into the shaded half by a cytochalasin-sensitive process; C, Ca^{2+} channels have clustered at the presumptive rhizoid pole and initiate growth of a network of actin filaments; D, Golgi vesicles bearing Ca^{2+} channels (among other things) are guided to the presumptive rhizoid pole, where they fuse with the plasma membrane; E, F, well-developed actin cables extending to the nucleus, rhizoid outgrowth has begun. (After Brawley and Robinson, 1985.)

After the point of rhizoid formation has been determined, the zygote divides mitotically in a plane transverse to the axis defined by the rhizoid (Fig. 11-33 B). The upper cell of the two-celled embryo divides vertically, whereas the lower divides transversely, thus forming a

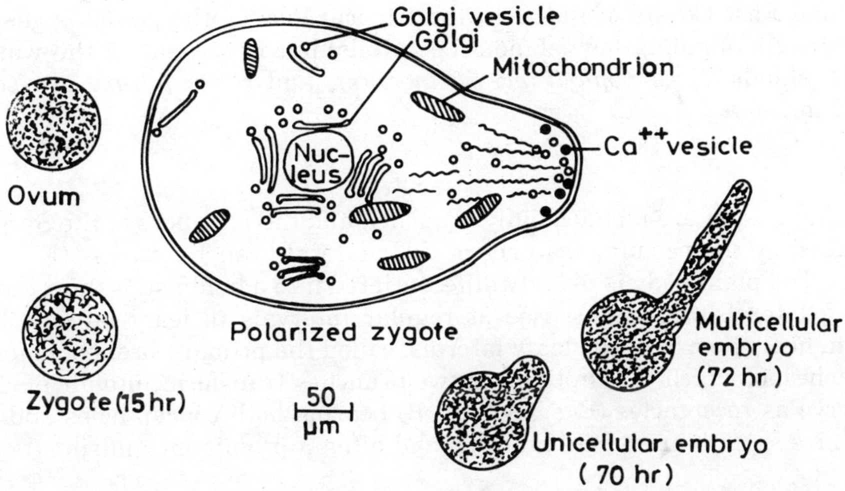

Fig. 11-35 Stages in shape transformation during early development of *Fucus distichus*. Outlines from polarized zygote (speculative sketch). Indications are that Golgi vesicles travel to the site of outgrowth, that mitochondria become axially oriented, and that several kinds of vesicles accumulate in the presumptive rhizoid. The "tracks" thought to guide vesicles to the site of exocytosis are especially speculative. The nucleus remains in the cell centre; chloroplasts (not shown) are dispersed throughout the cell. (After Harold, 1990.)

four-celled embryo (Fig. 11-33 C). The upper two cells, together with the median cell, divide and redivide transversely and periclinally, giving rise to a tissue differentiated into the medulla and cortex (Fig. 11-33 D). The lowermost cell of the quadrant from which the primary rhizoid originated also forms secondary rhizoids. With the growth of the embryo, there differentiates an apical cell in a small depression which forms a filamentous hair (Fig. 11-33 E). Subsequently, the cells adjacent to the hair also grow into hairs and form a tuft on the upper surface. This development is followed by degeneration of all the cells of the hair, except the basal cell of the first-formed hair. The basal cell finally functions as an apical initial of the *Fucus* thallus.

Family: Sargassaceae
Genus: *Sargassum*

Sargassum, like *Fucus*, is diploid and lacks an alternation of generations. The two genera differ mainly in their external morphology and in the number of eggs produced in an oogonium (eight in *Fucus* but one in *Sargassum*).

Occurrence

Sargassum, popularly called gulfweed, may be free-floating or attached to rocks. It grows abundantly in the tropical oceans of the Southern hemisphere: the Australian and Caribbean Coasts, the Gulf of Mexico, and the Sargasso Sea of the south central Atlantic. It is also found on the West and East Coasts of India. In the tropical Pacific, the genus is generally absent from the waters surrounding low islands (i.e., atolls) but is present in the waters of neighbouring high islands. *S. carpophyllum*, *S. cinereum*, and *S. ilicifolium* are some common species found in India.

Morphology

The thalli of *Sargassum* are monopodially branched and the members of the Sargassaceae are chiefly identified by the peculiar features of their lateral branch systems (Figs. 11-36, 11-37 A, B, 11-38 A). The plant body is usually differentiated into a holdfast, a short stipe, and much branched long laterals which give rise at regular intervals to leafy laterals bearing cryptoblasts. From near the axil of the leafy laterals, called the primary branch, emerges a second order of branches, of which the first one or two branches transform into air bladders and the remaining serve as receptacles (Fig. 11-39 A, B) bearing both conceptacles and cryptoblasts. The 'leaves' have smooth or serrate margins and often a prominent midrib.

Fig. 11-36 *Sargassum pallidum*, habit (after Yoshida, 1983).

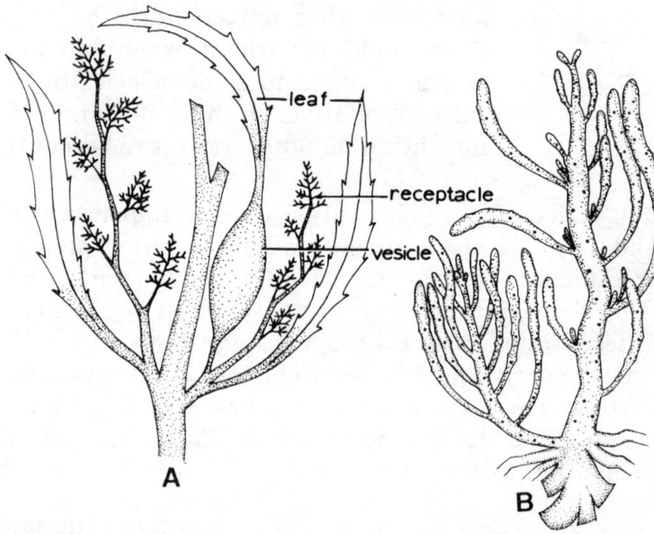

Fig. 11-37 *Sargassum*. A, *S. longifolium*, part of fertile plant; B, *S. swartzii*, part of plant (after Chauhan and Thivy, 1964).

S. polycystum can be 2 metres long. It is attached to the substratum by a dense rhizoidal basal system from which several erect branches arise. These erect branches in turn produce cylindrical secondary branches having Y-shaped projections. The leaf-like appendages can be 5 cm long and 1 cm broad. The terminal portions of mature plants are leafless but give rise to compact clusters of receptacles and tiny spherical air bladders.

A transverse section through a branch, leaf or stipe shows well marked differentiation into

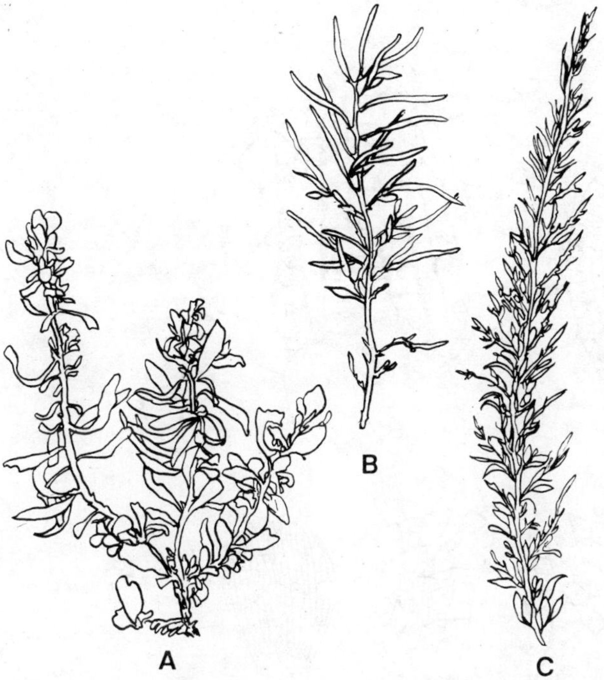

Fig. 11-38 *Sargassum miyabei*. A, young plant; B, male receptacles; C, part of female plant with receptacles. (After Yoshida, 1983.)

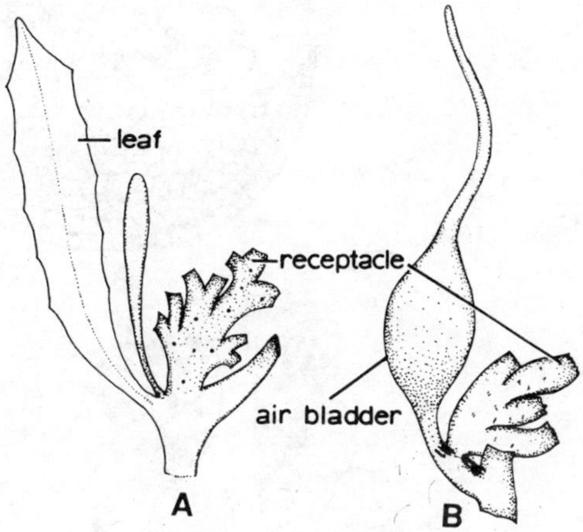

Fig. 11-39 *Sargassum swartzii*. A, B, parts of plants with receptacles (after Chauhan and Thivy, 1964).

three regions: meristoderm, cortex, and medulla. In some species, which are free-floating, the medulla may be almost absent. Unlike *Fucus*, the cortex of *Sargassum* contains neither mucilaginous cells nor hyphae. The air bladder consists of an epidermis, cortex, and a central hollow cavity filled with air.

As in *Fucus*, the growth and organization of the thallus is achieved through the activity of an apical cell with three cutting faces.

Reproduction

Vegetative *S. natans* and *S. hystrix*, which grow free-floating in the Sargasso Sea, are known to multiply exclusively by vegetative means. It is interesting that free-floating algae of salt marshes, e.g., *Pelvetia* and *Bostrychia*, also multiply vegetatively.

Sexual The Sargassum species are both dioecious and monoecious but, in contrast to *Fucus*, it forms special branches which bear fertile conceptacles (Fig. 11-40 A) or sterilc conceptacles (Fig. 11-40 B). The conceptacles and antheridia develop in the same manner as in *Fucus*; oogonial development (Fig. 11-40 C, D) also follows the same course up to the stage of formation of eight nuclei, but seven of these nuclei degenerate and the remaining nucleus, along with the oogonial cytoplasm, forms a single egg.

After maturation of the oogonium, the outer wall layer ruptures and the middle layer develops into a mucilaginous stalk which, while still attached to the mother plant, pushes the

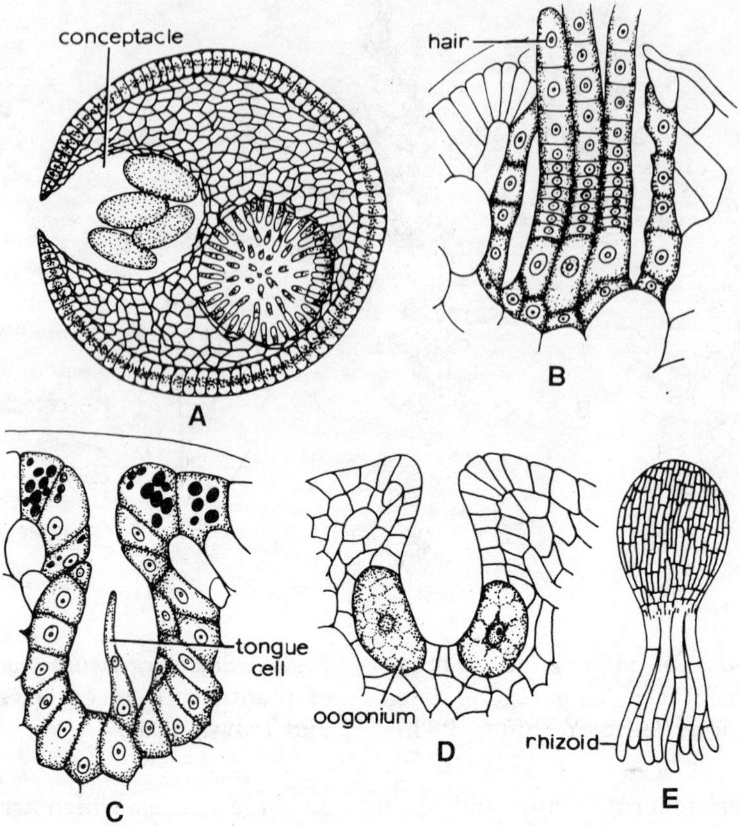

Fig. 11-40 *Sargassum*, some reproductive and developmental stages. A, *S. swartzii*, transverse section through rachide, showing compressed nature (after Chauhan and Thivy, 1964); B, *S. filipendula*, section of young cryptoblast; C, *S. filipendula*, section of young conceptacle; D, *S. linifolium*, section through young female conceptacle, showing embedded oogonia; E, *S. filipendula,* germling at rhizoidal stage.

entire oogonium through the ostiole to the exterior. Fertilization occurs inside the oogonium and even the resulting zygote starts germinating within the oogonial wall. The remaining features of sexual reproduction and the development of the embryo into a germling (Fig. 11-40 E) are similar to those of *Fucus*.

The salinity level, temperature, and nature and composition of the growth medium affect the growth of the young stages in culture. The young stages thrive best in cooler and high salinity waters. When the temperature is high and, at the same time, the salinity is low, the effect on young thalli is more detrimental than when these influences operate individually (De Wreede, 1978).

The mature ova of such brown algae as *Sargassum* secrete some sexual substances which attract the spermatozoids to the ova (Kajiwara *et al.*, 1980). Kajiwara *et al.* have found that the male gametes of *Sargassum horneri* show a strong positive response to four synthetic attractants, viz., 1,trans-3,cis-5-octatriene, 1,trans-3,trans-5-octatriene, 1,trans-3,trans-5-octatriene, and cis-2,cis-4,trans-6-octatriene. Most of these octatrienes are not naturally found in marine brown algae.

Population Ecology of Fucales

Fucoids reproduce through gametes and by vegetative propagation. Their eggs are quite large. Settlement is the initial post-sinking attachment of propagules to the substratum, while recruitment is the transition into one or more sizes or developmental stages.

Egg output of fucoids has been studied by several workers. A comprehensive study was that of Ang (1991) for *F. distichus*. About 5–15 × 10^6 eggs m^{-2} yr^{-1} were produced. The egg production estimates for fucoids are some orders of magnitude lower than those for spore production by kelps (Chapman, 1984), possibly because kelp spores are much smaller than fucoid eggs, and fecundity is inversely related to parental investment per propagule (Chapman, 1995).

Post-settlement mortality among microbenthic recruits of *Sargassum sinclairii* reduces the number of plants reaching visible size to 1500 m^{-2}, which is 5% of the settlement density (Chapman, 1995). *F. distichus* recruits arise only from zygotes (Ang, 1991). It is much easier to prepare a demographic budget of fecundity, settlement, and recruitment in fucoids than in other seaweeds. Even so, the microscopic size of propagules, settlers, and early recruits makes estimation procedures difficult.

In situations where the water column is fully turbulent, there is very little possibility of long-distance transport of propagules before they reach the bottom. The planktonic phase ends when a propagule contacts and attaches to the substratum. In *S. muticum* the settlement of propagules is negatively related to water flow velocity. Fucoid propagules are in a suitable size range for the filter feeders (mussels and barnacles) which share the habitat, but there are no data on propagule losses to these animals. Settled propagules become prey to grazers.

After settlement, fucoid propagules become members of the microbenthos. For some months they are not visible to the unaided eye and act as microrecruits (Ang, 1991). Grazing reduces the density of recruits of *A. nodosum* by a factor of >300 over one year (Lazo, 1992; Chapman, 1995). Even one-year-old plants are so small (up to 2 mm) that they can be easily grazed by epilithic molluscs.

Physical factors also exert strong effects on the demography of fucoid microrecruits. *A. nodosum* is conspicuously absent from wave-battered shores. Fucoid recruits enter the macrobenthos at a size of about 1 mm. Some of these plants pass through a series of developmental stages to achieve a size at which sexual maturity occurs. Most life-table budgets for fucoids have been based on age-specific survival. Since development is quite plastic, a small plant may be either old or young, depending on ecophysiological circumstances. Very small plants are unlikely to become reproductive, whatever their age, and it appears that survival is strongly size- rather than age-specific.

With increasing density a closed canopy of larger plants forms, reducing the light available to smaller plants whose growth rate slows or falls to zero below the compensation point for photosynthesis. At that stage herbivory or physical erosion can eliminate individuals from the population. Mortality rates should therefore be higher among small sub-canopy plants than among larger canopy-forming individuals. The sizes and densities of fucoid populations are strongly affected by grazing. Many experiments have shown an effect of herbivores on cover or biomass. For a demographic study, effects need to be shown in terms of density.

Species Interactions

In the intertidal rocky shores of the North Atlantic there are complex relationships among the fucoid species themselves and between fucoids, ephemeral algae, sessile filter-feeding animals, herbivores and even carnivores (since their prey interact directly with fucoids). In Australasia huge multispecies strands of fucaleans occur both in the subtidal and intertidal, but the information on their interaction ecology is quite meagre.

The NW Atlantic

In the NW Atlantic, fucoid algae rank low in the competitive hierarchy of sessile species on intertidal shores, even though they comprise most of the biomass and, in some areas, occur in such quantities that commercial harvesting occurs (Menge, 1976; Lubchenco, 1982). The long-lived perennial *Chondrus crispus* and short-lived ephemeral forms, e.g., *Ulva lactuca* and *Enteromorpha* spp., are competitively superior to fucoids (Lubchenco, 1982), and barnacles are competitively superior to *C. crispus*. If the competitive hierarchy is transitive, barnacles are superior space competitors to fucoids. Mussels also outcompete fucoids for space (Menge, 1976). Under these circumstances, how do fucaleans come to occupy so much space on rocky shores? It may be that the consumers so decimate populations of superior competitors that fucoids flourish. *C. crispus* is even more resistant than fucoids to grazing but is restricted to the low shore (by desiccation stress) where it excludes colonization of the larger brown algae. Periwinkles control ephemeral algae whereas whelks control filter feeders on the mid-shore. Fucoids appear to be protected against periwinkle grazing by the accumulation of repellent phlorotannins (Chapman, 1995).

Ephemeral algae are the preferred food of grazing periwinkles. For *Littorina obtusata* the preferred foods are fucoids, as it consumes about ten times more of *F. spiralis* than *Ulva* (Norton *et al.*, 1990). On the other hand, *L. littorea* preferentially consumes *Ulva* (Chapman, 1995). Smaller thalli of Fucales are also susceptible to snail grazing. The size escape from grazing in *Fucus vesiculosus* correlates with an increase in tissue phlorotannin concentration in the larger thalli.

The occurrence of a canopy of perennial fucoids strongly influences interactions on rocky shores, as it blocks the settlement of ephemeral algae and juvenile fucoids even when herbivores are absent (Lubchenco, 1986). This finding conflicts with the reports of Menge (1976). According to Lubchenco (1986), the average cover of fucoid canopy and open habitats determines the frequencies of important species interactions. The commonest interaction is canopy exclusion of ephemeral algae and germlings of perennial fucoids, and the second important interaction here is competition between ephemeral algae and fucoid germlings. Herbivory is less common.

The rocky shore presents a physiological gradient for marine plants, with a benign end closest to the sea and a stressful terrestrial end. Three species of *Fucus* occur on this gradient in Nova Scotia. *F. evanescens* grows only low on the shore. Above it, is a zone of *F. vesiculosus* and, at the top of the eulittoral, there is a zone of *F. spiralis*. These distributions occur on rock surfaces exposed to air at low tide. In addition, *F. distichus* occurs within tide pools of the upper eulittoral and littoral fringe.

Species which are good competitors are sometimes poorly defended against grazing because chemical defence being energetically costly can detract from competitive ability. *F. spiralis* is usually better protected against grazers than is *F. vesiculosus*. This accounts for the persistence of *F. spiralis* where *F. vesiculosus* (its superior competitor) is present.

Along the NE Atlantic, e.g., the Isle of Man, patellids on exposed shores prevent the development of fucoids. Although fucoids have a negative effect on the population of barnacles, the recruitment of plants seems to be enhanced by a barnacle cover, partly because barnacles limit the feeding efficiency of limpets. Usually strongly wave-exposed shores are dominated by populations of animals whereas sheltered shores are covered with a dense rockweed vegetation. The fucoid vegetation on sheltered coasts of the Isle of Man is structured into distinct zones of species on the shore gradient.

REFERENCES

Anderson, M.R., Cardinal, A., and Larochelle, J., An alternate growth pattern for *Laminaria longicruris*, *J. Phycol.*, **17**, 405–11 (1981).

Ang, P.O., Natural dynamics of a *Fucus distichus* (Phaeophyceae, Fucales) population, *Mar. Ecol. Prog. Ser.*, **78**, 71–81 (1991).

Asensi, A., Delepine, R., and Guglielmi, G., Nouvelles observations sur l'ultrastructure du plastidome des Pheophycees, *Soc. Phycol. France, Bull.*, **22**, 192–205 (1977).

Berkaloff, C. and Rousseau, B., Ultrastructure of male gametogenesis in *Fucus serratus* (Phaeophyceae), *J. Phycol.*, **15**, 163–73 (1979).

Boalch, G.T., Studies on *Ectocarpus* in culture. II. Growth and nutrition of a bacteria-free culture, *J. Mar. Biol. Ass.* (U.K.), **41**, 287–304 (1961).

Bolwell, G.P., Callow, J.A., Callow, M.E., and Evans, L.V., Cross fertilization in fucoid seaweeds, *Nature*, **268**, 626–27 (1977).

Bouck, G.B., The development and postfertilization fate of the eyespot and the apparent photoreceptor in *Fucus* sperm. *In* Fredrick, J.F. and Klein, R.M. (eds.) Phylogenesis and morphogenesis in the algae, *Ann. N.Y. Acad. Sci.*, **175**, 673–85 (1970).

Brawley, S.H., Fertilization in natural populations of the dioecious brown alga *Fucus ceranoides* and the importance of the polyspermy block, *Mar. Biol.*, **113**, 145–57 (1992).

Brawley, S.H., Wetherbee, R., and Quatrano, R.S., Fine structural studies of the gametes and embryo of *Fucus vesiculosus* L. (Phaeophyta), *J. Cell Sci.*, **20**, 233–71 (1976).

Brawley, S.H. and Robinson, K.R., Cytochalasin treatment disrupts the endogenous currents associated with cell polarization in fucoid zygotes: studies of the role of F-actin in embryogenesis, *J. Cell Biol.*, **100**, 1173–84 (1985).

Chapman, A.R.O., Reproduction, recruitment and mortality in two species of *Laminaria* in southwest Nova Scotia, *J. Exp. Mar. Biol. Ecol.*, **78**, 99–109 (1984).

Chapman, A.R.O., Functional ecology of fucoid algae: twenty-three years of progress, *Phycologia*, **34**, 1–32 (1995).

Chauhan, V.D. and Thivy, F., On the occurrence of some *Sargassum* species in Gujarat, *Phykos*, **3**, 19–25 (1964).

Clayton, M.N., Evolution and life histories of brown algae, *Bot. Mar.*, **31**, 379–87 (1988).

Clayton, M.N., Phylum Phaeophyta. *In* Margulis, L., Corliss, J.O., Melkonian, M., and Chapman, D.J. (eds.) Handbook of Protoctista, 698–714, Jones and Bartlett, Boston (1990).

De Wreede, R., Growth in varying culture conditions of embryos of three Hawaiian species of *Sargassum* (Phaeophyta, Sargassaceae), *Phycologia*, **17**, 23–31 (1978).

Dieck, I.T., Circannual growth rhythm and photoperiodic sorus induction in the kelp *Laminaria setchellii* (Phaeophyta), *J. Phycol.*, **27**, 341–50 (1991).

Evans, L.V., Distribution of pyrenoids among some brown algae, *J. Cell Sci.*, **1**, 449–54 (1966).

Evans, L.V., Callow, J.A., and Callow, M.E., The biology and biochemistry of reproduction and early development in *Fucus*. *In* Round, F.E. and Chapman, D.J. (eds.) Progress in Phycological Research, Vol. 1, 67–110, Elsevier, Amsterdam (1982).

Fritsch, F.E., The Structure and Reproduction of the Algae, Vol. II, Cambridge University Press, London (1945).

Galatis, B., Katsaros, C., and Mitrakos, K., Fine structure of vegetative cells of *Sphacelaria tribuloides* Menegh. (Phaeophyceae, Sphacelariales): with special reference to some unusual proliferations of the plasmalemma, *Phycologia*, **16**, 139–51 (1977).

Harold, F.M., To shape a cell: an enquiry into the causes of morphogenesis of microorganisms, *Microbiol. Rev.*, **54**, 381–431 (1990).

Hay, M.E., The functional morphology of turf-forming seaweeds: persistence in stressful marine habitats, *Ecology*, **62**, 739–50 (1981).

Henry, E.C. and Cole, K.M., Ultrastructure of swarmers in the Laminariales. I. Zoospores, *J. Phycol.*, **18**, 550–69 (1982a).

Henry, E.C. and Cole, K.M., Ultrastructure of swarmers in the Laminariales. II. Sperm, *J. Phycol.*, **18**, 570–79 (1982b).

Hori, T. and Ueda, R., The fine structure of algal chloroplasts and algal phylogeny. *In* Tokida, J. and Hirose, H. (eds.) Advance of Phycology in Japan, 11–42, Gustav Fischer Verlag, Jena (1975).

Kajiwara, T., Kodama, K., and Hatanaka, A., Male-attracting substance in a marine brown alga *Sargassum horneri*, *Naturwissenschaften*, **67**, 612–13 (1980).

Katsaros, C. and Galatis, B., Ultrastructural studies on thallus development in *Dictyota dichotoma* (Phaeophyta, Dictyotales), *Brit. Phycol. J.*, **20**, 263–76 (1985).

Kawai, H., Flagellar autofluorescence in brown algal swarmers and their phototactic responses, *Bot. Mag.*, Tokyo, **105**, 171–84 (1992a).

Kawai, H., A summary of the morphology of chloroplasts and flagellated cells in the Phaeophyceae, *Korean J. Phycol.*, **7**, 33–43 (1992b).

Kawai, H., Kubota, M., Kondo, T., and Watanabe, M., Action spectra for phototaxis in zoospores of the brown alga *Pseudochorda gracilis*, *Protoplasma*, **161**, 17–22 (1991).

Kawai, H., Müller, D.G., Fölster, E., and Häder, D.P., Phototactic responses in the gametes of the brown alga, *Ectocarpus siliculosus*, *Planta*, **182**, 292–97 (1990).

Kitayama, T., Kawai, H., and Yoshida, T., Morphological observations on *Sphacelaria californica* Sauvageau ex Setchell et Gardner (Sphacelariales, Phaeophyceae), new to Japan, *Jap. J. Phycol.* (Sorui), **39**, 189–93 (1991).

Kreimer, G., Kawai, H., Müller, D.G., and Melkonian, M., Reflective properties of the stigma in male gametes of *Ectocarpus siliculosus* (Phaeophyceae) studied by confocal laser scanning microscopy, *J. Phycol.*, **27**, 268–76 (1991).

Lazo, L., Demography of Harvested Populations of Ascophyllum nodosum, Ph.D. Thesis, Dalhousie University, Halifax, Canada (1992).

Lubchenco, J., Effects of grazers and algal competitors on fucoid colonization in tide pools, *J. Phycol.*, **18**, 544–50 (1982).

Lubchenco, J., Relative importance of competition and predation: early colonization by seaweeds in New England. *In* Diamond, J. and Case, T.J. (eds.) Community Ecology, 537–55, Harper and Row, New York (1986).

Lüning, K., Egg release in gametophytes of *Laminaria saccharina*: induction by darkness and inhibition by blue light and UV, *Brit. Phycol. J.*, **16**, 379–93 (1981).

Lüning, K., New frond formation in *Laminaria hyperborea* (Phaeophyta): a photoperiodic response, *Brit. Phycol. J.*, **21**, 269–73 (1986).

Lüning, K., Photoperiodic control of sorus formation in the brown alga *Laminaria saccharina*, *Mar. Ecol. Prog. Ser.*, **45**, 137–44 (1988).

Maier, I. and Müller, D.G., Chemotaxis in *Laminaria digitata* (Phaeophyceae), *J. Exp. Bot.*, **41**, 869–76 (1990).

Mann, K.H. and Chapman, A.R.O., Primary production of marine macrophytes. *In* Cooper, J.P. (ed.) Photosynthesis and Productivity in Different Environments, 207–33, Cambridge University Press, London (1975).

Manton, I., Some phyletic implications of flagellar structure in plants, *Adv. Bot. Res.*, **2**, 1–34 (1965).

McLachlan, J. and Bidwell, R.G.S., Effects of colored light on the growth and metabolism of *Fucus* embryos and apices in culture, *Can. J. Bot.*, **61**, 1993–2003 (1983).

Menge, B.A., Organization of the New England rocky intertidal community: the role of predation, competition and environmental heterogeneity, *Ecological Monographs*, **46**, 355–93 (1976).

Motomura, T., Ultrastructural study of sperm in *Laminaria angustata* (Laminariales, Phaeophyta), especially on the flagellar apparatus, *Jap. J. Phycol.*, **37**, 105–16 (1989).

Motomura, T., Ultrastructure of fertilization in *Laminaria angustata* (Phaeophyta, Laminariales) with emphasis on the behaviour of centrioles, mitochondria and chloroplasts of the sperm, *J. Phycol.*, **26**, 80–89 (1990).

Motomura, T. and Sakai, Y., The occurrence of flagellated eggs in *Laminaria angustata* (Phaeophyta, Laminariales), *J. Phycol.*, **24**, 282–85 (1988).

Muller, D.G., Generationswechsel, Kernphasenwechsel und Sexualität der Braunalge *Ectocarpus siliculosus* im Kulturversuch, *Planta*, **75**, 39–54 (1967).

Müller, D.G., Studies on reproduction in *Ectocarpus siliculosus*, *Soc. Bot. France, Memoires*, **1972**, 87–98 (1972).

Müller, D.G., Experimental evidence against sexual fusions of spores from unilocular sporangia of *Ectocarpus siliculosus* (Phaeophyta), *Brit. Phycol. J.*, **10**, 315–21 (1975).

Müller, D.G., Genetic affinity of *Ectocarpus siliculosus* (Dillw.) Lyngb. from the Mediterranean, North Atlantic and Australia, *Phycologia*, **18**, 312–18 (1979).

Müller, D.G. and Gassmann, G., Sexual hormone specificity in *Ectocarpus* and *Laminaria* (Phaeophyceae), *Naturwissenschaften*, **67**, 462 (1980).

Müller, D.G., Jaenicke, L., Donike, M., and Akintobi, T., Sex attractant in a brown alga: chemical structure, *Science*, **171**, 815–17 (1971).

Müller, D.G., Maier, I., and Gassmann, G., Survey on sexual pheromone specificity in Laminariales (Phaeophyceae), *Phycologia*, **24**, 475–84 (1985).

Norton, T.A., Hawkins, S.J., Manley, N.L., Wiliams, G.A., and Watson, D.C., Scraping a living: a review of littorinid grazing, *Hydrobiologia*, **193**, 117–38 (1990).

O'Kelly, C.J., The evolutionary origin of the brown algae: information from studies of motile cell ultrastructure. *In* Green, J.C., Leadbeater, B.S.C., and Driver, W.L. (eds.) The Chromophyte Algae: Problems and perspectives, 255–78, Clarendon Press, Oxford (1989).

O'Kelly, C.J. and Floyd, G.L., Absolute configuration analysis of the flagellar apparatus in *Giraudyopsis stellifer* (Chrysophyceae, Sarcinochrysidales) zoospores and its significance in the evolution of the Phaeophyceae, *Phycologia*, **24**, 263–74 (1985).

Oliviera, L. and Bisalputra, T., Ultrastructural and cytochemical studies on the nature and origin of the cytoplasmic inclusions of aging cells of *Ectocarpus* (Phaeophyta, Ectocarpales), *Phycologia*, **16**, 235–43 (1977).

Oltmanns, F. and Berthold, G., Über Scheinkopulation bei Ectocarpeen und anderen Algen, *Flora*, **83**, 398–410 (1987).

Papenfuss, G.F., Problems in the classification of the marine algae, *Svensk. Bot. Tidskr.*, **45**, 4–11 (1951).

Papenfuss, G.F., Problems in the classification of the marine algae, Proceedings of the VII International Botanical Congress, 822–23 (1953).

Parker, B.C. and Huber, J., Translocation in *Macrocystis*. II. Fine structure of the sieve tubes, *J. Phycol.*, **1**, 172–79 (1965).

Percival, E., Do the polysaccharides of brown and red seaweeds ignore taxonomy? *In* Irvine, D.E.G. and Price, J.H. (eds.) Modern Approaches to the Taxonomy of Red and Brown Algae, 47–62, Academic Press, London (1978).

Percival, E., The polysaccharides of green, red, and brown seaweeds: their basic structure, biosynthesis, and function, *Brit. Phycol. J.*, **14**, 103–17 (1979).

Peters, A.F., Taxonomic implications of gamete fusions in the parasitic brown alga *Herpodiscus durvillaeae*, *Can. J. Bot.*, **68**, 1398–1401 (1989).

Phillips, J.A., Reproduction in Southern Australian species of the Dictyotales (Phaeophyta), *Bot. Mar.*, **31**, 437–45 (1988).

Phillips, J.A. and Clayton, M.N., Biflagellate spermatozoids in the Dictyotales: the structure of gametes and gametangia in *Zonaria angustata* (Dictyotales, Phaeophyceae), *Phycologia*, **30**, 205–14 (1991).

Phillips, J.A. and Clayton, M.N., Flagellate spores in *Homoeostrichus olsenii* Womersley (Dictyotales, Phaeophyceae): the largest known motile reproductive cells of marine macroalgae, *Phycologia*, **33**, 415–19 (1994).

Prudhomme van Reine, W.F., Criteria used in systematic studies in the Sphacelariales. *In* Irvine, D.E.G. and Price, J.H. (eds.) Modern Approaches to the Taxonomy of Red and Brown Algae, 301–23, Academic Press, London (1978).

Reed, R.H., Davison, I.R., Chudek, J.A., and Foster, R., The osmotic role of mannitol in the Phaeophyta: an appraisal, *Phycologia*, **24**, 35–47 (1985).

Sanbonsuga, Y. and Neushul, M., Hybridization and genetics of brown algae. *In* Gantt, E. (ed.) Handbook of Phycological Methods: Developmental and cytological methods, 69–79, Cambridge University Press, London (1980).

Scagel, R.F., The Phaeophyceae in perspective, *Oceanogr. Mar. Biol. Ann. Rev.*, **4**, 123–94 (1996).

Smith, G.M., Cryptogamic Botany, Vol. I, Algae and Fungi, 2nd edn., McGraw-Hill, New York (1955).

Tanaka, J., A new species of *Spatoglossum* (*S. crassum* sp. nov.: Dictyotales, Phaeophyceae) from Japan, *Phycologia*, **30**, 574–81 (1991).

Van den Hoek, C. and Flintermann, A., The life history of *Sphacelaria furcigera* Kutz. (Phaeophyceae), *Blumea*, **16**, 193–242 (1968).

Wynne, M.J., Life history and systematic studies of some Pacific North American Phaeophyceae (brown algae), *Univ. Calif. Publ. Bot.*, **50**, 1–88 (1969).

Wynne, M.J. and Loiseaux, S., Recent advances in life history studies of Phaeophyta, *Phycologia*, **15**, 435–52 (1976).

Yoshida, T., Japanese species of *Sargassum* subgenus *Bactrophycus* (Phaeophyta, Fucales), *Jour. Fac. Sci.*, **13**, 99–246 (1983).

12 Chlorophyta

CLASS: CHLOROPHYCEAE

GENERAL CHARACTERS

The phylum Chlorophyta includes the three classes Chlorophyceae, Charophyceae, and Prasinophyceae.

These algae are eucaryotic and have, as in higher plants, the same pigments (chlorophyll-a, chlorophyll-b, various carotenes, and xanthophylls) in the same proportion. The pigments are located in definite chloroplasts. The excess photosynthates are commonly stored in the form of starch. The inner layer of the cell wall is usually but not always cellulosic. The flagella, when present, are usually two or four in number, equal in length, and of the whiplash type.

OCCURRENCE AND ECOLOGICAL AMPLITUDE

The Chlorophyceae comprise three main types of forms, namely, free-living, attached, and parasitic, and all or some of these types may be aquatic, amphibious, terrestrial or subaerial. Of the aquatic forms, the Ulvaceae and Siphonales are mostly marine, whereas the Conjugales and Oedogoniales are almost entirely freshwater.

Although the green algae are predominantly freshwater forms, quite a few species grow on the surface of or within moist soil, tree barks, moist and shaded rocks, and on a variety of other terrestrial and subaerial habitats. Species of *Trentepohlia* constitute some of the best known examples of subaerial algae, whereas those of *Cladophora* and some members of the Chaetophorales grow on the shells of molluscs in freshwater ponds and lakes. Some species of *Chlamydomonas* and *Characium* flourish on crustaceans, turtles or other aquatic animals.

Chlorochytrium lemnae is a space parasite (endophyte) in *Lemna*, whereas *Cephaleuros* and *Rhodochytrium* are true parasites. Species of *Trebouxia*, *Chlorella*, and *Trentepohlia* form symbiotic association with fungi in various lichens. Some unicellular green algae are regularly found within the epidermal tissues of certain lower animals.

In contrast to the Cyanophyta, the Chlorophyta are mostly cold water forms although some strains of *Chlorella* are known to be thermophilic. *Chlamydomonas* spp. and various chlorococcaleans occur in such abundance in snow that they impart to it a reddish colour. This is due to the haematochrome (mostly secondary carotenoids dissolved in oil) they possess.

Certain heterotrophs, e.g., *Polytoma*, and facultatively heterotrophic algae, e.g., *Chlamydomonas*, occur in sewage lagoons and other habitats rich in reduced organic compounds and organic acids. Such organisms are collectively called "acetate flagellates".

Some green algae having large cells, e.g., *Chara*, *Nitella*, *Hydrodictyon*, and *Valonia*, have been much used as experimental organisms in plant physiology, especially bioelectric phenomena. In these cells, potential differences have been shown to exist between the cell's interior and exterior, the latter usually being positive (*negative* in *Valonia*). The gradient of potassium ions appears to be responsible for this potential in *Hydrodictyon* and *Nitella*. In other algae, the potential is probably a result of an internal concentration gradient related to the protoplasmic contents.

Dunaliella is highly halotolerant, thriving in habitats ranging from weakly brackish waters to saturated brines. It is extremely interesting metabolically in that it combines a virtually impermeable cell membrane with a striking capacity to regulate glycerol levels; this combination produces a tightly controlled unicellular *milieu interieur* (see Levandowsky and Hutner, 1979). The fundamental metabolic characteristic of *Dunaliella* is its ability to regulate glycerol production in response to salinity.

RANGE OF THALLUS STRUCTURE

The thallus exhibits a wide variation in its habit and morphology, ranging from a motile or nonmotile cell through colonial, filamentous, parenchymatous, and siphoneous habits to the highly evolved heterotrichous filament. The highest type of specialization seems to have been attained in such genera as *Draparnaldiopsis* (Fig. 12-1) and *Chara* which have a highly differentiated, complicated, and organized thallus. However, no elaborate and bulky parenchymatous or pseudoparenchymatous forms, as are met with in the Laminariales and Fucales of the Phaeophyta, are found in the green algae. Simple, pseudoparenchymatous thalli are however known in the Siphonales.

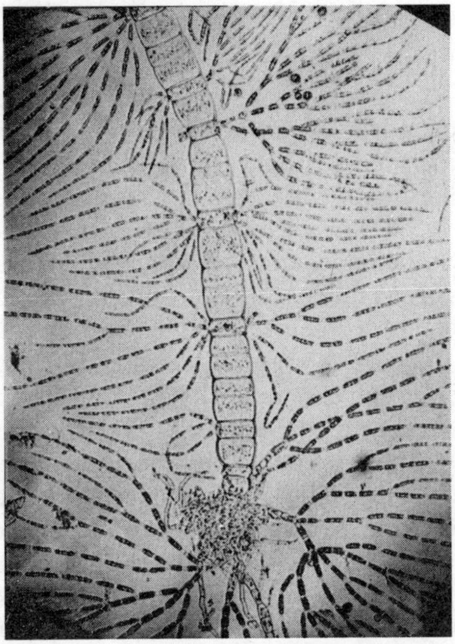

Fig. 12-1 *Draparnaldiopsis indica*, thallus showing long and short axial cells, branches, and basal region with rhizoids. (×225.) *Courtesy* Y.B.K. Chowdary.

CELL WALL

Except for a few primitive flagellate forms, the vast majority of green algae have a distinct, fairly rigid wall around their protoplast. The cell wall consists of two or three layers of which the inner may be either completely cellulosic, i.e., consisting of pure glucose residues, or a mixture of cellulosic and noncellulosic chains. Outside the inner cellulosic layer is a layer of pectose or mucilaginous substance. The latter is water-soluble and hence is continuously regenerated in aquatic species. The gelatinous wall layer may be impregnated with lime in some members of the Siphonales. In *Cladophora* and *Oedogonium*, a third chitinous layer may be laid down outside the pectose layer.

Since long, the chlorophytan cell walls have been supposed to be mainly cellulosic, but several recent researches have tended to disprove this belief. The cell walls of zoospores of *Chlamydomonas reinhardii* contain at least 5% nitrogen and have mainly pentoses and deoxyhexoses as the carbohydrate components, but neither glucose nor amino sugars (Jaenicke and Waffenschmidt, 1981). These cell walls are therefore not cellulosic but proteoglycan, and contain at least 25% protein.

The somatic cells of *Volvox carteri* lie embedded in, and are kept together, by a sheath material that mainly contains several proteoglycans; the carbohydrate content is chiefly made of arabinose, xylose, and mannose. Proteolytic and enzymatic processes are involved in the liberation of reproductive units in *Chlamydomonas* and *Volvox*. These enzymes have been named lysins by Jaenicke and Waffenschmidt (1981). These lysins are produced within the algal cells and then excreted into the ambient medium.

FLAGELLA

The motile vegetative cells and most zoospores and gametes generally have one, two, or four, and rarely many, anteriorly inserted whiplash flagella of equal length. These are associated with a neuromotor apparatus which connects them with a centrosome lying within or just outside the nucleus.

CELL STRUCTURE AND PROTOPLAST

The green algae are typically eucaryotic, having definite nuclei, chloroplasts, and mitochondria. A central vacuole is generally found in mature cells, with the cytoplasm confined to just inside the cell wall. In some species of *Spirogyra*, the vacuolar sap contains purple pigments which mask the green colour of the chloroplasts.

Most green algae have uninucleate cells but those of the Chlorococcales, Cladophorales, Siphonales, and *Sphaeroplea* are multinucleate (coenocytic). The nucleus has a double-layered porous nuclear membrane, one or more nucleoli, and centromeric chromosomes. Well developed complex nucleoli occur in the Conjugales and *Acetabularia*.

There is a great diversity in the number, morphology, and arrangement of the green algal chloroplasts, and this has been interpreted to suggest the manifestation of evolutionary tendencies among different orders of the phylum.

A single, cup-shaped or bowl-shaped chloroplast per cell, with one or a few pyrenoids, is characteristic of the Volvocales though rarely an axile stellate (*Chlamydomonas arachne*) or reticulate (*Sphaerella lacustris*) chloroplast may be found.

A single parietal chloroplast, usually having a single pyrenoid, is found in the Chlorococcales but *Trebouxia* has a single, lobed, axile chloroplast with one pyrenoid, whereas *Eremosphaera* has many, small, discoid chloroplasts devoid of pyrenoids.

A reticulate chloroplast with several pyrenoids is characteristic of *Hydrodictyon*, *Cladophora*, and the Oedogoniales, and a parietal ring-, collar- or girdle-shaped chloroplast containing a few pyrenoids is found in many Ulotrichaceae. A parietal chloroplast having a variable number of pyrenoids is also found in most of the Chaetophorales. In more advanced members of this order, e.g., *Draparnaldia* and *Draparnaldiopsis*, the main axes of central cells have a diminutive chloroplast restricted to the middle of the cell.

The Conjugales have three basic and common types of chloroplasts, viz., (1) a flat axile plate with several pyrenoids (*Mesotaenium* and *Mougeotia*); (2) a pair of axile stellate chloroplasts, each with a single pyrenoid (*Zygnema*); and (3) one or a few spiral, ribbon-shaped chloroplasts, each with many pyrenoids (*Spirogyra*).

Many discoid chloroplasts with or without pyrenoids are found in the Siphonales and Charales.

The pyrenoid of the green algae commonly consists of a proteinaceous core which is surrounded by minute plates of starch. It is often highly refractile.

The cells of the primitive, motile green algae commonly possess a pair of contractile vacuoles near the base of the flagella. The chloroplasts of motile cells generally also possess an eyespot near the anterior end.

The mitochondria, Golgi bodies, and endoplasmic reticulum characteristic of eucaryotic cells are also found in the cells of the Chlorophyta.

In the Volvocales, Oedogoniales, and Ulotrichales, the excess photosynthates are stored in the form of starch. Some Chlorococcales accumulate both starch and lipid, whereas most Siphonales and some Conjugales store fat.

CELL DIVISION

In the simple forms belonging to the Volvocales and Chlorococcales, cell division is linked with reproduction, but in most other green algae, it may be both vegetative and reproductive.

During nuclear division, all the four stages, i.e., prophase, metaphase, anaphase, and telophase, are evident. There are wide variations in the number and morphology of chromosomes but these seem to bear little, if any, taxonomic correlation or significance.

The green algae, except the Conjugales and some others, have centric chromosomes with localized centromeres in the median, submedian or terminal position. The Conjugales, on the other hand, have diffused centromeres. The wide range of variation in the chromosome number of different species is mostly due to aneuploidy although a few examples of polyploidy have also been reported.

The two modes of nuclear and cell division in the green algae are:

(1) The mitosis is intranuclear (with the nuclear envelope remaining closed at the metaphase) and is interrupted by spindle microtubules. A characteristic additional set of microtubules disposed transversely to the long axis of the spindle occurs at telophase and is termed the phycoplast. This latter structure facilitates cytokinesis either by furrowing (as in *Tetraedron*) or by cell plate formation (as in *Oedogonium*). At telophase, the daughter nuclei

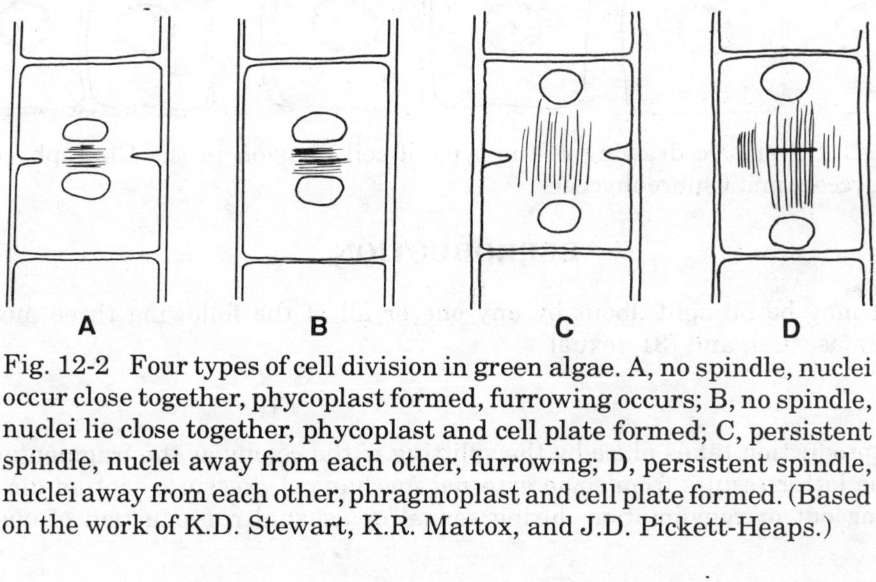

Fig. 12-2 Four types of cell division in green algae. A, no spindle, nuclei occur close together, phycoplast formed, furrowing occurs; B, no spindle, nuclei lie close together, phycoplast and cell plate formed; C, persistent spindle, nuclei away from each other, furrowing; D, persistent spindle, nuclei away from each other, phragmoplast and cell plate formed. (Based on the work of K.D. Stewart, K.R. Mattox, and J.D. Pickett-Heaps.)

tend to lie close together. Examples are *Ulothrix*, *Oedogonium*, *Draparnaldia*, *Fritschiella*, *Volvox*, and *Ulva*.

(2) The spindle and nuclear envelope are open. At telophase, the microtubules of the intranuclear spindle are persistent and phragmoplast is formed at cytokinesis during the progress of furrowing. Examples are *Coleochaete*, *Chara*, *Klebsormidium*, *Spirogyra*, and several land plants.

These general patterns of cell division are explained diagrammatically in Fig. 12-2. The general patterns of cell divisions in the three classes, Charophyceae, Ulvophyceae, and Chlorophyceae are illustrated in Fig. 12-3.

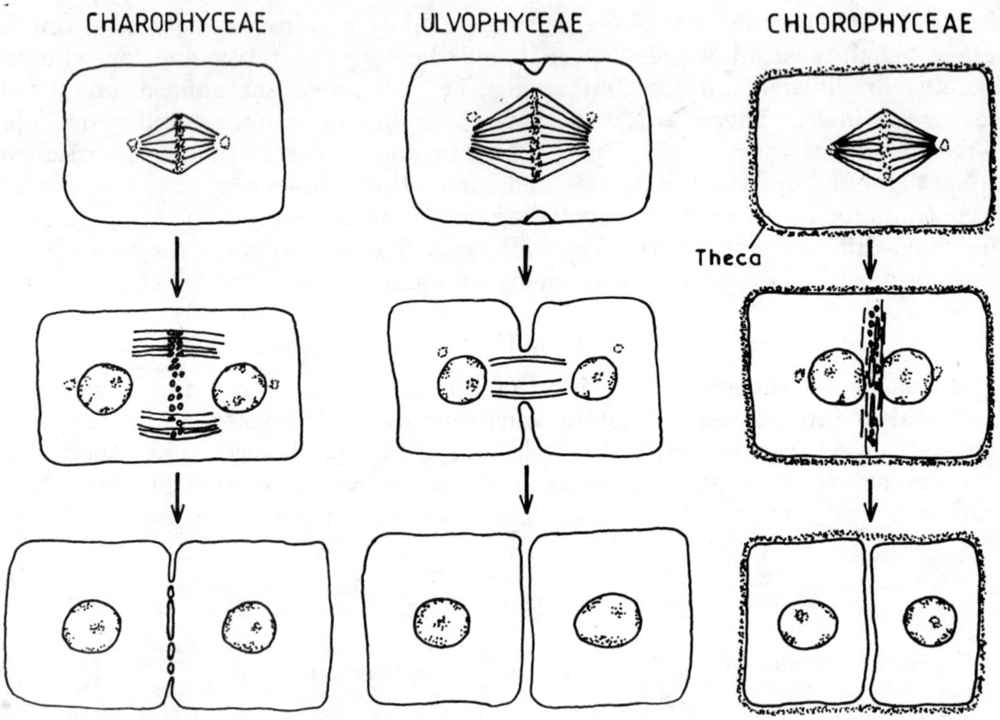

Fig. 12-3 Schematic drawing of the type of cell division in the Charophyceae, Ulvophyceae, and Chlorophyceae.

REPRODUCTION

Reproduction may be brought about by any one or all of the following three methods: (1) vegetative, (2) asexual, and (3) sexual.

Vegetative

Vegetative reproduction takes place by the splitting of the colony or the fragmentation of the filaments. The latter results from some external mechanical pressure, septum dissolution or from the dying out or consumption during sexual or asexual reproduction of one or a few intercalary cells of the filament. In *Ulothrix*, *Oedogonium* or *Sphaeroplea*, the number of filaments increases by occasional fragmentation of one filament into two, each of which then grows to adult size. The best known example is however *Stichococcus* in which the tendency to fragment is so strong and pronounced that as soon as the filament grows to the stage of four or six cells, fragmentation occurs so that filaments longer than 4–6 cells are seldom found.

Asexual

The commonest method of reproduction is by the repeated division of the protoplasts of certain cells. The daughter protoplasts are either transformed into motile and flagellate, commonly naked zoospores, or they round off into nonmotile aplanospores provided with true cell walls. The number of zoospores or aplanospores produced within a mother cell varies from one (*Oedogonium*), two, four or more (in many algae) to as many as several thousand in *Hydrodictyon*. These asexual cells may be produced either in ordinary, unmodified cells (*Ulothrix*) or in specially modified cells known as zoosporangia (*Trentepohlia*).

In many forms, zoospores are produced during the night and liberated in the morning. Their formation is most active during favourable growth periods when the alga is young and healthy. The formation of zoospores may sometimes be artificially induced by modifications of environmental conditions such as pH, temperature, light, and transference from flowing to still water.

The zoospores are liberated either by gelatinization of the parent cell wall or, more commonly, through one or more pores formed in the lateral walls. When liberated, they are generally naked and swarm around in this state for a few hours to a few days. They then come to rest and attach themselves to some substratum by their anterior ends, lose flagella, secrete a wall, and become quiescent for some time before growing into new individuals.

Sexual

Most green algae, except some Chlorococcales, reproduce sexually. In the Conjugales, the fusing gametes are amoeboid and nonflagellate, whereas in other orders, at least the male gamete is always flagellated.

The Chlorophyta exhibit wide variations in the kind and formation of their gametes. When the fusing gametes are morphologically identical and indistinguishable, they are known as isogametes; such isogamous reproduction is noticed, among others, in species of *Chlamydomonas*, *Ulothrix*, and *Zygnema*. When the fusing gametes are both motile and flagellate but unequal in size (as found in *Chlamydomonas braunii*, *Aphanochaete*, and others), they are termed anisogamous. Oogamous reproduction involves fusion between a small flagellate and actively motile male gamete (known as the antherozoid) and a large, nonmotile, nonflagellate, and passive female gamete, the ovum or oosphere. The ovum is generally produced singly within a specially differentiated and enlarged cell called the oogonium, e.g., *Oedogonium* and *Coleochaete*. The antherozoids are however many and are produced within an antheridium; in *Oedogonium*, nevertheless, only two antherozoids are produced per antheridium.

In *Spirogyra*, the fusing gametes, which are nonflagellate, are morphologically isogamous but physiologically anisogamous since one of them behaves as male and the other as female. *Sirogonium* provides an isolated example of morphological anisogamy in the order Conjugales since it forms a small male and large female gametangium.

The advancement in sexual reproduction, from isogamy through anisogamy to oogamy, seems to have been accompanied by a reduction in the number and an increase in the size of the female gametes. The evolution from isogamy to oogamy perhaps occurred independently in different orders of the green algae. Progressive evolutionary series illustrating the transition from isogamy to oogamy are met with in the coenobial Volvocales and in certain Chaetophoraceae, e.g., *Stigeoclonium*, *Aphanochaete*, *Chaetonema*, and *Coleochaete*.

With the exception of three species (*Chlorogònium oogamum*, *Carteria iyengarii*, and *Chaetonema irregulare*) in which the ovum is released from the oogonium prior to fertilization, in all others fertilization takes place while the ovum is still within the mother cell.

Generally, the two members of a pair of fusing gametes are derived from two different individuals, such individuals being termed heterothallic. A number of green algae are however homothallic; in these, fusion can take place between two gametes which have been derived from the same parent individual.

The zygote formed as a result of isogamous or anisogamous reproduction or conjugation is called zygospore, whereas that produced as a result of oogamous fertilization is termed oospore. In most haploid Chlorophyta, the diploid zygospore or oospore secretes a thick wall and becomes transformed into a resting cell. In the next favourable season, it germinates to produce one or more plants. On the other hand, in many marine Chlorophyta, some Cladophorales, and certain diploid forms, the zygote germinates directly into a vegetative plant.

Occasionally, some gametes, without fusion, may directly give rise to new plants, or may form resting cells known as parthenospores which subsequently produce new plants. Such parthenogenesis occurs in *Ulothrix* and certain other algae.

CONTROL OF SEXUAL MORPHOGENESIS

Sexuality induction in laboratory cultures of many green algae is often correlated with depletion of nitrate, ammonia or other nutrients in the culture medium. This is particularly so in the case of desmids and unicellular flagellates where the cells are often directly converted into gametes.

In many spp. of *Volvox*, male colonies produce some sex hormone, but in *V. dissipatrix*, the hormone is produced by both sexes. The sex hormones produced by most spp. of *Volvox* seem to be large glycoproteins.

In *Volvox* populations, both in nature and culture, the number of individuals in the population is increased exponentially by repeated formation of asexual spheroids. After some period of asexual propagation, sexual male spheroids may be produced spontaneously; they produce a hormone which induces more sexual spheroids, both male and female, eventually leading to the production of an entirely sexual population (see Miller and Starr, 1981). Interestingly, the addition of small amounts of L-glutamate to culture suspension of *V. capensis* induces sexual morphogenesis but only in the light (Miller and Starr, 1981). The light seems to function in some indirect and unknown manner in the above induction. Miller and Starr further noted great plasticity in the control of sexual morphogenesis in *V. capensis*, as borne out by their discovery that an inducing factor from nutrient broth plus old *Volvox* culture filtrate when added to the assay medium results in sexual induction in the dark.

PERENNATION

Certain green algae produce special resting stages which enable the alga to pass through adverse or unfavourable environmental conditions. Such resting cells may be vegetative (akinetes), asexual (hypnospores) or sexual (zygospores or oospores).

Akinetes are prominently differentiated and enlarged vegetative cells which become thick-walled and densely laden with food reserves to tide over adverse periods. In these akinetes, the spore wall fuses with that of the parent cell and a few additional wall layers are deposited outside the whole structure. Characteristic intercalary and terminal akinetes are found in species of *Pithophora*. Hypnospores are modified aplanospores that secrete specially thickened cell walls around them, e.g., in *Sphaerella* and *Protosiphon*.

In many Chlorophyceae, the only mode of perennation is by the formation of resting zygospores or oospores. The ordinary vegetative cells of *Pleurococcus*, *Trebouxia*, *Prasiola*, and certain other terrestrial or subaerial algae can perennate in this way, i.e., without the formation of any special stages.

LIFE CYCLE

Four main types of life cycle—haploid, diploid, isomorphic or homologous, and heteromorphic—are encountered in the green algae.

Ulothrix, *Pandorina*, *Coleochaete*, and *Oedogonium*, for example, are haploid, with the zygote representing the only diploid stage in the life cycle. In these, meiosis occurs during the first division of the zygote nucleus (Fig. 2-11).

In the diploid forms, such as many Siphonales and some Chlorococcales, the mature vegetative plant is diploid and meiosis occurs during the formation of gametes which represent the only haploid stage. The zygote germinates directly into the diploid plant.

The isomorphic life cycle involves an alternation between a haploid gametophyte and a diploid sporophyte, both of which are morphologically quite indistinguishable from each other. The haploid phase produces gametes that fuse to form the zygote which in turn germinates into a diploid sporophytic plant and produces zoospores without undergoing any meiotic division. Meiosis occurs during the formation of zoospores and hence they are haploid. These grow into haploid gametophytes (Fig. 2-17). This kind of alternation of generations is found in the Ulvaceae, many Cladophorales, and certain Chaetophorales, e.g., *Draparnaldiopsis* and *Fritschiella*.

Urospora, in which the two free-living alternating generations are morphologically dissimilar, provides an example of the heteromorphic life cycle.

A novel type of life cycle has been described in *Ulva mutabilis* by Hoxmark and Nordby (1974). The unusual characteristic feature is the occurrence of haploid meiosis that produces nonviable offspring. This alga has three main types of plant, viz., (1) normal, diploid sporophytes, formed by the fusion of two gametes; (2) haploid gametophytes, produced by haploid zoospores as a result of normal meiosis; and (3) novel type of parthenosporophytes, formed by the germination of gametes. The parthenosporophytes are of two different mating types, + and –. The former types go through normal meiosis at zoosporogenesis. But the minus-type parthenosporophytes show highly abnormal and erratic meiosis. This abnormal meiosis is actually a regularly occurring haploid meiosis that occurs only in the minus-type parthenosporophytes (Hoxmark and Nordby, 1974).

A detailed study of the life cycle of this species has shown that the fusion of gametes of + and – mating types produces a zygote which resorbs its flagella after settlement on some substratum. This zygote gives rise to a diploid sporophyte. Unfused gametes give rise to parthenosporophytes (+ and –). The + type parthenosporophyte somehow regulates its chromosome number to a diploid value, but the – type is unable to achieve this and hence remains haploid. Both the diploid and haploid parthenosporophytes form quadriflagellate zoospores. Of course, both + and – zoospores are also produced normally by the normal sporophyte of type (1). In contrast, the parthenosporophytes produce only one type of zoospore, viz., + type by the + parthenosporophyte, and – type by the – one. After some period of motility, the zoospores settle down on a substratum where they germinate directly into + and – gametophytes. These gametophytes are morphologically similar to the sporophyte generation. The gametes, unlike zoospores, are biflagellate, and are produced mitotically.

CLASSIFICATION

The use of the electron microscope has considerably added to our understanding of the micromorphology of the green algae. This study in conjunction with their chemical and physiological features has led many phycologists to propose different systems of classification of the Chlorophyta. These systems vary mainly in the degree of emphasis placed on a particular combination of phyletic characters.

Emphasizing the morphological and reproductive features, Fritsch (1935) proposed a widely accepted system of classification. He divided the green algae into nine orders (Volvocales, Chlorococcales, Ulotrichales, Cladophorales, Chaetophorales, Oedogoniales, Conjugales, Siphonales, and Charales). In this book, we have followed the same system of classification but have raised the Charales to the rank of a class (Charophyceae) coordinate with the Chlorophyceae. Thus, the Chlorophyta includes two classes of which the Chlorophyceae has eight orders, whereas the Charophyceae has a single order, the Charales. For convenience, we have included the prasinophytes as a third class, Prasinophyceae.

Two of the more widely followed systems of classification which may be mentioned here are those of Bold (1967) and Round (1971).

Bold, following some earlier workers, has raised the Charales to the rank of a phylum, the Charophyta. The division Chlorophycophyta includes only one class, the Chlorophyceae, having ten orders (Volvocales, Chlorosphaerales, Chlorococcales, Ulotrichales, Ulvales, Cladophorales, Siphonales, Dasycladales, Oedogoniales, and Zygnematales).

Round (1971) has divided the green algae (Chlorophyta *sensu* Fritsch) into three phyla containing six classes and 37 orders as follows:

Phylum: Chlorophyta

Class: Chlorophyceae

Orders: Chlamydomonadales, Volvocales, Polyblepharidales, Tetrasporales, Chlorodendrales, Chlorosarcinales, Chlorococcales, Ulotrichales, Codiolales, Ulvales, Prasiolales, Cylindrocapsales, Microsporales, Chaetophorales, Trentepohliales, Pleurococcales, Ulvellales

Class: Oedogoniophyceae

Order: Oedogoniales

Class: Zygnemaphyceae

Orders: Mesotaeniales, Zygnematales, Gonatozygales, Desmidiales

Class: Bryopsidophyceae

Orders: Cladophorales, Sphaeropleales, Acrosiphonales, Dasycladales, Siphonocladales, Chlorochytriales, Derbesiales, Codiales, Caulerpales, Dichotomosiphonales, Phyllosiphonales

Phylum: Prasinophyta

Class: Prasinophyceae

Orders: Pyramimonadales, Prasinocladales, Halosphaerales

Phylum: Charophyta

Class: Charophyceae

Order: Charales

Green algae are classified into orders or classes largely on the basis of their fine structure, the most widely used parameters being the structure of the flagellated cell and of mitosis/cytokinesis. A principal difference between flagellated reproductive cells of green algae occurs in the absolute orientation of their basal bodies. In one group, basal bodies the two basal bodies that carry microtubular flagellar roots) are displaced relative to one another into the 11/5 o'clock position (cells viewed from their flagella-bearing end), usually by a distance of one basal body diameter. Green algae having this type of basal body arrangement occur in the classes Ulvophyceae and Pleurastrophyceae *sensu* Mattox and Stewart (1984). In another group of green algae, basal bodies are either not displaced at all, or are displaced into the 1/7 o'clock position (Melkonian and Berns, 1983; Reize and Melkonian, 1988). This group is represented by the Chlorophyceae *sensu* Mattox and Stewart (1984). Reize and Melkonian (1988) have shown a strong correlation between basal body absolute orientations and other structural features of the flagellated cells and of the mitotic/cytokinetic system. This points to the key importance of the basal body orientation in green algal systematics.

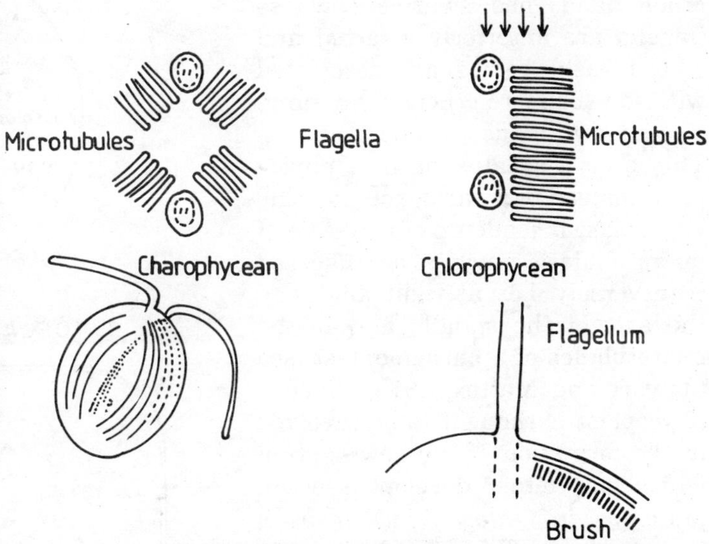

Fig. 12-4 Microtubular arrangement in the chlorophycean and charophycean zoospores.

Figure 12-4 compares the arrangement of microtubules in zoospores of Chlorophyceae and Charophyceae.

CYTOLOGICAL CLASSIFICATION OF GREEN ALGAE

After conducting an extensive survey of the processes of mitosis, cell division, and cytokinesis in several genera of the green algae, Pickett-Heaps (1967, 1969, 1972), Pickett-Heaps and

Marchant (1972), and Stewart and Mattox (1975) have suggested that, on the basis of comparative cytology, the green algae may be broadly divided into two distinct classes, the Charophyceae and the Chlorophyceae. The motile cells of the Charophyceae have laterally attached flagella whose basal bodies are associated with a single broad band of microtubules. In general, the mitosis and cytokinesis in *Chara* resemble those in angiosperms in two respects, viz., (1) the mitotic spindle is open, and (2) a phragmoplast proliferating from a persistent interzonal spindle is involved in cytokinesis. (The phragmoplast is a universal feature of higher plants.) As thus delimited, the class Charophyceae includes the orders Klebsormidiales, Zygnematales, Coleochaetales, and Charales.

The class Chlorophyceae, on the other hand, has swarmers whose flagella are anteriorly inserted and whose basal bodies are associated with four or more cruciately arranged narrow bands of microtubules. This class typically forms a phycoplast instead of a phragmoplast. The phycoplast is made up of a system of microtubules which are disposed transversely, i.e., at right angles to the axis of the spindle and to the microtubules of a phragmoplast (see Stewart and Mattox, 1975). Such a phycoplast is thought to be involved in the formation of the new septum which may either develop as a cell plate (as in *Oedogonium*) or as a furrow (as in *Tetraedron*). Another general feature of phycoplast-bearing algae is that the daughter nuclei tend to lie close to the developing septum; this is not so in those algae that have phragmoplasts. Stewart and Mattox include the following orders in their Chlorophyceae: Volvocales, Chlorococcales, Microsporales, Ulvales, Chaetophorales, and Oedogoniales. The Oedogoniales have a closed spindle and barrel-shaped plasmodesmata.

Studies on cytology and fine struc-

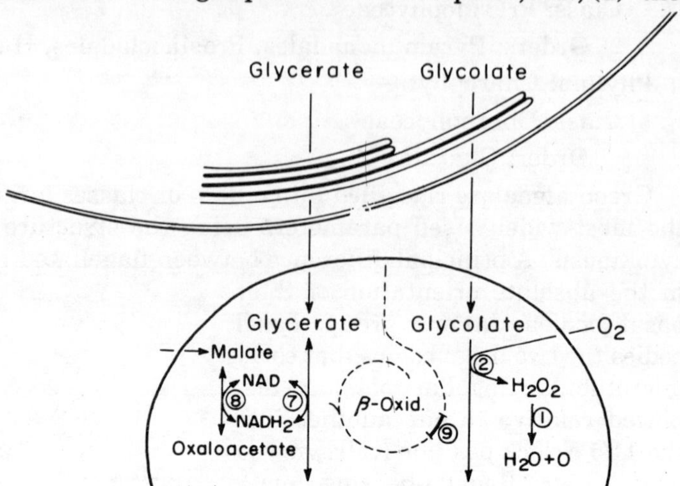

Fig. 12-5 Glycolate pathway in *Mougeotia*. 1–9, enzymes: 1, catalase; 2, glycolate oxidase; 3, alanine glyoxylate aminotransferase; 4, glutamate-glyoxylate aminotransferase; 5, serine hydroxymethyl transferase; 6, serine-pyruvate aminotransferase; 7, hydroxypyruvate reductase; 8, malate dehydrogenase; 9, hydroxyacyl-CoA dehydrogenase. (After Stabenau, 1984.)

ture have indicated that within the green algae, one line of evolution (the Chlorophyceae) probably led from a *Chlamydomonas*-like ancestor to the Volvocales, Chlorococcales, some Ulotrichales, Ulvales, Chaetophorales, and Oedogoniales. A second evolutionary line (the Charophyceae), which eventually gave rise to bryophytes and higher plants, probably arose from primitive flagellates and evolved into Conjugales, Klebsormidiales, Coleochaetales, and Charales. These views gain some support from biochemical data also. Thus, the Charophyceae seem to (1) contain the peroxisomal enzyme glycolate oxidase (see Fig. 12-5) (the higher plants also have this enzyme), and (2) have significant amounts of polyunsaturated C_{20} fatty acids. Their superoxide dismutase is more closely related to that of the higher plants (Kessler, 1984). (The Chlorophyceae typically contain glycolate dehydrogenase instead of glycolate oxidase.)

The bases on which the above cytological classification has been projected are illustrated in Table 12-1.

Table 12-1 Cytological comparison of some representative genera of green algae (after Pickett-Heaps, 1972)

Character	*Ulothrix, Stigeoclonium, Microspora*	*Klebsormidium*	*Spirogyra, Cosmarium, Micrasterias, Closterium*
Spindle	Closed or semiclosed	Open	Open
Centriole	+	+	−
Constancy of pole-chromosome distance during anaphase	−	+	±
Persistence of microtubules near nucleus after telophase	−	+	+
Persistence of interzonal microtubules for some time after telophase	−	+	±
Membranal coating of mitotic chromosomes	−	Occasional	Occasional
Phycoplast/collapse of spindle at telophase	+	−	−
Cleavage	−	+	+

GREEN ALGAL PHYLOGENY

Until a few decades ago, the green algae were considered as the products of three progressive lines of evolution: (1) the volvocine line which had evolved from a simple flagellate unicell, probably similar to *Chlamydomonas*, to larger colonies of differentiated cells, e.g., *Volvox*; (2) the chlorococcine (siphoneous) line, having multinucleate taxa with few or no cross walls demarcating the cells of a thallus (e.g., *Codium*, *Cladophora*); and (3) the tetrasporine (ulotrichalean) line thought to have evolved from uninucleate unicells into relatively complex filaments and tissue-like thalli bearing structures such as branches and rhizoids (e.g., *Fritschiella*). As the ulotrichalean line had the most complex thallus organization, it was thought to contain the ancestor of land plants (see McCourt, 1995). This view was based on morphological traits whose homologies were quite difficult to assess because cell shape, thallus form, plastid structure, etc., are evolutionarily convergent at higher levels. For example, multicellular filaments have evolved in several lineages (see Bold and Wynne, 1985). Electron microscopic researches in the past few decades yielded taxonomically more useful homologous characters for major groups of green algae, primarily relating to flagellar structure and cell division. These ultrastructural features were also nearly universally applicable to green algae (Mattox and Stewart, 1984). The work of Mattox and Stewart led to the reorganization of major groups and revision of the above three lines of evolution. These workers created a five-class system (Chlorophyceae, Micromonadophyceae, Pleurastrophyceae, Charophyceae, and Ulvophyceae). They agreed with the then prevailing view that green algae evolved from primitive motile unicells. Their major contribution was the classification of multicellular green algae based on the types of motile cells produced. According to them, the major classes had evolved as monophyletic groups from unicellular ancestors which happened to acquire a series of derived characteristics of flagellar roots and mitotic apparatuses (Fig. 12-6) (see McCourt, 1995).

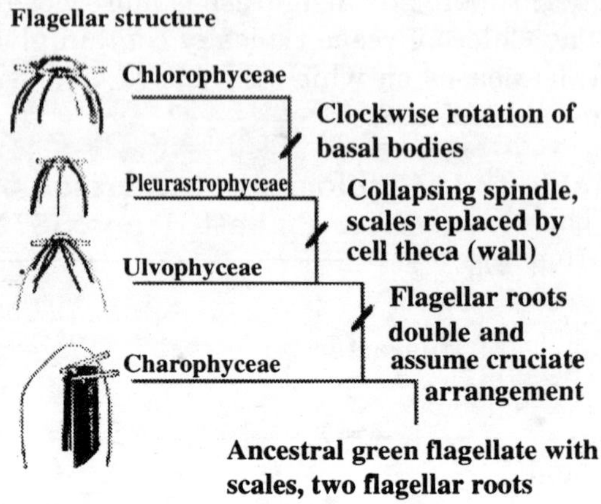

Fig. 12-6 Proposed phylogeny of Mattox and Stewart (1984) showing several character changes and motile cell structure of four of their five classes. (After McCourt, 1995.)

The last decade has seen striking advances in molecular biology some of which have been exploited by phycologists to test the proposal made by Mattox and Stewart. The relatively short 5S rRNA gene (120 base pairs) has been analyzed for this purpose. Some of the results have turned out to be in accord with traditional views of green algal evolution, viz., that *Chlamydomonas* was basal to all green plants, and *Nitella* was sister taxon to higher plants. Use has also been made of the small (18S) and large (26S) subunits of rRNA sequences or the rDNA encoding them. The Micromonadophyceae, comprising tiny, simple flagellate unicells, turned out to be an unnatural group because its defining characters were primitive and shared by other classes as well. Taxa in this class may perhaps be basal and primitive members of other main lineages.

The Pleurastrophyceae has turned out to be a fairly natural group. The Ulvophyceae includes many marine forms with multinucleate thalli (e.g., *Codium*), and also simpler filamentous types formerly classified in the Tetrasporales. The rDNA data alone do not support monophyly of this class but point to a close relationship between Ulvophyceae and Chlorophyceae—two groups with different flagellar basal body arrangements (McCourt, 1995).

Within the Chlorophyceae, some work done on the Chlorococcales has cast serious doubt on the validity of conventional groups. The small subunit rRNA genes have been used to test the monophyly of eight species of *Chlorella*. Considerable sequence differences were seen to exist among the species which did not form a monophyletic group when sequences were combined in a data set with those of other green algae.

Did simple, motile unicells evolve via several steps into larger, more complex colonies of differentiated cells culminating in *Volvox*? Ribosomal DNA sequences have suggested that colonial habit probably evolved several times in different lineages of the biflagellate unicell *Chlamydomonas*. This large genus contains hundreds of species and appears to be paraphyletic (see Glossary) with some members being more derived than their archetypal vegetative condition would suggest. A recent morphological analysis of nine genera of Volvocales indicated that several were paraphyletic and that traditional generic concepts may be defective (McCourt, 1995).

MOLECULAR PHYLOGENETICS AND LAND-PLANT ANCESTORS

The class Charophyceae is of special importance to theories on the origin of higher plants from green algae. It contains thallus types ranging from simple unbranched filaments (*Klebsormidium*, *Spirogyra*) and unicells to parenchymatous, erect branching forms (*Coleochaete*, *Chara*). Morphology of motile cells allies the class Charophyceae to bryophytes and vascular plants. There are ultrastructural, biochemical, and morphological data suggesting the placement of this class on the higher plant lineage. However, there are also some conflicts in details: (1) the placement of the Zygnematales on the tree, (2) the identity of the green algal sister taxon of higher plants, and (3) whether or not the Charophyceae are monophyletic (McCourt, 1995).

The placement of charophycean taxa on the lineage leading to higher plants has also received support from sequence data for nuclear and chloroplast genes. Similarities in cell division and biochemical features place the Zygnematales within the 'streptophyte' clade that includes charophycean algae and higher plants. Rearrangements of entire genes also give clues to the green algal land-plant connection. The discovery (by Baldauf and Palmer, 1990) that a protein elongation factor (called *tuf*A) has moved from the chloroplast to the nucleus in some Charophyceae (a transfer also exhibited by higher plants but not by other green algae) strongly supports the Charophyceae land-plant linkage, which is even further strengthened by the discovery of introns homologous to those of higher plants in each of two chloroplast tRNA genes in the Charales and *Coleochaete* (Fig. 12-6) (Manhart and Palmer, 1990). Only one of the introns occurs in the Zygnematales, and the absence of the second intron reinforces the hypothesis that the latter group may be more basal on the land plant lineage than either *Coleochaete* or the Charales (McCourt, 1995).

Some studies of rDNA sequences indicate that the Charophyceae may be paraphyletic in the sense that the Charales are more closely related to land plants than to other charophytes, but some other rDNA analyses suggest that the Charophyceae is a monophyletic group, with the entire class being sister taxon to the embryophytes (see Graham, 1993).

According to Bold and Wynne (1985), the chloroplast genome of green algae shows a greater diversity in size, structure, and gene content than that of higher plants. Thus, the inverted repeat is a nearly universal feature in land plants but is absent from the plastid genomes of *Coleochaete*, *Spirogyra*, and *Sirogonium*.

Within the Chlorophyta, the Prasinophyceae are the most ancient stock from which all structurally more complex Chlorophyta appear to have evolved. However, the evolutionary origin of the Prasinophyceae and therefore the whole phylum Chlorophyta is obscure. With the general acceptance of the serial endosymbiosis theory, it is believed that the Chlorophyta originated by a primary endosymbiotic event involving an oxygenic phototrophic procaryote and colourless flagellate (zooflagellate). Since there are no extant colourless mastigotes that resemble Prasinophyceae, the evolutionary history of the eucaryotic *host* is unknown. According to Mattox and Stewart (1984), the *ancestral green flagellate* was an asymmetric, complex cell that became structurally simplified after acquiring the photosynthetic endosymbiont. Melkonian (1984) regarded the structurally most simple Prasinophyceae (i.e., the Mamiellales) as more closely related to an *ancestral zooflagellate*.

SELECTED GENERA

Order: VOLVOCALES

The unicellular and colonial green algae with either a permanently motile, or a sedentary vegetative phase that is readily revertible to motility, are included in the Volvocales. On the basis of vegetative habit, this order has been divided into three suborders, namely, (1) the Chlamydomonadineae, comprising motile individuals; (2) the Tetrasporineae, consisting of palmelloid forms; and (3) the Chlorodendrineae, including dendroid species. The suborders Tetrasporineae and Chlorodendrineae have many *Chlamydomonas*-like characters, such as eyespot, contractile vacuoles, and chloroplast.

The Chlamydomonadineae includes four families distinguishable by cell wall morphology: the Chlamydomonadaceae have a cell wall made of glycoproteins rich in hydroxyproline as the main structural component; the Sphaerellaceae have a thickened gelatinous wall provided with a number of simple or branched processes and a chloroplast of variable morphology, generally containing one or more pyrenoids; the Polyblepharidaceae includes naked forms capable of exhibiting changes in the shape of the protoplast and provided with two or more flagella; and the Phacotaceae is characterized by cells that are usually enveloped in a calcified sheath or capsule separated from the cytoplasmic membrane by an intervening mucilaginous space.

The Volvocales includes many phytoflagellates which combine typically plant-like nutrition and autotrophy with an animal-like behaviour, responding rapidly and precisely to light and other stimuli. Like protozoa, the phytoflagellates show fundamental biophysical homologies with metazoan neuromuscular cells.

Family: Chlamydomonadaceae
Genus: *Chlamydomonas*

Occurrence

Most species of *Chlamydomonas* are freshwater forms, or grow in ditches, tanks, ponds, and lakes. Some are marine, whereas others occur in moist, terrestrial habitats. Quite a few grow in brackish water and in waters polluted with sewage or industrial waste. *Chlamydomonas* also occurs in airborne dust. *C. nivalis* accumulates large quantities of haematochrome and is found in snow in alpine and arctic regions, causing 'red snow'.

Nutrition

Most species are obligate phototrophs but *C. dysomos* is a facultative heterotroph and can grow in the dark in the presence of acetate as a carbon source.

Morphology

Light Microscopy

Chlamydomonas is a motile unicellular alga. It is generally oval but variations in its shape are also noticed. The cell is provided with a cellulosic wall and gives rise to two anteriorly inserted whiplash flagella, each originating from a basal granule located in the anterior papillate or nonpapillate region of the cytoplasm (Fig. 12-7). Two, rarely more, contractile vacuoles are found near the bases of the flagella, and a prominent cup- or bowl-shaped chloroplast is present in each cell. The chloroplast contains at its posterior end a pyrenoid with a starch sheath, and towards one side of its anterior end is found an eyespot. The single nucleus remains suspended in the colourless portion of the cytoplasm.

Glycoproteins rich in hydroxyproline constitute the main structural component of the cell wall. In the living cell, sheets or fragments of the glycoprotein tend to be rapidly deposited along the amorphous inner wall layer (Catt *et al.*, 1978). In these glycoproteins, the major sugar components are arabinose, galactose, and mannose (Roberts, 1979).

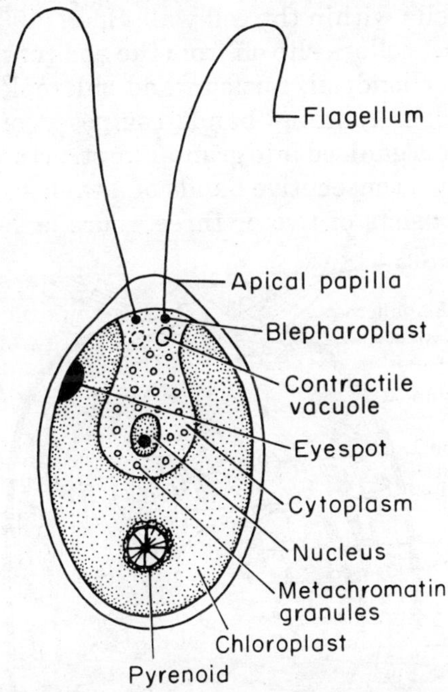

Fig. 12-7 *Chlamydomonas*, cell structure.

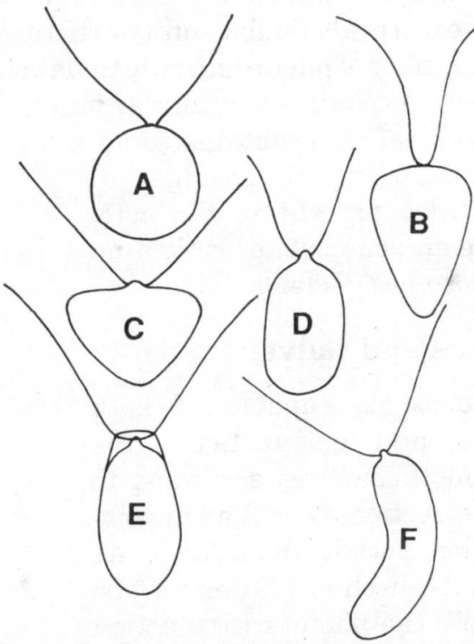

Fig. 12-8 *Chlamydomonas*, some cell shapes. A, *C. incerta*; B, *C. conica*; C, *C. gyroides*; D, *C. biconvexa*; E, *C. pseudocostata*; F, *C. lunata*. (After Ettl, 1965.)

Variability

Chlamydomonas exhibits great variability in cell shape (Fig. 12-8), insertion of flagella, cell wall, chromatophore (Fig. 12-9), pyrenoid, and in various other structural and reproductive features. A detailed study of such variability and the importance of such features in the taxonomic delimitation of different species has been described by Ettl (1965).

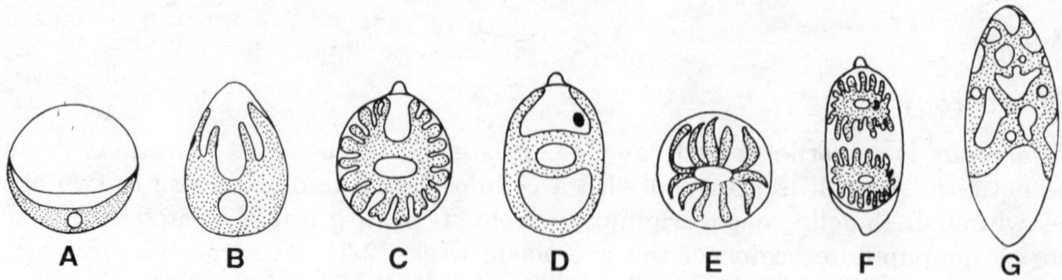

Fig. 12-9 *Chlamydomonas*, chloroplast morphology. A, *C. ametastatos*; B, *C. polydactyla*; C, *C. corrosa*; D, *C. regularis*; E, *C. arachne*; F, *C. zygnemoides*; G, *C. diffusa*. (After Ettl, 1965.)

Electron Microscopy

The flagellum shows the typical 9 + 2 arrangement of the component fibrils. In *C. reinhardii*, the flagella protrude through the cell wall via short tunnels lined with parallel arrays of cylindrical fibrils (Snell, 1983). These slits are lined with collars which contain the fibrils. These fibrillar cylinders are thought to permit free movement of the flagella within the cell wall. Snell (1983) has shown that during the initial stages of the mating intact collars slip off from the ends of the flagella when cell wall loss occurs. The cytoplasmic, mitochondrial, nuclear, and chloroplast membranes are all double unit structures. The chloroplast contains bands composed of a variable number of photosynthetic thylakoids which are not organized into grana-like structures (Fig. 12-10). A colourless, granular matrix separates the two consecutive bands of a thylakoid. The chloroplast also contains some DNA. The eyespot consists of two or three, more or less parallel rows of linearly arranged fat droplets. Also present in the cytoplasm are an endoplasmic reticulum and dictyosomes (Golgi bodies).

Phototaxis and Galvanotaxis

C. reinhardii is capable of both phototaxis and galvanotaxis; the cells orient themselves according to the light direction as well as in relation to the electric field lines. As shown by Nultsch (1979) and Dolle *et al.* (1987) the phototactic reaction depends on both fluence rate and Ca^{2+} concentration. Nultsch *et al.* (1986) showed that organic Ca^{2+} channel blockers, such as diltiazem and nimodipine, inhibit the phototactic response very specifically, without impairing the motility of the cells.

The cell rotates around its long axis. The photoreceptor pigment is

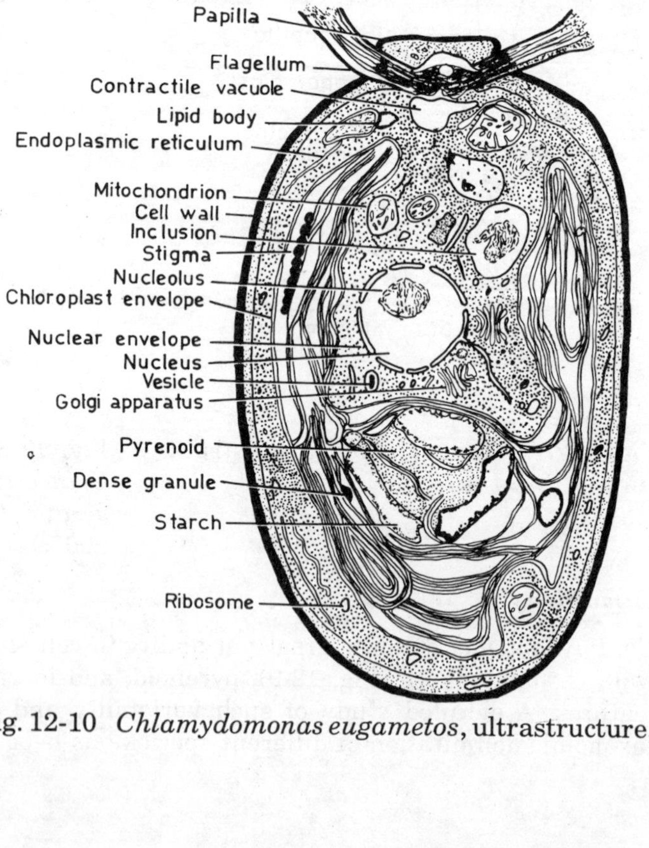

Fig. 12-10 *Chlamydomonas eugametos*, ultrastructure.

probably located in the plasmalemma or the outer chloroplast envelope or both. If the light comes from the side, the photoreceptor is periodically irradiated if it faces the light during rotation. Photons absorbed by the photoreceptor pigments appear to cause an excited state and, probably, a conformational change of the photoreceptor protein. Ca^{2+} channels located in the area of the plasma membrane overlying the stigma open, so that a Ca^{2+} influx results. The membrane responds with a local depolarization, and a subsequent electrotonic spread along the plasma membrane causes Ca^{2+} channels in the flagellar membrane to open. An axonemal flagellar component is activated, leading to a change of the synchrony of the flagellar beat. The result is a steering response with a phototactic reorientation of the cell with respect to the light direction.

Dolle and Nultsch (1988) have observed that *C. reinhardii* cells move towards the cathode. The galvanotactic orientation is also Ca^{2+}-dependent and specifically inhibited by diltiazem and nifedipine, without impairing the motility, thus excluding the possibility of an electrophoretical movement. These results show that galvanotaxis is a true directional sensory response to the electric stimulus. Dolle and Nultsch (1988) suggested that voltage-gated Ca^{2+} channels might be involved in this case.

Reproduction

Asexual During favourable environmental conditions, the alga discards its flagella and enters into a nonmotile phase, and its protoplast undergoes two, three or four successive mitotic divisions (all longitudinal) resulting in the production of four, eight or 16 uninucleate

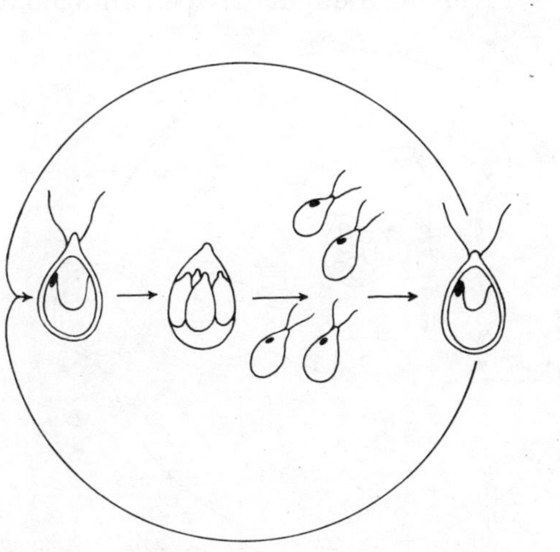

Fig. 12-11 *Chlamydomonas*, zoospore production.

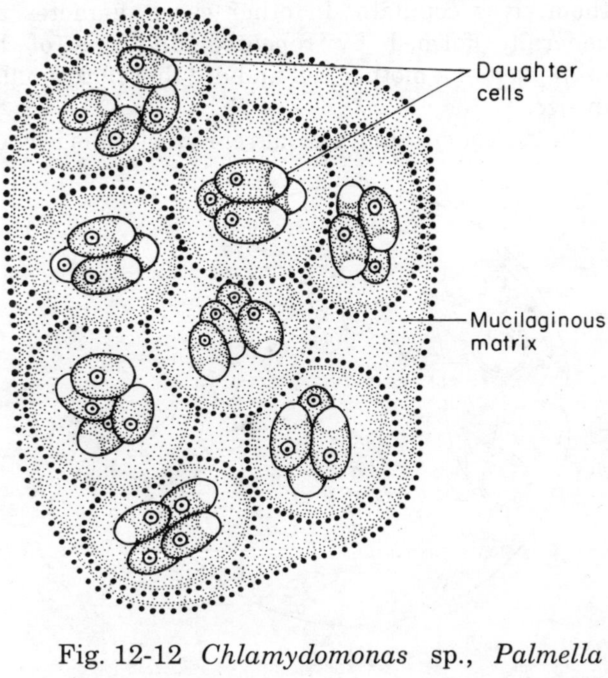

Fig. 12-12 *Chlamydomonas* sp., *Palmella* stage.

daughter protoplasts (Fig. 12-11). Each of these acquires a pair of flagella and a wall before being released from the mother cell through gelatinization or rupture of the mother wall. The zoospores gradually develop into mature *Chlamydomonas* cells.

Under adverse conditions, the daughter protoplasts, instead of growing into zoospores, continue to divide, each producing a group of 2–4 aplanospores within its own newly formed gelatinous wall. Meanwhile, the original parent wall also gelatinizes and the entire groups of aplanospores remain embedded within a common gelatinous matrix. Such a phase, which may be quite short-lived, is called a *Palmella* stage (Fig. 12-12). With the recurrence of a favourable growing period, each aplanospore changes into a zoospore which grows in size to become a *Chlamydomonas* plant. In *C. nivalis*, the aplanospores develop into hypnospores.

Sexual Sexual reproduction ranges from isogamy to oogamy (Figs. 12-13, 12-14 A, B), and the sexually reproducing alga may be homothallic (*C. gynogama*, *C. media*) or heterothallic (*C. reinhardii*). Anisogamy and oogamy have been described on the basis of observations with materials collected from natural habitats. Therefore, virtually nothing is known about the nature of the genetic or environmental factors controlling sexual reproduction in the anisogamous or oogamous species of *Chlamydomonas*. Much experimental work however has been carried out on the isogamously reproducing heterothallic species.

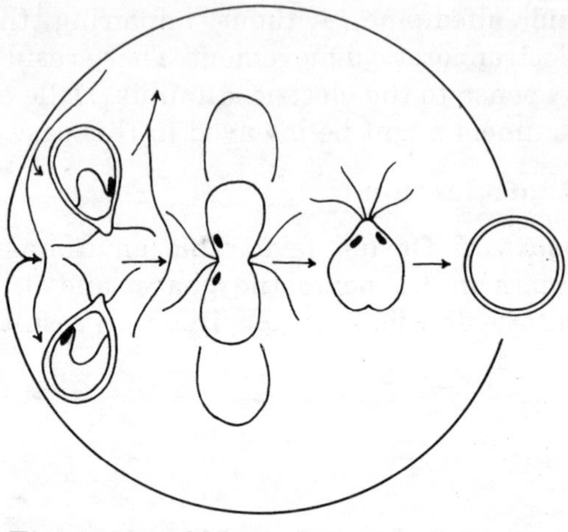

Fig. 12-13 *Chlamydomonas*, isogamy.

In heterothallic *C. moewusii*, adult individuals themselves copulate. In other cases, gametes are generally formed by repeated divisions of the protoplast of a mother cell and are therefore smaller in size.

In *C. debaryanum*, sexual reproduction is isogamous, involving a union between biflagellate

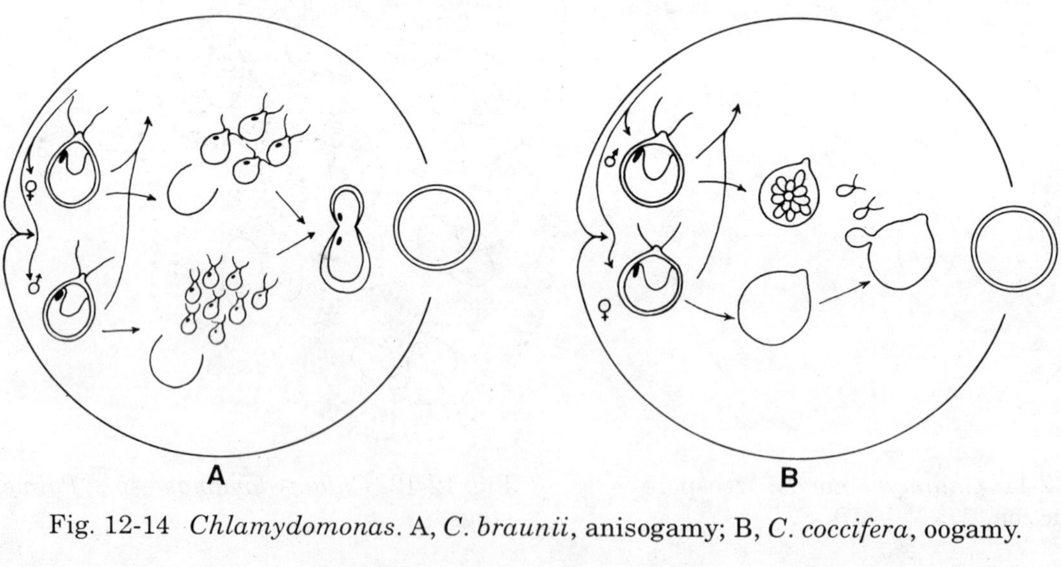

Fig. 12-14 *Chlamydomonas*. A, *C. braunii*, anisogamy; B, *C. coccifera*, oogamy.

gametes. *C. braunii* shows anisogamy (Fig. 12-14 A). The male zoogametes (microgametes) are smaller in size and are produced in greater numbers per cell than the female zoogametes (macrogametes). As a rule, the male cell produces eight microgametes, whereas the female produces only four macrogametes. This difference between two kinds of gametes is further advanced in the oogamous *C. coccifera* (Fig. 12-14 B) where the female cell, instead of dividing to produce gametes, discards its flagella and directly functions as an immobile female gamete, the egg. The male gametes, on the other hand, are produced by repeated divisions of the protoplast of the cell into 16 small, biflagellate microgametes.

A homothallic strain of *C. monadina* produces cells of three sizes. The largest are vegetative while the two smaller types can behave as gametes. In polar view, the macrogamete orients itself at right angle to the surface of the liquid medium, holding this position by its flagella outstretched at a 180° angle to each other in the surface microlayer (Rosowski and Hoshaw, 1988). The gametic flagella do not agglutinate. The anterior end of the microgamete penetrates the side of the macrogamete, with both gametes retaining their cell walls and flagella during the initial contact. Thereafter the smaller gamete forms an anterior papilla. The papillar wall fuses with the wall of the larger gamete and flagellar activity is lost. Although the macrogamete remains stationary prior to and during gametic union, it does not lose its flagella till the fusion of the protoplasts within the macrogametangium (Rosowski and Hoshaw, 1988).

The pulsation rates of contractile vacuoles in the macro- and microgametes are similar before gametic fusion. As soon as the gametic walls touch each other, the vacuolar pulsations in the microgamete increase from once every 40–50 seconds per vacuole to once every 30 sec. No change occurs in the pulsation rate in the macrogamete but that in the newly-formed zygote becomes once every minute. It appears that an increase in the rate of inflow of water into the microgamete acts as the driving force for its movement into the gametangium of the macrogamete.

Figure 12-15 illustrates the anisogamous sexuality and vacuolar activity in liquid culture.

Control of Sexuality

In *C. reinhardii* and *C. moewusii* (=*C. eugametos*), two main kinds of factors—genetic and environmental—are known to affect the onset and course of sexual reproduction.

Genetic factors A pair of sex-determining allelic genes designated + and – exist in the diploid zygote. The complementary genes segregate in the ratio of 1 : 1 during meiosis in the zygote, thus giving rise to one half + type and the other half – type individuals (Fig. 12-16). Mating can occur only between gametes of complementary sexes, i.e., + and –.

Environmental factors In general, nitrogen deficiency induces gametogenesis. Ammonium nitrogen is very specific in the inhibition of sexuality (Fig. 12-17). The male and female cells differ in their response to light; male gametes (– mating type) are produced in the presence of light, and female gametes (+ mating type) in its absence (Wiese, 1965). The presence of calcium is essential for mating. When cells of the + and – mating types are transferred into a medium deficient in nitrogen and low in other salts, the vegetative cells differentiate into gametes without undergoing any morphological change. The main detectable difference between vegetative cells and gametes is the differentiation of flagellar membranes. The agglutination or clumping of gametes occurs by adhesion of flagellar membranes. In *C. moewusii*, a fusing pair of opposite gametes is finally released from the clump with their flagellar membranes unattached to each other.

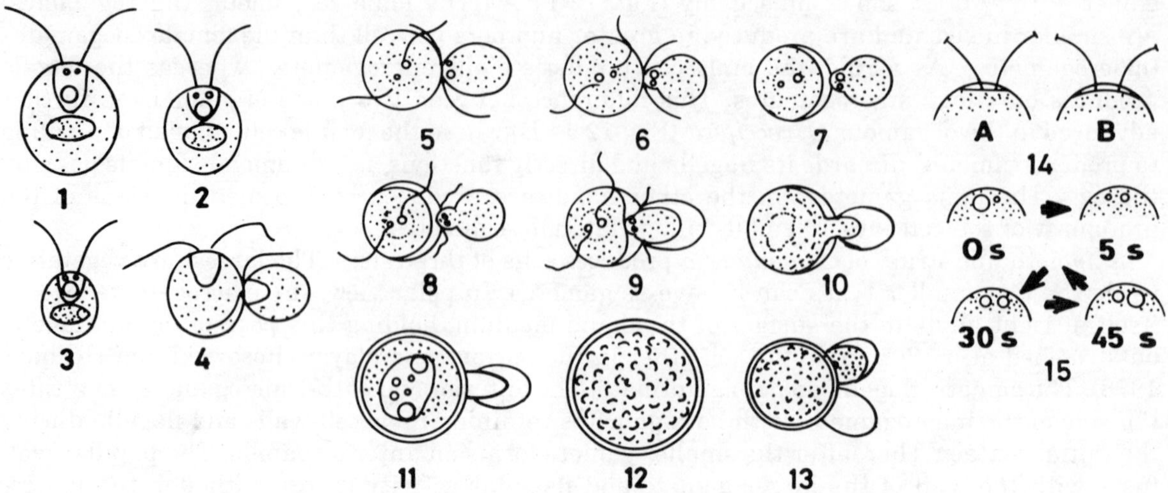

Fig. 12-15 *Chlamydomonas monadina*, sexual process and vacuolar activity. 1, an example of the largest motile cell observed in liquid cultures; never observed in sexual fusions, this cell is interpreted as strictly vegetative; note laterally elongated pyrenoid in the cup-shaped chloroplast; contractile vacuoles below the flagellar bases; nucleus anterior; median longitudinal optical view; 2, cell interpreted to be a macrogamete; median longitudinal optical view; 3, smallest cell observed in liquid cultures; interpreted to be a microgamete since cells of this size fuse with those of the size in 2; 4, lateral view of a microgamete pairing with the macrogamete from the side; 5–11, polar view of successive stages of gametic union: 5, same stage as 4; flagella of microgamete and macrogamete do not touch except by chance; 6, gametic walls fuse; flagella of the microgamete become nearly motionless; contractile vacuoles increase their rate of pulsation and a papilla forms on the microgamete; 7, protoplast of macrogamete contracts away from the point of contact of microgamete; 8, microgamete contracting posteriorly with its anterior penetrating the macrogametangium; 9, microgametoplast pressing against that of the macrogamete; flagella on the macrogamete are retained; 10, fusing gametes; flagella of the macrogamete disappear at the moment the gametic protoplasts fuse; 11, same stage one half an hour later than 10; protoplasts have fused; a second cell wall was secreted by the microgamete before it fused with the macrogametoplast; empty microgametangium remains on the wall of the macrogametangium; 12, mature floating zygospore; microgametangial wall is lost; 13, microgamete attempting fusion with recently formed zygote; successful microgamete has left an empty microgametangium; 14, anterior portions of microgametes before gametic union (A) and immediately before papilla formation (B); 15, sequence of vacuolar activity showing expansion and contraction of paired vacuoles in gametes or vegetative cells at rest (s = seconds). (After Rosowski and Hoshaw, 1988.)

Concanavalin A, which is a tetravalent lectin, causes isoagglutination of gametes of *Chlamydomonas*. This lectin attaches to the flagellar membranes, thereby causing a common bond between cells. McLean *et al.* (1981) have visually demonstrated the presence of Concanavalin A binding sites on the flagellar membrane surface. These sites are more dense on gametes than vegetative cells and they occur in clusters along the membrane. According

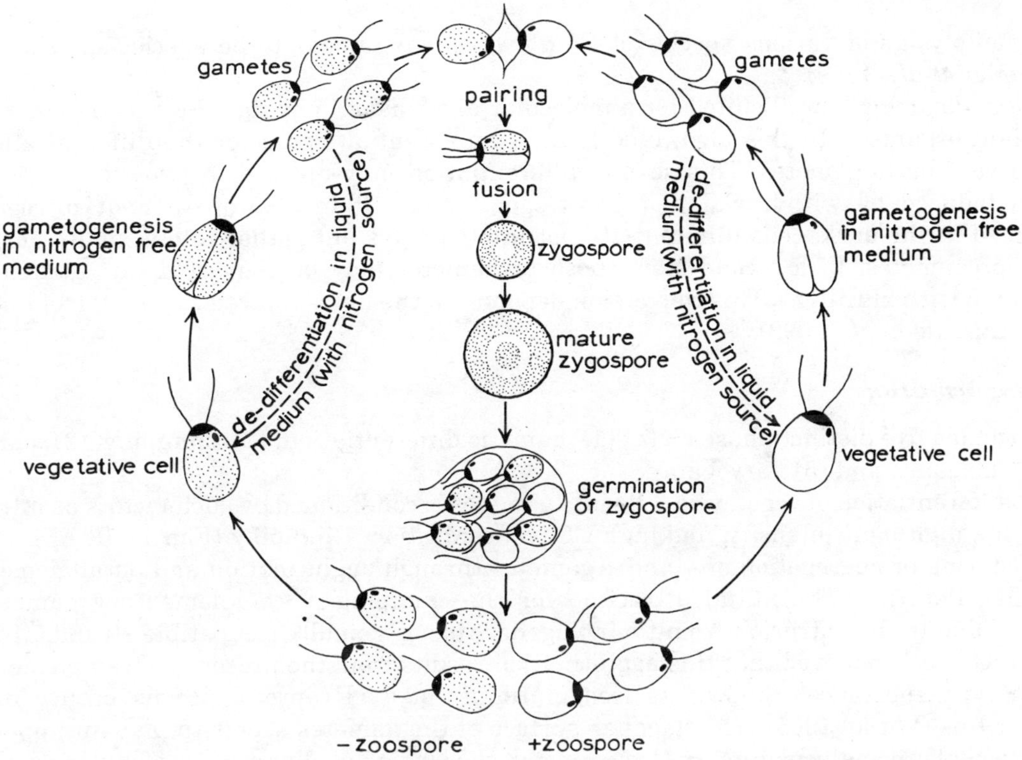

Fig. 12-16 *Chlamydomonas reinhardii*, experimental control of sexual cycle.

to McLean *et al.* (1981), the Concanavalin A binding sites are linked to the sexual process and move to the flagellar tip in response to gamete contact. It is possible that membrane tubulin constitutes one type of Concanavalin A binding site, or it may participate in the movements of the Concanavalin A sites.

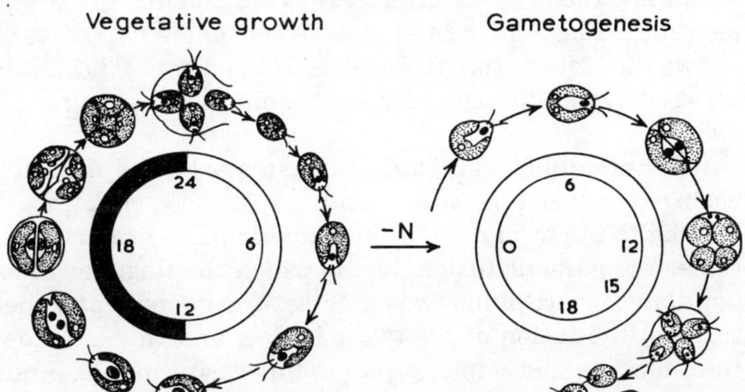

Fig. 12-17 *Chlamydomonas*, influence of environmental factors on vegetative growth and gametogenesis.

The cell wall of gametes of *C. reinhardii* is rich in glycoproteins. This wall becomes enzymatically lysed, prior to gametic fusion, by a gametic enzyme called autolysin. The gametic autolysin also acts on the cell wall of vegetative cells, producing wall-less protoplasts. The autolysin is a glycoproteinase enzyme that acts on its substrate, the inner layer of the cell wall. Waffenschmidt *et al.* (1989) raised polyclonal antibodies against the gametic autolysin and purified them. The purified immunoglobulins inhibit the enzyme activity. These immunoglobulins do not cross-react with the autolysin from vegetative cells.

The autolysins of various species of *Chlamydomonas* appear to be species-specific (Waffenschmidt *et al.*, 1989).

Chlamydomonas is well suited for a molecular analysis of light signal transduction chains in a plant organism. In this alga, blue light is an essential signal for the differentiation of vegetative cells to gametes. This sexual differentiation may proceed in two steps. The first step is induced by withdrawal of the nitrogen source. If incubation without nitrogen is performed in the dark, cells differentiate not into gametes but rather into sexually noncompetent pregametes. In a second step, these pregametes may be converted into gametes by irradiation with blue light. This conversion depends on the light-induced expression of nuclear genes (Buerkle *et al.*, 1993).

Zygote Formation

This includes five distinct phases, viz., (1) gametic differentiation, (2) clumping, (3) pairing, (4) plasmogamy, and (5) karyogamy.

The differentiation of vegetative cells into gametes is conditioned by such factors as nitrogen deficiency, high light intensity, and high CO_2 concentration. Clumping (Fig. 12-18 A) involves the clustering or aggregation of + and – gametes through agglutination and entanglement of their flagellar tips. The initial attraction for the clumping of complementary gametes is probably due to the extrusion from their flagellar tips of sexually compatible strands (Brown *et al.*, 1968). It is believed that this agglutination results from the presence of complementary mating type substances (known as isoagglutinins) of a glycoproteinaceous nature in the flagellar tips (Wiese, 1965). The flagellar surface of the gametes seems to play an important role in sexual cell agglutination. In *C. eugametos*, the whole flagellar surface of mating gametes has been shown to be involved in binding the gametes together (Mesland, 1977). This contrasts with vegetative cells whose flagella do not agglutinate.

The flagella of agglutinating cells change the pattern of their movement from the regular swimming beat to a strong twitching. This gives the gametic clumps a vibrating appearance. Flagellar adhesion between gametes serves three main functions, namely, (1) it allows the cells to sort themselves into pairs; (2) it maintains the cells in close proximity; and (3) it activates the cells for cell fusion, by forming a plasma papilla (Van den Ende *et al.*, 1988).

After clumping, the pairing phase starts: the individual gametes within a clump pair off, each pair consisting of a + and a – gamete still united at their flagellar tips. The factors leading to the formation of the gametic pairs are not known. Subsequent to the pairing phase comes the gametic fusion during which the flagellar union progresses downward towards the papillate surface of the two gametes. The gametic pair then establishes a connection or passage through the fusion of the two papillae, and this is followed by the release of flagellar union, thus making the gametic pair temporarily motile. Immediately after this, the flagella are discarded and the cytoplasmic fusion is followed by the fusion of the gametic chloroplasts. Blank *et al.* (1978) have shown that in zygotes of *C. reinhardii* the nuclear fusion precedes the fusion of the chloroplasts. Karyogamy follows plasmogamy, the two nuclei coming to lie in the equatorial region where they fuse.

In *C. eugametos*, complementary gametes of opposite mating type make chance contacts without chemoattraction. Mutual recognition takes place via the flagella (Demets *et al.*, 1988). The subsequent mating proceeds in three steps, namely:

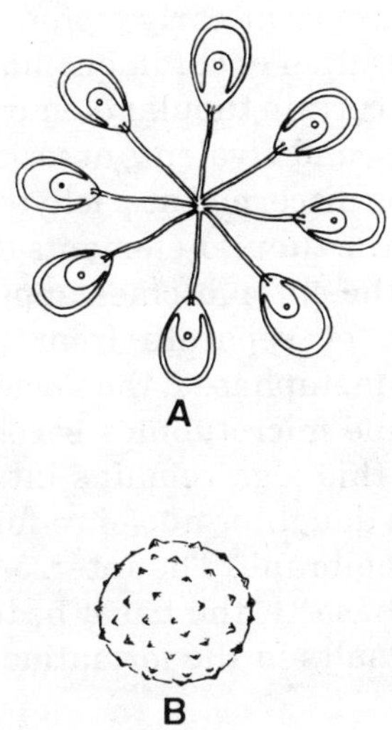

Fig. 12-18 *Chlamydomonas*. A, gametic clumping; B, zygote.

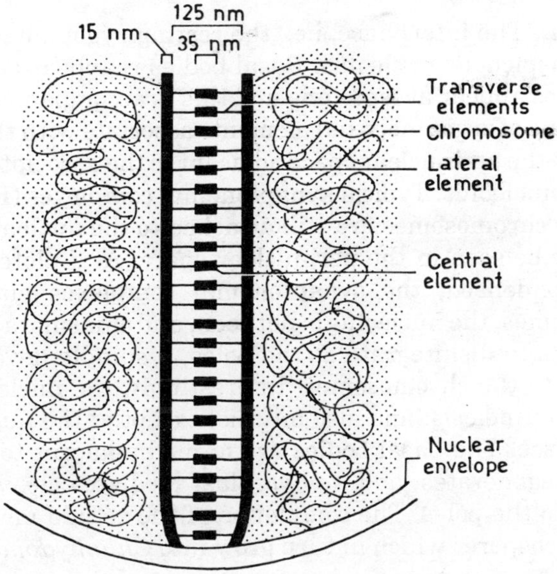

Fig. 12-19 *Chlamydomonas reinhardii*, synaptonemal complex in longitudinal section. Two lateral elements associate with bivalent chromosomes which are separated by central space (about 125 nm). Central element is present along specialized regions of synapsed bivalents. Transverse elements extend from lateral elements to central element. Synaptonemal complex is associated with nuclear envelope. (After Triemer and Brown, 1976.)

(1) Sexual agglutination The gametes stop swimming, adhere to each other by their flagella, and manoeuvre the cell apices into close proximity.

(2) Cell fusion The partners fuse by forming an interconnecting bridge. The resulting +/– tandem is called a vis-a-vis pair. After fusion, the flagella disadhere. Thereafter, swimming is resumed by the mating type + flagella but not by those of type –.

(3) Zygote formation After some hours of swimming, the vis-a-vis pair settles down and retracts its flagella. The two cell bodies then fuse completely to form a zygote.

The gametes can activate potential partners by forming agglutinin-rich vesicles which are then blebbed off from the flagella and shed into the ambient medium. During sexual agglutination, partner cells continuously inactivate the agglutinins of one another, but the inactivated agglutinins tend to be replaced by new copies (Demets *et al.*, 1988).

The mating competence and agglutinability of mt^+ cells of *C. eugametos* depends on light (Kooijman *et al.*, 1988). Light affects only the activity of the flagellar agglutinins (glycoproteins) but not that of the agglutinins on the cell surface.

Zygote Germination and Meiosis

The zygote (Fig. 12-18 B) forms a multilayered wall and perennates. Triemer and Brown (1976) have investigated the ultrastructural details of meiosis in germinating zygotes of *C.*

reinhardii. The interphase, i.e., the resting zygote, has ample starch, is densely granular, and has a conspicuous nucleolus. Basal bodies reappear either at interphase or at early leptotene. Axial cores appear at leptotene and this is accompanied by the condensation of chromonemata. By the time of zygotene, axial elements associate with the nuclear wall, certain tubular elements appear in the perinuclear space adjacent to the associated chromosomes, and bivalents associate with the nucleolus. Typical synaptonemal complexes (Fig. 12-19) can be discerned at pachytene when the chromosomes are still attached to the nuclear wall whereas the tubular elements can no longer be seen in the perinuclear space. At diplotene-diakinesis, the chromosomes appear highly condensed, the synaptonemal complexes either degenerate or separate from the chromosomes, the nucleolus is not seen, and chiasmata can be seen. By metaphase I, the nuclear wall tends to disintegrate at the poles, a spindle develops, and spindle microtubules become attached to the chromosomes. Interestingly, the nuclear envelope in this alga remains intact throughout meiosis (and also mitosis) except at the nuclear poles. The daughter nuclei re-form at telophase. The basal bodies are formed adjacent to the nuclear membrane. The interzonal spindle degenerates, and a phycoplast mediates cleavage. By metaphase II, the basal bodies migrate to the poles. The completion of the second meiotic division results in the formation of haploid zoospores which in turn grow into *Chlamydomonas* plants.

Life Cycle of Chlamydomonas reinhardii

C. reinhardii is a convenient experimental subject and some workers have grown it in synchronous culture. Since most of the cells in such cultures are at the same stage of division or development at any given time, uniformly homogeneous material can be obtained for the study of the sexual process at the molecular level.

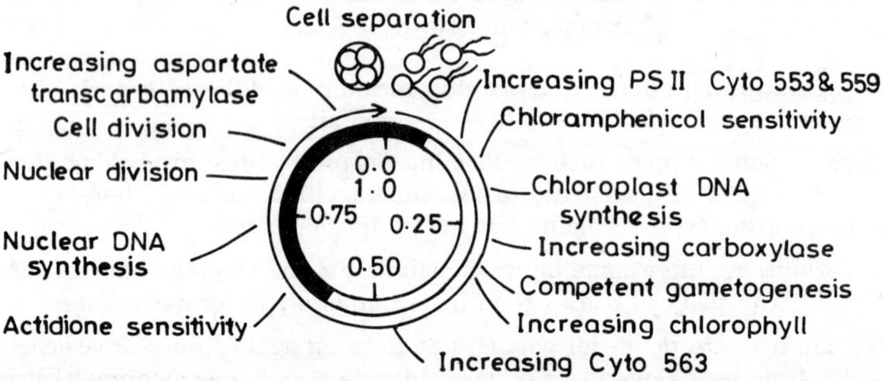

Fig. 12-20 *Chlamydomonas reinhardii*. Cell cycle map. Inner circle shows transition points for various inhibitors as determined from non-synchronous cultures in continuous light. For comparison, outer circle represents cell cycle events in 12 hr light : 12 hr dark synchronized cultures. Open bar, light phase; closed bar, dark phase. A 2-hr time period has been deleted in the synchronous cell cycle (in the dark phase) between cell division and cell separation. This period as well as the entire cycle is lengthened by about 2 hr in synchronous cultures as compared to nonsynchronous ones. (After Howell, 1974.)

A good way of synchronizing the cells is to expose them to alternating periods of light and darkness. The cell cycle of *C. reinhardii* as observed in light-dark synchronized cells is shown in Fig. 12-17. Here the cycle is 16 hr long, and the dark segment on the time scale represents the dark period of the synchronous cycle. Figure 12-20 shows the cell cycle map of *C. reinhardii*.

Genus: *Gonium*

Occurrence

It occurs free-floating in rain water pools, roadside ditches, and freshwater ponds.

Morphology

Species are small, saucer-shaped or plate-like coenobia (Fig. 12-21), each containing 4, 8, or 16 biflagellate, *Chlamydomonas*-like cells. The coenobium usually looks squarish in surface view. *G. pectorale* has four central cells and 12 peripheral cells (Fig. 12-21). The coenobium swims by somersaulting.

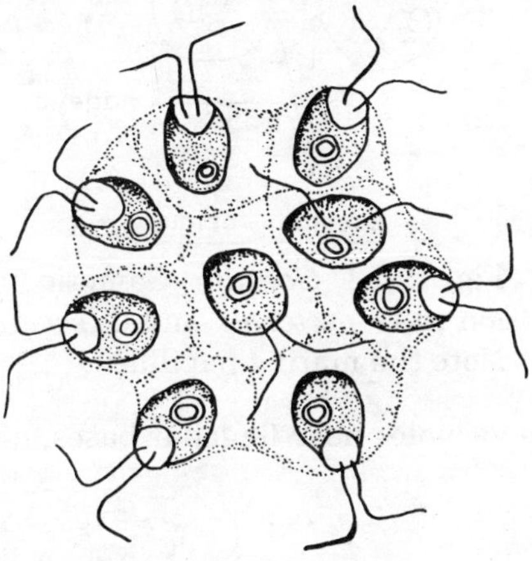

Fig. 12-21 *Gonium formosum*, coenobium.

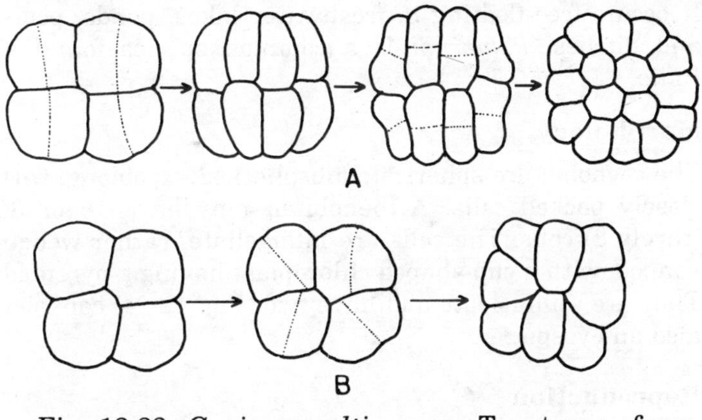

Fig. 12-22 *Gonium multicoccum*. Two types of embryogenesis. A, stages in formation of 16-celled daughter coenobium; B, stages in formation of 8-celled daughter coenobium. (After Nozaki and Kuroiwa, 1991.)

Reproduction

Vegetative It occurs from detached fragments of the coenobium. Figure 12-22 illustrates two types of embryogenesis in *G. multicoccum*.

Asexual All 16 cells can form daughter coenobia by longitudinal divisions.

Sexual *G. pectorale* is heterothallic and isogamous. Each cell produces and releases a biflagellate gamete. The plus and minus gametes fuse laterally. The zygote sheds off its flagella, secretes a thick wall, and perennates. Upon germination, it produces four biflagellate daughter cells, each of which then divides mitotically four times. In this way, four small, 16-celled daughter coenobia are produced. These gradually grow to normal size with maturity.

The gametes of *G. pectorale* bear mating papillae (Fig. 12-23) which initiate plasmogamy. In the 4-celled species, *G. sociale*, one of the two conjugating gametes bears a slender papilla at the flagellar base, whereas the other conjugant does not (Nozaki, 1986). In this species, plasmogamy is initiated by the union between the tip of the mating (unilateral) papilla of one gamete and the anterior part of the other gamete. In *G. pectorale*, plasmogamy is initiated when the tips of the two (bilateral) papillae unite.

The germinating zygote of *G. pectorale* gives rise to four biflagellate cells joined together in a colony. In contrast, in *G. sociale*, the four biflagellate cells emerging from the zygote do not remain joined together but are released individually and independently (Nozaki, 1986).

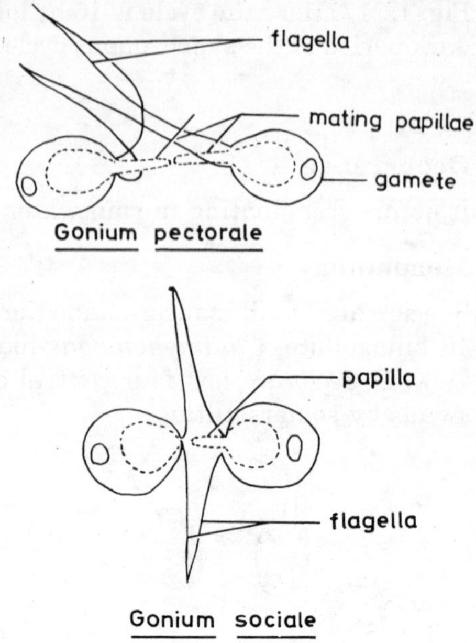

Fig. 12-23 *Gonium*. Gametic fusion in *G. pectorale* and *G. sociale*. Note the mating papillae.

Genus: *Pandorina*

Occurrence

It occurs free-floating in freshwater lakes, ponds, pools, and ditches. *P. morum* is a common species found in India.

Morphology

The coenobia are spherical, subspherical, or oblong, with closely packed cells. A coenobium may have 16 or 32 (rarely 8) cells. The cells are biflagellate, rather wedge-shaped, with a cup-shaped chloroplast having a pyrenoid. They are uninucleate and have two (Fig. 12-24) contractile vacuoles near flagellar bases, and also an eyespot.

Reproduction

Vegetative It can occur from detached parts of a coenobium.

Asexual All cells can produce daughter coenobia. The colony stops swimming. The cells withdraw their flagella and divide four times to form the daughter coenobia. These undergo inversion before being released.

Sexual It is heterothallic and slightly anisogamous. The gametes are biflagellate and fuse laterally or terminally. The quadriflagellate zygote comes to rest, sheds its flagella, perennates, and later germinates, producing a swarmer which develops into a new plant.

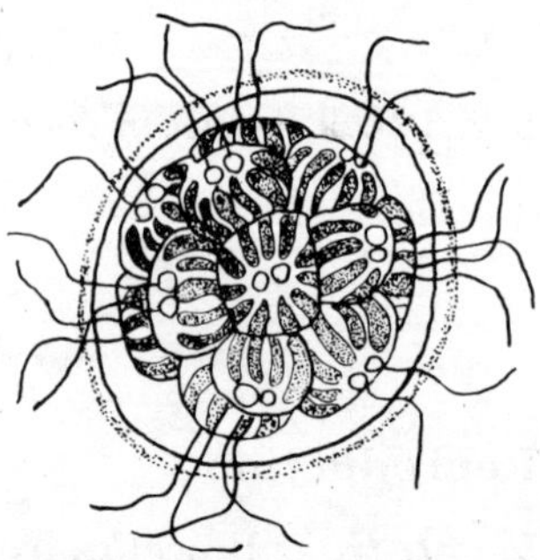

Fig. 12-24 *Pandorina morum*, coenobium.

Genus: *Eudorina*

Occurrence

It is a common inhabitant of freshwater ditches, pools, and ponds and in the plankton of soft water lakes.

Morphology

The alga forms motile coenobia which are ellipsoidal or spherical. Each coenobium (Fig. 12-25) has 32 or 64 globose cells embedded in mucilaginous matrix, and arranged in definite tiers of, for example, 4, 8, 8, 8, and 4 cells each. The cell structure is broadly similar to that of *Chlamydomonas*. The eyespots in the anteriorly located cells are usually better developed than those in the posterior cells.

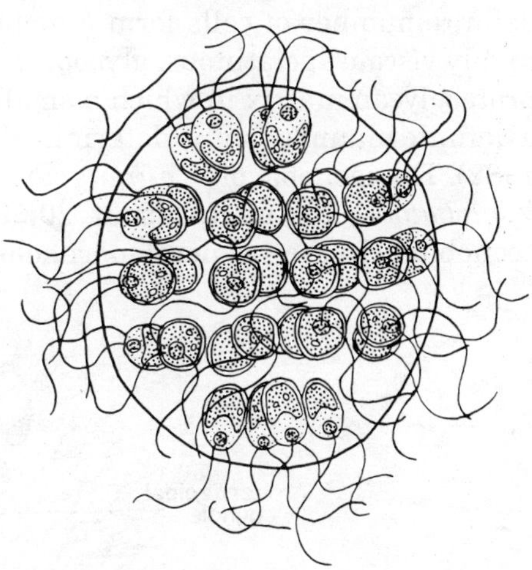

Fig. 12-25 *Eudorina elegans*, young coenobium.

Reproduction

Vegetative It is by fragmentation of coenobia.

Asexual The anterior (front) tiers of cells usually do not reproduce but remain sterile. The remaining cells can divide and produce daughter coenobia. The details of daughter coenobium formation are described under the next genus, *Volvox*.

Sexual *Eudorina* spp. are anisogamous or oogamous and usually heterothallic. In the male coenobia, each cell (except for the front 4) divides successively to form a flat or curved plate of 64 fusiform biflagellate antherozoids. Upon maturity, the entire group is released as a unit which separates into individual antherozoids in the vicinity of the female coenobium.

The cells (except the front 4) of the female colony enlarge slightly and function directly as female gametes. After fertilization, the zygote withdraws its flagella, secretes a thick, smooth wall and perennates. Later, it germinates by producing one or more zoospores meiotically. These give rise to new individuals.

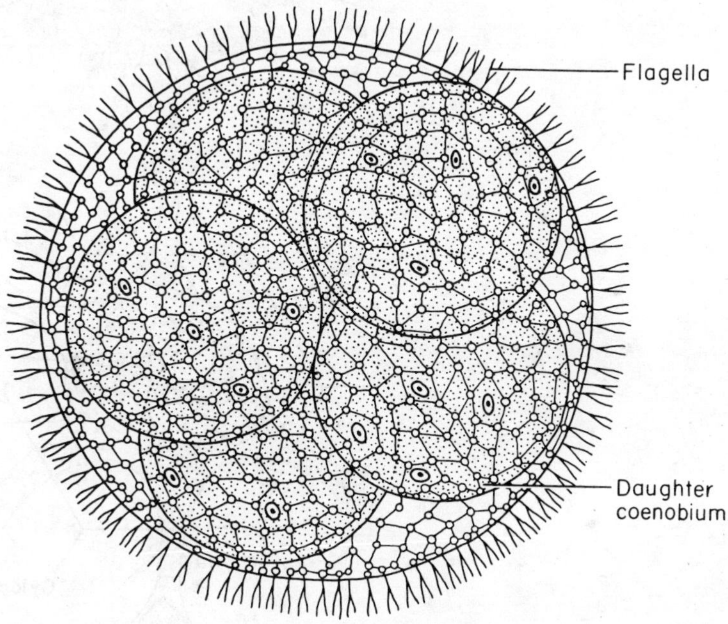

Fig. 12-26 *Volvox*, mature coenobium containing daughter coenobia.

Genus: *Volvox*

Occurrence

Volvox is a freshwater planktonic form occurring as green balls of pinhead size in temporary and permanent pools and ponds. The spring and rainy seasons are the usual periods of their active growth.

Morphology

The colonies (coenobia) generally have a spherical, oval or ellipsoidal contour and are motile; the movement is brought about by the joint action of the flagella (Fig. 12-26) of individual cells. A definite number of cells form a globular outer hull or syncytium which is held together by a highly viscous, gelatinous, glycoprotein sheath. This is filled with a mucilaginous polyglucan or proteoglycan matrix in which a small number of reproductive cells or gonidia are embedded in a definite manner that is determined by systematic cleavages during embryogenesis (Jaenicke, 1982). The coenobia of *V. aureus* (Fig. 12-27 A) are composed of 500–3000 cells, whereas those of *V. globator* have up to about 20,000 cells. Other species may have 500–50,000 cells per coenobium. In their general morphology, the individual cells of *Volvox* resemble *Chlamydomonas*

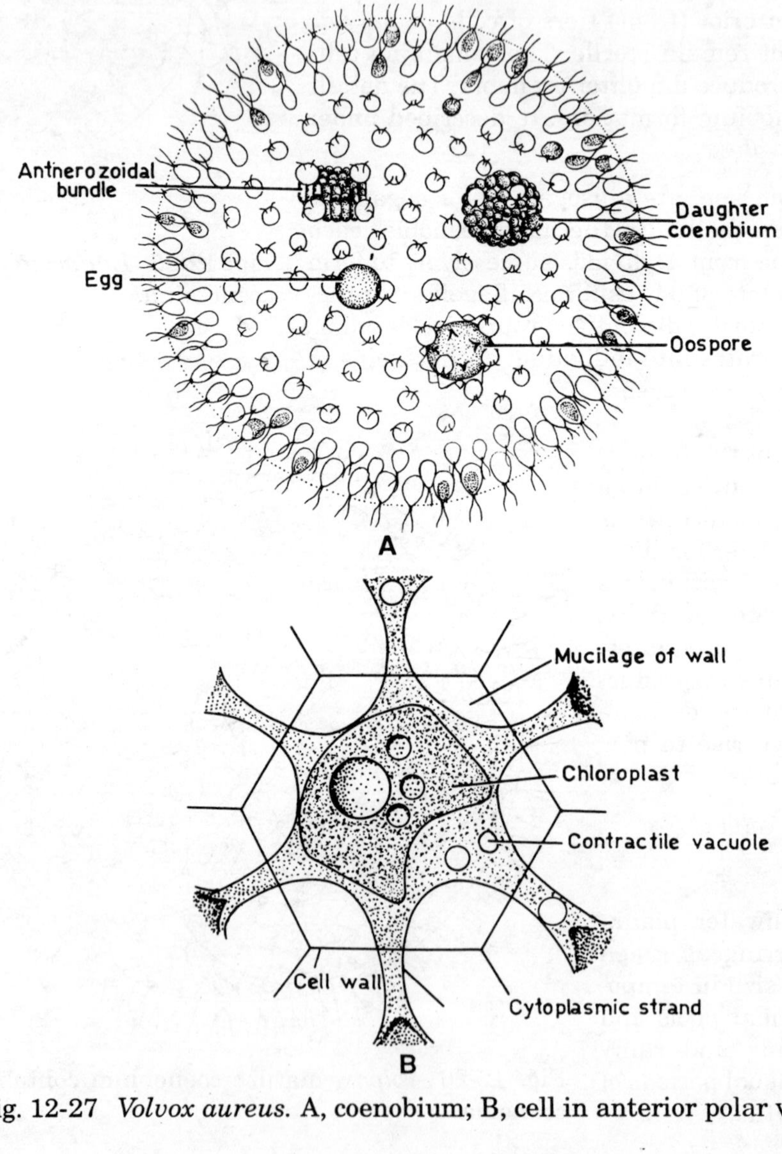

Fig. 12-27 *Volvox aureus.* A, coenobium; B, cell in anterior polar view.

and *Sphaerella* in that a cell has a pair of anteriorly inserted flagella and a cup-shaped or laminate chloroplast containing one or more pyrenoids. Two or more contractile vacuoles and an eyespot are found in the anterior region. The cells in the posterior region of the coenobium are usually larger than those in the anterior region. Most species have prominent cytoplasmic strands (Fig. 12-27 B) connecting the cells of a colony but *V. mononae* and *V. tertius* lack such connecting strands. The cells are uninucleate. *V. carteri* is an oval, hollow coenobium swimming with the anterior end ahead, while rotating around its longitudinal axis.

Reproduction

In contrast to *Chlamydomonas*, which discharges all its vital functions (including reproduction) and normally does not die, the cells of a *Volvox* colony show pronounced functional specialization.

Asexual Most of the cells of a coenobium are vegetative but a few in the posterior region are reproductive (gonidial); these enlarge and lose their flagella.

In a coenobium, 2–50 asexual gonidia are produced. Before they divide, the gonidia are slightly pushed into the interior of the colony. The gonidium divides mitotically several times in an exact cleaving pattern, giving rise to four puckered, quadrangled tetrads of cells that are disposed on top of each other; this symmetry probably is caused and maintained by a sticky sulphated glycoprotein (Jaenicke, 1982). The first two divisions are in planes perpendicular to each other (Fig. 12-28) but subsequent divisions are longitudinal. The daughter protoplasts at the eight-celled stage are in the form of a curved plate called the Plakea stage (Fig. 12-28). At the 16-celled stage, cells are arranged within the periphery of a hollow sphere with an opening towards the anterior end. The cell division phase in the developing coenobium continues until it

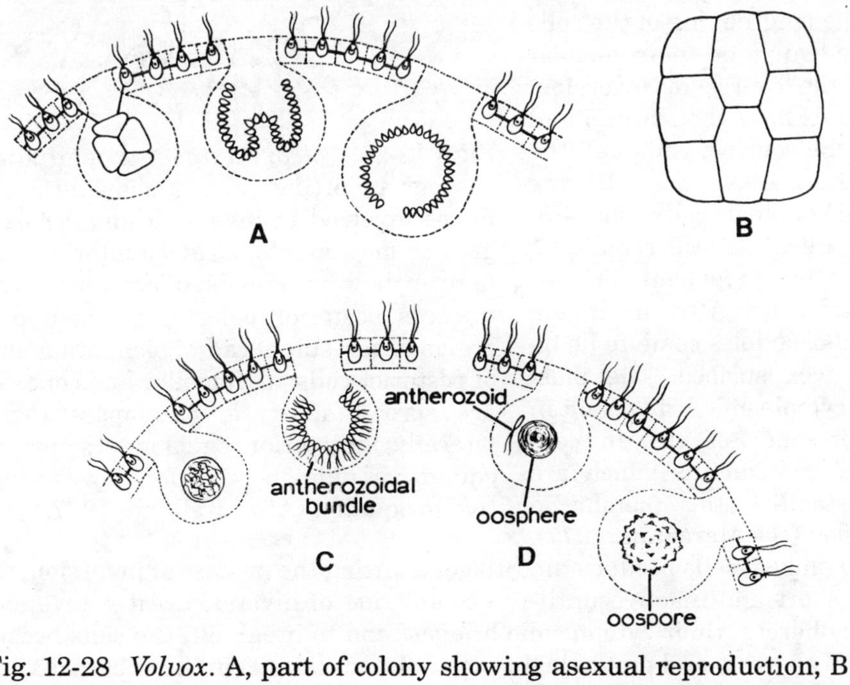

Fig. 12-28 *Volvox*. A, part of colony showing asexual reproduction; B, Plakea stage; C, D, stages in sexual reproduction. (After Smith, 1955.)

attains a specific number of cells. At the end of this phase, the peripheral row of almost spherically arranged cells, which are still naked, have their anterior ends pointing towards the centre of the developing coenobium. The coenobium then undergoes a complete inversion, i.e., inside-out turning, through the opening, with the consequence that the anterior ends of cells, which were previously facing the centre of the sphere, now face outward. Each cell of the daughter coenobium finally acquires a cell wall and a pair of flagella at its anterior end. The daughter coenobia are released after the disintegration of the parent coenobium.

The ultrastructural aspects and the morphogenetic mechanism of the inversion process have been studied by Pickett-Heaps (1970) and Kelland (1977). Active changes and deformities in the shape of individual cells in each embryo during the progress of inversion have been recorded by Kelland (see Fig. 12-29). Pickett-Heaps has seen microtubules in inverting cells and these microtubules could be involved at least in cell elongation.

Pickett-Heaps (1970) has made an ultrastructural study of coenobial differentiation and inversion in *Volvox*. At least the younger and developing cells are interconnected by means of cytoplasmic bridges which seem to function as channels of intercellular communication; though structurally different, these bridges are functionally analogous to the plasmodesmata of angiosperms.

Microtubules seem to play an important role in the lengthening of the cells and the broadening of their nuclear ends during the course of inversion. The plakeal cells have their nuclei and centrioles at the concave ends and the plastids at the convex faces. During inversion, all plakeal cells simultaneously elongate while still remaining interlinked by the cytoplasmic bridges at their plastid poles. After inversion, the nuclei and centrioles come to lie on the outer, convex surface. The plasmalemma of cytoplasmic bridges often shows the presence of certain concentric or spiral striations which are thought to stabilize the membrane during inversion (see Marchant, 1977).

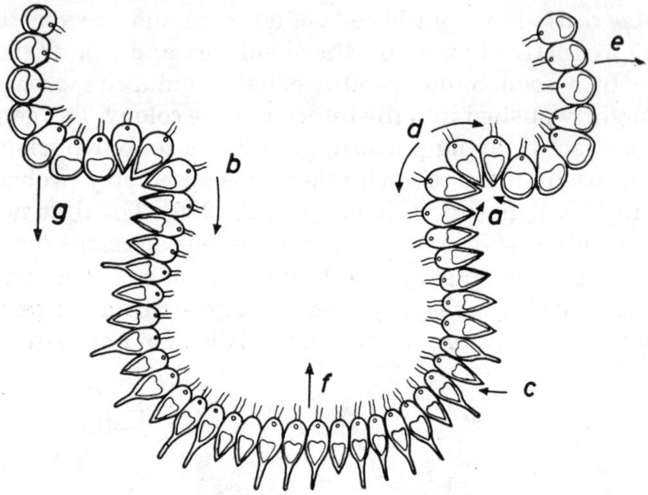

Fig. 12-29 *Volvox aureus*. Longitudinal sections through inverting embryo showing primary motive forces involved in inversion and resultant morphogenetic movements. a, at equatorial bend, cells adhere at their basal ends; b, bend moves from equator towards posterior pole; c, contraction of posterior region as a result of radial elongation and narrowing of posterior cells; d, flagellar ends of cells at equator are spread apart; e, phialopore region expands laterally; f, posterior region moves upward relative to equator; g, phialopore region moves downward relative to equator. (After Kelland, 1977.)

Though the plakeal cells produce their flagella during the process of inversion, these flagella remain quite short and inactive until the completion of inversion. After inversion, the cells are laterally adherent, their cytoplasmic bridges tend to break off, the cells become rounded, and the flagella elongate and protrude through a fluted channel in the sheath of the coenobium. The daughter coenobium is released after the parental coenobial sheath has gelatinized.

Sexual The timing of sexual reproduction is controlled by certain recognizable chemical switches. The vegetative cycle may be repeated indefinitely or until sexuality is induced. Reproduction is oogamous. Species reproducing sexually may be monoecious (*V. globator*) or dioecious (*V. aureus*). Since the monoecious forms are commonly protandrous, fertilization between antherozoids and eggs from different individuals is effected. The gonidium-like male and female cells are respectively called antheridia and oogonia. Gamete formation is triggered by a hormone, mostly produced by the males and excreted.

Each antheridium undergoes repeated cell divisions in a way similar to that in the development of an asexual gonidium into a daughter coenobium. A mass of naked, biflagellate fusiform antherozoids, ranging in number from 16 to 512 per antheridium, is ultimately produced (Fig. 12-28).

The vegetative cells destined to become oogonia enlarge, lose their flagella, and become rounded or flask-shaped, with much of the oogonial portion projecting into the interior of the colony. The entire contents of the oogonium finally form a single nonflagellate egg (Fig. 12-28) with a beak-like protrusion towards one side, through which the antherozoid enters the oogonium.

During fertilization, the entire mass of antherozoids is set free as a unit colony; this bundle remains intact until it approaches an egg. The individual antherozoids are then set free and one of them fuses with the egg, leading to the production of the oospore (Fig. 12-28). The oospore subsequently secretes a smooth or spiny wall of three layers; it also accumulates much haematochrome which colours the zygote orange-red. The oospore constitutes the perennating stage in the life history of *Volvox.*

During oospore germination, the two outer wall layers gelatinize and the inner layer forms a vesicle in which the zygote protoplast migrates. The zygote nucleus divides meiotically and, of the resulting four nuclei, three degenerate while the fourth uninucleate protoplast develops into a coenobium through asexual reproduction.

The alga is haploid with its diploid phase restricted to the zygote.

In several species, hormones act as signals between the sexes to initiate sexual differentiation (Starr, 1968). The fluid in which sperm bundles have been produced by *V. aureus* coenobia can be shown to cause the production of male colonies in populations which otherwise would have produced only asexual colonies.

Volvox hormones are species- or even variety-specific. Even when the hormones are harvested from males, they can induce both male and female colonies in those species where the females are recognizably different from young vegetative colonies. Only in *V. dissipatrix* has hormonal activity been recorded from a female clone, though its action resembles that of the male hormone. The hormones from *V. carteri* have been shown to be made of a glycoprotein consisting of about 60% protein (virtually lacking hydroxyproline) and 40% carbohydrate. Asexual daughter coenobia are produced in *Volvox* in successive generations. If during the development of embryos a species-specific sex hormone is present, then, instead of asexual colonies, sexual colonies are formed. In most species, only the male colonies (in dioecious species) produce this hormone, but both antheridial and oogonial colonies of *V. dissipatrix* can produce the same. One important contribution in this area is that of Starr *et al.* (1980) in which it is reported that L-glutamic acid stimulates development of sexual coenobia in *V. capensis*. This amino acid is produced as a natural product of the digestion of the glycoproteinaceous parental matrix at the time of release of daughter coenobia. When the level of L-glutamic acid reaches a certain threshold, sexuality is induced. Glutamate being a key intermediate or metabolite of nitrogen metabolism, its role in sexual induction in this case is highly significant, interesting, and surprising. Since it is effective in sexual morphogenesis at a fairly low concentration (10 μg/l)—too low to be effective as a metabolite—it seems that in this case the glutamic acid may be acting as some kind of messenger, but its precise site of action is unknown.

The genetical studies of *Volvox* have lagged behind those of *Chlamydomonas*. Huskey *et al*. (1979) produced several mutants of *V. carteri* and made a preliminary genetic analysis. All the mutants showed simple Mendelian segregation patterns and they could be allocated to 14 linkage groups. Unlike *Chlamydomonas* and *Eudorina* in which nonMendelian segregation patterns have been reported by several workers (Sager, 1972; Mishra and Threlkeld, 1968), no such patterns could be found in *Volvox*.

Work on genetic analysis of *Volvox carteri* has led to the hypothesis that a small number of loci act to cause differentiation between somatic and reproductive cell types. The patterns of cell-type-specific gene expression in wild-type and mutant embryos are consistent with this hypothesis which has now received support from the work of Schiedlmeier *et al.* (1994) on genetic transformation. These workers have attempted to transform *V. carteri* with various bacterial or plant selectable markers that were introduced by microinjection, electroporation, particle bombardment, UV-laser microbeam irradiation or agitation with glass beads. No transformation with heterologous selectable markers was achieved, possibly because of an inability of these algae to express heterologous genes, but successful transformation occurred with the availability of a homologous selectable marker (the recently cloned nitrate reductase-encoding gene of *V. carteri*, *nitA*, to complement a *nitA* mutation) (Schiedlmeier *et al.*, 1994).

Stable nuclear transformation could be achieved using the cloned *V. carteri* $nitA^+$ gene (which encodes nitrate reductase) to complement a $nitA^-$ mutation. Following bombardment of mutant cells with plasmid-coated gold particles, transformants able to utilize nitrate as a nitrogen source could be recovered. DNA analysis indicated that the plasmid integrated into the genome, often in multiple copies, at sites other than the *nitA* locus. Cotransformants were recovered with a frequency of 40–80% when cells were cobombarded with a selected and an unselected marker. Thus, *V. carteri* becomes one of the simplest multicellular organisms that is accessible to detailed molecular studies of genes regulating cellular differentiation and morphogenesis (Schiedlmeier *et al.*, 1994).

According to Koufopanou and Bell (1993), it is conceivable that the separation of soma from germa may have resulted as a specialization in source and sink, with somatic cells acting as sources, taking nutrients from the external environment and germ cells as sinks, utilizing nutrients to grow and reproduce. This hypothesis may be well tested in *Volvox*, where single germ cells can be cultured in isolation from the soma, thus serving both as source and sink, and their growth compared with that of germ cells with an intact soma where source and sink are separated into different cells. Such an experiment revealed that germ cells grown with an intact soma grew faster than those grown with disrupted soma or that were completely isolated, but the difference widened with increasing nutrient concentration as predicted by the source-and-sink hypothesis. The advantage, however, may not have sufficed to compensate fully for the initial investment in soma, especially in nutrient-poor habitats possibly due to the energetic cost of swimming. In nature, species with segregated soma are found in nutrient-rich lakes and ponds. In experimental farm ponds, the biomass of such species increases with eutrophication more than the biomass of related species without division of labour, suggesting an advantage consistent with the source-and-sink (Koufopanou and Bell, 1993).

Order: CHLOROCOCCALES

The Chlorococcales includes unicellular and colonial forms in which the vegetative thallus is nonmotile and no vegetative cell divisions occur. The vegetative cells lack flagella, contractile vacuoles, and eyespot. The colonial members arise as a consequence of the union of zoospores or autospores inside the parent cell wall or soon after their liberation from the parent cell. The thallus morphology, the features of asexual reproduction (zoosporic or nonzoosporic), and, to some extent, the tendency of the cells to become coenocytic have formed the basis of classification of the order into families; the main series of forms in this order, namely, the azoosporic Chlorococcales and the zoosporic Chlorococcales, are illustrated here with reference to the representative genera *Chlorella* and *Hydrodictyon*.

Family: Chlorellaceae
Genus: *Chlorella*

Occurrence

Chlorella is a cosmopolitan, ubiquitous alga occurring in freshwater, brackish water, and terrestrial habitats. *C. lichina* is an algal symbiont of the lichen *Calicium chlorina*. Some chlorellas, e.g., *Zoochlorella*, grow as symbionts in Hydra or other aquatic animals.

Morphology

Chlorella is unicellular nonmotile alga. The spherical, subspherical or ellipsoidal cells are bound by a true cellulosic wall. Each cell has a bell-shaped or cup-shaped parietal chloroplast with or without a pyrenoid (Fig. 12-30). There may be a hyaline cavity towards one side of the chloroplast and in this cavity, or in the colourless central cytoplasm, are located the single nucleus, the mitochondria, and the Golgi bodies. The photosynthetic thylakoids lack grana-like organization. Towards the end of the growth phase and the beginning of the reproductive phase, the cells become multinucleate.

The fine structure of *Chlorella* cell has been found to be highly plastic and polymorphic.

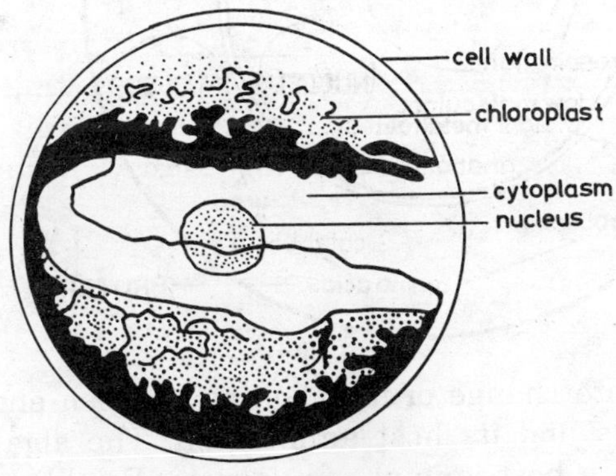

Fig. 12-30 *Chlorella*, cell structure.

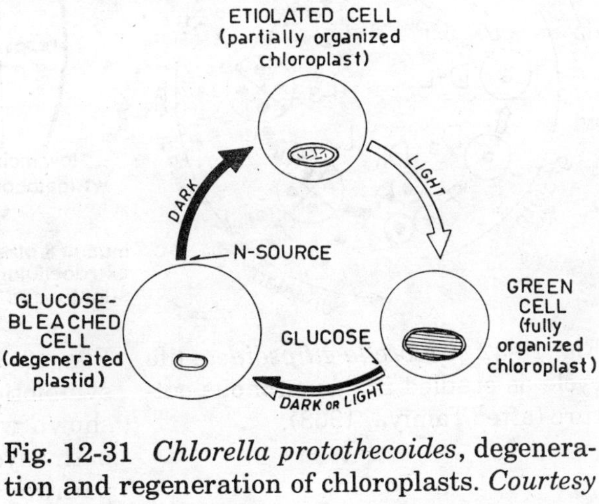

Fig. 12-31 *Chlorella protothecoides*, degeneration and regeneration of chloroplasts. *Courtesy* E. Hase.

Changes in environmental conditions such as light quality, duration and intensity, temperature and chemical composition of the growth medium greatly influence the micromorphology of the chloroplast (Fig. 12-31), pyrenoid, and cell wall.

The modern techniques of DNA hybridization and protein biochemistry have been applied to several strains of *Chlorella* with a view to delimiting morphologically ill-defined species. Kessler (1984) has done much work on biochemical taxonomy of *Chlorella*, based on a study of hydrogenase activity and the production of astaxanthin, canthaxanthin, and echinenone under nitrogen-deficient conditions. The cell walls of these strains which produce these carotenoids also contain another polymeric carotenoid, sporopollenin (Burczyk and Hesse, 1981).

Reproduction and Synchronous Culture

Chlorella reproduces exclusively by the formation of (normally four) asexual autospores. Motile cells, zoospores or gametes are not produced.

Tamiya (see Morimura, 1959) succeeded in synchronizing the population of *C. ellipsoidea* by subjecting the cell to alternating light-dark cycles. With the synchronous culture technique, four phases (Fig. 12-32) in the life cycle of *Chlorella* were identified, viz., (1) the growth phase, during which the autospores grow in size at the expense of the photosynthetic products; (2) the early ripening phase, when the cells of the growth phase prepare themselves for cell division; (3) the post-ripening phase, when the cells divide twice either in the dark or the light; and (4) the division phase, during which the parent wall gelatinizes or ruptures, liberating the autospores which in the very young stage are known as dark nascent cells (D_n).

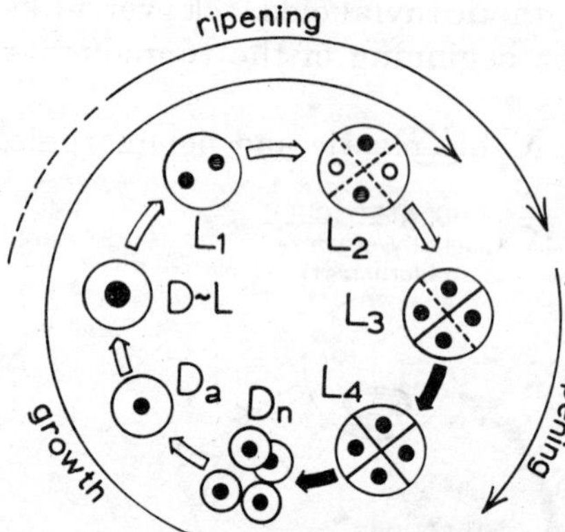

Fig. 12-32 *Chlorella ellipsoidea*, life cycle as studied in synchronous culture (after Tamiya, 1963).

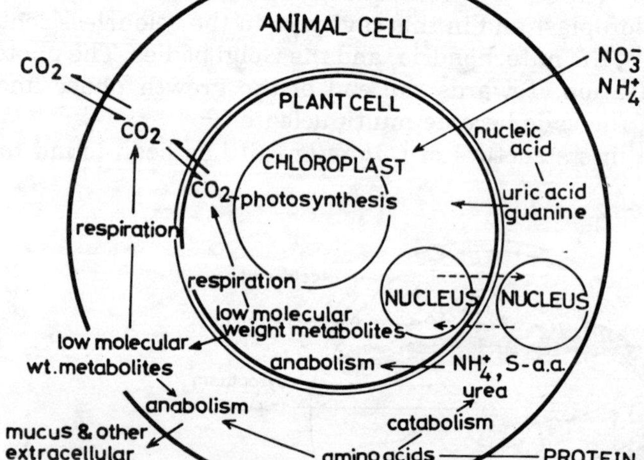

Fig. 12-33 Interchange of metabolites between endosymbiotic alga and its host animal cell. The alga is shown within a host animal cell vacuole. Established pathways are shown in solid arrows, whereas uncertain pathways are indicated by broken arrows. S-a.a., sulphur-containing amino acid. (After Trench, 1979.)

Symbiosis

Chlorohydra viridissima contains several cells of *Chlorella* within its endodermal cells. These green hydras can survive starvation much better and for longer periods than colourless, alga-free hydras. A significant amount of the carbon dioxide fixed by the algal cells during photosynthesis is transferred to the animal tissues. Figure 12-33 shows some metabolite exchanges between endosymbiotic algae, such as *Chlorella*, and their host animal cell.

Another animal that has endosymbiotic *Chlorella* is *Paramecium bursaria*. Here again, *Chlorella* contributes, at least partially, to its host's nutrition.

The symbiotic *Chlorella* cells, when cultured free from the host cells, sometimes release as much as 75 per cent of their photosynthate in the form of maltose, glucose, or glycollate into the ambient medium. Obviously, these could then be utilized by the host.

One puzzling aspect of the alga-animal symbiosis is the way in which the algal cells escape digestion. These cells do go into food vacuoles of the host. Probably, the composition of the membrane of the food vacuole changes at some stage so that it becomes a protective membrane around the algal cells. Alternatively, the cell wall or plasmalemma of the alga might undergo some similar change and then act as a protective covering.

The growth and early ripening phases are both light- and temperature-dependent, whereas the post-ripening and autospore liberation phases are only temperature-dependent. As shown in Fig. 12-32, the growth and early ripening phases are further subdivided into five stages distinguished on the basis of photosynthetic activity, DNA contents, and division performance in the dark. The D_a (dark active) cells are uninucleate, photosynthetically very active, and are derived from D_n cells. D~L (dark to light transitional) cells are also uninucleate but are larger in size and photosynthetically less active with comparatively higher DNA content than the D_a cells. L_1 cells are larger and have more DNA than D~L cells. All these cells, i.e., D_a, D~L, and L_1, fail to divide when they are incubated in the dark. The L_2 cells are binucleate and are capable of incipient division in the dark. L_3 cells always become tetranucleate when kept in the dark or the light and produce four autospores. L_4 cells are tetranucleate autospore mother cells which liberate the autospores or D_n cells, independent of light (L_1, L_2, L_3, L_4 are light cells).

The cell division of *Chlorella* has a specific requirement for sulphur because it cannot occur in its absence. Under photosynthetic conditions, it requires nitrogen in addition to a sulphur source, whereas in the dark the cell division can proceed normally with sulphur alone.

Kessler and Huss (1992) have emphasized the need to use correctly identified strains of *Chlorella* for physiological, biochemical, and biotechnological studies or applications. Table 12-2 shows the suitability of some species for research and biotechnology.

Family: Hydrodictyaceae
Genus: *Hydrodictyon*

Occurrence

Popularly known as "water net", *Hydrodictyon* grows in the plankton and benthos of freshwater ponds and lakes. The common species, *H. reticulatum* (Fig. 12-34), is found free-floating in certain ponds in spring and summer. It is sometimes so abundant that it almost covers the entire pond surface. Another species, *H. indicum* Iyengar, is common in India.

Morphology

Hydrodictyon is a macroscopic nonmotile coenobium consisting of a network of pentagons or

Table 12-2 Suitability of five species of *Chlorella* for research and biotechnology (after Kessler and Huss, 1992)

Problem or purpose	Suitable species				
	fusca	*saccharophila*	*sorokiniana*	*kessleri*	*vulgaris*
Hydrogen production	+				
Secondary carotenoids	+				
Acid tolerance		+			
Salt tolerance		+			
Temperature tolerance			+		
Mass culture					
Under normal conditions	+		+	+	+
In acid water		+		+	
In salt water		+			+
At high temperature	+		+	+	

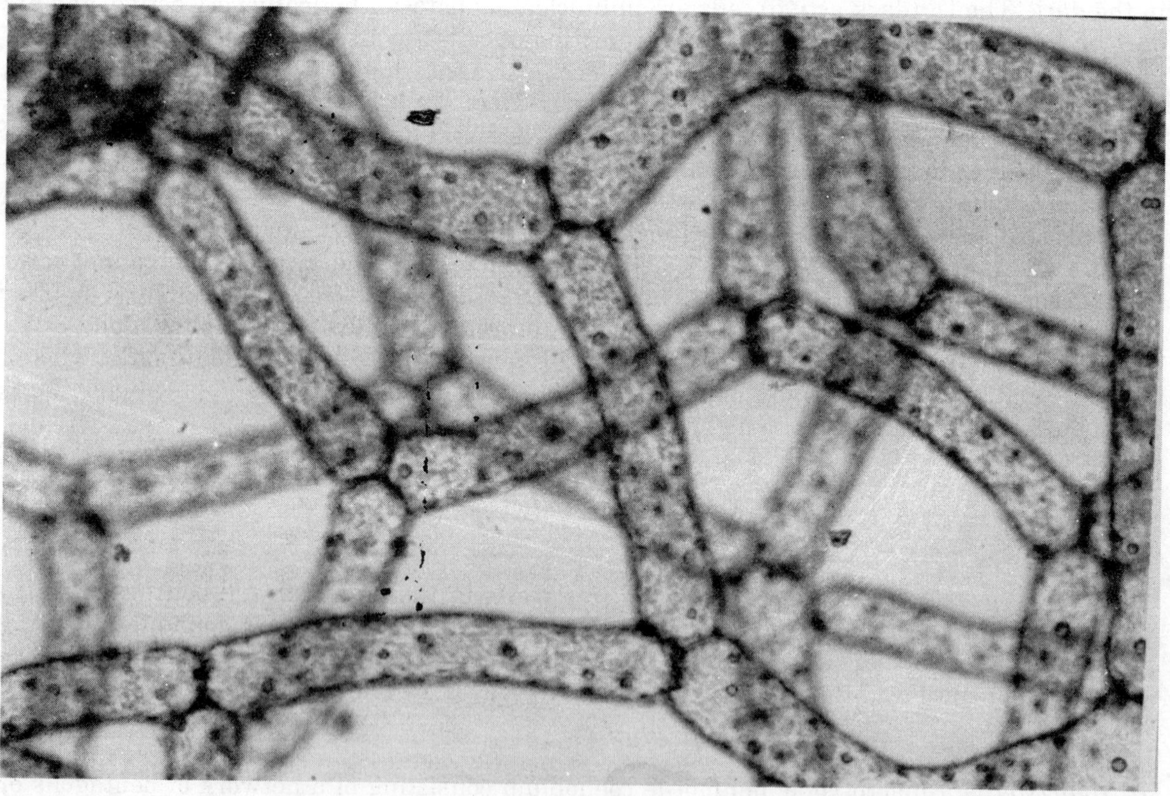

Fig. 12-34 *Hydrodictyon reticulatum*. (Approx. ×150.) *Courtesy* K. Ueda.

hexagons (Fig. 12-35 A, B) with each corner of the polygon resulting from the union of three large cylindrical cells (Fig. 12-35 C). Each coenobium is typically cylindrical, closed at both ends, and may consist of a few hundred to several thousand cells in different species. The mature coenobium may sometimes be as long as 30 cm. The young cells are generally uninucleate with a parietal, band-shaped chloroplast having a single pyrenoid. As the cells grow and enlarge, they become coenocytic and the band-shaped chloroplast becomes reticulate and forms many pyrenoids (Fig. 12-35 D). Mature cells, which may sometimes measure 2–3 mm in length, contain a large central vacuole which displaces the cytoplasm towards the periphery of the cell.

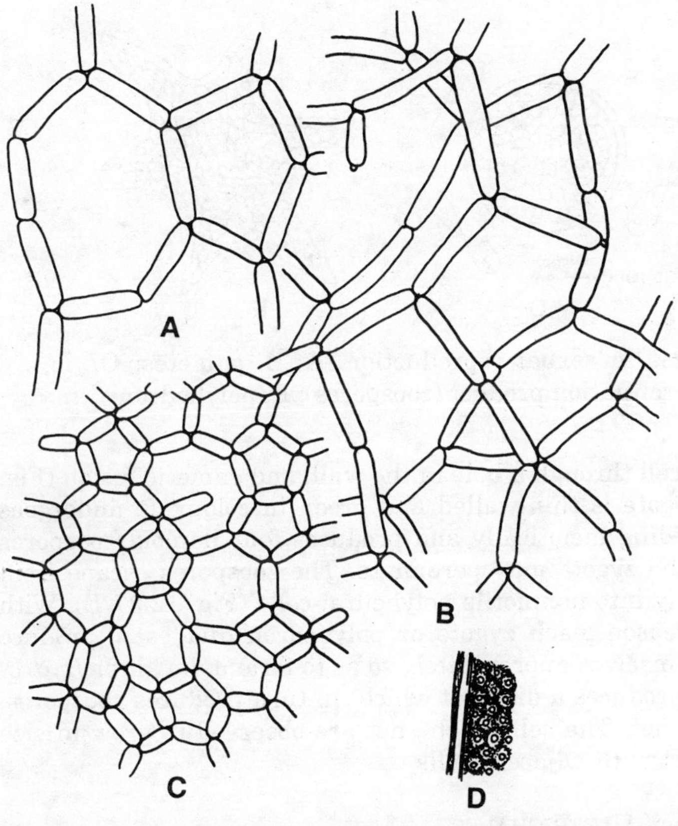

Fig. 12-35 *Hydrodictyon reticulatum*. A, B, parts of old coenobium; C, part of young coenobium; D, part of cell showing chloroplast with pyrenoids.

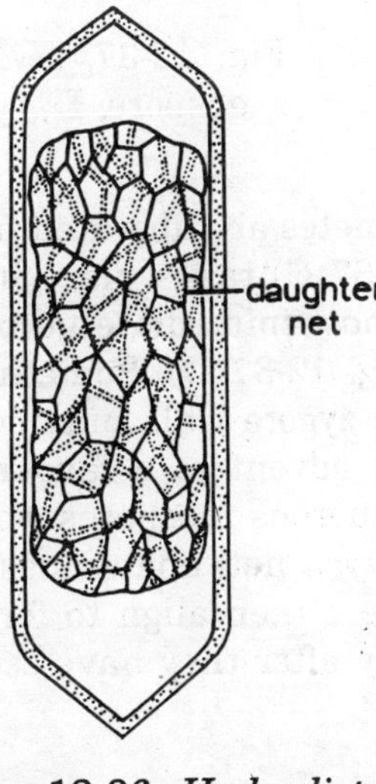

Fig. 12-36 *Hydrodictyon*, formation of new net within parent cell.

Reproduction

Vegetative Reproduction is sometimes effected by the fragmentation of a net into two or three nets.

Asexual Reproduction is brought about by the formation of a large number (up to 20,000) of tiny biflagellate zoospores within any vegetative cell of the thallus. These are not liberated but remain within the mother cell and for a short while may exhibit some movement. The flagella are then withdrawn and the zoospores elongate into tiny cylindrical cells which come together in groups of five or six and dispose themselves in such a manner as to form a characteristic miniature net of *Hydrodictyon* (Fig. 12-36). The parental cell wall ultimately softens, liberating the young *Hydrodictyon* coenobium which later grows to adult size without undergoing any cell division.

Sexual Reproduction is isogamous and involves the fusion of biflagellate isogametes (Fig. 12-37 A, B) formed in large numbers from ordinary vegetative cells. Unlike the zoospores, the

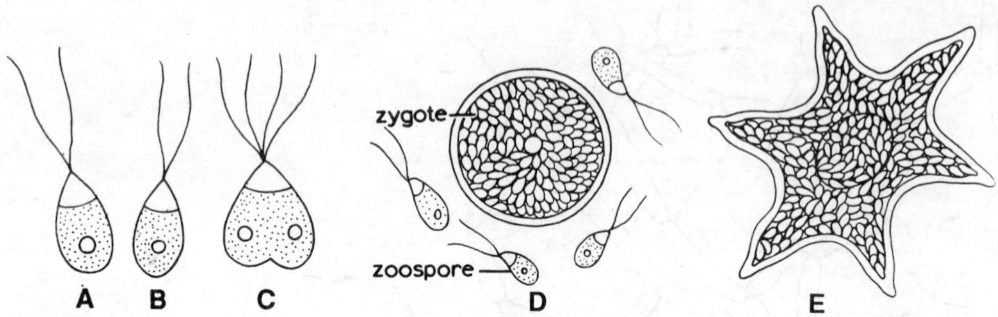

Fig. 12-37 *Hydrodictyon*, stages in sexual reproduction. A, B, gametes; C, zygospore; D, zygote with its germination product (zoospores); E, polyhedron.

gametes are liberated from the parent cell through a hole in the wall, and gametic fusion (Fig. 12-37 C) takes place in water. The zygote is thin-walled and green in colour. It undergoes almost immediate germination by dividing meiotically and produces four haploid zoospores (Fig. 12-37 D). Sometimes, however, the zygote may perennate. The zoospores escape from the zygote wall and develop individually into nonmotile polyhedral cells (Fig. 12-37 E). With the advent of a favourable growing season, each zygote or polyhedron divides to produce numerous zoospores which arrange themselves appropriately so as to form a daughter *Hydrodictyon* net. Sometimes, a polyhedron produces a disk net which in turn produces zoospores. These then align to form a cylindrical net. The cells of the net are observed to grow in size only after they have established contact with adjacent cells.

Order: ULOTRICHALES

The Ulotrichales includes unbranched filamentous and parenchymatous forms showing little structural or functional specialization among vegetative cells except that the lowest cell of the thallus may be modified to serve as an organ of anchorage. Depending on cell structure, the order has been classified into three suborders, the Ulotrichineae, the Prasiolineae, and the Sphaeropleineae. The Ulotrichineae have uninucleate cells with a single, parietal, band- or girdle-shaped chloroplast and are segregated into four families on the basis of wall structure and thallus organization: the Ulotrichaceae include simple filamentous forms with cells having a one-piece simple cell wall and a girdle-shaped chloroplast; the Microsporaceae have one filamentous genus in which the cell wall is composed of overlapping H-shaped pieces; in the Cylindrocapsaceae, the cells are elliptical with a thick, stratified wall and in old filaments some cells may divide obliquely so that some parts of the filament become multiseriate; the Ulvaceae contain forms with parenchymatous thalli and are retained in the Ulotrichineae because like *Ulothrix* their young stages are generally filamentous.

The suborder Prasiolineae with a single family Prasiolaceae includes only one membranous or thalloid genus *Prasiola* whose cells contain an axile stellate chloroplast.

The Sphaeropleineae is also a monogeneric suborder represented by *Sphaeroplea*, an unbranched filamentous alga made up of large coenocytic cells, each provided with several band-shaped or discoid chloroplasts.

The prevailing modes of sexual reproduction and life cycle are (1) isogamous and haploid (Ulotrichaceae and *Microspora*), (2) isogamous and isomorphic (Ulvaceae), and (3) oogamous and haploid (*Cylindrocapsa* and *Sphaeroplea*). *Prasiola* exhibits an interesting type of life cycle in that the thallus is either completely diploid, producing diploid zoospores, or is partly diploid and partly haploid, with the gametes being produced from the cells of haploid tissue (Cole and Akintobi, 1963). In certain species of *Prasiola*, patches of gametophytic tissue develop upon the diploid sporophyte (Fig. 12-38) after meiosis. In these, the relation between the diploid and haploid tissues seems to be one of parasitism since each type of tissue is a distinct unit. Members of this genus commonly grow in habitats enriched with bird droppings near coastal areas but *P. calophylla* occurs in habitats not experiencing nutrient enrichment from birds. It does not occur in highly saline habitats, but is common in Antarctic streams and on water-flushed ground. This alga has three distinct growth forms: uniseriate filaments, narrow ribbons, and expanded sheets (Fig. 12-39). Ribbons are found mostly on the lower surfaces of stones, and uniseriate filaments on the exposed surfaces of the stream beds of seasonal melt streams. Expanded sheets occur in slow-flowing water (Broady, 1989). Reproduction is by thallus fragmentation and by aplanospore formation. Fast-flowing, seasonal streams which receive their water from glaciers and icefields are favourable habitats for this species. It also occurs on terminal ice-faces of glaciers and as chasmoendolithic growths. Foliose thalli occur scattered over the surfaces of terminal walls of glaciers which slope at angles of up to 40° (Broady, 1989).

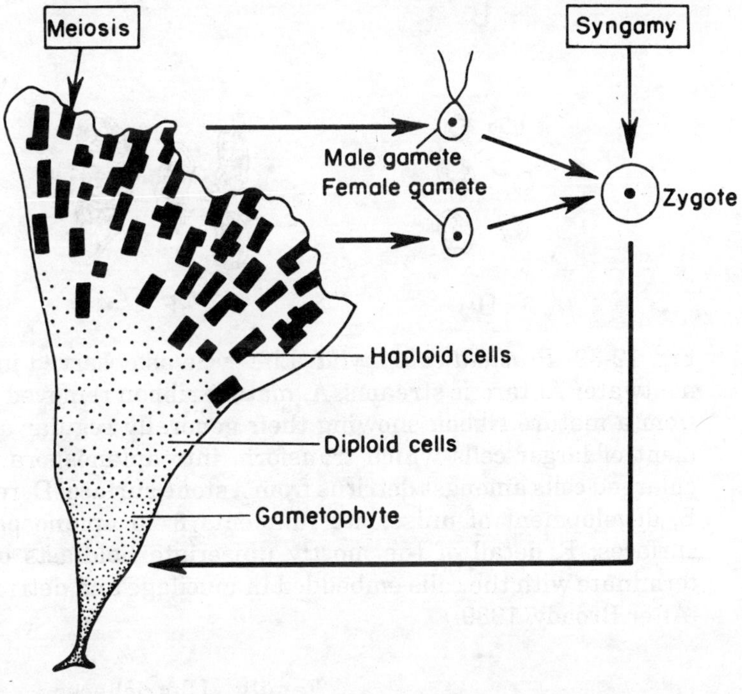

Fig. 12-38 *Prasiola*, occurrence of haploid and diploid cells on the same thallus. Life cycle is also shown.

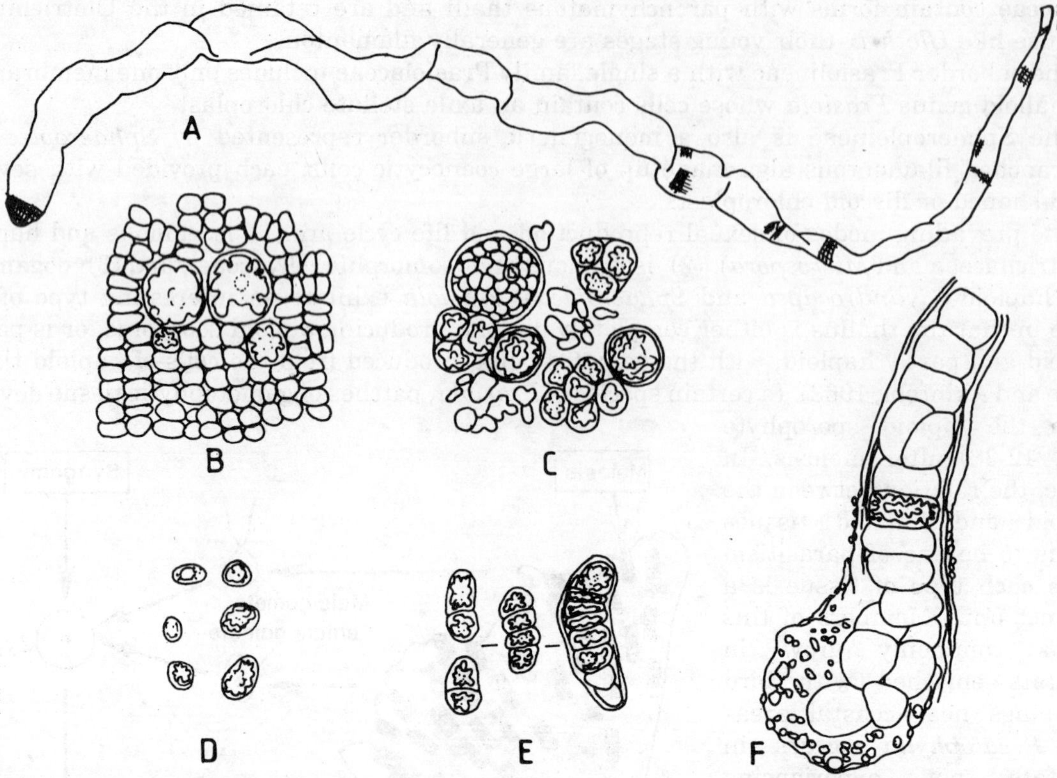

Fig. 12-39 *Prasiola calophylla*. Life cycle as observed in field material collected from meltwater Antarctic streams. A, mature ribbon removed from a stone; B, detail of cells from a mature ribbon showing their generally regular arrangement and the development of larger cells which transform into aplanosporangia; C, aplanosporangia and enlarged cells amongst detritus from a stone surface; D, recently released aplanospores; E, development of uniseriate filaments from aplanospores in algal crusts on stone surfaces; F, detail of the mostly uniseriate holdfasts of two mature ribbons which terminate with the cells embedded in mucilage and detritus attached to stone surfaces. (After Broady, 1989.)

Family: Ulotrichaceae
Genus: *Ulothrix*

Occurrence

Ulothrix occurs in flowing waters, ponds, pools, lakes, and in reservoirs where the water is continuously renewed. It also grows on stones and pebbles lying within the spray zone of waterfalls. When young, it generally grows attached to submerged objects. *U. zonata* is found in cold water streams, *U. flacca* is marine, and *U. implexa* is a lithophyte in estuaries (see Fig. 12-40).

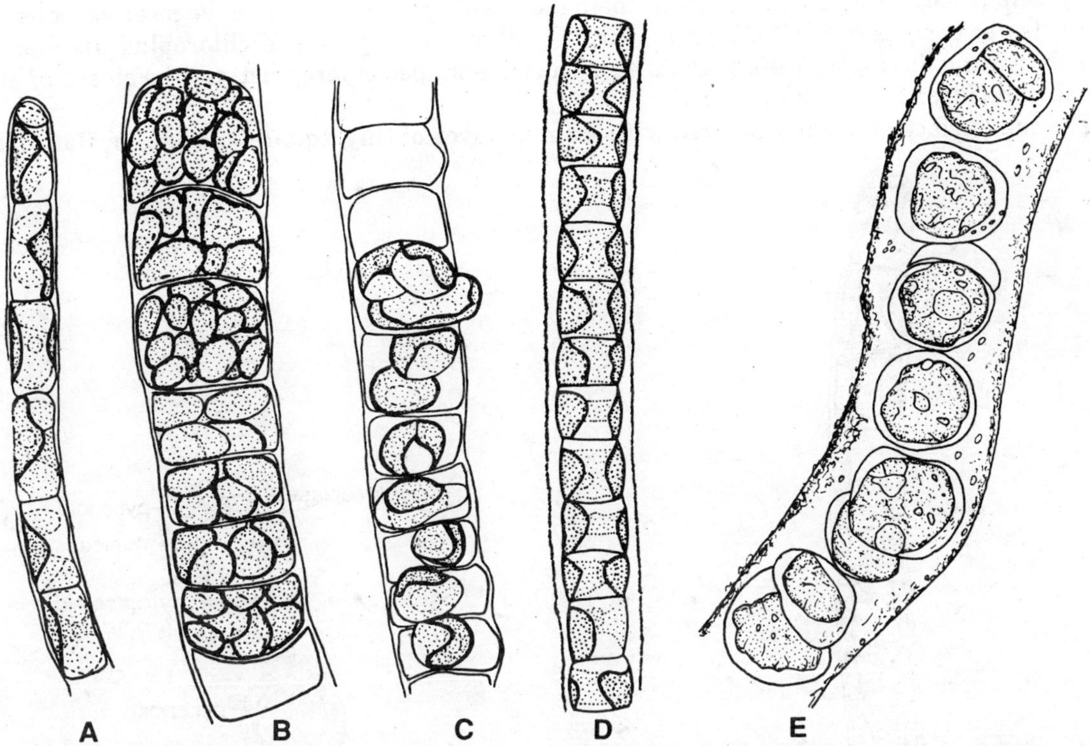

Fig. 12-40 *Ulothrix*. A–C, *U. implexa*: A, part of vegetative filament; B, filament with zoosporangia; C, filament with germinating aplanospores. D–E, *U. flacca*: D, part of vegetative filament; E, vegetative filament after prolonged exposure to adverse conditions. (After Lokhorst, 1978.)

G.M. Lokhorst of the Rijksherbarium, Leiden, has made a thorough and monographic study of the ecology, morphology, and life history of various species of *Ulothrix* (Lokhorst, 1978). The marine *U. speciosa* is fairly common in the littoral zone of the West European seashores. It generally prefers sheltered localities. It does not occur in the undergrowth of macroalgae on hard substrates, and is very rarely seen on animals, kelps or fucoids. *U. flacca* is a brackish water and marine species and is a common winter or spring alga in the littoral zone of the West European seashores. Unlike *U. speciosa*, it prefers localities exposed to wave action. It also grows epilithically on granite boulders, basalt blocks, pebbles, limestone, bitumen, and concrete. Some other habitats or substrata include fucoids and certain animals. It grows much better in open coastal areas than in brackish waters. *U. implexa* is a marine as well as a brackish water form. It is confined to hard substrata. In open areas, it prefers sheltered localities.

Morphology

The plant body is an unbranched uniseriate filament composed of short, cylindrical, quadrate or squarish cells (Figs. 12-40 A–D; 12-41) of which the basal cell is colourless and modified to function as a holdfast. When exposed to adverse environmental conditions, the protoplasts often shrink or appear abnormal and unhealthy (see Fig. 12-40 E). The growth is diffuse, every cell (except the basal holdfast) being capable of division. The vegetative cells are uninucleate, possess a cell wall, and a girdle-, collar- or ring-shaped chloroplast having one or more pyrenoids (Figs. 12-40 A–D; 12-41). The ring-shaped chloroplast may be closed or open at one end (Figs. 12-41; 12-42 A, B).

The cell surface is usually covered with a single layer of tiny, square or angular, flat scales.

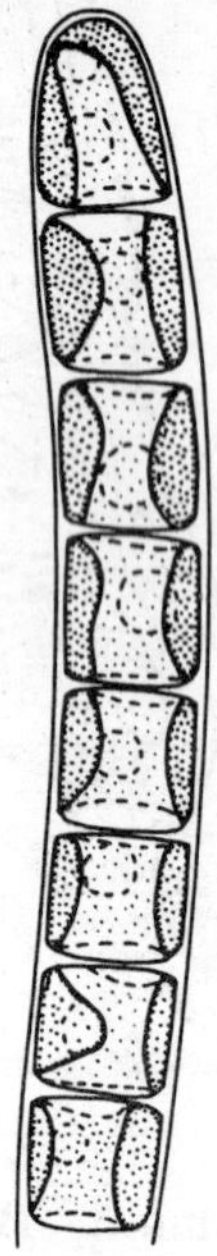

Fig. 12-41 *Ulothrix speciosa*, part of vegetative filament (after Lokhorst, 1978).

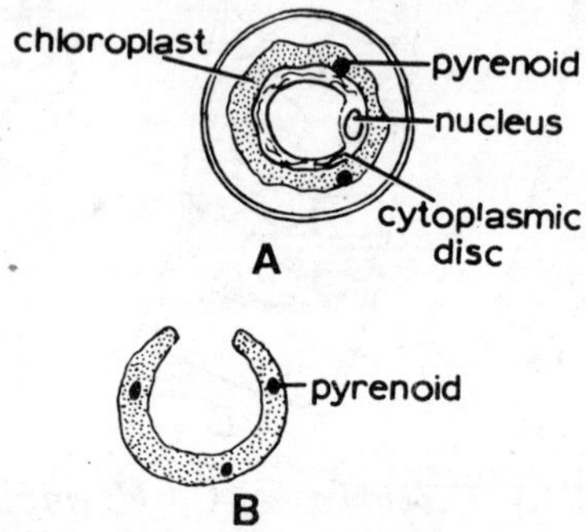

Fig. 12-42 *Ulothrix*. A, cross-section through cell with ring-shaped chloroplast; B, horseshoe-shaped chloroplast.

Reproduction

Vegetative A filament fragments into two or more pieces, each of which grows into a new plant.

Asexual Each cell, except the basal holdfast, produces up to eight, rarely 16, zoospores and usually there exists an apical-basal gradient in their formation. The mother protoplast divides mitotically, producing naked and stigmatic zoospores which morphologically resemble the unicellular Volvocales and are liberated from the parent cell through a pore in the lateral wall. Depending on the number of divisions, the mother protoplast may produce quadriflagellate macrozoospores, quadriflagellate microzoospores or biflagellate microzoospores. The liberated zoospores swim about for some time, anchor themselves to some solid object by their anterior ends, withdraw flagella, and secrete a cell wall. Each then divides into two cells, the lower forming the holdfast and the upper dividing and redividing to produce vegetative cells of the filament. The filaments formed from macrozoospores are much stronger and healthier than those derived from biflagellate microzoospores. Quadriflagellate microzoospores on germination produce intermediate filaments.

Asexual reproduction also takes place by aplanospores (Fig. 12-43 A). The daughter protoplasts, instead of forming zoospores, differentiate into nonmotile thin-walled aplanospores which may either be released from the parent cell or remain enclosed within it during the unfavourable growth period. With the onset of favourable periods, each aplanospore gives rise to a zoospore or germinates directly into a filament. Occasionally, *U. zonata* can form akinetes (see Fig. 12-43 B).

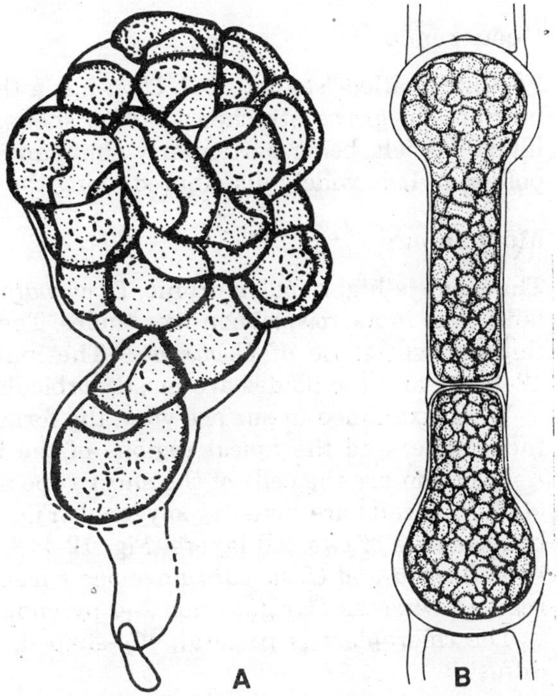

Fig. 12-43 *Ulothrix*. A, *U. flacca*, sporophyte with aplanospores; B, *U. zonata*, showing two akinetes. (After Lokhorst, 1978.)

Sexual Almost all the experimentally investigated species are sexually heterothallic, and gametic union always occurs between morphologically similar gametes of opposite, i.e., + and –, mating types. Up to 32 or 64 gametes per cell are formed and they resemble the biflagellate microzoospores in their mode of formation and morphology. The zygote is a thick-walled resting structure and on germination its nucleus divides by meiosis; during this time, the + and – sex factors segregate, giving rise to haploid zoospores or aplanospores, one-half of which are the + type and the other half the – type. Up to 16 zoospores or aplanospores may be produced from a germinating zygospore, though four is the usual number. A reduction in the chromosome number during germination of the zygote nucleus has been observed.

Upon escaping from the mother cell, both zoospores and gametes are enclosed in a distinct mucilaginous envelope or vesicle within which they sometimes show some movement.

The rare parthenogenetic development of a gamete into a vegetative filament and the occasional gamete-like behaviour of the biflagellate zoospores have also been recorded.

Contrary to the popular belief that *Ulothrix* is haplobiontic, Lokhorst (1978) had marshalled strong evidence for the heteromorphic diplobiontic life cycle in five species, e.g., *U. speciosa*, *U. flacca*, and *U. implexa*. In these, the zygote develops into an independent, unicellular, stalked sporophytic phase. The asexual spores formed meiotically by the sporophyte give rise to the haploid gametophytic filaments.

The reproductive response of various species to different photoperiods has been studied by several workers, including Lokhorst (1978). Most species produce their zoospores under short-day conditions, whereas gametogenesis is initiated or stimulated only under long-day conditions.

Family: Ulvaceae

The members of this family develop as uniseriate *Ulothrix*-like filaments whose cells later divide in more than one plane, so that the plants become flat, parenchymatous sheets or ribbons. These algae show isomorphic alternation of generations.

Genus: *Ulva*

Occurrence

Popularly called "sea lettuce", *Ulva* has a thin, leaf-like thallus, resembling a salad leaf. It is marine and grows attached to loose shells, pebbles, rocks, stones, and other objects in the intertidal belt, being particularly abundant in estuaries and coastal areas affected by sewage pollution. It is widely distributed along the Western Coast of India.

Morphology

The blade is highly polymorphic. *U. curvata* has markedly curved blades. *U. neapolitana* has lanceolate to narrow, ribbon-like blades. The blades of *U. lactuca* (Fig. 12-44 A) are stiffer and thicker than those of *U. curvata*. The margins of *U. lactuca* are entire or undulate (Fig. 12-44 A), and the blades are mostly orbicular.

When examined in surface view, the form and arrangement of the cells differ for the basal, the middle, and the apical regions of the blade. The lowermost cells are mostly rhizoidal. Above them are the cells of the short stipe and then the cells of the blade proper. In the main blade, the cells are usually polygonal (Fig. 12-44 B). Most species are distromatic, i.e., have blades made of two cell layers (Fig. 12-44 C).

U. lactuca and *U. curvata* have one pyrenoid per cell in most cells of the middle and apical regions, whereas *U. rigida* has 2–4 pyrenoids per cell in these regions.

The chloroplast is parietal, cup-shaped, with some lobes or arms. The thallus growth is diffuse.

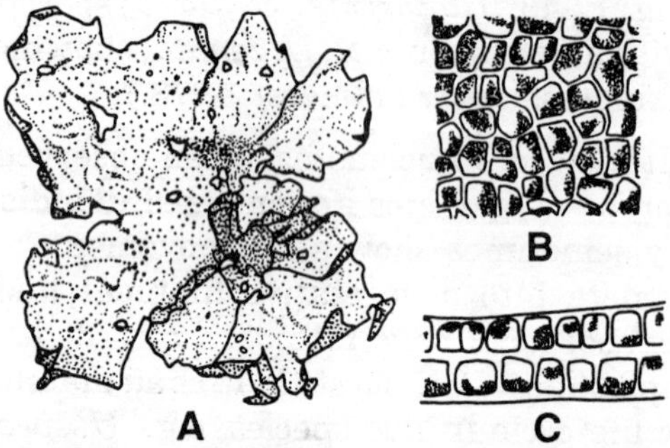

Fig. 12-44 *Ulva lactuca*. A, habit; B, surface view of part of thallus; C, transverse section of part of thallus.

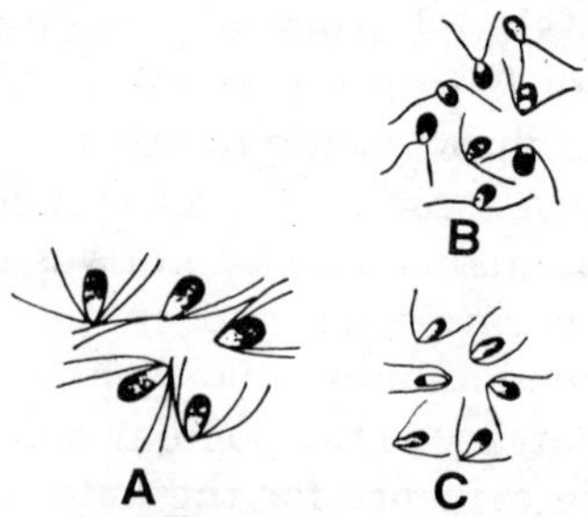

Fig. 12-45 *Ulva lactuca*, reproduction. A, zoospores; B, female gametes; C, male gametes.

Reproduction

Vegetative Vegetative propagation occurs from detached thallus fragments.

Asexual Asexual reproduction is by quadriflagellate zoospores (Fig. 12-45 A) produced meiotically by the sporophyte. These germinate and develop into gametophytes which are morphologically like the sporophyte.

Sexual The gametophytes produce iso- or anisogametes (Fig. 12-45 B, C) which fuse to form the zygote. This then develops into the sporophyte. The sequence of stages in the life history is shown in Fig. 12-46.

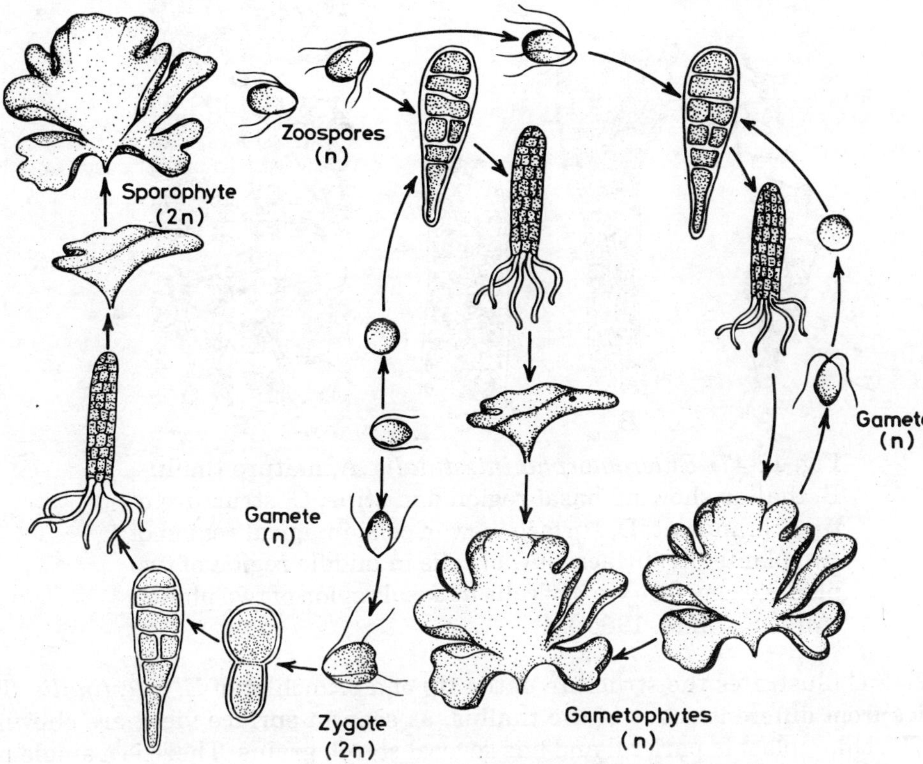

Fig. 12-46 *Ulva*, life cycle (note the isomorphic alternation of generations).

Genus: *Enteromorpha*

Occurrence

It grows both in marine and freshwater habitats, especially in alkaline streams. Some species are notorious ship-fouling algae worldwide.

Morphology

It forms hollow tubular thalli resembling the intestine. Some tubes are over 10 cm long. The tubes are attached to the substratum (e.g., rocks and ship hulls) by means of rhizoids arising from the cells of the basal region. The growth of the thallus is partly diffuse and partly apical.

The thallus of *E. intestinalis* is linear, oblong, or oblanceolate, mostly compressed, the two cell layers more or less adnate, leaving a hollow margin, or may be tubular and inflated. They may be unbranched (Fig. 12-47 A) or branched; in the latter case, the branches tend to be concentrated towards the basal region. The basal region is usually narrowed into a stipe (Fig. 12-47 B). *E. compressa* has strap-shaped thalli.

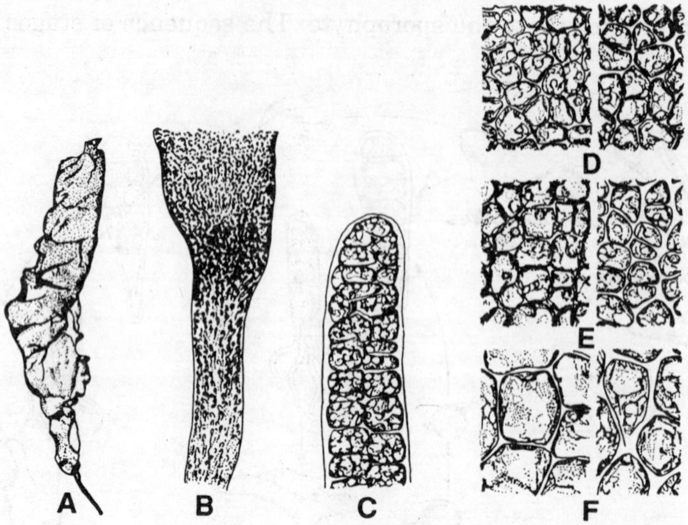

Fig. 12-47 *Enteromorpha intestinalis*. A, mature thallus; B, thallus showing basal region and stipe; C, structure of tip of branchlet; D, surface view of cells in apical region of two plants; E, surface view of cells in middle region of two plants; F, surface view of cells in basal region of two plants. (After Koeman, 1985.)

Figure 12-47 C illustrates the structure of the tip of a branchlet of *E. intestinalis*. The cells of this species from different zones of the thallus, as seen in surface view, are shown in Fig. 12-47 D–F. The chloroplast is parietal and has several starch grains. There is a single pyrenoid per cell.

Reproduction

Vegetative Vegetative reproduction occurs from detached fragments of thallus.

Asexual Asexual reproduction is brought about by quadriflagellate zoospores formed meiotically by the sporophytic plants.

Sexual Sexual reproduction occurs by anisogametes formed by the dioecious gametophytes. Some gametes can germinate without copulation.

Both gametes and zoospores are positively phototactic.

The development of the zygote, zoospores, and parthenogenetic gametes starts with the formation of a rhizoid. An upright uniseriate filament is then produced. Later, the filaments grow into the hollow cylinders which may or may not become compressed.

The life history resembles that of *Ulva*.

Family: Sphaeropleaceae
Genus: *Sphaeroplea*

The Sphaeropleaceae includes the interesting alga *Sphaeroplea*. This alga is like *Ulothrix* but is coenocytic and shows a special kind of oogamous reproduction.

Occurrence

It occurs in rain water pools and ditches, usually on both sides of railway lines.

Morphology

It is an unbranched uniseriate filamentous alga having long filaments, with unusually long cells (Fig. 12-48). Each cell contains many transverse cytoplasmic discs or septa separated from each other by large vacuoles. Each such cytoplasmic septum has a ring- or collar-shaped, typical ulotrichalean, chloroplast (Fig. 12-48) plus one or more nuclei. It is possible that *Sphaeroplea* may have evolved from a *Ulothrix*-like ancestor in which most of the cross walls between cells disappeared except for a few which remained, thus giving rise to the coenocytic condition with chloroplasts reminiscent of a *Ulothrix*.

The cross walls separating the long cells are often thick, conspicuous, but incomplete, and have prominent finger-like lobes (Fig. 12-49 A, B) and plugs. The cytoplasms of adjoining cells thus remain interconnected.

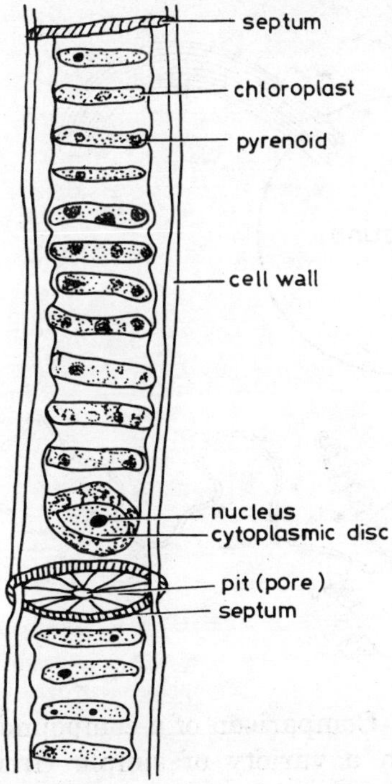

Fig. 12-48 *Sphaeroplea annulina*, part of filament.

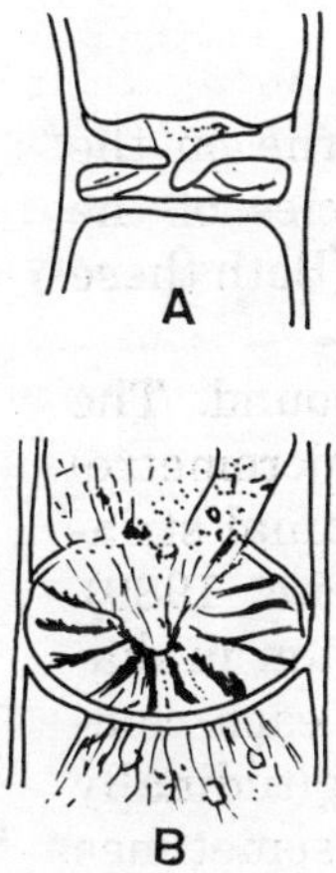

Fig. 12-49 *Sphaeroplea africana*. A, optical section of septum; B, surface view of septum.

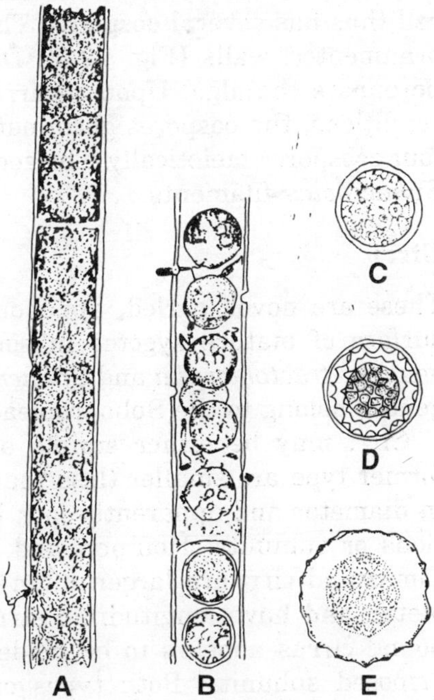

Fig. 12-50 *Sphaeroplea annulina*. A, formation and liberation of antherozoids; B, fertilization of oospheres and formation of oospores; C, multinucleate egg cell; D, oospore covered by primary membrane; E, mature oospore.

Reproduction

Vegetative Vegetative propagation occurs by filament fragmentation.

Asexual Asexual reproduction is not known.

Sexual *S. annulina* shows an interesting kind of oogamy. The antherozoids (Fig. 12-50 A) and ova (Fig. 12-50 B) are formed in large numbers in *unmodified* cells, not in specially differentiated gametangia. Thus, when compared to *Ulothrix*, the gametes of *Sphaeroplea* are much more advanced, being oogamous, but the gametangia remain at the same level as in *Ulothrix*.

Within a male cell or gametangium, progressive cleavage of the cytoplasm leads to the formation of numerous uninucleate protoplasts, each of which metamorphoses into a naked spindle-shaped biflagellate antherozoid. The antherozoids are liberated through pores in the walls of the gametangium.

In the female gametangium, the contents likewise divide into several ova (Fig. 12-50 B, C). The antherozoids enter the female gametangium through pores in its walls, and fertilize the ova. Each cell thus has several oospores. These develop thick, ornamented walls (Fig. 12-50 D, E) and serve to perennate the alga. Upon recurrence of favourable conditions, the oospores germinate, each producing four zoospores meiotically. The zoospores give rise to *Sphaeroplea* filaments.

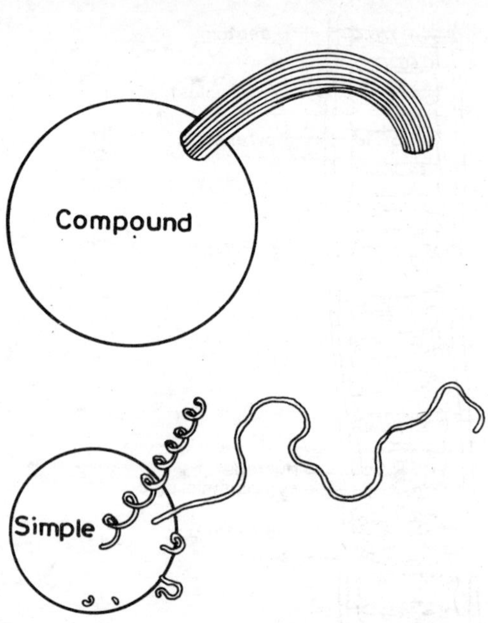

Fig. 12-51 Comparison of a compound cirrus with a variety of simple cirri (after Hoffman and Buchheim, 1989).

Cirri

These are novel, curled, appendages borne on the surface of mature zygotes in some species of the genera *Atractomorpha* and *Sphaeroplea*. (Both these genera belong to the Sphaeropleaceae.)

Cirri may be either simple or compound. The former type are smaller (less than 0.5 micrometre) in diameter and apparently lack longitudinal striations or subunits (Hoffman and Buchheim, 1989). Compound cirri are larger, often over 3 µm in diameter, and have longitudinal striations; each compound cirrus appears to be made of longitudinally disposed subunits. Both types of cirri sometimes occur on the same zygote. Cirri appear to lack mineralization and may be mainly organic in nature.

Figure 12-51 compares simple and compound cirri.

Order: CLADOPHORALES

The Cladophorales includes freshwater and marine filamentous algae, mostly branched, having large multinucleate cells which are thick-walled and possess reticulate chloroplasts and many pyrenoids. Most members occur in the relatively clean, flowing water of streams. These algae generally do not occur in absolutely quiet waters.

Reproduction takes place by fragmentation, by biflagellate or quadriflagellate zoospores, and by biflagellate isogametes. The life cycle generally involves an alternation between isomorphic generations.

Family: Cladophoraceae
Genus: *Cladophora*

Occurrence

A large genus with about 150 species, *Cladophora* occurs in diverse freshwater, brackish water, and marine habitats. The plants may be free-floating or attached to rocks, aquatic angiosperms or shells of molluscs. Some species grow so prolifically during spring and summer as to form dense mats, blankets or ropy aggregates, blocking and clogging the streams. Other species produce sponge-like balls in deep water. *C. glomerata* is a typical freshwater species often the most abundant filamentous alga found in streams throughout the world. *C. crispata* becomes attached to the walls of municipal water reservoirs. A massive growth of various species of *Cladophora* in canals impedes the flow of water through water distribution channels.

Most species prefer hard waters having relatively high pH (about 7.5 to 9.5).

Cladophora montagneana occurs commonly in tropical and temperate Central and Eastern America, Western Africa, and Western Australia. Its prolific development has caused serious environmental problems in shallow estuaries in Australia (Gordon *et al.*, 1985). The alga forms extensive aegagropiloid mats of loose-lying spheres on the estuary floor. The thalli are dark green, entangled, irregular aggregates up to 4 cm in diameter. Some spheres are densely branched.

Cladophora occurs in diverse marine and freshwaters and provides habitat and food for many organisms. Generally, *Cladophora* is an attached benthic alga, but it can occur as floating mats or as loose masses on soft substrates. Members of the genus may occur in ultraoligotrophic lakes (Stanford and Prescott, 1988) to highly eutrophic habitats, and they range from arctic to temperate marine waters. Some species in intertidal pools are capable of withstanding wide salinity variations and other species in saline lakes can survive up to 100% salinities (Borowitzka, 1981). It may well be the most ubiquitous macroalga in freshwaters worldwide (Dodds and Gudder, 1992). It can reach nuisance levels as a result of cultural eutrophication. Problems attributed to such blooms include clogging of water works, excessive diurnal swings in O_2, fouling of fish lines, unpleasant odours and appearance, lowering of property values, and danger of entanglement to young, inexperienced swimmers. Its metabolism and morphology are related to hydrodynamic conditions. Nitrogen and phosphorus are the most commonly reported limiting nutrients. *Cladophora* is a mid- to late-successional species in freshwater where it is grazer-resistant. In marine communities, however, it is an early opportunist and relatively palatable to invertebrates. *Cladophora* is colonized by a variety of epiphytes and motile animals because it can offer protection from predation, food (in the form of epiphytes) or a substrate that is anchored against flow disturbance. Species interactions that occur within *Cladophora* communities include (1) competition with other primary producers, (2) association with nitrogen-fixing epiphytes, (3) grazing on epiphytes by invertebrates, and (4) complicated foodwebs in marine intertidal and freshwater communities.

Morphology

Cladophora is profusely branched (Fig. 12-52) and, when young, is attached to the substratum by septate rhizoidal downgrowths from the basal region of the filaments or their lowermost cells (Fig. 12-53 A). The rhizoidal branches are often perennial and help in perennation of the alga through unfavourable conditions.

The cells are large, cylindrical, multinucleate, and have an elaborate chloroplast which may form a continuous reticulate network in younger cells but may become parietal in older ones (Fig. 12-53 B, C). In specimens collected from shaded habitats, the chloroplast occurs as a dense reticulum, whereas in those from well exposed localities, the chloroplasts are clearly separated from each other (Whitton, 1970). Many pyrenoids occur in the chloroplast. The cytoplasm is located centrally in the cell and contains many nuclei. Unlike most uninucleate plant and animal cells, in this alga, mitosis and cytokinesis are quite independent of each other and this is why the cells are multinucleate.

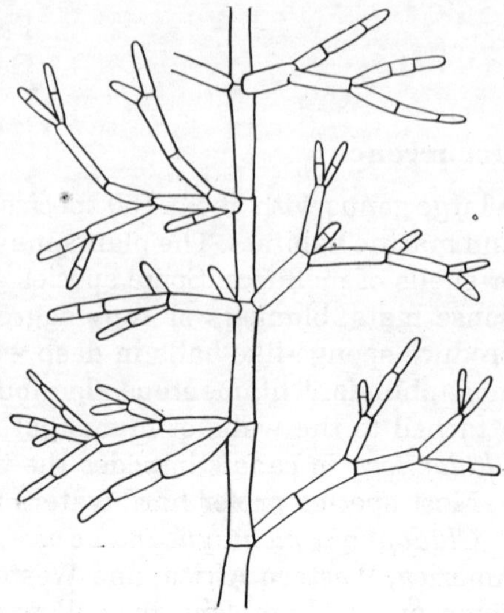

Fig. 12-52 *Cladophora longicellulata*, part of thallus.

The branching (see Fig. 12-54 A) of the thallus is usually dichotomous and rarely trichotomous. Alternate (lateral) branches are also known. The branches originate in a characteristic manner, just beneath the septum between two cells. A bulge appears near the upper end of a cell (Fig. 12-54 B, C). A portion of the cell contents of the parent cell passes into the bulge which is then cut off by a septum. This septum is parallel to the long axis of the filament and at right angles to the septum between the two parent cells. The cell bulge is then moved upward and outward as a result of the localized growth of the parent cell membrane just beneath the bulge. Consequently, the 90° angle between the new and old septa increases progressively (Fig. 12-54 D) until, in some cases, the two septa align in a straight line (Fig. 12-54 E). By this stage, the new bulge will have grown into a new cell or even a small branch and the mode of branching will appear dichotomous (Fig. 12-54 E) instead of lateral. Such a process of branch formation has been styled *evection* and is characteristic of many species. Occasionally, two such buds may be formed instead of one and then the branches will appear trichotomous.

Unlike *Ulothrix*, the mode of growth in *Cladophora* is both apical and intercalary. The relative extent of apical and intercalary growth in different species, however, varies widely; in *C. rivularis*, it is almost entirely intercalary.

The cell wall is thick, stratified, and composed of layers of microfibrils (mostly cellulosic) arranged at right angles to each other. The microfibrils of the lateral walls are often continued into those of the cross septa. The microfibrillar layers frequently become so compact with the amorphous layers that the lamellar details of the outer wall become obscure.

The branches appear coarse and stringy to the touch and, as there is little secretion of mucilage, they harbour many diatoms and other microorganisms as epiphytes.

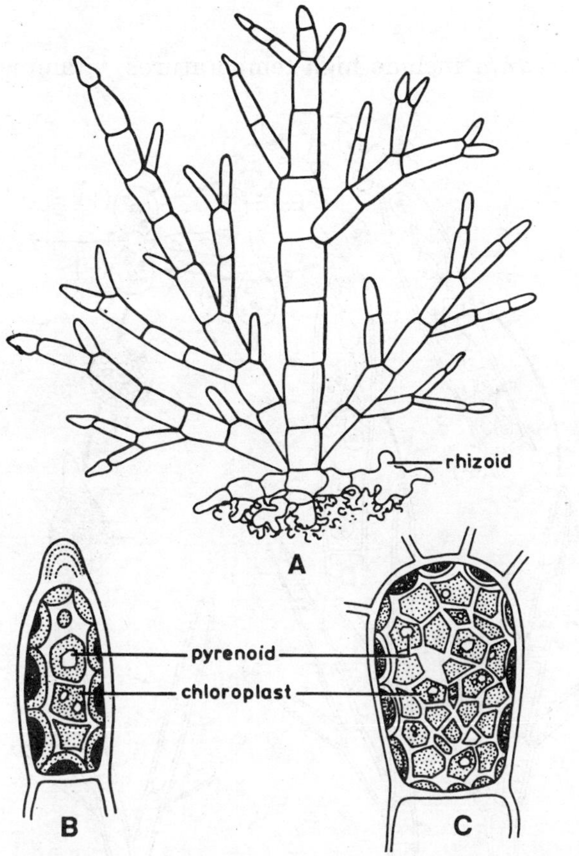

Fig. 12-53 *Cladophora jongianum*. A, habit; B, C, apical and intercalary cells with parietal chloroplasts.

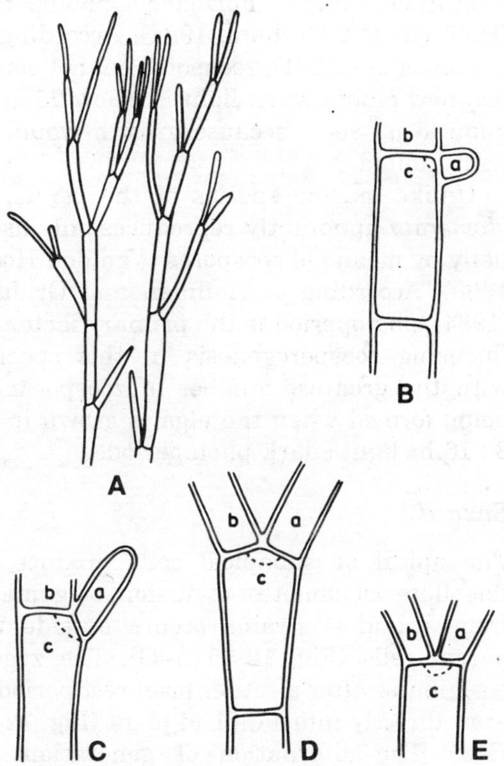

Fig. 12-54 *Cladophora*. A, branches; B–E, successive stages in evection.

Reproduction

Vegetative

A filament may fragment into two or more pieces, each of which may form a new plant. The smaller branches often become detached from the parent thallus and then grow into new plants.

Asexual

The protoplasts of apical or subapical cells break into uninucleate segments which are transformed into a biflagellate or quadriflagellate zoospore. Mature zoospores are released through pores formed in the lateral walls of the cells. Zoospore formation occurs in ordinary, unmodified cells.

After a period of motility and dispersal, the zoospores settle down on some substratum and germinate to give rise to *Cladophora* plants which are morphologically identical with the zoospore-producing parent thalli. The reduction division in some species has been observed to occur at the stage of zoospore formation.

Factors conducive to zoosporogenesis in *C. glomerata* include high temperatures, vitamin limitation, and shortened photoperiod (Hoffman and Graham, 1984). According to Lorenz *et al.* (1991), zoospores cannot establish new plants when light is below 25 µmol quanta m^{-2} sec^{-1} because growth would be light-limited.

Unlike marine species of the genus, *C. glomerata* apparently reproduces only asexually by means of zoospores (Van den Hoek, 1963). According to Hoffman and Graham (1984), photoperiod is the primary factor influencing zoosporogenesis in this species, with the greatest number of zoosporangia being formed when the alga is grown in an 8 : 16 hr light : dark photoperiod.

Sexual

The apical or subapical cells produce biflagellate isogametes. A fusion of gametes from + and – strains occurs outside the parent cells (Fig. 12-55 A–G). The zygote germinates after a rather brief rest period to grow directly into a diploid plant (Fig. 12-55 H–J). The alternation of generations in many species is isomorphic. However, *C. glomerata* shows a diplontic life cycle since the filaments are diploid and the gametes represent the only haploid stage. The zygote germinates directly into the diploid plant.

Fortnightly peak periods of gametogenesis and zygote formation have been reported for *Cladophora* and it is thought that such periodicity may be connected in some way with lunar tide cycles.

Many species have been shown to be polyploids. The number of nucleoli and chromocentres has also been correlated with the degree of polyploidy.

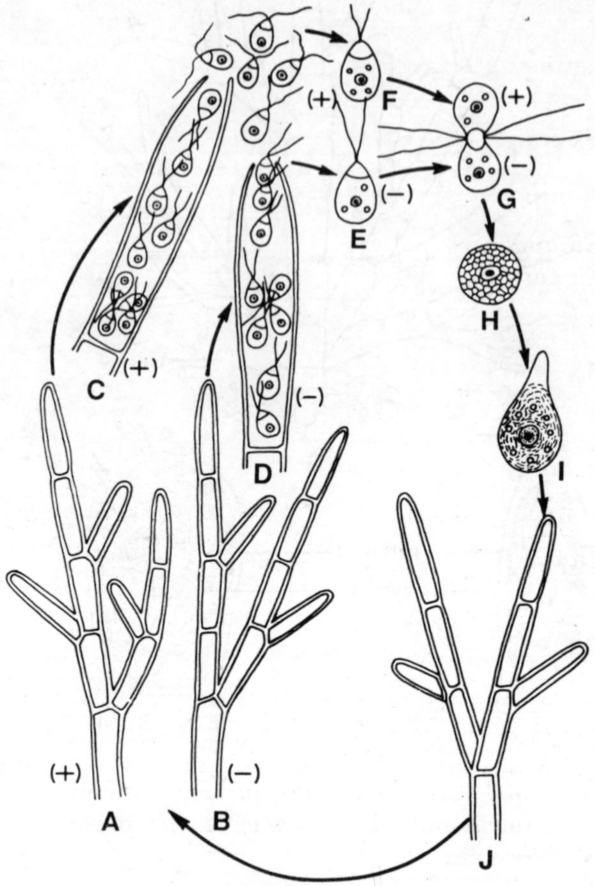

Fig. 12-55 *Cladophora*, sexual reproduction. A, B, gametophytic plants (+ and – strains); C, D, gamete formation and liberation; E, F, gametes of different mating types; G, fusion; H, zygote; I, J, germination of zygote and formation of new diploid filaments.

Seasonal Growth Cycle

Whitton (1970) has reviewed the seasonal growth behaviour of *C. glomerata* in eutrophic waters of temperate rivers. The perennating filaments attached to rocks start producing new branches in spring. After a maximum of growth and branch formation in summer, there is a slowing down of vegetative growth. A second period of rapid growth occurs in early autumn. It is believed that such growth occurs from zoospores produced the preceding summer. During late autumn, the upright parts of the thalli become detached, leaving behind the basal fragments still attached to rocks. Thick-walled akinetes are occasionally formed.

In standing water, on the other hand, the thalli and akinetes survive through winter at the bottom of the ponds under a layer of silt. Zoospore release occurs during May-June.

Species Interactions

Competition

Cladophora is usually a late- or mid-successional (climax) species in flowing freshwaters but an early-successional, opportunistic species in marine waters.

Cladophora itself can occur as an epiphyte on *Potamogeton pectinatus* and *Phragmites australis* increasing the susceptibility of *Phragmites* to breakage. When *Cladophora* decomposes, it releases an unknown type of water-soluble compound that inhibits formation of new shoots of *Phragmites* (Schröder, 1987).

C. glomerata is sometimes associated with the macrophyte *Elodea canadensis*. *C. glomerata* exerts negative effects on growth of both *Elodea* and *Potamogeton*, mainly as a result of competition for light.

Diseases

Patrick *et al.* (1983) have studied the biological control of freshwater *Cladophora*. Of the several grazers investigated (pond snail *Physa*, crayfish *Orconectes*, the tadpole *Rana*, the catfish *Ictalurus* and the fathead minnow *Pimephales*), none preferred *Cladophora*, but the fungus *Acremonium kiliense* had a detrimental effect on *C. glomerata*. The specificity of fungal pathogens varies. *Coenomyces* sp. can infect *Cladophora repens* and *Rhizoclonium* sp.

Grazing

Members of *Cladophora* are poor, nonpreferred food sources for freshwater grazers (Bronmark *et al.*, 1991). But in marine systems, in keeping with its position as an early-successional species, *Cladophora* is quite palatable (Lubchenco, 1978). Some taxa that graze *Cladophora* in marine and freshwaters are listed in Table 12-3.

Complex Species Interactions

Cladophora is often found associated with nitrogen-fixing organisms. Birch and Gabrielson (1984) showed that the biomass of marine *Cladophora* increases after decomposition of blooms of the nitrogen-fixing cyanobacterium *Nodularia spumigena*. Nitrogen fixation by cyanobacterial epiphytes on freshwater *Cladophora* also has been reported (Dodds, 1991).

Cladophora and phytoplankton often compete in lakes. The phytoplankton can intercept light, but benthic mats of filamentous periphyton can intercept nutrients from the sediments (Hansson, 1988).

Complex community interactions involving grazers, *Cladophora*, and its epiphytes occur in lotic communities. Quite often *Cladophora* offers protection from fish predation but not invertebrate predation (see Dodds and Gudder, 1992). Sometimes floods decrease the numbers of invertebrate grazers, potentiating *Cladophora* blooms during the next growing season. Midge larvae decrease algal biomass when they first colonize *Cladophora*, but the larvae stimulate growth later when they approach pupation, possibly by regenerating nutrients (Power, 1991). Chironomid larvae and mayfly nymphs that eat *Cladophora* have higher emergence rates and populations in floating mats than in attached streamers. Insects are less susceptible to fish predation in the floating masses, and floating *Cladophora* mats tend to provide thermally favourable microhabitats for insect growth and development (Power, 1990).

Table 12-3 Taxa known to consume *Cladophora* in marine and freshwater habitats (condensed from Dodds and Gudder, 1992)

Species	Comments
FRESHWATER	
Asellus aquaticus	Slow growth on *Cladophora* in laboratory experiments
Hydropsyche occidentalis, *Baetis tricaudatis*, *Hyalella azteca*, *Simulum argus*, *Argia vivida*, *Sigara* sp.	Present in gut contents
Theodoxus fluviatilis (Osteichthyes)	Lowered relative abundance of *Cladophora* in chambers
Orconectes propinquus (Decapoda)	Found in gut
Lymnaea spp. (Gastropoda)	Only when competing for food with tadpoles, diatoms preferred otherwise
Tilapia	As a food supplement
Brachycentrus occidentalis	Only after removing epiphytes
Agapetus celatus	Exclusion experiments
Macrobrachium rosenbergii	Freshwater prawn can grow on *Cladophora* in culture
MARINE	
Hermaeina smithi	May use chloroplasts symbiotically
Idotea chelipes	Laboratory feeding experiments
Idotea baltica	Older *Idotea baltica* eat *Cladophora*, younger prefer diatoms
Lymnaea peregra	Poor growth
Limapontia capitata	Several *Cladophora* spp. consumed

Many freshwater organisms (e.g., nematodes, caddis larvae, and isopods) prefer *Cladophora* as a substrate because it provides protection from larger predators. Small-mouthed salamander larvae (*Ambystoma texanum*) prefer *Cladophora* as a refuge from predation and because it is inhabited by increased levels of their isopod prey (Holomuzki, 1989).

Genus: *Pithophora*

Occurrence

It occurs in freshwater ditches, pools, and fallow fields in tropical and subtropical regions.

Morphology

The thallus is a branched filament attached to the substrata by means of rhizoids. The branches are usually solitary, sometimes opposite or dichotomous.

The cells are long, cylindrical, and multinucleate. The cytoplasm forms a lining layer enclosing a large central vacuole traversed by cytoplasmic strands. The chloroplast is single, parietal, reticulate, and has several pyrenoids.

Perennation

The usual mode of perennation is by the formation of prominent akinetes (Fig. 12-56). The protoplasmic contents shrink and migrate to the upper or distal end of the cell which may undergo some swelling. A cross wall delimits the swollen akinete from the rest of the mother cell. The akinete then develops a thick wall. A filament can form both intercalary and terminal akinetes. Sometimes, chains of akinetes develop. Upon resumption of favourable growth conditions, the akinete germinates by dividing transversely into two cells. One of these develops into a rhizoidal system and the other gives rise to the filament.

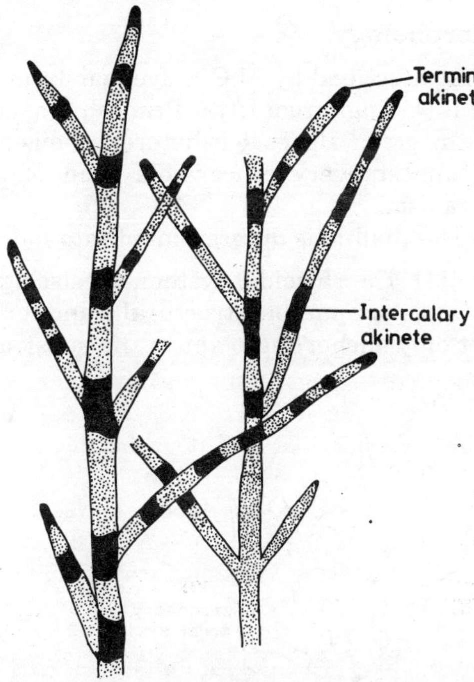

Fig. 12-56 *Pithophora* sp., thallus with intercalary and terminal akinetes.

Reproduction

Vegetative reproduction occurs by fragmentation. Asexual and sexual reproductions appear to be absent.

Order: CHAETOPHORALES

The heterotrichous habit, i.e., the differentiation of branching filaments into erect and prostrate systems, is the most outstanding singular feature of the order Chaetophorales. These plants may further be characterized by the frequent production of hairs (e.g., in Chaetophoraceae) or setae (e.g., Coleochaetaceae) or by the formation of differentiated reproductive organs such as sporangia and gametangia (e.g., Trentepohliaceae). The hairs have a single or a group of narrow elongated cells with well marked tapering apices, whereas the setae or bristles are the outgrowths of the wall with pointed ends. Certain members, e.g., the Trentepohliaceae, exhibit a marked terrestrial or subaerial tendency. *Fritschiella tuberosa* (Chaetophoraceae) is exclusively terrestrial.

Except for *Aphanochaete*, *Chaetonema*, and *Coleochaete*, other members of the Chaetophorales show isogamous sexual reproduction.

Family: Chaetophoraceae
Genus: *Fritschiella*

Occurrence

Fritschiella tuberosa Iyengar is an interesting monotypic tropical alga widespread in India, Nepal, South Africa, and many other countries. It grows in moist soils of drying-up rain water pools. It is either terrestrial or amphibious but generally does not grow in free water.

Morphology

First described by M.O.P. lyengar from South India, *Fritschiella* was later studied in detail by R.N. Singh from Uttar Pradesh. This alga is probably the most highly differentiated species of the green algae. It is heterotrichous and filamentous and is endowed with the potentiality of almost every conceivable kind of somatic advancement possible in a heterotrichous organism.

The thallus is differentiated into four distinct regions (Fig. 12-57 A):

(1) The rhizoidal system, consisting of colourless, branched or unbranched, multicellular rhizoids comparable structurally and functionally with the rhizoids of bryophytes. The rhizoids not only anchor the plant to the substratum but also serve to absorb soil nutrients.

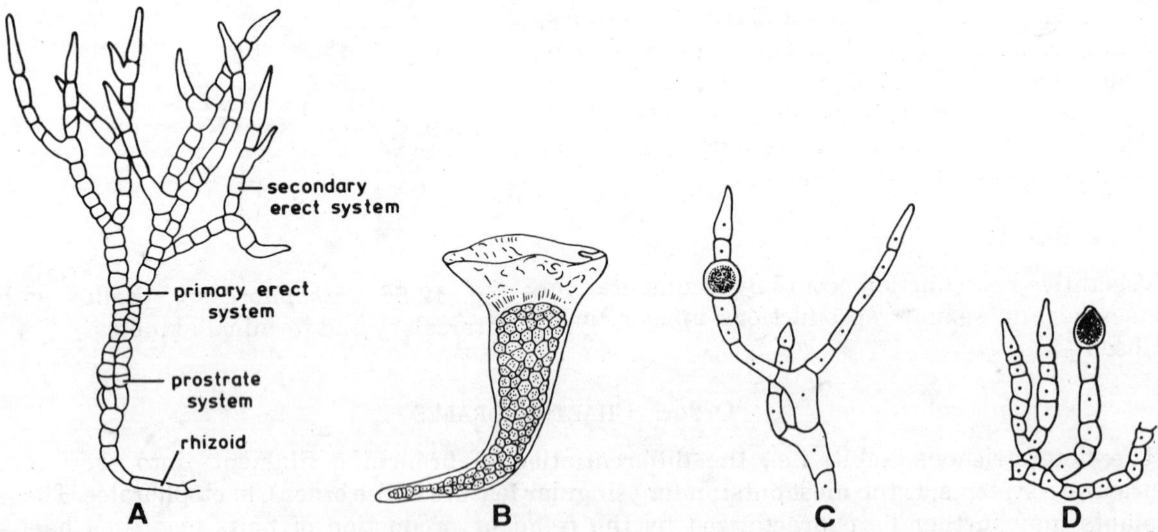

Fig. 12-57 *Fritschiella*. A, habit; B, funnel-shaped, perennating tuberous body; C, intercalary sporangium; D, terminal sporangium. (After Patel and Patel, 1969.)

(2) The prostrate system, composed of uniseriate or multiseriate (pseudoparenchymatous) clusters of rounded or irregular cells with dense contents (e.g., proteins, starch, and haematochrome). It is generally filamentous in the early stages of development in young plants. Sometimes, its filaments become further differentiated into nodal and internodal regions. The cells or filaments give rise on the lower side to rhizoids and on the upper side to the primary erect system. The cells or filaments are meant for food storage, perennation, and reproduction.

(3) The primary erect system, having uniseriate or biseriate cells (very similar to the cells of the prostrate system), partly photosynthetic and partly conducting in function.

(4) The secondary erect (projecting) system, consisting of freely branched uniseriate filaments with green, elongate, uninucleate cells, each having a parietal chloroplast with a few pyrenoids. This system is probably meant exclusively for photosynthesis.

The rhizoidal and prostrate systems are subterranean, being completely embedded beneath the surface of the soil. The primary erect system is generally partly embedded and partly projecting above ground level. The secondary erect or projecting system is fully exposed to light and air.

Perennation

During adverse periods, the erect and rhizoidal systems commonly degenerate and disappear and *Fritschiella* perennates by means of its prostrate system. Unmodified cells of the prostrate system tide over adverse periods as such but the nodal regions of the prostrate system, being capable of independent existence, may get detached from the parent thallus because of death and decay of internodal regions, and thus not only serve the function of perennation but also vegetative propagation. Yet another mode of perennation is by the formation of specially modified tuber-like bodies (Fig. 12-57 B) enclosed by cell walls having a dark and thick cuticle. Formed in the prostrate system, these tubers are commonly either funnel-shaped or club-shaped (Fig. 12-57 B). Each such tuber may be up to 1 mm in length.

Reproduction

Asexual Reproduction takes place by the formation of biflagellate or quadriflagellate zoospores, one or two of which normally emerge from a mother cell. Such zoospores are structurally similar to those of *Ulothrix*. Patel and Patel (1969) have recorded differentiated intercalary and terminal sporangia (Fig. 12-57 C, D) which are somewhat larger in size than the ordinary vegetative cells. However, the nature and fate of the products of such sporangia are not known.

Sexual An interesting feature of *F. tuberosa* is the combination of a highly differentiated vegetative thallus with an equally simple and primitive mode of sexual reproduction, viz., isogamy.

The life history of *F. tuberosa* has been described by Singh (1947) as an obligate alternation of isomorphic generations, with the gametophyte plants producing biflagellate isogametes; the zygote germinates into the sporophyte which in turn produces haploid zoospores after meiosis. Hopkins (1977) has failed to find such an obligate alternation of generations but has instead reported an asexual repeating of one generation; this species regularly forms one quadriflagellate zoospore per cell in all parts of the erect and prostrate systems.

Fritschiella has attracted considerable attention in connection with speculations on the algal ancestry of higher plants (see Singh, 1954). It has been strongly advocated that the ancestors of the early land plants were green algae very similar to the present day *Fritschiella*. The reason such ancestors are sought among the green algae is that the basic physiological, biochemical, and metabolic characteristics of the higher plants (from bryophytes onwards) can be compared only with those of the Chlorophyceae. *Fritschiella* was considered nearest to the hypothetical ancestors on the basis of its following attributes:

(1) terrestrial or amphibious habitat;

(2) rhizoidal system strongly resembling the rhizoids of bryophytes, both structurally and functionally;

(3) prostrate system being very much like the subterranean rhizomatous structures of certain pteridophytes and angiosperms;

(4) reproduction being mostly confined to prostrate system as in the Anthocerotales whose reproductive bodies are endogenous and embedded in the thallus;

(5) tropical distribution (it is widely believed that the first transmigrants were tropical forms); and

(6) high degree of thallus differentiation, indicating the existence of a strong potentiality for further elaboration in a chaetophoraceous alga in the direction of evolution of an early algal transmigrant form.

Stewart and Mattox (1975) have strongly opposed the foregoing view and have instead proposed that the land plants originated not from members of the Chlorophyceae but from ancestral forms of such extant genera as *Chara* and *Coleochaete* (i.e., class Charophyceae of Stewart and Mattox). This question is further discussed under the Charophyceae and under Green Algal Phylogeny.

Genus: *Stigeoclonium*

Occurrence

It occurs in well-aerated flowing water in drains, sewage channels, storm water streams, and in standing water, attached to rocks, stones, and aquatic macrophytes. It is a large genus with many species worldwide. *S. tenue*, *S. lubricum*, *S. attenuatum*, and *S. setigerum* are some of the species found in India.

Morphology

It is typically a heterotrichous alga with more or less equally well developed prostrate and erect systems of branching filaments (Fig. 12-58 A, B). From the basal system (Fig. 12-58 A, B) arise a number of erect filaments. These show alternate (*S. attenuatum*) or opposite (*S. flagelliformis*) manner. The branches usually terminate in long, colourless, multicellular hairs (Fig. 12-58 A). The growth of the upright filaments is diffuse, whereas that of the basal system is apical.

The cells are uninucleate, each with a parietal chloroplast having a few pyrenoids.

Reproduction

Vegetative It occurs by fragmentation of erect or prostrate filaments.

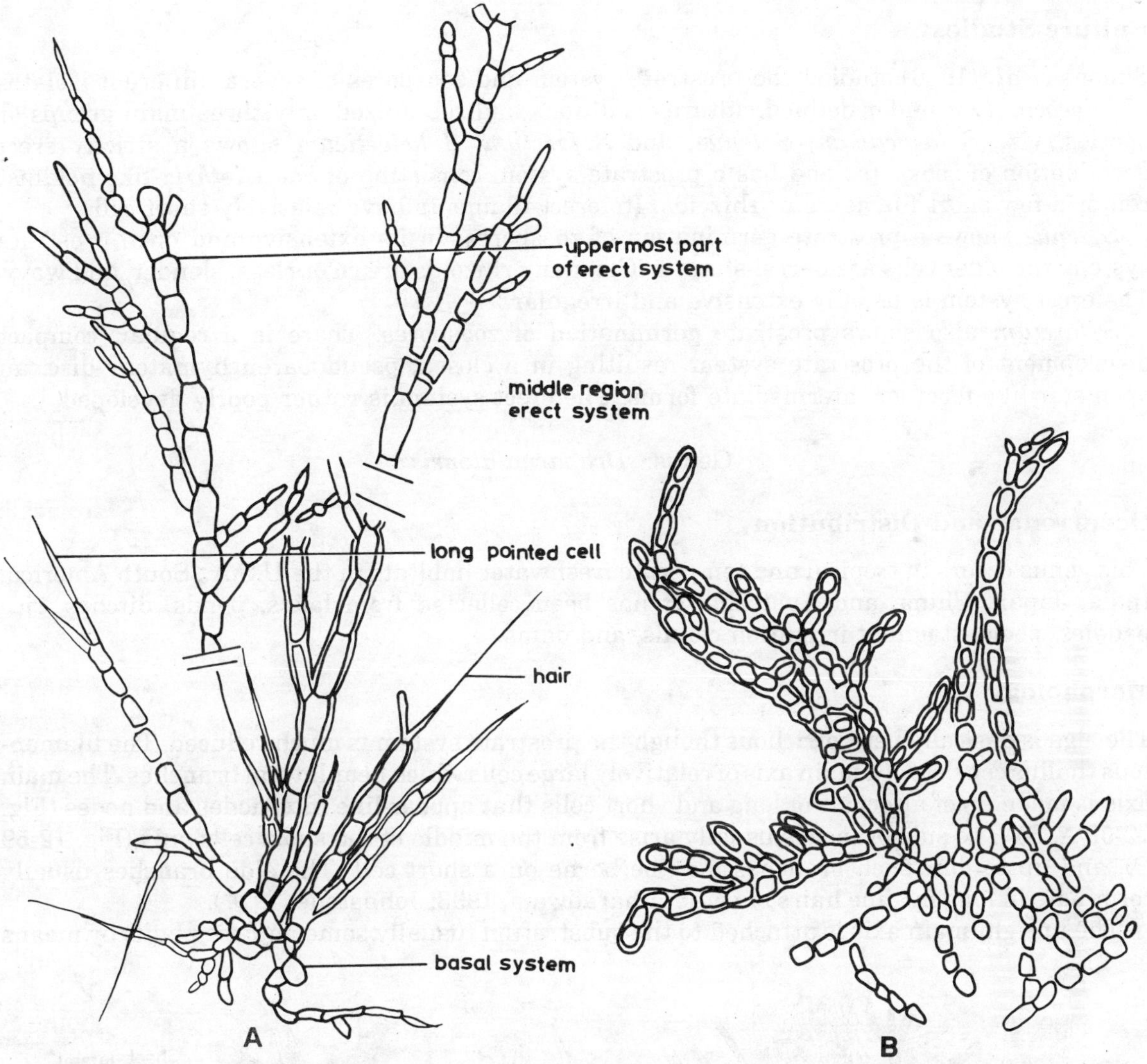

Fig. 12-58 *Stigeoclonium setigerum*. A, morphology of natural material showing heterotrichous habit; B, basal system as seen in one-month-old culture. *Courtesy* Y.B.K. Chowdary.

Asexual Quadriflagellate zoospores are produced singly in vegetative cells of the upright filaments. The zoospores are released through pores in the lateral wall. *S. amoenum* produces quadriflagellate macrozoospores and quadriflagellate microzoospores. After swarming for some time, the zoospores attach themselves by their anterior end to a substratum and germinate into new plants.

Sexual Isogametes are formed singly from some cells of erect filaments. They are usually biflagellate, rarely quadriflagellate. They fuse to form the zygote which develops into a new plant. The life history of most species is isomorphic.

Culture Studies

Simons *et al.* (1986) studied the prostrate system and zoospores of several different isolates of *Stigeoclonium* under defined culture conditions and recognized only three main groups or species, viz., *S. helveticum*, *S. tenue*, and *S. farctum*. *S. helveticum* shows a strictly erect germination of zoospores and has a prostrate system consisting of one *Ulothrix*-like holdfast cell or a few short filaments or rhizoids. Its erect filaments have relatively short cells.

S. tenue shows a prostrate germination of zoospores. In its extensive and open prostrate system, the older cells are barrel-shaped. The many rhizoids are colourless, slender, and wavy. The erect system is usually extensive and irregular.

S. farctum also shows prostrate germination of zoospores. There is a regular, compact development of the prostrate system resulting in a closed, pseudoparenchymatous disc, an open star-like form, or intermediate forms. The erect system is rather poorly developed.

Genus: *Draparnaldiopsis*

Occurrence and Distribution

This genus occurs in tropical and temperate freshwater habitats in the U.S.A., South America, India, Japan, China, and Australia. It has been collected from lakes, ponds, ditches, rice paddies, pools, stagnant irrigation canals, and dams.

Morphology

The alga is basically heterotrichous though the prostrate system is much reduced. The filamentous thallus consists of a main axis of relatively large cells which bear lateral branches. The main axis is made up of alternating long and short cells that appear like internodes and nodes (Fig. 12-59 A, B). The side branches usually arise from the middle of the short cells only (Fig. 12-59 C), and up to four such branches may be borne on a short cell. The side branches usually terminate in long hyaline hairs or setae (Bharadwaja, 1933; Johnstone, 1977).

The upright main axis is attached to the substratum (usually some aquatic plant) by means

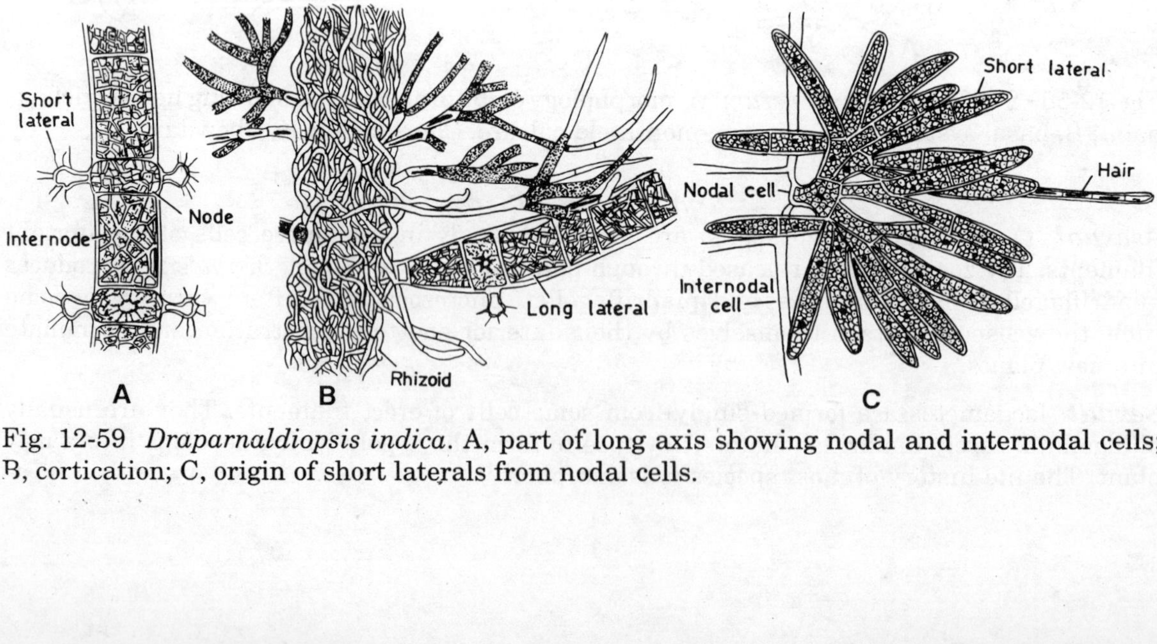

Fig. 12-59 *Draparnaldiopsis indica*. A, part of long axis showing nodal and internodal cells; B, cortication; C, origin of short laterals from nodal cells.

of multicellular rhizoidal branches arising from the basal cell. Similar branches also sometimes arise from other cells, forming a kind of cortex (Fig. 12-59 B) around parts of the main axis.

The branches arising from the nodal cells may either all be of limited growth or some may be of unlimited growth and others of limited growth. Those of unlimited growth repeat the structure of the main axis. The cells of those branches which are limited in growth are usually smaller than those of the main axis or unlimited branches.

The cells are uninucleate and contain a parietal chloroplast with several pyrenoids.

Reproduction

Asexual *D. indica* multiplies by the formation of aplanospores. Singh (1945) reported the formation of zoospores from the short laterals of the diploid plants of *D. indica*. Meiosis seems to occur during zoosporogenesis. The zoospores germinate into haploid, gametophytic plants (which are morphologically identical with the diploid sporophytes).

Sexual The gametophytic thalli produce isogametes which fuse to form a zygote. The latter in turn gives rise to the sporophytic generation.

The isomorphic alternation in *D. indica* described by Singh (1945) could not be confirmed by Johnstone (1977), and may accordingly be regarded as uncertain.

Family: Trentepohliaceae

This includes subaerial heterotrichous forms which form distinctive sporangia and gametangia. Hairs and setae are usually absent.

Cephaleuros virescens and *C. mycoidea* are parasitic on angiosperms. Some species cause the "red rust" disease of tea.

Genus: *Trentepohlia*

Occurrence

Most species are typically subaerial, growing in damp tropical and subtropical regions on walls, barks, leathery leaves, or rocks. The thallus usually looks orange red due to abundance of haematochrome. Some species occur in lichens.

Morphology

The alga is a branched, heterotrichous filament (Fig. 12-60). The branching in the erect filaments may be alternate, opposite, or unilateral. The growth is apical. In *T. umbrina*, the prostrate system is better developed than the erect system.

The cells are cylindrical, barrel-shaped, or moniliform. Their walls are thick, stratified, and cellulosic. The terminal cells are usually covered by pectose caps. The septa between adjoining cells often have a pore or pit and are penetrated by a protoplasmic strand. The young cells are uninucleate. The older cells become multinucleate. The cells contain several discoid or band-shaped parietal chloroplasts, lacking pyrenoids. They store much haematochrome.

Reproduction

Vegetative Most species are typically adapted to their subaerial way of life and propagate vegetatively by means of cellular dust which is dispersed by wind. The cells of the prostrate system separate from each other, round off, and form a powdery mass which is blown around by wind. Upon settlement, the cells germinate into new plants.

Sometimes, the cells of the prostrate system form thick-walled akinetes.

Asexual The zoospores are formed in specialized sporangia. The sporangia are ovoid or ellipsoid. They may be stalked or funnel-shaped.

Stalked sporangia (Fig. 12-60) are borne on erect filaments. At maturity, the entire sporangium becomes detached from its stalk and is blown away by wind. Upon settlement, its contents release quadriflagellate zoospores. These give rise to new plants.

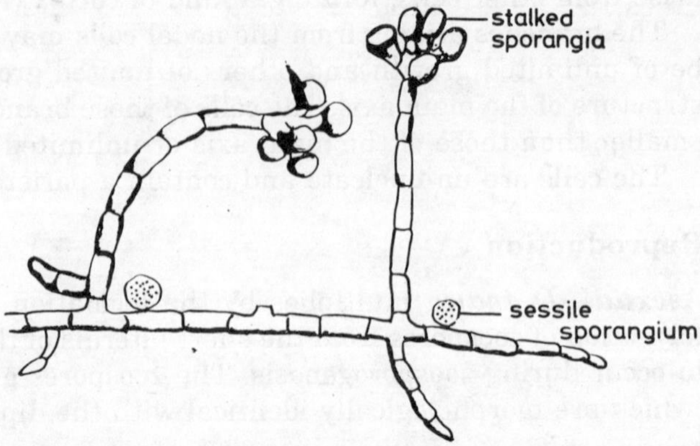

Fig. 12-60 *Trentepohlia* sp., part of thallus, showing sporangia.

The funnel-shaped sporangium is cut off from the distal portion of a cell by a transverse septum which lies between two superposed thickening rings. At maturity, the parent cell wall splits near the septum and the sporangium detaches. The nature and fate of the sporangial products are obscure.

Sexual The gametangia are sessile and do not become detached from the mother plant. They are usually but not exclusively borne on the prostrate filaments. They produce only biflagellate isogametes. Sometimes, these gametes give rise to new plants directly, without undergoing fusion, thus behaving as parthenogametes or asexual zoospores.

Family: Coleochaetaceae
Genus: *Coleochaete*

Occurrence

Coleochaete, the sole genus of the family Coleochaetaceae, has some 10 species which grow epiphytically on the leaves and stems of freshwater higher plants such as *Hydrilla* and *Potamogeton*, or as endophytes in *Nitella*.

Morphology

C. pulvinata (Fig. 12-61) is heterotrichous with the branched filaments of the erect system organized into a more or less hemispherical cushion. In *C. scutata* (Figs. 12-62 and 12-63), the erect system is absent and the prostrate system is discoid showing radial arrangement of its congregated branches; this gives rise to a pseudoparenchymatous disc which grows by means of apical (marginal) meristems. The branching of the thallus may result from lateral outgrowths or dichotomy of the apical meristems. The cells are uninucleate, and contain an irregular parietal chloroplast with one or two pyrenoids. The entire cell (including the flagella) is covered with a single layer of diamond-shaped scales arranged in regular rows (Sluiman, 1983). *Coleochaete* differs from other members of the Chaetophorales in its chromosome number and morphology.

Some or most of the cells of the thallus produce setae, each of which is composed of a

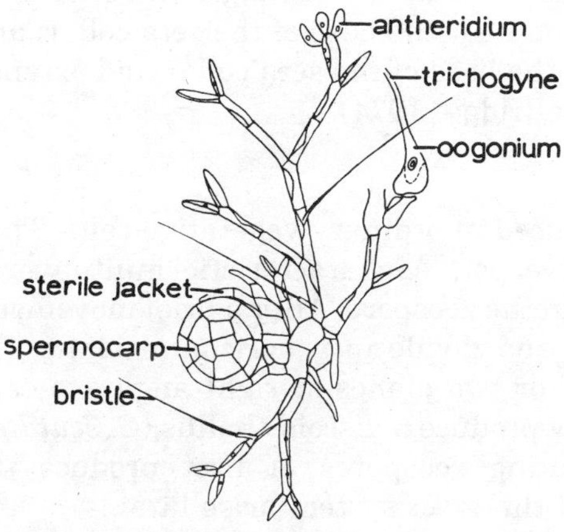

Fig. 12-61 *Coleochaete pulvinata*, habit.

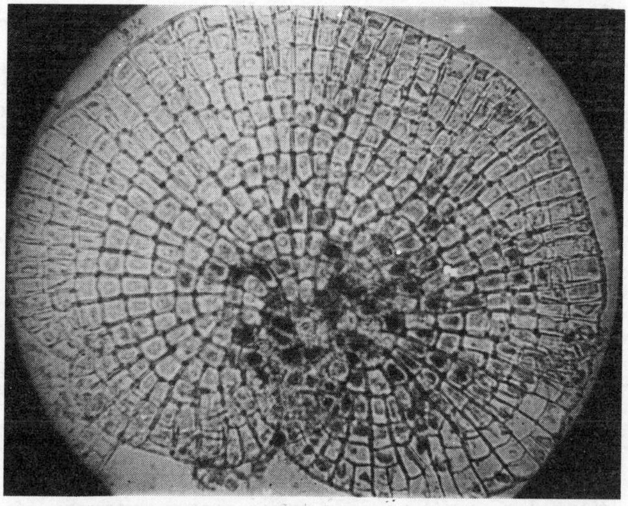

Fig. 12-62 *Coleochaete scutata*, habit of fertile material.

cytoplasmic thread completely or partially enclosed within a basal sheath (Fig. 12-64). The setae are generally regarded as outgrowths of the plasma membrane emerging through a pore in the cell wall. They readily break off after some time, leaving only the basal sheaths. The setae probably defend the alga against grazers, as broken setae exude a substance which repels potential grazers (Marchant and Pickett-Heaps, 1977).

The seta-bearing cells constitute a unique character of the family Coleochaetaceae. The seta-bearing cells of *C. scutata* differentiate from vegetative cells and represent up to 5 per

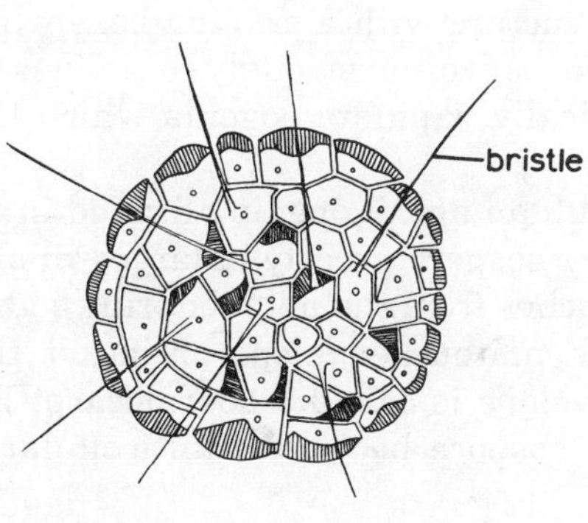

Fig. 12-63 *Coleochaete scutata*, habit.

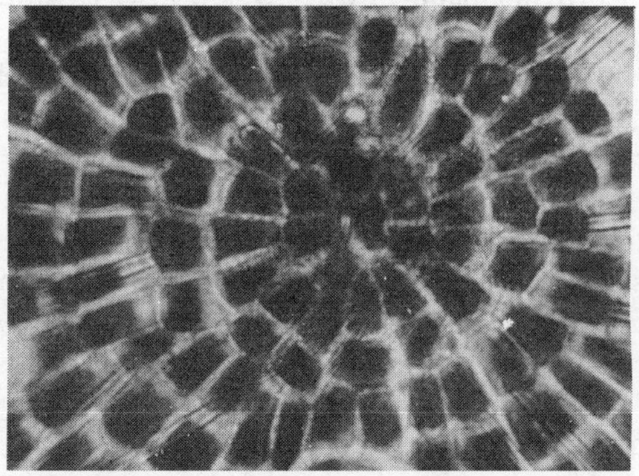

Fig. 12-64 *Coleochaete scutata*, part of colony showing sheathed setae. (×270.) *Courtesy* Y.B.K. Chowdary.

cent of the cells in a typical thallus (McBridge, 1974). They have the following modifications: (1) a tube-like extension of the cell wall, called the seta collar; (2) the seta proper, a thin membrane-bound structure originating from the cytoplasm but exuded through the seta collar; (3) the setasome, a granular body found in the cytoplasm near the base of the seta collar; and (4) a crescent-shaped chloroplast that revolves around the base of the seta collar and extends a diverticulum of its outer membrane into the seta (McBridge, 1974).

Reproduction

Asexual Single, ovoid, biflagellate zoospores are produced in ordinary vegetative cells. They possess a lateral chloroplast but are devoid of an eyespot. A characteristic multilayered structure, associated with the flagellar base, is present in the zoospore. After a brief movement, the zoospores withdraw their flagella, secrete a wall, and divide in a horizontal plane; the upper cell forms the seta and the lower divides in one or two planes at right angles to each other to form the primary initials which by their activity produce a discoid thallus (*C. scutata*). In heterotrichous forms (*C. pulvinata*), the germinating zoospores at first produce the branched prostrate system from which the branches of the erect system arise later.

Sexual *C. pulvinata* is monoecious, whereas *C. scutata* is dioecious. The sexuality is of an advanced oogamous type and is accompanied by a kind of fruit formation not found in any other green algae. The heterotrichous species bear the sex organs on the branches of the erect system.

In *C. pulvinata*, the antheridia are produced terminally on branches, sometimes on the same branch that bears an oogonium. The antheridial initials arise as colourless outgrowths from the terminal cells of a branch (Fig. 12-61) and one antheridium gives rise to a single minute biflagellate oval or spherical, naked gamete.

The antheridia of *C. scutata* (Fig. 12-65) are produced from some intercalary cells lying within the periphery of the thallus. At the time of antheridial formation, an intercalary cell divides into a number of daughter cells each of which finally differentiates into an antheridium. Occasionally, the antherozoids of *C. scutata* are green rather than colourless.

The oogonia of *C. pulvinata* are also produced terminally and singly but their seemingly lateral position is due to the growth and production of branches from the cells beneath the oogonium (Fig. 12-66). Each oogonium is a flask-shaped structure with a swollen base which contains an egg, and a slender neck or trichogyne. This type of oogonium strongly resembles the carpogonium of the Rhodophyta. Discoid species have typically papillate oogonia which lack trichogynes.

During fertilization, an antherozoid enters an egg through an apical opening formed in the trichogyne or in the papilla of the oogonium. The resulting oospore greatly enlarges in size, sometimes attaining a diameter of 150 μm, and certain branches from the neighbouring cells of a zygote grow out forming a rather loose pseudoparenchymatous envelope or jacket that completely encircles the oospore. The oospore plus the envelope is called a spermocarp (Fig. 12-67) which is analogous to an angiospermic fruit. The oospore becomes multicellular at maturity.

After perennation, when the oospore germinates, its nucleus divides meiotically and this is followed by a few mitotic divisions, producing a 16- to 32-celled structure. Each of these cells forms a biflagellate zoospore which grows into a new plant. *Coleochaete* is haploid, with an oospore representing the only diploid stage in the life cycle.

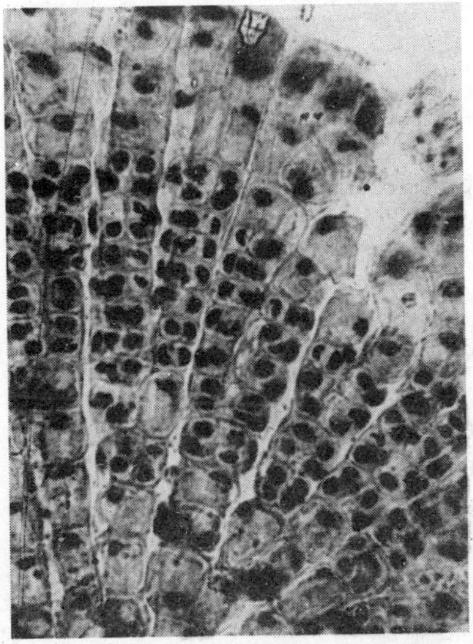

Fig. 12-65 *Coleochaete scutata*, part of thallus showing antheridia. (×145.) *Courtesy* Y.B.K. Chowdary.

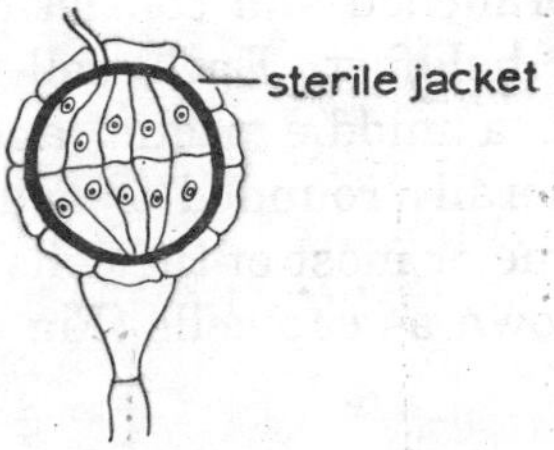

Fig. 12-66 *Coleochaete pulvinata*, spermocarp.

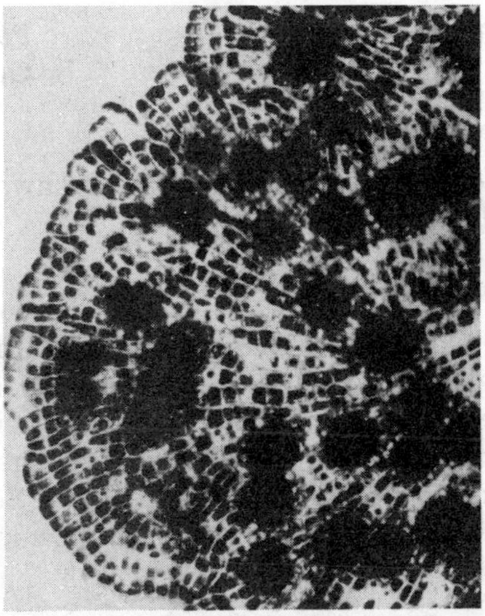

Fig. 12-67 *Coleochaete scutata*, part of thallus showing spermocarps. (×85.) *Courtesy* Y.B.K. Chowdary.

Coleochaete is unique among the green algae and similar to higher plants in that its zygote is retained on the parent thallus and undergoes further development there (Graham, 1984).

Order: OEDOGONIALES

The two main distinguishing features of the Oedogoniales are (1) the mode of cell division, leading to the formation of characteristic caps on certain cells; and (2) the production of multiflagellate zoospores or gametes.

The single family Oedogoniaceae comprises the three genera *Oedogonium*, *Bulbochaete*, and *Oedocladium* (Fig. 12-68) which differ from one another in thallus organization. *Oedogonium* is an unbranched, filamentous form which grows attached to the substratum when young but often becomes free-floating at maturity. *Bulbochaete* is a profusely branched alga with unilateral branches lying on alternate sides and almost every cell bearing a characteristic attenuated hair with a bulbous base; the terminal cells are generally provided with a pair of such hairs. *Oedocladium* is terrestrial and heterotrichous with a prostrate system bearing numerous branched, septate, and colourless rhizoids on its lower side and branches of the erect system on its upper side.

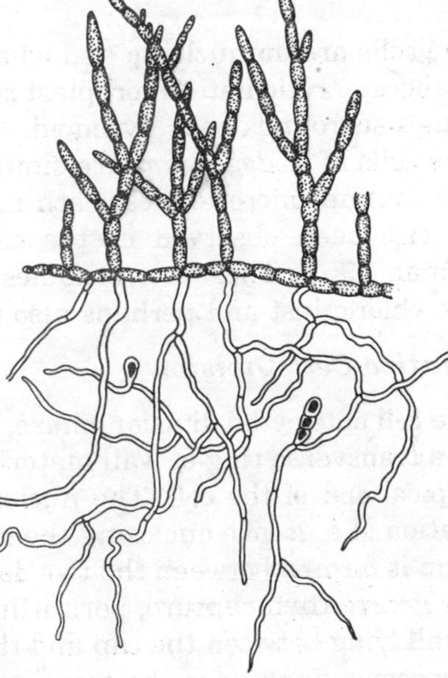

Fig. 12-68 *Oedocladium protonema*, rhizoids and two resting cysts.

Family: Oedogoniaceae
Genus: *Oedogonium*

Occurrence

Oedogonium is a widespread freshwater alga which grows epiphytically in ponds, pools, and shallow tanks.

Morphology

The filaments of *Oedogonium* are unbranched and consist of cylindrical cells except for the basal cell which is modified into a holdfast. Each cell is provided with a thick wall differentiated into an inner cellulosic, a middle pectic, and an outer chitinous layer. The terminal cells of the filaments are generally rounded or acuminate and the intercalary cells often show an apical-basal polarity. Some or most of the cells at the distal end exhibit parallel striations or annular scars and are known as cap cells (Fig. 12-69).

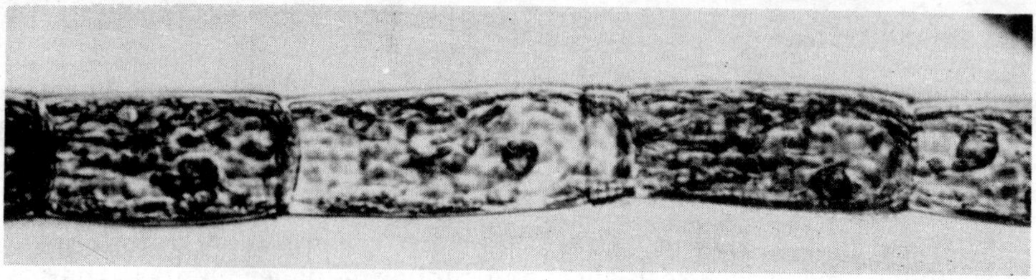

Fig. 12-69 *Oedogonium* sp., part of filament showing cap cells. (Approx. ×200.)

The cells are uninucleate and when mature have a central vacuole containing cell sap, and an elaborate, reticulate chloroplast containing many pyrenoids (Fig. 12-69). A sheath of starch granules surrounds each pyrenoid.

The cells of *Oedogonium* are similar to those of other green algae except that their chloroplasts contain microtubules, each made up of two helically wound subunits. Such elements have also been observed in the chloroplasts of zoospores, zoospore germlings, and eggs (Hoffman, 1967). These microtubules are said to provide structural support to the massive reticulate chloroplast and perhaps also to facilitate its growth and development.

Vegetative Cell Division

As the cell enters the division phase, the nucleus moves from the lateral position to the centre. Soon a transverse ring of wall material appears on the inner face of the lateral wall just below the apical end of the cell. The nuclear division, the growth of the ring in thickness, and the formation of a groove enclosing the growing ring occur concomitantly. An unattached floating septum is formed between the two daughter nuclei. The middle and outer wall layers external to the groove then rupture, permitting free elongation of the ring which forms a new piece of cell wall lying between the cap and the sheath. Ultimately, the floating septum moves upward and becomes fixed near the terminus of the old cell wall. The new cell has its wall formed from the thickened ring and the newly synthesized piece. The membranous striation of the ruptured parental wall at the anterior region of the upper daughter cell is the cap and the cell bearing it is known as a cap cell. The number of caps on a cell indicates the number of cell divisions that have taken place.

An ultrastructural study (Fig. 12-70) of the mode of cell division of *Oedogonium borisianum* (Hill and Michalis, 1968) has revealed that:

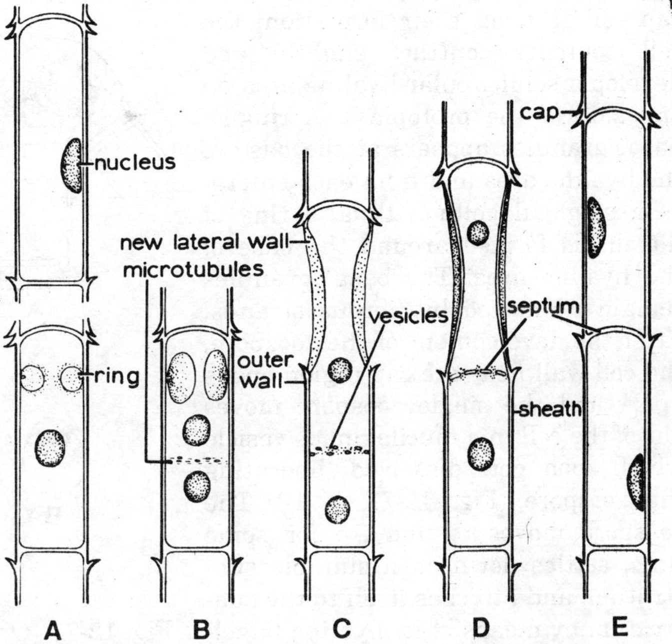

Fig. 12-70 *Oedogonium borisianum*, stages in cell division.

(1) The ring (Fig. 12-70 A) below the cap originates as a three-layered structure by a method that excludes the possibility of its origin from an infolding of the innermost wall layer.

(2) The ring grows in size with a gradual addition of vesicular material from the cytoplasm.

(3) The mother wall adjacent to the fully-formed ring splits off.

(4) The single, peripheral nucleus migrates to the centre and karyokinesis occurs. This is followed by the formation in the internuclear region of a row of microtubules (Fig. 12-70 B) in a plane parallel to that of the future cross wall.

(5) Concurrent with the development in (4) the ring expands into a cylinder (Fig. 12-70 C) which becomes the cuticle of the upper daughter cell. The septum, which for some time remains unattached to the lateral wall, later migrates upward to the base of the cylinder (Fig. 12-70 D).

(6) Following stage (5), a new lateral wall is formed between the cuticle and the plasmalemma of the upper daughter cell.

(7) The upward migrated transverse septum grows into a mature cross wall which unites with the newly formed wall on either side (Fig. 12-70 E).

The mode of cross wall formation rules out the possibility of cell division either by cytokinesis or by annular furrowing of the cytoplasm.

In a karyological study of sixteen taxa of *Oedogonium*, Srivastava and Sarma (1979) found the chromosome number (n) to range from 9 to 46. According to them, aneuploidy has played a stronger role than euploidy in the speciation of this genus, with some role also being played by chromosomal rearrangements.

Reproduction

Vegetative

Fragmentation is the usual method of propagation but under certain conditions *Oedogonium* may propagate also by akinete formation.

Asexual

Reproduction occurs by the formation of multiflagellate zoospores produced singly within a cap cell. During their formation, the cell contents contract slightly and develop a semicircular hyaline area on one side of the protoplast. A ring of basal granules appears at the base of the hyaline area and from each emerges a single flagellum; thus, a ring of flagella is formed around the base of the hyaline area. The basal granules remain connected by fibrous strands. After the development of the zoospore, the cell wall near the cap region opens apart and the single zoospore moves out of the cell in a mucilaginous vesicle which soon gets dissolved, liberating the zoospore (Fig. 12-71 A, B). The zoospore moves to and fro for some time, settles down on a suitable substratum, and attaches itself to the substratum by means of its hyaline flagellar end. Thereafter, the flagella are withdrawn and the quiescent zoospore elongates considerably. The attached end of the growing zoospore may differentiate into a smooth holdfast if the substratum is smooth and a lobed holdfast if the substratum is rough.

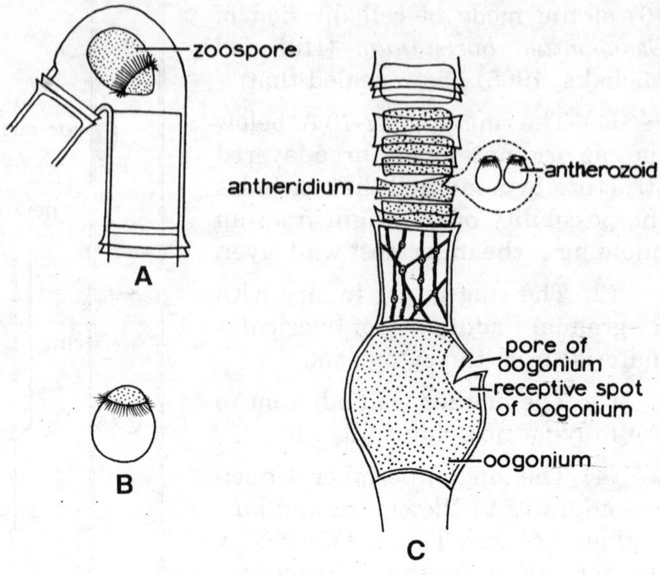

Fig. 12-71 *Oedogonium*. A, formation and liberation of zoospore; B, one zoospore with crown of flagella; C, oogamous reproduction in homothallic macrandrous species.

Sexual

Reproduction is oogamous and is of two kinds, viz., (1) macrandrous, and (2) nannandrous.

The macrandrous forms may be monoecious, producing antheridia and oogonia on the same plant (Fig. 12-71 C), or dioecious, producing antheridia and oogonia on different individuals. In the nannandrous forms, the sexual plants are dimorphic—the oogonia being formed in filaments of normal size, whereas the antheridia are produced in filaments, known as dwarf males (Fig. 12-72 A) or nannandria, which are extremely small and are always found attached to oogonia proper or to the underlying cell.

Macrandrous Forms

The antheridial mother cell may be terminal or intercalary. In either case, it divides vegetatively into an upper antheridial cell and a lower sister cell. The latter undergoes a series of vegetative divisions to produce a row of two or more antheridia. An antheridium may give rise to a single multiflagellate antherozoid or it may undergo a single transverse or vertical division followed by the transformation of each of the two daughter cells into an antherozoid. Although quite similar to the zoospores, the antherozoids are smaller and may have fewer flagella.

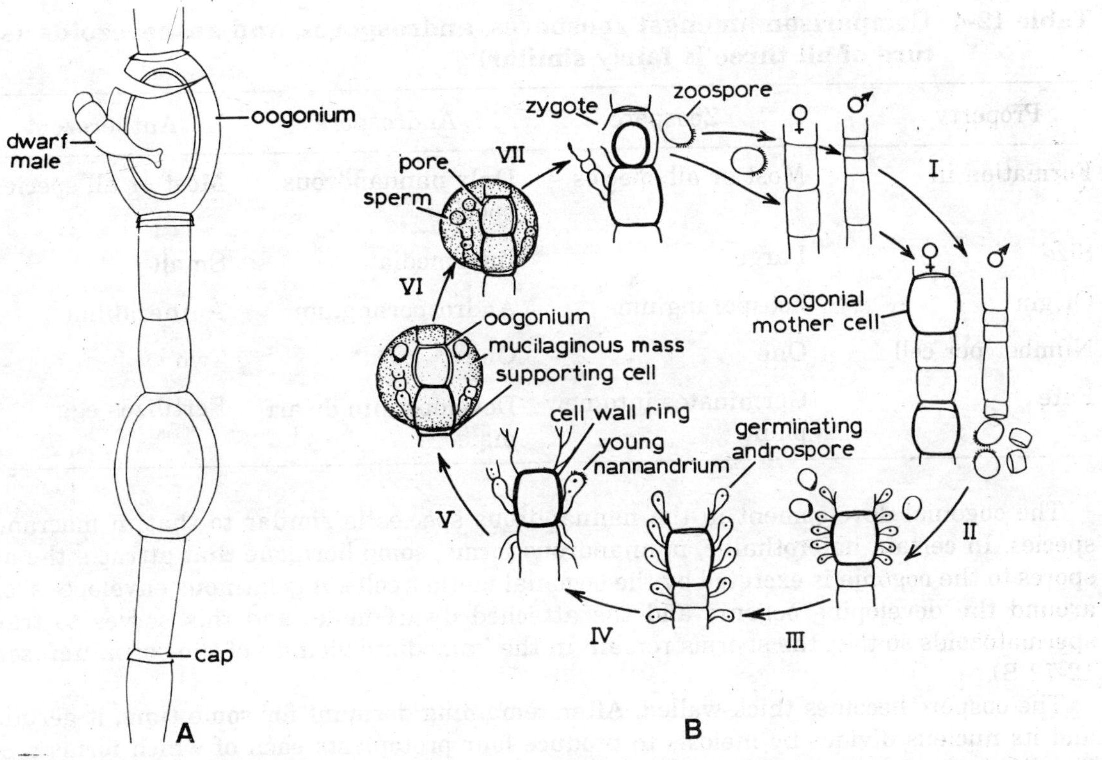

Fig. 12-72 *Oedogonium*. A, nannandrous species; B, life cycle of nannandrous species.

The oogonia are produced from cells that act as oogonial mother cells. Each of these cells divides into an upper cap cell functioning as oogonium proper, and a lower supporting cell. The latter may again behave as an oogonial mother cell, thus forming a row of two or more consecutive oogonia. Or, it may remain vegetative, in which case the oogonia are solitary. The oogonium, which is filled with reserve food, enlarges to some extent and assumes a more or less spherical shape. A colourless region, called the receptive spot, appears at one point near the side wall and through it an antherozoid finds its way into the egg.

Nannandrous Forms

Each dwarf male or nannandrium is a few-celled filament with a basal stalk cell and two to three antheridial cells. The dwarf males are derived from antherozoid-like zoospores, known as androspores, which are formed singly within antheridia-like cells called androsporangia. A species that bears both oogonia and androsporangia is designated gynandrosporous, whereas the one that bears them on different filaments is termed idioandrosporous. The changes that take place during the development of androsporangia and androspores are similar to those occurring in the production of antheridia and antherozoids. After their liberation from androsporangia, the androspores swim about for some time and then only one or a few of them may settle on an oogonium or a suffultory cell (Table 12-4). The androspore then germinates into a dwarf male. Each antheridium of the dwarf male commonly produces two antherozoids lying one above the other.

Table 12-4 Comparison amongst zoospores, androspores, and antherozoids (structure of all three is fairly similar)

Property	Zoospore	Androspore	Antherozoid
Formation in	Most or all species	Only nannandrous species	Most or all species
Size	Large	Intermediate	Small
Origin	Zoosporangium	Androsporangium	Antheridium
Number per cell	One	One	Two
Fate	Germinates into new plant	Develops into dwarf male	Fertilizes egg

The oogonial development in the nannandrous species is similar to that in macrandrous species. In certain heterothallic, nannandrous forms, some hormone that attracts the androspores to the oogonia is excreted by the oogonial mother cells. A gelatinous envelope is formed around the developing oogonia and the attached dwarf male, and this serves to trap the spermatozoids so that the sperms remain in the immediate vicinity of the oogonium (see Fig. 12-72 B).

The oospore becomes thick-walled. After remaining dormant for some time, it germinates and its nucleus divides by meiosis to produce four protoplasts each of which forms a multiflagellate zoospore which grows into a new haploid *Oedogonium* plant. In some heterothallic species, two of the four zoospores develop into male filaments, whereas the other two develop into female filaments.

The oogonial mother cell of *Oedogonium donnellii* produces a pheromone called circein which affects the behaviour and development of the androspore of *O. donnellii*: the androspore forms a sperm-producing dwarf male (Hill *et al.*, 1989). On the other hand, if the androspore is subjected to a nitrogen-rich environment (abundant nitrate or ammonium ions), it forms a vegetative male thallus that cannot be distinguished from the one which originally released the androspore. If exposed to neither circein nor increased nitrate/ammonium, the androspore enters a cycle of swimming androspore-cyst-swimming androspore. Treatments with inhibitors of transcription (actinomycin D) and translation (cycloheximide) indicate that androspore development into either a dwarf male or a vegetative filament requires several different phases of *de novo* synthesis of RNA and protein stimulated by circein or by nitrate ions (Hill *et al.*, 1989).

Genus: *Oedocladium*

Occurrence

It occurs in moist terrestrial habitats.

Morphology

It is a branched (Fig. 12-73 A) heterotrichous, filamentous alga made of uninucleate cylindrical cells. The septa are sometimes indistinct. The prostrate system is anchored to the soil by means of rhizoids.

The cells have a parietal reticulate chloroplast with many pyrenoids. Cell division occurs in the same way as described for *Oedogonium* and involves the formation of caps.

Reproduction

Vegetative Vegetative propagation occurs by fragmentation of erect or prostrate filaments.

Asexual Asexual reproduction is similar to that in *Oedogonium*. The zoospores and androspores are multiflagellate. *O. carolinianum* forms chains of androsporangia (Fig. 12-73 B).

Sexual Sexual reproduction is advanced oogamous type, with the oogonia (Fig. 12-73 A) and antheridia being borne on the same or different filaments. Species may be macrandrous or nannandrous (Fig. 12-73 B). The antherozoids are multiflagellate.

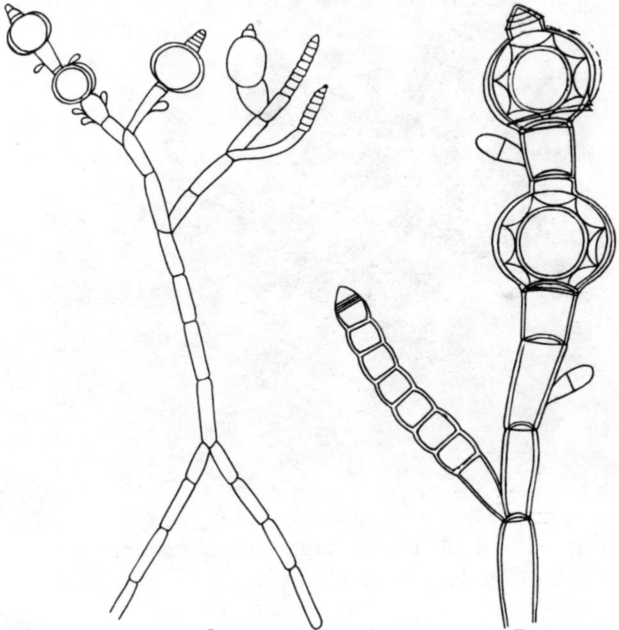

Fig. 12-73 *Oedocladium* sp. A, habit; B, androsporangia and oogonia.

Order: CONJUGALES

The Conjugales includes both unicellular and simple, unbranched filamentous forms which differ from other green algae in (1) elaboration or complexity of chloroplast; (2) absence of flagellated stages; and (3) occurrence of sexual reproduction through conjugation, involving the fusion of amoeboid gametes.

The cells commonly have a few, large and elaborate chloroplasts which are in the form of (1) a flat axile plate, as in *Mesotaenium* and *Mougeotia*; (2) a pair of axile stellate chloroplasts, as in *Cylindrocystis* and *Zygnema*; and (3) one or more spiral, ribbon-like chloroplasts, as in *Spirotaenia* and *Spirogyra*. The unicellular forms, popularly known as "desmids" (Figs. 12-74, 12-75 A), contain an axile (rarely parietal) chloroplast.

With rare exceptions, the chloroplasts contain large and well defined pyrenoids. The cells have a single, conspicuous, centrally located nucleus. Many members have an unusually large number of rather small-sized chromosomes.

The usual methods of reproduction are vegetative and sexual; rarely, asexual reproduction occurs by the formation of akinetes and aplanospores.

Vegetative multiplication in the unicellular desmids is brought about by cell division. In filamentous forms, fragmentation is often attended by the formation of special types of septa which may be replicate or semireplicate.

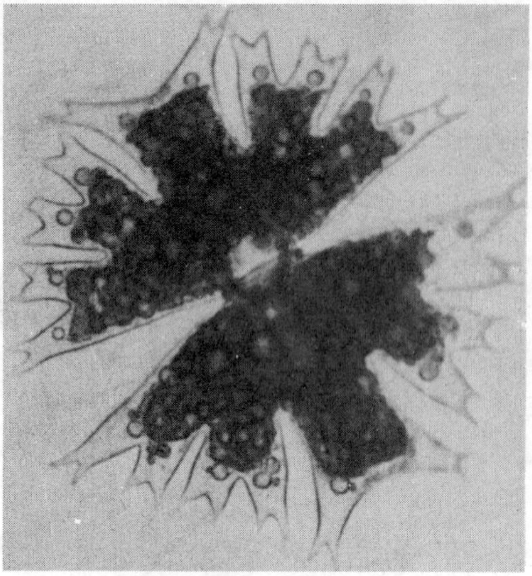

Fig. 12-74 *Micrasterias* sp. (Approx. ×200.) *Courtesy* K. Ueda.

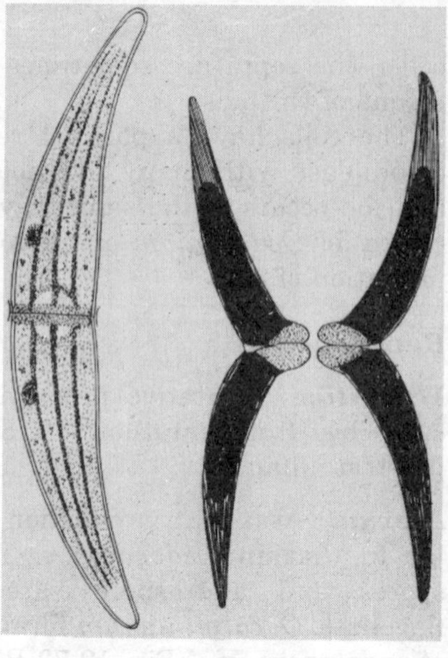

Fig. 12-75 *Closterium* sp. A, cell; B, conjugation.

Sexually, the unicellular Conjugales (Fig. 12-75 B) reproduce by the formation of a papillate bridge between two cells through which the contents of one, designated male, pass into the other, termed female. The contents of both the conjugating cells may sometimes pass into a conjugation tube and gametic fusion may take place within the tube (Fig. 12-76) rather than within one of the two cells.

Fig. 12-76 *Closterium ehrenbergii*, conjugation and zygospore formation. (Approx. ×100.) *Courtesy* K. Ueda.

Some important nuclear characteristics of the Conjugales are (1) complex nucleolus, with much internal differentiation resulting from the presence of nucleolar organizing regions of specific chromosomes, as in the interphase nuclei; (2) polycentric chromosomes; and (3) parallel disjunction of daughter chromosomes at anaphase in many species.

The nucleolar organizing chromosomes of the Conjugales are unique in that the secondary constrictions remain invisible though some satellite segments are often discernible at some stages of mitosis.

Most species of *Spirogyra*, *Mougeotia*, and *Zygnema* have minute, dot-like chromosomes, but in *S. crassa*, the chromosomes are often longer than 10 μm.

Polyploidy has been demonstrated in several genera, e.g., *Spirogyra*, *Zygnema*, and *Mougeotia*, and filament width shown to be a function of ploidy level (Hoshaw and Hull, 1981).

Some mating types of desmids such as *Closterium* grow restricted to a rather narrow geographical area. When this area expands beyond a certain limit, a postzygotic isolating mechanism, such as hybrid sterility (or at least weakness), tends to develop gradually between the allopatric populations of the same species. This can help speciation (Ichimura, 1982).

In *Closterium ehrenbergii*, distinct mating types are recognized on the basis of ability to produce zygospores in laboratory intercrossings. These mating groups, in nature, are reproductively isolated by various isolating mechanisms, e.g., ecological and sexual isolation (prezygotic) and/or hybrid weakness (postzygotic), besides geographical isolation. Ichimura (1982) postulates that the above isolating mechanisms support the biological integrity of each mating group by preventing hybridization, especially between sympatric mating groups.

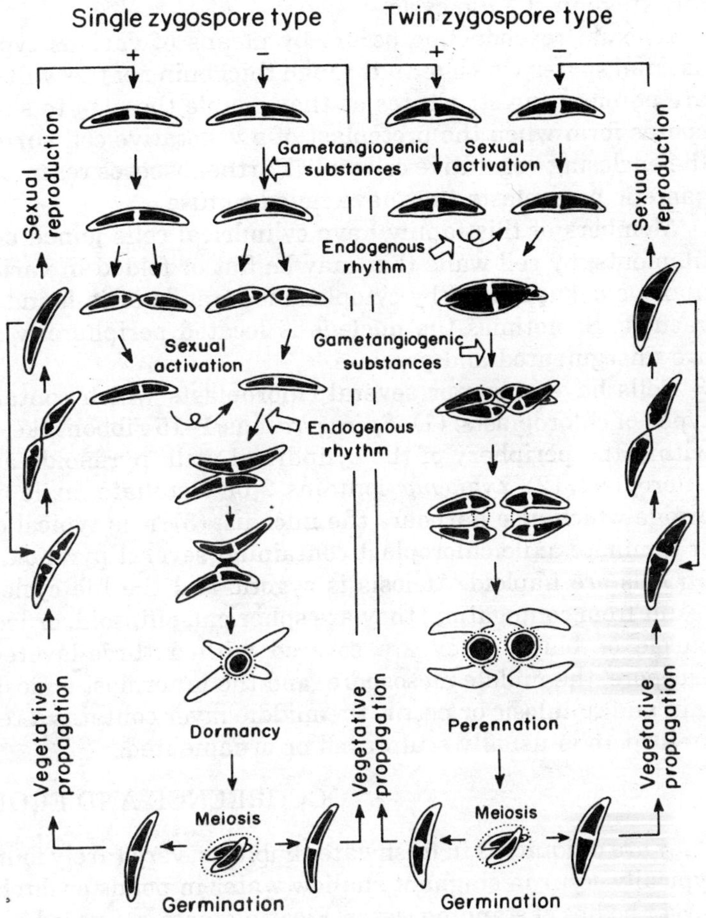

Fig. 12-77 *Closterium*, life cycle showing form changes and some regulatory factors (after Ichimura, 1982).

Figure 12-77 illustrates the life cycle of this interesting desmid, showing some morphological changes and the possible controlling factors involved.

Hoshaw and McCourt (1988) prefer to call the Conjugales as "Zygnematales". The order Zygnematales contains three families: Zygnemataceae (filamentous); Mesotaeniaceae (saccoderm desmids); and Desmidiaceae (placoderm desmids). Desmids are unicellular. Hoshaw and McCourt have reviewed the work done on the Zygnemataceae since about 1965. Some salient findings are summarized below.

FAMILY: ZYGNEMATACEAE

GENERAL CHARACTERS

The most distinctive feature is the process of conjugation. Two nonflagellate amoeboid gametes from the same or different filaments fuse to form a zygote. The gametes are formed in vegetative cells joined by a conjugation tube. Neither flagella nor their rudiments occur at any stage in the life cycle.

Asexual reproduction occurs by means of various types of specialized cells. Akinetes are asexual spores which form through thickening of the walls of a normal vegetative cell. Akinetes are perennating structures as they enable the alga to survive prolonged dry periods. Aplanospores form when the protoplast of a vegetative cell shrinks and forms a new cell wall inside the enclosing vegetative cell wall. Parthenospores resemble aplanospores but are derived from gametic protoplasts that have failed to fuse.

Members of this family have cylindrical cells joined end to end, in uniseriate unbranched filaments, by cell walls that may be flat or folded in various ways. Cells are uninucleate; the nucleus is suspended by cytoplasmic strands or is found in a cytoplasmic bridge in a central vacuole. Sometimes the nucleus is located peripherally next to the cell wall. The cell walls are unsegmented and poreless.

Cells have single or several chloroplasts which contain pyrenoids. There are three basic types of chloroplasts: (1) *Spirogyra* has 1–15 ribbon-like, parietal chloroplasts that are coiled within the periphery of the cylindrical wall; pyrenoids are scattered along the length of the chloroplast; (2) *Zygnema* contains 2 or 4 stellate, axile chloroplasts linked by a cytoplasmic bridge which also harbours the nucleus; (3) it is typical of *Mougeotia* which has a single flat or laminate axile chloroplast containing several pyrenoids.

Cells are haploid. Meiosis is zygotic and the life cycle is haplobiontic. Diploid zygospores result from conjugation; they are spherical, ellipsoid, or lenticular and may look brown, yellow, purple or black. They are covered with a three-layered conspicuous wall: the outermost exospore, the middle mesospore, and the innermost endospore. The outer and inner layers are thin and cellulosic or pectic, the middle layer contains a resistant material, sporopollenin. The mesospore is usually sculptured or ornamented.

OCCURRENCE AND ECOLOGY

They are ubiquitous in freshwater habitats, very rarely found in saline or brackish waters. They typically occur in stagnant shallow water in ponds or ditches, as well as in flowing waters and larger bodies of standing water. Floating mats composed of several species are common. Surface mats contain many air bubbles formed as a result of active photosynthesis: the pH in the mats often exceeds 10 in the centre even when the pH of the ambient water is only around 7.

Zygogonium occurs in acidic water (pH around 3–4). Whereas placoderm desmids often grow as nuisance blooms, this is rare in the Zygnemataceae (Hoshaw and McCourt, 1988).

Certain aquatic fungi belonging to the Phycomycotina parasitize Zygnemataceae, often inflicting much damage or even causing death. Natural populations of Zygnemataceae are, however, usually not devastated by fungi. The chytrid *Rhizophydium sphaerocarpum* is pathogenic to some strains of *Spirogyra*. An amoeba, *Nuclearia delicatula* pushes its pseudopodia into injured or damaged cells of *Spirogyra* but not *Zygnema* (Cann, 1986).

PHYTOCHROME AND CHLOROPLAST MOVEMENT

In *Mougeotia* the single laminate chloroplast rotates about the long axis of the cell to change the amount of surface area exposed to light. In low light, its large flat side faces the light. In bright light, the narrow edge profile faces the light.

Chloroplast movement in *Mougeotia* can be induced by exposure to light for less than a microsecond, after which it slowly reorients itself in the dark. This implies that light perception and chloroplast response are decoupled in this alga and the two component aspects of chloroplast movement may be studied separately. Phytochrome is the chief photoreceptor involved in the low-intensity response (Hoshaw and McCourt, 1988). Exposure to a pulse of red light induces chloroplast reorientation; if red light is followed by far-red, no such response occurs. The action spectrum of the low-intensity response has a maximum in red light but the high intensity response has a peak in the blue region of the spectrum. The high intensity response (i.e., the edge towards light source) requires either continuous light or repeated pulses of light. During movement, the chloroplast edges bend and often become lobed. Microfilaments, probably made of actin, connect the edges to the plasma membrane and are involved in the binding and lobing phenomena.

Chloroplast movement is by no means the only photoresponse in which phytochrome is involved. Phytochrome plays a role in other such responses in the Zygnemataceae. In *Spirogyra*, rhizoid differentiation is stimulated by red light but inhibited by far-red. Phytochrome may be involved in cell division in *Spirogyra*.

CYTOLOGY

The Zygnemataceae show unique nuclear features. The nucleolus has a complex internal differentiation in the form of nucleolar organizing tracks. It disorganizes during prophase to produce some nucleolar material which associates with chromosomes during the division cycle. Chromosomes usually lack a single, localized centromere and are polycentric or have a diffuse centromere; such chromosomes show a parallel separation at anaphase.

The Interphase Nucleus

In *Spirogyra* and *Sirogonium* the nucleus is suspended by cytoplasmic strands in a central vacuole. In *Mougeotia* it is flattened against the plate-like chloroplast midway between the cell poles.

In *Spirogyra* the nucleolus consists of a granular region and a fibrillar region adjacent to the nucleolar organizing chromosome. This fibrillar region is made of ribonucleoprotein and is called the *nucleonema* (Hoshaw and McCourt, 1988). In *S. submargaritata* the nucleolar organizer of the nucleolar organizing chromosome always remains within the nucleolus.

Mitosis and Cytokinesis

The metaphase nuclei of *Spirogyra* have gaps at the polar regions in the nuclear envelope through which many microtubules extend into the nucleus. These microtubules may help proper positioning of the chromosomes on the equatorial plate at metaphase. At anaphase, logitudinally aligned microtubules form a sheath surrounding the spindle in a manner suggestive of a phragmoplast. Wall microtubules may sometimes move to the spindle at preprophase and back to the wall at telophase. Cytokinesis begins at early anaphase and involves septum growth and cell-plate growth. When interzonal strands join the septum, longitudinal microtubules are present in these strands and in the cytoplasm near the edge of the septum. Many vesicles lie scattered in the cytoplasm. After some time, a row of these vesicles becomes associated with the septum edge. According to Ueda *et al.* (1986), small vesicles in the metaphase spindle of *Spirogyra* fuse to form the nuclear envelope.

According to Hoshaw and Wells (1982), mitosis in *Sirogonium melanosporum* is similar to that in *Spirogyra*. The chromosomes are rod-shaped. Cells have 1 or 2 nucleoli and two nucleolar organizing chromosomes. Nucleolar organizing tracks and nucleolar substance are present, and chromosomes undergo parallel separation at anaphase. The nuclei usually contain 25 chromocentres. The nuclear envelope remains intact at metaphase. Cytokinesis involves a septum and cell plate which are associated with a ring of granules in the centre of the dividing cell. Figures 12-78 and 12-79 illustrate nucleolar chromosome formation and mitosis.

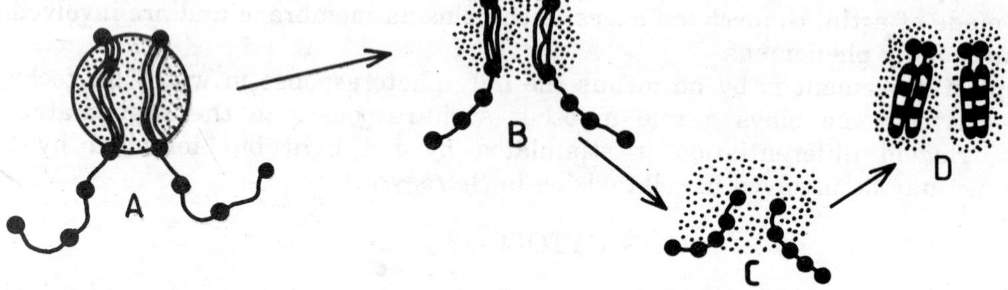

Fig. 12-78 *Sirogonium melanosporum*. Formation of nucleolar organizing chromosome. A, two nucleolar organizing tracks surrounded by nucleolar substance inside nucleolus; B, shortened nucleolar chromosome in nucleolar substance from disorganized nucleolus; C, nucleolar chromosomes surrounded by nucleolar substance; D, paired chromatids of nucleolar chromosomes surrounded by nucleolar substance; the chromatids have terminal satellites as well as nucleolar organizing regions. (After Hoshaw and Wells, 1982.)

Pickett-Heaps and Wetherbee (1987) detected a rudimentary phragmoplast formation and absence of anaphase A in *Mougeotia*.

Systematics and Phylogeny

Mattox and Stewart (1984) divided the Chlorophyta into five classes based primarily on the structure and orientation of flagellar roots in motile cells. Out of the five classes, the Charophyceae was considered to be the closest to higher plants. The Zygnemataceae and other conjugating green algae (i.e., desmids) were included in the Charophyceae even though the conjugating algae lack any flagellated cells. They were placed in the Charophyceae on the basis of their other similarities such as the mode of cell division, phragmoplast formation, and the nature of the interzonal spindle. Like other phragmoplast-forming green algae, *Spirogyra* and the saccoderm desmid *Netrium* use glycolate oxidase to oxidize glycolate; this contrasts with the phycoplast-producing algae in which the enzyme concerned is glycolate dehydrogenase. The location of these two enzymes also differs: the oxidase is found in spherical microbodies whereas the dehydrogenase occurs in mitochondria. The enzymology of urea degradation also resembles that in Charophyceae; the Charophyceae (and Ulvophyceae) have urease whereas the Chlorophyceae has urea amidolyase. *Zygnema cylindricum* and some desmids have been found to employ urease rather than urea amidolyase (Hoshaw and

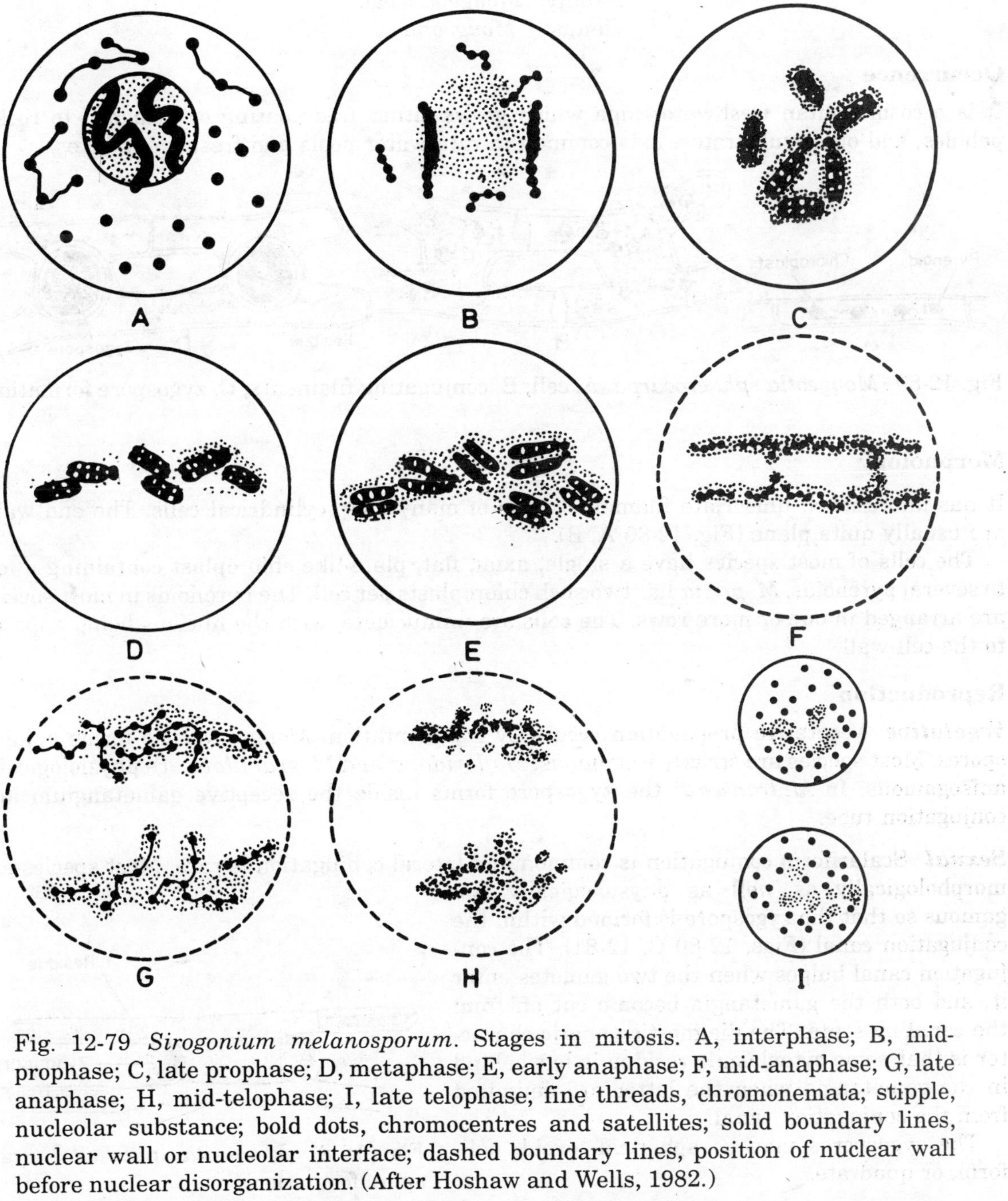

Fig. 12-79 *Sirogonium melanosporum*. Stages in mitosis. A, interphase; B, mid-prophase; C, late prophase; D, metaphase; E, early anaphase; F, mid-anaphase; G, late anaphase; H, mid-telophase; I, late telophase; fine threads, chromonemata; stipple, nucleolar substance; bold dots, chromocentres and satellites; solid boundary lines, nuclear wall or nucleolar interface; dashed boundary lines, position of nuclear wall before nuclear disorganization. (After Hoshaw and Wells, 1982.)

McCourt, 1988). Though the above data support a phylogenetic link of the conjugating green algae with the Charophyceae, the data are based only on a few taxa and many more species need to be examined.

Family: Mougeotiaceae
Genus: *Mougeotia*

Occurrence

It is a cosmopolitan freshwater alga which grows either free-floating or attached to rocks, pebbles, and other substrates. It is common in rain water pools and freshwater lakes.

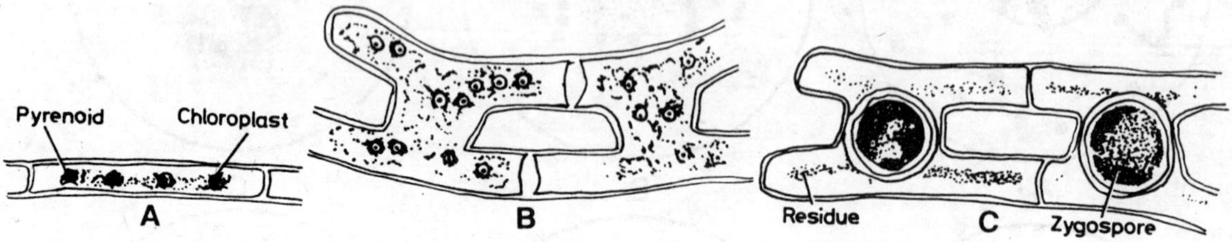

Fig. 12-80 *Mougeotia sphaerocarpa*. A, cell; B, conjugating filaments; C, zygospore formation.

Morphology

It has unbranched uniseriate filaments made of many long, cylindrical cells. The end walls are usually quite plane (Fig. 12-80 A, B).

The cells of most species have a single, axial, flat, plate-like chloroplast containing a few to several pyrenoids. *M. prona* has two such chloroplasts per cell. The pyrenoids in most species are arranged in one or more rows. The cells are uninucleate, with the nucleus being apposed to the cell wall.

Reproduction

Vegetative Vegetative propagation occurs by fragmentation. *Mougeotia* also forms aplanospores. Most species are strictly isogamous. *M. floridana* and *M. granulata* are physiologically anisogamous. In *M. transeaui* the zygospore forms inside the receptive gametangium and conjugation tube.

Sexual Scalariform conjugation is common and lateral conjugation is rare. Most species are morphologically as well as physiologically isogamous so that the zygospore is formed within the conjugation canal (Figs. 12-80 C, 12-81). The conjugation canal bulges when the two gametes enter it, and both the gametangia become cut off from the canal by septa. The diagnostic generic character is that some cytoplasmic residue is left behind in the gametangia when the latter are delimited from the conjugation canal.

The zygospores may be spherical, ovoid, doliform, or quadrate.

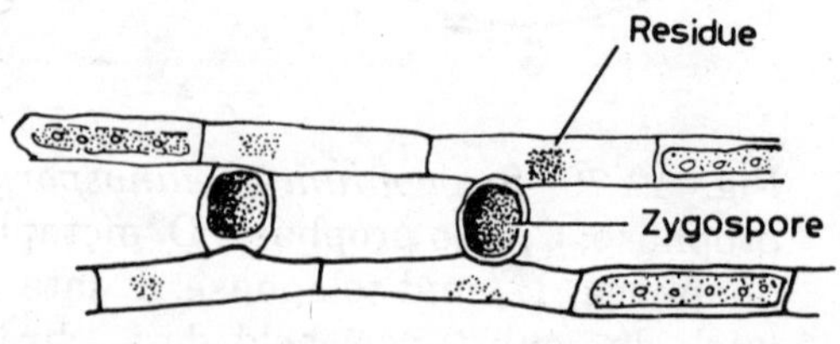

Fig. 12-81 *Mougeotia pulchella*, zygospore formation.

Family: Zygnemaceae
Genus: *Spirogyra*

Occurrence

A freshwater, submerged (or free-floating) alga, *Spirogyra* occurs in various water bodies of both a temporary and permanent nature. The filaments are slimy to touch because of an outer mucilaginous wall layer.

Morphology

The plant body is an unbranched filament (Fig. 12-82) consisting of a uniseriate row of cylindrical cells with the basal cell frequently developing into a branched, or highly lobed, anchoring organ in those species that grow attached to the substratum. The cell wall consists of two layers, an inner cellulosic and an outer pectic layer. The septa between the cells may be plane, semireplicate or replicate and, as in higher plants, their formation is always followed by the secretion of a cellulosic layer along both their sides. A large vacuole containing tanniferous vesicles lies in the centre of the cell. The cytoplasm forms a thin layer lining the

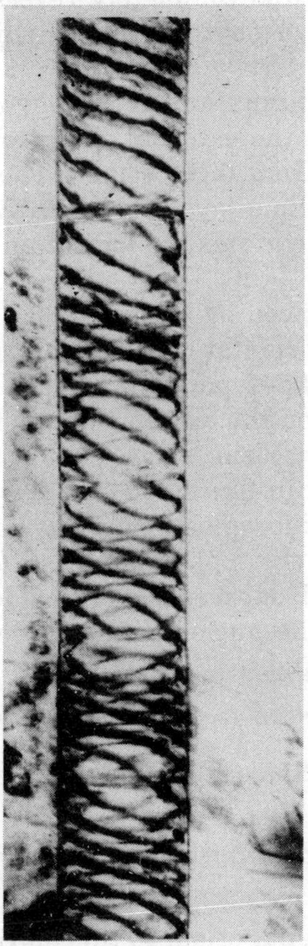

Fig. 12-82 *Spirogyra* sp., part of filament. (Approx. ×150.)

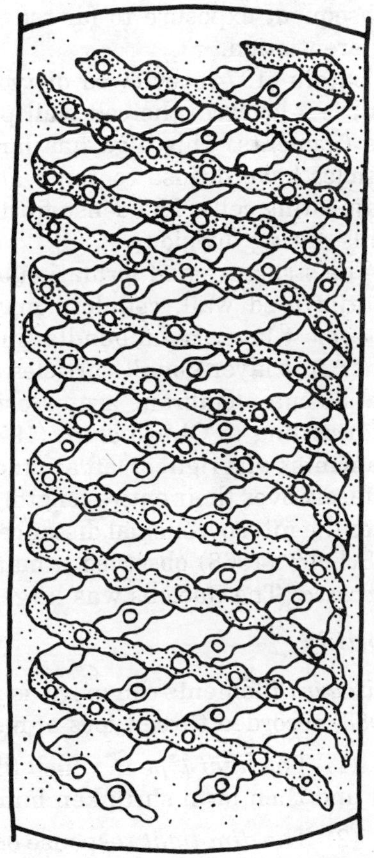

Fig. 12-83 *Spirogyra verruculosa*, vegetative cell.

cell wall, and the single nucleus situated in the central part of the cell is connected with the peripheral cytoplasm through a number of radiating cytoplasmic strands. One or more helical or spiral, ribbon-shaped chloroplasts, with smooth or serrated margins and containing several pyrenoids, each ensheathed with starch grains, are present in the cell (Fig. 12-83).

According to Dawes (1965), in *Spirogyra* (1) the inner layer of the cell wall as also the wall of the conjugation tube consist of cellulose I microfibrils; (2) the chloroplast contains photosynthetic bands, each consisting of 4–12 thylakoids, numerous starch ensheathed pyrenoids, and pyrenoid-like bodies lacking starch sheath (karyoids or protopyrenoids); and (3) the cells have other organelles such as a nucleus with a complex nucleolus, numerous Golgi bodies and mitochondria, and an endoplasmic reticulum.

Some species found in freshwater streams grow attached by means of rhizoids occurring in the form of small or large protuberances, or rods of rosettes. In a physiological study of rhizoid formation in *Spirogyra fluviatilis*, Nagata (1973) has observed that, in laboratory cultures, rhizoid formation was restricted to the terminal cells of a filament. Of the various stimuli inducing rhizoid formation, light proved to be the most important since no rhizoids could be initiated in the dark. Red light was much more effective in inducing rhizoid differentiation than green or blue light. The fact that the effect of red light was completely reversed by subsequent exposure to far-red light indicates the involvement of phytochrome in rhizoidal differentiation.

Lacalli (1974) reviewed dictyosome function during cell wall formation in *Spirogyra*. The wall is 4-layered: the cell wall proper, and three outer layers in the external slime covering the filaments. This alga has large and small vesicles derived from dictyosomes. The large vesicles have diffuse contents and help maintain the external slime layer of vegetative and conjugating cells. The dense fibrillar material in small vesicles facilitates the formation of cell walls during division.

The structure and formation of cell wall layers has been described by Herth (1983). In the multilayered wall, cellulose microfibrils show three different orientations: random in the outermost layer, axial bundles in the middle layer, and bundle of 5–6 microfibrils each in the innermost layer. Small particles arranged in hexagonal rosettes on the extraplasmatic face of the plasma membrane are associated with the formation of microfibrils.

According to Ohiwa *et al.* (1976) the cell wall grows helically in *Spirogyra* and *Zygnema*: filaments twist right or left around the long axis as they grow. The chloroplasts of *Spirogyra* grow diffusely over their entire length. Pyrenoids do not migrate in the chloroplast but arise *de novo* after the interpyrenoidal distance in the diffusely-growing chloroplast exceeds a critical length.

Schölm (1968) observed a marked diurnal change in size of the nucleus and nucleolus in *S. crassa*. The nucleus was largest at noon and smallest at midnight.

Motility

Spirogyra filaments can move as a result of secretion of pectic mucilage. Tanaka and Matsuura (1983) recorded three types of movement:

(1) The *light-type* in which filaments exposed to about 1400 lux after a dark period spread out and then form shrunken bundles.

(2) The *dim-light* response occurs after exposure to 200 lux light period. In this movement the filaments form shrunken, loose aggregates at first and then spread out, thus reversing the sequence of events observed in the *light-type* movement.

(3) *Intermediate*-type movements result at around 750 lux during the first few hours and are succeeded by type-1 (light-type) movements.

The membrane potential in *Spirogyra* also changes in response to light. This response occurs only when at least a part of the chloroplast is present.

Movements of filaments appear to depend on the rate of photosynthesis. For instance when filaments are exposed to strong light (over 3000 lux) in the presence of DCMU, they show *dim-light* or intermediate-type movement rather than the light-type (Tanaka and Matsuura, 1983).

Spirogyra can show any or all of the following types of movements: positively phototrophic, positively or negatively gravitropic, spiral curling, and straightening.

Species Concept

Conventionally, species are described on the basis of morphological characteristics of field-collected materials. These morphospecies are open to question in view of widespread occurrence of polyploidy.

Allen (1958) first discovered the emergence of polyploid forms within clonal cultures of *S. pratensis*. She observed that a homogeneous culture containing filaments of uniform width in course of time gave rise to two markedly wider classes of filaments which were polyploids. The starter culture contained 11–15 chromosomes per cell, the next wider class had 26–30, and the widest had 56–60 chromosomes per cell. She called this series of three filament types a *species complex*. This term connotes an erroneous analogy with a *polyploid complex* in higher plants (Grant, 1981) in which polyploid complexes are a consequence of hybridization between two distinct species. Simons (1987) used the term *species complex* while referring to a group of co-occurring species whose taxonomic descriptions differed only in quantitative traits, but he was dealing with algal populations in natural field material and did not imply any ploidal differences between filament populations.

Nuclear Cytology

Of the polycentric (having several centromeres) chromosomes, invariably two or more chromosomes, termed nucleolar organizing chromosomes (Fig. 12-84 A–E), contain a distinct nucleolus organizing region (Fig. 12-84 A). During nuclear division, the nucleoli disappear (Fig. 12-84 B–E) by metaphase and reappear by interphase. The interphase nucleolus is highly differentiated, containing nucleolar organizing region in a highly coiled form. This region remains coated with a deeply stainable substance known as the organizing track. The complex nucleolus results from the fusion of a number of nucleoli depending on the number of nucleolus organizing chromosomes.

Reproduction

Vegetative This is the most common method of reproduction and involves fragmentation of filaments.

Sexual Species showing lateral conjugation (Fig. 12-85) are homothallic, whereas those exhibiting scalariform conjugation are generally heterothallic. In scalariform conjugation (Fig. 12-86), the filaments of + and – strains associate in pairs and in each pair the side walls of some, or all, cells facing each other form papillate outgrowths. The latter extend towards each other and finally fuse, thus establishing a conjugation canal. The entire protoplasmic contents

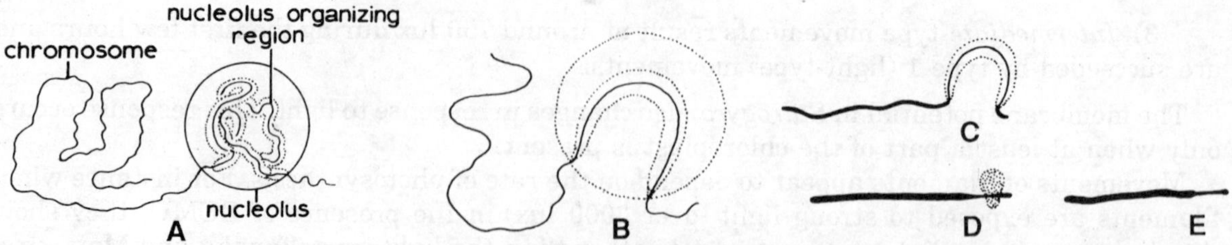

Fig. 12-84 *Spirogyra*, stages in nucleolar organization. A, coiled nucleolar organizing region of chromosome inside nucleolus at interphase; B, uncoiling and contraction of nucleolar organizing chromosome at early prophase; C–D, dispersal of nucleolus at middle and late prophase; E, disappearance of nucleolus. (After Godward, 1966.)

of the – type cell go into the + type through the canal by means of amoeboid movement (Fig. 12-87). When the conjugation begins, the two filaments are in contact with each other. As the papillae of the conjugation canal are formed and grow to form the canal, the two mating filaments are pushed away from each other. It has been observed that during the formation of the conjugation tube, one papillate outgrowth penetrates into the other. The dissolution of the cross wall at the junction of the two papillae is affected by the formation in the cytoplasm of a large number of vesicles or contractile vacuoles which migrate to the junction and release substances that dissolve the cross wall (Dawes, 1965).

After the completion of conjugation, one of the two fusing filaments has empty cells and the other contains dark, spherical or oval structures—the zygotes. This type of sexual reproduction involving migration of the – gamete into the + is physiologically anisogamous even though the two fusing gametes are morphologically isogamous. In some species, the contents of both – and + cells move into the conjugation tube and the fusion between gametes takes place within the conjugation canal. Such species are morphologically as well as physiologically isogamous.

In lateral conjugation (Fig. 12-85), the septum at the point of its attachment with either side of the lateral wall dissolves and the lateral wall bulges out slightly, thus creating a passage between the adjacent cells. Soon, the contents of one cell start exhibiting amoeboid movement and finally move into the next cell through a narrow lateral passage. If the filaments are examined at this stage, empty cells are seen in the male and zygote containing cells in the female.

Rarely, some cells of a filament may act as male and others as female with respect to another member of a filament pair. In this case, each of the conjugating filaments contains male as well as female cells (Fig. 12-88). It has also been reported that three filaments A, B, and C (instead of two) may conjugate, with the central filament B behaving as male towards A and as female towards C.

The zygospore is always a three-layered, thick-walled structure. It germinates after perennation and its nucleus divides by meiosis. Three of the resulting four nuclei degenerate and the surviving uninucleate protoplast undergoes repeated transverse divisions, giving rise to a single *Spirogyra* filament (Fig. 12-89).

Grote (1977a, b) studied the sexual cycle in *S. majuscula*. Initial attachment between conjugating filaments occurs by means of mucilaginous threads which hold the filaments together but are torn by papillar growth until filaments are held together by conjugation tubes only. According to Grote, conjugation tube formation is induced by the chemical interaction between agglutinated filaments.

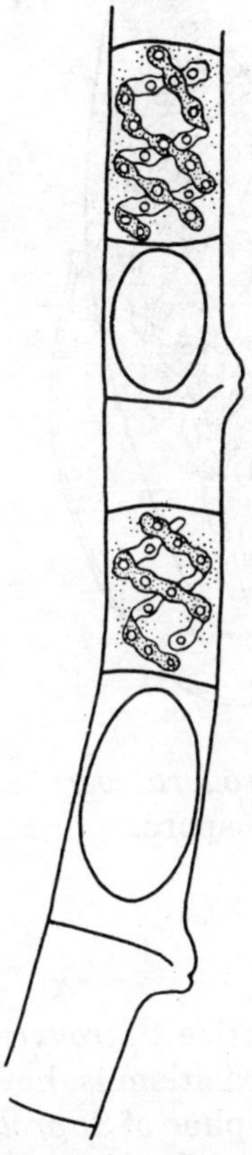

Fig. 12-85 *Spirogyra biformis*, lateral conjugation (after Yamagishi, 1966).

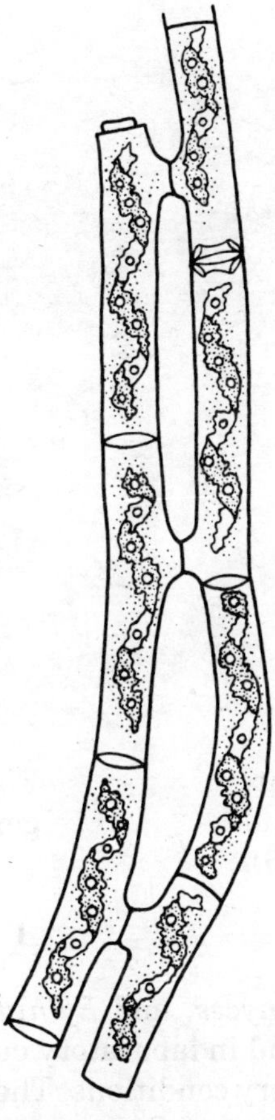

Fig. 12-86 *Spirogyra inflata*, scalariform conjugation (after Yamagishi, 1966).

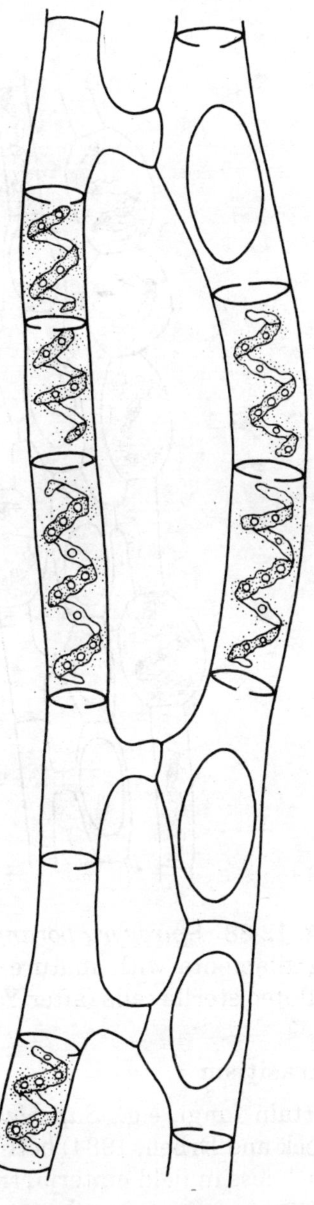

Fig. 12-87 *Spirogyra micropunctata*, conjugating filaments (after Yamagishi, 1966).

According to Simons *et al.* (1984), nitrogen depletion and light intensity are the two major factors in the induction of conjugation and zygospore formation in many species. They listed the following range of conditions as being conducive to conjugation: pH 7–9, temperature 10–25°C, light intensity 100–27,000 lux, daylength neutral or long-day, and nitrogen depletion (0–1 mg per litre).

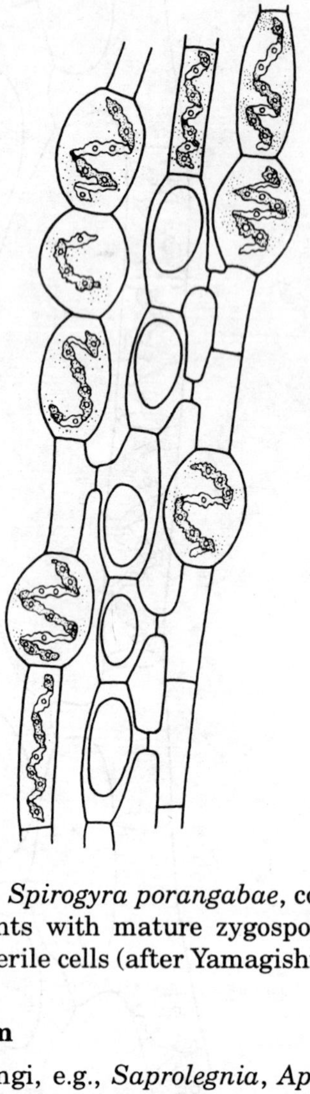

Fig. 12-88 *Spirogyra porangabae*, conjugating filaments with mature zygospores and bullated sterile cells (after Yamagishi, 1966).

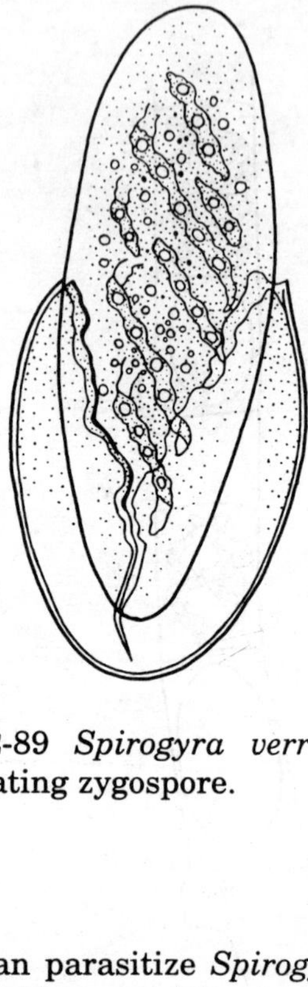

Fig. 12-89 *Spirogyra verruculosa*, germinating zygospore.

Parasitism

Certain fungi, e.g., *Saprolegnia*, *Aphanomyces*, and *Pythium*, can parasitize *Spirogyra* spp. (Beck and Erben, 1984) both in the field and in laboratory culture. The parasitism is, however, much less in field material than in laboratory conditions. The vegetative hyphae of *Saprolegnia asterophora* growing from infected filaments of *Spirogyra* invade the neighbouring, healthy filaments, thus causing infection. The hyphae also extend within the host alga from cell to cell with the disintegration of cellular contents and the penetration of algal septa. The fungus later reproduces sexually by forming 10–40 oogonia external to the host filament. These oogonia develop on short hyphae produced at right angles from intrafilament hyphae. From near an oogonium up to three small antheridia are formed and coil around the oogonial stalk. Each oogonium produces one or two oospores, following fertilization.

The fungal infection often distorts the spiral arrangement of the chloroplasts in the host, and its pyrenoids also disintegrate.

Genus: *Zygnema*

Occurrence

Commonly found free-floating in ponds and streams, *Zygnema* is a widely distributed fresh-water alga. Sometimes, it may grow submerged, living entirely under water attached to stones, pebbles, and other objects. *Z. terrestre* is terrestrial.

Morphology

Like *Spirogyra*, *Zygnema* also is filamentous and unbranched. It differs from *Spirogyra* mainly in its plastid morphology. The cells of *Zygnema* contain a pair of axile stellate chloroplasts (Fig. 12-90), each harbouring a single central pyrenoid with radiating starch grains. The cells are uninucleate and the single nucleus lies embedded in the middle of the cytoplasm that separates the two chloroplasts. The nucleus contains one nucleolus with one nucleolar organizing chromosome.

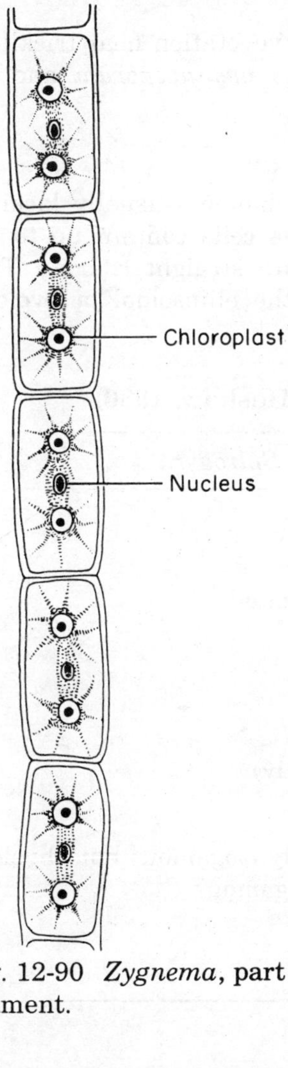

Fig. 12-90 *Zygnema*, part of filament.

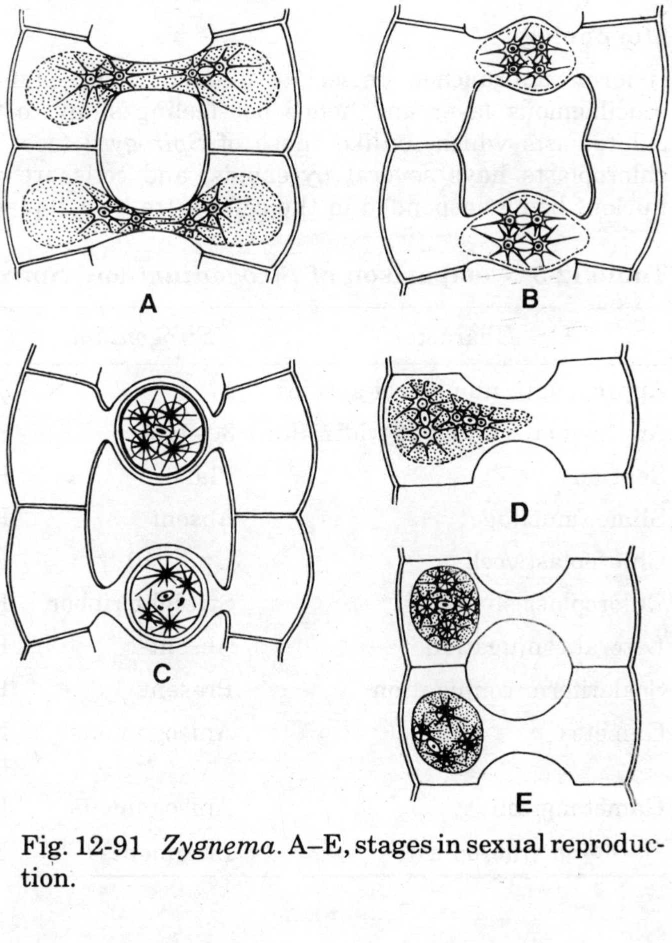

Fig. 12-91 *Zygnema*. A–E, stages in sexual reproduction.

Reproduction

Vegetative Reproduction is brought about by the fragmentation of the filament. *Z. terrestre* and *Z. giganteum* form thick-walled akinetes.

Asexual No zoospores are produced. *Z. spontaneum* reproduces by aplanospores.

Sexual It is always morphologically isogamous. Most species are physiologically isogamous (Fig. 12-91 A–C) but some are anisogamous (Fig. 12-91 D, E). Both scalariform and lateral conjugation are known.

Perennation

Some species can perennate and survive desiccation by means of akinetes and also by their thick-walled zygotes.

Genus: *Sirogonium*

Occurrence

It is a freshwater alga which grows in dense masses among damp vegetation near trickling water, shallow water bodies, or in lagoons, pools, and ditches. *S. melanosporum* and *S. sticticum* are common in paddy fields.

Morphology

It forms unbranched uniseriate filaments with plane septa, the filaments usually lacking mucilaginous layer and hence not feeling slimy to the touch. The cells contain up to 10 chloroplasts which, unlike those of *Spirogyra* (see Table 12-5), are straight ribbons. The chloroplasts have several pyrenoids, and cells are uninucleate, the ellipsoidal or ovoidal nucleus being suspended in the cell centre by cytoplasmic strands.

Table 12-5 Comparison of *Sirogonium* and *Spirogyra* (after Hoshaw, 1986)

Character	*Sirogonium*	*Spirogyra*
Approximate number of species	17	320
Approximate filament width (μm)	30–110	8–200
Septum	Plane	Plane or replicate
Slime (mucilage)	Absent	Present
Chloroplasts/cell	Up to 10	Up to 15
Chloroplast shape	Straight ribbon	Helical ribbon
Lateral conjugation	Absent	Present (usually)
Scalariform conjugation	Present	Present
Gametes	Anisogamous	Morphologically isogamous but physiologically anisogamous
Gametangium	Anisogamous	Isogamous
Germling chloroplasts	Fragments	Ribbons

Species have two nucleolar organizing chromosomes. During mitosis in several species, the nucleolar organizing chromosomes are derived partly from the organizer tracks in the nucleolus and partly from the karyoplasm, while all other chromosomes develop from the karyoplasm (Harada, 1981). The nucleolar organizing chromosomes have also been seen in the diplotene (meiosis) stage of *S. melanosporum*.

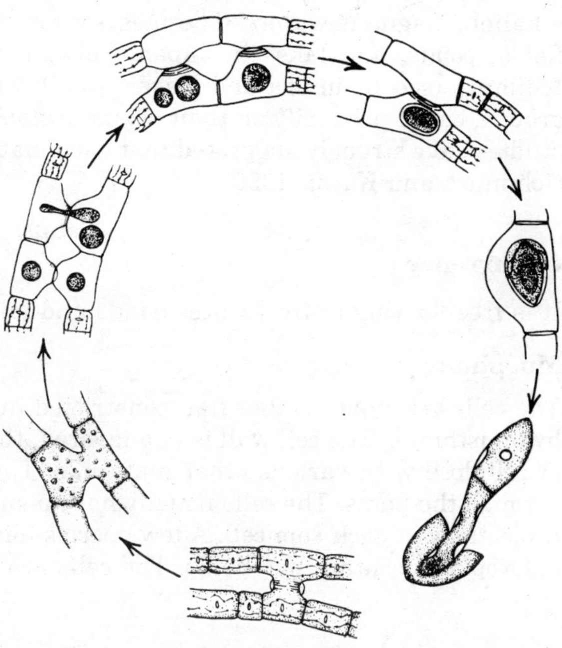

Fig. 12-92 *Sirogonium*, life history.

Reproduction

Vegetative Vegetative propagation is by filament fragmentation.

Sexual *S. floridanum* is homothallic (Hoshaw, 1986). Two filaments come in contact and adhere to each other (i.e., genuflect). The ordinary vegetative cells metamorphose into progametangia which in this species form papillae at genuflection. The progametangia then divide once or twice, producing male or female gametangia plus one or two sterile cells. In these respects, *Sirogonium* is distinctly different from *Spirogyra* in which the gametangia are morphologically isogamous. In *Sirogonium*, the male gametangia are smaller than female (Fig. 12-92). *Sirogonium sticticum* and *S. melanosporum* are also homothallic and anisogamous. Production of zygospores occurs on an irregular schedule.

Prior to gamete formation, the chloroplasts of the gametangia tend to fragment. The gametangial protoplasts contract and become anisogametes, the male gametes usually maturing before the female. The male gamete moves into the female gametangium where it fuses with the larger, female gamete. Thus, the zygotes form in the female gametangium, not in the conjugation tube. However, unlike *Spirogyra*, a distinct conjugation tube is absent in *Sirogonium* (Table 12-5). The zygospores are thick-walled, accumulate oil, and develop ornamentation of their wall. The zygospores of *S. melanosporum* are ellipsoidal, whereas those of *S. floridanum* are somewhat ovoidal.

The germination of zygospores occurs after some period of perennation. The zygospore wall dehisces and the germling grows out as an elongate body which divides, yielding a filament of *Sirogonium*. Figure 12-92 shows the life cycle of *Sirogonium*.

Family: Desmidiaceae

The desmids are some of the most beautiful of the freshwater unicellular algae known. They are highly symmetrical, being abundant in the plankton of soft, clean, slightly acidic waters. Their cell wall is made of two pieces and has pores. Each cell consists of two symmetrical halves called semicells which may be interlinked by a connecting zone called isthmus. The nucleus lies in this isthmus. *Closterium* (Figs. 12-75, 12-76) is an unconstricted desmid, whereas *Cosmarium* is constricted.

Closterium ehrenbergii is a cosmopolitan desmid which grows in slightly eutrophic and alkaline, stagnant waters. The biosystematics of many populations of this alga from paddy fields, ponds, and lakes in Japan, Taiwan, Nepal, and Australia have been studied by T. Ichimura (see Ichimura and Kasai, 1995), who have recognized more than a dozen mating groups, based primarily on their sexual isolation. Morphological, cytological, and reproductive studies have strongly suggested that each mating group of *C. ehrenbergii* is a biological species (Ichimura and Kasai, 1990).

Genus: *Cosmarium*

Occurrence

It is free-floating in freshwater ponds and lakes.

Morphology

The cells are small, rather flat, constricted into two symmetrical semicells (Fig. 12-93) joined by an isthmus. The cell wall is two-layered, the inner being cellulosic and the outer a complex of cellulose with various other materials. The wall is porous and some mucilage is secreted through the pores. The cells usually have a single, large, axile chloroplast with some radiating projections in each semicell. A few species have two or four chloroplasts in each semicell. The chloroplasts contain pyrenoids. The cells are uninucleate.

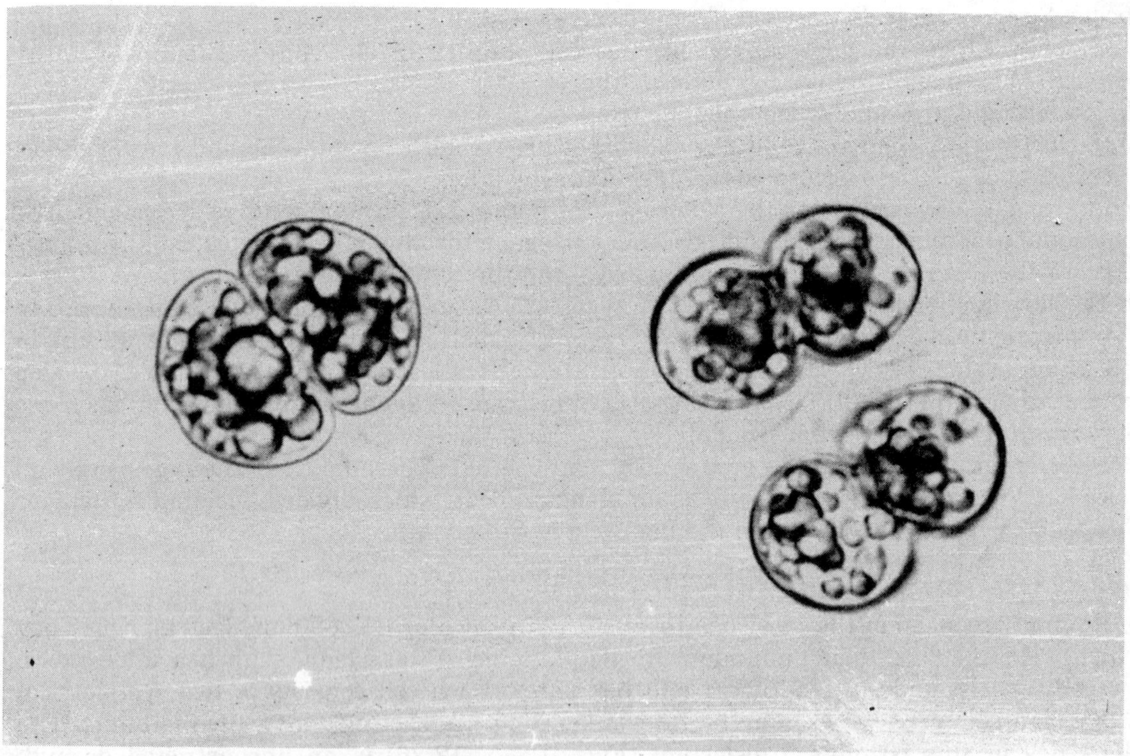

Fig. 12-93 *Cosmarium* sp. (Approx. ×150.)

Reproduction

Vegetative Vegetative propagation occurs by cell division (Fig. 12-94) involving nuclear division, isthmus elongation, constriction, and separation of the daughter cells in which one semicell is derived from the mother cell and the other is formed afresh.

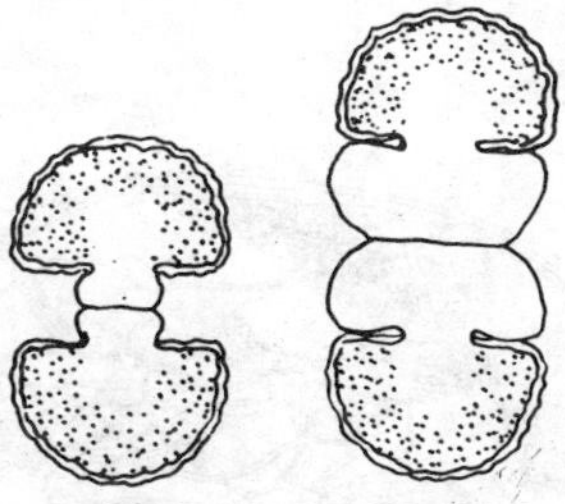

A B

Fig. 12-94 *Cosmarium*. A–B, stages in cell division.

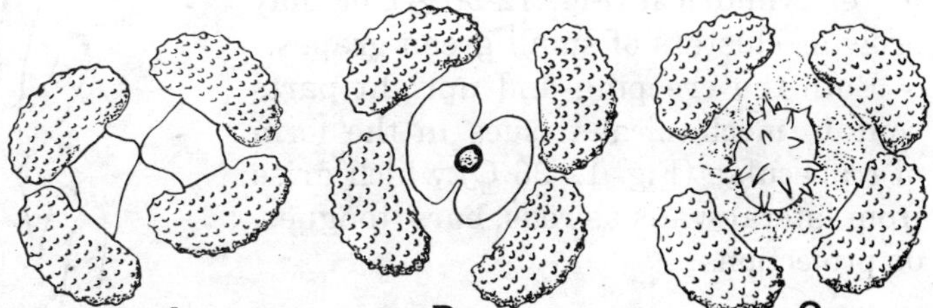

A B C

Fig. 12-95 *Cosmarium*, stages in conjugation.

Sexual Two entire cells, behaving as gametes, conjugate (Fig. 12-95 A–C). The isthmus regions of the conjugants break. The semicells gape apart (Fig. 12-95 A, B) to facilitate the amoeboid migration of both the gametic protoplasts towards each other. They meet and fuse midway between the two (Fig. 12-95 C) cells. Thus, *Cosmarium* shows morphological as well as functional isogamy.

The zygospore perennates and later germinates. Its nucleus divides meiotically to form four nuclei out of which two degenerate and the remaining two give rise to new cells.

Order: SIPHONALES

This includes macroscopic and coenocytic algae which, with the exception of *Protosiphon*, are all marine.

Fritsch (1935) included several families and many genera in his Siphonales. Some of his families have been raised to independent orders by most other algologists.

The thalli of the Siphonales are composed of coenocytic siphoneous filaments involving rhizoidal branches, prostrate creeping portions, and erect fronds. The filaments contain many discoid chloroplasts and nuclei but lack septa. The chloroplasts lie around a central vacuole.

Many genera are known as fossils from the Ordovician onwards.

Vegetative propagation occurs by fragmentation. Asexual reproduction is usually lacking. Sexual reproduction is by delimitation of gametangia which produce iso- or anisogametes. The mature plants are diploid, and meiosis occurs at gametogenesis.

Family: Caulerpaceae
Genus: *Caulerpa*

Occurrence

It is widespread in tropical and subtropical coasts, inhabiting the littoral zone on rocks, corals, and sandy substrata.

Morphology

It has long creeping, branched, stolon-like strands (Fig. 12-96 A, B) or "rhizomes" which give off rhizoids here and there. The rhizoids anchor the plant to the substratum (Fig. 12-96 B). The stolons produce upright fronds which may be leaf-like (Fig. 12-97) or cylindrical (Fig. 12-96 A), or may grow as clusters of small green grapes.

Both the creeping and upright parts contain mechanical tissues in the form of trabeculae (Fig. 12-96 C) which arise from lateral walls as rods, bars, tongues, or projections.

Reproduction

Vegetative Vegetative propagation is by detachment of erect fronds or stolons.

Sexual Sexual reproduction is anisogamous. The gametes are formed within the erect portion. Most species are heterothallic. Upon escape through pores, the gametes fuse, and the resulting zygote tends to germinate into the new plant without undergoing any resting phase.

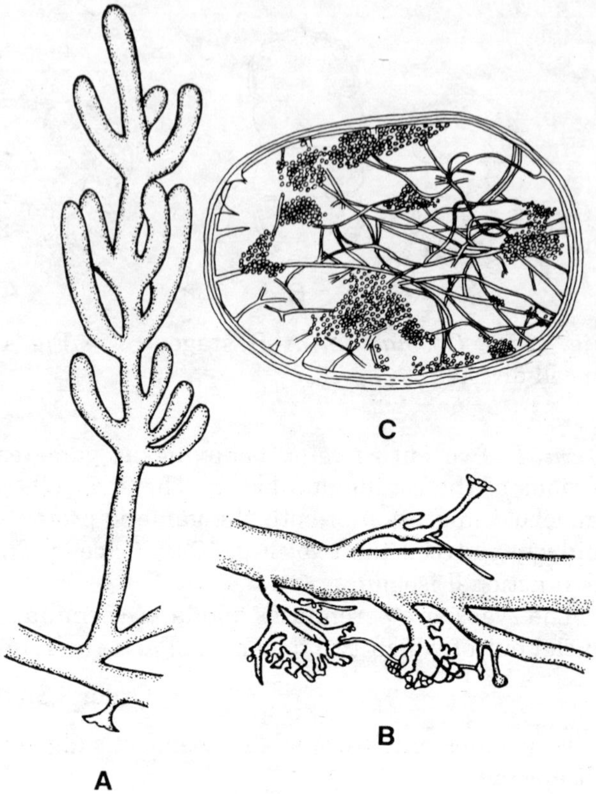

Fig. 12-96 *Caulerpa fastigiata*. A, part of stolon showing attaching disc; B, stolon with rhizoids terminating in coralloid discs; C, transverse section through stolon showing trabeculae, stratified wall, and starch grains.

Family: Codiaceae
Genus: *Codium*

Occurrence

It is a common inhabitant of the littoral and sublittoral zones of both temperate and tropical coasts.

Morphology

It has large, extensively branched (mostly dichotomous) thalli (Fig. 12-98 A). The plant has a central core of continuous medullary filaments. Many of these filaments bend outward and bear club-shaped swellings at their ends; the swollen outgrowths (Fig. 12-98 B) are called utricles and make up the cortex of the thallus. The septa are rare or lacking. Some species have their utricles bearing internal wall thickenings at the apex, whereas other species lack such thickenings.

Each utricle contains several discoidal chloroplasts lacking pyrenoids, and also many nuclei.

Reproduction

Vegetative Vegetative propagation occurs from detached fragments.

Sexual Sexual reproduction is by anisogametes formed within small gametangia cut off as lateral outgrowths from the utricles (Fig. 12-98 B). The gametes come out of the gametangial apex through a lid-like pore. Species may be monoecious or dioecious. The plant is diploid.

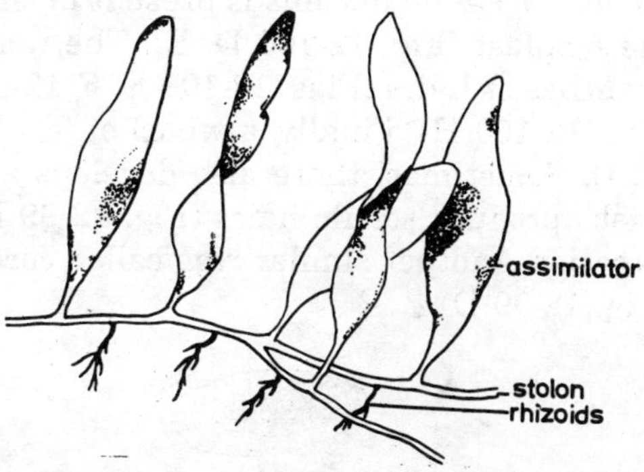

Fig. 12-97 *Caulerpa prolifera*, habit.

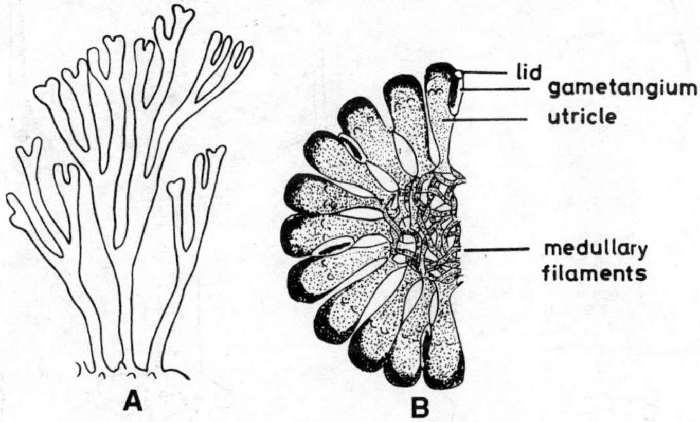

Fig. 12-98 *Codium tomentosum*. A, habit; B, part of transverse section of branch showing utricles and gametangia.

Family: Dasycladaceae
Genus: *Acetabularia*

Occurrence

It occurs in tropical and temperate coasts commonly in the littoral zone. It grows attached to shells, corals, or rocks and stones.

Morphology

Popularly called the Mermaid's Wine goblet, the alga is a beautiful stalked saucer-like disc (Fig. 12-99 A) or umbrella (Fig. 12-99 B) and has been much used in biochemical experiments designed to elucidate the role of the nucleus in cellular control processes. It can reach a height of over 10 cm.

The plant is attached by means of a lobed rhizoidal holdfast (Fig. 12-99 C). In the young stage, the single nucleus is present in this holdfast. The upright tubular stalk grows out from the holdfast (Fig. 12-100 D, E). The upright axis gives rise successively to whorls of lateral branches or hairs (Figs. 12-100 E, F, 12-99 D), most of which are shed off as the axis elongates (Fig. 12-100 H). Finally, a whorl of fertile rays develops at the apex of the stalk (Fig. 12-100 H, I). Sometimes, there also develops a ring of knobs at the base of the fertile rays. These knobs produce sterile hairs (Fig. 12-99 D), the whole aggregate being designated the corona superior. Another similar ring called corona inferior sometimes develops below the fertile disc (Fig. 12-99 D).

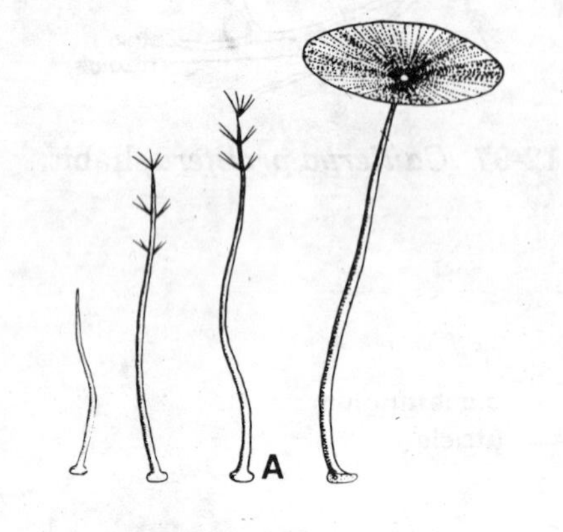

Fig. 12-99 *Acetabularia*. A, four plants of different ages; B, disc or umbrella of gametangia; C, lobed holdfast containing the single nucleus; D, fertile rays, hairs, corona superior, and corona inferior (h, hairs; ci, corona inferior; st, sterile hairs).

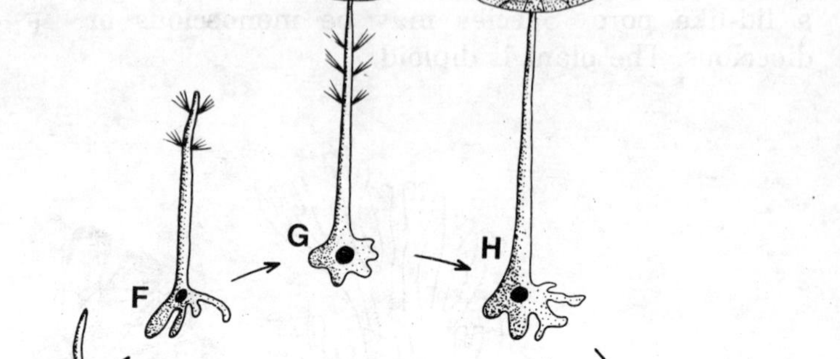

Fig. 12-100 *Acetabularia*. A–I, stages in life history.

Reproduction

The single diploid nucleus enlarges and divides repeatedly. Many of the daughter nuclei pass into the developing cysts within the fertile rays (gametangia). Within each gametangium, the protoplast cleaves off into uninucleate portions that become covered by a thick wall, forming cysts. The cyst wall contains a cap-like lid (Fig. 12-100 B). Within the cyst, the single nucleus undergoes repeated divisions, the last division being meiotic (Fig. 12-100 A). The isogametes develop from the haploid nuclei and come out of the cyst through the apical pore by lifting off the lid. They fuse (Fig. 12-100 C), and the zygote develops into the new plant (Fig. 12-100 D–H).

Figure 12-101 illustrates the life cycle of *A. acetabulum*.

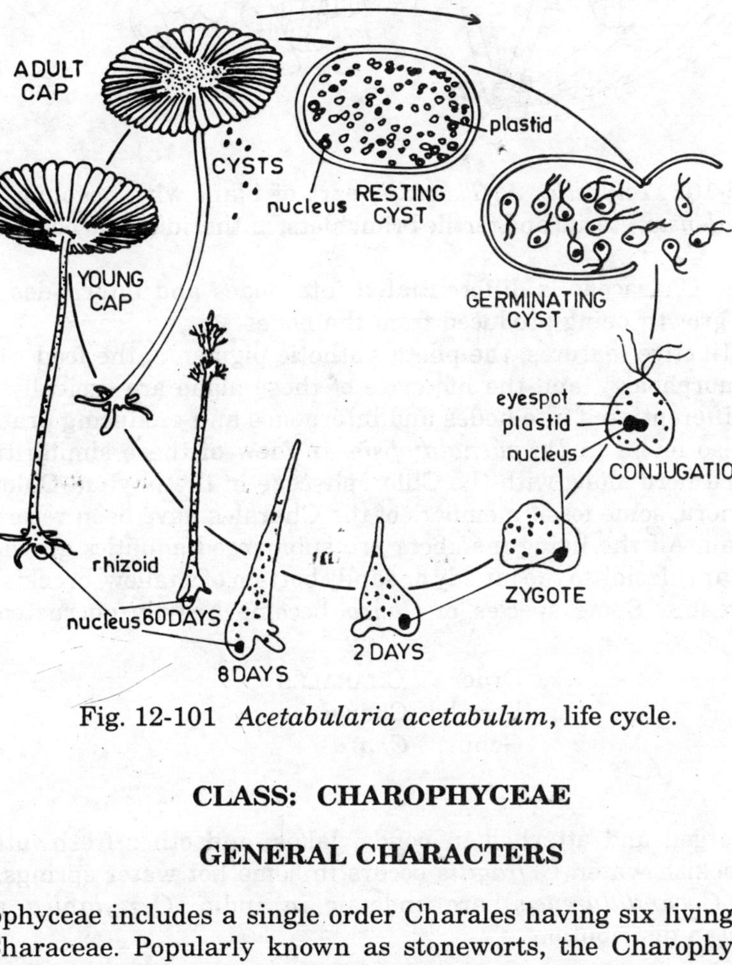

Fig. 12-101 *Acetabularia acetabulum*, life cycle.

CLASS: CHAROPHYCEAE

GENERAL CHARACTERS

The class Charophyceae includes a single order Charales having six living genera, all placed in the family Characeae. Popularly known as stoneworts, the Charophyceae constitutes a distinctive and isolated group of highly differentiated and elaborately organized green thallophytes which—because of their uncertain affinities—have presented greater difficulties in classification than any other group of plants. The class is characterized by such distinguishing features as (1) enclosure of the antheridia and oogonia by jackets of sterile cells; (2) biflagellate and spiral-shaped nature of the antherozoids; (3) nonformation of zoospores; and (4) germination of the zygote into a protonemal stage, the latter giving rise to a mature plant. Figure 12-102 A, B illustrates the structure of a charophyte.

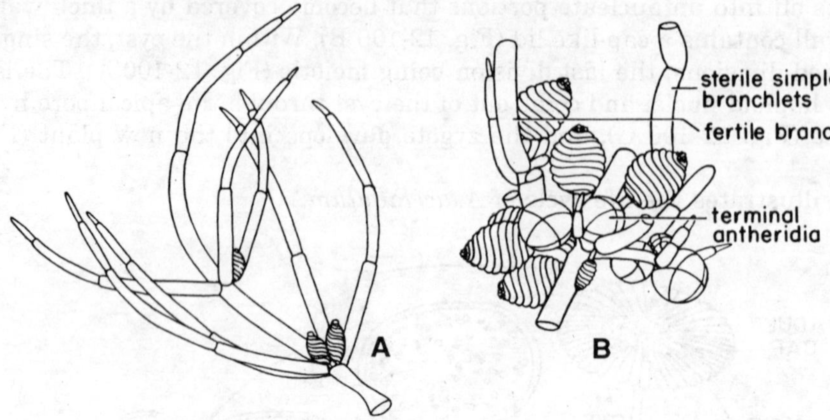

Fig. 12-102 *Tolypella*. A, *T. boldii*, part of plant with oogonia; B, *T. canadensis*, sterile and fertile branchlets, antheridia, and oogonia.

The thallus of the Characeae is differentiated into nodes and internodes with whorls of branches of limited growth being produced from the nodes.

Despite these distinctive features, the photosynthetic pigments, the food reserves, the cell wall, the flagellar morphology, and the life cycle of these algae are typically chlorophytean. Further, a thallus differentiated into nodes and internodes and producing branches only from the nodal cells is also found in *Draparnaldiopsis*. In view of these similarities, the Charophyceae are classified here along with the Chlorophyceae in the phylum Chlorophyta.

Besides living genera, some fossil members of the Charales have been recorded from as far back as the Devonian. All the living members are submerged aquatics growing attached by means of multicellular rhizoids to the muddy or sandy bottom of shallow, brackish or freshwater lakes, ponds or streams. Some species of *Chara* become heavily encrusted with calcium carbonate.

Order: CHARALES
Family: Characeae
Genus: *Chara*

Occurrence

Chara grows submerged and attached in ponds, lakes, and other freshwater habitats. *C. baltica* grows in brackish water. *C. fragilis* occurs in some hot water springs. A few species (e.g., *C. nuda* and *C. vandalurensis*) are endemic in India. *C. zeylanica* and *C. braunii* exemplify cosmopolitan distribution.

Morphology

Usually 6–10 inches tall, the main axis and branches of *Chara* are differentiated into nodes and internodes (Fig. 12-103 A). Commonly, the internodal segments in many species have the

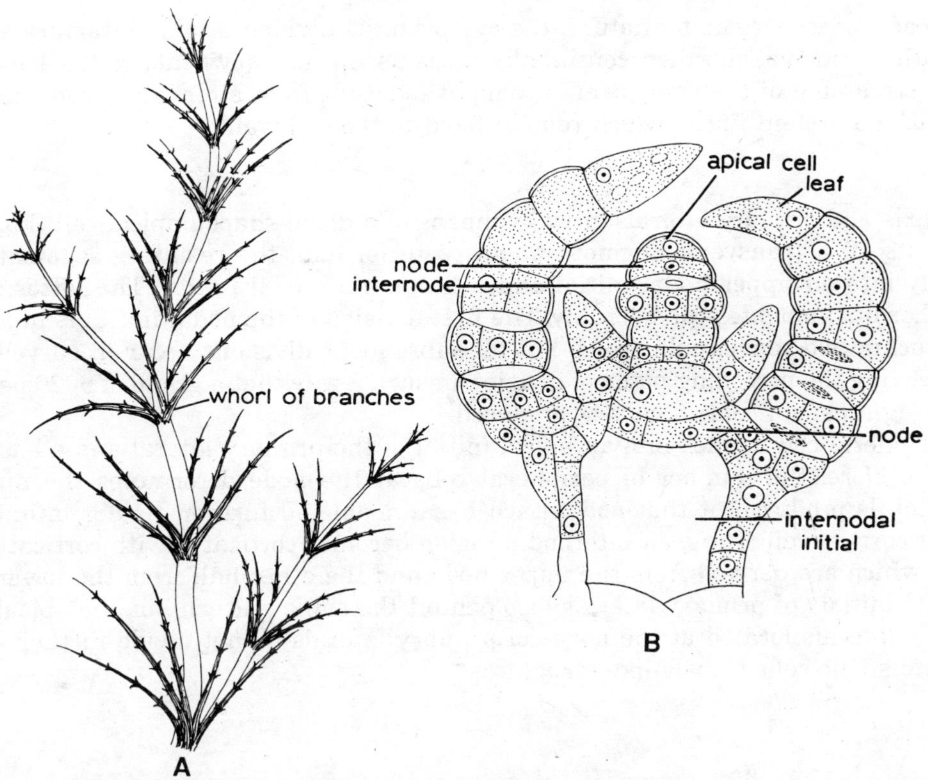

Fig. 12-103 *Chara*. A, part of vegetative thallus showing habit; B, vertical section through apex of thallus.

same diameter (width) regardless of whether found in the apical part or the basal parts of the plant. Each node bears a whorl of several branches and consists of a pair of central cells surrounded by a peripheral group of 6–20 cells. The internode is always composed of a single elongate cell which may be corticated. The corticating cells are also long and are derived from both the upper and lower nodes. Branched multicellular rhizoids are formed from the lowermost one or two nodes. The branches of the first order, produced from the nodes of the main axis, are known as primary laterals. These are also called laterals of limited growth because of the cessation of growth in these branches after they have formed a few nodes and internodes. Single-celled branches called secondary laterals arise from the nodes of primary laterals. Sometimes, from near the axils of the oldest whorls of the primary laterals (pseudo-axillary position), branches of unlimited growth emerge with the same degree of differentiation as found in the main axis.

Cell Structure

The nodal cells contain dense cytoplasm, a single nucleus, and a few discoid or elliptical chloroplasts, but in the internodal cells, there is a large central vacuole, hundreds of nuclei, and many discoid chloroplasts, the latter two occupying the peripheral cytoplasmic region. The chloroplast lacks a pyrenoid.

On the basis of its streaming nature, the cytoplasm is divided into a stationary exoplasm and a rotating endoplasm which continually streams up and down along the longitudinal plane. The streaming of the cytoplasm is thought to result from alternating contraction and expansion of the protein fibrils which remain fixed to the cell wall.

Growth

The main axis and primary laterals grow by means of a dome-shaped apical cell (Fig. 12-103 B) which cuts off a transverse segment at its posterior end; the resulting segment divides transversely into an upper nodal initial and a lower internodal initial. The latter does not divide further but elongates considerably. The first division of the nodal initial is in a vertical plane producing two semicircular cells, but all subsequent divisions occur in curved planes, each intersecting the preceding plane of division in such a way that a group of 6–20 peripheral cells enclosing a pair of central cells is produced.

Each peripheral cell divides into an apical initial of the primary lateral and a basal nodal cell and, therefore, the number of peripheral cells at the node determines the number of primary laterals produced at that node. Each basal nodal cell further divides into an upper and a lower cortical cell. Thus, an internodal region becomes corticated with corticating cells, one-half of which are derived from the upper node and the other half from the lower node.

The nodal initials of primary laterals also exhibit the same pattern but the apical initials of secondary laterals located at the nodes of primary laterals do not divide further and only elongate into single-celled, scale-like structures.

Reproduction

Vegetative

Some means of vegetative propagation are by the formation of bulbils upon rhizoids (Fig. 12-104 A) and on lower nodes (Fig. 12-104 B) of cells, or by the formation of protonemal outgrowths derived from the nodes. Reproduction in some cases takes place by means of amylum stars (Fig. 12-104 C) which are stellate aggregates of cells densely filled with starch grains and produced from the lower nodes.

Sexual

All species of *Chara* show a highly advanced type of oogamy. The antheridial filaments are borne within a structure called the globule, whereas the oogonium is present within the nucule. Both are situated at the base of secondary laterals (Fig. 12-105 A).

A mature globule is a hollow spherical body and consists of an outer, a middle, and an inner group of cells termed, respectively, shield cells, manubrial cells, and capitulum cells (Fig. 12-105 B). A capitulum generally divides and gives rise to a group of two to four secondary head cells or capitula from each of which is produced a pair of antheridial or spermatogenous filaments (Fig. 12-105 B). Each cell of the spermatogenous filament forms a spiral biflagellate sperm (Fig. 12-105 C, D). In an electron microscope study of *C. corallina* Moestrup (1970) has reported the presence of scales on the flagella of its spermatozoids. The cells of spermatogenous filaments generally divide synchronously.

The nucule is an oblong structure consisting of five spirally coiled tube cells which form a sterile envelope around the oogonium and of five-lobed corona cells that project beyond the apex of the oogonium (Fig. 12-105 A).

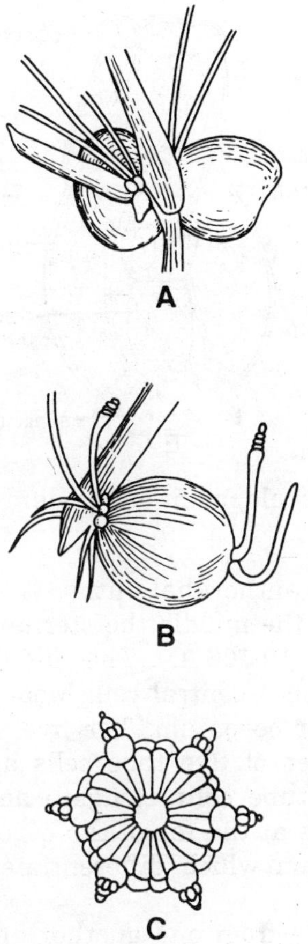

Fig. 12-104 *Chara*. A, *C. aspera*, root bulbil; B, *C. baltica*, stem bulbil; C, *C.* sp., amylum star.

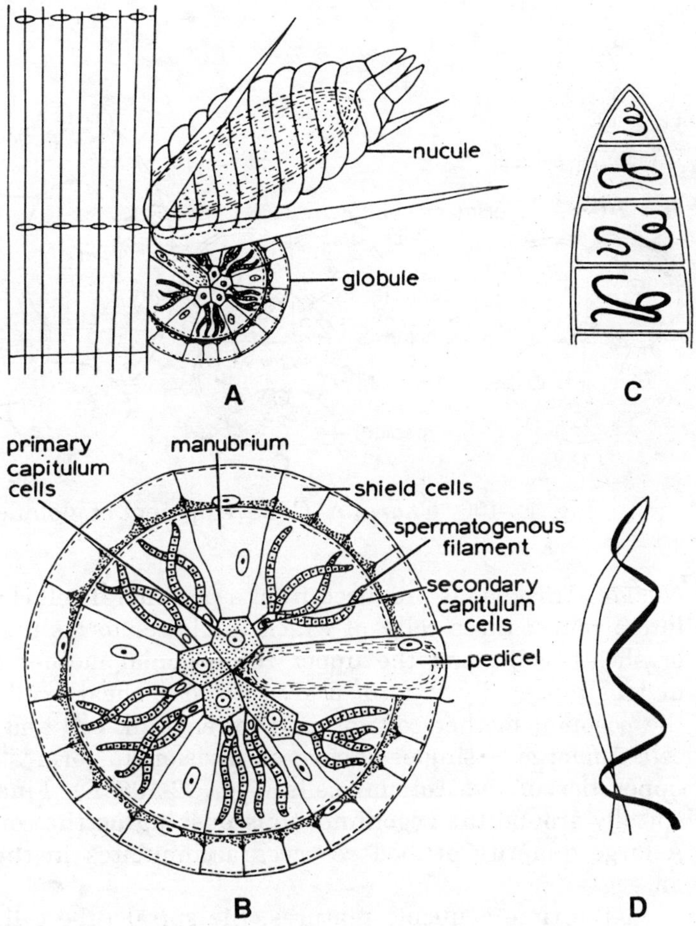

Fig. 12-105 *Chara*. A, portion of plant bearing nucule and globule; B, structure of mature globule; C, spermatogenous filament; D, biflagellate spiral sperm.

Development of Sex Organs

Globule This develops from an adaxial peripheral cell at the node of a primary lateral. This cell divides into two, the lower forming the pedicel and the upper acting as an antheridial initial (Fig. 12-106 A). The latter divides thrice to give rise to an octant stage. Each cell of the octant undergoes two periclinal divisions resulting in a radial row of three cells (Fig. 12-106 B, C) with the outer cell functioning as the shield cell, the middle as the manubrium, and the inner as the primary head cell. Subsequently, the shield cells expand laterally and the manubria elongate vertically. By this time, the primary head cell has already divided and the resulting secondary head cells bifurcate vertically into a pair of cells, each developing into a spermatogenous filament. In a mature globule, the large number of spermatogenous filaments radiate in the hollow cavity.

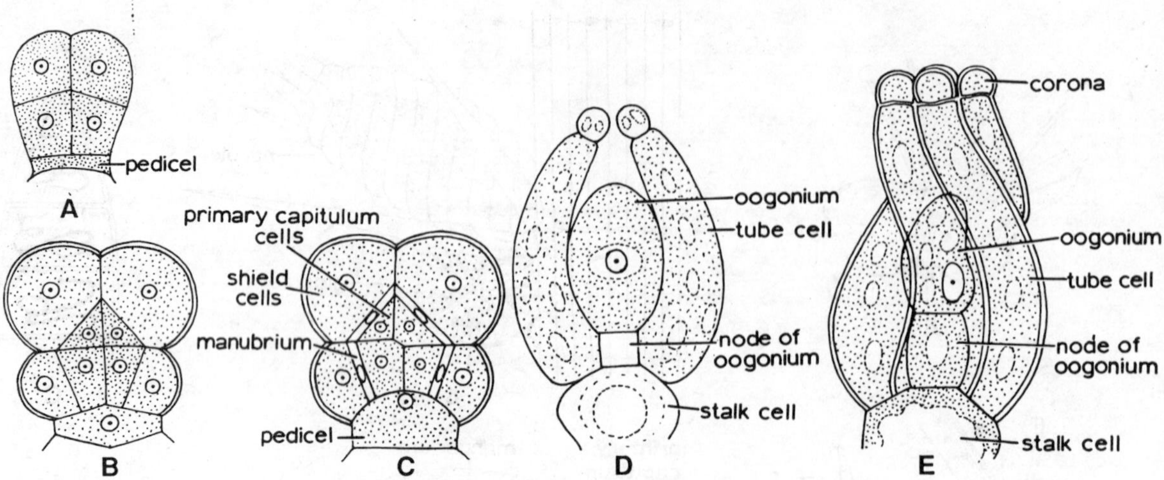

Fig. 12-106 *Chara.* A–C, development of globule; D–E, development of nucule.

Nucule This also is produced from a peripheral cell close to the antheridial initial. It divides into a row of three cells, of which the lower forms the pedicel, the middle the sterile jacket or sheath cells, and the upper the oogonial mother cell (Fig. 12-106 D). The middle cell divides repeatedly to form a group of five sheath cells enclosing a central cell. Meanwhile, the oogonial mother cell forms a lower stalk cell and an upper oogonium. The five sheath cells undergo a single transverse division to form a lower tier of five tube cells and an upper tier of five coronal cells (Fig. 12-106 E). Finally, the tube cells elongate and coil spirally around the oogonium, thus pushing up the coronal cells at the top of the oogonium. A large quantity of food reserves accumulates in the oogonium which differentiates into an egg.

At the time a nucule matures, the spiral tube cells separate from one another and the resulting space in between them provides an opening for the entrance of sperms, one of which finds its way inside the oogonium and fuses with the ovum.

The wall of the zygote thickens and after perennation the oospore germinates; the nucleus migrates to the anterior region where it probably divides meiotically. A septum is then laid down forming a uninucleate upper cell and a degenerative, trinucleate lower cell (Fig. 12-107 A). The upper cell undergoes one mitotic division in a vertical plane. Of the two daughter cells, one acts as the protonemal initial and the other as the rhizoidal initial. These initials form the filamentous protonema and the colourless rhizoids respectively (Fig. 12-107 B), both with nodes and internodes. The plant arises from one of the appendages borne on the second node of the protonema.

Because of the suspected occurrence of meiosis during the germination of the zygote (and not during gametogenesis), the life cycle of *Chara* is believed to be haplontic.

Pickett-Heaps (1967, 1968) has found that mitosis and cytokinesis in *Chara* broadly resemble those in higher plants in that the mitotic spindle is open and the cytokinesis is effected by a phragmoplast that proliferates from an interzonal spindle which persists at telophase. The cell division in *Chara* also resembles that in *Coleochaete*.

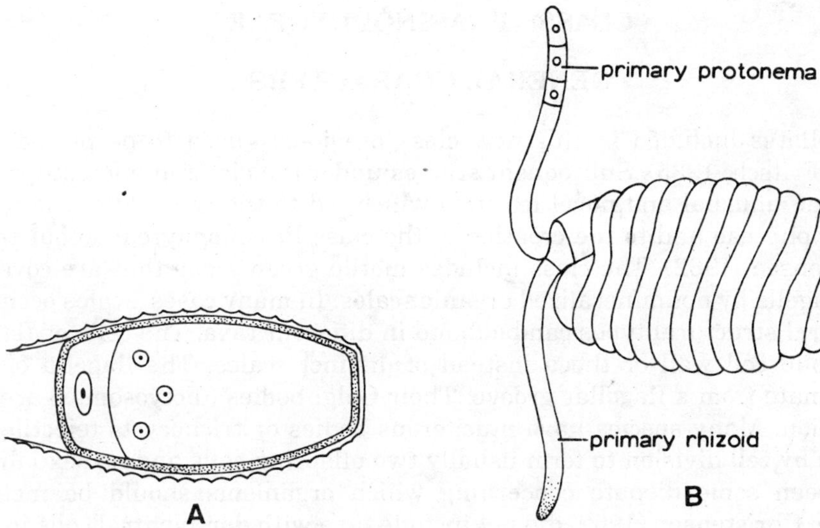

Fig. 12-107 *Chara*. A, longitudinal section of germinating oospore showing nuclear division; B, surface view of germinating oospore. (After Smith, 1955.)

Phylogeny

This has long been a hotly debated subject and the available fossil records are of little help in suggesting any clues to the origin of this class. In respect of photosynthetic pigments, food reserves, cell wall composition, flagellar morphology of spermatozoids, and zygote germination, the Charophyceae resemble the Chlorophyceae. The differentiation of the main filament into nodal and internodal cells, the formation of corticating filaments, the production of lateral branches of limited growth, and the participation of the laterals of limited growth in reproduction are features shared also by the chaetophoralean genus *Draparnaldiopsis*. These traits have been emphasized by many phycologists to suggest a possible derivation of the Charophyceae from the Chaetophorales (Desikachary and Sundaralingam, 1962). But the apical growth and the complex nature of the male and female sex organs discount any possible origin of the Charophyceae from the Chaetophorales. Papenfuss (1955) on the basis of parallelism in the development of sex organs has emphasized an affinity between bryophytes and the Charophyceae. Bold (1967) considers that morphologically the sex organs of the Charophyceae are in no way different from those of bryophytes.

Origin of Land Plants

According to Stewart and Mattox (1975), the ancestry of archegoniates should be traced from the Charales and also possibly from *Coleochaete*-like algae. This view is based on the following points of resemblance between the Charales and the archegoniate plants: (1) presence of phragmoplast; (2) presence in motile cells of a multilayered structure (MLS) associated with the flagellar base strikingly similar to the MLS and the flagellar base found in the antherozoids of bryophytes; (3) occurrence of glycolate oxidase; (4) identical microtubular cytoskeletons of the spermatozoids; (5) protection of gametangia by sterile cells; and (6) apparent similarity between the plant bodies (of course, the archegoniates are not thalloid).

CLASS: PRASINOPHYCEAE

GENERAL CHARACTERS

The algal flagellates included in this new class previously used to be placed in the order Volvocales (see Fritsch, 1935). Subsequent studies under the electron microscope revealed the existence of some unusual and novel features which led to the removal of the prasinophytes from the Chlorophyceae and to the creation of the class Prasinophyceae about three decades ago (see Christensen, 1962). The class includes motile green algae that are covered on their cell body and flagella by nonmineralized organic scales. In many cases, scales occur in multiple layers and several structural types can be found in different taxa. The cells of *Tetraselmis* are covered by a solid cell wall or theca instead of distinct scales. The flagella of these green flagellates originate from a flagellar groove. Their Golgi bodies (dictyosomes) are located in a parabasal position. Many species have muciferous bodies or trichocysts (ejectile organelles). Reproduction is by cell division to form usually two offspring cells and no sexuality is known.

There has been some dispute concerning which organisms should be included in the Prasinophyceae. Christensen (1962) did not include taxa with dorsiventral cells in the Prasinophyceae but created a new class, the Loxophyceae, for these genera (e.g., *Micromonas*, *Nephroselmis* and *Pedinomonas*). Other authors did not recognize the Loxophyceae and usually include the above-named genera in the Prasinophyceae (Norris, 1980) or in another class, Micromonadophyceae (Mattox and Stewart, 1984). In 1982, Moestrup resurrected the class Loxophyceae and included three genera as possible members (*Monomastix*, *Pedinomonas*, and *Scourfieldia*). These three genera lack scales on their flagella (indeed two, *Pedinomonas* and *Scourfieldia*, also lack them on their cell bodies). These three genera differ considerably from the Prasinophyceae in fine structure and also differ greatly among themselves. Melkonian (1990) therefore does not agree with the proposal of Moestrup (1982). He excludes *Pedinomonas* and *Monomastix* from the Prasinophyceae and includes 13 genera (about 120 species) distributed over four orders (Mamiellales, Pseudoscourfieldiales, Chlorodendrales, and Pyramimonadales) in the class.

The Prasinophyceae are largely marine (but some are found in brackish and freshwater habitats. *Mesostigma* is exclusively freshwater. Members of the order Mamiellales are conspicuous in the oceanic picoplankton.

Asexual resting cysts are common. Especially interesting are the large phycoma stages in the genera *Halosphaera*, *Pachysphaera*, and *Pterosperma*. The phycoma has a bilayered cell wall, the outer layer probably containing sporopollenin. It grows to a size many times larger than that of the original flagellate alga. This growth is accompanied by division within the phycoma of cell organelles, which eventually separate into numerous motile cells. The prasinophyte *Tetraselmis convolutae* is an extracellular endosymbiont in the tissues of the acoel flatworm *Convoluta roscoffensis*.

In *Tetraselmis* and *Scherffelia*, cell body scales fuse after exocytosis to form a compact cell wall or theca. *Micromonas* lacks scales. Four other structural aspects characterize motile cells in the Prasinophyceae: (1) parallel kinetosomes (basal bodies); (2) tubular flagellar hairs (hair-scales) in two opposite rows along the flagella (exception: *Mesostigma*); (3) a depression or groove at the flagellar insertion; and (4) location of Golgi bodies is parabasal, viz., close to the kinetosomes (Melkonian, 1990).

The prasinophytes occur in freshwater, brackish water, and marine habitats. Most species are unicellular and some form palmelloid stages. The cell may be uni-, bi-, or quadriflagellate. Most prasinophytes which may be motile, coccoid, or palmelloid share the following characters:

(1) The flagella (4 or less) arise from an apical pit. They have a coating of scales as well as hairs. The flagella are thicker than those of the Chlorophyceae. The flagellar scales are arrayed in two layers in some species, e.g., *Prasinocladus marinus*. The flagella are equal in length and anteriorly inserted. In *P. marinus*, the flagellar bases are arranged in a row, the flagella are half the body length and are usually directed forward in swimming. The uniflagellate and biflagellate species usually have laterally attached flagella and a groove or depression in the attachment region.

(2) The motile cell is covered with one to several characteristic layers of organic scales. Some species tend to have a flexible noncellulosic theca in place of the scales. The scales may sometimes be siliceous rather than organic.

(3) A special kind of fibrous band connects the flagellar bases to the chloroplast and nuclear envelope.

(4) The pyrenoid is penetrated by extensions from the cytoplasm or even the nuclear envelope.

(5) Two contractile vacuoles situated at the anterior end empty into the apical depression.

(6) Prominent dictyosomes are found above the nucleus on either side of the flagellar bases. The number of dictyosomes appears to be characteristic for different genera or species.

(7) The flagellar scales and hairs are produced in a scale reservoir, whereas the body scales originate in vesicles of the Golgi apparatus.

(8) The eyespot forms part of the chloroplast.

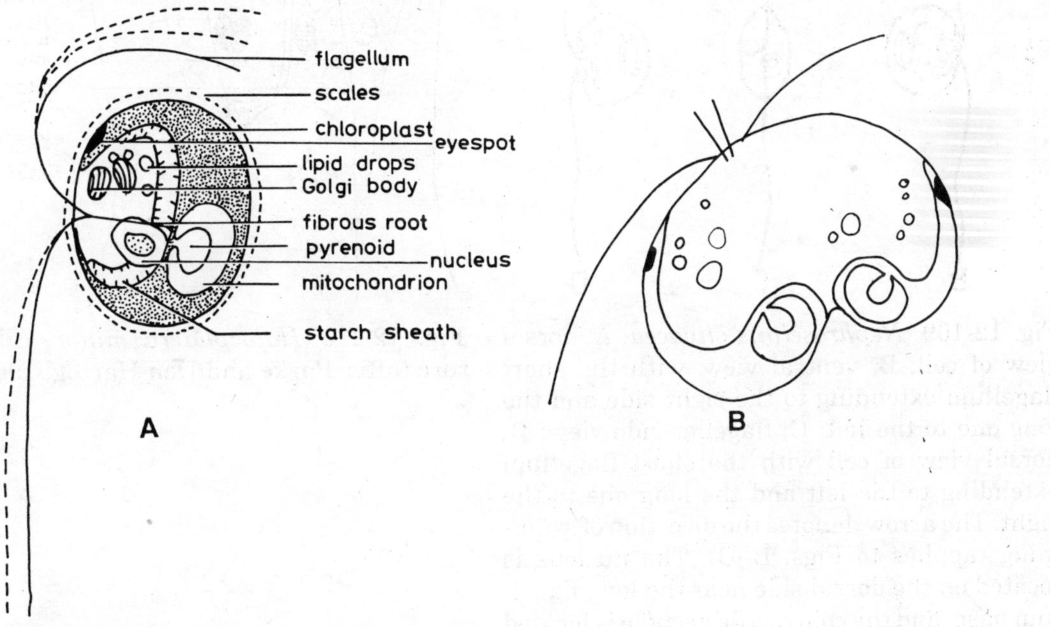

Fig. 12-108 *Heteromastix rotunda*. A, mature cell; B, dividing cell. (After Manton *et al*., 1965.)

(9) The pigmentation is broadly similar to that in the Chlorophyceae. Some prasinophytes also have such additional pigments as micronone (in *Micromonas*) and siphonein (in *Pyramimonas* and *Heteromastix*) (Fig. 12-108 A) (see Ricketts, 1970). *Micromonas* contains some chlorophyll-c (Wilhelm *et al.*, 1986) besides chlorophyll-a and -b. It also contains a novel type of carotenoid, called prasinoxanthin (Foss *et al.*, 1984), which appears to be functionally similar to siphonoxanthin. *Micromonas* appears to be the first organism containing chlorophyll-b which uses three different chlorophylls at the same time for light harvesting (Wilhelm *et al.*, 1986).

(10) Starch, mannitol, and certain lipid bodies are the customary storage products.

(11) The zoospores tend to be formed in pairs.

(12) Sexual reproduction is mostly unknown, and the proliferation tends to occur by

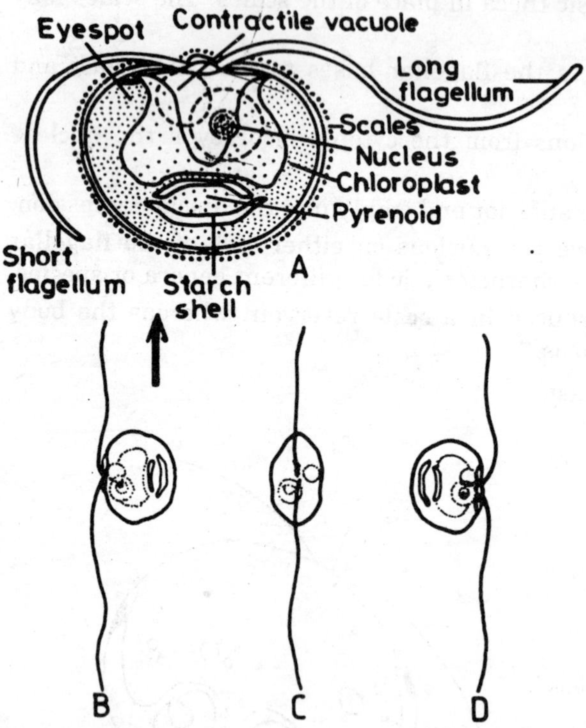

Fig. 12-109 *Nephroselmis olivacea*. A, dorsal view of cell; B, ventral view, with the short flagellum extending to the right side and the long one to the left; C, flagellar-side view; D, dorsal view of cell with the short flagellum extending to the left and the long one to the right. The arrow denotes the direction of swimming (applies to Figs. B–D). The nucleus is located on the dorsal side near the long flagellum base, and the contractile vacuole is located on the ventral side near the short flagellum base. (After Suda and Watanabe, 1989.)

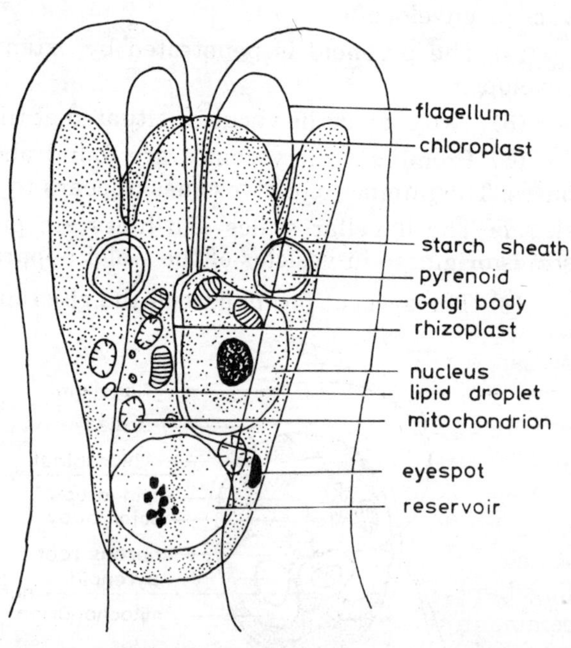

Fig. 12-110 *Halosphaera minor*, cell structure (after Parke and Den Hartog, 1965).

longitudinal division (Fig. 12-108 B). However, Suda and Watanabe (1989) have demonstrated a specialized sexual process in *Nephroselmis olivacea*. The alga is heterothallic. Plus and minus gametes are morphologically isogamous but functionally dissimilar. The minus gametes settle on the substratum by their ventral side whereas the plus gametes attach to the dorsal side of the minus gametes near the flagellar base of the plus gamete. The mature zygotes are spherical. Upon germination, they release two biflagellate cells, each having two pyrenoids. These cells divide into four vegetative cells, each with a single pyrenoid. Figure 12-109 shows a vegetative cell of *N. olivacea* from different planes.

(13) A nonmotile cyst phase alternates with the flagellated cells. In *Halosphaera* (Fig. 12-110), only the motile phase can persist as an independent form reproducing asexually by fission.

(14) The trichocysts show some ejectile property (e.g., *Pyramimonas* and *Halosphaera*).

(15) The apparent ease of fossil formation. This may be due to the presence of resistant, sporopollenin-containing cell walls. Several fossil prasinophytes resembling *Pachysphaera* and *Pterosperma* are known.

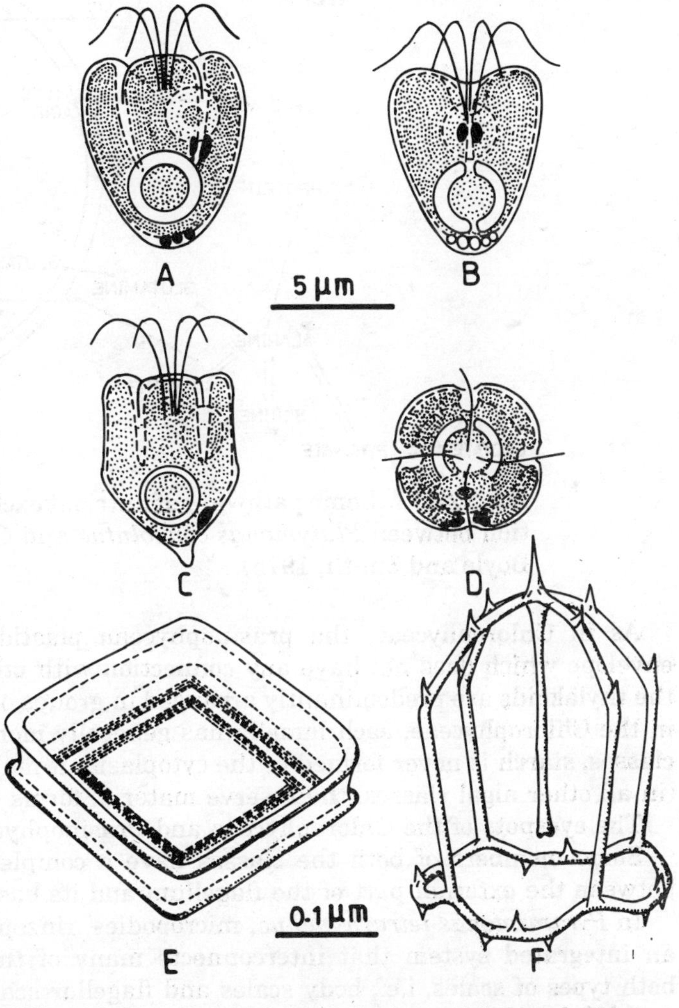

Fig. 12-111 *Pyramimonas mitra*. Schematic drawings of live cells, showing the major organelles and variation in cell shape. Large scales cover the body. The box-shaped type forms the inner layer outside the flagellar pit, the crown scale type forms the outer layer.

Most Prasinophyceae form two or more kinds of periplastic (body) scales which differ morphologically from the flagellar scales. The flagellar scales commonly form a compact mosaic of minute penta- or hexagonal scales which are commonly further overlaid by scales of other shapes. Some species of *Pyramimonas* (Fig. 12-111) and a few other prasinophytes form large outer flagellar scales, each having a characteristic, centrally attached, adnate spine, but no such spines are carried by the body scales. *Dolichomastix* interestingly has a simple periplast made up of monomorphic, rimless plate scales which resemble the flagellar scales (see Manton, 1977). This genus also lacks adnate spines and its scaly flagella are unusually long and flexible.

Platymonas convolutae lives symbiotically with the worm *Convoluta roscoffensis*. Figure 12-112 shows some interactions between the alga and the worm.

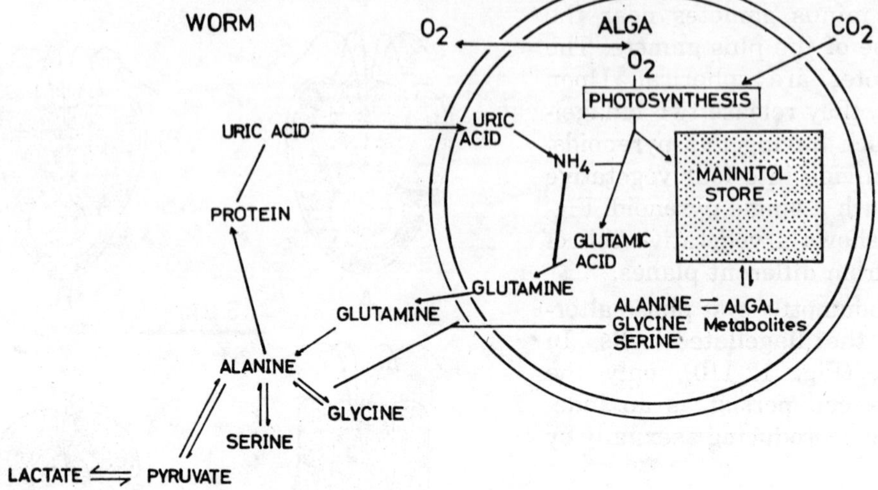

Fig. 12-112 Some pathways of nutrient exchanges in symbiotic association between *Platymonas convolutae* and *Convoluta roscoffensis* (after Boyle and Smith, 1975).

As in Chlorophyceae, the prasinophycean plastids are bounded by a two-membraned envelope which does not have any connection with other cell organelles. Within the plastid, the thylakoids are predominantly arranged in groups of threes in the Prasinophyceae whereas in the Chlorophyceae, each lamella has generally more than three thylakoids. In both these classes, starch is never formed in the cytoplasm; it may only be formed within the chloroplast (in all other algal classes, the reserve material forms outside the plastid in the cytoplasm).

The eyespots of the Chlorophyceae and Prasinophyceae seem to be of the same type.

Some members of both the classes have a complex stellate body in the transition zone between the external part of the flagellum and its basal body.

In *Pyramimonas tetrarhynchus*, microbodies, rhizoplasts, and endoplasmic reticulum form an integrated system that interconnects many of the cellular organelles. In this species, both types of scales, i.e., body scales and flagellar scales, can be formed together within the same Golgi cisterna (Walne and Moestrup, 1977). It has been estimated that each cell of *P. tetrarhynchus* may form about 350,000 small underlayer scales and about 20,000 longer and complex scales.

It has generally been believed that the algae belonging to the Prasinophyceae constitute a primitive group. The work of Stewart *et al.* (1974) on the cytology and cell division of *Platymonas subcordiformis* seems to dispel this belief. In this alga, the interzonal spindle collapses at telophase and a system of transversely disposed microtubules develops between the nuclei. These microtubules occur at right angles to the axis of the recent spindle and are collectively called the phycoplast. The function of the phycoplast seems to be to facilitate the development of the new septum. Neither of these two features (viz., collapse of spindle, and the phycoplast) can be considered primitive. Later studies have revealed that the organisms included in the Prasinophyceae differ in respect of their cytological, nuclear, and cytokinetic attributes, and probably constitute a heterogeneous, undefinable, and unnatural assemblage. Thus, *Pedinomonas minor* seems to have a persistent interzonal spindle.

The primitive green algae were classified into the classes Loxophyceae and Prasinophyceae by Christensen (1966). With the subsequent availability of data on their fine structure, Norris (1980) merged the two classes into one, heterogeneous assemblage called the Prasinophyceae. Later, Moestrup (1982) separated the scale-bearing species of this assemblage and regarded them to constitute the Prasinophyceae. Mattox and Stewart (1984) again lumped together the scaly and the non-scaly members into the heterogeneous group Prasinophyceae. But Moestrup and Throndsen (1988) again defended the classification of the scaly green flagellates into the single class Prasinophyceae, while leaving unresolved the issue of classifying the non-scaly members. Thus, the term Prasinophyceae has meant different things to different phycologists.

Mantoniella squamata is presently considered to be one of the most primitive green plants (Moestrup, 1990). It is a tiny marine, picoplanktonic flagellate. In fact, according to Van den Hoek *et al.* (1988), a *Mantoniella*-like cell is *the* most primitive green plant. The body and flagellar surfaces of *M. squamata* are covered by characteristic scales that resemble a spider's web. The cells also contain certain trichocyst-like organelles.

The flagellar scales are somewhat elongated and, when undisturbed, are arranged in rows with the long axis in the longitudinal direction of the flagellum. These scales appear to be heptaradial: seven major radial spokes divide the scale into segments, and each segment is subdivided by a slightly shorter radial spoke terminating at the central ring of perforations. Six (sometimes five) concentric rows of bars divide the scale further, resulting in its characteristic web-like appearance. Thus, the scale shows a ring of 7 central perforations, one of which is often larger than the others, surrounded by five or six rings of about 14 perforations (Moestrup, 1990).

The body scales are of two distinct types. The most numerous are the large subquadrangular octaradial scales. The smaller, tetraradial body scales are much less numerous.

The mitotic process in the uniflagellate scaly alga *Mantoniella squamata* is unlike that in other prasinophytes. The cell enlarges and its single chloroplast and pyrenoid divide. As the cell elongates, the single Golgi body, the single mitochondrion, and the two basal bodies divide. The replicated basal bodies and flagella separate as the nucleus enlarges. A Golgi body is located at each spindle pole. The basal bodies lie within invaginations of the nucleus antapical to the poles (see Barlow, 1977).

Phycologists have been divided over the question of what rank (whether class or phylum) should be assigned to the prasinophytes. Some authorities have created a separate phylum (Prasinophyta) to accommodate these algae. However, we believe that the points of resemblance between the Chlorophyceae and the Prasinophyceae (broadly similar pigmentation, eyespots, chloroplast structure, cellulosic cell wall, deposition of starch in the plastid, and certain similarities in cell division and cytokinesis) are strong enough not to warrant a phylum status for the prasinophytes. They are therefore treated as a separate class within the phylum Chlorophyta. Norris (1982) has found evidence for some phylogenetic resemblances amongst the various algae included in the Prasinophyceae. He defends the grouping of these organisms in this class and believes that this most primitive class of the phylum Chlorophyta may have evolved from certain flagellate chromophytes.

PEDINOPHYCEAE

On the basis of his study of the fine structure of the tiny jumping flagellate, *Pedinomonas mikron*, Moestrup (1991) created a new class of green algae, called the Pedinophyceae.

Since *P. mikron* was found to differ significantly from *P. minor* in respect of behaviour and flagellar apparatus, *P. mikron* was raised to a separate genus and named *Resultor* (Fig. 12-113). Pedinophyceae is characterized by its typical flagellar apparatus, mitosis, and cytokinesis. The flagella show the 11/5 orientation (on the dial of a clock) otherwise typical of Ulvophyceae and Pleurastrophyceae, but they are arranged end to end as in the Chlorophyceae. The flagellar root system is asymmetric and includes a rhizoplast which emerges from the base of one flagellum but then associates with a microtubular root from the second basal body.

The mitosis appears to be closed and the spindle is persistent. Neither phycoplast nor phragmoplast is formed during cytokinesis.

The eyespot (Fig. 12-113) is located at the opposite end of the cell (from the flagella) and adjacent to the pyrenoid, reminiscent of the arrangement in the most primitive taxa of the Prasinophyceae. However, members of Pedinophyceae lack prasinoxanthin that occurs in many Prasinophyceae.

According to Moestrup (1989), the primitive green algae include the classes Prasinophyceae and Pedinophyceae; he considers the class Micromonadophyceae *sensu* Stewart and Mattox as being synonymous with the Prasinophyceae.

The representative examples of Pedinophyceae are *Pedinomonas*, *Resultor*, and *Scourfieldia*.

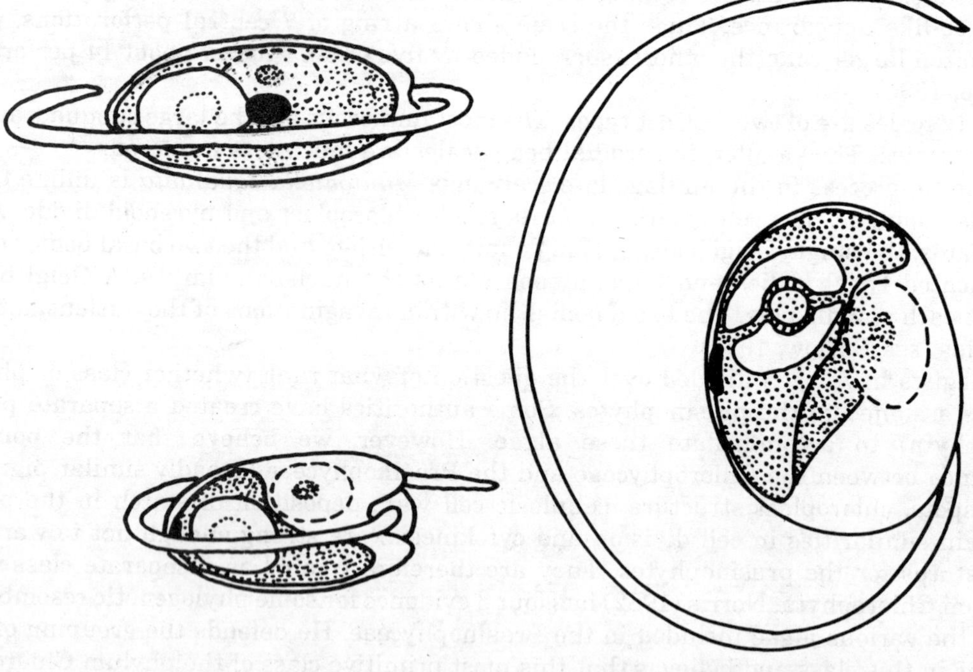

Fig. 12-113 *Resultor mikron*. A cell seen from three different angles. (After Moestrup, 1991.)

REFERENCES

Allen, M.A., The biology of a species complex in *Spirogyra*, Ph.D. Thesis, Indiana University, Bloomington (1958).

Baldauf, S.L. and Palmer, J.D., Evolutionary transfer of the chloroplast *nif.* gene to the nucleus, *Nature*, **344,** 262–65 (1990).

Barlow, S., Fine structure and cell division of the scale-covered uniflagellate *Mantoniella squamata* (Chlorophyta-Prasinophyceae), *J. Phycol.*, Suppl. Abst. No. 18, p. 5 (1977).

Beck, S.J. and Erben, K., Facultative parasitism of *Spirogyra* sp. (Chlorophyta) by *Saprolegnia asterophora* and *Pythium gracile* (Eumycota, Oomycetes), *J. Phycol.*, **20**, 13–19 (1984).

Bharadwaja, Y., A new species of *Draparnaldiopsis*, *New Phytol.*, **32**, 165–74 (1933).

Birch, P.B. and Gabrielson, J.O., *Cladophora* growth in the Peel-Harvey estuarine system following blooms of the cyanobacterium *Nodularia spumigena*, *Bot. Mar.*, **27**, 165–71 (1984).

Blank, R., Grobe, B., and Arnold, C.G., Time sequence of nuclear and chloroplast fusions in the zygote of *Chlamydomonas reinhardii*, *Planta*, **138**, 63–64 (1978).

Bold, H.C., Morphology of Plants, Harper and Row, New York (1967).

Bold, H.C. and Wynne, M.J., Introduction to the Algae: Structure and reproduction, 2nd edn., Prentice-Hall, Englewood Cliffs, New Jersey (1985).

Borowitzka, L.J., The microflora: adaptations to life in extremely saline lakes, *Hydrobiologia*, **81**, 33–46 (1981).

Boyle, J.E. and Smith, D.C., Biochemical interactions between the symbionts of *Convoluta roscoffensis*, *Proc. Roy. Soc.* (London), **189B**, 121–35 (1975).

Broady, P.A., The distribution of *Prasiola calophylla* (Carmich.) Menegh. (Chlorophyta) in Antarctic freshwater and terrestrial habitats, *Antarctic Science*, **1**, 109–18 (1989).

Bronmark, C., Rundle, S.D., and Erlandsson, A., Interactions between freshwater snails and tadpoles: competition and facilitation, *Oecologia*, **87**, 8–18 (1991).

Brown, R.M. (Jr.), Johnson, O.P.S.C., and Bold, H.C., Electron and phase contrast microscopy of sexual reproduction in *Chlamydomonas moewusii*, *J. Phycol.*, **4**, 100–120 (1968).

Buerkle, S., Gloeckner, G., and Beck, C.F., *Chlamydomonas* mutants affected in the light-dependent step of sexual differentiation, *Proc. Natl. Acad. Sci.* (USA), **90**, 6981–85 (1993).

Burczyk, J. and Hesse, M., The ultrastructure of the outer cell wall layer of *Chlorella* mutants with and without sporopollenin, *Plant Syst. Evol.*, **138**, 121–37 (1981).

Cann, J.P., The feeding behavior and structure of *Nuclearia delicatula* (Filosea: Aconchulinida), *J. Protozool.*, **33**, 392–96 (1986).

Catt, J.W., Hills, G.J., and Roberts, K., Cell wall glycoproteins from *Chlamydomonas reinhardii*, and their self assembly, *Planta*, **138**, 91–98 (1978).

Cole, K.M. and Akintobi, S., The life cycle of *Prasiola meridionalis*, *Can. J. Bot.*, **41**, 661–68 (1963).

Christensen, T., Botanik, Systematisk Botanik, Vol. II, *Alger*. Munksgaard, Kobenhaven (1962).

Christensen, T., Alger. *In* Böcher, T.W., Lange, M., and Sorensen, T. (eds.) Systematisk Botanik, Vol. 3, No. 3, Munksgaard, Copenhagen (1963).

Christensen, T., Alger. *In* Böcher, T.W., Lange, M., and Sorensen, T. (eds.) Botanik, Vol. 2, Systematisk Botanik, 2nd edn., 1–180, Munksgaard, Copenhagen (1986).

Dawes, C.J., An ultrastructural study of *Spirogyra*, *J. Phycol.*, **1**, 121–27 (1965).

Demets, R., Tomson, A.M., Homan, W.L., Stegwee, D., and Van den Ende, H., Cell-cell adhesion in conjugating *Chlamydomonas* gametes: a self-enhancing process, *Protoplasma*, **145**, 27–36 (1988).

Desikachary, T.V. and Sundaralingam, V.S., Affinities and interrelationships of the Characeae, *Phycologia*, **2**, 9–16 (1962).

Dodds, W.R., Community interactions between the filamentous alga *Cladophora glomerata* (L.) Kützing: its epiphytes and epiphyte grazers, *Oecologia*, **85**, 572–80 (1991).

Dodds, W.R. and Gudder, D.A., The ecology of *Cladophora*, *J. Phycol.*, **28**, 415–27 (1992).

Dolle, R. and Nultsch, W., Effects of calcium ions and of calcium channel blockers on galvanotaxis of *Chlamydomonas reinhardii*, *Bot. Acta*, **101**, 18–23 (1988).

Dolle, R., Pfau, J., and Nultsch, W., Role of calcium ions in motility and phototaxis of *Chlamydomonas reinhardii*, *J. Plant Physiol.*, **126**, 467–73 (1987).

Ettl, H., Über systematische Probleme in der Gattung *Chlamydomonas*, *Phycologia*, **5**, 61–70 (1965).

Foss, P., Guillard, R.R.L., and Liaaen-Jensen, S., Prasinoxanthin: a chemosystematic marker for algae, *Phytochemistry*, **23**, 1629–33 (1984).

Fritsch, F.E., The Structure and Reproduction of the Algae, Vol. I, Cambridge University Press, London (1935).

Godward, M.B.E. (ed.), The Chromosomes of the Algae, Edward Arnold, London (1966).

Gordon, D.M., Van den Hoek, C., and McComb, A.J., An aegagropiloid form of the green alga *Cladophora montagneana* Kutz. (Chlorophyta, Cladophorales) from Southwestern Australia, *Bot. Mar.*, **27**, 57–65 (1985).

Graham, L.E., *Coleochaete* and the origin of land plants, *Am. J. Bot.*, **71**, 603–608 (1984).

Graham, L.E., Origin of Land Plants, Wiley, New York (1993).

Grant, V., Plant Speciation, 2nd edn., Columbia University Press, New York (1981).

Grote, M., Untersuchungen zum Kopulationsverlauf bei der Grunalge *Spirogyra majuscula*, *Protoplasma*, **91**, 71–82 (1977a).

Grote, M., Über die Auslosung der generativen Fortpflazung unter kontrollierten Bedingungen bei der Grunalge *Spirogyra majuscula*, *Z. Pflanzenphysiol.*, **83**, 95–107 (1977b).

Hansson, I.A., Effects of competitive interactions on the biomass development of planktonic and periphyton algae in lakes, *Limnol. Oceanogr.*, **33**, 121–28 (1988).

Harada, A., Cytological studies on *Sirogonium*. I. Mitosis in *S. sticticum* and *S. melanosporum*, *Jap. J. Phycol.*, **29**, 23–29 (1981).

Herth, W., Arrays of plasma-membrane "rosettes" involved in cellulose microfibril formation of *Spirogyra*, *Planta*, **159**, 347–56 (1983).

Hill, G.J.C., Cunningham, M.R., Byrne, M.M., Ferry, T.P., and Halvorson, J.S., Chemical control of androspore morphogenesis in *Oedogonium donnellii* (Chlorophyta, Oedogoniales), *J. Phycol.*, **25**, 368–76 (1989).

Hill, J.C. and Michalis, L., An ultrastructural study of the vegetative cell division in *Oedogonium borisianum*, *J. Phycol.*, **4**, 261–71 (1968).

Hoffman, J.P. and Graham, L.E., Effects of selected physicochemical factors on growth and zoosporogenesis of *Cladophora glomerata* (Chlorophyta), *J. Phycol.*, **20**, 1–7 (1984).

Hoffman, L.R., Observations on the fine structure of *Oedogonium*. III. Microtubular elements in the chloroplasts of *O. cardiacum*, *J. Phycol.*, **3**, 212–21 (1967).

Hoffman, L.R., *Atractomorpha echinata* gen. et sp. nov.: a new anisogamous member of the Sphaeropleaceae (Chlorophyceae), *J. Phycol.*, **19**, 76–86 (1983).

Hoffman, L.R. and Buchheim, M.A., Zygote appendages (cirri): a new structural feature in the Sphaeropleaceae (Chlorophyceae), *J. Phycol.*, **25**, 149–59 (1989).

Holomuzki, J.R., Predation risk and macroalga use by the stream-dwelling salamander *Ambystoma texanum*, *Copeia*, **1**, 22–28 (1989).

Hopkins, A.W., Feulgen microspectrophotometric investigation of the life history of *Fritschiella tuberosa* (Chlorophyceae), *J. Phycol.*, **13**, 321–23 (1977).

Hoshaw, R.W., Sexual cycles and their implications for systematics in *Sirogonium* (Zygnemataceae, Chlorophyta), *Phycologia*, **25**, 371–78 (1986).

Hoshaw, R.W. and Hull, H.M., Ploidy and speciation in the Zygnemataceae, *J. Arizona Acad. Sci.*, **16**, 20–21 (1981).

Hoshaw, R.W. and McCourt, R.M., The Zygnemataceae (Chlorophyta): a twenty-year update of research, *Phycologia*, **27**, 511–48 (1988).

Hoshaw, R.W. and Wells, C.V., Systematics of the Zygnemataceae (Chlorophyceae). IV. Nuclear cytology of *Sirogonium melanosporum*, a species with large chromosomes, *Trans. Amer. Microscop. Soc.*, **101**, 276–86 (1982).

Howell, S.H., An analysis of cell cycle controls in temperature sensitive mutants of *Chlamydomonas reinhardii*, *Nature New Biol.*, **240**, 264–67 (1974).

Hoxmark, R.C. and Nordby, O., Haploid meiosis as a regular phenomenon in the life cycle of *Ulva mutabilis*, *Hereditas*, **76**, 239–50 (1974).

Huskey, R.J., Griffin, B.E., Cecil, P.O., and Callahan, A.M., A preliminary genetic investigation of *Volvox carteri*, *Genetics*, **91**, 229–44 (1979).

Ichimura, T., Isolating mechanisms in speciation of *Closterium*, *Jap. J. Phycol.*, **30**, 332–43 (1982)

Ichimura, T., Geographical distribution and isolating mechanisms in the *Closterium ehrenbergii* species complex (Chlorophyceae, Closteriaceae). *In* Hara, H. (ed.) Origin and

Evolution of Diversity in Plants and Plant Communities, 295–303, Academia Scientific Books, Tokyo (1985).

Ichimura, T. and Kasai, F., Mating systems and speciation in haplontic unicellular algae, desmids. *In* Kawano, S. (ed.) Biological Approaches and Evolutionary Trends in Plants, 195–201, Academic Press, London (1990).

Ichimura, T. and Kasai, F., Morphological variation and zygotic defective mating-type plus in a population of *Closterium ehrenbergii* (Desmidiales, Chlorophyta) from Boest Brook, Denmark, *Phycologia*, **34**, 45–50 (1995).

Jaenicke, L., *Volvox* biochemistry comes of age, *Trends in Biochem. Sci.*, **7**, 61–64 (1982).

Jaenicke, L. and Waffenschmidt, S., Liberation of reproductive units in *Volvox* and *Chlamydomonas*: proteolytic processes, *Ber. Deutsch. Bot. Ges.*, **94S**, 375–86 (1981).

Johnstone, I.M., *Draparnaldiopsis*: filamentous green alga (Chlorophyta, Chaetophoraceae) requiring vitamin B_{12}, *Phycologia*, **16**, 183–87 (1977).

Kelland, J.H., Inversion in *Volvox* (Chlorophyceae), *J. Phycol.*, **13**, 373–78 (1977).

Kessler, E., A general review on the contribution of chemotaxonomy to the systematics of green algae. *In* Irvine, D.E.G. and John, D.M. (eds.) Systematics of the Green Algae, 391–407, Academic Press, London (1984).

Kessler, E. and Huss, V.A.R., Comparative physiology and biochemistry and taxonomic assignment of the *Chlorella* (Chlorophyceae) strains of the culture collection of the University of Texas at Austin, *J. Phycol.*, **28**, 550–53 (1992).

Koeman, R.R.T., The Taxonomy of *Ulva* Linnaeus, 1753, and *Enteromorpha* Link, 1820 (Chlorophyceae), in the Netherlands, Drukkerij van Denderen, Groningen, Netherlands (1985).

Kooijman, R., Wildt, P.D., Homan, W.L., Musgrave, A., and Van den Ende, H., Light affects flagellar agglutinability in *Chlamydomonas eugametos* by modification of the agglutinin molecules, *Plant Physiol.*, **86**, 216–23 (1988).

Koufopanou, V. and Bell, G., Soma and germ: an experimental approach using *Volvox*, *Proc. Roy. Soc.* (London), **B254**, 107–13 (1993).

Lacalli, T., Golgi function and cell wall formation in the Conjugales, *Rev. Can. Biol.*, **33**, 125–33 (1974).

Levandowsky, M. and Hutner, S.H. (eds.), Biochemistry and Physiology of Protozoa, Vol. 1, 2nd edn., Academic Press, New York (1979).

Lokhorst, G.M., Taxonomic studies on the marine and brackish-water species of *Ulothrix* in Western Europe, *Blumea*, **24**, 191–299 (1978).

Lorenz, R.C., Monaco, M.F., and Herdendorf, C.E., Minimum light requirements for substrate colonization by *Cladophora glomerata*, *J. Great Lakes Res.*, **17**, 536–42 (1991).

Lubchenco, J., Plant species diversity in a marine intertidal community: importance of herbivore food preference and algal competitive abilities, *Am. Nat.*, **112**, 23–39 (1978).

Manhart, J.R. and Palmer, J.D., The gain of two chloroplast tRNA introns marks the green algal ancestors of land plants, *Nature*, **345**, 268–70 (1990).

Manton, I., *Dolichomastix* (Prasinophyceae) from arctic Canada, Alaska and South Africa: a new genus of flagellates with scaly flagella, *Phycologia*, **16**, 427–38 (1977).

Manton, I., Rayns, D.G., Ettl, H., and Parke, M., Further observations on green flagellates with scaly flagella: the genus *Heteromastix* Korshikov, *J. Mar. Biol. Ass.* (U.K.), **45**, 241–51 (1965).

Marchant, H.J., Colony formation and inversion in the green alga *Eudorina elegans*, *Protoplasma*, **93**, 325–39 (1977).

Marchant, H.J. and Pickett-Heaps, J.D., Ultrastructure, development and cytoplasmic rotation of setae-bearing cells of *Coleochaete scutata*, *J. Phycol.*, **13**, 28–36 (1977).

Mattox, K.R. and Stewart, K.D., Classification of the green algae: a concept based on comparative cytology. *In* Irvine, D.E.G. and John, D.M. (eds.) The Systematics of Green Algae, 29–72, Academic Press, London (1984).

McBridge, G.E., The seta-bearing cells of *Coleochaete scutata* (Chlorophyceae, Chaetophorales), *Phycologia*, **13**, 271–85 (1974).

McCourt, R.M., Green algal phylogeny, *TREE*, **10**, 159–63 (1995).

McLean, R.J., Katz, K.R., Sedita, N.J., Menoff, A.L., Laurendi, C.J., and Brown, R.M. (Jr.), Dynamics of Concanavalin A binding sites on *Chlamydomonas moewusii* flagellar membranes, *Ber. Deutsch. Bot. Ges.*, **94S**, 387–400 (1981).

Melkonian, M., Flagellar apparatus ultrastructure in relation to green algal classification. *In* Irvine, D.E.G. and John, D.M. (eds.) Systematics of the Green Algae, 73–120, Academic Press, London (1984).

Melkonian, M., Phylum Chlorophyta: Class Prasinophyceae. *In* Margulis, M., Corliss, J.O., Melkonian, M., and Chapman, D.J. (eds.) Handbook of Protoctista, 600–607, Jones and Bartlett, Boston (1990).

Melkonian, M. and Berns, B., Zoospore ultrastructure in the green alga *Friedmannia israelensis*: an absolute configuration analysis, *Protoplasma*, **114**, 67–84 (1983).

Mesland, D.A.M., Flagellar surface morphology of *Chlamydomonas eugametos*, *Protoplasma*, **93**, 311–23 (1977).

Miller, C.E. and Starr, R.C., The control of sexual morphogenesis in *Volvox capensis*, *Ber. Deutsch. Bot. Ges.*, **94S**, 357–72 (1981).

Mishra, N.C. and Threlkeld, S.F.H., Genetic studies in *Eudorina*, *Genet. Res.*, **11**, 21–31 (1968).

Moestrup, O., The fine structure of mature spermatozoids of *Chara corallina*: with special reference to microtubules and scales, *Planta*, **93**, 295–308 (1970).

Moestrup, O., Flagellar structure in algae: a review, with new observations particularly on the Chrysophyceae, Phaeophyceae (Fucophyceae), Euglenophyceae, and *Reckertia*, *Phycologia*, **21**, 427–528 (1982).

Moestrup, O., Scale structure in *Mantoniella squamata*, with some comments on the phylogeny of the Prasinophyceae (Chlorophyta), *Phycologia*, **29**, 437–42 (1990).

Moestrup, O., Further studies of presumedly primitive green algae, including the description of Pedinophyceae class nov. and *Resultor* gen. nov., *J. Phycol.*, **27**, 99–133 (1991).

Moestrup, O. and Throndsen, J., Light and electron microscopical studies on *Pseudoscourfieldia marine*: a primitive scaly green flagellate with posterior flagella, *Can. J. Bot.*, **66**, 1415–34 (1988).

Morimura, Y., Synchronous culture of *Chlorella*. I. Kinetic analysis of the life cycle of *Chlorella ellipsoidea* as affected by changes of temperature and light intensity, *Pl. Cell Physiol.*, **1**, 49–62 (1959).

Nagata, Y., Rhizoid differentiation in *Spirogyra*, *Pl. Cell Physiol.*, **14**, 531–54 (1973).

Norris, R.E., Prasinophytes. *In* Cox, E.R. (ed.) Developments in Marine Biology, 85–145, Phytoflagellates, Vol. 2, Elsevier, New York (1980).

Norris, R.E., Prasinophyceae: Introduction and bibliography. *In* Rosowski, J.R. and Parker, B.C. (eds.) Selected Papers in Phycology. II. 740–46, Phycological Society of America, Lawrence, Kansas (1982).

Nozaki, H., Sexual reproduction in *Gonium sociale* (Chlorophyta, Volvocales), *Phycologia*, **25**, 29–35 (1986).

Nozaki, H. and Kuroiwa, T., Morphology and sexual reproduction of *Gonium multicoccum* (Volvocales, Chlorophyta) from Nepal, *Phycologia*, **30**, 381–93 (1991).

Nultsch, W., Effect of external factors on phototaxis of *Chlamydomonas reinhardii*. III. Cations, *Arch. Microbiol.*, **123**, 93–99 (1979).

Nultsch, W., Pfau, J., and Dolle, R., Effects of calcium channel blockers on phototaxis and motility of *Chlamydomonas reinhardii*, *Arch. Microbiol.*, **144**, 393–97 (1986).

Ohiwa, T., Tazawà, M., and Kamiya, N., Spiral cell wall growth in Zygnemataceae, *Bot. Mag.*, Tokyo, **89**, 267–75 (1976).

Papenfuss, G.F., Classification of the Algae. *In* A Century of Progress in the Natural Sciences, Proceedings of the California Academy of Sciences, California, pp. 115–224 (1955).

Parke, M. and Den Hartog, I., Three species of *Halosphaera*, *J. Mar. Biol. Ass.* (U.K.), **45**, 537–57 (1965).

Patel, R.J. and Patel, N.J., On *Fritschiella tuberosa* Iyengar from Vallabh Vidyanagar (Gujarat), *Jour. Gujarat Univ.*, **12**, 242–45 (1969).

Patrick, R., Rhyne, C.F., Richardson, R.W., III, Larson, R.A., Bott, T.T., and Rogenmuser, K., The potential for biological controls of *Cladophora glomerata*, United States Environmental Protection Agency, EPA 600/3-83-065, 153 (1983).

Pickett-Heaps, J.D., Ultrastructure and differentiation of *Chara* sp. II. Mitosis, *Austr. J. Biol. Sci.*, **20**, 883–94 (1967).

Pickett-Heaps, J.D., Ultrastructure and differentiation of *Chara* sp. IV. Spermatogenesis, *Austr. J. Biol. Sci.*, **21**, 655–90 (1968).

Pickett-Heaps, J.D., The evolution of the mitotic apparatus: an attempt at comparative ultrastructural cytology in dividing plant cells, *Cytobios*, **3**, 257–80 (1969).

Pickett-Heaps, J.D., Some ultrastructural features of *Volvox*: with special reference to the phenomenon of inversion, *Planta*, **90**, 174–90 (1970).

Pickett-Heaps, J.D., Cell division in *Klebsormidium subtillissimum* (formerly *Ulothrix subtillissima*) and its possible phylogenetic significance, *Cytobios*, **6**, 167–83 (1972).

Pickett-Heaps, J.D. and Wetherbee, R., Spindle function in the green alga *Mougeotia*: absence of anaphase A correlates with postmitotic nuclear migration, *Cell Motility Cytoskeleton*, **7**, 68–77 (1987).

Pickett-Heaps, J.D. and Marchant, H.J., The phylogeny of green algae: a new proposal, *Cytobios*, **6**, 255–64 (1972).

Power, M.E., Benthic turfs vs floating mats of algae in river food webs, *Oikos*, **58**, 67–79 (1990).

Power, M.E., Shifts in the effects of tuft-weaving midges on filamentous algae, *Amer. Midland Naturalist*, **125**, 275–85 (1991).

Reize, I.B. and Melkonian, M., Absolute orientations of basal bodies in green algae evaluated by light microscopy, *Botanica Acta*, **101**, 192–95 (1988).

Ricketts, T.R., The pigments of the Prasinophyceae and related organisms, *Phytochemistry*, **9**, 1835–42 (1970).

Roberts, K., Hydroxyprotein: its asymmetric distribution in a cell wall glycoprotein, *Planta*, **146**, 275–79 (1979).

Round, F.E., The taxonomy of the Chlorophyta. II, *Brit. Phycol. J.*, **6**, 235–64 (1971).

Sager, R., Cytoplasmic Genes and Organelles, Academic Press, New York (1972).

Schiedlmeier, B., Schmitt, R., Muller, W., Kirk, M.M., Gruber, H., Mages, W., and Kirk, D.L., Nuclear transformation of *Volvox carteri*, *Proc. Natl. Acad. Sci.* (USA), **91**, 5080–5084 (1994).

Schölm, H.E., Über tagesperiodische Anderungen der sichtbaren Flache von Nucleus und Nucleolus einheimischer Susswasseralgen und ihre Beeinflussbarkeit, *Protoplasma*, **66**, 393–401 (1968).

Schröder, V.R., Reed decay at Lake Constance (Untersee) observations and investigations, *Arch. Hydrobiol. Suppl.*, **76**, 53–99 (1987).

Simons, J., *Spirogyra* species and accompanying algae from dune waters in the Netherlands, *Acta Bot. Neerland.*, **36**, 13–31 (1987).

Simons, J., Van Beem, A.P., and De Vries, P.J.R., Induction of conjugation and spore formation in species of *Spirogyra* (Chlorophyceae: Zygnematales), *Acta Bot. Neerland.*, **33**, 323–34 (1984).

Simons, J., Van Beem, A.P., and De Vries, P.J.R., Morphology of the prostrate thallus of *Stigeoclonium* (Chlorophyceae, Chaetophorales) and its taxonomic implications, *Phycologia*, **25**, 210–20 (1986).

Singh, R.N., Nuclear phases and alternation of generations in *Draparnaldiopsis indica* Bharadwaja, *New Phytol.*, **44**, 118–29 (1945).

Singh, R.N., *Fritschiella tuberosa* Iyengar, *Ann. Bot.*, **11**, 159–64 (1947).

Singh, R.N., *Fritschiella tuberosa* and the algal ancestry of higher plants, Proceedings of the VIII International Botanical Congress, pp. 1–4 (1954).

Sluiman, H.J., The flagellar apparatus of the filamentous green alga *Coleochaete pulvinata*: absolute configuration and phylogenetic significance, *Protoplasma*, **115**, 160–75 (1983).

Smith, G.M., Cryptogamic Botany, Vol. I, Algae and Fungi, 2nd edn., McGraw-Hill, New York (1955).

Snell, W.M., Characterization of the *Chlamydomonas reinhardii* flagellar collar, *Cell Motility*, **3**, 273–80 (1983).

Srivastava, S. and Sarma, Y.S.R.K., Karyological studies on the genus *Oedogonium* Link (Oedogoniales, Chlorophyceae), *Phycologia*, **18**, 228–36 (1979).

Stabenau, H., Microbodies in different algae. *In* Wiessner, W., Robinson, D., and Starr, R.C. (eds.) Compartments in Algal Cells and Their Interaction, 183–90, Springer-Verlag, Berlin (1984).

Stanford, J.A. and Prescott, G.W., Limnological features of a remote alpine lake in Montana, including a new species of *Cladophora* (Chlorophyta), *Journal of the North American Benthological Society*, **7**, 140–51 (1988).

Starr, R.C., Cellular differentiation in *Volvox*, *Proc. Natl. Acad. Sci.* (USA), **59**, 1082–88 (1968).

Starr, R.C., O'Neil, R., and Miller, C.E., L-Glutamic acid as a mediator of sexual morphogenesis in *Volvox capensis*, *Proc. Natl. Acad. Sci.* (USA), **77**, 1025–28 (1980).

Stewart, K.D. and Mattox, K.R., Comparative cytology, evolution and classification of the green algae with some consideration of the origin of other organisms with chlorophylls a and b, *Bot. Rev.*, **41**, 104–35 (1975).

Stewart, K.D., Mattox, K.R., and Chandler, C.D., Mitosis and cytokinesis in *Platymonas subcordiformis*: a scaly green monad, *J. Phycol.*, **10**, 65–79 (1974).

Suda, S. and Watanabe, M.M., Evidence for sexual reproduction in the primitive green alga *Nephroselmis olivacea* (Prasinophyceae), *J. Phycol.*, **25**, 596–600 (1989).

Tamiya, H., Cell differentiation in *Chlorella*. *In* Fogg, G.E. (ed.) Sympos. Cell Differentiation, *Soc. Exptl. Biol.*, **17**, 188–214 (1963).

Tanaka, K. and Matsuura, M., Studies on the growth and development in *Spirogyra*. IV. A close relationship between and diurnal movement pattern and the photosynthetic rates of *Spirogyra* filaments, *Jap. J. Phycol.*, **31**, 24–27 (1983).

Trench, R.K., The cell biology of plant-animal symbiosis, *Ann. Rev. Plant Physiol.*, **30**, 485–531 (1979).

Triemer, R.E. and Brown, R.M. (Jr.), Ultrastructure of meiosis in *Chlamydomonas reinhardii*, *Brit. Phycol. J.*, **12**, 23–44 (1976).

Ueda, K., Abhayavardhani, P., and Noguchi, T., Formation of the nuclear envelope during mitotic anaphase in *Spirogyra*, *Bot. Mag.*, Tokyo, **99**, 301–308 (1986).

Van den Ende, H., Klis, F.M., and Musgrave, A., The role of flagella in sexual reproduction of *Chlamydomonas eugametos*, *Acta Bot. Neerl.*, **37**, 327–50 (1988).

Van den Hoek, C., Revision of the European species of *Cladophora*, E.J. Brill, Leiden (1963).

Van den Hoek, C., Stam, W.T., and Olsen, J.L., The emergence of a new chlorophytan system and Dr. Kornmann's contribution thereto, *Helgolander Meeresunters.*, **42**, 339–83 (1988).

Waffenschmidt, S., Kuhne, W., and Jaenicke, L., Immunological characterization of gamete autolysins in *Chlamydomonas reinhardii*, *Botanica Acta*, **102**, 73–79 (1989).

Walne, P.L. and Moestrup, O., Ultrastructure and scale formation in the type species of *Pyramimonas*, *J. Phycol.*, Suppl. Abst. No. 413, p. 71 (1977).

Whitton, B.A., Biology of *Chadophora* in freshwaters, *Water Research*, **4**, 457–76 (1970).

Wiese, L., On sexual agglutination and mating type substances (gamones) in isogamous heterothallic Chlamydomonads. I. Evidence of the identity of the gamones with the surface components responsible for sexual flagellar contact, *J. Phycol.*, **1**, 46–54 (1965).

Wilhelm, C., Lenartz-Weiler, I., Wiedemann, I., and Wild, A., The light-harvesting system of a *Micromonas* species (Prasinophyceae): the combination of three different chlorophyll species in one single chlorophyll protein complex, *Phycologia*, **25**, 304–12 (1986).

Yamagishi, T., Studies on the genus *Spirogyra* collected in Japan, *Sci. Reports Tokyo Kyoiku Daigaku*, **12**, 73–105 (1966).

13 Ecology

HABITATS

In general, the algae grow and survive in an extraordinary range of habitats: from scorching hot springs to snowy peaks; from slow-growing lichens to the lining of the mouth of the clam, *Tridaena*.

The vast majority of algae are aquatic, especially occurring on the surfaces of water and moist habitats. Any moist surface that is exposed to sunlight will support the growth of some algae.

Rock faces, rock debris, concrete buildings, footpaths, cooling towers of power plants and other industrial plants, and tree barks are some of the terrestrial habitats colonized by algae. Leaves of many plants in tropical countries also harbour algal growth on their surfaces. Virtually all soils are inhabited by microalgae. Some algae (e.g., *Chlamydomonas nivalis*) occur on permanent ice and snow. Others live in hot springs (e.g., *Mastigocladus*).

The tropical rice field is one of the most suitable habitats for diverse blue-green algae, e.g., *Aulosira*, which grow luxuriantly in the microaerobic and reducing conditions in these fields.

Many algae colonize sewage disposal beds and filters of water works, playing an important role in the cleansing of water. In temporary water pools, algal flagellates and certain soil algae proliferate.

Along seacoasts, the rocks and wet or submerged silt and sand constitute good sites for colonization by algae (Fig. 13-1). The algae also grow on submerged plants and animals. In fact, ecologically algae are the most widespread of the photosynthetic plants, constituting the bulk of the carbon assimilating, floating microscopic cells in the sea and in freshwaters (phytoplankton). They are the primary producers over three-fourths of the earth's surface.

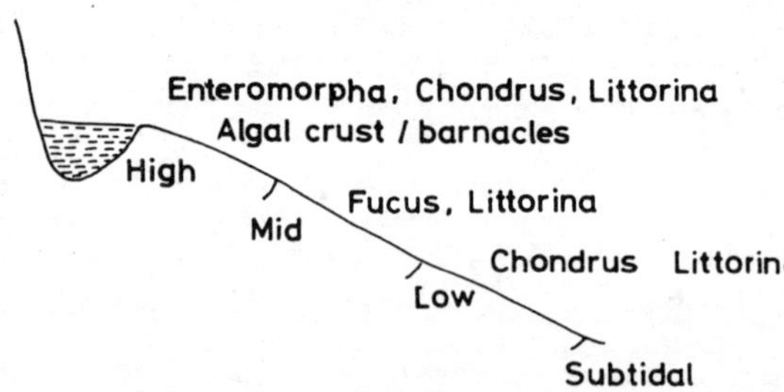

Fig. 13-1 Zonation of some common inhabitants on a rocky intertidal zone of seashore in U.S.A. (after Lubchenco, 1980).

In running waters, discharge patterns assume fundamental significance by influencing both gross morphology and stream bed characteristics, which in turn determine the range of habitats available for colonization by algae. Periodicity of flooding is critical in allowing or preventing the establishment of stable communities.

Subtidal algae are those that inhabit some substratum below lowest astronomical tide. These algae are always submerged.

A change in incoming solar radiation is the major factor driving seasonal environmental change. With radiation, the relationship of seasonal change to latitude is obviously very strong, except in the polar regions where there is a constant 100% change. Only at less than 10° latitude is the change small. Between incoming radiation and subtidal algae is found the atmosphere, with its variable weather, and sea water, with its variable transparency (Kain,

1989). At higher latitudes there tends to be more extensive cloud cover in winter; this strengthens the latitudinal effect on incoming radiation. Water transparency varies from place to place and season to season. Light penetration is deeper in summer than in winter. Of course, changes in radiation also affect temperature.

Table 13-1 summarizes certain important factors affecting algae and how they may or may not change with season. The table shows that only light is clearly related to latitude.

Table 13-1 Principal seasonal factors affecting subtidal algae (after Kain, 1989)

Seasonal change	Latitudinal correlation
Light	Strong
Temperature	Weak
Nutrients	None
Disturbance	Perhaps

According to Kain (1987), some subtidal algal species can *anticipate* favourable seasons whereas others *respond* to them. Lüning and Dieck (1989) have termed these algae as Type 2 and Type 1, respectively. Type 1 (season-responders) grow and reproduce while the going is good, i.e., the environment is favourable. Season anticipators grow and reproduce in a strategic annual rhythm suitable for the species; in these, growth occurs as a response to a trigger and not as a response to favourable environmental conditions.

The growth rate of a responder tends to be strongly correlated with light. In contrast, even when irradiance is maximal, the growth of an anticipator is slower than otherwise warranted. Here, any excess organic matter synthesized is stored for the rainy day, to be used for growth in low light during the winter when nutrients are not limiting. The best example for this kind of behaviour is met with in *Laminaria hyperborea* (Lüning, 1971).

The benthic algae grow at the bottom of water bodies, either attached to stones and pebbles (epilithic), mud or sand (epipelic), plants (epiphytic) or animals (epizoic).

The algae found in deserts may live in or on soil, on the lower surfaces of stones and pebbles, and in rock fissures. A few can even penetrate within rocks (e.g., *Hyella*).

Some algae (e.g., *Chlorella*) live endozoically in diverse animals, e.g., protozoa, coelenterates, molluscs, and worms. Zooxanthellae thrive in association with corals in reef communities. *Platymonas* is intimately associated with the flatworm *Convoluta roscoffensis*. *Basicladia* grows attached to turtles and *Characium* to mosquito larvae. Some examples of endophytic algae are *Nostoc* in *Anthoceros*, *Anabaena* in *Azolla*, and *Coleochaete nitellarum* in *Nitella*.

Some algae parasitize certain plants or animals (Table 13-2). *Cephaleuros* parasitizes tea (*Thea sinensis*) and *Ceratocolax* is parasitic on *Phyllophora*. Many red algae show parasitic tendencies.

Certain green (e.g., *Trebouxia*, *Chlorella*) and blue-green (*Nostoc*) algae form symbiotic associations with fungi in several lichens.

Table 13-2 Examples of epiphytic/parasitic algae

Epiphyte/Parasite	Host
Ceramium codicola	*Codium fragile*
Polysiphonia lanosa	*Ascophyllum nodosa*
Smithora naiadum	*Zostera*
Porphyra nereocystis	*Nereocystis luetkeana*
Janczewskia gardneri	*Laurencia spectabilis*
Choreonema thuretii	*Jania rubens*
Harveyella mirabilis	*Rhodomela* spp.
Callocolax globulosis	*Calophyllis flabellulata*
Ceratocolax hartzii	*Phyllophora membranifolia*
Cephaleuros virescens	*Thea sinensis*
Phyllosiphon arisari	*Arisaema*
Dictyosiphon eckmanii	*Scytosiphon* sp.
Bangia ciliaris	*Chaetomorpha* sp.
Notheia anomala	*Hormosira* sp., *Xiphophora* sp.

PARASITIC ALGAE

Some species of the Rhodophyta are parasitic (Table 13-2). They infect red algal hosts only and often seem to be closely related to their hosts; sometimes, the parasite and host belong to the same family. Despite close phylogenetic relations, however, some ultrastructural differences are sometimes seen between the parasite and the host. For instance, freshly released spores of the parasite *Janczewskia morimotoi* contain immature chloroplasts devoid of phycobilisomes and having 6–8 thylakoids, and at certain stages, the apical cells of this parasitic species have chloroplasts with numerous thylakoids as well as phycobilisomes. In the apical cells of the host *Laurencia nipponica*, the chloroplasts always contain 4 or more thylakoids and phycobilisomes. Whereas most stages of the host *Laurencia* have phycobilisomes, this is not so for most stages of its parasite *Janczewskia* (Nonomura and West, 1980).

PATHOGENIC ALGAE

Several pathogens attack algae, and some pathogenic algae can infect certain living organisms. A green alga causes lymphadenitis in cattle (Rogers *et al.*, 1980) and certain other green algae attack angiosperms or cause pathogenesis in molluscs (Naidu, 1971). Morse *et al.* (1977, 1981) have reported that a siphonaceous chlorophyte is associated with tumorous growths in sea fans (*Gorgonia*). Another chlorophyte (*Entocladia endozoica*) appears to cause abnormal growths in corals of the genus *Pseudoplexaura*; this alga *E. endozoica* belongs to the family Ulvellaceae of the order Ulvales (Goldberg *et al.*, 1984). The natural habitat of this alga is the skeleton of the gorgonian coral (*Pseudoplexaura* spp.). Host tissues respond to the presence of *E. endozoica* by producing a capsule made primarily of scleroprotein skeleton and secondarily of calcareous spicules. This skeletal capsule blocks the contact of the alga with host tissue but has to pay a price for such blockade; the skeleton loses much of its tensile strength as well as elasticity. The coral colony breaks apart at the site of the weakened skeleton, thereby exposing the algal filaments to relatively high light fields and to the low nitrogen sea water; these conditions induce the algae to reproduce. Later, the damaged host tissue regenerates and re-seals the capsule with the result that the enclosed algae resume their vegetative growth. It appears that some host-derived amino acids (especially cystine or tyrosine) are involved in regulating reproduction of *Entocladia* (Goldberg *et al.*, 1984).

COMMUNITIES

A community essentially means a collection of species living together on a particular habitat. It is made of populations, each population denoting a collection of individuals of a single species. An association may be defined as an assemblage of species that recurs under comparable ecological conditions in different places. The species within an association interact intimately amongst themselves, although only some species (or even a single species) may be the dominants/subdominants.

Disturbance is an important determinant of community structure and dynamics (Sousa, 1984). Communities are not static but change both structurally and physiologically during succession. This means that disturbance effects may vary with developmental state. Examples of such dependence are found in the effects of wave disturbance on marine intertidal (Paine and Levin, 1981) and freshwater microalgal (Luttenton and Rada, 1986) communities. Community response to disturbance also varies spatially. Environmental patchiness within an ecosystem may affect community structure and function in ways that strengthen or reduce resistance and/or alter the rate and pattern of post-disturbance recovery (Peterson and Stevenson, 1992).

Benthic algal communities in streams are periodically subjected to high-discharge events (Biggs and Close, 1989; Stevenson, 1990). These communities can change considerably in structural and physiological properties (Peterson and Stevenson, 1992) during succession. Thus the degree to which disturbance affects community structure and function can depend both upon disturbance timing as well as intensity.

Lotic algal communities are affected by current (Lamb and Lowe, 1987) which may also influence their response to disturbance. Current can influence algal immigration, emigration, and reproduction as well as attachment strength and community physiognomy. Current-related differences in algal community structure and physiology may sometimes translate into differences in resistance and resilience (Peterson and Stevenson, 1992).

Changes in dominance occurring during benthic algal succession in streams are driven by shifts from species that immigrate rapidly, or those that persist through disturbance but are poor competitors, to species that compete well under conditions of resource limitation within high-density, late successional algal mats (Peterson and Grimm, 1992). In flowing waters, where spatial heterogeneity in current maintains a diversity of habitats and temporal variation in discharge results in periodic disturbance, both of these alternatives represent viable ecological strategies. Variation in disturbance frequency and intensity affects successional patterns, species-dominance hierarchies, and species diversity (Petraitis *et al.*, 1989).

Peterson and Stevenson (1992) have compared the effects of disturbance timing on resistance and resilience of epilithic algal communities growing in fast and slow current outdoor experimental stream channels in Kentucky, U.S.A. that were either left undisturbed (control) over 33 days following a simulated spate, or were subjected to an additional spate after either 9, 18, 27, or 33 days. On day 33, all channels were subjected to a final spate to assess effects of short-term disturbance history on resistance, independently of seasonal influences. Succession proceeded from a sparsely populated community dominated by a small, monoraphid diatom (*Achnanthes minutissima*) immediately after the initial spate, to dominance by dense floating mats of *Mougeotia*, *Spirogyra*, and *Synedra* spp. by day 21–24. Resistance was generally lower in slow-current communities, both in terms of cell-density reduction and displacement of taxonomic structure, than in fast-current communities. Resistance in slow-current communities varied temporally. Slow-current communities with high predisturbance phaeophytin content (an indicator of algal senescence) also changed most in diatom assemblage structure across the final spate. No such relationship was noted in fast current, suggesting that autogenic factors influenced communities in slow current more than those in fast. Resilience was higher in slow-current communities than in fast current, with disturbed communities reaching biomass and taxonomic structure similar to controls after 3–9 days. High resilience in slow current resulted from enhanced reproduction in some populations following spate-induced biomass reduction and presumed release from nutrient and light limitation, and low shear stress relative to fast current channels where biomass accrual was limited by current. Interactions between disturbance timing, successional state, and habitat affect the susceptibility of epilithic algal communities to disturbance and probably influence temporal and spatial heterogeneity in stream ecosystems (Peterson and Stevenson, 1992).

In biological oceanography whereas physical scientists focus first on the 90% similarities among their systems before they pursue the 10% dissimilarity, marine biologists mainly deal with the minute dissimilarities and often tend to give a much less consideration to the strong similarities (Jumars, 1993). Some marine biologists feel that species may be the *noise* of community ecology and that seemingly unpredictable variance of individual species becomes general and predictable when one considers functional groups of organisms; functional groups being defined by a few general and important organismal features such as body plan, behaviour or life history (Hay, 1994).

The foundations of modern community ecology have rested on studying the unique attributes of each species. However, notwithstanding the strong impact and utility of these studies, it has been argued that several species within a community may be so similar as to be functionally equivalent (Sale, 1991; Peters, 1991). According to Hay (1994), if functional groups are based on some ecologically meaningful characteristics then a way may be paved of productively using both the species-specific and the functional-group approaches. The latter approach may be used to see more clearly the large ecological forces that cause changes in distribution, abundance, and diversity of functional groups; and one could then focus critically on the species-specific differences important in determining interactions within a functional group (Hay, 1994).

Feldmann (1937) classified the algal life forms on the basis of their mode of overwintering. He classified algae into (1) annual algae, i.e., those which are found throughout the year, forming one or several generations per year, their zygotes or spores germinate immediately; and (2) perennial algae, i.e., those in which the complete frond is perennial.

The annual algae were subdivided into Ephemerophyceae, Eclipsiophyceae, and Hypnophyceae. *Enteromorpha* exemplifies the Ephemerophyceae which grow confined to one period of the year and are present during the remaining period in a microscopic vegetative phase.

The Eclipsiophyceae, exemplified by many Phaeophyceae, are present during the remaining period as a resting stage. The Hypnophyceae includes many desmids, but it is not known how long desmids persist in nature.

The perennial algae were subdivided into four classes, viz., Phaeophyceae (frond erect, e.g., *Fucus*), Chamaeophyceae (frond a crust, e.g., *Lithophyllum*), Hemiphanerophyceae (only part of the frond persists for several years and part of the erect frond is persistent, e.g., *Cystoseira*), and Hemicryptophyceae (only the basal portion is persistent, e.g., *Cladostephus*).

Round (1981) has proposed that these four classes be renamed to end in phycon. Thus, the new names would be Ephemerophycon, Eclipsiophycon, Hypnophycon, and Hemicryptophycon.

SIZES

The mean spherical diameter of majority of phytoplankton species ranges from about 2 μm to 200 μm (Dussart, 1965). The biomass of phytoplankton cells varies from about 15–15,000 μm^3 $cell^{-1}$. The small cells have a high area/volume ratio and tend to be subspherical or globular, whereas the large cells having a low area/volume ratio are usually irregular in shape.

Dussart (1965) termed the 2–20 μm organisms as nannoplankton, 20–200 μm organisms as microplankton, though other workers have used different ranges (see Malony, 1980). Depending on the mesh size of the plankton net used, the smaller cells which pass through the net have been loosely called nannoplankton, whereas those that are retained by a net have been called the netplankton. Usually, the nannoplankton are more abundant and more productive than the netplankton, especially in oceanic waters where the dominant species consist of the solitary motile coccolithophorids, and the naked dinoflagellates. In contrast, coastal waters and continental shelf tend to be richer in netplankton, e.g., large, chain-forming diatoms and dinoflagellates. An analogous situation prevails in freshwater: oligotrophic lakes are usually rich in nannoplankton, whereas netplankton dominates in eutrophic lakes (Kalff, 1972).

It appears that microzooplankton (<200 μm) and invertebrate larvae mainly feed on the smaller, nannophytoplankton (Beers and Stewart, 1971; Jorgensen, 1966). In contrast, macrozooplankton (e.g., particle grazing copepods) selectively eat large particles when presented with multisized algae (Gaudy, 1974).

The cell size also influences the sinking and suspension of phytoplankton population (Smayda, 1970). The small cells or colonies usually have lower sinking rates as compared to those of bigger organisms. High area/volume ratios facilitate suspension and increase the residence time of small cells in the upper illuminated layers of water. A low area/volume ratio, in contrast, is conducive to sinking and exposes the organisms to environmental gradients. In some cases, this can be advantageous if the alga sinks from a nutrient-depleted upper layer to a nutrient-rich deeper layer of water, for instance.

PHYTOPLANKTON AS PART OF A COMMUNITY

Though turbulence plays an extremely important part in the life of the phytoplankton, it has to be emphasized that the observed activities in a natural water sample are those of a whole community and not just some organisms or only turbulence.

Phytoplankton is customarily regarded as the base of the trophic structure of the pelagic ecosystem and dominant in biomass and metabolic activity. In recent years it has become evident that heterotrophic bacterioplankton is usually commensurate with phytoplankton in biomass and that the chemical environment of the phytoplankton must be largely determined by the activities of this other fraction. The picophytoplankton rely on regeneration of mineral nutrients via bacteria and phagotrophic flagellates and the bacteria in turn depend on the release of extracellular products by phytoplankton. There is the rather paradoxical situation that by releasing organic matter phytoplankton stimulates its chief competitors for scarce mineral nutrients. Bjornsen (1988) regarded such release as an inevitable loss by passive diffusion and described the bacteria as ectoparasites rather than mutualists.

ALGAE AS ECOLOGICAL INDICATORS

Though most workers tend to use micro- and macrofauna for assessment of water quality stress, recent years have seen some interest in algae for this purpose (see Schubert, 1984). The algae occupy a unique position among primary producers: they constitute an important link in the food chain and are essential to the economy of marine and freshwater environments as food organisms. The factors influencing rise, fall, and changes in algal populations, their interactions with other organisms, and the effects of man upon their habitat are prominent ecological problems. Some algae are now being increasingly used in laboratory bioassays with a view to gaining relevant information about the availability of nutrients and other chemicals to algae and their different stimulatory and inhibitory effects. The importance of the use of algal bioassays as indicators of ecological changes is being gradually established. Synchronously growing cultures of the green alga *Selenastrum* are used in a standard algal assay test for freshwater system. A qualitative approach, based on some particular group of algae, such as the blue-greens, or diatoms, can often be employed in direct toxicity or taste, odour, and filter clogging problems. In marine habitats, some seaweed species can be used as bioindicators of pollution. Seaweeds are strong bioaccumulators of minerals and their use as continuous sampling monitors for pollutants in coastal waters is now becoming fairly popular (see Schubert, 1984).

Some algae are suitable organisms for monitoring heavy metals in water (Rai *et al.*, 1981; Whitton, 1975). Whitton recommends *Cladophora glomerata*, *C. fracta*, and *Lemanea fluviatilis* as indicator organisms for field work.

Certain industrial establishments in the U.S.A. now routinely use algal bioassays for determining the changes in N and P loading, effects on streams receiving effluents, and monitoring of heavy metals and pesticides.

INDIAN WORK ON FRESHWATER ALGAE

The phytoplankton and periphyton communities have been studied in some Indian rivers, e.g., Ganga, Yamuna, Hooghly, Cauvery, Gomati, Sone, and Moosi. Very few detailed studies have been made on any single river, and the published work is more of the nature of preliminary surveys and isolated research here and there.

In general, the prevailing temperatures as well as light intensity are fairly high in many parts of the Indian plains, and these are conducive to good growth of algae. The pH values of most Indian rivers exceed 7 and may be as high as 9. Some rivers, e.g., Jhelum, have hard water with total alkalinity values of more than 60 ppm. The Gomati has carbonate content varying from 0 ppm to 43 ppm with the higher values prevailing in winter and late summer and the lower values during the monsoons and early summer (Prasad and Singh, 1980). The sewage polluted zones of the Gomati have higher concentrations of bicarbonates as compared to nonpolluted parts. A similar relation holds for chloride content also, and some workers feel that high chloride content in a river may be a good indicator of pollution. The dissolved oxygen concentration tends to show an inverse relation with organic or sewage pollution, reaching the lowest values (around 0) in heavily polluted water (Tiwari, 1983).

Increasing pollution is generally accompanied by decrease in the nitrate content of many river waters but in some cases the nitrate content increases with increasing pollution. Discharge of sewage into a river often causes a rise in the ammonia concentration of its water. The magnesium content of the Gomati ranges from 6 ppm to 50 ppm, the higher values obtaining in sewage polluted water, especially during summer. Sewage pollution also causes high total hardness in water.

The work done on river algae has tended to show that, in general, the density of total algae is highest in August-October and in February-March, and is lowest in May to August.

The largest number of studies on Indian algae have been made on the blue-green algae. These are characteristic of waters receiving high nutrient inputs, yet the maximum in algal biomass occurs when the dissolved nutrient concentrations are low. The blue-greens have a high affinity for phosphorus and can outcompete other algae when nutrients are low (Shapiro, 1973). Most workers have found that these algae grow best at high temperatures when the organic matter availability is high and the dissolved oxygen is low. This last point has assumed much significance during the past few years when the pre-eminent role of anaerobic conditions in the growth and multiplication of several blue-greens was properly appreciated.

In the Gomati, the blue-green algae are negatively correlated with total hardness, diatoms, and Euglenophyceae, but are positively related with low transparency and the calcium and ammonia contents of the water.

Unlike the Cyanophyceae, the Chlorophyceae grow better in low organic matter and high dissolved oxygen. The desmids and Chlorococcales seem to be favoured by high temperature, high light intensity, low oxidizable organic matter, low nitrate content, and low sewage pollution. The green algae tend to predominate during the winter and early summer and are scarce during the monsoons.

The Bacillariophyceae (diatoms) commonly attain their maximum in December-January and are scarce during monsoons and summer. In the Ganga, a higher summer maximum and a lower winter maximum have been reported. The diatoms seem to be favoured by low prevailing temperatures. Silica is generally believed to be another important factor regulating diatom numbers, but the work of Prasad and Singh (1980) does not support this conclusion. In the Hooghly, the planktonic diatoms have been found to be inversely related to the phosphate content of water but directly related to dissolved oxygen content.

Pollution phycology has attracted much interest in recent years and some research findings are now available for Indian waters. The algal communities of the river Moosi have been surveyed with reference to pollution status of river zones with special reference to such parameters as temperature, organic matter, dissolved oxygen content, nitrate content, iron content, and current speed. Sewage contamination is indicated by the dominance of such algae as *Oscillatoria*, *Stigeoclonium*, *Pinnularia*, *Cyclotella*, *Nitzschia*, and *Navicula*. Mildly polluted zones have *Gomphonema*, and oxygen-rich waters harbour *Achnanthes*.

Some important lakes and several village ponds, temple tanks, and other standing water bodies have also been surveyed. The Ramgarh Tal and Suraha Tal, both in Uttar Pradesh, are the best studied examples of lakes. In these lakes, the water pH prevails between 8 and

10 and the waters remain quite rich in nitrates and phosphates. The highly alkaline waters also, in general, tend to be richer in total dissolved solids as compared to less alkaline waters. The chloride content of many lentic waters increases in summer and falls in winter.

In general, phosphates do not limit algal growth in Indian water bodies, though their concentration fluctuates in different seasons, being low in winter and high in the monsoons. The phosphate content of water often becomes very low, coinciding with the maximum development of a blue-green algal bloom; in such a system, the phosphate present in water moves from the water into the algal cells, from where, of course, it may be recycled when the cells die.

The nitrate content of various lakes and ponds has been found to vary considerably. Ramgarh Tal has 0.008–0.89 ppm. The higher values are realized immediately after floods and rainfall. In a Hyderabad pond, the nitrate content can sometimes exceed 10 ppm. Still higher values have been recorded from some ponds in South India.

With the prevailing atmospheric temperatures being rather high, the dissolved oxygen content of lentic water tends to remain low, the actual values ranging from zero ppm to 12 ppm in different areas and seasons. When the dissolved oxygen is low, the ammonia content tends to increase. Likewise, soluble organic matter tends to be inversely related to dissolved oxygen.

In general, strongly alkaline waters are infested with thick algal blooms, especially during the summer months. In the Ramgarh Tal, one phytoplankton maximum occurs in Sept-Oct and another in Dec-Jan. The Suraha Tal shows a single peak in Feb. In both cases, the total phytoplankton goes hand in hand with suspended solids.

The Kashmir State has oligotrophic lakes that show ephemeral thermal stratification and are poor in phytoplankton. But some parts of these lakes are now experiencing eutrophication. In the eutrophic Dal Lake, the peak growth of diatoms occurs in Jan-Feb, of green algae in Aug, of euglenoids and Dinophyceae in Aug-Sept, and of blue-greens in Oct. Out of all these various groups, the diatoms are commonly dominant, sometimes exhibiting a second, smaller peak in October.

SOIL ALGAE

The algae constitute an important component of the soil microflora. They act as a reserve for plant nutrients, influence soil structure, influence the activities of other organisms, and contribute to the organic carbon and fixed nitrogen status of the soil through their photosynthesis and nitrogen fixation.

Many soil algal species are ubiquitous in distribution and there are no characteristic algal associations formed in any particular geographical region or soil type in the world. In general, the blue-green algae do not occur in soils of pH less than 4. Many green and other eucaryotic algae, however, can grow in soils of pH less than 4, as well as in soils of higher pH.

Solar radiation, water, and temperature are the more important abiotic factors regulating the distribution, metabolism, and life histories of soil algae, whereas ionic factors, e.g., pH, redox potential, and soil texture are somewhat less important factors (Metting, 1981).

In the soil profile, most algal growth is thought to be confined to the upper few mm or cm, and the subterranean flora mainly includes resting stages or inactive cells carried along with the seepage water, agricultural activity, root growth, or soil animals. Several workers have recorded the microstratification of algal populations within the upper few mm or cm of soil profiles, rocks, or gravel deposits (see Friedmann and Galun, 1974; Metting, 1981). The upper 1.5 cm zone of various British soils harbours diverse populations of several green and yellow-green algae (Broady, 1979).

In semiarid environments, examination of soil has shown that the upper surface tends to be colonized mainly by the Cyanophyceae (0–2 cm), whereas the greatest cell numbers of Chlorophyceae and Bacillariophyceae occur at 4–6 cm depths (Nordin and Blinn, 1972). More recent work of Schubert (1984) on the same soils previously studied by Nordin and Blinn (1972) has shown that soil algae fluctuate with the growing season and soil profile.

The Cyanophyceae dominate in deserts, forming surface crusts. The Oscillatoriaceae are common in cultivated and noncultivated desert in Arizona, whereas the other cyanophytes are common in virgin or fallow areas (Cameron, 1963). In the lsraeli Negev desert, Friedmann *et al.* (1967) found the Chlorophyceae to be dominant, and the blue-greens, yellow-greens, and diatoms to be less common. In the coastal areas of Texas, the green and blue-green algae are the most common and most diverse (Dykstra *et al.*, 1975). In several tropical regions, *Chlamydomonas* spp. are ubiquitous, and *Schizothrix calcicola* is one of the most common blue-greens.

Filamentous cyanophytes are some of the most abundantly occurring forms in the polar regions of the Antarctica. The algae also constitute an important component of tundra soil (Cameron *et al.*, 1978). The upper 2 cm of tundra soil contains many green, blue-green, and yellow-green algae. In India, Marathe (1969) studied the algal flora of cultivated soils from Jalgaon and found that these soils were quite poor in supporting algal populations.

The algae are important in stabilizing the soil through aggregation of soil particles. They contribute to soil nutrients, especially nitrogen. Crusts of Cyanophyceae aid in the retention of silt and clay that produce a rearrangement of soil particles. These crusts greatly increase organic carbon and nitrogen contents of the soil, improve water infiltration, decrease erosion, and furnish a suitable habitat for seed germination (see Starks *et al.*, 1981).

Studies of several workers on the ecogenesis of the Surtsey Island, Iceland, formed by volcanic eruption in 1963, have demonstrated that the blue-green algae are the primary colonizers but are soon succeeded by coccoid green algae.

The terrestrial blue-greens and other soil algae show good adaptations to live and grow in those climates and microenvironments in which available water is the main limiting factor, and some soil algae can survive very long periods without water. In soils other than those in which water is the primary limiting factor, algal growth is largely influenced by the temperature range. Species of *Stichococcus*, *Microcoleus*, and *Schizothrix* have a marked capacity to resist extremely low temperatures (even –150°C) in crushed soil. Likewise, many soil algae when dry can tolerate abnormally high temperatures; thus, *Scytonema* is known to tolerate short exposure to 110°C, whereas *Spongiochloris typica* cells can survive a year in air-dried soil that has been dried in an oven at 100°C (see Trainor and McLean, 1964).

Neutral and weakly or moderately alkaline soils provide good conditions for the development of blue-green algae; these algae and some diatoms can tolerate fairly high ionic strengths. Nitrogen-fixing blue-green algae generally grow better and fix more nitrogen in water-logged soils as compared to oxidizing or aerobic soils (Fogg *et al.*, 1973).

According to McCann and Cullimore (1979), various pesticides influence soil algae both *in vitro* and *in vivo*. Pre-emergent herbicides tend to affect the range of algal genera and the number of algal cells present at a time of accelerating algal activity in the soil. These herbicides produce a more adverse effect on algal growth rates than do post-emergent herbicides. The blue-greens, which are mainly surface inhabitants, are particularly vulnerable.

Nutritionally, most soil algae appear to be photoautotrophic but some are photoauxotrophic. Whereas the former group can synthesize all their organic compounds from inorganic materials, using energy from sunlight, the photoauxotrophic algae can utilize sunlight as energy source but are unable to manufacture all their organic compounds from inorganic materials. Some soil algae are facultatively photoheterotrophic or chemoheterotrophic (Khoja and Whitton, 1971). Good examples of facultative photoheterotrophy are met with among the blue-green algae and the diatoms. Many chlorophytan and xanthophytan algae are facultatively chemoheterotrophic.

Parker (1960, 1961) has discussed the various types of biotic interactions of algae with other organisms. These phenomena include amensalism, competition, commensalism, protocooperation, parasitism, and neutralism. One good example of such biotic interacting systems is furnished by the system comprising the nitrogen-fixing blue-green algae, other microorganisms (Fig. 13-2), and the paddy plants, in a tropical paddy field. Another well known example of biotic interaction is that involving *Azotobacter* and other bacteria that grow within the mucilage sheaths of such blue-green algae as *Rivularia* and *Nostoc*.

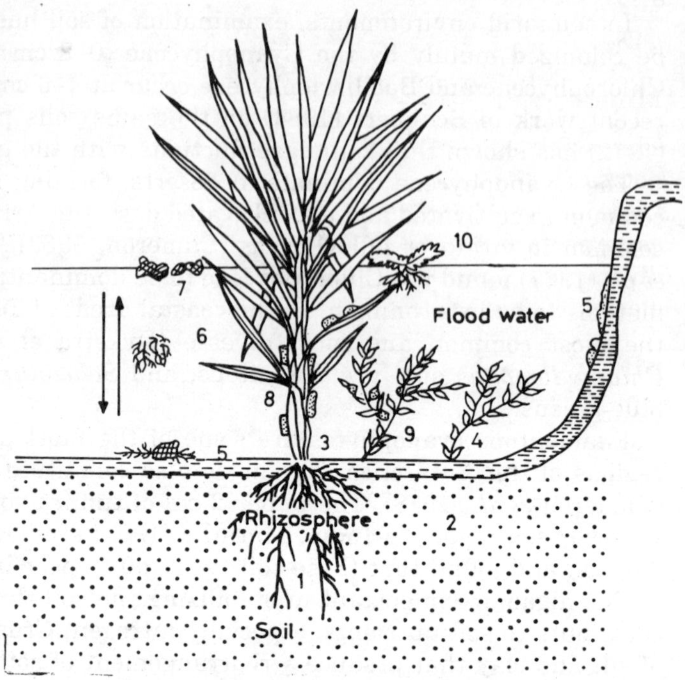

Fig. 13-2 Environment and nitrogen fixation in a rice field. 1–4, N_2-fixing bacteria: 1, associated with roots; 2, in soil; 3, epiphytic on rice; 4, epiphytic on weeds. 5–9, cyanobacteria: 5, at soil-water surface; 6, free-floating; 7, at air-water interface; 8, epiphytic on rice; 9, epiphytic on weeds. 10, *Azolla*. (After Roger and Watanabe, 1986.)

Soil algae act as energy sources for protozoa, nematodes, snails, insects, and earthworms. *Pinnularia*, *Navicula*, *Calothrix*, *Phormidium*, and other algae have been recorded from the guts of earthworms (Atlavinyte and Pociene, 1974). The decomposition products of dead algae are used as nutrients by saprophytic microbes.

ALGAE AS INDICATORS OF SOIL FERTILITY

Moisture, temperature, light, soil texture, and the chemical composition of the soil are some important factors which influence the growth of soil algae. The physical characteristics are governed by the relatively stable conditions of climate and/or natural soil structure. The chemical quality of the soil is determined by its composition and biota but may also be influenced by agricultural practices. Fertilizers added to the soil change the balance of mineral nutrients, and pesticide use may result in an accumulation of toxic residues. The composition of the soil microflora may also be altered; this may be undesirable in view of the fact that microorganisms have an important role in soil fertility. Some aspects of soil chemistry governing algal growth are the following.

Mineral Nutrients

The nutritional requirements of the algae for the major elements (calcium, magnesium, potassium, carbon, nitrogen, phosphorus, sulphur) are the same as those of higher plants. Certain trace elements (iron, manganese, silicon, zinc, copper, cobalt, molybdenum) are also essential. The availability of these nutrients has an important influence on both algal species diversity and biomass (assuming that moisture, temperature, and light are not limiting). Some elements may be limiting (usually P) or inhibitory.

pH

Nearly neutral or slightly alkaline soils support the most varied algal flora. Members of the Chlorophyceae are usually found in soils of a wide pH range. The Bacillariophyceae and the Cyanophyceae are less well represented in acid soils. Growth of blue-greens is extremely rare below a pH of 5. This probably accounts for the abundance of blue-greens in arid soils which are all alkaline.

Both the nutrient status of the soil and its pH can change greatly by the application of fertilizers. The quality of the soil and the algae populations is also affected by the introduction of toxicants into the soil. The most important of these are the pesticides.

Pesticides

Many soil algae are susceptible to pesticides, especially herbicides (Table 13-3).

ALGAL ASSAY FOR SOIL QUALITY

Chemical determination of soil elements, and particularly of pesticides, is frequently time-consuming and expensive, requiring elaborate extraction procedures and analytical techniques. In contrast, algal assays generally require limited amount of equipment and can be conducted rapidly and simply. Also chemical procedures generally determine the total concentration in the soil of the material in question. This amount is not necessarily that available for uptake by the plant, and consequently does not provide information concerning its potential toxicity (of pesticides, etc.) or benefits (from plant nutrients) to plant growth. These determinations may therefore be less useful than bioassays in evaluating the quality of the soil as it affects agriculture. However, bioassays can often fail to distinguish between related chemicals, for example, pesticides and their transformation products.

For an assay procedure to be accepted as a standard, it must be simple, reliable, and inexpensive. Consequently, methods that involve either filter paper placed on the surface of the soil or implanted microscope slides are preferable to more elaborate procedures. The assay organism should preferably be isolated from the soil and have the following properties:

(1) The ability to tolerate a wide range of environmental conditions.

Table 13-3 Toxicity of some pesticides to soil algae (condensed from Pipe and Schubert, 1984)

Pesticides	Toxicity level							
	*In vivo**				*In vitro*			
	1	2	3	4	1	2	3	4
Picloram, siduron, 2,4,S-T, TCA, methabenzthiazuron	+							
Diuron, monuron		+						
Atrazine, linuron, mancozeb, metribuzin, pentachlorophenol, TCA			+					
2,4-D, simazine				+				
Barban, ceresan, chloranils, 2,4-D, diphenamid, malathion, solan, vapam					+			
Diquat, fenuron, fluometuron, linuron, metribuzin, monuron, neburon						+		
Amitrol-T, atrazine, BHC, 2,4-D, dalapon, dinoseb, diquat, paraquat, picloram, propanil, simazine, TCA							+	
Amitrol-T, atronzine, bromoxynil, ceresan, DDT, diquat, methoxeychlor, siduron, 2,4,S-T								+

*1, no toxicity; 2, toxic to some algae at less than 0.1 ppm; 3, toxic to some algae at field application levels of 0.1–5 ppm; 4, toxic to most algae at more than 5 ppm.
Some pesticides fall into different classes because a wide range of results have been reported by different workers.

(2) A growth potential correlating closely with that of algae indigenous to the sample being examined.

(3) A growth potential varying widely with different environments.

(4) Qualities permitting accurate and rapid monitoring of its growth.

SUCCESSION

The algae contribute to soil formation as well as to the fertility of mature soils. They are often the first organisms to colonize bare rocks or other newly-created or exposed substrata. They enhance the weathering of silicates by promoting water retention and by creating weakly acidic conditions as a result of their photosynthesis. Lithophytic algae are greatly influenced by moisture content, insolation, and the nature of the substrate. In highly arid regions, succession is often arrested at the stage of primary colonization by algae, mosses, and lichens. The alga *Gloeocapsa* is the commonest genus found in chasmolithic communities in flint and plutonic rocks and endolithic microhabitats in African deserts. In contrast, most dolomitic and calcareous substrates are dominated by filamentous blue-greens and coccoid green algae.

The algae also contribute greatly to organic carbon and nitrogen levels in secondary community succession. According to Metting (1981), there are no algal species which operate specifically as pioneer algae in secondary succession but some instances are known where seasonal variations within algal communities occur in response to agricultural operations or other disturbances; one good example of this is the annual succession of algae in tropical rice fields.

PRODUCTIVITY AND PRODUCTION

Primary algal productivity is the rate at which algae synthesize organic matter during photosynthesis. Of the gross (total) primary productivity, some portion is respired during metabolism, another portion is excreted as organic carbon, and the remainder increases the algal biomass. The latter two fractions make up the net primary production that is available to the rest of the community. In land plants, about one-half of the fixed carbon may be lost through respiration but this loss is much less in algae in view of the fact that, unlike higher plants, the algae have very little heterotrophic (nonphotosynthetic) tissue. The amount of carbon excreted by phytoplankton is commonly less than 20% of net productivity (Fogg, 1983); this value may be higher in some marine algae.

Primary productivity is usually expressed as gram carbon m^{-2} day^{-1}, or gram carbon m^{-3} day^{-1}, or as kcal m^{-2} yr^{-1}.

Productivity is not to be confused with standing crop biomass; the latter does not consider the time factor and the usually high growth rates of algae. In an algal bloom that has exhausted the ambient nutrient supply, for instance, standing crop is often high though productivity is low. Conversely, in a planktonic system with abundance of grazers, the standing crop of algae can be quite low even with a high specific growth rate and productivity; this occurs because of a rapid turnover of nutrients (Harlin and Darley, 1988).

Productivity is sometimes expressed in terms of yield, as gram m^{-2} day^{-1}. Maximum yields are usually obtained at intermediate densities and growth rates because maximum growth rates tend to occur at lower densities; at high densities, the growth rate becomes low because of increased competition for nutrients and light (Harlin and Darley, 1988). In fact it is these two factors that are probably most important determinants of algal productivity in nature. Changes in irradiance and nutrient supply, along with temperature changes, lead to seasonality in both primary and secondary productivity (Harlin and Darley, 1988). Algal growth is necessarily limited to surface waters due to the fairly rapid attenuation of light energy in the water column. However, some benthic seaweeds are capable of growing in the extremely low light, as they live 200 metres deep in the ocean, at 0.01% of the ambient surface irradiation (Littler *et al.*, 1985). In some subtropical oceanic areas, nutrient limitation is responsible for the low primary productivity values; in general, nitrogen tends to be limiting in marine ecosystems whereas phosphorus is more often limiting in freshwaters. (Silicon deficiency appears to be important in limiting spring blooms of diatoms both in marine and freshwater systems.)

During 1980s seaweed ecologists noted that algal morphology and anatomy were correlated with such important characteristics as productivity, thallus longevity, and susceptibility to herbivory. This allowed seaweeds to be placed into polyphyletic functional groups with similar ecological characteristics, and often with similar responses to perturbations such as turbulence, desiccation or herbivory. These functional groups differed from guilds in being based on those morphological traits which influenced ecological performance, rather than on similarity in resource use.

It appears that productivity and disturbance potential may have a disproportionately strong effect on the structure of algal communities and that these structuring processes impinge on seaweeds in a form-specific manner. Productivity potential of a site is determined by factors contributing to the maximum possible rate of biomass production (light, nutrients, desiccation, and turbulence). Disturbance potential is likewise determined by factors controlling the maximum possible rate of biomass loss.

The algae increase soil fertility through their photosynthesis and nitrogen fixation. Some estimates of primary production by soil algae range from 0.5–1.4 tons of organic matter per hectare in a Russian soil, to 6 tons of organic matter per million pounds of soil in an American soil (see Metting, 1981).

Nitrogen fixation by soil algae has been well studied in Japan, India, the Philippines, U.K., former U.S.S.R., U.S.A., and several other countries. Henriksson *et al.* (1975) found that at least in laboratory experiments, Swedish temperate soils possessed a greater nitrogen fixation capacity (about 2 μ gram nitrogen fixed/gram soil/hr) as compared to Indian tropical soils (0.45 μ gram nitrogen fixed/gram soil/hr). According to these workers, temperate soils, whether cultivated or not, also harbour more active populations of nitrogen-fixing algae as compared to tropical soils. The growth of nitrogen-fixing algae is generally greater and better on moistener soils in both tropical and temperate soils.

Inoculation of paddy fields with nitrogen-fixing algae is known to increase yields of rice by as much as 30 per cent in China, Vietnam, Japan, Egypt, former U.S.S.R., and India.

The algae are also known to improve (or reclaim) certain barren (alkaline or saline) soils in India (Singh, 1961). Natural algal succession in sugarcane and maize fields as well as grasslands is quite important as a source of green manure. Several workers have studied the effects of insecticides and herbicides on soil algae and have reported inhibitory, stimulatory, or no influence of these biocides. Commonly, herbicides and fungicides inhibit algal growth and multiplication but insecticides usually do not. Some algae absorb or decompose biocides (see Wright, 1978). Thus, species of *Chlorella* are known to absorb and metabolize 2,4-D, dieldrin, lindane, malathion, parathion, etc. The algae are now being increasingly utilized as bioassay organisms for anticipating crop response to both fertilizers and biocides because of their biochemical similarity to angiosperms and their faster growth (Metting, 1981).

RIVER PERIPHYTON METABOLISM

Periphyton is the complex of algae, bacteria, fungi, polysaccharides, enzymes, and detritus. It can process organic material and fix energy by photosynthesis. Geology, climate, stream morphology, and season determine the relative importance of the periphyton in the flow of organic energy in undisturbed lotic ecosystems. Human impacts affect water quality and hydrodynamics, and hence the metabolism of periphyton (Uehlinger and Brock, 1991).

A frequently used method to assess periphyton primary productivity and respiration is to enclose periphyton samples in transparent respiration chambers and to monitor the change in dissolved O_2, CO_2, or to measure the flux of radiotracers, typically ^{14}C or ^{32}P. A modification of the chamber method has been developed by Uehlinger and Brock (1991) and has the potential for application to different systems.

The system (Fig. 13-3) consists of several continuous-flow-through respiration chambers, which can be operated simultaneously. Chamber volume and throughput rate can be adjusted to optimize differences in oxygen concentration. Measurements can be performed with either artificial or natural substrata. Extrapolation of chamber data to the real system is affected by the assessment and simulation of *in situ* conditions of light and current patterns and by the high variability in biomass and activity. It is likely that future developments in automation of chamber operation and data analysis result in a standardized and simple procedure for metabolic measurements.

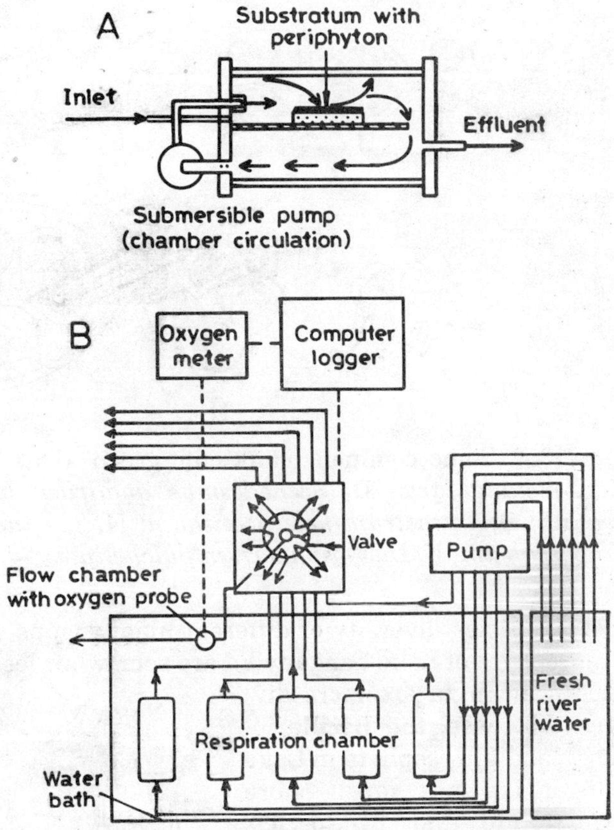

Fig. 13-3 A, sketch of the flow-through respiration chamber; B, sketch of apparatus for measuring periphyton metabolism. (After Uehlinger and Brock, 1991.)

PHYTOPLANKTON

Phytoplankton is mainly made of euplankton, i.e., the permanently floating community of the open water. Some accidental plankters may be washed into the plankton and are called pseudoplankton or tychoplankton. The floating community at the water-air interface is called the neuston. Trypton or obioseston comprises those floating organisms which develop on suspended particulate organic matter or detritus. Seston refers to both the living plankton and the trypton.

The algae constitute an important and sizable fraction of the plankton (Fig. 13-4) in lakes both in tropical and temperate zones. Many studies have been made on the phytoplankton, hydrology, and productivities of Lake Victoria, Lake Tanganyika, Lakes Huron, Erie, and Ontario, Lake Superior, Lake George, and several other large lakes throughout the world (Talling, 1966; Lewis, 1978a, b; Hecky and Kling, 1981). Some 50–100 species of phytoplankton have been recorded in the tropical lakes of insular Southeast Asia. In general, the chrysophytes are rare or absent in most tropical lakes but these algae do occur in Lake Tanganyika, possibly because of the fairly oligotrophic status of the latter as compared to the eutrophic status of many other tropical lakes. Both chrysophytes and cryptophytes are abundantly represented in the plankton of the markedly oligotrophic lakes of northwestern Ontario in Canada.

The eucaryotic algae include both flagellated and nonflagellated forms, the latter being more dominant in both freshwater and marine phytoplankton than the flagellated algae, especially in species larger than 10 μm. The diatoms, for instance, constitute the most important and dominant algae in both freshwater and marine habitats, whereas the desmids and chlorococcalean green algae are equally important in many freshwater habitats.

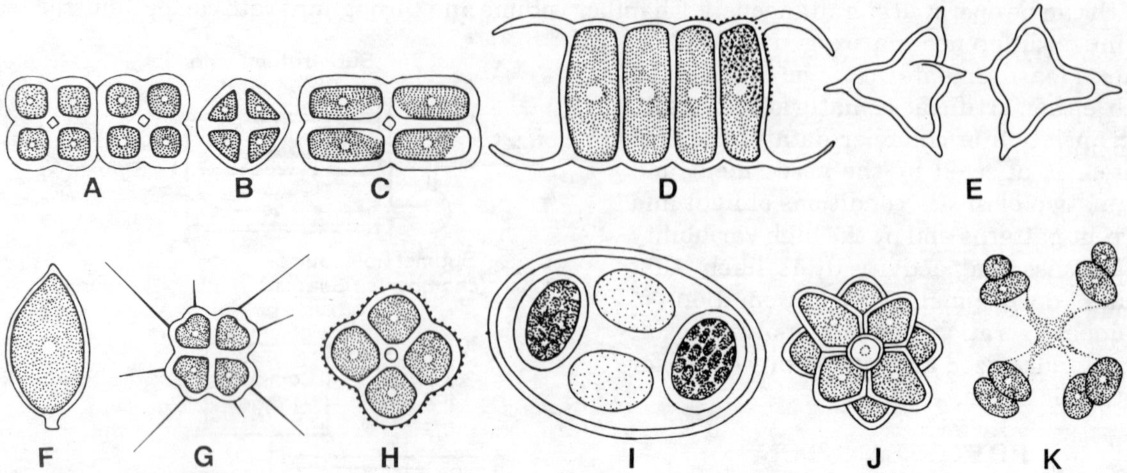

Fig. 13-4 Some common planktonic green algae. A, *Crucigenia quadrata*; B, *C. tetrapedia*; C, *C. rectangularis*; D, *Scenedesmus quadricauda*; E, *Tetraedron regulare*; F, *Characium braunii*; G, *Tetrastrum heteracanthum*; H, *T. punctatum*; I, *Oocystis elliptica*; J, *Coelastrum proboscideum*; K, *Dictyosphaerium pulchellum*.

The species diversity of different algal groups varies in different lakes. For instance, the Chlorophyta of Lake Tanganyika are somewhat less diverse than that of Lake Lanao, whereas the Cyanophyta are more diverse. Likewise, the Bacillariophyta and Chrysophyta in Lake Tanganyika are much more diverse (18 and 13 species, respectively) than those (4 and 1) in Lake Lanao (Hecky and Kling, 1981).

Planktonic desmids normally occur only in calcium-poor waters. However, algal distributions are governed not by one but by a combination of factors. Thus, calcium content also depends on pH and the bicarbonate content of water.

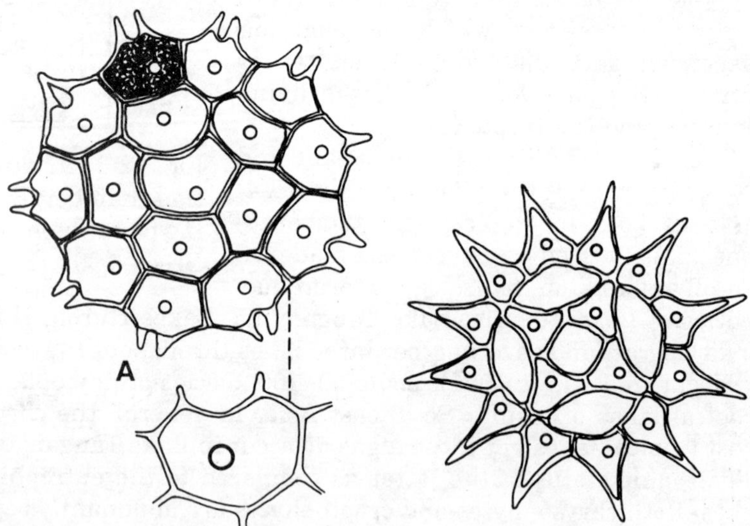

Fig. 13-5 *Pediastrum*, a common planktonic alga. A, *P. boryanum*, coenobium; B, *P. boryanum*, cell; C, *P. simplex*, coenobium.

The diatom *Fragilaria capucina* grows better when the Ca : Mg ratio exceeds 1 and the monovalent : divalent ionic ratio is low. In contrast, some species of *Synura* grow better when mono : di ratio is high and concentration of local solids is low.

The diatoms are often abundant in calcareous waters with mono : di ratio of less than 1.5.

The work on Russian fish ponds has illustrated the relative importance of K or Na. The addition of potassium phosphate changes the dominance of algal population from blue-greens to desmids. The addition of sodium phosphate disintegrates the colonies of *Microcystis* and *Aphanizomenon*, but this does not happen when potassium phosphate is applied.

Although most eutrophic lakes are dominated by cyanophycean blooms, some are dominated by the Chlorococcales. For instance, Lake Arreso in Denmark is a highly eutrophic, shallow lake of some 40 km^2 area, mean depth 3 m, unstratified except when covered by ice, and in which nitrogen and phosphorus are never limiting phytoplankton growth. This lake is dominated throughout the year by chlorococcalean green algae such as *Chlorella vulgaris*, *Scenedesmus* spp., and *Pediastrum* spp. (Fig. 13-5 A–C). Although cyanophyceans such as *Anabaena flos-aquae* and *Aphanothece clathrata* are also common, especially in August and September, they never dominate over the Chlorococcales. Cryptomonads, dinoflagellates, chrysophytes, and desmids are very rare, if found at all. Some diatoms occur but are quite less frequent. The important question that arises is: why is such a highly eutrophic lake a green algal lake and not a blue-green algal lake? While discussing this, Shapiro (1973) demonstrated that the dominance of phytoplankton in a nutrient-rich pond could be switched from blue-greens to Chlorococcales by adding free CO_2 and by lowering the pH of the water. In Lake Arreso, carbon is never limiting and therefore the pH generally remains rather low (i.e., below the optimum pH range for blue-greens). Reynolds and Walsby (1975) stated that chlorococcaleans tend to oust blue-green algae in nutrient-rich lakes with a high ratio between lake circumference and its volume. Possibly, the pH in such lakes remains stabilized by means of atmospheric CO_2 because of a large ratio between surface area and lake volume.

The mean concentrations of chlorophyll-a give a good indication of the biomass of phytoplankton in the euphotic zones of lakes, and are commonly estimated by limnologists to get an idea of the phytoplankton in a lake. These concentrations tend to be low in oligotrophic lakes and high in eutrophic ones. Some reported concentrations (approximate) for different lakes are: 3 mg/m^3 in Lake Victoria, 1.8 mg/m^3 in Lakes Huron, Erie, and Ontario, and 0.9 mg/m^3 in Lakes Superior and Tanganyika. Lake Tanganyika shows a greater relative annual range between maximum and minimum phytoplankton and chlorophyll-a concentrations than other tropical lakes and the temperate Great lakes. Chlorophyll-a ranges from 0.1 mg/m^3 to 4.5 mg/m^3 in the euphotic zone and between 0.2 and 20.4 in surface waters, whereas the phytoplankton biomass ranges from 25–1570 mg/m^3 in the euphotic zone. The annual mean concentrations are among the lowest known, 140 mg/m^3 for phytoplankton biomass and 1.2 mg/m^3 for chlorophyll-a (Hecky and Kling, 1981).

Studies of seasonal cycles and succession of phytoplankton also furnish valuable information about a lake. In Lake Tanganyika, the seasonal cycle of phytoplankton in the euphotic zone has been divided into three phases, based on algal abundance and species succession and coinciding with corresponding phases of annual thermal stratification. These three phases are (1) low biomass and stable species composition from mid-February through April; (2) intermediate biomass with species replacements among the chrysophytes and diatoms from May through mid-September; and (3) highest biomass accompanied by pronounced waxing and waning of *Anabaena* and certain other algae from mid-September through November (Hecky and Kling, 1981). In this lake, the phytoplankton biomass can be as low as 60 mg/m^3 during the phase of stable stratification and can become as high as 930 mg/m^3 at the end of the period of deep mixing. *Nitzschia* and other diatoms attain their abundance only during the period of mixing, while *Anabaena* sp. and other blue-greens become prominent at times of surface warming.

A broadly similar pattern has been reported for Lake Victoria (Talling, 1966) but there are a few differences also. For instance, the only flagellate recorded from Victoria is *Ceratium*, whereas a *Melosira* found abundantly in Victoria is absent in Tanganyika. Lake Victoria has abundant populations of diatoms and large filamentous blue-greens throughout the year but in Tanganyika, these populations were mostly seasonal, virtually vanishing for most part of the year. Another difference relates to desmids which are more prominent in Victoria than in Tanganyika.

When the same lake is studied by different workers and at different times, the data obtained for a particular parameter often differ. Some recent estimates of primary production and biomass in some tropical lakes are those of Hecky and Fee (1981) and are given in Table 13-4.

Table 13-4 Annual averages of biomass, daily integral production, and algal growth rate for euphotic zones of some well studied tropical lakes (from Hecky and Fee, 1981)

Lake	Biomass (gram carbon/m²)	Daily integral production (gram carbon/m²/day)	Growth rate (*K*/day)	
			Mean	Range
Tanganyika	0.59	0.8	0.9	0.1–3.1
Lanao	1.47	1.7	0.56	0.15–2.0
Titicaca	2.4	1.45	0.47	0.16–0.56
George	30	4.5	0.14	?

Rather curiously, though Lake Tanganyika is fairly oligotrophic and harbours a rather low algal biomass, its fish production is quite high. The lake shows an anomalously high carbon efficiency transfer from primary production to fish production (Hecky and Fee, 1981). The basis underlying this high efficiency is not clearly understood. According to Oglesby (1977), annual primary production is a better predictor of annual fish yields from lakes than any other relationship between yield and environmental variables, but his conclusion is not accepted by Hecky and Fee as it fails to account for the unusually high yields of fishes coupled with rather low primary production values.

The reproductive rate of a local algal population is ultimately determined by the combined net effect of limiting nutrients, major ions, pH, and other physical factors. Nutrients constitute one of the major variables controlling phytoplankton community structure and biomass. The relationship between phosphorus concentration and chlorophyll (Dillon and Rigler, 1974) suggests that *phosphorus*, *nitrogen*, and *silicon* often become limiting resources. Phosphorus additions to lakes increase algal *biomass*, whereas the proportions of such added nutrients as N and P dramatically influence the algal species composition.

In freshwater habitats, phytoplankton population dynamics are greatly affected by the availability of P and other nutrients (Fig. 13-6). Phosphorus is the key biomass-limiting nutrient in many lakes, and kinetic studies (e.g., Rhee, 1972) have demonstrated that heterotrophic bacteria are better competitors than are phytoplankton for dissolved inorganic

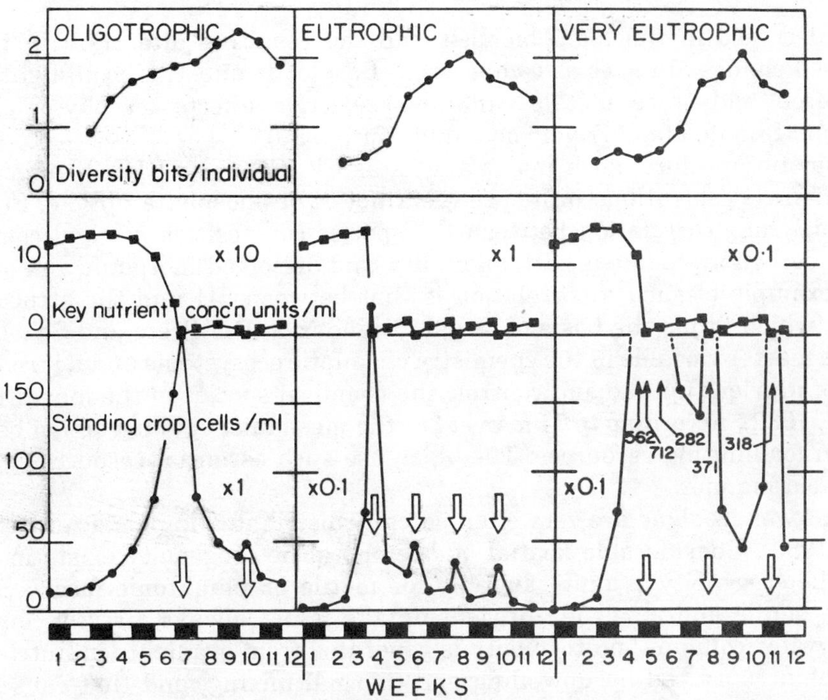

Fig. 13-6 Model to explain phytoplankton diversity in different trophic level systems. Downward pointing hollow arrows indicate times at which nutrient limitation occurs; x denotes key nutrient (usually phosphorus). (After Moss, 1973.)

orthophosphate (Brown *et al.*, 1981). In environments where the concentrations of essential nutrients fluctuate, it becomes difficult to identify any single nutrient which limits the growth rate and biomass of the microplankton community; in such fluctuating or nonsteady state systems, regulation of the plankton growth is mainly controlled by multiple nutrients simultaneously. Brown *et al.* have shown that productivity of some eucaryotic phytoplankton is maximized only when organic carbon is low and the environment is periodically perturbed by mineral nutrients.

Excess inputs of phosphorus cause eutrophication in many freshwater lakes. Understanding the kinetics of P-limited growth and P uptake in phytoplankton can contribute much to our knowledge of how the algae respond to environmental changes and nutrient fluctuations. It is a common belief that interspecific differences in kinetic parameters for nutrient-limited uptake or growth regulate seasonal succession, dominance, and coexistence of species in the phytoplankton community (Gotham and Rhee, 1981). Feedback regulation of nutrient uptake seems to be a common adaptive mechanism in planktonic algae. According to Gotham and Rhee, the growth rate of several common phytoplankton species is a function of total cell phosphorus. Interspecific differences in the effects of feedback regulation on nutrient uptake can contribute significantly to species interactions in nutrient-limited environments.

Edmondson and Lehman (1981) studied the reverse kind of situation in Lake Washington, i.e., sewage was diverted, leading to *decreased* inputs of P in the lake. This resulted in the concomitant decrease in the algal biomass and the resulting alteration in the N : P ratio likewise caused changes in species composition. Besides N and P, silicon, light, and, in some cases, even iron and trace metals can have selective effects on phytoplankton species (Huntsman and Sunda, 1980; Zavenboom and Mur, 1980).

Besides osmotic pressure, such major anions as Cl^-, SO_4^{--}, and HCO_3^- affect algal growth rates and cation concentrations influence the kinetics of phosphate uptake. Several workers have recorded strong correlation between the species composition of algal communities and the inorganic carbon system (e.g., pH, alkalinity, and dissolved inorganic and organic C). The best known example of such a correlation is that between pH and the structure of diatom communities, which forms the basis of Nygaard's indexes (Del Prete and Schofield, 1981). In fact, pH is the master variable in the chemistry of aquatic ecosystems and it strongly influences the kinetics of nutrient uptake and controls the chemical species of the ions utilized by algae (Tilman *et al.*, 1982). According to Tilman *et al.*, the mechanism of interaction between species is competition for limiting resources. The algae use such essential resources as light, P, and N in a threshold manner.

Nutrients as well as algae are very often patchily distributed in pelagic environments (Wall and Briand, 1980). Considerable spatial and temporal heterogeneity exists in such environments. This heterogeneity is quite suitable for motile or planktonic forms. Several phytoplankters are motile and in algae, nutrient uptake is not always directly coupled to reproduction. In a water column, heterogeneity is generated from gradients in nutrients and light, from the patchiness caused by upwelling and thermal mixing, and that caused by fish and zooplankton excretion and *in situ* decay of organisms.

Many unicellular green algae are important as sewage purifiers in oxidation ponds. Most sewage treatment ponds have a characteristic volvocalean/chlorococcalean flora, with the Volvocales (mostly flagellates) developing first and being later replaced by the Chlorococcales. Different types of treatment ponds commonly harbour the following typical algal forms:

(1) Lightly loaded ponds and polluted village ponds develop blooms of *Microcystis* in summer and a mixed chlorococcalean community at other times.

(2) Highly polluted ponds with low ammoniacal nitrogen have a chlorococcalean community which at certain times is replaced by *Closterium* and *Cyclotella*.

(3) Ponds with a high biochemical oxygen demand and high ammoniacal nitrogen usually have euglenoids dominating.

(4) Ponds with a high biochemical oxygen demand and moderate or low ammoniacal nitrogen tend to support communities containing species of *Chlorella*, *Selenastrum*, *Ankistrodesmus* and *Scenedesmus*.

STOCHASTIC GEOMETRY AND PLANKTON ECOLOGY

The most fundamental linkages in ecosystem dynamics are trophodynamic. A trophodynamic theory requires a framework based upon interorganism or interparticle distance, and essential component relating trophodynamics and the kinetic environment. It is typically assumed that interparticle distances are drawn from a random distribution, even though particles are known to be distributed in patches. Both random and patch-structure interparticle distances have been analyzed by Rothschild (1992) using the theory of stochastic geometry; he has discussed some aspects of stochastic geometry—point processes and random closed sets (RCS)—useful for studying plankton ecology. For point-process theory, the interparticle distances, random-distribution order statistics, transitions from random to patch structures, and second-order moment functions have been described (Rothschild, 1992). For RCS-theory, the volume fractions, contact distributions, and covariance functions are given. Applications of stochastic-geometry theory relate to nutrient flux among organisms, grazing, and coupling between turbulent flow and biological processes. The theory shows that particles are statistically closer than commonly assumed, substantially resolving the troublesome issues of autotroph-heterotroph nutrient exchange; that the microzone notion can be extended by RCS; that patch structure can substantially modify predator-prey encounter rates, even though the number of prey is fixed; and that interparticle distances and the RCS covariance function provide a fundamental coupling with physical processes (Rothschild, 1992).

Stochastic geometry has some applications in the study of plankton ecology, especially molecular-nutrient flux and grazing. Rates of nutrient flux among organisms are a function of the diffusive properties of nutrient molecules and the distance between donor organisms and acceptor cells. The interparticle distance can be studied in terms of point processes and random closed sets (RCS). Many particles are statistically much closer to one another than believed hitherto. This is because the reported distances are based upon mean distances; these both under- and overestimate the actual distance of most particles. A large number of particles are found at distances less than the mean distance. The close proximity of donors and acceptors implies a commonplace nutrient exchange between donor and acceptor cells at greater than diffuse background levels. Stochastic geometry is used to sharpen the notion of the probability distribution of interparticle distance. RCS can be used to develop a geometric foundation for the study of microzones or relatively high concentrations of nutrients surrounding a nutrient donor (Rothschild, 1992).

The main groups of plankton may be classified by size and density. Large zooplankton are about 100 μm in diameter and occur at densities of 10^{-2} individuals per cm^3. Large phytoplankton are of the order of 100 μm in diameter and occur at densities of 100 individuals per cm^3. Picoplankton are about 1 μm in diameter and occur at densities of 10^6 individuals per cm^3.

The densities enable computing the nearest neighbour distance (NND) for each major group. These are plotted in Fig. 13-7. Picoplankton have an interparticle distance of only roughly 10^{-3} cm, whereas the diameter of a large zooplankton is about 10^{-1} cm. Therefore, the large zooplankton and picoplankton are in *continual contact*.

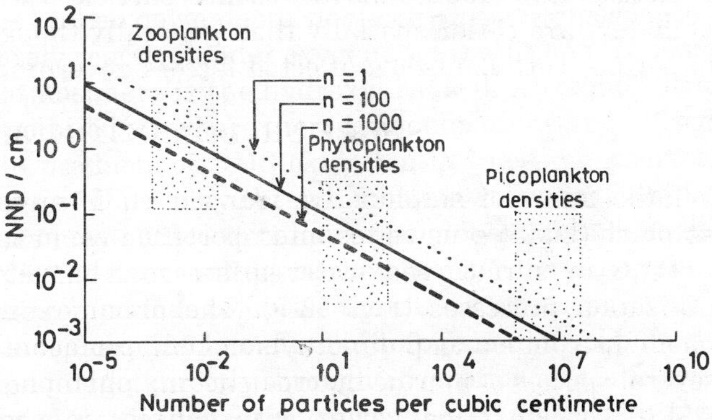

Fig. 13-7 Nearest neighbour distance (NND) as a function of particle density. The line corresponding to $n = 1$ is the conventional NND. The lines corresponding to $n = 100$ and $n = 1000$ are MNNDs for $n = 100$ and $n = 1000$, respectively. Typical ranges of numerical densities (which generally do not overlap) are shown for zooplankton, phytoplankton, and picoplankton. MNND, minimum mean distance to the nearest neighbour. (After Rothschild, 1992.)

The relatively large size of the zooplankton and the relatively small interparticle distance of the picoplankton suggests that large zooplankton might contribute nutrients to picoplankton at rates higher than otherwise expected.

The entire transfer process would be even more efficient if the zooplankton had an efficient way of finding the phytoplankton patches. There exists some possibility that catabolizing picoplankton may provide directional guidance for grazing zooplankton, even though the picoplankton are too small to be ingested by larger zooplankton (Rothschild, 1992). The basic idea is that phytoplankton exudates are metabolized by picoplankton and that picoplankton catabolites provide a more efficient directional sense to chemotactic zooplankton regarding their orientation toward phytoplankton patches. The phytoplankton release organic molecules, the molecules are ingested, then catabolized by picoplankton, and finally the diffused picoplankton catabolites are detected at relatively high concentrations by grazer chemoreceptors, which are almost in direct contact with the picoplankton cells. In other words, the picoplankton serve as chemical *repeaters* and enable detection of the presence and direction of a phytoplankton patch at a greater range than if the grazers were using only the phytoplankton exudates for chemotactic spatial clues (Rothschild, 1992).

Gerritsen and Strickler (1977) discussed the dynamics of grazers and the phytoplankton cells upon which they feed; this depends largely upon grazer-phytoplankton-cell encounter rates. The encounter rates have generally been estimated on the assumption that prey are distributed at random relative to the predator. However, because plankton are generally distributed patchily, the assumption of randomness generates a misleading view of grazer-phytoplankton trophodynamics (Rothschild, 1992).

The effects of turbulent flow on particles depend on both the density of particles and their relative motion. The complex interrelationships depend upon how the particles are distributed in the flow field; the specifics of the flow; and the swimming or other behaviour of the particle.

Rothschild's (1992) analysis of interparticle nutrient flux and grazing suggests that many plankters are closer spatially than generally thought. It seems that spatial distributions are important turbulent-flow affected factors governing nutrient flux among organisms.

SULPHUR, PLANKTON, AND THE CLIMATE

Volatile forms of sulphur are transferred from sea to land via the atmosphere. Dimethyl sulphide (DMS) constitutes an important link in this process.

DMS in surface sea water arises from a network of production, transformation, and utilization processes (Fig. 13-8). The precursor of DMS in sea water is the tertiary sulphonium compound β-dimethylsulphoniopropionate (DMSP), which has been identified in several species of marine macroalgae and phytoplankton (see Malin *et al.*, 1992). Intracellular DMSP concentration varies with salinity in some phytoplankton species suggesting an osmoregulatory role. DMSP is the nitrogen analogue of glycine betaine, a quaternary ammonium compound, which is involved in osmoregulation in some plant cells. Marine phytoplankton probably switches to DMSP production under conditions of nitrogen limitation (Turner *et al.*, 1988).

DMS is thought to be directly excreted into sea water by algal cells. Relatively little DMS is found in growing cultures but during the declining and stationary phases DMS and dissolved DMSP concentrations increase greatly (Turner *et al.*, 1988). DMSP is ubiquitous in sea water.

DMS can be photoxidized to dimethyl sulphoxide (DMSO) in sea water in the presence of photosensitizing compounds, and the rate of loss of DMS via this route appears to be about the same order as the emission rate of DMS to the atmosphere. DMSO seems to be widely distributed in the marine environment.

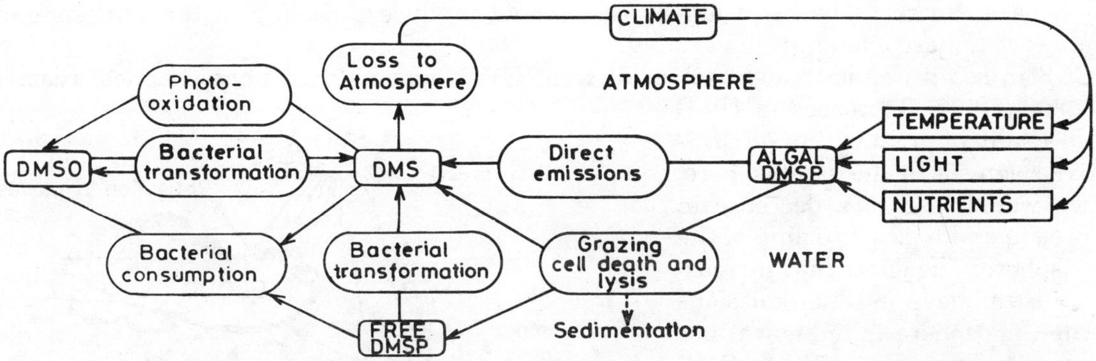

Fig. 13-8 The marine biogeochemical cycle of dimethyl sulphide (DMS); production, transformation, and utilization pathways that may ultimately influence the quantity of DMS lost to the atmosphere. (After Malin *et al.*, 1992.)

Loss of DMS to the atmosphere represents a small fraction of the potential marine pool. Following emission to the atmosphere, DMS undergoes rapid dilution and is subject to chemical transformations such that it has a short lifetime of hours to days.

THE ATMOSPHERIC CHEMISTRY OF DMS

Following emission from sea water, DMS is broken down photochemically in the troposphere. It is a high energy compound that is moderately reactive under oxygenated conditions. The main daytime oxidizing agent for DMS in the atmosphere is the hydroxyl radical. At night, nitrate radicals can be important, particularly in polluted air where there is enough ozone and nitrogen oxides for NO_3^- radicals to form. The main products of DMS oxidation in the atmosphere are generally SO_2/SO_4^{2-}. The oxidation products of DMS play three important roles in the atmosphere. First, a flux of DMS from the oceans may suffice to balance the global sulphur budget. Secondly, DMS oxidation products are acidic and hence influence the pH of aerosols and rain. In areas remote from fossil fuel burning, these compounds comprise the chief sources of acidity.

Lastly, DMS oxidation can affect the atmosphere via formation of sulphate aerosol particles, which not only alter the planetary radiation budget directly through absorption and scattering, but also indirectly as the main source of cloud-condensation nuclei (CCN) in remote areas (Malin *et al.*, 1992).

DMS chemistry essentially operates in the troposphere. Sulphur is also very important in the stratosphere, which influences the earth's radiation budget. A major source of this aerosol is believed to be carbonyl sulphide (COS) (Khalil and Rasmussen, 1984).

DMS AND GLOBAL CHANGE

Aerosol particles undoubtedly affect the earth's climate (Houghton *et al.*, 1990). According to Charlson *et al.*, 1987, the algal DMS/CCN/cloud albedo link may be a climate-regulating mechanism. Their hypothesis is that warming of the atmosphere and surface oceans, due to an increase in greenhouse gases or solar heat input, would lead to enhanced production of DMS by algae. This would result in a greater flux of the gas across the sea surface, elevation in atmospheric SO_4^{2-}, and a corresponding increase in CCN number density. The final outcome would be an increase in cloud albedo that would produce a cooling of the atmosphere to counteract the assumed initial warming.

COS in sea water is thought to result from UV-B light-induced photochemical reactions (Andreae, 1990). Increases in UV-B could result in greater flux of COS-derived aerosol to the stratosphere, which would lead to a decrease in insolation and hence a cooling of the troposphere. The effect that increased UV-B will have on DMS emissions to the atmosphere is unknown, but *Phaeocystis pouchetii*, a prolific DMS producer, secretes a pigment that screens out UV-B (Marchant *et al.*, 1991). Preferential survival of this species might result in increased DMS emissions.

Figure 13-9 illustrates the important interactions of marine phytoplankton with the oceans, atmosphere, and iron.

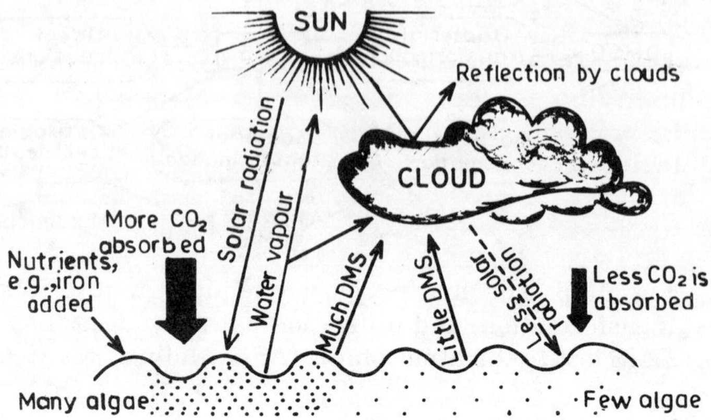

Fig. 13-9 Interactions of marine phytoplankton with the oceans, atmosphere, and iron.

THE CRITICAL DEPTH CONCEPT

The concept of critical depth was developed by Sverdrup (1953) to explain the onset of the spring bloom of phytoplankton. It pointed the way to a biological oceanography based securely on an appreciation of the dynamics of the physical environment (Mills, 1989). The principle can explain seasonal and geographic variations in oceanic productivity. The critical depth concept has proved useful in analyses of variations in duration of growing season in estuarine, coastal, and open ocean habitats (Sinclair *et al.*, 1981), of the enhancement of biological productivity associated with physical fronts in tidally mixed environments (Pingree *et al.*, 1976), and of marked difference between North Atlantic and North Pacific oceans in the manifestation of a spring bloom (Frost, 1987).

The importance of basin- and global-scale models of plankton dynamics has greatly increased by the contemporary need to understand the role of the ocean in controlling climate (Platt *et al.*, 1991). At the same time, the development of satellite-based oceanography has provided the means to test the predictions of physical-biological models on synoptic scales (Sathyendranath *et al.*, 1991). Furthermore, the phasing of the spring phytoplankton bloom relative to the phasing of life history events elsewhere in the pelagic ecosystem is now believed to have profound significance for larval survival in exploited fish populations (Cushing, 1975).

Platt *et al.* (1991) have combined an analytical solution for the daily rate of primary production per unit surface area with currently plausible estimates of phytoplankton loss, to provide an analytical model for critical depth. They have deduced an exact expression for the critical depth, and examined its sensitivity to variations in several parameters. They have shown that the critical depth criterion is a necessary, but not a sufficient, condition for the initiation of a phytoplankton bloom.

Platt *et al.* have found an exact expression for the critical depth in terms of a generalized, biomass-specific, loss term. The loss term is calculated as the sum of contributions from algal respiration and excretion, grazing by micro- and macrozooplankton, and sedimentation. The respiratory costs of algal growth and metabolism dominate the generalized loss term. From the information used to calculate critical depth, it is possible to deduce the rate of increase in algal biomass (or, equivalently, the net production) for the mixed layer. As long as the growth rate is positive, the Sverdrup criterion is respected. This leads to a characteristic time scale for the development of a bloom. When the time scale is short relative to the time between mixing by storms, a bloom can be expected to occur (Platt *et al.*, 1991).

THE IDEAL PHYTOPLANKTON ORGANISM

Suspension may be achieved by an organism either having zero excess density, or having a sinking rate less than the upward vertical component of turbulent motion in the water, or having active motility. Except for some cyanobacteria, *Botryococcus* and a few other algae, phytoplankton cells have a density which is greater than that of the water and several highly successful kinds are nonmotile. For most phytoplankton, the problem thus is that of adjusting sinking rate to a value suited to the prevailing turbulent mixing in a particular water body. For cells or colonies less than about 0.5 mm in diameter, flow is laminar rather than turbulent. For spherical objects the rate of fall is proportional to the square of the radius so that for suspension purposes the smaller the organism, the better it is.

Absorption of photosynthetically radiant energy is also a complicated matter, involving *inter alia* a size factor (Fogg, 1991). Pigments are more efficient in absorption if they are packaged in small cells rather than in large ones; the specific absorption coefficient at the chlorophyll absorption maximum in the red is about six times greater for cells of 1 μm diameter as compared with those of 100 μm diameter when concentrations of chlorophyll per unit volume of water are equal. Thus, again, there is an advantage for a phytoplankton alga in being small. Near the water surface, intensities of both visible and ultraviolet radiation are often damaging. On the other hand, it would appear to be a good strategy to have the photosynthetic system adjusted to function optimally at depths where vertical mixing is least and nutrient concentrations higher, that is, at the bottom of the photic zone. Many phytoplankton forms appear to be adapted in this way, with their photosynthesis becoming light saturated at comparatively low irradiance and with concomitant susceptibility to photoinhibition (Fogg, 1991).

Efficiency in uptake of scarce nutrients is essential for success in most natural waters. Over distances of about 100 μm molecular diffusion rather than eddy diffusion is the dominant process transporting materials to cells (Fogg, 1991).

Some parameters which describe growth, destruction, and movement of phytoplankton are tabulated in Table 13-5.

Much variation can be ascribed to shape, structure, and physiological history, but overall it seems that relative growth rate and biomass-specific rates of photosynthesis decrease with increasing cell size (Reynolds, 1984a; Harris, 1986). Picoplankton dominates in all types of oligotrophic water. Similar ability of smaller forms (up to 8 μm) to outcompete larger ones (100–200 μm) under conditions of low nutrient supply has been reported in experimental enclosures in the sea (Takahashi *et al.*, 1982).

Table 13-5 Parameters describing growth, destruction, and movement of phytoplankton (after Imboden, 1990)

Characteristic or parameter	Typical range
Growth rate	0.1–1 day^{-1}
Nutrient uptake rate	1–100 day^{-1}
Respiration/mineralization rate	0.01–0.1 day^{-1}
Sinking rate	0.1–1 m day^{-1} (extreme values, 0–10 m day^{-1})
Active movement of zooplankton	Up to 30 m half-day^{-1}
Time of photoresponse*	0.02–0.5 hr
Time of photoadaptation	
From dark to light	4–6 hr
From light to dark	2–6 wk

*The term *photoresponse* is used for the response of photosynthetic rate P to changing light intensity I along a fixed $P(I)$-curve. In contrast, *photoadaptation* is the biological adjustment to variable light conditions of changes, such as in photosynthetic pigments and chemical composition of the plankton cell, which eventually lead to a new $P(I)$-curve.

PHOTOSYNTHETIC ADAPTATIONS OF PICOPHYTOPLANKTON

The picophytoplankton consists mainly of coccoid cyanobacteria, possibly of some free-living prochlorophytes (Chisholm *et al.*, 1988), and a diversity of eucaryotes, perhaps mainly chlorophytes and prasinophytes. The typical physiological state of picophytoplankton is one of adaptation to low irradiance. The oft-recorded lower concentrations of picoplankton in surface waters, as compared with deeper water, may be partly due to photoinhibition and partly due to other factors such as nutrient availability and predation (Fogg, 1991).

ULTRAPLANKTON

The ultraplanktonic community comprises of both pico- and nannoplankton. The composition of this community appears to be much the same in all types of water and in all parts of the world (Stockner, 1988). It includes heterotrophic bacteria, phototrophic picoplankton, nannoplanktonic flagellates, and virus particles (Fogg, 1987; Proctor and Fuhrman, 1990).

Azam and Ammerman (1984) visualized this community as having structure. The metabolic activity of individual cells produces sustained gradients in concentrations of metabolites around them and Azam and Ammerman calculated that, if its boundary is put at the distance at which the concentration of a released substance falls to 10% of that at the cell surface, then the activity domain of a 20 μm diameter cell has a radius of 100 μm. For a cell of 2 μm diameter, the radius would be 10 μm. Thus, the activity domains of the phototrophs do not overlap and most of the heterotrophic bacteria will be found outside the enriched microzones, if uniform distribution is assumed. The ultraplanktonic community is quite dynamic. The generation times of the microorganisms concerned are short. *In situ* measurements of rates of growth for picophytoplankton have values ranging from 2.7–160 hr with a mode around 16 (Stockner and Antia, 1986). Mortality rates are equally high and, according to Proctor and Fuhrman (1990), 30% of cyanobacterial and 60% of heterotrophic mortality is due to viral infection.

Excretion from healthy algal cells may provide as much as 50% of the carbon required for bacterial production (Nalewajko *et al.*, 1980; Reimann, 1983). Further contributions to the labile dissolved organic fraction come from release during feeding by phagotrophic flagellates and the release of soluble organic matter following viral lysis of bacteria and cyanobacteria appears to be considerable (Proctor and Fuhrman, 1990). Turnover times for dissolved organic substances such as glucose and amino acid are often high. Undoubtedly most of the uptake is bacterial.

The cycling of inorganic nutrients is linked with the release and utilization of organic matter. Indeed, the rapid cycling of nitrogen which occurs in the euphotic zone is largely carried out by the ultraplanktonic community (Fogg, 1982). The flagellate component is more active in mineral recycling than the bacteria. Anderson *et al.* (1986) reported that in grazing experiments in batch cultures the marine flagellate *Paraphysomonas imperforata* was responsible for the bulk of phosphorus regeneration whereas bacteria made a negligible contribution. In a lake water from the euphotic zone in summer, Jürgens and Güde (1990) found 62% of the particulate and 40% of the total phosphorus bound by bacteria.

The picophytoplankton appear to be the main beneficiaries of the regeneration of nitrogen and phosphorus.

The time scales of processes in the ultraplanktonic community lie in the range of microseconds to hours.

The standing stocks of picoplankton are determined primarily by predation rather than by nutrient supply. Although numbers of coccoid cyanobacteria are somewhat greater in eutrophic than in oligotrophic waters the proportion which they form of the total phytoplankton biomass falls (Stockner, 1988).

The ultraplankton constitutes a dynamic, self-contained equilibrium community in view of its photosynthetic primary production, in which the population densities of the component species are set by the kinetics of their trophic relationships rather than by the input of materials from outside (Fogg, 1991). "High efficiencies of uptake and rapid cycling of mineral elements enable the community to function at low ambient nutrient concentrations and to hold sufficient amounts of scarce nutrients to permit rapid multiplication. Since the organisms are so small as to sediment at a negligible rate, or, if larger are motile, loss of nutrients by sedimentation does not occur and the community is potentially capable of maintaining itself indefinitely in surface waters" (Fogg, 1991).

According to Fogg (1991), the ultraplankton is restricted because it can only respond to increased availability of nutrients or energy supply to a limited extent by increases in population density, thus activating a feedback mechanism by favouring the flagellates (which prey on the primary producers) and enhancing rate of turnover rather than accumulation of phototrophic biomass. However, the loss of competitive ability which accompanies increase in size of individual organisms matters less if nutrients are abundantly available and larger size confers immunity against predatory nannoflagellates. A new order of phytoplanktonic existence is thus possible, one in which nutrient limitation and sedimentation become major hazards and in which turbulence rather than molecular diffusion becomes a dominant factor (Fogg, 1991).

There is a corresponding profound discontinuity in the phytoplankton in the size range of 10–20 μm. Organisms smaller than this tend to be of rather uniform and simple form and those larger are usually of varied and elaborate shapes. Sournia (1982) commented on this discontinuity by stating: 'most phytoplankton populations consist of a relatively large- and a relatively small-sized component, which differ from each other in many respects (if not all respects), namely: sampling and counting techniques, abundance, taxonomic composition, diversity, motility, and physiology'. Ultraplankton are simple spheres, ovoids or rods, whereas microplankton display an enormous variety and intricacy of cell shape and, often, combination of cells into colonies of specific form. These differences are illustrated particularly clearly amongst the cyanobacteria, in which the picoplanktonic forms are unicellular, simple in shape, and less than 3 μm in maximum dimensions, whereas the others are larger in cell size, multicellular, usually filamentous and characteristically forming colonies visible to the naked eye (Fogg, 1987). Differences are discernible in organelles as well as in general cell shape. In the nannoplankton there is a predominance of flagellated forms, including the phototrophic as well as phagotrophic kinds, but there is a scarcity of motile cells in the size range 10–30 μm, then with increase in size beyond this, an abundance of flagellated forms especially among the dinoflagellates (Fogg, 1991). According to Fogg (1991), in the domain of laminar flow, motility is useful in catching prey and in gaining access to niches enriched with nutrients whereas in the domain of turbulence it also gives the advantages of movement into water masses with better illumination or higher nutrient concentrations and in counteracting sedimentation. The larger planktonic cyanobacteria nearly all contain gas vacuoles, which in a different way serve the same ends as do flagella in Dinophyceae, but the picoplanktonic forms do not.

PHYSIOLOGICAL ECOLOGY OF MICROPHYTOPLANKTON

The demerits of larger size lie mainly in less efficient uptake of nutrients and in liability to sedimentation into darkness. Rather than grazing, nutrient supply or turbulence appear to be the dominant factors controlling increase of the larger phytoplankton (Fogg and Thake, 1987).

The rates of sedimentation, flotation, and swimming achievable by microplankton enable them to move through the water column of the photic zone in times commensurate with those of cell division. In many cases, turbulent diffusion is the dominant process transporting dissolved substances. The maximization of nutrient flux depends on steepening of the concentration gradient across the unstirred layer of water (the diffusion barrier) surrounding the cell. This can be achieved either by shortening the distance from the cell at which the concentration in the bulk medium is reached, or by keeping the concentration at the cell surface rather low. A cell may control the effective viscosity of the water surrounding it through surface electrical properties which influence the number of layers of water molecules in its vicinity. Plankton algae are usually electronegative.

Zooplankton, fish, mammals, and birds by producing excreta enrich the water locally and it is likely that algal cells absorb nutrients sufficiently quickly from such patches to give them some competitive advantage. Nutrient-depleted algal cells may, in fact, take up ammonium and phosphate ions extremely rapidly.

Reynolds (1984a) and Fogg and Thake (1987) have reviewed the various features of microplankton which might reduce sinking rate and hence loss by sedimentation. One of the elaborations of form associated with reduced sinking rate are the long delicate bristles on mature colonies of *Pediastrum boryanum* (Gawlick and Millington, 1988). Chain formation does not seem to be an adaptation reducing sinking rate although it may be regarded as a means of achieving a size advantageous in discouraging predators whilst giving a lower sinking rate than a sphere of equal volume. The relation between sinking velocity and chain length has been investigated by Davey and Walsby (1985) for *Anabaena* sp. Sinking velocities of *Anabaena* increased with chain length. Among methods of reducing the mean specific gravity of a cell the most effective is gas vacuole production by cyanobacteria. Selective accumulation of ions seems to be of importance only as a means of controlling buoyancy in a few of the largest phytoplankton forms. Actively growing cells are more buoyant than slowly growing ones and limitation of photosynthetic uptake of carbon dioxide increases sinking rate. Living cells of many species have lower sinking rates than similar killed cells (see Fogg, 1991).

THE AQUEOUS MEDIUM

Although water is an excellent solvent, some elements necessary for algal growth occur in extremely low concentrations, and phytoplankton growth sequesters what is available into particulate form that can settle down in the bottom sediment. Phytoplankton lives a precarious existence in a narrow zone between shortage of some essential mineral nutrients above, and lack of light below (Fogg, 1991).

Since it controls both access to light and distribution of nutrients, water movement is a crucial factor in the life of phytoplankton (Margalef, 1978). This movement is a continuum from ocean currents down to molecular motion but the following four regions in the spectrum have been distinguished (see Harris, 1986):

(1) Large-scale rotational stirring motion commensurate with the water body itself, caused by external forces and experiencing unequal velocity fluctuations along the three space axes.

(2) Turbulent mixing brought about by medium sized eddies with velocities approximately equal in all directions and with turbulent energy cascading from large to small eddies.

(3) A transition range with smaller eddies whose properties depend on the viscosity of the fluid as well as on the rate of energy dissipation.

(4) The region of molecular motion in which viscosity is the only determining factor and energy is finally dissipated as heat.

The kinds of motion each have important but different consequences for phytoplankton. The large scale motions have been the focus of classical physical oceanography and limnology and can be described by deterministic mathematical expressions. The smaller scale turbulence can be analyzed statistically but is one of the least understood areas of classical physics. The range of complicated nonlinear behaviour in water bodies is rich in bifurcations which lead to the development of spatiotemporal chaos (Moore and Weiss, 1990). The transition of such eddies with turbulent flow to the realm of laminar flow and molecular motion mostly depends on shear rate and viscosity. The ratio of these is expressed in the Reynolds number for flow defined as $R_1 = puL/n$, where p = density, u = velocity, L = a characteristic length dimension, and n = viscosity (Hutchinson, 1967). The critical value of R_1 for water lies between 500 and 2000; below 500 flow is laminar and above 2000 it is turbulent. This transition appears to be important for phytoplankton and, to some extent, it may be under biological control but the lack of relevant rheological and shear rate data from natural water bodies makes mathematical modelling uncertain (Jenkinson, 1986).

Light, mineral nutrients, temperature, and water movement are by no means the only physico-chemical factors in the aquatic environment that affect the life of phytoplankton. Dissolved organic matter is also important. It occurs in concentrations of 5–10 mg per litre in most sea- and freshwaters and consists of polymeric material that forms complexes with inorganic ions and thus modifies their biological impact. Such material probably does not provide much energy in the photic zone but on photochemical breakdown it can yield pyruvate which is used by microorganisms (Kieber *et al.*, 1989). However, in most waters, there are found low concentrations of labile and biologically active substances such as organic acids, sugars, amino acids, nucleotides, and vitamins. The concentrations of these substances are of little significance; but their rate of turnover is very high and this makes them important.

In regard to the basic features of the physiological ecology of the phytoplankton there is no essential difference between fresh- and salt waters (Fogg and Thake, 1987).

TURBULENCE

Turbulent fluid motion may be defined as an irregular condition of flow in which the various quantities of the flow, e.g., velocity and pressure show a random variation in time and space. In contrast to the turbulent motion, which occurs at relatively high velocities, the orderly streamlined flows at low velocities are termed as laminar flows (Papoutsakis, 1991). The question of whether a flow is turbulent or laminar is determined not only by the velocity which characterizes the flow, but also by the viscosity of the fluid and the geometry of the flow field. These quantities may be combined into a single dimensionless quantity known as the Reynolds number (*Re*), defined as

$$R = \frac{\text{(a characteristic flow dimension)(a characteristic flow velocity)}}{\text{(kinematic fluid viscosity)}}$$

Equation $R = nd_i^2/V$ gives a specific definition of R for agitated vessels based on the impeller diameter d_i. Here the characteristic dimension is d_i, and the characteristic velocity is nd_i, where n is the rate of impeller rotation. The kinematic viscosity of a fluid (V) is the ratio of the fluid viscosity to the fluid density. For each specific definition of R, the numerical values of R indicate whether the flow is laminar or turbulent.

In turbulent flow, the kinetic energy is transferred from a part of the fluid to the other part predominantly by the motion of eddies; eddies are swirling pockets of fluid. When the motion of these eddies is the same in all directions at various points in the flow field, the turbulent flow is referred to as isotropic. When the transfer rate of kinetic energy is the same at all points in the turbulent field, the turbulence is homogeneous. In other cases, it is in-homogeneous, as is the case in the turbulent flows of agitated vessels (Papoutsakis, 1991).

Figure 13-10 shows the energy spectrum of isotropic turbulence, $E(k, t)\,dk$ is the energy per unit fluid mass contained in eddies that correspond to wave numbers between k and $k + dk$, where t is time. The inverse of the wave number characterizes the eddy sizes, so the eddy size decreases as the wave number increases. At higher wave numbers, within the inertial and energy dissipation ranges, the properties of turbulence are independent of the conditions of generation of turbulence. It is predominantly in the energy dissipation range that the kinetic energy of the fluid is dissipated as heat (Papoutsakis, 1991).

Turbulence in the aquatic environment plays a crucial role in the life of phytoplankton by influencing their access to light and nutrients. Organisms below about 20 μm in linear dimensions (the ultraplankton) are suited to existence in a domain in which molecular diffusion rather than eddy diffusion is the predominant agency transporting materials to and from cells. Turbulence is important in the placing of the water containing this community in the light field but the rapid exchanges by molecular diffusion which small size makes possible allow the establishment of a self-contained and highly dynamic community of phototrophs, viruses, heterotrophic bacteria, and phagotrophic flagellates in which materials are cycled with little loss by sedimentation or transfer to higher trophic levels (Fogg, 1991). In this equilibrium system, population densities are determined by internal dynamics rather than by nutrient input. Larger phytoplankton escape from control by grazing of flagellates but suffer the penalties of inefficiency in uptake, so that they can only develop when concentrations of nutrients are relatively high. They also have sedimentation as a factor additional to water movement to remove them from the photic zone. Availability of nutrients and transport into darkness both closely depend on turbulence and the highly variable nature of this compels microplankton to be opportunistic, able to grow and multiply only when a transient niche with suitable nutrient concentrations, irradiance, and turbulence characteristics presents itself. Equilibrium is never achieved. There are radical differences, not only in size but in morphology, physiology, and ecological strategy, between the phototrophs of the equilibrium ultraplanktonic system and those of the nonequilibrium microplanktonic community. According to Fogg (1991), the microphytoplankton may be divided into two main types according to ecological strategy. One, typified by the larger diatoms, is nonmotile and depends on sufficient mixing to maintain it in the photic zone. The other, typified by the dinoflagellates and gas-vacuolate cyanobacteria, is most successful when the water column is sufficiently stable to allow it to use its motility or buoyancy control to position itself for best access to light and nutrients. The communities of mixed and stratified waters may follow each other in the same water body in seasonal succession or exist side by side when a tidal mixing front forms in a shallow sea. In highly turbulent waters which otherwise mix too deeply to allow net photosynthesis, a population may be held in a favourable position for growth by the formation of eddies. Always the interactions between phytoplankton and the other kinds of organisms in the plankton have to be borne in mind, those with bacteria being particularly significant when the overall activity of a planktonic community is being considered (Fogg, 1991).

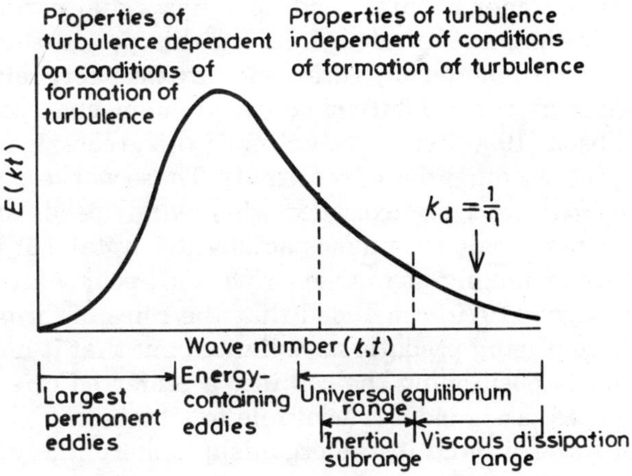

Fig. 13-10 Aspects of turbulence (after Papoutsakis, 1991).

SMALL-SCALE TURBULENCE AND PHYTOPLANKTON

Small-scale turbulence (over a few millimetres, for seconds of time) can be of crucial importance for the growth and survival of some species. Pollingher and Zemel (1981) reported that whereas wind during the day did not affect the division rate of *Peridinium cinctum* in Lake Kinneret, wind during the first part of the night had an inhibitory effect. These dinoflagellates appear to be sensitive when in the premitotic and mitotic stages of cell division, which under natural conditions has a diel periodicity with a maximum during the first part of the night. Turbulence during this period thus causes mortality. Increases of growth rate seen with increasing turbulence are probably related to increased rates of transport to the cell, whereas the inhibition occurs from mechanical damage by viscous stresses. Thomas and Gibson (1990) tentatively ranked the green algae, cyanobacteria, diatoms, and dinoflagellates in increasing order of sensitivity. These workers reported that the threshold values for damage to *Gonyaulax* are exceeded when wind speeds are greater than 1.54–2.06 ms^{-1}.

Small-scale turbulence accelerates uptake of nutrients by microplankton besides playing a part in mixing of nutrient-rich and -poor water can also damage some algae mechanically. Smayda (1970) concluded that the roles of form elaboration in slowing down sinking and in discouraging predators are limited but that it might be involved in promoting nutrient uptake and in positioning the cell into a preferred orientation or rotation when in motion. Reynolds (1984a) assigned a crucial role to a high coefficient of form resistance; by resisting movement of water around it, the organism is more likely to remain within a given flow and be carried along by it.

THE PHYTOPLANKTON POPULATIONS OF MIXED AND STABILIZED WATERS

Striking qualitative differences occur between the phytoplankton floras of mixed and stratified waters. The former have diatoms as the characteristic component whereas the latter are dominated by dinoflagellates and/or gas-vacuolate cyanobacteria. Margalef (1978) gave values in terms of eddy diffusion coefficients for the degrees of turbulence preferred, 2–100 cm^2 sec^{-1} for diatoms, 0.02–1 cm^2 sec^{-1} for dinoflagellates. There is some parallel here to the distinction between '*r*-selected' species, characteristic of unstable environments and with a major strategy lying in having high growth rate, and '*K*-selected' species, for which survival depends on obtaining scarce resources in a complex and stable community. These have mainly been distinguished in terrestrial communities; the application of *r* and *K* theory to phytoplankton has been discussed by Kilham and Kilham (1980) and Harris (1986).

The distinction between mixed and stratified waters is valid for both salt- and freshwaters and is as apparent in the seasonal succession in a discrete water body as it is in the two water masses coexisting on either side of a front. Reynolds *et al.* (1984), who carried out experiments in a large limnetic enclosure in which nutrients were added to avoid limitation, were able to switch the phytoplankton between one type and the other by imposing 3- to 4-week cycles of mixing and restratification. Diatoms and desmids grew rapidly in the periods of mixing whereas gas-vacuolate cyanobacteria and the dinoflagellate *Ceratium* showed the opposite tendency. Diatoms cannot swim, depend on mixing to keep them in the photic zone, and can cope with wide variation in irradiance. On the other hand, dinoflagellates can swim, and gas-vacuolate cyanobacteria can move up and down the water column; both have narrower ranges of tolerance to irradiation and thus can only be successful if the water column is reasonably stable. The biological advantage which a dinoflagellate has in a suitable environment is well illustrated by *Ceratium hirundinella*. In calm weather it shows a general pattern of upward migration during the day and descent during the night, with an avoidance of the surface especially in bright sunshine. This behaviour maximizes photosynthesis and enables cells to recharge with nutrients in deeper waters when the surface layer becomes depleted. Together with immunity to a large extent from grazers and fungal parasites, it allows *Ceratium* to achieve a biomass density of up to 370 mg chlorophyll-a m^{-2}, which exceeds that of most other kinds of phytoplankton. The thick-walled cysts which it forms enable it to overwinter in bottom deposits and their germination in spring provides a substantial inoculum for the next year's growth.

Figure 13-11 illustrates a possibility matrix showing the most likely phytoplankton assemblages as a function of nutrients and mixing.

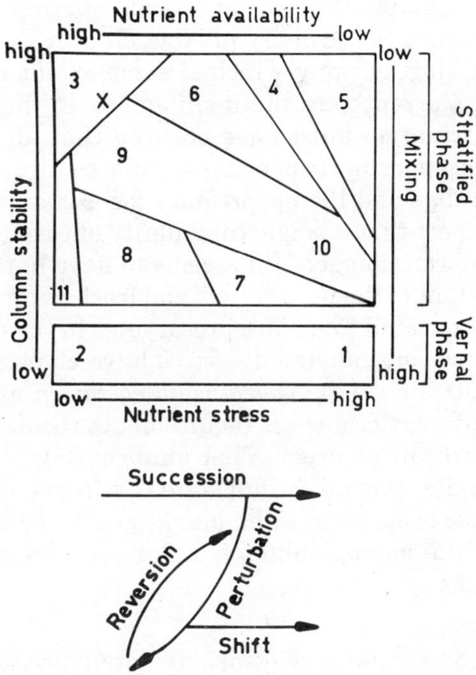

Fig. 13-11 Reynolds possibility matrix showing the most likely phytoplankton assemblages as a function of nutrients and mixing. The lower figure indicates the direction of motion in response to perturbation and tends to indicate the likely sequence of events. Community classification: 1, *Asterionella*, *Melosira italica*; 2, *Asterionella*, *Stephanodiscus astraea*; 3, *Eudorina*, *Volvox*; 4, *Sphaerocystis*; 5, *Chrysophytes*; 6, *Anabaena*, *Aphanizomenon*; 7, *Tabellaria*, *Fragilaria*, *Staurastrum*; 8, *Melosira granulata*, *Fragilaria*, *Closterium*; 9, *Microcystis*; 10, *Ceratium*; 11, *Pediastrum*, *Coelastrum*; 12, *Oscillatoria agandhii*. X, Opportunists. (After Reynolds, 1980.)

EFFECTS OF TURBULENCE ON HORIZONTAL DISTRIBUTION

Turbulence can affect horizontal as well as vertical distribution of phytoplankton. Horizontal displacements are more extensive than those in the vertical direction. Mixing rates may be kilometres per day horizontally as compared with a few metres vertically. However, they are less important for the phytoplankton. The persistence of concentrated patches will depend on whether the rate of increase of the population is sufficient to compensate for loss by turbulent dispersion. The larger the patch better it will be able to maintain itself since losses will depend on the area of the interface with the surrounding water but the total population increase will be a function of volume (Fogg, 1991).

Continuous measurement of chlorophyll by the *in vivo* fluorescence technique from ships has shown considerable variation in horizontal distribution on the 10–100 km scale. Power spectral analyses of such data suggest connection between patchiness and turbulence (Platt and Denman, 1980).

EFFECTS OF LARGE-SCALE ROTATIONAL STIRRING

The main effects of large-scale stirring on phytoplankton are manifested in the variations in intensity of primary production over the oceans, which reflect the transport of nutrients, and in biogeography, which to some extent reflects the transport of species.

Currents are the main agents in the dissemination of marine phytoplankton and oceanic circulation must have ensured that all but the most recently evolved species will have had the opportunity of being inoculated into all parts. Given the geological age of the phytoplankton groups and the opportunity for exchange of genetic information which must exist, one might expect that a single community of cosmopolitan species would have evolved. As far as present information goes this seems to have happened at the picoplankton level, even, perhaps, to the extent of the floras of sea and freshwater being similar, but with the reservation that eucaryotic forms tend to replace procaryotes in the colder waters (Fogg, 1991). At the microplankton level, however, individual species have characteristic distributions. A few seem to be cosmopolitan but some, e.g., *Skeletonema costatum* are differentiated into genetically distinct strains with different ecological requirements (Gallagher, 1982). Most are confined to Arctic, Antarctic or tropical sea areas. That uniformity in distribution has not been achieved must be attributed to the nonequilibrium state that pervades the microphytoplanktonic community. Hutchinson's (1961) paradox of the plankton arrived at the correct conclusion, namely, that the community of the microplankton is a nonequilibrium system (Fogg, 1991).

BLOOMS

Phytoplankton blooms are often predictable features of marine and freshwater habitats. Blooms appear after certain hydrobiological changes including enhanced terrigenous runoff, water column turnover, upwelling, and increased thermal stratification, coupled with temperature and light conditions conducive to growth and multiplication of biomass (Fogg, 1969; Reynolds and Walsby, 1975). These changes lead to nutrient enrichment of near-surface waters supporting blooms. As a result, the synergistic impacts of optimal physical and chemical conditions can determine blooming frequencies and magnitudes (Paerl, 1988).

Upon examining combinations of environmental conditions most likely to elicit nuisance blooms, commonalities and analogous situations become more apparent among coastal marine (dinoflagellate dominated), estuarine (dinoflagellate and cyanobacteria dominated), and freshwater (cyanobacteria dominated) ecosystems (Paerl, 1988). A combination of the following hydrological, chemical, and biotic factors will most likely lead to bloom-sensitive waters: a horizontally distinct water mass; a vertically stratified water column; warm weather conditions, as typified by dry monsoon tropical climates and summer seasons in temperate zones; high incident photosynthetically active radiation; enhanced allochthonous organic matter loading; enhanced allochthonous inorganic nutrient loading; adequate availability of essential metals, supplied by terrigenous inputs or upwelling; suitability of underlying sediments for resting cysts or akinetes; algal-bacterial synergism, which exerts positive impact on algal nutrient cycling; algal-micrograzer synergism, which also stimulates nutrient cycling without consumption of filamentous and colonial nuisance taxa; and selective (for non-nuisance taxa) activities of macrograzers such as crustaceans and fish larvae (Paerl, 1988).

There are certain manifestations of blooms that universally translate as nuisances. Three basic nuisance classes are attributable to certain bloom-forming phytoplankton taxa, viz., (1) some water quality deterioration; (2) chronic or intermittent health hazards, including toxicity; and (3) losses of aesthetic and recreational value of affected waters. Nuisance conditions falling in category (1) may include physico-chemical alteration of water, such as hypolimnetic deoxygenation; adverse biotic impacts resulting from toxicity of the bloom-formers; reduction or elimination of benthic biota due to altered chemical conditions in sediments; reduction of *desirable* algal or higher plant species due to decreases in water transparency; and resultant trophic impacts due to altered or undesirable food characteristics of bloom species, including distaste, mechanical constraints to ingestion, and toxicity, all leading to shifts from plankton-based food webs to benthic or detrital ones (Paerl, 1988). Category (2) encompasses growth stimulation of pathogenic organisms. Category (3) includes a wide variety of undesirable aesthetic impacts including foul odours and bad tastes associated with blooms; water discolouration; and poor fishing and boating characteristics.

Table 13-6 summarizes the physiological and ecological characteristics of selected taxa of cyanobacterial and dinoflagellate nuisance blooms.

OCEANS AS CARBON SINK

It has generally been believed that the supply of dissolved inorganic carbon (DIC) does not limit oceanic primary productivity, as its concentration in sea water exceeds that of other plant nutrients such as nitrate and phosphate by two and three orders of magnitude, respectively. But the bulk of oceanic new production and a major fraction of vertical carbon flux is mediated by a few diatom genera whose ability to use DIC components other than CO_2 is unknown. Riebesell *et al.* (1993) have shown that under optimal light and nutrient conditions, diatom growth rate can in fact be limited by the supply of CO_2.

Dissolved inorganic carbon in sea water exists in three interchangeable forms: CO_2, HCO_3^-, and CO_3^{2-}. Despite its low concentration, CO_2 is the main source of inorganic carbon for phytoplankton growth in the natural environment. Whereas some microalgae tested can use bicarbonate, common marine diatoms use only dissolved CO_2 (Riebesell *et al.*, 1993).

In view of the large pool of DIC in sea water, the CO_2 supply limits growth rate but not the total biomass of a diatom bloom after exhaustion of nitrate and phosphate. But as the rate of biomass build-up by a bloom is a function of both algal growth rate and grazing, the biomass attained during the bloom is directly proportional to the growth rate (Raymont, 1980). Because the magnitude of particle sinking is a function of algal biomass concentration, higher algal growth rates stimulate vertical carbon flux and enhance remineralization depth (Riebesell *et al.*, 1993). Enhanced output by the biological pump affects the vertical distribution of inorganic nutrients in the ocean, transferring nutrients from the surface to the deep ocean. Thus the ocean's capacity to sequester carbon by the biological pump may well be positively correlated with atmospheric CO_2 concentrations (Riebesell *et al.*, 1993).

The significance of the oceans as a sink for atmospheric CO_2 is currently of great interest because of its effects on the likely global warming. Net removal of CO_2 from the atmosphere occurs both by chemical and biological processes. Biological removal occurs by the sedimentation of the biomass produced by photosynthetic microorganisms; this carries the fixed carbon down to the depth of the ocean. Nitrogen and phosphorus needed for new production (that is, extra to those recycled by decomposition through the upper levels of the ocean) come from upwelling from the deep ocean. But how can CO_2 be limiting? Over 95 per cent of carbon fixation in phytoplankton is by the photosynthetic carbon-fixation reaction mediated by the enzyme Rubisco (ribulose bisphosphate carboxylase), which can use only CO_2. CO_2 is also

Table 13-6 Some cyanobacterial and dinoflagellate nuisance bloom-forming tax and their properties (modified from Paerl, 1988)

Genus	Preferred habitat	Bloom characters	Toxic properties (Example)
CYANOBACTERIA*			
Anabaena	Rivers	Surface scums; dispersed colonies	VFDF (anatoxin A); (*A. flos-aquae*)
Lyngbya		Suspended filaments; flakes	Toxic; gastrointestinal disorders
Microcystis	Rivers	Surface scums; dispersed colonies	SDF-FDF (peptides); (*M. aeruginosa*)
Nodularia	Oligohaline estuaries	Surface scums; dispersed colonies	Toxic; nature of toxin unknown
Oscillatoria	Mesotrophic lakes, rivers, oligohaline estuaries	Subsurface layers and dispersed filaments	Toxic; gastrointestinal disorders
DINOFLAGELLATES†			
Amphidinium	Physically stable near-shore marine waters		Choline-like toxin
Exuviella	Coastal regions (Japan)		Hepato-neuro-toxins
Gonyaulax	Coastal waters in tropical and subtropical waters		Saxitoxin; paralytic shellfish poisoning
Gymnodinium	Coastal waters (Mexico, English Channel)		Neurotoxin; hemolytic toxins; paralytic
Noctiluca	Coastal Korea and Japan		Toxin ammoniacal (?)
Peridinium	Freshwater systems		Nature of toxin poorly known

Notes: *All 5 genera of cyanobacteria occur in eutrophic lakes and ponds.
†All 6 genera of dinoflagellates form red tides and are toxic to fish.
(SDF, slow death factor; FDF, fast death factor, VFDF, very fast death factor.)

the substrate for the carboxylase (phosphoenol-pyruvate carboxylase) responsible for most of the remaining C fixation by diatoms. The bulk of dissolved inorganic carbon in the oceans is, however, in the form of bicarbonate. So one possible limitation on the use of the apparent excess inorganic carbon is the rate at which bicarbonate is converted to CO_2 (Raven, 1993).

Biological membranes are quite permeable to gaseous CO_2 and hence allow inorganic C entry by CO_2 diffusion across the plasmalemma and plastid-envelope membranes. Aquatic plants have a constraint on CO_2 supply to the outer surface of the plasmalemma: the lower diffusion coefficient of CO_2 in water than in air. This constraint is partially offset by conversion of HCO_3^- to CO_2 within diffusion range of the plasma membrane (see Raven, 1993).

The work of Riebesell *et al.* (1993) on laboratory cultures of three species of oceanic diatoms suggests that any decrease in free CO_2 concentration in bloom conditions, of CO_2 fixation by Rubisco faster than CO_2 is resupplied from the atmosphere, would reduce the rate of primary production. Riebesell *et al.* also found that the rate of inorganic C uptake was not greater than could be explained by diffusion of CO_2 and uncatalyzed conversion of HCO_3^- to CO_2. The inorganic C utilization by the three diatoms may thus be accounted for by diffusive supply of CO_2 to the cell surface without extracellular catalysis of the HCO_3^- to CO_2 conversion.

Some microalgae can use HCO_3^- (HCO_3^- use being defined as photosynthetic inorganic C assimilation in excess of what can be explained by uncatalyzed extracellular conversion of HCO_3^- to CO_2 with subsequent CO_2 uptake). HCO_3^- use may involve extracellular catalysis of HCO_3^- to CO_2 conversion with subsequent CO_2 uptake or active HCO_3^- influx. Bicarbonate use is widespread in microalgae, although its extent, like that of CO_2 active transport, may have been overestimated for marine photosynthetic microorganisms growing in air-equilibrated sea water (Raven, 1993).

The results obtained by Riebesell *et al.* are consistent with inorganic C limitation of growth rate in *new production* conditions in the ocean.

IRON LIMITATION

De Baar *et al.* (1995) have tested the suggestion that iron is a limiting nutrient for plankton productivity and consequent CO_2 drawdown by looking at natural levels of productivity in regions of the Southern Ocean with differing iron abundance. In some parts of the Antarctic circumpolar current (ACC), upwelling of deep waters supplies sufficient iron to the surface to sustain moderate primary production but not to permit blooms to develop. In contrast, within the fast-flowing, iron-rich jet of the polar front (PF), spring blooms produced phytoplankton biomass an order of magnitude greater than that in southern ACC waters, leading to CO_2 undersaturation. The plankton-rich PF waters were sharply delineated from adjacent iron-poor waters, indicating that iron availability was the critical factor in blooming (De Baar *et al.*, 1995).

They recorded strong maxima in iron and phytoplankton, and the consequent CO_2 undersaturation, at the PF relative to the ACC, showing that the iron hypothesis holds good for this unperturbed ecosystem. In contrast, although similar maxima for iron and chlorophyll-a have been observed in a natural plume downstream of the Galapagos Islands, no significant effects of CO_2 were found. Moreover, in the equatorial Pacific experiments, pulsed addition of iron causes only a small and transient CO_2 response whereas the natural continuous supply of iron in the PF produces a strong response (De Baar *et al.*, 1995).

On Fe enhancement when ocean water is placed in incubation bottles, plankton doubling-rates increase and, provided that the light regime is adequate and grazing is modest, blooms develop. Blooms act as an important vehicle for export of carbon into the deep sea (the biological pump) and associated drawdown of CO_2 from the atmosphere.

EUTROPHICATION

Eutrophication is usually defined to mean lake enrichment owing to any and all nutritive substances. The term has come to connote something undesirable, but this view is loaded with prejudice, for eutrophication is not necessarily always undesirable. If a lake becomes less eutrophic, this can sometimes lead to losses of certain species of plants or animals, and such losses are against the objectives of the conservationists. On the other hand, too much eutrophication also can cause such losses.

Another common statement that waters do become more eutrophic with increasing age is again not necessarily always true.

The meanings of the terms eutrophication and pollution overlap to some extent but, in general, pollution denotes the addition of harmful or directly toxic materials, whereas eutrophication involves enrichment with nontoxic nutrients. Thus, the discharge of *raw* sewage into a lake is described by everybody as pollution, but it also satisfies the definition of eutrophication. On the other hand, the discharge of *treated* sewage that has been well oxygenated and has become mineralized into harmless plant nutrients cannot be called pollution—it is best labelled as eutrophication.

The chief causes of eutrophication are sewage and agricultural fertilizers. Nitrogen and phosphorus are the main nutrients in sewage, occurring mainly as nitrates and phosphates. A substantial fraction of the nitrate content of rivers comes from land drainage, but this does not apply to phosphates which mostly or entirely come from sewage and detergents. This is because, unlike nitrate, phosphate does leach off easily from soil or land.

Table 13-7 compares the algal characteristics of some oligotrophic and eutrophic lakes.

Table 13-7 Examples of commonly recorded algae in plankton of oligotrophic and eutrophic lakes (note that some species occur in both types of lake)

Phytoplankton	Lake	
	Oligotrophic	Eutrophic
Desmids	*Cosmarium, Staurastrum, Staurodesmus*	
Diatoms	*Cyclotella comta, Tabellaria, Fragilaria crotonensis*	*Asterionella, Fragilaria crotonensis, Stephanodiscus, Melosira*
Dinoflagellates	*Peridinium* spp., *Ceratium*	*Peridinium bipes, Glenodinium, Ceratium*
Chlorococcales	*Oocystis*	*Scenedesmus, Pediastrum*
Cyanophyceae		*Aphanizomenon, Microcystis, Anabaena, Oscillatoria rubescens*

The productivity of algal populations is the chief foundation on which the aquatic food webs rest. Depending on size, this autotrophic algal community can be divided into two broad groups, viz., the net plankton and the nannoplankton. Individuals of the net plankton are retained by a 64 μm mesh net, whereas the nannoplanktonic organisms pass through such nets. Filter feeding herbivores mainly ingest the nannoplankton.

It used to be a general belief that the relative productivities of the net and nannoplankton are proportional to their relative biomasses; thus, if nannoplankton made up some 30 per cent of the biomass, it contributed 30% of the production. Recent studies have discounted this theory and it is now believed that the nannoplankton are more productive per unit biomass than the net plankton (Gelin, 1975; Ostrofsky and Peairs, 1981). This modern view is based on the argument that nutrient uptake is a surface phenomenon and in lake water, which constitutes a quite dilute medium, any increase in surface area : volume ratio conferred by small size would be competitively advantageous.

The plankton of freshwater lakes generally consists of multispecies representatives from up to 7–10 taxonomic divisions. However, the relative proportions of the species of different divisions fluctuate with changing habitat factors and nutrient levels in a lake; representatives of certain divisions dominate the community biomass at various times of a year. Temperate lakes conspicuously show vernal and autumnal abundance of diatoms.

Many lakes contain large-sized diatoms as a dominant component of their net plankton. These diatoms and other chlorophyll-c containing algae are, in general, photosynthetically less efficient than many smaller green algae such as *Chlorella* (Dunstan, 1973), especially under low light intensities.

NUTRIENT LIMITATION OF PHYTOPLANKTON GROWTH

Assimilatory uptake of NO_3^- by phytoplankton is a major nitrate-consuming process in lakes. The traditional view on nutrient limitation of phytoplankton growth has been that phosphorus is basically limiting in most kinds of natural lakes (Elser *et al.*, 1990), whereas nitrogen may be periodically limiting in lakes receiving unbalanced anthropogenic loads of P and N (i.e., eutrophic lakes). However, a rather close balance between P and N limitation can occur also in undisturbed lakes with long water retention times. In such lakes, the phytoplankton productivity depends strongly on internal recycling of nutrients and therefore a rather balanced supply of P and N is to be expected. One group of lakes with long water retention and readily acidified are the oligotrophic headwater lakes located on slowly weathered bedrock and nutrient-poor deposits. When acidification is not due to atmospheric input of nitrogen, this type of acidified lake can be expected to be one in which there is a close balance between P and N limitation (Gahnström *et al.*, 1993).

If a phytoplankton community becomes N-limited, a shift from nonnitrogen-fixing to nitrogen-fixing phytoplankton species may be expected. There may occur a shift from non-blue-green to blue-green species in acidified lakes (Schindler *et al.*, 1985) but nitrogen-fixing blue-greens have never dominated in such waters. Thus, the shift from eucaryotic algae to blue-greens in acidified lakes is probably not due to N deficiency. In eutrophic lakes this type of shift may be due to lowered N : P ratios. Blue-greens (both nitrogen-fixing and non-fixing) are often found to dominate when total-N : total-P ratios (by weight) are below 29 : 1. However, although acidified lakes normally have high N : P ratios, the late summer phytoplankton community is often dominated by blue-greens, hence the nutrient ratio hypothesis cannot explain the observed species shift.

Almost all types of phytoplankton can assimilate NO_3^-, NO_2^- or NH_4^+; many species can also utilize organic forms of N. In most experiments with algal monocultures, NH_4^+ is preferred as a nitrogen source by most species, because it can be assimilated with low energy costs. Little is known, however, about the ability of different species in a natural community to compete for various sources of nitrogen. Blue-greens have been regarded as poor competitors for NO_3^- and will be outcompeted by other phytoplankton in nitrate-rich environments. On the other hand, blue-greens are good at competing for NH_4^+ and tend to dominate in ammonium-rich environments. Therefore, a reduced transfer of NH_4^+ to NO_3^- in acidified lakes may lead to dominance shifts from eucaryotic algae to nonnitrogen-fixing blue-greens. In the phytoplankton community, dominance shifts due to altered nitrogen chemistry in acidified lakes may, in turn, affect the entire pelagic food chain since cyanophytes are generally of little nutritional value to herbivorous zooplankton (Lampert, 1987).

Changes in cloud cover are among the critical uncertainties in projections of future climate (Dickinson, 1989). Increased frequency of cloudy days has strong implications for deep-water phytoplankton that account for substantial primary production in oligotrophic and mesotrophic lakes during summer stratification (St. Amand and Carpenter, 1993). Deep-water algae show high rates of nutrient supply by eddy diffusion from the hypolimnion, but they are often limited by grazers, low temperatures, or low light. If global warming reduces vertical mixing (McCormick, 1990), the metalimnion is likely to become a more important habitat for phytoplankton. Increased cloud cover may reduce surface irradiance to the point that algae cannot maintain a positive carbon balance in deep, nutrient-rich water. If photosynthesis were restricted to nutrient-poor surface waters, primary production would decrease by factors of two to three (Carpenter *et al.*, 1992).

EUTROPHICATION AND RED TIDES

Ho and Hodgkiss (1993) have discussed the appearance and significance of red tides in Tolo Harbour, Hong Kong, which has suffered these tides since the early seventies. Tolo Harbour, a semienclosed embayment in the northeastern waters, is most affected by the events. In keeping with the increases in population, and thus in nutrient load, red tide in Tolo Harbour has been a consequence as well as a process of eutrophication. Tolo Harbour could be of particular importance in red tide research because both the landlocked geometry of the embayment and the dramatic changes of environmental conditions as a result of rapid economic growth are of special significance for studying the mechanisms of red tide formation. Red tides in inner Tolo peak in March to May annually. This relates to replenishment of bottom nutrients into surface water due to climatic changes during this period. The increasing number of red tide occurrences is accompanied by an increase in the variety of species and a change in population dominance with dinoflagellates gradually replacing diatoms. In 1988, for example, a red tide caused by *Gonyaulax polygramma* persisted there for more than three months. The maximum concentration of *G. polygramma* reached 23,000 cells per ml and several fish kills due to deoxygenation during night hours were recorded. In recent years, low levels of paralytic shellfish poisoning (PSP) ranging from a trace to 600 mouse units per kilogram tissue of green lipped mussel have also been detected in Hong Kong waters.

The raw field data showed that there was a continuous increase of inorganic nitrogen and inorganic phosphorus within the water column of inner Tolo Harbour for the period from 1982–1989. However, the rate of annual increase in soluble total nitrogen (TN) concentration was slightly lower than that of soluble total phosphorus (TP). Thus, there was a gradual decrease in the N : P ratio in inner Tolo Harbour. The inorganic N : P ratio was 20.3 in 1983 but fell to 11.05 in 1989. This decrease in the N : P ratio can be attributed to certain pollution control measures in which the nitrogen load was reduced. The growths of most of the causative organisms of red tide (Table 13-8) were however optimized in a low N : P ratio of 6–15, as indicated by bottle bioassay in the laboratory. Whilst the primary objective of the Tolo Harbour Action Plan was to tackle eutrophication problems caused by diatoms, the increased prominence of dinoflagellates and small flagellates may have been a result of neglecting phosphorus control in the Tolo Harbour Action Plan. There was a negative correlation between red tide occurrences and the sea water N : P ratios. Increasingly, whenever there was a drop in the annual sea water N : P ratio, the annual red tide occurrence correspondingly increased. The results provided strong evidence that phosphorus was the primary limiting factor for a major portion of the red tide causative organisms in Tolo Harbour. The changes in the ratio of the nitrogen to phosphorus contents suggested that a relatively low N : P ratio is usually optimal for the outbreaks of red tide (Ho and Hodgkiss, 1993).

Table 13-8 Optimal N : P (atomic) ratios for the growth of the various red tide causative organisms (Source: Ho and Hodgkiss, 1993)

Causative species	Optimal N : P ratio for growth
Ceratium furca	12–22
Gonyaulax polygramma	4–8
Gymnodinium nagasakiense	11–16
Noctiluca scintillans	8–14
Prorocentrum dentatum	6–13
Prorocentrum minimum	4–13
Prorocentrum sigmoides	4–15
Prorocentrum triestinum	8–15
Scrippsiella trochoidea	6–13
Cryptomonas spp.	12–20
Prymnesium spp.	6–12
Olisthodiscus sp.	4–15
Skeletonema costatum	15–30
Alexandrium catenella	15–30
Mesodinium rubrum	No significant response to N : P ratio

Several reports on the problems of red tide in the South China Sea have also noted that phosphorus was the primary limiting factor for dinoflagellate blooms (Cheong *et al.*, 1988; Huang, 1989). Thus, it appears that the nontoxic red tides occurring in coastal and estuarine environments of the West Pacific Subtropical Region are principally limited by nutrient enrichment and, in particular, phosphorus.

According to Bellinger (1979), if inorganic nitrogen was greater than 0.1 mg l^{-1} and phosphate greater than 0.02 mg l^{-1} the water body (mainly freshwater) would be subjected to ill effects from eutrophication. In Tolo Harbour, when dissolved nitrogen was greater than 0.1 mg l^{-1} and dissolved phosphorus greater than 0.02 mg l^{-1}, the red tides were seen. This is thus a special nutritional requirement for coastal, nontoxic red tides in the territorial waters of Hong Kong, and possibly may be the general criterion for red tides in other subtropical estuarine environments.

SPECIES SUCCESSION

Many workers have studied the pattern of seasonal fluctuations in phytoplankton succession in various lakes. A few basic processes seem to play the major role in controlling the general successional sequence in lakes. Two broad types of factors, called allogenic and autogenic, are involved in these processes. The allogenic factors include water chemistry, temperature, turbulence, etc. The autogenic factors include the species competition, predation, parasitism, allelopathy, and other similar biotic factors.

Both growth rates and loss rates of a species are important factors determining phytoplankton succession. In recent years, the emphasis of research seems to have shifted to temperature effects on the physiology of resource utilization (Mechling and Kilham, 1982; Yoder, 1979). According to Tilman *et al.* (1982), the major pattern of algal seasonal succession can be explained by the interactions between supplies of N, P, Si, and temperature. Possibly, temperature affects mainly the maximal growth rate of a species, not its half-saturation constant for a nutrient. Tilman *et al.* further suggest that the trophic structure of aquatic ecosystems plays an important role in phytoplankton ecology. Resource competition among algal species, pH, and temperature are the main factors controlling the composition of phytoplankton communities. Tilman *et al.* are of the opinion that instead of concentrating on causes of species diversity, researchers should emphasize seasonal population dynamics and succession.

Species successions have a major role in phytoplankton dynamics and in coupling the algal communities to higher trophic levels. Such successions involve continuous community reorganization, and they occur irrespective of the indigenous flora, biogeographic regime, water mass, stage or type of annual phytoplankton cycle. Succession is usually defined as a change in species composition within a given water mass, resulting from changing physical, chemical, and biotic factors within that water mass (Smayda, 1980). In true succession, autochthonous populations are involved, whereas 'sequential' changes result from the entry of allochthonous populations.

Many algal classes are represented in the phytoplankton of lakes, rivers, and oceans; and diatoms, dinoflagellates, and coccolithophorids are pre-eminent in marine waters. Diatoms tend to dominate in colder, nutrient-rich waters. Coccolithophorids are dominant in warmer nutrient-poor waters, and dinoflagellates are somewhat intermediate in general environmental preference.

A common observation is the seasonal progression from diatom dominated communities to those dominated by coccolithophorids or dinoflagellates. Several species of motile algae usually follow the initial dominance of nonmotile species. In temperate coastal waters, there is usually a spring bloom of diatoms that is followed in summer by one of dinoflagellates. In warm, nutrient-poor oceanic waters (e.g., the Sargasso Sea), coccolithophorids and other flagellates exhibit prolonged community dominance (Fig. 13-12).

Smayda (1980) is of the view that the most fundamental of the phytoplankton successional patterns, with regard to ecological consequences, is species succession (Fig. 13-13); this succession is characterized by the (1) co-occurrence of many species for varying durations and at different times, (2) exhibition generally by each species of a population maximum, with the maximal abundance varying among the different species, and (3) demonstration of concurrent peaks by several species.

Unlike succession in terrestrial habitats (where a pioneer plant community slowly evolves through several seres to a climax), that in water bodies usually involves frequent, unpredictable changes in composition and abundance of species, including reversals to pre-existing communities. Further, whereas terrestrial succession is very slow, lasting over several decades, that of planktonic community is usually annual.

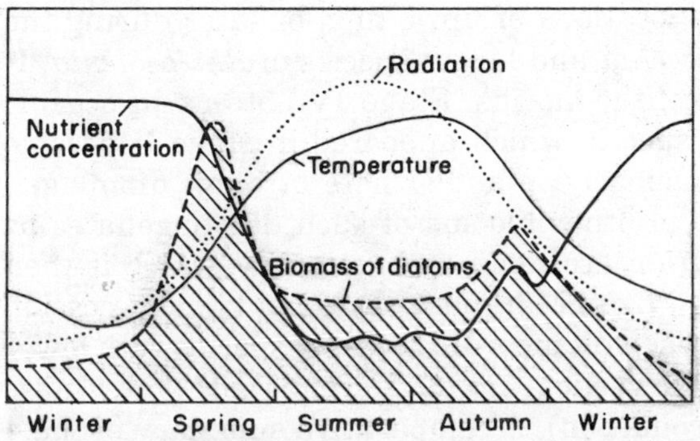

Fig. 13-12 Seasonal biomass changes in diatom population with associated changes in radiation, temperature, and nutrient concentration, in euphotic zone of ocean (after Tait, 1968).

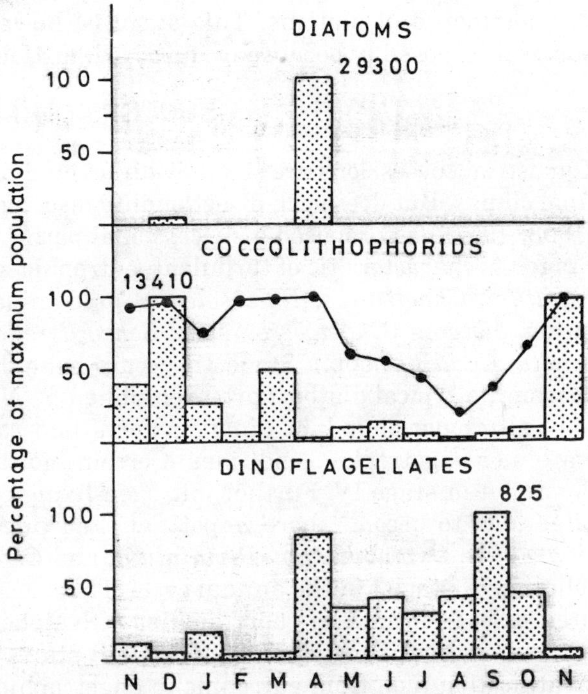

Fig. 13-13 One-year succession profile of diatoms, coccolithophorids, and dinoflagellates, showing their relative maxima in surface water (up to 10 metre deep) of Sargasso Sea, 22 km southeast of Bermuda, in 1957–58. Concentrations are shown as percentage of maximum observed concentration of each group. Curve in coccolithophorid panel represents % of total population of *Emiliania huxleyi*. (After Hulburt *et al.*, 1960.)

SARGASSO SEA

These subtropical waters lie in the centre of the great North Atlantic Eddy, with surface temperatures ranging between 18°C and 30°C. Hulburt *et al*. (1960) studied the phytoplankton cycle near Bermuda. Coccolithophorids, especially *Emiliania huxleyi*, dominate throughout the year. Dinoflagellates were never abundant and did not exhibit any distinct species succession. To a small extent, the same was true of diatoms. Stage I of phytoplankton succession in this sea occurs during May-October and comprises sparse populations. During this stage, dominance passed (temporarily) from coccolithophorids to dinoflagellates, but species abundance and diversity remained more or less unchanged (Hulburt *et al*., 1960). The breakdown of the summer thermocline in November signalled the start of stage II in which *Emiliania huxleyi* dominated. Stage III commenced with the onset of thermal stratification in April, during which the elevated nutrient levels, increase in light intensity, etc., favoured the dominance of diatoms. This stage is, however, quite brief and involves limited species succession, possibly because of quick exhaustion of nutrients.

SUCCESSION AS A PATHWAY

Terrestrial successions are strongly directional progressing through various seral stages to the final climax. But does such directionality also apply to succession in aquatic habitats? Margalef (1958, 1967) has proposed a successional pathway for aquatic systems, consisting of 4 stages. Stage I is characteristic of turbulent, eutrophic waters, and small-celled diatoms (*Skeletonema costatum*, *Chaetoceros*, *Rhizosolenia*) predominate. Stage II has more mixed community of larger diatoms (*Chaetoceros* spp., *Schroederella*) and dinoflagellates (*Prorocentrum*, *Scrippsiella*, *Ceratium* spp.). Stage III occurs near the locations of upwelling, or later during the season. Its typical diatoms are exemplified by *Nitzschia* and larger species of *Rhizosolenia*. It may also have abundant dinoflagellates and coccolithophorids. Stage IV obtains in oceanic waters or oligotrophic conditions. Certain motile species which appeared in stage II become dominant in stage IV. Further, nitrogen-fixing cyanobacteria and/or heterotrophic dinoflagellates tend to become more important. Red tide and other blooms of such dinoflagellates as *Gonyaulax*, *Gymnodinium*, *Peridinium*, and *Ceratium* are common in stage IV, which is then followed by stage I in the annual cycle. Thus, according to Margalef, phytoplankton succession progresses from smaller-celled species with high area : volume ratio to larger species with lower ratios, and then on to flagellates. It usually starts with vertical mixing and ends with water mass stratification (i.e., from eutrophic to oligotrophic condition). A comparative summary of the 4 stages proposed by Margalef is given in Table 13-9.

Table 13-9 Summary of Margalef's four stages of species succession in aquatic bodies

Parameter	I*	II	III	IV†
Cell surface : cell volume ratio	1.0	0.5	0.3	Very low
Pigment ratio ($O.D._{430}/O.D._{665}$)‡	2.5–3.5	3–4	?	Over 40
Typical algae	Small diatoms, small flagellates	*Chaetoceros* sp., coccolithophorids, small dinoflagellates	Round and big diatoms and dinoflagellates	Large dinoflagellates, coccolithophorids
Division rate	1 or more/day	A few days	?	About 1/week
Cell density/ml	10^2–10^3	10^1–10^2	?	10^1

*This stage corresponds to stage III in Sargasso Sea (Hulburt *et al.*, 1960).

†This stage corresponds to stages II and I in Sargasso Sea (Hulburt *et al.*, 1960).

‡O.D., optical density.

In the Caribbean Sea, dinoflagellate bioluminescence gives a prominence and elegance to the species successions. These bioluminescent blooms are commonly caused by virtually unialgal *Pyrodinium bahamense* (Seliger *et al.*, 1970). In some places, other dinoflagellates such as *Ceratium* spp. and *Peridinium divergens* also occur in small numbers, besides the dominant *Pyrodinium bahamense*.

Little is known about the factors controlling the sudden appearance of such red tide blooms. Even during periods when the numbers of dinoflagellates are quite low, they are eaten by shellfish. The shellfish themselves are immune to the toxin produced by these algae, but the shellfish which have fed on toxic dinoflagellates are hazardous to human beings which eat the shellfish. Though the toxin is of no apparent advantage to the dinoflagellates, it may well be a factor in producing blooms. The toxin kills fish and other animals which degenerate and release nutrients which in turn may stimulate the growth and multiplication of dinoflagellates.

Three important habitats for marine planktonic communities are the estuarine, coastal, and oceanic habitats. Table 13-10 compares the general properties of the phytoplankton of these habitats.

Table 13-10 General comparison of marine phytoplankton communities in estuarine, coastal, and oceanic habitats

Property	Habitat		
	Estuarine	Coastal	Oceanic
Nutrient content	High	Variable	Low
Turbulence	High	Variable	Low
Time scale of variability	Days	Weeks	Months
Vertical velocity (cm/sec)	?	10^{-2}–10^{-4}	10^{-4}–10^{-5}
Margalef succession type*	Stage I	Stages II-III	Stage IV
Productivity	High	Variable	Low
Food web complexity	Low	Intermediate	High
Skeletization	Slight	Frequent (SiO_2)	Common ($CaCO_3$)
Growth rate	High	Moderate	Low
Cell density (per litre)	10^6 or more	10^3–10^5	Up to 10^3
Major algal groups	Flagellates, small diatoms	Diatoms	Coccolithophorids, dinoflagellates
Typical species	*Skeletonema costatum*, *Leptocylindrus danicus*, *Detonula confervacea*	*Thalassiosira nitzschioides*, *Skeletonema costatum*, *Rhizosolenia alata*	*Coccolithus huxleyi*, *Trichodesmium thiebautii*, *Mastogloia rostratum*

*See Table 13-9.

There is some indication that the disappearance of dinoflagellate blooms in nature may be brought about by certain bacteria; several marine dinoflagellates are known to harbour bacteria endosymbiotically.

FACTORS REGULATING SPECIES SUCCESSION

Allogenic, autogenic, and sequential factors influence species succession. The former include those over which the algae have no control and are exemplified by salinity, temperature, light, turbulence, and anthropogenic substances. The autogenic factors, in contrast, can be controlled significantly either by algae or by other trophic levels. Nutrients, water quality, life cycle characteristics, allelochemicals, and predation are examples of autogenic factors. The mean sequential factor is represented by the introductions and translocations of populations by hydrographic disturbances and their accompanying environmental modifications. Some of the above factors overlap and may not always be mutually exclusive. For instance, phytoplankton population density is an autogenic factor but it can influence light intensity which is an allogenic factor. Sinking rate cannot be strictly defined as being either autogenic or allogenic.

The influence exerted by a certain factor on species succession is a function of the extent to which the populations may adapt physiologically to changes in that factor. Algal species, for instance, can adapt to sun- or shade-forms, can alter their phosphorus requirements by luxury uptake, etc.

PERIODICITY

Most phytoplankton populations are rather short-lived and exhibit a marked seasonal periodicity. Sometimes, a particular algal species suddenly becomes dominant in phytoplankton, maintains its abundance for 2–4 weeks, and then just as suddenly disappears. There are two chief ways in which the inoculum of this species originates. In some cases, the species occurs in the water body in very small numbers throughout the year as, for example, *Asterionella formosa* (Fig. 13-14) in Lake Windermere. Alternatively, the cells may be brought afresh into the lake with inflowing water or they may be resuspended from bottom sediments or grow from perennating zygospores, etc. The second possibility seems to operate in the case of *Melosira italica* (see Lund, 1965).

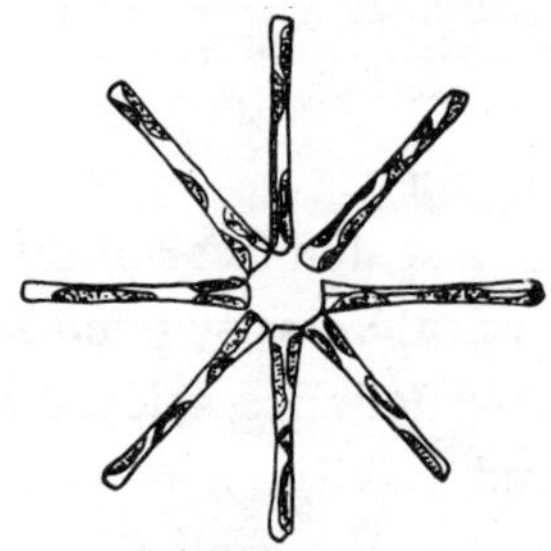

Fig. 13-14 *Asterionella formosa*, habit.

Many workers have undertaken researches to find out what factors enable the species to grow abundantly and how do they control the population density of the species. Physical, chemical, and biological factors are involved in these processes and all these factors interact together in complex ways. Important physical factors include light, temperature, turbulence, turbidity. The chief chemical factors are inorganic and organic nutrients and growth substances, and the major biotic factors include parasitism, predation, and competition. When most of these factors are favourable for a particular species, it grows prolifically and forms blooms.

The importance of physico-chemical factors in regulating phytoplankton periodicity has been best demonstrated in the case of the well-known phenomenon of the spring maximum of diatoms in temperate waters. In this case, increasing temperature and light intensity are the chief factors involved in the spring blooming of diatoms, whereas increasing silica levels produce the same effect in summer (see Golterman, 1975).

In Lake Windermere, the smallest nannoplanktonic algal species are also abundant in the spring but their periodicity is mainly due to grazing, due to their capacity for heterotrophic growth, and by the competition for nutrients. Within a lake, the environment need not be and is not uniform. The distributions of algal species and their predators are never homogeneous and the same applies to light penetration and nutrient supply. Most algal species have at least one parasite species which can afflict it, and most algae are grazed—the nannoplankton by crustaceans and rotifers, and the netplankton by protozoans. The crustaceans and rotifers engulf the algal cells, whereas the protozoans enter the cells and ingest them or attach themselves to the alga and use their contents (Golterman, 1975). Predation is another important factor that regulates algal populations. It can affect the outcome of competition between two populations and can prevent a competitive exclusion as well as destroy a potential coexistence situation. Sometimes, predation involves some selectivity; selectivity occurs when the ratio of attack rates of a predator on two prey populations is not equal to the ratio of the densities of the prey populations.

In natural waters, the growth *rate* of many diatoms is probably limited by phosphate availability, whereas their *yield* is chiefly limited by silicate.

Turbulence of water seems to be the main factor involved in the seasonal cycle of *Melosira italica* (Lund, 1965), although its importance is disputed by Golterman (1975), especially for some situations. In temperate lakes, diatoms are commonly dominant in early spring and tend to be succeeded by green flagellates in late spring which in turn are succeeded by cyanobacteria in summer. In such lakes, cryptomonads are abundant throughout the year, and sometimes a second diatom peak occurs in late summer in which *Ceratium* is the species concerned.

Phosphate content in water is another factor regulating the algal population density. In some lakes, both phosphate and nitrate may limit growth (Bush and Welch, 1972); these lakes tend to support chiefly cyanobacteria such as *Aphanizomenon*, *Anabaena*, and *Coelosphaerium*. In general, blue-green algae dominate in lakes where N : P ratios are low, whereas other classes of algae dominate where these ratios are high. Similarly, in certain lakes, silica and phosphorus are the main limiting nutrients; in these, diatoms are rare when Si : P ratios are low and diatoms dominate when these ratios are high.

When attacked by parasites, the host algal populations are greatly decreased in numbers, sometimes as much as 90 per cent. In this respect, parasitism differs from grazing; in the latter case, instead of a steep reduction in the host population, an equilibrium tends to be established between the grazer and the algal populations. Certain desmid populations are subject to parasitism. Many rotifers graze nannoplanktonic algae. In natural waters, cyanobacteria are probably less grazed than green algae; this may be one reason why cyanobacteria frequently form blooms (Arnold, 1971).

Aquatic ecosystems are much more complex than is commonly realized. There has been a general tendency to emphasize the role of a single factor, such as nutrient limitation of phytoplankton. Relatively small shifts in components further up the food web produce significant effects on algal population dynamics (Porter, 1976). Many physiological ecologists tend to believe that communities can be represented by such unspecific entities as chlorophyll-a or particulate carbon. But the immense range of organization and life cycles of phytoplankters disprove such an erroneous attitude. Nutrients do give important clues to the size of final yields but we need to study several other factors also if we are to form a coherent and meaningful picture of the totality of phytoplankton species composition, succession, and productivity (Jewson *et al.*, 1981). The importance of one such additional factor, viz., loss rates, considered in conjunction with factors limiting growth rate and final yield has been emphasized in a recent study on diatoms by Jewson *et al.* (1981). These workers have measured certain factors controlling the growth and decline of a diatom crop (*Melosira italica* and *Stephanodiscus astraea* mainly) in a large, well mixed eutrophic lake, Lough Neagh, lreland. The increase in chlorophyll ceased when soluble reactive phosphorus became depleted, while biomass continued to increase until silica became undetectable. The net population growth rate was quite high, reaching 4% per day, whereas losses due to washout (less than 0.5%), parasitism (4% infestation by chytrids), and grazing by *Cyclops* and other zooplankters remained rather low. More than 90% of the population of *Melosira* and *Stephanodiscus* rapidly sedimented during calm weather at the time of nutrient limitation. In the sediment, the diatom crops persisted for certain periods (around a month or more) after which they were attacked by benthic animals and only about 1% of the population could survive through to the following year. The numbers, density, distribution, and activity of the benthic fauna not only influence algal populations directly (by determining whether cells are trapped in sediments or return to the water column), but also indirectly by affecting nutrient recycling.

At least for diatoms, light and silica are two very important factors. The former controls initiation of a net increase in population size and the rate of population increase, whereas the cessation of diatom growth is controlled by silica depletion. In those situations where silica supplies are adequate, sedimentation can become a critical factor and a major determinant of succession (Knoechel and Kalff, 1978; Kalff and Knoechel, 1978).

DIEL PERIODICITY

The chemical composition and pigmentation in phytoplankton populations often show regular diel periodicities (Eppley *et al.*, 1967; Frempong, 1981). Based on diel observations on Esthwaite Water, a productive English lake, Frempong (1981) has shown the sensitivity of different indexes of biomass and physiological state to short-term environmental perturbations. These indexes may respond to such perturbations in "no-diel", "pseudo-diel" or "true-diel" variations. Frempong found that the order of sensitivity of the various indexes, as indicators of diel periodicity, was carbohydrate-related ratios chlorophyll-a : carbon; carbon : nitrogen; carotenoids : chlorophyll-a. Seasonal background greatly influences the diel variability in these indexes.

Ryther *et al.* (1961) have shown that concentrations of nitrate and phosphate exhibit diel variations in certain lakes, whereas Frempong (1981) has shown the same phenomenon with respect to ammonium nitrogen. Possibly, the same holds good for certain other nutrients also.

Pseudo-diel variations do not result from any real changes in cellular composition but rather reflect shifts in the ratios for the particulate material due to biomass redistribution. True-diel variations reflect physiological differentiation in response to environmental changes, e.g., in light intensity or quality.

Cyclomorphosis

Certain diatoms, dinoflagellates, and many zooplanktonic species exhibit a characteristic seasonal polymorphism in respect of their body sizes (Hutchinson, 1967). A similar seasonal variation in filament length of *Oscillatoria redekei* has been reported by Gibson (1975). This regular seasonal cycle is not related to the seasonal fluctuations in the biomass of *O. redekei,* but occurs in step with the nutrient concentrations in lake water. In an Irish lake, the mean filament length rose to a peak in May and fell sharply in June-July. A second peak occurred in August and was followed by a second decline in winter. Such seasonal changes show considerable parallel with corresponding changes in phosphate and nitrate contents of the water and also its pH. Thus, nitrate and phosphate become depleted by the spring outburst of the phytoplankton and the pH rises due to CO_2 utilization in photosynthesis. After this period, the alga is stressed by phosphorus limitation and its filaments become short. Conversely, when the phosphate and nitrate concentrations in lake water begin to rise, the filaments also become longer.

Another possibility pertains to the adaptive significance of filament length in relation to the sinking rates of the organism. Since short filaments sink more slowly than long ones, filament shortening during the warm water period may promote suspension of filaments in water as opposed to their sinking.

CLASSIFICATION

Taylor (1980) has classified the phytoplanktonic algae into the following groups:

Kingdom: Prokaryota (cells have one DNA-containing compartment and 70S ribosomes)
- Division: Cyanophyta
  - Class: Cyanophyceae (cyanophytes)

Kingdom: Eukaryota (cells with at least two DNA-containing compartments, 80S cytoplasmic ribosomes)
- Division: Pyrrhophyta
  - Class: Dinophyceae (dinoflagellates)
- Division: Cryptophyta
  - Class: Cryptophyceae (cryptomonads)
- Division: Chrysophyta
  - Class: Prymnesiophyceae (Haptophyceae, prymnesiomonads)
  - Class: Chrysophyceae (chrysomonads)
  - Class: Bacillariophyceae (diatoms)
  - Class: Raphidophyceae (Chloromonadophyceae, chloromonads)
- Division: Xanthophyta
  - Class: Xanthophyceae (xanthophytes)
- Division: Eustigmatophyta
  - Class: Eustigmatophyceae (eustigmatophytes)
- Division: Euglenophyta
  - Class: Euglenophyceae (euglenoids)
- Division: Chlorophyta
  - Class: Prasinophyceae (prasinomonads)
  - Class: Chlorophyceae (green algae)

A more recent classification, relating to marine phytoplankton, is that proposed by Chretiennot-Dinet *et al.* (1993). These authors classify the phytoplankton into the following 17 classes. The names of classes are given below:

Chlorarachniophyceae
Chlorophyceae
Chrysophyceae
Cryptophyceae
Cyanophyceae
Diatomophyceae
Dictyochophyceae
Dinophyceae
Euglenophyceae
Eustigmatophyceae
Micromonadophyceae
Pedinophyceae
Prasinophyceae
Prymnesiophyceae
Raphidophyceae
Rhodophyceae
Tribophyceae

PARADOX OF THE PLANKTON

Lakes (Fig. 13-15) and oceans are anisotropic environments whose ecosystems are organized along the axis defined by light and gravity, and they have vertical gradients in light, oxygen, nutrients, and redox potential. Such gradients exhibit daily or seasonal fluctuations that are not exactly the same in adjacent water bodies. This lack of synchrony between fluctuations in adjacent columns of water constitutes an important source of horizontal variability in the plankton populations.

In studies of plankton populations, diversity of populations is a useful parameter. The spectrum of diversity is often related to the spectra of turbulent diffusion and of covariance

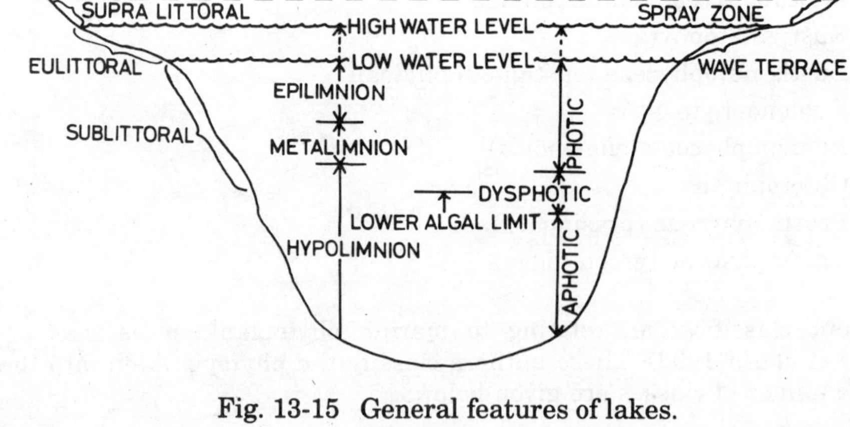

Fig. 13-15 General features of lakes.

in the distribution of species (Margalef, 1979). In the particular case studied by Margalef in the Mediterranean Sea, dinoflagellates dominated in summer in stratified water near the surface, and moderately diversified communities exhibited continuum with increasing diversity as the sampling space is increased. In more turbulent and fertile spots, diatoms dominated and there was high diversity in small spots because of mixing. In these small regions, diversity does not further increase with increasing size of the sample, and the populations tend to be fairly similar over large extensions as a result of mixing. This example recalls to mind the "paradox of the plankton" mentioned by Hutchinson (1961).

Algal populations inhabiting a common environment compete for nutrients and other environmental resources such as light. In nature, single, one-species populations do not exist but occur as mixtures of several different populations of algae, bacteria, fungi, and other organisms, the different populations interacting in diverse ways. Some populations excrete certain chemicals into the environment and these chemicals may be toxic to their competitors.

Most algae are osmotrophic, i.e., they obtain their mineral salts from the water or soil by a molecule-to-molecule or ion-by-ion transfer to the chemicals across their cell membranes. Different populations of osmotrophic algae compete for resources of inorganic nutrients. A few algae, e.g., some cryptomonads, are phagotrophic as they ingest and digest particulate matter and then absorb the products of digestion.

Competition between algal populations can involve two different kinds of interaction. Firstly, mineral salts and light may be absorbed from the common environment, and the resulting reduction of these resources decreases the net growth rates of the competing populations. This kind of interaction is called competition (Fig. 13-16). Secondly, the populations may release certain chemicals that exert toxic or inhibitory effects on other populations. Fredrickson and Stephanopoulos (1981) designated this second type of interaction as "antagonism" if the toxicity and inhibitory effects are mutual, and "amensalism" if only one of the two populations produces a toxin whereas the other does not.

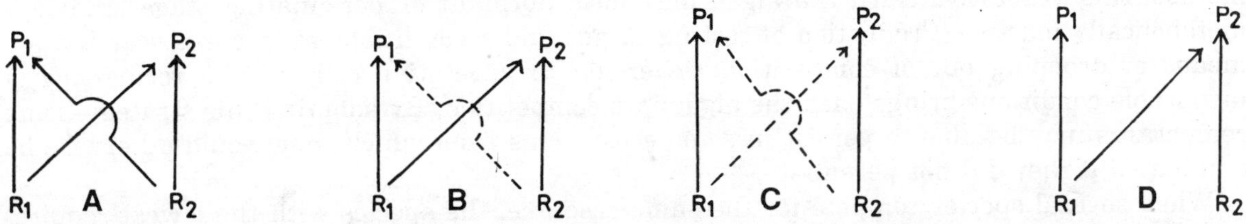

Fig. 13-16 Four instances of pure competition involving two populations (P_1 and P_2) and two resources (R_1 and R_2). Solid arrow indicates that resource exerts dynamical effect on population; dashed arrow means there is no such dynamical effect. (After Fredrickson and Stephanopoulos, 1981.)

Competition in nature is seldom, if ever, pure and simple; pure and simple competition means that there is only one nutrient whose availability influences the growth rates of the populations, and competition for this particular nutrient is the only interaction between the populations. Competition between two populations tends to eliminate one of the two populations from the common habitat, and this is particularly true when competition is mainly for a single resource and when the populations do not otherwise interact. However, in natural habitats, many factors mitigate the severity of competition and hence competitors do often coexist.

Limnologists have repeatedly stated that complete competitors cannot coexist, but this theoretical concept is belied by the so-called paradox of the plankton; it is a well established fact that many species of phytoplankton which compete for the limited amounts of nutrients present in many water bodies, can and do persist in the relatively homogeneous environments of large lakes. Theoretically, one would expect that one species alone would outcompete all others so that in a final equilibrium state the multispecies assemblage would reduce to a single-species population. Hutchinson (1961) suggested that competitive exclusion may not occur in a spatially homogeneous ecosystem having periodic time-varying inputs, and the pure and simple competitors therein may actually coexist (Fredrickson and Stephanopoulos, 1981). Recent researches have demonstrated that some kinds of periodic disturbances of a spatially homogeneous system can permit pure and simple competitors to coexist in a limit cycle. However, some workers believe that periodic disturbance of inputs to a spatially homogeneous system cannot by itself explain the coexistence of large number of species on a few limiting resources (see Fredrickson and Stephanopoulos, 1981). The common approach to resolving this paradox of the plankton is to invoke the heterogeneity of the environmental conditions. Environmental heterogeneity may involve discontinuous changes in environmental conditions at the boundaries between homogeneous subenvironments, or it may involve certain continuous changes within a system that is not divided into discrete subsystems. Some important factors that can influence and perturb such a system include agitation, nutrient mixing, motility of cells or flagellated stages, and chemotactic responses.

Another explanation that is sometimes advanced to resolve the paradox of the plankton points to the existence of numerous resources that exert dynamic effects in a system. There are also certain other factors which allow competitors to coexist. The algae of different classes sometimes utilize light energy of different wavelengths and hence can coexist. When the environmental conditions become adverse for the growth and multiplication of actively metabolizing vegetative cells, the algae may form dormant or perennating stages that are metabolically inactive. Production of resting stages under conditions of resource scarcity is a means of dropping out of competition; reversion to vegetative cells at the recurrence of favourable conditions brings back the algae into competition. By adopting this strategy, some competitors may be able to persist in some ecosystems from which they would otherwise be eliminated if they did not perennate.

When several species compete for the same resource, the species with the lowest requirement becomes the best competitor (i.e., is superior to others) at equilibrium (Tilman, 1977; Hansen and Hubbell, 1980). This species competitively displaces all others, independent of the initial densities of the competitors. This theoretical expectation has recently been experimentally verified by Tilman *et al.* (1981) in the case of certain nutrient-limited competition experiments with *Asterionella formosa* and *Synedra ulna* at temperatures from 8°C to 24°C. Silicate growth kinetics of temperature adapted *Asterionella* and *Synedra* predicted that *Asterionella* should competitively displace *Synedra* below 20°C, and *Synedra* should displace *Asterionella* above 20°C. These predictions turned out to be correct.

According to Tilman *et al.* (1981), the addition of spatial structure to a simple model of resource competition provides an equilibrium solution to the paradox of the plankton. The same effect is achieved by the addition of nonequilibrium conditions to simple models of resource competition. There have been a number of theoretical demonstrations recently

(Armstrong and McGehee, 1980; Levins, 1979) that many more species can coexist than there are limiting resources; in other words, the coexistence of numerous algal species can no longer be considered paradoxical. Tilman *et al.* have argued that it is incorrect to state that a particular lake is phosphorus- or nitrogen-limited. In fact, it is the individual algae (not lakes) that may be limited by a particular nutrient. Tilman *et al.* believe that the "paradox of the plankton" propounded by Hutchinson (1961) can now be safely dismissed as a dead issue.

The traditional view of a lake as constituting a homogeneous environment has turned out to be inadequate for understanding the diversity of coexisting species. New light has been shed on Hutchinson's (1961) paradox of the plankton by certain recent techniques that allow for the resolution of small-scale processes (Reynolds, 1984b). The field of research called 'dynamic biological limnology' (Legendre and Demers, 1984) deals with the coupling of biological and hydrodynamic processes.

The scale of vertical mixing processes shows large variations from minutes to days (Imboden, 1990). Consequently, algae are subject to a wide range of variation in light intensity. Under conditions of strong mixing the light climate as experienced by algae might change from bright surface light to near total darkness within minutes. The response of the rate of photosynthesis subsequent to changes in light intensity is affected by delays and complex temporal dynamics (e.g., Marra, 1980).

Most of the mathematical models for photosynthesis, however, are static and do not take the dynamic aspects into account. They describe a fixed relationship between the rate of photosynthesis and the light intensity; they fail to describe the response of photosynthesis under variable light conditions.

The model DYPHORA (DYnamic model for the PHOtosynthetic Rate of Algae) designed by Pahl-Wostl (1992) does take these dynamics into account by introducing two characteristic response times for the biological processes: (1) the effect of light inhibition having a time scale of minutes to a few hours, and (2) the time lag of the rate of photosynthesis for increasing light intensities having a time scale of seconds to minutes. The importance of the dynamic relative to the static description of photosynthesis depends on the time scales of the changes in the environment and the biological response, becoming significant when the time scales are comparable (Pahl-Wostl, 1992).

PRIMARY PRODUCTION

BIOMASS AND PHOTOSYNTHETIC CAPACITY (P_{max})

Maximum biomass ranges from about 26 mg/m^3 in Lake Biwa, Japan, to over 2100 mg/m^3 in Lake Aranga, Udi, Ethiopia (measurements as chlorophyll-a values). The values above 400 mg/m^3 are, however, generally rare and involve cyanobacteria.

Much work has been done on the contribution of phytoplankton to productivity in lakes, but very little is known about the role and significance of the smaller algae, less than about 15 μm in size, which collectively constitute the ultraplankton and which occur in pelagic waters in lakes along with the larger phytoplankton. Ultraplankton is known to supply proportionately more of the total phytoplankton production than is accounted for by its fraction of the total biomass (Ross and Duthie, 1981). Still smaller flagellates (microplankton, not exceeding 10 μm) are predominant in oceanic biomass and play an important role in community metabolism (Pomeroy and Johannes, 1968). The micro- and ultraplankton algae are also generally believed to show a fairly high photosynthetic efficiency. Especially in oligotrophic lakes, the micro- and ultraplankters assume an increasingly important role and they seem to be more abundant in oligotrophic than eutrophic lakes. According to Ross and Duthie (1981), as much as 47% of total phytoplankton biomass in the extremely oligotrophic Canadian Lake Matamec is constituted by the ultraplankton which, however, accounts for about 70% of the primary production in this lake. They found that the photosynthetic efficiency of the ultraplankton was about 2.5 times greater than that of the phytoplankton component, and attributed this differential efficiency to the differences in the surface-to-volume ratios between the smaller and the larger algal species (Ross and Duthie, 1981).

P_{max} is the maximum specific rate of gross photosynthesis reached at high irradiances, expressed per biomass unit of chlorophyll-a. These values on particular days can range from 0.5–38 mg oxygen/mg chlorophyll-a/hr for various lakes. A similar range for annual mean values is from about 3.2 for a lake in Alaska to 33 for Lake Chad.

DENSITY-DEPENDENT EFFECTS

According to D.W. Schindler and others, photosynthesis increases linearly with biomass or cell volume of phytoplankton in the lakes studied, and J.F. Talling found a similar linear relation between photosynthesis and chlorophyll-a. In contrast, several workers have noted that photosynthesis per unit biomass *decreases* with increasing biomass, measured either as chlorophyll-a or cell volume. It seems that both these situations may operate in different lakes/areas.

SEASONAL PATTERN OF PHOTOSYNTHESIS

In many temperate lakes, daily integral photosynthesis is limited by the daily totals of irradiance in water and by nutrients for much of the summer. The changes from winter to summer usually lead to the highest photosynthetic rates of the year which level off as nutrients are exhausted.

BIOMASS CHANGES AND NET PHOTOSYNTHESIS

The classical picture of biomass changes in lake phytoplankton shows a spring maximum (usually of diatoms and chrysomonads) and a second maximum (usually of green or blue-green algae in the summer or of diatoms in late summer), both being controlled primarily by nutrient limitations, once the winter limitations of light and temperature are overcome.

In the tropics, seasonal changes are usually insignificant. Here the ratio of maximum : minimum biomass usually does not exceed 5, in contrast to about 30 for many temperate lakes.

ANNUAL NET PRODUCTION RELATIONS

The annual net production of phytoplankton is less than 15 gram carbon/m^2/yr above 59° latitude; between 40° and 59°, most lakes have net production below 35. At still lower latitudes, many data are not available (very few lakes studied), but are all above 35 gram carbon/m^2/yr.

TROPHIC STATE

Most oligotrophic lakes have up to above 25 gram carbon/m^2/yr. The eutrophic lakes exceed

75 gram carbon/m^2/yr. The lowest value recorded is 1 gram carbon/m^2/yr for Alaska ponds, and the highest (over 2600 gram carbon/m^2/yr) is for Lake Marius in Egypt.

In high latitudes, light is more important as a limiting factor, whereas in lower latitudes, factors related to nutrient availability become more critical in determining phytoplankton production.

PHYTOPLANKTON PRODUCTION AND BIOTIC VARIABLES

Phytoplankton biomass and chlorophyll-a correlate well with each other and with phytoplankton production.

The best estimates of phytoplankton production are obtained when latitude, precipitation, and thermocline depth are considered together with chlorophyll-a concentration. Over 90% of the total variation in phytoplankton production can be accounted for by these variables.

Brylinsky (1980) has found that surprisingly phosphate and nitrate concentrations in lake water do not correlate well with phytoplankton production. This is probably related to the *variable turnover* rate of these nutrients rather than to their standing stock value. Schindler (1977) points out that determining the concentration of PO_4^{--} and NO_3^- in lake water is a poor indicator of their *dynamics* and a poor predictor of production in the growing season (spring). The inverse relationship between productivity and biomass on the one hand, and some properties of the phytoplankton, on the other, is illustrated in Fig. 13-17.

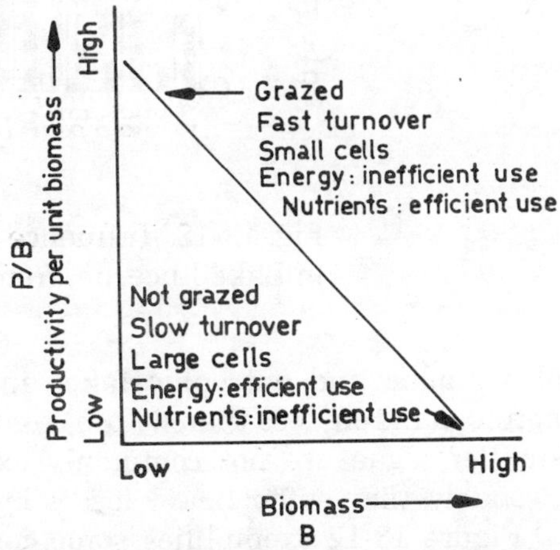

Fig. 13-17 Inverse relationship between productivity and biomass with some properties of the phytoplankton (after Harris, 1986).

PHYTOPLANKTON DYNAMICS

The phytoplankton of north temperate zone typically consists of 100 to several hundred spp. The early attempts to relate spp. composition to lake trophic state sought to determine suitable *indicator species* or quotients of the number of species present in certain taxonomic groupings that would reflect this trophy. Such indices are little used today because of taxonomic difficulties and because these indexes depend only on the number of species, not their abundances. The *Shannon* diversity index, for example, cannot be applied to phytoplankton because it depends more on the taxonomic competence of an investigator rather than on the nature of the ecosystem.

Changes in the nutrient content of the water affect primarily the dynamics of plankton and not their mean annual biomass (Fig. 13-18). At higher nutrient levels the variations between spring maximum, clear water period and summer maximum increase greatly. These variations are also an indication of the coupling within the nutrient chain.

BIOMASS

The mean summer biomass ranges from about 100–100,000 mg/m^3 wet weight, between most

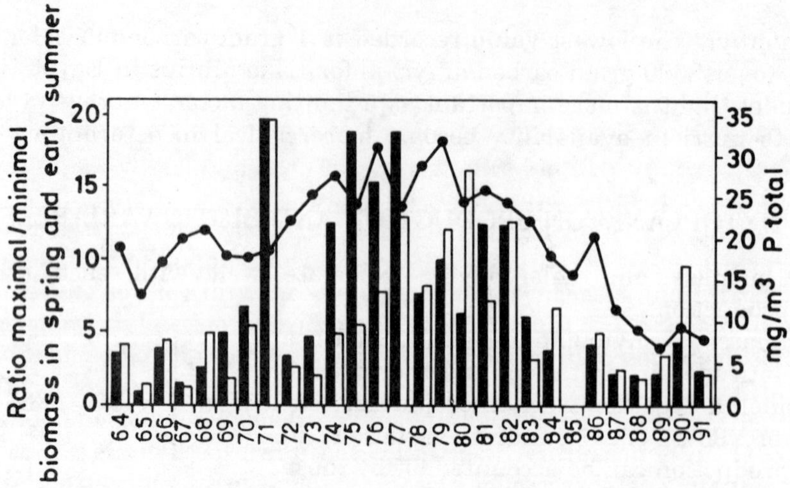

Fig. 13-18 Influence of zooplankton on algal biomass dynamics in Lake Lucerne, from 1964–1991 (after *EAWAG News*, 1993).

oligotrophic and eutrophic lakes in the north temperate zone. In oligotrophic lakes, the nannoplankton (less than 64 μm) contribute most of the biomass on an annual basis, but these smaller algae are not commonly examined by limnologists and they rarely form blooms. Probably, they suffer heavy losses by grazing, etc.

Figure 13-12 exemplifies some commonly observed changes in the biomass of diatoms in different seasons. The corresponding fluctuations in nutrient concentration, radiation, and temperature are also shown. These relationships are, however, not universal but vary from place to place. The figure shows only one typical example.

PRODUCTION RATES

The annual gross production varies from about 4 gram carbon/m^2/yr in the most oligotrophic lakes to around 700 gram carbon/m^2/yr in the most eutrophic.

The production rate of phytoplankton (chiefly *Oscillatoria* sp. and *Spirulina platensis*) in Lake Nakuru, Kenya, has been estimated to be about 15 kcal/m^2/day (Fig. 13-19) (Vareschi, 1977). This figure also illustrates the energy flow through this lake ecosystem. The biomass of algae is estimated as 2250 kcal/m^2.

INTERRELATION BETWEEN ABIOTIC VARIABLES

Most abiotic variables relate to climate factors, lake morphometry, and lake chemistry. The water temperature and daylength range are closely related to latitude. The mean depth is related to morphometry. The phytoplankton production chiefly depends on two major factors, viz., (1) solar energy, and (2) nutrients.

In general, phytoplankton production shows *strongest* correlations with variables related to solar energy input, moderate correlations with those related to water chemistry, and weak correlations with variables related to morphometry. Latitude shows a very high correlation with phytoplankton production.

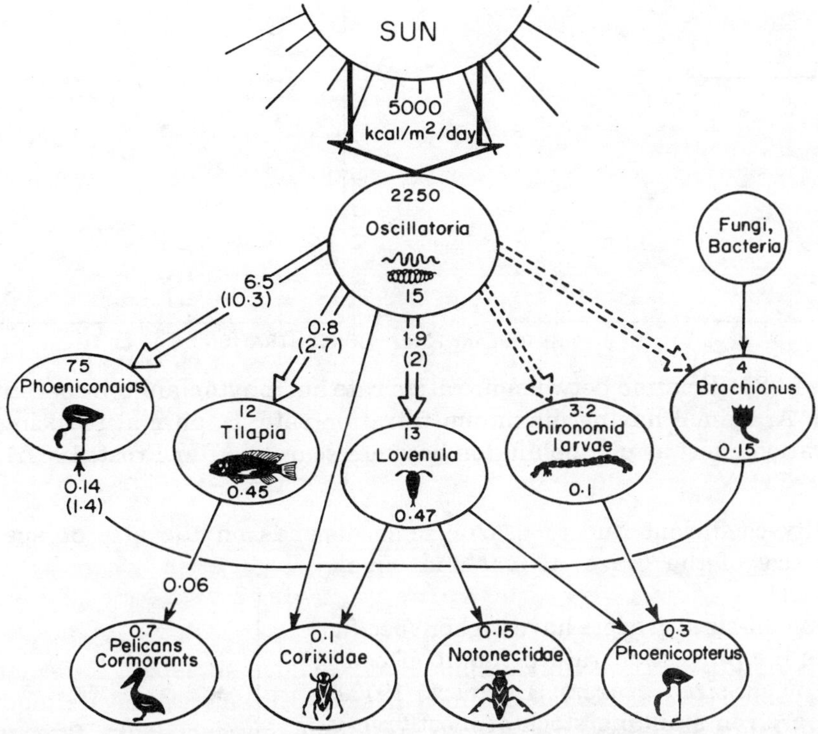

Fig. 13-19 Energy flow in ecosystem of Lake Nakuru, Kenya. Upper numbers indicate biomass (kcal/m^2) and lower, production (kcal/m^2/day). Arrows represent energy flow, upper number on each arrow being mean consumption rate (kcal/m^2/day) and lower (in parentheses), maximal consumption rate. All numbers are rough approximations. (After Vareschi, 1977.)

GRAZING

Grazing of phytoplankton by zooplankton is often a major factor determining phytoplankton abundance and it sometimes determines the timing and magnitude of phytoplankton peaks in lakes and oceans. Cells of different types or sizes may be grazed at different rates, and the species composition of a phytoplankton community can change as a consequence of grazing. The grazing rate inter alia depends on abundance of phytoplankton because many grazers remove algal cells from water by filtration. This means that changes in filtration rate reflect the feeding strategy of the grazer. Two possible and likely feeding strategies of a planktonic filter feeding grazer are shown in Fig. 13-20.

At low phytoplankton concentrations, a grazer of type A (in Fig. 13-20) produces a constant mortality which generally permits the phytoplankton population to grow despite being grazed. Grazers of type B cause a progressively lower mortality, or stop feeding altogether when phytoplankton concentration becomes too low.

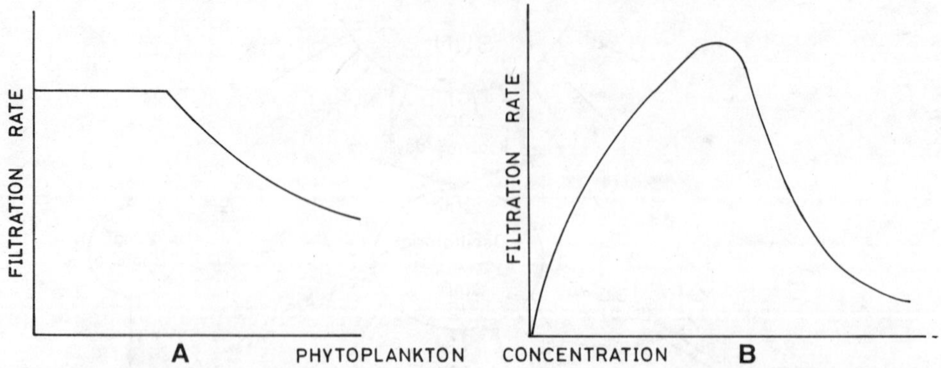

Fig. 13-20 Relation between filtration rate and phytoplankton concentration. A, animal having maximum filtration rate; B, animal reducing its filtration effort as phytoplankton becomes scarce. (After Frost, 1981.)

The mortality coefficient due to grazing also depends on the size or species of phytoplankton and size of the grazer (Nival and Nival, 1976) (Fig. 13-21).

Commonly, small-sized grazers have higher specific ingestion rates (i.e., ingestion rate per unit of body weight) than bigger-sized grazers (Lampert, 1977). Consequently, a given standing stock of mostly very small grazers exerts a proportionally larger grazing mortality on a phytoplankton community than the same standing stock of much larger consumers.

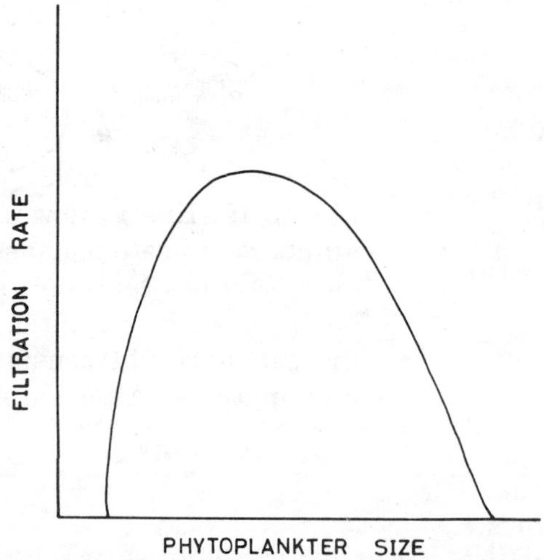

Fig. 13-21 Relation between filtration rate of planktonic filter feeding grazer and size of phytoplankter ingested.

The effect of grazers is not restricted to grazing alone, for they may also contribute indirectly to the growth of phytoplankton by recycling dissolved nutrients through their excretion of metabolites. Phosphorus recycling is especially important in many freshwater ecosystems, whereas nitrogen recycling is especially important in oceans. Under optimal feeding conditions, consumers excrete nitrogen equivalent to about one-third of ingested nitrogen (Corner and Davies, 1971). According to Porter (1976), there exists an intimate link between grazing, nutrient recycling by grazers, and phytoplankton growth. He opined that grazers provide nutrients to certain type of algae, resistant to digestion by grazers, while the algae pass unharmed through the digestive tract of the grazer.

Predicting the outcome of species interactions is a major goal in community ecology. Although a large number of field experiments have been performed, there have been no attempts to explain quantitative variation in the outcome of comparable species manipulations across habitats. For planktonic communities, much is known about the effects of consumers on lower trophic levels. Sarnelle (1992) has made predictions about how the magnitude of herbivore effects on phytoplankton should vary across a gradient of enrichment using two simple predator-prey models. These predictions were then compared with data on the effects of herbivore manipulations from a survey of field experiments in temperate lakes. He focussed on patterns across an enrichment gradient, since this serves to integrate resource (bottom-up) and consumer (top-down) control. The objective was to account for variation in the results of field experiments and test a simple hypothesis about the interaction between grazers and phytoplankton across an enrichment gradient.

Leibold's (1990) survey of field manipulations of nutrients and predators in lakes indicates that the presence of *Daphnia* is a critical factor. However, even within the subset of experiments having *Daphnia* as a dominant grazer, responses of total phytoplankton biomass to grazer manipulation vary over more than an order of magnitude from one lake to the next (Vanni, 1984); Sarnelle's analysis focusses on the prediction of these quantitative effects of *Daphnia* manipulation.

The interaction between the planktonic herbivore *Daphnia* and its phytoplanktonic prey has attracted the attention of those attempting to predict the equilibrium biomass of organisms of each trophic level with simple models (Arditi and Ginzburg, 1989; Leibold, 1990). Much of this work has concentrated on ways that two-species, Lotka-Volterra models of exploitation can be modified to obtain the prediction that phytoplankton biomass should increase with nutrient enrichment. Two-species, Lotka-Volterra models of exploitation generally predict that, at equilibrium, enrichment will increase the biomass of the consumer, while the biomass of the resource is unaffected. In contrast, there is a vast amount of data from numerous lakes that clearly shows mean phytoplankton biomass (usually measured as chlorophyll-a) to be positively related to phosphorus level (Peters, 1986). In addition, strong responses of phytoplankton biomass to anthropogenic increases in phosphorus supply rate have been well documented (Schindler and Fee, 1974; Edmondson and Lehman, 1981). Some of the responses of algal biomass to enrichment can surely be attributed to time lags in the numerical response of herbivores to increased algal growth rates.

Several modifications of two-species exploitation models have been proposed to reconcile observed and predicted algal responses to enrichment. In general, algal biomass will increase if the herbivore's feeding rate and/or assimilation efficiency decline with enrichment, or if the herbivore's death rate increases with enrichment (Walters *et al.*, 1987). Declines in feeding rate and assimilation efficiency may result from increases in grazing-resistant algae with enrichment. The effects of these so-called "inedible" algae on predictions of equilibrium biomass have already been explored in detail (Leibold, 1990). Sarnelle (1992) quantified algal responses to *Daphnia* manipulation as an Algal Response Factor (ARF), defined as total algal biomass in the low-*Daphnia* treatment divided by total algal biomass in the high-*Daphnia* treatment. Total phosphorus (TP) concentration was used as an index of algal carrying capacity, ranging from 10 to 460 µg/l over the 22 experiments surveyed. The Algal Response Factor ranged from 1 to 40 and was a positive, linear function of TP:

$$\text{ARF} = -0.14 + 0.08(\text{TP}),\ r^2 = 0.81:$$

$$\log \text{ARF} = -0.81 + 0.83(\log \text{TP}),\ r^2 = 0.75.$$

Thus, algal carrying capacity, as quantified by TP, explains much of the variation in *Daphnia* effects on total algal biomass across lakes.

The survey results supported the prediction of the simpler model, a two-species, Lotka-Volterra model of pure exploitation. Incorporating the additional complexity of inedible algae into this model did little to improve its predictive power. The conclusion that inedible algae are not of major importance to the prediction of *Daphnia* effects across an enrichment gradient was supported by a survey of *Daphnia* effects on the proportionate biomass of inedible algae. There was no evidence that *Daphnia* grazing typically favours dominance by inedible algae at equilibrium in highly enriched lakes.

Sarnelle's results suggest that the well-established positive relationship between TP and equilibrium algal biomass in lakes is more likely to be a consequence of increases in *Daphnia*'s death rate with enrichment, rather than decreases in *Daphnia*'s feeding and assimilation rates. When zooplanktivorous fish are rare, *Daphnia* should be able to prevent phytoplankton biomass from responding to nutrient addition at equilibrium. As a consequence, the success of biomanipulation in eutrophic lakes should critically depend upon the effectiveness of strategies aimed at reducing zooplanktivory.

The results of field experiments on *Daphnia* effects have important implications for the application of top-down, biomanipulation techniques to reduce algal biomass in lakes. Biomanipulation produces relatively small effects on algal biomass at TP levels below 15 µg/l. It does not seem possible to reduce algal biomass in mesotrophic lakes to levels found in oligotrophic lakes. Even in mesotrophic lakes, however, substantial improvements in water clarity can be achieved (Mazumder *et al.*, 1990). This is due to a curvilinear relationship between

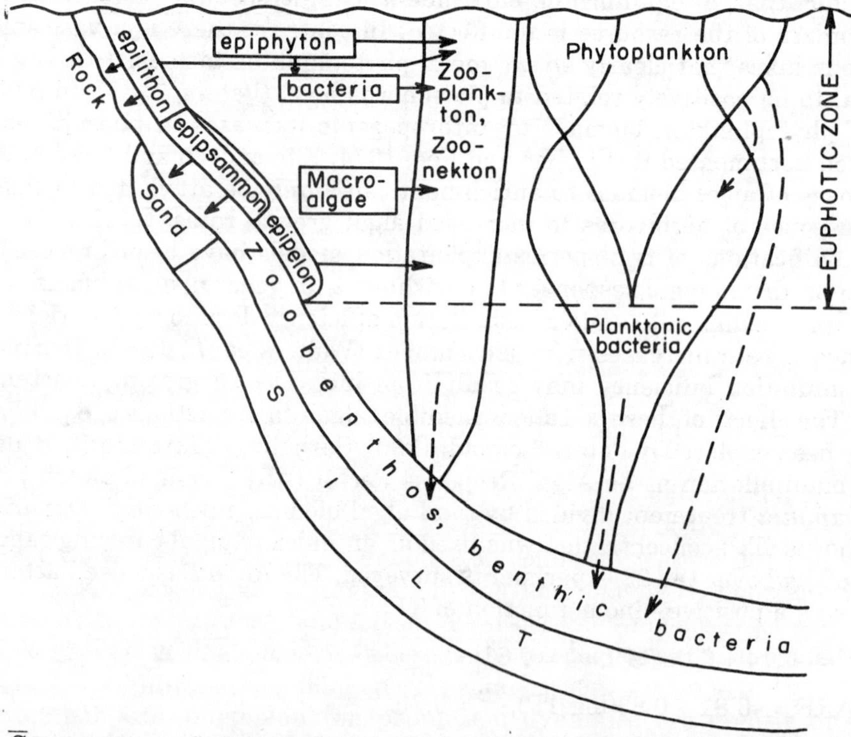

Fig. 13-22 Some common habitats of algae and other organisms in lakes and sea. Solid lines represent grazing pathways of energy flow; dashed lines show detrital pathways. (Modified from Round, 1981.)

algal biomass and transparency (Tilzer, 1988), and the well-known fact that the same algal biomass will result in a higher transparency if the size of the algal particles increases. In contrast, algal biomass in hypereutrophic takes can be reduced to mesotrophic levels given a sufficient decrease in predatory mortality on *Daphnia*. Lakes that will show the greatest effects of biomanipulation are those that are most heavily impacted by nutrient inputs, i.e., those most likely to require restorative measures. Given that the effects of *Daphnia* on total algal biomass are reasonably predictable, the success of biomanipulation depends upon the effectiveness of strategies aimed at reducing the biomass of zooplanktivorous fish. The evidence that zooplanktivory is favoured by enrichment, however, suggests that eutrophic lakes may be quite resistant to manipulations of trophic structure at this level. Partial removal of zooplanktivores or addition of piscivorous fish may produce only transitory effects (Sarnelle, 1992).

The influence of grazing on growth of phytoplankton is most obvious in seasonally variable environments where grazer pressure is temporally variable. Grazers usually respond to phytoplankton blooming by increasing their own numbers, but their population growth lags behind phytoplankton growth to some extent because of the time required for adult grazers to mature and for their nonfeeding stages to develop. Most temperate zone plankton communities show striking seasonal variations in phytoplankton abundance because the stocks of consumers decline to such fairly low levels in unfavourable periods that they cannot control the explosive growth of the phytoplankton in the spring. In contrast, those aquatic communities which do not experience marked seasonal fluctuations do not exhibit striking variations in stocks of phyto- and zooplankton (Frost, 1981). In these latter situations, phytoplankton abundance is regulated by fairly equal influences of nutrient supply, turbulence, grazing, and various other factors, none of which usually becomes significantly more or less important than some other factor.

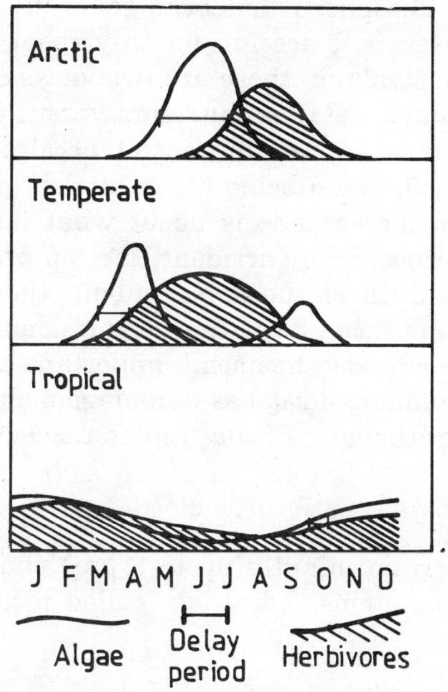

Fig. 13-23 Seasonal variations in phytoplankton and herbivorous zooplankton (hatched area) in different latitudes. The horizontal bar indicates the delay period between the increases of phytoplankton and zooplankton. (After Cushing, 1959.)

Figure 13-22 illustrates some common habitats of algae and other organisms.

Some seasonal variations in phytoplankton and herbivorous zooplankton occur in different latitudes. These are illustrated in Fig. 13-23.

ANIMALS AS DISPERSERS OF ALGAE

Sea urchins, molluscs, amphipods, filter feeders, and herbivorous fishes feed on aquatic algae, many of which are digested but a few can survive digestion. These survivors are dispersed by the mobile animals through their excreta.

Paya and Santelices (1989) reported that small individuals of the clingfish *Sicyases sanguineus* consume as many as 18 species of marine algae in Chile. Out of these some, e.g., *Enteromorpha* can survive digestion. *E. compressa* and *Gelidium chilense* survived by tissue regeneration when offered as food to the fish in the laboratory and *E. compressa* also showed some stimulation in swarmer formation.

Fishes are highly mobile algal grazers, especially in tropical waters. They tend to forage and rest in subtidal habitats experiencing considerable sedimentation and accumulation of some animal faeces (Bray *et al.*, 1981). They appear to play a role in the dispersal of those algae which have survived digestion.

Phosphorus has been generally accepted to be the dominant limiting nutrient in lakes but it seems to account for only about 50% of algal biomass. As for the role of grazing of algae by zooplankton, there are two views of what are the dominant factors controlling phytoplankton abundance (i.e., nutrients versus grazing). There has been much recent debate on top-down versus bottom-up control of algae biomass. The situation is further complicated by the zooplankton being eaten by fish (planktivores) and the latter by bigger fish (piscivores). The trophic cascade is about what happens to the lower trophic levels when one disturbs, on purpose or by accident, the top predators within a lake (Carpenter and Kitchell, 1993).

Much of the debate about the trophic cascade has focussed on whether it is generally applicable or whether it is a dominant process controlling algal abundance in all lakes. This debate also has some important applied ramifications as believers in its relevance advocate biomanipulation as a management tool. Clearly there is a strong need to test the applicability or otherwise of the trophic cascade hypothesis to a wide variety of lakes all over the world.

PICOPLANKTON

Certain minute (up to 2 μm) phototrophic organisms occur in both marine and freshwater ecosystems. These are called picoplankton (Stockner, 1988). The algal picoplankton is now

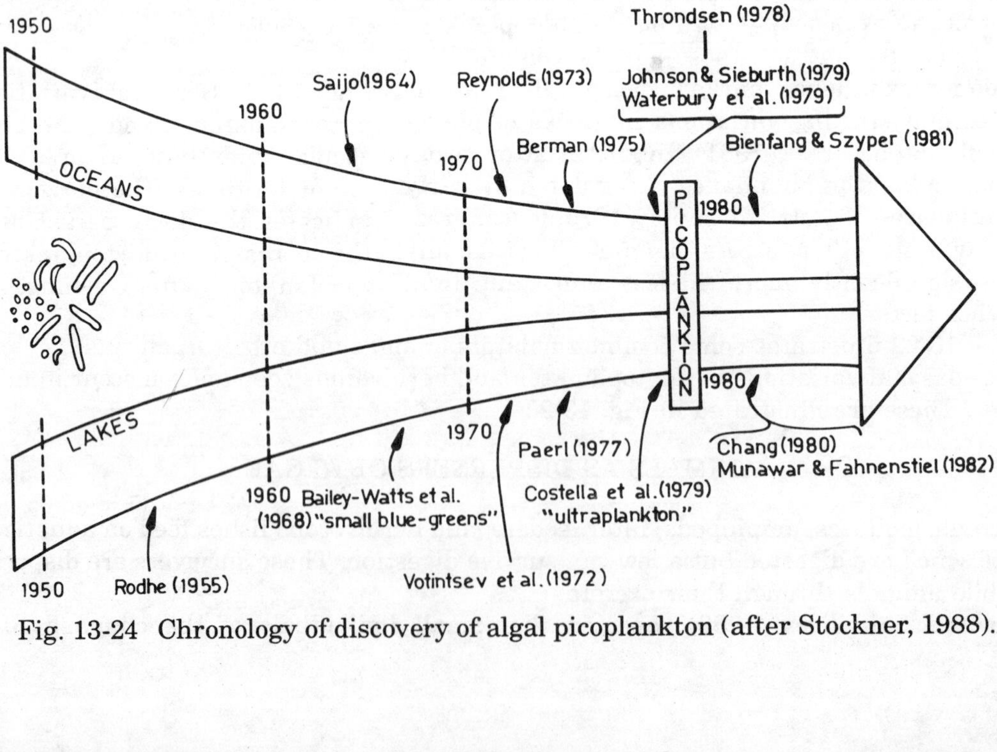

Fig. 13-24 Chronology of discovery of algal picoplankton (after Stockner, 1988).

known to constitute a ubiquitous component of the microbial plankton communities. This component contributes substantially to the total biomass of phytoplankton, and in nutrient-poor waters can be responsible for up to around 80 per cent of the total carbon production. The pico-algae are grazed by flagellates, ciliates, rotifers, copepods, and other metazoans, and thus contribute to the flow of energy to higher trophic levels (Stockner, 1988).

Figure 13-24 shows the chronology of discovery of picoplankton. Although some incidental reports of the existence of some minute organisms in the plankton appeared during 1950–1977, the finding that minute chroococcoid cyanobacteria were ubiquitous in the oceans was independently reported by Johnson and Sieburth (1979) and Waterbury *et al.* (1979). By now, the pico-algae are known to occur in all the major oceans of the world except the Black and Red Seas. The algal picoplankton has also been recorded from several European and American lakes.

Some examples of marine picoplankton include *Chlorella nana*, *Nannochloris* spp., *Micromonas pusilla, Dolichomastix lepidota*, and *Hillea marina*. The freshwater picoplankton is exemplified by *Cyanodictyon reticulatum*, *Synechococcus* sp., *Chlorella minutissima*, *Stichococcus* spp., and *Rhodomonas pygmaea*.

BENTHOS

Those communities which grow attached at the bottom of a water body comprise the benthos. The algae grow on those (Fig. 13-22) benthic habitats where some light penetrates. Rhizobenthos includes those species which are attached by means of rhizoids to the sediment, e.g., *Chara, Halimeda, Codium*, and *Bryopsis*. Haptobenthos is that which grows adnate to solid surfaces. It can be subdivided into epiphyton (e.g., *Oedogonium* and *Coleochaete* grow epiphytically on reeds and aquatic plants) and epilithon (e.g., *Rivularia* growing on submerged stones and pebbles), epipsammon (certain microalgae growing on sand), epizoon (those growing on animals). Periphyton denotes growths on artificial substrata.

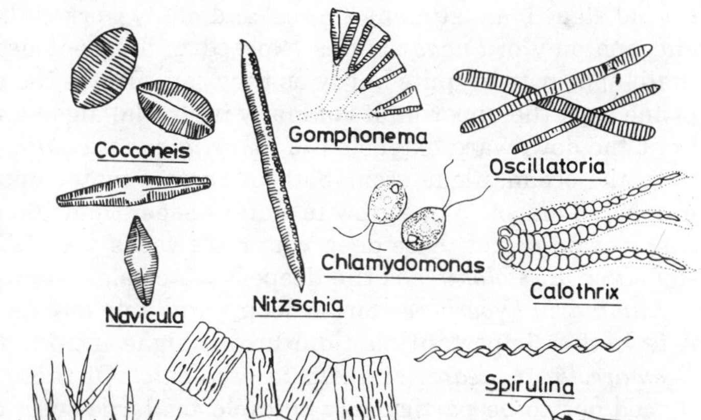

Fig. 13-25 Some typical benthic algae. Of these, some are benthic only in certain developmental stages, e.g., *Chlamydomonas*.

There are certain organisms that show creeping movement on sediments; these can be designated herpobenthic. Likewise, endobenthic communities live and bore into solid substrata, e.g., *Hyella*. Metaphyton refers to those species which are loosely associated often in some mucilage secreted by epiphyton but lack attachment structures and consequently can be easily washed off the epiphyton. They occur both in freshwater and marine environments, often forming extensive communities.

Figure 13-25 illustrates some representative benthic algae.

MARINE ALGAE

DISTRIBUTION

Fucoid algae blanket many shores, and many workers have compared the growth, morphology, and anatomy of *Fucus* species exposed to different degrees of wave action. Some individual thalli appear to be quite hardy as they can survive the waves. Climatic conditions periodically prune back the upper limits of many intertidal algae and physical as well as biotic factors can limit the downward extension of *Pelvetia canaliculata*.

In the ocean, algae occur both in surface water and along the shore attached to rocks. A number of marine algae grow in water deeper than 100 metres, especially in the Pacific Ocean. A few examples of these deep water seaweeds are *Callymenia*, *Codium latum*, and *Ecklonia stolonifer*. *E. stolonifer* is the deepest water alga known (about 200 metres deep).

Laminaria hyperborea forms deep water kelp forests in the Atlantic along the British Coast. A few other important subtidal brown algae include *L. saccharina*, *Saccorhiza polyschides*, *Desmarestia aculeata*, and *Alaria esculenta*. Of these, *L. saccharina* and *A. esculenta* have turned out to be particularly suitable for large-scale cultivation in underwater kelp farms. *Saccorhiza polyschides* also grows well in these farms but is too easily dislodged and also has a lower organic content.

Encrusting coralline algae inhabit some of the hardest substrata within the photic zone, in some cases covering up to 90% of the rock surface under the canopy of *Hedophyllum sessile* in the boreal northeastern Pacific. In this area, the vertical zonation and spatial distribution of coralline algae in intertidal habitats is governed by desiccation, wave action, and shading from the larger brown algae. The upper parts of the intertidal are dominated by *Corallina vancouveriensis*. In tide pools and beneath the canopy of *Hedophyllum*, *Lithophyllum* and *Lithothamnion* are abundant. Most of the primary substratum in the lower intertidal is occupied either by laminarialean holdfasts or by calcareous crusts of coralline red algae (Steneck and Paine, 1986).

The distribution of a large number of tropical marine algae extends from the West Indies to East Africa.

Some examples of genera whose distribution ranges from the Caribbean westward into the Pacific and Indian Oceans include *Dictyosphaeria*, *Chamaedoris*, *Neomeris* (Chlorophyta), *Turbinaria*, *Rosenvingea* (Phaeophyta), and *Eucheuma*, *Martensia*, and *Amansia* (Rhodophyta). All these genera show a discontinuity in their distribution in the Atlantic Ocean (Papenfuss, 1972). One possible barrier to an eastward migration of the Caribbean genera may be the Gulf Stream which, according to Papenfuss, carries the algae northward into colder waters where most of them die.

Womersley (1972) recognizes three basic algal zones on the coasts of South Australia: (1) the upper zone of turf-forming red algae, e.g., *Pterocladia* and *Corallina*; (2) the middle zone of large kelps, e.g., *Ecklonia*, *Sargassum*, and *Cystoseira*; and (3) the lower zone of large-sized red algae, e.g., *Plocamium* and *Phacelocarpus*.

When the coastal waters are rough, the upper zone is fairly wide but it is quite narrow in calm water areas or may even be altogether absent.

An array of morphologies and life history strategies exist to increase the fitness of marine macroalgae in the presence of environmental disturbances such as periodic desiccation at low tide, temperature stresses, hydrodynamic shear forces created by waves and currents, sand-scouring abrasion or burial, and herbivory. Littler and Littler (1984) have identified several functional form groups that differ in external morphology, internal anatomy, and texture. These range from the most herbivore resistant, tough and crustose group to the soft, more herbivore susceptible groups. These morphological groups tend to range in resistance to grazing from sea urchins and fishes depending on their texture.

Figure 13-26 illustrates the relationship between osmotic resistance and the adaptation of various algae to their mode of life in the sea.

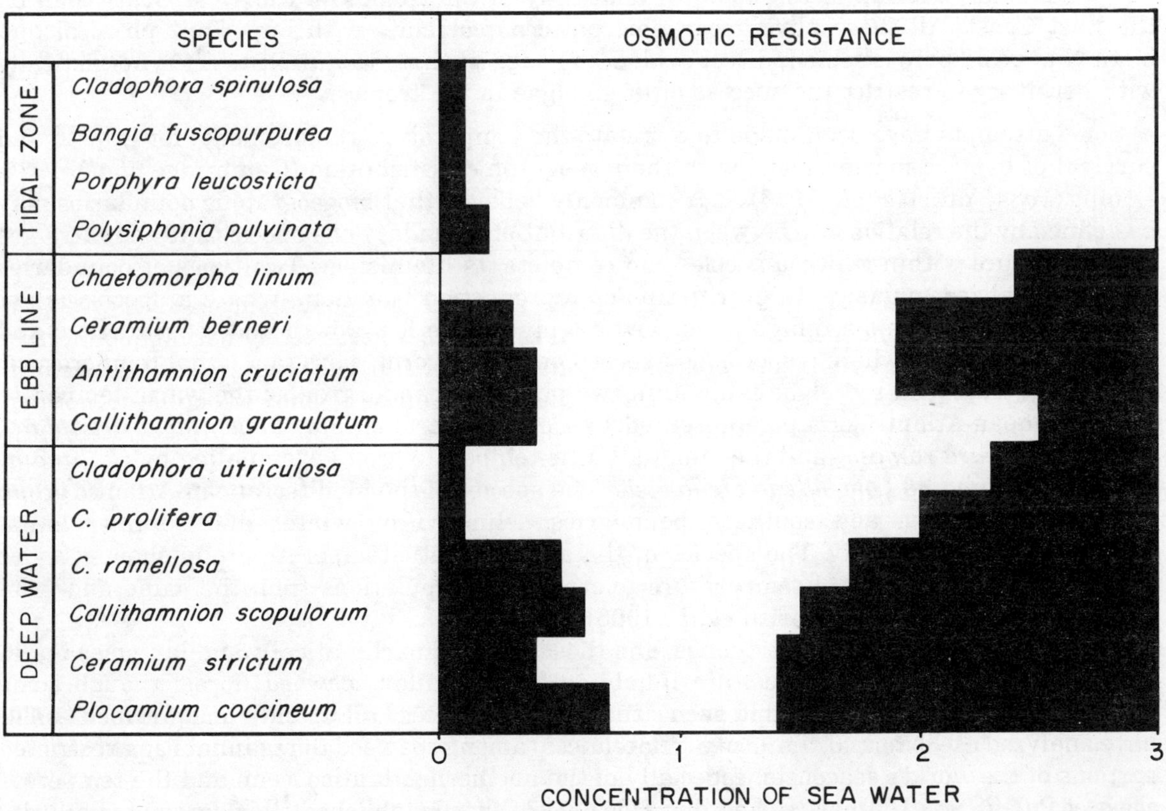

Fig. 13-26 Sensitivity of certain algae from different ocean depths to osmotic pressure of water. White areas denote survival; black areas indicate dead after 24 hr. Concentration increments: 0.2 means 2 parts sea water plus 8 parts freshwater; at 3.0, the concentration of solutes in sea water triples, by evaporation to one-third of volume. (After Biebl, 1962.)

BIOGEOGRAPHY

There are striking changes in biogeographic patterns of marine algal distribution, diversity, biomass, and morphology along latitudinal gradients (Gaines and Lubchenco, 1982). Some agents regulating species distributions are physical parameters, dispersal, competition, predation, mutualism, and other biotic interactions. Predation by herbivorous molluscs, echinoderms, crustaceans, and fishes strongly influences patterns of algal biogeography.

On the basis of extensive work done on the East and West Coasts of U.S.A., Gaines and Lubchenco (1982) describe the following 4 latitudinal algal patterns:

(1) The algal diversity peaks occur in temperate latitudes for the West Coast but in the tropics for the East Coast.

(2) The proportion of calcified species increases and that of blades declines relative to branched fleshy or filamentous species, in tropical versus temperate latitudes.

(3) The proportion of small plants increases in the tropics.

(4) The large thalli decline more dramatically in the tropics on the West Coast than on the East Coast. All these phycogeographic patterns correlate with important physical and biotic changes. There is some indirect evidence to suggest that low nutrients act synergistically with herbivory to restrict the success of large algae in the tropics.

Some attempts have been made to correlate the temperature requirements for growth and survival of benthic marine algae with their geographic distribution (Cambridge *et al.*, 1984; Lüning, 1984; Yarish *et al.*, 1986). It is commonly believed that biogeographic boundaries may be defined by the relationship between the distribution boundary of a species and the extremes of temperature within which a species can complete its life history. Two types of boundaries can be visualized, namely, (1) growth and/or reproduction boundary, where a species is not exposed every year to a too high or too low a temperature for growth and reproduction; and (2) lethal boundary, where a species is exposed once in several years to a lethal temperature. Some West European red algae fall within two phytogeographic groups: the warm-temperate Mediterranean-Atlantic group represented by *Calliblepharis ciliata*, *Lomentaria articulata*, and *Cryptopleura ramosa*, and the amphiatlantic-temperate group exemplified by *Callithamnion tetragonum* and *Lomentaria orcadensis*. The species of the Mediterranean-Atlantic group have their northern and southern boundaries delimited by winter and summer lethal temperatures, respectively. The species of the amphiatlantic-temperate group show ecotypic differentiation in respect of temperature tolerance for populations from the same and from either side of the Atlantic (Yarish *et al.*, 1986).

The coasts in different climatic zones, and those situated in climatically similar zones but in different oceans or hemispheres, are inhabited by dissimilar seaweed floras, though some species or genera may be shared in such situations. Santelices (1980) and Van den Hoek (1984) have analyzed the extent of similarity (relatedness) among seaweed floras inhabiting restricted portions of the world's seacoasts, especially of the northern Atlantic Ocean and the temperate coast of Pacific South America. Van den Hoek (1984) has established the degree of similarity between red algal floras in each pair of 22 climatically defined biogeographic regions. Based on such studies, he proposed the following seven divisions of the red algal seaweed flora: (1) a rich tropical warm temperate Tethyan group, (2) a group consisting of some depauperate extensions of the group in (1), (3) a temperate North Pacific group, (4) a group composed of the Arctic cold temperate North Atlantic flora and the Northeast Atlantic warm temperate flora, (5) an Antarctic cold temperate southern hemisphere group, (6) a group made up of the two highly individual Southeast Atlantic flora (South Africa) and Southwest Pacific flora (South Australia and North New Zealand), and (7) a group comprising the depauperate warm temperate Southeast Pacific flora. He found that though the northern and southern hemisphere temperate and polar floras are quite unrelated, they nevertheless share several cool water genera which have successfully crossed the adverse tropical belt. Further, he believes that the floras of South Africa and Southern Australia owe their richness and individuality to a long isolation and a continued residence in warm temperate conditions with small seasonal fluctuations.

ZONATION

The variability in the distribution and zonation of the attached or benthic marine seaweeds in different oceans and regions of the world is much greater than that in case of freshwater algae. The Pacific Ocean is richer in algal species than the Atlantic. Australia is especially rich in kelps. The coasts of western India, Japan, New Zealand, Southeast Australia, and Southwest Africa also harbour a rich diversity of algal species.

A variety of physico-chemical and biological factors influence the distribution and composition of marine algal communities. The nature of substratum (chemical composition, location, texture, water holding capacity), light (periodicity, intensity, wavelength), temperature, and rainfall are some of the important physical factors involved. Important chemical factors include salinity, macronutrients, micronutrients, vitamins and growth factors, extracellular products, and pollution load, if any.

Biotic factors play a vital role in the distribution of seaweeds.

Removal of limpets from a part of seashore often results in a dramatic colonization of that part with seaweeds. Limpets are known to control the abundance of intertidal algae and, if sufficiently abundant, can keep the shore virtually free of seaweeds. Further, in the absence of excessive interspecific competition, seaweed species can not only survive but even thrive over a much greater vertical range than they normally occupy. Recent researches have revealed complex and subtle interactions among the fucoids, limpets, and barnacles that grow on British shores.

The chief biotic factors include competition from such organisms as parasites, epiphytes, symbionts, endophytes, and grazers, diseases, and the beneficial or harmful effects of various organisms on the availability and utilization of nutrients, space or light. In addition to the above, the distribution of seaweed communities is profoundly influenced by the periodicity and amplitude of tides, by currents, upwellings, storms, and winds. The responses of the phenotype to the environment are often most marked in perennial seaweeds.

Zonation in India

The vertical distribution of seaweeds along the seacoast with reference to the nature of the tides, extent of intertidal zone, and the gradient of shore, etc., is called zonation. The Indian Coast generally has mixed tides and fairly narrow intertidal zones. In general, the tidal range is greater in the West Coast (especially the Gujarat-Saurashtra Coast) than in the East Coast.

The sandy shores in the Eastern Coast near Visakhapatnam and Mahabalipuram have some outcrops of boulders or rocks which show two distinct zones of algae, viz., a sublittoral zone of species of *Gracilaria*, *Grateloupia*, *Hypnea*, *Liagora*, and a littoral zone with *Enteromorpha compressa*, *Chaetomorpha* sp., *Ectocarpus* sp., and *Cladophora* sp.

Rocky ledges and sand-covered areas with underlying sandstone or limestone boulders sometimes become exposed during very low tides; these habitats are commonly dominated by *Enteromorpha* sp., as in Porbandar and Veraval (see Krishnamurthy, 1977).

Rocky coasts with high cliffs, common along the West Coast, tend to have mostly some blue-green algae and some sublittoral algae.

The East Coast along South India and the archepelagos of Andaman and Nicobar Islands have sublittoral coral formations with uneven, sand-covered surface. These have mostly *Gelidium*, *Gelidiella*, and *Ulva*.

A supralittoral fringe, a midlittoral fringe, and an infralittoral fringe can be demarcated in the intertidal zone along the Visakhapatnam Coast (see Umamaheshwararao and Sreeramulu, 1964). Out of these three belts, the first is devoid of algae, the second develops regular bands of such dominant algae as *Chaetomorpha antennina*, *Ulva fasciata*, *Enteromorpha compressa*, *Porphyra vietnamensis*, and *Chnoospora minima*. Other common algae found in this fringe include *Liagora erecta* and *Bangiopsis subsimplex*. Certain perennial seaweeds, e.g., *Gracilaria* sp., *Sargassum vulgare*, *S. illicifolium*, *S. tenerrimum*, *S. turneri*, and *Jania* sp., are characteristic inhabitants of the infralittoral fringe. This fringe also harbours good growths of *Caulerpa taxifolia*, *C. racemosa*, *Padina tetrastromatica*, *Grateloupia filicina*, *G. lithophila*, *Rosenvingea* sp., *Sphacelaria furcigera*, and certain species of *Dictyota*, *Zonaria*, *Cladophora*, *Chaetomorpha*, *Boodlea*, *Hypnea*, *Centroceras*, and *Wrangelia*.

On this coast, two peak development periods of various green, brown, and red seaweeds are June to August and November to December.

The intertidal zone of the Mahabalipuram Coast has been divided into four zones, viz., (1) the *Gracilaria-Grateloupia* zone, (2) the *Chaetomorpha* zone, (3) the *Ectocarpus* zone, and (4) the *Enteromorpha* zone (see Srinivasan, 1946).

The following belts are generally encountered on the West Coast:

(1) Supralittoral It is a zone of brownish-black blue-green algae with species of *Lyngbya*, *Pleurocapsa*, and *Calothrix* dominating. In this belt, the shallow pools contain *Ectocarpus*.

(2) Eulittoral The green belts of *Ulva* and *Enteromorpha* occur in the upper eulittoral. The shallow pools have *Hypnea valentiae* and *Laurencia obtusa*, while the deep pools tend to harbour *Acanthophora*, *Caulerpa scalpelliformis*, *Laurencia hypnoides*, and *Hypnea musciformis*.

The lower eulittoral zone contains a belt of *Colpomenia*, *Iyengaria*, *Hydroclathrus* (Fig. 13-27), *Gelidium*, *Polysiphonia*, and *Ceramium* spp. in mixed combinations. The shallow pools abound in species of *Caulerpa*, *Halimeda*, and *Udotea*, whereas the deep pools have *Dictyopteris*, *Cystophyllum*, *Sargassum*, and *Padina*.

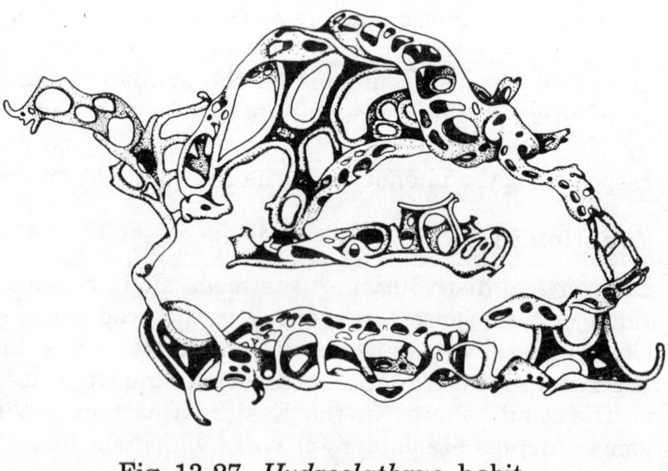

Fig. 13-27 *Hydroclathrus*, habit.

(3) Sublittoral Species of *Champia*, *Codium*, *Caulerpa*, and *Chondria* are dominant in this zone.

ALGAE IN THE SERVICE OF GLOBAL ENVIRONMENT

The recent upsurge of worldwide interest in several aspects of environmental phycology (see Fogg and Thake, 1987; Rai *et al.*, 1994) not only attests to the profound importance of algae in local, regional, and global environmental problems but has also contributed to a much better appreciation of their services to aquatic and atmospheric environments besides, of course, the well-known role of the blue-green algae in the nitrogen economy of paddy fields (Singh, 1961; Venkataraman, 1972). The most important of these services relates to the photosynthetic carbon fixation and oxygen evolution by oceanic phytoplankton (Kumar and Kumar, 1997). Besides the terrestrial forests, the marine phytoplankton is the major sink for the greenhouse gas carbon dioxide. Any decrease or loss of phytoplankton caused, say, by the increased incidence of ultraviolet-β radiation resulting from stratospheric ozone depletion may have adverse impacts not only on the world's fish harvests (a food-chain effect) but also on global warming (Häder *et al.*, 1995). According to Fogg (1990), global warming might produce some drastic rearrangements of flora, fauna, and fishing grounds in some sea areas but the overall oceanic productivity may not change significantly.

A clear connection between marine algae and climate has become apparent in recent years. It occurs through the production of a compound which breaks down to release volatile dimethyl sulphide (DMS) and acrylic acid. DMS is a key substance in the global sulphur cycle. Its oxidation products influence atmospheric acidity, cloud formation, and the earth's temperature. The compound in question is dimethylsulphoniopropionate (DMSP), which is synthesized by algae to help maintain their osmotic balance with sea water. The chief sources of DMSP in the natural environment are marine phytoplankton blooms, where high levels of primary production and biomass occur on a time-scale of weeks (Malin, 1997).

ALGAE AS ECOSYSTEM ENGINEERS

There are many organisms, including algae, that play a role in the creation, modification and maintenance of habitats—activities that do not involve direct trophic interactions between species but are nevertheless important and quite common. These organisms are called ecosystem engineers. They directly or indirectly modulate the availability of resources to other species by causing physical state changes in biotic or abiotic materials (Jones *et al.*, 1994).

Blooms of marine phytoplankton scatter and absorb light in upper layers of the ocean. This enhances warming of surface waters that can initiate the development of a thermocline. Freshwater phytoplankton in lakes also intercepts light in upper water column, smaller algae being more effective as compared to larger species. Light interception leads to shallower mixing depth, lower metalimnetic temperatures and lower heat content of water column (Jones *et al.*, 1994).

Cyanobacterial communities in deserts and arid lands also act as engineers by exuding mucilaginous organic compounds. These compounds glue the cells, organic matter, and soil particles together to form microphytic crumbs. The slimy exudates change infiltration, percolation, retention and evaporation of water and reduce soil erosion (Mazumder *et al.*, 1990).

Crustose coralline algae such as *Lithophyllum* found in coral reefs overgrow and cement together detritus on outer algal ridge of barrier reef. This tends to break force of water and protect corals against strong wave action (Anderson, 1992).

GIGANTIC EXPERIMENTS ON OCEANIC MICROALGAE

An open ocean ecosystem experiment has been conducted to answer a puzzling question: Why do vast regions of the oceans have high concentrations of N and P and yet support low phytoplankton biomass? One hypothesis is that phytoplankton of these regions is limited by iron. Bottle experiments are not suitable for testing this hypothesis because corrections for zooplankton grazing cannot be made properly and also there is a high probability of contaminating the bottles with traces of iron. With a view to overcoming these limitations, the first open ocean fertilization experiment, called IRONEX, was carried out in the equatorial Pacific (see Carpenter *et al.*, 1995). Dissolved iron was added to an unenclosed 64 km^2 patch of water so as to increase the ambient concentration 100-fold. It was found that photosynthetic efficiency increased within the first 24 hr, and by the third day, chlorophyll concentration as well as primary productivity had increased three times. Increased photosynthesis caused a small though significant drawdown of CO_2 in the surface waters but was not sufficient enough to produce detectable changes (decline) in nutrients. This short term experiment did not indicate whether the modest productivity increase and negligible impact on N and P levels resulted from the disappearance of available Fe, increased zooplankton grazing, or the short duration of the experiment. In the follow-up IRONEX II, multiple additions of iron, over several days, were used to simulate natural iron input, and both zooplankton grazing rates and concentrations of other potentially limiting nutrients were monitored (Coale *et al.*, 1996). The huge phytoplankton bloom formed by the relief of iron limitation was not checked by either grazing or secondary nutrient limitation, thus strongly supporting the view that the high nitrate low-chlorophyll condition of these waters is caused by iron limitation of algal growth (Coale *et al.*, 1996; La Roche *et al.*, 1996). IRONEX II showed increases in all phytoplankton groups, with diatoms showing the greatest increase in biomass over ambient (about 85 times). The smaller algae were less affected, with *Synechococcus* (1 micron) and red fluorescing picoplankton (less than 2 microns) only doubling in biomass. The principal results of IRONEX II were the following:

(1) Specific growth rate (cell division rate) of the phytoplankton doubled, phytoplankton abundance increased by over 20 times, and nitrate concentration declined by half. Diatoms dominated.

(2) Indicators of phytoplankton photosynthetic capacity (e.g., light absorption) showed immediate and sustained increases.

(3) As the bloom developed, the partial pressure of CO_2 in the centre of the patch decreased rapidly, reducing the ocean-to-atmosphere CO_2 flux by 60 per cent (Frost, 1996).

It can therefore be concluded that mesoscale iron fertilization experiments bring out not only the feasibility but also utility of engineering efforts in the open ocean.

Some have suggested that fertilization of the entire Southern ocean with Fe could sequester substantial quantities of atmospheric CO_2, delaying predicted greenhouse warming of the earth to a modest degree. Debates about the feasibility, wisdom, and ethics of such climate engineering are greatly affected by our knowledge of the response of oceans to nutrient enrichment. Experiments like IRONEX can contribute something towards this effort.

REFERENCES

Anderson, O.K., Goldman, J.C., Caron, D.A., and Dennett, M.R., Nutrient cycling in a microflagellate food chain. III. Phosphorus dynamics, *Mar. Ecol. Prog. Ser.*, **31**, 47–55 (1986).

Anderson, R.A., Diversity of eukaryotic algae, *Biodiv. Conser.*, **1**, 267–92 (1992).

Andreae, M.O., Ocean-atmosphere interactions in the global biogeochemical sulfur cycle, *Mar. Chem.*, **30**, 1–29 (1990).

Arditi, R. and Ginzburg, L.R., Coupling in predatorprey dynamics: ratio-dependence, *J. Theor. Biol.*, **139**, 311–26 (1989).

Armstrong, R. and McGehee, R., Competitive exclusion, *Am. Nat.*, **116**, 151–70 (1980).

Arnold, D.E., Ingestion, assimilation, survival and reproduction by *Daphnia pulex* fed seven species of blue-green algae, *Limnol. Oceanogr.*, **16**, 906–20 (1971).

Atlavinyte, O. and Pociene, C., The effect of earthworms and their activity on the amount of algae in the soil, *Pedobiologia*, **13**, 445–55 (1974).

Azam, F. and Ammerman, J.W., Cycling of organic matter by bacterioplankton in pelagic marine ecosystems: microenvironmental considerations. *In* Fasham, M.J.R. (ed.) Flows of Energy and Materials in Marine Ecosystems, 345–60, Plenum Press, New York (1984).

Bailey-Watts, A.E., Bindloss, M.E., and Belcher, J.H., Freshwater primary production by a blue-green alga of bacterial size, *Nature*, **220**, 1344–45 (1968).

Beers, J.R. and Stewart, G.L., Microzooplankters in the plant communities of the upper waters of the eastern tropical pacific, *Deep Sea Res.*, **18**, 861–83 (1971).

Bellinger, E.G., The response of algal populations to change in lake water quality. *In* James, A. and Evison, L. (eds.) Biological Indicators of Water Quality, 9–27, Wiley, Chichester (1979).

Berman, T., Size fractionation of natural aquatic populations associated with autotrophic and heterotrophic carbon uptake, *Mar. Biol.*, **33**, 215–20 (1975).

Biebl, R., Temperaturresistenz tropische Meeresalgen, vergleichen mit jener von Algen in temperierten Meeresgebieten, *Bot. Mar.*, **4**, 241–54 (1962).

Bienfang, P.K. and Szyper, J.P., Phytoplankton dynamics in the subtropical Pacific Ocean off Hawaii, *Deep Sea Res.*, **28**, 981–1000 (1981).

Biggs, B.J.F. and Close, M.E., Periphyton biomass dynamics in gravel bed rivers: the relative effects of flow and nutrients, *Freshwater Biol.*, **22**, 209–31 (1989).

Bjornsen, P.K., Phytoplankton exudation of organic matter: why do healthy cells do it?, *Limnol. Oceanogr.*, **33**, 151–54 (1988).

Bray, R.N., Miller, A.C., and Geesey, G.C., The fish connection: a trophic link between planktonic and rocky communities?, *Science*, **214**, 204–205 (1981).

Broady, P.A., Qualitative and quantitative observations on green and yellow green algae in some English soils, *Brit. Phycol. J.*, **14**, 151–60 (1979).

Brown, E.J., Button, D.K., and Lang, D.S., Competition between heterotrophic and autotrophic microplankton for dissolved nutrients, *Microbiol. Ecol.*, **7**, 199–206 (1981).

Brylinsky, M., Estimating the primary productivity of lakes and reservoirs. *In* LeCren, E.D. and Lowe-McConnell, R.H. (eds.) The Functioning of Freshwater Ecosystems, 411–53, Cambridge University Press, London (1980).

Bush, R.M. and Welch, E.B., Plankton association and related factors in a hypertrophic lake, *Water Air Soil Pollution*, **1**, 257–74 (1972).

Cambridge, M., Breeman, A.M., Van Osterwijk, R., and Van den Hoek, C., Temperature responses of some North Atlantic *Cladophora* species (Chlorophyceae) in relation to their geographic distribution, *Helgolander Meeresunters*, **38**, 349–63 (1984).

Cameron, R.E., Algae of Southern Arizona. I. Introduction: blue-green algae, *Rev. Algol.*, **6**, 282–318 (1963).

Cameron, R.E., Knox, A.D., and Morelli, F.A., The role of algae in tundra soil. *In* Tieszen, L.L. (ed.) Vegetation and Production Ecology of an Alaskan Arctic Tundra, 207–27, Springer-Verlag, New York (1978).

Carpenter, S.R., Fisher, S.G., Grimm, N.B., and Kitchell, J.F., Global change and freshwater ecosystems, *Ann. Rev. Ecol. Syst.*, **23**, 119–39 (1992).

Carpenter, S.R. and Kitchell, J.F. (eds.), Who's eating who, then?, *TREE*, **9**, 450–51 (1993).

Carpenter, S.R., Chisholm, S.W., Krebs, C.J., Schindler, D.W., and Wright, R.F., Ecosystem experiments, *Science*, **269**, 324–27 (1995).

Chang, V.T.P., Zwei neue *Synechococcus*-Arten aus dem Zurichsee, *Schweiz. Z. Hydrol.*, **42**, 247–54 (1980).

Charlson, R.J., Lovelock, J.E., Andreae, M.O., and Warren, S.G., Oceanic phytoplankton, atmospheric sulphur, cloud albedo and climate, *Nature*, **326**, 655–61 (1987).

Cheong, S.T., Heung, K.S., Chen, K.W., and Tsang, T.M., Observations on a red tide in Xiamem Port West, *Acta Oceanologica Sinica*, **10**, 602–608 (1988).

Chisholm, S.W., Olson, R.J., Zettler, E.R., Goericke, R., Waterbury, J.B., and Welschmeyer, N.A., A novel free-living prochlorophyte abundant in the oceanic euphotic zone, *Nature*, London, **334**, 340–43 (1988).

Chretiennot-Dinet, M.J., Sournia, A., Ricard, M., and Billard, C., A classification of the marine phytoplankton of the world from class to genus, *Phycologia*, **32**, 159, 79 (1993).

Coale, K.H., Johnson, K.S., Fitzwater, S.E., and 16 other authors, A massive phytoplankton bloom induced by an ecosystem scale iron fertilization experiment in the equatorial Pacific Ocean, *Nature*, **383**, 495–501 (1996).

Corner, E.D.S. and Davies, A.G., Plankton as a factor in the nitrogen and phosphorus cycles in the sea, *Adv. Mar. Biol.*, **9**, 101–204 (1971).

Costella, A.C., Shortreed, K.S., and Stockner, J.G., Phytoplankton fractionation studies in Great Central Lake, British Columbia: a nutrient-enriched sockeye salmon (*Onchorhynchus nerka*) nursery lake, *Fish. Mar. Serv. Tech. Rep.*, **880**, 27 p. (1979).

Cushing, D.H., The seasonal variation in oceanic production as a problem in population dynamics, *J. Cons.*, **24**, 455–64 (1959).

Cushing, D.H., Marine Ecology and Fisheries, Cambridge University Press, Cambridge (1975).

Davey, M.C. and Walsby, A.E., The form resistance of sinking algal chains, *Brit. Phycol. J.*, **20**, 243–48 (1985).

De Baar, H.J.W., De Jong, J.T.M., Bakker, D.C.E., Loscher, B.M., Veth, C., Bathmann, U., and Smetacek, V., Importance of iron for plankton blooms and carbon dioxide drawdown in the Southern Ocean, *Nature*, **373**, 412–15 (1995).

Del Prete, A. and Schofield, C., The utility of diatom analyses of lake sediments for evaluating acid precipitation effects on dilute lakes, *Arch. Hydrobiol.*, **91**, 332–40 (1981).

Dickinson, R.E., Uncertainties of estimates of climate change: a review, *Climate Change*, **15**, 5–14 (1989).

Dillon, P.J. and Rigler, F.H., The phosphorus-chlorophyll relationship in lakes, *Limnol. Oceanogr.*, **19**, 767–73 (1974).

Dussart, B.H., Les differentes categories de plancton, *Hydrobiologia*, **26**, 72–74 (1965).

Dunstan, W.M., A comparison of the photosynthesis: light intensity relationship in phylogenetically different marine microalgae, *J. Exp. Mar. Biol. Ecol.*, **13**, 181–87 (1973).

Dykstra, R.F., MacEntee, F.J., and Bold, H.C., Some edaphic algae of the Texas Coast, *Texas J. Sci.*, **26**, 171–77 (1975).

EAWAG News, **34**, 12–16 (1993).

Edmondson, W.T. and Lehman, J.T., The effect of changes in the nutrient income on the condition of Lake Washington, *Limnol. Oceanogr.*, **26**, 1–29 (1981).

Elser, J.J., Marzolf, E.R., and Goldman, C.R., Phosphorus and nitrogen limitation of phytoplankton growth in the freshwaters of North America: a review and critique of experimental enrichments, *Can. J. Fish. Aquat. Sci.*, **47**, 1468–77 (1990).

Eppley, R.W., Holmes, R.W., and Paasche, E., Periodicity in cell division and physiological behaviour of *Ditylum brightwellii*: a marine planktonic diatom during growth in light-dark cycles, *Arch. Microbiol.*, **56**, 305–23 (1967).

Feldmann, J., Recherches sur lá vegetation marine de lá Mediterrannee, lá cote des Alberes, *Rev. Algol.*, **10**, 1–339 (1937).

Fogg, G.E., The physiology of an algal nuisance, *Proc. Roy. Soc.* (London), **B173**, 175–89 (1969).

Fogg, G.E., Nitrogen cycling in sea waters, *Phil. Trans. Roy. Soc.* (London), **B296**, 511–20 (1982).

Fogg, G.E., The ecological significance of extracellular products of phytoplankton photosynthesis, *Bot. Mar.*, **26**, 3–14 (1983).

Fogg, G.E., Marine planktonic cyanobacteria. *In* Fay, P. (ed.) The Cyanobacteria, 393–414, Elsevier Science Publishers, Amsterdam (1987).

Fogg, G.E., Changing productivity of the oceans in response to a changing climate, *Annals of Botany*, **67** (Suppl. 1), 57–60 (1990).

Fogg, G.E., The phytoplanktonic ways of life, *New Phytol.*, **118**, 191–232 (1991).

Fogg, G.E., Stewart, W.D.P., Fay, P., and Walsby, A.E., The Blue-green Algae, Academic Press, London (1973).

Fogg, G.E. and Thake, B., Algal Cultures and Phytoplankton Ecology, University of Wisconsin Press, Madison (1987).

Fredrickson, A.G. and Stephanopoulos, G., Microbial competition, *Science*, **213**, 972–79 (1981).

Frempong, E., Diel periodicity in the chemical competition of lake phytoplankton, *Arch. Hydrobiol.*, **92**, 457–95 (1981).

Friedmann, E.I. and Galun, M., Desert algae, lichens and fungi. *In* Brown, G.W. (Jr.) (ed.) Desert Biology. II, Academic Press, New York (1974).

Friedmann, E.I., Lipkin, Y., and Ocampa-Paus, R., Desert algae of the Negev (Israel), *Phycologia*, **6**, 185–200 (1967).

Frost, B.W., Grazing. *In* Morris, I. (ed.) The Physiological Ecology of Phytoplankton, 465–91, Blackwell, Oxford (1981).

Frost, B.W., Grazing control of phytoplankton stock in the open subarctic Pacific Ocean: a model assessing the role of mesozooplankton, particularly the large calanoid copepods *Neocalanus* spp., *Mar. Ecol. Ser.*, **39**, 49–68 (1987).

Frost, B.W., Phytoplankton bloom on iron rations, *Nature*, **383**, 475–76 (1996).

Gahnström, G., Blomqvist, P., and Fleischer, S., Are key nitrogen fluxes changed in the acidified aquatic ecosystem?, *Ambio*, **22**, 318–24 (1993).

Gaines, S.D. and Lubchenco, J., A unified approach to marine plant herbivore interactions. II. Biogeography, *Ann. Rev. Ecol. Syst.*, **13**, 111–38 (1982).

Gallagher, J.C., Physiological variation and electrophoretic banding patterns of genetically different seasonal populations of *Skeletonema costatum* (Bacillariophyceae), *J. Phycol.*, **18**, 148–62 (1982).

Gaudy, R., Feeding four species of pelagic copepods under experimental conditions, *Mar. Biol.*, **25**, 125–41 (1974).

Gawlick, S.R. and Millington, W.F., Structure and function of the bristles of *Pediastrum boryanum* (Chlorophyta), *J. Phycol.*, **24**, 474–82 (1988).

Gelin, C., Nutrients, biomass and primary productivity of nanoplankton in eutrophic Lake Vombjson, Sweden, *Oikos*, **26**, 121–39 (1975).

Gerritsen, J. and Strickler, J.R., Encounter probabilities and community structure in zooplankton: a mathematical model, *J. Fish. Res. Board Can.*, **34**, 73–82 (1977).

Gibson, C.E., Cyclomorphosis in natural populations of *Oscillatoria redekei* Van Goor, *Freshwater Biol.*, **5**, 279–89 (1975).

Goldberg, W.M., Makemson, J.C., and Colley, S.B., *Entocladia endozoica* sp. nov., a pathogenic chlorophyte: structure, life history, physiology, and effects on its coral host, *Biol. Bull.*, **166**, 368–83 (1984).

Golterman, H.L., Physiological Limnology, Elsevier, Amsterdam (1975).

Gotham, I.J. and Rhee, G.Y., Comparative kinetic studies of phosphate-limited growth and phosphate uptake in phytoplankton in continuous culture, *J. Phycol.*, **17**, 257–65 (1981).

Häder, D.P., Worrest, R.C., Kumar, H.D., and Smith, R.C., Effects of increased solar ultraviolet radiation on aquatic ecosystems, *Ambio*, **24**, 174–80 (1995).

Hansen, S.R. and Hubbell, S.P., Single nutrient microbial competition: agreement between experimental and theoretically forecast outcomes, *Science*, **207**, 1491–93 (1980).

Harlin, M.W. and Darley, W.M., The algae: an overview. *In* Lembi, C.A. and Waaland, J.R. (eds.) Algae and Human Affairs, 3–27, Cambridge University Press, Cambridge (1988).

Harris, G.P., Phytoplankton Ecology, Chapman and Hall, London (1986).

Hay, M.E., Species as 'noise' in community ecology: do seaweeds block our view of the kelp forest?, *TREE*, **9**, 414–16 (1994).

Hecky, R.E. and Fee, E.J., Primary production and rate of algal growth in Lake Tanganyika, *Limnol. Oceanogr.*, **26**, 532–47 (1981).

Hecky, R.E. and Kling, H.J., The phytoplankton and protozooplankton of the euphotic zone of Lake Tanganyika: species composition, biomass, chlorophyll content and spatio-temporal distribution, *Limnol. Oceanogr.*, **26**, 548–64 (1981).

Henriksson, E., Henriksson, L.E., and DaSilva, E.J., A comparison of nitrogen fixation by algae of temperate and tropical soils. *In* Stewart, W.D.P. (ed.) Nitrogen Fixation by Free-living Microorganisms, Vol. 6, 199–206, Cambridge University Press, London (1975).

Ho, K.C. and Hodgkiss, I.J., Macronutrients in Tolo Harbour and their Relations to Red Tides, *EMECS Newsletter*, No. 4, 10–11, Hyogo (1993).

Houghton, J.T., Jenkins, G.J., and Ephraums, J.J. (eds.), Climate Change: the IPCC Scientific Assessment, Cambridge University Press, Cambridge (1990).

Huang, N.M., The distribution of chlorophyll-a in Daya Bay and its affecting factors, *Acta Oceanologica Sinica*, **11**, 769–79 (1989).

Hulburt, E.H., Ryther, J.H., and Guillard, R.R.L., The phytoplankton of the Sargasso Sea off Bermuda, *J. Cons., CIEM*, **25**, 115–28 (1960).

Huntsman, S.A. and Sunda, W.G., The role of trace metals in regulating phytoplankton growth. *In* Morris, I. (ed.) The Physiological Ecology of Phytoplankton, 285–328, University of California Press, Berkeley (1980).

Hutchinson, G.E., The paradox of the plankton, *Am. Nat.*, **95**, 137–46 (1961).

Hutchinson, G.E., A Treatise on Limnology, Vol. II, Wiley, New York (1967).

Imboden, D.M., Mixing and transport in lakes: mechanisms and ecological reference. *In* Tilzer, M. and Serruya, C. (eds.) Large Lakes: Ecological structures and functions, 47–80, Springer-Verlag, New York (1990).

Jenkinson, I.R., Oceanographic implications of non-newtonian properties found in phytoplankton cultures. *Nature*, London, **323**, 435–37 (1986).

Jewson, D.H., Rippey, B.H., and Gilmore, W.K., Loss rates from sedimentation, parasitism, and grazing during the growth, nutrient limitation and dormancy of a diatom crop, *Limnol. Oceanogr.*, **26**, 1045–56 (1981).

Johnson, P.W. and Sieburth, J. McN., Chroococcoid cyanobacteria in the sea: a ubiquitous diverse phototrophic biomass, *Limnol. Oceanogr.*, **24**, 928–35 (1979).

Jones, C.G., Lawton, J.L., and Shachak, M., Organisms as ecosystem engineers, *Oikos*, **69**, 373–86 (1994).

Jorgensen, C.B., Biology of Suspension Feeding, Pergamon Press, Oxford (1966).

Jumars, P.A., Concepts in Biological Oceanography, Oxford University Press, Oxford (1993).

Jürgens, K. and Güde, H., Incorporation and release of phosphorus by planktonic bacteria and phagotrophic flagellates, *Mar. Ecol. Prog. Ser.*, **59**, 271–84 (1990).

Kain, J.M., Seasonal growth and photoinhibition in *Plocamium cartilagineum* (Rhodophyta) off the Isle of Man, *Phycologia*, **26**, 88–99 (1987).

Kain, J.M., The seasons in the subtidal, *Brit. Phycol. J.*, **24**, 203–15 (1989).

Kalff, J., Netplankton and nanoplankton production and biomass in a north temperate zone lake, *Limnol. Oceanogr.*, **17**, 712–20 (1972).

Kalff, J. and Knoechel, R., Phytoplankton and their dynamics in oligotrophic and eutrophic lakes, *Ann. Rev. Ecol. Syst.*, **9**, 475–95 (1978).

Khalil, M.A.K. and Rasmussen, R.A., Global sources, life-times and mass balances of carbonyl sulfide (COS) and carbon disulphide (CS_2) in the earth's atmosphere, *Atmos. Environ.*, **18**, 1805–13 (1984).

Khoja, T. and Whitton, B.A., Heterotrophic growth of blue-green algae, *Arch. Microbiol.*, **79**, 280–82 (1971).

Kieber, D.J., McDaniel, J., and Mopper, K., Photochemical source of biological substrates in sea water: implications for carbon cycling, *Nature*, London, **341**, 637–39 (1989).

Kilham, P. and Kilham, S.S., The evolutionary ecology of phytoplankton. *In* Morris, I. (ed.) The Physiological Ecology of Phytoplankton, 571–96, Blackwell Scientific Publications, Oxford (1980).

Knoechel, R. and Kalff, J., An *in situ* study of the productivity and population dynamics of five freshwater planktonic diatom species, *Limnol. Oceanogr.*, **23**, 195–218 (1978).

Krishnamurthy, V., Some general consideration on zonation of marine algae on the Indian Coasts. *In* Proceedings Seminar on Sea Salt and Plants, 219–33, Bhavnagar (1977).

Kumar, H.D. and Kumar, S., Global and General Environment, Anmol Publications, New Delhi (1997).

La Roche, J., Boyd, P.W., McKay, R.M.L., and Geider, R.J., Flavodoxin as an *in situ* marker for iron stress in phytoplankton, *Nature*, **383**, 802–805 (1996).

Lamb, M.A. and Lowe, R.L., Effects of current velocity on the physical structuring of diatom (Bacillariophyceae) communities, *Ohio Journal of Science*, **87**, 72–78 (1987).

Lampert, W., Studies on the carbon balance of *Daphnia pulex* de Geer as related to environmental conditions, *Arch. Hydrobiol.*, Suppl., **48**, 310–35 (1977).

Lampert, W., Laboratory studies on zooplankton-cyanobacteria interactions, *N.Z.J. Mar. Freshw. Res.*, **21**, 483–90 (1987).

Legendre, L. and Demers, S., Towards dynamic biological oceanography and limnology, *Can. J. Fish. Aquat. Sci.*, **41**, 2–19 (1984).

Leibold, M., Resource edibility and the effects of predators and productivity on the outcome of trophic interactions, *Am. Nat.*, **134**, 922–49 (1990).

Levins, R., Coexistence in a variable environment, *Am. Nat.*, **115**, 765–83 (1979).

Lewis, W.M. (Jr.), A compositional, phytogeographical and elementary structural analysis of the phytoplankton in a tropical lake: Lake Lanao, Philippines, *J. Ecol.*, **66**, 213–26 (1978a).

Lewis, W.M. (Jr.), Dynamics and succession of the phytoplankton in a tropical lake: Lake Lanao, Philippines, *J. Ecol.*, **66**, 849–80 (1978b).

Littler, M.M. and Littler, D.S., Relationships between macroalgal functional form groups and substrata stability in a subtropical rocky intertidal system, *J. Exp. Mar. Biol. Ecol.*, **74**, 13–34 (1984).

Littler, M.M., Littler, D.S., Blair, S.M., and Norris, J.N., Deepest known plant life discovered on an uncharted seamount, *Science*, **227**, 57–59 (1985).

Lubchenco, J., Algal zonation in the New England rocky intertidal community: an experimental analysis, *Ecology*, **61**, 333–44 (1980).

Lund, J.W.G., The ecology of the freshwater phytoplankton, *Biol. Rev.*, **40**, 231–93 (1965).

Lüning, K., Seasonal growth of *Laminaria hyperborea* under recorded underwater light conditions near Helgoland. *In* Crisp, D.J. (ed.) Proceedings of the IVth European Symposium, 347–61, University Press, Cambridge (1971).

Lüning, K., Temperature tolerance and biogeography of seaweeds: the marine algal flora of Helgoland (North Sea) as an example, *Helgolander Meeresunters*, **38**, 305–17 (1984).

Lüning, K. and Dieck, I.T., Environmental triggers in algal seasonality, *Bot. Mar.*, **32** (1989).

Luttenton, M.R. and Rada, R.G., Effects of disturbance on epiphytic community architecture, *J. Phycol.*, **22**, 320–26 (1986).

Malin, G., Sulphur, climate and the microbial maze, *Nature*, **387**, 857–58 (1997).

Malin, G., Turner, S.M., and Liss, P.S., Sulfur: the plankton/climate connection, *J. Phycol.*, **28**, 590–97 (1992).

Malony, T.C., Algal size. *In* Morris, I. (ed.) The Physiological Ecology of Phytoplankton, 433–63, Blackwell, Oxford (1980).

Marathe, K., Studies on soil algae of India. II. Soil algae from the cultivated fields of Jalgaon, *J. Univ. Bombay*, **38**, 69–72 (1969).

Marchant, H.J., Davidson, A.T., and Kelly, G.J., UV-B protecting compounds in the marine alga *Phaeocystis pouchetii*, *Mar. Biol.*, **109**, 391–95 (1991).

Margalef, R., Temporal succession and spatial heterogeneity in phytoplankton. *In* Buzzati-Traverso, A.A. (ed.) Perspectives in Marine Biology, 323–49, University of California Press, Berkeley (1958).

Margalef, R., Succession in marine populations, *Advg. Frontiers Pl. Sci.*, **2**, 137–88 (1967).

Margalef, R., Life-forms of phytoplankton as survival alternatives in an unstable environment, *Oceanologica Acta*, **1**, 493–509 (1978).

Margalef, R., The organisation of space, *Oikos*, **33**, 152–59 (1979).

Marra, J., Vertical mixing and primary production. *In* Falkowski, P.G. (ed.) Primary Productivity in the Sea, 121–37, Plenum Press, London (1980).

Mazumder, A., Taylor, W.D., McQueen, D.J., and Lean, D.R.S., Effects of fish and plankton on lake temperature and mixing depth, *Science*, **247**, 312–15 (1990).

McCann, A.E. and Cullimore, D.R., Influence of pesticides on the soil algal flora, *Residue Reviews*, **72**, 1–31 (1979).

McCormick, M.J., Potential changes in thermal structure and cycle of Lake Michigan due to global warming, *Trans. Am. Fish. Soc.*, **119**, 183–94 (1990).

Mechling, J.A. and Kilham, S.S., Temperature effects on silicon limited growth of the Lake Michigan diatom *Stephanodiscus minutus* (Bacillariophyceae), *J. Phycol.*, **18**, 199–205 (1982).

Metting, B., The systematics and ecology of soil algae, *Bot. Rev.*, **47**, 195–312 (1981).

Mills, E.L., Biological Oceanography: An early history, 1870–1960, Cornell University Press, Ithaca (1989).

Moore, D.R. and Weiss, N.O., Dynamics of double convection, *Phil. Trans. Roy. Soc.* (London), **A332**, 121–34 (1990).

Morse, D.E., Morse, A., and Duncan, H., Algal tumors in the Caribbean seafan *Gorgonia ventalina*, *Internat. Coral Reef Sympos.*, **1**, 623–29 (1977).

Morse, D.E., Morse, A., Duncan, H., and Trench, R.K., Algal tumors in the Caribbean Octocorallian, *Gorgonia ventalina*. II. Biochemical characterization of the algae, and first epidemiological observations, *Bull. Mar. Sci.*, **31**, 399–409 (1981).

Moss, B., Diversity in freshwater phytoplankton, *Amer. Midland Naturalist*, **90**, 341–55 (1973).

Munawar, M. and Fahnenstiel, G.L., The abundance and significance of ultraplankton and microalgae at an offshore station in central Lake Superior, *Can. Tech. Rep. Fish. Aquat. Sci.*, **1153**, 1–13 (1982).

Naidu, K.S., Infection of the giant scallop *Placopecten magellinicus* from Newfoundland with an endozoic alga, *J. Inverteb. Pathol.*, **17**, 145–57 (1971).

Nalewajko, C., Lee, K., and Fay, P., Significance of algal extracellular products to bacteria in lakes and in cultures, *Microbial Ecol.*, **6**, 199–207 (1980).

Nival, P. and Nival, S., Particle retention efficiencies of an herbivorous copepod *Acartia clausi* (adult and copepodite stages): effects on grazing, *Limnol. Oceanogr.*, **21**, 24–38 (1976).

Nonomura, A.M. and West, J.A., Ultrastructure of the parasite *Janczewskia morimotoi* and its host *Laurencia nipponica* (Ceramiales, Rhodophyta), *J. Ultrastruct. Res.*, **73**, 183–98 (1980).

Nordin, R.N. and Blinn, D.W., Analysis of a saline tallgrass prairie ecosystem. IV. Preliminary investigations on soil algae, *N. Dak. Acad. Sci.*, **25**, 8–17 (1972).

Oglesby, R.T., Relationship of fish yield to lake phytoplankton standing crop production, and morphoedaphic factors, *J. Fish. Res. Board*, **34**, 2271–79 (1977).

Oliver, R.L. and Walsby, A.E., Direct evidence for the role of light-mediated gas vesicle collapse in the buoyancy regulation of *Anabaena flos-aquae* (cyanobacteria), *Limnol. Oceanogr.*, **29**, 879–86 (1984).

Ostrofsky, M.L. and Peairs, H.J., The relative photosynthetic efficiency of *Asterionella formosa* Hass. (Bacillariophyta) in natural plankton assemblages, *J. Phycol.*, **17**, 230–33 (1981).

Paerl, H.W., Ultraphytoplankton biomass and production in some New Zealand lakes, *J. Mar. Freshwater Res.*, **11**, 297–305 (1977).

Paerl, H.W., Nuisance phytpolankton blooms in coastal, estuarine, and inland waters, *Limnol. Oceanogr.*, **33**, 823–47 (1988).

Pahl-Wostl, C., Dynamic versus static models of photosynthesis, *Hydrobiologia*, **238**, 189–96 (1992).

Paine, R.T. and Levin, S.A., Intertidal landscapes: disturbance and the dynamics of a pattern, *Ecological Monographs*, **51**, 145–78 (1981).

Papenfuss, G.F., On the geographical distribution of some tropical marine algae. *In* Nisizawa, K. (ed.) Proceedings of the VII International Seaweed Symposium, 45–51, University of Tokyo Press, Tokyo (1972).

Papoutsakis, E.T., Fluid mechanical damage of animal cells in bioreactors, *TIBTECH*, **9**, 427–37 (1991).

Parker, B.C., Experimental Investigations of the Relationships of Certain Soil Algae with Their Associated Microorganisms (Ph.D. thesis), University of Texas, Austin (1960).

Parker, B.C., Facultative heterotrophy in certain soil algae from the ecological viewpoint, *Ecology*, **42**, 380–86 (1961).

Paÿa, I. and Santelices, B., Microalgae survive digestion by fishes, *J. Phycol.*, **25**, 186–88 (1989).

Peters, R.H., The role of prediction in limnology, *Limnol. Oceanogr.*, **31**, 1143–59 (1986).

Peters, R.H., A Critique for Ecology, Cambridge University Press, Cambridge (1991).

Peterson, C.G. and Grimm, N.B., Temporal variation in enrichment effects during periphyton succession in a nitrogen-limited desert stream ecosystem, *Journal of the North American Benthological Society*, **11**, 20–36 (1992).

Peterson, C.G. and Stevenson, R.J., Resistance and resilience of lotic algal communities: importance of disturbance timing and current, *Ecology*, **73**, 1445–61 (1992).

Petraitis, P.S., Latham, R.E., and Niesenhaum, R.A., The maintenance of species diversity by disturbance, *Q. Rev. Biol.*, **64**, 393–418 (1989).

Pingree, R.D., Holligan, P.M., Mardell, G.T., and Head, R.N., The influence of physical stability in spring, summer and autumn phytoplankton blooms in the Celtic Sea, *J. Mar. Biol. Ass.* (U.K.), **56**, 845–73 (1976).

Pipe, A.E. and Schubert, L.E., The use of algae as indicators of soil fertility. *In* Algae as Ecological Indicators, 213–33, Academic Press, London (1984).

Platt, T. and Denman, K., Patchiness in phytoplankton distribution. *In* Morris, I. (ed.) The

Physiological Ecology of Phytoplankton, 413–31, Blackwell Scientific Publications, Oxford (1980).

Platt, T., Bird, D.F., and Sathyendranath, S., Critical depth and marine primary production, *Proc. Roy. Soc.* (London), **B246**, 205–17 (1991).

Pollingher, U. and Zemel, E., *In situ* and experimental evidence of the influence of turbulence on cell division processes of *Peridinium cinctum* forma *westii* (Lemm.) Lefevre, *Brit. Phycol. J.*, **16**, 281–87 (1981).

Pomeroy, L.R. and Johannes, R.E., Occurrence and respiration of the ultraplankton in the upper 500 meters of the ocean, *Deep Sea Res.*, **15**, 381–91 (1968).

Porter, K.G., Enhancement of algal growth and productivity by grazing zooplankton, *Science*, **192**, 1332–34 (1976).

Prasad, B.N. and Singh, Y., Algal hydrobiology in India, *Proc. Natl. Acad. Sci.* (India), **50B**, 271–300 (1980).

Proctor, L.M. and Fuhrman, J.A., Viral mortality of marine bacteria and cyanobacteria, *Nature*, London, **343**, 60–62 (1990).

Rai, L.C., Gaur, J.P., and Kumar, H.D., Phycology and heavy metal pollution, *Biol. Rev.*, **56**, 99–151 (1981).

Rai, L.C., Gaur, J.P., and Soeder, C.J. (eds.), Algae and Water Pollution, Schweizerbartsche, Stuttgart (1994).

Raven, J.A., Limits on growth rates, *Nature*, **361**, 209–10 (1993).

Raymont, E.G., Plankton and Productivity in the Oceans, Pergamon Press, Oxford (1980) .

Reimann, B., Biomass and production of phyto- and bacterio-plankton in eutrophic Lake Tystrup, Denmark, *Freshwater Biol.*, **13**, 389–98 (1983).

Reynolds, C.S., Growth and buoyancy of *Microcystis aeruginosa* Kutz. emend. Elenkin in a shallow eutrophic lake, *Proc. Roy. Soc.* (London), **B184**, 29–50 (1973).

Reynolds, C.S., Phytoplankton periodicity: the interactions of form, function and environmental variability, *Freshwater Biol.*, **14**, 11–142 (1984a).

Reynolds, C.S., The Ecology of Freshwater Phytoplankton, Cambridge University Press, Cambridge (1984b).

Reynolds, C.S. and Walsby, A.E., Water blooms, *Biol. Rev.*, **50**, 437–81 (1975).

Reynolds, C.S., Wiseman, S.W., and Clarke, M.J.O., Growth- and loss-rate responses of phytoplankton to intermittent artificial mixing and their potential application to the control of planktonic algal biomass, *Journal of Applied Ecology*, **21**, 11–39 (1984).

Reynolds, N., The estimation of the abundance of ultraplankton, *Brit. Phycol. J.*, **8**, 135–46 (1973).

Rhee, G.Y., Competition between an alga and an aquatic bacterium for phosphate, *Limnol. Oceanogr.*, **17**, 505–14 (1972).

Riebesell, U., Wolf-Gladrow, D.A., and Smetacek, V., Carbon dioxide limitation of marine phytoplankton growth rates, *Nature*, **361**, 249–51 (1993).

Rodhe, W., Productivity: can plankton production proceed during winter darkness in subarctic lakes?, *Int. Ver. Theor. Angew. Limnol. Verh.*, **12**, 117–22 (1955).

Roger, P. A. and Watanabe, I., Technologies for utilizing biological nitrogen fixation in wetland rice: potentialities, current usage, and limiting factors, *Fertilizer Res.*, **9**, 39–77 (1986).

Rogers, R.J., Cannole, M.D., Norton, J., Thomas, A., Ladds, P.W., and Dickson, J., Lymphadenitis of cattle due to infection with green algae, *J. Comp. Pathol.*, **90**, 1–9 (1980).

Ross, P.E. and Duthie, H.C., Ultraplankton biomass, productivity, and efficiency in Lac Matamee: a Precambrian Shield Lake, *J. Phycol.*, **17**, 181–86 (1981).

Rothschild, B.J., Application of stochastic geometry to problems in plankton ecology, *Phil. Trans: Roy. Soc.* (London), **B336**, 225–37 (1992).

Round, F.E., The Ecology of Algae, Cambridge University Press, London (1981).

Ryther, J.H., Menzel, D.W., and Vaccaro, R.F., Diurnal variation in some chemical and biological properties of Sargasso Sea, *Limnol. Oceanogr.*, **6**, 149–53 (1961).

Saijo, Y., Size distribution of photosynthesizing phytoplankton in the Indian Ocean, *J. Oceanogr. Soc. Jpn.*, **19**, 187–89 (1964).

Sale, P.F., The Ecology of Fishes on Coral Reefs, Academic Press, London (1991).

Santelices, B., Phytogeographic characterization of the temperate coast of Pacific South America, *Phycologia*, **19**, 1–12 (1980).

Sarnelle, O., Nutrient enrichment and grazer effects on phytoplankton in lakes, *Ecology*, **73**, 551–60 (1992).

Sathyendranath, S., Gouveia, A.D., Shetye, S.R., Ravindran, P., and Platt, T., Biological control of surface temperature in the Arabian Sea, *Nature* (London), **349**, 54–56 (1991).

Schindler, D.W., Evolution of phosphorus limitation in lakes, *Science*, **195**, 260–62 (1977).

Schindler, D.W. and Fee, E.J., Experimental lakes area: whole-lake experiments in eutrophication, *J. Fish. Res. Board*, **31**, 937–53 (1974).

Schindler, D.W., Mills, K.H., Malley, D.F., Findlay, D.L., Shearer, J.A., Davies, I.J., Tumer, M.A., Linsey, G.A., and Cruikshank, D.R., Long-term ecosystem stress: the effects of years of experimental acidification on a small lake, *Science*, **228**, 1395–1401 (1985).

Schubert, L.E. (ed.), Algae as Ecological Indicators, Academic Press, London (1984).

Seliger, H.H., Carpenter, J.H., Loftus, M., and McElroy, W.D., Mechanisms for the accumulation of higher concentrations of dinoflagellates in a bioluminescent bay, *Limnol. Oceanogr.*, **15**, 234–45 (1970).

Shapere, A. and Wilczek, F., Geometry of self-propulsion at low Reynolds number, *Journal of Fluid Mechanics*, **198**, 557–85 (1989).

Shapiro, J., Blue-green algae: why they become dominant?, *Science*, **179**, 382–84 (1973).

Sinclair, M., Subba Rao, D.V., and Couture, R., Phytoplankton temporary distributions in estuaries, *Oceanogr. Acta*, **4**, 239–46 (1981).

Singh, R.N., Role of Blue-green Algae in the Nitrogen Economy of Indian Agriculture, Indian Council of Agricultural Research, New Delhi (1961).

Smayda, T.J., The suspension and sinking of phytoplankton in the sea, *Oceanogr. Mar. Biol. Ann. Rev.*, **8**, 353–612 (1970).

Smayda, T.J., Phytoplankton species succession. *In* Morris, I. (ed.) The Physiological Ecology of Phytoplankton, 493–570, Blackwell, Oxford (1980).

Sournia, A., Form and function in marine phytoplankton, *Biol. Rev.*, **57**, 347–94 (1982).

Sousa, W.P., The role of disturbance in natural communities, *Ann. Rev. Ecol. Syst.*, **15**, 353–92 (1984).

Srinivasan, K.S., Ecology and seasonal succession of the marine algae at Mahabalipuram (Seven Pagodas) near Madras, *Ind. Bot. Soc.*, M.O.P. Iyengar Commemoration Volume, 267–78 (1946).

St. Amand, A. and Carpenter, S.R., Metalimnetic phytoplankton dynamics. *In* Carpenter, S.R. and Kitchell, J.F. (eds.) Trophic Cascades in Lakes, Cambridge University Press, Cambridge (1993).

Starks, T.L., Schubert, L.E., and Trainor, F.R., Ecology of soil algae: a review, *Phycologia*, **20**, 65–80 (1981).

Steneck, R.S. and Paine, R.T., Ecological and taxonomic studies of shallow-water encrusting Corallinaceae (Rhodophyta) of the boreal north-eastern Pacific, *Phycologia*, **25**, 221–40 (1986).

Stevenson, R.J., Benthic algal community dynamics in a stream during and after a spate, *Journal of the North American Benthological Society*, **9**, 277–88 (1990).

Stockner, J.G., Phototrophic picoplankton: an overview from marine and freshwater ecosystems, *Limnol. Oceanogr.*, **33**, 765–75 (1988).

Stockner, J.G. and Antia, N.J., Algal picoplankton from marine and freshwater ecosystems: a multidisciplinary perspective, *Can. J. Fish. Aquat. Sci.*, **43**, 2472–2503 (1986).

Sverdrup, H.U., On conditions for the vernal blooming of phytoplankton, *J. Cons. Perm. int. Explor. Mer.*, **18**, 287–95 (1953).

Tait, R.V., Elements of Ecology, Butterworths, London (1968).

Takahashi, M., Koike, I., Iseki, K., Bienfang, P.K., and Hattori, A., Phytoplankton species' responses to nutrient changes in experimental enclosures and coastal waters. *In* Grice, G.D. and Reeve, M.R. (eds.) Marine Mesocosms, 333–40, Springer-Verlag, New York (1982).

Talling, J.F., The annual cycle of stratification and phytoplankton growth in Lake Victoria (East Africa), *Int. Revue ges. Hydrobiol.*, **51**, 545–621 (1966).

Taylor, F.J.R., Basic biological features of phytoplankton cells. *In* Morris, I. (ed.) The Physiological Ecology of Phytoplankton, 3–55, Blackwell, Oxford (1980).

Thomas, R.H. and Walsby, A.E., The effect of temperature on recovery of buoyancy by *Microcystis*, *J. Gen. Microbiol.*, **132**, 1665–72 (1986).

Thomas, W.H. and Gibson, C.H., Effects of small-scale turbulence on microalgae, *Journal of Applied Phycology*, **2**, 71–77 (1990).

Throndsen, J., Productivity and abundance of ultra- and nannoplankton in Oslofjorden, *Sarsia*, **63**, 273–84 (1978).

Tilman, D., Resource competition between planktonic algae: an experimental and theoretical approach, *Ecology*, **58**, 338–48 (1977).

Tilman, D., Kilham, S.S., and Kilham, P., Phytoplankton community ecology: the role of limiting nutrients, *Ann. Rev. Ecol. Syst.*, **13**, 347–72 (1982).

Tilman, D., Mattson, M., and Langer, S., Competition and nutrient kinetics along a temperature gradient: an experimental test of a mechanistic approach to niche theory, *Limnol. Oceanogr.*, **26**, 1020–33 (1981).

Tilzer, M.M., Secchi disk-chlorophyll relationships in a lake with highly variable phytoplankton biomass, *Hydrobiologia*, **162**, 163–71 (1988).

Tiwari, D., Pollution Phycology of the Varanasi Frontage of the River Ganges (Ph.D. thesis), Banaras Hindu University, Varanasi (1983).

Trainor, F.R. and McLean, R.J., A study of a new species of *Spongiochloris* introduced into sterile soil, *Am. J. Bot.*, **51**, 57–60 (1964).

Turner, S.M., Malin, G., Liss, P.S., Harbour, D.S., and Holligan, P.M., The seasonal variation of dimethyl sulfide and dimethylsulfoniopropionate concentrations in near-shore waters, *Limnol. Oceanogr.*, **33**, 364–75 (1988).

Uehlinger, U. and Brock, J.T., The assessment of river periphyton metabolism: A method and some problems. *In* Whitton, B.A., Rott, E., and Friedrich, G. (eds.) Use of Algae for Monitoring Rivers. E. Rott, Institut für Botanik, Universitat Proceedings of Internat. Sympos. held at Dusseldorf, Germany 26–28 May 1991. Published by E. Rott, Inst. f. Botanik AG Hydrobotanik, Universitat Innsbruck, Austria, 175–81 (1991).

Umamaheshwararao, M. and Sreeramulu, T., An ecological study of some intertidal algae of the Visakhapatnam Coast, *J. Ecol.*, **52**, 595–616 (1964).

Utkilen, H.C., Skulberg, O.M., and Walsby, A.E., Buoyancy regulation and chromatic adaptation in planktonic *Oscillatoria* species: alternative strategies for optimising light absorption in stratified lakes, *Archiv für Hydrobiologie*, **104**, 407–17 (1985).

Van den Hoek, C., Worldwide latitudinal and longitudinal seaweed distribution patterns and their possible causes, as illustrated by the distribution of Rhodophytan genera, *Helgolander Meeresunters*, **38**, 227–57 (1984).

Vanni, M.J., Biological control of nuisance algae by *Daphnia pulex*: experimental studies, pages 151–156 in Lake and reservoir management, Proceedings of the Third Annual Conference of the North American Lake Management Society, American Lake Management Society, Washington, D.C. (1984).

Vareschi, E., Biomasse und Fressrate der Zwergflamingoes in Lake Nakuru (Kenia), *Verh. Dtsch. Zool. Ges.*, p. 41 (Abst.) (1977).

Venkataraman, G.S., Algal Biofertilizers and Rice Cultivation, Today and Tomorrow Publishers, New Delhi (1972).

Votintsev, K.K., Meshceryakova, A.I., and Popovskaya, G.I., The importance of ultra-nanoplanktonic algae in the primary production of Lake Baikal in the summer, *Gidrobiol. Zh.*, **8**, 21–27 (1972).

Wall, D. and Briand, F., Spatial and temporal overlap in lake phytoplankton communities, *Arch. Hydrobiol.*, **88**, 45–57 (1980).

Walters, C.J.E., Krause, W.E., Neill, T., and Northcote, T.G., Equilibrium models for seasonal dynamics of plankton biomass in four oligotrophic lakes, *Can. J. Fish. Aquat. Sci.*, **44**, 1002-1017 (1987).

Waterbury, J.B., Watson, S.W., Guillard, R.R.L., and Brand, L.E., Widespread occurrence of a unicellular, marine, planktonic cyanobacterium, *Nature*, **277**, 293–94 (1979).

Waterbury, J.B., Willey, J.M., Franks, D.G., Valois, F.W., and Watson, S.W., A cyanobacterium capable of swimming motility, *Science, New York*, **230**, 74–76 (1985).

Whitton, B.A. (ed.), River Ecology, University of California Press, Berkeley (1975).

Womersley, H.B.S., Aspects of the distribution and ecology of subtidal marine algae on Southern Australian Coasts. *In* Nisizawa, K. (ed.) Proceedings of the VII International Seaweed Symposium, 52–54, University of Tokyo Press, Tokyo (1972).

Wright, S.J.L., Interactions of pesticides with microalgae. *In* Hill, I.R. and Wright, S.J.L. (eds.) Pesticide Microbiology, Academic Press, London (1978).

Yarish, C., Breeman, A.M., and Van den Hoek, C., Survival strategies and temperature responses of seaweeds belonging to different biogeographic distribution groups, *Bot. Mar.*, **29**, 215–30 (1986).

Yoder, J.A., Effect of temperature on light-limited growth and chemical composition of *Skeletonema costatum* (Bacillariophyceae), *J. Phycol.*, **15**, 362–70 (1979).

Zavenboom, W. and Mur, L.R., N_2-fixing cyanobacteria: why they do not become dominant in Dutch hypertonic lakes?, *Dev. Hydrobiol.*, **2**, 123–30 (1980).

14 Applied Phycology

INTRODUCTION

With the phenomenal increase in urban population and industrial growth during the past few decades, some of the major problems of a basic nature confronting mankind are those of quantity and quality of food, feed, drinking water, disposal of sewage and industrial wastes, and proper conservation of soils and water. Suitably controlled algal growth can provide positive help in tackling these problems.

There are many ways in which the algae can be used, but the most promising bases for immediate further increase of microalgae production are those in which the algae are obtained as byproducts rather than as main products as, for instance, *Spirulina* as a byproduct of soda manufacture from carbonate brine in Mexico, or the algal mixtures obtained as byproducts of urban sewage treatment processes in Israel. Continued efforts to evolve suitable algal technology with a view to reducing the costs of production should see a more widespread application and commercialization of edible algae (Soeder, 1980).

The algae and their products find a conspicuous usage in maritime countries where most people use some algae or algal products daily, either directly or indirectly.

In the Far East and the Pacific Islands, people eat seaweeds such as *Porphyra*, *Laminaria*, *Undaria*, *Gracilaria* (Fig. 14-1), *Alaria* (Fig. 14-2), and *Asparagopsis*. In Hawaii, about 50 species of algae are eaten. Worldwide, over 160 species are commercially important food sources, mostly belonging to the Rhodophyta, Phaeophyta, and Chlorophyta, and a few (about 8 species) belonging to the Cyanophyta.

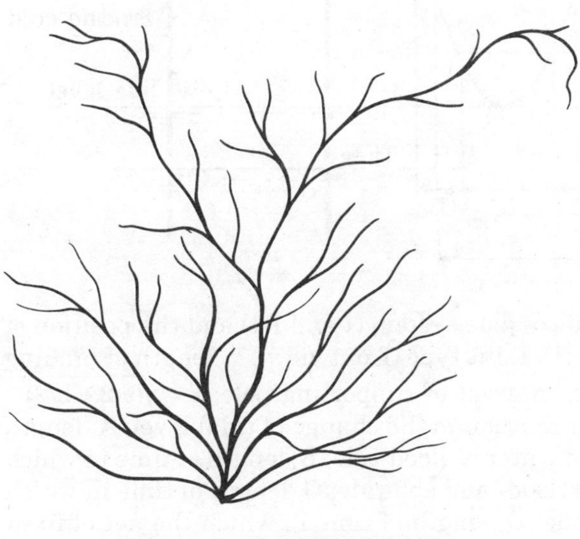

Fig. 14-1 *Gracilaria*, habit.

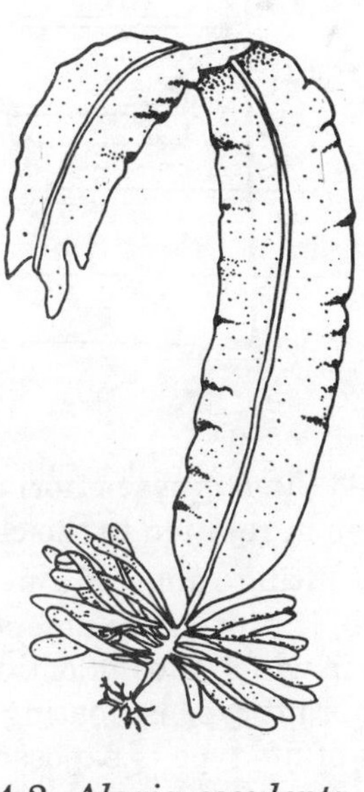

Fig. 14-2 *Alaria esculenta*, plant with sporophylls near its base.

Some species of *Nostoc*, *Aphanothece*, and *Spirulina* exemplify the important freshwater or terrestrial blue-green algae that are edible. Of these, the most important is *Spirulina* which is mass-cultured in Mexico, Taiwan, and India for its especially high protein content (up to about 65%) and nutritional value. The majority of the Indian population is vegetarian and *Spirulina* can be a good meat substitute for these people.

Examples of edible green algae include *Ulva*, *Enteromorpha*, *Monostroma*, and the unicellular *Chlorella*. Taiwan cultivates *Chlorella* on a mass scale, producing over 1500 tons dry weight annually.

SEAWEED MARICULTURE (MARINE AGRONOMY)

Two important examples of edible brown seaweeds are *Laminaria* spp. and *Undaria pinnatifida*.

Perhaps the most important of all the edible seaweeds is the red alga *Porphyra* (called *nori* in Japan). Over 60,000 hectares in Japan are used for cultivating this seaweed. The mariculture of seaweeds employs two primary approaches, viz., use of (1) concrete blocks, and (2) bamboo-cum-rope network. In (1), concrete blocks are placed on the sea floor to enhance seaweed growth. In (2), small or large fragments of the seaweed (or its spores) are colonized on ropes (Figs. 14-3, 14-4, and 14-5) which are cultured on raft-like networks of bamboos and

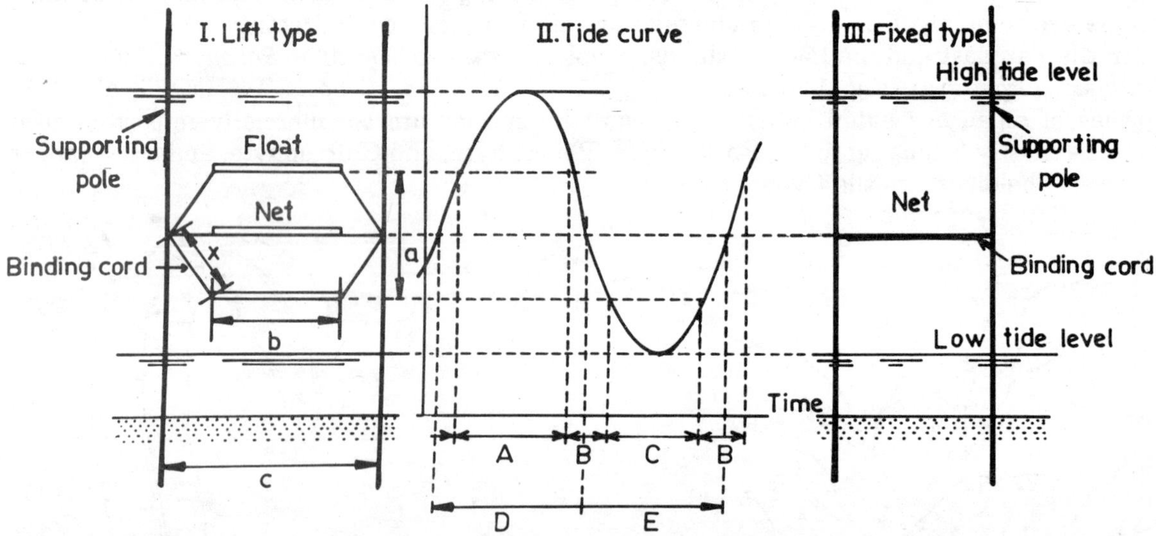

Fig. 14-3 Two types of nori cultivating apparatus of pole system (I and III) and the position of nori-nets in relation to the change of tidal level (II). I, lift type (front view). x: length of binding cord, a: lifting range of a net, b: width of net, c: interval of supporting pole; $x = \sqrt{(c/2 - b/2)^2}$, $c > x + b$; II, tide curve and position of nori-net in relation to the change of tidal level; A, length of time in which the net of lift type is immersed in water at flood-tide; B, length of time in which the net of lift type is floating on water surface at flood- and ebb-tide; C, length of time in which the net of lift type is exposed in the air at ebb-tide; D, length of time in which the net of fixed type is immersed in water at flood-tide; E, length of time in which the net of fixed type is exposed in the air at ebb-tide; III, fixed type (front view).

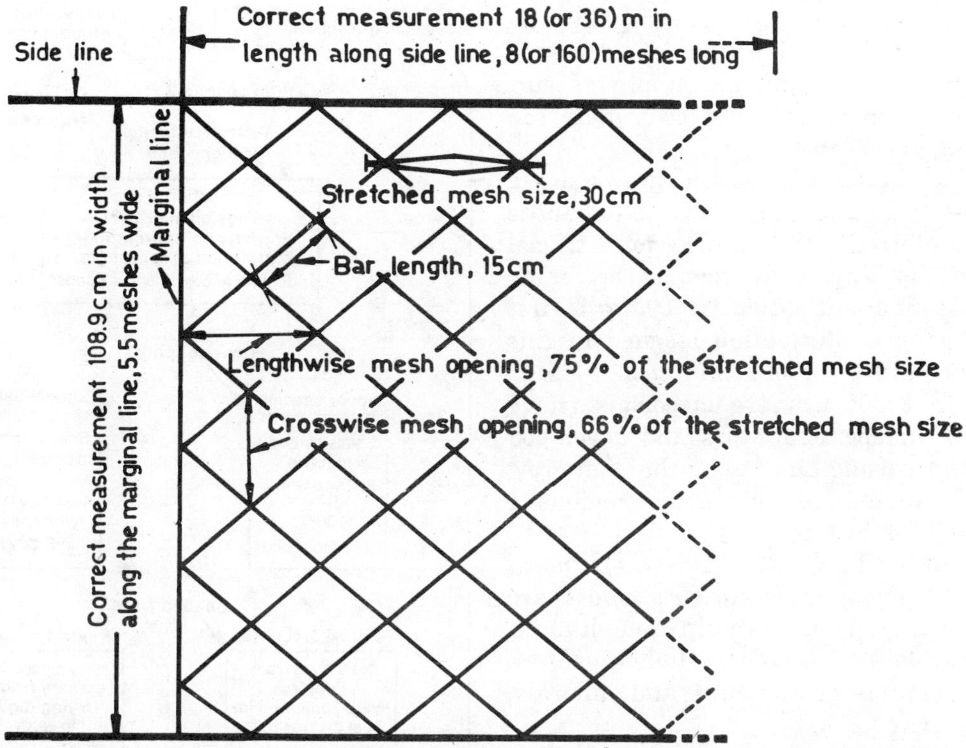

Fig. 14-4 Structure of the nori-net used as substrate for nori cultivation.

held at various depths along the seashore. The farming of *Porphyra* in Japan (Figs. 14-6, 14-7) is a well-developed industry. When mature, the *Porphyra* plants are harvested, dried, pressed into sheets, and marketed. These sheets are used in soups and sushi.

Seaweeds can not only be cultivated along the seashore but also on vast areas of the open ocean. This new concept involves huge networks of some 20 metre deep plastic pipes (ocean farms) emplaced in the surface waters of the oceans. These pipes provide substrata for seaweed attachment. Sea water is rather deficient in nitrate and phosphate, but this problem can be overcome by wave- or wind-powered pumping or upwelling of deeper nutrient-rich waters to the surface layers through vertical pipes extending to depths of over 100 metres (Wilcox, 1982).

PRACTICAL CULTURE METHODS IN THE SEA

In some instances, the threads on which the juvenile fronds have been artificially grown are wrapped around plastic ropes (diameter 1.5 cm) and stretched (spread) in the sea. In others, the threads are cut into short pieces which are twisted into plastic rope at intervals of 10–15 cm and attached either to floating buoys or to concrete or steel structures fixed to the bottom of the sea.

In 1945, a Japanese named Yōshirō Ōtsuki, who was living in China, devised a system of artificially cultivating *Laminaria* along the Chinese coast, where it occurs naturally in some parts. He remained in China until 1953, improving, popularizing, and perfecting this system. Zoospores settled on cords suspended directly in the sea; and gametophytes survived the summer even in areas where sea water was warm (30°C).

Undaria (wakame), which grows in a natural state in many parts of the Japanese coast, is preferred (to *Laminaria*) for artificial cultivation in Japan. It seemed better to establish sound cultivation for *Undaria* first and then apply information learned in this way to the cultivation of *Laminaria*.

Since the 1960s, Chinese phycologists have done good, independent work and developed methods for raising *Laminaria* that can grow even in the temperate and warmer regions of the East China Sea.

In Canada and the U.K., *Palmaria palmata* (dulse) and *Chondrus crispus* (Irish moss) are often eaten directly as a protein- and vitamin-rich vegetable. In fact, most edible algae are quite rich in proteins, vitamins, and minerals, including iodine.

In the Philippines, *Enteromorpha* spp. (Fig. 14-8), *Caulerpa racemosa, Gelidiella acerosa, Laurencia* spp., and *Gracilaria* spp. are eaten raw as salad; *Ulva lactuca* and *Gelidiella acerosa* are cooked with vegetables; *Porphyra crispata* is mixed in soups; and a dessert is made from *Gracilaria* spp. mixed with sugar and cocoanut milk.

In Korea, laver (*Porphyra*) has been cultivated for 15 centuries and it constitutes an important marine commodity exported abroad. *P. tenera* and *P. yezoensis* are the two important species. These are cultivated both in Korea and Japan. Both these species form abundant neutral spores which make it possible to harvest more than one crop in a single season. The annual harvest of nori (laver) in Japan exceeds $120 million and constitutes Japan's most valuable marine product. The lipids of nori mainly have some highly unsaturated fatty acids and also some antioxygenic factor that checks the formation of

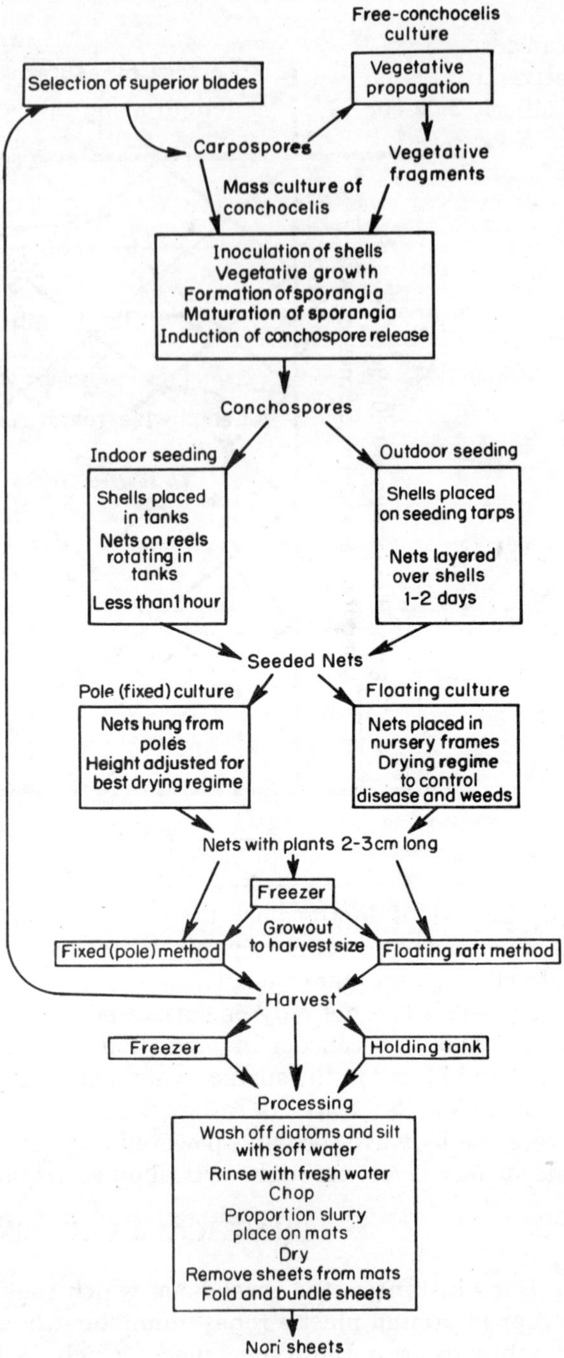

Fig. 14-5 Flowchart of *Porphyra* mariculture starting from thallus and conchocelis stage to processed nori sheets (after Mumford and Miura, 1988).

rancid odours even after prolonged storage. *P. linearis* is another useful species that has an attractive, pleasing flavour because of the high content of several amino acids and of isofloridoside.

Eucheuma is being artificially cultivated in the Philippines on nylon threads hung in seacoast in areas away from typhoon-prone localities.

Fig. 14-6 *Porphyra* farming in Japan. Floating cultivation. *Courtesy* M. Ohno.

Fig. 14-7 *Porphyra* farming in Japan. Pole system. *Courtesy* M. Ohno.

Laminaria is extensively cultivated in China and Japan (Figs. 14-9, 14-10, 14-11, and 14-12).

Mass Culture of *Conchocelis*

In February or March, mature *Porphyra* fronds producing carpospores are placed in tanks filled with sea water together with oyster shells.

Growth of *Conchocelis* is stimulated by sufficient sunlight and fertilizers when the tank-water temperature is less than 15°C. Water is circulated continuously.

Tanks are shaded when the water temperature exceeds 20°C. Light is reduced to 150 lux at the peak of summer, when water temperatures rise above 25°C. This keeps *Conchocelis* dormant. At this time, conchospores begin to appear; but the high temperatures prevent the growth of filaments.

When water temperatures drop to about 25°C, 8 or 10 hours of sunlight a day (short-day treatment) are permitted so as to allow conchospores to grow to maturity.

In September or October (water temperature 20–22°C), conchospores in oyster shells grow vigorously. At this time, artificial sowing for the production of *Porphyra* fronds is performed in either of the two following ways:

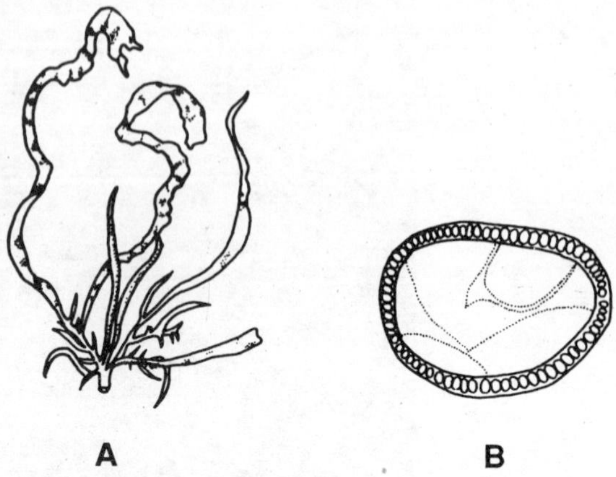

Fig. 14-8 *Enteromorpha linza*. A, habit; B, transverse section through basal part of thallus.

(1) Large numbers of the conchospore-producing oyster shells are placed in net bags or other open work containers among the artificial substrates (net farms) directly in the sea.

(2) The conchospore-producing oyster shells and the substrate nets are placed together in large tanks containing constantly circulating sea water.

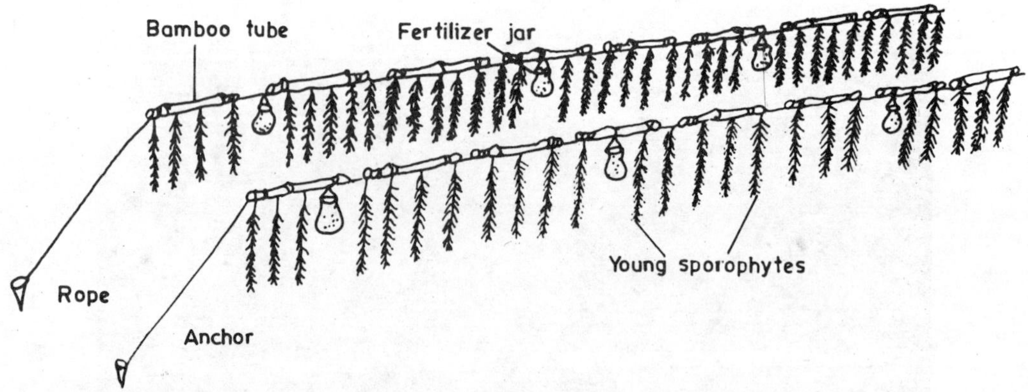

Fig. 14-9 Single-line bamboo rafts used for kelp cultivation in China. The porous earthenware jars are filled with fertilizer that seeps out into the ocean. (After Cheng, 1969.)

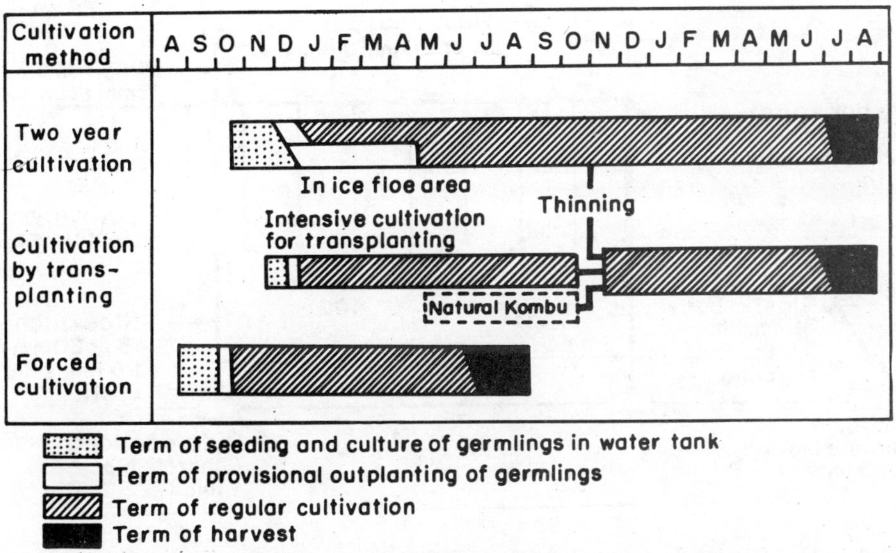

Fig. 14-10 Major seasonal events in the two-year cultivation method, the forced cultivation method, and the transplanted seedstock method of rearing edible kelp (after Kawashima, 1984).

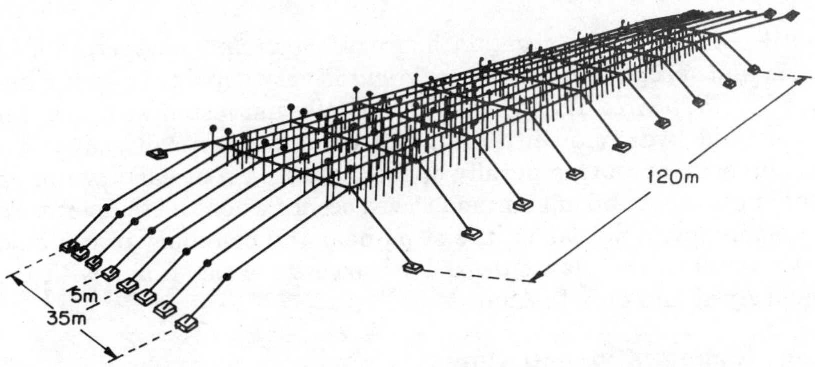

Fig. 14-11 General kelp farm arrangement (after Kawashima, 1984).

Harvesting and Farming

It is advisable to harvest seaweeds before they are old because once spores have formed, the fronds become tough, change colour, and lose taste. For the species accustomed to cold climates, a temperature of 10°C to 15°C is optimum, and, for warm water species, from 20°C to 25°C is best.

Sublittoral species can be harvested at any time. The lowest spring tides are the best time to harvest littoral algae; these occur for three or four days when the moon is full or before appearance of the new moon.

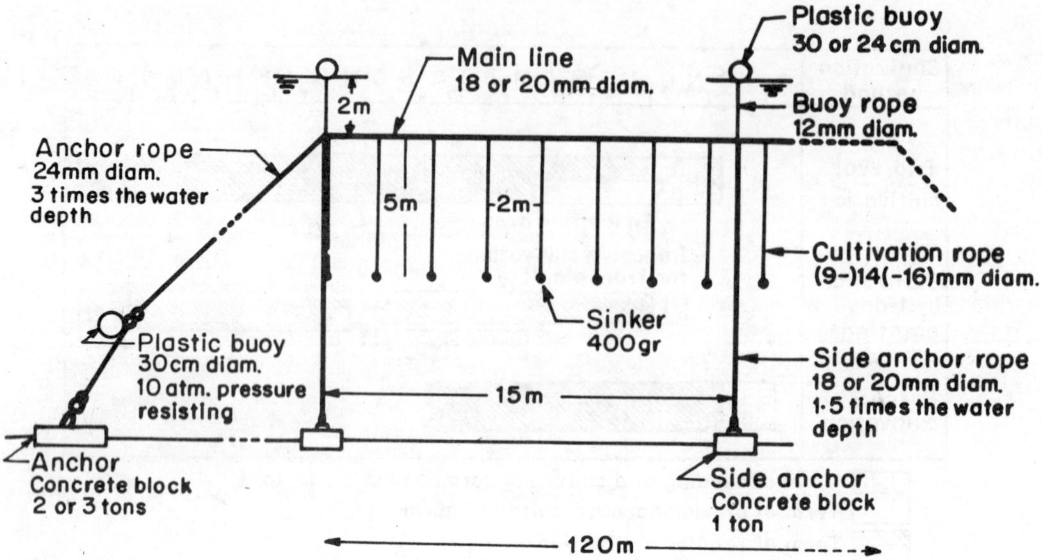

Fig. 14-12 Detail of kelp farm structure showing arrangement of vertical ropes (after Kawashima, 1984).

Monostroma and Enteromorpha

Some widely utilized green sea vegetables are *Monostroma oxyspermum, Enteromorpha prolifera, E. linza,* and species of *Ulva. Monostroma* is very popular in Japan and is cultivated in the same ways as *Porphyra.* These algae are usually harvested in winter months.

Undaria pinnatifida (wakame) in the wild is an annual brown seaweed limited to the temperate seas. Juvenile sprouts generally appear in autumn or early winter. Mature fronds appear in winter and spring, and maximum growth occurs when the temperatures are between 10°C and 15°C. Sporophylls appear on the stipe near the boundary of the blade; and spores are produced. Above 20°C, the plants degrade. Harvest seasons differ with the region: from February through April and July to August.

Mass Culture of Gametophytes in Tanks

The asexual spores produced by the sporophytes of Laminariales develop into tiny filamentous gametophytes. The female gametophytes form one-cell eggs; the male ones form spermatozoids. The fertilized egg germinates into a macroscopic sporophyte, which grows into the adult body. The latter produces zoospores, which can be collected by placing pieces of mature fronds in a tank of sea water together with convenient plastic threads on which the zoospores soon settle. The pieces of frond should be removed in a day since, if left in the water too long, they produce a polluting, brown, mucus-like substance. Developing male and female gametophytes are mass-cultured directly in the tank. At maturity they produce eggs and spermatozoids and ultimately juvenile sporophytes visible to the naked eye. Finally juvenile fronds appear on the plastic threads. These are transplanted into the sea and numerous juvenile fronds appear in about a week. They soon mature and can then be harvested (Fig. 14-13).

Environmental conditions determine the time when juvenile sporophytes may be transplanted into the sea. Water temperature is the most important condition, since the fronds tend to die at a temperature exceeding 20°C. For best results, either of the following is taken to control conditions in the tanks so that the juvenile fronds are ready at the time when the marine environmental conditions are optimum:

(1) Water temperature is controlled at between 5°C and 8°C and the tanks are shaded and kept dark so that juvenile fronds remain dormant until October (Fig. 14-13 A).

(2) Gametophytes are kept dormant during July and August when the water temperature rises above 25°C and 30°C by lighting the tank dimly (Fig. 14-13 B). Beginning in September, conditions favourable to the formation of eggs and spermatozoids and for fertilization of eggs are available.

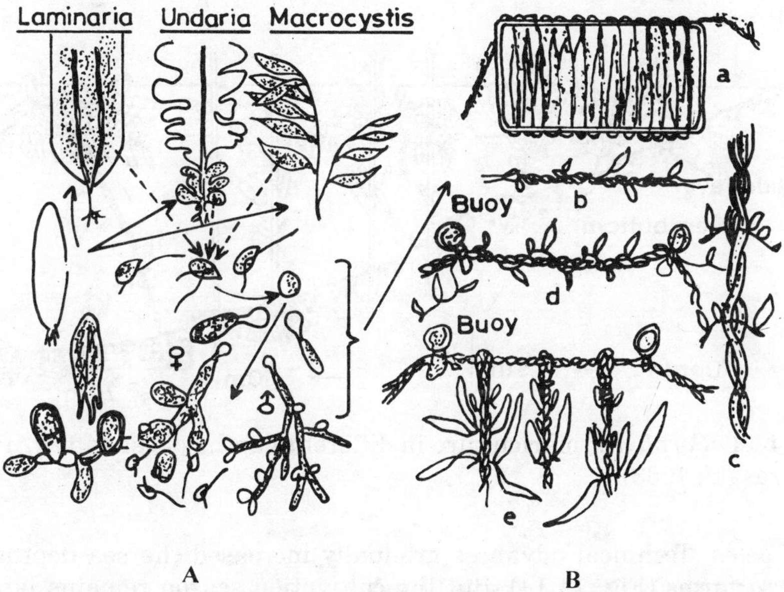

Fig. 14-13 Mass culture of laminarialean gametophytes in tanks. A, gametophyte culture at proper temperature; B, gametophyte collector for tank culture. (After Arasaki and Arasaki, 1983.)

Since it is somewhat harder to keep the juvenile fronds dormant, the method (2) is more practical.

Laminaria releases zoospores in the cool season between October and December, when the water temperature is about 15°C (the same reproductive period applies to many Laminariales species including *Eisenia, Ecklonia,* and *Alaria*). In gametophyte mass-culture tanks, the temperature may easily be kept lower than 20°C; and juvenile fronds will appear in the winter-spring season, when sea water is not too warm. If growth of *Laminaria* juvenile fronds is retarded at temperatures between 5°C and 6°C when they are from 2–3 centimetres long, they will grow well when transplanted into the sea. In general, mass artificial cultivation of *Laminaria* is easier than that of *Undaria*.

Several decades ago bamboo or tree branches and trunks were used to grow *Porphyra* but material limitations prevented its cultivation in water more than five metres deep. The only part of even the longest bamboo branches to which *Porphyra* fronds could attach themselves was the upper one metre, which corresponds to the intertidal level. Finally, once put in place, these branches and trunks are difficult to move. Bamboo branches or plastic poles have been set up and nets of palm-fibre yarn or synthetic fibre are hung on them. This produced a horizontal substrate on which small fronds could grow. This system became popular over six decades ago. During the 1970s, further improvement occurred in the form of floats for the

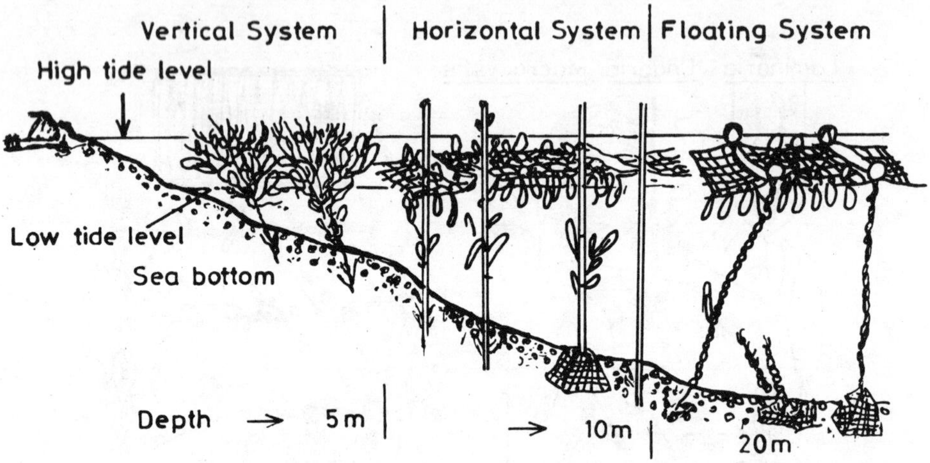

Fig. 14-14 *Porphyra*, mariculture in different depths of sea (after Arasaki and Arasaki, 1983).

nets instead of poles. Technical advances gradually increased the sea depths that could be used for *Porphyra* farms (Fig. 14-14). But the cultivation season remains largely unaltered. The substrates are set in place from late September to mid October, when the water temperature is 20°C to 22°C. Harvests are made until the end of March. Though fronds continue to develop into April, they are too short to be suitable for production of sheet nori. The substrates are removed either then or at the end of the cultivation period. *Porphyra* disappears in the summer (Arasaki and Arasaki, 1983).

Undaria pinnatifida is an edible seaweed popular in Japan. It grows on rocks and reefs and is artificially grown extensively by the following methods:

(1) Stone deposition on the sea bottom within the range of natural *Undaria.* The stones become colonized soon. Stones may also be placed along with cultured sporophylls. In some cases, stones are first placed along with sporophylls and after the zoospores have attached on the stones, they are placed in the sea.

(2) Sporophyll deposition may be practised with the objective other than transplantation. The sporophylls are placed in the twists and coils of a rope or tied to it. The ropes are then sunk by sinkers to the sea bottom.

When sporophylls are deposited with the idea of transplantation, they are first placed in a habitat where *Undaria* is naturally growing well, and then transplanted at other places in the sea bottom.

(3) The zoospores are allowed to settle on nets in tanks or in a live well on a boat. The nets are then sunk by sinkers to the sea bottom and the germlings allowed to grow into adult thalli.

The zoospores are usually sown directly on the materials used for rearing the thalli. Spun yarns (about 4 mm in diameter) of hemp palm or coil yarn and of synthetic fibres are the substrates of choice for cultivating *Undaria* (Saito, 1975). The spore-collectors are hung from a raft in the sea. The culture of the germlings is continued until the water temperature falls to 20°C or less and until the sporophytes or the young thalli are produced.

Figure 14-15 illustrates the cultivating apparatus for *Undaria*.

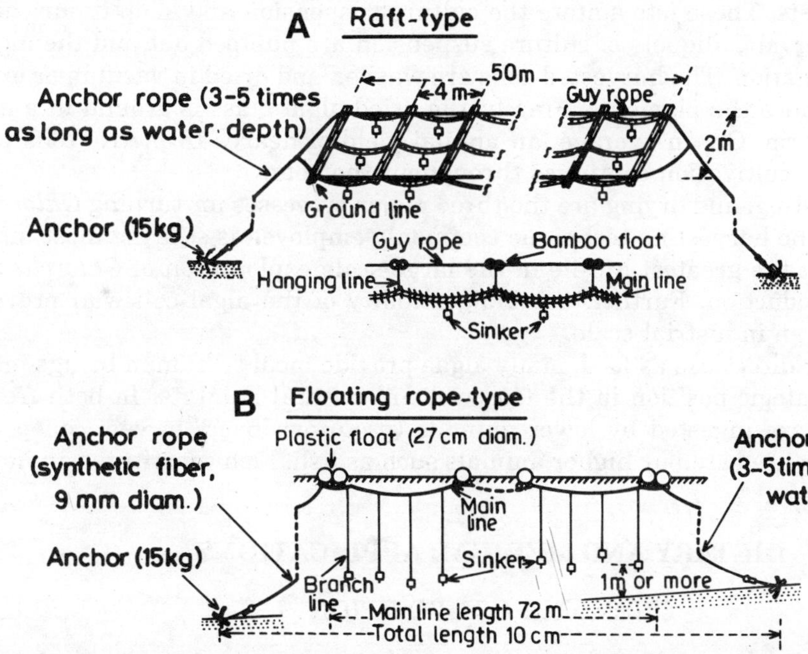

Fig. 14-15 *Undaria* cultivation system. A, raft-type; B, floating rope-type. (After Saito, 1975.)

By autumn, the ropes or yarns become densely covered with *Undaria* plants. The yarns are wound around a rope of Manila hemp or synthetic fibres, at suitable intervals, or cut into short pieces and inserted in the twists of the ropes. The latter are then placed in the sea supported by floats in rough water. *Undaria* is now widely cultivated in the open sea on floating ropes; earlier it used to be grown mostly in calm bays on simple rafts.

Harvesting is done from March through June or July. The ropes are hauled up from the sea and their attached thalli are cut off by means of a sickle.

Although *Porphyra* has been in use as a supplementary diet in Japan for a long time, its restriction to marine habitat, slow growth rate, and relatively poor vitamin and protein content make it a less favourable algal food than *Chlorella*. The latter grows very fast under different conditions and therefore a much greater number of crops can be harvested. It is also richer in protein and lipid content than *Porphyra* and contains a wider variety as well as a higher concentration of vitamins. The nutritional value of *Chlorella* is comparable to that of a mixture of soybeans and spinach. Simple growth requirements, production of little waste material, and high growth rate are the features that have encouraged the mass cultivation of *Chlorella* in Germany, Japan, and the U.S.A.

Chlorella grows actively in culture when provided with sunlight (or artificial light), CO_2, and mineral nutrients. Provision has also to be made for frequent or continuous agitation of the culture suspension so as to prevent the cells from settling down, and to ensure a proper distribution of nutrients, CO_2, and light. The open circulation system of mass culture devised by Tamiya (1960) in Japan consists of an open, shallow culture pond containing rotating pipes with numerous fine jets. These jets agitate the culture suspension and keep it enriched with CO_2. At frequent intervals, aliquots of culture suspension are pumped out and the algal cells harvested by centrifugation. The harvested cells are washed and dried in vacuum or extracted with methanol to remove the pigments. Finally, the dried algal mass is ground in a mill and stored in powdered form. On an average, an annual yield of nearly 13 metric tons per acre can be expected if the cultivation continues throughout the year.

Cultivation, harvesting, and drying are the three major processes for turning *Chlorella* into foodstuffs. Of these, the harvesting technique commonly employed is still the most inefficient and expensive so that the greatest hurdle in the large scale exploitation of *Chlorella* as food is its high cost of production. Further, the indigestibility of the algal cell wall prevents its direct use as food on an industrial scale.

In addition to their direct use as food, many algae provide meal to human beings indirectly by virtue of their strategic position in the food webs in natural habitats. In both fresh- and marine water, algae are ingested by lower animals (protozoa, insect larvae, copepods, and rotifers) which in turn are eaten by higher animals such as fish. Fish constitutes an important source of protein.

DIETARY AND MEDICAL APPLICATIONS

CHEMICAL COMPOSITION

Seaweeds are rich in carbohydrates (50–60 per cent of dry weight) (see Table 14-1), minerals (up to 25 per cent), and vitamins. In addition, they contain characteristic mucilages.

PROTEIN CONTENT

Nitrogen content of edible seaweeds ranges from 1.5 to 7.6 per cent (dry weight). When raw protein is calculated by multiplying nitrogen content by 6.25, the protein range becomes from 10 to 48 per cent (Table 14-2).

Amino acids in these proteins are about the same as those in ordinary proteins, and the amino-acid composition is actually better than that of land plants. Interestingly, this amino-acid composition closely resembles ovalbumin (egg-white protein). In general, animal experiments and experiments on artificial digestion indicate that alkaline-extracted seaweed proteins—especially from such old Japanese favourites as Asakusa-nori (*Porphyra tenera*), and matsumo (*Heterochordaria abietina*, recently renamed *Analipus japonicus*)—are both good and highly nutritive.

Table 14-1 Approximate chemical composition of some edible seaweeds (unit grams) (after Arasaki and Arasaki, 1983)

Seaweed (per 100 g)	Water	Raw proteins	Fat	Carbohydrates	Fibre	Ash
Ulva sp.	15	24	0.6	42	5	14
Enteromorpha sp.	4	21	0.3	61	7	7
Eisenia bicyclis	19	7.5	0.1	51	10	12
Heterochordaria abietina (*Analipus japonicus*)	13	19	0.4	40	6	17
Undaria pinnatifida	16	13	2	48	4	18
Laminaria sp.	18	7	2	49	5	19
Gracilaria sp.	13	8	0.05	58	3	18
Chondrus crispus	16	11	3	55	2	14
Porphyra tenera	12	31	0.6	39	6	10

Table 14-2 Nitrogen contents of some seaweeds (condensed from Arasaki and Arasaki, 1983)

Algae	Nitrogen (%)
Enteromorpha compressa	1.98
Enteromorpha linza	3.09
Ulva pertusa	3.26
Ulva lactuca	2.38
Eisenia bicyclis	1.82
Analipus japonicus	3.80
Laminaria japonica	2.47
Chondrus ocellatus	4.37
Chondrus crispus	1.80
Gelidium amansii	3.25
Gymnogongrus flabelliformis	4.31
Porphyra tenera	7.63

Extracts obtained from seaweeds by means of a 70 per cent aqueous-alcohol contain amino acids, peptides, nucleic acids, and such sugar alcohols as mannitol, sorbitol, and dulcitol.

Several free amino acids in fairly large amounts are found in seaweed ethanolic extracts. This includes some special amino acids peculiar to seaweeds (see Table 14-3). Habitat and seasonal variation have an effect on the content of amino acids and peptides in seaweeds.

Table 14-3 Amino-acid composition of proteins in some seaweeds and ovalbumin (g of amino acid–N/100 g of protein-N) (after Arasaki and Arasaki, 1983)

Amino acid	*Ulva pertusa*	*Eisenia bicyclis*	*Undaria pinnatifida*	*Porphyra tenera*	*Grateloupia turuturu*	*Ovalbumin*
Tryptophan	0.3	1.3	0.8	1.3	0.8	1.0
Lysine	4.5	7.8	4.3	4.5	4.3	7.7
Histidine	4.0	4.0	2.7	1.4	1.8	4.1
Arginine	14.9	18.6	7.5	16.4	15.8	11.7
Aspartic acid	6.5	5.0	5.6	7.0	5.7	6.2
Threonine	3.1	2.3	2.4	4.0	3.0	3.0
Serine	3.0	2.3	2.8	2.9	2.8	6.8
Glutamic acid	6.9	7.6	5.1	7.2	6.3	9.9
Proline	4.0	4.5	2.8	6.4	5.1	2.8
Glycine	5.2	6.5	4.4	7.2	5.0	3.4
Alanine	6.1	7.0	4.8	7.4	5.5	6.7
Cysteine	1.2	0.7	0.5	0.3	0.7	1.4
Valine	4.9	5.9	4.1	6.4	4.9	5.4
Methionine	1.6	2.4	2.2	1.7	1.7	3.1
Isoleucine	3.5	4.4	2.9	4.0	4.4	4.8
Leucine	6.9	7.3	5.1	8.7	6.3	6.2
Tyrosine	1.4	2.1	1.6	2.4	0.9	1.8
Phenylalanine	3.9	4.0	3.7	3.9	3.7	4.1
Total	82.9	93.6	63.3	93.1	74.3	90.1
N %	13.2	10.6	11.6	13.6	14.4	15.8

Nonprotein free amino acids in the cells include β-alanine, α- and γ-aminobutyric acid, taurine, 2-aminocapylic acid, ornithine, citrulline, lanthionine, phenylserine, and hydroxyproline (Table 14-4). In *Porphyra tenera*, alanine makes up about 25 per cent of the total free amino acids and probably accounts for the faintly sweet taste.

Table 14-4 Composition of amino acids in ethanolic extracts from some seaweeds (mg % dry weight)

Amino acid	*Ulva pertusa*	*Enteromorpha linza*	*Undaria pinnatifida*	*Sargassum confusum*	*Chondria crassicaulis*
Alanine	17.7	23.8	617	278	71.4
Alloisoleucine	0	0	2.7	0	0
Arginine	2.5	1.9	36.5	1.6	trace
Aspartic acid	4.4	13.7	5.4	27.5	87.1
Chondrine	28.7	43.0	41.0	22.8	193
Citrulline	0	0	0	0	0
Cysteic acid	35.5	13.1	4.8	3.7	13.3
D-Cysteinolic acid	152	73.4	1.9	2.2	57.4
Glutamic acid	31.8	55.0	89.8	28.5	49.5
Glycine	9.1	5.2	455	3.7	29.1
Histidine	0	0	2.1	0	3.3
Isoleucine	3.7	5.8	11.2	9.7	6.4
Leucine	6.6	6.8	19.6	14.3	5.3
Lysine	0.9	0.8	34.6	0	3.6
Methionine	0	0	1.7	0	trace
Ornithine	0	0	0	4.0	0
Phenylalanine	4.1	3.8	9.2	11.3	0
Proline	40.0	51.1	156	24.2	50.8
Serine	11.9	33.7	64.4	51.6	12.9
S-Hydroxymethyl-L-homocysteine	0	0	0	0	0
Taurine	1.8	2.0	11.8	9.7	14.5
Threonine	5.7	3.8	90.3	12.0	12.0
Tryptophan	2.4	1.4	5.8	8.0	12.6
Tyrosine	2.1	2.1	10.1	7.5	0
Valine	3.5	3.9	11.1	14.0	7.6

FATS AND LIPIDS

Though the fat content of seaweeds is low (approximately 1 per cent dry weight), the fatty acid composition differs from that of ordinary plant oils only in that there are more unsaturated than saturated fatty acids in it. The main fatty acid is oleic acid. Palmitic acid is the main saturated fatty acid, but myristic and stearic acids are also present. Non-saponificating substances—sterols and lipid-soluble vitamins—seem to play a greater role as compared to neutral fatty acids in algae than they do in land plants.

VITAMINS

High vitamin and mineral contents are the outstanding nutritional features of sea vegetables. Table 14-5 compares their vitamin contents with those of a few other foods (Arasaki and Arasaki, 1983).

Table 14-5 Vitamin content in sea vegetables and other foods (after Arasaki and Arasaki, 1983)

Content per 100 g	A (IU)	B_1 (mg)	B_2 (mg)	Niacin (mg)	C (mg)	B_6 (μg)	B_{12} (μg)	Folic acid (μg)
Dry seaweeds	20,400 to	0.12 to	0.89 to	2.6 to				
Porphyra tenera	44,500	0.25	1.24	10	20	1.04	13–29	8.8
Ulva sp.	960	0.06	0.03	8.0	10		6.3	11.8
Enteromorpha sp.	500	0.04	0.52	1.0	10		1.3	42.9
Eisenia bicyclis	50	0.02	0.02	2.6	0			
Laminaria sp.	430	0.08	0.32	1.8	11	0.27	0.3	
Undaria pinnatifida	140	0.11	0.14	10.0	15			
Tomato	200	0.08	0.03	0.3	20	0.11	0	28
Spinach	2,600	0.12	0.30	1.0	100	0.18	0	140
Apple	5	0.02	0.03	0.2	5	0.03	0	5
Cabbage	10	0.05	0.05	0.2	44	0.16	0	90

Asakusa-nori (*Porphyra tenera*) is a virtual storehouse of vitamins with a vitamin A content twenty times that of green peppers and ten times that of spinach. Its vitamin C content is about the same as that of tomatoes but four times that of apples. In addition, it provides ample vitamin B_1. The better the colour and flavour of the nori the higher its vitamin content. Since dried or toasted nori must be stored away from sunlight and in a dry place it does not lose its vitamin C.

MINERALS

Sea vegetables contain more minerals (7–38% of dry weight) than any other kind of food. All of the minerals required by human beings are present in seaweeds in sufficient amounts.

The high amount of calcium in sea vegetables, if fully effective nutritionally, would make them the richest food after milk. Should its utilization turn out to be as good as that in milk, sea vegetables will become an important source of calcium (Table 14-6).

Table 14-6 Calcium content in sea vegetables and other foods (after Arasaki and Arasaki, 1983)

Dry seaweeds	mg %	Other foods	mg %
Undaria pinnatifida	1,300	Sesame seed	1,100
Eisenia bicyclis	1,170	Dried sardine	330
Analipus japonicus	890	Soybean	190
Laminaria sp.	800	Milk	100
Ulva sp.	730	Spinach	98
Enteromorpha sp.	600	Egg	65
Porphyra tenera	470	Cabbage	24

The iron content of sea vegetables ranges from two to more than ten times that of egg yolk and spinach. *Enteromorpha* has about 105 mg % whereas *Porphyra tenera* has about 20 mg %. (It should be noted that sesame seeds have only 16 mg %.)

IODINE

Since the Japanese eat lots of seaweeds that are rich in iodine, salt is not iodized in Japan. One gram of kombu kelp daily would provide the 0.1–0.2 milligram required by a normal adult or the 0.2 milligram needed by children and pregnant women. Table 14-7 gives the iodine content of some seaweeds.

Table 14-7 Iodine content of some seaweeds (approximate)

Seaweeds (dry)	Content (mg %)
Laminaria sp.	190–470
Eisenia bicyclis	95–56
Sargassum confusum	275–325
Undaria pinnatifida	15–35
Gelidium sp.	150–170
Chondrus ocellatus	1.0–1.2
Porphyra tenera	0.5

FLAVOUR AND TASTE

When growing in the sea, sea vegetables have only a weak flavour that is produced by free iodine and certain sulphur compounds such as dimethyl sulphide.

Volatile elements in decomposing seaweeds give off certain odours and tastes (Table 14-8).

Table 14–8 Some volatile components of seaweeds (after Arasaki and Arasaki, 1983)

	Ulva pertusa	*Entero-morpha*	*Laminaria* sp.	*Sargassum* sp.	*Porphyra tenera*
Dimethyl sulphide	+	+	±	–	–
Methylmercaptan	–	–	+	+	+
Trimethylamine	+	+	+	+	+
Formic acid	+	+	+	+	+
Acetic acid	+	+	+	+	+
Acrylic acid	+	+	–	–	–
Propionic acid	+	+	+	+	+
Butyric acid	+	+	+	+	+
Isovaleric acid	+	+	+	+	+
N-caproic acid	+	+	+	+	+
Caprylic acid	+	+	+	+	+
Myristic acid	+	+	+	+	+
Palmitic acid	+	+	+	+	+
Linoleic acid	+	+	+	+	+
P-cresol	+	+	+	+	+
Furfural	+	+	+	+	+
Methyl furfural	+	+	+	+	+
N-valeraldehyde	+	+	+	+	+
Benzaldehyde	+	+	+	+	+
Furfuryl alcohol	+	+	+	+	–
D-limonene	+	+	+	+	+
Geraniol	+	+	+	+	+
Pinene	+	+	+	+	+
Terpinolene	+	+		+	+

ORGANIC ACIDS

The flavours of many seaweeds are caused by such organic acids as formic, propionic, acetic, isovalerianic, caproic, and myristic. Unsaturated fatty acids give them their characteristic taste.

AMINO ACIDS

The contents and types of amino acids, e.g., glycine and alanine (sweet) and leucine, isoleucine, and valine (slightly bitter) also impart some flavour to seaweeds. Alcoholic extracts of Asakusa-nori are rich in glutamic acid, alanine, and taurine. Those of *Undaria pinnatifida* contain a great deal of alanine and glycine, whereas *Laminaria japonica* has glutamic acid and aspartic acid.

EXAMPLES OF EDIBLE SEAWEEDS

Laminaria japonica (Kombu)

This is used in the preparation of stock to serve as the basis for many other foods. Monosodium glutamate, aspartic acid, alanine, mannitol, and iodine account for the flavour of *Laminaria japonica*. Kombu should not be boiled long because this can release unpleasant-tasting inorganic magnesium, calcium, and sulphuric acid into the water.

Porphyra tenera (Asakusa-nori)

The complex taste of Asakusa-nori results from two nucleic acids (5′-guanylic acids) and several amino acids (glutamic, alanine, glycine, and taurine). Taurine and alanine are present in large amounts. Alanine produces the slightly sweet taste of the fresh fronds.

ALGAE AS FOOD FOR CRUSTACEANS

Arnold (1971) compared the food values of *Anacystis, Synechococcus, Anabaena*, and other cyanobacteria with that of certain green algae when used as feed for *Daphnia pulex*. He found that the cyanobacteria were much inferior to *Chlorella, Ankistrodesmus*, and *Chlamydomonas*. The reproduction rate of *Daphnia* fed with cyanobacteria was always lower than that fed on green algae. The different species of cyanobacteria used in feeding trials showed considerable differences in respect of their individual effects on ingestion, assimilation, and reproduction rate of *Daphnia*. Some of the cyanobacteria were even toxic. Whereas *Synechococcus cedrorum* caused the highest survival rate of *Daphnia, S. elongata* inhibited the daphnid's reproduction, possibly because it was not ingested. In the case of *Anacystis nidulans,* the ingestion was quite high but assimilation was low.

Some limnologists have observed that filtering Crustacea prefer to ingest certain types of phytoplankton cells rather than others. Porter (1973) conducted grazing experiments with several different classes of algae and found that *Anabaena affinis* and *A. flos-aquae* were among the species which were not ingested by crustaceans. In Lake George (South Africa), however, it has been reported that *Microcystis, Anabaenopsis*, and a few other cyanobacteria can be digested and assimilated but do not constitute an optimal diet for herbivores at all stages of their life cycles (Greenwood and Lund, 1973).

In a study of distribution and feeding of larval Chironomidae in a British gravel-pit lake, Titmus and Badcock (1981) found that only *Tanypus* larvae ate some cyanobacteria, whereas *Chironomus, Cryptochironomus,* and *Procladius* did not ingest any cyanobacteria. Analyses of the gut contents of the larvae of chironomids revealed that *Chironomus* and *Polypedilum* larvae fed mainly on detritus, whereas their cyanobacterial content was less than 2%. *Tanypus* larvae had 45% *Synedra,* 34% *Navicula*, 11% cyanobacteria, and 6% other algae. *Procladius* larvae fed mainly on small crustaceans (about 90%) and about 8% on algae which did not include any cyanobacteria. *Cryptochironomus* fed virtually exclusively on oligochaetes.

FODDER AND FERTILIZER

Alaria, Laminaria, Palmaria, and some other seaweeds have been used directly as fodder for livestock in Europe. More commonly, seaweed meal or powder is supplemented to the regular diet of cattle, pigs, sheep, fish, and poultry. Certain brown seaweeds, e.g., *Laminaria, Fucus,* and *Ascophyllum,* are the common ingredients of this seaweed meal.

Gracilaria meal can be profitably supplemented (up to 5%) to the feed of chicks and laying hens.

The algal mixture obtained as byproduct of sewage treatment process, and the protein-rich freshwater alga *Spirulina* grown on wastewater can be fed to fishes, poultry, and cattle to improve their health and productivity. For this purpose, *Spirulina* has been successfully cultivated in wastewater in Lucknow, Nagpur, and Varanasi. The work done at the National Botanical Research Institute in Lucknow (Fig. 14-16) has shown that the biomass of *Spirulina* grown on sewage water is free from pathogenic bacteria, enteroviruses, amoebae or worms. Even if one-fifth of the conventional animal feeds are substituted by mass-grown microalgae, it causes a significant improvement in the health and milk yield of cattle.

One great advantage of *Spirulina* is that its cultivation does not require any fertile or arable land. In India, we have thousands of hectares of barren wasteland that is either too dry or too saline/alkaline to sustain conventional agriculture. In these areas, *Spirulina* cultivation can be attempted in shallow tanks or ponds lined with polythene sheeting and filled with wastewater.

The Irish collect and use *Fucus* as manure on a large scale. In India, a comparative study of the yield of 'bhindi' (*Abelmoschus esculentus*) grown separately on a mixture of cow dung and wood ash manure, and on seaweed manure, indicated the superiority of the latter (Thivy, 1960). The seaweed manure however is poorer in nitrogen and phosphorus than the farmyard manure. The blue-green algae, which are rich in nitrogen and phosphorus, are better fertilizers than seaweeds. In tropical countries, the bottom mud of dried up ponds is regularly used as manure in crop fields; the manurial value is mostly due to the high content of blue-green algae. A suitably blended mixture of seaweed and cyanophycean manures (e.g., bloom of *Microcystis*) may serve as an ideal fertilizer and this can relieve the acute shortage of fertilizers in developing countries.

The fertility of natural habitats benefits from algal growth in many other ways as well. Many algae found in such habitats are believed to produce considerable amounts of extracellular substances, including organic acids, amino acids, and polypeptides which chelate organic and inorganic ions and maintain them in a state readily available to plants. The extracellular products also serve as sources of carbon and nitrogen for other microorganisms that regulate the overall balance of soil nitrogen, sulphur, phosphorus, and carbon.

In respect of the nitrogen status of natural habitats, the nitrogen-fixing blue-green algae deserve special mention. These algae grow luxuriantly in tropical habitats, e.g., rice fields.

Fig. 14-16 *Spirulina platensis*, cultivation in sewage for animal feed, at National Botanical Research Institute, Lucknow. *Courtesy* M.R. Ahmad.

The experiments conducted with *Tolypothrix tenuis* in Japan and with *Aulosira fertilissima* in India have shown that the yield of paddy is substantially increased following the inoculation of fields with these algae. The algologists at the Central Rice Research Institute, Cuttack (India), inoculated rice fields with four species of nitrogen-fixing blue-green algae; the grain yield increased by nearly 30 per cent.

Over 15 genera of free-living blue-green algae (e.g., *Anabaena*, *Cylindrospermum*, *Nostoc*, *Aulosira*, *Scytonema*, *Oscillatoria*, *Plectonema*, and *Aphanothece*) are known to fix nitrogen. Their contribution to the nitrogen fertility is especially important in flooded soils (e.g., rice fields) where the prevailing microaerobic or anaerobic conditions are highly conducive to nitrogenase activity in the blue-green algae. In Japan and the Philippines, in nonfertilized flooded plots, net gains of soil nitrogen range from 20–70 kg N/ha/year (Watanabe and Roger, 1984). Fertilization with phosphorus and potassium increased these gains greatly. Some 25–30% of the nitrogen fixed by the blue-green algae is taken up by the rice plants (Watanabe and Roger, 1984).

Some information is available on the effects of agronomical practices on blue-green algae in rice fields. Land preparation and management seem to have only incidental effects, and appear not to interfere with the establishment and activity of inoculated blue-green algae. The blue-green algae are generally more resistant to insecticides and pesticides than other algae and can tolerate pesticide levels obtaining in the field. In fact, insecticides tend to suppress the animals which graze on blue-green algae and this enables these algae to establish large populations.

The application of nitrogenous fertilizer usually inhibits the fixation of nitrogen by the blue-green algae in rice fields. However, if urea granules are placed deep (rather than broadcast at the surface of water), the growth and nitrogen fixation of blue-greens are usually not inhibited (Roger *et al.*, 1980). Since the growth of nitrogen-fixing blue-green algae in rice fields is generally limited by phosphorus deficiency, the application of some phosphate stimulates these algae.

The Indian Agricultural Research Institute, New Delhi, has evolved the technology of growing a mixed blue-green algal community of nitrogen fixers and distributing them to farmers for artificial inoculation in fields for increasing biological nitrogen fixation. This technology has proved successful in several areas where the indigenous blue-green algal flora is not very rich. In U.P. and Bihar, where luxuriant growths of blue-greens occur after the rains, such technology is not very suitable.

Cyanobacteria are unique in the sense that both photosynthesis and nitrogen fixation often occur in the same organism or even the same cell. It is this dual capacity to fix carbon as well as nitrogen that makes cyanobacteria attractive as sources of nitrogenous biofertilizer. The rice field cyanobacteria generate ammonium ions by using sunlight, air, and water. Some of the fixed ammonium appears to be released into the ambient water, thereby enriching it in fixed nitrogen. Attempts are being made to produce mutants in which the fixed nitrogen, i.e., ammonium, is leaked out of the cells into the medium, rather than being metabolized within the cell (Stewart *et al.*, 1987). Another desirable goal is to produce amino acid-liberating mutants of nitrogen-fixing cyanobacteria.

One main problem in the biofertilizer technology is that nothing is known about the survival of the introduced algae in the field or the outcome of their competition with the native residents, or to what extent they are vulnerable to grazing or predation. For use in the field, it is desirable to have suitable strains or mutants that continue to fix nitrogen unaffected by the presence of nitrogenous fertilizers. Another desirable feature is that the strains should be resistant to commonly used herbicides, to salinity, and to desiccation (Stewart *et al.*, 1987).

In agriculture, seaweeds act as useful soil conditioner, fertilizer, and green manure. The manurial value is due to the high content of potassium salts, micronutrients, and growth substances (chiefly cytokinins). Soil acidity can be reduced by adding calcareous seaweeds, e.g., *Lithothamnion*. Seaweeds are widely used as liquid fertilizers in gardens, greenhouses, and a variety of such crops as tomatoes, potatoes, corn, and citrus fruit (Stephenson, 1981). In the Gulf of Kutch, where over 10 tons of harvestable *Sargassum* are available annually, liquid extract is made from this seaweed and used to fertilize several crops (Sarma *et al.*, 1984).

In the Sambhar Salt Lake in Rajasthan (India), cartloads of algal mats consisting of

Anabaenopsis and *Spirulina* are produced annually, from September to December, and are employed by local farmers as manure.

SEAWEEDS AS ANIMAL FEED

In ancient times, seaweeds used to be fed to horses, cattle, sheep, and pigs in France, Scotland, Ireland, Norway, and other countries. In Norway, *Alaria esculenta* was fed to cows (Jensen, 1972). These days seaweed meal made mainly from *Ascophyllum nodosum* is being fed to animals in many coastal and maritime countries. This meal contains up to 20% of its weight in such minerals as Na, K, I, Zn, and S. Its protein content varies from about 4% to 10% and carbohydrates (alginates, fucoidin, cellulose, mannitol, laminarin) constitute some 50% of the weight. It has a variety of vitamins.

ALGAE AND FISH NESTS

The algal thalli, mainly of *Tiffaniella*, *Pterosiphonia*, and *Murrayellopsis*, are used by goldfish (*Hypsypops rubicunda*) to build nests upon which the eggs are laid (Foster, 1972). The fish seems to avoid bringing sexually mature thalli into the nest but mainly uses the vegetative thalli. The nest can be quite conspicuous against the background of animal-encrusted rocks, especially in the fish breeding season. When the breeding season is over, a slow deposit of detritus accumulates on the nests and some sessile animals begin to attach on to the nests. According to Foster, nest building occurs as a result of the fish's clearing activity along with normal recruitment of turf species into the cleared areas from surrounding populations. The fish also weeds out nonturf forming organisms from the nest site.

The blue-green algae grow well in ponds or soils and help decrease their salinity and pH and increase their nitrogen, phosphorus, and organic matter content. However, to achieve any worthwhile and lasting improvement, it is necessary to remove the algae from the soil since otherwise they would recycle the absorbed salts back into the soil (Kumar, 1983). An alternative strategy is not to dig ponds but to create ponds by enclosing the usar soil all round with earthen embankments so as to encourage waterlogging during the rainy season. When good growth of algae has occurred, they are removed by microstraining or filtration. A few such cycles of algal growth and removal can make the soil fit at least for the cultivation of paddy.

POLLUTANT-GLEANING

The microalgae take up heavy metals in industrial effluents by accumulating the toxic metals within their cells. Thus, they act as waste traps (Rai *et al.*, 1981). They can then be harvested to remove the toxic compounds from the water. Zinc, mercury, cadmium, copper, uranium, and lead are some metal ions that can accumulate as much as several thousand fold in microalgae. Pesticides and other pollutants can also so accumulate in algal cells. The algae which have accumulated toxic metals or pollutants may be utilized as biomass for biogas production or, in some selected cases, as feed for animals.

SPIRULINA

Spirulina (Fig. 14-16) is an exceptionally important blue-green alga in view of its high nutritional value both for humans and animals. The alga occurs naturally in several highly saline and alkaline lakes (pH 9.4 to 11.0) in Africa, Mexico, and elsewhere. The Kanembou people around Lake Tchad in Africa and the Mexican inhabitants near Lake Texcoco have collected *Spirulina* from the lakes and eaten it since time immemorial. The alga is a veritable protein concentrate (around 60–70% of dry weight is crude protein) and its crude lipids vary from about 9–15% (dry weight basis) (Ciferri, 1983). It is quite rich in isoleucine, leucine, phenylalanine, tyrosine, and valine, but is comparatively deficient in sulphur containing amino acids. This deficiency can be balanced by including whole grain cereals such as wheat or barley in the diet, as is done by the Kanembou and the Aztecs. According to Richmond and Preiss (1980), 20 g of dried *Spirulina* can be easily produced per m^2 per day, amounting to an annual protein yield of 50,000 kg per hectare; this figure is much higher than the maximum yield of animal protein (less than 200 kg) per hectare per year.

Some other nutritional merits of *Spirulina* include lack of toxicity, low nucleic acid content (about 4%), and its lipids being chiefly made of unsaturated fatty acids that do not produce cholesterol. These properties make *Spirulina* a good health food for patients of coronary illness and obesity. Much work on the commercial and nutritional exploitation of mass-grown *Spirulina* has been done at the Central Food Technological Research Institute, Mysore (Venkataraman, 1983), and using indigenous methods of cultivation, yields of 8–12 g/m^2/day have been obtained. When grown in a clean water system by adding chemical fertilizers, the production costs go up but the alga can be used as food for humans.

In Lucknow, the alga is grown in sewage water supplemented with sodium bicarbonate, in rectangular cemented ponds of 30 m × 5 m, each containing 20,000 litres of sewage medium to a depth of 15 cm. Compressed air is bubbled. Luxuriant growth occurs 2–3 weeks after inoculation. The alga is harvested by filtration through polyester or nylon mesh cloth, and sun-dried before use as highly nutritive animal feed.

S. subsalsa grows prolifically (along with *Arthrospira platensis* and *Anabaenopsis arnoldii*) in brine beds in Sambhar Salt Lake in Rajasthan. These algae form thick crusts on the surface of brine in salt beds. The thick algal mats are manually removed, allowed to dry in heaps, and then auctioned to farmers who use them as fertilizer in fields of maize or wheat.

The varied systems of *Spirulina* production and the uses to which the alga can be put are illustrated in Fig. 14-16.

MASS CULTURE AND YIELD OF MICROALGAE

The Japanese *Chlorella* ponds involve sophisticated clean culture and costly operations where mass cultures are seeded from sterile stocks and grown under fairly controlled conditions by automatic devices. The algal biomass is harvested by centrifugation, washed, and freeze-dried (Kawaguchi, 1980). This practice contrasts with the wastewater systems, being adopted in India and other developing countries (using *Spirulina* instead of *Chlorella*); in these systems, diluted sewage or other wastewater is used as the culture medium for growing algae-bacteria mixtures, in small ditches. In Mysore and Chennai, dense blooms of *Spirulina*, contaminated with some eubacteria, thrive on the residues of fermented cow dung exposed to sunlight in shallow ditches and stirred occasionally by a broom. The resulting biomass is harvested by cloth filtration and dried in the sun. One notable advantage of the Indian practice is that the water left behind after the harvesting of the biomass is quite clean and, of course, the cost of algal biomass produced is cheaper than that produced in clean culture systems.

A variant of the Indian method is followed in China where *Chlorella* is mass cultured on pig manure.

Scenedesmus and *Coelastrum* are being mass cultured in Germany, Israel, Japan, Thailand, and some other countries. These, as also the *Spirulina* grown in India, are particularly easy to harvest by filtration.

Crude protein is the chief valuable component of microalgal biomass (Table 14-9).

Table 14-9 Composition of drum-dried, mass-grown *Scenedesmus acutus* and *Spirulina maxima*, in per cent of matter, and comparison of their protein productivity with a few other protein sources (after Soeder and Pabst, 1970; Aaronson and Dubinsky, 1982)

Component	*Chlorella*	*Scenedesmus*	*Spirulina*	Clover leaf	Wheat
Crude protein		50–60	56–62		
Protein yield (kg/ha/yr)	35,000	25,000	39,000	1680	300
Carbohydrates		10–17	16–18		
Lipids		12–14	2–3		
Nucleic acids		3.5–4.5	3.5–4.5		

Besides the components listed, the algae contain vitamins and minerals.

Table 14-10 Approximate average yield of mass-grown microalgae (condensed and modified from Soeder, 1980; Aaronson and Dubinsky, 1982)

Alga	Place/Country	Average net yield (dry matter) (gram dry weight/m^2/day)	
		Clean outdoor culture	Sewage based algal-bacterial system
Scenedesmus	Rupite (Rumania)	25–30	
Scenedesmus	Dortmund (Germany)	15–28	
Scenedesmus	Bangkok (Thailand)	18	47
Scenedesmus	Tokyo (Japan)	14	
Scenedesmus	Trebon (Czechoslovakia)	12–25	
Spirulina	Bangkok	18	
Spirulina	Trujillo (Peru)	28	
Chlorococcales	Haifa (Israel)		41
Chlorococcales	Gainesville (U.S.A.)		30
Chlorella	Tokyo	4–28	
Diatoms	Woods Hole (U.S.A.)	10–13	
Chlorella	Jerusalem (Israel)	12–60	

The mass-grown *Scenedesmus* has a spinach-like taste, whereas *Spirulina* has a flavour resembling that of some boiled mushrooms.

The yields of algae vary from country to country and also depend on whether they are cultured in clean water or wastewater media (see Table 14-10).

PHYCOCOLLOIDS

The largest commercial use of seaweeds (apart from their use as food in Oriental countries) is as a source of alginic acid, agar, and carrageenan. These colloids are widely used in food, pharmaceutical, textile, and cosmetic industries. All three compounds are in fact cell wall polysaccharides.

Alginates are calcium and sodium salts of alginic acid. Alginic acid is a complex polyuronic polymer made of β-1,4-linked D-mannuronic and L-guluronic acid units (Fig. 14-17). Alginic acid is insoluble in water but can absorb large volume of water. Alginates are nontoxic, highly viscous, and form gels readily, thus finding use as thickeners in food industry. Alginates are used as a stabilizer in ice cream, milk, and fruit squashes, and as a gelling or thickening agent for jams, jellies, and sauces. The paper industry uses it as a surface sizing and coating agent. Other uses are as fireproofing of fabrics, textile, paint industries, etc. Figure 14-18 shows how alginates are manufactured.

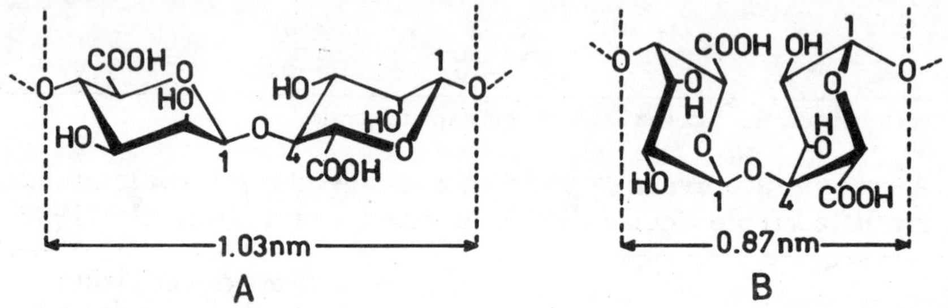

Fig. 14-17 Alginic acid molecule. A, mannuronic; B, guluronic acid residues.

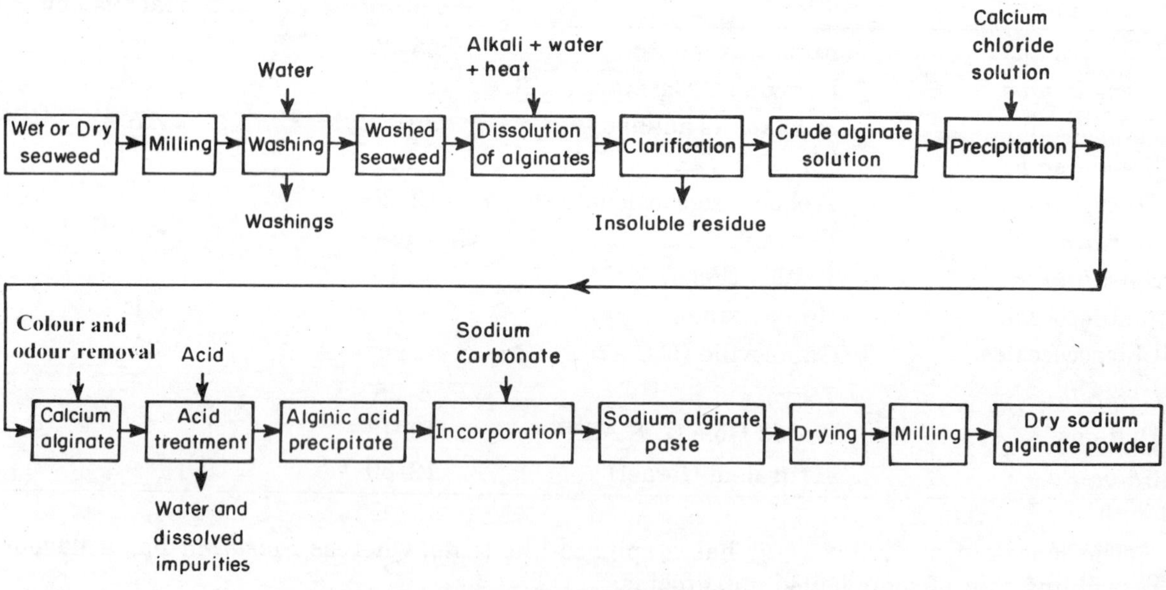

Fig. 14-18 A typical alginate manufacturing process.

In Europe and the U.S.A., alginates come from *Macrocystis*, *Laminaria*, and *Ascophyllum*. The principal sources in India are *Sargassum* and *Turbinaria*.

Agar and carrageenan are both galactans, made of galactose units. Agar is obtained from members of the Gracilariaceae and Gelidiaceae, whereas carrageenan is extracted from certain algae belonging to the Hypneaceae (Fig. 14-19), Phyllophoraceae, Solieraceae, and Gigartinaceae. The chief source of carrageenan is *Eucheuma* spp. in the Philippines, and *Chondrus crispus* in Canada. Its principal use is in dairy industry but is also used in shampoos, cosmetics, pharmaceutics, brewing and leather industries.

The primary sources of agar are *Gelidium*, *Gracilaria*, *Pterocladia*, and *Ahnfeltia*. In India, *Gelidiella acerosa* is the principal agar-yielding alga. The most important application of agar is as a bacteriological medium and for growing cell cultures and microorganisms in the laboratory. Lesser uses are in food and pharmaceutical industries as stabilizing and protective agents in icings, as preservative in canned meats and fish, and as clarifying agent in the manufacture of beer and wine.

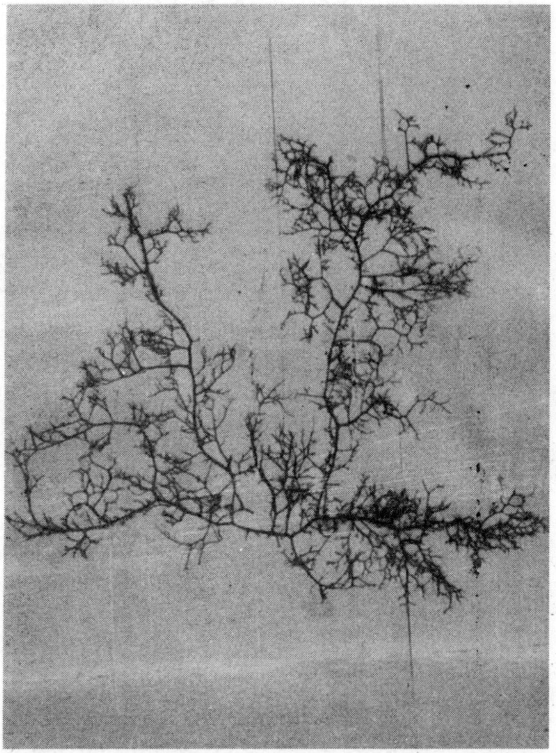

Fig. 14-19 *Hypnea valentiore*, material from Veraval. *Courtesy* K. Rama Rao.

Agarose is a highly purified form or low-charged fraction of agar. It has some acidic sulphate groups which make it valuable in biomedical applications, electrophoresis, gel diffusion, filtration, immunological and separation techniques, and as overlay for plaque formation in virus studies. Figure 14-20 shows the structural units of sulphated galactans.

ENERGY AND CHEMICALS

In coastal areas, seaweeds may be used in biogas plants, either separately or mixed with cow dung, to produce methane. *Sargassum tenerrimum* has been found to be quite suitable for use in biogas plants in Bhavnagar (Sarma *et al.*, 1984).

Since time immemorial, such kelps as *Laminaria* have been harvested to obtain soda and potash used in making soap, glass, porcelain, and alum (Chapman and Chapman, 1980). Kelps have also been used for extracting iodine, ammonia, charcoal, acetone, organic acids, mannitol, laminarin, fucoidin, and funori.

Diatomite is made of the siliceous cell walls (frustules) of fossil diatoms. It is used as a powder for cleaning and polishing metals, in the preparation of dynamite, and the filtration of liquids in the sugar refining and brewing industries. Fossil coccolithophorids are used as chalk.

The unicellular, halophilic green alga *Dunaliella* produces glycerol as the major photosyn-

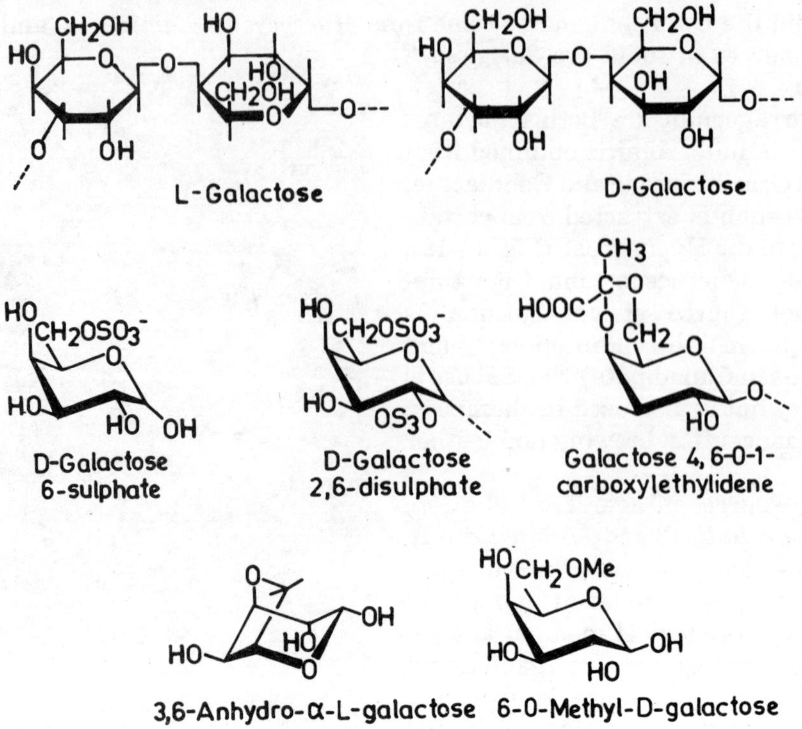

Fig. 14-20 Structural units of sulphated galactans.

thate. This alga is an ideal organism for biosolar energy conversion in many arid zones, as highly saline water is readily available in such areas. The residue remaining after glycerol extraction is rich in protein and β-carotene and can be used as a good feed. This alga lacks a cellulose cell wall. When grown in presence of 5 M NaCl, its intracellular glycerol concentration can rise to about 50% (about 7 M). The alga synthesizes glycerol under hypertonic conditions and eliminates glycerol under hyptonic conditions, both processes occurring independently of protein synthesis (Ben-Amotz and Arnon, 1983).

At certain stages of its development, *Botryococcus braunii* (Fig. 14-21 A–C) produces large amounts of hydrocarbons including long-chain fatty acids. In the resting state, the cells accumulate carotenoids and appear yellowish-orange. At this stage, the unsaponifiable lipids often increase to 75% of the dry weight (Bachofen, 1982). Salinity profoundly affects the lipid content of *Botryococcus* cells; increase of salinity from 0 to 6% increases the lipid content from about 35% to 50% (dry weight).

Another recent and novel approach involves the use of *Spirulina* for methane production. When mixed with sewage sludge, *S. maxima* biomass greatly increases the performance of anaerobic digesters. A mixture of sewage sludge and *Spirulina* doubles the methane yield (Samson and LeDuy, 1983). Not only this but the algal biomass alone can also be used as the sole substrate of anaerobic digestion for producing methane. Mechanical (ultrasonic) and thermochemical pretreatments of the *Spirulina* biomass fed into the anaerobic digesters increased the solubility of the biomass and stimulated the activity of acid forming bacteria (Samson and LeDuy, 1983).

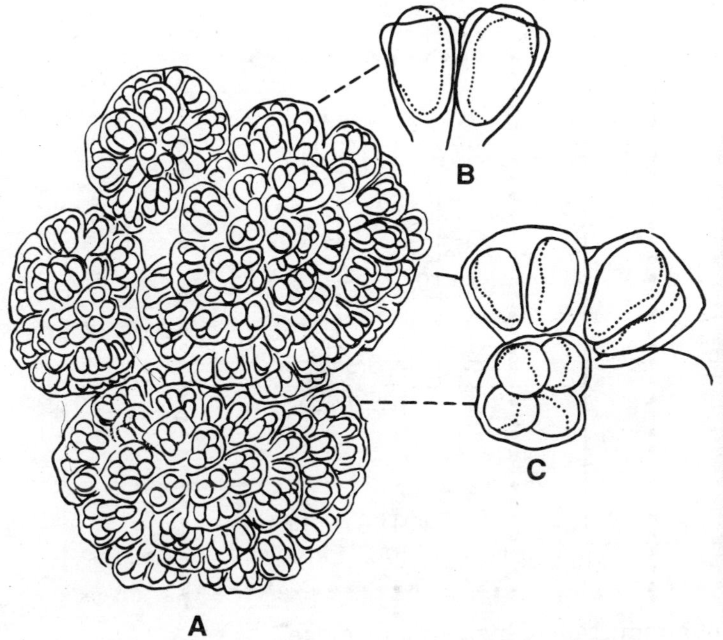

Fig. 14-21 *Botryococcus braunii*. A, colony; B, C, a few cells from different parts of the colony.

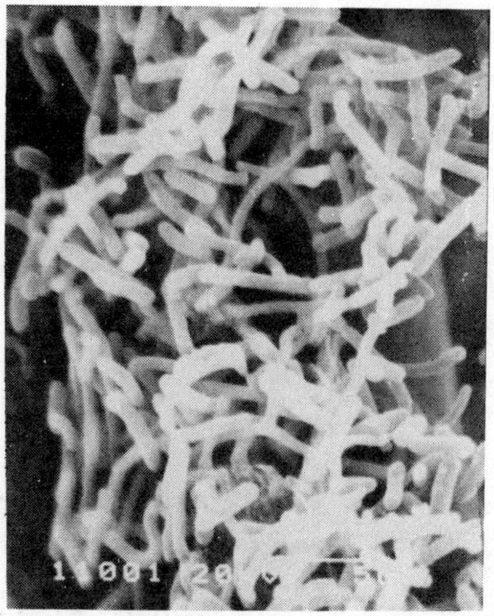

Fig. 14-22 *Anacystis nidulans*.

The unicellular cyanobacterium *Anacystis nidulans* (Fig. 14-22) has been used for sustained photoproduction of ammonia from nitrate—a remarkable process for the conversion of solar energy into chemical form (Ramos *et al.*, 1982). This is achieved by inhibiting the enzyme glutamine synthetase with the glutamate analogue methionine sulphoximine. The cells treated with this inhibitor continue to produce ammonia at high rates with fairly high efficiency. Ammonia is valuable as a fuel and fertilizer.

HYDROGEN PRODUCTION

Several algae produce hydrogen (Fig. 14-23) which has received much attention in recent years as a clean type of fuel. Strains of *Chlorella*, *Scenedesmus*, *Synechococcus*, *Microcystis*, *Oscillatoria*, and others produce hydrogen at fairly high rates; though some of the hydrogen is again taken up by the cells. The strain Miami BG7 of *Oscillatoria* is particularly suitable as it lacks the uptake of hydrogenase which catalyzes the uptake of hydrogen by the cells. This enzyme has an adverse effect on the net yield of hydrogen gas (Phlips and Mitsui, 1986). Phlips and Mitsui observed that immobilization of the strain Miami BG7 with agar significantly improves the rate and duration (sustainability) of hydrogen production as compared to that by free cell suspensions. The rates of hydrogen production of about 12 microlitres H_2 per mg dry weight per hour were recorded and hydrogen production could be sustained for three weeks. Immobilization also conferred some resistance against environmental fluctuations and adapted the cells to outdoor light conditions. Limiting the supply of combined nitrogen to the algal cells greatly enhanced the rate of hydrogen photoproduction. This enhancement was accompanied by a concomitant decrease in oxygen production.

Certain marine cyanobacteria have been used for hydrogen photoproduction from salt water

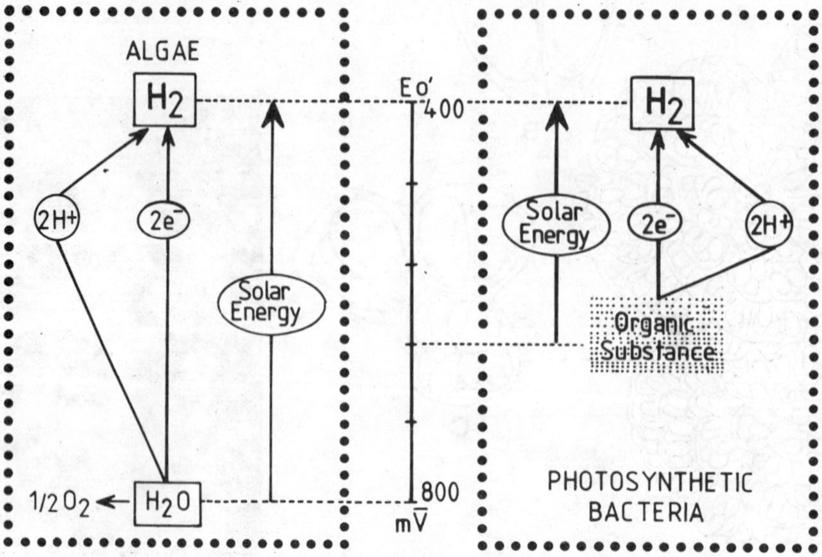

Fig. 14-23 Photoproduction of hydrogen by algae.

over a one month period, using both free cells and immobilized cells both indoors and outdoors. This work has been done by Mitsui and associates at the Rosenstiel School of Marine and Atmospheric Sciences in Miami, Florida, U.S.A. Mitsui has also developed a prototype floating hydrogen production system using a cyanobacterium.

WASTELAND RECLAMATION

The occurrence of alkaline and saline 'usar' soils is widespread in many parts of India. Thousands of hectares of fertile land are being lost to agriculture annually because of salinity caused by canal irrigation. Many arid and desert areas are, however, advantageous for cultivation of unconventional crops such as algae. The water available in most arid areas is highly saline. The temperature and light conditions in these areas are quite suitable for algal growth. Algal cultivation requires shallow ponds (not exceeding 25–30 cm in depth) dug over large, flat stretches of vacant land; large tracts of such land are abundantly available in desert areas.

ALGAE AND MEDICINE

Certain algae or their products cause disease in humans, whereas others are useful in curing human diseases. Several tropical and subtropical seaweeds have curative powers, whereas some microalgae can cause adverse effects in animals as well as humans.

MEDICAL USES OF ALGINATE

Alginic acid has the following two medical uses.

Radiography Contrast Agent

Barium sulphate, the contrast agent in radiography for the diagnosis of diseases of the digestive tract, precipitates rapidly since it does not dissolve well in water. The propylene glycol ester of alginic acid effectively ensures uniformity and stability of barium sulphate suspension, making the acid useful in X-ray photography.

Calcium Alginate Wools

Alginic acid is the source of calcium alginate wools, which are used as hemostatic agents in surgery and dentistry. They are easy to sterilize and have no side effects.

FOLK MEDICINE

In the Orient, Russia, and Europe, various algae have long been used as cures and treatments for a wide range of pathological conditions. The following attributes may be noted for some seaweeds (Arasaki and Arasaki, 1983):

Laminaria japonica	Effective either charred or pickled; helpful against neuroses and palsy when strips are placed in bathwater; lowers hypertension and is good for edema
Eisenia bicyclis	Effective against gynaecological diseases
Undaria pinnatifida	Cleanses blood after childbirth
Nemacystus decipiens	Effective against swellings
Porphyra sp.	Effective against beriberi
Digenea simplex	An anthelmintic
Chondrus crispus	Effective against respiratory ailments
Enteromorpha sp.	Effective against haemorrhoids and stomach diseases

ALGAE AS CAUSATIVE AGENTS

The colourless, yeast-like green alga *Prototheca* is the best known example of a disease-causing alga. *P. wickerhamii* and *P. zopfii* cause protothecosis. Patients afflicted with protothecosis have defective leucocytes and often suffer from bursitis and skin lesions. Treatment with amphotericin B, with or without tetracycline, effectively cures protothecosis (Venezio *et al.*, 1982).

In Sweden, some persons working with diatomaceous earth suffer from algal silicosis, i.e., irritation of the lungs caused by fine silica particles. In Japan, some cases of goitre have been attributed to the consumption of diet rich in seaweeds. Arsenic poisoning can occur if too much of seaweed is eaten.

Lyngbya majuscula causes dermatitis, manifested as a skin rash followed by blistering. *Fragilaria striatula* and *Cladophora* spp. also cause dermatitis and itching in fishermen (Hashimoto, 1979). Mittal *et al.* (1979) found that in Delhi, several patients of naso-bronchial allergies showed positive skin reactions to *Lyngbya major*. Species of *Chlorella*, *Oscillatoria*, *Anabaena*, and other algae are strongly suspected to be potent allergens that cause asthma in Venezuela, U.S.A., and other countries (Stein and Borden, 1984).

Some algae produce toxins (Figs. 14-24, 14-25) that are ultimately ingested by humans. Certain dinoflagellates, e.g., *Pyrodinium* and *Protogonyaulax*, produce toxin that causes fish

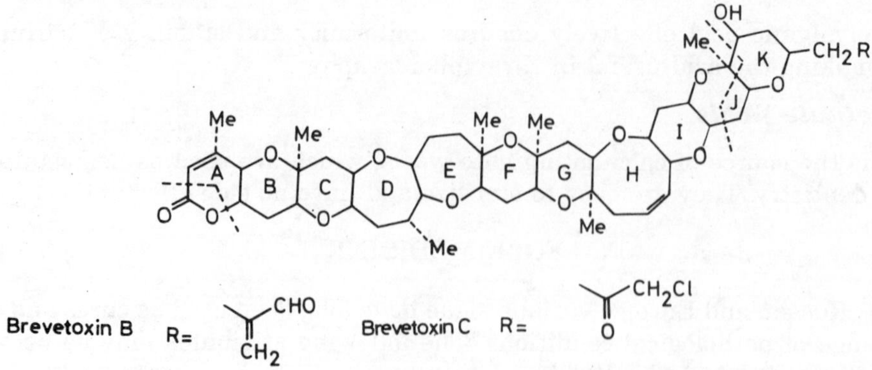

Fig. 14-24 *Gymnodinium brevis*, toxin structure

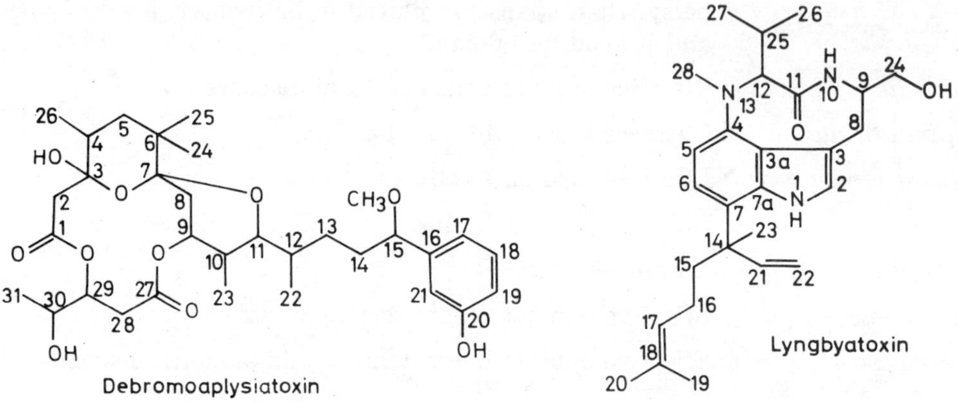

Fig. 14-25 Structure of dermatitis-inducing cyanobacterial toxins.

and shellfish to become toxic to birds and mammals. These dinoflagellate toxins cause neurological and muscular disorders in humans (Hashimoto, 1979), and paralytic shellfish poisoning in mammals which have eaten the affected shellfish. The paralytic shellfish toxins chiefly block sodium influx by inhibiting nerve transmission impulses (Steidinger, 1983). Sometimes, a mammal dies of suffocation within a few hours of consuming poisonous shellfish.

The alga *Prymnesium parvum* (Fig. 14-26) secretes toxins which cause fish mortalities in brackish water. These toxins can lyse human erythrocytes.

The toxic blue-green alga *Microcystis aeruginosa* is grazed by fish in which the toxin becomes concentrated. When humans eat that fish, they can develop neuromuscular disorders. Species of *Anabaena*, *Oscillatoria*, and *Schizothrix* produce a lipopolysaccharide endotoxin which probably causes gastrointestinal disorders (Carmichael, 1981). Of course, toxic blue-green algae are known to cause death of cattle, sheep, birds, and other animals.

Thousands of humans living in the South Pacific islands and the Caribbean are afflicted annually by the ciguatera disease caused by toxic dinoflagellates (Ragaelis, 1984). This disease is most prevalent in the tropics between 35°N and 34°S latitudes. The disease is chiefly caused by the algivorous surgeon fish and parrot fish, which graze on such dinoflagellates as

Gambierdiscus toxicus, *Amphidinium carterae*, and *Prorocentrum* spp. (Carmichael, 1986). *Prorocentrum concavum* and *Gambierdiscus toxicus* appear to be the major contributors of ciguatera toxins to the Caribbean reef and inshore ecosystems.

The toxins produced by freshwater cyanobacteria contain alkaloids or peptides. The alkaloid toxins are quick acting neurotoxins which paralyze peripheral skeletal muscles and respiratory muscles, resulting in death from respiratory failure. These toxins are produced by several species of *Anabaena*.

Peptide toxins which act as hepatotoxins are mainly produced by *Microcystis aeruginosa*. These toxins destroy the hepatocyte membrane, causing haemorrhagic shock and death. The most frequently recorded symptoms produced by *Microcystis* toxins are the swollen, blood engorged liver with haemorrhagic necrosis and the mildly oedematous lungs.

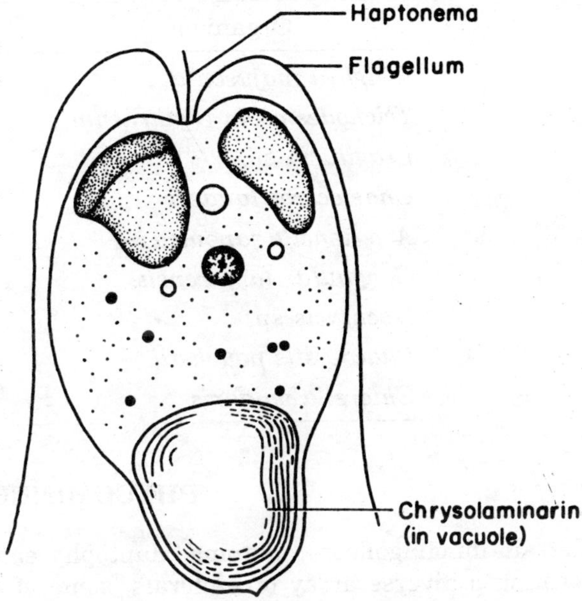

Fig. 14-26 *Prymnesium*, cell structure.

The dinoflagellates produce toxins that cause paralytic shellfish poisoning (PSP). Important symptoms of PSP are neurological derangement and appear rather quickly, often within half an hour of ingesting contaminated shellfish. Death can occur from respiratory paralysis within about 12 hr of illness and is preceded by such symptoms as nausea, vomiting, weakness, and muscular paralysis.

BENEFICIAL ALGAE

The positive aspects of algae in medicine involve such uses as vermifuge, anaesthetic, antipyretic, cough remedy, wound healing, thirst quenching, and treatments for gout, gallstones, goitre, hypertension, bowel movement and skin diseases (Hoppe, 1979). Some constituents of seaweeds show antibiotic activity (Glombitza, 1979; Hashimoto, 1979).

Chlorella produces chlorellin (Table 14-11) and *Phaeocystis pouchetii* acrylic acid. Ehresmann *et al.* (1979) have shown that aqueous extracts from *Cryptosiphonia woodii* and *Farlowia mollis* inhibit the herpes simplex virus. Kainic acid, produced by *Digenea*, is a very effective vermifuge (anthelmintic).

In China, decoctions of *Sargassum* and *Laminaria* are often used to treat cancer (Yamamoto *et al.*, 1974).

Dried stipes of *Laminaria* are currently popular in obstetrical and gynaecological practices.

The vermifuge kainic acid is employed as a useful diagnostic tool in understanding the nature of seizure in epilepsy.

The phycocolloids extracted from selected species of brown and red seaweeds serve as useful pharmaceutical compounds. Carrageenan is used in cough syrups. Fucoidin and agar are used as binding agents for medical tablets. Agar is a blood anticoagulant. Alginate and carrageenan are used as dental molds.

Table 14-11 Some antibiotic producing algae (condensed from Glombitza, 1979)

Organism	Compound or Antibiotic
Lyngbya majuscula	Terpene, carbohydrates
Trichodesmium erythraeum	Terpene, carbohydrates
Fragilaria sp.	Peptides
Chaetoceros lauderi	Polysaccharides
Asterionella japonica	Nucleotides, fatty acids
Gonyaulax tamarensis	Terpene, carbohydrates
Isochrysis sp.	Terpene, carbohydrates
Phaeocystis pouchetii	Acrylic acid
Chlorella vulgaris	Chlorellin

PHYCOMINERALIZATION

Certain dinoflagellates, diatoms, Haptophyceae, green, brown, and red algae are capable of forming a diverse array of minerals, some of which cannot be formed inorganically in the biosphere. These algae precipitate minerals. Out of a total of 31 different biogenic minerals identified so far, about 12 are synthesized by algae. Carbonate minerals (e.g., calcite and aragonite) are the most widely utilized bioinorganic constituents. Calcite is synthesized by dinoflagellates, haptophytes, Rhodophyta, Charophyta, and the siphoneous green algae. The Phaeophyta, Rhodophyta, and Chlorophyta (including Siphonales) synthesize aragonite. Opal (silica) is deposited by diatoms and barite (sulphates) is synthesized by members of the Charophyta. Some siphoneous green algae also deposit oxalates (e.g., whewellite). The alga *Galaxaura obtusata* forms a beautiful intercellular array of aragonite crystals.

The products of phycomineralization are often quite diverse. They may be formed, resorbed, modified, or redeposited. Some or all of these products/processes may have had some impact on the biosphere.

Most algae, especially greens and browns, form minerals by bulk extracellular and/or intercellular mineral deposition, without the elaboration of any elaborate organic matrices (see Lowenstam, 1981). The initial precipitates may differ from the form in which they are finally stabilized, or during development of the alga, one mineral may substitute for another. Biogenic minerals commonly have attributes by which they can be distinguished from their inorganic counterparts.

ALGAL NUISANCES AND INDICATORS OF POLLUTION

While moderate growths of algae in water bodies are beneficial in oxygenating the water and preventing putrefaction of organic matter, excessive growths create serious nuisance and are bad for the aquatic animals.

The major cause of proliferation of nuisance algae is the nutrient enrichment or eutrophication of lentic (standing) water bodies. Phosphorus is the most important nutrient involved in eutrophication. Reductions of phosphorus input greatly aid the nuisance algae control. Much of the phosphorus in water bodies comes from the sewage discharged into them. Diversion or stoppage of sewage discharge into a lake often leads to significant reduction in the growth of nuisance algae. Some examples of nuisance algae include the blooms of *Oscillatoria* and *Microcystis*. Some of the nuisance algae are toxic to cattle and other animals.

Laboratory studies on algal indicators have included bioassays and field studies. Bioassay is done mainly with the green alga *Selenastrum capricornutum*. Field studies have either involved the use of a single algal species, e.g., *Cladophora glomerata*, as a pollution indicator, or have attempted to assess the usefulness of an entire algal community in indicating pollution. Certain artificial substrates are placed in a river or lake and the algal communities which colonize these substrates are then studied with reference to the load of such pollutants as sewage, heat, metals, petroleum products or biocides (Lowe and Gale, 1980).

ALGAL WEEDS

Algal populations that cause adverse effects are referred to as nuisance or, in the case of macrophytic forms, "weedy" algae.

Examples of weedy algae are encountered by a person who steps out on a boat dock to fish and instead pulls up a wad of charoid algae, or whose boat motor becomes choked with filamentous algal mats. Weedy algae, both macrophytic and microphytic forms, occur not only in freshwaters but also in marine systems. Examples include the green alga *Codium* that infests shellfish beds, the biofouling organisms that attach to ship hulls, and the unicellular algal blooms that retard growth of seaweeds in confined aquaculture systems (Lembi *et al.*, 1988).

The two major growth forms of freshwater macrophytic algae are filamentous mat formers and charoids. Mat-forming algae are typically found in shallow water where they may be free-floating (e.g., *Pithophora, Spirogyra, Hydrodictyon*) or attached, primarily as epiphytic or epilithic forms. Epilithic algae (e.g., *Cladophora, Ulothrix, Stigeoclonium*) commonly attach to rocks; epiphytic algae (e.g., *Oedogonium*) attach to macrophytes.

Free-floating forms are generally restricted to static waters such as ponds and sheltered littoral areas of lakes. Attached forms occupy a much wider range of habitats. Attached algae can become detached from their substrates and, because of their positive buoyancy when oxygen bubbles are trapped in the mat, form free-floating rafts of algal material. These mats, in various stages of senescence and decomposition, may then move downstream or wash up on beaches and shorelines. Epiphytic algae are frequently protected from washout in a flowing system by remaining entangled in the foliage of rooted macrophyte beds.

Charoid algae are seldom problems in deep, open water areas but can obstruct the uses of ponds, canals, and shallow areas of lakes where the plants extend to the water surface.

Some genera of cyanobacteria include species that form mats (e.g., *Oscillatoria, Lyngbya, Phormidium*). Species of *Phormidium* attach to cement linings of swimming pools.

Excessive growths of macrophytic algae, either alone or in combination with vascular plants, impair swimming, fishing, and boating.

These algae restrict and reduce the efficiency of culture and harvest activities in fish culture ponds. They often compete with phytoplankton, thus reducing the base of the aquatic food chain.

Cladophora, Stigeoclonium, Oedogonium, and *Ulothrix* create problems in irrigation canals by attaching to concrete canal linings, thus reducing both flow rate and capacity. Mats that break away from the linings float downstream where they foul pump inlets, irrigation siphons, and sprinkler heads (Hansen *et al.*, 1984). *Cladophora glomerata* is a major problem in some water delivery systems.

Algal mats often house or provide shelter for noxious insects such as mosquito larvae and flies. Filamentous algae have been reported to harbour snails that cause schistosomiasis. Although macrophytic algae themselves do not appear to be a major food source for macro-invertebrates, their attached algae can be grazed by invertebrates as can their detrital remains. The charoid algae are excellent habitats for both littoral invertebrates and fish.

Some carnivorous fishes consume small amounts of filamentous algae and *Chara*. Bluegills grow best in aquariums when their diet of oligochaetes or mealworm larvae is supplemented with dried *Chara*.

Macrophytic algae appear to invade sites in which submerged vascular plants have been chemically or mechanically removed, a situation that is easily achieved in small and shallow manmade bodies of water.

Pithophora and *Lyngbya* contain some species of free-floating macrophytes which pose problems in the management of shallow lakes and ponds, including fish ponds. The filaments of the mats are tightly intertwined, producing thick clumps of floating vegetation. Both *Pithophora* and *Lyngbya* are very difficult to control with copper sulphate or simazine and hence cause more serious management problems than such algicide-susceptible filamentous genera as *Spirogyra* and *Oedogonium* found in similar habitats (Lembi *et al.*, 1988).

Environmental conditions for free-floating algae are considerably different from those for attached forms. Water flow is generally minimal so that replenishment of essential resources may not be continuous. A free-floating alga is subject to movement that can range from buoyancy at the surface, to sinking below the photic depth, to complete washout from the system. Water level fluctuations in static bodies of water which might, for example, lead to stranding of the alga above the water line in summer are not uncommon. Thus, the alga must be adapted to survive an inconstancy of environmental conditions (Lembi *et al.*, 1988).

Most free-floating macrophytic algae begin growth in the spring on the bottom sediments from overwintering spores/zygotes in the case of annual forms (e.g., *Spirogyra*) or from overwintering filaments in perennial forms (e.g., *Pithophora*, which also germinates from akinetes). As oxygen bubbles become trapped in the filaments, the mats rise to the surface to form streamers from the bottom, some portions of which break off to form free-floating rafts.

Although *Pithophora* also can be found below the surface, some mats settling into light-limited zones may not regain buoyancy and eventually die due to low photosynthetic production. However, photosynthesis in both *Lyngbya* and *Pithophora* appears to be well adapted to low light conditions. *Pithophora* can survive up to about 2 months in complete darkness without significant loss of chlorophyll.

In the dense mats and intertwined filaments of *Pithophora*, *Lyngbya*, and *Cladophora*, the interior of the mat must present a unique environment in terms of light, temperature, nutrients, and pH, which could have an impact on associated epiphytes and invertebrates. It is known that the light compensation point for photosynthesis in *Pithophora* is reached between 8 mm and 10 mm beneath the mat surface. Net negative energy balance plus decomposition of filaments within the mats might release nutrients. That would affect not only associated organisms but also the growth of outer mat edges, a situation that would be especially critical in late summer under nutrient-limiting conditions.

The impact of mat morphology on management practices, such as algicide treatments, could be significant. For example, the lack of light penetration into the mat can alter the activity of light-activated algicides such as simazine. According to Whitton (1970), the lack of penetration of mats by copper sulphate was a major factor in the observed copper tolerance of *Cladophora* in the field, even though the cells themselves were highly susceptible.

Alteration of environmental conditions such as nutrient reduction or darkness is the most effective management tool for macroalgae. Significant biomass reductions can result from nutrient reduction practices. However, sites in which nutrient reduction is not currently a feasible option or is a long-term project (e.g., irrigation and drainage systems in which water is drawn from a large watershed, confined aquaculture systems, and shallow lakes and ponds impinged by nonpoint sources of nutrients) may require more direct approaches for the removal of algae to insure use of the water.

Anderson and Dechoretz (1984) list six active ingredients of the algicides commonly used for algae control: copper, simazine, endothall, acrolein, diquat, and chlorine. Of these, copper sulphate pentahydrate is the most commonly used in "natural" bodies of water and, with the exception of trout habitat, copper can be used in waters intended for fishing, aquaculture, livestock watering, irrigation, and swimming. In contrast, simazine, endothall, and diquat have time restrictions (ranging from 24 hr to 1 yr) on various uses of water after treatment. Both acrolein and chlorine are highly toxic to fish and are limited to use in irrigation water conveyance systems and in swimming pools and municipal water treatment facilities, respectively (Lembi *et al.*, 1988).

Mechanical harvesters have been used successfully in place of or in conjunction with aquatic herbicides for submerged weed control. Epiphytic algae are commonly harvested along with the vascular plants. Harvesters are seldom used alone for free-floating algae although they may be used successfully in enclosed areas where the algae cannot float away. The major disadvantages of mechanical harvesters for floating-mat algae control include their inability to move in waters less than 1 m deep.

Some organisms used for macroalgal control include waterfowl (ducks, geese, and swans), snails, crayfish, and herbivorous fish such as *Tilapia* and grass carp (*Ctenopharyngodon idella*). Almost all of these organisms have limitations for widespread use including the potential for increased nutrient pollution (waterfowl), narrow thermal range for survival (snails, *Tilapia*), and the large numbers of animals required to reduce algae growth adequately (crayfish). The most widely used biocontrol agent at the present time is the sterile triploid grass carp (Cassini and Caton, 1986).

ALGAE AND WATER POLLUTION

The algae produce both positive and negative effects in polluted water. Sometimes, pollution leads to enrichment of plant nutrients in water and this selectively stimulates the growth of some algal species producing massive surface growths or "blooms" which in turn spoil the water quality. Certain algae flourish in water polluted with sewage or organic wastes, playing important role in "self-purification" of the body of water. Some selected types of algae found in polluted water can be used as indicators of pollution. In many temperate countries, polluted water algae often include certain strains toxic to man or animals drinking that water.

Some important pollutants of water bodies include fertilizing materials such as sewage and organic wastes, municipal garbage, effluents from dairies, milk plants, tanneries, slaughter houses, and paper mills. Discharge of hot water from factories and effluents containing heavy metals from various industries also cause pollution.

While most algae become troublesome when present in abundance in a water body, there are some species which cause problems even when present in small numbers. Good examples of the latter kind include *Synura*, *Synedra*, *Tabellaria*, and *Melosira*. The presence of a few cells of *Synura* is sufficient to impart bad taste and foul smell to the water (see Table 14-12). Likewise, even small numbers of the diatoms *Synedra*, *Tabellaria*, and *Melosira* greatly reduce the length of filter runs in water supplies.

Table 14-12 Some important algae which impart odour and taste to water (condensed from Palmer, 1980)

Genus	Odour(s)	Taste	Tongue sensation
Anacystis	Grassy, septic	Sweet	
Aphanizomenon	Grassy, nasturtium, septic	Sweet	Dry
Chlamydomonas	Musty, grassy, fishy, septic	Sweet	Slick
Ceratium	Fishy, septic	Bitter	
Dinobryon	Violet, fishy		Slick
Fragilaria	Geranium, musty		
Gomphosphaeria	Grassy	Sweet	
Melosira	Geranium, musty		Slick
Peridinium	Cucumber, fishy		
Synedra	Grassy, musty		Slick
Synura	Muskmelon, cucumber, spicy, fishy	Bitter	Dry, metallic, slick

Many species of algae can produce water blooms. The most frequently involved genera include *Microcystis*, *Anabaena*, *Aphanizomenon*, *Oscillatoria*, *Hydrodictyon*, *Chlorella*, *Ankistrodesmus*, *Synedra*, *Cyclotella*, *Synura*, *Euglena*, and *Chlamydomonas*. Not all of the bloom-forming species are planktonic.

Some filamentous green algae, e.g., *Spirogyra*, *Zygnema*, and *Cladophora*, form mats or blankets at the water surface which serve as breeding sites for gnats and midges.

Nonflowing water bodies, e.g., lakes and reservoirs, become eutrophic when they contain excess plant nutrients. The word pollution is frequently used in connection with flowing water and also with lakes and reservoirs, at least when the pollutants added do not stimulate increased growth of algae (Palmer, 1980). Thus, a lake could be polluted with acids and sulphates and debris from mining operations, and could become eutrophic with sewage. With a river, the term pollution would more often be used for both conditions.

Examples of algae involved in eutrophication are *Microcystis, Anabaena, Rivularia, Oscillatoria.* In some cases, *Cladophora*, *Spirogyra*, and diatoms occur profusely in eutrophic water.

Pollution points to a situation where the condition is potentially harmful to human health or is capable of interfering with the water use. After sewage or organic effluent has polluted a stream or river, the algae present react in a manner that is of great importance. During the course of natural purification, the algae oxygenate the water. The species and numbers of algae found in the sewage-polluted portion of a stream are different from those present in the unpolluted portion above the sewer discharge. With the progressive decomposition of sewage in the stream, the numbers, and kinds of microorganisms change until eventually the flora and fauna in the newly purified water become fairly similar to those found upstream.

In most organically polluted water bodies, *Euglena viridis*, *Oscillatoria tenuis*, *O. limosa*, and *Nitzschia palea* tend to be dominant.

SEWAGE DISPOSAL

Sewage consists of water-borne domestic and industrial waste which is fairly rich in dissolved or suspended organic and inorganic constituents, but very poor in oxygen. It harbours a number of faecal and other anaerobic bacteria, some of which may be pathogenic. The sewage has to be treated before its disposal for two main reasons. Firstly, the anaerobic digestion of sewage produces stinking and offensive odours. Secondly, the contamination of potable water with sewage infested raw material is potentially a rich source for inorganic nutrients such as nitrogen, phosphorus, potassium, and sulphur. This aspect of sewage assumes considerable importance in view of the fact that many developing countries are facing an acute shortage of inorganic fertilizers on the one hand and an explosive population increase on the other.

Sewage oxidation ponds have been created for bringing about its complete oxidation into mineral components. Such ponds support luxuriant growth of unicellular algae, e.g., *Chlorella, Chlamydomonas, Scenedesmus*, and *Euglena*. These help in the bacterial decomposition of sewage by providing oxygen; in addition, they recover the mineral nutrients from sewage which would otherwise have been lost in the effluent.

In streams polluted with sewage, algae and bacteria act together in purifying the water. The algae use the nitrate, phosphate, and other nutrients present in sewage, growing and multiplying rapidly. Since they photosynthesize, they oxygenate the water. Sewage polluted water is quite low in dissolved oxygen because bacteria use up the oxygen when they decompose the organic wastes. Algal photosynthesis provides the oxygen needed by the bacteria to thrive and continue their decomposer activity. During decomposition, nitrates, ammonia, phosphate, and other mineral nutrients are released from the wastes and these nutrients are in turn absorbed by the algae. The end result of this bacteria-algae cooperation is that the organic wastes are broken down and the water is purified.

The algae also play an important role in sewage stabilization ponds. Trickling filters, activated sludge systems, and lagoon systems are the three commonly used methods for treatment of municipal sewage. If sewage is allowed to remain in an oxidation stabilization pond for 20–30 days, it can be sufficiently purified, through algal-microbial action, to be used for irrigation in crop fields.

Some important genera of algae encountered in sewage stabilization ponds are *Chlorella, Ankistrodesmus, Scenedesmus, Euglena, Chlamydomonas, Oscillatoria, Micractinium*, and *Anacystis*.

Sewage algae have also been used as animal feed, as manure, and for ingestion by fish fingerlings in fish ponds. Figure 14-27 illustrates the design of a simple chamber for growing algae in sewage effluent. The main limitation is the lack of a cheap and effective harvesting technique.

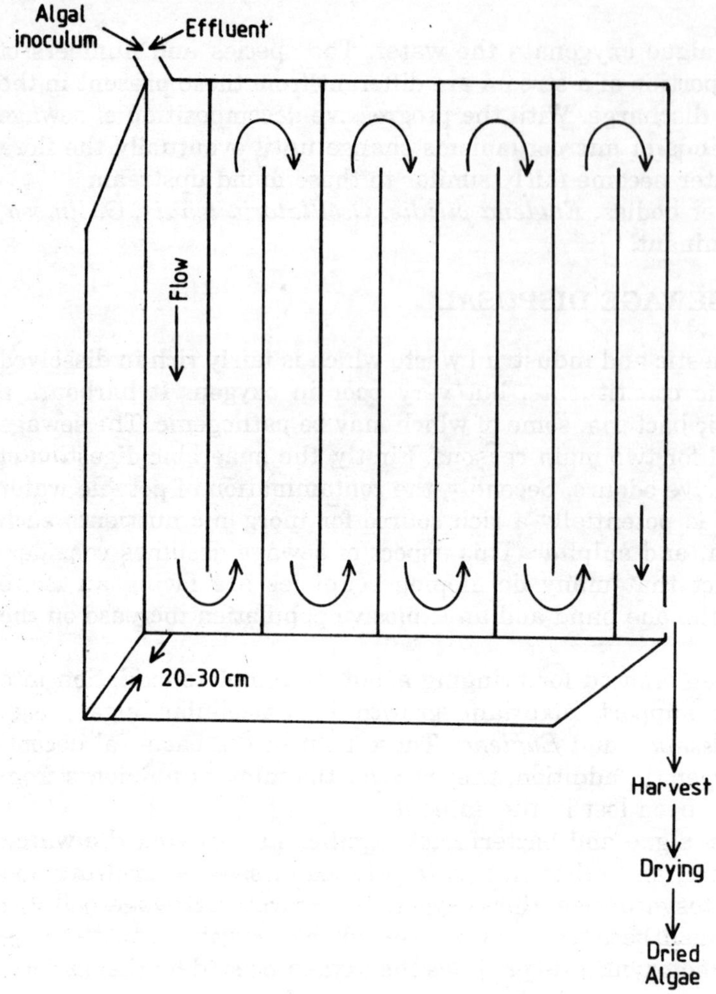

Fig. 14-27 A simple chamber for growing algae in sewage effluent. A series of baffles are arranged with a gentle slope to facilitate the desired flow.

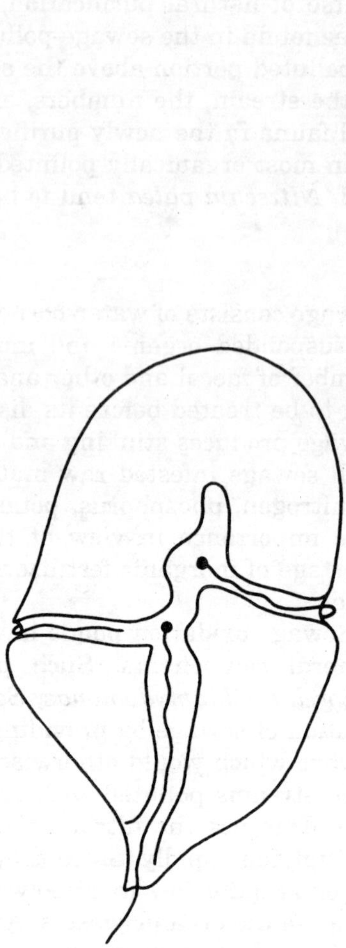

Fig. 14-28 *Gymnodinium*.

TOXICITY

The planktonic algae sometimes produce water blooms in which cell densities are so high as to impart a reddish, yellowish-brown, or bluish-green colour to the water. Some of these organisms show considerable toxicity. Toxic algae occur both in oceans and limnic habitats. The marine toxic species belong almost exclusively to the dinoflagellates (Fig. 14-28), whereas the freshwater toxin producers are mostly cyanobacterial forms (see Table 14-13).

The microscopic planktonic algae of the world's oceans form critical food for filter-feeding bivalve shellfish (oysters, mussels, scallops, clams) as well as the larvae of some crustaceans and finfish. Usually the proliferation of plankton algae is therefore beneficial for aquaculture and fisheries. However, in some situations, algal blooms can have a negative impact causing severe economic losses to aquaculture, fisheries, and tourism operations and having major environmental and human health impacts (Hallegraeff, 1992). Among about 5000 species of living marine phytoplankton, some 300 species can occasionally occur in such large numbers that they obviously discolour the surface of the sea (so-called *red tides*), while only about 40 species can produce potent toxins that find their way through fish and shellfish to humans (Table 14-14).

Table 14-14 summarizes three different types of harmful algal bloom problems, together with representative examples of causative algal species, ranging from dinoflagellates, diatoms,

Table 14-13 Some toxic planktonic algae and their properties (after Kremer, 1981)

Habitat	Alga	Toxin	Property/Mode of toxin action
Freshwater	*Microcystis aeruginosa*	Microcystin	Hepatotoxic (to liver)
	Anabaena flos-aquae	Anatoxin A, B, C, or D	Neurotoxic
	Aphanizomenon flos-aquae	Saxitoxin	Neurotoxic
	*Prymnesium parvum**	Prymnesin	Neurotoxic
Marine	*Lyngbya gracilis*	Debromoaplysiatoxin	Dermatitis
	Gonyaulax catenella	Saxitoxin	Neurotoxic
	G. tamarensis	Gonyautoxin	Neurotoxic
	Gymnodinium spp.	Not named	Neurotoxic
	*Prymnesium parvum**	Prymnesin	Neurotoxic

*This toxic alga belongs to the class Haptophyceae and occurs in limnic, brackish, and marine habitats.

Table 14-14 Different types of harmful algal blooms (after Hallegraeff, 1992)

Species which produce harmless water discolourations but can sometimes grow so dense that they cause indiscriminate kills of fish and invertebrates due to oxygen depletion
Examples: *Gonyaulax polygramma, Noctiluca scintillans, Scrippsiella trochoidea, Trichodesmium erythraeum*

Species which produce potent toxins that can find their way through the food chain to humans, causing gastrointestinal and neurological illnesses, such as:

Paralytic shellfish poisoning (PSP)
Examples: *Alexandrium* spp., *Gymnodinium catenatum*, *Pyrodinium bahamense*
Diarrhetic shellfish poisoning (DSP)
Examples: *Dinophysis* spp., *Prorocentrum lima*
Amnesic shellfish poisoning (ASP)
Examples: *Nitzschia pungens* f. *multiseries*, *N. pseudoseriata*
Ciguatera fishfood poisoning
Examples: *Gambierdiscus toxicus*
Neurotoxic shellfish poisoning (NSP)
Example: *Gymnodinium breve*
Cyanobacterial toxin poisoning
Examples: *Anabaena flos-aquae*, *Microcystis aeruginosa*, *Nodularia spumigena*

Species which are nontoxic to humans, but harmful to fish and invertebrates (especially in intensive aquaculture systems) by damaging or clogging their gills
Examples: *Chaetoceros convolutus, Gymnodinium mikimotoi, Chrysochromulina polylepis, C. leadbeateri, Prymnesium parvum, P. patelliferum, Heterosigma akashiwo, Chattonella antiqua*

prymnesiophytes, and raphidophytes to cyanobacteria. The diversity of chemical structures of algal toxins is illustrated in Fig. 14-29. Often, there is no clear-cut correlation between algal concentrations and their potential harmful effects. Dinoflagellate species such as *Dinophysis* and *Alexandrium* (=*Gonyaulax*) can contaminate shellfish with toxins, even at low cell concentrations. *Chrysochromulina* produces only moderate biomass levels but has a very high toxic potency.

Table 14-15 lists the clinical symptoms of various types of fish and shellfish poisoning.

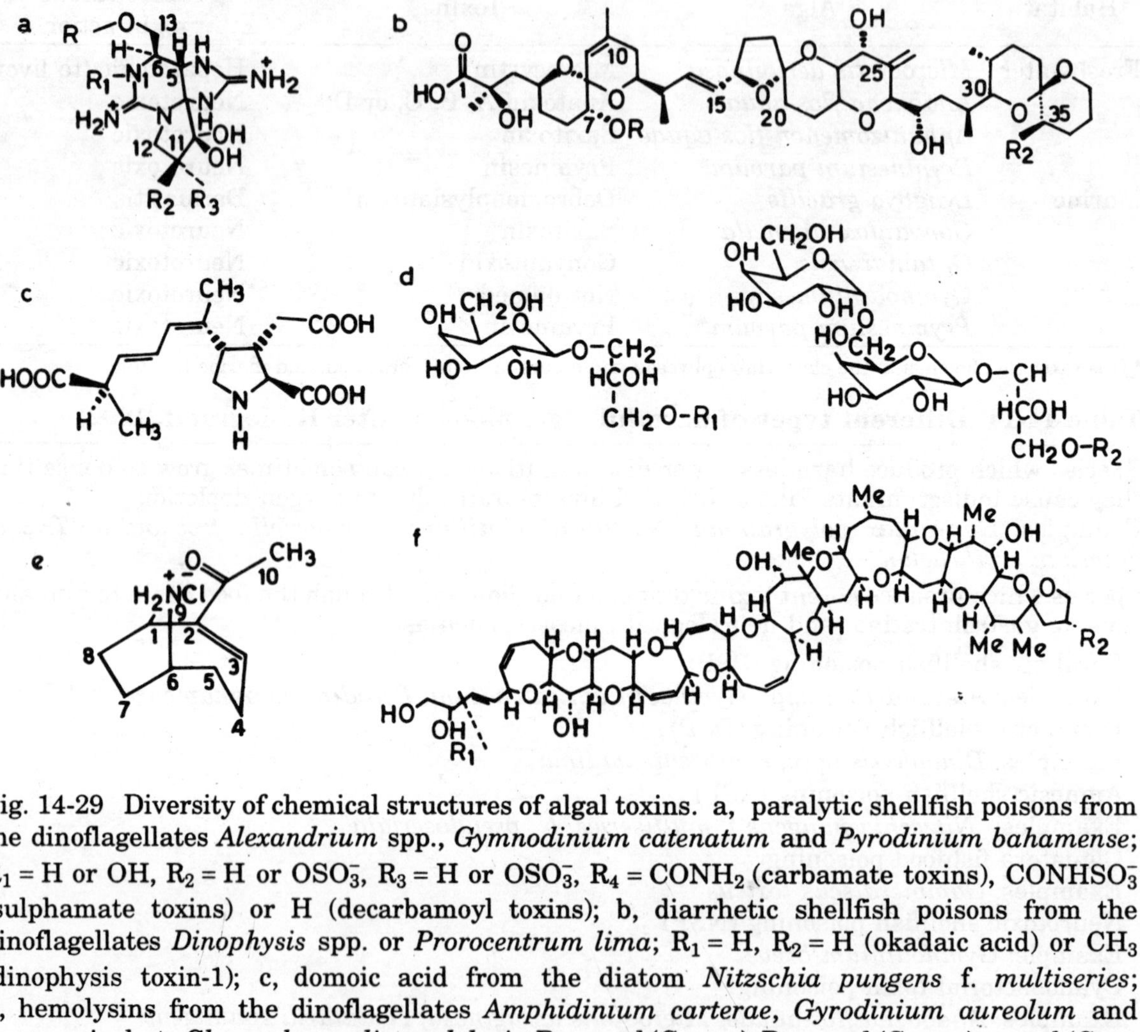

Fig. 14-29 Diversity of chemical structures of algal toxins. a, paralytic shellfish poisons from the dinoflagellates *Alexandrium* spp., *Gymnodinium catenatum* and *Pyrodinium bahamense*; R_1 = H or OH, R_2 = H or OSO_3^-, R_3 = H or OSO_3^-, R_4 = $CONH_2$ (carbamate toxins), $CONHSO_3^-$ (sulphamate toxins) or H (decarbamoyl toxins); b, diarrhetic shellfish poisons from the dinoflagellates *Dinophysis* spp. or *Prorocentrum lima*; R_1 = H, R_2 = H (okadaic acid) or CH_3 (dinophysis toxin-1); c, domoic acid from the diatom *Nitzschia pungens* f. *multiseries*; d, hemolysins from the dinoflagellates *Amphidinium carterae*, *Gyrodinium aureolum* and prymnesiophyte *Chrysochromulina polylepis*; R_1 = acyl ($C_{18:4w3}$); R_2 = acyl ($C_{18:4w3}$) or acyl ($C_{18:5}$, $C_{20:5}$) or acyl ($C_{20:5}$); e, anatoxin-a from the cyanobacterium *Anabaena flos-aquae*; f, ciguatoxin from the dinoflagellate *Gambierdiscus toxicus*; R_1 = CH_2 = CH—, R_2 = H (*Gambierdiscus*) or OH (moray eels). (After Hallegraeff, 1992.)

Table 14-15 Clinical symptoms of various types of fish and shellfish poisoning (after Hallegraeff, 1992)

Paralytic shellfish poisoning (PSP)	Diarrhetic shellfish poisoning (DSP)	Amnesic shellfish poisoning (ASP)	Ciguatera
Causative organism			
Alexandrium spp.; *Gymnodinium catenatum*; *Pyrodinium bahamense*	*Dinophysis acuminata*; *Dinophysis fortii*	*Nitzschia pungens* f. *multiseries*; *Nitzschia pseudodelicatissima*; *Nitzschia pseudoseriata*	*Gambierdiscus toxicus*; some unidentified species
Symptoms			
Mild Case			
Within half an hour: tingling sensation around lips, spreading to face and neck; prickly sensation in fingertips and toes; headache, dizziness, nausea, vomiting, diarrhoea	After a few hr: diarrhoea, nausea, vomiting, abdominal pain	After 3–5 hr: nausea, vomiting, diarrhoea, abdominal cramps	Symptoms develop within a day of eating fish; gastrointestinal symptoms: diarrhoea, abdominal pain, nausea, vomiting
Extreme Case			
Muscular paralysis; respiratory difficulty; choking sensation; death through respiratory paralysis may occur within a day of ingestion	Chronic exposure may promote tumour formation in the digestive system	Decreased reaction to deep pain; dizziness, hallucinations, confusion; short-term memory loss; seizures	Neurological symptoms: numbness and tingling of hands and feet; cold objects feel hot to touch; difficulty in balance; low heart rate and blood pressure; rashes; sometimes death through respiratory failure
Treatment			
Stomach pumping and artificial respiration	Recovery after 3 days irrespective of medical treatment		No antitoxin or specific treatment available; neurological symptoms may last for months and years; calcium and mannitol help relieve symptoms

While harmful algal blooms, in a strict sense, are completely natural phenomena which have occurred throughout recorded history, in the past two decades the public health and economic impacts of such events have increased in frequency, intensity, and geographic distribution. One example is the increased global distribution of PSP. Until 1970, PSP-producing dinoflagellate blooms (of *Alexandrium* (*Gonyaulax*) *tamarense* and *Alexandrium* (*Gonyaulax*) *catenella*) were only known from temperate waters of Europe, North America, and Japan (Dale and Yentsch, 1978). By 1990, PSP was well documented from throughout the Southern Hemisphere, in South Africa, Australia, India, Thailand, and other countries (Fig. 14-30). Other species of *Alexandrium*, such as *A. cohorticula* and *A. minutum*, as well as

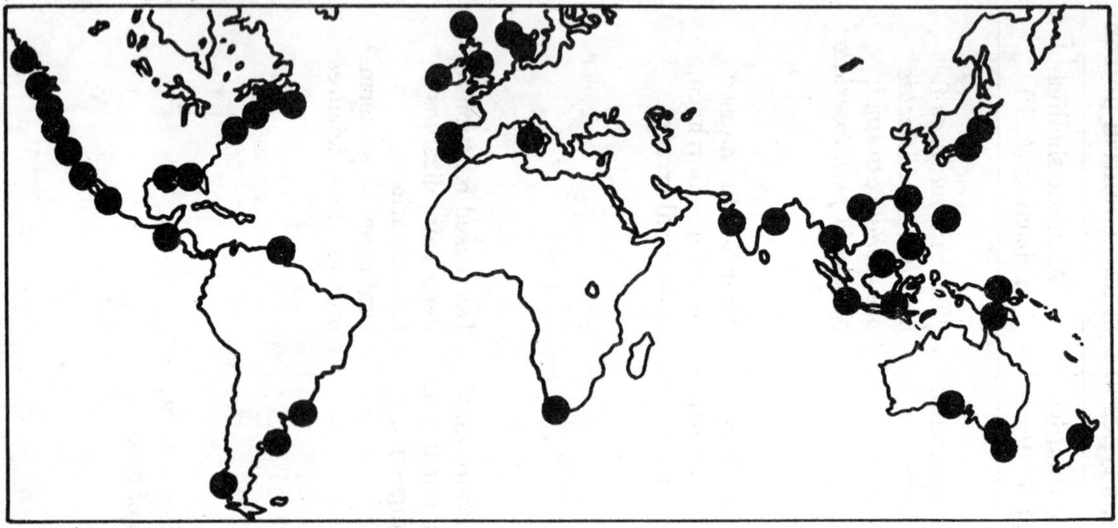

Fig. 14-30 Known world distribution of paralytic shellfish poisoning in 1990 (after Hallegraeff, 1992).

Gymnodinium catenatum and *Pyrodinium bahamense* var. *compressum*, have now also been implicated (Hallegraeff, 1992).

According to Shumway (1990) and Hallegraeff (1992), there are four explanations for the recorded increase of algal blooms: increased scientific awareness of toxic species; increased utilization of coastal waters for aquaculture; stimulation of plankton blooms by cultural eutrophication and/or unusual climatological conditions; and transport of dinoflagellate resting cysts either in ships' ballast water or associated with movement of shellfish stocks from one area to another.

Many toxic cyanobacterial blooms have been found to exhibit highly variable toxicity. Some factors which influence the observed variability include differences in algal species or strain composition in a bloom, growth conditions, age of the bloom, production, accumulation, inactivation or destruction of toxins, and presence and strain composition of bacteria. Some bacteria depress toxin secretion in *Anabaena flos-aquae* (Carmichael and Gorham, 1977).

Colonies of this alga seem to include both toxic and nontoxic filaments and this may partly explain the oft-observed toxicity variability in this organism.

Microcystis aeruginosa, Anabaena flos-aquae, and *Aphanizomenon flos-aquae* are the most important toxin producing blue-green algae which may, however, occur as toxic or nontoxic populations or substrains in natural habitats. Henning and Kohl (1981) have shown that in German lakes, the toxic effects produced by *Microcystis aeruginosa* depend on the degree of decomposition or disintegration of the cells. Sometimes, the toxicity of the same strain differs from lake to lake. *M. aeruginosa* contains two effective toxic principles, called the fast death factor and the slow death factor. The former is a cyclic peptide called microcystine and causes rapid death (within 4 hours) of the animals who ingest the alga, whereas the slow death factor causes death only after a longer period.

Henning and Kohl (1981) have studied the toxicity of the water blooms caused by *M. aeruginosa* in German lakes. Two types of symptoms can be distinguished: animals dying within 4 hours had their livers badly affected and suffered acute respiratory failure. Animals which died long after ingesting the toxic algae showed different type of symptoms and their livers were not damaged. They just sat stiffly and refused food or water until death occurred. They secreted something sticky at their eyelids which became agglutinated, and their blood vessels of the intestines were greatly congested.

Scavenging of shoreline deposits of neurotoxic benthic cyanobacteria by dogs has resulted in deaths at some freshwater lakes in Scotland. The buoyant growth habit of the common toxic planktonic species of *Microcystis*, *Anabaena*, *Aphanizomenon*, *Nodularia*, and *Oscillatoria* form scums in lakes and ponds during calm weather, so that an acutely toxic dose of cyanobacterial toxins can be presented to animals in a smaller volume than their daily water requirement. Animal poisonings due to the ingestion of toxic scum or concentrated bloom occur as a result of contact with toxic planktonic scums and blooms. Dogs lick adherent material from their coats; this has in a few cases (see Codd *et al.*, 1992) contributed to the ingestion of lethal doses of hepatotoxic *Nodularia spumigena* after swimming in water containing scum.

British scientists (see Codd *et al.*, 1992) investigated dog poisonings that occurred rapidly after ingestion of neurotoxic benthic cyanobacteria accumulating along the margins of Scottish lakes. Benthic *Oscillatoria* spp. and the cyanobacterial neurotoxin anatoxin-a have been identified in scums and dog stomach contents. Visits to the sites of the poisonings showed that the accumulations of toxic cyanobacteria were highly localized.

If some of the toxic planktonic algae happen to be ingested either along with drinking water or during swimming, they may cause various disease syndromes. For example, *Anabaena* and *Microcystis* cause gastric trouble; *Gymnodinium brevis* (Fig. 14-28) produces respiratory disorders, and *Lyngbya* and *Chlorella* are responsible for certain skin infections.

Burkholder *et al.* (1992) report the discovery of a microscopic, unicellular organism which, at one stage in its remarkable life cycle, secretes a powerful toxin which kills fish: most unusually, the organism uses dying fish to its nutritional advantage. The organism is a photosynthetic dinoflagellate, which lurks dormant on the seabed until live fish approach. Within minutes, it excysts, releasing a motile, vegetative stage which swims, grows and swarms within the water column. The toxic vegetative cells extend a tongue-like organelle, the peduncle, which attaches to and sucks the contents from fragments of fish tissue. There it secretes a potent, water-soluble neurotoxin which kills fish. In one episode, about a million menhaden (*Brevoortia* sp.) were killed (Smayda, 1992). Several hours later, the dinoflagellate cells encyst, sink to the bottom sediments and await another fish. Neither the chemical nature of the neurotoxin nor the broader distribution of the dinoflagellate is known. It may well be widespread and may have been responsible for many of the enigmatic fish kills in coastal regions (Burkholder *et al.*, 1992).

Red tides (which may in fact be red, green, yellow or brown) are of course one manifestation of blooms of phytoplankton, population explosions undergone by dinoflagellates, diatoms and several other groups of photosynthetic microalgae. According to Smayda (1992), such blooms have underpinned marine foodwebs for three billion years, but the red-tide blooms of nutritionally inadequate or toxic species have less benign effects. In more recent times there has been an apparent increase in bloom frequency and spread of noxious species; the occurrence of toxicity in species that had been thought to be harmless; and several reports of catastrophic mass deaths of marine mammals, fish, and invertebrates (see Sherman *et al.*, 1989).

Recently a previously undescribed mode of feeding (termed desmotrophy) by a toxic, photosynthetic phytoplankter on other phytoplankton has been reported (see Smayda, 1992). This toxic flagellate, also lethal to fish, invertebrates and macroalgae, produces membrane-puncturing compounds which allow it to extract nutrients from its prey (Smayda, 1992).

With the possible exception of desmotrophy, phytoplankton toxins have not been reported to have a nutritional role; rather, they may serve as chemical deterrents against predation, even protecting shellfish which have sequestered them during feeding. By contrast, the dinoflagellate described by Burkholder *et al.*, 1992, does derive nutritional gain during its kill—it digests fish tissue to which it attaches by means of its peduncle. Another difference between the biology of this dinoflagellate and that of other toxin producers lies in the surprising effect of phosphorus. The addition of phosphate, unlike nitrate or ammonia, stimulates the growth of gametes, whereas it is the limitation of this nutrient that is implicated in toxigenesis in other species (see Graneli *et al.*, 1991; Smayda, 1992).

A recent outbreak of toxic algal bloom (*Chrysochromulina* cf. *leadbeateri*) occurred during May-June 1991 in Norway. It was accompanied by an extensive mortality of fish (Atlantic salmon, *Salmo salar*) in fish farms. The alga produced toxin(s) with acute effects on *in vivo* and *in vitro* tests (Aune *et al.*, 1992).

PARASITISM

Certain algae parasitize such aquatic invertebrates as *Stentor*, *Paramecium*, *Hydra*, snails, sponges, and mussels. The algae involved mostly belong to the genera *Chlorella* or *Zoochlorella* and occasionally *Carteria*, *Protococcus*, *Coccomyxa*, and *Chlamydomonas*. Some aquatic algae infest the gills of fish, obstructing the latter's breathing. Species of the dinoflagellate *Oodinium* parasitize freshwater fishes and marine tunicates.

Species of the parasitic green alga *Cephaleuros* cause red rust of tea and inflict heavy economic losses by seriously affecting the yield of tea.

EFFECTS ON AQUATIC ANIMALS

The excessive growth of certain algae (*Microcystis aeruginosa*) in a body of water often results in severe depletion of oxygen in the habitat. This leads to mass mortality of fish due to suffocation. Sometimes, high temperature and bright sunshine result in massive disintegration of algal blooms, releasing into the medium their noxious components. Choking of the gills of fish by these algae is also partly responsible for their death.

BIOFOULING

Some algae cause fouling of substrates, by opportunistic colonization, both in freshwater and marine habitats. Any objects submerged in water become quickly colonized by microalgae and bacteria. Diatoms attach to a variety of substrates including surfaces coated with toxic paints. Rapid colonization is known to occur on inshore rocks, pilings, on oil platforms, boats, ship hulls, and buoys (Terry and Edyvean, 1984). Fouling on ship hulls results in increase in frictional resistance, leading to loss of speed and increased fuel consumption. Species of *Enteromorpha* and *Ectocarpus* are the most common ship-fouling algae. *Enteromorpha* is usually the dominant alga found on copper-containing antifouling paints, whereas *Ectocarpus* dominates on paints containing organometallic biocides. Species of *Amphora*, *Achnanthes*, and *Stauroneis* grow both on paints containing copper or organo-tin.

Cooksey and Cooksey (1986) have studied the adhesion of fouling diatoms to surfaces of submerged substrates, with special reference to their ecological role in the nutrient dynamics of the biofilm. According to Cooksey and Cooksey, vesicles produced in the Golgi apparatus and containing some polysaccharide-proteinaceous material are transported to the cell membrane (Fig. 14-31) near the raphe canal. They fuse with the membrane and secrete their

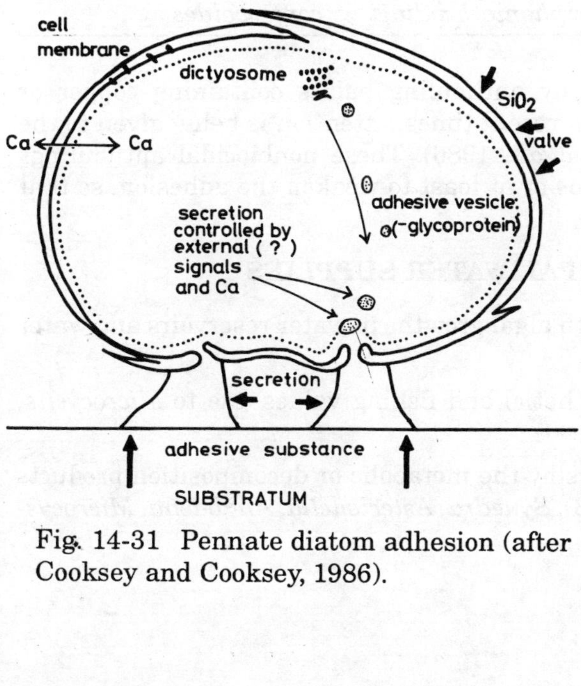

Fig. 14-31 Pennate diatom adhesion (after Cooksey and Cooksey, 1986).

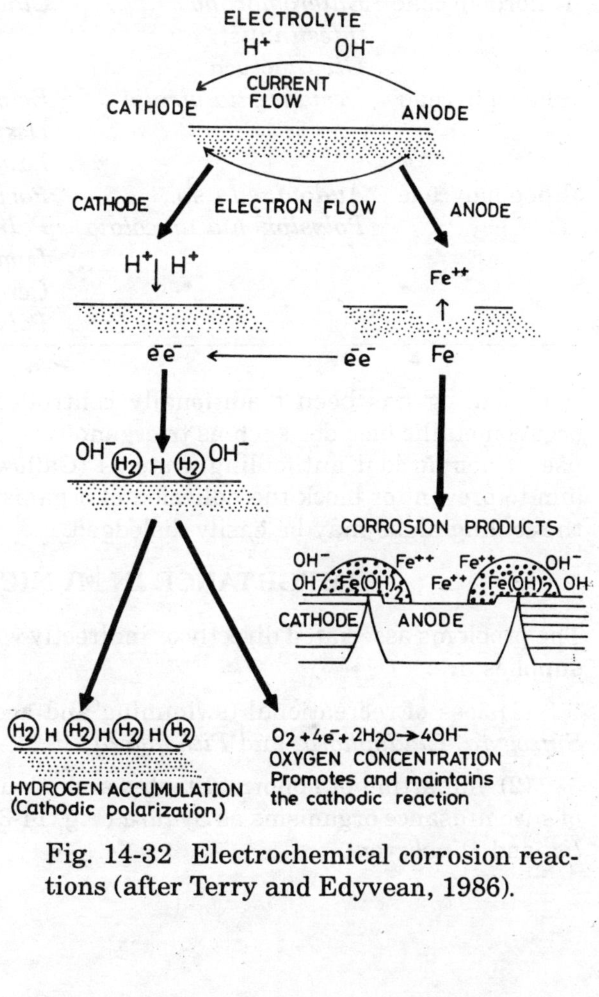

Fig. 14-32 Electrochemical corrosion reactions (after Terry and Edyvean, 1986).

contents. It is this secreted material that allows the cell to adhere to the substratum. There is some indication of the involvement of a glycoprotein and also calcium in this material (Cooksey and Cooksey, 1986).

Algal fouling can cause serious problems in offshore gas extraction operations, as all installations become rapidly colonized by fouling algae. Some of the problems include (1) obscuring the underlying substratum and hindrance in inspection; (2) increase in hydrodynamic loading; and (3) corrosion. Thus, the algae can corrode the underlying steel in offshore installations (see Fig. 14-32) by influencing and modifying the oxygen concentration, changing the pH, or producing metabolites which create a more aggressive electrolyte (Fig. 14-32). The fundamental electrochemical nature of corrosion suggests that a decrease in oxygen concentration would reduce the cathodic reaction, thereby leading to a corresponding reduction in corrosion (Terry and Edyvean, 1986).

Some common algae recorded from offshore installations are listed in Table 14-16.

Table 14-16 Some algae recorded on offshore installations in North Sea (after Terry and Picken, 1986)

Class	Widespread	Common	Less common
Chlorophyceae	*Enteromorpha intestinalis*, *Ulva lactuca*	*Cladophora* spp.	*Chaetomorpha* spp., *Spongomorpha* spp.
Phaeophyceae	*Desmarestia viridis*	*Ectocarpus* spp., *Desmarestia ligulata*, *Laminaria digitata*	*Pilayella littoralis*, *Laminaria hyperborea*
Rhodophyceae	*Audouinella* sp., *Polysiphonia urceolata*	*Porphyra* sp., *Palmaria palmata*, *Lomentaria* spp., *Ceramium rubrum*, *Polysiphonia brodiaei*	*Bangia atro-purpurea*, *Gelidium* spp., *Plumaria elegans*, *Rhodomela confervoides*

Biofouling has been traditionally controlled by antifouling paints containing copper or organometallic biocides such as triorgano-tins. In recent times, attention is being given to the use of nonbiocidal antifouling systems (Callow *et al.*, 1986). These nonbiocidal antifoulings aim to prevent or block the adhesion of organisms or at least to weaken the adhesion, so that the fouling algae may be easily dislodged.

IMPORTANCE IN MUNICIPAL WATER SUPPLIES

The problems associated directly or indirectly with algal growths in water reservoirs and water supplies are:

(1) loss of recreational (swimming and aesthetic) and fishing values due to *Microcystis*, *Spirogyra*, *Cladophora*, and *Pithophora*;

(2) imparting of abnormal tastes and odours by the metabolic or decomposition products of such nuisance organisms as *Synura* (Fig. 14-33), *Synedra*, *Asterionella*, *Anabaena*, *Microcystis*, and *Dinobryon*;

(3) clogging of water filters by *Oscillatoria*, *Spirogyra*, and certain diatoms, thereby shortening the filter runs leading to serious economic losses;

(4) colouration of such waters, for example, by *Chlorella*, *Chlamydomonas*, *Euglena*, and *Oscillatoria*;

(5) spoilage of the product quality of the food, pharmaceutical, and pulp industries using such waters;

(6) production of toxic substances;

(7) corrosion of concrete and metallic walls of pipes and boilers by carbonic, oxalic, and silicic acids excreted by, for example, *Anacystis* and *Chaetophora*;

(8) interference with water purification; and

(9) changes in the pH, CO_2, and bicarbonate and oxygen content of such waters.

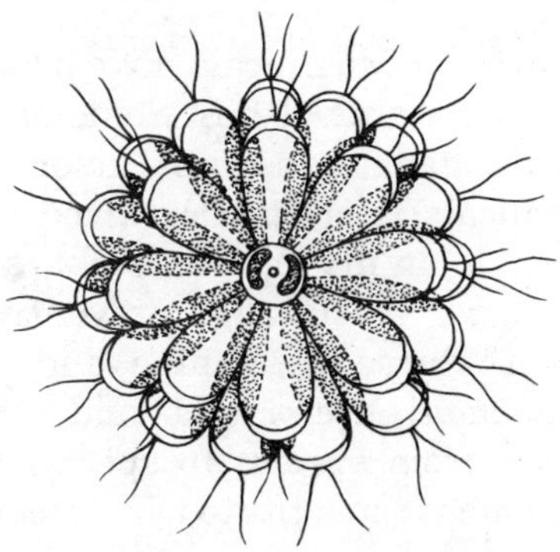

Fig. 14-33 *Synura uvella*, habit.

In water treatment plants, the raw water is chlorinated in order to kill algae and other microorganisms. However, even this water is sometimes not completely free of algae since some of them are chlorine resistant and their presence may alter its quality and potability.

The only useful purposes the algae serve in water supplies are that they (1) maintain aerobic conditions by checking putrefaction of organic substances, and (2) reduce the total hardness of water by consuming bicarbonates and the nearly-insoluble carbonates.

CONTROL OF UNDESIRABLE SPECIES

BIOLOGICAL CONTROL

The virus, cyanophage LPP-1, and several other phycoviruses (e.g., LPP-2, SM-1, N-1, and AS-1) infect various blue-green algae and could conceivably be employed to control their growth in surface water since they cause lysis of the sensitive forms. Recently, the eucaryotic algae *Chlorella* and *Sirodotia* have also been reported to be attacked by phycoviruses. The addition of virus particles to cultures of susceptible algae results in a considerable increase in virus titres and a rapid fall in algal cell numbers (see Safferman, 1973).

A better method for algal control consists in introducing suitable crustaceans or fish fingerlings into the water body. These animals feed on algae either directly or indirectly, and may be harvested for food at maturity.

In some cases, algal growth in ponds may be controlled by introducing the floating angiosperm *Lemna* which shades the water below. This shading in turn inhibits the algae.

Another promising method of controlling toxic blue-green algae is to introduce certain chrysophytes such as *Ochromonas danica* which have been shown to engulf and digest the cells of such blue-green algae as *Microcystis aeruginosa*, in mixed cultures. Up to four cyanobacterial cells have been seen within the cytoplasm of a single cell of *Ochromonas*. The phagocytic cells of *Ochromonas* have high acid phosphatase activity.

Gymnodinium helveticum (dinoflagellate) shows nonselective and nonpredatory phagotrophy and these cells contain various algae including blue-greens inside them (Irish, 1979).

CHEMICAL CONTROL

A variety of chemicals have been tested for controlling the growth of algae in swimming pools or other water bodies. Some of these chemicals include copper sulphate, chlorine, potassium permanganate, sodium arsenite, and sodium pentachlorophenate. The efficacy of these chemicals is often short-lived and some of them can have adverse side effects. The dosage depends on pH and other characteristics of the water to be treated and on the concentration of algae. A suitable preventive agent that keeps the algae in check is chlorophenyl-dimethylurea. Ethionine and 2,5-dichloro-3,4-dinitrothiophene are selectively algicidal to *Anabaena*, *Microcystis*, and other cyanophytes. The response of algae to copper sulphate varies from species to species (Table 14-17). Some promising algicides such as antibiotics, quinones, substituted hydrocarbons, and phenols are not in common use because of their higher cost.

Table 14-17 Examples of algae that are highly sensitive or highly resistant to copper sulphate (after Palmer, 1980)

Highly susceptible	Highly resistant
Anabaena, Anacystis, Rivularia, Aphanizomenon, Gomphosphaeria	*Calothrix, Symploca*
Hydrodictyon, Oedogonium, Rhizoclonium, Spirogyra, Ulothrix	*Ankistrodesmus, Chara, Dictyosphaerium, Nitella, Pithophora, Scenedesmus, Coelastrum*
Asterionella, Cyclotella, Fragilaria, Melosira, Dinobryon, Synura, Uroglenopsis, Volvox	*Pandorina, Eudorina*

The quinone 2,3-dichloro-1,4-naphthoquinone is more selectively toxic to many bloom-forming cyanophytes than to other algae. This chemical can be effectively used to control water blooms caused by the blue-green algae, especially in the summer. The rate of application is 1 ppm.

In algal cultures, copper toxicity is determined not by the total copper concentration present but by the cupric ion activity (Sunda and Lewis, 1978). In natural water bodies also, McKnight (1981) has shown that the concentration of the free copper ion determines the toxic response of the phytoplankton. She has used copper sulphate to treat a late summer dinoflagellate bloom caused by *Ceratium hirundinella*. The dinoflagellate population decreased by about 90% one day after the addition of copper sulphate to the water reservoir, and was succeeded by the green alga *Nannochloris* sp. With the growth of this and other green algae, the primary productivity in the reservoir decreased initially but its pretreatment level was restored in about 10 days. She also found that the two green algal species tolerated much higher concentrations of cupric ion than the dinoflagellate, both in the field and in laboratory culture experiments.

REFERENCES

Aaronson, S. and Dubinsky, Z., Mass production of microalgae, *Experientia*, **38**, 36–40 (1982).

Anderson, L.W.J. and Dechoretz, N., Laboratory and field investigations of a potential selective algicide, PH.4062. *J. Aquat. Plant Management,* **22**, 67–75 (1984).

Arasaki, S. and Arasaki, T., Low Calorie, High Nutrition Vegetables from the Sea, Japan Publications, Inc., Tokyo (1983).

Arnold, D.E., Ingestion, assimilation, survival and reproduction by *Daphnia pulex* fed seven species of blue-green algae, *Limnol. Oceanogr.*, **16**, 906–20 (1971).

Aune, T., Skulberg, O.M., and Underdal, B., A toxic phytoflagellate bloom of *Chrysochromulina* cf. *leadbeateri* in coastal waters in the North of Norway, *Ambio.*, **21**, 471–74 (1992).

Bachofen, R., The production of hydrocarbons by *Botryococcus braunii*, *Experientia*, **38**, 47–49 (1982).

Ben-Amotz, A. and Arnon, M., Accumulation of metabolites by halotolerant algae and its industrial potential, *A. Rev. Microbiol.*, **37**, 95–119 (1983).

Burkholder, J.M., Noga, E.J., Hobbs, C.H., and Glasgow, H.B. (Jr.), New 'phantom' dinoflagellate is the causative agent of major estuarine fish kills, *Nature*, **358**, 407–10 (1992).

Callow, M.E., Pitchers, R.A., and Milne, A., The control of fouling by non-biocidal systems. *In* Evans, L.V. and Hoagland, K.D. (eds.) Algal Biofouling, 145–58, Elsevier, Amsterdam (1986).

Carmichael, W.W. (ed.), The Water Environment: Algal toxins and health, Plenum Press, New York (1981).

Carmichael, W.W., Algal toxins, *Adv. Bot. Res.*, **12**, 47–101 (1986).

Carmichael, W.W. and Gorham, P.R., Factors influencing the toxicity and animal susceptibility of *Anabaena flos-aquae* (Cyanophyta) blooms, *J. Phycol.*, **13**, 97–101 (1977).

Cassini, J.R. and Caton, W.E., Efficient production of triploid grass carp (*Ctenopharyngodon idella*) utilizing hydrostatic pressure, *Aquaculture*, **55**, 43–50 (1986).

Chapman, V.J. and Chapman, D.J., Seaweeds and Their Uses, 3rd edn., Chapman and Hall, London (1980).

Ciferri, O., *Spirulina*: the edible microorganism, *Microbiol. Rev.*, **5**, 60–70 (1983).

Codd, G.A., Edwards, C., Beattie, K.A., Barr, W.M., and Gunn, G.J., Fatal attraction to cyanobacteria?, *Nature*, **359**, 110–11 (1992).

Cooksey, K.E. and Cooksey, B., Adhesion of fouling diatoms to surfaces: some biochemistry. *In* Evans, L.V. and Hoagland, K.D. (eds.) Algal Biofouling, 41–53, Elsevier, Amsterdam (1986).

Dale, B. and Yentsch, C.M., Red tide and paralytic shellfish poisoning, *Oceanus*, **21**, 41–49 (1978).

Ehresmann, D.W., Deig, E.F., and Hatch, M.T., Antiviral properties of algal polysaccharides and related compounds. *In* Hoppe, H.A., Levring, T., and Tanaka, Y. (eds.) Marine Algae in Pharmaceutical Science, 294–302, Walter de Gruyter, Berlin (1979).

Foster, M.S., The algal turf community in the nest of ocean gold fish, *Hypsypops rubicunda*. *In* Nisizawa, K. (ed.) Proceedings of the VII International Seaweed Symposium, 55–60, University of Tokyo Press, Tokyo (1972).

Glombitza, K.W., Antibiotics from algae. *In* Hoppe, H.A., Levring, T., and Tanaka, Y. (eds.) Marine Algae in Pharmaceutical Science, 303–42, Walter de Gruyter, Berlin (1979).

Graneli, E., Sundstrom, B., Edler, L., and Anderson, D.M. (eds.), Toxic Marine Phytoplankton, Elsevier, New York (1991).

Greenwood, P.H. and Lund, J.W.G., A discussion on the biology of an equatorial lake: Lake George, Uganda, *Proc. Roy. Soc.*, **184B**, 277–346 (1973).

Hallegraeff, G.M., A review of harmful algal blooms and their apparent global increase, *Phycologia*, **32**, 79–99 (1992).

Hansen, G.W., Oliver, F.E., and Otto, N.E., Herbicide Manual, U.S. Department of the Interior, Bureau of Reclamation, Denver, CO. (1984).

Hashimoto, Y., Marine Toxins and Other Bioactive Marine Metabolites, Japan Scientific Societies Press, Tokyo (1979).

Henning, M. and Kohl, J.G., Toxic blue-green algae water blooms found in some lakes in the German Democratic Republic, *Int. Revue ges. Hydrobiol.*, **66**, 553–61 (1981).

Hoppe, H.A., Marine algae and their products and constituents in pharmacy. *In* Hoppe, H.A., Levring, T., and Tanaka, Y. (eds.) Marine Algae in Pharmaceutical Science, 25–119, Walter de Gruyter, Berlin (1979).

Irish, A.E., *Gymnodinium helveticum* Penard (*F. Achroum* Skuja): a case of phagotrophy, *Brit. Phycol. J.*, **14**, 11–15 (1979).

Jensen, A., The nutritive value of seaweed meal for domestic animals. *In* Nisizawa, K. (ed.) Proceedings of the VII International Seaweed Symposium, 7–14, University of Tokyo Press, Tokyo (1972).

Kawaguchi, K., Microalgae production systems in Asia. *In* Shelef, G. and Soeder, C.J. (eds.) Algae Biomass, 25–33, Elsevier, Amsterdam (1980).

Kawashima, S., Kombu cultivation in Japan for human foodstuff, *Jap. J. Phycol.*, **32**, 379–94 (1984).

Kremer, B.P., Toxische Planktonalgen, *Naturwissenschaften*, **68**, 101–109 (1981).

Kumar, H.D., Algae and rural development, Presidential address, Proceedings of the All India Applied Phycological Congress, pp. 1–10, Kanpur (1983).

Lembi, C.A., O'Neal, S.W., and Spencer, D.F., Algae as weeds: economic impact, ecology and management alternatives. *In* Lembi, C.A. and Waaland, J.R. (eds.) Algae and Human Affairs, 455–81, Cambridge University Press, Cambridge (1988).

Lowe, R.L. and Gale, W.F., Monitoring river periphyton with artificial benthic substrates, *Hydrobiologia*, **69**, 235–44 (1980).

Lowenstam, H.A., Minerals formed by organisms, *Science*, **211**, 1126–31 (1981).

McKnight, D., Chemical and biological processes controlling the response of a freshwater ecosystem to copper stress: a field study of the $CuSO_4$ treatment of Mill Pond Reservoir, Burkington, Massachusetts, *Limnol. Oceanogr.*, **26**, 518–31 (1981).

Mittal, A., Agrawal, M.K., and Shivpuri, D.N., Respiratory allergy to algae-clinical aspects, *Ann. Allergy*, **42**, 253–56 (1979).

Mumford, T.F. (Jr.) and Miura, A., *Porphyra* as food: cultivation and economics. *In* Lembi, C.A.

and Waaland, J.R. (eds.) Algae and Human Affairs, 87–117, Cambridge University Press, Cambridge (1988).

Palmer, C.M., Algae and Water Pollution, Castle House Publications, London (1980).

Phlips, E.J. and Mitsui, A., Characterization and optimization of hydrogen production by a salt water blue-green alga *Oscillatoria* sp. Miami BG7. II. Use of immobilization for enhancement of hydrogen production, *Int. J. Hydrogen Energy*, **11**, 83–89 (1986).

Porter, K.G., Selective grazing and differential digestion of algae by zooplankton, *Nature*, **244**, 179–80 (1973).

Ragaelis, E.P. (ed.), Seafood Toxins, American Chemical Society, Washington, D.C. (1984).

Rai, L.C., Gaur, J.P., and Kumar, H.D., Phycology and heavy metal pollution, *Biol. Rev.*, **56**, 99–151 (1981).

Ramos, J.L., Guerrero, M.G., and Losada, M., Sustained photo-production of ammonia from nitrate by *Anacystis nidulans*, *Applied* and *Environmental Microbiol.*, **44**, 1020–25 (1982).

Richmond, A. and Preiss, K., The biotechnology of alga culture, *Interdiscip. Sci. Rev.*, **5**, 60–70 (1980).

Roger, P.A., Kulasooriya, S.A., Tirol, A.C., and Croswell, E.T., Deep placement: a method of nitrogen fertilizer application compatible with algal nitrogen fixation in wetland rice soils, *Plant and Soil*, **57**, 137–42 (1980).

Safferman, R.S., Phycoviruses. *In* Carr, N.G. and Whitton, B.A. (eds.) The Biology of Blue-green Algae, 214–37, Blackwell, Oxford (1973).

Saito, Y., *Undaria*. *In* Tokida, J. and Hirose, H. (eds.) Advance of Phycology in Japan, 304–20, W. Junk, The Hague (1975).

Samson, R. and LeDuy, A., Influence of mechanical and thermochemical pretreatments on anaerobic digestion of *Spirulina maxima* algal biomass, *Biotechnol. Lett.*, **5**, 651–82 (1983).

Sarma, Y.S.R.K., Chandarana, R.B., Ramavat, B.K., and Tarwadi, S.J., Utilization of seaweed for liquid fertilizer energy and poultry feed. *In* Proceedings Seminar on Sun, Sea and Shore, 90–91, Bhavnagar (1984).

Sherman, K., Alexander, L.M., and Gold, B.D. (eds.), Food Chains, Yields, Models and Management of Large Marine Ecosystems, Westview, Boulder (1989).

Shumway, S.E., A review of the effects of algal blooms on shellfish and aquaculture, *Journal of the World Aquaculture Society*, **21**, 65–104 (1990).

Smayda, T.J., A phantom of the ocean, *Nature*, **358**, 374–75 (1992).

Soeder, C.J., Massive cultivation of microalgae: results and prospects, *Hydrobiologia*, **72**, 197–209 (1980).

Soeder, C.J. and Pabst, W., Gesichtspunkte zur Verwendung von Tier und Mensch, *Ber. Deutsch. Bot. Ges.*, **83**, 607–25 (1970).

Steidinger, K.A., A re-evaluation of toxic dinoflagellate biology and ecology. *In* Round, F.E. and Chapman, D.J. (eds.) Progress in Phycological Research, Vol. 2, 1147–88, Elsevier, Amsterdam (1983).

Stein, J.R. and Borden, C.A., Causative and beneficial algae in human disease conditions: a review, *Phycologia*, **23**, 485–501 (1984).

Stephenson, J.W., The effects of a seaweed extract on the yield of a variety of field and glasshouse crops. *In* Fogg, G.E. and Jones, W.E. (eds.), *Proc. Intl. Seaweed Sympos.*, **8**, 740–44 (1981).

Stewart, W.D.P., Rowell, P., Kerby, N.W., Reed, R.H., and Machray, G.C., N_2-fixing cyanobacteria and their potential applications, *Phil. Trans. Roy. Soc.* (London), **317B**, 245–58 (1987).

Sunda, W.G. and Lewis, J.A., Effect of complexation by natural organic ligands on the toxicity of copper to a unicellular alga, *Monochrysis lutheri*, *Limnol. Oceanogr.*, **23,** 870–76 (1978).

Tamiya, H., Role of algae as food. *In* Proceedings of Symposium Algology, 379–89, Indian Council of Agricultural Research, New Delhi (1960).

Terry, L.A. and Edyvean, R.G.J., Influences of microalgae on corrosion of structural steel. *In* Lewis, J.R. and Mercer, A.D. (eds.) Corrosion and Marine Growth on Offshore Structures, 38–44, Ellis Horwood, Chichester (1984).

Terry, L.A. and Edyvean, R.G.J., Recent investigations into the effects of algae on corrosion. *In* Evans, L.V. and Hoagland, K.D. (eds.) Algal Biofouling, 211–29, Elsevier, Amsterdam (1986).

Terry, L.A. and Picken, G.B., Algal fouling in the North Sea. *In* Evans, L.V. and Hoagland, K.D. (eds.) Algal Biofouling, 179–92, Elsevier, Amsterdam (1986).

Thivy, F., Seaweed utilization in India. *In* Proceedings of Symposium Algology, 345–65, Indian Council of Agricultural Research, New Delhi (1960).

Titmus, G. and Badcock, R.M., Distribution and feeding of larval Chironomidae in a gravel-pit lake, *Freshwater Biol.*, **11**, 263–71 (1981).

Venezio, F.R., Lavoo, E., Williams, J.E., Zeiss, C.R., Caro, W.A., Mangkornkanok-Mark, M., and Phair, J.P., Progressive cutaneous protothecosis, *Am. J. Clin. Path.*, **77**, 485–95 (1982).

Venkataraman, L.V., Blue-green Alga *Spirulina*, Department of Science and Technology, New Delhi (1983).

Watanabe, I. and Roger, P.A., Nitrogen fixation in wetland rice fields. *In* Subba Rao, N.S. (ed.) Current Developments in Biological Nitrogen Fixation, 237–76, Oxford and IBH, New Delhi (1984).

Whitton, B.A., Toxicity of zinc, copper, and lead to Chlorophyta from flowing waters, *Arch. Microbiol.*, **72**, 353–60 (1970).

Wilcox, H.A., The ocean as a supplier of food and energy, *Experientia*, **38**, 31–35 (1982).

Yamamoto, I., Nagumo, T., Yagi, K., Tominaga, H., and Aoki, M., Antitumor effects of seaweeds. I. Antitumor effect of extracts from *Sargassum* and *Laminaria*, *Japan J. Exp. Med.*, **44**, 543–46 (1974).

Further Reading

Abbott, I.A. and Dawson, E.Y., How to Know the Seaweeds?, 2nd edn., Wm. C. Brown, Dubuque (1978).

Abbott, I.A., Foster, M.S., and Eklund, L.F., Pacific Seaweeds Aquaculture, Institute of Marine Resources, La Jolla (1980).

Akatsuka, I. (ed.), Introduction to Applied Phycology, SPB Academic Publishing, The Hague (1991).

Bardach, J.E., Ryther, J.H., and McLarney, W.O., Aquaculture: The farming and husbandry of freshwater and marine organisms, Wiley-Interscience, New York (1972).

Belcher, H. and Swale, E., A Beginner's Guide to Freshwater Algae, HMSO, London (1976).

Belcher, H. and Swale, E., An Illustrated Guide to River Phytoplankton, HMSO, London (1979).

Bellinger, E.G., A Key to Common British Algae, Institution of Water Engineers and Scientists, London (1980).

Bird, C.J. and Ragan, M.A. (eds.), Proceedings of the XI International Seaweeds Symposium, W. Junk, The Hague (1984).

Boney, A.D., Phytoplankton, 2nd edn., Edward Arnold, London (1989).

Bonotto, S., Kefeli, V., and Puiseyux-Dao, S. (eds.), Developmental Biology of *Acetabularia*, Elsevier, Amsterdam (1979).

Brook, A.J., The Biology of Desmids, Blackwell, Oxford (1981).

Bryant, D.A. (ed.), The Molecular Biology of Cyanobacteria, Kluwer Academic Publishers, Dordrecht (1994).

Carefoot, T. and Simpson, R.D., Seashore Ecology, University of Queensland Press, St. Lucia, Australia (1985).

Carr, N.G. and Whitton, B.A. (eds.), The Biology of Cyanobacteria, Blackwell, Oxford (1982).

Chapman, A.R.O., Biology of Seaweeds: Levels of organization, University of Park Press, Baltimore (1979).

Christensen, T., Algae: A taxonomic survey, Aio Tryk, Odense (1980).

Cole, K.M. and Sheath, R.G. (eds.), Biology of the Red Algae, Cambridge University Press, Cambridge (1990).

Cox, E.R. (ed.), Phytoflagellates, Elsevier, New York (1980).

Dawes, C.J., Marine Botany, Wiley-Interscience, New York (1981).

Dodge, J.D., Marine Dinoflagellates of the British Isles, HMSO, London (1982).

Dring, M.J., The Biology of Marine Plants, Edward Arnold, London (1982).

Drouet, F., Revision of the Nostocaceae with Constricted Trichomes, *Nova Hedwigia*, **57**, 1–258 (1978).

Duddington, C.L., Beginner's Guide to Seaweeds, Drake, New York (1971).

Evitt, W.R., Sporopollenin Dinoflagellate Cysts: Their morphology and interpretation, American Association of Stratigraphic Palynologists Foundation, Dallas, Texas (1985).

Fitzgerald, G., Algicides, University of Wisconsin Water Resources Center, Madison (1971).

Flügel, E. (ed.), Fossil Algae, Springer-Verlag, Berlin (1977).

Fogg, G.E. and Thake, B., Algal Cultures and Phytoplankton Ecology, 3rd edn., University of Wisconsin Press, Madison (1987).

Gantt, E. (ed.), Handbook of Phycological Methods: Developmental and cytological methods, Cambridge University Press, London (1980).

Goff, L.J. (ed.), Algal Symbiosis: A continuum of interaction strategies, Cambridge University Press, London (1983).

Goldman, C.R. (ed.), Primary Productivity in Aquatic Environments, University of California Press, Berkeley (1965).

Guiry, M.D. and Blunden, G. (eds.), Seaweed Resources in Europe: Uses and potential, Wiley, Chichester (1991).

Hara, H. (ed.), Origin and Evolution of Diversity in Plants and Plant Communities, Academia Scientifica Books, Tokyo (1985).

Hillson, C.J., Seaweeds, Pennsylvania State University Press, Philadelphia (1977).

Hope, A.B. and Walker, N.A., The Physiology of Giant Algal Cells, Cambridge University Press, London (1975).

Hoppe, H.A., Levring, T., and Tanaka, Y. (eds.), Marine Algae in Pharmaceutical Science, Walter de Gruyter, Berlin (1979).

Hori, T. (ed.), An Illustrated Atlas of the Life History of Algae, Vols. 1–3, Uchida Rokakuho Publishers, Tokyo (1993, 1994).

Humm, H.J. and Wicks, S.B., Introduction and Guide to the Marine Blue Green Algae, Wiley-Interscience, Somerset (1980).

Imai, T. (ed.), Aquaculture in Shallow Seas: Progress in shallow sea culture, Balkema, Rotterdam (1978).

Irvine, L.M., Seaweeds of the British Isles. I. Rhodophyta, British Museum of Natural History, London (1983).

Irvine, D.E.G. and John, D.M. (eds.), Systematics of the Green Algae, Academic Press, London (1984).

Irvine, D.E.G. and Price, J.H. (eds.), Modern Approaches to the Taxonomy of Red and Brown Algae, Academic Press, London (1978).

John, J., The Diatom Flora of the Swan River Estuary, Western Australia, Cramer, Vaduz (1983).

Kapraun, D.F., An Illustrated Guide to the Benthic Marine Algae of Coastal North Carolina. I. Rhodophyta, University of North Carolina Press, Chapel Hill (1980).

Kashyap, A.K. and Kumar, H.D. (eds.), Recent Advances in Phycology. Proc. of Internat. Phycotalk Symposium, Rastogi Publications, Meerut (1993).

Kemp, P.F., Sherr, B.F., Sherr, E.V., and Cole, J.J. (eds.), Handbook of Methods in Aquatic Microbiol Ecology, Lewis, Boca Raton (1993).

Krauss, R.W. (ed.), The Marine Plant Biomass of the Pacific Northwest Coast: A potential economic resource, Oregon State University Press, Corvallis (1977).

Kristiansen, J. and Andersen, R.A. (eds.), Chrysophytes: Aspects and problems, Cambridge University Press, London (1986).

Kumar, H.D., Algal Cell Biology, 2nd edn., Affiliated East-West Press, New Delhi (1989).

Kumar, H.D. (ed.), Phycotalk, Vols. I and II, Rastogi Publications, Meerut (1989, 1990).

Kumar, H.D. and Singh, H.N., A Textbook on Algae, 4th edn., East-West Press, New Delhi (1995).

Lawson, G.W. and John, D.M., The Marine Algae and Coastal Environment of Tropical West Africa, Cramer, Vaduz (1982).

Lee, J.J., Hutner, S.H., and Bovee, E.C. (eds.), An Illustrated Guide to the Protozoa, Society of Protozoologists, Lawrence, Kansas (1985).

Lee, T., The Seaweed Handbook: An illustrated guide to seaweeds from North Carolina to the Arctic, Marines Press, Boston (1977).

Lembi, C.A. and Waaland, J.R. (eds.), Algae and Human Affairs, Cambridge University Press, Cambridge (1988).

Lewin, R.A. (ed.), The Genetics of Algae, University of California Press, Berkeley (1976).

Lind, E.M. and Brook, A.J., A Key to the Commoner Desmids of the English Lake District, Freshwater Biological Association, Scientific Publication No. 42, Ambleside (1980).

Lobban, C.S., Harrison, P.J., and Duncan, M.J., The Physiological Ecology of Seaweeds, Cambridge University Press, London (1985).

Lobban, C.S. and Wynne, M.J. (eds.), The Biology of Seaweeds, Blackwell, Oxford (1981).

Lüning, K., Seaweeds: Their environment, biogeography, and ecophysiology, Wiley-Interscience, New York (1990).

Margulis, L., Symbiosis in Cell Evolution: Life and its environment on the early earth, Freeman, San Francisco (1981).

Margulis, L., Corliss, J.O., Melkonian, M., and Chapman, D.J., The Handbook of Protoctists, Jones and Bartlett, Boston (1987).

Margulis, L. and Schwartz, K.C., Five Kingdom: An illustrated guide to the phyla of life on earth, Freeman, San Francisco (1982).

Martinez, M.R., A Checklist of Blue-green Algae of the Philippines, National Institute of Biotechnology and Applied Microbiology (Marcos Foundation), Laguna, Philippines (1984).

Marvan, P., Pribil, S., and Lhotsky, O. (eds.), Algal Assays and Monitoring Eutrophication, Schweizerbartsche, Stuttgart (1979).

Mitsui, A., Miyachi, S., San Pietro, A., and Tamura, S. (eds.), Biological Solar Energy Conversion, Academic Press, New York (1977).

Morris, I. (ed.), The Physiological Ecology of Phytoplankton, Blackwell, Oxford (1980).

Norse, E.A. (ed.), Global Marine Biological Diversity: A strategy for building conservation into decision making, Island Press, Washington (1993).

Parish, J.H. (ed.), Developmental Biology of Prokaryotes, University of California Press, Berkeley (1979).

Prescott, G.W., The Diatoms, Coward, McCann and Georghegan, New York (1977).

Prescott, G.W., How to Know the Freshwater Algae?, 3rd edn., Wm. C. Brown, Dubuque (1978).

Prescott, G.W., Bicudo, C.E.D.M., and Vinyard, W.C., A Synopsis of North American Desmids, University of Nebraska Press, Lincoln (1982).

Rai, L.C., Gaur, J.P., and Soeder, C.J. (eds.), Algae and Water Pollution, Special Vol. 42 of *Archiv für Hydrobiologie*, E. Schweizerbartsche Verlagsbuchhandlung, Stuttgart (1994).

Rogers, L.J. and Gallon, J.R. (eds.), Biochemistry of the Algae and Cyanobacteria, Clarendon Press, Oxford (1988).

Ryther, J.H., Fuels from marine biomss, *Oceanus*, **22**, 48–58 (1979).

Sandgren, C.D. (ed.), Growth and Reproductive Strategies of Freshwater Phytoplankton, Cambridge University Press, Cambridge (1988).

Schleifer, K.H. and Stackebrandt, E. (eds.), Evolution of Prokaryotes, Academic Press, London (1984).

Schwimmer, M. and Schwimmer, D., The Role of Algae in Plankton and Medicine, Grune and Stratton, New York (1955).

Sieburth, J.M., Sea Microbes, Oxford University Press, New York (1979).

Smayda, T.J. and Shimizu, Y. (eds.), Toxic Phytoplankton Blooms in the Sea, Proceedings of the Fifth International Conference on Toxic Marine Phytoplankton, Newport, Rhode Island, 28 Oct.–1 Nov. 1991, Elsevier, Amsterdam (1993).

Sournia, A., Phytoplankton Manual, UNESCO, Paris (1978).

Spector, D.L. (ed.), Dinoflagellates, Academic Press, Orlando (1984).

Steele, J.H., Spatial Pattern in Plankton Communities, Plenum Press, New York (1977).

Stewart, W.D.P. (ed.), Algal Physiology and Biochemistry, Blackwell, Oxford (1974).

Tappan, H., The Paleobiology of Plant Protists, Freeman, San Francisco (1980).

Tarapchak, S.J. and Stoermer, E.F., Phytoplankton of Lake Michigan, Argonne National Laboratory, Argonne (1976).

Taylor, F.J.R. (ed.), The Biology of Dinoflagellates, Blackwell, Palo Alto, Calif. (1987).

Tokida, J. and Hirose, H. (eds.), Advance of Phycology in Japan, W. Junk, The Hague (1975).

Tomas, C.R. (ed.), Marine Phytoplankton: A guide to naked flagellates and coccolithophorids, Academic Press, San Diego (1993).

Toomey, D.F. and Babcock, J.A., Precambrian and Paleozoic Algal Carbonates, West Texas: Southern New Mexico, Colorado School of Mines, Colorado (1983).

Trainor, F.R., Introductory Phycology, Wiley, New York (1978).

Trench, R.K., Physiology, ultrastructure and biochemistry of cyanellae, *Prog. Phycol. Res.*, **1**, 257–87 (1982).

Tseng, C.K. (ed.), Common Seaweeds of China, Science Press, Beijing (1983).

Tseng, C.K. (ed.), Proceedings of the Joint China-U.S. Phycology Symposium, Science Press, Beijing (1983).

Venkataraman, G.S., Algal Biofertilizers and Rice Cultivation, Today and Tomorrow's Printers and Publishers, New Delhi (1972).

Venkataraman, L.V. and Becker, E.W., Biotechnology and Utilization of Algae: The Indian experience, Department of Science and Technology, New Delhi (1985).

Vinyard, W.C., Diatoms of North America, Mad River Press, Eureka (1980).

Wiessner, W., Robinson, D., and Starr, R.C. (eds.), Compartments in Algal Cells and Their Interaction, Springer-Verlag, Berlin (1984).

Werner, D. (ed.), The Biology of Diatoms, Blackwell, Oxford (1977).

Wetzel, R.L. (ed.), Methods and Measurements of Periphyton Communities: A review, ASTM Special Technical Bulletin, Baltimore (1979).

Womersley, H.B.S., The Marine Benthic Flora of Southern Australia. I. Government Printer, Canberra, South Australia (1984).

Wray, J.L., Calcareous Algae, Elsevier, Amsterdam (1977).

Yentsch, C.S. and Taylor, D.L., Red Tides, Harvard University Press, Boston (1982).

Zajic, J.E. (ed.), Properties and Products of Algae, Plenum Press, New York (1970).

Glossary

abaxial. Located in a position away from axis of plant.

acronematic. Flagella with slender and smooth surface and ending in thin hair.

acyl lipid. Lipids joined to acids through anhydride bonds.

adaxial. Located on the side next to main axis.

akinete. Vegetative cell that becomes converted into thick-walled nonmotile resting spore; wall of cell becomes wall of spore.

algicide. Substance highly toxic to algae.

algicolous. Living on or attached to algae.

algin. One or more polysaccharides in intercellular spaces of tissues of larger Phaeophyceae; composed of D-mannuronic and L-guluronic acids.

alginate. General term for salts of alginic acid, especially Na salts.

allelic genes. Number of genes occupying the same locus on linkage group or chromosome.

allelopathy. Harmful direct or indirect effect of one organism on another by production of a chemical which escapes into environment.

allophycocyanin. One of three biliprotein pigments of Rhodophyceae, Cyanophyceae, and Cryptophyceae; photosynthetically active and contains chromophore phycocyanobilin.

α-granules. Submicroscopic granules rich in glycogen and found in cells of blue-green algae.

alternation of generations. Life history phase which contains alternation of gamete-producing stage (gametophyte) with meiospore-producing stage (sporophyte); frequently, alternation of multicellular diploid stage with multicellular haploid stage (generations may be isomorphic or heteromorphic).

alveola(e). Elongated chamber running from axial or central part of valve to margin, opening to inside of cell by large opening and with perforate outer layer.

amoeboid. Like an amoeba in locomotion or nutrition; creeping motion accompanied by changes in body shape.

amphiesma. Outer cell covering in dinoflagellates; includes peripheral vesicles, associated microtubules, and all thecal plates and membranes.

amylopectin. Storage polysaccharide composed of α-1,4 glucoside linkages, with α-1,6-linked side chains; also known as "branching factor" of starch; stains red-purple with I_2KI.

amyloplast. A colourless starch forming or storing plastid; a type of leucoplast.

amylose. Protein of storage polysaccharide starch, composed of α-1,4 glucoside linkages (not branched); stains blue with I_2KI.

anaerobe. Organism growing or active in absence of free oxygen.

anastomosing. Plants or plant parts intermittently joining and separating to form network.

androsporangium. Sporangium producing androspore.

androspore. Antherozoid-like zoospore formed singly in androsporangium; produces dwarf male filament, as in Oedogoniaceae.

aneuploidy. Chromosome number less or more than exact multiple of haploid number.

anisogamy. Union between two morphologically dissimilar gametes.

annular. Ring-like.

antapical. Away from apex; basal.

anterior. In or towards front.

antheridium. Uni- or multicellular male gametangium.

antherozoids. Sperms; male gametes.

anticlinal. Pertaining to pattern of cell division which occurs in direction perpendicular to circumference of suface. Anticlinal cell divisions lead to increase in circumference of plant part.

aplanogametes. Nonflagellate gametes showing amoeboid movement.

aplanospore. Nonmotile spore in which spore wall is not derived from wall of its parent cell.

apogamy. Development of diploid sporophyte from haploid gametophyte without fertilization.

apomeiosis. Nuclear division without meiosis, in a cell which normally divides by meiosis.

archegonium. Multicellular female gametangium producing egg and consisting of neck and venter; includes sterile cells in addition to fertile egg.

areolae. Cavity-like depressions, each covered with perforated membrane, the sieve membrane.

armored. Having articulated plates or thecae, as in some members of Dinophyceae.

asexual. Lack of apparent sexual organs.

assimilator. Upright leaf-like part of some siphonaceous green algae.

atmophytic. Of plants existing in subaerial habitats; on or in soil, rocks, wood, snow, or ice.

autospores. Nonmotile spores resembling parent cell in shape and structure.

autotrophic. Capable of producing required food substances from inorganic raw materials.

auxiliary cell. Cell that receives nucleus from zygote and then produces gonimoblast filaments in red algae.

auxospore. Cell that enlarges greatly to offset diminution by vegetative cell division; in most cases, a zygote.

auxotrophic. Nutrition in which externally produced organic compounds such as amino acids and vitamins are required.

axenic culture. Pure culture; containing only one species or strain; bacteria-free.

axile. Situated along the axis; axial; e.g., chloroplast of *Mougeotia* (Chlorophyceae).

axoneme. Shaft of flagellum consisting of microtubules and surrounded by plasma membrane.

basal body. Organelle from which flagella and cilia arise.

benthos. Algae growing at bottom of sea or lakes.

β-granules. Granules of proteinaceous nature confined to Cyanophyceae.

bifurcate. Divided into two parts; forked.

biomass. Total amount of living organisms present at any one time; commonly expressed as g or kcal/m^2 or m^3.

bipartite flagella. Flagella having distal part (usually 1/3 to 1/8) thinner than proximal region; thinner part of flagellum consisting of central pair of microtubules and plasmalemma covering.

bipinnate. Twice pinnate; bearing on axes pinnate leaflets that grow opposite each other on main stem.

biseriate. Arranged in two rows.

blepharoplast. Granule lying at base of flagellum; gives rise to one flagellum.

bloom. Profuse development of one or a few species of algae in water body.

boreal. Usually pertaining to colder waters of Northern Hemisphere.

brackish. Having salt content less than that of ocean; usually applied if salt content is between 2 and 20 parts per thousand.

bristle. Long, thin cytoplasmic projection through pectic layer of certain algae.

bulbil. Small group of cells cut off from thallus; group functions as vegetative reproductive unit.

byssoid. Very slender and resembling a cobweb.
caducous. Seasonally shed.
caespitose. Matted or tangled; tufted habit.
calcareous. Impregnated with lime.
calciphile. Organism which grows well in areas rich in calcium salts.
calciphilic. Pertaining to organisms well adapted to calcium-rich water.
calciphobe. Organism which grows poorly in areas high in calcium salts.
callose. Polysaccharide consisting chiefly of a β-1,3-linked glucoside found in sieve cells and elements of Laminariales (Phaeophyceae).
canaliculi. Tubular canals present on valve surface of diatoms.
capitate. Having enlargement or head at one end.
capitulum. Cell in antheridium of çharophytes from which antheridial filaments arise.
carboxysome. Polygonal granule composed of ribulose bisphosphate carboxylase.
carotene. General name for orange-yellow isoprenoid polyene plant pigments, containing only carbon and hydrogen.
carotenoids. General name for pigments of carotene and xanthophyll type; yellow, orange, or red pigments composed of eight linearly joined isoprenoid units, widespread among all organisms.
carpogonium. Female gametangium in red algae; consists of swollen base and elongated neck or trichogyne.
carposporangia. Single-celled structures borne on minute, parasitic carposporophytic generation in Rhodophyta; these sporangia produce nonmotile carpospores.
carpospore. Spore produced within carposporangium of red algae.
carposporophyte. Carpospore-producing second generation plant of red algae; parasite on female gametophyte, arising directly or indirectly from zygote.
carrageenan. Commercially marketed sulphated galactan phycocolloid obtained from Rhodophyceae, usually from Gigartinales; also spelled carragheen.
catenate. Series of cells arranged end to end in bead-like chain.
cellular. Organisms made of conventional units of structure and function known as cells, each containing several proteins and both DNA and RNA; differ from **acellular** entities which have very few proteins and either DNA or RNA but not both together.
central nodule. Wall thickening in centre of valve in diatoms.
centric. Pertaining to diatoms that are circular in valve view and have radial symmetry.
centrosome. Polar body at each pole of dividing cell; spindle is seen to diverge from these bodies.
chasmolithic. Living in rock fissures.
chemoautotroph. Organism which obtains energy from oxidation of reduced inorganic compounds, and cell carbon primarily from CO_2.
chemotaxis. Motile response to chemical stimulus.
chitin. Polysaccharide composed of β-1,4-linked acetylglucosamine units and found in exoskeletons of certain arthropods as well as in walls of some members of Chlorophyceae, in threads secreted by some diatoms, and some fungi.
chloroplast. Double membrane-bounded semiautonomous organelle of cytoplasm of eucaryotes and characterized by internal chlorophyll containing lamellar structure (thylakoids) embedded in protein-rich stroma; capable of light-dependent photophosphorylation and photosynthetic CO_2 fixation; contains DNA and RNA.
chromatic adaptation. Capacity of some algae to synthesize pigments that are complementary to quality of available light. Also known as **Gaidukov phenomenon**.
chromatid. One or two identical halves of

chromosome.

chromatophore. Plastid containing chlorophyll-a and other pigments but not chlorophyll-b.

chromocentres. Feulgen-positive bodies of unknown function found on chromosomes of Phaeophyta.

chrysolaminarin. Leucosin; food reserve of Chrysophyta.

cingulum. Transverse groove (girdle) of dinoflagellate; in diatoms, portion of girdle associated with single valve which lies perpendicular to valve face.

circadian rhythm. Repeated occurrence of natural phenomenon, e.g., cell division, photosynthesis, and bioluminescence, with periodicity of about 24 hours.

cistron. Functional unit of gene which codes for single polypeptide.

clathrate. Having net-like appearance.

clone. Group of individuals produced asexually from single individual.

coccoid. Pertaining to habit; nonmotile unicells.

coccolith. External calcitic microcrystalline plate or disc formed by many coccolithophorids (Prymnesiophyceae).

coenobial. See **coenobium**.

coenobium. Colony consisting of definite number of cells arranged in specific manner.

coenocytic. Multinucleate cell.

colligate. Septum showing H-shaped structure.

colonial. Habit showing number of cells held together within envelope.

colony. Loose organization of similar cells which have developed together from single, original parent plant or cell. Each cell is potentially capable of life activities independent of others in the colony.

competition. Negative biological interaction between two or more individuals that occurs when a necessary resource is in limited supply relative to organisms' demands.

conceptacles. Cavity-like depressions on receptacle of Fucales that contain gametangia.

conjugation. Sexual union in Conjugales involving fusion between amoeboid gametes.

contractile vacuoles. Organelles of osmoregulation; also thought to play role in excretion of waste material.

coralline. Frequently used to refer to calcareous Rhodophyceae of Corallinaceae.

corona. Crown, especially applied to cluster of cells at distal end of oogonium in Charophyceae.

cortex. That tissue of a more or less solid alga which lies beneath epidermis, i.e., between epidermis and medulla.

corticated. Convex or outer layer(s) of small cells covering that produced directly by apical cell.

corticolous. Term given to those algae which live on bark of trees.

cosmopolitan. Found in most or all parts of world.

costae. Thickened regions of valve that separate rows of areolae one from the other.

crenulate. Wavy with small teeth or scallops.

cruciate. Having shape of cross, as in the case where contents of tetrasporangium are oriented at right angles to each other.

cryophilic. Organisms which live optimally at temperatures below 5°C.

cryoplankton. Plankton of polar or cold regions.

cryptoblasts, cryptostomata. Sterile conceptacles found in Fucales.

cuneate. Wedge-shaped.

cuticle. Structureless, amorphous layer bounding outer surface of some algae.

cyanelle. Photosynthetic organelle equivalent to chloroplast but resembling a unicellular blue-green alga; endosymbiont reduced to status of chloroplast within eucaryotic cell.

cyanophage. Virus that infects certain blue-green algae.

cyanophycin granules. Proteinaceous food reserve occurring in granular form in cells of blue-green algae.

cyst. Resting cells with thick envelope.

cystocarp. Fruiting body of red algae; aggregate structure consisting of carposporangia and sterile covering cells.

cytokinesis. Process of cell division.

cytopharyngeal. Pertaining to cytopharynx, i.e., gullet reservoir, and vacuoles in *Euglena*.

cytosome. Apparatus used in certain euglenoids for ingestion of food particles.

dendroid. Tree-like habit with much branching. In certain colonial algae, tree-like habit is achieved by repeated branching of mucilaginous stalks.

derepression. Release of inhibition of enzyme synthesis.

desmoschisis. Sometimes called "vegetative cell division" (*sensu* Fritsch); division of cells in which parental wall forms part of wall of cellular progeny.

developmental. Changes that organism undergoes during its vegetative or body organization.

diaminopimelic acid. Amino acid with two amino groups; has definite chemical structure.

diatomaceous earth. Deposit composed largely of walls of fossil diatoms.

dichotomy. Repeatedly bifurcating pattern of branching.

dictyosomes. Vesicular structures of unknown functions found in cytoplasm of eucaryotic cells. Also known as **Golgi bodies**.

diffuse. Pertaining to growth in which every vegetative cell is capable of growth and division.

diffused centromeres. Chromosome containing many scattered centromeres along its length.

dimorphic. Where gametophytic and sporophytic generations are morphologically distinct.

dioecious. Location of male and female sex organs on separate plants.

diplobiontic. Type of life history having two free-living morphological phases.

diplohaplont. Where diploid and haploid generations alternate successively.

diplont. Diploid plant in which the only haploid stage consists of gametes.

diplostichous. Type of axis cortication in Charophyceae in which there is a secondary columnar cell for each primary cortical cell.

distal. Opposite of basal.

distichous. Arranged in two vertical rows, along opposite sides of axis.

distromatic. Condition where thallus is two cells thick.

doliform. Cask- or barrel-shaped.

dormant. Not growing or germinating; resting.

dorsiventral. Having recognizable dorsal and ventral surfaces.

dystrophic. Lakes with water having very low lime content and very high humus content; bog lakes with coloured water and limited nutrients.

ecad (ecotype; ecophene). Growth form determined by ecological or habitat conditions; purely somatic (noninheritable) modification.

echinate. Spiny.

ecotype. Genetic race or strain of species which has developed morphological response to its environment; synonym, **ecad**.

ectocarpin. Hormone produced by female gametes of brown alga *Ectocarpus*, causing clustering and accumulation of sperms at hormone source.

edaphic. Referring to algae that live on or in soil or sediments.

ejectosome. Term introduced for the unique trichocysts of Cryptophyceae and Prasinophyceae; helically wound ribbon which is ejected by sudden unrolling; after discharge, the wound bands of two connected components form tubular threads.

eleutheroschisis. Cellular division in which walls of cellular products are entirely new and free of parent cell.

encapsulated. Pertaining to habit; sac-like covering enclosing organism.

endemic. Native to certain region.

endolithic. Living inside rock.

endophyte. Plant living within another plant.

endoplasmic reticulum. Fine tubular or vesicular structures traversing cytoplasm of eucaryotic cells.

endospore. Internally formed thin-walled spores of Cyanophyta, analogous to aplanospores.

endozoic (endozootic). Living within tissues of animal but not necessarily parasitic.

epicone. Anterior part of dinoflagellate cell.

epidaphic. Living on soil surface.

epilithic. Living attached to rock.

epipelic. Living on (or in) fine sediment.

epipsammic. Living attached to sand grains.

epitheca. Larger half of diatom frustule which covers smaller half (**hypotheca**).

epizoic. Growing attached to outer surface of animals.

eucaryota. Cellular organisms, in which genetic, respiratory, and photosynthetic apparatuses are organized into nucleus, mitochondrion, and chromatophore, respectively.

euphotic zone. That upper layer of water receiving sufficient light for photosynthesis to occur.

euryhaline. Tolerating broad range of salinity.

eurythermal. Tolerating broad range of temperature.

eutrophic. Pertaining to habitats rich in nutrients and organic matter for growth of algae and other plants and microorganisms.

evection. Pushing one branch or part above, or into greater prominence than, another.

exogenous. Formed at surface; arising from without.

exospores. Spores produced externally or outwardly as in Cyanophyta; analogous to aplanospores.

extrusome. Extrusive organelle, membrane-bound, located in cortical cytoplasm and readily discharged when subjected to wide range of stimuli.

eyespot. Red-coloured spot (**stigma**) generally believed to have visual function.

facultative. Occasional; incidental; can live under different conditions of life.

falcate. Sickle-shaped.

false branching. Branching resulting from degeneration of cell in loop or from growth of free ends of trichome through filament sheath, as in some blue-green algae.

fenestrate. Having several openings.

fibrillar. Bearing hairs or fibres which are more or less parallel and not matted.

filamentous. Thread-like photosynthetic plants.

flagella. Fine, thread-like structures by activity of which cells move.

frustule. Cell wall of diatom composed of two overlapping thecae (epitheca and hypotheca).

fucoidin. Calcium salt of a carbohydrate ethereal sulphate believed to be useful as blood anticoagulant.

fucosan vesicles. Sac-like structures in cells of brown algae; contain phenolics and tannins.

funori. Commercially produced phycocolloid of some Rhodophyceae, used as glue.

fusiform. Spindle-shaped.

gamete. Sex cell; two gametes of opposite sex unite to form zygote.

gamone. Chemical involved in effecting sexual union; in *Chlamydomonas*, complementary contact sex substances.

gas vacuoles. Gas-filled cavities in cells of certain planktonic blue-green algae which disappear when subjected to pressure. Also known as **pseudovacuoles**.

geminate. Paired.

geniculum. Uncalcified region between segments of articulated coralline algae (Rhodophyceae).

girdle. Transverse groove containing one flagellum as seen in dinoflagellates; in diatoms, portion of frustule between epivalve and hypovalve including epicingulum and hypocingulum.

girdle view. Side view of diatom that reveals junction of epitheca and hypotheca.

globule. Male reproductive organs of Charales having jacket of sterile cells around fertile cells; analogous to antheridium.

glomerule. Clustér of branches at node, as in *Batrachospermum*.

glucosamine. Glucose derivative containing amino group at second carbon of six-carbon molecule.

glycolipids. Compounds made of lipids and galactose.

gonidium. Thick-walled asexual reproductive cell.

gonimoblasts. Filaments formed from zygote in red algae; bear carposporangia.

gonospores. Spores produced following meiosis; also called meiospores.

gregarious. Grouped closely together; clustered.

gullet. Misleading term referring to anterior invagination in Euglenophyceae and Cryptophyceae; term implies invagination is concerned with food ingestion, which is generally not the function; "reservoir" is preferred.

gynandrosporous. Species bearing both oogonia and androsporangia on the same filament.

gyrogonite. Fossilized oospore of charophytes.

habit. General form or aspect or mode of growth of plant.

habitat. Natural place of growth of alga or plant.

haematochrome. Orange or red oily pigment related to carotene and present in resting cells and eyespots of certain algae.

haplobiont. Organism having only one vegetative stage; may be in either diplont or haplont.

haplobiontic. With only one separate multicellular generation in life history.

haplont. Haploid plant in which the only diploid stage is confined to zygote.

haplostichous. In Charophyceae, cortication in which no secondary cells accompany primary cortical cells; in Phaeophyceae, uniaxial vegetative types (versus polystichous or multiaxial types).

hapteron(a). Multicellular outgrowth at basal end of certain Laminariales (Phaeophyceae), branched and root-like.

haptonema(ta). Thread-like organelle which may coil and uncoil and may act as holdfast in Prymnesiophyceae; has outer sheath of 3 concentric membranes and inner circle of 6 or 7 microtubules.

haustorium. Cellular process serving parasite as organelle of attachment, and as means for food absorption from host tissues.

heterocyst. Specialized enigmatic cell found in certain blue-green algae.

heterodynamic flagella. Flagella with dissimilar patterns of motion and/or function.

heterokaryosis. Association of nuclei of different genetical constitutions in vegetative cell.

heteromorphic. Life cycle involving alternation between morphologically dissimilar generations.

heteroplastidy. Having two kinds of plastids.

heterothallic. Self-incompatibility; sexual

fusion occurs only between gametes of different parentage or plants.

heterothallism. Condition where an organism will not reproduce sexually in clonal culture.

heterotrichous. Thallus differentiated into prostrate and erect system of branching filaments.

heterotroph. Organism capable of utilizing exogenous organic compounds as energy sources for growth.

heterotrophic. Organisms dependent on exogenous organic sources for their metabolism and growth.

holdfast. Single cell or group of cells that acts as organ of attachment.

holocarpic. Phenomenon in which entire alga is transformed into gametangium.

hologamy. Fusion of mature individuals, i.e., mature individuals directly act as gametes.

holophytic. Plant-like mode of nutrition involving photosynthesis.

holozoic. Feeding like animals by ingesting solid food.

homodynamic flagella. Flagella with similar patterns of motion and function.

homothallic. Self-compatible; fusion can occur between gametes derived from the same plant.

hormocyst. Thick-walled hormogonium or multicellular akinete found in a few blue-green algae.

hormogone. Short piece of trichome consisting of undifferentiated vegetative cells which are moniliform; hormogonium is generally motile and meant for propagation.

host. Plant that gives nourishment to parasite or just mechanical support or shelter to epiphyte.

hypnospore. Thick-walled spore; meant for perennation.

hypotheca. Inner and smaller valve of diatom frustule.

hystichosphere. Fossilized encysted stage of dinoflagellates which may be highly ornamented.

idioandrosporous. Species bearing androsporangia and oogonia on separate filaments.

in situ. Describes conditions that occur in natural environment of an organism or refers to physiological experiments performed in field under natural conditions.

insolation. Incoming solar radiation.

intercalary. Growth pattern in which newly formed cells are produced between two existing cells, e.g., of filament.

intercalary band. That element of cingulum, different in structure or form from distal elements; also called copula; may form bands of silica or scales which extend inward to form septa.

intergeniculum. Calcified segment between uncalcified joints or nodes in stem or plant body, e.g., in *Chara* (Charophyceae) and *Ceramium* (Rhodophyceae).

internode. Space between two joints or points of attachment; in a filament, it is part of a cell between two end walls.

intertidal. Between low and high tide levels.

in vitro. Describes laboratory experimentation using cell-free extracts or organs or organelles that have been removed from a living organism.

in vivo. Describes conditions or laboratory experimentation with cells, tissues, organs or whole organisms.

iridescent. Glowing; shining; reflecting different hues when seen from various angles.

isogamy. Fusion between morphologically and physiologically similar gametes.

isomorphic. Life cycle involving alternation between two morphologically similar generations.

isoprenoid. Compound composed of isoprene units, e.g., carotenoids and steroids.

isthmus. Cytoplasmic region between 2 cell halves (semicells) as in desmids formed as a result of cytoplasmic restriction.

juvenile. Small; not yet well developed or fully mature; not having adult traits.

juxtaposed. Side by side.

karyogamy. Fusion of nuclei.

karyokinesis. Process of nuclear division.

keel. Ridge present on valves of some pennate diatoms (Bacillariophyceae).

kelp. Common name for some of the larger Phaeophyceae (e.g., Laminariales).

labiate process. Siliceous tube or opening which projects inward from valve surface in certain diatoms and terminates in longitudinal slit surrounded by two lip-like structures; the tube may also extend outward from valve surface.

lacustrine. Growing in lakes.

lamella(e). Middle lamella between plant cell walls (formerly used to denote photosynthetic closed membrane sacs now called thylakoids).

lamellate (lamellose). Made up of layers joined together.

laminarin. Polysaccharide food reserve in brown algae.

lateral conjugation. Conjugation involving conjugation tubes linking gametes from adjacent cells in the same filament, as in certain *Spirogyra* spp. (Chlorophyceae).

lentic. Living in standing water.

leucosin. Highly refractile polysaccharide with β-1,3 linkages which forms food reserve in Chrysophyta and Xanthophyta; chemically similar to laminarin; sometimes also called chrysolaminarin.

lorica(e). Noncellulosic shell-like structure housing an organism and having openings for organelles of locomotion.

lotic. Living in running water.

lunate. Crescent-shaped.

macrandrous. Filaments producing antheridia similar in size and morphology to those producing oogonia; sexually monomorphic plants, as in *Oedogonium*.

mantle. Outermost portion of valve in diatoms which is bent at approximately 90° and connected to girdle.

manubrium. Columnar cell that connects pedicel to shield cell in antheridia of Charophyceae.

marl. Calcareous deposit formed by such algae as *Chara* and some cyanophytes.

mastigoneme. Hair-like appendage on some flagella.

mating type. Individuals of heterothallic species which are isogamous and readily participate in sexual reproduction; an isogamete is termed "+" or "–" rather than male or female.

matrix. Enveloping or surrounding material, generally mucilaginous.

medulla. Central portion of axis, organ, or plant body.

meiospores. Spores formed after meiosis in zygote.

meristoderm. Meristematic surface layer of tissue.

mesocaryotic. Description of nucleus of dinoflagellates and euglenoids in which chromosomes typically persist in elongate, condensed, discrete condition throughout cell cycle.

microfibril. Any small, usually submicroscopic fibrillar entity in cell, e.g., in cellulose in 5–70 nm wide threads of crystalline anhydrous cellulose I, found in many algal cell walls.

micrometre. μm, unit of measurement equal to 10^{-6} m; earlier term, micron (μ).

microtubules. Small (15–26 nm) tube-shaped bodies found in cytoplasm of most cells; they are made of helically arranged protein dimers; present in cilia, flagella, spindles, and other such organelles; they are believed to be contractile, skeletal, and/or transporting in function.

mitochondria. Cytoplasmic double-membraned organelles concerned with energy release in respiration.

mitospores. Spores formed after mitosis;

may be haploid or diploid.

mixotroph. Photoautotroph which is capable of utilizing organic compounds; also a facultative heterotroph.

moniliform. Arranged like string of beads.

monoecious. Plant bearing both male and female sex organs on the same individual.

monomorphic. Formation of only one kind of plant in life cycle.

monophyletic group. An ancestor and all of its descendants. In a typical cladistic analysis the ancestor is not specified either because it is not available or is not easily identifiable. Nevertheless, one may assign taxa to monophyletic groups based on the presence of shared, derived traits or synapomorphies.

monostromatic. Condition in which thallus is only one-cell layer thick.

monotrichous. Having single flagellum.

motile. Capable of independent movement by means of flagella or some other device.

muciferous body. Organelle which contains mucilage in Euglenophyceae, Dinophyceae, Chrysophyceae, and Prymnesiophyceae.

mucopeptides. Compounds made of carbohydrates and amino acids; carbohydrates are N-acetylglucosamine and N-acetyl muramic acid; amino acids are glutamic acid, alanine, glycine, aspartic acid, lysine, and diaminopimelic acid.

multiaxial. Formation of main axis of thallus by group of branched filaments.

multiplicative. Process leading to increase in number of an organism or its cells.

multiseriate. Having more than one row of cells.

muramic acid. Glucosamine derivative containing carboxyethyl group at 3-0 position, e.g., 3-0-carboxyethyl-D-glucosamine.

nannandrous. Sexually dimorphic plants as in Oedogoniaceae with dwarf male.

nannoplankton. Plankton with dimensions 2–20 μm.

necridium. Dead or degenerated cell in cyanophytes which is commonly site of branch formation.

nemathecium. Superficial reproductive sorus, in some Florideophycidae (Rhodophyceae).

nematocyst. Structurally complex ejectile organelle found in certain dinoflagellate genera; also called *cnidocyst*.

neritic. Marine biome where land masses extend outward as continental shelves.

neustonic. Term given to those organisms (including algae) living at air-water interface.

nitrogenase. Enzyme concerned with conversion of molecular nitrogen into ammonia.

nitrogen fixation. Conversion of dinitrogen gas (N_2) into a combined form (e.g., NH_3, NH_4).

node. Point or area of axis where branching or leafing occurs. In filament, it is location of septum.

nucleolar organizing chromosome. Chromosome concerned with formation of nucleolus.

nucleomorph. Membrane organelle in perichloroplastic compartment of Cryptophyceae with suggested role of subsidiary genome.

nucule. Female reproductive organ of Charales.

nurse cell. Cell laden with reserve food and borne near carpogonium in red algae.

obligate. Essential or necessary; not facultative.

obovate. Inversely egg-shaped, i.e., broader at distal end.

obpyriform. Inversely pear-shaped.

ocellus. Eyespot or photoreceptor with associated lens-like organelle.

oligotrophic. Habitats relatively poor in nutrients.

ontogenetic. Pertaining to development of individual organism through its various stages.

ontogeny. Development of organism.

ooblast. Connecting filament through which zygote nucleus migrates from carpogonium to auxiliary cell in Rhodophyta.

oogamy. Fusion of motile sperm with large passive nonmotile egg.

osmotroph. Organisms which absorb nutrients in soluble form through plasma membrane.

ostiole. Opening or pore of conceptacle of Fucales.

ovoid. Like hen's egg.

ovum. Female, nonmotile gamete or egg cell.

oxidation pond. Enclosure for sewage designed to promote digestion of sewage with help of oxygen released by algae during photosynthesis.

palisade. Erect cylindrical cells laterally united into compact tissue.

palmella stage. Temporarily nonmotile sedentary stage in life history of certain motile algae; cells remain passive and embedded in gelatinous matrix.

palmelloid. Palmella-like habit.

pantonematic. Flagellum in which surface is covered with hair-like appendages.

paraflagellar body. Swelling on emergent flagellum of certain Euglenophyceae near the point in reservoir where two flagella meet; thought to be photoreceptor for phototaxis; parabasal body.

paraphyletic group. A group that does not include all of the descendants of a common ancestor.

paraphysis. Sterile filament borne near reproductive structure; paraphysis is hair-like and may be branched or unbranched.

parasexual. Organisms showing genetic recombination not involving regular alternation between karyogamy and meiosis.

parasporangia. Sporangia whose protoplast divides into more than four spores but at least first division is mitotic; commonly found in Rhodophyta.

parenchymatous. Pertaining to tissue composed of thin-walled and living cells.

parietal. Positioned against inner wall of cell.

parthenogenetically. Pertaining to mode of development in which female gamete germinates without undergoing fertilization.

parthenospore. Spore which develops from unfertilized gamete and has thick wall.

pectinate. Resembling a comb.

pelagic. Living unattached in open sea, e.g., *Sargassum natans*.

pellicle. Outer bounding membrane found in cells lacking cell wall; resembles but is not equivalent to firm cell wall.

pennate. Describes diatoms in Pennales that are characterized generally as having elongate cells with ornamentation of valves arranged in a more or less bilateral symmetry.

pericarp. Urn-shaped sterile envelope surrounding cystocarp or carposporophyte.

pericentral cell. One of a ring of cells cut off from and surrounding central axis in some red algae.

periclinal. Parallel with circumference.

periphyses. Sterile, branched or unbranched, hair-like cells growing from conceptacle but not closely associated with reproductive organ.

periphyton. Microalgae associated with or growing attached to stems, twigs, and culms of larger aquatic plants.

periplast. Delicate protective covering of flagellates that lack cell wall.

phagotroph. Organism which ingests solid food particles.

phenology. Study of periodic (seasonal) phenomena usually in relation to abiotic factors.

photic zone. Zone of water throughout which photosynthetically useful light penetrates; situated above aphotic zone.

photoautotroph. Autotroph which derives

its energy from light; phototroph.

photoheterotroph. Heterotrophic organism which uses light to supplement its energy needs beyond those of heterotrophy.

photoreceptor. Site or molecule where light energy is absorbed.

phototaxis. Movement oriented in response to light.

phragmoplast. Parallel arrangement of microfibrils to spindle axis at telophase; cell plate is deposited across these microfibrils.

phycobilisomes. Particles containing phycobilin, phycocyanin, and phycoerythrin pigments.

phycobiont. Algal component of lichen.

phycoplast. Arrangement of microfibrils perpendicular to spindle axis and at equator of cell at telophase.

phylogeny. Racial history or evolutionary development of species.

pit connection. Cytoplasmic strand connecting two adjoining cells through pit in their respective cell walls.

placenta. Composite, often conspicuous, multinucleate cell produced when carpogonium fuses with auxiliary cell and other sterile cells in Rhodophyta; gonimoblasts may develop from this placenta.

placoderm desmids. Desmids which have two semicells frequently joined by narrow isthmus; pores are normally present in cell walls.

plakea stage. Curved plate-like, eight-celled stage in development of coenobium.

plane. Pertaining to septa with smooth, flat surface.

planktonic. Floating in water.

plasmalemma. Living membrane separating protoplasm of cell from cell wall.

plasmodesmata. Cytoplasmic strands connecting adjoining cells and linking cytoplasm.

plasmogamy. Fusion of cytoplasmic materials (usually also associated with fusion of nuclear materials) as in formation of zygote.

plethysmothallus. Microscopic, ectocarpoid filament arising from zoospore and serving as accessory method of reproducing sporophyte generation vegetatively or by formation of reproductive bodies in Phaeophyta.

polar nodule. Wall thickening at the two poles in diatom frustule.

polyeder. Tetrahedral stage in some organisms which form zoospores, e.g., in *Pediastrum* and *Hydrodictyon* (Chlorophyceae).

polyhedral bodies. Polygonal particles found in cells of blue-green algae; their function and chemistry are not known.

polyphosphate granules. Polymers of inorganic phosphate stored in algal cells; occur in granular form.

polyphyletic. Refers to groups whose members, although descended from a common ancestor, are each more closely related to taxa outside the designated group.

polyploidy. Cells containing three, four or more times the haploid number of chromosomes.

polysiphoneous. Consisting of definite number of pericentral cells cut off from and surrounding each cell in axial cell row; consisting of several coherent longitudinal rows of cells.

polysporangium. Sporangium containing more than four spores; at least first division is meiotic.

polystichous. Mode of branching in which branches are inserted on axis in various planes or ranks.

procarp. Carpogonium and auxiliary cell or cells when they are members of common branch system.

procaryota. Cellular organisms lacking membrane-bound genetic, photosynthetic, and respiratory organelles.

profundal zone. Deep region of water body below the light controlled region of photosynthetic plants.

propagule. Few-celled branch serving as means of vegetative propagation, as in Sphacelariales.

prostrate. Lying flat on substratum.

protandrous. Hermaphrodite organisms in which male reproductive structure matures earlier than female.

protonema. Juvenile, often filamentous or vesicular, stage in life history of plant.

proximal. Opposite of distal; nearest to point of origin or attachment.

pseudoparenchymatous. Collection of cells, filaments or hyphae forming tissue that resembles parenchyma.

pseudoraphe. False raphe; longitudinal space on valve of diatom bounded on both sides by striae.

punctae. Perforations in wall of diatoms.

pyriform. Pear-shaped, with broad end towards base.

quadrate. Squarish; four-sided or rectangular.

raphe. Longitudinal cleft seen on valve surface of diatom.

receptacle. Tip of branch of thallus bearing conceptacles as in Fucales.

recombinants. Offspring with new combination of genes different from either parent.

red tide. Describes a bloom and/or dense concentration of phytoplankton, usually dinoflagellates, that absorb more light than surrounding water and reflect wavelengths of light from yellow to red or brown; such a bloom is often associated with toxins that can kill fish and can cause illness or death in humans (see **saxitoxin**); the phenomenon is not associated with ocean tides.

regeneration. Vegetative development from dormant or old part of thallus, often stimulated by breakage, senescence or wounding.

replicate. Septum showing two circular infoldings, one on either side.

repression. Inhibition of enzyme synthesis.

reproductive. Processes leading to continuation of species or races.

revolute. Rolled back from apex or margin.

rhizopodia. Unicellular organisms capable of forming pseudopodia or false feet for locomotion or anchorage.

rhizopodial. Type of habit in which unicellular organisms form pseudopodia as locomotory organs.

saccoderm desmid. Desmid with unpitted walls, and without semicells.

saprobic. Pertaining to organisms that feed on decaying organic matter.

satellite chromosomes. Short segments of chromosomes constricted from rest of chromosomes.

saxicolous. Growing on rocks or rocky substrata.

saxitoxin. Highly toxic neurotoxin(s) produced by some *Gonyaulax* and *Pyrodinium* spp. (Dinophyceae) that cause paralytic shellfish poisoning (PSP) in humans.

scalariform. Ladder-like arrangement.

scute cell. Shield cell or wall cell of charophyte antheridium.

sedentary. Stationary and attached, whether stalked or sessile.

segregative cell division. Type of cell division characteristic of green algal order Siphonocladales in which protoplast is cleaved into spherical masses which then proceed to expand and function as independent entities.

semicell. One of two half-cells of placoderm desmid, which is a mirror image of the other half-cell; the two parts often connected by isthmus.

semireplicate. Only one side of septum wall showing circular infolding.

separation disc. Breakage area in filamentous Cyanophyceae caused by death of cell; frequently point of liberation of hormogonium.

sessile. Attached directly to substratum; not stalked.

seston. Particulate matter in free water.

silicalemma. Triple membrane system concerned with deposition of silica walls in diatoms.

simultaneous division. Nuclear and cytoplasmic division occurring concurrently.

siphoneous. Tubular thallus in algae lacking septa or cross walls during vegetative phase of growth.

spermatium. Nonflagellated naked male gamete of red algae.

spermocarp. Fruiting body consisting of sterile jacket of cells around fertilized oogonium, as in *Coleochaete*.

sporophyte. Usually diploid, spore producing phase of life history.

statospore. Resting spore in Chrysophyceae often with ornamented siliceous wall; endogenously formed (sexual or asexual); stomatocyst.

stenohaline. Tolerant of narrow range of salinity.

stenothermal. Tolerant of narrow range of temperature.

stephanokont. Condition in which swarmers have crown of flagella, e.g., in *Oedogonium*.

sterile. Vegetative; lacking reproductive organs.

stichidium. Inflated or expanded specialized branch bearing tetrasporangia in some Rhodophyceae.

stichonematic. Type of flagellum with single row of mastigonemes.

stigma. Eyespot or red spot of flagellates found within cell near or inside chromatophore. Believed to have regulatory function in cell motility.

stipe. Stalk; portion of kelp between holdfast and blade.

stochastic. Based on probabilities, in which prediction is not a single fixed number but a range of possible numbers; random.

stomatocyst. Endogenous resting spore with silicified wall (Chrysophyceae).

stratified. Layered.

stromatolite. Laminated structures formed by certain filamentous Cyanophyceae and bacteria as a result of deposition of carbonates and/or trapped sediments.

subaerial. Referring to habitats well raised above soil surface, e.g., tree barks, rocks, and stones.

sublittoral. Bottom or benthic region of ocean; usually refers to deeper or inshore layers of sea water below lowest tide.

substratum. Surface or object upon or within which organism is growing.

successive division. Nuclear and cytoplasmic divisions occurring one after the other.

sulcus. Longitudinal furrow in hypocone of members of Dinophyceae; annular groove between valve mantle and girdle of some members of Bacillariophyceae.

supporting cell. Cell that gives rise to carpogonial branch.

supralittoral. Beyond reach of highest tide on seashore; spray zone.

swarmer. Flagellated reproductive cell whether gamete or spore.

synaptonemal complex. Characteristic structures corresponding to bivalents in meiotic nuclei and seen under electron microscope.

synistome. 1–2 distinct regions of fibrillar material, organized into alternating dense or less dense regions, between or around pairs of flagella in quadriflagellate prasinophytes.

syntagmic germination. Formation of single thallus by germination of several tetraspores within tetrasporangium in Rhodophyta.

synzoospore. Compound, multiflagellate, and multinucleate asexual spore found in *Vaucheria*.

tetraspore. One of four nonmotile haploid spores formed in tetrasporangium in red algae.

tetrasporophyte. Diploid phase producing tetraspores by meiotic division in tetrasporangium.

thalloid. Like plant or alga that is not differentiated into roots, stem, and leaves.

thallus. Relatively undifferentiated plant body that is not divided into roots, stem, and leaves.

theca(e). Solid outer wall; it may be a wall with plates as in Dinophyceae; valve of diatom (Bacillariophyceae).

thermophile. Organism which lives at high temperatures.

thylakoid. Structural unit of lamellar system forming double membrane disc; photosynthetic lamella.

torulose. Knobby or twisted.

trabeculae. Anastomosing projections of wall material which traverse central vacuole and cytoplasm, e.g., in *Caulerpa*.

transcription. Process in which DNA is copied into messenger RNA.

transduction. Process of genetic recombination in which DNA of donor bacterium is carried to recipient by virus.

transformation. Process of genetic recombination in bacteria affected by incorporation of naked DNA from donor bacterium.

trichoblast. Filamentous lateral outgrowth, consisting of single row of unpigmented cells, usually branched, borne from surface thallus layer.

trichogyne. Hair-like, receptive, prolongation of carpogonium with which spermatium fuses.

trichome. Row of cells without investing sheath (as in Cyanophyta); any sterile filamentous branch arising from thallus (as in algal divisions other than Cyanophyta).

trichothallic. Intercalary growth in which meristem is located at base of a hair.

true branching. Branched by lateral division of cell in main filament.

trumpet hyphae. Long tubular achlorophyllous cells of medulla found in brown algae; conduct water and nutrients.

tychoplankton. Benthic microorganisms accidentally suspended in water column usually by turbulence or other disturbance.

tylacanthous. Cortication in Charophyceae in which primary, spine bearing cortical cells are larger than secondary cells.

unarmored. Lacking a cell covering composed of polysaccharide plates or valves (Dinophyceae).

unduliseptate. Septum with wavy margins.

uniaxial. Plant axis made of single filament or its branches.

unilocular. Pertaining to sporangia borne on sporophyte generation in Phaeophyta; unilocular sporangia not divided into separate chambers but produce numerous spores, by meiosis, in the single chamber of sporangium, spores produced being haploid.

uniseriate. Arranged in single row or series.

urseolate. Shaped like pitcher.

utricle. Small sac-shaped filament, e.g., in *Codium*.

vacuolar apparatus. Includes two kinds of organelles, viz., contractile vacuoles and cytopharyngeal apparatus consisting of gullet, reservoir, and a number of small contractile vacuoles surrounding reservoir.

vacuole. Small, usually spherical space within cell, bounded by membrane and containing fluid sap.

valve. One of two parts of diatom theca; the other is the connecting band.

valve view. Top surface of epitheca or hypotheca of diatom.

vegetative. Formation of plant body lacking reproductive structures or organs.

ventral. Lower or inner side.

verrucose. Knobby or warty.

vesicle. Small bladder-like sac filled with

gas.

water bloom. Luxuriant growth of one or a few species of algae in water, often imparting colour to water.

whorl. Group of similar organs radiating from node.

whorled. Surrounding axis or branch in a ring.

zonate. Division of tetrasporangium in three parallel planes so that tetraspores appear arranged in linear row.

zoogamete. Motile flagellate gamete.

zoospore. Motile flagellated asexual cell.

zygospore. Thick-walled resistant spore resulting from union of gametes; thick-walled zygote.

Author Index

Subject Index

Generic Index